HBJ MILLER

COMPREHENSIVE

GAAP GUIDE

1992

A comprehensive restatement
of all current promulgated

GENERALLY ACCEPTED ACCOUNTING PRINCIPLES

MARTIN A. MILLER, C.P.A.

HBJ PROFESSIONAL PUBLISHING
HBJ MILLER ACCOUNTING PUBLICATIONS, INC.

Harcourt Brace Jovanovich, Publishers
SAN DIEGO   NEW YORK   LONDON

The publisher has not sought nor obtained approval of this publication from any other organization, profit or non-profit, and is solely responsible for its contents.

Miller Comprehensive GAAP Guide
is a trademark of Harcourt Brace Jovanovich, Inc.

ISBN: 0-15-601810-1 (hardcover)
ISBN: 0-15-601809-8 (softcover)
ISBN: 0-15-500043-8 (college edition)
ISSN: 0734-8355

Printed in the United States of America

TABLE OF CONTENTS

Specialized Industry Accounting Principles

Foreword

This *Comprehensive GAAP Guide* contains all the promulgated and many of the nonpromulgated accounting principles in use today. Each promulgated pronouncement is thoroughly reviewed in a comprehensive format that is easy to assimilate and understand. Many chapters contain in-depth illustrations on the application of the specific accounting principle. Pronouncements covering the same subject matter have been compiled and incorporated in a single chapter regardless of the date of their origin.

Important nonpromulgated accounting principles have been integrated throughout the text in an effort to give the reader a more complete perspective of the specific subject matter.

Perhaps the most important feature of this comprehensive guide to accounting principles is its readability. The utmost care has been exercised to avoid incomprehensible language. Sentence structure has been deliberately simplified as much as possible to foster the maximum comprehension in a minimum period. Illustrations are used generously to demonstrate the applicability of specific concepts and principles, and observation paragraphs are utilized to stress important information.

No attempt is made to resolve apparent errors and conflicts in the promulgated pronouncements. However, these items are objectively brought to the reader's attention.

An innovative Disclosure Index has been provided which contains both required and recommended disclosures currently in use. This index has been designed to assist the preparer or reviewer of financial statements in determining whether necessary disclosures have been made.

A Note from the Publishers

Martin A. Miller, author of the GAAP Guide, *died in August of 1991. Marty set the standard for our industry when he conceived of the* GAAP Guide, *a standard we have incorporated into all of our publications. We will miss Marty's contributions, and we will strive to maintain the same level of excellence he expected.*

The 1992 edition of the GAAP Guide *was prepared by L. Harold Levinson. Harold has worked with HBJ Miller Accounting since its inception and is a frequent contributor to the* GAAP Guide *Update Service. Harold is a professor of law at Vanderbilt University. He is a CPA and an attorney, and practiced each profession before entering law teaching. In addition, he has written numerous scholarly and professional publications.*

Cross-Reference

ORIGINAL PRONOUNCEMENTS TO
COMPREHENSIVE GAAP GUIDE CHAPTERS

This locator provides instant cross-reference between an original pronouncement and the chapter(s) in this publication where such pronouncement appears. Original pronouncements are listed chronologically on the left and the chapter(s) in which the pronouncement appears in this GAAP GUIDE on the right. Where an original pronouncement has been superseded, cross-reference is made to the succeeding pronouncement.

ACCOUNTING RESEARCH BULLETINS

(Accounting Research Bulletins (ARB) 1–42 were revised, restated or withdrawn at the time ARB No. 43 was issued.)

ORIGINAL PRONOUNCEMENT   GAAP GUIDE REFERENCE

ARB No. 43 (Restatement and Revision
of Accounting Research Bulletins)

Chapter 1-A:
Unrealized Profit   Installment Method of Accounting, p. **20.01**
Capital Surplus   Stockholders' Equity, p. **38.01**
Consolidated Statements   Consolidated Financial Statements, p. **5.01**
Treasury Stock   Stockholders' Equity, p. **38.01**
Receivables—Officers & Employees   Current Assets and Current Liabilities, p. **8.01**
Donated Stock   Stockholders' Equity, p. **38.01**

Chapter 1-B:
Profits or Losses—Treasury Stock   Stockholders' Equity, p. **38.01**

Chapter 2-A:
Comparative Statements   Consolidated Financial Statements, p. **5.01**

Chapter 2-B:
Combined Statement—Income & Surplus   Superseded by APB-9

Chapter 3-A:
Current Assets and Current Liabilities Current Assets and Current Liabilities, p. **8.01**

Chapter 3-B:
Application of U.S. Government Securities
to Federal Taxes   Superseded by APB-10

Cross-Reference

ACCOUNTING PRINCIPLES BOARD OPINIONS

Cross-Reference

APB Opinion No. 4
Accounting for the Investment Credit

Investment Tax Credit, p. **25.01a**
Investment Tax Credit, p. **25.01b**

APB Opinion No. 5
Reporting of Leases in Financial Statements
of Lessees

Superseded by FASB-13

APB Opinion No. 6
Status of Accounting Research Bulletins

Portions of this Opinion superseded by APB-
11, 16, 17, 26, and FASB-8. The balance of this
Opinion appears in the following chapters:
Stockholders' Equity, p. **38.01**
Current Assets and Current Liabilities, p. **8.01**
Depreciable Assets and Depreciation, p. **11.01**

APB Opinion No. 7
Accounting for Leases in Financial Statements
of Lessors

Superseded by FASB-13

APB Opinion No. 8
Accounting for Costs of a Pension Plan

Superseded by FASB-87

APB Opinion No. 9
Reporting the Results of Operations

Portions of this Opinion superseded by
APB-15, 16, 20, 30, and FASB-16. The balance
of this Opinion appears in :
Results of Operations, p. **36.01**

APB Opinion No. 10
Omnibus Opinion—1966

Portions of this Opinion superseded by
APB-14, 16, and 18. The balance of this
Opinion appears in the following chapters:

Income Taxes, p. **19.01a**
Income Taxes, p. **19.01b**
Stockholders' Equity, p. **38.01**
Installment Method of Accounting, p. **20.01**

APB Opinion No. 11
Accounting for Income Taxes

Portions of this Opinion superseded by
APB23 and FASB-9. The balance of this
opinion appears in Income Taxes, p. **19.01a**

APB Opinion No. 12
Omnibus Opinion—1967

Portions of this Opinion superseded by
APB-14 and FASB-106. The balance of this
Opinion appears in the following chapters:
Deferred Compensation Contracts, p. **10.01**
Depreciable Assets and Depreciation, p. **11.01**
Stockholders' Equity, p. **38.01**
Interest on Receivables and Payables, p. **22.01**

APB Opinion No. 13
Amending Paragraph 6 of APB-9, Application
to Commercial Banks

Results of Operations, p. **36.01**

APB Opinion No. 14
Accounting of Convertible Debt and Debt
Issued with Stock Purchase Warrants

Convertible Debt, p. **7.01**

ACCOUNTING PRINCIPLES BOARD STATEMENTS

FINANCIAL ACCOUNTING STANDARDS BOARD STATEMENTS

FASB Statement No. 11
Accounting for Contingencies—Transition
Method   Contingencies, p. **6.01**

FASB Statement No. 12
Accounting for Certain Marketable
Securities   Marketable Securities, p. **28.01**

FASB Statement No. 13
Accounting for Leases   Leases, p. **26.01**

FASB Statement No. 14
Financial Reporting for Segments of a
Business Enterprise   Segmental Reporting, p. **37.01**

FASB Statement No. 15
Accounting by Debtors and Creditors for
Troubled Debt Restructurings   Troubled Debt Restructuring, p. **40.01**

FASB Statement No. 16
Prior Period Adjustments   Results of Operations, p. **36.01**

FASB Statement No. 17
Accounting for Leases—Initial Direct Costs   Rescinded by FASB-91

FASB Statement No. 18
Financial Reporting for Segments of Business
Enterprises—Interim Financial Statements   Segmental Reporting, p. **37.01**

FASB Statement No. 19
Financial Accounting and Reporting by Oil
and Gas Producing Companies   Oil and Gas Producing Companies, p. **75.01**

FASB Statement No. 20
Accounting for Forward Exchange Contracts   Superseded by FASB-52

FASB Statement No. 21
Suspension of the Reporting of Earnings per
Share and Segment Information by
Nonpublic Enterprises   Earnings Per Share, p. **13.01**
                                                        Segmental Reporting, p. **37.01**

FASB Statement No. 22
Changes in the Provisions of Lease
Agreements Resulting from Refunding of
Tax-Exempt Debt   Leases, p. **26.01**

FASB Statement No. 23
Inception of the Lease   Leases, p. **26.01**

FASB Statement No. 24
Reporting Segment Information in Financial
Statements That Are Presented in Another
Enterprise's Financial Report   Segmental Reporting, p. **37.01**

FASB Statement No. 39

Financial Reporting and Changing Prices:
Specialized Assets—Mining and Oil and Gas   Superseded by FASB-89

FASB Statement No. 40

Financial Reporting and Changing Prices:
Specialized Assets—Timberlands and
Growing Timber   Superseded by FASB-89

FASB Statement No. 41

Financial Reporting and Changing Prices:
Specialized Assets—Income-Producing Real
Estate   Superseded by FASB-89

FASB Statement No. 42

Determining Materiality for Capitalization
of Interest Cost   Interest Costs Capitalized, p. **22.51**

FASB Statement No. 43

Accounting for Compensated Absences   Current Assets and Current Liabilities, p. **8.01**

FASB Statement No. 44

Accounting for Intangible Assets of Motor
Carrier   Intangible Assets, p. **21.01**

FASB Statement No. 45

Accounting for Franchise Fee Revenue   Franchise Fee Revenue, p. **60.01**

FASB Statement No. 46

Financial Reporting and Changing Prices:
Motion Picture Films   Superseded by FASB-89

FASB Statement No. 47

Disclosure of Long-Term Obligations   Long-Term Obligations, p. **27.51**

FASB Statement No. 48

Revenue Recognition When Right of Return
Exists   Revenue Recognition, p. **36.51**

FASB Statement No. 49

Accounting for Product Financing
Arrangements   Product Financing Arrangements, p. **33.01**

FASB Statement No. 50

Financial Reporting in the Record and Music
Industry   Record and Music, p. **53.01**

FASB Statement No. 51

Financial Reporting by Cable Television
Companies   Cable Television, p. **51.01**

FASB Statement No. 52

Foreign Currency Translation   Foreign Operations and Exchange, p. **16.01**

Cross-Reference

FASB Statement No. 66
Accounting for Sales of Real Estate

Real Estate-Recognition of Sales, p. **81.01**

FASB Statement No. 67
Accounting for Costs and Initial Rental
Operations of Real Estate Projects

Real Estate Costs and Initial Rental
Operations, p. **80.01**

FASB Statement No. 68
Research and Development Arrangements

Research and Development Costs, p. **35.01**

FASB Statement No. 69
Disclosures about Oil and Gas Producing
Activities

Amended by FASB-89

FASB Statement No. 70
Financial Reporting and Changing Prices:
Foreign Currency Translation

Superseded by FASB-89

FASB Statement No. 71
Accounting for the Effects of Certain Types
of Regulation

Regulated Industries, p. **85.01**

FASB Statement No. 72
Accounting for Certain Acquisitions of
Banking or Thrift Institutions

Intangible Assets, p. **21.01**
Business Combinations, p. **3.01**
Bank and Thrift Institutions, p. **45.01**

FASB Statement No. 73
Reporting a Change in Accounting for
Railroad Track Structures

Accounting Changes, p. **1.01**

FASB Statement No. 74
Accounting for Special Termination Benefits
Paid to Employees

Superseded by FASB-88

FASB Statement No. 75
Deferral of the Effective Date of Certain
Accounting Requirements for Pension
Plans of State and Local Governmental
Units

Pension Plan Financial Statements, p. **31.51**

FASB Statement No. 76
Extinguishment of Debt

Extinguishment of Debt, p. **14.51**

FASB Statement No. 77
Reporting by Transferors for Transfers of
Receivables with Recourse

Transfer of Receivables With Recourse, p. **39.51**

FASB Statement No. 78
Classification of Obligations That Are
Callable by the Creditor

Current Assets and Current Liabilities, p. **8.01**

FASB Statement No. 79
Elimination of Certain Disclosures for Business
Combinations by Nonpublic Enterprises

Business Combinations, p. **3.01**

FASB Statement No. 92
Regulated Enterprises—Accounting for
Phase-in Plans

Regulated Industries, p. **85.01**

FASB Statement No. 93
Recognition of Depreciation by Not-for-
Profit Organizations

Depreciable Assets and Depreciation, p. **11.01**

FASB Statement No. 94
Consolidation of all Majority-owned
Subsidiaries

Consolidated Financial Statements, p. **5.01**

FASB Statement No. 95
Statement of Cash Flows

Cash Flow Statement, p. **4.01**

FASB Statement No. 96
Accounting for Income Taxes

Income Taxes, p. **19.01b**
Investment Tax Credit, p. **25.01b**

FASB Statement No. 97
Accounting and Reporting by Insurance
Enterprises for Certain Long-Duration
Contracts and for Realized Gains and
Losses from the Sale of Investments

Insurance Enterprises, p. **65.01**

FASB Statement No. 98
Accounting for Leases:
• Sale-Leaseback Transactions
  Involving Real Estate
• Sales-Type Leases of Real Estate
• Definition of Lease Term
• Initial Direct Costs of Direct
  Financing Leases

Leases, p. **26.01**
Real Estate—Recognition of Sales, p. **81.01**

FASB Statement No. 99
Deferral of the Effective Date of
Recognition of Depreciation by
Not-for-Profit Organizations

Depreciable Assets and Depreciation, p. **11.01**

FASB Statement No. 100
Accounting for Income Taxes—
Deferral of the Effective Date
of FASB Statement No. 96

Income Taxes, p. **19.01b**

FASB Statement No. 101
Regulated Enterprises—Accounting for
the Discontinuation of Application
of FASB Statement No. 71

Regulated Industries, p. **85.01**

FASB Statement No. 102
Statement of Cash Flows—Exemption of
Certain Enterprises and Classification
of Cash Flows from Certain Securities
Acquired for Resale

Cash Flow Statement, p. **4.01**

FINANCIAL ACCOUNTING STANDARDS BOARD INTERPRETATIONS

ORIGINAL PRONOUNCEMENT   GAAP GUIDE REFERENCE

Cross-Reference

FASB Interpretation No. 31
Treatment of Stock Compensation Plans in
EPS Computations — Stock Issued to Employees, p. **39.01**

FASB Interpretation No. 32
Application of Percentage Limitations in
Recognizing Investment Tax Credit — Investment Tax Credit, p. **25.01a**

FASB Interpretation No. 33
Applying FASB Statement No. 34 to Oil
and Gas Producing Operations Accounted
for by the Full Cost Method — Oil and Gas Producing Companies, p. **75.01**

FASB Interpretation No. 34
Disclosure of Indirect Guarantees of
Indebtedness of Others — Contingencies, p. **6.01**

FASB Interpretation No. 35
Criteria for Applying the Equity Method of
Accounting for Investments in Common Stock — Equity Method, p. **14.01**

FASB Interpretation No. 36
Accounting for Exploratory Wells in
Progress at the End of a Period — Oil and Gas Producing Companies, p. **75.01**

FASB Interpretation No. 37
Accounting for Translation Adjustments
upon Sale of Part of an Investment in a
Foreign Entity — Foreign Operations, and Exchange, p. **16.01**

FASB Interpretation No. 38
Determining the Measurement Date for
Stock Option, Purchase, and Award
Plans Involving Junior Stock — Stock Issued to Employees, p. **39.01**

FINANCIAL ACCOUNTING STANDARDS BOARD TECHNICAL BULLETINS

> FASB Technical Bulletins are issued by the Staff of the Financial Accounting
> Standards Board to provide timely guidance on specific accounting questions.
> Technical Bulletins are not approved by the FASB and are not considered
> promulgated GAAP. However, if a majority of the Board objects to the issuance
> of a Technical Bulletin, it is not issued.

ORIGINAL PRONOUNCEMENT	GAAP GUIDE REFERENCE
Technical Bulletin 79-1 Purpose and Scope of FASB Technical Bulletins and Procedures for Issuance	No reference

Cross-Reference

Technical Bulletin 79-2
Computer Software Costs   Superseded by FASB-86

Technical Bulletin 79-3
Subjective Acceleration Clauses in Long-Term
Debt Agreements   Current Assets and Current Liabilities, p. **8.01**

Technical Bulletin 79-4
Segment Reporting of Puerto Rican
Operations   Segmental Reporting, p. **37.01**

Technical Bulletin 79-5
Meaning of the Term "Customer" As It
Applies to Health Care Facilities under
FASB Statement-14   Segmental Reporting, p. **37.01**

Technical Bulletin 79-6
Valuation Allowances Following Debt
Restructuring   Troubled Debt Restructuring, p. **40.01**

Technical Bulletin 79-7
Recoveries of a Previous Writedown under a
Troubled Debt Restructuring Involving a
Modification of Terms   Troubled Debt Restructuring, p. **40.01**

Technical Bulletin 79-8
Applicability of FASB Statements 21 and 23
to Certain Brokers and Dealers in Securities   Financial Reporting and Changing Prices,
                                             p. **15.51**

Technical Bulletin 79-9
Accounting in Interim Periods for Changes in
Income Tax Rates   Income Taxes, p. **19.01a**
                                             Income Taxes, p. **19.01b**

Technical Bulletin 79-10
Fiscal Funding Clauses in Lease Agreements   Leases, p. **26.01**

Technical Bulletin 79-11
Effect of a Penalty on the Term of a Lease   Rescinded by FASB-98

Technical Bulletin 79-12
Interest Rate Used in Calculating the Present
Value of Minimum Lease Payments   Leases, p. **26.01**

Technical Bulletin 79-13
Applicability of FASB Statement-13 to
Current Value Financial Statements   Financial Reporting and Changing Prices,
                                             p. **15.51**

Technical Bulletin 79-14

Upward Adjustment of Guaranteed Residual
Values   Leases, p. **26.01**

Technical Bulletin 79-15

Accounting for Loss on a Sublease Not
Involving the Disposal of a Segment   Leases, p. **26.01**

Technical Bulletin 79-16

Effect of a Change in Income Tax Rate on the
Accounting for Leveraged Leases   Leases, p. **26.01**

Technical Bulletin 79-17

Reporting Cumulative Effect Adjustment
from Retroactive Application of FASB
Statement-13   Leases, p. **26.01**

Technical Bulletin 79-18

Transition Requirement of Certain FASB
Amendments and Interpretations of FASB
Statement-13   Leases, p. **26.01**

Technical Bulletin 79-19

Investors Accounting for Unrealized Losses
on Marketable Securities Owned by an
Equity Method Investee   Marketable Securities, p. **28.01**

Technical Bulletin 80-1

Early Extinguishment of Debt through
Exchange for Common or Preferred Stock   Extinguishment of Debt, p. **14.51**

Technical Bulletin 80-2

Classification of Debt Restructurings by
Debtors and Creditors for Troubled Debt
Restructurings   Troubled Debt Restructuring, p. **40.01**

Technical Bulletin 81-1

Disclosure of Interest Rate Futures Contracts
and Forward and Standby Contracts   Rescinded by FASB-80

Technical Bulletin 81-2

Accounting for Unused Investment Tax
Credits Acquired in a Business Combination
Accounted for by the Purchase Method   Investment Tax Credit, p. **25.01a**

Technical Bulletin 81-3

Multi-employer Pension Plan Amendments
Act of 1980   Pension Plans—Employers, p. **30.01**

Technical Bulletin 81-4

Classification as Monetary or Nonmonetary
Items   Superseded by FASB-89

Technical Bulletin 85-4

Accounting for Purchases of Life Insurance   Current Assets and Current Liabilities, p. **8.01**

Technical Bulletin 85-5

Issues Relating to Accounting for Business
Combinations, including

- Costs of Closing Duplicate Facilities of
  An Acquirer   Business Combinations, p. **3.01**
- Stock Transactions between Companies
  under Common Control   Business Combinations, p. **3.01**
- Downstream Mergers   Business Combinations, p. **3.01**
- Identical Common Shares for a Pooling
  of Interests   Business Combinations, p. **3.01**
- Pooling of Interests by Mutual and
  Cooperative Enterprises   Business Combinations, p. **3.01**

Technical Bulletin 85-6

Accounting for a Purchase of Treasury Shares
at a Price Significantly in Excess of the Current
Market Price of the Shares and the Income
Statement Classification of Costs Incurred in
Defending against a Takeover Attempt   Stockholders' Equity, p. **38.01**

Technical Bulletin 86-1

Accounting for Certain Effects of the
Tax Reform Act of 1986   Income Taxes, p. **19.01a**

Technical Bulletin 86-2

Accounting for an Interest in the Residual
Value of a Leased Asset   Leases, p. **26.01**

Technical Bulletin 87-1

Accounting for a Change in Method of
Accounting for Certain Postretirement
Benefits   Rescinded by FASB-106

Technical Bulletin 87-2

Computation of Loss on an Abandonment   Regulated Industries, p. **85.01**

Technical Bulletin 87-3

Accounting for Mortgage Servicing Fees and
Rights   Mortgage Banking Industry, p. **70.01**

Technical Bulletin 88-1

Issues Relating to Accounting for Leases

- Time Pattern of the Physical Use of the
  Property in an Operating Lease   Leases, p. **26.01**
- Lease Incentives in an Operating
  Lease   Leases, p. **26.01**
- Applicability of Leveraged Lease
  Accounting to Existing Assets of the
  Lessor   Leases, p. **26.01**
- Money-Over-Money Lease Transactions   Leases, p. **26.01**
- Wrap Lease Transactions   Leases, p. **26.01**

Technical Bulletin 88-2
Definition of a Right of Setoff   Current Assets and Current Liabilities, p. **8.01**

Technical Bulletin 90-1
Accounting for Separately Priced Extended
Warranty and Product Maintenance Contracts   Revenue Recognition, p. **36.51**

FINANCIAL ACCOUNTING STANDARDS BOARD EXPOSURE DRAFTS

> Exposure Drafts are published by the Financial Accounting Standards Board to provide a
> tentative position with respect to financial accounting issues. These publications are not
> official promulgations and are included in the *GAAP Guide* for informational purposes
> only.

EXPOSURE DRAFT	GAAP GUIDE REFERENCE
Offsetting of Amounts Related to Certain Contracts: An Interpretation of APB Opinion No. 10 and FASB Statement No. 105	Current Assets and Current Liabilities, p. **8.01** Financial Instruments, p. **15.01**
Disclosures About Market Value of Financial Instruments	Financial Instruments, p. **15.01**
Accounting for Income Taxes— Deferral of the Effective Date of FASB Statement No. 96: An Amendment of FASB Statement No. 96	Income Taxes, p. **19.01b**
Accounting for Income Taxes	Income Taxes, p. **19.01b**
Accounting for Contributions Received and Contributions Made and Capitalization of Works of Art, Historical Treasures, and Similar Assets	Nonmonetary Transactions, p. **29.01** Revenue Recognition, p. **36.51**

ACCOUNTING CHANGES

Overview

The promulgated GAAP on accounting changes are as follows:

APB-20,   Accounting Changes

FASB-3,   Reporting Accounting Changes in Interim Financial Statements

FASB-32,   Specialized Accounting and Reporting Principles and Practices in AICPA Statements of Position and Guides on Accounting and Auditing Matters

FASB-56,   Designation of AICPA Guide and Statement of Position (SOP) 81-1 on Contractor Accounting and SOP 81-2 Concerning Hospital Related Organizations as Preferable for Purposes of Applying APB-20

FASB-73,   Reporting A Change in Accounting for Railroad Track Structures

FASB-83,   Designation of AICPA Guides and Statement of Position on Accounting by Brokers and Dealers in Securities, by Employee Benefit Plans, and by Banks as Preferable for Purposes of Applying APB Opinion 20

FASB Interpretation-1,   Accounting Changes Related to the Cost of Inventory

FASB Interpretation-20,   Reporting Accounting Changes under AICPA Statements of Position

The promulgated GAAP apply to a full set of financial statements prepared in conformity with GAAP. In addition, the promulgated GAAP specifically do not alter or amend any accounting change made in conformity with industry audit guides issued by the AICPA in the past or in the future.

> **OBSERVATION:** *Because the SEC rejected the successful efforts accounting method for oil and gas producing companies which is embodied in FASB-19, FASB-19 was subsequently amended in February 1979 by FASB-25.*
>
> *FASB-25 specifically states that for the purposes of the promulgated GAAP on accounting changes (APB-20) the provisions of FASB-19 pertaining to the successful efforts method remain in*

effect. Therefore, since FASB-19 expresses a preference for the successful efforts method of accounting and rejects other methods, an enterprise that changes to any method other than the successful efforts will have the burden of justifying such change (APB-20).

Types of Accounting Changes

Accounting changes are broadly classified as (1) changes in an accounting principle, (2) changes in an accounting estimate, and (3) changes in the reporting entity.

The correction of an error in previously issued financial statements is not an accounting change.

Changes in Accounting Principles

There is a presumption that once adopted, an accounting principle should not be changed in accounting for events or for transactions of a similar nature. The pervasive principle of *consistency* enhances the utility of financial statements.

An accounting principle may be changed if the alternative principle is preferable (rule of preferability).

An accounting change should not be made for a single transaction or for a transaction or event in the past that has been terminated or is nonrecurring.

A change in an accounting principle is the result of changing from one acceptable accounting principle to another acceptable accounting principle. A change in an accounting practice or method is also considered a change in accounting principle. Because the current or future effects of a change in an accounting estimate cannot be separated from an accounting principle, a change in an accounting estimate that is recognized in part or entirely by a change in an accounting principle should be reported as a change in an accounting estimate. For example, a change to expensing from deferring a cost because its future benefits have become doubtful involves both a change in an accounting principle and a change in an estimate, which are inseparable. These types of changes are reported as a change in an accounting estimate.

A change in, or a new, promulgated GAAP or the issuance of an industry audit guide by the AICPA constitutes sufficient support for a change in an accounting principle. Other changes in an accounting principle must be justified by the company making the change.

FASB-32 specifies that the specialized accounting and reporting principles which appear in certain AICPA Statements of Position and guides on accounting and auditing matters are *preferable accounting principles* for the purposes of justifying a change in accounting principle under APB-20 (Accounting Changes).

The following industry audit guides and one Statement of Position (SOP) were expressly excluded from FASB-32 because they, in the opinion of the FASB, do not contain any specialized accounting and/or reporting principles:

1. SOP 75-4, Presentation of Disclosure of Financial Forecasts
2. The Auditor's Study and Evaluation of Internal Control in EDP Systems
3. Audits of Service-Center-Produced Records
4. Computer Assisted Audit Techniques
5. Medicare Audit Guide

In addition, FASB-32 excludes the industry and audit guide entitled "Audits of State and Local Governmental Units," and SOP 75-3 (Accruals of Revenues and Expenditures by State and Local Governmental Units). The specialized accounting principles and practices for state and local governmental units are promulgated by the Governmental Accounting Standards Board (GASB).

FASB-32 also states that future Statements of Position and guides on accounting and auditing matters, if acceptable to the FASB and after appropriate due process, may become additional preferable accounting principles (PAP).

FASB-56 and FASB-83 cover the following AICPA publications that contain preferable accounting principles and practices and that were issued subsequent to FASB-32:

- Audit and Accounting Guide for Construction Contractors
- Statement of Position 81-1 (Accounting for Performance of Construction-Type and Certain Production-Type Contracts)
- Statement of Position 81-2 (Reporting Practices Concerning Hospital-Related Organizations)
- Statement of Position 83-1 (Reporting by Banks of Investment Securities Gains or Losses)
- Industry Audit Guide (Audits of Banks, 1983)
- Audit and Accounting Guide (Audits of Brokers and Dealers in Securities, 1985)
- Audit and Accounting Guide (Audits of Employee Benefit Plans, 1983)

For the purposes of making an accounting change (APB-20), the specialized accounting principles and practices that appear in the above AICPA publications are designated as *preferable* in accordance with the provisions of FASB-32. In other words, FASB-56 and FASB-83 extend the provisions of FASB-32 to the above AICPA publications.

The following borderline areas are not considered a change in an accounting principle:

1. A principle, practice, or method adopted for the first time on new or previously immaterial events or transactions
2. A principle, practice, or method adopted or modified because of events or transactions that are clearly different in substance
3. Changing from an accelerated depreciation method to straight line at a planned point in the life of an asset, provided the plan is made at the time of adoption of the accelerated method and the policy is consistently applied

A change in the composition of the elements of cost (material, labor, and overhead) included in inventory is an accounting change that must be justified on the basis of the rule of preferability (FASB Interpretation-1).

The FASB has delegated to the AICPA the power to issue Statements of Position on how to report accounting changes (FASB Interpretation-20).

The following are the more common changes in accounting principles:

1. A change in the method of pricing inventory, such as LIFO to FIFO or FIFO to LIFO
2. A change in the method of depreciating previously recorded assets, such as from a straight line to an accelerated method or from an accelerated to a straight-line method
3. A change in the method of accounting for long-term construction-type contracts, such as from the percentage-of-completion method to the completed-contract method or from the completed-contract method to the percentage-of-completion method

As mentioned earlier, a change in an accounting principle to effectuate a change in an accounting estimate is not considered a change in an accounting principle. It is considered a change in an accounting estimate.

Reporting a Change in an Accounting Principle

Although the presumption is that once an accounting principle has been adopted it should not be changed, when a change is necessary it should be recognized by including the cumulative effect of the change in the net income of the period of change, and not by restating the financial statements of prior periods. The cumulative effect of a change in an accounting principle is equal to the total direct effects (less related taxes) that the change has on prior periods. For example, if the total direct effects of a change in a depreciation method has the effect of increasing prior years' income by $100,000 and if the current year's tax rate is 50%, the cumulative effect of the change in the depreciation method is $50,000. Indirect effects (nondiscretionary effects) are included in the cumulative effect only if they are to be recorded on the books as a result of the change in accounting principle. Direct and indirect effects are discussed more fully later in this chapter.

The effect of a change in an accounting principle for the current period is not included in the cumulative effect, but the net income for the current period is reported by using the newly adopted accounting principle.

Although the cumulative effect is not an extraordinary item, it is shown in the income statement net of related tax effects between extraordinary items and net income, as follows:

Income before extraordinary items (includes the effect of a change in an accounting principle for the current year)	$XX,XXX
Extraordinary items *(Note:_____)*—net of related tax effects	X,XXX
Cumulative effect of a change in an accounting principle (includes the effect of a change in an accounting principle for prior years)—net of related tax effects	X,XXX
Net income	$XX,XXX

Earnings per share shown on the face of the income statement should include the per share amount attributable to the cumulative effects of the accounting change (net of related taxes).

At this juncture, it may be well to establish the fact that the promulgated GAAP provide some exceptions to the rule of not restating prior-year financial statements in accounting for a change in an accounting principle. The following specific items are exceptions to the general rule, and prior-period financial statements which are presented for comparative purposes must be retroactively restated in reporting a change in an accounting principle:

1. Change from LIFO method of inventory pricing to another method
2. Change in accounting for long-term construction-type contracts
3. Change to or from the "full cost" method of accounting in the extractive industries
4. One-time change for closely held corporations in connection with a public offering of its equity securities, or when such a company first issues financial statements (a) for obtaining additional equity capital from investors, (b) for effecting a business combination, or (c) for registering securities
5. Change from the retirement-replacement-betterment method of accounting for railroad track structures to the depreciation method of accounting (FASB-73)

> **OBSERVATION:** *FASB-73 amends paragraph 27 of APB-20 to specify that a change from the retirement-replacement-betterment method of accounting for railroad track structures to the depreciation method of accounting shall be accounted for by restating all prior-period financial statements that are presented for comparative purposes.*

In computing the cumulative effect of a change in an accounting principle, the *direct effects* of the change are always included, but the *nondiscretionary effects* (indirect effects) are included only if they are being recorded on the books as a result of the change. Direct effects of a change in accounting principle are those adjustments which are necessary to apply the change to all affected prior periods. Nondiscretionary effects (indirect) are *secondary effects* that sometimes arise from applying the newly adopted accounting principle to the prior years involved in the change. In other words, nondiscretionary effects are those which are caused by the direct effects. For example, a change from an accelerated depreciation method to the straight-line method will directly affect the net income of the prior periods in which the accelerated method was used. However, profit-sharing expense, incentive compensation costs, and royalties based on net income are affected only if the base on which they were computed (net income, income before extraordinary items, etc.) is changed. Therefore, when income of a prior period is changed by a direct effect of a change in an accounting principle, it may result in a nondiscretionary effect. If the nondiscretionary effect is to be recorded on the books as a result of the change in accounting principle, it is included in the cumulative effect. For example, if in prior years a manager had been receiving a bonus of 10% of net income, and a change in an accounting principle affects the prior years' bonuses, a nondiscretionary effect results. If an adjustment is to be made to the manager's bonus in the current year (recorded on the books), the nondiscretionary effects, less related taxes, are included in the calculation of the cumulative effect of the change in an accounting principle. However, if the company is owed money by the manager as a result of the bonus adjustment and the company does not intend to collect, the nondiscretionary effect is not included in the cumulative effect, because it is not recorded on the books.

When a change in an accounting principle involves depreciation, an adjustment must be made to the accumulated depreciation account. Assume that a change in an accounting principle involves a change from an accelerated method to the straight-line method for a particular asset. The direct effect of such a change is the difference in depreciation expense for all prior years in which the particular asset was depreciated. For discussion purposes, let us assume that the difference in the depreciation methods resulted in an increase to prior years' income of $100,000. Thus, the cumulative effect of the change in depreciation methods, before related taxes, is $100,000. If the current year's tax rate is 50%, deferred taxes would have to be adjusted for the tax on the $100,000 cumulative effect. The journal entry to record the cumulative effect of a change in an accounting principle and its related tax effect is as follows:

Accumulated depreciation	$100,000	
Deferred taxes		$50,000
Cumulative effect of a change in accounting principle		50,000

The debit to accumulated depreciation increases by $100,000 the net depreciable base of the fixed asset. The credit of $50,000 to the cumulative effect of a change in an accounting principle appears in the current year's income statement between extraordinary items and net income.

When an accounting change from FIFO to LIFO is made in pricing inventory, it may be impossible to compute the cumulative effect. In this and other situations where the cumulative effect cannot be determined, the disclosure of the cumulative effect is omitted. However, the amount of the effect in the current year and its per share information should be disclosed in a footnote. The reason for omitting the cumulative effect should also be fully disclosed.

A new depreciation method may be adopted for newly acquired long-lived assets and all future assets of the same class. This does not constitute a change in an accounting principle under the promulgated GAAP. However, if the new depreciation method is applied to previously acquired long-lived assets of the same class, a change in an accounting principle occurs.

A new depreciation method may be adopted for newly acquired long-lived assets and future assets of the same class and at the same time, older long-lived assets of the same class may be depreciated under a different method. This type of change in an accounting principle does not require an adjustment, but APB-20 does require disclosure. A description of the change and its effect on income before extraordinary items and on net income of the period of change, along with related per share data, must be disclosed.

A change in an accounting principle may occur, and for some reason only the current year's income statement is presented. In this event, the regular and pro forma amounts and related per share data for the preceding period must be disclosed in a footnote to the financial statements.

If an accounting change is considered immaterial in the year of change but is reasonably expected to become material in subsequent periods, it should be fully disclosed in the year of change.

In reporting a change in an accounting principle in the income statement, the presentation is broken down into a *regular* portion and a *pro forma* portion. The *regular* portion discloses in total amounts (1) income before extraordinary items and cumulative effect of a change in an accounting principle, (2) extraordinary items, (3) cumulative effect on prior years of the change in accounting principle, and (4) net income, which is the total of the first three items.

For the current year, income before extraordinary items and cumulative effect of a change in an accounting principle are determined by using the newly adopted accounting principle. Extraordinary items are disclosed in the usual manner. The cumulative effect on prior years of the change in accounting principle for the current year must be calculated. For the purposes of APB-20, the cumulative effect consists of the direct effects (less related taxes) that the newly adopted accounting principle has on all prior years and any indirect effects that are actually recorded on the books as a result of the change. Another method of determining the cumulative effect of a change in an accounting principle is the difference between (1) retained earnings at the beginning of the year of change and (2) retained earnings that would have been reported at the beginning of the year if the new accounting principle had been used in prior years.

The last item for the current year (regular portion) is *net income*, which is a total of the first three items already discussed. In addition, both primary and fully diluted per share data must be disclosed for (1) income before extraordinary items and cumulative effect of a change in an accounting principle, (2) extraordinary items, (3) cumulative effect on prior years of a change in an accounting principle, and (4) net income.

Any prior years included for comparative purposes in the *regular portion* presentation are disclosed at their previously reported amounts.

The *pro forma* portion of the income statement presentation includes (1) income before extraordinary items, (2) net income, and (3) related per share data for both primary and fully diluted earnings. For comparative purposes *pro forma* information must be disclosed for the current period and all prior periods presented. The *pro forma* portion is presented as if the newly adopted accounting principle had always been used. Thus, the direct effects (less related taxes) of the newly adopted accounting principle and the indirect effects (less related taxes) are used in determining the *pro forma* amounts. However, the indirect effects are used only if they are to be recorded on the books. As discussed previously, indirect effects such as profit sharing, incentive compensation, or royalties arise as a result of a direct effect. Net income is changed by the direct effect, which in turn may create an indirect effect because it is based on the determination of net income. The cumulative effect of a change in an accounting principle does not appear at all in the *pro forma* presentation. The following illustrates the *regular* and *pro forma* presentations required by APB-20:

Regular portion:	*19X1*	*19X2*
Income before extraordinary item(s) and cumulative effect of a change in an accounting principle	$XX,XXX	$XX,XXX
Extraordinary item(s) [describe]	(X,XXX)	X,XXX
Cumulative effect on prior years (to December 31, 19X1) of a change in an accounting principle	X,XXX	—
Net income	$XX,XXX	$XX,XXX
Per share amounts—no dilution: Income before extraordinary item(s) and cumulative effect of a change in an accounting principle	$X.XX	$X.XX
Extraordinary item(s)	(.XX)	.XX
Cumulative effect on prior years (to December 31, 19X1) of a change in an accounting principle	.XX	—
Net income per share—primary	$X.XX	$X.XX
Per share amounts—fully diluted: Income before extraordinary item(s) and cumulative effect of a change in an accounting principle	$X.XX	$X.XX
Extraordinary item(s)	(.XX)	.XX
Cumulative effect on prior years (to December 31, 19X1) of a change in an accounting principle	.XX	—
Net income per share—fully diluted	$X.XX	$X.XX
Pro forma portion:		
Income before extraordinary item(s), assuming accounting change is applied retroactively	$XX,XXX	$XX,XXX
Earnings per share—no dilution	$ X.XX	$ X.XX
Earnings per share—fully diluted	$ X.XX	$ X.XX
Net income	$XX,XXX	$XX,XXX
Earnings per share—no dilution	$ X.XX	$ X.XX
Earnings per share—fully diluted	$ X.XX	$ X.XX

Note: As required by GAAP, extraordinary items and the cumulative effect on prior years are both shown on financial statements net of any related tax.

The nature, justification, and preferability (if applicable) of a change in an accounting principle and its effects on income should be clearly disclosed in the financial statements of the period in which the change is made.

For all changes in accounting principles where there is no restatement of prior-period financial statements, the following should be observed:

1. Prior-period comparative financial statements should be presented as previously reported.

2. The cumulative effect of changing to a new accounting principle should be made in net income of the period of the change and should be shown in the income statement between extraordinary items and net income. The effect of the change is *not* an extraordinary item, but should be reported in a similar manner.

   The amount of cumulative effect to be reported is the difference between (a) retained earnings at the beginning of the period of change and (b) retained earnings at the beginning of the period of change adjusted for the retroactive cumulative effect of the new accounting change, including related income tax effect.

3. The earnings per share information on the face of the income statement should include the per share amount of the cumulative effect of the change.

4. The earnings per share (primary and diluted) for income before extraordinary items and net income should be shown on the face of the income statement for all periods presented.

Reporting Accounting Changes—Interim Periods

The cumulative effect of an accounting change is always included in net income of the first interim period, regardless of in which period during the year the accounting change occurs. If the accounting change occurs in other than the first interim period, the current and prior-period interim statements should be restated to include the newly adopted accounting principle. However, the cumulative effect of the change in an accounting principle is included only in the net income of the first interim period.

When the cumulative effects of a change in an accounting principle cannot be determined, the *pro forma* amounts cannot be computed. In this event, as mentioned earlier, the cumulative effect and *pro forma* amounts are omitted. However, the amount of the effect of adopting the new accounting principle and its per share data for each interim period and year-to-date amounts must be disclosed in a footnote to the financial statements, along with the reasons for omitting the cumulative effect and *pro forma* information.

Publicly traded companies that do not issue separate fourth-quarter reports must disclose in a note to their annual reports any effect of an accounting change made during the fourth quarter. This is similar to other disclosure requirements of publicly traded companies that do not issue fourth-quarter interim reports.

The following disclosures concerning a cumulative effect-type accounting change should be made in interim financial reports:

1. The nature and justification of the change should be made in the interim period in which the new accounting principle is adopted.
2. The effects of the accounting change on income from continuing operations, net income, and related per share data for both should be made:
   a. In the interim period in which the change is made
   b. In each, if any, prior interim period
   c. In each, if any, restated prior interim period
   d. In year-to-date and last twelve-months-to-date financial reports that include the adoption of the new accounting principle
   e. In interim financial reports of the fiscal year, subsequent to the interim period in which the accounting change was adopted
3. The *pro forma* effects of the accounting change on income from continuing operations, net income, and related per share data should be made:
   a. For the interim period in which the change is made
   b. For any interim period of prior fiscal years for which financial information is presented
   c. In year-to-date and last twelve-months-to-date financial reports that include the adoption of a new accounting principle

If no interim periods of prior fiscal years are presented, footnote disclosure for the corresponding interim period of the immediate fiscal year in which the accounting change occurred should be made for actual and *pro forma* income from continuing operations, net income, and related per share data.

Cumulative Effect vs Retroactive Restatement

An accounting change occurs when an enterprise changes from one acceptable accounting principle or practice to another acceptable accounting principle or practice. For example, a change from the LIFO method of pricing inventory to the FIFO method is an accounting change. However, a change from an unacceptable accounting principle or practice to an acceptable principle or practice is a correction of an error and not an accounting change.

APB-20 (Accounting Changes) requires some types of accounting changes to be reported in comparative financial statements by the *restatement method* and other types to be reported by the *cumulative effect method*. Under either method, the most important thing is to communicate to the users of the financial statements that an accounting change has occurred and to disclose the nature and effect of the change in principle or practice.

The cumulative effect method and retroactive restatement method both require exactly the same information. The total effect (direct and indirect) of the accounting change on all prior periods must be known. This total effect in a restatement is charged or credited to beginning retained earnings in the year of change. In the cumulative effect method the total effect appears in the income statement of the year of change as a separate item immediately above net income. Under both methods, the newly adopted accounting principle or practice is used in determining net income of the year of change (current period).

In order to retroactively restate a particular prior year, the details of any effects of the change in accounting principle on that particular year must be available. If this information is not available, that particular prior year cannot be retroactively restated. In applying the cumulative effect method, the details of any effects of the change in accounting principle on a particular year must also be available to determine the *pro forma* income statement presentation that is required by APB-20. Thus, if you cannot restate a particular prior year, you cannot determine the *pro forma* presentation required by APB-20.

When using the cumulative effect method, APB-20 requires a regular and *pro forma* presentation of (a) income before extraordinary items, (b) extraordinary items, (c) cumulative effect of a change in accounting principle, and (d) net income. The *pro forma* presentation discloses the above four income statement items and related per share amounts on the basis that the financial statements presented were retroactively restated.

In addition, the cumulative effect of a change in an accounting principle may be omitted under APB-20 if it is impossible to compute. In this event, the effects of the change, in the year of change, must be disclosed along with an explanation as to why the cumulative effect was omitted.

Existing GAAP (APB-9) require that net income include all items of profit and loss recognized during a period, except prior period adjustments. Prior period adjustments bypass the income statement and are charged or credited directly to retained earnings. Retroactive restatement of a financial statement is accounted for in the same manner as a prior period adjustment. Thus, retroactive restatement bypasses the income statement, and retained earnings is charged or credited. However, the restated financial statements reflect all of the details of the revision.

In applying the cumulative effect method, the total effects of the change in accounting principle for all prior periods is reflected in the income statement of the year of change. Thus, under the cumulative effect method, the income statement is not bypassed.

The type of modification, or modification and qualification, that must be made to the opinion paragraph of the standard auditor's report to account for a change in an accounting principle depends upon whether the cumulative effect or the retroactive restatement method is used to report the change. If the retroactive restatement method is used to report the change in accounting principle, the opinion paragraph is modified by including a statement that *consistency has been achieved after giving retroactive effect to the change*. In this event, the modification does not result in a qualification of the auditor's opinion because consistency has been achieved. If the "cumulative effect" method is used to report the change in accounting principle, the opinion paragraph of the auditor's report is modified by including a statement that the "accounting principles have been applied on a consistent basis, except for the specific change which is referred to in the opinion paragraph." In this event, the modification to the opinion paragraph results in a qualification of the auditor's opinion because consistency has not been achieved. The following examples illustrate the appropriate wording of the opinion paragraph of the auditor's report.

Financial statements restated:

> . . . in conformity with generally accepted accounting principles applied on a consistent basis after giving retroactive effect to the change, with which we concur, in the method of reporting investment values described in Note 1 to the financial statements.

Financial statements not restated:

> . . . in conformity with generally accepted accounting principles applied on a consistent basis except for the change, with which we concur, in the method of determining depreciation of plant properties as described in Note C to the financial statements.

Changes in an Accounting Estimate

A change in an accounting estimate is usually the result of new events, changing conditions, more experience, or additional information, any of which requires the revision of previous estimates.

Estimates are necessary in determining uncollectible receivables, salvage values, useful lives, provisions for warranty, and a multitude of other items involved in preparing financial statements.

A change in a depreciation method for a previously recorded asset is a change in accounting principle, but a change in the estimated useful life or salvage value of a previously recorded asset is a change in an accounting estimate.

Reporting a Change in an Accounting Estimate

A change in an accounting estimate *should not* be accounted for by restatement of prior years' financial statements. The effect of the change in accounting estimates should be accounted for (1) in the period of change, if the change affects only that period or (2) in the period of change and future periods, if the change affects both.

A change in an accounting estimate caused in part or entirely by a change in an accounting principle should be reported as a change in an accounting estimate.

Disclosure should be made in current-period financial statements of the effects of a change in an accounting estimate on income before extraordinary items, net income, and related per share data.

If a change in an accounting estimate affects future periods, the effect on income before extraordinary items, net income, and the related per share information should be disclosed in the income statement.

Ordinary accounting estimates for uncollectible accounts or inventory adjustments, made each period, do not have to be disclosed unless they are material.

Reporting a Change in an Entity

Restatement of prior years' financial statements is necessary when an accounting change results in financial statements that are actually statements of a different reporting entity.

All prior and current periods presented should be restated to reflect financial information for the new reporting entity.

Full disclosure should be made describing the nature of the change and the reason for it.

Changes in income before extraordinary items, net income, and related earnings per share should be adequately disclosed.

Reporting Corrections of Errors

Prior-period errors in financial statements discovered subsequently should be reported as prior-period adjustments. FASB-16 limits prior-period adjustments to:

1. Corrections of errors in financial statements of prior periods
2. Adjustments resulting from the realization of income tax benefits of preacquisition operating-loss carryforwards of purchased subsidiaries

Errors result from mistakes in mathematics and application of an accounting principle or from misjudgment in the use of facts. A change in an accounting estimate is the result of new information, changing conditions, more experience, or additional information that requires the revision of previous estimates. A change from an unacceptable accounting principle to a generally accepted one is a correction of a prior-period error (APB-20).

The nature of the error and the effect of its correction on income before extraordinary items, net income, and the related per share data must be fully disclosed in the period the error is discovered and corrected.

Financial Summaries

The presentation of accounting changes, including *pro forma* amounts, in financial summaries, including five-year summaries, should be presented in the same way as presented in the primary financial statements (APB-20).

Comprehensive Illustration

The following is a comprehensive illustration of presenting a change in an accounting principle.

At the end of 19X9, a company decides to change from an accelerated method of recording depreciation on plant equipment to the straight-line method. The direct effect of this change is $600,000 (19X9—$100,000; 19X8—$60,000; 19X7—$100,000; 19X6—$140,000; 19X5 and prior—$200,000). The indirect items (nondiscretionary) affected by the change in an accounting principle are an incentive bonus plan and royalties, which are 10% of the annual net income. Any adjustment for indirect effects is to be recorded on the books. Income tax rates are 50%. The company has 1,000,000 shares of common stock outstanding, and the comparative income statements for 19X9 and 19X8 reflect the following without any adjustments for the accounting change:

	19X9	19X8
Income before extraordinary item(s)	$2,400,000	$2,200,000
Less: Extraordinary item(s) *(Note:____)*	70,000	—
Net income	$2,330,000	$2,200,000
Primary earnings per share before		
extraordinary item(s)	$ 2.40	$ 2.20
Extraordinary item(s)	(0.07)	—
Net income	$ 2.33	$ 2.20

The following adjustments are needed in the previous information to account for the change in the accounting principle:

Regular Portion

1. For the current year (19X9), income before extraordinary items and cumulative effect of a change in an accounting principle is calculated as follows:

Before adjustment	$2,400,000
Adjustment for direct effects ($100,000)	
less taxes (50%)50,000	
Adjustment for indirect effects	
(10% of $100,000 less 50% taxes)	(5,000)
As adjusted	$2,445,000

> **Note:** Incentive bonuses and royalties of $240,000 had already been recorded on the books (10% of $2,400,000). However, the adjustment for the direct effects results in a net increase of $50,000 to income. Thus, the net indirect effects of $5,000 must be included in the calculation. The net indirect effects of $5,000 reduces income because it is an expense (incentive bonus and royalties).

2. Extraordinary items are presented in the usual manner and require no adjustment.
3. The cumulative effect on prior years of the change in an accounting principle is computed as follows:

Direct effect of the change in accounting principle on all years except the current year	$500,000
Less: 50% taxes	(250,000)
Indirect effect of the change in accounting principle on all years except the current year	(50,000)
Less: 50% taxes	25,000
Net cumulative effect on prior years	$225,000

> **Note:** Both direct and indirect effects are included because indirect effects are to be recorded on the books for the current year.

4. Any prior years presented are disclosed at their previously reported amounts.

Pro Forma Portion

1. The pro forma portion is presented as if the newly adopted accounting principle had always been used. In addition, indirect effects of the change are considered if they are to be recorded on the books.
2. For current year (19X9), income before extraordinary items is calculated as follows:

Before adjustment	$2,400,000
Adjustment for direct effects ($100,000) less taxes (50%)	50,000
Adjustment for indirect effects (10% of $100,000 less 50% taxes)	(5,000)
As adjusted	$2,445,000

Note: Incentive bonuses and royalties of $240,000 had already been recorded on the books (10% of $2,400,000). However, the adjustment for the direct effects results in a net increase of $50,000 to income. Thus, the net indirect effects of $5,000 must be included in the calculation. The net indirect effects of $5,000 reduces income because it is an expense (incentive bonus and royalties).

3. For the prior year presented (19X8), income before extraordinary items is calculated as follows:

Before adjustment	$2,200,000
Adjustment for direct effects ($60,000) less taxes (50%)	30,000
Adjustment for indirect effects (10% of $60,000 less 50% taxes)	(3,000)
As adjusted	$2,227,000

Note: Incentive bonuses and royalties of $220,000 had already been recorded on the books (10% of $2,200,000). However, the adjustment for the direct effects results in a net increase of $30,000 to income. Thus, the net indirect effects of $3,000 must be included in the calculation. The net indirect effects of $3,000 reduces income because it is an expense (incentive bonus and royalties).

The statement presentation for our illustration, taking into consideration the effects of the change in using a different depreciation method is:

	19X9	19X8
Income before extraordinary item(s) and cumulative effect of a change in accounting principle	$2,445,000	$2,200,000
Extraordinary item (*Note: ___*)	(70,000)	—
Cumulative effect on prior years (to December 31, 19X8) of changing to a different depreciation method (*Note: ___*)	225,000	—
Net income	$2,600,000	$2,200,000
EPS before extraordinary item(s)	$ 2.45	$ 2.20
Extraordinary item	(0.07)	—
Cumulative effect on prior years (to December 31, 19X8) of changing to a different depreciation method	.22	—
Net income	$ 2.60	$ 2.20

Pro forma amounts assuming the
new depreciation method is applied
retroactively:

Income before extraordinary item(s)	$2,445,000	$2,227,000
Earnings per share	$ 2.45	$ 2.23
Net income	$2,375,000	$2,227,000
Earnings per share	$ 2.38	$ 2.23

The company in the above illustration had no dilutive securities. Thus, the presentation for fully diluted EPS is omitted.

ACCOUTING POLICIES

Overview

The source of promulgated GAAP for disclosure of accounting policies is APB-22 (Disclosure of Accounting Policies). APB-22 specifically states that its provisions be followed by nonprofit entities. However, unaudited interim reports for companies which have not changed their accounting policies since the end of the preceding fiscal year need not disclose accounting policies in such interim reports.

> **OBSERVATION:** Unaudited reports issued for internal use only and certain other special reports, apparently would not have to comply with APB-22.
>
> The promulgated GAAP states that it does not supersede any other promulgated GAAP issued previously.

Background

All financial statements that purport to present financial position, results of operations, and cash flows in accordance with GAAP must comply fully with the provisions of APB-22.

Significant Accounting Policies

The preferable presentation of disclosing accounting policies is in the first footnote of the financial statements, under the caption "Summary of Significant Accounting Policies." APB-22 specifically states this preference, but mentions the need for flexibility in the matter of formats.

The requirement of the promulgated GAAP is that a description of all significant accounting policies of a reporting entity should be included as an integral part of the financial statements. Basis of consolidation, depreciation methods, amortization of intangibles, inventory pricing, recognition of profit on long-term construction-type contracts, and recognition of revenue from franchising and leasing operations are the examples described in the opinion. However, disclosure of accounting policies, should not be duplicated if presented elsewhere as an integral part of the financial statements. In disclosing accounting policies it may become necessary to refer to items presented elsewhere in the report, such as in the case of a change in an accounting principle which requires specific treatment.

> **OBSERVATION:** *FASB Technical Bulletin 82-1 requires the disclosure of the sale or purchase of tax benefits through tax leases.*

Disclosure

Both the accounting principle and the method of applying such a principle should be disclosed. Informed professional judgment is necessary to select for disclosure those principles which materially affect the financial position, results of operations, and changes in financial position. However, accounting principles and their method of application in the following areas are considered particularly important:

1. A selection from existing acceptable alternatives
2. The areas peculiar to a specific industry in which the entity functions
3. Unusual and innovative application of GAAP

Comprehensive Illustration

The following are comprehensive illustrations of the disclosure of significant accounting policies.

Principles of consolidation The consolidated financial statements include the assets, liabilities, revenues, and expenses of all significant subsidiaries. All significant intercompany transactions have been eliminated in consolidation. Investments in significant companies which are 20% to 50% owned are carried at equity in net assets and the corporation's share of earnings is included in income. All other investments are carried at cost or less.

Fixed assets and depreciation Fixed assets are carried at cost. Expenditures for replacements are capitalized, and the replaced items are retired. Maintenance and repairs are charged to operations. Gains and losses from the sale of fixed assets are included in income.

Depreciation is calculated on a straight-line basis utilizing U.S. Internal Revenue Service estimated lives. The corporation and its subsidiaries use other depreciation methods (generally accelerated) for tax purposes where appropriate.

Inventories Inventory values are stated at the lower of cost or market using the last-in, first-out (LIFO) method for substantially all qualifying domestic inventories and the average cost method for other inventories.

Income taxes Provision has been made for deferred income taxes where differences exist between the period in which transactions, principally related to depreciation, affect taxable income and the period in which they enter into the determination of income in the financial statements. The investment tax credit is deferred and amortized over the average life of the fixed assets by reductions in the provision for income taxes.

Pension plan It is the policy of the company and its consolidated subsidiaries to fund pension costs as accrued. Prior service costs are amortized over varying periods not exceeding 40 years.

Patents, trademarks, and goodwill Amounts paid for purchased patents and for securities of newly acquired subsidiaries in excess of the fair value of the net assets of such subsidiaries have been charged to patents, trademarks, and goodwill. The portion of such amounts determined to be attributable to patents is amortized over their remaining lives and the balance is amortized over the estimated period of benefit but not more than 40 years.

Earnings per share Earnings per share is based on the weighted-average number of shares of common stock outstanding in each year. There would have been no material dilutive effect on net income per share for 19X1 or 19X2 if convertible securities had been converted and if outstanding stock options had been exercised.

BUSINESS COMBINATIONS

Overview

The promulgated GAAP for business combinations are covered by APB-16 (Accounting for Business Combinations), which has been amended by FASB-38 (Accounting for Preacquisition Contingencies of Purchased Enterprises), and FASB-79 (Elimination of Certain Disclosures for Business Combinations by Nonpublic Enterprises).

Both incorporated and unincorporated entities are covered by APB-16. However, certain types of transactions are not covered by APB-16, as follows:

1. Acquisition of any minority interests in a subsidiary (APB-16 does require the use of the purchase method for this type of transaction.)
2. Creation by a corporation of a newly formed corporation for the purpose of transferring the corporation's net assets to the newly formed corporation
3. Transfer of net assets or the exchange of shares of stock between companies under common control

FASB Technical Bulletin 85-5 was issued to provide guidance on certain issues relating to business combinations (APB-16). The titles to the issues covered by FASB:TB 85-5 are:

- Costs of Closing Duplicate Facilities of an Acquirer
- Stock Transactions between Companies under Common Control
- Downstream Mergers
- Identical Common Shares for a Pooling of Interests
- Pooling of Interests by Mutual and Cooperative Enterprises

Each of the above issues relating to business combinations is addressed in this chapter.

Background

A business combination occurs when one entity combines its resources with part or all of the resources of another entity with the object of eliminating any duplication.

The purchase method of accounting for a business combination reflects the acquisition of one company by another. The difference, if any, between the fair value of the identifiable net asset purchased and the amount paid is recorded as goodwill. The acquiring company reports the results of operations of the acquisition from the date it is acquired.

The pooling-of-interests method of accounting for a business combination reflects the union of ownership between the entities involved. The pooling is accomplished primarily by the issuance of common voting stock of the acquiring company. Goodwill is never recorded in a pooling of interests, because the assets and liabilities of the companies involved are carried forward at their recorded amounts. Results of operations are restated for prior periods as if the entities involved had always been combined.

Purchase Method

Business combinations accounted for by the purchase method are recorded at cost. The determination of cost is usually based on the fair value of the property acquired or the fair value of the property given up, whichever is more clearly evident. An asset acquired for cash is recorded at the amount disbursed. In an exchange of assets where no cash is involved, cost is determined by the fair value of the assets given up or received, whichever is more clearly evident. If stock is issued in exchange for assets, cost is determined by the fair value of the assets acquired, which is tantamount to the consideration received for the stock issued.

> **OBSERVATION:** *FASB Technical Bulletin 84-1 concludes that the acquisition of the results of an R&D arrangement through the issuance of capital stock should be accounted for at the fair value of the stock issued, or at the fair value of the consideration received, whichever is more clearly evident.*

The cost of a liability assumed in a business combination is the present value of the amount that will eventually be paid. The difference between the fixed rate of debt securities assumed and the effective or current yield rate for comparable securities should be recorded as a premium or a discount (APB-21).

The market price of traded securities is usually clear evidence of fair value. However, the market price of a traded security issued in a business combination may have to be adjusted for the quantity issued, price fluctuations, and issue costs. A good barometer for fair value may be the average market price for a period before and after the business combination. In addition, independent appraisals are frequently useful in determining fair value.

Registration and issuing costs of equity securities issued in a business combination accounted for by the purchase method are deducted from the fair value of such securities. All direct costs of the acquisition are included as part of the total cost of the acquisition.

The recorded cost of an acquisition is equal to the determinable amount of cash and other net assets that are unconditionally surrendered at the date of acquisition. Any contingent additional consideration is fully disclosed in the financial statements but is not recorded as a liability. Contingently issuable debt or equity securities are not shown as outstanding until the contingency is definitely resolved. The fact that contingently issuable debt or equity securities are held by an independent escrow agent does not alter the treatment that such securities are not considered outstanding.

Contingent considerations may be based on maintaining or achieving specific earning levels over future periods or may be based on a security's maintaining or achieving a specific market price.

When a contingent consideration based on earnings is achieved, the acquiring company records the current fair value of the additional consideration. At this juncture, it is more than likely that the increase in the cost of the acquisition will be in the form of goodwill. In this event, the goodwill should be amortized over the remaining life of the acquired asset, but in no event more than 40 years (APB-17).

When a contingent consideration based on maintaining or exceeding a specific market price for the securities issued to consummate the acquisition is not achieved, the acquiring company will have to issue additional securities in accordance with the contingency arrangements. The issuance of the additional contingency securities is based on their then-current fair value but does not increase the overall cost of the acquisition, because the recorded cost of the original securities issued is reduced by the same amount. The only item that changes is the total number of shares issued for the acquisition. An example will clarify the situation.

A issues 1,000 shares of its common stock to a seller for an acquisition. The market price of the stock, at the date of the sale, was $12 per share, and A guarantees that, at the end of two years, if the market price is less than $12 per share, it will issue additional shares to make up any difference. Under the agreed-upon conditions A deposits 500 shares of stock with an independent escrow agent.

In accordance with the promulgated GAAP (APB-16), A records the acquisition at $12,000 ($12 per share x 1,000). At the end of the two years the market price of the stock is $10 per share, and the escrow agent delivers 200 shares to the seller in accordance with the seller's instructions. The remainder of the shares is returned to A.

A records the issuance of the 200 additional shares at the current market price of $10 per share for a total of $2,000, and correspondingly reduces the original stock issued to $10 per share, or a total of $10,000. The total acquisition price remains $12,000, and only the number of shares issued changes from 1,000 to 1,200.

In the event that debt securities are issued in an acquisition and that subsequently additional debt securities are issued as contingent consideration, the reduction in the value results in the necessity to record a discount on the debt securities. Discounts arising in this manner are amortized over the life of the securities, commencing from the date the additional securities are issued.

Contingent consideration that provides compensation for services or use of property are accounted for as expenses of the appropriate period on resolution of the contingency.

Interest or dividends paid or accrued on contingent securities during the contingency period are accounted for in the same manner as the underlying security. Therefore, interest expense or dividend distributions on contingent securities are not recorded until the contingency is resolved. In the event a contingency is resolved which results in the payment of an amount for interest or dividends on the contingent securities, that amount is added to the cost of the acquisition at the date of distribution.

When a savings and loan association is acquired in a business combination accounted for by the purchase method, the assets and liabilities acquired are recorded at their fair values on the date of acquisition. This is called the *separate valuation* method, as opposed to the *net spread* method, which values the purchase as a whole, based on the spread between interest rates received on the mortgage portfolio and interest rates paid on savings accounts. The net spread method is unacceptable for purposes of GAAP.

> **OBSERVATION:** *FASB-72 concludes that goodwill arising in the acquisition of a troubled banking or thrift institution should be*

amortized over a relatively short period because of the uncertainty about the nature and extent of the estimated future benefit related to the goodwill.

In applying the separate valuation method, receivables are recorded at their present values, using appropriate current interest rates, less allowances for uncollectibility and collection. Payables are recorded at the present values of amounts to be paid, determined at appropriate current interest rates.

Any portion of the purchase price that cannot be assigned to specifically identifiable tangible and intangible assets acquired, less liabilities assumed, shall be recorded as goodwill. Goodwill must be amortized by the straight-line method (APB-17), unless both the following conditions are met:

1. Part or all of the recorded goodwill includes one or more of the following factors which could not be separately determined:
   a. Capacity of existing savings accounts and loan accounts to generate future income and/or additional business or new business
   b. Nature of territory served
2. The anticipated benefits to be received from the factors in 1 above are expected to decline over their estimated lives

Only in those cases where both of the above conditions are met can accelerated methods be used to amortize the purchased goodwill (FASB Interpretation-9).

Allocating cost The total cost of an acquisition must be allocated to the individual assets acquired. Each identifiable asset is assigned a cost equal to its fair value. Contingent assets and liabilities are allocated a portion of the total cost of a purchased acquisition, if certain conditions are met (FASB-38). Independent appraisals and/or subsequent sales of acquired assets may provide evidence of fair value. Some methods of determining values are:

1. Inventories—Net realizable value less a reasonable profit, except raw materials, which should be valued at current replacement cost
2. Receivables—Present value of the amount that will be received, less an allowance for uncollectible accounts

3. Marketable securities—Net realizable value
4. Plant and equipment—Appraised values in accordance with intended use
5. Liabilities—Present value of the amount to be paid

An acquiring corporation should allocate costs to assets received and liabilities assumed as follows:

1. All identifiable assets and liabilities should be assigned a portion of the total cost based on fair value at the date of acquisition.
2. Any excess of cost over the amount assigned to identifiable assets less liabilities should be recorded as goodwill.
3. In the event that the assignable fair values of net assets acquired exceed the cost (sometimes referred to as negative goodwill), the noncurrent assets acquired (excluding long-term investments in marketable securities) should be reduced proportionately. Excess of net assets over cost (negative goodwill) should not be recorded unless all the noncurrent assets acquired (excluding long-term investments in marketable securities) have been reduced to zero.

The cost of a business combination accounted for by the purchase method includes the *direct costs* of acquisition (paragraph 76 of APB-16). Liabilities and commitments for expenses of closing a plant that is being acquired in an acquisition are direct costs of the acquisition and are recorded at the present values of amounts to be paid (paragraph 88i of APB-16). However, the cost incurred in closing facilities already owned by the acquiring company, which happens to duplicate other facilities that are being acquired in a business combination accounted for by the purchase method, are not recognized as part of the cost of acquisition (FASB Technical Bulletin 85-5).

Only out-of-pocket or incremental direct costs that are incurred in effecting the business combination are included in the cost of the acquisition (Accounting Interpretation No. 33 of Business Combinations). Direct out-of-pocket or incremental costs that are capitalized include finders' fees and fees paid to outside consultants for accounting, legal, engineering investigations, and appraisals (Accounting Interpretation No. 33 of Business Combinations). Other direct costs that are incurred in a business combination accounted for by the purchase method that are internal and recurring must be expensed as incurred.

Indirect and general expenses that are related to a business combination accounted for by the purchase method are deducted as incurred in determining net income (paragraph 76 of APB-16). Registration and issuing costs of equity securities issued in a business combination accounted for by the purchase method are deducted from the fair value of such securities (paragraph 76 of APB-16). Costs incurred in unsuccessful business combination negotiations are also deducted as incurred (Accounting Interpretation No. 33 of Business Combinations).

Acquisition of pension plan assets and liabilities   FASB-87 (Employers' Accounting for Pensions) amends APB-16 to provide that the assets and liabilities of a pension plan acquired by the purchase method of accounting shall no longer be accounted for in accordance with the provisions of APB-16 (paragraph 88h), but shall be accounted for in accordance with paragraph 74 of FASB-87, which is discussed below.

When a single-employer defined benefit pension plan is acquired as part of a business combination accounted for by the purchase method, an excess of the projected benefit obligation over the plan assets shall be recognized as a liability and an excess of plan assets over the projected benefit obligation shall be recognized as an asset. The recognition of a new liability or new asset by the purchaser, at the date of a business combination accounted for by the purchase method, results in the elimination of any (a) previously existing unrecognized net gain or loss, (b) unrecognized prior service cost, and (c) unrecognized net obligation or net asset that existed at the date of initial application of FASB-87.

In subsequent periods, the differences between the purchaser's net pension cost and contributions will reduce the new liability or new asset recognized at the date of combination to the extent that the previously unrecognized net gain or loss, unrecognized prior service cost, or unrecognized net obligation are considered in determining the amounts of contributions to the plan. In addition, the effects of an expected plan termination or curtailment shall be considered by the purchaser in calculating the amount of the projected benefit obligation at the date of a business combination accounted for by the purchase method.

FASB-106 makes a similar amendment to APB-16 relating to the purchase of assets and liabilities of a postretirement benefit plan other than pensions, discussed in the chapter entitled "Postretirement Benefits Other Than Pensions."

Contingent assets and liabilities   A portion of the total cost of acquiring an enterprise under the purchase method must be allocated to contingent assets, contingent liabilities, and contingent impairments of assets, if any, provided that the following conditions are met:

a. It is probable that the contingent item existed at the consummation date of the business combination accounted for by the purchase method.

b. After the consummation date, but prior to the end of the *allocation period* the facts in *a.* above are confirmed.

c. The amount of the asset, liability, or impairment can be reasonably estimated.

If the above conditions are met, a portion of the total cost of acquiring an enterprise under the purchase method must be allocated to any contingent items (FASB-38).

The *allocation period* is the period that is required by the purchaser to identify and quantify the acquired assets and assumed liabilities for the purposes of allocating the total cost of the acquisition in accordance with APB-16. The allocation period will not usually exceed one year from the closing date of the purchase transaction (FASB-38).

After the allocation period is over, any subsequent adjustments for contingent items must be included in net income of the period in which the adjustment is recognized. In other words, adjustments for contingent items arising from a purchased acquisition are charged to net income if they occur after the end of the allocation period.

FASB-38 is effective for adjustments that are determined in fiscal years beginning after December 15, 1980.

Disclosure for the Purchase Method

The following disclosures should be made in the period in which a business combination occurs and is accounted for by the purchase method:

1. Name, brief description, and total cost of the acquisition
2. Method of accounting, that is, the purchase method
3. Period for which results of operations of the acquisition are included in the income statement (usually starts at the date of acquisition)
4. Description of the plan for amortization of acquired goodwill
5. Other pertinent information such as contingent payments, options, or other commitments
6. Combining several minor acquisitions for disclosure purposes is acceptable

The following supplemental information should be disclosed in the notes to the financial statements of an acquiring company in the year of acquisition:

1. Results of operations for the current period, combining the acquisition as though it were acquired at the beginning of the period.
2. If comparative statements are presented, results of operations should include the acquisition as though it were acquired at the beginning of the comparative statement period.

> *OBSERVATION:* *FASB-79 (Elimination of Certain Disclosures for Business Combinations by Nonpublic Enterprises) provides that the above supplemental information does not have to be disclosed by nonpublic enterprises. For the purposes of FASB-79, a nonpublic enterprise is an enterprise other than one (a) whose debt or equity securities are traded in a public market on a stock exchange or in the over-the-counter market or (b) whose financial statements are filed with a regulatory agency in preparation for the sale of any class of securities.*

Purchase versus Pooling-of-Interests

A purchase of assets is accounted for differently from a purchase of a stock interest. In both cases, however, goodwill or negative goodwill can arise. A pooling-of-interests is accounted for in the same way whether there is an exchange of stock for stock or of stock for net assets. In addition, goodwill or negative goodwill is never recorded in a pooling-of-interests.

Purchase of assets   In the purchase of assets, goodwill is equal to the difference between the purchase price paid and the fair value of the identifiable net assets acquired. If the purchase price paid exceeds the fair value of the identifiable net assets acquired, the goodwill is positive and is recorded on the books as an asset. If the purchase price paid is less than the fair value of the identifiable net assets acquired, the goodwill is negative and it may or may not be recorded on the books as a deferred credit. Identifiable net assets are equal to the fair value of the acquired identifiable assets less the fair value of the assumed liabilities.

On July 1, 19X7, Jones Company sold all its net assets and business to Smith Corporation for $415,000. The following is Jones Company's balance sheet as of July 1, 19X7:

Balance Sheet

Cash	$ 20,000
Accounts receivable	72,000
Allowance for doubtful accounts	(8,000)
Inventory	120,000
Plant and equipment	260,000
Total assets	$464,000
Accounts payable	$ 60,000
Accrued expenses	5,000
Mortgage payable—plant	120,000
Common stock	200,000
Retained earnings	79,000
Total liabilities and equity	$464,000

Additional Information:

Confirmation of the accounts receivable revealed that $10,000 were uncollectible.

The physical inventory count was $138,000 (fair value).

The fair value of the plant and equipment was $340,000.

The journal entry to record the investment on the books of Smith Corporation is:

Investment in Jones Co. (100%)	$415,000	
Cash		$415,000

The computation of goodwill involved in the transaction is:

Computation of Goodwill

Assets	$464,000
Liabilities ($60,000 + $5,000 + $120,000)	185,000
Total	$279,000
Additional uncollectibles	(2,000)
Increase in inventory	18,000
Increase in plant and equipment	80,000
Adjusted net assets	$375,000
Cost of purchase	415,000
Goodwill	$ 40,000

Assume that the purchase price was $350,000.

Adjusted net assets	$375,000
Cost of purchase	350,000
Negative goodwill	$ 25,000

Negative goodwill is not recorded, because noncurrent assets (plant and equipment) are reduced to $315,000.

Negative goodwill should never be recorded unless all the noncurrent assets acquired, except long-term investments in marketable securities, have been proportionately reduced to zero.

If after reducing the noncurrent assets (except long-term investment in marketable securities) to zero a credit still remains, it should be classified as a deferred credit (excess of acquired stock over cost) and should be amortized to income over the period that is expected to benefit, but not to exceed 40 years (APB-17).

Goodwill may not be written off as a lump sum to capital surplus or retained earnings, nor be reduced to a nominal amount, at or immediately after acquisition.

Purchase of a stock interest The percentage of book value acquired is subtracted from the purchase price, and any residue is goodwill or negative goodwill.

ABC Corporation purchased for $1,500,000 90% of the common stock and 50% of the preferred stock of XYZ Corporation. At the date of acquisition, XYZ Corporation's stockholders' equity was:

Stockholders' Equity

Common stock, 100,000 shares, $5 par, all authorized, issued, and outstanding	$ 500,000
5% preferred stock, 10,000 shares, all authorized, issued, and outstanding	1,000,000
Paid-in capital	200,000
Retained earnings	300,000
Total stockholders' equity	$2,000,000

The computation of the goodwill involved in the transaction is:

Computation of Goodwill

	Minority Interests (10%)	Preferred Stock	ABC Corporation (90%)
Common stock	$ 50,000		$ 450,000
Preferred stock		$500,000	500,000
Paid-in capital	20,000		180,000
Retained earnings	30,000		270,000
Totals	$100,000	$500,000	$1,400,000
Cost of 90% common and 50% preferred			1,500,000
Goodwill			$ 100,000

The journal entry to record the transaction is:

Investment in XYZ Corporation	$1,500,000	
Cash		$1,500,000

Goodwill of $100,000 was involved.

Goodwill is not necessarily the difference between cost and the book value of an investment, unless the book value is equal to the fair value of the underlying assets. The underlying assets represented by an investment must be individually assigned a fair value at the date of acquisition, and if the assigned fair values are less than the amount of the investment, the difference is goodwill. For consolidation purposes, the acquisition of a stock investment may be considered the purchase price paid for an interest in the underlying net assets of a business.

It must be remembered that if any excess of cost over acquired book value is allocated to depreciable or amortizable assets, the depreciation or amortization expense of subsequent periods must be increased to spread the amount of such excess over the remaining life of the assets.

If after assigning values to the underlying assets of an investment there is resulting goodwill, it must be amortized over a period of 40 years or less, starting from the date of the acquisition of the investment. *However, since consolidating adjustments and eliminations are never posted on the books, it is necessary to reduce the beginning consolidated retained earnings, in the years subsequent to the first year, by the amount of depreciation or amortization of prior years.*

Assuming that P was amortizing $10,000 of the excess of cost over book value (goodwill) over a 10-year period, the consolidated adjustment for the second full year would be:

Consolidated retained earnings	$1,000	
Amortization, current year	1,000	
Excess of cost over book value		$2,000

Goodwill should not be recorded where it is obvious that the underlying asset in a stock interest purchase or the net assets in a straight asset purchase are undervalued. Any excess cost over book value at the date of acquisition should be assigned specifically to these undervalued assets.

When any excess cost over book value (goodwill) is assigned to specific assets, it must be depreciated or amortized on the consolidated working papers.

Excess cost over book value of $25,000 is assigned (1) $5,000 to a parcel of land and (2) $20,000 to the building located on the land. The building has a 20-year life, and the following adjusting journal entry must be made on the consolidated working papers (assume one full year):

Land	$ 5,000	
Building	20,000	
Investment account		$25,000
Depreciation	$ 1,000	
Accumulated depreciation		$ 1,000

Since consolidated adjusting journal entries are never posted on the books, this journal entry must be repeated each year.

In the final year, when the building is completely depreciated, the following entry is made on the consolidated working papers:

Accumulated depreciation	$20,000	
Fixed asset–building		$20,000

The entry for the land remains and is repeated each year on the consolidated working papers as long as the land is part of the assets of the consolidated group.

All transactions for cash or stock are purchases except the exchange, by the acquirer, of common voting stock for 90% or more of the common voting stock or all of the net assets of the seller (pooling-of-interests).

In other words, all transactions are purchases except those which qualify as a pooling-of-interests.

In a purchase, operations of the investee are taken into consideration by the investor, from the date of the purchase. There is no retroactive restatement of any financial statements.

Different Classes of Capital Stock

The main point to remember in computing a parent's investment in a subsidiary is to isolate those elements of the subsidiary's stockholders' equity to which the parent company is actually entitled. For instance, if the subsidiary had minority interests, they would have to be excluded in computing the parent's investment. Other items that must be considered are different classes of stock, dividends in arrears, and liquidating dividends. If another class of stock is participating, it must share in the retained earnings of the subsidiary to the extent of its participation. If another class of stock is cumulative as to dividends and dividends are in arrears, the amount of dividends in arrears must be deducted from retained earnings before determining the parent's interest in the subsidiary's stockholders' equity.

The following are guidelines for preferred stock issues:

1. Nonparticipating and noncumulative preferred stocks require no apportionment of retained earnings.
2. Nonparticipating and cumulative preferred stocks require an apportionment only to the extent of any dividends in arrears.
3. Participating preferred stock requires an apportionment of retained earnings, under all circumstances. The apportionment is made on the basis of the total dollar amount of the par or stated values of the securities involved.

On January 1, 19X7, P acquires for $5,200,000 80% of the common stock and 60% of the 5% preferred stock of S. On the date of acquisition the stockholders' equity of S consisted of:

	Shares	*Dollars*
Common stock ($1 par)	1,000,000	$1,000,000
5% preferred stock ($100 par) nonparticipating and cumulative	50,000	5,000,000
3% preferred stock ($10 par) fully participating and noncumulative	200,000	2,000,000
Retained earnings		2,000,000

The 5% preferred stock has a liquidating preference value of $105 per share and dividends of $350,000 are in arrears. Determine the parent's share of the subsidiary's stockholders' equity as of the date of acquisition.

<u>Apportionment of Retained Earnings</u>

Total retained earnings	$2,000,000
Less: Dividends in arrears—Preferred	350,000
Balance	$1,650,000
Less: Liquidating preference dividend $5	250,000
Balance	$1,400,000
Less: 20% minority interest	280,000
Balance to apportion	$1,120,000
3% preferred, 2/3	746,667
Balance to P Company	$ 373,333

The 3% preferred stock ($10 par) participates fully with the common stock ($1 par) in the earnings of the company. The apportionment is made on the basis of the total par or stated value dollar amounts of the common and 3% preferred, which are $1,000,000 and $2,000,000, respectively. Therefore, the apportionment of retained earnings after all adjustments is 1/3 to common shareholders and 2/3 to the 3% participating preferred shareholders.

<u>Computation of P's Investment</u>

	Minority Interests 20%	5% Preferred	Participating Preferred	P Company 80%
Common stock	$200,000			$ 800,000
5% preferred		$5,000,000		
3% preferred–participating			$2,000,000	
Retained earnings	280,000		746,667	373,333
Dividend–arrears		350,000		
Liquidating dividend		250,000		
Totals	$480,000	$5,600,000	$2,746,667	$1,173,333
60% of preferred to P		3,360,000		3,360,000
Totals	$480,000	$2,240,000	$2,746,667	$4,533,333
Cost of 80% of common and 60% of preferred				5,200,000
Goodwill				$ 666,667

Acquisition of Stock Directly from Subsidiary

Sometimes a stock interest is acquired directly from the investee. That is, a subsidiary will sell some of its own capital stock to another company. In this event, it must be remembered that the amount paid for capital stock must be added to the stockholders' equity before determining the acquirer's stock interest.

Company S had 100,000 shares of $1 par capital stock outstanding ($100,000) and $60,000 of retained earnings. On January 1, 19X7, Company S authorized an additional 200,000 shares of capital stock ($1 par) and sold them to P Company for $250,000. Determine P Company's stock interest in S Company.

Computation of S Company's Stockholders' Equity

Common stock ($1 par) (300,000 shares)	$300,000
Paid-in capital—common	50,000
Retained earnings	60,000
Total	$410,000

Computation of P's Investment in S

	Minority Interest 33 1/3%	P Company 66 2/3%
Common stock	$100,000	$200,000
Paid-in capital	16,667	33,333
Retained earnings	20,000	40,000
Totals	$136,667	$273,333
Cost of P's 66 2/3%		250,000
Negative goodwill		$ 23,333

Step-by-Step Acquisition

A corporation may acquire a subsidiary in more than one transaction. In this case, any goodwill or negative goodwill involved must be computed at the time of each step-by-step transaction. When control is achieved, it is necessary to adjust to the equity method any earlier step acquisition accounted for by the cost method. The result of this treatment is that the parent's portion of the undistributed earnings of the subsidiary for the period prior to achieving control is added to the investment account of the parent.

Assume that Company P acquired an interest in Company S in two steps: (1) acquired 20% of the outstanding common stock for $200,000; and (2) the following year acquired an additional 60% for $500,000. At the dates of acquisition, the equity book value for Company S was $900,000 and $1,100,000 respectively.

Computation of Excess of Cost over Book Value

First Acquisition

Cost of 20% acquired	$200,000
20% of equity book value of $900,000	180,000
Excess of cost over book value (goodwill)	$ 20,000

Second Acquisition

Cost of 60% acquired	$500,000
60% of equity book value of $1,100,000	660,000
Excess of book value over cost (negative goodwill)	($160,000)

Actually, as of the date of the second acquisition, Company P had an investment of $700,000 for 80% of Company S. Company S at the second acquisition date had an equity book value of $1,100,000, and Company P's 80% is $880,000, for which it paid $700,000. If Company P had recorded its first acquisition of 20% by the equity method, it would have recorded its 20% of the $200,000 increase in Company S's book value (assuming that no dividends or other distributions were made to Company P by Company S). Thus the adjusted equity in Company S on the books of Company P would include the original $200,000 purchase price plus 20% of the $200,000 increase in book value (from $900,000 to $1,100,000) or a total of $220,000 ($180,000 + $40,000). The cost of the second acquisition of 60% for $500,000 and the adjusted basis for the 20% at $220,000 equals $720,000, which represents 80% of $1,100,000, or $880,000. The difference of $160,000 is the excess of book value over cost (negative goodwill) indicated by the computation for the second acquisition of 60%.

Stock Exchanges – Companies Under Common Control

In an exchange of stock between two of its subsidiaries, one or both of which is partially owned, a parent company should account for its minority interest at historical cost, if the minority shareholders are not a party to the exchange transaction (FASB Technical Bulletin 85-5). Under this circumstance, the minority interest remains outstanding and is not affected by the transaction. FASB Technical Bulletin 85-5 also reconfirms that the acquisition of all or part of a minority interest between companies under common control, regardless of how acquired, is never considered a transfer or exchange by the companies under common control (Accounting Interpretation No. 39 of APB-16).

The term *business combination* does not apply to the transfer of net assets or the exchange of shares between companies under common control (paragraph 5 of APB-16). Therefore, the acquisition of some or all of the stock held by minority shareholders of a subsidiary is not a business combination. However, paragraph 43 of APB-16 prescribes exactly how such a transaction should be reported. Under paragraph 43 of APB-16, the acquisition of some or all of the stock held by minority stockholders of a subsidiary, whether acquired by the parent, the subsidiary itself, or another affiliate, should be accounted for by the purchase method (fair value). Under this circumstance, the minority interest is affected by the transaction and the result is that a new minority interest is created in a different subsidiary. Accounting Interpretation No. 26 of APB-16 describes the following transactions in which purchase accounting applies: (a) a parent company exchanges its common stock or assets or debt for common stock held by minority shareholders of its subsidiary, (b) the subsidiary buys as treasury stock the common stock held by minority shareholders, or (c) another subsidiary of the parent exchanges its common stock or assets or debt for common stock held by the minority shareholders of an affiliated subsidiary.

Pooling-of-Interests Method

The purchase method and the pooling-of-interests method are both acceptable in accounting for business combinations, but not as alternatives. A business combination either qualifies for the pooling-of-interests method or is treated as a purchase. *Part-purchase and part-pooling of the same business combination is unacceptable* (APB-16).

> **OBSERVATION:** *The promulgated GAAP requirements for using the pooling-of-interests method are detailed and quite restrictive.*

Conditions for the Pooling-of-Interests Method

1. Each of the combining companies must be autonomous and not have been a subsidiary or division of another corporation within two years before the plan of combination is initiated.

The initiation date is the *earlier of:*

   a. The date of public announcement, or notification to the shareholders of any one of the combining companies, the major terms of the plan including the ratio of exchange or a formula which provides for the ratio of exchange
   b. The date that shareholders of the company being acquired are notified directly or by newspaper advertisement of the exchange offer (APB Interpretation of APB-16)

A new company, incorporated within the last two years, qualifies unless it was in any way a successor to a company that would not have been considered autonomous.

It is irrelevant whether a parent company or any of its wholly owned subsidiaries distribute voting common stock to effect a combination, as long as the condition of autonomy is met.

> **OBSERVATION:** *Although the promulgated GAAP specifically states "wholly owned subsidiary," an APB interpretation (non-promulgated) suggests that substantially all the subsidiary's outstanding voting stock be owned by the parent and under no circumstances would less than 90% be considered substantially all.*

A judicial order to divest is an exception to the rule, and both the divesting company and the acquiring company will be considered autonomous.

2. At the date of initiation and at the date of consummation of the plan of combination, each combining company is independent of each other combining company. An intercorporate investment of 10% or less of the total outstanding voting common stock of any combining company is acceptable and will not impair the independence test.

An exchange by a partially owned subsidiary of its common stock for the outstanding voting stock of its parent (a *downstream merger*) does not qualify as a pooling-of-interests, because it fails to meet the independence rule (FASB Technical Bulletin 85-5).

In addition, the term *business combination* does not apply to the transfer of net assets or the exchange of shares between companies under common control (paragraph 5 of APB-16). Therefore, the exchange by a partially owned subsidiary of its common stock for the outstanding voting common stock of its parent (a downstream merger) cannot be accounted for as a business combination. However, paragraph 43 of APB-16 prescribes exactly how such a transaction should be reported. Under paragraph 43 of APB-16, the acquisition of some or all of the stock held by minority stockholders of a subsidiary, whether acquired by the parent, the subsidiary itself, or another affiliate, should be accounted for by the purchase method (fair value).

Accounting Interpretation No. 26 of APB-16 specifically requires that purchase accounting be applied to downstream mergers. Under Accounting Interpretation No. 26, the exchange by a partially owned subsidiary of its common stock for the outstanding voting stock of its parent should be accounted for as if the parent had exchanged its common stock for common stock held by minority shareholders of its subsidiary. Purchase accounting is applied whether a subsidiary acquires its parent or a parent acquires the minority interest of the subsidiary, because the end result is a single shareholder group. Furthermore, if a new corporation exchanged its common stock for the common stock of the parent and the common stock of the subsidiary held by the minority shareholders, the accounting treatment would be the same.

> **OBSERVATION:** *The promulgated GAAP provides that if a company held as an investment a minority interest of 50% or less on October 31, 1970, and initiates a plan of combination within five years after that date, the resulting combination could be accounted for as a pooling-of-interests, provided all other provisions of the promulgated GAAP were complied with. This section is referred to as the "grandfather clause," and the five-year limitation was deleted by FASB-10.*

3. After a plan is initiated, it must be completed within one year in accordance with a specific plan, or completed in a single transaction.

> **OBSERVATION:** *A pooling-of-interests is, in essence, a combining of existing shareholders' voting common stock in which the separate shareholder interests lose their identity, resulting in the mutual combination of risks and rights.*
>
> *Any change in the exchange ratio or terms thereof creates a new initiation date for the plan of combination. Any change in the*

relative voting rights that result in preferential treatment for some common stockholder groups is incompatible to a pooling-of-interests.

Litigation or proceedings of a governmental authority that delay the completion of a plan of combination are excepted from the one-year rule, providing they are beyond the control of any of the combining companies.

4. At the consummation date of the plan the acquiring company offers and issues its majority class of stock (voting rights) for no less than 90% of the *voting common stock interests* of the combining company being acquired. The 90% or more of the voting common stock interests being acquired is determined at the date the plan is consummated.

> **OBSERVATION:** *An APB Interpretation, which is not promulgated GAAP, suggests that the consummation date is the date the assets are transferred to the issuing company.*

This requirement of 90% or more of the voting common stock interests being acquired at consummation date can be related to the requirement that intercorporate investments of 10% or less, in any company being acquired, is acceptable for the independence rule (see condition 2 above).

The determination of whether the acquiring company acquires 90% or more of the outstanding voting common stock interests at the date of consummation excludes the following shares of the company being acquired:

a. Any shares acquired for any form of consideration and held at the date of initiation of the plan of combination by the acquiring parent or its subsidiaries

b. Any shares acquired and held after the date of initiation by the acquiring parent or its subsidiaries, except those shares acquired by the issuance of the acquiring company's own voting stock

> **OBSERVATION:** *In other words, intercorporate investments in the company being acquired, except those acquired by the issuance of voting common stock after the date of initiation, are excluded in calculating the number of voting common stock interests that are exchanged at the consummation date.*

> *The larger the intercorporate investment an acquirer has in an acquisition that was acquired prior to the initiation date, the more difficult the 90% will be to achieve.*

An investment in the voting common stock of the acquiring company held by a company being acquired must be restated in an equivalent number of shares of the company being acquired. The equivalent number of shares is determined by the exchange ratio of the plan of combination and then deducted from the number of voting common shares actually exchanged on the consummation date. The resulting number of shares of the company being acquired must equal 90% or more of its total outstanding voting common shares at the date of consummation.

B has 100,000 shares of voting common stock outstanding and owns an investment in A of 1,000 shares of voting common stock. A initiated a plan of combination to acquire B by offering four shares of its voting common stock (majority class) for each share of B's voting common stock. At the date of consummation, 91,000 shares of B's stock are tendered to A. However, the 1,000 shares of voting common stock of A held by B must be restated into an equivalent amount of B's stock in accordance with the exchange ratio of four to one, which equals 250 shares. In other words, at consummation date B is theoretically the owner of 250 shares of its own stock when restated in terms of the exchange ratio. The 250 shares are deducted from the 91,000 shares tendered, which equals 90,750 shares, and then compared to 90% of the outstanding voting common stock of B at the date of consummation, which in this case is 90,000 shares (90% of 100,000).

As a result, A's acquisition of 91,000 shares is restated to 90,750 shares, which meets the 90% requirement, and the transaction can be accounted for as a pooling-of-interests.

When two or more companies are acquired in a plan of combination, each condition necessary for a pooling-of-interests must be met by each company. However, 90% of each combining company must be exchanged for voting common stock of the acquiring company. Intercompany investments between any of the combining companies are excluded in calculating whether 90% or more of the voting common stock interests are exchanged, but are included in computing the total amount of voting common stock interests outstanding.

A plan of combination may not include a pro rata cash distribution but may within limits include a cash distribution for fractional shares and for shares purchased from dissenting shareholders. Cash may also be used in a plan of combination to retire, or redeem, callable debt and equity securities.

A transfer of all the net assets at the date the plan is consummated in exchange for voting common stock (majority class) of the acquiring company qualifies as an exchange of substantially all (90% or more) of the *voting common stock interests*.

Although the requirement is for *all the net assets* of the company being acquired, temporary cash, receivables, and marketable securities may be retained to settle liabilities, disputed items, or contingencies. In a net asset transaction, both voting common stock and other stock may be issued by the acquiring company, if the company whose net assets are being acquired has both voting common stock and other stock outstanding. However, the voting common stock and other stock must be issued in proportion to the voting common stock and other stock outstanding, of the company being acquired, at the date of consummation of the plan of combination.

In determining the independence rule (see condition 2 above) in an exchange of voting common stock for net assets, intercorporate investments of 10% or less are evaluated in terms of the issuing company's voting common stock, as follows:

a. The number of voting common shares being issued at the date of consummation for all the net assets is allocated between outstanding voting common stock and the other outstanding stock if any. The net assets being acquired should include any intercorporate investment in the acquiring company.

b. A ratio is computed between the number of shares of voting common stock outstanding, at the date of consummation, for the company whose net assets are being acquired, and the number of voting common shares of the acquirer allocated (in a above) to the acquisition of voting common stock interests.

c. An intercorporate investment of the issuer in the voting common stock of the company whose assets are being acquired is restated in equivalent shares of the ratio computed in b above.

d. An intercorporate investment in the issuing company by the company whose net assets are being acquired is not restated, because the number of shares is already stated in terms of the issuing company's stock.

e. In order to meet the 90% test, all intercorporate investments (when restated in terms of the stock of the issuing company) cannot exceed 10% of the number of issued shares of voting common stock allocated and issued for the acquisition of the voting common stock interests being acquired.

P owns 12,000 shares of S's voting common stock that was acquired prior to initiation date. P issues 100,000 shares of its voting common stock to acquire all the net assets of S, which include 1,000 shares of P's voting common stock. The 100,000 shares of P's stock is allocated 70% to outstanding voting common stock and 30% to other outstanding stock. S has 210,000 shares of voting common stock outstanding.

P has allocated 70,000 (70% of 100,000) shares of its stock to acquire the 210,000 shares of S's voting common stock at the consummation date. This results in a ratio of one share of P for three shares of S.

The 12,000 shares of S that are owned by P are converted to 4,000 shares of P. The 1,000 shares of P that are owned by S are already stated in P's stock. The 4,000 equivalent shares and the 1,000 shares of P equal 5,000 shares and are compared to 10% of the 70,000 shares of P's voting common stock that have been allocated for the acquisition of the voting common stock interests in S. The 5,000 equivalent shares of P are less than the 10% of the 70,000 shares allocated by P for the acquisition and thus the combination qualifies for a pooling of interests.

---

5. No changes in the equity interests of the voting common stock of any combining company may be made in contemplation of a pooling-of-interests. This restriction is for a period beginning two years prior to the initiation date of the plan of combination and for the period between the initiation date and the consummation date.

Normal distributions based on earnings and/or prior policy are permitted.

The organizational form of a mutual or cooperative enterprise does not have equity interests of voting common stock. The conversion of a mutual or cooperative enterprise to equity interests of voting common stock represents a change in the form of organization, not a change in the equity interests of voting common stock. Therefore, the conversion of a mutual or cooperative enterprise to stock ownership within two years before a plan of combination is initiated or between the dates a combination is initiated and consummated does not preclude accounting for such a combination as a pooling-of-interests (FASB Technical Bulletin 85-5).

6. The reacquisition of voting common stock by any combining company is allowed except for purposes of business combinations. In addition, any reacquisition of voting common stock between the initiation and the consummation dates must be no more than a normal amount.

A normal amount of reacquired shares is determined by reference to a company's pattern of reacquisition prior to the initiation of a plan of combination.

A systematic pattern of reacquisition of voting common stock established for stock option or compensation plans is permitted.

After a plan is initiated, the acquisition of voting common stock of the issuing company by any combining company is considered the same as if the issuing company reacquired its own shares.

The important point in this provision of APB-16 is that shares are not reacquired in substance or form to effect a business combination.

7. Each common stockholder to a plan of combination must receive a voting common stock interest exactly in proportion to his or her voting common stock interest prior to the combination.

A business combination cannot be accounted for as a pooling-of-interests if the issuer retains a right of first refusal to repurchase the shares issued in certain circumstances, even if the shares issued are identical to other outstanding common shares (FASB Technical Bulletin 85-5).

Generally, restrictions imposed on the sale of stock to the public in compliance with governmental regulations do not violate the provisions of APB-16, providing that subsequent to the combination the issuer has started the process of registering the stock or had agreed to register the stock (Accounting Interpretation No. 11 of Business Combinations).

8. The common stockholders to a plan of combination must receive the voting rights they are entitled to and must not be deprived or restricted in any way from exercising those rights.

9. The entire plan of combination must be effectuated on the date of consummation.

This provision prohibits contingent shares that are to be issued at a later date, except for contingently issuable shares which will be used to adjust differences in amounts represented at consummation date by management. These differences are recorded as an adjustment to combined stockholders' equity and reflected in net income of the period of resolution or as a prior-period adjustment of the correction of an error of a prior period.

10. After the combination is consummated, any transaction, implied or explicit, that is inconsistent with the combining of the interests of the common stockholders counteracts the effect of combining stockholders' interests.

Application of the Pooling-of-Interests Method

All the conditions for a pooling-of-interests must be met before a business combination can be accounted for as such. The mechanics of applying the pooling-of-interests method are:

1. At the date the combination is consummated, assets, liabilities, and stockholders' equity are combined and recorded at historical cost in conformity with GAAP.
2. If an acquiring company issued treasury stock to effect part or all of a plan of combination, the treasury stock must first be treated as though it were retired (gain or loss is recorded), and then it is considered the same as any other previously unissued shares.
3. Intercorporate investments in the acquiring company are treated as treasury stock in combined financial statements. Intercorporate investments, other than in the acquiring company stock, are treated as retired stock of the combination.
4. All financial statements for the period in which the combination occurred should be reported as though the combination occurred at the beginning of the period.
5. Prior-year financial statements should be restated on a combined basis.
6. Expenses relating to the combination are expenses of the combined group and should be deducted from combined net income. Examples of such expenses are registration fees, finders' and consultants' fees, and costs and losses resulting from combining the separate companies.
7. If within two years after a combination, a material profit or loss results from the disposal of a significant portion of the assets of the previously separate companies, full disclosure, as an extraordinary item (net of tax effects), should be made in the combined financial statements.
8. Prior to the consummation date of a plan of combination, the investment on the books of the acquiring company (investor)

should be accounted for by the equity method, if acquired for voting common stock, and at cost if the investment was acquired for cash.

Under the pooling-of-interests method, the cost of an acquisition is the total par or stated value of the capital stock issued by the acquirer to effect the combination. This amount is debited to an investment account and the appropriate capital stock account is credited. Fair values are ignored and goodwill is never recorded in a pooling-of-interests.

In a consolidated balance sheet the capital stock account will always be equal to the total par or stated value of the outstanding shares of the acquiring company. Therefore, the first adjustment to the investment account on the consolidated working papers is to eliminate the capital stock account of the acquired company. If the capital stock account of the acquired company exceeds the debit in the investment account (not usually likely), any balance is transferred to combined contributed capital by debiting the capital stock account and crediting combined contributed capital.

It is much more likely that the debit in the investment account will exceed the capital stock account of the acquired company. In this event, the excess is debited to any other contributed capital account of the acquired company and if an excess still exists, the balance is debited to consolidated retained earnings. Obviously, no amount should exist in the investment account after these adjustments.

Disclosure for Pooling-of-Interests Combinations

The following disclosures should be made to the financial statements in the period in which the pooling occurs:

1. Brief description of the companies combined
2. Method of accounting for the combination, that is, the pooling-of-interests method
3. Description and amount of shares of stock issued to effect the combination
4. Details of the results of operations for each separate company, prior to the date of combination, that are included in the current combined net income
5. Description of the nature of adjustments in net assets of the combining companies to adopt the same accounting policies
6. If any of the combining companies changed their fiscal year

as a result of the combination, full disclosure should be made of any changes in stockholders' equity that were excluded from the reported results of operations.

7. Revenue and earnings previously reported by the acquiring company should be reconciled with the amounts shown in the combined financial statements.

8. Any plan of combination that has been initiated but not consummated at a balance sheet date must be fully disclosed, including the effects of the plan on combined operations and any changes in accounting methods.

In the period that a pooling-of-interests is consummated, recurring intercompany transactions should be eliminated to the greatest extent possible from the beginning of the period. However, nonrecurring intercompany transactions involving long-term assets and liabilities need not be eliminated, but in that event they should be fully disclosed (APB-16).

CASH FLOW STATEMENT

Overview

FASB-95 (Statement of Cash Flows) requires that a *statement of cash flows* be included as part of a full set of general purpose financial statements that are externally issued by any business enterprise. FASB-95 supersedes APB-19, which had required the inclusion of a statement of changes in financial position as part of a full set of general purpose financial statements. All business enterprises are required to comply with the provisions of FASB-95 except not-for-profit organizations.

FASB-102 was issued to provide exemptions from the provisions of FASB-95 to (a) certain employee benefit plans that report their financial information in accordance with FASB-35 (Accounting and Reporting by Defined Benefit Pension Plans) and (b) highly liquid investment companies that meet certain conditions. Employee benefit plans and investment companies that meet the conditions specified in FASB-102 are not required to include a statement of cash flows as part of their complete financial presentation.

FASB-102 also provides that cash receipts and cash payments resulting from transactions in certain securities, other assets, and loans acquired specifically for resale must be classified as *operating cash flows* in a statement of cash flows. The cash receipts and cash payments required by FASB-102 to be classified as operating cash flows result from acquisitions and sales of (a) securities and other assets that are acquired specifically for resale and are carried at market value in a trading account and (b) loans that are acquired specifically for resale and are carried at market value or the lower of cost or market value.

FASB-102 is effective for financial statement issued on or after March 1, 1989, and earlier application of the provisions of FASB-102 is encouraged. Restatement of comparative amounts in earlier period financial statements in order to comply with the provisions of FASB-102 is required.

FASB-104 amends FASB-95 to permit banks, savings institutions, and credit unions to report net cash flows from certain transactions instead of gross cash flows required by the provisions of FASB-95. FASB-104 also amends FASB-95 by allowing an enterprise that meets certain conditions, to classify the cash flow of a hedging transaction and the cash flow of its related hedged item in the same category of cash flow (operating activity, investing activity, or financing activity).

Background

Over the years, problems had developed in preparing statements of changes in financial position in accordance with the provisions of APB-19. There was a significant lack of comparability between different statement presentations because under APB-19, *funds* could be defined as either cash, cash and temporary investments, quick assets, or working capital. Another problem was the diversity of statement formats that was permitted by APB-19. Many felt that APB-19 did not contain clear objectives for preparing the statement of changes in financial position.

FASB-95 represents the latest effort of the accounting profession to improve the preparation of cash flow statements. Based on a four-to-three vote of the seven-member Financial Accounting Standards Board, FASB-95 is effective for annual financial statements for fiscal years ending on or after July 16, 1988.

FASB-95 contains a rigid set of guidelines, which contrasts with the flexibility that was permitted under APB-19. The new cash flow statement requires that an enterprise report its *gross* cash receipts and cash payments from operating, investing, and financing activities. In addition, the statement of cash flows must also contain a clear explanation of the changes in cash and cash equivalents for the period.

Statement of Cash Flows—General

Under the provisions of FASB-95, a statement of cash flows shall clearly specify the amount of net cash provided or used by an enterprise during a period from (a) operating activities, (b) investing activities, and (c) financing activities. The statement of cash flows shall clearly indicate the net effect of those cash flows on the enterprise's cash and cash equivalents. A reconciliation of beginning and ending cash and cash equivalents shall be included in the statement of cash flows. FASB-95 also requires that the statement of cash flows contain separate related disclosures about all investing and financing activities of an enterprise that affect its financial position but do not directly affect its cash flows during the period.

Descriptive terms such as *cash* or *cash and cash equivalents* shall be used in the statement of cash flows and ambiguous terms such as *funds* shall not be used. A statement of cash flows shall contain an explanation of the change during the period in an enterprise's cash and cash equivalents. The total amounts of cash and cash equivalents at the beginning and end of the period shown in the statement of cash flows shall be the same amounts of cash and cash equivalents at the beginning and end of the period that were previously reflected in the statement of changes in financial position.

Under FASB-95, cash equivalents are short-term, highly liquid investments that are (a) readily convertible to known amounts of cash and (b) so near their maturities that they present insignificant risk of changes in value because of changes in interest rates. As a general rule, only investments with original maturities of three months or less qualify as cash equivalents. Examples of items commonly considered to be cash equivalents are Treasury bills, commercial paper, money market funds, and federal funds sold.

> **OBSERVATION:** *An enterprise shall disclose its policy for determining which items are treated as cash equivalents. Any change in that policy shall be accounted for as a change in accounting principle and shall be effected by restating financial statements of earlier years that are presented for comparative purposes. FASB-95 does not specify the accounting treatment of amounts in bank accounts that are unavailable for immediate withdrawal, such as compensating balances in the bank account of a borrower. Apparently these amounts should be treated as cash, with disclosure of any material restrictions on withdrawal. This treatment is provided by SEC Regulation S-X, Rule 5-02 (1).*

Gross and net cash flows   As a general rule, FASB-95 requires an enterprise to report the gross amounts of its cash receipts and cash payments on the statement of cash flows. The gross amounts of cash receipts and cash payments are usually presumed to be more relevant than net amounts. However, it may be sufficient in some circumstances to report the net amount of certain assets and liabilities instead of their gross amounts. Under FASB-95, the net changes during a period may be reported if knowledge of the gross cash receipts and payments is not necessary to understand the enterprise's operating, investing, and financing activities.

The net changes during a period may be reported for those assets and liabilities in which turnover is quick, amounts are large, and maturities are short. Items that qualify for net reporting because their turnover is quick, their amounts are large, and their maturities are short are cash receipts and cash payments pertaining to (a) investments (other than cash equivalents), (b) loans receivable, and (c) debt, providing that the original maturity of the asset or liability is three months or less.

Banks, savings institutions, and credit unions   Instead of reporting gross amounts of cash flows on their statements of cash flows, as required by FASB-95, banks, savings institutions, and credit unions are permitted by the provisions of FASB-104 to report net amounts of cash flows that result from (a) deposits and deposit withdrawals with other financial institutions, (b) time deposits accepted and repayments of deposits, and (c) loans to customers and principal collections of loans. This provision of FASB-104 gives an enterprise the following choices in reporting cash flows on its statement of cash flows:

1. To report the gross amount of all cash receipts and disbursements
2. To report the net cash flows in the limited situations allowed by FASB-95, such as loans with maturities of three months or less, and to report gross amounts for all other transactions
3. If the enterprise is a bank, savings institution, or credit union, to report net cash flows in the limited situations allowed by FASB-104, such as time deposits, and to report gross amounts for all other transactions
4. If the enterprise is a bank, savings institution, or credit union, to report net cash flows in the situations allowed by FASB-95 and also those allowed by FASB-104, and to report gross amounts for all other transactions.

> **OBSERVATION:** *The choices outlined above may produce a serious lack of comparability among the statements of cash flows of various enterprises.*

If a consolidated enterprise includes a bank, savings institution, or credit union that uses net cash reporting as allowed by FASB-104, the statement of cash flows of the consolidated enterprise must separately report (a) the net cash flows of the financial institution and (b) the gross cash receipts and cash payments of other members of the consolidated enterprise, including subsidiaries of a financial institution that are not themselves financial institutions.

OBSERVATION: *The above provision requires separate reporting of net cash flows and gross cash flows in a consolidated statement, if the net cash flows are allowed by FASB-104. It would seem desirable, along similar lines, to require separate reporting of net cash flows and gross cash flows, if the net cash flows are allowed by the exceptions contained in FASB-95, such as loans with maturities of three months or less. However, neither FASB-95 nor FASB-104 expressly require separate reporting in these situations.*

FASB-104 is effective for annual statements of cash flows for fiscal years ending on or after June 16, 1990. Earlier application is permitted. If an enterprise applies any provision of FASB-104 (whether by early application or after the effective date), the enterprise must restate or reclassify comparative amounts in financial statements for earlier periods.

Classification of cash receipts and cash payments   Under the provisions of FASB-95, cash receipts and cash payments result from transactions involving either operating activities, investing activities, or financing activities. An enterprise is required by FASB-95 to classify its cash receipts and cash payments shown in its statement of cash flows into operating activities, investing activities, or financing activities. As a general rule, each cash receipt or cash payment is required to be classified according to its source (operating, investing, or financing) without regard to whether it arose as a hedge of another item. However, an exception to this general rule is provided for hedging transactions by paragraph 7b of FASB-104 which amends footnote 4 of FASB-95. The amendment provides that the cash flow of a hedging transaction may be classified in the same category as the cash flow of its related hedged item, provided that the enterprise (a) discloses this accounting policy and (b) reports the gain or loss on the hedging instrument in the same accounting period as the offsetting gain or loss on the hedged item. Thus, the cash flow from a hedging transaction and the cash flow from its related hedged item may both be classified in the same category of cash flow (operating, investing, or financing), provided that the accounting policy is disclosed and the gain or loss on both transactions is recognized in the same accounting period.

An amendment to FASB-95 by FASB-102 provides that cash receipts and cash payments must be classified as operating cash flows in a statement of cash flows when such cash receipts and cash payments result from the acquisition or sale of (a) securities and other assets that are acquired specifically for resale and carried at market value in a trading account and (b) loans that are acquired specifically for resale and carried at market value or the lower of cost or market value. However, the cash receipts and cash payments from the sale of loans originally acquired as investments shall be classified as investing cash flows in a statement of cash flows, regardless of any subsequent change in the purpose of holding those loans.

Investing Activities—Include making and collecting loans and acquiring and disposing of debt or equity instruments and property, plant, and equipment and other productive assets; that is, assets held for or used in the production of goods or services by the enterprise (other than materials that are part of the enterprise's inventory).

Under the provisions of FASB-102, the following cash flows are classified as operating cash flows instead of investing cash flows: (1) cash receipts and cash payments resulting from originations, purchases, and sales of loans that are acquired specifically for resale and carried at market value or the lower of cost or market value and (2) cash receipts and cash payments resulting from purchases and sales of securities and other assets that are acquired specifically for resale and carried at market value in a trading account. Cash receipts and cash payments from the sale of loans originally acquired as investments shall be classified as investing cash flows in a statement of cash flows, regardless of any subsequent change in the purpose of holding those loans.

Financing Activities—Include obtaining resources from owners and providing them with a return on, and return of, their investment; borrowing money and repaying amounts borrowed, or otherwise settling the obligation; and obtaining and paying for other resources obtained from creditors on long-term credit.

Operating Activities—Include all transactions and other events that are not defined as investing or financing activities. Operating activities generally involve producing and delivering goods and providing services. Cash flows from operating activities are generally the cash effects of transactions and other events that enter into the determination of income.

> **OBSERVATION:** *Cash received from sales of inventory to customers is classified as cash from operating activities, whether received at the time of sale or collected at some other time, on open account or on a note (short-term, long-term, or installment). Similarly, cash paid to suppliers for inventory is classified as cash used for operating activities, whether paid at time of purchase or paid at some other time, on open account or on a note (short-term, long-term, or installment).*

The appropriate classification for a cash receipt or a cash payment that can qualify for more than one cash flow activity shall be the activity that is likely to be the predominant source of cash flows for that item. For example, the acquisition and sale of equipment used by an enterprise or rented to others are generally investing activities. However, if the intention of an enterprise is to use or rent the equipment for a short period of time and then sell it, the cash receipts and cash payments associated with the acquisition or production of the equipment and the subsequent sale shall be considered as cash flows from operating activities.

Foreign currency cash flows An enterprise with foreign currency translations or foreign operations shall report, in its statement of cash flows, the reporting currency equivalent of foreign currency cash flows using the exchange rates in effect at the time of the cash flows. An appropriately weighted average exchange rate for the period may be used in lieu of the actual currency rates at the dates of the cash flows, providing that the results are substantially the same. The effect of exchange rate changes on cash balances held in foreign currencies shall be reported in the statement of cash flows as a separate part of the reconciliation of the change in cash and cash equivalents during the period.

Exemption for certain employee benefit plans FASB-102 provides an exemption from the provisions of FASB-95 for (a) defined benefit pension plans that present their financial information in accordance with FASB-35 and (b) other employee benefit plans that present their financial information similar to that required by FASB-35, including those employee benefit plans that present their plan investments at fair value. Thus, these employee benefit pension plans are not required to include a statement of cash flows in their financial presentations. However, FASB-102 encourages all employee benefit pension plans to include a statement of cash flows as part of their financial presentation in those circumstances in which such a statement would provide relevant information concerning a plan's ability to meet its future obligations.

Exemption for certain investment companies   FASB-102 was issued to provide for certain exemptions from the provisions of FASB-95 (Statement of Cash Flows). One of these exemptions provides that certain investment-type entities that meet all of the conditions specified in FASB-102 are not required to include a statement of cash flows as part of their complete financial presentation in accordance with GAAP. The entities entitled to this exemption are as follows:

a.   Investment companies that are subject to the registration and regulatory requirements of the Investment Company Act of 1940 (1940 Act)

b.   Investment enterprises that have essentially the same characteristics as investment companies subject to the 1940 Act

c.   Common trust funds, variable annuity accounts, or similar funds maintained by a bank, insurance company, or other enterprise in its capacity as a trustee, administrator, or guardian for the collective investment and reinvestment of moneys

Under FASB-102, the investment type entities specified above are not required to include a statement of cash flows in their financial presentations, provided that they meet all of the following conditions:

a.   Substantially all investments owned by the enterprise were highly liquid during the period covered by the financial statements (highly liquid investments include, but are not limited to, marketable securities and other assets that can be sold through existing markets).

b.   Substantially all of the investments owned by the enterprise are carried at market value including securities for which market value is calculated by the use of matrix pricing techniques (described in the AICPA audit and accounting guide entitled *Audits of Investment Companies*). Securities that do not meet this condition are those for which (a) market value is not readily ascertainable and (b) fair value must be determined in good faith by the board of directors of the enterprise.

c. Based on averaged debt outstanding during the period, the enterprise had little or no debt in relation to average total assets. (For purposes of FASB-102, average debt outstanding generally may exclude obligations from (a) redemption of shares by the enterprise, (b) unsettled purchases of securities or similar assets, or (c) written covered options.)

d. A statement of changes in net assets must be provided in the enterprise's financial presentation.

Content and Form of Statement of Cash Flows

A statement of cash flows shall separately disclose the amount of net cash provided or used during a period from an enterprise's (a) operating activities, (b) investing activities, and (c) financing activities. The effect of the total amount of net cash provided or used during a period from all sources (operating, investing, and financing) on an enterprise's cash and cash equivalents shall be clearly disclosed in a manner that reconciles beginning and ending cash and cash equivalents.

In reporting cash flows from *operating activities* in the statement of cash flows, FASB-95 encourages but does not require an enterprise to use the *direct method*. Enterprises that do not use the direct method to report their cash flows from operating activities shall use the *indirect method* (also referred to as the reconciliation method). There is no difference in reporting the cash flows from investing and financing activities, regardless of whether the direct or indirect method is used.

A presentation of a statement of cash flows by the direct method will reflect the gross amounts of the principal components of cash receipts and cash payments from operating activities, such as cash received from customers and cash paid to suppliers and employees. On the other hand, a presentation of a statement of cash flows by the indirect method will reflect net income and the adjustments necessary to reconcile net income to net cash for the period. Using the direct method, the amount of net cash provided from or used by operating activities during the period is equal to the difference between the total amount of gross cash receipts and the total amount of gross cash payments arising from operating activities. Using the indirect method, the amount of net cash provided from or used by operating activities during the period is determined by making the necessary adjustments to reconcile net income of the period to the amount of net cash of the period. A statement of cash flows presented by either the direct method or the indirect method shall clearly reflect the amount of net cash flow provided or used by operating activities during a period.

> **OBSERVATION:** *An enterprise may use an alternate method of computation to arrive at the amounts shown in a statement of cash flows. For example, when preparing a direct method statement of cash flows, an enterprise may make an alternate computation to determine the amount of cash received from customers; i.e., it may start with total sales for the period and adjust that figure for the difference between beginning and ending accounts receivable.*

Direct method FASB-95 requires enterprises using the direct method of reporting the amount of net cash flow provided from or used by operating activities to present separately, at a minimum, in their statement of cash flows, the following principal components of operating cash receipts and operating cash payments:

- Cash collected from customers, including lessees, licensees, and other similar receipts
- Interest and dividends received
- Any other operating cash receipts
- Cash paid to employees and other suppliers of goods or services including suppliers of insurance, advertising, and other similar cash payments
- Any other operating cash payments, including interest paid, income taxes paid, and other similar cash payments

The provisions of FASB-95 encourage, but do not require, an enterprise to include in its statement of cash flows other meaningful detail pertaining to its cash receipts and cash payments from operating activities. For example, a retailer or manufacturer might decide to subdivide cash paid to employees and suppliers into cash payments for costs of inventory and cash payments for selling, general, and administrative expenses.

> **OBSERVATION:** *The use of the direct method is encouraged by FASB-95 because it reflects the gross amounts of the principal components of cash receipts and cash payments from operating activities, while the indirect method does not.*

Indirect method Enterprises that choose not to provide information about major classes of operating cash receipts and cash payments by the direct method as encouraged by FASB-95 shall indirectly determine and report the same amount of net cash flow from operating activities by reconciling net income to net cash flow (the indirect or reconciliation method). The adjustments necessary to reconcile net income to net cash flow are made to net income to remove (a) the effects of all deferrals of past operating cash receipts and cash payments, such as changes during the period in inventory, deferred income and the like, and all accruals of expected future operating cash receipts and cash payments, such as changes during the period in receivables and payables, and (b) the effects of all items whose cash effects are investing or financing cash flows, such as depreciation, amortization of goodwill, and gains or losses on sales of property, plant, and equipment and discontinued operations (which relate to investing activities), and gains or losses on extinguishment of debt (which is a financing activity).

Reconciliation of net income to net cash flow Regardless of whether an enterprise uses the direct or indirect method of reporting net cash flow from *operating* activities, FASB-95 requires that a reconciliation of net income to net cash flow be provided in the statement of cash flows. The reconciliation of net income to net cash flow from operating activities should provide information about the net effects of operating transactions and other events that affect net income and operating cash flows in different periods. That reconciliation shall separately reflect all major classes of reconciling items. For example, major classes of deferrals of past operating cash receipts and cash payments and accruals of expected future operating cash receipts and payments, including at a minimum changes during the period in receivables and payables pertaining to *operating* activities, shall be separately reported. Enterprises are encouraged to provide further breakdowns of those categories that they consider meaningful. For example, changes in trade receivables for an enterprise's sale of goods or services might be reported separately from changes in other operating receivables.

If the indirect method is used to report net cash flow from operating activities, FASB-95 requires the separate disclosure of the amounts of interest paid (net of amounts capitalized) and income taxes paid during the period. If an enterprise uses the direct method, the reconciliation of net income to net cash flow from operating activities shall be provided in a separate schedule (that is, separate from the statement of cash flows).

If an enterprise uses the *indirect* method, the reconciliation may be *either* included within and as part of the statement of cash flows or provided in a separate schedule, with the statement of cash flows reporting only the net cash flow from operating activities. If the reconciliation is included within and as part of the statement of cash flows, all adjustments to net income to determine net cash flow from operating activities shall be clearly identified as reconciling items.

> **OBSERVATION:** *The indirect method of reporting net cash flow from operating activities and the reconciliation of net income to net cash flow required by FASB-95 are similar presentations, except that the reconciliation requires that all reconciling items be clearly identified and that amounts of interest paid (net of amounts capitalized) and income taxes paid during the period be separately disclosed. Both presentations start with net income and include reconciling adjustments that are made to net income to arrive at net cash flow provided or used in operations. An enterprise may simply combine both presentations into one reconciliation of net income to net cash flow provided or used in operations.*

Noncash investing and financing activities   FASB-95 requires that related disclosures to the statement of cash flows contain information about all investing and financing activities of an enterprise during a period that affect recognized assets or liabilities but that do not result in cash receipts or cash payments. The related disclosures may be either narrative or summarized in a schedule, and they shall clearly relate the cash and noncash aspects of transactions involving similar items. Examples of noncash investing and financing transactions are: Converting debt to equity; acquiring assets by assuming directly related liabilities, such as purchasing a building by incurring a mortgage to the seller; obtaining an asset by entering into a capital lease; and exchanging noncash assets or liabilities for other noncash assets or liabilities. Only the cash portion of a part-cash, part-noncash transaction shall be reported in the statement of cash flows.

Cash flow per share   An enterprise is prohibited by FASB-95 from reporting any amount representing cash flow per share in its financial statements.

Effective date and transition FASB-95 is effective for annual financial statements for fiscal years ending on or after July 16, 1988. Earlier application of the provisions of FASB-95 is encouraged. In its initial year of application, FASB-95 does not have to be applied in financial statements of interim periods; however, cash flow information for those interim periods shall be restated if reported with annual financial statements for that fiscal year. Retroactive restatement of earlier years' financial statements for comparative purposes is encouraged, but not required.

Changes to the Standard Auditor's Report

In April 1988, Statement on Auditing Standards No. 58 (SAS-58) was issued because of several new developments in auditing standards. SAS-58 prescribes the following new form of the auditor's standard report that provides for the new statement of cash flows and eliminates the old statement of changes in financial position:

We have audited the accompanying balance sheets of X Company as of December 31, 19X2 and 19X1, and the related statements of income, retained earnings, and cash flows for the years then ended. These financial statements are the responsibility of the Company's management. Our responsibility is to express an opinion of these financial statements based on our audits.

We conducted our audits in accordance with generally accepted auditing standards. Those standards require that we plan and perform the audit to obtain reasonable assurance about whether the financial statements are free of material misstatement. An audit includes examining, on a test basis, evidence supporting the amounts and disclosures in the financial statements. An audit also includes assessing the accounting principles used and significant estimates made by the management, as well as evaluating the overall financial statement presentation. We believe that our audits provide a reasonable basis for our opinion.

In our opinion, the financial statements referred to above present fairly, in all material respects, the financial position of X Company as of December 31, 19X2 and 19X1, and the results of operations and its cash flows for the years then ended in conformity with generally accepted accounting principles.

Financial Institutions—Implementation Problems

Cash is the "product" of financial institutions, and their cash turnover is much greater than that of nonfinancial enterprises. As a result, some financial institutions may encounter problems in implementing the provisions of FASB-95.

Up to the time that FASB-95 was issued, financial institutions, especially commercial banks, reported only the net change in investments, loans, and deposit accounts in their financial statements. A change in this type of reporting is necessary because FASB-95 requires the presentation of gross cash receipts and payments for *investing and financing transactions* with original maturities of over three months. The requirement that gross amounts be presented will result in some financial institutions presenting very large cash flows, even in the trillions of dollars. On the other hand, a net presentation is permitted by FASB-95 for transactions in which a financial institution:

a. Is substantively holding or disbursing cash on behalf of its customers (such as for customer checking accounts)
b. Presents cash flows related to investments, loans, and certificates of deposits that have original maturities of less than three months (**Note**: Demand and credit card receivables will meet this provision even though they may remain outstanding for longer periods.)

It will probably be easier for financial institutions to develop systems that capture the gross cash flows of all transactions regardless of maturity rather than keep track of only those cash flows with maturities of three months or less. In addition, information concerning gross cash flows for earlier years may not be available and some financial institutions will not be able to restate prior years in the year they adopt FASB-95.

Although FASB-95 does not address specialized industries, it does cover a few specialized transactions that will affect financial institutions, such as (a) interest credited directly to deposit accounts, (b) revolving lines of credit, and (c) leveraged leases.

Interest credited directly to deposit accounts—Financial institutions shall account for interest credited directly to deposit accounts as an operating cash payment. Savings and loan associations, in particular, may have to change their statement presentations because many of them present interest credited to savings accounts as a noncash expense when reconciling net income and net cash provided by operations.

Revolving lines of credit—Commercial banks will have to present the gross cash receipts and payments related to revolving lines of credit, unless the loans are supported by notes with a maturity of three months or less.

Leveraged lease accounting—In accounting for leveraged leases, enterprises will have to show separately the individual cash flows related to the investment, the debt incurred, principal payments received under the lease, and principal payments made on the debt. This is true despite the fact the investments in the leased asset and related debt are presented net in the balance sheet.

Comprehensive Illustration*

Financial institutions   As a result of the amendments to FASB-95 by FASB-102, care must be exercised in classifying cash receipts and cash payments associated with investments in loans and securities. The main effect of FASB-102 impacts the statements of cash flows of financial institutions. For example, the cash receipts and cash payments associated with securities that are carried in *trading accounts* by banks, brokers, and dealers in securities must be classified as cash flows from operating activities. On the other hand, if securities are acquired for investment purposes, the related cash receipts and cash payments must be classified as cash flows from investing activities. Loans are given similar treatment. The cash receipts and cash payments associated with mortgage loans that are held for resale by a bank or mortgage broker must be classified as cash flows from operating activities. However, if the mortgage loans are held for investment purposes, the related cash receipts and cash payments must be classified as cash flows from investing activities.

* Adapted with permission from the *Journal of Accountancy*, copyright © 1988 by the American Institute of Certified Public Accountants, Inc.

The purpose of the comprehensive illustration that follows is to demonstrate the basic procedure in preparing a statement of cash flows. Ordinarily, a statement of cash flows would contain the current year and the immediate prior year for comparison purposes. However, to keep the illustration uncluttered and as simple as possible, only the current year is shown, and, in addition, the provisions of FASB-102 have been excluded from the illustration. Thus, the statement of cash flows that is shown in the following illustration is for enterprises other than financial institutions.

The starting point for the preparation of a Statement of Cash Flows, in accordance with the provisions of FASB-95, is the computation of the increases and decreases in balance sheet accounts from the previous period to the current period. After all of the increases and decreases have been calculated, each one must be analyzed to determine its effect, if any, on the net cash provided or used in either the operating, investing, or financing activities of the enterprise. If an increase or decrease consists of more than one transaction, each one must be separately analyzed. In addition to the Cash Flow Worksheet, which depicts the increases and decreases in the balance sheet accounts from one period to another, a condensed income statement is necessary.

Reference numbers have been parenthesized throughout this illustration to allow the reader to follow each transaction from its original source to the place it appears on the statement of cash flows. Both a statement of cash flows prepared by the indirect method and a statement of cash flows prepared by the direct method are illustrated.

This Comprehensive Illustration consists of the following documents listed in the order of their appearance:

Cash Flow Worksheet—This worksheet reflects the increases and decreases in the balance sheet accounts of the AAA Accounting Corporation from 19X1 to 19X2. A condensed statement of income of the AAA Accounting Corporation also appears on this worksheet. Reference numbers are parenthesized.

Schedule of Transactions—This schedule contains a separate analysis of each increase and decrease that appears on the Cash Flow Worksheet. As mentioned above, all reference numbers are parenthesized.

Consolidated Statement of Cash Flows (Indirect Method)—Prepared in accordance with the provisions of FASB-95.

Consolidated Statement of Cash Flows (Direct Method)—Prepared in accordance with the provisions of FASB-95. Also, illustrates how cash flow information for the direct method can be obtained by alternative methods.

Cash Flow Worksheet:

AAA Accounting Corporation
Cash Flow Worksheet
December 31, 19X2

	Increase or (Decrease)	Purchase of XYZ Co.	Increase or (Decrease) Without XYZ
ASSETS			
Cash & cash equivalents	$ 1,500	$ 300 (1)	$ 1,200 (4)
Accounts receivable—net	9,000	2,000	7,000
Notes receivable	(7,000)		(7,000)
Inventories	6,000	3,000	3,000 (10)
Prepaid expenses	1,000		1,000 (11)
Property, plant, & equipment	17,000	10,000	7,000
Accumulated depreciation & amortization	(5,000)		(5,000)
Investment in affiliated companies	2,100		2,100
Intangible assets	1,400	2,000	(600) (19)
	$26,000	$17,300 (2)	$ 8,700
LIABILITIES & EQUITIES			
Short-term notes payable—banks	$ (4,000)		$ (4,000)
Accounts payable & accrued expenses	5,350	$1,500	3,850
Long-term debt	14,000	7,800	6,200
Capital lease obligations	1,600		1,600
Deferred income taxes	1,000		1,000 (30)
Common stock	3,000		3,000
Retained earnings	5,050		5,050
	$26,000	$ 9,300 (3)	$16,700

Income Statement

Sales	$150,000	(33)
Other income	10,000	(34)
Costs of sales	(122,000)	(35)
Selling & administrative	(15,400)	(36)
Depreciation & amortization	(8,600)	(37)
Equity in net income of investees	3,000	(38)
Gain on sale of equipment	2,500	(39)
Interest expense	(5,500)	(40)
Income tax expense	(6,000)	(41)
Net income	$ 8,000	(42)
Dividends paid to shareholders	(2,950)	(43)
	$ 5,050	

Note: References are parenthesized.

Schedule of Transactions:

AAA Accounting Corporation
Schedule of Transactions
For Year Ending December 31, 19X2

1.   *Acquisition of XYZ Company*   During 19X2, AAA purchased the common stock of XYZ Company for $8,000 cash. The purchase price was allocated based on these fair values of XYZ's assets and liabilities at the date of acquisition:

Cash	$ 300	
Accounts Receivable	2,000	
Inventory	3,000	
Property, plant, & equipment	10,000	
Goodwill & other intangible assets	2,000	
Accounts payable & accrued expenses	(1,500)	
Long-term debt	(7,800)	
	$ 8,000	
Assets acquired	$17,300	(2)
Less: Liabilities assumed	9,300	(3)
Cash paid	$ 8,000	
Less: Cash acquired in transaction	300	(1)
Net assets acquired, excluding cash	$ 7,700	

2. *Accounts receivable*   Accounts receivable net of allowances of $900 in 19X2 and $500 in 19X1 were $29,000 and $20,000 at December 31, 19X2 and 19X1 respectively. AAA wrote off $350 in bad debts and recognized a provision for losses on receivables (in selling & administrative expense) of $750.

Accounts receivable 12/31/X2	$29,000	
Accounts receivable 12/31/X1	20,000	
Increase in accounts receivable	$ 9,000	
Less: Accounts receivable acquired from XYZ	2,000	
Increase in accounts receivable without XYZ	$ 7,000	(5)
Add back provision for bad debts	750	(6)
Increase in accounts receivable before bad debts	$ 7,750	(7)

3. *Accounts payable & accrued expenses*   Accounts payable and accrued expenses were $33,000 and $27,650 on December 31, 19X2 and 19X1, respectively. Included are accruals for income taxes payable of $3,500 and $3,000 and for interest payable of $2,300 and $2,000.

Accounts payable & accrued expenses 12/31/X2	$33,000	
Accounts payable & accrued expenses 12/31/X1	27,650	
Increase in accounts payable & accrued expenses	$ 5,350	
Less: Accounts payable & accrued expenses from XYZ Co.	1,500	
Increase in accounts payable & accrued expenses	$ 3,850	
Increase consists of:		
Increase in accrual for income taxes	$ 500	(22)
Increase in accrual for interest payable	300	(23)
Increase in accounts payable from 19X1 to 19X2	3,050	(24)
Total increase	$ 3,850	

4. *Notes receivable*   AAA collected principal of $2,500 on an installment note receivable related to a product sale and $4,500 on a note receivable from a prior year's sale of a plant.

Payment received on installment note receivable	$ 2,500	(8)
Payment received on prior year's sale of plant	4,500	(9)
Decrease in notes receivable	$ 7,000	

5. *Capital lease obligation*   AAA entered into a capital lease for equipment with a fair value of $2,000. Principal payments on this and other lease obligations amounted to $400 during the year.

New capital lease	$ 2,000	(28)
Principal payments on new capital lease	400	(29)
Increase in capital lease obligations	$ 1,600	

6. *Long-term debt*   AAA borrowed $9,000 on a long-term basis during the year and made payments of $1,800 on long-term debt.

Increase in long-term debt	$14,000	
Less: Assumed in the XYZ acquisition	7,800	
Increase in long-term debt without XYZ	$ 6,200	
Increase consists of:		
New long-term borrowing	$ 9,000	(25)
Repayment of long-term borrowing	(1,800)	(26)
Conversion of common stock (see #12)	(1,000)	(27)
Increase in long-term debt without XYZ	$ 6,200	

7. *Short-term revolving credit agreement*   AAA borrowed $5,500 and repaid $9,500 under a revolving credit agreement with an original maturity of one year. At the time of the agreement, AAA signed a single note with a one-year term for the maximum amount available.

Proceeds—borrowings revolving line of credit	$ 5,500	(20)
Repayments—borrowings revolving line of credit	(9,500)	(21)
Decrease in short-term notes payable to banks	$ 4,000	

8. *Dividend from affiliated company*   An affiliate paid AAA a $900 dividend. It was accounted for using the equity method of accounting.

Increase in equity in net income of investees	$ 3,000	(17)
Dividend received from equity investee	(900)	(18)
Increase in investment in affiliated companies	$ 2,100	

9. *Sale of equipment & construction of warehouse*   AAA received $6,500 from the sale of equipment, which had a book value of $4,000 and originally cost $7,000. In addition, AAA built a warehouse for $12,000 (including $300 of capitalized interest).

Purchase of property, plant, & equipment	$12,000 (12)
Original cost of equipment sold	(7,000) (13)
Acquisition of equipment under capital lease	2,000 (14)
Increase in property, plant, & equipment	$7,000

10. *Depreciation & amortization expense*   AAA's 19X2 depreciation expense and amortization of intangibles were $8,000 and $600 respectively.

Depreciation expense for 19X2	$ (8,000) (15)
Accumulated depreciation on equipment sold	3,000 (16)
Decrease in accumulated depreciation account	$ (5,000)
Amortization of intangible assets	$ (600) (19)
Decrease in intangible assets	$ 600
Total depreciation & amortization expense	$ 8,600 (37)

11. *Deferred income taxes*   AAA's 19X2 provision for deferred taxes was $1,000.

Provision for deferred income taxes	$ 1,000
Increase in deferred income taxes	$ 1,000 (30)

12. *Common stock issued*   In 19X2, AAA issued $3,000 of additional common stock ($2,000 for cash and $1,000 upon the conversion of debt).

Sale of common stock for cash	$ 2,000 (31)
Issuance of common stock-conversion of debt	1,000 (32)
Increase in common stock	$ 3,000

13. *Dividends paid to shareholders*   AAA paid dividends of $2,950 to shareholders in 19X2.

Dividends paid to shareholders	$ 2,950 (43)

14. *Cash & cash equivalents*   Cash & cash equivalents were $7,500 and $6,000 on December 31, 19X2 and 19X1, respectively.

Cash & cash equivalents December 31, 19X2	$ 7,500
Cash & cash equivalents December 31, 19X1	6,000
Increase in cash & cash equivalents	$ 1,500 (1) + (4)

Indirect Method:

AAA Accounting Corporation
Consolidated Statement of Cash Flows
(Indirect Method)
Increase (Decrease) in Cash and Cash Equivalents
For the Calendar Year Ended December 31, 19X2

Cash flows from operating activities:

Net income		(42)	$ 8,000
Adjustments to reconcile net income to net cash provided by operating activities:			
Depreciation and amortization	(15) + (19)	$ 8,600	
Provisions for doubtful accounts receivable	(6)	750	
Provision for deferred income taxes	(30)	1,000	
Undistributed earnings of affiliate	(17) + (18)	(2,100)	
Gain on sale of equipment	(39)	(2,500)	
Payment received on installment sale of product	(8)	2,500	
Changes in operating assets and liabilities net of effects from purchase of XYZ Company:			
Increase in accounts receivable	(7)	(7,750)	
Increase in inventory (Note 1)	(10) + (11)	(4,000)	
Increase in accounts payable and accrued expenses (Note 1)	(22) + (23) + (24)	3,850	
Total adjustments to net income			350
Net Cash Provided by Operating Activities			$ 8,350

Cash flows from investing activities:

Purchase of property, plant, & equipment	(12)	$(12,000)	
Purchase of XYZ Company (net of cash acquired)	(2) – (3) – (1)	(7,700)	
Proceeds from sale of equipment (Note 2)	(13) – (16) + (39)	6,500	
Payment received on note for sale of plant (Note 2)	(9)	4,500	
Net Cash Provided (Used) by Investing Activities			$ (8,700)

Cash flows from financing activities:

Proceeds from revolving line of credit	(20)	$5,500
Principal payments on revolving line of credit	(21)	(9,500)
Principal from long-term borrowings	(25)	9,000
Principal payments on long-term borrowings	(26)	(1,800)
Principal payment on capital lease obligation	(29)	(400)
Proceeds from sale of common stock	(31)	2,000
Dividends paid	(43)	(2,950)
Net Cash Provided (Used) by Financing Activities		1,850
Net Increase (Decrease) in Cash and Cash Equivalents		$ 1,500
Cash and Cash Equivalents— beginning of year		6,000
Cash and Cash Equivalents— end of year		$7,500

Supplement disclosures of cash flow information:

- *Accounting policy note:* The company considers all highly liquid investments with a maturity of three months or less at the date of acquisition, to be "cash equivalents."

- *Debt or property, plant & equipment note:* (Note 3) During 19X2, the company incurred interest cost of $5,800 [(40) + $300 capitalized), including $300 capitalized. Interest paid was $5,500 [$5,800 – (23)] during 19X2. (See Note 4).

- *Income tax note:* (Note 3) The company made income tax payments of $4,500 [(41) – (30) – (22)] during 19X2.

- *Acquisitions note:* (Note 3) In connection with the acquisition of all of the common stock of XYZ Co. for $8,000 [(2)–(3)], the company acquired assets with a fair value of $17,300 (2) and assumed liabilities of $9,300 (3).

- *Leases note:* (Note 3) During 19X2, the company incurred a capital lease obligation of $2,000 (28) in connection with lease agreements to acquire equipment.

- *Shareholders' equity note:* (Note 3) On June 11, 19X2, the company called for redemption of all 5.75% convertible debentures outstanding. Debenture holders of securities with a carrying amount of $1,000 [(27), (32)] elected to convert the debentures into 20,000 shares of common stock.

Note 1—FASB-95 requires separate presentation of changes in inventory, in receivables, and in payables relating to operating activities. The idea is to allow users to estimate amounts that would be reported when using the direct method of reporting. It is probably acceptable to present line items that include other reconciling items (in this case the changes in prepaid expenses and accrued expenses) as long as all the items combined would affect a single line item under a direct-method presentation.

Note 2—It is probably acceptable to combine these cash receipts into a single line item, such as "proceeds from sales of property, plant and equipment."

Note 3—The location of this disclosure is not specified by FASB-95. Many enterprises will probably decide to present the disclosures required by FASB-95 in existing notes discussing related matters.

Note 4—Alternatively, interest paid (net of interest capitalized) of $5,200 ($5,500 – $300).

Direct Method:

AAA Accounting Corporation
Consolidated Statement of Cash Flows
(Direct Method)

Increase (Decrease) in Cash and Cash Equivalents
For the Calendar Year Ended December 31, 19X2

Cash flows from operating activities:

Cash received from customers (see separate computation)		$144,750
Cash paid to suppliers and employees (see separate computation)		(137,600)
Cash dividend received from affiliate	(18)	900
Other operating cash receipts	(34)	10,000
Interest paid in cash (net of amounts capitalized)	(40) – (23)	(5,200)
Income taxes paid in cash	(41) – (30) – (22)	(4,500)
Net Cash Provided (Used by Operating Activities)		$ 8,350

Computation of cash received from customers during the year:

Sales		(33)	$ 150,000
Collection of installment payment for sale of product		(8)	2,500
			$ 152,500
Gross accounts receivable—beginning of year	$20,500		
Accounts receivable acquired in XYZ deal	2,000		
Accounts receivable written off	(350)		
Gross accounts receivable—end of year	(29,900)		
Excess of new accounts receivable over collections from customers		(7)	(7,750)
Cash received from customers during the year			$ 144,750

Computation of cash paid to suppliers and employees during the year:

Cost of sales		(35)	$ 122,000
Selling & administrative expenses	(36)	$15,400	
Noncash expenses (provision for bad debts)	(6)	(750)	
Net expenses requiring cash payments			$ 14,650
Consolidated increase in inventory		$ 6,000	
Inventory acquired in purchase of XYZ Co.		(3,000)	
Net increase in inventory from AAA's operations		(10)	3,000
Increase in prepaid expenses		(11)	1,000
Adjustments-changes in accounts payable & accrued expense:			
Balance—beginning of year		$27,650	
Amounts related to income taxes and interest at beginning of year		(5,000)	
Accounts payable & accrued expenses assumed in purchase of XYZ Co.		1,500	
Balance—end of year		(33,000)	
Amounts related to income taxes and interest at end of year		5,800	
Amounts charged to expense but not paid during the year			(3,050)
Cash paid to suppliers & employees during the year			$ 137,600

CONSOLIDATED FINANCIAL STATEMENTS

Overview

The promulgated accounting standards and reporting principles for consolidated financial statements, combined financial statements, and comparative financial statements are:

ARB-43, Chapter 1A, Rules Adopted by Membership
ARB-43, Chapter 2A, Comparative Financial Statements
ARB-51, Consolidated Financial Statements (as amended)
FASB-94, Consolidation of all Majority-owned Subsidiaries

ARB-43, Chapter 1A, contains six rules that were adopted by the professional organization of certified public accountants in 1934. Rule three is concerned with consolidated financial statements. The thrust of this rule is that a subsidiary company's retained earnings created prior to the date of its acquisition cannot be considered part of the consolidated retained earnings of the parent company and its subsidiaries. Furthermore, any dividends declared out of such retained earnings cannot be included in the net income of the parent company.

ARB-43, Chapter 2A discusses the desirability of presenting comparative financial statements in annual reports, because such a presentation is likely to provide much more information than non-comparative statements.

ARB-51, as amended by FASB-94, is the main source of promulgated GAAP relating to consolidated financial statements. Under ARB-51, a consolidated financial statement represents the results of operation, statement of cash flows, and financial position of a single entity. They are presumed to be more meaningful than separate statements.

FASB-94 amends ARB-51 to require, with few exceptions, a parent company to consolidate all of its majority-owned subsidiaries. To effectuate this amendment, it was necessary to make amendments to APB-18 (Equity Method of Accounting for Investments in Common Stock) and ARB-43, Chapter 12 (Foreign Operations and Foreign Exchange). FASB-94 also amends ARB-51 to require a parent company to disclose summarized information about the assets, liabilities, and results of operations of majority-owned subsidiaries that were previously unconsolidated for fiscal years 1986 and 1987 that, for fiscal years ending after December 15, 1988, are required to be consolidated under the provisions of ARB-51 (as amended). However, a parent company may elect to present separate financial statements for these majority-owned subsidiaries instead of summarized financial information.

FASB-94 is effective for financial statements covering fiscal years ending on or after December 16, 1988. Although application of the provisions of FASB-94 to interim financial statements of the year of adoption is not required, comparative financial statements for earlier periods, including those of the year of adoption, shall be retroactively restated when FASB-94 is first applied.

> **OBSERVATION:** *Implementation of FASB-94 will drastically change the financial statements of some affected enterprises, and may make some enterprises appear to be in violation of the provisions of loan covenants or other obligations, which require the enterprises to maintain certain financial ratios. Expert legal and financial advice should be obtained.*

Considerable nonpromulgated GAAP exist for consolidated financial statements, especially in the area of reporting and types of presentations.

Background

Consolidated financial statements represent the results of operation, statement of cash flows, and financial position of a single entity. Under GAAP (ARB-51), consolidated financial statements are presumed to present more meaningful information than separate financial statements and must be used in substantially all cases in which a parent directly or indirectly controls the majority voting interest (over 50%) of a subsidiary. Consolidated financial statements should not be used in those circumstances in which (a) the parent's control of the subsidiary is temporary, or (b) there is significant doubt concerning the parent's ability to control the subsidiary.

Retained earnings of a purchased subsidiary at the date of acquisition are never treated as part of consolidated retained earnings. The retained earnings, other capital accounts, and capital stock of a purchased subsidiary at the date of acquisition represent the book value that must be eliminated in preparing consolidated statements.

A parent company should not exclude a majority-owned subsidiary from consolidation because it has a different fiscal year. For consolidation purposes, a subsidiary can usually prepare financial statements that correspond with its parent's fiscal period. If a subsidiary's fiscal year is within three months or less of its parent's fiscal year, it is acceptable to use those fiscal-year financial statements for consolidation purposes, providing that adequate disclosure is made of any material events occurring within the intervening period.

Prior to its amendment by FASB-94, paragraph 3 of ARB-51 provided that consolidated financial statements may be more meaningful if subsidiaries with *nonhomogeneous* operations were excluded from the consolidation. Most subsidiaries with nonhomogeneous operations were either in the finance, insurance, or real estate industries. Paragraph 3 of ARB-51 resulted in some parent companies excluding subsidiaries with nonhomogeneous operations from their consolidated financial statements while other parent companies included them. This practice has been criticized because (a) similar enterprises were applying different consolidation policies and (b) significant amounts of assets, liabilities, revenues, and expenses were omitted from the parent's consolidated financial statements. The omission of the liabilities of subsidiaries with nonhomogeneous operations has become a significant factor in the explosion of *off-balance sheet financing.*

As a result of the issuance of FASB-94, a subsidiary with nonhomogeneous operations can no longer be excluded from consolidation on the basis that its operations are unrelated to the rest of the consolidated group.

Majority-Owned Subsidiaries

ARB-51, as amended by FASB-94, requires that all investments in which a parent company has a controlling financial interest represented by the direct or indirect ownership of a majority voting interest (more than 50%) shall be consolidated, except those in which (a) control of the subsidiary is temporary, or (b) significant doubt exists regarding the parent's ability to control the subsidiary. For example, a subsidiary in legal reorganization or bankruptcy is controlled by the receiver or trustee and not by the parent company.

> **OBSERVATION:** *When an enterprise changes from using the equity method to preparing consolidated financial statements for nonhomogeneous subsidiaries, as required by FASB-94, this change*

*will not alter the net income **bottom line**. The change may, however, radically affect other items on the financial statements, as well as the ratios derived from these items. As a result, the change may make some enterprises appear to be in violation of the provisions of loan covenants or other obligations that require the enterprise to maintain ratios at specified levels.*

Enterprises, creditors, and others should obtain expert legal and financial advice on the impact of FASB-94. A major issue is whether an enterprise's compliance with pre-existing loan covenants should continue to be determined under prior GAAP. If the answer is "yes," an enterprise will have to prepare pro forma financial statements in accordance with prior GAAP, for the limited purposes of demonstrating compliance with pre-existing loan covenants, even though financial statements for other purposes will be prepared in accordance with FASB-94.

FASB-94 also added a new paragraph 19 to ARB-51 which requires a parent company to disclose summarized information concerning the assets, liabilities, and results of operations (or separate financial statements) for all majority-owned subsidiaries that were previously unconsolidated for fiscal years 1986 and 1987 that are consolidated for fiscal years ending after December 15, 1988, in accordance with FASB-94.

> **OBSERVATION**: *FASB-94 implies that enterprises should continue to disclose this information on every financial statement for the indefinite future. If the FASB wishes to terminate this type of disclosure, presumably it will promulgate a new statement.*

FASB-94 amends Chapter 12 of ARB-43 by deleting paragraphs 8 and 9 (Consolidation of Foreign Subsidiaries), which had permitted the exclusion from consolidation of majority-owned foreign subsidiaries because of foreign currency and/or exchange restrictions. This amendment narrows the exception for a majority-owned foreign subsidiary from one that permits exclusion from consolidation of any or all foreign subsidiaries to one that effectively eliminates distinctions between foreign and domestic subsidiaries (paragraph 9 of FASB-94). Thus, a majority-owned subsidiary must be consolidated unless significant doubt exists regarding the parent's control of the subsidiary or the parent's control is temporary. FASB-52 (Foreign Currency Translation) contains special rules for translating foreign currency financial statements of foreign subsidiaries that operate in countries with highly inflationary economies.

FASB-94 amends APB-18 by removing the requirement of APB-18 to report unconsolidated majority-owned subsidiaries by the equity method. In addition, FASB-94 eliminates the provisions of APB-18 applying to "parent-company financial statements prepared for issuance to stockholders as the financial statements of the primary reporting entity."

> **OBSERVATION:** *FASB-94 totally prohibits the use of the equity method of accounting for investments in majority-owned subsidiaries. This is the combined result of paragraph 15.d and paragraph 13 of FASB-94. Paragraph 15.d states that the limitations on the use of consolidated statements (temporary control or doubtful control) are also limitations on the use of the equity method. Accordingly, when these limitations apply, the equity method is prohibited by paragraph 15.d. When these limitations do not apply, the equity method is prohibited by paragraph 13, which requires consolidated financial statements.*
>
> *The equity method is still applicable under existing GAAP in those circumstances in which an investor owns less than a majority of the investee. FASB-94, paragraphs 15.a and 15.e mentions the equity method as being appropriate for investments in common stock of corporate joint ventures.*

A majority-owned subsidiary may not be consolidated if significant doubt exists regarding the parent's control of the subsidiary or the parent's control of the subsidiary is temporary. Since FASB-94 prohibits the use of the equity method of accounting in these circumstances, it appears that the cost method of accounting should be used.

Accounting and Reporting On Subsidiaries

The common stock or net assets of a subsidiary may be purchased (1) for book value, (2) in excess of book value, and (3) for less than book value. If purchased for more than book value, there may be resulting goodwill; if purchased for less than book value, there may be a resulting deferred credit, sometimes referred to as negative goodwill.

When a subsidiary is acquired by the purchase method in more than one transaction, each purchase should be determined on a step-by-step basis and consolidation is usually not made until control (more than 50%) is achieved. In the year that control is achieved, the percentage amount of net income from the purchased subsidiary will probably vary. For example, if a parent company purchased 25% of a subsidiary at the end of a quarter of a year, the income from the subsidiary that the parent would include in its income would be 0% at the end of the first quarter, 25% at the end of the second quarter, 50% at the end of the third quarter, and 75% at the end of the last quarter. (Income from a purchased acquisition accrues subsequent from the date of acquisition.) ARB-51 suggests two methods for the inclusion of income from a subsidiary in periods where there are several purchases. The preferable method usually is to include the subsidiary in the consolidation as if it had been acquired at the beginning of the period, and to deduct at the bottom of the consolidated income statement the net income of the subsidiary that does not accrue to the parent.

> **OBSERVATION:** *Apparently, when using this method, all the revenue and expense accounts of the subsidiary remain in the consolidated income statement, since only the net income that the parent is not entitled to is deducted from the consolidated net income at the bottom of the statement.*

The other method suggested is to include in the parent's consolidated income statement only the subsidiary's revenue and expenses subsequent to the date of acquisition.

In the disposal of a subsidiary during the year, ARB-51 suggests that it may be preferable to omit from the consolidated income statement all details of the operation of the subsidiary and to show only the equity of the parent in the earnings of the subsidiary, prior to disposal, as a separate item in the consolidated income statement (the equity method).

Consolidated financial statements are prepared in the same manner for a pooling-of-interests as they are for a purchase. In the purchase method, fair values are assigned to identifiable assets and any excess cost is recorded as goodwill. In a pooling-of-interests, the cost of an acquisition is the total par or stated value of the capital stock issued by the acquiring company and goodwill is never recorded.

Combined Financial Statements

Consolidated financial statements are usually justified on the basis that one of the consolidating entities exercises control over the affiliated group. When there is no such control, combined financial statements may be used to accomplish the same results. A company controlled group of companies, or a group of unconsolidated subsidiaries that could otherwise not be consolidated, should utilize combined financial statements. Combined financial statements are prepared on the same basis as consolidated financial statements, except that a controlling interest is not included.

Comparative financial statements Comparative financial statements reveal much more information than noncomparative statements and furnish useful data about differences in the results of operations for the periods involved or in the financial position at the comparison dates.

Consistency is a major factor in creating comparability. Prior-year amounts and classifications must be, in fact, comparable with the current period presented, and exceptions must be clearly disclosed.

Consolidation versus Equity Method

The only difference between the equity method of accounting for investments in common stocks and consolidated financial statements is the amount of detail reported. Under both methods all intercompany transactions are eliminated. In consolidated financial statements the details of all entities to the consolidation are reported in full. In the equity method the investment is shown as a single amount in the investor balance sheet, and earnings or losses are generally shown as a single amount in the income statement. This is the reason why the equity method is frequently referred to as *one-line consolidation*.

Consolidated Work Papers

The difference between regular work papers for a single business and consolidated work papers is that the adjustments on the regular work papers will be journalized and posted to the books, whereas eliminations and adjustments made on consolidated work papers *are never posted to the books of the individual companies.*

Intercompany Transactions

Sales and purchases   The gross amount of all intercompany sales and/or purchases is eliminated on the consolidated work papers. When the adjustment has already been made in the trial balance for ending inventory the eliminating entry is made against cost of sales. When the adjustment has not been made for ending inventory the eliminating entry is made against the purchase account.

Receivables and payables   Intercompany receivables and payables include:

1.   Accounts receivable and accounts payable
2.   Advances to and from affiliates
3.   Notes receivable and notes payable
4.   Interest receivable and interest payable

The gross amount of all intercompany receivables and payables is eliminated on the consolidated work papers. Care must be exercised where a receivable is discounted with one of the consolidated companies (no contingent liability). If the balance sheet reflects a discounted receivable with another affiliate, it must be eliminated by a debit to discounted receivables and a credit to receivables. However, if one affiliate discounts a receivable to another affiliate, who in turn discounts it to an outsider, a real contingent liability exists, which must be shown on the consolidated balance sheet.

Unrealized profits in inventory   Regardless of any minority interests, all (100%) of any intercompany profits in inventory must be eliminated on the consolidated work papers if such inventory profits are represented by assets within the group. If the inventory containing intercompany profits has been disposed of to outsiders, no adjustment need be made. If the adjustment for intercompany profits in inventory is not made, consolidated net income is overstated and the consolidated ending inventory is overstated.

P Company purchased $200,000 and $250,000 of merchandise in 19X1 and 19X2, respectively, from its subsidiary S at 25% above cost. As of December 31, 19X1 and 19X2, P had on hand $25,000 and $30,000 of merchandise purchased from S. The following is the computation of intercompany profits:

Computation of Intercompany Profits

Beginning inventory	$ 25,000	=	125%
Cost to S	20,000	=	100%
Intercompany profit	$ 5,000		25%
Ending inventory	$ 30,000	=	125%
Cost to S	24,000	=	100%
Intercompany profit	$ 6,000		25%

The adjustment is different for a consolidated balance sheet than for a consolidated income statement, because a consolidated balance sheet reflects only the ending inventory, whereas a consolidated income statement usually shows both the beginning and ending inventories. For a consolidated balance sheet only, the consolidated adjusting entry is:

Retained earnings	$6,000	
Inventory		$6,000

For a consolidated income statement the following adjustments are necessary:

Sales—S Company	$250,000	
Purchases—P Company		$250,000
To eliminate intercompany sales and purchases.		
Consolidated retained earnings	$ 5,000	
Purchases or cost of sales		$ 5,000
To reverse consolidated adjustment of 12/31/X1.		
Purchases or cost of sales	$ 6,000	
Inventory—ending		$ 6,000
To eliminate intercompany profit in ending inventory.		

The adjustment to consolidated retained earnings was necessary because on the prior year's consolidated work papers the intercompany profit was eliminated. Remember, consolidated adjustments and eliminations are never posted to the books of the individual companies. Therefore the beginning inventory for P still reflected the prior year's intercompany inventory profits from S.

If merchandise containing an intercompany inventory profit is reduced from the purchase price to market value and the reduction is equal to, or more than, the actual intercompany inventory profit, no further reduction is made. For example, if merchandise costing one affiliate $10,000 is sold to another affiliate for $12,000, who reduces it to market value of $11,000, the consolidated working paper adjustment for unrealized intercompany inventory profits should be only $1,000.

Minority interests do not affect the adjustment for unrealized intercompany profits in inventories. However, consolidated net income and minority interests in the net income of a subsidiary are affected, because the reduction or increase in beginning or ending inventory of a partially owned subsidiary does affect the determination of net income.

Unrealized intercompany losses in inventory are accounted for in the same manner as unrealized profits, except that they have the opposite effect.

Profits or losses on sales and/or purchases prior to an affiliation are never recognized as a consolidated adjustment.

Unrealized profits in long-lived assets   Regardless of any minority interests, all (100%) of any intercompany profits on the sale and/or purchase of long-lived assets between affiliates is eliminated on the consolidated work papers.

When one affiliate constructs or sells a long-lived asset to another affiliate at a profit, the profit must be eliminated on the consolidated work papers. As with unrealized intercompany profits or losses in inventory, minority interests do not affect any consolidated adjustment for profits in intercompany sales of long-lived assets between affiliates. However, net income of the subsidiary involved in the intercompany profit on a long-lived asset is affected, which in turn affects consolidated net income and minority interests.

In consolidating a subsidiary in a regulated industry, intercompany profits are not eliminated on manufactured or constructed facilities for other members of the consolidated group, to the extent that they are equivalent to a reasonable return on investment as established by industry practice.

If a nondepreciable asset is involved in an intercompany profit on a long-lived asset, the profit is eliminated by a debit to either retained earnings, in the case of an adjusted consolidated balance sheet, or to gain on sale, in the case of a consolidated income statement.

Depreciable assets require the same adjustment for intercompany profit as nondepreciable long-lived assets, and an adjustment must also be made for any depreciation recorded on the intercompany profit.

An 80%-owned subsidiary sells to its parent for $100,00 a piece of machinery that cost $80,000. The sale was made on July 1, 19X1, and consolidated statements are being prepared for December 31, 19X1. The parent depreciates machinery over 10 years on a straight-line basis and recorded one-half a year's depreciation on the purchased machinery.

The first entry eliminates the $20,000 of intercompany profit, as follows:

Gain on sale of machinery	$20,000	
Machinery		$20,000

Since the parent company has recorded one-half a year's depreciation on the machinery, the following additional entry is made:

Accumulated depreciation	$1,000	
Depreciation expense		$1,000

Because consolidated eliminations and adjustments are never posted to any books, in the second year the following entries are made:

Retained earnings	$20,000	
Machinery		$20,000

To eliminate intercompany profit on prior year's sale of machinery.

Accumulated depreciation	$ 3,000	
Retained earnings		$ 1,000
Depreciation expense		2,000

To eliminate the $2,000 depreciation expense on intercompany profit on the sale of machinery and to eliminate the $1,000 depreciation expense for prior year's depreciation.

The process of eliminating the depreciation expense on the intercompany profit on the sale of long-lived assets continues until the asset is fully depreciated, and thereafter until the asset is disposed of or retired. In the example, the following entry would be made every year on the consolidated work papers after the asset is fully depreciated and before it is disposed of or retired.

Accumulated depreciation	$20,000	
Retained earnings		$20,000

An affiliate that makes an intercompany profit on the sale of long-lived assets to another affiliate may pay income taxes on the gain. This occurs usually when the affiliated group does not file consolidated tax returns and the gain cannot be avoided for tax purposes. In such cases, the intercompany profit on the sale should be reduced by the related tax effects in computing the consolidated adjusting entry.

Intercompany bondholdings   Intercompany bonds purchased by an affiliate are treated in the year of acquisition as though they have been retired. Any gain or loss is recognized in the consolidated income statement for the year of acquisition.

The amount of gain or loss on an intercompany bond purchase is the difference between the unamortized bond premium or discount on the books of the issuer and the amount of any purchase discount or premium.

An intercompany gain or loss on bonds cannot occur when an affiliate makes the purchase directly from the affiliated issuer, because the selling price will be exactly equal to the cost.

An affiliate purchases $20,000 face value 6% bonds from an affiliated issuer for $19,500.

On the affiliated investor's books the following entry is made:

Investment in bonds	$19,500	
Cash		$19,500

On the affiliated issuer's books the entry is:

Cash	$19,500	
Discount on bonds payable	500	
Bonds payable		$20,000

The consolidated elimination is:

Bonds payable	$20,000	
Discount on bonds payable		$ 500
Investment in bonds		19,500

An intercompany gain or loss on bonds cannot occur when the purchase price is exactly the same as the carrying value on the books of the affiliated issuer.

The following conditions must exist for an affiliated investor to realize a gain or loss on intercompany bondholdings:

1. The bonds are already outstanding.
2. The bonds are purchased outside the affiliated group.
3. The price paid is different from the carrying value of the affiliated issuer.

Company S acquires $50,000 of face amount 6% bonds from an outsider. These bonds were part of an original issue of $300,000 made by the parent of Company S. The purchase price was $45,000, and the bonds mature in four years and nine months. Interest is payable on June 30 and December 31, and the purchase was made on March 31.

The journal entry on the books of Company S to record the purchase is:

Investment in bonds	$45,000	
Accrued interest receivable	750	
Cash		$45,750

On the consolidated working papers at the end of the year the following entries are made:

Investment in bonds	$ 5,000	
Gain on intercompany bondholdings		$5,000
To adjust the investment in bonds to face amount and record the gain.		

Bonds payable—Co. P	$50,000	
Investment in bonds—Co. S		$50,000

To eliminate intercompany
bondholdings.

Interest income—Co. S	$ 2,250	
Interest expense—Co. P		$ 2,250

To eliminate intercompany interest
on bonds that was actually earned.

Interest income—Co. S	$ 788	
Investment in bonds		$ 788

To eliminate amortization of $5,000
discount on bonds recorded on Co. S
books. (9/57 of $5,000 = $788)

Accrued interest payable	$ 1,500	
Accrued interest receivable		$ 1,500

To eliminate accrued interest payable
on 12/31/XX by Co. P, and the accrued
interest receivable on 12/31/XX by
Co. S.

This example contains all the possible adjustments except for an issuer's premium or discount. Assume the following additional information on the original issue:

Face amount	$300,000
Issued at 96	288,000
Date of issue	1/1/70
Maturity date	1/1/80

Company S had purchased its $50,000 face amount when the issue had four years and nine months left to maturity.

On the parent company's books this discount is being amortized over the life of the bond issue at the rate of $1,200 per year ($12,000 discount divided by ten years).

An adjustment must be made on the consolidated work papers to eliminate the portion of the unamortized bond discount existing at the date of purchase that is applicable to the $50,000 face amount purchased by Company S.

Total discount on issue	$12,000
1/6 applicable to Co. S purchase	$ 2,000
Amount of discount per month ($2,000 divided by 120 months)	$ 16.67
Four years and nine months equal 57 months x $16.67	$ 950

The amount of unamortized bond discount on Co. P books applicable to the $50,000 purchase made by Company S was $950 at the date of purchase. This $950 would have entered into the computation of the gain or loss on intercompany bondholdings. In the example the gain or loss on intercompany bondholdings of $5,000 would have been reduced by $950 ($4,050) and the following additional consolidated elimination would have been made:

Gain or loss on inter- company bondholdings	$950	
Unamortized bond discount		$950

Intercompany dividends   Intercompany dividends must be eliminated on the consolidated work papers. Consolidated retained earnings should reflect the accumulated earnings of the consolidated group arising since acquisition which has not been distributed to the shareholders of, or capitalized by, the parent company. In the event that a subsidiary capitalizes earnings arising since acquisition by means of a stock dividend, or otherwise, a transfer to capital surplus is not required in consolidating.

Intercompany stockholdings   If a subsidiary holds stock of its parent, it is treated as "treasury stock" on the consolidated balance sheet and subtracted from consolidated stockholder's equity.

Income Tax Considerations

Income taxes must be deferred on any intercompany profits where the asset still exists within the consolidated group. However, if consolidated tax returns are filed, no adjustment need be made for deferred income taxes, because intercompany profits are eliminated in computing the consolidated tax liability.

Minority Interests

Consolidated financial statements are prepared primarily for the benefit of creditors and shareholders.

Minority interests in net income are deducted to arrive at consolidated net income. However, minority interests are theoretically limited to the extent of their equity capital, and losses in excess of minority interest equity capital are charged against the majority interest. Subsequently, when the losses reverse, the majority interests should be credited with the amount of minority interest losses previously absorbed before credit is made to the minority interests.

Computing minority interests in a complex father-son-grandson affiliation may be demonstrated by using the following diagram.

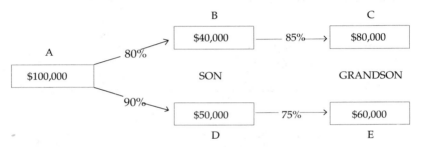

The computations of minority interests and consolidated net income follow:

	E	D	C	B	A
Net income	$60,000	$50,000	$80,000	$ 40,000	$100,000
75% to D	(45,000)	45,000			
		$95,000			
90% to A		(85,500)			85,500
85% to B			(68,000)	68,000	
				$108,000	
80% to A				(86,400)	86,400
Minority interests	$15,000	$ 9,500	$12,000	$ 21,600	
Consolidated net income					$271,900

In a situation where a subsidiary owns shares of the parent company, consolidated net income may be found algebraically, as the following illustration depicts:

Company	Unconsolidated income	
A	$40,000	A, the parent, owns 80% of B
B	20,000	B owns 70% of C
C	10,000	C owns 20% of A

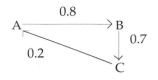

Let A = A's *consolidated basis* net income
B = B's *consolidated basis* net income
C = C's *consolidated basis* net income

The figures and relationships can be put into algebraic form so as to compute *consolidated net income.*

$$A = 40,000 + 0.8B$$
$$B = 20,000 + 0.7C$$
$$C = 10,000 + 0.2A$$

Solving for *A*, we have:

$$A = 40,000 + 0.8\ (20,000 + 0.7C)$$
$$A = 40,000 + 16,000 + 0.56C$$
$$A = 56,000 + 0.56C$$
$$A = 56,000 + 0.56\ (10,000 + 0.2A)$$
$$A = 56,000 + 5,600 + 0.112A$$
$$0.888A = 61,600$$
$$A = 69,369$$

Since 20% of the parent, A, is owned by an outsider, C, only 80% of A is used as consolidated net income.

$69,369 × 0.8 = $55,495 = consolidated net income

Disclosure

The consolidation policy should be fully disclosed on the financial statements or in footnotes to the statements.

Disclosure of minority interests   The *parent company theory* is used in practice almost exclusively for disclosing minority interests in a consolidated balance sheet. Under the parent company theory, minority interests are *not* considered part of stockholders' equity and are disclosed in the consolidated balance sheet between the liability section and the stockholders' equity section. Where minority interests are insignificant and do not warrant a separate classification in the consolidated balance sheet, some enterprises have seen fit to disclose minority interests among other liabilities. Minority interests in consolidated net income are shown as a deduction of consolidated net income.

Under the *entity theory*, minority interests are disclosed within and as part of the consolidated stockholders' equity section of the consolidated balance sheet. Although the entity theory has much more theoretical support, it is seldom used in practice.

CONTINGENCIES

Overview

Accounting for contingencies is covered by FASB-5 (Accounting for Contingencies) which amends ARB-50 (Contingencies); FASB Interpretation-14 (Reasonable Estimation of the Amount of a Loss); and FASB Interpretation-34 (Disclosure of Indirect Guarantees of Indebtedness of Others). FASB Technical Bulletin 81-2 has been issued to provide guidance on preacquisition contingencies (FASB-38).

The conditions for accrual of a loss contingency in FASB-5 do not amend any other requirement to accrue a particular type of loss expense in any other existing promulgated GAAP. In particular, the following items are specifically excluded from the scope of FASB-5:

1. APB-12, as it pertains to deferred compensation
2. APB-25, Accounting for Stock Issued to Employees
3. Accounting for other employment-related costs, such as group insurance, vacation pay, workmen's compensation, and disability benefits.

Background

A contingency is an existing condition, situation, or set of circumstances involving varying degrees of uncertainty that may, through one or more related future events, result in the acquisition or loss of an asset or the incurrence or avoidance of a liability, usually with the concurrence of a gain or loss. The resulting gain or loss is referred to as a *gain contingency* or a *loss contingency.*

The existence of a loss contingency may be established on or before the date of the financial statements, or after the date of the financial statements but prior to the issuance date of the financial statements. After a loss contingency is established, the probability of its developing into an actual loss must be evaluated. Accounting for a loss contingency is based upon the degree of probability that one or more future events will occur which will result in an actual loss. On the other hand, gain contingencies are never recorded on the books of an entity until they are actually realized, although footnote disclosure in the financial statements may be necessary.

Loss contingencies may arise from the risk of exposure resulting from the following list of items, which is not all-inclusive:

- Collectibility of receivables
- Property loss by fire, explosion, or other hazards
- Expropriation of assets
- Pending or threatened litigation, claims or assessments
- Product warranties or defects
- Catastrophe losses of property

Not all uncertainties in the accounting process are contingencies, as that term is used in FASB-5. Depreciable assets have a reasonably estimated life, and depreciation expense is used to systematically allocate the cost of the asset over its estimated useful life. Estimates, such as depreciation and similar accrued amounts, are not uncertainties as described in FASB-5.

Classification of a Loss Contingency

A loss contingency will develop into an actual loss only upon the occurrence of one or more future events, whose likelihood of occurring may vary significantly. Under the provisions of FASB-5, the likelihood that a loss contingency will develop into an actual loss must be classified as either (a) probable (likely to occur), (b) reasonably possible (halfway between *probable* and *remote*), or (c) remote (slight chance of materializing).

Accounting and Reporting a Loss Contingency

Depending upon whether it is classified as probable, reasonably possible, or remote, a loss contingency may have to be either (a) accrued as a charge to income as of the date of the financial statements, (b) disclosed by footnote in the financial statements, or (c) not disclosed at all.

The following two conditions must be met for a *loss contingency* to be accrued as a charge to income as of the date of the financial statements:

- It is *probable* that as of the date of the financial statements an asset has been impaired or a liability incurred, based on information available before the actual issuance date of the financial statements.

It is implicit in this condition that it must be *probable* that one or more future events will occur to confirm the loss.

- The amount of loss can be reasonably estimated.

> **OBSERVATION:** *If a loss contingency is classified as probable and only a range of possible loss (similar to a minimum-maximum) can be established, then the* **minimum** *amount in the range should be accrued, unless some other amount within the range appears to be a better estimate (FASB Interpretation-14).*

If an exposure to a loss exists in excess of the amount accrued in accordance with the above provisions of FASB-5, and the amount of the excess exposure is classified as *probable* or *reasonably possible*, financial statement disclosure of the excess loss contingency is required by FASB-5. The disclosure shall contain a description of the nature of the excess loss contingency and the range of possible loss (similar to a minimum-maximum), or include a statement that no estimate of the loss can be made.

If one or both conditions for the accrual of a loss contingency are not met and the loss contingency is classified as *probable* or *reasonably possible*, financial statement disclosure of the loss contingency is required by FASB-5. The disclosure shall contain a description of the nature of the loss contingency and the range of possible loss (similar to a minimum-maximum), or include a statement that no estimate of the loss can be made.

Loss contingencies arising after the date of the financial statements A loss contingency that is classified as *probable* or *reasonably possible*, which occurs after the balance sheet date but before the issuance date of the financial statements, may have to be disclosed to avoid misleading financial statements. If professional judgment deems this type of disclosure necessary, the disclosure shall contain a description of the nature of the loss contingency and the range of possible loss (similar to a minimum-maximum), or include a statement that no estimate of the loss can be made. On the other hand, it may be desirable to disclose this type of loss contingency by supplementing the historical financial statements with pro forma statements reflecting the loss as if it occurred at the date of the financial statements.

Allowance for uncollectible receivables For the purposes of GAAP, accounts receivable must be reported at their net realizable value. Net realizable value is equal to the gross amount of the receivables less an estimated allowance for uncollectible accounts.

Under FASB-5, a contingency exists if, at the date of its financial statements, an enterprise does not expect to collect the full amount of its accounts receivable. Under this circumstance, an accrual for a loss contingency must be charged to income if both of the following conditions are met:

- It is *probable* that as of the date of the financial statements an enterprise does not expect to collect the full amount of its accounts receivable, based on information available before the actual issuance of the financial statements.
- The amount of loss contingency (uncollectible receivables) can be *reasonably estimated*.

If both of the above conditions are met, an accrual for the estimated amount of uncollectible receivables must be made even if the uncollectible receivables cannot be specifically identified. An enterprise may base its estimate of uncollectible receivables on its prior experience, the experience of other enterprises in the same industry, the debtor's ability to pay, and/or an appraisal of current economic conditions. A significant uncertainty exists in the ultimate collection of accounts receivable if an enterprise is unable to reasonably estimate the amount of its uncollectible receivables. If a significant uncertainty does exist in the collection of the receivables, the installment sales method, cost-recovery method, or some other method of revenue recognition shall be used (paragraph 12 of APB-10).

In the event that one or both conditions for the accrual of a loss contingency on uncollectible receivables are not met and the loss contingency is classified as *probable* or *reasonably possible*, the nature of the loss contingency and the range of the possible loss (similar to a minimum-maximum), or a statement that no estimate of the loss can be made, must be disclosed in the financial statements.

Product or service warranty obligation A product or service warranty obligation is a contingency under the provisions of FASB-5, because of the potential claims which may result from the warranty. If both of the conditions for the accrual of a loss contingency are met, an accrual for the estimated amount of a warranty obligation must be made even if the warranty obligation cannot be specifically identified. An enterprise may base its estimate of a warranty obligation on its prior experience, the experience of other enterprises in the same industry, and/or an appraisal of current economic conditions. If an enterprise is unable to reasonably estimate the amount of its warranty obligation and the range of possible loss is wide, significant uncertainty exists as to whether a sale should be recorded. If a

significant uncertainty does exist in estimating a warranty obligation, a sale shall not be recorded and the installment sales method,
cost-recovery method, or some other method of revenue recognition
shall be used (paragraph 12 of APB-10).

In the event that one or both conditions for the accrual of a loss
contingency are not met and a loss contingency is classified as *probable* or *reasonably possible*, the nature of the loss contingency and the
range of possible loss (similar to a minimum-maximum), or a statement that no estimate of the loss can be made, must be disclosed in
the financial statements.

If a dealer offers a separately priced extended warranty or product
maintenance contract, the applicable GAAP is provided by FASB
Technical Bulletin 90-1, discussed in the chapter entitled "Revenue
Recognition."

Litigation, claims or assessments If both conditions for the accrual
of a loss contingency are met, an accrual for the estimated amount of
pending or threatened litigation and actual or possible claims or
assessments is required by FASB-5. Some of the factors that should
be considered in determining whether the conditions for accrual
have been met are the (a) nature of the litigation, claim or assessment, (b) progress of the case, including progress after the date of the
financial statements but before the issuance date of the financial
statements, (c) opinions of legal counsel, and (d) management's
intended response to the litigation, claim or assessment.

In the event that one or both conditions for the accrual of a loss
contingency are not met and a loss contingency is classified as *probable* or *reasonably possible*, the nature of the loss contingency and the
range of possible loss (similar to a minimum-maximum), or a statement that no estimate of the loss can be made, must be disclosed in
the financial statements.

Unasserted Claims or Assessments

An *unasserted claim* is one which has not been asserted by the claimant because the claimant has no knowledge of the existing claim or
does not elect to assert the existing claim. If it is *probable* that an
unasserted claim will be asserted by the claimant and it is *probable* or
reasonably possible that an unfavorable outcome will result, the
unasserted claim must be disclosed in the financial statements.
However, if these conditions are not met, disclosure is not required
for unasserted claims or assessments where apparently the potential
claimant has no knowledge of the claim's existence.

Disclosure of Remote Loss Contingencies

As a general rule, financial statement disclosure of loss contingencies that have a *remote* possibility of materializing is not required by FASB-5. However, loss contingencies that may occur as the result of a *guarantee* must be disclosed in the financial statements, even if they have a *remote* possibility of materializing.

Guarantees to repurchase receivables or related property, obligations of banks under letters of credit or *stand-by agreements*, guarantees of the indebtedness of others, and unconditional obligations to make payments are examples of the types of guarantee contingencies which must be disclosed even if they have a *remote* possibility of materializing. FASB-5 requires that the nature and amount of the guarantee be disclosed in the financial statements. In addition, consideration should be given to disclosing the amount, if estimable, that can be recovered in the event the guarantor is called upon to satisfy the guarantee.

FASB Interpretation-34 (Disclosure of Indirect Guarantees of Indebtedness of Others) was issued to clarify that the term *guarantee of indebtedness of others* (paragraph 12 of FASB-5) includes both direct and indirect guarantees.

In both a direct and indirect guarantee of indebtedness of others, three parties are involved: (1) the debtor, (2) the creditor, and (3) the guarantor. In a direct guarantee, the guarantor agrees to make payment directly to the creditor if the debtor fails to do so. The guarantee runs directly from the guarantor to the creditor. Thus, the creditor has a direct claim against the guarantor if the debtor defaults. In an indirect guarantee, the guarantor agrees to transfer funds to the debtor if a specified event occurs. The guarantee runs directly from the guarantor to the debtor, but the creditor is an indirect beneficiary of the guarantee. Thus, the creditor has an indirect claim against the guarantor because he may exercise the debtor's claim against the guarantor in the event of default. After the guarantor transfers the funds to the debtor, they may become available to the creditor. (The preceding definitions are based on paragraph 2 of FASB Interpretation-34, which is further clarified by paragraph 9, Appendix A, of FASB Interpretation-34.)

> **OBSERVATION:** *FASB Interpretation-34 states that the funds transferred to the debtor will become legally available to creditors. However, this does not necessarily mean that any creditor will actually receive the transferred funds. The agreement may specifically require the debtor to use the funds for purposes other than the*

payment of creditors. For example, the agreement may require that the debtor retain the transferred funds in order to maintain its working capital at or above a specified minimum.

Another possibility is that competing creditor claims may be made against the transferred funds, in which event litigation may be the only solution.

FASB Interpretation-34 describes the following agreements as indirect guarantees of indebtedness of others:

- A guarantor is obligated to transfer funds to a debtor if a specific event occurs. The funds transferred must be legally available to the debtor's creditors, who also expressly have the right to enforce the terms of the agreement in the event of default.
- A guarantor is obligated to transfer funds to a debtor if the debtor's income, working capital, and/or coverage of fixed charges are not maintained at specified amounts.

Thus, one must conclude that an indirect guarantee of the indebtedness of another, for the purposes of FASB Interpretation-34, must involve, among other factors, a transfer of funds from the guarantor to the debtor. However, paragraph 3 of FASB Interpretation-34, further clarifies the situation. Paragraph 3 states that the term "guarantees of indebtedness of others" in paragraph 12 of FASB-5, "includes" those indirect guarantees described in FASB Interpretation-34. The use of the word "includes" in this context may mean "includes, but is not limited to." If this is correct, other types of indirect guarantees of indebtedness of others that do not involve the "transfer of funds" should be disclosed in accordance with FASB-5 when professional judgment warrants such disclosure.

FASB Interpretation-34 makes no mention of who must disclose indirect guarantees of indebtedness of others in accordance with FASB-5. It is obvious that until the indirect guarantee is actually enforced, the guarantor must disclose the *remote* loss contingency that would result from the enforcement of the guarantee. However, there may be circumstances in which professional judgment may require disclosure, by the debtor and/or creditor, of indirect guarantees which have not yet been enforced.

> **OBSERVATION:** *Apparently, the Financial Accounting Standards Board recognized the need for clarification of indirect guarantees of indebtedness of others because some enterprises were*

*interpreting paragraph 12 of FASB-5 to cover only direct guaran-
tees. Thus, indirect guarantees, in some instances, were not being
properly disclosed. FASB Interpretation-34 was probably issued to
clarify and correct this situation.*

Disclosure of Noninsured Property

An enterprise may be underinsured or not insured at all against the
risk of future loss or damage to its property by fire, explosion, or
other hazard. The fact that an enterprise's property is underinsured
or not insured at all constitutes an existing uncertainty as defined by
FASB-5. However, the absence of insurance does not mean that an
asset has been impaired or a liability incurred as of the date of the
financial statements. Therefore, FASB-5 does not require financial
statement disclosure of noninsurance or underinsurance of possible
losses, but specifically states that it does not discourage this practice.

Reporting Gain Contingencies

Gain contingencies should be disclosed in the financial statements
by footnote, but should not be reflected in income, because doing so
might result in recognizing revenue prior to its realization. Care
should be exercised in disclosing gain contingencies to avoid misleading implications as to the recognition of revenue prior to its
realization (ARB-50).

Appropriation of Retained Earnings

FASB-5 does not prohibit an enterprise from appropriating specific
amounts of retained earnings for potential loss contingencies. However, the amount of appropriated retained earnings must be reported within the stockholders' equity section of the balance sheet,
clearly identified as an appropriation of retained earnings. In addition, the following rules must be observed:

1. No costs or losses shall be charged against the appropriated
   retained earnings and no part of the appropriated retained
   earnings may be transferred to income or in any way used to
   affect the determination of net income for any period.
2. The appropriated retained earnings shall be restored intact to
   retained earnings when the appropriation is no longer considered necessary.

Preacquisition Contingencies (FASB-38)

A portion of the total cost of acquiring an enterprise under the purchase method (APB-16) must be allocated to contingent assets, contingent liabilities, and contingent impairments of assets, provided that the following conditions are met:

- It is probable that the contingent item existed at the consummation date of the business combination.
- After the consummation date, but prior to the end of the "allocation period" it is confirmed that the contingent item did exist at the consummation date of the business combination.
- The amount of the asset, liability, or impairment can be reasonably estimated.

If the above conditions are met, a portion of the total cost of acquiring an enterprise under the purchase method must be allocated to any contingent items (FASB-38).

The *allocation period* is the period that is required by the purchaser to identify and quantify the acquired assets and assumed liabilities for the purposes of allocating the total cost of the acquisition in accordance with APB-16.

Any adjustment for contingent items arising from a purchase transaction that occurs after the end of the "allocation period" is included in net income of the period in which the adjustment is recognized.

CONVERTIBLE DEBT

Overview

APB-14 establishes the promulgated GAAP for reporting the issuance of convertible debt and debt issued with stock purchase warrants. The issuance of any debt security not explicitly discussed in APB-14 should be accounted for in accordance with the substance of the transaction (APB-14).

For the purpose of applying APB-14, the time of issuance of a debt security is the date on which an agreement as to the terms of the debt security is reached and announced, even though the agreement may be subject to the subsequent approval of the stockholders and/or directors of the enterprise.

FASB-84 establishes the method of accounting and reporting that should be applied to certain conversions of convertible debt that are induced by the debtor. Under FASB-84, an *induced conversion* of convertible debt is one in which the original conversion privileges are changed, or additional consideration is paid, to induce the holder of the convertible debt to convert to the equity securities of the debtor.

FASB-84 amends APB-26 (Early Extinguishment of Debt) to provide that induced conversions of convertible debt that were previously covered by APB-26 are now covered by the provisions of FASB-84.

Background

Convertible debt is convertible into the common stock of the issuer or an affiliated enterprise, and because of the conversion option, a debtor can generally issue convertible debt at a lower interest rate than comparable nonconvertible debt. Most convertible debt is *callable* at the option of the debtor and is generally subordinated to nonconvertible debt. The characteristics of convertible debt are:

- The issue price is not significantly greater than the face amount.
- The interest rate is lower than the interest rate on an equivalent, but not convertible, security.
- The initial conversion price is greater than the market value of the underlying security.

- The conversion price does not change (except pursuant to certain antidilutive considerations).
- The security is usually callable by the issuer.
- The debt is usually subordinate to the nonconvertible debt of the issuer.

Issuance of convertible debt   A convertible debt security may be issued with a conversion feature that is physically inseparable from, and part of, the convertible debt security, or with a separate conversion feature, such as a deductible stock purchase warrant.

Under current accounting practice (APB-14), the economic substance of an inseparable conversion option is not recognized at the time the convertible debt is issued, because none of the issuance proceeds from the convertible debt are allocated to the conversion option. APB-14 requires that all of the issuance proceeds be credited to the liability account for the convertible debt after accounting for any related bond discount or premium.

Under current accounting practice (APB-14), the economic substance of a separate conversion option is recognized, because a portion of the issuance proceeds from the debt is allocated to the conversion option. The portion of the issuance proceeds allocated to the separate conversion option is based on the relative fair value of the convertible debt and conversion option on their date of issuance. Thus, the convertible security itself is credited at par or face value, the detachable warrant is credited at market value, and the discount or premium is the residual amount required to balance the cash received.

Xeta Corporation issues $10,000 of 5% convertible preferred stock with a detachable common stock warrant to purchase one share of Xeta's common stock at a specified price. At the time of issuance, the quoted market price of the convertible stock was $97 per share, and the stock warrants were quoted at $2 each. The proceeds of the sale to Xeta Corporation were $9,900. The transaction is accounted for as follows:

Cash	$9,900	
Discount on 5% convertible preferred stock	300	
5% Convertible preferred stock		$10,000
Paid-in capital (stock warrants)		200

The difference between the face amount of the 5% convertible preferred stock and the value of the warrants that were recorded on the books ($10,000 + $200 = $10,200) less the amount of cash proceeds received from the sale ($9,900) is equal to the discount ($300).

OBSERVATION: *Proper recognition of the economic substance of the issuance of convertible debt requires that a portion of the proceeds from the issuance of the debt be allocated to the conversion option and credited to paid-in capital. This is exactly the method of accounting that was required by prior promulgated GAAP (APB-10). However, APB-10 was superseded by APB-14, which does not give recognition to the economic substance of a conversion option that is inseparable from its regulated convertible security, but does recognize the economic substance of a conversion option that is separable from its related convertible security. Thus, under APB-14, accounting for the issuance of convertible debt with an insepa-rable conversion option is different than accounting for the issu-ance of convertible debt with a separate conversion option.*

Conversions of convertible debt   Once a separate conversion fea-ture is issued, such as a detachable stock purchase warrant, it is usually separately traded from its related convertible debt security. The separate conversion feature has its own market price, and con-version requires (a) the surrender of the conversion feature, and (b) the payment of any other consideration required by the terms of the warrant.

Under current accounting practice (APB-14), when a separate conversion feature, such as a detachable stock purchase warrant, is exercised and converted into equity securities of the debtor, in accor-dance with the original conversion terms, no gain or loss is recog-nized on the transaction. The amount previously credited to paid-in capital for the conversion feature at issuance is debited, the amount of cash received, if any, is recorded, and the par value of the capital stock issued and the appropriate credit to capital stock in excess of par is recorded. The following is an illustration of such a transaction.

Ace Corporation previously issued convertible debt securities with detachable stock purchase warrants. A credit of $10 for each warrant was recorded in paid-in capital at the date of issuance, representing the relative market value of each warrant. There was no discount or premium on the issuance of the convertible debt with detachable stock purchase warrants. Each stock purchase warrant was convertible into 50 shares of Ace Corporation's $1 par value common stock, upon the payment of $200 and the surrender of the warrant. Assuming that one warrant was exercised, the journal entry would be:

Cash	$200	
Paid-in capital (stock warrants)	10	
Capital stock ($1 par value)		$ 50
Capital in excess of par (common stock)		160

Thus, under current accounting practice, the conversion of a separate conversion feature, such as a detachable stock purchase warrant, is accounted for as an equity transaction, and no gain or loss is recorded.

In order to exercise a conversion feature that is physically inseparable from, and part of, a convertible debt security, the entire security must be surrendered, and the debt is retired by the debtor.

Under current accounting practice (APB-14), when a convertible debt security with an inseparable conversion feature is converted into equity securities of the debtor in accordance with the original conversion terms, no gain or loss is recognized on the transaction. The convertible debt security is surrendered by the holder and the debt is retired by the debtor. The following is an illustration of such a transaction.

Blue Corporation has outstanding $20,000,000 of 14% convertible bonds, with an unamortized bond premium balance of $800,000. Each $1,000 bond is convertible into ten shares of Blue Corporation's $5 par value common stock. On April 1, 19X1, all of the convertible bonds were converted by the bondholders.

14% Convertible bonds payable	$20,000,000	
Unamortized bond premium	800,000	
Common stock ($5 par x 200,000)		$ 1,000,000
Capital in excess of par (common stock)		19,800,000

Under current accounting practice, no gain or loss is recognized on the conversion of convertible bonds to common stock if the conversion is made in accordance with the original conversion terms.

Extinguishments of debt APB-26 applies to all extinguishments of debt made before or at maturity, except debt that is extinguished through a troubled debt restructuring (FASB-15). APB-26 covers the *extinguishment* of convertible debt but does not cover convertible debt that is *converted* to the equity securities of the debtor in accordance with the original conversion terms in the debt agreement. Thus, it is important to distinguish the difference between an extinguishment of debt and the conversions of debt.

FASB Technical Bulletin 80-1 states that APB-26 applies to all early extinguishments of debt effected by the issuance of common or preferred stock, including redeemable and fixed-maturity preferred stock, unless the extinguishment is a troubled debt restructuring (FASB-15) or a *conversion* by the holder pursuant to conversion privileges contained in the original debt issue.

> **OBSERVATION**: *An accounting interpretation of APB-26 dated March 1973, states that "APB Opinion No. 26 does not apply to a conversion of debt nor does the Opinion specify the accounting for conversion of debt. In practice, however, the carrying amount of the debt, including any unamortized premium or discount, is credited to the capital accounts upon conversion to reflect the stock issued and no gain or loss is recognized."*

An extinguishment of debt is the reacquisition of debt prior to, or at, the maturity date of the debt. Under APB-26, all extinguishments of debt are basically alike, and accounting for such transactions should be the same, regardless of the method used to achieve the extinguishment. Thus, there should be no difference in accounting for an extinguishment of debt by (a) cash purchase, (b) exchange of stock for debt, (c) exchange of debt for debt, and (d) any other method (see paragraph 19 of APB-26).

Gain or loss on the extinguishment of debt is the difference between the total reacquisition cost of the debt and the net carrying amount of the debt on the date of the extinguishment. Under APB-26, gain or loss on the extinguishment of debt is recognized immediately, in the period of extinguishment, and, if material, is reported as an extraordinary item, net of related tax effects (FASB-4).

Inducements to convert Generally, convertible debt is issued in anticipation that it will be converted into equity securities, and that the issuer will not have to pay the face amount of the debt at its maturity date. Although most convertible debt issues provide for the issuance of common equity shares upon conversion, the terms of a convertible debt security may provide for the issuance of preferred or other type of equity security upon conversion. When an enterprise converts debt to common equity shares, the liability for the debt is eliminated and the number of common equity shares outstanding is increased, which affects the computation of earnings per share (EPS). When debt is converted to common equity shares, the pretax net income of the enterprise also increases by the amount of interest expense that was previously paid on the convertible debt.

Convertible debt is generally converted by a holder when the market value of its underlying equity securities into which the debt can be converted exceeds the face amount of the debt. If a convertible bondholder does not convert, the issuer may exercise the call provision in the debt to force conversion.

Convertible debt is usually not converted when the market value of its underlying equity securities is less than the face amount of the debt. Under this circumstance, the issuer may either (a) exercise the call provision in the debt and pay the bondholders the face amount of the convertible debt or (b) offer the bondholders an inducement to convert which exceeds the original conversion terms.

Induced Conversions of Convertible Debt

FASB-84 applies to conversions of convertible debt in which the original conversion terms are changed by the debtor to induce the holder of the convertible debt to convert to equity securities of the debtor. Changes in the original conversion terms may include (a) the reduction of the original conversion price to increase the number of shares of equity securities received by the bondholder, (b) the issuance of warrants or other securities, or (c) the payment of cash or some other type of consideration.

FASB-84 applies only to induced conversions that (a) are exercisable for a limited period of time and (b) include the issuance of no less than the number of shares of equity securities required by the original conversion terms for each convertible bond converted. Thus, for each convertible bond that is converted, the debtor must issue, at a minimum, the amount of equity securities required by the original conversion terms.

For the purposes of applying FASB-84, it makes no difference whether the holder of the convertible debt legally exercises, or does not legally exercise, the original contractual conversion privileges.

> *OBSERVATION: FASB-84 applies only to those induced conversions that are offered for a "limited period of time." Unfortunately, the term "limited period of time" is not explained adequately.*

Example 1 of Appendix A of FASB-84 appears to indicate that 60 days is considered a limited period of time. Example 2 indicates that 30 days is considered a limited period of time. However, paragraph 32 of FASB-84 seems to indicate that a "limited period of time" may even be longer than 60 days.

In an induced conversion of convertible debt under FASB-84, a debtor does not recognize any gain or loss on the amount of equity securities that are required to be issued under the original conversion terms for each convertible bond converted. However, the fair value of any equity securities or other consideration paid or issued by the debtor, which exceeds the amount of equity securities required to be issued for each convertible bond converted under the original conversion terms, shall be recognized as an ordinary expense on the date the inducement offer is accepted by the bondholder. In other words, the fair value of any incremental consideration that is incurred by the debtor in an induced conversion shall be recognized as an ordinary expense on the date the inducement offer is accepted by a bondholder.

> **OBSERVATION**: *If 500 different bondholders accepted an inducement offer on 40 different days during the "limited period of time" allowed by FASB-84, a separate computation of the fair value of the incremental consideration may be required if the fair value of the debtor's common stock changes from day to day.*

CALCULATION OF INCREMENTAL CONSIDERATION

Black Corporation has outstanding one hundred 10% Convertible Bonds due on December 31, 19X1. Each $1,000 bond is convertible into 20 shares of Black Corporation $1 par value common stock. To induce bondholders to convert to its common stock, Black Corporation increases the conversion rate from 20 shares per $1,000 bond to 25 shares per $1,000 bond. This offer was made by Black Corporation for a limited period of 60 days commencing March 1, 19X2.

On April 1, when the market price of Black's common stock was $60, one bondholder tendered a $1,000 convertible bond for conversion. Under FASB-84, the amount of incremental consideration is equal to the fair value of the additional five shares of Black Corporation's common stock on April 1. Thus, the amount of incremental consideration is $300 (5 shares x $60 per share).

The journal entry to record the transaction is:

Convertible bonds payable	$1,000	
Debt conversion expense	300	
Common stock ($1 par value)		
($1 x 25 shares)		$ 25
Capital in excess of par		
(common stock)		1,275

The incremental consideration paid or issued by a debtor may also be calculated as the difference between (a) the fair value of the equity securities and/or other consideration required to be issued under the original terms of the conversion privilege and (b) the fair value of the equity securities and/or other consideration that is actually issued.

Market value of securities based on inducement	
(25 x $60)	$1,500
Market value of securities based on original terms	
(20 x $60)	1,200
Fair value of incremental consideration	$ 300

> **OBSERVATION:** *If, on April 2, when the market price of Black's common stock was $62, another bondholder tendered a $1,000 convertible bond for conversion the amount of incremental consideration, under the provisions of FASB-84 would be $310 (5 shares x $62 per share).*

Effective date and transition   FASB-84 is effective for induced conversions of convertible debt that are offered by the debtor on or after April 1, 1985. As with most promulgated GAAP, earlier application of the provisions of FASB-84 is encouraged.

An accounting change which results from the initial application of FASB-84 shall be made by the retroactive restatement of all comparative financial statements presented. In addition, the financial statements of the year of change shall disclose the nature of any restatement and its effect on income before extraordinary items, net income, and related per share amounts, for each year presented.

CRITIQUE OF FASB-84

Induced Conversions of Convertible Debt

There is a significant difference between extinguishment accounting and conversion accounting. As a rule, gain or loss is recognized in extinguishment accounting, while no gain or loss is recognized in conversion accounting. Extinguishment accounting results in the *extinguishment* of a debt, while conversion accounting results in the issuance of equity securities and the *retirement* of a debt. Although FASB-84 refers to both extinguishment and conversion accounting, it does not distinguish between the two methods.

Under FASB-84, the amount of equity securities issued under the original conversion terms is accounted for as a conversion and no gain or loss is recognized, but the market value of any additional conversion inducement is accounted for as an ordinary expense (as opposed to an extraordinary expense). If the additional inducement consists of equity securities, the market value of such securities is credited to capital stock, and if necessary to capital in excess of par, with an offsetting debit to debt conversion expense. If the additional inducement consists of assets other than the debtor's equity securities, the market value of such assets is credited with an offsetting debit to debt conversion expense.

Paragraph 23 of FASB-84, which contains the basis for the above conclusions, is quoted below:

> In a conversion pursuant to original conversion terms, debt is extinguished in exchange for equity pursuant to a pre-existing contract that is already recognized in the financial statements and no gain or loss is recognized upon conversion. Unlike a conversion pursuant to original terms, in an induced conversion transaction the enterprise issues shares or pays assets in excess of those provided in the preexisting contract between the parties. The Board believes that the enterprise incurs a cost when it gives up securities or assets pursuant to a previous obligation and that the cost of those securities or assets should be recognized.

When an enterprise gives up *assets* or increases its *liabilities* to induce the conversion of its convertible debt to its equity securities, there is no question that a cost is incurred. However, serious doubt exists whether an enterprise incurs a cost when it gives up its own *equity securities* as an inducement for the conversion of convertible debt.

Paragraph 65 of FASB Concept Statement No. 3 states that expenses represent outflows or other using up of assets or incurrences of liabilities (or a combination of both) during a period. There is no outflow or other using up of assets or incurrence of liabilities when, as a conversion inducement, an enterprise issues its equity securities and records their fair market value as debt conversion expense. The debt conversion expense that is required to be recorded in an induced conversion under FASB-84 does not represent any outflow of assets or the incurrence of any liabilities, unless capital stock is considered an asset. However, since it is widely held that a corporation cannot own part of itself, a corporation's own capital stock should not be considered a corporate asset. Paragraph 43 of FASB Concept Statement No. 3 defines equity, which includes capital stock, as "the residual interest in the assets of an entity that remains after deducting its liabilities." Thus, capital stock cannot be both an asset and part of equity.

Generally, the issuance of capital stock increases an enterprise's assets or decreases its liabilities, and increases the number of capital shares outstanding. The principal amount of a convertible debt issue does not change, regardless of the number of equity shares that are issued in a conversion. When capital stock is issued in a transaction that does not affect the assets or liabilities of an enterprise, only the number of outstanding shares of capital stock is increased, which simply dilutes the equity of the individual shareholders.

FASB-84 also overlooks the fact that the issuance of capital stock is a capital transaction, and under current accounting practice, capital transactions should not enter into the income determination of an enterprise (APB-9). FASB-84 requires that an enterprise record the market value of its capital stock that is issued to induce the conversion of convertible debt, along with an offsetting debit to debt conversion expense. The credit to capital stock increases stockholders' equity, and the debit to debt conversion expense for the same amount is included in determining income for the period. The ultimate effect of the debt conversion expense is to decrease retained earnings (stockholders' equity) in the same amount originally credited to capital stock (stockholders' equity). The net result of this capital transaction is (a) an increase in the number of shares of capital stock outstanding, and (b) the transfer of the fair market value of the capital stock issued to induce the conversion from retained earnings to capital stock, and if necessary, capital in excess of par. Thus, the total assets, total liabilities, and total equity of an enterprise are not changed by the capital transaction required by FASB-84.

> **OBSERVATION:** *Ordinarily, a corporation does not recognize a gain or loss when it exchanges its equity securities for property or money (IRC Sec. 1032). Thus, it appears that the debt conversion*

> *expense created by the capital transaction advocated by FASB-84
> would not be tax deductible.*

The debt conversion expense that is recorded under the provisions of FASB-84 does not generate an economic loss to an enterprise, because it does not result in the outflow of any assets or the incurrence of any liabilities. It is the individual stockholders of an enterprise that suffer the economic loss from the accounting required by FASB-84. First, the number of shares issued in a conversion reduces the primary earnings per share of an enterprise which may affect the value of the individual stockholder's investment. Secondly, the debt conversion expense may reduce primary earnings per share even further and, if significant, this reduction in earnings per share may affect the market price of the enterprise's stock. Thus, it is the individual stockholder, not the enterprise, that may suffer economic loss as a result of the provisions of FASB-84.

FASB-84 may encounter some legal problems with the Model Business Corporation Act (MBCA), which has been adopted by many states. Section 19 of the MBCA apparently requires that the consideration for the issuance of capital shares be paid in cash, tangible or intangible property, or in services actually performed for the corporation. It is not clear whether debt conversion expense will qualify as consideration for the issuance of capital stock. In addition, Section 17 of the MBCA appears to require that the consideration for the shares issued in a conversion of debt shall be the principal sum of, and accrued interest on, the debt.

Under current accounting practice, capital transactions are not included in the determination of the income of an enterprise, but are required to be adequately disclosed in the financial statements. Thus, current accounting practices for capital transactions would seem to require that the conversion of debt to equity be accounted for as a conversion, whether or not the original conversion privileges are exercised or additional equity securities are offered by the debtor. In this event, conversion accounting should be applied, and no gain or loss recognized on the capital transaction. Conversion accounting for induced conversions was recommended by some of the respondents to the exposure draft for FASB-84. Paragraph 26 of FASB-84, which reflects this position, is quoted below:

> Some respondents stated that no cost should be recognized on induced conversions of convertible debt instruments. They recommended that the original and incremental consideration be accounted for in the same manner as a conversion pursuant to original conversion terms. They reasoned that

changes in the number of shares issuable to satisfy a preexisting obligation do not change the nature of that obligation and also noted that gains and losses are not recognized by an enterprise in certain types of transactions involving issuance of shares of ownership.

Applying the Provisions of FASB-84

Under FASB-84, if the original conversion terms require the issuance of 50 shares of $1 par value common stock for each $1,000 convertible bond, and the debtor issues, as an additional inducement to convert, five additional shares of its common stock with a total market value of $100 ($20 per share), a loss is recognized on the market value of the additional common stock. The following illustrates the journal entry for such a transaction:

Convertible bond payable	$1,000	
Debt conversion expense ($20 x 5)	100	
Capital stock ($1 par) ($1 x 55 shares)		$ 55
Capital in excess of par (common stock)		1,045

As mentioned previously, the debt conversion expense of $100 creates a loss of $100, which decreases retained earnings (stockholders' equity) by the same amount. The net effect of the transaction is that $100 of retained earnings is converted into $100 of capital stock and capital in excess of par (common stock). If conversion accounting is followed for the same transaction, the results are exactly the same, except there is no loss, and no transfer of retained earnings to capital stock and capital stock in excess of par (common stock). The following illustrates the journal entry for such a transaction:

Convertible bond payable	$1,000	
Capital stock ($1 par) ($1 x 55 shares)		$ 55
Capital in excess of par (common stock)		945

Under conversion accounting, the capital stock issued in the conversion is recorded at the net carrying amount of the debt which is being converted and no gain or loss is recognized on the transaction. The market value of the capital stock is ignored.

If the additional inducement consists of assets other than the debtor's equity securities, the market value of such assets is credited with an offsetting debit to debt conversion expense. Thus, if the original conversion terms require the issuance of 50 shares of $1 par value common stock for each $1,000 convertible bond, and the debtor pays an additional inducement of $100 in cash or $100 in market value of other assets, a loss is recognized in the amount of $100. The following illustrates the journal entry for such a transaction:

Convertible bond payable	$1,000	
Debt conversion expense	100	
Capital stock ($1 par)		$ 50
Capital in excess of par (common stock)		950
Cash or other assets		100

An economic loss occurs when the additional inducement paid by a debtor in an induced conversion is in the form of cash or other assets. The effect of the payment of the $100 cash inducement in the above journal entry (a) decreases cash by $100, (b) creates a loss of $100 (debt conversion expense), and (c) has no effect on the capital stock accounts. The $100 loss results in a $100 decrease in retained earnings (stockholders' equity), which is not offset by any other amount.

CURRENT ASSETS AND CURRENT LIABILITIES

Overview

The primary source of promulgated GAAP concerning current assets and current liabilities is ARB-43, Chapter 3A. Other related promulgated GAAP included in this chapter are:

ARB-43, Chapter 1A, Receivables from Officers, Employees, or Affiliated Companies

ARB-43, Chapter 3A, Current Assets and Current Liabilities

FASB-6, Classification of Short-Term Obligations Expected to Be Refinanced

FASB-43, Accounting for Compensated Absences

FASB-78, Classification of Obligations That Are Callable by the Creditor

FASB Interpretation-8, Classification of a Short-Term Obligation Repaid Prior to Being Replaced by a Long-Term Security

FASB Technical Bulletin 79-3 was issued to provide guidance in accounting for long-term obligations that contain subjective acceleration clauses. FASB Technical Bulletin 85-4 provides guidance on accounting for purchases of life insurance.

Operating Cycle

In the ordinary course of business there is a continuing *circulation of capital* within the current assets. For example, with a manufacturer, cash is expended for materials, labor, and factory overhead that are converted into finished inventory. After being sold, the inventory is usually converted into a trade receivable and, on collection of receivable, is converted back to cash. The average time elapsing between expending the cash originally and receiving the cash back from the trade receivable is called an *operating cycle*. *One year* is used as a basis for segregating current assets when the operating cycle occurs more frequently than once a year. When the operating cycle is *longer than one year*, as with the lumber, tobacco, and distillery businesses, then the longer period should be used as the operating cycle. *In the event that a business clearly has no operating cycle, the one-year rule is used.*

The classification of current assets and current liabilities for a specific company is directly related to the company's operating cycle.

Frequently, businesses have a *natural business year*, at the end of which the company's activity, inventory, and trade receivables are at their lowest point.

Current Assets

Resources that are reasonably expected to be realized in cash, sold, or consumed (prepaid items) during the normal operating cycle of a business are classified as current assets. Current assets are sometimes called circulating or working assets, and cash that is restricted as to withdrawal or use for other than current operations should not be classified as a current asset.

There are several basic categories of current assets:

Cash   Includes money in any form, for example, cash on deposit, cash awaiting deposit, and cash funds available for use.

Secondary cash resources   The most common type of secondary cash resources are marketable securities.

Inventories   Include merchandise, raw materials, work in process, finished goods, operating supplies, and ordinary maintenance material and parts.

Receivables   Include accounts receivable, notes receivable, and receivables from officers and employees. To be classified as current assets, all these must become due within the current operating cycle.

Prepaid expenses   Include prepaid insurance, interest, rents, taxes, advertising, and operating supplies. Prepaid expenses are not converted into cash; and if they are not paid in advance, they would require the use of current assets during the operating cycle.

Current assets do not always represent their present realizable cash value. Accounts receivable, net of allowances for uncollectible accounts, are effectively stated at the amount of cash estimated as realizable. Supplementary information should be disclosed that reveals the basis on which current assets are stated and an indication of the method of determining the cost.

Current Liabilities

Current liabilities are obligations whose liquidation is reasonably expected to require the use of current assets or the creation of other current liabilities.

There are several basic types of current liabilities:

Obligations for items that have entered the operating cycle, which include trade payables and accrued liabilities such as wages and taxes.

Other debt that is expected to be liquidated during the current operating cycle, which includes short-term notes and the currently maturing portion of long-term debt.

Prepayments that include collections received in advance of services, for example, prepaid subscriptions and other deferred revenues.

Accruals which include estimates of accrued amounts that are expected to be required to cover expenditures within the year for known obligations (1) when the amount can be determined only approximately (provision for accrued bonuses payable) or (2) where the specific person(s) to whom payment will be made is (are) unascertainable (provision for warranty of a product).

Current liabilities should not include a contractual obligation falling due at an early date that is expected to be refinanced or refunded and is not reasonably expected to require the use of current assets or the creation of other current liabilities.

When appropriate, current liabilities should be recorded at their present values of the amounts to be paid.

Offsetting Assets and Liabilities

Offsetting is the display of a recognized asset and a recognized liability as one net amount on a financial statement. If the amount of the recognized asset and the amount of the recognized liability are exactly the same, the net or combined amount of both would be zero and as a result, no amount would appear on the financial statement. On the other hand, derecognition of an asset or extinguishment of a liability usually results in the removal of that asset or liability from the financial statement. Derecognition and extinguishment generally result in the recognition of a gain or loss.

Under existing GAAP, the offsetting of assets and liabilities for financial statement presentation purposes is considered unacceptable, unless a legal right of setoff exists (paragraph 7 of APB-10). For example, certain securities may be purchased from the U.S. Government, which by their terms are acceptable for the payment of taxes. The purchase of such securities is, in substance, an advance payment of taxes that will become payable in the near future. In this event, a legal right of setoff exists and the securities may be deducted (offset) from the related taxes payable in the statement of financial position.

Paragraph 7 of APB-10 (Omnibus Opinion—1966) states as follows:

1. It is a general principle of accounting that the offsetting of assets and liabilities in the balance sheet is improper except where a right of setoff exists. Accordingly, the offset of cash or other assets against the tax liability or other amount owing to governmental bodies is not acceptable except in the circumstances described in paragraph 3 below.

2. Most securities now issued by governments are not by their terms designed specifically for the payment of taxes and, accordingly, should not be deducted from taxes payable on the balance sheet.

3. The only exception to this general principle occurs when it is clear that a purchase of securities (acceptable for the payment of taxes) is in substance an advance payment of taxes that will be payable in the relatively near future, so that in the special circumstances the purchase is tantamount to the prepayment of taxes. This occurs at times, for example, as an accommodation to a local government and in some instances when governments issue securities that are specifically designated as being acceptable for the payment of taxes of those governments.

FASB Technical Bulletin 88-2 was issued to define the term *right of setoff*, which appears in paragraph 7 of APB-10 (Omnibus Opinion—1966). A right of setoff is the legal right of a debtor, by contract or otherwise, to discharge part or all of a debt against an amount owed to the debtor by another party. According to FASB Technical Bulletin 88-2, the following conditions must be met by a debtor to establish that a right of setoff exists:

a. The amount owed to each party is determinable.
b. The debtor has the legal right to set off part or all of a debt it owes against an amount owed to the debtor by another party.
c. The debtor intends to set off.
d. The debtor's right of setoff is enforceable at law.

If all of the above conditions are met, a debtor may offset a related asset and liability and report the net amount in its statement of financial position. For purposes of applying FASB Technical Bulletin 88-2, a financial institution shall not consider cash on deposit as an amount owed to the depositor.

FASB Technical Bulletin 88-2 does not address nonrecognition (derecognition) of assets and liabilities and does not modify the accounting treatment prescribed by any accounting pronouncement that results in offsetting or in a presentation in a statement of financial position that is similar to the effect of offsetting.

FASB Technical Bulletin 88-2 is effective for transactions entered into on or after January 1, 1989. Earlier application of this Technical Bulletin is encouraged for unissued annual financial statements. Retroactive restatement of previously issued financial statements for periods prior to January 1, 1989 (the effective date of FASB:TB 88-2) is also encouraged.

> **OBSERVATION:** *As of the date of this publication, an Exposure Draft (ED) was outstanding, entitled* Offsetting of Amounts Related to Certain Contracts: An Interpretation of APB Opinion No. 10 and FASB Statement No. 105. *This ED would incorporate the guidance contained in FASB Technical Bulletin 88-2 and would add a new interpretation regarding the offsetting of certain types of financial instruments. The ED is summarized at the end of the chapter entitled "Financial Instruments."*

Working Capital

Working capital is the excess of current assets over current liabilities, and it indicates the relative liquidity of an enterprise.

Changes in each element of working capital   The changes in each element of working capital are the increases or decreases in each current asset and current liability over the amounts in the preceding year, as follows:

	19X1	19X2	Increase or (Decrease)
Current Assets			
Cash	$10,000	$ 15,000	$ 5,000
Accounts receivable	25,000	35,000	10,000
Inventory	50,000	60,000	10,000
Prepaid expenses	1,000	500	(500)
Total current assets	$86,000	$110,500	$24,500
Current Liabilities			
Accounts payable	$10,000	$15,000	$ 5,000
Notes payable-current	20,000	15,000	(5,000)
Accrued expenses	1,000	1,500	500
Total current liabilities	$31,000	$31,500	$ 500
Net working capital	$55,000	$79,000	
Increase or decrease in working capital			$24,000

The *current ratio,* or *working capital ratio,* is a measure of current position and is useful in analyzing short-term credit.

The current ratio is computed by dividing the total current assets by the total current liabilities.

	19X1	19X2
Current assets	$650,000	$525,000
Current liabilities	250,000	225,000
Working capital	$400,000	$300,000
Current ratio	2.6 : 1	2.3 : 1

The *acid-test ratio* is determined by dividing the *cashlike* assets by total current liabilities. The cashlike assets consist of cash, receivables, and marketable securities. Only receivables and securities *convertible into cash* should be included, and restricted cash and securities should be excluded.

	19X1	19X2
Cash	$ 200,000	$ 150,000
Marketable securities	400,000	350,000
Receivables, net	800,000	600,000
Total cashlike assets	$1,400,000	$1,100,000
Total current liabilities	$ 600,000	$ 500,000
Acid-test ratio	2.3 : 1	2.2 : 1

Receivables

For the purposes of GAAP, accounts receivable must be reported in the financial statements at net realizable value. Net realizable value is equal to the gross amount of receivables less an estimated allowance for uncollectible accounts.

Under FASB-5 (Contingencies), a contingency exists if, at the date of its financial statements, an enterprise does not expect to collect the full amount of its accounts receivable. Under this circumstance, an accrual for a loss contingency must be charged to income, if both of the following conditions exist:

- It is *probable* that as of the date of the financial statements an asset has been impaired or a liability incurred, based on subsequent available information prior to the issuance of the financial statements, and
- The amount of the loss can be *reasonably estimated*.

If both of the above conditions are met, an accrual for the estimated amount of uncollectible receivables must be made even if the uncollectible receivables cannot be specifically identified. An enterprise may base its estimate of uncollectible receivables on its prior experience, the experience of other enterprises in the same industry, the debtor's ability to pay, or an appraisal of current economic conditions. A significant uncertainty may exist in the ultimate collection of the receivables if an enterprise is unable to reasonably estimate the amount that is uncollectible. If a significant uncertainty exists in the ultimate collection of the receivables, the installment sales method, cost-recovery method, or some other method of revenue recognition should be used (paragraph 12 of APB-10). In the event that both of the above conditions for accrual are not met and a loss contingency is at least *reasonably possible*, certain financial statement disclosures are required by FASB-5.

Two common procedures of accounting for bad debts are (a) the direct write-off method and (b) the allowance method. However, for the reasons discussed below, the direct write-off method is not acceptable for the purposes of GAAP.

Direct write-off method   This method recognizes a bad debt expense only when a specific account is determined to be uncollectible. The weaknesses of the direct write-off method are:

1. Bad debt expense is not *matched* with the related sales.
2. Accounts receivable are always overstated, because no attempt is made to account for the unknown bad debts included therein.

Allowance method   A percentage of each period's sales or ending accounts receivable is estimated to eventually prove uncollectible. Consequently, the amount determined is charged to bad debts of the period and the credit is made to a valuation account such as allowance for doubtful accounts. When specific accounts are written off, they are debited to the allowance account, which is periodically recomputed.

Bad debts may be estimated as a percentage of sales or of accounts receivable. For financial statement purposes, unearned interest and finance charges are deducted from the related receivable. This is necessary in order to state the receivable at its current realizable value.

Discounted notes receivable arise when the holder endorses the note (with or without recourse) to a third party and receives a sum of cash. The difference between the amount of cash received by the holder and the maturity value of the note is called the discount. If the note is discounted with recourse, the assignor remains contingently liable for the ultimate payment of the note when it becomes due. If the note is discounted without recourse, the assignor assumes no further liability.

The account called discounted notes receivable is a contra account which is deducted from the related receivables for financial statement purposes.

The following is the procedure for computing the proceeds of a discounted note:

1. Compute the total maturity value of the note, including interest due at maturity.
2. Compute the discount amount (the maturity value of the note multiplied by the discount rate for the time involved).
3. The difference between the two amounts (1 minus 2) equals the proceeds of the note.

A $1,000 90-day 10% note is discounted at a bank at 8% when 60 days are remaining to maturity.

Maturity—$1,000 x 102.5% (1/4 of 10% plus face)	$1,025.00
Discount—$1,025 x 1.333% (1/6 of 8%)	13.66
Proceeds of note	$1,011.34

Factoring

Factoring is a process by which a company can convert its receivables into cash by assigning them to a factor either with or without recourse. *With recourse* means that the assignee can return the receivable to the company and get back the funds paid if the receivable turns out to be uncollectible. *Without recourse* means that the assignee assumes the risk of any losses on collections. Under factoring arrangements, the customer may or may not be notified.

Pledging

Pledging is the process whereby the company uses existing accounts receivable as collateral for a loan. The company retains title to the receivables but pledges that it will use the proceeds to pay the loan.

Cash Surrender Value of Life Insurance

The proceeds of a life insurance policy usually provide some degree of financial security to one or more beneficiaries named in the policy. Upon death of the insured, the insurance company pays the beneficiary the face amount of the policy, less any outstanding indebtedness.

From an economic standpoint, insurance is a method which is used to spread a specific risk among many individuals. The insurance company assumes the specific risk, such as death, and charges a premium based on actuarial calculations. In the case of death, mortality tables have been established which take into consideration the frequency of deaths among individuals of various age groups. The premiums collected by the insurance company are used to pay current benefits and costs, and the balance is invested to yield investment income. Theoretically, if an individual dies in the year that the mortality tables predict, the accumulated net premiums collected by the insurance company, plus the investment earned on the accumulated premiums, should be sufficient to pay the face amount of the policy and still leave a profit for the insurance company.

Insurable interest   An owner of an insurance contract must have an insurable interest in the insured individual in order for the contract to be valid. An insurable interest in life insurance need only exist at the time the policy is issued, while an insurable interest in property insurance must exist at the time of a loss. An insurable interest is a test of financial relationship. A wife may insure the life of her husband, an employer the life of an employee, a creditor the life of his debtor, and a partner the life of a copartner.

A life insurance contract contains the name of the owner of the policy, the name of the insured individual, and the name of the beneficiary who receives the insurance proceeds upon the death of the insured individual. A life insurance contract may have more than one owner and more than one beneficiary. The rights of an owner of a life insurance contract include the right to change the beneficiary, the right to borrow on the policy, and the right to surrender the policy to the insurance company for its cash value. The beneficiary of a life insurance contract has the right to receive the proceeds of the policy upon the death of the individual insured by the contract. An irrevocable beneficiary is one that cannot be changed by the owner of the insurance policy. As a rule, a beneficiary does not have the right to borrow against the insurance policy, change the name of the beneficiary, or surrender the policy to the insurance company for its cash value.

Accounting for purchases of life insurance   FASB Technical Bulletin 85-4 provides guidance on accounting for purchases of life insurance. An investment in a life insurance policy should be accounted for at the amount that can be realized by the owner of the policy as of the date of its statement of financial position. Generally, the amount that can be realized from a life insurance policy is the amount of its cash surrender value. The increase in the cash surrender value of an insurance policy for a particular period should be recorded by the owner of the policy as an asset on its statement of financial position. The insurance expense for the same period is the difference between the total amount of premium paid and the amount of increase in the cash surrender value of the policy (FASB:TB 85-4).

> **OBSERVATION:** *Compliance with the provisions of FASB:TB 85-4 is required by all entities that purchase life insurance in which the entity is* **either** *the owner or beneficiary of the insurance contract (see Footnote 1 to FASB:TB 85-4). Although they may be the same individual or entity, the owner and the beneficiary of an insurance contract have different contractual rights. As a rule, the beneficiary has only the right to receive the proceeds of the insurance policy upon the death of the insured individual named in the policy. Ownership rights to an insurance contract vest solely with the owner of the policy and include the right to borrow against the policy, the right to surrender the policy for its cash value, and the right to change the beneficiary. Thus, FASB:TB 85-4 is in error by requiring an individual or entity which is solely the beneficiary and not the owner of an insurance policy to report the cash surrender value of the policy as an asset on its statement of financial position. Only an entity that is either the owner or the owner/beneficiary of an insurance policy should comply with the provisions of FASB:TB 85-4.*

An enterprise is the owner and sole beneficiary of a $200,000 life insurance policy on its president. The annual premium is $16,000. The policy is starting its fourth year, and the schedule of cash values indicates that at the end of the fourth year the cash value increases $25 per thousand. The enterprise pays the $16,000 premium, and the journal entry to record the transaction is as follows:

Life insurance expense – officers	$11,000	
Cash surrender value – life insurance policy	5,000	
Cash		$16,000

The cash surrender value of a life insurance policy is classified either as a current or noncurrent asset in the policy owner's statement of financial position, depending upon the intentions of the policy owner. If the policy owner intends to surrender the policy to the insurer for its cash value within its normal operating cycle, the cash surrender value should be classified as a current asset in the statement of financial position. If there is no intention of cashing in the policy's cash value within the normal operating cycle of the policy owner, the cash surrender value should be classified as a noncurrent asset in the statement of financial position.

Computing Life Insurance Expense

The insurance expense is always the difference between the premium paid (cash) and the increase in the cash surrender value of the policy.

Disclosure

Current assets and current liabilities should be clearly identified in the financial statements, and the basis of determining the amounts stated should be fully disclosed. The following are the more common disclosures that should be made for current assets and current liabilities in the financial statements or in footnotes thereto:

1. Method of valuing current marketable securities (FASB-12)
2. Classification of inventories and the method used (FIFO, LIFO, average cost, etc.)
3. Restrictions on current assets
4. Current portions of long-term obligations
5. Description of accounting policies relating to current assets and current liabilities

Accounts receivable and notes receivable from officers, employees, or affiliated companies, if material, must be reported separately in the financial statements (ARB-43, Chapter 1A).

Current Obligations Expected to Be Refinanced

FASB-6 and FASB Interpretation-8 establish the promulgated GAAP for reclassifying a short-term obligation (current liability) that is expected to be refinanced into a long-term liability, or stockholders' equity. In other words, if a company intends to refinance a short-term obligation into a classification other than current liability, prior to the issuance of the financial statements, it may be allowed to do so at the balance sheet date, even though the refinancing has not occurred. The actual intent to refinance, supported by an agreement which meets certain requirements (discussed below) are prerequisites for the reclassification.

The promulgated GAAP (FASB-6) applies only to those companies that issue classified balance sheets. A classified balance sheet reflects current assets and current liabilities separately for easy determination of working capital and to make the financial presentation more meaningful. Because of the specialized nature of some industries (stock brokers, real estate agents, stock life insurance companies, etc.) unclassified balance sheets are presented and therefore are not affected by the promulgated GAAP.

A short-term obligation should be excluded from current liabilities if the company intends to refinance it on a long-term basis and the intent is supported by either of the following conditions:

1. The actual issuance, after the date of the balance sheet but prior to the issuance of the financial statements, of a long-term obligation or equity security whose proceeds are used to retire the short-term obligation—in essence, the conversion of short-term obligation into a long-term obligation or equity.

    The amount of short-term obligations which can be reclassified cannot exceed the actual proceeds received from the issuance of the new long-term obligation.

    If equity securities are issued, the short-term obligation is excluded from current liabilities but is not included in stockholders' equity.

    OBSERVATION: *The promulgated GAAP (FASB-6) is silent on what classification to use to report the newly issued equity securities on the financial statements.*

2. Prior to the issuance of the financial statements the company has entered into an agreement that enables it to refinance a short-term obligation on a long-term basis. The terms of the agreement must be clear and unambiguous and must contain the following provisions:

    a. The agreement may not be cancelled by the lender or investor (company can cancel), and it must extend beyond the normal operating cycle of the company. (If the company has no operating cycle or the operating cycle occurs more than once a year, then the one-year rule is used.)

> b. At the balance sheet date and at its issuance, the company was not in violation, nor was there any information that indicated a violation, of the agreement.
>
> c. The lender or investor is expected to be financially capable of honoring the agreement.

The amount of short-term obligation which can be excluded from the current liabilities cannot exceed the amount of available refinancing covered by the established agreement. The amount must be adjusted for any limitations in the agreement which indicate the full amount obtainable will not be available to retire the short-term obligations. In addition, if the agreement indicates that the amount available for refinancing will fluctuate, then the most conservative estimate must be used. If no reasonable estimate can be made, then the agreement does not fulfill the necessary requirements and the full amount of current liabilities must be presented.

An enterprise may seek alternative financing sources besides those in the established agreement. However, if alternative sources do not materialize, the company must intend to borrow from the source in the agreement.

> **OBSERVATION**: *If the terms of the agreement allow the prospective lender or investor to set interest rates, collateral requirements, or similar conditions that are unreasonable to the company, the intent to refinance may not exist.*

Any *rollover agreements* or *revolving credit agreements* must meet the above provisions to enable a company to classify the related short-term obligations.

> **OBSERVATION**: *Long-term obligations that contain subjective acceleration clauses are not covered by FASB-6. A subjective acceleration clause is one in which the lender can unilaterally accelerate a long-term loan. For example, the loan agreement might state that "if, in the opinion of the lender, the borrower experiences recurring losses or liquidity problems, the lender may accelerate part or all of the loan balance . . . "*
>
> *FASB Technical Bulletin 79-3 was issued to provide guidance in accounting for long-term obligations that contain subjective acceleration clauses. If it is probable that the subjective acceleration clause will be exercised, the amount of the long-term obligation*

which is likely to be accelerated should be classified as a current liability. On the other hand, if it is reasonably possible that the subjective acceleration clause will be exercised, footnote disclosure may be all that is necessary. Finally, if the possibility of subjective acceleration is remote, no disclosure may be necessary. Professional judgment is necessary to determine what type of disclosure is required for long-term obligations containing subjective acceleration clauses.

The financial statements must contain a footnote disclosing the amount excluded from current liabilities and a full description of the financial agreement and new obligations incurred or expected to be incurred or the equity securities issued or expected to be issued.

Classification of Callable Obligations

FASB-78 establishes the promulgated GAAP for the current/non-current classification in the debtor's balance sheet of obligations that are payable on demand or callable by the creditor. FASB-78 does not address the creditor's balance sheet classification of demand or callable obligations. FASB-78 is applicable to obligations reported in classified balance sheets and to footnote disclosures of maturities of obligations reported in both classified and unclassified balance sheets. FASB-78 does not alter treatment of *subjective acceleration clauses* in long-term debt arrangements which is presently covered by FASB Technical Bulletin 79-3.

Background Several existing GAAP cover the balance sheet classifications of assets and liabilities into current and noncurrent categories. FASB-6 and FASB Interpretation-8 are concerned with an enterprise's intentions to refinance a current liability into a long-term liability or stockholders' equity. FASB-6 and FASB Interpretation-8 are discussed elsewhere in this chapter.

Chapter 3A of ARB-43 provides that current assets are those that are *reasonably expected* to be realized in cash, sold, or consumed (prepaid items) during the normal operating cycle of an enterprise. Current liabilities are obligations whose liquidation is *reasonably expected* to require the use of current assets, or the creation of other current liabilities during the normal operating cycle of an enterprise. The concept of an enterprise's normal operating cycle is discussed elsewhere in this chapter.

Under the provisions of Chapter 3A of ARB-43, the classification of current assets and current liabilities depends on an enterprise's normal operating cycle, which may be one year or a period longer than one year. Those assets that are reasonably expected to be realized in cash, sold, or consumed during the normal operating cycle of an enterprise are classified as current. Those liabilities whose liquidation is reasonably expected to require the use of current assets, or the creation of other current liabilities, during the normal operating cycle of an enterprise are classified as current. Under Chapter 3A of ARB-43, professional judgment must be used to analyze the substance of the transaction underlying each asset and liability to determine those that shall be classified as current and those that shall be classified as noncurrent.

Long-term obligations that contain subjective acceleration clauses are not covered by FASB-6, FASB Interpretation-8, or Chapter 3A of ARB-43. A subjective acceleration clause is one that permits the lender to unilaterally accelerate part or all of a long-term obligation. For example, the debt agreement might state that "if, in the opinion of the lender, the borrower experiences recurring losses or liquidity problems, the lender may at its sole discretion accelerate part or all of the loan balance..."

FASB Technical Bulletin 79-3 was issued to provide guidance in accounting for long-term obligations that contain subjective acceleration clauses. If it is *probable* that the subjective acceleration clause will be exercised by the creditor, the amount of the long-term obligation which is likely to be accelerated shall be classified as a current liability by the debtor. On the other hand, if it is *reasonably possible* that the subjective acceleration clause will be exercised by the creditor, footnote disclosure may be all that is required. Finally, if the possibility of subjective acceleration is *remote*, no disclosure may be required. Professional judgment is necessary to determine what type of disclosure, if any, is necessary for long-term obligations which contain subjective acceleration clauses.

> **OBSERVATION:** *The probable, reasonably possible, and remote criteria used in FASB Technical Bulletin 79-3 were originally used in FASB-5 (Contingencies). Under FASB-5,* **probable** *means that the event is likely to occur and* **remote** *means that the event has little chance of occurring.* **Reasonably possible** *represents a likelihood that is halfway between probable and remote.*

An *objective acceleration clause* in a long-term debt agreement is one that contains objective criteria that must be used by the creditor as the basis for calling part or all of the loan, such as a specified minimum amount of working capital or net worth requirement. In a long-term debt agreement, it is not unusual to find both objective and subjective acceleration clauses.

In the event of a violation of an objective acceleration clause, most long-term obligations become immediately callable by the creditor, or become callable after a grace period that is specified in the loan agreement. When this occurs, the creditor can demand payment of part or all of the loan balance, in accordance with the terms of the debt agreement.

Classifying callable obligations   The provisions of FASB-78 must be applied by a debtor to all obligations reported in classified balance sheets and to all disclosures concerning maturities of obligations in both classified and unclassified balance sheets. Once the maturity date of an obligation is determined in accordance with the provisions of FASB-78, the debtor shall apply its normal operating cycle to determine whether the obligation shall be classified as current or noncurrent.

FASB-78 is applied to a classified balance sheet to determine whether the obligation should be classified as current or noncurrent for balance sheet purposes. FASB-78 is applied to both classified and unclassified balance sheets to determine the maturity dates of obligations disclosed by footnotes. For example, an unclassified balance sheet may contain footnote disclosures of the maturity dates of obligations, in spite of the fact that the obligations are not classified in the unclassified balance sheet, or may not be separately identified from other obligations in the unclassified balance sheet.

A creditor may have waived the right to demand payment on a specific obligation for a period that extends beyond the debtor's normal operating cycle. In this event, the debtor shall classify the obligation as a noncurrent liability.

> *OBSERVATION: FASB-78 does not indicate the form in which the creditor's waiver must appear, or the manner in which an independent auditor should verify the existence of such a waiver. Sound professional judgment will generally require a written waiver by the creditor, supported by appropriate language in the management representation letter. In addition, a written opinion from the client's legal counsel is highly desirable as a means of verifying the existence of any waiver, and is essential if the client wishes to rely on an oral waiver by the creditor.*

At the date of the debtor's balance sheet, an obligation may, by its terms, be payable on demand. In this event, FASB-78 requires that the obligation be classified as a current liability, unless the creditor has waived the right to demand payment for a period that extends beyond the debtor's normal operating cycle. A violation of an objective acceleration clause in a long-term debt agreement may exist at the date of the debtor's balance sheet. FASB-78 requires that such an obligation be classified as a current liability at the debtor's balance sheet date unless:

1. The creditor has waived the right to demand payment for a period that extends beyond the debtor's normal operating cycle, or
2. The debtor has cured the violation after the balance sheet date, but prior to the issuance date of the financial statements, and the obligation is not callable for a period that extends beyond the debtor's normal operating cycle.

OBSERVATION: FASB-78 appears to offer a debtor an opportunity to delay the issuance of its financial statements long enough to coincide with the date that a violation is cured and thus avoid classifying the obligation as a current liability.

A long-term debt agreement may provide for a grace period which commences after the occurrence of a violation of an objective acceleration clause. FASB-78 requires that such an obligation be classified as a current liability at the debtor's balance sheet date, unless:

1. The creditor has waived the right to demand payment for a period that extends beyond the debtor's normal operating cycle, or
2. The debtor has cured the violation after the balance sheet date, but prior to the issuance date of its financial statements, and the obligation is not callable by the creditor for a period that extends beyond the debtor's normal operating cycle, or
3. The unexpired grace period extends beyond the debtor's normal operating cycle.

OBSERVATION: Under ARB-43, Chapter 3A, the classification of a long-term obligation that was or became payable on demand

> *depended on whether the debtor **reasonably expected** the creditor to require payment within the debtor's normal operating cycle. Thus, under ARB-43, Chapter 3A, the pervasive accounting principle of substance over form governed the classification of the long-term obligation. In applying the provisions of ARB-43, Chapter 3A, professional judgment was required to determine the substance of the transaction.*
>
> *FASB-78, which amends ARB-43, Chapter 3A, requires that an obligation be classified as current or noncurrent, based solely on whether the legal terms of the loan agreement require payment within the debtor's normal operating cycle. Thus, applying FASB-78 should be easy, because no professional judgment is required, and the substance of the transaction can be ignored.*

FASB-78 is effective for balance sheet classification of obligations for fiscal and interim periods that begin on or after December 16, 1983. Earlier application of FASB-78 in previously unissued financial statements is encouraged. Retroactive restatement of previously issued financial statements to conform with the provisions of FASB-78 is permitted, but not required.

Compensated Absences

FASB-43 (Accounting for Compensated Absences) is the promulgated GAAP that cover employees' compensated absences and is concerned only with the proper accrual of the liability for compensated absences rather than the allocation of such costs to interim accounting periods. FASB-43 does not apply to the following:

1. Severance or termination pay
2. Stock or stock options issued to employees
3. Deferred compensation
4. Postretirement benefits
5. Group insurance, disability pay, and other long-term fringe benefits
6. Certain sick pay benefits that accumulate

Compensated absences arise from employees' absences from employment because of illness, holiday, vacation, or other reasons. When an employer expects to pay an employee for such compensated absences, a liability for the estimated probable future payments must be accrued if all the following conditions are met:

1. The employee's right to receive compensation for the future absences is attributable to services already performed by the employee.
2. The employee's right to receive the compensation for the future absences is vested, or accumulates.
3. It is probable that the compensation will be paid.
4. The amount of compensation is reasonably estimable.

The fact that an employer meets the first three conditions and not the fourth condition must be disclosed in the financial statements.

Vested rights are those which have been earned by the employee for services already performed. Thus, vested rights are not contingent on any future services by the employee and are an obligation of the employer even if the employee quits or is fired. Rights that accumulate are nonvesting rights to compensated absences that are earned and can be carried forward to succeeding years. Rights that accumulate increase an employee's benefits in one or more years subsequent to the year in which they are earned. For the purposes of FASB-43, it makes no difference whether a limit is imposed on the amount of accumulated rights that can be carried forward to future years. For example, if accumulated vacation days can be partially or fully carried forward for use in succeeding years, the employer should accrue a liability equal to the probable number of vacation days the employee will likely use. However, an employer does not have to accrue a liability for nonvesting rights to compensated absences that expire at the end of the year in which they are earned, because they do not accumulate.

Nonvesting sick pay benefits that accumulate and can be carried forward to succeeding years are given special treatment by FASB-43. An employer generally does not have to accrue a liability for such sick pay benefits, as he does for other nonvesting rights that accumulate. This is an exception to the general rule in FASB-43. If payment of nonvesting accumulating sick pay benefits depends on the future illness of the employee, an employer does not have to accrue a liability for such payments. The reasons cited in FASB-43 for this exception are (1) the cost/benefit rule, (2) the materiality rule, and (3) the reliability of estimating the days an employee will be sick in succeeding years. This exception does not apply in circumstances where the employer pays the sick pay benefits even though the employee is not actually sick. Thus, where an employer pays nonvesting accumulated sick pay benefits to employees even though their absences from work are not caused by illness, or if sick pay benefits are allowed to be taken as *terminal leave*, the employer should accrue a liability for such payments. Under these circumstances, such payments cannot be considered to be sick pay benefits for the purposes of FASB-43. An employer's general policy for the payment of nonvesting accumulating sick pay benefits should govern the accounting for such payments.

FASB-43 is effective for fiscal years ended on or after December 16, 1981, and earlier application is encouraged.

FASB-43 requires that accounting changes resulting from the adoption of its provisions shall be made retroactively, that financial statements of the year of change shall disclose the nature of any restatement, and that its effect on sales, income before extraordinary items, net income, and related per share amounts for each year shall be restated.

> **OBSERVATION**: *The recognition of a change in an accounting principle, such as FASB-43, through the retroactive restatement of the financial statements violates existing GAAP, because the effects of the change are charged directly to retained earnings and thus bypass the income statement. A change in an accounting principle, such as FASB-43, should be accounted for by including the cumulative effects of the change in net income of the year of change (APB-20). The effects of a retroactive restatement are charged directly to retained earnings, as is prior-period adjustment. FASB-16 clearly limits prior-period adjustments to (1) a correction of an error in a prior-period statement or (2) an adjustment for the realization of certain preacquisition tax benefits. Finally, APB-9 requires that net income include all items of income and expense, except (1) prior-period adjustments, (2) dividends, and (3) capital transactions.*

If retroactive restatement of the financial statements is not practicable, FASB-43 permits the use of APB-20 in accounting for the effects of the change in accounting principle resulting from the adoption of FASB-43.

CURRENT VALUE ACCOUNTING

Overview

There is no promulgated GAAP on current value accounting, and its general use for basic financial statements is prohibited under existing GAAP. However, like general price-level information, current value data may be utilized to supplement the historical cost financial statements required by GAAP.

Background

Current value accounting deals with the measurement of profits and the valuation of a business entity during periods of inflation.

In current value accounting, historical costs are replaced by current values that attempt to measure what a company would receive if it disposed of its assets. Thus, current value accounting violates the going-concern concept of GAAP in that it is based on liquidation values.

Current Value Methods

The major problem in current value accounting is the measurement of current values. The two most commonly used methods are the entry value system and the exit value system.

The entry value system is based on cost of replacement or reproduction. Replacement cost is the estimated cost of acquiring new and equivalent property at current prices after adjusting for depreciation, and may be approximated through the use of a specific price index. Reproduction cost is the estimated cost of producing new and equivalent property at current prices after adjusting for depreciation.

The exit value system is usually based on net realizable value in the ordinary course of business, or sometimes on discounted future cash flow. Net realizable value is the estimated selling price of the asset less any costs to complete or dispose. Discounted future cash flow is the present value of estimated cash inflows, or cost savings, discounted at an appropriate rate of interest.

Monetary and Nonmonetary Items

To apply current value accounting methods, it is necessary to separate assets and liabilities into monetary and nonmonetary, in the same manner as in general price-level information.

Monetary assets or liabilities are fixed in terms of currency and are usually contractual claims. Since these amounts are fixed, there is usually no need to restate monetary assets and liabilities. Examples of monetary assets and liabilities are cash, accounts and notes receivable, and accounts and notes payable.

Nonmonetary assets or liabilities are those other than monetary assets or liabilities. Nonmonetary assets are generally restated for changes in current value. Examples of nonmonetary assets and liabilities are inventory, investments in common stock, property, plant and equipment, liability for advance rent collected, and common stock.

Because monetary assets are stated in fixed amounts of currency, they represent the amount of cash that is expected to be realized by them in the near future. Therefore, monetary assets are effectively stated at their net realizable value and do not usually have to be restated for current value financial statements.

Nonmonetary assets are not stated in fixed amounts of currency and thus do not reflect their net realizable value. Therefore, nonmonetary assets must be restated to their present current worth for current value financial statements.

Holding Gains

Regardless of the current value method used, holding gains will arise.

A holding gain is the difference between the current value of an asset and its historical cost. Realized holding gains result from the disposal of an asset, either by sale or use, during an accounting period. Unrealized holding gains result from increases in current values of assets during an accounting period in which such assets are retained by the entity.

Controversy exists as to whether holding gains should be reported in the current value income statement or in a separate statement of changes in holding gains.

Current Value Income

Under the current value concept, current operating income is the result of deducting from actual revenues the cost of goods sold and other expenses based on current values. Realized income is determined by adding realized holding gains to net operating income (current operating income less income taxes). Current value income is obtained by adding unrealized holding gains to realized income. The following illustration shows the steps required to determine current value income.

Revenues (actual)
Less: Current value of cost of goods sold and other expenses
Current operating income
Less: Income taxes
Net operating income
Plus: Realized holding gains
Realized income
Plus: Unrealized holding gains
Current value income

The following example illustrates the computation of current value income.

Fair Value, Inc., paid $1,200,000 in December 19X6 for certain of its inventory. In December 19X7, one half of the inventory was sold for $1,000,000, when the replacement cost of the original inventory was $1,400,000. *Ignoring income taxes*, what amount should be shown as the total gain resulting from the above facts in a current fair value accounting income statement for 19X7?

The computation of current value income is as follows:

Proceeds of sale	$1,000,000
Less: Current value of inventory sold (1/2 of $1,400,000)	700,000
Current operating income	$ 300,000
Plus: Realized holding gain—Inventory ($700,000 current value – $600,000 historical cost)	100,000
Realized income	$ 400,000
Plus: Unrealized holding gains—Inventory	100,000
Current value income	$ 500,000

Comprehensive Illustration

This comprehensive illustration compares traditional historical cost accounting to the current value method of accounting.

Balance Sheet

Assets	Historical cost	Current value
Current assets:		
Cash	$ 1,700	$ 1,700
Accounts receivable	5,500	5,500
Investments	200	200
Inventory	2,500	3,000
Fixed assets:		
Plant	4,000	5,000
Accumulated depreciation	(400)	(500)
Total assets	$13,500	$14,900

Liabilities		
Current liabilities	$ 5,000	$ 5,000
Stockholders' equity:		
Common stock	4,000	4,000
Retained earnings	4,500	2,900
Revaluation reserve		3,000
Total liabilities and stockholders' equity	$13,500	$14,900

Comments:

Under the current value accounting method, the monetary assets and liabilities are not restated, because they represent amounts fixed in terms of currency. However, the nonmonetary assets and liabilities (inventory, plant, and stockholders' equity) are restated to their net realizable values.

Statement of Income

	Historical cost		Current value	
Sales		$13,000		$13,000
Cost of goods sold		4,000		5,500
Gross margin		$ 9,000		$ 7,500
Less Expenses:				
Depreciation	$200		$ 250	
Others	600	800	600	850
Income before taxes		$ 8,200		
Current operating income				$ 6,650
Less: Provision for taxes		4,100		4,100
Net income		$ 4,100		
Net operating income				$ 2,550
Realized holding gains applicable to:				
Sale of inventory			$1,500	
Depreciation of plant			50	1,550
Realized income				$ 4,100
Unrealized holding gains applicable to:				
Replacement at cost of inventory at year end			$ 500	
Undepreciated value of plant			950	1,450
Current value income				$ 5,550

Comments:

Under the traditional historical cost method, net income is $4,100, whereas current value income is $5,550. Both methods use actual sales, but the current value method uses current values (replacement cost) in computing cost of goods sold and other expenses. In periods of inflation, gross margins will usually be less than under historical cost accounting, because current values are used.

Net income under historical cost accounting is always equal to realized income under current value accounting. In other words, historical cost accounting net income always includes realized holding gains. Holding gains are always separately identified in current value income statements. The only difference in dollar amounts between the two methods is unrealized holding gains. A current value income statement will reflect all unrealized holding gains, whereas these unrealized gains are never included in an historical cost income statement.

The provision for income taxes is the same for both historical cost and current value income statements. Depreciation expense is computed on the current value of an asset for current value accounting, whereas historical cost is used for historical cost purposes.

Statement of Changes in Revaluation Reserve (Holding Gains)

Revaluation reserve (holding gains), beginning of the year:		—
Realized holding gains applicable to:		
Inventory sold	$1,500	
Depreciation on plant (5% of $1,000)	50	$1,550
Unrealized holding gains applicable to:		
Inventory at year end	$ 500	
Undepreciated value of plant	950	1,450
Total revaluation reserve (holding gains)		$3,000

Comments:
The revaluation reserve (which is shown on the balance sheet as $3,000) is a stockholder's equity account which reflects the difference between historical cost and current value.

Statement of Retained Earnings

	Historical cost	Current value
Beginning balance	$ 400	$ 400
Add: Net income	4,100	
Current value income		5,550
Total	$4,500	$5,950
Less: Backlog depreciation		50
Revaluation reserve		3,000
Ending retained earnings	$4,500	$2,900

Comments:
Backlog depreciation (sometimes referred to as the *amortization gap*) is the difference between accumulated depreciation under historical cost and accumulated depreciation based on current value.

DEFERRED COMPENSATION CONTRACTS

Overview

The main source of promulgated GAAP for deferred compensation contracts is APB-12, paragraphs 6–8, as amended by FASB-106. If individual deferred compensation contracts, as a group, are tantamount to a pension plan, they should be accounted for in accordance with the GAAP on pension plans, discussed in the chapter entitled "Pension Plans—Employers."

If individual deferred compensation contracts are, as a group, tantamount to a plan for postretirement benefits other than pensions, they should be accounted for in accordance with the GAAP on postretirement benefits, discussed in the chapter entitled "Postretirement Benefits Other Than Pensions."

> **OBSERVATION:** *Professional judgment will be required to determine whether individual contracts are tantamount to a plan.*

This chapter discusses the accounting for individual deferred compensation contracts which are not tantamount to a plan, either for pensions or for postretirement benefits other than pensions.

Background

According to APB-12, deferred compensation contracts should be accounted for on an individual basis for each employee. If a deferred compensation contract is based on current and future employment, only the amounts attributable to the current portion of employment should be accrued.

If a deferred compensation contract contains benefits payable for the life of a beneficiary, the total liability should be based on the beneficiary's life expectancy or on the estimated cost of an annuity contract that would provide sufficient funds to pay the required benefits.

The total liability for deferred compensation contracts is determined by the terms of each individual contract. The amount of the periodic accrual, computed from the first day of the employment contract, must total no less than the then present value of the benefits provided for in the contract. The periodic accruals should be made systematically over the active term of employment.

A deferred compensation contract provides for the payment of $50,000 per year for five years, beginning one year after the end of the employee's 10-year contract. A 10% interest rate will be assumed.

We must find the present value for the five $50,000 payments at the end of 10 years, as follows:

Present value of $50,000 in five years	$ 31,045
Present value of $50,000 in four years	34,150
Present value of $50,000 in three years	37,565
Present value of $50,000 in two years	41,320
Present value of $50,000 in one year	45,455
Total present value of benefits at end of employment	$189,535

We now know that $189,535 must be accumulated over 10 years to have available the funds required to pay the benefits in accordance with the contract. We must find the amount of the annual accrual that earning 10% interest will total $189,535 at the end of 10 years. This may be found by using the formula for the value of an annuity due, as follows:

$$A = R\left[\sum (1 + i)^n\right]$$
$$\$189{,}535 = \$10{,}811$$

The annual accrual is $10,811.

FASB-106 amends APB-12 on the method of accruing an employer's obligation under deferred compensation contracts that are not tantamount to a plan for pension or other postretirement benefits. FASB-106 requires the employer to make periodic accruals, so that the cost of the deferred compensation is attributed to the appropriate years of an employee's service, in accordance with the terms of the contract between the employer and that employee.

The employer should make the attribution in a systematic and rational manner. By the time an employee becomes fully eligible for the deferred compensation specified in the contract, the accrued amount should equal the then present value of the expected future payments of deferred compensation.

The following two examples illustrate the accruals required by FASB-106. In the first example, the employee must remain in service for a number of years in order to become eligible for the deferred compensation. In the second example, the employee becomes eligible in the same year the contract is signed.

Example 1: *Employee must remain in service for a number of years in order to become eligible.*

A deferred compensation contract with a newly hired employee provides for a payment of $100,000 upon termination of employment, provided the employee remains in service for at least 4 years.

The employer should make annual accruals during each of the first 4 years of this employee's service, to recognize the portion of deferred compensation cost attributable to each of these years. In order to make these annual accruals, the employer should start by making reasonable assumptions about (1) the employee's anticipated retirement date and (2) the discount rate for making computations of present value.

If the employer assumes that the employee will remain in service for a total of 9 years (including 5 years after becoming fully eligible for the deferred compensation), and the discount rate is 8%, the present value of the $100,000 deferred compensation at the end of the 4th year will be $68,058 (present value of $100,000 payable at the end of 5 years @ 8% discount).

Accruals should be made for each of the first 4 years, so that the balance in the accrued liability account at the end of the 4th year will be $68,058. The simplest way to accomplish this will be on a straight-line basis, as follows:

Accrued amount anticipated at end of 4th year	$68,058
Annual accrual during each of first 4 years (1/4 of $68,058)	$17,015

This computation will result in the recognition of $17,015 deferred compensation cost during each of the first 4 years of the employee's service. The balance in the accrued liability account at the end of the

4th year, when the employee is eligible to terminate and collect the deferred compensation, will be $68,058, the present value of the $100,000 deferred compensation payable 5 years later. (The 5 years represent the anticipated total service of 9 years, minus the 4 years already served.)

Next, assume the employee remains in service throughout the 5th year and is still expected to complete the 9-year term originally anticipated. The accrued liability should be adjusted as of the end of the 5th year to reflect the present value of the deferred compensation, which will be $73,503 (present value of $100,000 payable at the end of 4 years @ 8% discount).

The cost recognized for the 5th year will therefore be $5,445, determined as follows:

Accrued amount at end of 5th year	$73,503
Accrued amount at end of 4th year	68,058
Cost recognized in 5th year	$ 5,445

Example 2: *Employee becomes eligible in same year contract is signed.*

An employee is hired on January 1, 19X2. The contract provides for a payment of $20,000 upon termination of employment, provided the employee remains in service for at least 6 months. The employer anticipates the employee will remain in service for 3 years. The assumed discount rate is 8%.

The employee is still in service at the end of calendar year 19X2. Having completed at least 6 months of service, the employee is eligible to terminate and collect the deferred compensation. The accrual as of December 31, 19X2, is $17,147, the present value of $20,000 payable at the end of 2 years @ 8% discount. (The 2 years represent the originally anticipated service of 3 years, minus the one year of 19X2 already served.) The entire amount of the accrual is recognized as a deferred compensation cost in calendar year 19X2, since the employee achieved full eligibility by the end of the year.

If the employee remains in service throughout 19X3 and all assumptions remain unchanged, the amount of the accrued liability as of December 31, 19X3, should be adjusted to $18,519, the present value of $20,000 at the end of 1 year @ 8% discount.

The cost recognized in 19X3 is therefore $1,372, determined as follows:

Accrued amount at end of 19X3	$18,519
Accrued amount at end of 19X2	17,147
Cost recognized in 19X3	$ 1,372

The amendment of APB-12 by FASB-106 is effective for fiscal years beginning on or after March 16, 1991. If this amendment requires an employer to change its method of accounting for existing deferred compensation contracts, the method of accounting for the transition depends on the type of benefits the contracts provide.

If the contracts provide postretirement health or welfare benefits, employers should apply the general transition provisions and effective dates of FASB-106, discussed in the chapter entitled "Postretirement Benefits Other Than Pensions."

If the contracts do not provide postretirement health or welfare benefits, employers should recognize the transition as the effect of a change in accounting principle (under APB-20, para. 17-21).

DEPRECIABLE ASSETS AND DEPRECIATION

Overview

This chapter brings together the promulgated GAAP relating to depreciable assets and depreciation, in addition to nonpromulgated GAAP of importance.

The following is the promulgated GAAP discussed in this chapter:

ARB-43, Chapter 9A, Depreciation and High Costs
ARB-43, Chapter 9C, Emergency Facilities
APB-6, paragraph 17, Depreciation on Appreciation
APB-6, paragraph 20, Declining-Balance Depreciation
APB-12, paragraphs 4 and 5, Disclosure of Depreciable Assets and Depreciation

FASB-93 (Recognition of Depreciation by Not-for-Profit Organizations) was issued to require that not-for-profit organizations recognize the cost of using up long-lived tangible assets in general purpose external financial statements. [Note: In September 1988, the FASB extended the effective date of FASB-93 from fiscal years beginning on or after May 16, 1988, to fiscal years beginning on or after January 1, 1990.]

Background

The basic principle of matching revenue and expenses is applied to long-lived assets that are not held for sale in the ordinary course of business. The systematic and rational allocation used to achieve "matching" is usually accomplished by depreciation, amortization, or depletion, according to the type of long-lived asset involved.

Asset Cost

The basis of accounting for depreciable fixed assets is cost, and all normal expenditures of readying an asset for use should be capitalized. However, unnecessary expenditures that do not add to the utility of the asset should be charged to expense. An expenditure for repairing a piece of equipment that was damaged during shipment should be charged to expense.

Razing and removal costs (less salvage value) of structures located on land purchased as a building site are added to the cost of the land. Land itself is never depreciated.

> **OBSERVATION:** *Promulgated GAAP (ARB-43) requires that assets be recorded at cost, except in the case of quasi-reorganizations (corporate readjustments) in which it is permissible to write up or write down assets to market values (APB-6).*
>
> *When price-level accounting methods are used as supplemental statements, the distortion of assets and related depreciation resulting from inflation is somewhat ameliorated.*

Salvage Value

Salvage or residual value is an estimate of the amount that will be realized at the end of the useful life of a depreciable asset. Frequently, depreciable assets have little or no scrap value at the end of their estimated useful life and, if immaterial, the amount(s) may be ignored.

Estimated Useful Life

The estimated useful life of a depreciable asset may differ from company to company or industry to industry. A company's maintenance policy will affect the longevity of a depreciable asset.

> **OBSERVATION:** *Total utility of an asset, expressed in time, is called the **physical life.** The utility of an asset to a specific owner, expressed in time, is called the **service life.***

Valuation of Assets

Under specific circumstances, assets may be valued in the following ways:

Historical costs   The actual amount paid at the date of acquisition, including all normal expenditures of readying an asset for use.

Replacement cost   The amount that it would cost to replace an asset. Frequently, replacement cost is the same as fair value.

Fair market value   The price at which a willing seller would sell to a willing buyer, neither under any compulsion to buy or to sell.

Present value   The value today of something due in the future.

General price-level restatement   The value of an asset restated in terms of current purchasing power.

Self-Constructed Fixed Assets

When a business constructs a long-lived asset for its own use, the following procedure should be observed:

1. All *direct costs* should be included in the total cost of the asset, which should be capitalized.
2. *Fixed overhead costs* should not be included unless they are increased by the construction of the asset.
3. *Interest costs* may or may not be capitalized as part of construction cost of the fixed assets.

> **OBSERVATION:** *Interest costs that are material must be capitalized on certain qualifying assets under the provisions of FASB-34. (See chapter entitled "Interest Costs Capitalized.")*

Write-Up of Assets to Appraisal Values

GAAP prohibit the write-up of fixed assets to market or appraisal values. However, although prohibiting such a procedure, GAAP state that if fixed assets are written up to market or appraisal values, depreciation should be based on the written-up amounts (ARB-43).

Improvement of Depreciable Assets

Expenditures that increase the capacity of operating efficiency of an asset, if they are substantial, should be capitalized. Minor expenditures are usually treated as period costs even though they may have the characteristics of capital expenditures. When the cost of improvements is substantial or when there is a change in the estimated useful life of an asset, depreciation charges for future periods should be revised on the basis of the new book value and the new estimated remaining useful life.

The revision of the estimated useful life of an asset is measured prospectively and accounted for in the current and future periods. No adjustment is made to prior depreciation.

A machine that originally cost $100,000 was being depreciated (no salvage value) over ten years, using the straight-line method. At the beginning of the fifth year $20,000 was expended, which considerably improved the operating efficiency of the machine and extended its useful life four years.

Original cost	$100,000
Less: Four years' depreciation	40,000
Balance (adjusted)	$ 60,000
New expenditures	20,000
New depreciable base	$ 80,000
Useful life (6 + 4) in years	10
Amount of annual depreciation	$ 8,000

Kinds of Depreciation

Physical depreciation is related to a depreciable asset's wear and deterioration over a period.

Functional depreciation arises from obsolescence or inadequacy of the asset to perform efficiently. Obsolescence may arise when there is no further demand for the product that the depreciable asset produces or from the availability of a new depreciable asset that can perform the same function for substantially less cost.

Depreciation Methods

The goal of a depreciation method should be to provide for a reasonable, consistent matching of revenue and expense, by systematically allocating the cost of the depreciable asset over its estimated useful life.

The actual accumulation of depreciation in the books is accomplished by using a *contra* account, called accumulated depreciation or allowance for depreciation.

The amount subject to depreciation is the difference between cost and residual or salvage value and is called the *depreciable base.*

Straight line   *Straight-line depreciation* is determined by the formula:

$$\frac{\text{Cost less salvage value}}{\text{Estimated useful life}} = \text{annual depreciation}$$

Estimated useful life is usually stated in time periods, such as years or months.

Units of production   The *units-of-production method* relates depreciation to the estimated production capability of an asset and is expressed in a rate per unit or hour.

The formula is:

$$\frac{\text{Cost less salvage value}}{\text{Estimated units or hours}} = \text{rate per unit}$$

A machine is purchased at a cost of $85,000 and has a salvage value of $10,000. It is estimated that the machine has a useful life of 750,000 hours.

$$\frac{\$85,000 - \$10,000}{750,000} = \$.10 \text{ per hour depreciation}$$

The units-of-production method is used in situations where the usage of the depreciable asset varies considerably from period to period, and in those circumstances in which the service life is more a function of use than passage of time.

Sum of the years' digits   The *sum-of-the-years'-digits method* is one of the accelerated methods of depreciation that provides higher depreciation expense in the early years and lower charges in later years.

To find the sum of the years' digits, the digit of each year is progressively numbered and then added up. The sum of the years' digits for a five-year life would be:

$$5 + 4 + 3 + 2 + 1 = 15$$

For four years:

$$4 + 3 + 2 + 1 = 10$$

For three years:

$$3 + 2 + 1 = 6$$

When dealing with an asset with a long life, it is necessary to use the general formula for finding the sum of the years' digits:

$$S = N \left(\frac{N + 1}{2} \right)$$

To find the sum of the years' digits for an asset with a 50-year life:

$$S = 50 \left(\frac{50 + 1}{2} \right)$$

$$S = 50(25 \ 1/2)$$
$$S = 1{,}275 \text{ sum of the years' digits for 50 years}$$

The sum of the years' digits becomes the denominator, and the digit of the highest year becomes the first numerator. For example, the first year's depreciation for a five-year life would be 5/15 of the depreciable base of the asset.

Assume that an asset cost $11,000, has a salvage value of $1,000, and has an estimated useful life of four years.

The first step is to determine the depreciable base:

Cost of asset	$11,000
Less: Salvage value	1,000
Depreciable base	$10,000

The sum of the years' digits for four years is:

$$4 + 3 + 2 + 1 = 10$$

The first year's depreciation is 4/10, the second year's 3/10, the third year's 2/10, and the fourth year's 1/10, as follows:

4/10 of $100,000	=	$ 4,000
3/10 of $10,000	=	3,000
2/10 of $10,000	=	2,000
1/10 of $10,000	=	1,000
Total depreciation		$10,000

When an asset is placed in service during the year, the depreciation expense is taken only for the portion of the year that the asset is used. For example, if an asset (of a company on a calendar-year basis) is placed in service on July 1, only six months' depreciation is taken. In our preceding illustration the six months' depreciation expense would be 1/2 of 4/10, or $2,000. If this occurs, then the second year's depreciation expense is calculated as follows:

1/2 of 4/10 of $10,000	=	$2,000
1/2 of 3/10 of $10,000	=	1,500
Depreciation expense second year	=	$3,500

Declining balance   The most common of these accelerated methods is the *double-declining-balance method*, although other alternative (lower than double) methods are acceptable. Under double-declining balance, the first year's depreciation is double the straight-line rate. In succeeding years, the same percentage is applied to the remaining book value. No allowance is made for salvage, because the method always leaves a remaining balance, which is treated as salvage value. However, the asset should not be depreciated below the estimated salvage value.

An asset costing $10,000 has an estimated useful life of 10 years. Using the double-declining-balance method, the expense is computed as follows.

First, the regular straight line method percentage is determined, which in this case is 10% (10-year life). This amount is doubled to 20% and applied each year to the remaining book value, as follows:

Year	Percentage	Remaining book value	Depreciation expense
1	20	$10,000	$2,000
2	20	8,000	1,600
3	20	6,400	1,280
4	20	5,120	1,024
5	20	4,096	819
6	20	3,277	655
7	20	2,622	524
8	20	2,098	420
9	20	1,678	336
10	20	1,342	268
Salvage value		1,074	

Had the preceding illustration been 1 1/2 times declining balance (150%), the rate would have been 15% of the remaining book value.

In the illustration above, if the asset (of a company on a calendar-year basis) had been placed in service on July 1, the first year's depreciation would have been $1,000 (1/2 of $2,000), and the second year's depreciation would have been 20% of $9,000 (remaining value after the first year), or $1,800.

The declining-balance method is one that meets the requirements of being systematic and rational. If the expected productivity or revenue-earning power of the asset is relatively greater during the early years of its life, or where maintenance charges tend to increase during later years, the declining-balance method may provide the most satisfactory allocation of cost. That conclusion also applies to other methods, including the sum-of-the-years' digits method, that produce substantially similar results (paragraph 205a of FASB-96).

Cost Recovery Method

The cost recovery method, also known as the sunk-cost theory, is used in situations where recovery of cost is undeterminable or very questionable. The procedure is simply that all cost is recovered before any gain is recognized. The cost recovery method is also used for questionable receivables.

Other Types of Depreciation

Replacement depreciation The original cost is carried on the books, and the replacement cost is charged to expense in the period the replacement occurs.

Retirement depreciation The cost of the asset is charged to expense in the period it is retired.

Present-value depreciation Depreciation is computed so that the return on the investment of the asset remains constant over the period involved.

Promulgated GAAP dictates that depreciation should systematically and rationally allocate the cost of an asset over its estimated useful life. Straight-line, sum-of-the-years'-digits, and declining-depreciation methods are considered acceptable, providing they are systematic and rational. For financial accounting purposes, companies should not use depreciation guidelines or other tax regulations issued by the IRS, but should estimate useful lives and calculate depreciation expense according to generally accepted procedures. When depreciation for tax purposes differs from depreciation for financial accounting purposes, income tax allocation (FASB-96) should be used.

In periods of inflation, depreciation charges based on historical cost of the original fixed asset may not reflect current price levels, and hence may not be an appropriate matching of revenues and expenses for the current period. In 1953, promulgated GAAP (ARB-43) took the position that it was acceptable to provide an appropriation of retained earnings for replacement of fixed assets, but not acceptable to depart from the traditional cost method in the treatment of depreciation, because a radical departure from the generally accepted procedures would create too much confusion in the minds of the readers of financial statements. Although inflation has become quite serious in recent years, depreciation based on historical cost remains the official, promulgated accounting principle.

Depletion

Cost depletion is the basic method of computing a deduction for depletion. An estimate is made of the amount of natural resources to be extracted, in units or tons, barrels, or any other measurement. The estimate of total recoverable units is then divided into the total cost of the depletable asset, to arrive at a depletion rate per unit. The annual depletion expense is the rate per unit times the number of units extracted during the fiscal year. If at any time there is a revision of the estimated number of units that are expected to be extracted, a new unit rate is computed. The cost of the natural resource property is reduced each year by the amount of the depletion expense for the year.

Disclosure

Allowances for depreciation and depletion should be deducted from the assets to which they relate (APB-12).

The following disclosures of depreciable assets and depreciation should be made in the financial statements or notes thereto:

1. Depreciation expense for the period
2. Balances of major classes of depreciable assets by nature or function
3. Accumulated depreciation allowances by classes or in total
4. The methods used, by major classes, in computing depreciation

> **OBSERVATION:** *Promulgated GAAP (APB-12) requires that the above disclosures be made in the financial statements or in footnotes. In addition, the effect of a change from one depreciation method to another must be disclosed (APB-20).*

Depreciation—Not-for-Profit Organizations (FASB-93)

> [**Note:** In September 1988, the FASB extended the effective date of FASB-93 from fiscal years beginning on or after May 16, 1988, to fiscal years beginning on or after January 1, 1990.]

FASB-93 establishes financial accounting and reporting standards that require all not-for-profit organizations to recognize the depreciation of long-lived assets in general purpose external financial statements. FASB-93 also makes it mandatory for not-for-profit organizations to disclose information about depreciable assets and depreciation in the same manner as required by paragraph 5 of APB-12 (Omnibus Opinion – 1967).

Since FASB-93 requires the recognition of depreciation of long-lived assets in general purpose external financial statements of not-for-profit organizations, certain provisions relating to depreciation that are found in the documents listed below are no longer acceptable accounting principles and cease to be specialized accounting principles under FASB-32 (Specialized Accounting and Reporting Principles and Practices in AICPA Statements of Position and Guides on Accounting and Auditing Matters);

- *Audits of Colleges and Universities,* an AICPA Industry Audit Guide, which permits but does not require depreciation of certain assets (chapter 2, page 10).
- *SOP 78-10, Accounting Principles and Reporting Practices for Certain Nonprofit Organizations,* an AICPA Statement of Position, which exempts certain long-lived tangible assets from depreciation (paragraph 108).

The measurement, recognition, or financial statement display of depreciable assets and/or any related depreciation are not addressed by FASB-93.

FASB-93 requires that not-for-profit organizations recognize periodic depreciation expense on all of their long-lived tangible assets. FASB-93 also requires the same financial statement disclosure pertaining to depreciable assets and depreciation as that required by paragraph 5 of APB-12 (Omnibus Opinion – 1967). That financial statement disclosure is as follows:

- The amount of depreciation expense for the current period
- Balances of major classes of depreciable assets, by nature or function, at the balance sheet date
- Accumulated depreciation, either by major classes of depreciable assets or in total, at the balance sheet date
- A general description of the method(s) used in calculating depreciation for major classes of depreciable assets

FASB-93 does not require the recognition of depreciation on individual works of art or historical treasures whose economic benefits or service potentials diminish very slowly over extended periods of time, resulting in extraordinarily long estimated useful lives. FASB-93 requires that verifiable evidence exist demonstrating that (i) the asset individually has cultural, aesthetic, or historical value that is worth preserving perpetually and (ii) the holder has the technological and financial ability to protect and preserve essentially undiminished the service potential of the asset and is doing that.

> **OBSERVATION:** *It is not clear whether the provisions of FASB-93 that pertain to the depreciation of individual works of art and historical treasures are to be applied only to not-for-profit organizations or to both profit and not-for-profit organizations.*

Effective date and transition   FASB-93 is effective for financial statements issued for fiscal years beginning on or after January 1, 1990, and earlier application of FASB-93 is encouraged.

Financial statements of prior years that are presented for comparison purposes shall be retroactively restated to conform to the provisions of FASB-93. FASB-93 shall be applied by adjusting the opening net asset balance of the earliest year presented, or if no prior years are presented for the year in which FASB-93 is first applied. The financial statements of the period in which FASB-93 is first applied shall disclose the nature of any restatement and its effect on the change in net assets for each period presented.

Retroactive application of the provisions of FASB-93 requires estimates of useful lives and salvage values of all recognized long-lived tangible assets. Information that has become available after acquisition of the assets may be considered in making those estimates.

DEVELOPMENT STAGE ENTERPRISES

Overview

FASB-7 establishes the current promulgated GAAP for accounting and reporting by development stage enterprises in all industries. It supersedes FASB Interpretation-5 in the area of research and development for development stage enterprises, and does not alter or amend any other promulgated or nonpromulgated GAAP. Promulgated GAAP in this area specifically state that FASB-7 does not alter nonpromulgated GAAP with respect to:

a. An established business in expansion phases
b. Extractive industries in exploration or development stages
c. Real estate firms developing properties

Applying FASB-7 to financial statements of established operating companies is covered by FASB Interpretation-7, which is covered later in this chapter.

Background

A development stage company is one in which principal operations have not commenced or principal operations have generated an insignificant amount of revenue. During the development stage, a company devotes most of its activities toward establishing a new business. (For example, building production facilities or acquiring operational assets, training personnel, developing markets, etc.)

Accounting and Reporting

A development stage company must issue the same basic financial statements as any other enterprise, and such statements should be prepared in conformity with GAAP. A development stage company should follow GAAP in determining whether operating costs should be expensed, capitalized, or deferred. In the case of a subsidiary or a similar type of enterprise, this determination is made within the context of the entity presenting the financial statements. Thus, it would be possible to expense an item on the financial statements of a

subsidiary and capitalize the same expense on the financial statements of the parent company (FASB Interpretation-7). For example,
if a subsidiary purchases a machine that will be used only for
research and development, it would expense the cost of the item in
the year of acquisition. However, the parent company could capitalize the same machine, if in its normal course of business such a
machine has an alternative future use.

Disclosure

The bulk of FASB-7 concentrates on establishing the disclosure requirements for a development stage company. The financial statements must disclose the following:

1. Accumulated losses should be described as "deficit accumulated during the development stage."
2. The income statement should show revenues and expenses
   for each period being presented and should also present a
   running cumulative total of both amounts from the company's inception. This provision also applies to dormant
   companies that have been reactivated at the development
   stage. In such cases, the totals begin from the time that development stage activities are initiated.
3. The statement of changes in financial position should reflect a
   cumulative total of the sources and uses of funds from the
   company's inception and amounts for the current period.

   The statement of changes in financial position need be presented only when required by promulgated GAAP. That is, it
   can be omitted if the financial statements are for internal use
   only or if they are prepared for a special purpose.
4. A separate statement of stockholders' equity shall be issued
   and shall contain the following information:
   a. The date and number of shares of stock (or other secu-
      rities) issued for cash or other consideration and the
      dollar amount assigned.
   b. For each issuance of capital stock involving noncash
      consideration, a description of the nature of the con-
      sideration and the basis for its valuation.

A company can combine separate transactions of equity securities, provided that the same type of securities, consideration per
equity unit, and type of consideration are involved and the transactions are made in the same fiscal period.

Modification of the statement of stockholders' equity may be required for a combined group of companies that form a development stage company or for an unincorporated development stage entity.

> **OBSERVATION:** *Promulgated GAAP does not indicate the types of modifications that might be necessary.*

5. The financial statements shall be identified as those of a development stage company and contain a description of the proposed business activities.
6. The first year that the company is no longer in the development stage, the financial statements shall indicate that in the prior year it was in the development stage. If the company includes prior-year figures for comparative purposes, the cumulative amounts required in 2 and 3 above should not appear.

When a development stage company which is a subsidiary adopts a new accounting principle, the parent should also reflect this accounting change by making the necessary adjustments on its financial statements in compliance with APB-20 (FASB Interpretation-7). Any such adjustments and related income tax effects should be recorded and disclosed.

EARNINGS PER SHARE

Overview

The main source of promulgated GAAP for earnings per share is APB-15, which has been amended by FASB-55 (Determining Whether a Convertible Security is a Common Stock Equivalent) and by FASB-85 (Yield Test for Determining whether a Convertible Security Is a Common Stock Equivalent).

The promulgated GAAP apply to financial statements of corporations prepared in conformity with GAAP whose capital structure comprises common stock, including common stock equivalents, and/or senior securities. In this respect, the promulgated GAAP excludes mutual companies that do not have common stock, such as mutual savings banks, credit unions, cooperatives, and other similar entities. Also specifically excluded from the promulgated GAAP are registered investment companies, government-owned corporations and nonprofit entities.

In addition, statements prepared for special purposes, wholly owned subsidiaries and parent companies that accompany consolidated financial statements are not covered by the promulgated GAAP for obvious reasons.

Nonpublic Enterprise (FASB-21)

A nonpublic enterprise is an enterprise other than one:

1. Whose debt or equity securities are traded in a public market
2. That is required to file financial statements with the SEC

An enterprise loses its status as nonpublic when it issues financial statements in preparation for the sale of any class of securities in a public market.

A public market is a foreign or domestic stock exchange or an over-the-counter market.

A nonpublic enterprise is not required to disclose earnings per share (APB-15), or segment information (FASB-14), in a complete set of separately issued financial statements. The nonpublic enterprise may be a subsidiary, a joint venture, or any other investee.

If the nonpublic enterprise elects to disclose earnings per share or segment information, it must comply with the disclosure requirements of GAAP. It may not disclose this information on an arbitrary basis.

Background

Earnings per share (EPS) or loss per share (LPS) is an important measure of performance for all users of financial statements, and should appear prominently on the face of the income statement for all periods presented. Earnings-per-share data should be consistent with the captions shown on the income statement, but EPS for continuing operations and EPS for net income are mandatory.

> **OBSERVATION:** *Although EPS for extraordinary items is not required, it is strongly recommended by APB-15 and APB-30. EPS for discontinued operations and the resulting gain or loss on the disposal of a segment may or may not be presented (APB-30).*
>
> *EPS for the cumulative effects of an accounting change is required by APB-20 and APB-30.*

If prior-period dollar amounts on an income statement have been restated as a result of a prior-period adjustment, the EPS data must also be restated, and the *effects* of such a restatement in per share amounts should be disclosed in the financial statements in the year of restatement.

When common stock equivalents or other dilutive securities cause a dilution in one of the EPS data presented on the face of the income statement, and at the same time cause an antidilutive effect in another EPS data presented on the same income statement, all the EPS data presented should be computed using the common stock equivalents or other dilutive securities, regardless of the dilution (APB-30).

In reporting the cumulative effects of an accounting change, two presentations of EPS data for each caption presented are required. The regular presentation includes the primary and fully diluted EPS (1) for the current year reflecting the new accounting principle and its cumulative effect on prior years and (2) for any prior years as previously presented. The *pro forma* presentation includes the primary and fully diluted EPS (1) for the current year reflecting the new accounting principle and (2) for any prior years presented, restated to include the effect of the new accounting principle (APB-20). (See the chapter entitled "Accounting Changes" for illustration of presentation.)

A *dual presentation* is the presentation of EPS data for both primary and fully diluted earnings per share. This information indicates the minimum and maximum levels of dilution for current earnings. GAAP requires that primary and fully diluted EPS be given equal prominence on the income statement.

If a conversion takes place during or after a current period (up to the issuance date of the financial report) that would have materially affected primary EPS if such conversions were included in primary EPS from the beginning of the period or from the date of issuance, if later, supplemental information reflecting the retroactive effect should be furnished in a footnote. Under no circumstances should such retroactive effect be included in EPS data on the face of the income statement.

Common Stock Equivalents

The concept of common stock equivalents (CSE) is essential to an understanding of reporting EPS in accordance with GAAP. The concept is based on the principle of *substance over form*, in that, although certain securities are not actually common stock, the terms and/or conditions under which they were issued usually contain provisions that enable the holder to become a common stockholder. For example, the holder of participating preferred stock is usually entitled to share in the earnings of a corporation when the earnings exceed a specified level. If the corporation has excellent earnings, the value of the participating preferred stock will undoubtedly increase, and its owner has a share in the earnings potential of the business. At the same time, the earnings potential of the common stockholder is decreased, usually as to dividends and possible price appreciation on his shares. This is the concept of *dilution*.

Consequently, the auditor wishes to identify and disclose the substance of these dilutive securities by disclosing their effect on the earnings of the common shareholder. Neither the conversion to common stock nor the imminence of conversion is a prerequisite to a security being considered a CSE.

The determination that a security is (or is not) a CSE is made at the time the security is issued and is based on conditions that existed at the time of issuance. Once a security has been classified as a CSE, it should not be changed thereafter as long as the security is outstanding. If a security is deemed to be a CSE and identical securities are subsequently issued, the identical securities must be classified as CSE.

> *OBSERVATION: In determining the "time of issuance" of a security for the purposes of CSE, all pertinent facts must be considered. The time of issuance is generally the date on which the terms*

of the offering were reached and announced even though they are
subject to the approval of directors, stockholders, or others.

If a security is not classified as a CSE at the time of issuance but is subsequently reclassified as a CSE, it is excluded from primary EPS but included in computing fully diluted EPS (primary EPS and fully diluted EPS are discussed below).

Common stock equivalents are used only in respect in EPS, and the designation does not effect any other accounting treatment or financial statement presentation.

The following are common types of CSE:

Stock options, warrants, and similar instruments   Stock options, warrants, and other similar instruments should be considered CSE *at all times*. These types of security arrangements usually have no cash yield and their right to obtain common stock usually dictates their value.

Convertible debt and convertible preferred stock   FASB-55 and FASB-85 amend APB-15 (Earnings Per Share) by establishing new criteria for computing the yield test for determining whether a convertible security is a common stock equivalent. FASB-55 replaces the "prime interest rate" with the "average Aa corporate bond yield" as the basis for computing the yield test, and FASB-85 changes the "cash yield test" to an "effective yield test." Thus, under APB-15 as amended by FASB-55 and FASB-85, a convertible security is considered a common stock equivalent if its *effective yield* at the date of its issuance is less than 66 2/3% of the then *current average Aa corporate bond yield*. The effective yield to maturity and, if any, the effective yield to all "call" dates must be computed, and the lowest effective yield is used for determining whether the convertible security is a common stock equivalent.

The average Aa corporate bond yield that is used on the date of issuance is determined by reference to the average Aa corporate bond yield for a brief period (about one week) prior to the issuance date of the convertible security.

In computing the effective yield of a convertible security, FASB-85 establishes the following rules:

1. The stated amount of annual interest or dividend payments, and any "original" or "call" premium or discount must be included in computing the effective yield of a convertible security. In computing effective yield, interest shall be compounded on a semiannual basis for bonds issued in the United States. For bonds that are sold or issued in other countries,

interest shall be compounded on the same basis as publicly traded bonds in that particular country. Put options or changing conversion rates shall not be included in computing the effective yield.

2. The effective yield to maturity and, if any, the effective yield to all "call" dates must be computed, and the lowest effective yield is used for determining whether the convertible security is a common stock equivalent.

3. If a convertible security does not have a maturity date, the effective yield shall be computed as the ratio of the stated annual interest or dividend payments to the market price of the convertible security at the date of its issuance.

4. The effective yield of a convertible security with adjustable interest or dividend payments shall be based on its scheduled formula adjustments and formula information at issuance date.

On January 1, 19X1, Ace Company received proceeds of $95,000 from the sale of $100,000 of 12% Convertible Bonds at an original discount of 5%. The term of the bonds is 10 years, and interest is payable semi-annually on June 30 and December 31 of each year. On January 1, 19X6 (5 years), the bonds are callable at 102. The average Aa corporate bond yield for the immediate prior week from the date of issuance of the convertible securities was 21%. The effective yield on the bonds to the call date and to maturity are computed as follows:

Interest compounded semiannually at 12% for one year on $100,000	$12,360
Amount of proceeds from bond sale	$95,000
Effective yield to maturity ($12,360/$95,000)	13.01%
Interest for 5 years (5 × $12,360)	$61,800
Amount of call premium (2%)	2,000
Total	$63,800
Divided by five years ($63,800/5 years)	$12,760
Amount of proceeds from bond sale	$95,000
Effective interest rate to call date ($12,760/$95,000)	13.43%

Under FASB-85, the effective yield to maturity is used to determine whether the convertible security qualifies as a common stock equivalent because it is less than the effective yield to the call date. Thus, the convertible security is classified as a common stock equivalent, since the effective yield to maturity of 13.01% is less than 66 2/3% of the average Aa corporate bond yield (21%), which is 14.00%.

Moody and *Standard & Poor* are the two major bond rating organizations in the United States. An Aa bond rating indicates bonds of high quality which are very likely to be repaid (principal and interest) by the issuer. Many financial institutions issue bond yield information regularly and enterprises should encounter no difficulty in obtaining the "average Aa corporate bond yield." However, there are many different types of bond ratings and related bond yields, and care should be exercised to make sure that the correct information is obtained.

If convertible securities are sold or issued outside the United States, the most comparable *long-term yield* in the foreign country should be used instead of the "average Aa corporate bond yield."

FASB-85 is effective for convertible securities issued on or after April 1, 1985. Convertible securities issued prior to April 1, 1985, may be, but are not required to be, accounted for in accordance with FASB-85 if financial statements for the year have not been issued. Retroactive application of the provisions of FASB-85 to previously issued annual financial statements is permitted. The restated financial statement of the year of change shall disclose the nature of the restatement and its effect on income before extraordinary items, net income, and related per share amounts for each year presented.

A convertible security issued prior to the promulgation of FASB-55 (February 1982) shall be considered a common stock equivalent if, at the time of its issuance, its effective yield is less than 66 2/3% of the then current prime interest rate.

Participating securities   If a participation feature includes a share in the earnings potential of the corporation on substantially the same basis as that of the common shares, such participating securities are generally classified as CSE.

Contingent shares   Contingent issuable shares depend on some future event or on certain conditions being met.

Generally, contingently issuable shares should not be considered CSE unless the contingent event has been attained as of the reporting date for the EPS. The following general rules apply to contingent issuable shares.

Attainment or maintenance of a certain level of earnings   (1) If the level is currently being attained, the contingent shares should be considered CSE for both primary and fully diluted earnings. (2) If the attainment or maintenance contingency is above the present level of earnings, the contingent shares should be considered CSE only for the purpose of fully diluted earnings, in which case earnings for the period are adjusted to the specified earning level before computing EPS. Prior-period EPS should not be restated to reflect the year-to-year effect of the above changes.

Contingent on future market price   CSE for both primary and fully diluted earnings should be considered only for the number of contingent shares that would be issued based on the market price at the close of the period being reported on. Prior-period EPS is restated to reflect the market price changes from year to year.

Both future earnings and future market price   Some contingent issuable shares are conditioned on both future earnings and a future market price. Under these conditions only the number of shares that would be issuable by meeting both conditions at the end of the period being reported on should be considered CSE for both primary and fully diluted earnings. Prior-period EPS is restated to reflect the change in the number of shares from year to year.

Some options, warrants, and other CSE are not convertible until some future date. Usually these securities receive no cash dividends, derive their worth solely from their conversion feature, and thus can be considered CSE depending on the time they become directly convertible. If they can be converted within five years after the period being presented, they are CSE for both primary and fully diluted EPS; if they can be converted before ten years but after five, they are used only in fully diluted EPS calculations; any conversion after ten years can be ignored on the basis of its questionable relevance to the current period (APB-15).

Shares placed in escrow accounts that are contingently returnable shall be accounted for in the same manner as contingently issuable shares, for the purposes of computing EPS.

Sometimes subsidiaries issue convertible securities, options, warrants, or common stock that are in the hands of the public, which should be considered CSE from the standpoint of consolidated and parent company financial statements for the purpose of computing EPS. In this event, the subsidiary should compute its EPS in accordance with the promulgated GAAP, and then the consolidated group or parent company would compute its proportionate share of the subsidiary's primary and/or fully diluted EPS based on the number of shares held. In other words, the consolidated group or parent company would include as income from the subsidiary only an amount equal to the number of shares held in the subsidiary multiplied by the subsidiary's primary and/or fully diluted EPS computed in accordance with GAAP.

Sometimes a subsidiary will issue a security that is convertible into parent company stock, or issue options or warrants to purchase parent company stock. In this case, the options and warrants should be considered CSE by the parent company in computing consolidated and parent company primary and fully diluted EPS. However, subsidiary securities convertible into parent company stock must be evaluated to determine whether they are CSE and enter into the computation of the parent company's primary EPS, or whether they are not CSE and enter only into the parent company's computation of fully diluted EPS. The test for CSE in this case is the same as that for any other convertible security: If at the time of issuance, a convertible security has terms or conditions that make it a CSE, and its effective yield at the date of issuance is less than 66 2/3% of the average Aa corporate bond yield, the convertible security should be considered a CSE.

Although most dividends are reported as historical facts for the purposes of EPS, stock dividends, splits or reverse splits should be presented in terms of the current equivalent number of common shares outstanding at the date of declaration. When this procedure is used, the basis for reporting such dividends should be fully disclosed. In this connection, presenting data as to dividends per share following a pooling-of-interests creates a disclosure problem. Therefore, in such cases it is usually preferable to disclose the dividends per share by the principal constituent on a historical basis, and in addition, the amount per equivalent share, or the total amount, for the other constituents in the pooling for each period, along with adequate disclosure of all pertinent facts. In all cases, where dividends are reported on other than a historical basis, full disclosure of such basis should be made in the financial statements or footnotes thereto.

CSE Materiality

If the dilution in EPS from all CSE is less than 3%, the dilution may be ignored (APB-15). This is an application of the basic principle of materiality.

The rule is that "common stock equivalents that in the aggregate dilute EPS by less than 3% need not be taken into consideration."

However, in order to determine the 3% rule, primary and fully diluted EPS must be computed without and with the CSE.

Antidilution

If the inclusion of a CSE has the effect of increasing EPS or of decreasing LPS (loss per share), such CSE should be excluded from the EPS computation. As a result, a CSE may enter into the determination of primary EPS in one year and not another, because once a security has been classified as a CSE it always retains that status.

The following example illustrates the effects of antidilution.

During January the XYZ Company issued 10,000 shares of 100 par value 5% preferred stock when the average Aa corporate bond yield was 7%. The preferred shares were sold for $110 per share and were convertible into five shares of common stock. XYZ Company also had 300,000 shares of common stock outstanding at the beginning of the year. Net income was $220,000. What was the EPS for XYZ Company for the year?

Computation of Weighted Average Shares

Common stock outstanding, beginning of year	300,000
CSE-Preferred stock (issued for less than 2/3 of the average Aa corporate bond yield)	50,000
Weighted average shares	350,000

Adjustments to Net Income

Net income	$220,000
Less: Preferred dividends	50,000
Adjusted	$170,000
EPS, assuming conversion ($220,000 ÷ 350,000)	$ 0.63
EPS, assuming no conversion ($170,000 ÷ 300,000)	$ 0.57

* *Note*: EPS with conversion is antidilutive and is not used.

Computation of Preferred Stock Yield

The effective yield is determined by dividing the initial issuance price into the stated amount of interest. The preferred stock was sold at issuance for $110 per share and the stated interest was 5%:

$$\$5 \div \$110 = 0.0454 = 4.5\%$$

The result of this computation indicates that the effective yield at the date of issuance was 4.5%. The effective yield is compared to 2/3 of the average Aa corporate bond yield for the week prior to the date of issuance, which was 4.7%:

$$2/3 \text{ of } 7\% = 0.0466 = 4.7\%$$

The effective yield of 4.5% was less than 2/3 of the 7% average Aa corporate bond yield (4.7%) for the week prior to the date of issuance, which makes the preferred stock a CSE. However, because of its antidilutive effect, the preferred stock is not used.

Simple Capital Structures

A corporation with a simple capital structure is one that consists of only capital stock, or which includes no potentially dilutive CSE that could dilute EPS by more than 3% in the aggregate.

For organizations with simple capital structures, the presentation of EPS in the income statement should appear as follows:

	19XX	*19XX*
Income before extraordinary items	$XX,XXX	$XX,XXX
Extraordinary items (describe)	XXX	—
Net income	$XX,XXX	$XX,XXX
Earnings per common share:		
Income before extraordinary items	$ X.XX	$ X.XX
Extraordinary item (Note 1)	.XX	—
Net income per share	$ X.XX	$ X.XX

EPS data are presented before and after extraordinary items. The per share amounts for extraordinary items are arrived at simply by subtraction.

Complex Capital Structures

For organizations with complex capital structures the procedure for determining EPS requires that the auditor gather information regarding various outstanding securities, use that information in computing two EPS figures (which is called a dual presentation), and then present the two EPS amounts with equal prominence on the face of the income statement. The captions for the two EPS figures are "Earnings per common share and common stock equivalents" and "Earnings per common share—assuming full dilution."

The first of these captions is referred to as *primary earnings* and the second as *fully diluted earnings*. The difference between primary EPS and fully diluted EPS is that primary EPS considers only securities that are common stock or CSE, whereas fully diluted EPS indicates the maximum dilution.

Under both methods, antidilutive securities are excluded. Antidilutive securities are those which have the effect of increasing EPS or reducing loss per share.

Three types of securities that might enter into the computation of fully diluted EPS are:

1. Senior stock or debt that is convertible but not a CSE
2. Options or warrants
3. Contingently issuable shares

The difference between primary and fully diluted EPS is whether the securities are CSE. Only CSE enter into primary EPS, whereas all potentially dilutive securities are part of fully diluted EPS.

Dual Presentation of Net Income

A dual presentation includes primary EPS and fully diluted EPS. Only CSE enter into the computation of primary EPS, whereas CSE plus any other dilutive securities enter into the computation of fully diluted EPS.

Any securities that increase EPS are excluded from all computations. These types of securities are called *antidilutive* and either increase EPS or decrease LPS (loss per share).

Primary EPS = common stock + CSE
Fully diluted EPS = primary EPS + additional dilutive securities

Weighted Average Shares

Computations of EPS are based on the weighted number of shares outstanding for each period presented. A separate computation of the weighted number of shares outstanding must be made for primary EPS and fully diluted EPS.

The following example for ABC Company demonstrates how the weighted average shares are determined.

Common stock outstanding, 1/1/77	200,000 shares
Preferred stock (convertible into 2 shares of common stock), outstanding 1/1/77	50,000 shares
Convertible debentures (convertible into 100 shares of common stock for each $1,000 bond)	$100,000

On March 31, ABC reacquired 5,000 shares of its own common stock.

On May 1, ABC converted 20,000 shares of preferred stock into common.

On July 1, ABC converted $50,000 of convertible debentures into common stock.

On September 30, ABC reacquired 5,000 shares of its common stock.

Computation of Weighted Average Shares

1. Common stock outstanding, 1/1/77	200,000
2. Common stock reacquired, 3/31/77	(3,750)
3. Conversion of preferred stock on 5/1/77	26,667
4. Conversion of convertible debentures on 7/1/77	2,500
5. Common stock reacquired on 9/30/77	(1,250)
Total weighted average shares, 1977	224,167

1. Common stock outstanding   Since the 200,000 shares of common stock were outstanding for the entire year, all the shares are included in the weighted average shares.

2. Common stock reacquired   On March 31, 1977, 5,000 shares were reacquired, which means that 9/12 of the year they were not outstanding. Since the 5,000 shares are already included in the 200,000 shares (1 above), we must deduct that portion which was not outstanding during the full year. Thus, 9/12 of the 5,000 shares, or 3,750 shares, should be excluded from the computations, which means that only 196,250 of the 200,000 shares were outstanding for the full year.

3. Conversion of preferred   On May 1, 1977, 20,000 shares of the preferred were converted into common stock. Since the conversion rate is 2 for 1, an additional 40,000 shares were outstanding from May 1 to the end of the year. Thus, 8/12 of the 40,000 shares, or 26,667 shares, should be included in the weighted average shares outstanding for the year.

4. Conversion of convertible debentures   On July 1, 1977, $50,000 of the convertible debentures were converted into common stock. The conversion rate is 100 shares for each $1,000 bond, which means that the $50,000 converted consisted of fifty $1,000 bonds, or 5,000 shares of common stock. Since the conversion was on July 1, only 6/12 of the 5,000 shares (2,500) are included in the weighted average shares outstanding for the year.

5. Common stock reacquired   5,000 additional shares out of the 200,000 shares outstanding at the beginning of the year were reacquired on September 30, which means that for 3/12 of the year they were not outstanding. Thus, 3/12 of 5,000 shares, or 1,250 shares, must be excluded from the computation of weighted average shares outstanding for the year.

The weighted average number of shares must be used so as to reflect the period in which each security affected operations.

Any stock splits or stock dividends (or reverse splits or dividends) must be retroactively recognized in all periods presented in the financial statements. A stock split or stock dividend should be recognized if it occurs after the close of the period but before issuance of the financial statements. If this situation occurs, it must be fully disclosed in the statements. Also, as mentioned previously, the dividends per share must be reported in terms of the equivalent number of shares outstanding at the time the dividend is declared.

Before computing EPS a company must subtract from net income any earnings pledged to senior security holders. If such a security is cumulative preferred, all dividends, whether the company has earnings to cover them or not, must be deducted from net income. In the case of a net loss, the loss is increased by the amount of cumulative dividends in arrears. If the senior security stipulates that dividends are limited to earnings, then adjustments are obviously made to the extent of available earnings.

A company adjusts noncumulative interest or dividends only to the extent they are accruable or declared.

All the above adjustments must be given adequate disclosure in the financial statements or footnotes thereto.

As mentioned earlier, it is possible for a security to be dilutive with respect to one of the EPS figures presented in the financial statements and at the same time be antidilutive to another. In such an instance the effects of such a security should be included in all EPS calculations.

Treasury Stock Method

When potential dilution from stock options and similar instruments is less than 20% of the number of common shares outstanding, the treasury stock method is used to compute the dilution.

When the market price of the underlying stock exceeds the exercise price for substantially all of three consecutive months, the treasury stock method is used to determine the amount of dilution.

The treasury stock method assumes that the stock options or similar instruments are exercised and the money received by the company is used to purchase as much common stock on the open market as possible. The average market price is used for primary EPS and the ending market price is used for fully diluted EPS, unless the average market price is higher. The amount of stock that cannot be purchased because of the lack of money is considered additional outstanding shares, which could have a dilutive effect on EPS. The computations are made by quarters in the year, unless the market price is relatively stable during the year, in which case one computation for the year can be used. The formula to compute CSE for stock options and similar instruments is:

$$\text{Number of shares} - \left[\frac{\text{number of shares} \times \text{exercise price}}{\begin{array}{c}\text{average market price*}\\ or \\ \text{ending market price**}\end{array}}\right] = \begin{array}{c}\text{additional shares}\\ \text{outstanding}\end{array}$$

* Average market price is used for primary EPS.

** Ending market price is used for fully diluted EPS, unless average market price is higher.

OBSERVATION: *Frequently an option or similar instrument is excluded from the computation of primary EPS, but must be included in the determination of fully diluted EPS.*

The following problem illustrates how the incremental shares by quarters are computed for stock options and similar instruments.

A company has 10,000 stock options outstanding, which are exercisable at $60 each. Given the market prices below, determine the incremental shares by quarters, and the number of shares that should be included for both primary and fully diluted EPS.

	Quarters			
	1	*2*	*3*	*4*
Average market price	56	64	70	68
Ending market price	60	68	72	64

The formula for determining the incremental shares by quarters for primary EPS using the *average market price* is as follows:

$$\text{1st quarter } 10,000 \; - \; \frac{10,000 \times \$60}{\$56} \; = \; 0^*$$

$$\text{2nd quarter } 10,000 \; - \; \frac{10,000 \times \$60}{\$64} \; = \; 625$$

$$\text{3rd quarter } 10,000 \; - \; \frac{10,000 \times \$60}{\$70} \; = \; 1,429$$

$$\text{4th quarter } 10,000 \; - \; \frac{10,000 \times \$60}{\$68} \; = \; 1,176$$

Total incremental shares by quarters	=	3,230
Divided by 4 quarters	=	808

* The exercise price of $60 is higher than the average market price.

The reason why we divide by four quarters is that four quarters entered into our computation. The 808 shares must be included in the computation of primary EPS.

The computation of fully diluted EPS uses the *ending market price* unless the average market price is higher.

$$\text{1st quarter } 10{,}000 \quad - \quad \frac{10{,}000 \times \$60}{\$60} \quad = \quad 0^*$$

$$\text{2nd quarter } 10{,}000 \quad - \quad \frac{10{,}000 \times \$60}{\$68} \quad = \quad 1{,}176$$

$$\text{3rd quarter } 10{,}000 \quad - \quad \frac{10{,}000 \times \$60}{\$72} \quad = \quad 1{,}667$$

$$\text{4th quarter } 10{,}000 \quad - \quad \frac{10{,}000 \times \$60}{\$68 \ \ (\text{Note 1})} \quad = \quad 1{,}176$$

Total incremental shares by quarters =	4,019
Divided by 4 quarters =	1,005

* The exercise price of $60 is the same as the ending market price.

Note 1. Since the average market price is higher in the fourth quarter, it is used.

The computation of the incremental shares by quarters when divided by the number of quarters involved gives us the number of shares that could not be purchased with the proceeds from the hypothetical exercise of all the stock options. The computation could be determined by just dividing either the average or ending market price (whichever is applicable) into the hypothetical funds received by the exercise of the stock options, and whatever number of shares cannot be purchased are considered additional outstanding shares.

Under the treasury stock method, the funds that would have been received from the exercise of the options or similar instruments are calculated and:

1. The amount calculated as received is applied as if the funds were used to purchase common stock at the *average market price during the period*, except that for *fully diluted EPS* the market price at the end of the year is used, *if it is higher than the average market price*.
2. All options are considered to be exercised as at the beginning of the period (or time of issuance, if later).
3. Any remaining shares of common stock that theoretically could not be purchased because of the lack of funds are considered outstanding and are added to the total outstanding shares of common stock used to compute EPS.

The theory behind the treasury stock method is that any number of shares of common stock that could have been purchased on the open market with the exercised price funds from the options or similar instruments are not additional outstanding stock and have no dilutive effect on EPS.

The treasury stock method is not used for options and similar instruments that contain a provision which permits or requires the holder to pay part or all of the exercise price by tendering debt or other security of the issuer. The amount of dilution caused by these options and similar instruments is determined by the "if converted" method, which is discussed later in this chapter.

Modified Treasury Stock Method

When the number of shares of common stock that can be purchased with the hypothetical funds from the exercise of the options or similar instruments exceeds 20% of the number of common shares outstanding, the modified treasury stock method is used to determine the dilution, if any.

A maximum of 20% of the outstanding number of common shares may be purchased with the money received from the hypothetical exercise of all the stock options and similar instruments involved.

If any hypothetical money is still left after purchasing the 20% maximum, it is applied as follows (hypothetically):

1. Reduction of existing debt
2. Investment in short-term paper

Net income is adjusted for any interest expense (income) saved or created by 1 and 2, and the related tax effects are taken into consideration.

The following problem demonstrates how the modified treasury stock method is used in those situations where the stock options outstanding exceed 20% of the authorized and issued common stock.

Assume the following data:

Common stock	500,000 shares
Stock options (exercisable at $28)	120,000 shares
6% debt outstanding	$500,000
Net income	$400,000
Average and year-end market price of common stock	$30
Tax rate	50%

What is the primary EPS?

Since the number of stock options exceeds 20% of the total outstanding shares before exercise, the modified treasury stock method must be used.

The first step is to assume that all outstanding stock options are exercised.

Proceeds of exercise of options (120,000 x $28)   <u>$3,360,000</u>

The next step is to apply the proceeds as follows:

1. To purchase the maximum (20%) amount of common stock in the open market at either (a) the average market price in the case of primary EPS computation or (b) the ending market price or the average market price, whichever is higher, in the case of fully diluted EPS computations.
2. If any of the hypothetical funds remain after purchasing the maximum (20%) amount of common stock on the open market, they are applied:
    a. First, to reduce any long-term debt of the enterprise,
    b. Secondly, to purchase short-term paper (hypothetically)

In this problem the application of the proceeds would be:

Application of Proceeds

Purchase of maximum 100,000 shares (20%)	$3,000,000
Reduction in 6% debt	360,000
Total application of proceeds	$3,360,000

After the excess funds are applied to the reduction of $360,000 of 6% long-term debt, we must compute what effect this has on net income, because interest expense is hypothetically reduced by the reduction of the long-term debt.

Adjustment to Income

Net income	$400,000
Add: Net reduction of interest on 6% debt, less 50% taxes (0.06 x $360,000 x 0.5)	10,800
Adjusted net income	$410,800

Since 120,000 stock options were outstanding and we were restricted to purchasing 100,000 (20% maximum), the remaining 20,000 shares must be considered outstanding for the computations of both primary and fully diluted EPS.

Adjustment to Common Stock

Common stock outstanding	500,000
Additional shares (120,000 − 100,000)	20,000
Adjusted common stock	520,000
Primary EPS ($410,800 ÷ 520,000)	$ 0.79

The last item we must check is whether the addition of the stock options to the computation of primary EPS has had an antidilutive effect. This is determined by computing primary EPS without the stock options, as follows:

Primary EPS before options ($400,000 ÷ 500,000)	$0.80

Since primary EPS excluding the stock options is higher than it is including them, there is no antidilutive effect. However, in this case the dilutive effect is less than the 3% materiality rule and can be ignored.

The following is a summary of the steps in the modified treasury stock method.

1. The regular treasury stock method is followed except that a maximum of 20% of the outstanding number of common shares may be theoretically purchased.
2. The regular steps are followed for the treasury stock method.
3. Any remaining theoretical funds are applied in the following order:
    a. Reduction of any borrowings
    b. Investment in short-term government or commercial paper
    c. Recognition of any tax effect of a and b
4. The total effect of all steps are aggregated; if the net effect is dilutive, it is recognized in EPS.

If-Converted Method

Convertible debt and convertible preferred stock are considered common stock equivalents (CSE) if their effective yield, at the date of issuance, is less than 2/3 of the then current average Aa corporate bond yield.

When convertible debt or convertible preferred stock is CSE and enter into primary EPS, or when these same types of securities are not CSE but enter into the computation of fully diluted earnings, the *if-converted* method is used to determine dilution.

The principal objective of the if-converted method is to adjust net income for the effects of including a security in primary or fully diluted EPS. These adjustments are usually preferred dividends or interest on convertible securities.

> **OBSERVATION:** *Nondiscretionary items that would have been made on the basis of net income, such as profit-sharing expense, royalties, and investment credits, must also be taken into consideration.*

The if-converted method assumes that convertible issues are converted at the beginning of the year or at issuance date, if later.

Some convertible debt and preferred stock require the holder to pay a stipulated amount of cash on conversion. The treasury stock method is used to account for any cash received when the if-converted method is used. However, theoretical stock purchases are assumed only if the market price exceeds the exercise price or if the exercise price is less than market because the convertible security is selling at a discount.

It stands to reason that if you are going to consider one of these types of securities a CSE, the applicable dividend and interest must be added back to net income, *if either was previously deducted.*

The following example illustrates the application of the if-converted method.

X Company has outstanding 100,000 shares of common stock and $500,000 in 6% debentures convertible into 10 shares for each $1,000 bond. The convertible debentures are CSE, and net income for the year was $100,000. What is primary EPS, assuming a 50% tax rate?

Primary shares outstanding:	
Common stock	100,000
Convertible debentures (500 x 10)	5,000
Total primary shares—outstanding	105,000
Primary net income:	
Net income	$100,000
Add back interest on bonds, less	
tax effects (0.06 x $500,000) x 0.5)	15,000
Total primary net income	$115,000
Primary EPS (with conversion)	
($115,000 ÷ 105,000 shares)	$ 1.10

Once again we must check to see whether the inclusion of the convertible debentures in the computation of primary EPS is antidilutive, by comparing primary EPS computed with the bonds to primary EPS computed without the bonds, as follows:

Primary EPS (without conversion)	
($100,000 ÷ 100,000 shares)	$1.00

Primary EPS with conversion of the convertible bonds ($1.10) is more than primary EPS without the conversion ($1) and is therefore antidilutive.

In the above example, assume that instead of the convertible debenture, there were 10,000 shares of 3% preferred stock ($100 par) convertible into five shares for each share of preferred. What is the primary EPS?

Primary shares outstanding:	
Common stock	100,000
Convertible preferred (10,000 × 5)	50,000
Total primary shares	150,000
Primary net income (with conversion)	$100,000

No adjustment is made when considering preferred stock as CSE, because dividends are deducted from net income.

Primary net income (without conversion):	
($100,000 – $30,000 for preferred dividends)	$ 70,000
Primary EPS (with conversion):	
($100,000 ÷ 150,000 shares)	$ 0.67
Primary EPS (without conversion)	
($70,000 ÷ 100,000 shares)	$ 0.70

Primary EPS with conversion is *not antidilutive* and is therefore used.

The *if-converted method* recognizes that the holders of a convertible bond or other debt instrument may share in equity (through conversion to common stock) or in debt (from holding the bond), but not in both. Many convertible securities are such that in order to convert to common stock, the holder must surrender his security.

In summary, convertible issues of this type that are CSE are assumed to be converted as at the beginning of the period (or at the date of issuance, if later), and the following steps are taken:

1. Net income must be recomputed to reflect the conversion of these securities from the beginning of the period. Interest

charges and other expenses attributable to the convertible issues, along with any preferred dividends, must be taken into consideration in recomputing net income.

2. EPS is computed on the basis of the amount of common stock that would have been outstanding if these types of convertible securities were converted as at the beginning of the period (or at the date of issuance, if later).

Some warrants and convertible securities require a cash payment on conversion. In these cases, if the market price of the underlying stock exceeds the exercise price or if the security being converted is selling for a discount that results in an exercise price lower than the market price of the underlying common stock, then (1) the theoretical proceeds should be applied in accordance with the treasury stock method *and* (2) the if-converted method should apply as to the retirement or conversion of such warrants or convertible securities.

Two-Class Method

Although the *two-class method* is considered inappropriate when other acceptable methods can be used, it may be necessary in the case of *participating securities and two classes of common stock*.

Under the *two-class method*, CSE are treated as common stock, but with a dividend rate different from that of the common stock, there is no conversion of any convertible securities, and:

1. No use of theoretical proceeds is considered.

2. All required distributions to senior securities, CSE, and common stock are assumed to be deducted from net income.

3. The remaining amount is divided by the CSE and common shares, after adding back distributions under 2 above to arrive at primary EPS.

Loss per Share

Loss per share is generally based on the number of outstanding common shares, and any assumption of conversion would be antidilutive because the loss is spread over more shares, thereby reducing the loss per share.

Business Combinations

Shares issued in a combination accounted for by the *purchase method* are accounted for in the EPS calculation from the date of the acquisition. When the *pooling method* is used, the calculation is based on the total weighted average number of shares of the constituent firms, adjusted to the equivalent shares of the surviving company.

The difference in treatment is based on the difference between the purchase method, in which results of operations appear in the parent's net income only from the date of acquisition, and the pooling method, in which results are "pooled" for all periods presented.

> **OBSERVATION:** *As mentioned previously, data as to dividends per share following a pooling-of-interests may create a disclosure problem. In such cases, it is usually preferable to disclose on a historical basis the dividends per share paid by the principal constituent of the pooling and the amount of dividends per equivalent share, or the total amount of dividends, for the other constituents in the pooling. This type of presentation should be made for each period presented, along with adequate disclosure of all the pertinent facts.*
>
> *In all cases, where dividends are reported on other than a historical basis, full disclosure of such basis is required in the financial statements or footnotes thereto.*

Disclosure

Disclosure should be made of all pertinent rights and privileges of the various security holders, including dividend and liquidation preferences, participation rights, call prices and dates, and conversion and exercise prices.

The bases on which primary and fully diluted EPS have been calculated should be disclosed in a schedule or a footnote to the financial statements. This disclosure should include the identification of any CSE in determining primary and fully diluted EPS, describe all assumptions used, and reveal the number of shares issued on conversion, exercise, or otherwise during the most recent annual fiscal period and any subsequent periods presented.

It may be desirable to provide clear-cut computations or reconciliations of each security entering into the computation of primary and fully diluted EPS. However, this type of information which shows the historical amount of outstanding common shares should not be shown on the face on the income statement.

A company should also disclose, preferably in a footnote, the effect of any recapitalization. For instance, if common stock is sold and the proceeds are used to retire preferred stock or bonds, supplemental EPS information should be supplied, showing the effects of such a transaction if it had occurred at the beginning of the period.

The following specific disclosures mentioned in this chapter are repeated here for convenience:

1. EPS should appear prominently on the face of the income statement for all periods presented.

2. The effects of prior-period EPS restated in per share amounts should be disclosed in the financial statements in the year of restatement.

3. If CSE or conversions occur during or after a current period that would have materially affected primary EPS, supplemental information reflecting the retroactive effect should be furnished in a footnote, if such CSE had been included in the computation of EPS for the current period. Under no circumstances should such retroactive effect be actually included in EPS data on the face of the income statement.

4. When stock dividends, splits, or reverse splits are presented in terms of the current equivalent number of common shares outstanding, as they should be, the basis for reporting such dividends should be fully disclosed.

5. A stock dividend, split, or reverse split that occurs after the close of a period but before issuance of the financial statements should be retroactively recognized in all periods presented in the financial statements. Full disclosure of the fact must be made in the financial statements or footnotes thereto.

6. All adjustments made to net income for the computation of EPS must be adequately disclosed.

Comprehensive Illustration

The following problem illustrates the application of all the components of determining EPS in accordance with the promulgated GAAP (APB-15).

Assume the following information for Black Corporation for 19X2 and 19X1. On the basis of this information compute the primary and fully diluted EPS for 19X2 and 19X1. Show your computation by supporting schedules in good form.

Common stock ($1 par) issued prior to 19X1	1,000,000 shs.
Common stock ($1 par) issued for cash, 7/1/X2	100,000 shs.
Stock options to acquire one share of $1 common for $50 issued 1/1/70 expire 1/1/80	100,000 shs.
3% preferred stock ($100 par) convertible into 1.5 shares of $1 common. Sold at par (3/1/X0) when the average Aa corporate bond yield was 7%	200,000 shs.
6% debentures issued at par 4/1/X2, convertible into 15 shares of $1 common for each $1,000 bond. The debentures are not CSE.	$500,000

Market price of common stock ($1 par):

	Average	Ending
19X2	64	66
19X1	48	47

Income tax rate: 50%

	19X2	19X1
Income before extraordinary item	$3,200,000	$2,600,000
Extraordinary item	(400,000)	(600,000)
Cumulative effect of a change in accounting for depreciation	100,000	—
Net income	$2,900,000	$2,000,000

Computation of Weighted Average Shares

	19X2	19X1
Common stock ($1 par)	1,000,000	1,000,000
Common stock ($1 par) issued 7/1/X2 equivalent shares (100,000 × 6/12)	50,000	—
Stock option (CSE) (Schedule A)	21,875	—
3% Preferred stock (CSE) (Schedule B)	300,000	300,000
Primary weighted average shares	1,371,875	1,300,000
Stock options (Schedule A)	2,368	—
Convertible debentures (Schedule C)	5,625	—
Fully diluted weighted average shares	1,379,868	1,300,000

Schedule A—Computation of CSE, Stock Options

19X2—Primary EPS (use average market price = 64)

$$100{,}000 \quad - \quad \frac{100{,}000 \ \times \ \$50}{\$64} \quad = \quad \underline{\underline{21{,}875}}$$

19X2—Fully diluted EPS (use ending market price = 66, unless average is higher = 64)

$$100{,}000 \quad - \quad \frac{100{,}000 \ \times \ \$50}{\$66} \quad = \quad 24{,}243$$

Less included in primary EPS (above)	21,875
Additional shares for fully diluted EPS	2,368

19X1—The average and ending market prices are less than the $50 exercise price, which results in no CSE.

Schedule B—Computation of CSE, Preferred Stock

Because the effective yield (3%) is less than 2/3 of the average Aa corporate bond yield of 7% (2/3 of 7% = 4.67%) at the date of issue, the preferred stock is a CSE.

200,000 shares x 1.5 (conversion rate) = 300,000

Schedule C—Convertible Debenture Dilution

The 6% convertible debentures are not CSE, because they were issued to yield 6%, which is more than 2/3 of the average Aa corporate bond yield (2/3 of 7% = 4.67%). However, they do enter into the computation of fully diluted EPS because of their potential dilution (convertibility).
Issued 4/1/X2 and convertible into 15 shares per $1,000.

Fully converted (500 x 15)	7,500
Issued 4/1/X2 (7,500 x 9/12)	5,625

Antidilution test—3% preferred stock:

	19X2	19X1
Without preferred:		
Net income	$2,900,000	$2,000,000
Less: Preferred dividends ($3 × 200,000)	600,000	600,000
Adjusted	$2,300,000	$1,400,000
Weighted average shares (1,000,000 + 50,000 + 21,875)	1,071,875	1,000,000
Primary EPS without conversion	$ 2.15	$ 1.40
With preferred:		
Net income	$2,900,000	$2,000,000
Weighted average shares	1,371,875	1,300,000
Primary EPS, with conversion	$ 2.11	$ 1.54

Antidilution test—6% convertible debentures:

	19X2
Without conversion:	
Net income	$2,900,000
Weighted average shares (1,000,000 + 50,000 + 21,875 + 300,000 + 2,368)	1,374,243
Fully diluted EPS without conversion	$2.11
With conversion:	
Net income	$2,900,000
Plus: Interest expense ($500,000 × 6% × 9/12 × 50% tax rate)	11,250
Adjusted net income	$2,911,250
Weighted average shares (1,374,243 + 5,625)	1,379,868
Fully diluted EPS with conversion	$2.11

Statement Presentation

	19X2	19X1
Income before extraordinary item	$3,200,000	$2,600,000
Extraordinary item (Note _____)	(400,000)	(600,000)
Cumulative effect of change in accounting principle (depreciation)	100,000	—
Net income	$2,900,000	$2,000,000

Earnings per share and common stock equivalents:

Income before extraordinary item	$	2.33	$	2.00
Extraordinary item (Note _____)		(0.29)		(0.60)
Cumulative effect of change in accounting for depreciation		0.07		—
Net income	$	2.11	$	1.40
Shares outstanding		1,371,875		1,000,000

Earnings per share assuming full dilution:

Income before extraordinary item	$	2.33	$	2.00
Extraordinary item (Note_____)		(0.29)		(0.60)
Cumulative effect of change in accounting for depreciation		0.07		—
Net income	$	2.11	$	1.40
Shares outstanding		1,379,868		1,000,000

Comments:

1. In 19X1 the preferred stock was excluded from primary and fully diluted EPS because it was antidilutive ($1.40 versus $1.54).

2. Any CSE that in the aggregate dilutes EPS (primary or fully diluted) by less than 3% can be ignored (materiality rule). In this comprehensive illustration the aggregate dilution of the CSE included in the computation of EPS was greater than 3% ($2.19 - $2.11 = $.08 or 3.65%).

NOTE: The pro forma presentation required for a change in an accounting principle has been excluded from the above illustration for the sake of brevity.

EQUITY METHOD

Overview

The promulgated GAAP for the equity method of accounting for investments in common stock is APB-18 (as amended) and FASB Interpretation-35 (Criteria for Applying the Equity Method of Accounting for Investments in Common Stock). In addition, Statement of Position 78-9 (Accounting for Investments in Real Estate Ventures) covers the application of the equity method of accounting to unincorporated real estate ventures.

FASB-13, paragraph 31, requires that subsidiaries whose principal business is leasing property to its parent company should be consolidated and the equity method is unacceptable.

> **OBSERVATION:** *The original pronouncements published by the FASB indicate that paragraph 31 of FASB-13 has been superseded by FASB-94. This supersedure cannot be found anywhere in the text of FASB-94.*

The promulgated GAAP extends the use of the equity method to investments in common stock of corporate joint ventures and certain other investments in common stock. The promulgated GAAP does not cover investment companies registered under, or those which would be included in, the Investment Company Act of 1940, or nonbusiness entities, such as individual, trusts, and estates.

> **OBSERVATION:** *An investor's qualifying assets, for the purposes of capitalizing interest costs under FASB-34, shall include equity funds, loans, and advances made to investees accounted for by the equity method, provided that the investee (a) is undergoing activities necessary to start its planned principal operations and (b) the activities include the use of funds to acquire qualifying assets for its operations (FASB-58). For further discussion, see the chapter entitled "Interest Costs Capitalized."*

Background

Domestic and foreign investments in common stocks and corporate joint ventures should be presented in consolidated financial statements on the *equity basis* by an investor, whose investment in the voting stock, although less than control, gives it the ability to *exercise significant influence over the operating and financial policies* of the investment.

The equity method of accounting may not be used to account for majority-owned subsidiaries in consolidated financial statements (see FASB-94).

Under the equity basis of accounting for investments in common stock, consolidated net income during a time period includes the parent company's proportionate share of the net income reported by the investee for the periods subsequent to acquisition. *The effect of this treatment is that net income for the period and stockholder's equity at the end of the period are the same as if the companies had been consolidated.* Any dividends received are treated as adjustments of the amount of the investment under the equity basis.

When appropriate, investors should use the equity method to account for investments in common stock, corporate joint ventures, and in other common stock investments (domestic and foreign) in which ownership is less than 50%.

It is presumed, absent evidence to the contrary, that an investment (directly or indirectly) of less than 20% of the voting stock of an investee indicates lack of significant influence, and the use of the equity method or consolidated statements is not required.

It is assumed, absent evidence to the contrary, *that an investment (directly or indirectly) of 20% or more of the voting stock of an investee indicates the ability to exercise significant influence and control, and the equity method or consolidated statements, whichever is more meaningful, is required for a fair presentation.*

The 20% ownership is based on current outstanding securities that have voting privilege. Potential ownership and voting privileges should be disregarded.

Presumption of Significant Influence

In order to establish a uniform application of the equity method, the presumption in APB-18 is that, absent evidence to the contrary, an investment (direct or indirect) of 20% or more of the voting stock of an investee indicates that the investor has the ability to exercise significant influence over the operating and financial policies of the investee. Evidence that the investor has such significant influence over the investee includes the following:

1. Investor has representation on the board of directors of the investee.
2. Investor participates in the policy-making process of the investee.
3. Material intercompany transactions occur between the investor and the investee.
4. Interchange of managerial personnel between the investor and the investee.
5. Technological dependency of the investee on the investor.
6. Extent of ownership of the investor in relation to the concentration of other shareholders.

The determination of the investor's influence in an investment may be difficult to reach and the application of sound judgment may frequently be necessary. However, the presumption is that significant influence does exist in an investment of 20% or more, unless sufficient evidence to the contrary outweighs the presumption.

> **OBSERVATION:** *There is also a presumption in APB-18 that significant influence does not exist in an investment of less than 20%. However, APB-18 makes it perfectly clear that this presumption may be overcome by enough evidence to the contrary. Thus, significant influence over the operating and financial policies of an investment of less than 20% can occur.*

In an investment of 20% or more, enough evidence may exist to demonstrate that the investor cannot exercise significant influence over the operating and financial policies of the investee. Thus, the presumption of significant influence in investments of 20% or more may be overcome by sufficient evidence.

The following conditions may indicate that an investor is unable to exercise significant influence over the operating and financial policies of an investee:

1. The investee opposes the investment and files a lawsuit or complaint, indicating that the investor does not have significant influence.

2. An agreement is executed between the investee and the investor which indicates that significant influence does not exist.

   *OBSERVATION: These types of agreements are generally referred to as **standstill agreements** and are frequently used to settle disputes between and investor and an investee. They may contain information as to whether the investor can or cannot exercise significant influence over the investee. The following are some of the typical provisions of the standstill agreement:*

   a. *The investee agrees to use its best efforts to obtain representation for the investor on its board of directors.*
   b. *The investor agrees not to seek representation on the investee's board of directors.*
   c. *The investee may agree to cooperate with the investor.*
   d. *The investor may agree to limit its ownership in the investee.*
   e. *The investor may agree not to exercise its significant influence over the investee.*
   f. *The investee may acknowledge or refute the investor's ability to exercise significant influence.*

   If a standstill agreement contains provisions indicating that the investor has given up some significant rights as a shareholder, the agreement is regarded, under FASB Interpretation-35, as a factor in determining that the equity method should not be used.

3. Significant influence is exercised by a small group of shareholders representing majority ownership of the investee.
4. The investor attempts, but cannot obtain, the financial information that is necessary to apply the equity method.

   OBSERVATION: The Codification of Statements on Auditing Standards (AU332.09) states that, "The refusal of an investee to furnish necessary financial data to the investor is evidence (but not necessarily conclusive evidence) that the investor does not have the ability to exercise significant influence over operating and financial policies of the investee such as to justify the application of the equity method of accounting for investments in 50% or less owned companies in accordance with the provisions of APB-18."

5. The investor attempts and fails to obtain representation on the investee's board of directors.

> **OBSERVATION:** *FASB Interpretation-35 implies that the investor must actually try to obtain financial information or try to obtain representation on the investee's board. It seems logical that the same effect should result in the event that the investor had prior knowledge that he would fail in these attempts and, therefore, did not even attempt them.*

Many other factors, not listed above, may affect an investor's ability to exercise significant influence over the operating and financial policies of an investee. An investor must evaluate all existing circumstances to determine whether factors exist that overcome the presumption of significant influence in an investment of 20% or more of an investee.

> **OBSERVATION:** *On the other hand, an investor must also evaluate existing circumstances in an investment of less than 20% of an investee. The presumption that significant influence does not exist in an investment of less than 20% may be overcome by factors that indicate that significant influence does exist.*
>
> *If there is not enough evidence to reach a definitive conclusion at the time that the investment is made, it may be advisable to wait until more evidence becomes available.*

FASB Interpretation-35 is effective for fiscal years ending on or after June 15, 1982, and earlier application is encouraged. Accounting changes caused by the application of FASB Interpretation-35 shall not be accounted for as accounting changes (APB-20). Instead, accounting changes required by FASB Interpretation-35 shall be accounted for in accordance with the provisions of paragraphs 19 (l) and (m) of APB-18 (Equity Method), as follows:

1. If an investment in voting stock falls below the 20% level, or other factors indicate that the investor can no longer exercise significant influence, the presumption is that the investor has lost the ability to exercise significant influence and control, in which case the equity method should be discontinued. The carrying amount at the date of discontinuance becomes the cost of the investment. Subsequent dividends are accounted for by the cost method from the date the equity method was discontinued.
2. An investor who, because of other factors, obtains significant influence or who acquires more than 20% ownership in an

investee after having had less than 20% *must retroactively adjust its accounts to the equity method on the basis of a step-by-step acquisition of an investment.* In this event, at the date of each step in the acquisition, the carrying value of the investment must be compared with the underlying net assets of the investee to determine whether goodwill (positive or negative) is involved.

Cost Method

The cost method is generally used when ownership is less than 20%. The original investment under the cost method is recorded at cost, and income is recognized from dividends received out of accumulated earnings earned after the date of acquisition.

Dividends received out of accumulated earnings prior to the date of acquisition are recorded as a return of investment and reduce the cost of the investment.

Certain factors, such as continuing operating losses, may indicate that a substantial decline in the value of the investment has occurred. If such a decline is not temporary, it should be recognized in the accounts.

Special rules apply to the cost method when it is used to account for unconsolidated subsidiaries (see the chapter entitled "Consolidated Financial Statements").

Equity Method

Under the equity method the original investment is recorded at cost and is adjusted periodically to recognize the investor's share of earnings or losses after the date of acquisition. *Dividends received reduce the basis of the investment.* Continuing operating losses from the investment may indicate the necessity for an adjustment in the basis of the investment in excess of those recognized by the application of the equity method.

An investor's share of earnings or losses from its investment is usually shown as a *single amount* (called a *one-line consolidation*) in the income statement, after the following adjustments:

1. Intercompany profits and losses are eliminated, unless realized, in the same manner as if the investee were consolidated.
2. Any difference between the underlying equity in net assets of the investee and the cost of the investment should be accounted for on a consolidated basis. Therefore, goodwill should be amortized over a period of 40 years or less.

3. The investment should be shown in the investor's balance sheet as a single amount and earnings or losses should be shown as a single amount (one-line consolidation) in the income statement, *except for the investor's share of (a) extraordinary items and (b) prior-period adjustments, which should be shown in the income statement separately.*

4. Capital transactions of the investee that affect the investor's share of stockholders' equity should be accounted for on a consolidated basis.

5. Gain or loss is recognized when an investor sells the common stock investment, *equal to the difference between the selling price and the carrying amount of the investment at the time of sale.*

6. If the investee's financial reports are not timely enough for an investor to apply the equity method, the investor should use the most recent available financial statement, and the lag in time created should be consistent from period to period.

7. Other than temporary declines, a decrease in an investment should be recognized in the books of the investor.

8. Losses on an investment decrease the basis of the investment, which may not be reduced below zero, at which point the use of the equity method should be discontinued, unless the investor has guaranteed obligations of the investee or is committed to provide financial support. The investor should resume the equity method when the investee subsequently reports net income and the net income exceeds the investor's share of any net losses not recognized during the period of discontinuance.

9. Dividends for cumulative preferred stock of the investee must be deducted first before the investor's share of earnings or losses is computed, whether the dividend was declared or not.

10. An investor who acquires more than 20% ownership in an investee after having had less than 20% *must retroactively adjust its accounts to the equity method on the basis of a step-by-step acquisition of a subsidiary.* In this event, at the date of each step in the acquisition, the carrying value of the investment must be compared with the underlying net assets of the investee to determine whether goodwill (positive or negative) is involved.

OBSERVATION: When restating financial statements of prior periods, interest cost capitalized in accordance with FASB-58 shall not be changed. Thus, if an unconsolidated investee is subsequently consolidated in the investor's financial statements as a result of increased ownership or a voluntary change by the reporting entity, interest costs capitalized in accordance with FASB-58 shall not be changed if restatement of financial statements is necessary. For further discussion of the capitalization of interest costs on equity funds, loans, and advances made by an investor to an investee accounted for by the equity method, see the chapter entitled "Interest Costs Capitalized."

11. If an investment in voting stock falls below the 20% level, the presumption is that the investor has lost the ability to exercise significant influence and control, in which case the equity method should be discontinued. The carrying amount at the date of discontinuance becomes the cost of the investment. Subsequent dividends are accounted for by the cost method from the date the equity method was discontinued.

12. An investor's shares of earnings or losses from an investment accounted for by the equity method is based on the outstanding shares of the investee without regard to common stock equivalents (APB-15).

13. The equity method should not be used for investments of a temporary nature, for foreign investments subject to controls and restrictions, and for those investments in which the investor does not have significant influence over the financial and administrative policies of the investee.

> **OBSERVATION:** *It is interesting to note that the cost method and the equity method are both bookkeeping and reporting methods. For example, a company may account for an investment by the cost method and prepare financial statements on the equity method. On the other hand, consolidation would more likely be classified as a reporting method. The amount of detail reported in the financial statements is the main difference between the equity method and consolidation.*

Disclosure

Full disclosure must be made for investments accounted for by the equity method and should include:

1. The name of the investment
2. The percentage of ownership

3. The accounting policies of the investor in accounting for the investment
4. The difference between the carrying value of the investment and the underlying equity in the net assets, and the accounting treatment of such difference
5. The quoted market price of the investment, except if it is a subsidiary
6. If material, a summary of the assets, liabilities, and results of operations presented as a footnote or as separate statements
7. The material effect on the investor of any convertible securities of the investee

If the equity method is not used for an investment of 20% or more, disclosure should be made of the name of the investment and reason(s) why the equity method was not used. Conversely, if the equity method is used for an investment of less than 20%, disclosure should be made of the name of the investment and reason(s) why the equity method was used.

In evaluating the extent of disclosure, the investor must weigh the significance of the investment in relation to its financial position and results of operations.

Unincorporated Real Estate Ventures

The thrust of Statement of Position 78-9 is to extend the provisions of APB-18 (Equity Method) to unincorporated real estate ventures. Thus, if an investor includes an investment in a real estate venture in its financial statements prepared in conformity with GAAP, the real estate venture should generally be accounted for in accordance with APB-18. Regulated investment companies and other enterprises that must account for their investments at quoted market value or fair value are not required to comply with SOP 78-9.

The promulgated GAAP on the equity method of accounting (APB-18) applies only to investments held in the form of common stock. APB-18 does not cover investments in unincorporated businesses such as general partnerships, limited partnerships and investments held as undivided interests. In November 1971, an AICPA staff interpretation of APB-18 concluded that many aspects of the equity method were, in fact, quite appropriate in accounting for investments in certain unincorporated entities.

The preferable accounting principles expressed in SOP 78-9 confirm that unincorporated investments in noncontrolled real estate ventures should, as a general rule, be accounted for and reported under the equity method. The exposure to joint and several liability and the special income tax considerations of nonincorporated joint ventures are the principal differences cited by SOP 78-9 between corporate joint ventures and nonincorporated joint ventures. Some of the special problems which may arise in applying the equity method to unincorporated real estate ventures which are not controlled are covered by SOP 78-9 and are discussed below.

Many unincorporated joint ventures are not taxable entities for income tax purposes and the tax liability is usually passed on to the individual partners or investors. In this event, the temporary (timing) difference, if any, is the difference between income or loss recorded by a partner or investor using the equity method and the partner's or investor's share of distributable taxable income or loss reported by the unincorporated joint venture.

As mentioned previously the equity method is used in those situations where the partner or investor can exercise significant influence over the operating and financial policies of the unincorporated investee, which is presumed to occur when the investment is 20% or more of the investee. However, in those situations where an investor, directly or indirectly, controls (usually 50% or more) an investee, a parent-subsidiary relationship exists and consolidated financial statements are required (see FASB-94). On the other hand, a limited partner's interest may be so insignificant that little, if any, influence can be exerted over the operating and financial policies of the limited partnership. When this, or a similar situation exists, it may be appropriate for the limited partner or investor to account for its investment by the cost method.

A general partner of a limited partnership should not use the equity method to account for its investment, if the limited partnership agreement provides for control of the partnership by the general partners. On the other hand, a limited partner may be in control, if it holds over 50% interest in the limited partnership.

The equity method should be used in accounting for undivided interests in real estate ventures provided that some level of joint control exists between the owners. Some level of joint control is usually present in most real estate ventures owned by undivided interests. Joint control exists where the approval of two or more owners is required to finance, develop, operate or sell the real property. An undivided interest in the assets, liabilities, revenue and expenses of a real estate venture may be present if joint control does not exist and each undivided interest is liable only for indebtedness it incurs, is entitled only to its pro-rata share of income, and is liable only for its pro-rata share of expenses.

Accounting for losses   Losses in excess of amounts invested, including loans and advances, should be recorded by partners or investors in real estate ventures in which they are jointly and severally liable. Such excess losses should be reported as a liability on the balance sheet of the partner or investor.

Sometimes a partner or investor is unable to bear its share of losses in a real estate venture and the other partners or investors may become liable. Accounting for this type of loss by a partner or investor is governed by the promulgated GAAP on contingencies (FASB-5). Therefore, if it is probable that a partner or investor in a real estate venture will have to bear a proportionate share of another partner's or investor's losses, the loss should be recorded. However, the partner or investor who is unable to bear the loss should still continue to record the losses on its books until the liability for payment has been terminated by agreement or operation of law.

Purchased goodwill   The excess of cost of a real estate investment over the fair value of the underlying net assets (tangible and intangible) should be recorded as goodwill. Purchased goodwill should be amortized by systematic charges to income over the period to be benefited, but not to exceed 40 years (APB-17).

Capital transactions with a real estate venture   The amount of cash contributed by a partner or investor for the formation of a real estate venture should be recorded as an investment provided that all partners or investors contribute cash. A partner or investor who contributes real estate as a capital investment in a real estate venture should record as its investment the carrying cost of the real estate contributed. No profit should be recognized on a transaction that is, in economic substance, a capital contribution to a real estate venture.

Under all circumstances, a partner or investor who sells real estate to a real estate venture must comply with all of the applicable provisions of the industry accounting guide entitled "Accounting for Profit Recognition on Sales of Real Estate."

In the event a partner or investor contributes real estate to a real estate venture as a capital contribution and simultaneously receives a sum of cash from the venture which does not have to be reinvested back into the venture, the transaction is in substance an exchange to the extent of the amount of cash received. Thus, a partner or investor should recognize a profit on the amount of cash received.

The carrying amount of real estate contributed as capital by a partner or investor may exceed the proportionate amount of interest received in the venture compared to cash contributions by other partners or investors. In this event, the partner or investor contributing the real estate should recognize a loss on the transaction to the extent that a cash contribution for the same interest in the venture exceeds the carrying amount of the real estate.

Services or intangibles contributed to a real estate venture by a partner or investor should be accounted for in the same manner as that of a wholly-owned investment.

Interest income on partners' or investors' loans and advances to a real estate venture should be deferred if one of the following conditions exists:

1. The collectibility of the principal amount of the loans and advances or any remaining interest payments is in doubt.
2. The other partners or investors in the real estate venture are not reasonably expected to bear their share of present or future losses.

The entire amount of interest income accrued on loans and advances to a real estate venture should be recorded as earned if both of the above conditions do not exist but a third condition exists as follows:

3. The partner or investor has recorded its proportionate share of income or loss from the venture (equity method), which included interest expense on loans and advances.

If none of the above three conditions exist, a portion of the interest income on loans and advances should be deferred. The percentage of interest income which must be deferred is equal to the partner's or investor's percentage interest in the real estate venture.

If a real estate venture capitalizes costs of services performed by a partner or investor, the partner or investor may recognize profit on the services performed, but only to the extent of outside interests in the real estate venture and if:

1. The form and substance of the transaction are basically the same.
2. No significant uncertainties exist pertaining to completion of performance by the partner or investor, and to the total costs involved, and other partners or investors are reasonably expected to be able to share their portion of any present or future losses.

Similarly, if a partner or investor capitalizes costs of services performed by the real estate venture, the partner's or investor's share of the venture's profit on the services performed should be recorded as a reduction of the capitalized costs.

If a real estate venture sells real estate to a partner or investor, the partner's or investor's share of the venture's profit on the sale should be recorded as a reduction of the cost of the real estate purchased and not recognized as profit.

Conclusion

The basis of recording income from investments accounted for by the cost method is dividends arising from earnings after the date of acquisition. Dividends are frequently unrelated to the earnings or losses of an investment, because some companies pay dividends in excess of earnings and sometimes when there are no earnings at all. These types of shortcomings of the cost method make it difficult to relate earnings to the proper periods.

The market value method recognizes both dividends received and changes in the market price of the investment. Dividends received are included as income from the investment, as is the increase or decrease in the market value of the investment. The carrying amount of the investment in the balance sheet is the market value of the investment on that date. Thus the market value method more clearly reports the economic substance of holding the investment.

The promulgated GAAP requires that the equity method be used for domestic and foreign noncontrolled investments in voting common stock. The equity method is used in those situations where the investor can exercise significant influence over the investee, which is presumed to occur when the investment is 20% or more of the investee. Under the equity method, dividends are credited to the investment account and are not considered income, and after all the necessary eliminating entries are made, the investor periodically records its share of the investee's net income as a debit to the investment account and a credit to income from the investment. The eliminating entries are the same as would be made for consolidated financial statements, including amortization of goodwill, if necessary. The equity method is usually called "one-line consolidation," because the investment is shown in the balance sheet as one amount and the income is likewise shown in the income statement, except for the extraordinary items and prior period adjustments. Gain or loss on investment accounted for by the equity method is the difference between the sales price and the carrying value of the investment on the date of sale. If a decline of the value of an investment accounted for under the equity method is other than temporary, it is recorded as a loss in the period it occurs.

The basic difference between consolidation and the equity method is the amount of detail reported in the financial statements.

Comprehensive Illustration

Cost method   The original investment is recorded at cost in an investment account. Additions to, or returns of, the original investment are also recorded at cost in the investment account. Dividends received out of accumulated earnings prior to acquisition are recorded as a return of investment. *All other dividends are recorded as dividend income.*

The recording of dividends as dividend income is the major difference between the cost and the equity methods.

Equity method   This method is exactly the same as the cost method except:

1. Dividends received are credited to the investment account and are not considered income.
2. The investor periodically records its share of the investee's net income by a debit to the investment account and a credit to income from subsidiary. Goodwill is amortized over a period of 40 years or less.

On December 31, 19X1, LKM Corporation acquired a 90% interest in Nerox Company for $700,000. Total stockholders' equity on the date of acquisition consisted of capital stock (common $1 par) of $500,000 and retained earnings of $250,000. During 19X2, Nerox Company had net income of $90,000 and paid a $40,000 dividend.

Cost method:

Investment in Nerox (90%)	$700,000	
Cash		$700,000
Cash	$ 36,000	
Dividend income		$ 36,000

On December 31, 19X2, the investment account on the balance sheet would show $700,000 and the income statement would show $36,000 dividend income:

Equity method:

Investment in Nerox (90%)	$700,000	
Cash		$700,000
Cash	$ 36,000	
Investment in Nerox (90%)		$ 36,000
Investment in Nerox (90%)	$ 81,000	$ 625
Net income from 90% subsidiary	625	81,000

The debit of $81,000 to the investment account represents 90% of the $90,000 of net income for Nerox Company for 19X2. The credit of $625 to the investment account represents amortization of goodwill of $25,000 which is assumed to be amortized over the maximum period of 40 years ($700,000 purchase price less 90% of $750,000 ($675,000) book value = $25,000 goodwill).

On December 31, 19X2, the investment account on the balance sheet would show $744,375 ($700,000 + $81,000 – $625 – $36,000), and the income statement would show $80,375 net income from 90% subsidiary.

The basic difference between the cost and equity methods of accounting for a stock investment is that the cost method records dividends as dividend income and the equity method does not record dividend income, but does record as income the proportionate share of the investee's net income.

Converting from Cost Method to Equity Method

Under the cost method the investment account is debited only with the cost of the stock acquired. Dividends received on the stock acquired are credited to dividend income and are reported in net income for the period. An exception occurs when dividends are received out of accumulated earnings prior to the date of the acquisition of the investment, which are recorded as a reduction of the investment and not as dividend income. Under the equity method the investment account changes to reflect the book value that the stock acquired actually represents. The difference between the two methods will always be the actual book value that the stock acquired represents less any dividends received that were reported as dividend income.

P acquires a 30% stock interest in S for $45,000. Stockholders' equity of S at the date of acquisition consisted of $100,000 of capital stock and retained earnings of $50,000 for a total of $150,000. During the year, S had net income of $30,000 and paid to P a dividend of $3,000 out of current earnings.

Cost method:

P will record in an investment account its investment in S of $45,000 and will report the $3,000 dividend as dividend income in determining its net income for the year. P's investment account at the end of the year will still show a balance of $45,000, the original investment.

Equity method:

P will record as income 30% of the $30,000, or $9,000, as its share of the net income of S for the year, as follows:

Investment in S	$9,000	
Income from S		$9,000

When the $3,000 dividend was received during the year, the entry was:

Cash	$3,000	
Investment in S		$3,000

P's investment in S at the end of the year was $51,000 as follows:

Original investment	$45,000
Add 30% of S's net income	9,000
Total	$54,000
Less: Dividend received	3,000
Investment at end of year	$51,000

The $51,000 investment at the end of the year should exactly agree with P's 30% interest in S at the end of the year, as follows:

Stockholders' equity, beginning of year	$150,000
Add net income for year	30,000
Total	$180,000
Less: Dividend paid (P received $3,000, which represents 30%; thus 100% = $10,000)	10,000
Stockholders' equity, end of year	$170,000
P's investment of 30% of $170,000	$ 51,000

EXTINGUISHMENT OF DEBT

Overview

The following current promulgated GAAP that address the extinguishment of debt are discussed in this chapter:

APB-26, Early Extinguishment of Debt

FASB-4, Reporting Gains and Losses from Extinguishment of Debt

FASB-64, Extinguishments of Debt Made to Satisfy Sinking-Fund Requirements

FASB-76, Extinguishment of Debt

Technical Bulletin 80-1, Early Extinguishment of Debt Through Exchange for Common or Preferred Stock

Technical Bulletin 84-4, In-Substance Defeasance of Debt

APB-26 covers the extinguishment of all debt, whether early or not, except debt that is extinguished through a troubled debt restructuring (FASB-15), and convertible debt that is converted to equity securities of the debtor, which is covered by FASB-84 (see chapter entitled "Convertible Debt"). The classification of gain or loss on the extinguishment of debt is covered by FASB-4, which has been amended by FASB-64.

FASB-76 amends APB-26, to specify the criteria which shall be applied by a debtor in determining when an extinguishment of debt has occurred for the purposes of recognizing gain or loss on the extinguishment of debt. Under the provisions of FASB-76, certain in-substance defeasance transactions that were accounted for as extinguishments of debt under SOP 78-5 (Accounting for Advance Refundings of Tax-Exempt Debt) continue to be accounted for in the same manner.

FASB Technical Bulletin 80-1 deals with the issuance of equity securities in exchange for the extinguishment of debt.

FASB Technical Bulletin 84-4 provides guidance in the application of those provisions of FASB-76 (Extinguishment of Debt) that relate to (a) an instantaneous in-substance defeasance, (b) addressing remoteness of risk of trust assets, and (c) an in-substance defeasance of callable debt.

Background

An extinguishment of debt is the reacquisition of debt prior to or at the maturity date of the debt. Gain or loss on the extinguishment of debt is the difference between the total reacquisition cost of the debt and the net carrying amount of the debt on the date of extinguishment.

Most debt agreements issued in recent years contain a *call provision* and a *defeasance provision*. A call provision grants the issuer (debtor) the right to "call in" part or all of a debt before its scheduled maturity date, usually in exchange for a premium price. A defeasance provision allows the issuer to legally satisfy the debt and obtain a release of lien without necessarily retiring the debt. Thus, in a defeasance transaction the old debt is legally satisfied which results in the culmination of the earning process and recognition of gain or loss. In a nondefeasance transaction, there is no satisfaction of the old debt, no culmination of the earning process, and no gain or loss is recognized. However, under certain conditions a nondefeasance transaction may be accounted for as an in-substance defeasance, in which gain or loss is recognized, but the old debt is not legally satisfied. In an in-substance defeasance transaction, assets are deposited in a trust account for the sole purpose of paying the interest and principal on the outstanding debt as they become due, but the debt is not legally satisfied.

Accounting for Advance Refundings of Tax-Exempt Debt (SOP 78-5) was issued in 1978 by the AICPA to provide guidance in accounting for advance refundings of tax-exempt debt. When a defeasance transaction occurred in the advance refunding of tax-exempt debt, SOP 78-5 provided that the debtor had extinguished the debt and gain or loss on the extinguishment should be recognized. When a nondefeasance transaction occurred in the advance refunding of tax-exempt debt, SOP 78-5 provided that the debtor had not legally satisfied the debt and no gain or loss could be recognized. In addition, if certain conditions were met, a nondefeasance transaction could be accounted for as in-substance defeasance transaction, in which gain or loss was recognized, even though the old debt was not legally satisfied.

When a refunding is desired because of lower interest rates or some other reason, the old debt issue may not be callable for several years. This is the usual circumstance for an advance refunding. In an advance refunding, a new debt issue is sold to replace the old debt issue that cannot be called. The proceeds from the sale of the new debt issue are used to purchase high grade investments which are placed in an escrow account. The earnings from the investments in the escrow account are used to pay the interest and/or principal payments on the existing debt, up to the date that the existing debt can be called. On the call date of the existing debt, whatever remains in the escrow account is used to pay the call premium, if any, and all remaining principal and interest due on the existing debt.

In a well-publicized transaction early in 1982, Exxon Corporation purchased enough U.S. government securities to generate a cash flow sufficient to pay, on a timely basis, the interest and principal on six outstanding Exxon debt issues. Exxon deposited the U.S. governmental securities in an irrevocable trust that was created for the sole purpose of paying the principal and interest on the six debt issues. Exxon removed the debt issues and the government securities from its balance sheet and reported an after-tax gain of $132 million from this "in-substance defeasance" of its debt. The gain on the extinguishment of debt was reported on Exxon's financial statements for calendar year 1982, accompanied by an unqualified report from Price Waterhouse dated February 28, 1983.

In its "Action Alert" dated August 11, 1982, the Financial Accounting Standards Board (FASB) temporarily prohibited the recognition of an extinguishment of debt, unless the debtor had no further legal obligation with respect to the debt. At the same time, the FASB announced its intention of looking into the possibility of relaxing this standard, so as to allow the extinguishment of debt in some special circumstances where the debtor remains liable on the debt. The FASB noted that SOP 78-5 (Advance Refundings of Tax-Exempt Debt) allowed the extinguishment of debt with regard to tax-exempt debt in some circumstances where the debtor remained liable.

In November 1983, the FASB issued FASB-76 (Extinguishment of Debt), resulting from the study which had been announced at the time of the 1982 *Action Alert*. FASB-76 allowed the extinguishment of debt and the resulting recognition of gain or loss in some situations where the debtor remains liable, and this applied not only to the tax-exempt debt covered by SOP 78-5, but to all types of debt, whether taxable or tax-exempt. In order to qualify under FASB-76, the debtor must irrevocably place cash or other essentially risk-free monetary assets in a trust, solely for the purpose of satisfying the interest and principal payments on the debt. In addition, the possibility that the debtor will be required to make further payments must be remote.

Questions arose in 1984, as to whether FASB-76 allows extinguishment of debt by an instantaneous type of in-substance defeasance, in which an enterprise borrows at one interest rate and at the same time invests in other securities that yield a higher interest rate. The instantaneous nature of this type of transaction distinguishes it from the Exxon type of defeasance, in which Exxon purchased new securities to be placed in trust for the payment of preexisting Exxon debt. The proposed instantaneous in-substance defeasance transaction was for an enterprise to borrow by issuing zero coupon bonds in European bond markets, and at about the same time, to purchase U.S. Treasury bonds yielding a higher rate of interest. The U.S. Treasury bonds would be placed in an irrevocable trust created for the sole purpose of paying the zero coupon bonds. Finally, the U.S. Treasury bonds and the zero coupon bonds would be removed from the balance sheet and the gain on the extinguishment of debt would be reported in the enterprise's financial statements.

This type of instantaneous in-substance defeasance clearly conforms to the literal provisions of FASB-76. The FASB determined, however, that this instantaneous in-substance defeasance does not conform to the spirit of FASB-76. The result was FASB Technical Bulletin 84-4, issued on October 17, 1984, with earlier application encouraged for transactions in fiscal years for which annual financial statements have not previously been issued. In essence, Technical Bulletin 84-4 amends FASB-76 by prohibiting an in-substance defeasance if the assets that the debtor places in trust were acquired at about the time that the debt was incurred, or were acquired as part of a series of investment activities that were initiated at about the time that the debt was incurred.

Accounting for Extinguishments of Debt

Under APB-26 (Early Extinguishment of Debt), all extinguishments of debt prior to maturity are basically alike, and accounting for such transactions should be the same, regardless of the method used to achieve the extinguishment. Therefore, there should be no difference in accounting for an extinguishment of debt by (a) cash purchase, (b) exchange of stock for debt, (c) exchange of debt for debt, or (d) any other method.

Gain or loss on the extinguishment of debt is the difference between the reacquisition price and the net carrying amount of the debt on the date of the extinguishment.

Reacquisition price   The amount paid for the extinguishment. Includes call premium and any other costs of reacquiring the portion of the debt which is being extinguished.

Net carrying amount   The amount due at the maturity of the debt, adjusted for any unamortized premium or discount and any other costs of issuance (legal, accounting, underwriter's fees, etc.)

Note: When extinguishment is achieved through the exchange of securities, the reacquisition price is the total present value of the new securities being issued.

> *OBSERVATION: FASB Technical Bulletin 80-1 defines the term* **stock** *as any class of equity security, including redeemable and/or fixed maturity preferred stock. In addition, the Technical Bulletin requires that the gain or loss be based on either the value of the stock issued in exchange or the value of the debt that is being extinguished, whichever is more clearly evident.*

When Debt is Extinguished

Under the provisions of FASB-76, debt shall be considered extinguished for financial reporting purposes in the following circumstances:

1. On the date the debtor pays the debt to the creditor or on the date the debtor reacquires the debt in the public securities market.

2. On the date the debtor is *legally* released as the primary obligor under the debt and it is *probable* that the debtor will not be required to make future payments as guarantor of the debt. Under this provision of FASB-76, it makes no difference whether the creditor has been paid in full or not.

   > **Note:** This provision of FASB-76 covers those situations where a debtor is legally released as the *primary obligor* on a debt, and at the same time agrees to remain secondarily liable on the same debt.

   > *OBSERVATION: Direct and indirect guarantees of indebtedness of others, even if they have a remote possibility of materializing, must be disclosed in accordance with FASB-5 (Contingencies). Thus, any situation in which the debtor is released as the primary obligor under a debt, but remains contingently liable as a guarantor under the debt, must be appropriately disclosed in the financial statements of the debtor in accordance with FASB-5.*

3. On the date the debtor places cash or certain other assets (see below) in an irrevocable trust for the sole purpose of servicing the interest and principal payments of debt with specified

maturities and fixed schedule payments, and there is only a *remote* possibility that the debtor will be required to make any other future payments on the debt. In this circumstance, *remote* means that it is *unlikely* that the debtor will have to make any future payments on the debt.

This provision of FASB-76 covers in-substance defeasance transactions, which were previously covered by the AICPA Statement of Position 78-5. Under this provision of FASB-76, it makes no difference whether the debtor is or is not legally released as primary obligor on the debt.

Only debt with specified maturities and fixed payment schedules can be extinguished under this provision of FASB-76. Debt cannot be extinguished under this provision of FASB-76 unless the debt service requirements can be determined in advance. Thus, debt with variable terms, such as floating interest rates, does not qualify for this type of extinguishment.

Convertible debt cannot be extinguished under the in-substance defeasance provision of FASB-76 because the debt and the conversion option are inseparable, and because there will be no obligation to pay if the debentures are converted.

FASB Technical Bulletin 84-4 provides that callable debt may be extinguished under the in-substance defeasance provisions of FASB-76, provided that there is only a *remote* possibility that the debtor will exercise the call option. In the event the debtor does plan to exercise the call option at a specific future date, the debtor must irrevocably revise the maturity date of the debt to coincide with the intended call date of the debt. In this event, the cash flow from the assets in the irrevocable trust must be structured to approximately coincide, in timing and amount, with the revised scheduled interest and principal payments of the debt.

FASB Technical Bulletin 84-4 takes the position that most of the criteria for the extinguishment of debt are clearly specified in FASB-76, and any deviation from the specified criteria is not permitted. The Technical Bulletin suggests that a debtor use its judgment in those areas not specifically covered by FASB-76.

Based on the issuance of FASB-76, the SEC issued Financial Reporting Release No. 15, containing the following additional clarifications of certain provisions of FASB-76, which SEC reporting companies should observe:

a. An appropriate trustee is one that meets the eligibility requirements of the Trust Indenture Act of 1939 [Sections 310(a)(1) and 310(a)(2)]

b. An irrevocable trust is defined as a trust ". . . designed so that neither the corporation nor its creditors or others can rescind or revoke it, or obtain access to the assets."

c. An assessment is required to determine the likelihood of the debtor's being required to make future payments with respect to the debt, not only because of an inadequacy of trust assets, but also because of an acceleration of the debt's maturity as a result of a violation of a covenant of the debt issue or under cross-default provisions, or a violation of a covenant of another debt issue.

Instantaneous in-substance defeasance is prohibited The use of an in-substance defeasance to extinguish debt in accordance with the provisions of FASB-76 is prohibited by FASB Technical Bulletin 84-4 under any of the following circumstances:

a. The assets that a debtor places in an irrevocable trust to consummate an in-substance defeasance of debt are acquired "at about the time that the debt is incurred."

b. The assets that a debtor places in an irrevocable trust to consummate an in-substance defeasance of debt are acquired as part of a series of investment activities that are initiated "at about the time that the debt is incurred." A series of investment activities includes the purchase of assets or entering into a purchase agreement or futures contract "at about the time that the debt is incurred."

c. The assets that a debtor places in an irrevocable trust to consummate an in-substance defeasance of debt are acquired "at about the time that the debt is incurred" pursuant to a forward contract.

> **Note**: FASB Technical Bulletin 84-4 refers to each of the above transactions as an "instantaneous in-substance defeasance."

According to FASB Technical Bulletin 84-4, an "instantaneous" type of defeasance of debt is considered a "borrow-and-invest activity" which, in effect, hedges the debtor against the risk of changes in interest rates. Furthermore, the gain or loss on a borrow-and-invest activity reflects principally the difference in interest rates that existed in different markets on the same date that the debt was issued, while the gain or loss on previously outstanding debt reflects the difference between the interest rate that was issued and the interest rate that existed on the date that the debt was extinguished.

> **OBSERVATION:** *The key term in FASB Technical Bulletin 84-4 is "at about the time the debt is incurred." However, the Technical Bulletin gives absolutely no indication as to what this term means.*

Allowable trust assets Only monetary assets that are essentially risk free as to the collection of interest and principal may be placed in an irrevocable trust for the payment of the debt that is being extinguished. The monetary assets must be denominated in the same currency in which the debt is payable. Essentially risk-free monetary assets that are denominated in U.S. currency shall be limited to the following:

1. Direct obligations of the U.S. government
2. Obligations that are guaranteed by the U.S. government
3. Securities that are backed by U.S. government obligations under a collateral arrangement which provides that in the event of a default, interest and principal on the collateral flow immediately through to the holder of the security

Timing and amount of trust assets The maturity dates of the essentially risk-free monetary assets that are placed in the irrevocable trust must approximately coincide, in timing and amount, with the scheduled interest and principal payments on the debt that is being extinguished. In other words, the monetary assets held by the irrevocable trust must provide sufficient cash flow to approximately coincide with the timing and amount of the scheduled interest and principal payments on the debt that is being extinguished.

> **OBSERVATION:** *Under FASB-76, if a monetary asset can be paid before its scheduled maturity date, it is not essentially risk free as to the timing of the collection of its interest and principal and therefore cannot be owned by the irrevocable trust.*

Costs of administrating trust Earnings from reinvesting trust assets and the expected costs of administrating the irrevocable trust, such as trustee fees and related costs, shall be considered in computing the total amount of essentially risk-free monetary assets which will be required by the trust to pay the expected administration costs and to satisfy, in a timely manner, all scheduled interest and principal payments of the debt being extinguished.

Any obligation for trustee fees, taxes on trust income, and other trust expenses that are incurred directly by the debtor shall be accrued in the period in which the debt is recognized as extinguished.

Partial in-substance defeasance transactions Although in-substance defeasance transactions usually involve the entire debt issue, partial in-substance defeasance transactions are permitted by FASB-76. In this event, the amount of debt which is recognized as extinguished is either (a) a pro rata portion of all remaining interest and principal payments on the debt issue or (b) the principal and interest payments for a specific debt instrument with a specified scheduled maturity (paragraph 36 of FASB-76). Thus, a partial in-substance defeasance consisting only of interest payments or only of principal payments cannot be recognized by a debtor.

Disclosures for irrevocable trust If a debtor places assets that are essentially risk free in an irrevocable trust to extinguish a specific debt in accordance with FASB-76, the debtor shall disclose the following information in its financial statements for as long as the specific debt remains outstanding:

1. A general description of the transaction
2. The total amount outstanding at the end of the period
3. The total amount that is considered extinguished at the end of the period

FASB-76 is effective for extinguishments of debt that occur on or after January 1, 1984. The provisions of FASB-76 may be retroactively applied to previously *issued* annual financial statements, and earlier application of FASB-76 is encouraged in *unissued* annual financial statements.

Gain or Loss

The gain or loss on the extinguishment of debt is recognized immediately, in the year of extinguishment, and, if material, is reported as an extraordinary item, net of related tax effects (FASB-4). However, certain gains or losses on extinguishment of debt are not classified as extraordinary items. Under the provisions of FASB-64, gains or losses from the extinguishment of debt made within one year to meet sinking fund requirements shall not be classified as extraordinary items, but shall be included in income from continuing operations. This would also apply to any debt that has the same characteristics as sinking fund requirements, such as a required annual extinguishment of a specific percentage of outstanding debt prior to its maturity. However, gains or losses from the maturation of serialized debt are classified as extraordinary items, because under FASB-4 serial debt does not have the same characteristics as debt pursuant to sinking fund requirements.

> **OBSERVATION**: *FASB-64 is effective for all extinguishments of debt made on or after October 1, 1982. FASB-64 may be applied to previously unissued annual financial statements, but retroactive application of FASB-64 to previously issued annual financial statements is not permitted.*

Appropriate accounting recognition should be given to any stated or unstated rights or privileges arising from an extinguishment of debt.

Gains or losses on the extinguishment of debt should not be amortized over future periods.

In the early extinguishment of a debt, the recorded value of the new debt should not be affected in any way by the amount of the old debt.

Refunding of Tax Exempt Debt (FASB-22)

If a change in a lease occurs as a result of a refunding by the lessor of tax-exempt debt and (1) the lessee receives the economic advantages of the refunding, (2) the revised lease qualifies and is classified either as a capital lease by the lessee or as a direct financing lease by the lessor, the change in the lease shall be accounted for on the basis of whether or not an extinguishment of debt has occurred, as follows:

1. Accounted for as an extinguishment of debt:

   a. The lessee adjusts the lease obligation to the present value of the future minimum lease payments under the revised agreement, using the effective interest rate of the new lease agreement. Any gain or loss shall be treated as a gain or loss on an early extinguishment of debt.

   b. The lessor adjusts the balance of the minimum lease payments receivable and the gross investment in the lease (if affected) for the difference between the present values of the old and new or revised agreement. Any gain or loss shall be recognized in the current period.

2. Not accounted for as an extinguishment of debt:

   a. The lessee accrues any costs connected with the refunding that it is obligated to reimburse to the lessor. The interest method is used to amortize the costs over the period from the date of the refunding to the call date of the debt to be refunded.

b. The lessor recognizes as revenue any reimbursements to be received from the lessee for costs paid related to the debt to be refunded over the period from the date of the refunding to the call date of the debt to be refunded.

Disclosure

Gains or losses from the early extinguishment of debt which are classified as extraordinary items should be disclosed in the financial statements or in properly cross-referenced footnotes thereto, as follows:

1. A description of the transaction, including the sources, if identifiable, of any funds used to extinguish the debt
2. The income tax effect for the period of extinguishment
3. The gain or loss per share, net of any related income taxes

Comprehensive Illustration

On December 31, 1985, a corporation decides to retire $500,000 of an original issue of $1,000,000 8% debentures, which were sold on December 31, 1980, at a price of 98 and are callable at 101. The legal and other costs for issuing the debentures was $30,000. Both the original discount and the issue costs are being amortized over the 10-year life of the issue. What gain or loss is recognized on this early extinguishment of debt?

Amount of original expenses of issue	$30,000
Amount of original discount (2% of $1,000,000)	$20,000
Amount of premium paid for redemption (debentures callable at 101, 1% of $500,000)	$ 5,000
Date of issue	12/31/80
Date of maturity	12/31/90
Date of redemption	12/31/85

Interest on debentures is irrelevant.

Computation discussion If the original legal and other expenses of $30,000 are being amortized over the 10-year life of the issue and five years have elapsed since that date, one-half of these expenses have already been amortized, leaving a balance of $15,000 at the date of redemption. However, only one-half of the outstanding debentures is being retired, which leaves $7,500 to account for in the computation of gain or loss.

The original discount of $20,000 (debentures sold at 98) is handled exactly the same as the legal and other expenses. Since one-half of the discount has already been amortized, leaving a $10,000 balance at the date of redemption, and since only one-half of the issue is being redeemed, this leaves $5,000 more that must go into the computation of gain or loss.

Obviously, any time that a security is redeemed at a premium, the amount of premium must also enter into the computation of gain or loss. In this case, the premium is $5,000.

Since there is no other relevant information in the problem relating to gain or loss, the following items enter into the final computation:

Original-issue expenses relating to retired debentures	$ 7,500
Original discount relating to the retired debentures	5,000
Premium paid for redemption	5,000
Loss on redemption of $500,000 of debentures	$17,500

FINANCIAL INSTRUMENTS

Overview

FASB-105 establishes accounting and reporting standards for financial statement disclosure of financial instruments with (a) off-balance-sheet risk of accounting loss and (b) significant individual or group concentrations of credit risk. The provisions of FASB-105 apply to *all* entities, including not-for-profit organizations. The scope of FASB-105 does not include the recognition, measurement, or classification of financial instruments in financial statements. FASB-105 also amends paragraph 9 of FASB-77 (Reporting by Transferors for Transfers of Receivables with Recourse).

FASB-105 is effective for financial statements issued for fiscal years ending on or after June 16, 1990.

Background

Enterprises and/or individuals frequently acquire assets or liabilities by written contract. Under current accounting practice, exchanges between enterprises or individuals are usually recorded when the actual transfer of resources, services, and/or obligations occurs. If a significant period elapses between the execution and subsequent performance of a contract, a problem may arise as to when, if at all, the assets and/or liabilities created by the contract should be recognized by the contracting parties. Under existing accounting standards, assets and/or liabilities that are created by a contract may not be recognized to their full extent in the financial statements or they may not be recognized at all. These assets and liabilities are referred to as off-balance-sheet items.

There has been an explosion of different types of financial instruments in recent years which has resulted in a significant information gap. The newly developed financial instruments include interest rate swaps, forward contracts, interest rate caps and floors, repurchase agreements, and various forms of financial guarantees. FASB-105 has been promulgated to close the information gap on off-balance-sheet financial instruments and to provide disclosure of the potential accounting loss associated with off-balance-sheet items.

An off-balance-sheet accounting loss occurs when an entity disposes of an asset or liability, and the amount of the ultimate loss exceeds the net recorded amount, if any, of the asset or liability.

FASB-105 represents the first phase of a project devoted to financial statement disclosure of information relating to financial instruments. The first phase covers *all* types of entities, including not-for-profit organizations, and addresses the disclosure of information about (a) the extent, nature, and terms of financial instruments with off-balance-sheet credit or market risk and (b) significant concentrations of credit risk for *all* financial instruments. The second phase of this project will address disclosure of information about credit, market, and liquidity risk for all financial instruments. Subsequent phases may cover the recognition and measurement issues relating to financial instruments.

One of the major purposes for the issuance of FASB-105 was to bring the level of financial statement disclosure of information about financial instruments with off-balance-sheet risk at least up to that of existing disclosure requirements for on-balance-sheet instruments (paragraph 87 of FASB-105).

Definitions

FASB-105 contains a broad definition of the term *financial instrument* to cover the multitude of different types of financial instruments in use today and those that are expected to be developed in the future. Under the provisions of FASB-105, a *financial instrument* is defined as cash, evidence of an ownership interest in an entity, or a contract that meets the following criteria:

a. The contract contains a contractual obligation (unconditional or conditional) that requires one entity either to (i) deliver cash to the second entity, (ii) deliver another financial instrument to the second entity, or (iii) exchange financial instruments with the second entity on potentially unfavorable terms to the first entity.

b. The contract grants a contractual right (unconditional or conditional) to the second entity either to (i) receive cash from the first entity, (ii) receive another financial instrument from the first entity, or (iii) exchange other financial instruments with the first entity on potentially favorable terms to the second entity.

A financial instrument contract may contain unconditional rights and obligations or conditional rights and obligations. A right or obligation is unconditional when nothing but the passage of time is necessary for the right or obligation to mature. On the other hand, a conditional right or obligation is one that matures only on the occurrence of one or more events that are specified in the contract.

An on-balance-sheet accounting loss occurs when an asset is sold, exchanged, or disposed of otherwise, and the amount of the ultimate loss does not exceed the net recorded amount of the asset. For example, an ultimate loss of $10,000 or less on an asset with a net recorded amount of $10,000 on the date of disposition is an on-balance-sheet accounting loss and the maximum risk of accounting loss is the net recorded amount of the asset. On the other hand, an asset, such as a financial instrument, may have conditional rights and/or obligations that expose its owner to a risk of accounting loss that exceeds the net recorded amount of the asset. An off-balance-sheet accounting loss occurs when an asset or liability is sold, exchanged, or disposed of otherwise, and the amount of the ultimate loss exceeds the net recorded amount of the asset or liability. For example, an ultimate loss of more than $10,000 on an asset with a net recorded amount of $10,000 on the date of disposition is an off-balance-sheet accounting loss and the maximum risk of accounting loss exceeds the net recorded amount of the asset or liability.

An entity may be exposed to a risk of accounting loss in connection with financial instruments that have never been recognized as assets or liabilities in the statement of financial position. For example, gain or loss on certain forward interest rate agreements is not recognized until the settlement date of the contract, unless a loss is incurred at an earlier date. This type of financial instrument has a potential off-balance-sheet risk of accounting loss.

FASB-105 defines *financial instruments with off-balance-sheet risk of accounting loss* as those in which the risk of loss, *even if remote*, exceeds the amount recognized, if any, in the financial statements. FASB-105 defines an *accounting loss* as a loss that arises from exposure to credit risk and market risk which may have to be recognized as a direct result of conditional rights and obligations in the financial instrument's contract. The risk of accounting loss associated with a financial instrument includes (a) the failure of another party to perform in accordance with the contract terms (credit risk), (b) future changes in market prices that increase or decrease the value of the financial instrument (market risk), and (c) theft or physical loss of the financial instrument. Examples of financial instruments with off-balance-sheet risk of accounting loss are loan commitments, letters of credit, financial guarantees, interest rate caps and floors, obligations to repurchase receivables sold, futures contracts, and interest rate swaps.

Financial Instruments Excluded from FASB-105

FASB-105 requires the disclosure of (a) the extent, nature, and terms of financial instruments with off-balance-sheet risk, (b) the credit risk of financial instruments with off-balance-sheet risk, and (c) the concentrations of credit risk in financial instruments with or without off-balance-sheet risk of accounting loss.

There are two groups of financial instruments that are excluded or partially excluded from the above disclosure requirements of FASB-105. The first group is excluded from *all* of the disclosure requirements of FASB-105 and the second group is excluded from the disclosure of (a) the extent, nature, and terms of financial instruments with off-balance-sheet risk and (b) the credit risk of financial instruments with off-balance-sheet risk.

The following is the first group of financial instruments which are excluded from *all* of the disclosure requirements of FASB-105, regardless of whether the instrument is written or held:

- *Most insurance contracts*—Other than financial guarantees and investment contracts, all insurance contracts that are discussed in FASB-60 (Accounting and Reporting by Insurance Enterprises), and FASB-97 (Accounting and Reporting by Insurance Enterprises for Certain Long-Duration Contracts and for Realized Gains and Losses from the Sale of Investments)

- *Long-term obligations subject to FASB-47*—All unconditional purchase obligations that are subject to the disclosure requirements of FASB-47 (Disclosure of Long-Term Obligations) (Note: All unconditional purchase obligations that are *not* subject to to FASB-47 are subject to FASB-105.)

- *Pension, insurance, stock options, etc.*—Employers' and plans' obligations for pension benefits, postretirement health care and life insurance benefits, employee stock option and stock purchase plans, and other forms of deferred compensation arrangements, as defined in FASB-35 (Accounting and Reporting by Defined Benefit Pension Plans), FASB-87 (Employers' Accounting for Pensions), FASB-81 (Disclosure of Postretirement Health Care and Life Insurance Benefits), FASB-43 (Accounting for Compensated Absences), APB-25 (Accounting

for Stock Issued to Employees), and APB-12 (Omnibus Opinion—1967)

- *Pension plan financial instruments*—Financial instruments of a
  pension plan, including plan assets, when subject to the accounting and reporting requirements of FASB-87 (Note: Pension
  plan financial instruments, except obligations for pension benefits, *are included* in the scope of FASB-105, if the financial
  instruments are subject to the accounting and reporting provisions of FASB-35 (Accounting and Reporting by Defined Benefit
  Plans)

- *Extinguished debt subject to FASB-76*—In-substance defeasance of
  debt subject to the disclosure requirements of FASB-76 (Extinguishment of Debt) and any assets held in trust in connection
  with an in-substance defeasance of debt

The financial instruments in the second group are *excluded* from
disclosure requirements (a) and (b) of FASB-105 (above), but are not
excluded from complying with disclosure requirement (c), which
requires the disclosure of the concentration of credit risk in financial
instruments with or without off-balance-sheet risk of accounting
loss. The following are the financial instruments in the second group:

- *Lease contracts*—Lease contracts as defined in FASB-13 (Accounting for Leases)

- *Accruals denominated in foreign currency*—Accounts and notes
  payable and other financial instruments that result in accruals
  or other amounts denominated in a foreign currency and included in the balance sheet at translated or remeasured amounts
  under FASB-52 (Foreign Currency Translation), EXCEPT obligations under (i) financial instruments that have
  off-balance-sheet risk from other risks in addition to foreign
  exchange risk (such as a commitment to lend foreign currency
  or an option written to exchange foreign currency for a bond
  that either is or is not denominated in a foreign currency) and
  (ii) foreign currency exchange contracts (such as a forward
  exchange contract, a currency swap, a foreign currency futures
  contract, or an option to exchange currencies)

The financial statement disclosures of financial instruments that
are required by FASB-105 are in addition to all other financial statement disclosures of financial instruments that are required by other
existing GAAP.

Disclosure of Extent, Nature, and Terms of Financial Instruments with Off-Balance-Sheet Risk

Financial instruments with off-balance-sheet risk of accounting loss are those in which the risk of loss, even if remote, exceeds the amount, if any, recognized in the financial statements. Examples of financial instruments with off-balance-sheet risk of accounting loss are interest rate swaps, futures contracts, obligations to repurchase receivables sold, interest rate caps and floors, financial guarantees, letters of credit, and loan commitments.

> **OBSERVATION:** *FASB-5 (Contingencies) requires the financial statement disclosure of the nature and amount of guarantees, even if they have a remote possibility of materializing. Guarantees to repurchase receivables, obligations under letters of credit or stand-by agreements, guarantees of indebtedness of others, and unconditional obligations to make payments are examples of guarantee contingencies that must be disclosed even if it is remotely possible that they will occur. Disclosure of both direct and indirect guarantees of the indebtedness of others is required by FASB Interpretation-34.*

Except for those financial instruments that are excluded or partially excluded from the disclosure requirements of FASB-105, the following information about each class of all other financial instruments with off-balance-sheet risk should be disclosed by an entity in its financial statements or notes thereto:

- The face or contract amount (or the notional amount if there is no face or contract amount)
- The nature and terms, including at a minimum, a discussion of credit and market risk, cash requirements of the instrument, and the related accounting policies

The face, contract, notional, or principal amount should be disclosed by class (category) of financial instrument with off-balance-sheet risk, in the financial statements or footnotes thereto. Classification of financial instruments with off-balance-sheet risk should be based on those classes of financial instruments with off-balance-sheet risk that have developed over the years in various financial and regulatory reports and, as a result, have become generally accepted.

The nature and terms of each class of financial instrument with off-balance-sheet risk of accounting loss should be disclosed in the financial statements or footnotes thereto, including a discussion of credit risk, market risk, cash requirements, and related accounting policies. The discussion of credit risk should include an evaluation of the possibility that another party will fail to perform in accordance with the financial instrument contract. The discussion of market risk should include an evaluation of the possibility that the value of the financial instrument may increase or decrease as a result of future changes in market prices. The cash requirements, if any, of each class of financial instrument with off-balance-sheet risk of accounting loss should also be disclosed.

FASB-105 also requires a discussion of the accounting policies related to financial instruments with off-balance-sheet risk of accounting loss. An entity's accounting policies should be disclosed in accordance with APB-22 (Disclosure of Accounting Policies). Under the provisions of APB-22, the preferable presentation of disclosing accounting principles is in the first footnote of the financial statements, under the caption "Summary of Significant Accounting Policies." APB-22 requires that both the accounting principle(s) and the method(s) of applying them be disclosed. However, accounting principles and the method of applying them in the following areas are considered particularly important by APB-22: (a) a selection from existing acceptable alternatives, (b) the areas peculiar to a specific industry in which the entity functions, and (c) unusual and innovative application of GAAP.

Disclosure of Credit Risk of Financial Instruments with Off-Balance-Sheet Credit Risk

Financial instruments with off-balance-sheet risk of accounting loss are those in which the risk of loss, even if remote, exceeds the amount, if any, recognized in the financial statements. Examples of financial instruments with off-balance-sheet risk of accounting loss are interest rate swaps, futures contracts, obligations to repurchase receivables sold, interest rate caps and floors, financial guarantees, letters of credit, and loan commitments.

Except for those financial instruments with off-balance-sheet risk of accounting loss that are excluded or partially excluded from the disclosure requirements of FASB-105, the following information about each class of all other financial instruments with off-balance-sheet credit risk should be disclosed by an entity in its financial statements or notes thereto:

- The maximum amount of accounting loss that would be incurred if any party failed completely to perform according to the terms of the financial instrument with off-balance-sheet risk, even if this is a remote possibility, and the collateral or other security for the amount due, if any, was absolutely worthless (in other words, a "worst case" scenario)
- The entity's existing policy for determining the amount of collateral or other security required to support financial instruments subject to credit risk, information about the entity's access to that collateral or other security, and the nature and a brief description of the collateral or other security (in other words, an entity's policy for requiring security and a brief description of the security supporting financial instruments with off-balance-sheet risk of accounting loss)

FASB-105 encourages the disclosure of additional information about the extent of the collateral because it may provide a better indication of the extent of credit risk.

Disclosure of Concentrations of Credit Risk of All Financial Instruments

Except for those financial instruments that are completely excluded from the disclosure requirements of FASB-105, an entity should disclose the following information for all *significant* individual or group concentrations of credit risk associated with all owned financial instruments that both have and do not have off-balance-sheet risk of accounting loss:

- Information that identifies the activity, region, or economic characteristics of each significant concentration of credit risk

    > OBSERVATION: *The FASB did not define the terms* **significant** *or* **concentrations** *because it found "persuasive the view that management judgment about concentrations and significance is in and of itself useful information" (paragraph 102 of FASB-105).*

- The maximum amount of accounting loss that would be incurred if the individual or group that makes up the concentration of credit risk failed completely to perform according to the terms of the financial instrument contract, even if this is a remote possibility, and the collateral or other security for the amount due, if any, was absolutely worthless (in other words, a "worst case" scenario)

- The entity's existing policy for determining the amount of collateral or other security required to support financial instruments subject to credit risk, information about the entity's access to that collateral or other security, and the nature and a brief description of the collateral or other security (in other words, an entity's policy for requiring security and a brief description of the security supporting the financial instruments)

Individual concentrations of credit risk may exist in a specific industry or in a particular region. The following is an example of a business with a concentration of credit risk in a specific region: A retailer who sells merchandise on credit in its three stores located in Larkinsville is exposed to a concentration of credit risk confined geographically to the city of Larkinsville. The following is an example of a business with a regional concentration of credit risk in a specific industry: ABC Corporation's business activity is with customers located within the state of Georgia and as of December 31, 19XX, ABC's accounts receivables from companies in the semiconductor industry were $22 million. Under the provisions of FASB-105, ABC Corporation is exposed to a regional concentration of credit risk in the amount of $22 million from companies in the semiconductor industry in the State of Georgia.

Group concentrations of credit risk exist if two or more parties are engaged in similar activities and have similar economic characteristics, so that a change in economic or other conditions would cause similar effects on the ability of each of these parties to meet its contractual obligations. For example, an entity's trade accounts receivable from various companies in the same industry is a group concentration of credit risk.

> **OBSERVATION:** *One way an entity may significantly reduce the cost associated with determining and reporting industry or regional concentrations of credit risk is to include the information in a description of its activities. A description of the principal activities of an entity could include the disclosure of its industry and/or regional concentrations of credit risk which should be sufficient to meet the requirements of FASB-105. For example, information about concentrations of credit risk may be adequately disclosed by a local retail store in a description of the store's business, location, and policy for granting credit to local customers.*

Effective Date and Transition

FASB-105 is effective for financial statements of fiscal years ending on or after June 16, 1990. The disclosures required by FASB-105 do not have to be included in comparative financial statements that are presented for fiscal years prior to the effective date of FASB-105.

EXPOSURE DRAFT

The following material is based on two Exposure Drafts (ED), one entitled *Disclosures About Market Value of Financial Instruments* and the other entitled *Offsetting of Amounts Related to Certain Contracts: An Interpretation of APB Opinion No. 10 and FASB Statement No. 105.* These EDs are outstanding as of the date of this publication. There may be significant differences between the EDs discussed below and the official FASB Statements when they are promulgated. Thus, the reader is cautioned to compare carefully the material in these EDs with the official pronouncements when they become available.

Disclosures About Market Value of Financial Instruments

This Exposure Draft would require disclosure of the market value of all financial instruments for which it is practicable to estimate market value, whether or not the financial instruments are recognized in the statement of financial position. The following types of financial instruments are specifically excluded:

1. Obligations for pension benefits, other postretirement benefits, employee stock option and stock purchase plans, and other forms of deferred compensation. (Other FASB Statements already require disclosure of market value of some of these financial instruments.)
2. Substantively extinguished debt and the related assets held in trust
3. Insurance contracts, other than financial guarantees and investment contracts
4. Lease contracts
5. Warranty obligations

Disclosure would be based on quoted market prices if available, or on management's best estimate in other situations where estimates are practicable.

If it is not practicable to estimate market value, the ED would require disclosure of the following:

1. The carrying amount, interest rate, maturity, and other characteristics of the financial instrument
2. The reasons why it is not practicable to estimate market value
3. Whether the entity believes the carrying amount (a) approximates market value, (b) is significantly more than market value, or (c) is significantly less than market value

The ED would generally be effective for financial statements for fiscal years ending after December 15, 1991, but the effective date would be one year later for enterprises with less than $100 million in total assets.

Offsetting of Amounts Related to Certain Contracts: An Interpretation of APB Opinion No. 10 and FASB Statement No. 105

This Exposure Draft (ED) provides guidance about offsetting certain types of assets and liabilities on the statement of financial position. The ED incorporates all of FASB Technical Bulletin 88-2 (Definition of a Right of Setoff) and adds new material on the question of offsetting assets and liabilities relating to various types of contracts, such as forward contracts, interest rate and currency swaps, financial options, interest rate caps, collars and floors, swaptions, and similar contracts. The issue arises when an enterprise recognizes the market value of these contracts, or an accrued receivable or payable arising from them, without recognizing at the same time the notional amounts or the amounts to be exchanged.

The ED would prohibit an entity from offsetting, on the statement of financial position, the market value of contracts in a loss position against the market value of contracts in a gain position, unless a legal right of setoff exists. The underlying rationale is that the recognized market values of these contracts are assets and liabilities in their own right, and are therefore governed by the general rule against offsetting unless a legal right of setoff exists. The ED rejects the view, taken by some dealers, that the recognized values of these contracts are valuation accounts.

To illustrate the principle that offsetting is allowed if a legal right of setoff exists, the ED notes that an entity may report a single amount on the statement of financial position, representing the net market position of all recognized contracts, provided all of the contracts were executed with the same counterparty under a master netting agreement which includes a legal right of setoff.

This ED would become effective for financial statements for periods ending on or after December 16, 1992.

FINANCIAL REPORTING AND CHANGING PRICES

Note: Compliance with the guidelines provided by FASB-89 (Financial Reporting and Changing Prices) is voluntary, not mandatory, for financial statements issued after December 2, 1986.

Overview

FASB-33, issued in 1979, required certain large enterprises to disclose the effects of inflation. A number of later FASB Statements and Technical Bulletins provided additional guidance on this matter.

FASB-89 declares that such disclosure is now encouraged, but not required.

FASB-89 was promulgated by a four-to-three vote of the seven-member Financial Accounting Standards Board and is effective for financial reports issued after December 2, 1986.

An appendix to FASB-89 provides guidelines on the disclosure of the effects of inflation. These guidelines are substantially the same as prior FASB pronouncements, except that the new guidelines are not mandatory.

FASB-89 supersedes the pronouncements listed below relating to financial reporting and changing prices:

FASB-33, Financial Reporting and Changing Prices

FASB-39, Financial Reporting and Changing Prices: Specialized Assets—Mining and Oil and Gas

FASB-40, Financial Reporting and Changing Prices: Specialized Assets—Timberlands and Growing Timber

FASB-41, Financial Reporting and Changing Prices: Specialized Assets—Income-Producing Real Estate

FASB-46, Financial Reporting and Changing Prices: Motion Picture Films

FASB-54, Financial Reporting and Changing Prices: Investment Companies

FASB-69 (Paragraphs 35-38), Disclosures about Oil and Gas Producing Activities

FASB-70, Financial Reporting and Changing Prices: Foreign Currency Translation

FASB-82, Financial Reporting and Changing Prices: Elimination of Certain Disclosures

FASB Technical Bulletin 81-4, Classification as Monetary or Nonmonetary Items

FASB-89 also amends FASB Technical Bulletin 79-8 (Applicability of FASB Statements 21 and 33 to Certain Brokers and Dealers in Securities) to delete any reference to FASB-33.

Monetary Assets and Liabilities

Assets and liabilities are called *monetary items* if their amounts are fixed by contract or otherwise in terms of numbers of dollars. Cash, accounts and notes receivable in cash, and accounts and notes payable in cash are examples of monetary items.

Monetary items automatically gain or lose general purchasing power during inflation or deflation as a result of changes in the general price-level index. For example, a holder of a $10,000 promissory note executed 10 years ago and due today will receive exactly $10,000 today, in spite of the fact that $10,000 in cash today is worth a lot less than $10,000 in cash was worth 10 years ago.

Nonmonetary Assets and Liabilities

Assets and liabilities that are not monetary items are called *nonmonetary items.* Inventories, investment in common stocks, property, plant equipment, and deferred charges are examples of nonmonetary items. Holders of nonmonetary items may lose or gain with the rise or fall of the general price-level index if the nonmonetary item does not rise or fall in proportion to the change in the price-level index. In other words, a nonmonetary asset or liability is affected (a) by the rise or fall of the general price-level index and (b) by the increase or decrease of the fair value of the nonmonetary item. For example, the purchaser of 10,000 shares of General Motors common stock 10 years ago was subject (a) to the decrease in purchasing power and (b) to the rise in the fair value of his stock. If the decrease in purchasing power exactly offsets the increase in the price of the stock, the purchaser is, in effect, in the same economic position today as he or she was 10 years ago.

Net Monetary Position

The difference between monetary assets and monetary liabilities at any specific date is the net monetary position. The net monetary position may be either positive (monetary assets exceed monetary liabilities) or negative (monetary liabilities exceed monetary assets).

In periods in which the general price-level index is rising (inflation), it is advantageous for a business to maintain a net negative monetary position. The opposite is true during periods in which the general price-level index is falling (deflation). In periods of inflation, a business that has a net negative monetary position will experience general price-level gains because it can pay its liabilities in a fixed number of dollars that are declining in value as time goes by. In periods of inflation, a business that has a net positive monetary position will experience general price-level losses because the value of the dollar is declining.

Some assets and liabilities have characteristics of both monetary and nonmonetary items. Convertible debt, for example, is monetary in terms of its fixed obligation, but nonmonetary in terms of its conversion feature.

The determination of whether an item is monetary or nonmonetary is made as of the balance sheet date. Therefore, if convertible debt has not been converted as of that date, it should be classified as a monetary item. Additionally, a bond receivable held for speculation would be classified as nonmonetary because the amount that will be received when the bond is sold is no longer fixed in amount, as it would be if the same bond were held to maturity.

> **OBSERVATION**: *FASB-89 (paragraphs 96 through 108) contains a table that reflects the monetary-nonmonetary classification of most assets and liabilities.*

Current Cost Accounting

Current cost accounting is a method of measuring and reporting assets and expenses associated with the use or sale of assets at their current cost or lower recoverable amount at the balance sheet date or at the date of use or sale. Current cost/constant purchasing power accounting is a method of accounting based on measures of current cost of lower recoverable amounts in units of currency that each have the same general purchasing power. For operations for which the U.S. dollar is the functional currency, the general purchasing power of the dollar is used. For operations for which the functional currency is other than the U.S. dollar, the general purchasing power of either (a) the dollar or (b) the functional currency is used (see FASB-52, Foreign Currency Translation).

Determining Current Costs

Current cost is the current cost to purchase or reproduce a specific asset. Current reproduction cost must contain an allocation for current overhead costs (direct costing not permitted).

The current cost of inventory owned by an enterprise is the current cost to purchase or reproduce that specific inventory. The current cost of property, plant, and equipment owned by an enterprise is the current cost of acquiring an asset that will perform or produce in a manner similar to the owned asset.

An enterprise may obtain its current cost information internally or externally, including independent appraisals, and may apply the information to a single item or to groups of items. An enterprise is expected to select the types of current cost information that are most appropriate for its particular circumstances. The following types and sources of current cost information may be utilized by an enterprise:

1. Current invoice prices
2. Vendor firms' price lists, quotations, or estimates
3. Standard manufacturing costs that reflect current costs
4. Unit pricing, which is a method of determining current cost for assets, such as buildings, by applying a unit price per square foot of space to the total square footage in the building
5. Revision of historical cost by the use of indexation, based on:
    (i) externally generated price indexes for the services or goods being restated or
    (ii) internally generated indexes for the services or goods being restated

Depreciation methods Depreciation methods, useful lives, and salvage values used for current cost purposes should be the same as those used for historical cost purposes. If historical cost computations already include an allowance for changing prices, then a different method may be used for current cost purposes. However, any material differences should be disclosed in the explanatory notes to the supplementary information.

Recoverable amounts   Recoverable amounts are reductions that represent additional write-downs during a current period, from the current cost amount to a lower recoverable amount. These reductions reflect a permanent decline in the value of inventory, or property, plant, and equipment. Recoverable amounts may be determined by reference to net realizable values or values in use.

Net realizable value   Net realizable value is the expected amount of net cash or other net equivalent to be received from the sale of an asset in the regular course of business. Net realizable value should be used only if the specific asset is about to be sold.

Value in use   Value in use is the total present value of all future cash inflows that are expected to be received from the use of an asset. Value in use should be used only if there is no immediate intention to sell or otherwise dispose of the asset. Value in use should be estimated by taking into consideration an appropriate discount rate that includes an allowance for the risk involved in the circumstances.

Income tax expense   Income tax expense and the provision for deferred taxes, if any, are not restated in terms of current cost and are presented in the supplementary information at their historical cost. Disclosure should be made in the supplementary information to the effect that income tax expense for the current period is presented at its historical cost.

Minimum Supplementary Information

Under FASB-89, an enterprise is encouraged to disclose certain minimum supplementary information for each of its five most recent years (Five-Year Summary of Selected Financial Data). In addition, if income from continuing operations as shown in the primary financial statements differs significantly from income from continuing operations determined on a current cost/constant purchasing power basis, certain additional disclosures relating to the components of income from continuing operations for the current year should also be disclosed.

The minimum supplementary information encouraged by FASB-89 should be disclosed in average-for-the-year units of constant purchasing power. The Consumer Price Index for All Urban Consumers (CPI-U) should be used to restate the current cost of an item in average-for-the-year units of constant purchasing power. Alternatively, an enterprise may disclose the minimum supplementary information in dollars having a purchasing power equal to that of dollars of the base period used in calculating the CPI-U (currently 1967). The level of the CPI-U used for each of the five most recent years should be disclosed.

An enterprise is encouraged to disclose the following minimum supplementary information for the five most recent years:

- Net sales and other operating revenue
- Income from continuing operations on a current cost basis
- Purchasing power gain or loss on net monetary items
- Increase or decrease in the current cost or lower recoverable amount of inventory and property, plant, and equipment, net of inflation
- Aggregate foreign currency translation adjustment on a current cost basis, if applicable
- Net assets at the end of the year on a current cost basis
- Income per common share from continuing operations on a current cost basis
- Cash dividends declared per common share
- Market price per common share at year-end
- Average level of the Consumer Price Index for All Urban Consumers

Each of the above disclosures included in the five-year summary of selected financial data is discussed below.

Net sales and other operating revenue   Net sales and other operating revenue for each of the five most recent years is restated in average-for-the-year units of constant purchasing power using the CPI-U.

Income from continuing operations on a current cost basis   Income from continuing operations on a current cost basis for each of the five most recent years is computed in accordance with FASB-89 and then restated in average-for-the-year units of constant purchasing power using the CPI-U. For purposes of the minimum supplementary information, only certain items that are included in income from continuing operations in the primary financial statements have to be adjusted to compute income from continuing operations on a current cost basis. Under FASB-89, the following items should be adjusted to compute income from continuing operations on a current cost basis:

a. *Cost of goods sold*—must be determined on a current cost basis or lower recoverable amount at the date of a sale or at the date on which resources are used on or committed to a specific contract.

b. *Depreciation, depletion and amortization*—must be determined on the basis of the average current cost of the assets' service potentials or lower recoverable amounts during the period of use.

c. *Gain or loss on the sale, retirement, or write-down of inventory, property, plant, and equipment*—is equal to the difference between the value of the consideration received or the written-down amount and the current cost or lower recoverable amount of the item prior to its sale, retirement, or write-down.

All other revenue, expenses, gains, and losses that are included in the primary financial statements are not adjusted in computing income from continuing operations on a current cost basis. Thus, these items are included in income from continuing operations on a current cost basis using the same amounts that appear in the primary financial statements.

Income tax expense that is included in the primary financial statements is not adjusted in computing income from continuing operations on a current cost basis. Thus, income tax expense is included in income from continuing operations on a current cost basis using the same amount that appears in the primary financial statements. Disclosure must be made in the minimum supplementary information to the effect that income tax expense for the current period is presented at its historical cost.

Purchasing power gain or loss on net monetary items Purchasing power gain or loss on net monetary items for each of the five most recent years is computed and then restated in average-for-the-year units of constant purchasing power using the CPI-U. The purchasing power gain or loss on net monetary items is determined by restating in units of constant purchasing power the opening and closing balances of, and transactions in, monetary assets and monetary liabilities.

Increase or decrease in inventory, property, plant, and equipment at current costs The increase or decrease in current costs for inventory and property, plant, and equipment for each of the five most recent years must be restated in average-for-the-year units of constant purchasing power using the CPI-U. The increase or decrease in the current cost amounts of inventory and property, plant, and equipment represents the difference between the measures of the assets at their entry dates for the year and the measures of the assets at their exit dates for the year. The entry date is the beginning of the year of the date of acquisition, whichever is applicable. The exit date is the end of the year or the date of use, sale, or commitment to a specific contract, whichever is applicable.

The increase or decrease in the current cost amounts of inventory, property, plant, and equipment for the five-year summary is reported after the effects of each year's general inflation. The increase or decrease in the current cost amounts of inventory and property, plant, and equipment for the current year is reported both before and after the effects of general inflation.

Aggregate foreign currency translation adjustment (if applicable) Aggregate foreign currency translation adjustment (if applicable) for each of the five most recent years is computed on a current basis and then restated in average-for-the-year units of constant purchasing power using the CPI-U.

Current cost information for operations measured in a foreign functional currency is measured either (a) after translation and based on the CPI-U (the translate-restate method) or (b) before translation and based on a broad-based measure of the change in the general purchasing power of the functional currency (the restate-translate method). In this event, the same method must be used for all operations measured in foreign functional currencies, and the same method must be used for all periods presented. Appendix A of FASB-89 contains illustrative calculations of current cost/constant purchasing power information.

Net assets at end of each fiscal year   For purposes of the minimum supplementary information required by FASB-89, net assets at the end of each fiscal year are equal to all of the net assets appearing in the basic historical cost financial statements except that inventories, property, plant, and equipment are included at their current costs or at a lower recoverable amount. (Total net assets at historical cost minus inventories, property, plant, and equipment at historical cost, plus inventories, property, plant, and equipment at current costs or lower recoverable amount, equals net assets as encouraged by FASB-89.) The amount computed for net assets at end of each fiscal year is then restated in average-for-the-year units of constant purchasing power using the CPI-U.

Where comprehensive restatement of financial statements is made in lieu of the minimum supplementary information, net assets for the five-year summary of selected financial data may be reported at the same amount shown in the comprehensive restated financial statements.

Income per common share from continuing operations on a current cost basis   Income per common share from continuing operations for each of the five most recent years is computed and then restated in average-for-the-year units of constant purchasing power using the CPI-U. Income per common share from continuing operations on a current cost basis is found by dividing the outstanding number of shares of common stock into the total restated income from continuing operations on a current cost basis.

Cash dividends declared per common share   Cash dividends declared per common share for each of the five most recent years are restated in average-for-the-year units of constant purchasing power using the CPI-U.

Market price per common share at year-end   Market price per common share at year-end for each of the five most recent years is restated in average-for-the-year units of constant purchasing power using the CPI-U.

Average level of CPI-U   The average level of CPI-U for each of the five most recent years shall be disclosed in a note to the minimum supplementary information. If an enterprise presents comprehensive current cost/constant purchasing power financial statements measured in year-end units of purchasing power, the year-end level of the CPI-U for each of the five most recent years shall be disclosed.

Explanatory disclosures   An enterprise should provide an explanation of the disclosures encouraged by FASB-89 and a discussion of their significance in the circumstances of the enterprise. These explanatory statements should be sufficiently detailed so that a user who possesses reasonable business acumen will be able to understand the information presented.

Additional Disclosures for the Current Year

If income from continuing operations as shown in the primary financial statements differs significantly from income from continuing operations determined on a current cost/constant purchasing power basis, certain other disclosures for the current year are encouraged by FASB-89 in addition to the minimum supplementary information. The additional disclosures for the current year are as follows:

- Income from continuing operations for the current year on a current cost basis
- Separate amounts for the current cost or lower recoverable amount at the end of current year of (a) inventory, and (b) property, plant, and equipment
- Increase or decrease in current cost or lower recoverable amount before and after adjusting for the effects of inflation of (a) inventory, and (b) property, plant, and equipment
- The principal types and sources of information used to calculate current cost for the current year
- The differences, if any, in depreciation methods, useful lives, and salvage values used in the primary financial statements and the depreciation methods, useful lives, and salvage values used in the disclosure of current cost information for the current year

Each of the additional disclosures listed above are separately discussed in the following paragraphs.

Income from continuing operations for the current year on a current cost basis Income from continuing operations for the current year on a current cost basis is computed in accordance with FASB-89 and then restated in average-for-the-year units of constant purchasing power using the CPI-U. The information for income from continuing operations for the current year on a current cost basis should be presented in either a *statement format*, or a *reconciliation format*, which discloses all adjustments between the supplementary information and the basic historical cost financial statements (see illustrations in Appendix A of FASB-89). The same categories of revenue and expense that appear in the basic historical cost financial statements should be used for the presentation of income from continuing operations for the current year on a current cost basis. Account classifications may be combined if they are not individually significant for restating purposes, or if the restated amounts are approximately the same as the historical cost amounts.

Income from continuing operations for the current year on a current cost basis does not include (a) the purchasing power gain or loss on net monetary items, (b) the increase or decrease in the current cost or lower recoverable amount of inventory and property, plant, and equipment, net of inflation, and (c) the translation adjustment (if applicable). However, an enterprise may include this information after the presentation of income from continuing operations for the current year on a current cost basis (see illustrations in Appendix A of FASB-89).

Only certain items that are included in income from continuing operations in the primary financial statements have to be adjusted to compute income from continuing operations for the current year on a current cost basis. Under FASB-89, the following items must be adjusted to compute income from continuing operations for the current year on a current cost basis:

a. *Cost of goods sold*—must be determined on a current cost basis or lower recoverable amount at the date of sale or at the date on which resources are used on or committed to a specific contract

b. *Depreciation, depletion and amortization*—must be determined on the basis of the average current cost of the assets' service potentials or lower recoverable amounts during the period of use.

c. *Gain or loss on the sale, retirement, or write-down of inventory, property, plant, and equipment*—is equal to the difference between the value of the consideration received or the written-down amount and the current cost or lower recoverable amount of the item prior to its sale, retirement, or write-down

All other revenue, expenses, gains and losses that are included in the primary financial statements are not adjusted and may be disclosed as one in computing income from continuing operations for the current year on a current cost basis. Thus, these items are included in income from continuing operations for the current year on a current cost basis using the same amounts that appear in the primary financial statements.

Income tax expense that is included in the primary financial statements is not adjusted in computing income from continuing operations for the current year on a current cost basis. Thus, income tax expense is included in income from continuing operations for the current year on a current cost basis using the same amount that appears in the primary financial statements. Disclosure must be made in the minimum supplementary information to the effect that income tax expense for the current period is presented at its historical cost.

Separate amounts for the current cost or lower recoverable amount at the end of the current year of (a) inventory, and (b) property, plant, and equipment The current costs or lower recoverable amounts of inventory and of property, plant, and equipment at the end of the current year must each be disclosed as a separate item after the presentation of income from continuing operations for the current year on a current cost basis (see illustrations in Appendix A of FASB-89).

Increase or decrease in current cost or lower recoverable amount before and after adjusting for the effects of inflation of (a) inventory, and (b) property, plant, and equipment The increase or decrease in the current cost or lower recoverable amount before and after the effects of inflation must be separately disclosed for inventory and for property, plant, and equipment.

The principal types and sources of information used to calculate current costs for the current year The principal types and sources of information used to calculate current costs for the year must be disclosed in an explanatory note to the current cost information. The explanatory note should be sufficiently detailed so that a user who possesses reasonable business acumen will be able to understand the information presented.

The differences, if any, in depreciation methods, useful lives, and salvage values used in (a) the primary financial statements and (b) the disclosure of current cost information for the current year Depreciation methods, useful lives, and salvage values should be the same for current cost purposes as for historical cost purposes. If historical cost computations already include an allowance for changing prices, then a different method may be used for current cost purposes. However, any material differences must be disclosed in the explanatory note to the supplementary information.

Specialized Assets

Timberlands, growing timber, mineral ore bodies, proved oil and gas reserves, income-producing real estate, and motion picture films are classified as specialized assets. Specialized assets are considered unique, and the determination of their current costs is frequently difficult, if not impossible. For example, the current cost of an existing oil field may be difficult to determine because the oil field is one of a kind and cannot be duplicated. Yet, the definition of current cost is the current cost to purchase or reproduce the specific asset, and the current cost of property that is owned is the current cost of acquiring an asset that will perform or produce in a manner similar to that of the owned property.

FASB-89 provides special rules for determining the current costs of specialized assets. As a substitute for the current cost amounts and related expenses of timberlands and growing timber, income-producing real estate, and motion picture films, the historical cost amounts of such specialized assets may be adjusted for changes in specific prices by the use of a broad index of general purchasing power.

In the event an enterprise estimates the current cost of growing timber and timber harvested by adjusting historical costs for changes in specific prices, the historical costs may include either (a) only costs that are capitalized in the primary financial statements or (b) all direct costs of reforestation and forest management, even if such costs are not capitalized in the primary financial statements. Reforestation and forest management costs include planting, fertilization, fire protection, property taxes, and nursery stock.

Mineral resource assets   The requirements for determining the current cost amounts for mineral resource assets are flexible because there is no generally accepted approach for measuring the current cost of finding mineral reserves. In determining the current cost amounts of mineral resource assets, FASB-89 permits the use of specific price indexes applied to historical costs, market buying prices, and other statistical data to determine current replacement costs. FASB-89 encourages the disclosure of the types of data or information that are used to determine current cost amounts.

For enterprises that own significant mineral reserves, the following information on owned mineral reserves, excluding oil and gas, is encouraged to be disclosed for each of the five most recent years:

1. The estimated amount of proved or proved and probable mineral reserves on hand at the end of the year. A date during the year is acceptable, but the date must be disclosed.
2. The estimated quantity of each significant mineral product that is commercially recoverable from the mineral reserves in 1. above. The estimated quantity may be expressed in percentages or in physical units.
3. The quantities of each significant mineral produced during the year. In the case of ores, the quantity of each significant mineral produced by milling or similar processes must also be disclosed.
4. The quantity of mineral reserves (proved or proved and probable) purchased or sold in place during the year.
5. The average market price of each significant mineral product. If transferred within the enterprise, the equivalent market price prior to further use should be disclosed.

In classifying and detailing the above information, current industry practices should prevail.

The following procedures shall be used in determining the quantities of mineral reserves that should be reported:

1. In consolidated financial statements, 100% of the quantities of mineral reserves attributable to both the parent company and all consolidated subsidiaries shall be reported regardless of whether a subsidiary is partially or wholly owned.
2. In a proportionately consolidated investment, an investor shall include only its proportionate share of the investor's mineral reserves.
3. Mineral reserve quantities attributable to an investment accounted for by the equity method shall not be included at all. However, if significant, the mineral reserve quantities should be reported separately by the investor.

FASB-89 contains the following definitions relating to mineral resource assets:

> **Mineral resource assets** Assets that are directly associated with and derive value from all minerals extracted from the

earth. Such minerals include oil and gas, ores containing ferrous and nonferrous metals, coal, shale, geothermal steam, sulphur, salt, stone, phosphate, sand, and gravel. Mineral resource assets include mineral interests in properties, completed and uncompleted wells, and related equipment and facilities, and other facilities required for purposes of extraction (FASB Statement No. 19, *Financial Accounting and Reporting by Oil and Gas Producing Companies*, paragraph 11). The definition does not cover support equipment, because that equipment is included in the property, plant, and equipment for which current cost measurements are required by this appendix [FASB-89].

Proved mineral reserves   In extractive industries other than oil and gas, the estimated quantities of commercially recoverable reserves that, on the basis of geological, geophysical, and engineering data, can be demonstrated with a reasonably high degree of certainty to be recoverable in the future from known mineral deposits by either primary or improved recovery methods.

Probable mineral reserves   In extractive industries other than oil and gas, the estimated quantities of commercially recoverable reserves that are less well defined than proved.

FOREIGN OPERATIONS
AND EXCHANGE

Overview

The major promulgated GAAP on Foreign Currency Translation is FASB-52, which supersedes the following prior GAAP:

- FASB-8, Accounting for the Translation of Foreign Currency Transactions and Foreign Currency Financial Statements
- FASB-20, Accounting for Forward Exchange Contracts
- FASB Interpretation-15, Translation of Unamortized Policy Acquisition Costs by a Stock Life Insurance Company

FASB Interpretation-37 (Accounting for Translation Adjustments upon Sale of Part of an Investment in a Foreign Entity) clarifies paragraph 14 of FASB-52 in that a sale of an investment in a foreign entity includes a partial, as well as a complete, sale or other disposition of an ownership interest in a foreign investment.

FASB-52 covers the translation of foreign currency financial statements for the purposes of consolidation, combination, or reporting by the equity method (APB-18), and the translation of foreign currency transactions, including forward exchange contracts.

FASB-52 also amends paragraph 13 of APB-22 (Disclosure of Accounting Policies) by deleting the words "translation of foreign currencies" as an example of disclosure "commonly required with respect to accounting policies." Thus, APB-22 no longer requires the disclosure of foreign currency translations. However, FASB-52 does require specific disclosures of foreign currency translations.

Background

Business transactions and foreign operations that are recorded in a foreign currency must be restated in U.S. dollars in accordance with generally accepted accounting principles.

Transactions occur at various dates, and since the abandonment of the gold standard, exchange rates have tended to fluctuate considerably. Before an attempt is made to translate the records of a foreign operation, the records should be in conformity with GAAP. In addition, if the foreign statements have any accounts stated in a currency other than their own, they must be converted into the foreign statement's currency before translation into U.S. dollars or any other reporting currency.

The two major areas involved in foreign currency translations are:

I. The accounting and reporting of foreign currency transactions, including forward exchange contracts

II. The translation of foreign currency financial statements for the purposes of consolidation, combination, or reporting on the equity method (one-line consolidation)

A brief survey of FASB-52 follows:

1. Foreign currency financial statements must be in conformity with GAAP before they are translated.

2. Assets, liabilities, and operations of an entity must be expressed in the functional currency of the entity.

3. The functional currency of an entity is the currency of the primary economic environment in which the entity operates.

4. If a foreign entity's books of record are not kept in the functional currency, they must be remeasured into the functional currency prior to translation.

5. The current rate of exchange shall be used to translate the assets and liabilities of a foreign entity from its functional currency into the reporting currency.

6. The weighted-average exchange rate for the period shall be used to translate revenue, expenses, and gains and losses of a foreign entity from its functional currency to the reporting currency.

7. The current rate of exchange shall be used to translate changes in financial position other than those items found in the income statement, which are translated at the weighted-average exchange rate for the period.

8. Gain or loss on the translation of foreign currency financial statements is not recognized in current net income but is reported as a separate component of stockholders' equity. However, if remeasurement from the recording currency to the functional currency is necessary prior to translation, gain or loss on remeasurement is recognized in current net income.

9. The amounts accumulated in the separate component of stockholders' equity are realized on the sale or substantially complete liquidation of the investment in the foreign entity.

10. The financial statements of a foreign entity in a country that has had cumulative inflation of approximately 100% or more over a three-year period (highly inflationary) must be remeasured into the functional currency of the reporting entity.

11. A foreign currency transaction is one that requires settlement in a currency other than the functional currency of the reporting entity.

12. Gains or losses from foreign currency transactions are recognized in current net income, except for:

    a. Gain or loss on a designated and effective economic hedge of a net investment in a foreign entity

    b. Gain or loss on certain long-term intercompany foreign currency transactions

    c. Gain or loss on a designated and effective economic hedge of a firm identifiable foreign currency commitment which meets certain conditions

13. Taxable foreign exchange gains or losses that do not appear in the same period in taxable income and either (a) financial accounting income (books) or (b) a separate component of stockholders' equity (books) are temporary (timing) differences for which deferred taxes must be provided in accordance with existing GAAP (FASB-96).

14. Certain specific disclosures are required by FASB-52.

Translation Objectives

FASB-52 establishes accounting and reporting standards for (1) foreign currency transactions and (2) translation of foreign currency financial statements that are included by consolidation, combination, or the equity method in a parent company's financial statements. Foreign financial statements must conform to U.S. generally accepted accounting principles before they can be translated into dollars.

An important objective in translating foreign currency is to preserve the financial results and relationships that are expressed in the foreign currency. This is accomplished by using the *functional currency* of the foreign entity. The functional currency is then translated into the *reporting currency* of the reporting entity. FASB-52 assumes that the reporting currency for an enterprise is U.S. dollars. However, the reporting currency may be a currency other than U.S. dollars.

> **OBSERVATION**: *Perhaps the ultimate objective of translating foreign transactions and financial statements would be to produce the same results that each individual underlying transaction would have produced on the date it occurred, if it had then been recorded in the reporting currency.*

Functional Currency

FASB-52 requires that the assets, liabilities, and operations of an entity be measured in terms of the functional currency of that entity. The functional currency is the currency of the primary economic environment in which an entity generates and expends cash. The functional currency is generally the currency of the country in which the entity is located. However, the functional currency of a foreign operation may be the same as a related affiliated enterprise, if the foreign operation is a direct and integral component or extension of the related affiliated enterprise.

For the purposes of determining functional currency under FASB-52, foreign operations may be broken down into two models. The first model is the self-contained foreign operation, located in a particular country, whose daily operations are not dependent on the economic environment of the parent's functional currency. This type of foreign operation primarily generates and expends foreign currency; the net cash flows that it produces in foreign currency may be reinvested, or converted and distributed to its parent company. The functional currency for this type of foreign operation is its foreign currency.

The second model of foreign operation is usually a direct and integral component or extension of the parent company's operation. Financing is usually in U.S. dollars and is frequently supplied by the parent. The purchase and sale of assets are usually made in U.S. dollars. In other words, the daily operations of this type of foreign operation are dependent on the economic environment of the parent's currency. In addition, the changes in the foreign operation's individual assets and liabilities directly affect the cash flow of the parent company. The functional currency for this type of foreign operation is the U.S. dollar.

In the event that the facts in a given situation do not clearly identify the functional currency, the determination rests on the judgment of management. The FASB has developed the following guidelines, based on certain indicators, that should be considered in determining the functional currency of a foreign operation:

Cash Flow Indicators

The foreign operation's cash flows are mostly in foreign currency which does not directly affect the parent company's cash flows. Under these circumstances, the functional currency is the foreign currency.

The foreign operation's cash flows directly affect the parent company's cash flows on a current basis and are usually available for remittance through intercompany account settlement. Under these circumstances, the functional currency is the parent company's currency.

Sales Price Indicators

The foreign operation's sales prices for its products are primarily determined (on a short-term basis) by local competition, or local government regulation, and not by exchange rate changes. Under these circumstances, the functional currency is the foreign currency.

The foreign operation's sales prices for its products are mostly responsive (on a short-term basis) to exchange rate changes, such as worldwide competition and prices. Under these circumstances, the functional currency is the parent company's currency.

Sales Market Indicators

The foreign operation has an active local sales market for its products, although there also may be significant amounts of exports. Under these circumstances, the functional currency is the foreign currency.

The foreign operation's sales market is mostly in the parent's country, or sales contracts are mostly made in the parent company's currency. Under these circumstances, the functional currency is the parent company's currency.

Expense Indicators

The foreign operation's costs of production (labor, material, etc.) or service are mostly local costs, although there may also be imports from other countries. Under these circumstances, the functional currency is the foreign currency.

The foreign operation's costs of production or service, on a continuing basis, are primarily costs for components obtained from the parent's country. Under these circumstances, the functional currency is the parent company's currency.

Financing Indicators

Financing for the foreign operation is in foreign currency, and funds generated by the foreign operation are sufficient to service debt obligations. Under these circumstances, the functional currency is the foreign currency.

Financing for the foreign operation is provided by the parent company or is obtained in U.S. dollars. Funds generated by the foreign operation are insufficient to service its debt. Under these circumstances, the functional currency is the parent company's currency.

Intercompany Transactions

There is little interrelationship between the operations of the foreign entity and the parent company, except for competitive advantages, such as trademarks, patents, etc. Intercompany transactions are of a low volume. Under these circumstances, the functional currency is the foreign currency.

There is an extensive interrelationship between the operations of the foreign entity and the parent company. Intercompany transactions are numerous. Under these circumstances, the functional currency is the parent company's currency.

The functional currency of a foreign entity must be used consistently from one fiscal year to another, unless significant changes in economic facts and circumstances dictate a change.

> **OBSERVATION:** *A change in functional currency is accounted for as a change in an accounting estimate. Thus, the change is accounted for in the period of change and/or future periods (prospectively).*
>
> *If a change in functional currency occurs, the translation adjustments for prior periods are not removed from the separate component of stockholders' equity. Thus, the translated amounts of nonmonetary assets at the end of the period prior to the change in functional currency become the accounting basis for subsequent periods.*

After the functional currency of a foreign entity is determined, the financial statements must be remeasured in the functional currency before translation can be made under FASB-52. In other words, the functional currency is first determined. Then, the accounts and records and resulting financial statements of the foreign entity must be remeasured in the functional currency. Next, the financial statements are translated into the functional currency of the reporting entity. Usually, the functional currency of a foreign entity is either (1) the foreign currency of the country in which the foreign entity is located, (2) the foreign currency of a related affiliate, or (3) the U.S. dollar.

If the foreign entity's financial statements are already stated in terms of its functional currency, translation can be made under the provisions of FASB-52. The translation provisions of FASB-52 are discussed later. However, if the foreign entity's financial statements are not stated in the functional currency, the financial statements must be remeasured into the functional currency before they can be translated. The remeasurement of the foreign entity's financial statements into the functional currency is required by FASB-52 prior to translation. Remeasurement of the financial statements shall be made in accordance with the provisions of FASB-52, and shall produce the same results as if the entity's accounts and records had always been maintained in the functional currency.

> **OBSERVATION:** *For example, if a foreign entity's books of record are kept in French francs and the functional currency is British pounds, the books of record must be remeasured into British pounds before the financial statements can be translated into the functional currency of the reporting entity. Any translation gain or loss from French francs to British pounds is included in the remeasured net income.*

The remeasurement process required by FASB-52 is the same as that which was required by FASB-8 (Temporal Method), except for deferred income taxes and deferred life insurance policy acquisition costs. Thus, *exchange adjustments resulting from the remeasurement process are included in the determination of remeasured net income.* Deferred income taxes and deferred life insurance policy acquisition costs are remeasured using the current rate of exchange, instead of the historical exchange rate, which was required by FASB-8. The following is a brief review, using FASB-52 terminology, of the translation provisions of FASB-8. They are relevant under FASB-52 only for the remeasurement process from the recording currency to the functional currency, prior to translation from the functional currency to the reporting currency.

There are two categories of exchange rates that may be used in remeasuring financial statements. Historical exchange rates are those which existed at the time of the transaction, and the current exchange rate is the rate that is current at the date of remeasurement.

Monetary assets and liabilities are those which are fixed in amount, such as cash, accounts receivable, and most liabilities. Under FASB-8, all monetary assets and liabilities are translated at the current rate of exchange. All other assets, liabilities, and stockholders' equity are remeasured by reference to money price exchanges based on the type of market and time. FASB-8 describes the four types of money price exchanges as follows:

1. *Past purchase exchange*—the historical or acquisition cost, because it is based on the actual past purchase price

2. *Current purchase exchange*—the replacement cost, because it is measured by the current purchase price of a similar resource

3. *Current sale exchange*—the market price, because it is based on the current selling price of the resource

4. *Future exchange*—the present value of future net money receipts, discounted cash flow, or the discounted net realizable value, because it is based on a future resource

All other assets, liabilities, and stockholders' equity are remeasured based on the four money price exchanges, as follows:

1. Accounts based on past purchase exchanges (historical or acquisition cost) are remeasured at historical exchange rates.

2. Accounts based on current purchase, current sale, and future exchanges are remeasured at the current exchange rate.

Revenue and expense transactions are remeasured at the average exchange rate for the period, except those expenses related to assets and liabilities, which are remeasured at historical exchange rates. For example, depreciation and amortization are remeasured at historical exchange rates, the rate that existed at the time the underlying related asset was acquired.

The following is a comprehensive list of assets, liabilities, and stockholders' equity items and their corresponding remeasurement rates under FASB-8:

	Remeasurement Rates	
	Current	*Historical*
Cash (in almost all forms)	X	
Marketable securities—at cost		X
Marketable securities—at market	X	
Accounts and notes receivable	X	
Allowance for receivables	X	
Inventories—at cost		X
Inventories—at market, net realizable value, selling price	X	
Inventories—under fixed contract price	X	
Prepaid expenses		X
Refundable deposits	X	
Advances to subsidiaries	X	
Fixed assets		X
Accumulated depreciation		X
Cash surrender value—life insurance	X	
Intangible assets (all)		X
Accounts and notes payable	X	
Accrued expenses	X	
Accrued losses on firm commitments	X	
Taxes payable	X	
All long-term liabilities	X	
Unamortized premium or discount on long-term liabilities	X	
Obligations under warranties	X	
Deferred income		X
Capital stock		X
Retained earnings		X
Minority interests		X

Note: FASB-52 requires the current rate of exchange to be used for remeasuring deferred income taxes and deferred life insurance policy acquisition costs. In other respects, remeasurement under FASB-52 follows the above tabulation of exchange rates, derived from FASB-8.

As previously mentioned, revenue and expenses not related to any balance sheet items are remeasured at the average currency exchange rate for the period. The average may be based on a daily, weekly, monthly, or quarterly basis or on the weighted-average rate for the period, which will probably result in a more meaningful conversion. Revenue and expense items that are related to a balance sheet account, such as deferred income, depreciation, and beginning and ending inventories, are remeasured at the same exchange rate as the related balance sheet item.

In remeasuring the lower-of-cost-or-market rule, the remeasured historical cost is compared to the remeasured market, and whichever is lower in functional currency is used. This may require a write-down in the functional currency from cost to market, which was not required in the foreign currency financial statements. On the other hand, if market was used on the foreign statements and in remeasuring to the functional currency market exceeds historical cost, the write-down to market on the foreign statements will have to be reversed before remeasuring, which would then be done at the historical rate. Once inventory has been written down to market in remeasured functional currency statements, the resulting carrying amount is used in future translations until the inventory is sold or a further write-down is necessary. This same procedure is used for assets, other than inventory, that may have to be written down from historical cost.

The reason for the above procedure in applying the lower-of-cost-or-market rule in remeasuring foreign financial statements is that exchange gains and losses are a consequence of remeasurement and not of applying the lower-of-cost-or-market rule. This means that remeasured market is equal to replacement cost (market) in the foreign currency remeasured at the current exchange rate, except that:

1. Remeasured market cannot exceed net realizable value in foreign currency translated at the current exchange rate.
2. Remeasured market cannot be less than 1 above, reduced by an approximate normal profit translated at the current exchange rate.

For remeasurement purposes, the current exchange rate is the one in effect as of the balance sheet date of the foreign statements. Therefore, if the parent company's financial statements are at a date different from the date(s) of its foreign operation(s), the exchange rate in effect at the date of the foreign subsidiary's balance sheet is used for remeasurement and translation purposes.

Any translation adjustment arising from the remeasurement process is included in remeasured net income. In other words, any gain or loss resulting from the remeasurement process which is required by FASB-52 is included in net income in the remeasured financial statements.

After the foreign entity's financial statements are remeasured in the functional currency, they are ready for translation. If the functional currency of a foreign entity is the U.S dollar and the reporting currency of the parent is also the U.S. dollar, there will be no translation adjustment.

Translation of Foreign Operations—Highly Inflationary Economies

FASB-52 defines a highly inflationary economy as one in which the cumulative inflation over a three-year consecutive period approximates one hundred percent (100%). In other words, the inflation rate in an economy must be rising at the rate of about 35% per year for three consecutive years to be classified as highly inflationary.

For the purposes of FASB-52, a foreign entity in a highly inflationary economy does not have a functional currency. The functional currency of the reporting entity is used as the functional currency of the foreign entity in a highly inflationary economy. Thus, the financial statements for a foreign entity in a highly inflationary economy must be remeasured into the functional currency of the reporting entity. The remeasurement process required by FASB-52 is the same as that which is required for a foreign entity's financial statements that are not expressed in the functional currency. This remeasurement process, which was discussed in the prior section entitled "Functional Currency," is the same as that which was required by FASB-8 (Temporal Method), except for deferred income taxes and deferred life insurance policy acquisition costs.

> **OBSERVATION**: *Apparently, exchange adjustments resulting from the remeasurement process for foreign entities in highly inflationary economies must be included in the determination of remeasured net income, rather than reported as a separate component of stockholders' equity. Paragraph 11 of FASB-52 is not clear on this point, but does state that the remeasurement process must be done in accordance with paragraph 10.*

The International Monetary Fund (IMF) of Washington, D.C., publishes monthly statistics on international inflation rates. After the financial statements of a foreign entity in a highly inflationary economy are expressed in the functional currency of the reporting entity, they are ready for translation. However, since the financial statements are now expressed in the reporting currency, there will be no translation adjustment.

Translation of Foreign Currency Statements

Foreign currency financial statements must be in conformity with GAAP before they are translated into the functional currency of the reporting entity. FASB-52 covers the translation of financial statements from one functional currency to another for the purposes of consolidation, combination, or the equity method of accounting. Translation of financial statements for any other purpose is beyond the scope of FASB-52.

> **OBSERVATION:** *If the functional currency of a foreign operation is the same as its parent, there will be no need for translation. A translation adjustment will only occur if the foreign operation's functional currency is a functional currency different from that of its parent.*

The translation of foreign currency financial statements to the functional currency of the reporting entity does not produce realized exchange gains or losses. Instead, the gains or losses are considered unrealized and are recorded and reported as a separate component of stockholders' equity. In the year that FASB-52 is first applied, the beginning balance of the separate component of stockholders' equity should be equal to the difference between the net assets translated under FASB-8 and the net assets translated at the current exchange rate.

> **OBSERVATION:** *Paragraph 12 of FASB-52 states that "All elements of financial statements shall be translated by using a current exchange rate." This statement is obviously not correct because common stock, paid-in capital, donated capital, retained earnings, and similar items are not translated at the current exchange rate. Translation of these elements of the financial statements is made exactly as they were translated under FASB-8, as follows:*
>
> **Capital Accounts** *are translated at their historical exchange rates when the capital stock was issued, or at the historical exchange rate when the capital stock was acquired.*

Retained Earnings *are translated at the translated amount at the end of the prior period, plus the translated amount of net income for the current period, less the translated amount of any dividends declared during the current period.*

Assets and liabilities should be translated from the foreign entity's functional currency to the reporting entity's functional currency using the current exchange rate at the balance sheet date of the foreign entity. If a current exchange rate is not available at the balance sheet date of the foreign entity being translated, the first exchange rate available after the balance sheet date shall be used.

Revenue, expenses, and gains and losses should be translated from the foreign entity's functional currency to produce the approximate results that would have occurred if each transaction had been translated using the exchange rate in effect on the date that the transaction was recognized. Since the separate translation of every single transaction is impractical, an appropriate weighted-average exchange rate for the period should be used.

Gains or losses on the translation of foreign currency financial statements for the purposes of consolidation, combination, or reporting on the equity method are not included in current net income. All adjustments resulting from the translation of foreign currency financial statements must be recorded and reported as a separate component of stockholders' equity. Thus, these adjustments are treated as unrealized gains and losses, similar to unrealized gains and losses of noncurrent marketable securities (FASB-12).

The translation process embodied in FASB-52 includes the following steps:

1. Financial statements must be in conformity with U.S. GAAP prior to translation.
2. The functional currency of the foreign entity must be determined.
3. The financial statements must be expressed in the functional currency of the foreign entity. Remeasurement of the financial statements into the functional currency may be necessary. Gains or losses from remeasurement are included in remeasured current net income.
4. If the foreign entity operates in a country with a highly inflationary economy, its financial statements must be remeasured into the functional currency of the reporting entity.
5. The functional currency financial statements of the foreign entity are translated into the functional currency of the re-

porting entity using the current rate of exchange method. Gains or losses from translation are not included in current net income.

Realization of Separate Component of Stockholders' Equity

Upon part, complete, or substantially complete sale or upon complete liquidation of an investment in a foreign entity, a *pro rata* portion of the accumulated translation adjustments attributable to that foreign entity, which have been recorded as a separate component of stockholders' equity, shall be included in determining the gain or loss on the sale or other disposition of that foreign investment (FASB Interpretation-37). Thus, if an enterprise sells a 50% ownership interest in a foreign investment, 50% of the accumulated translation adjustments related to that foreign investment shall be included in determining the gain or loss on the sale of the 50% ownership interest.

FASB Interpretation-37 is effective for the sale of part of a foreign investment that is consummated on or after July 1, 1983, with earlier application encouraged in previously unissued financial statements. Retroactive restatement of previously issued financial statements is not required, but is permitted.

> **OBSERVATION:** *Any required provision for the permanent impairment of a foreign investment should be determined before translation and consolidation (see Appendix C, paragraph 118, of FASB-52). Apparently, this means that the amounts accumulated in the separate component of stockholders' equity for a specific foreign investment are not included in determining whether the investment has become permanently impaired.*

The separate component of stockholders' equity account for a foreign investment may contain amounts from the following sources:

1. Translation adjustments
2. Deferred income taxes related to items in the separate component of stockholders' equity
3. Gain or loss on an economic hedge of a net investment in a foreign entity
4. Gain or loss on intercompany foreign currency transactions of a capital or long-term nature

5. Under certain conditions, amounts deferred under FASB-8 on a forward exchange contract that hedged an identifiable foreign currency commitment of a nonmonetary asset

Foreign Currency Transactions

A foreign currency transaction is one that requires settlement in a currency other than the functional currency of the reporting entity. As a general rule, gains and losses on foreign currency transactions are recognized in current net income. However, the following foreign currency transactions, which are discussed later, may require different treatment than that afforded all other foreign currency transactions:

1. Gain or loss resulting from a foreign currency transaction that is designated as an economic hedge of a net investment in a foreign entity
2. Gain or loss resulting from intercompany foreign currency transactions of a capital nature or long-term financing nature, between an investor and investee where the investee entity is consolidated, combined, or accounted for by the equity method by the investor
3. Forward exchange contracts

If the exchange rate changes between the time a purchase or sale is contracted for and the time actual payment is made, a foreign exchange gain or loss will result. For example, if goods were purchased for 100,000 pesos when the rate of exchange was 10 pesos to a dollar, the journal entry in dollars would be:

Purchases	$10,000	
Accounts payable		$10,000

Assuming that when the goods are paid for, the exchange rate is 12:1, the journal entry in dollars would be:

Accounts payable	$10,000	
Cash		$ 8,333
Foreign exchange gain		1,667

The $8,333, at a 12:1 exchange rate, can purchase 100,000 pesos. The difference between the $8,333 and the original recorded liability of $10,000 is a foreign exchange gain.

A foreign exchange gain or loss must be computed at each balance sheet date on all recorded foreign transactions that have not been settled. The difference between the exchange rate that could have been used to settle the transaction at the date it occurred, and the exchange rate that can be used to settle the transaction at a subsequent balance sheet date, is the gain or loss on the foreign currency transaction, which is recognized in current net income. Generally, the current exchange rate is the rate that is used to settle a transaction on the date it occurs, or on a subsequent balance sheet date.

> **OBSERVATION:** *FASB-52 retains most of the provisions of FASB-8 regarding foreign currency transactions. The major difference is in the definition of a hedge of an identifiable foreign currency commitment, which is discussed in a later section.*

Forward Exchange Contracts

A forward exchange contract is a foreign currency transaction. A forward exchange contract is an agreement to exchange, at a future specified date and rate, currencies of different countries. Generally, a forward exchange contract is entered into either as a hedge or for speculation. Gains or losses on all foreign exchange contracts and foreign currency transactions are usually recognized in net income of the period in which the exchange rate changes. Gains and losses that are exceptions to this general rule are deferred and are discussed in a later section.

FASB-52 specifies two methods of determining gain or loss on forward exchange contracts, depending upon whether the contract is (1) a hedge (whether or not deferred) or (2) speculative.

Hedge contracts   Gain or loss is the difference between the balance sheet date spot exchange rate and the spot exchange rate at the inception of the contract, multiplied by the principal amount of foreign currency.

Speculative contracts   Gain or loss is the difference between the contracted forward exchange rate and the forward exchange rate available for the remaining maturity of the contract, multiplied by the principal amount of foreign currency.

> **OBSERVATION:** *The spot or forward exchange rate last used to measure gain or loss on a forward exchange contract for an earlier*

period may be used for either hedge or speculative contracts, if necessary.

The discount or premium involved in a forward exchange contract is the difference between the contract rate and the spot rate on the date of purchase, multiplied by the principal amount of foreign currency. Discounts and premiums are disposed of as follows:

Identifiable hedges   Either separately accounted for and amortized to net income over the life of the contract, or not separately accounted for and recognized as part of the total gain or loss on the identifiable transaction.

Hedge of net investment   Either separately accounted for and amortized to net income over the life of the contract, or not separately accounted for and recognized as part of the total gain or loss on the transaction.

All other contracts   Discounts and premiums are separately accounted for and amortized to net income over the life of the forward exchange contract.

Deferred Foreign Currency Transactions

Certain gains and losses on forward exchange contracts and certain types of foreign currency transactions are not included in current net income but are either (1) reported in the separate component of stockholders' equity, along with translation adjustments or (2) included in the overall gain or loss of the related foreign currency transaction. These deferred gains and losses may be classified as follows:

1. Gain or loss on a designated and effective economic hedge of a net investment in a foreign entity
2. Gain or loss on certain long-term intercompany foreign currency transactions
3. Gain or loss on a designated and effective economic hedge of a firm identifiable foreign currency commitment

Gain or loss on a forward exchange contract or foreign currency transaction that is intended and effective as an economic hedge of a net investment in a foreign entity is not recognized in current net income. Instead, the gain or loss is recorded and reported as a separate component of stockholders' equity. The foreign currency transaction must be designated and effective as an economic hedge of a net investment in a foreign entity. The accounting required by FASB-52 commences with the designation date of the transaction.

> **OBSERVATION:** *As an example of a foreign currency transaction intended to be an economic hedge of a net investment in a foreign entity, take the case of a U.S. parent company with a net investment in a Greek subsidiary that borrows Greek currency in the amount of its net investment in the Greek subsidiary. The U.S. company designates the loan as an economic hedge of its net investment in the Greek subsidiary. In other words, the U.S. parent computes its net investment in the foreign currency of its foreign subsidiary and then borrows the same amount of foreign currency as the amount of its net investment. In this event, if the net investment in the foreign subsidiary declines because of a change in exchange rates, the change is made up in the foreign currency loan. The U.S. company can buy a larger amount of the subsidiary's foreign currency with fewer U.S. dollars. When the net investment in the foreign subsidiary and the loan in the foreign currency of the foreign subsidiary are both translated into U.S. dollars, the change in the net investment in the foreign subsidiary (an asset) should be approximately equal to the change in the foreign currency loan, except for taxes, if any. Thus, the foreign currency loan acts as a hedge against any increase or decrease in the net foreign investment that is attributable to a change in the exchange rate. FASB-52 requires that both translated amounts be recorded and reported in a separate component of stockholders' equity. However, if the translated amount of the foreign currency loan (after taxes, if any) exceeds the translated amount of the net investment in the foreign subsidiary that was hedged, the gain or loss that is allocable to the excess must be included in net income, and not recorded and reported as a separate component of stockholders' equity.*

Gains or losses on intercompany foreign currency transactions of a capital or long-term nature are not included in current net income, but are reported in the separate component of stockholders' equity, along with translation adjustments. The entities involved in the intercompany foreign currency transactions reported in this manner must be consolidated, combined, or accounted for by the equity method. Gain or loss on intercompany foreign currency transactions that are not of a permanent nature are included in net income.

Gain or loss on a forward exchange contract or foreign currency transaction that is intended and effective as a hedge of a firm identifiable foreign currency commitment is deferred and included in the overall gain or loss from the firm identifiable foreign currency commitment. However, a loss shall not be deferred if it is estimated that the loss would be recognized in later periods. Thus, any loss that is expected to be recognized in later periods cannot be deferred. The foreign currency transaction must be firm, and must be designated and effective as a hedge of a foreign currency commitment. The accounting required by FASB-52 commences with the designation date of the transaction.

> **OBSERVATION:** *For example, a U.S. company purchases a large piece of equipment from a Mexican company for 100,000 pesos when the exchange rate is 10:1 (ten pesos to 1 dollar). Delivery of the equipment will be made in one year, at which time the purchase price must be paid in Mexican pesos. In order to hedge against the rise or fall in the exchange rate of the Mexican peso, the U.S. company purchases, for $1,000, a forward exchange contract to purchase 100,000 Mexican pesos in one year at the exchange rate of 10:1. At the end of six months, financial statements are prepared and the exchange rate of Mexican pesos is 12:1. Thus, at the end of six months, the cost of the equipment in U.S. dollars is $8,333, or 100,000 Mexican pesos, while at the date of purchase the cost in U.S. dollars was $10,000 or 100,000 Mexican pesos. The company has protected itself against an exchange rate change and at the end of the year will receive 100,000 Mexican pesos from the forward exchange contract upon payment of $10,000. However, at the interim six-month date, there is a loss on the forward exchange contract of $2,667 ($1,667, plus the cost of the forward exchange contract of $1,000). This loss cannot be deferred if the total cost of the asset, including the deferred loss on the forward exchange contract, is expected to exceed the estimated net realizable value of the asset.*

For the purposes of FASB-52, the amount of the forward exchange contract or foreign currency transaction cannot exceed the amount of the firm identifiable foreign currency commitment. If the amount of the transaction exceeds the amount of firm commitment, the gain or loss pertaining to the excess amount over the commitment may be deferred only to the extent that the transaction provides a hedge on an after-tax basis. Where gain or loss pertaining to amounts in excess of the foreign currency commitment is deferred, it is included as an offset to the related tax effects in the period in which such tax effects are recognized. Gains or losses in excess of the amount of commitment on an after-tax basis cannot be deferred. In addition, any gains or losses on a forward exchange contract or foreign currency transaction that are attributable to a period after the transaction date of the related commitment cannot be deferred.

Deferred gain or loss on a hedge of a foreign currency commitment that is sold or terminated is not recognized until the related identifiable transaction is consummated, unless the identifiable transaction is reasonably expected to result in a loss.

The major differences between FASB-52 and FASB-8 concerning a hedge of an identifiable foreign currency commitment are depicted in the following chart:

FASB-8 and 20	FASB-52
Covered forward exchange contracts only.	Covers all "designated" and "effective" hedges.
Life of the forward contract must extend from foreign currency commitment date to anticipated transaction date or later.	Commences at the "designation date."
Foreign currency commitment must be firm and noncancelable.	Foreign currency commitment must be firm.
Forward contract must be for the same currency as the identifiable commitment.	No rule, by Appendix C (paragraph 130) of FASB-52 suggests a hedge in another currency under certain conditions.

Deferred Taxes

Temporary differences are taxable transactions that do not appear in financial accounting income (books) and taxable income (tax return) in the same reporting period. Under existing GAAP (FASB-96 and APB-23), deferred taxes are provided for temporary (timing) differences. Thus, a reporting entity must determine its provision for deferred taxes to include taxable foreign currency transactions and taxable translation adjustments that are included in financial accounting income (books) and taxable income (tax return) in different reporting periods.

FASB-52 requires that deferred taxes be provided on taxable foreign currency transactions and taxable translation adjustments of foreign currency financial statements, regardless of whether the exchange gain or loss is charged to current net income or recorded and reported as a separate component of stockholders' equity. Thus, all taxable foreign exchange gains or losses that do not appear in the same period in taxable income and either (1) financial accounting income or (2) the separate component of stockholders' equity are temporary differences, for which deferred taxes must be provided. The amount of the deferred taxes should be determined in accordance with existing GAAP.

> **OBSERVATION:** *There is a presumption in GAAP that all undistributed earnings of a subsidiary (domestic or foreign) will eventually be transferred to the parent company. Unless this presumption is overcome, the undistributed earnings included in a parent's consolidated income will result in a temporary difference, and a provision for deferred taxes may be necessary. This same presumption exists for corporate joint ventures and investments accounted for by the equity method. Thus, unless this presumption is overcome by sufficient evidence to the contrary, a parent or investor will have to provide for deferred taxes on taxable translation adjustments that are included in financial accounting income and taxable income in different periods.*

Intraperiod income tax allocation should be disclosed in the financial statements in accordance with FASB-96. The total income tax expense for a period should be properly allocated to (1) income before extraordinary items, (2) extraordinary items, (3) adjustments of prior periods, and (4) direct entries to other stockholders' equity accounts. Therefore, the portion of income tax expense for a period that is attributable to items in the separate component of stockholders' equity should be allocated to the separate component of stockholders' equity, and should not appear as an increase or decrease of income tax expense for the period. In other words, deferred taxes related to items in the separate component of stockholders' equity account are charged or credited to the separate component of stockholders' equity account.

> **OBSERVATION:** *All aspects of income tax allocation are complicated, and these provisions of FASB-52 will require careful application to the specific facts of each situation. In particular, intercompany transactions of a long-term nature and the discontinuation of a foreign operation may present peculiar problems.*

Elimination of Intercompany Profits

The exchange rate to be used to eliminate intercompany profits shall be the rate that existed on the date of the intercompany transaction. FASB-52 permits the use of approximations and/or averages as long as they are reasonable.

> *OBSERVATION: Intercompany profits occur on the date of sale or transfer. Thus, the exchange rate on the date of sale or transfer should be used to determine the amount of intercompany profit to be eliminated.*

Exchange Rates

The balance sheet date of the foreign entity which is consolidated, combined, or accounted for by the equity method is used for translation purposes, if different from the balance sheet date of the reporting entity. Thus, the current exchange rate for the translation of foreign currency financial statements is the rate in effect on the balance sheet date of the foreign entity which is being translated. If a current exchange rate is not available at the balance sheet date of the foreign entity being translated, the first exchange rate available after the balance sheet date should be used. The exchange rate used for dividend remittances, if available, shall be used to translate foreign currency financial statements.

> *OBSERVATION: If a preference or penalty rate is used to translate intercompany transactions and the dividend remittance exchange rate is used for all other translation, a difference may arise in the intercompany receivables and payables. In this event, the difference shall be accounted for as a receivable or payable until the difference is eliminated by settlement of the transaction.*

Conditions may exist where it will be prudent to exclude a foreign entity from financial statements which are consolidated, combined, or accounted for by the equity method. Disruption of a foreign operation caused by internal strife or severe exchange restrictions may make it impossible to compute meaningful exchange rates. Under these circumstances, it is best to include earnings of a foreign operation only to the extent that cash has been received in unrestricted funds (ARB-43). Adequate disclosure should be made of any foreign subsidiary or investment that is excluded from the financial statements of the parent or investor. This may be accomplished by separate supplemental statements or a summary describing the important facts and information (ARB-43).

For foreign currency transactions, the exchange rate that existed on the date of the transaction should be used for translation purposes. A foreign currency transaction is one that requires settlement in a currency other than the functional currency of the reporting entity. A foreign exchange gain or loss must be computed at each balance sheet date on all recorded foreign currency transactions that have not been settled. The difference between the exchange rate that could have been used to settle the transaction at the date it occurred and the exchange rate that can be used to settle the transaction at a subsequent balance sheet date is the gain or loss on the foreign currency transaction.

> **OBSERVATION:** *More frequently than not, the current exchange rate is the rate that could have been used to settle the transaction at the date it occurred; the current exchange rate at a subsequent balance sheet date is usually the rate used to settle a transaction at a subsequent balance sheet date.*

Financial statements should not be adjusted for a change in rate subsequent to the date of the financial statements. However, disclosure of such a rate change, if significant, may be required under the disclosure provisions of FASB-52.

Use of Averages and/or Approximations

Since detailed compliance may require significant record keeping, the promulgated GAAP (FASB-52) permits the use of averages and/or reasonable approximations, providing the results do not differ materially from the prescribed standards.

Financial Statement Disclosure

The aggregate transaction gain or loss that is included in determining net income for the period, including gain or loss on forward exchange contracts, shall be disclosed in the financial statements or footnotes thereto.

> **OBSERVATION:** *Transaction gains or losses of dealers in foreign exchange may be accounted for as dealer gains or losses, instead of transaction gains or losses under FASB-52.*

An analysis of the changes in the separate component of stockholders' equity account for cumulative translation adjustments for the period shall be disclosed in either (1) a separate financial statement or (2) notes to the financial statements, or (3) be included as part of a stockholders' equity or a similar statement. The following is the minimum information that must be disclosed in the analysis:

1. Beginning and ending cumulative balances
2. The aggregate increase or decrease for the period from translation adjustments and gains and losses from (a) hedges of a net investment in a foreign entity and (b) long-term intercompany transactions
3. The amount of income taxes for the period allocated to translation adjustments
4. The amount of translation adjustment transferred to net income during the period as a result of a sale or complete or substantially complete liquidation of a foreign investment

Disclosure of exchange rate changes and related effects on foreign currency transactions that occur subsequent to the balance sheet date should be disclosed, if the effects are material. No adjustment should be made to the financial statements for exchange rate changes that occur subsequent to the balance sheet date.

Effective Date and Transition

FASB-52 shall be initially applied from the start of an enterprise's fiscal year and is effective for fiscal years commencing on or after December 15, 1982, although earlier compliance is encouraged. Financial summaries for periods prior to the effective date may be restated to comply with FASB-52. In the year of first compliance, the nature of any restatement and its effect on (1) income before extraordinary items, (2) net income, and (3) related per share data for each period restated must be disclosed. However, if the prior period is not restated, the disclosure of income before extraordinary items and net income is permitted on a *pro forma* basis.

> **OBSERVATION:** *To the extent practicable, financial statements restated for prior periods should contain all of the disclosures required by FASB-52.*

Gain or loss on forward exchange contracts, which under FASB-8 hedged an identifiable foreign currency commitment, shall be included in the opening balance of the separate component of stockholders' equity if the following conditions are met:

1. The forward exchange contract is canceled at the time FASB-52 is first applied.

2. The foreign currency commitment must involve the right to receive proceeds from the use or sale of nonmonetary assets that were translated at historical exchange rates under FASB-8.
3. The amount that can be included in the opening balance of the separate component of stockholders' equity may not exceed the amount of the related offsetting adjustment to the non-monetary assets.

> **OBSERVATION:** *For example, an enterprise has an operating lease or take-or-pay contract that represents the right to receive proceeds from the use or sale of a nonmonetary asset. Assume that the transaction qualified as an identifiable foreign currency commitment and the enterprise purchased a forward exchange contract to hedge the commitment, in accordance with the provisions of FASB-8. If the foreign exchange contract is canceled at the time that FASB-52 is first applied, any amounts that would have been deferred under the provisions of FASB-8 (up to the amount attributable to the related nonmonetary asset) shall be included in the opening balance of the separate component of stockholders' equity.*

In the year that FASB-52 is first applied, the beginning balance of the separate component of stockholders' equity is equal to the difference between the beginning net asset translated at the current exchange rate at the beginning of the period. In addition, as discussed above, gain or loss on forward exchange contracts, which under FASB-8 hedged an identifiable foreign currency commitment, shall also be included in the opening balance of the separate component of stockholders' equity, if they meet the necessary conditions.

The difference between the historical exchange rate and the current exchange rate for deferred income taxes and insurance policy acquisition costs that arise as a result of remeasuring a foreign entity's financial statements shall be reported as an adjustment of the opening balance of retained earnings.

> **OBSERVATION:** *In the event that a foreign entity's financial statements did not have to be remeasured because they were already expressed in its functional currency, the difference between the historical exchange rate and the current exchange rate for deferred income taxes and insurance policy acquisition costs would be reflected in the opening balance of the separate component of stockholders' equity.*

If an enterprise first applies FASB-52 for fiscal years ending on or before March 31, 1982, disclosure in the year of change shall be made in the financial statements of the effects of adopting FASB-52 on (a) income before extraordinary items, (b) net income, and (c) related per share data. Subsequent to March 31, 1982, these disclosures for the year of change are not required.

Comprehensive Illustration

The following is an illustration of how an enterprise should determine the beginning balance of the separate component of stockholder's equity.

DETERMINING THE BEGINNING BALANCE OF THE SEPARATE COMPONENT OF STOCKHOLDERS' EQUITY ACCOUNT

	Beginning of the Year			Beginning of the Year		
	Functional currency	FASB-52 exchange rates	U.S. dollars	Functional currency	Current exchange rates	U.S. dollars
Current Assets						
Cash	F 1,000	C*1.25	$ 800	F 1,000	C 1.25	$ 800
Accounts receivable	4,000	C 1.25	3,200	4,000	C 1.25	3,200
Inventory	10,000	H†2.00	5,000	10,000	C 1.25	8,000
Total	F15,000		$ 9,000	F15,000		$12,000
Property, plant, & equipment	F75,000	H 1.50	$50,000	F75,000	C 1.25	$60,000
Total assets	F90,000		$59,000	F90,000		$72,000
Current Liabilities						
Current Liabilities	F20,000	C 1.25	$16,000	F20,000	C 1.25	$16,000
Deferred income taxes	5,000	H 2.00	2,500	5,000	C 1.25	4,000
Long-term obligations	20,000	C 1.25	16,000	20,000	C 1.25	16,000
Total liabilities	F45,000		$34,500	F45,000		$36,000
Net assets (equals stockholders' equity)	F45,000		$24,500	F45,000		$36,000

COMPUTATION OF THE BEGINNING BALANCE OF THE SEPARATE COMPONENT OF STOCKHOLDERS' EQUITY ACCOUNT

Net assets at beginning of the year at current exchange rate $36,000

Net assets at beginning of the year at FASB-52 rates $24,500

Beginning balance of separate component of stockholders' equity $11,500

C* = Current exchange rate. H† = Historical exchange rate.

GENERAL PRICE-LEVEL CHANGES

Overview

Most information about restating financial statements for general price-level changes is contained in APB Statement-3, which was issued in June 1969. APB Statements are not considered promulgated GAAP.

Background

The degree of inflation or deflation in an economy may become so great that conventional statements lose much of their significance, and general price-level statements clearly become more meaningful.

The unit of measure is the basic difference between historical and general price-level financial statements. General price-level financial statements do not represent replacement cost or an appraisal value, but merely represent what historical-cost statements reflect in general purchasing power, as at a specific date. GAAP used in historical-cost financial statements are also used in general price-level financial statements. Changes in the general price level are measured in terms of index numbers; the base year is given the index number of 100, and changes are expressed as percentages of the base year.

General

It is important to remember that general price-level adjusted statements are based on historical cost. The process of restatement simply converts the historical dollars into dollars of current purchasing power. Statements are adjusted to reflect the price level at the *end* of the current period.

Historically, the rate of inflation in the United States has not been significant enough to cause serious erosion of the *unit of measure principle*. However, the double-digit inflation of recent years has caused some to question the usefulness of historical-cost financial statements.

The price-level adjustment process consists of restating historical-cost financial statements into common dollars.

Monetary Assets and Liabilities

For purposes of general price-level accounting assets and liabilities are called *monetary items* if their amounts are fixed by contract or otherwise in terms of numbers of dollars. Cash, accounts and notes receivable in cash, and accounts and notes payable in cash are examples of monetary items.

Monetary items automatically gain or lose general purchasing power during inflation or deflation as a result of changes in the general price-level index. For example, a holder of a $10,000 promissory note executed 10 years ago and due today will receive exactly $10,000 today, in spite of the fact that $10,000 in cash today is worth a lot less than $10,000 in cash was worth 10 years ago. Such losses or gains of this nature are called *general price-level gains or losses*. Although monetary assets and liabilities are *not restated* on a general price-level balance sheet, the general price-level gains and losses are calculated and are recognized in the general price-level income statement.

Nonmonetary Assets and Liabilities

Assets and liabilities that are not monetary items are called *nonmonetary items* for purposes of general price-level accounting. Inventories, investments in common stocks, property, plant, equipment, and deferred charges are examples of nonmonetary items. Holders of nonmonetary items may lose or gain with the rise or fall of the general price-level index if the nonmonetary item does not rise or fall in proportion to the change in the price-level index. In other words, a nonmonetary asset or liability is affected (1) by the rise or fall of the general price-level index and (2) by the increase or decrease of the fair value of the nonmonetary item. For example, the purchaser of 10,000 shares of General Motors common stock 10 years ago was subject (1) to the decrease in purchasing power and (2) to the rise in the fair value of the stock. If the decrease in purchasing power exactly offsets the increase in the price of the stock, the purchaser is, in effect, in the same position today as he was 10 years ago (that is, monetarily).

By means of the general price-level index nonmonetary items are *restated* to current purchasing power at the end of the reporting period. The difference produced by the restatement of nonmonetary items does not represent replacement cost or current values, but presents the historical cost in terms of current purchasing power.

Inventory purchased at the end of a period, although a nonmonetary item, may well be already stated at approximately the general purchasing power at the end of a period.

Net Monetary Position

The difference between monetary assets and monetary liabilities, at any specific date, is the net monetary position. The net monetary position may be either positive (monetary assets exceed monetary liabilities) or negative (monetary liabilities exceed monetary assets).

In periods in which the general price-level index is rising (inflation), it is advantageous for a business to maintain a net negative monetary position. The opposite is true during periods in which the general price-level index is falling (deflation). In periods of inflation, a business which has a net negative monetary position will experience general price-level gains, because it can pay its liabilities in a fixed number of dollars that are getting cheaper as time goes by. A net positive monetary position during periods of inflation results in a general price-level loss, because the value of the dollar is declining.

Some assets and liabilities have characteristics of both monetary and nonmonetary items. Convertible debt, for example, is monetary in terms of its fixed obligation, but nonmonetary in terms of its conversion feature.

The determination of whether an item is monetary or nonmonetary is made as at the balance sheet date. Therefore, if convertible debt has not been converted as of that date, it should be classified as a monetary item. Additionally, a bond receivable held for speculation would be classified as nonmonetary, because the amount that will be received when the bond is sold is no longer fixed in amount, as it would be if the same bond was held to maturity.

Price Indexes

Price-level changes are measured by price indexes. Price indexes are stated in percentages to a base year, which is assigned a value of 100.

By using a price index, dollars of general purchasing power in one period can be restated to dollars of general purchasing power of another period. The formula for restating dollars of one period to those of another is :

$$\frac{\text{New index (converting to)}}{\text{Old index (converting from)}}$$

For example, assume that the current ending price index is 120, and a parcel of land was purchased for $10,000 in a year when the price index was 80. The conversion would be:

$$\frac{120}{80} \quad \times \quad \$10,000 \; = \; \$15,000$$

This conversion should not be interpreted to mean that the land is worth $15,000. What it means is that, historically, the purchasing power needed to buy the land is equal to $15,000 in terms of the dollar represented by the new price index.

Restating can be made in either direction—to current purchasing power or to purchasing power of a prior year.

In the United States the best price index for restating financial statements is the Gross National Product Implicit Price Deflator, which is *not* a specific-goods price index, but a broad index of general price changes.

General Price-Level Gain or Loss

Monetary items automatically gain or lose general purchasing power as a result of changes in price indexes. Assume that a comparative balance sheet showed cash of $10,000 and notes payable of $20,000 at both balance sheet dates in a year when the price index went from 110 to 117. Obviously, the current year's $10,000 in cash cannot purchase what the prior year's $10,000 in cash could. Using our formula the conversion of the current year to general price levels would be:

$$\frac{117}{110} \quad \times \quad \$10,000 \; = \; \$10,636$$

The $636 is a loss in the general purchasing power of the cash as measured by the change in the price indexes.

On the other hand, the current year's $20,000 of notes payable will be paid with cheaper dollars than the prior year's $20,000 in notes payable:

$$\frac{117}{110} \quad \times \quad \$20,000 \; = \; \$21,272$$

The $1,272 ($21,272 – $20,000) is a gain in the general purchasing power, because the liability will be paid with dollars of less general purchasing power.

If our hypothetical company had no other monetary assets and liabilities besides the cash of $10,000 and notes payable of $20,000, it would have a net general price-level gain of $636 ($1,272 – $636 = $636) for the year.

A change in the price index from one period to another can be expressed as a percentage. When the index moves from 110 to 117, it has increased 7 points, or 6.36% (7/110 = 6.36). Applying this percentage increase to the $10,000 cash and $20,000 notes payable in the preceding example:

$10,000 x 6.36%	=	($ 636)
$20,000 x 6.36%	=	1,272
Net price-level gain for the period		$ 636

Note that price-level increases arising from assets cause a price-level *loss*, whereas price-level increases arising from liabilities cause a price-level *gain*.

Instead of computing a gain or loss on each individual monetary item, it is easier to calculate the net monetary position. In our last example, the net monetary position (negative) was $10,000 ($10,000 in cash less $20,000 notes payable). We can now restate the beginning net monetary position for the change in the price index and then subtract the actual net monetary position at the end of the period, as follows:

Net monetary position (negative)

$10,000 x $\dfrac{117}{110}$	$10,636
Less: Ending net monetary position	10,000*
Net general price-level gain	$ 636

* $10,000 cash less the $20,000 notes payable on the current year's balance sheet

Advantages of Restatement

Advantages of general price-level financial statements are:

1. The dollar is not stable, and changes in its monetary value should be reflected in financial statements in order to produce more realistic information.

2. General price-level financial statements provide more mean-ingful information in terms of current economic conditions.
3. Management's effectiveness in periods of inflation or defla-tion can be more readily determined.
4. General price-level balance sheets more clearly approximate current values.

Disadvantages of Restatement

Disadvantages of general price-level financial statements are:

1. Historical-dollar financial statements are based on verifiable information.
2. There is no general agreement as to which price-level index to use and how it should be applied.
3. Most assets and liabilities that have been recently acquired are already valued close to current price levels.
4. Historical costs have been employed traditionally over many years with satisfactory results.

Schedule of General Price-Level Gain or Loss

Our previous discussion has been oversimplified in order to demon-strate the nature of general price-level gains or losses.

In reality, a business will have many transactions that cause a change in net monetary assets or liabilities. Cash and credit sales increase the net monetary position; purchases, operating expenses, and cash dividends decrease the net monetary position. Deprecia-tion and amortization have no effect on the net monetary position. The procedure for preparing a schedule of general price-level gain or loss is:

1. Determine the net monetary position (positive or negative) at the beginning of the period (usually the monetary assets less the monetary liabilities at the end of the prior period) ad-justed to the general price-level index at the end of the period.
2. Add all increases in net monetary items from all sources (sales, miscellaneous revenue, proceeds from the sale of fixed assets, proceeds from the issuance of debt or stock, etc.), adjusted to the general price-level at the end of the period.

3. Deduct all decreases in net monetary items from all sources (expenditures for purchases, operating expenses, acquisition of assets, miscellaneous expenses, and the retirement of debt or stock), adjusted to the general price-level index at the end of the period.

4. Arrive at the *estimated* net monetary position at the end of the period, which is the difference between steps 1, 2, and 3 above.

    (1 + 2 − 3) = estimated net monetary position at the end of the period

5. Compute the *actual* net monetary position at the end of the period (monetary assets less monetary liabilities), and subtract this from the estimated net monetary position calculated in step 4.

    Note: The difference between the estimated net monetary items at the end of the period and the actual net monetary items at the end of the period is the general price-level gain or loss for the period. If the estimated net monetary items exceed the actual, a loss results. If the estimated net monetary items are less than the actual, a gain results.

This price-level gain or loss is shown in the income statement as the item immediately preceding net income.

General Price-Level Financial Statements

The following are general rules for preparing price-level adjusted financial statements:

1. All financial statements presented, including those of prior years, are restated to the purchasing power of the dollar at the most recent balance sheet date. This is called "rolling over" the previously restated statements. The prior restated statements are simply restated again to the current price level. This serves two purposes. It converts last year's statements into current-year dollars (comparability), and it translates last year's ending retained earnings into current-year dollars for use in the current-year statement of retained earnings.

2. Sales and expenses incurred evenly throughout the year are converted by using the average general price index for the year.
3. The inventory method (FIFO, LIFO, etc.) will dictate the price index to use for restating inventory.
4. Depreciation is restated by using the price index of the related asset.
5. Buildings, equipment, and other fixed assets are restated by using the price index existing at the time of their purchase.
6. Common stock is restated by using the price index existing at the time the stock was issued.

Comprehensive Illustration

The following comprehensive problem illustrates how financial statements are restated for general price-level changes.

ABC Corporation's financial statements for the year ended December 31, 19X2, are shown below:

ABC Corporation
Balance Sheet

As of December 31, 19X2

Cash	$100,000
Accounts receivable	200,000
Inventory (FIFO)	50,000
Fixed assets	250,000
Total assets	$600,000
Accounts payable	$ 70,000
Common stock	200,000
Retained earnings	330,000
Total liabilities and equity	$600,000

ABC Corporation
Income Statement
For the year ended December 31, 19X2

Sales		$900,000
Cost of goods sold:		
Beginning inventory	$ 50,000	
Add: Purchases	700,000	
Total	750,000	
Less: Ending inventory	50,000	
Cost of goods sold		700,000
Gross profit		200,000
Operating expenses:		
Depreciation		20,000
Other		80,000
Total operating expenses		100,000
Income before taxes		100,000
Income tax expense		20,000
Net income		$ 80,000

Relevant price indexes	
Beginning of year	104
End of year	108
Average	106
Fixed assets acquired	92
Formation of company	90

Additional data:

The company's net monetary position at December 31, 19X1, was $130,000. Inventories are priced on a FIFO basis.

The first step in this problem is to compute the amount of the general price-level gain or loss.

The essence of creating the schedule of general price-level gain or loss is to compare the monetary items at year end with the amount at which the items would have been stated if they were nonmonetary items.

The steps in preparing this schedule for ABC Corporation are explained below.

1. The net monetary position at the beginning of the year (December 31, 19X1) is given as $130,000. Restate this to current dollars as follows:

$$\$130,000 \times \frac{108}{104} = \$135,000$$

The beginning index of 104 is used because this is the net monetary position at the *beginning* of the period.

2. Assemble all increases in monetary items and convert them, using the appropriate index.

Increases:

Sales	$900,000
Total increases	$900,000
Factor	108/106
Adjusted sales	$916,981

The average index of 106 is used because sales are assumed to occur evenly through the year.

3. Assemble all decreases in monetary items and convert them, using the appropriate index.

Decreases:

Purchases	$700,000
Other expenses	80,000
Income tax expense	20,000
Total decreases	$800,000
Factor	108/106
Adjusted expenses	$815,094

The average index of 106 is used because purchases and expenses, including income tax expense, are assumed to be incurred evenly through the year.

4. The net estimated monetary position at year end is calculated as follows:

Net monetary position—beginning	$135,000
Plus: Increases	916,981
Less: Decreases	(815,094)
Net estimated monetary position— ending	$236,887

5. The actual net monetary position at the end of the period is calculated from actual amounts appearing on the balance sheet for the end of the period, as follows:

Monetary assets:

Cash	$100,000
Accounts receivable	200,000
Total actual monetary assets	300,000

Monetary liabilities:

Accounts payable	70,000
Total actual monetary liability	70,000
Net monetary position (positive)	$230,000

The general price-level gain or loss can now be calculated as follows:

Actual net monetary items	$230,000
Estimated net monetary items	236,887
General price-level gain (loss)	($ 6,887)

Since the estimated net monetary position exceeds the actual net monetary position, there is a loss.

The work papers for the restatement of the financial statements of ABC Corporation follow:

ABC Corporation
Income Statement
For the year ended December 31, 19X2

	Historical	Conversion Factor	Adjusted
Sales	$ 900,000	108/106	$916,981
Cost of goods sold:			
Beginning inventory	50,000	108/104	51,923
Add: Purchases	700,000	108/106	713,208
Total	750,000		765,131
Less: Ending inventory	50,000	108/108	50,000
Cost of goods sold	700,000		715,131
Gross profit	200,000		201,850
Operating expenses:			
Depreciation	20,000	108/92	23,478
Other	80,000	108/106	81,509
Total	100,000		104,987
Net income before taxes	100,000		96,863
Income tax expense	20,000	108/106	20,377
Net income	$ 80,000		76,486
General price-level gain (loss)			(6,887)
Net income—adjusted for changes in general price levels			$ 69,599

Schedule of General Price-Level Gain (Loss)

Historical		Converted for Price-Level Changes
$130,000	Beginning net monetary position [index at beginning of year (104) index at end of year (108) = conversion factor 108/104]	$135,000
900,000	Increases in monetary items during the year: sales $900,000 [average index during the year (106), index at end of year (108) = conversion factor 108/106]	916,981
(800,000)	Decreases in monetary items during the year: purchases $700,000, other expenses $80,000, income tax expense $20,000 [average index during the year (106), index at end of year (108) = conversion factor 108/106]	(815,094)
230,000	Ending net estimated monetary position	236,887
230,000	Ending actual net monetary position*	230,000
—	General price-level gain or (loss)	($ 6,887)

*Monetary assets—end of period	$300,000
Less: Monetary liabilities–end of period	70,000
Actual net monetary position- end of period	$230,000

ABC Corporation
Balance Sheet
As of December 31, 19X2

	Historical	Conversion Factor	Adjusted
Cash	$100,000	108/108	$100,000
Accounts receivable	200,000	108/108	200,000
Inventory	50,000	108/108	50,000
Fixed assets	250,000	108/92	293,478
Total assets	$600,000		$643,478
Accounts payable	$ 70,000	108/108	$ 70,000
Common stock	200,000	108/90	240,000
Retained earnings	330,000		333,478
Total liabilities and equity	$600,000		$643,478

Note: Only the nonmonetary assets and liabilities are restated on the general price-level balance sheet. The changes in the net monetary assets and liabilities have already been taken into account in the general price-level income statement as a general price-level gain or loss.

GOVERNMENT CONTRACTS

Overview

The promulgated GAAP covering government contracts are as follows:

ARB-43, Chapter 11A, Cost-Plus-Fixed-Fee Contracts
ARB-43, Chapter 11B, Renegotiation
ARB-43, Chapter 11C, Terminated War and Defense Contracts

Background

More frequently than not, government contracts are performed under a cost-plus-fixed-fee (CPFF) arrangement which provides for possible renegotiation, if the contracting officer for the government believes that excess profits were made by the contractor. These contracts usually also provide that the government may terminate the contract for its convenience at any time.

CPFF Contracts

Cost-plus-fixed-fee contracts generally provide that the government pay a fixed fee in addition to all costs involved in fulfilling the contract. The contract may include the manufacture of a product or only the performance of services, and the government may or may not withhold a specified percentage of the interim payments until completion of the entire contract. Furthermore, CPFF contracts are usually cancellable by the government, and when such contracts are terminated the contractor is entitled to reimbursement for all costs, plus an equitable portion of the fixed fee.

One of the main problems in accounting for CPFF contracts is when profits should be recognized. As a general rule, profits should not be recognized until the right to full payment becomes unconditional, which is usually when the product has been delivered and accepted or the services fully rendered (completed-contract method).

However, when CPFF contracts extend over several years, the completed-contract method may be utilized; the percentage-of-completion method is acceptable, provided that costs and profits can be reasonably estimated and realization of the contract is reasonably assured.

An advance payment by the government may not be offset as a payment on account, unless it is expected to be applied as such with reasonable certainty. A distinction should be made in the balance sheet between unbilled costs and fees and billed amounts. In the event that an advance is offset, it must be clearly disclosed.

Renegotiation

Renegotiation involves the adjustment of the original selling price or contract. Since the government makes renegotiation adjustments an integral part of a contract, a provision for such probable adjustments is necessary. This provision for renegotiation should be based on the contractor's past experience or on the general experience of the particular industry, and it is shown in the income statement as a reduction of the related sales or income. If a reasonable estimate cannot be made, disclosure of the inability to provide for renegotiation should be fully disclosed in the financial statements or footnotes thereto. The provision for renegotiation is reported as a current liability in the balance sheet.

In those unusual cases where collection is not reasonably assured, it may be preferable to employ the installment-sale or cost-recovery method in accounting for a government contract.

When a provision for renegotiation is made in a particular year and the subsequent final adjustment differs materially, the difference should be shown in the income statement of the year of final determination.

Disclosure

When a significant part of a company's business is derived from government contracts, such disclosure should be made in the financial statements or footnotes thereto, indicating the uncertainties involved and the possibility of renegotiation in excess of the amount provided. In addition, the basis of determining the provision for renegotiation should be disclosed (prior experience, industry experience, etc.).

Terminated War and Defense Contracts

This section of the promulgated GAAP deals with both fixed-price and cost-plus-fixed-fee contracts. It addresses the problems involved in the termination of a government contract by the government but does not cover terminations resulting from default of the contractor.

The determination of profit or loss on a terminated government contract is made as of the effective date of termination. This is the date that the contractor accrues the right to receive payment on that portion of the contract which has been terminated.

Although most government contracts provide for a minimum profit percentage formula in the event agreement cannot be reached, the amount of profit to be reported in the case of termination for the convenience of the government is the difference between all allowable costs incurred and the amount of the termination claim.

If it is impossible to determine a reasonable estimate of the termination claim for reporting purposes, full disclosure of this fact should be made by footnote to the financial statements, which should describe the uncertainties involved. In other words, those parts of the termination claim which can be reasonably ascertained should be reported, and those which cannot be reasonably ascertained should be described in a footnote to the financial statements.

Termination claims should be classified as current assets. Prior to termination notice, advances received should be deducted from termination claims receivable for reporting purposes. Loans received on the security of the contract or termination claim should be separately shown as current liabilities.

The cost of items included in the termination claim that are subsequently reacquired by the contractor should be recorded as a new purchase, and the amount should be applied as a reduction of the termination claim. These types of reductions from the termination claim are generally referred to as *disposal credits*.

Disclosure

Material amounts of termination claims should be classified separately from other receivables in the financial statements.

Termination claims should be stated at the amount estimated as collectible, and adequate provision or disclosure should be made for items of a controversial nature.

Claims against the government, if material, should be segregated from other receivables.

INCOME TAXES
IMPORTANT NOTICE

In December 1987, FASB-96 (Accounting for Income Taxes) was issued to supersede APB-11 (Accounting for Income Taxes). FASB-96 was scheduled to become effective for fiscal years beginning after December 15, 1988, and earlier adoption was encouraged.

As a result of numerous complaints from major industrial enterprises regarding the complexity and cost of implementing the provisions of FASB-96, the Financial Accounting Standards Board (FASB) issued FASB-100, deferring the effective date of FASB-96 by one year to December 15, 1989. FASB-103 granted a further deferral of two years to December 15, 1991, with earlier application encouraged.

Two Exposure Drafts (ED) are outstanding as of the date of this publication. One of the outstanding EDs would defer the effective date of FASB-96 for one more year, until fiscal years beginning after December 15, 1992, with earlier application permitted. The other outstanding ED would supersede FASB-96 and would be effective for fiscal years beginning after December 15, 1992. If the FASB meets its own schedule for issuing final Statements based on these two outstanding EDs, FASB-96 will be superseded without ever having gone into effect, although some enterprises have elected its early application.

Until the FASB issues a new Statement superseding FASB-96, an enterprise may account for income taxes by (i) continuing to apply the provisions of APB-11 or (ii) electing early adoption of FASB-96.

This edition of the *GAAP Guide* contains coverage of both APB-11 and FASB-96. The provisions of APB-11 appear in chapter 19.01a and the provisions of FASB-96 appear in chapter 19.01b.

Highlights of the outstanding Exposure Draft are summarized at the end of chapter 19.01b and are noted in the Disclosure Index.

Because of the status of APB-11 and FASB-96, it was also necessary to include two chapters entitled "Investment Tax

Credit" in this issue of the *GAAP Guide*. Chapter 25.01a contains coverage of the accounting standards relating to investment tax credits as they existed prior to the amendments by FASB-96. Chapter 25.01a should be used by those enterprises that are continuing to apply the provisions of APB-11 to account for income taxes. Chapter 25.01b contains coverage of the accounting standards relating to investment tax credits as they existed after the amendments by FASB-96. Chapter 25.01b should be used by those enterprises that are electing early adoption of the provisions of FASB-96.

INCOME TAXES

Overview

The present promulgated GAAP on income taxes, which are covered herein, consist of the following:

APB-10, paragraph 6, Tax Allocation Accounts—Discounts

APB-10, paragraph 7, Offsetting of Securities Against Taxes Payable

APB-11, Accounting for Income Taxes

APB-23, Accounting for Income Taxes—Special Areas

APB-24, Accounting for Income Taxes—Investments in Common Stocks Accounted for by the Equity Method

FASB-31, Accounting for Tax Benefits Related to U.K. Tax Legislation Concerning Stock Relief

FASB-37, Balance Sheet Classification of Deferred Income Taxes

FASB Interpretation-18, Accounting for Income Taxes in Interim Periods

FASB Interpretation-22, Applicability of Indefinite Reversal Criteria to Timing Differences

FASB Interpretation-29, Reporting Tax Benefits Realized on Disposition of Investments in Certain Subsidiaries and Other Investees

FASB Technical Bulletin 86-1 (FASB:TB 86-1) was issued on October 27, 1986, to provide guidance on recognizing and reporting the effects of the Tax Reform Act of 1986.

Background

One of the basic principles in accounting is that business entities are presumed to continue in existence unless liquidation is imminent (going-concern principle). Therefore, a business currently subject to income taxes will ordinarily continue to pay such taxes in the future. Income tax expense is an important determinant of net income, and must be identified to, and measured with, the appropriate accounting periods.

Income for federal tax purposes and financial accounting income frequently differ. Obviously, income for federal tax purposes is computed in accordance with the prevailing tax laws, whereas financial accounting income is determined in accordance with GAAP. In such a case, a company will have two different income tax liabilities: one for income tax purposes and the other for financial accounting purposes. This disparity is caused by timing differences.

Timing Differences

Timing differences are merely transactions that do not appear in financial accounting income and taxable income in the same reporting period. For example, accelerated depreciation for tax purposes and straight-line depreciation for financial accounting purposes create a timing difference in that taxable income will be different from financial accounting income in the same period. There are two types of timing differences:

1. Those which always reverse themselves in one or more future periods
2. Those which never reverse themselves, or permanent differences

Comprehensive interperiod income tax allocation includes the effects of timing differences in computing income tax expense for a period. This process balances the tax liability and income tax expense for a period by the use of tax deferrals and accruals.

Transactions that cause timing differences   There are four basic causes of timing differences:

1. Income that is included in taxable income, after it has already been included in financial accounting income
   (*Example*: Installment sales are reported for tax purposes as they are collected, but in financial accounting the total income is recognized in the period the sale is made, so collections on the installment sale are included in taxable income, after the entire sale was recognized by financial accounting in the year of sale.)
2. Income that is included in taxable income before it is included in financial accounting income
   (*Example*: Rents collected in advance must be included in

taxable income, but in financial accounting such rents are recognized only in the periods in which they are earned.)

3. Expenses deducted for taxable income after they have already been deducted for financial accounting income

   (*Example*: Provision for estimated product warranty is not deductible in computing taxable income, but such provision is made in financial accounting at the time a sale is made.)

4. Expenses deducted for taxable income before they are deducted for financial accounting purposes

   (*Example*: Accelerated depreciation is allowed in computing taxable income, but in financial accounting the straight-line method is usually used to more properly match revenue with its expired costs.)

Some timing differences reduce income taxes that would otherwise have to be paid, whereas other timing differences may increase income taxes.

> **OBSERVATION**: *The Tax Equity and Fiscal Responsibility Act of 1982 (TEFRA) provides that a taxpayer may elect to either (a) claim the full investment tax credit (ITC) and reduce the basis of the property by one-half of its related ITC, or (b) claim an ITC that is reduced by two percentage points and not reduce the basis of the related property.*
>
> *FASB Technical Bulletin 83-1 requires that the reduction in the basis of property by one-half of its related ITC (as may be required by TEFRA) must be accounted for as a timing difference in accordance with APB-11. Thus, deferred income taxes must be accrued in connection with the reduction of the basis of property in the same manner as deferred taxes are accrued in connection with a timing difference. See the section in Chapter 25.01 entitled "Reduction in basis of property" for more information.*

Permanent differences   Permanent differences arise from special tax laws regarding exempt income, dividends received exclusions, and certain other special deductions that, after taken, are permanent. Since permanent differences do not affect subsequent periods, no interperiod tax allocation need be made to account for them.

Permanent differences are either (a) nontaxable, (b) nondeductible, or (c) special tax allowances. Examples are:

1. Tax-exempt interest (municipal, state)
2. Proceeds from life insurance on officers
3. Amortization of goodwill
4. Life insurance premiums when corporation is beneficiary
5. Certain fines, bribes, kickbacks, etc.
6. Dividends received deduction for corporations
7. Excess percentage depletion over cost depletion

Bad debt allowances of savings and loan associations, and policyholders' surplus of stock life insurance companies that create a difference between taxable income and pretax financial accounting income are usually considered permanent differences, because the company controls the events that create the tax consequence. However, if circumstances dictate that income taxes will be paid because of a reduction in the bad debt allowance or in policyholders' surplus, a tax expense should be accrued on such reductions in the period they occur. In effect, these reductions do create a timing difference when they occur and should not be accounted for as an extraordinary item.

Disclosure of bad debt allowances and policyholders' surplus should be made in the financial statements or in footnotes, as follows:

Bad debt allowance (reserves)

1. The purpose of the allowance account and the rules and regulations pertaining thereto
2. The fact that income taxes may become payable if the allowance account is used for other purposes
3. The total amount of the allowance account for which income taxes have not been accrued

Policyholders' surplus

1. Treatment of the policyholders' surplus under the provisions of the IRC
2. The fact that income taxes may become payable if the company taxes specific action, which should be appropriately described
3. The total amount of policyholders' surplus for which income taxes have not been accrued

These disclosure requirements also apply to the parent company of the savings and loan association or the stock life insurance company.

Operating Losses

Under present tax regulations an operating loss of a period may be carried back or forward and may be applied as a reduction of income in those periods permitted by the tax laws. In such a case, the taxable income and the financial accounting income will change for the periods that the loss is carried back or forward.

If an operating loss is carried forward, the tax effects are not recognized because there is no assurance that they will be realized. For example, a loss carryforward would decrease the amount of taxes due in a certain future period, but if the company continues to lose money, there will be no profits to offset the carryforward and it may never be utilized. However, when the tax benefits of a loss carryforward are recognized in full or in part in subsequent periods, it is reported as an extraordinary item.

If an operating loss is carried back, the tax effect will certainly be realized in the form of a claim for taxes previously paid.

There is only one exception to not recognizing the effects of a loss carryforward. The tax effects of a loss carryforward may be realized in the books of accounts *providing that the realization is assured beyond any reasonable doubt.* In this event, in determining the results of operations for those periods the potential tax benefit (deferred tax credit) is recognized in the period(s) that gave rise to the loss. Estimates of the tax benefit should be based on the tax rates that are expected to exist at the time of realization. Any difference between the estimated amount and that received is applied as an adjustment of the tax expense of the period in which the benefit is received. Realization of a loss carryforward is assured beyond any reasonable doubt if the following conditions exist:

1. The company has been reasonably profitable over a long period or has experienced occasional losses which were subsequently offset by taxable income.
2. The loss carryforward is the result of an isolated, nonrecurring, and identifiable source.
3. Realization of future taxable income is large enough to offset the loss carryforward and will occur within the period allowed under tax law.

If tax benefits of loss carryforwards have not been recognized by a purchased subsidiary prior to the date of acquisition, they are recorded as assets purchased if realization is assured beyond any reasonable doubt. If they have not been recognized prior to the acquisition date, they are recognized when actually realized and treated as a retroactive adjustment of the purchase transaction. In this event, operating results for periods subsequent to the purchase may have to be retroactively adjusted if the affected balance sheet items have been subject to amortization.

A similar situation arises for loss carryforwards arising prior to a quasi-reorganization where realization is assured beyond a reasonable doubt. Under these circumstances, a previously unrecognized loss carryforward is recorded as an asset at the date of reorganization. If realization is not assured, the tax benefits of a loss carryforward are recognized when actually realized, and added to contributed capital, on the basis that the benefits are attributable to loss periods prior to the quasi-reorganization.

All other unused tax deductions and/or credits that may be carried back and forward in determining taxable income except investment tax credits are handled in the same manner as operating losses. That is, if realization is assured beyond any reasonable doubt, the tax deduction or credit is recognized for financial accounting purposes (books). As a general rule, investment tax credits may not be recognized even though their realization is assured beyond any reasonable doubt. However, in using the *with-and-without* method of computing deferred taxes, investment tax credits are recognized for financial accounting purposes (books) prior to their realization for tax return purposes (see the chapter entitled "Investment Tax Credits").

The tax effects of any realizable loss carryback should be recognized in the determination of the loss period net income. A claim of refund for past taxes will result and is shown on the balance sheet as a separate item (from other deferred taxes) and classified as either current or noncurrent. In the income statement, the claim of refund for past taxes is shown as a reduction of income tax expense for the current period.

When the tax effects of a carryback loss are not recognized (when prior years already are losses) and at the same time a net deferred tax credit exists, an adjustment may have to be made. In such a case, the deferred tax credits should be (1) eliminated to the extent of the tax effect of the resulting loss carryforward or (2) amortized over the period of the resulting loss carryforward. If in subsequent periods the loss carryforward is realized, in part or in whole, the prior adjustments to the deferred tax credits will have to be readjusted or reinstated at the then current tax rates. This procedure is similar to the offsetting of unused investment tax credits against existing net deferred tax credits required by FASB Interpretation-25 (see the chapter entitled "Investment Tax Credits").

Timing Differences—Special Areas

There is a presumption that all undistributed earnings of a subsidiary (domestic and foreign) will eventually be transferred to the parent. Unless the presumption is overcome, the undistributed earnings included in a parent's consolidated income will result in a timing difference, which should be recognized in the accounts. In addition, corporate joint ventures and investments in common stocks accounted for by the equity method present the same problem as a subsidiary in regard to timing differences and should be accounted for in the same manner.

> **OBSERVATION**: *Undistributed earnings of a subsidiary include those of a domestic international sales corporation (DISC) that qualify for tax deferral.*

An investor's proportionate share of operating losses from a subsidiary which files separate income tax returns, a joint venture, or an investment in common stock accounted for by the equity method, is accounted for in the same manner as other operating losses (see 19.04). As a result, an operating loss of this type is included in the investor's income or loss for the period, but is not treated as a timing difference unless it is realizable beyond any reasonable doubt. The journal entry to record the investor's proportionate share of an investee's operating loss is a debit to a loss account which appears on the income statement and a credit to the investment account. As a result, a difference is created between the accounting and tax basis of the investment. In addition, no deferred taxes are provided for, unless the operating loss is realizable beyond a reasonable doubt. Should the operating loss become realizable beyond a reasonable doubt a tax benefit is realized at that time. Because of the difference between the accounting and tax basis, a tax benefit will also be realized upon the ultimate disposition of the investment. FASB Interpretation-29 requires that these tax benefits be included as part of the gain or loss on the disposition of the investment. The result is that the tax benefit is given the same classification as the gain or loss on the investment (continuing operations, extraordinary item, disposal of a segment, etc.). Any significant variation in the usual relationship between income tax expense and pretax accounting income must be disclosed in the financial statements (APB-11).

> **OBSERVATION**: *There is a mistake in paragraph 3 of FASB Interpretation-29. The reference to paragraph 63(c) of APB-11 should be paragraph 62(c). There is no paragraph 63(c).*

Indefinite reversal criteria   The presumption that all undistributed earnings of a subsidiary or corporate joint venture will be eventually distributed to the parent may be overcome by sufficient evidence that the subsidiary or corporate joint venture has invested or will invest such earnings indefinitely, or that they will be remitted in a tax-free liquidation—all in accordance with a specific plan. In the event the plans change and earnings will be remitted in the forseeable future, the parent company should accrue as an expense of the current period the appropriate income tax expense. If the reverse occurs, where income taxes were accrued and the undistributed earnings will not be distributed in the foreseeable future, the parent company should adjust income tax expense of the current period. In either case, the adjustment of income tax expense should not be accounted for as an extraordinary item.

> *OBSERVATION: Under the provisions of the Tax Reform Act of 1984, qualified earnings of a Domestic International Sales Corpo-ration (DISC) that are not distributed to a stockholder(s), on or before December 31, 1984, are to be treated as previously taxed income, and thus, will be exempt from federal income taxes. As a result, deferred income taxes on undistributed earnings of a DISC that have been recorded on the books of a stockholder will have to be adjusted if the earnings are not expected to be distributed in a taxable transaction before January 1, 1985. FASB Technical Bulletin 84-2 provides that the adjustment to deferred taxes should be recognized as a reduction of income tax expense, in one interim period of the current year. The effect of the adjustment on income tax expense should be disclosed and may be shown as a separate component of income tax expense.*
>
> *FASB Technical Bulletin 84-2 is effective for financial statements and interim financial information issued after September 30, 1984, for fiscal years ending after July 18, 1984 (the enactment date of the Tax Reform Act of 1984). Earlier application is permitted, but not required. Interim financial information issued after September 30, 1984, for fiscal years ending after July 18, 1984, should be retroactively restated, if necessary.*

The indefinite reversal criteria for investments in common stock accounted for by the equity method depend upon those interests that control the investment. Only the controlling interest (50% or more) of an investment in common stocks accounted for by the equity method, can determine that undistributed earnings will be reinvested for an indefinite period. The fact that the equity method presumes that an investor has the ability to exercise significant influence over the investee if the investor owns 20% or more control, is irrelevant in considering the indefinite reversal criteria.

Corporate joint ventures may be permanent or have a limited life depending on the nature of the venture. GAAP (APB-18) require that corporate joint ventures, of less than 50% control, be accounted for by the equity method.

Changes in investment   An investment (usually 50% or more) in a subsidiary may change to the extent that a subsidiary relationship no longer exists, and the equity method (20% to 49% control) or the cost method (less than 20% control) must be applied. In the event that a subsidiary changes to an investment in common stock accounted for by the equity method, the investor should recognize income taxes on its share of the current earnings of the investee in accordance with the equity method. If, previous to the change in an investment from a subsidiary to one accounted for by the equity or cost method, the parent had not accrued income taxes because of the indefinite reversal criteria, it should then accrue income taxes on the undistributed earnings in the period that it becomes apparent that part or all of the undistributed earnings will be remitted. This accrual should not be accounted for as an extraordinary item.

Deferred income taxes resulting from undistributed earnings of a subsidiary, corporate joint venture, and an investment in common stock accounted for by the equity method should be considered in accounting for a sale or other disposition of the underlying investment.

An investment in common stock accounted for by the equity method may fall below the 20% ownership that is presumed to indicate significant control, or may rise to 50% or more, which indicates that it has become a subsidiary. If the investment becomes a subsidiary, the deferred income taxes, if any, previously accrued should be included in the income of the parent only as dividends are received that exceed the parent's share of earnings subsequent to the date of becoming a subsidiary. If the investment falls below 20% ownership, the deferred income taxes previously accrued should be included in income only as dividends are received that exceed the allocable share of earnings subsequent to the date the investment fell below 20%.

In the event of a sale or other disposition of an investment in common stock accounted for by the equity method, deferred taxes attributable to the investment should be taken into consideration.

Railroad gradings and tunnel bores   Income tax benefits resulting from the amortization of railroad gradings and tunnel bores are timing differences for which comprehensive interperiod tax allocation must be made (FASB Interpretation-18).

U.S. steamship companies Present promulgated GAAP do not cover deposits in capital construction funds or statutory reserves of U.S. steamship companies complying with the Merchant Marine Act of 1970.

Measuring timing differences Difficulties in measuring timing differences in these special areas do not justify ignoring the accrual of income taxes. Estimates and assumptions should be used that include all available related tax planning, tax credits, and deductions. Parent companies' income tax expense should also include a provision, if any, for taxes that would have been withheld if the undistributed earnings had been remitted as dividends.

The determination of whether the undistributed earnings of an investment in common stock accounted for by the equity method will be realized in dividends, the sale or other disposition, or a combination of both, must be made on the basis of the facts and circumstances of each individual investment. If it is determined that the undistributed earnings will be realized in dividends, the accrued income taxes should be based on any available dividend-received deduction, foreign-tax credit, and other tax credits or deductions that may be applicable in the circumstances. On the other hand, if the ultimate disposition will be realized by the sale of the investment, the accrued income taxes should be based on capital gain rates, if applicable, recognizing all other available credits and deductions.

The operating losses of a subsidiary, a joint venture, and an investment in common stock accounted for by the equity method are accounted for in the same manner as other operating losses previously mentioned.

Reporting the Effects of the Tax Reform Act of 1986

FASB Technical Bulletin 86-1 (FASB:TB 86-1), issued on October 27, 1986, provides guidance on recognizing and reporting the effects of the Tax Reform Act of 1986.

FASB:TB 86-1 specifies that the aggregate tax effects of any retroactive provision of the Tax Reform Act of 1986 should be recognized as a component of income tax expense and reported in the financial statements of the interim and annual periods that include the date of enactment of the Act (October 22, 1986). An enterprise should provide financial statement disclosure of the effects on income tax expense resulting from any retroactive provision of the Tax Reform Act of 1986.

An enterprise should not adjust its balance sheet amount of deferred charges or credits that were previously established in an annual period, prior to the effective date of the changes in the Act, except as required by existing pronouncements. In addition, an enterprise should not adjust the amount of net deferred tax credits that were previously offset by investment tax credits, even though the Tax Reform Act of 1986 specifies a reduction in the amount of the allowable carryforward for investment tax credits.

The prospective provisions of the Tax Reform Act of 1986 should not be recognized prior to their effective dates, except as required by existing pronouncements. The estimated annual effective tax rate should include the effect of any provision of the Tax Reform Act of 1986 that becomes effective during that annual period, beginning with the interim period that includes the effective date of the provision.

> **OBSERVATION**: *For the purposes of FASB Technical Bulletin 86-1, a retroactive provision includes any prospective provision of the Tax Reform Act of 1986 that is administratively implemented to be effective as of the beginning of an enterprise's fiscal year that is prior to October 22, 1986.*

FASB Technical Bulletin 86-1 is effective on October 22, 1986, for interim and annual periods ending on or after January 1, 1986. Previously issued financial information for such interim and annual periods should be restated to conform to the provisions of FASB Technical Bulletin 86-1, when such financial information is next reported.

Deferred Tax Method

The deferred tax method of allocating income taxes should be used (APB-11) and is considered the most useful and practical approach to interperiod allocation. The promulgated GAAP (APB-11) have rejected the use of other methods.

Under the deferred tax method, income taxes payable are computed twice: once on the amount that excludes any transaction causing a timing difference and once on the amount that includes the transaction causing a timing difference. The difference between the two income taxes payable is the deferred income tax for the period for that particular timing difference.

The promulgated GAAP (ABP-11) states that "The tax effect of a timing difference should be measured by the differential between income taxes computed with and without inclusion of the transaction creating the difference between taxable income and pretax accounting income." Taxable income is further defined as "the excess of revenues over deductions or the excess of deductions over revenue to be reported for income tax purposes for a period . . . except that deductions do not include loss carryforwards or loss carrybacks."

The following is an illustration of the with-and-without method of computing deferred income taxes as required by APB-11.

Assume the following facts for the XYZ Corporation for its calendar year ended December 31, 19XX:

- $362,500 allowable investment tax credit for the current year
- $1,000,000 of pretax financial accounting income (books)
- $200,000 of net timing differences which reduce taxable income
- 40% tax rate for the current period
- The maximum investment tax credit may not exceed the taxpayer's first $25,000 of tax liability, plus 90% of the tax liability over $25,000

Discussion

Income tax expense is computed on all taxable items included in pretax financial accounting income. In this example, all items included in financial accounting income are eventually taxable.

There are no permanent differences in this example. In any event, permanent differences do not affect subsequent periods because they do not reverse in future periods, and no interperiod tax allocation need be made to account for them. Therefore, if a permanent difference is taxable, it is included in computing income tax expense (books) for the period. If a permanent difference is nontaxable, it is excluded in computing income tax expense for financial accounting purposes.

The first computation in solving this example illustration is to determine income tax expense on pretax financial accounting income (books) and the current income tax liability on taxable income (tax return), as follows:

Income Tax Expense on Pretax Financial Accounting Income:

Pretax financial accounting income	$1,000,000
Rate of tax	40%
Income tax expense before allowable investment tax credit	400,000
Allowable investment tax credit [$25,000 plus 90% of ($400,000 less $25,000)]	362,500
Income tax expense (books)	$ 37,500

Current Income Tax Liability on Taxable Income:

Pretax financial accounting income	$1,000,000
Less: Timing difference	200,000
Taxable income	800,000
Rate of tax	40%
Income tax liability before allowable investment tax credit	320,000
Allowable investment tax credit [$25,000 plus 90% of ($320,000 less $25,000)]	290,500
Current income tax liability	$ 29,500

The $8,000 difference between income tax expense of $37,500 (books) and the current income tax liability of $29,500 (tax return) is the deferred tax expense on the net timing difference of $200,000, computed as follows:

Net timing difference	$ 200,000
Rate of tax	40%
Income tax expense before allowable investment tax credit	80,000
Allowable investment tax credit (90% of $80,000)	72,000
Deferred tax expense on timing difference	$ 8,000

The journal entry to record the income tax expense for the current period and the deferred taxes is:

Income tax expense—current	$29,500	
Income tax expense—deferred	8,000	
Current tax liability		$29,500
Deferred taxes		8,000

The provision for income taxes in the income statement for the current period would appear as follows:

Provision for income taxes:

Current	$29,500
Deferred	8,000
Total provision for income taxes	$37,500

Analysis of Solution:

From a practical standpoint, interperiod tax allocation is basically an accrual or prepayment process. In the above example, XYZ Corporation had $200,000 more pretax financial accounting income (books) than it showed on its tax return. Perhaps the reason for the difference was that for book income the straight-line method of depreciation was being used and for tax return purposes they used an accelerated method. The fact is that they showed $200,000 more income per books than on their tax return and for that reason taxes computed on book income was $8,000 more than that reflected on the tax return. The credit of $8,000 to deferred taxes is actually an accrual of income taxes which will have to be paid in the future when the timing difference reverses itself.

It must be realized that a timing difference can either increase or decrease taxable income. In the illustration of the XYZ Corporation, suppose that the $200,000 timing difference arose because of rental income collected in advance. Advance rental income is taxable when received for tax purposes, but would be excluded from financial accounting income (books) because it would not be income for the current period. In that case, pretax financial accounting income would only be $800,000 and taxable income $1,000,000. Instead of accruing the tax on the $200,000 timing difference, XYZ would in fact have to prepay it. The computations using the with-and-without method follow:

Income Tax Expense on Pretax Financial Accounting Income:

Pretax financial accounting income	$ 800,000
Rate of tax	40%
Income tax expense before allowable investment tax credit	320,000
Allowable investment tax credit [$25,000 plus 90% of ($320,000 less $25,000)]	290,500
Income tax expense	$ 29,500

Current Income Tax Liability on Taxable Income:

Pretax financial accounting income	$ 800,000
Add: Timing difference	200,000
Taxable income	1,000,000
Rate of tax	40%
Income tax liability before allowable investment tax credit	400,000
Allowable investment tax credit [$25,000 plus 90% of ($400,000 less $25,000)]	362,500
Current income tax liability	$ 37,500

The $8,000 difference between income tax expense of $29,500 (books) and the current income tax liability of $37,500 (tax return) is the deferred tax expense on the net timing difference of $200,000. However, this time the journal entry will reflect that the $8,000 of deferred taxes is actually a prepayment of future taxes, as follows:

Income tax expense—current	$37,500	
Deferred taxes	8,000	
Income tax expense—deferred		$ 8,000
Current tax liability		37,500

The provision for income taxes in the income statement for the current period would appear, as follows:

Provision for income taxes:

Current	$37,500
Deferred	(8,000)
Total provision for income taxes	$29,500

The *short-cut* approach which determines the deferred tax by applying the current tax rate to the transaction causing the timing difference works most of the time. However, in some instances involving the effect of the investment credit, foreign tax credit, and operating losses, the short-cut approach does not theoretically work.

Timing differences may be considered individually or in groups of similar timing differences, which may be further determined by the gross change or net change method. However, the tax effect in all cases is based on a differential calculation of taxes involved.

> **OBSERVATION:** *Where a company is subject to more than one tax rate, the U.S. tax rate is usually increased by an equivalent percent, to take into consideration taxes imposed by other jurisdictions.*

Individual method   The tax effect of a timing difference is computed separately on each timing difference.

Gross change method   For each group of similar timing differences a computation is made for the tax effects of originating differences based on the current tax rate, and for the tax effects of reversing differences at the tax rate reflected in the account.

Net change method   A single computation is made at current tax rates for the net cumulative tax effect of both originating and reversing differences occurring during a period for a particular similar group.

Groups of similar timing differences are determined on the basis of those arising from the same kind of transaction, such as depreciation, installment sales, and warranties.

Once a method for determining the tax effects of timing differences is selected, it must be consistently applied, because a change would probably require a consistency exception in the auditor's report.

Deferred taxes are amortized as the timing differences reverse in periods subsequent to their origination.

The total of all deferred federal income tax charges and all deferred federal income tax credits should be offset and the resulting net figure used for balance sheet purposes. (This does not include a claim of refund or offsets to future taxes arising from net operating loss carrybacks and carryforwards, which should be shown in separate accounts and classified as either current or noncurrent.)

Matching Concept

The principle of matching income tax expense with the related financial accounting income is the objective of comprehensive interperiod tax allocation.

ABC Construction Co. uses the completed-contract method for tax purposes and the percentage-of-completion method for financial accounting purposes. The realized gross profit recognized on one four-year contract was $5,000, $6,000, $7,000, and $12,000. Assuming a 50% tax rate in effect for the four years, tax allocation would be:

	1	*2*	*3*	*4*
Income	$5,000	$6,000	$7,000	$12,000
50% taxes	2,500	3,000	3,500	6,000
Net income	$2,500	$3,000	$3,500	$ 6,000

The journal entry the first three years was:

Income tax expense	$XXX	
Deferred taxes		$XXX

In the fourth year, when the contract was completed and appeared on the tax return, the journal entry was:

Income tax expense	$6,000	
Deferred taxes	9,000	
Income tax liability		$15,000

The matching concept includes accruing deferred taxes on undistributed earnings of subsidiaries, corporate joint ventures, and investment in common stock accounted for by the equity method. There is a presumption that these types of undistributed earnings will be paid, and deferred taxes should be accrued in the period such earnings are earned.

Control over the subsidiary, joint venture, or investment can determine that distributions of earnings will not be made or postponed indefinitely. Under these circumstances, deferred taxes need not be accrued.

Intraperiod Tax Allocation

Existing promulgated GAAP (APB-11) requires intraperiod tax allocation to contain the relationship between income tax expense and:

1. Income before extraordinary items
2. Extraordinary items
3. Prior-period adjustments
4. Direct entries to other stockholders' accounts

Intraperiod tax allocation merely involves associating the income tax expense involved with each of the above categories, which are usually shown *net of tax* in the income statement.

When an operating loss occurs, the tax effects should be associated with it in the period of occurrence.

Discounting Tax Allocation Accounts

Under present promulgated GAAP (APB-10), deferred taxes should not be accounted for on a discounted basis.

Offsetting—Taxes Payable

As a general rule the offsetting of assets and liabilities in the balance sheet is unacceptable unless a right of offset exists.

When securities that are specifically acceptable as payment for taxes are purchased, a right of offset exists, and such securities may be deducted from the related taxes payable on the balance sheet.

Income Taxes—Interim Periods

The promulgated GAAP for interim financial reporting (APB-28) requires that taxes for interim periods be determined in accordance with the existing promulgated GAAP for accounting for income taxes (APB-11). In addition, promulgated GAAP requires that an estimated annual effective tax rate be established and used, which includes anticipated investment tax credits, foreign tax credits, percentage depletion, capital gain rates, and all other available tax planning alternatives used in determining ordinary income or loss. At the end of each interim period during the year, this effective tax rate is revised, if necessary, to the best current estimates of the annual effective tax rate.

The interim-period tax is determined by applying the established estimated annual effective tax rate to the year-to-date ordinary income or loss, and subtracting the previous interim year-to-date tax on the ordinary income or loss. Ordinary income or loss is defined as income or loss from continuing operations before a provision for income taxes, excluding significant unusual or nonrecurring items. This excludes extraordinary items, discontinued operations, and cumulative effects of changes in an accounting principle. Income tax is defined to include both current and deferred taxes.

The estimated annual effective tax rate shall include only the tax benefit of a loss that has already been realized, or future realization is assured beyond any reasonable doubt. Therefore the year-to-date tax benefit of a loss shall not exceed benefits that have already been realized or those for which future realization is assured beyond any reasonable doubt.

The estimated annual effective tax rate should include an adjustment for existing net deferred credits, if an estimated ordinary loss is projected for a fiscal year or the year-to-date ordinary loss exceeds the entire projected loss for the year, and if all or part of the tax benefit of the loss will not be realized or realization is not assured beyond a reasonable doubt. The adjustment to the existing net deferred credits is the lesser of:

1. The unrecognized tax benefits of the loss
2. The net deferred tax credits that would otherwise be amortized during the carryforward period of the loss

Adjustments to net deferred credits should be included in computing the maximum tax benefit for year-to-date amounts.

The adjustment to the net deferred credits should be cumulatively reinstated in subsequent periods at the then current tax rates when the loss carryforward is realized in whole or in part.

The following illustration reflects the computation of the estimated annual effective tax rate and its application.

A business estimates $1,000,000 of ordinary income for the year and anticipated realizable tax credits of $100,000. The income tax rate is 50%. Seasonable patterns in the fourth quarter assure the realization of the tax benefits beyond any reasonable doubt.

Tax on ordinary income (50%)	$500,000
Less: Anticipated credits	100,000
Net tax to be provided	$400,000
Estimated annual effective tax rate ($400,000 required tax divided by $1,000,000 income)	40%

Based on the estimated annual effective tax rate, the quarterly computations of taxes might appear as:

Period	Estimated Results Quarter	Estimated Results Cumulative	Estimated Tax Rate	Provision For Taxes Quarter	Provision For Taxes Cumulative
1	($ 200,000)	($ 200,000)	40%	($ 80,000)	($ 80,000)
2	100,000	(100,000)	40%	40,000	(40,000)
3	150,000	50,000	40%	60,000	20,000
4	950,000	1,000,000	40%	380,000	400,000
	$1,000,000			$400,000	

If a reliable estimate cannot be made for the annual effective tax rate, the actual year-to-date annual effective tax rate should be used. If a reliable estimate of part of the ordinary income or loss, or of the related tax (or benefit), cannot be made, it should be reported in the interim period in which it actually occurs.

Significant, unusual, or extraordinary items that are reported separately net of their related tax effects are recognized in the interim period in which they occur. The related tax on these items is the difference between the tax on year-to-date ordinary income including the item and the tax on year-to-date ordinary income excluding the item.

Assume the same facts as those in the preceding illustration; assume also that the business incurs a tax-deductible significant unusual extraordinary loss in the third quarter of $200,000, the benefit (50%) for which is assured beyond any reasonable doubt, because the loss can be carried back.

Since the estimated annual effective tax rate is unaffected under these circumstances, the tax on ordinary income or loss is the same, and the computation of the estimated annual effective tax rate is not reproduced.

Period	Income Ordinary	Income Extraordinary	Provision for Taxes Ordinary	Provision for Taxes Extraordinary
1	($ 200,000)		($ 80,000)	
2	100,000		40,000	
3	150,000	($200,000)	60,000	($100,000)
4	950,000		$380,000	
	$1,000,000	($200,000)	$400,000	($100,000)

If the $200,000 tax-deductible unusual extraordinary loss in the third quarter was not realizable beyond any reasonable doubt, it would appear only in the third and succeeding periods to the extent that it could offset ordinary income for the year to date.

The tax benefit of a loss from significant, unusual, and extraordinary items or discontinued operations shall not be recognized until it is realized or realization is assured beyond a reasonable doubt. Realization is assured beyond a reasonable doubt by:

1. Offsetting year-to-date ordinary income
2. Offsetting taxable income from unusual, extraordinary, discontinued operations, or items credited directly to stockholders' equity accounts
3. Carrying back the loss to prior years
4. Future taxable income that is almost certain to occur shortly, especially from seasonable patterns of revenue

If all or part of such losses are not realized, and previously reported net deferred tax credits exist that would have been amortized during the carryforward period, the net deferred tax credits should be amortized in the same manner as previously stated.

The provision for taxes on income or loss from operations of a discontinued segment prior to measurement date, and the gain or loss on disposal of the discontinued operations, is determined (as stated earlier) by the difference between the tax on year-to-date ordinary income or loss including such items and the tax on year-to-date ordinary income or loss excluding the items. Thereafter the provision for taxes shall not be recomputed, but should be divided into two components: (1) for the remaining ordinary income or loss and (2) for the income or loss from operations of the discontinued segment. A revised estimated annual effective tax rate and resulting tax benefits is then recomputed for the remaining ordinary income or loss.

The following illustration depicts how a discontinued segment is accounted for:

A business estimates ordinary income of $1,000,000 for the year and tax credits of $100,000 that are realizable beyond any reasonable doubt. Income tax rates are 50%. The estimated annual effective tax rate is as follows:

Tax on pretax ordinary income (50%)	$500,000
Less: Anticipated credits	(100,000)
Net tax to be provided	$400,000
Estimated annual effective tax rate ($400,000 ÷ $1,000,000)	40%

The first two quarters appear as:

	Estimated Results			Provision for Taxes	
Period	Quarter	Cumulative	Rate	Quarter	Cumulative
1	$200,000	$200,000	40%	$ 80,000	$ 80,000
2	250,000	450,000	40%	100,000	180,000

During the third quarter the decision to discontinue a division of the company was made. The results of operations for the continuing divisions of the company and for the discontinued division are as follows:

	Revised	Discontinued Division	
Quarter	Ordinary Income	Operations	Loss on Disposal
1	$ 250,000	($ 50,000)	
2	350,000	(100,000)	
3	500,000	(100,000)	($550,000)
4 (Estimated)	500,000		
Total for Year	$1,600,000	($250,000)	($550,000)

The only assumptions that have changed for the estimated annual effective tax rate is that $20,000 of the $100,000 in tax credits was related to the discontinued operations. The recomputation of the estimated annual effective tax rate is:

Tax on ordinary income (50% of $1,600,000)	$800,000
Less: Anticipated tax credits	80,000
Net tax to be provided	$720,000
Estimated annual effective tax rate ($720,000 ÷ $1,600,000)	45%

The quarterly amounts, based on the revised ordinary income and estimated annual effective tax rate are:

Period	Estimated Results Quarter	Cumulative	Rate	Provision for Taxes Quarter	Cumulative
1	$ 250,000	$250,000	45%	$112,500	$112,500
2	350,000	600,000	45%	157,500	270,000
3	500,000	1,100,000	45%	225,000	495,000
4	500,000	1,600,000	45%	225,000	720,000
	$1,600,000			$720,000	

The computation of the tax benefit attributable to the discontinued division for the first two quarters is the difference between the tax on year-to-date ordinary income or loss including the discontinued division, and the tax on the year-to-date ordinary income or loss, excluding the discontinued division, as follows:

Quarter	Tax on Ordinary Income Previously Computed	Recomputed	Tax Benefit, Discontinued Div.
1	$ 80,000	$112,500	($32,500)
2	100,000	157,500	(57,500)
Totals	$180,000	$270,000	($90,000)

The third-quarter tax benefits for (1) the loss from operations and (2) the provision for the disposal of the discontinued division are computed on the revised estimated annual income with and without the effects of the discontinued division, as follows:

	Discontinued Division Loss on Operations	Loss on Disposal
Estimated revised ordinary income	$1,600,000	$1,600,000
Discontinued division loss on operations	250,000	
Discontinued division loss on disposal		550,000
Total	$1,350,000	$1,050,000

Tax at regular tax rate (50%)	$ 675,000	$ 525,000
Anticipated credits—continuing operations	(80,000)	(80,000)
Taxes—after effect of discontinued division	$ 595,000	$ 445,000
Previously computed taxes for year	720,000	720,000
Tax benefit—discontinued division	($ 125,000)	($ 275,000)
Less: Tax benefits recognized in first two quarters	(90,000)	—
Tax benefit for third quarter	($ 35,000)	($ 275,000)

The $20,000 in tax credits related to the discontinued division have not been recognized on the assumption that they will not be realized.

The tax benefit of a prior year's operating loss carryforward is recognized as an extraordinary item (APB-11) to the extent that offsetting income is available in each interim period.

The cumulative effect of a change in an accounting principle on the beginning-of-the-year retained earnings is reported in the first interim period of the fiscal year (FASB-3). The related income tax effects are computed as though the new accounting principle had been applied retroactively to all affected prior periods (APB-20). When the change is made in other than the first interim period, the prechange interim periods are restated by applying the newly adopted accounting principle to those prechange interim periods. The tax or tax benefits for the prechange interim periods is then recomputed on the year-to-date and annual estimated amounts, modified only for the effect of the change in accounting principle.

Businesses subject to tax in more than one taxing jurisdiction shall compute one overall estimated annual effective tax rate, except:

1. Ordinary income (loss) and related tax (benefit) shall be excluded in computing the estimated annual effective tax rate and interim-period tax (benefit) in any jurisdiction that anticipates an ordinary loss for the year, or has an ordinary loss for the year-to-date, for which a tax benefit cannot be recognized.

2. Ordinary income (loss) and related tax (benefit) shall be excluded in computing the estimated annual effective tax rate and interim-period tax (benefit) in any foreign jurisdiction

where reliable estimates cannot be made. In this event, the tax (benefit) on ordinary income (loss) shall be recognized in the interim period in which it is reported.

Changes resulting from new tax laws should be reflected in a revised estimated annual effective tax rate for the first interim period affected.

Full disclosure should be made of any significant difference in the usual relationship between income tax expense and pretax accounting income, arising from the application of the promulgated GAAP for accounting for income taxes in interim periods.

> **OBSERVATION**: *FASB Technical Bulletin 79-9 reaffirms the fact that the effect of a change in tax rates during an interim period be reflected in a revised estimated annual effective tax rate. The revised annual effective tax rate is applied to pretax income for the year to date at the end of the interim period in which the change in tax rate took effect. If the effects are material, previous interim periods of the current fiscal year should be restated and any adjustment accounted for as a prior-period adjustment in accordance with FASB-16.*

Disclosure

Balance sheet accounts relating to tax allocations are of two types:

1. Deferred charges and deferred credits arising from timing differences
2. Claim of refunds for past taxes or offsets to future taxes arising from the tax effects of carrybacks and carryforwards

Deferred income tax charges and credits must be disclosed in classified balance sheets as either current or noncurrent. APB-11 requires that all current amounts (debits and credits) be presented in the balance sheet as one net current amount and that all noncurrent amounts (debits and credits) be presented in one net noncurrent amount. The problem that arises is determining when a deferred tax charge or credit is current and when it is noncurrent. FASB-37 (Balance Sheet Classification of Deferred Income Taxes) contains the criteria that must be used in determining whether a deferred tax charge or credit is current or noncurrent. The general rule depends on whether or not a deferred tax charge or credit is related to an asset or liability. If a relationship exists between a deferred tax charge or credit and an asset or a liability, then the current or noncurrent classification is exactly the same as the related asset or liability. If no relationship exists between the deferred tax charge or credit and an asset or liability, then the current or noncurrent classification is determined by reference to the normal operating cycle of the business. The timing differences that do reverse within the normal operating cycle of a business are classified as current and those timing differences that reverse after the normal operating cycle period are classified as noncurrent (FASB-37).

A deferred tax charge or credit is related to an asset or liability if reduction of the asset or liability would cause the underlying timing difference to reverse. In other words, the timing difference automatically reverses as a result of the reduction in the related asset or liability. A reduction of the related asset can arise as a result of amortization, sale, or other realization of the asset. A reduction of the related liability can arise as a result of amortization, or other satisfaction of the liability. The following examples demonstrate how deferred tax charges and credits are classified for balance sheet presentation:

1. For tax purposes, a company uses an accelerated method of depreciation for a fixed asset, but for financial statement purposes the straight-line method is used.

   The sale of the fixed asset will cause a reduction in the fixed asset which will automatically reverse the underlying timing differences. In other words, the related timing differences will reverse as a result of the reduction in the fixed asset. Thus, the deferred income taxes that resulted from the two depreciation methods are related to the fixed asset. In this event, the deferred income taxes are classified exactly the same as the related fixed asset. If the fixed asset is classified noncurrent then the income taxes must also be classified as noncurrent. If the fixed asset was classified as 20% current and 80% noncurrent, then the deferred income taxes must be classified as 20% current and 80% noncurrent.

2. For tax purposes a company uses the installment sales method, but for financial statement purposes, sales are reported when the goods are delivered.

   The collection of the installment receivables is a reduction of the asset which causes the underlying timing differences to reverse. Thus, the deferred income taxes are related to the installment receivables (an asset) and they both must be classified exactly the same. If 30% of the installment receivables are current because of the normal operating cycle of the business then 30% of the related deferred taxes are also classified as current.

3. For tax purposes, a company uses the completed-contract method for reporting profits on construction contracts, but for financial statement purposes the percentage-of-completion method is used.

    The timing differences arising between the two methods of reporting profits will only reverse when the contracts are completed. Billing, collection, or retention of funds do not cause the timing differences to reverse. Thus, the deferred income taxes are not related to an asset or liability. Under these circumstances the deferred taxes are classified as current or noncurrent based on when they reverse. Those timing differences which reverse within the normal operating cycle of the business are classified as current and the balance is classified as noncurrent.

Claims for refunds and offsets to future taxes from the tax effects of carrybacks and carryforwards are classified as current or noncurrent on the basis of their expected realization during the current operating cycle.

The amounts and expiration dates of all operating-loss carryforwards not previously recognized should be disclosed, including those amounts which will be credited to deferred tax accounts.

All other significant unused deductions or credits including expiration dates should be fully disclosed.

The components of income tax expense for the period should be disclosed in the results of operations as:

1. Taxes estimated to be payable
2. Tax effects arising from timing differences
3. Tax effects of operating losses

In addition, as stated earlier, the income tax expense should be allocated to (1) income before extraordinary items, (2) extraordinary items, and (3) tax effects of any prior-period adjustments (see Intraperiod Tax Allocation section).

The tax benefit of an operating-loss carryforward that has not been recognized previously should be reported as an extraordinary item in the period in which it is realized.

The amount of tax effects of prior-period adjustments and direct entries to stockholders' equity should be disclosed.

Deferred taxes should not be included in the stockholders' equity section of a balance sheet or in the valuation of assets or liabilities.

Significant differences between taxable income and pretax accounting income and material variations between income tax expense and pretax accounting income should be fully disclosed unless apparent in the financial statements or from the nature of the entity's business activities.

Where income taxes have not been accrued on undistributed earnings because of the indefinite reversal criteria, the financial statements should contain a declaration of intention to reinvest the undistributed earnings or a statement that they will be remitted in the form of a tax-free liquidation, whichever is applicable. In addition, the cumulative amount of undistributed earnings for which income taxes have not been recognized should be disclosed.

United Kingdom Tax Benefits (FASB-31)

Recent changes in the tax law of the United Kingdom have created a potential six-year recapture period for the *stock relief* deduction. For companies affected by this new legislation, any tax benefits arising from the stock relief deduction shall be deferred, unless it is *probable* that recapture of the tax benefits will not occur during the six-year recapture period (FASB-31). If, in a subsequent period, it is determined that a previously recorded deferred tax benefit will not be recaptured because of a change in circumstances, then the tax benefit should be recognized in that period as a reduction of income tax expense. The reverse is also true. If, in a subsequent period, it is determined that a previously recognized tax benefit will be recaptured because of a change in circumstances, it should be deferred in that period by increasing income tax expense (FASB-31).

When the above requirements are initially included in interim financial statements, the recognition of previously deferred tax benefits shall be reported as an item of income tax expense for that interim period only, and shall not be classified as an extraordinary item. For subsequent interim reporting periods, adjustments due to changed circumstances shall be included as an adjustment of the estimated annual effective tax rate for the interim period in which circumstances change.

Tax benefits that are deferred under the provisions of FASB-31 are not timing differences and should be classified on the balance sheet based on the estimated recapture period (FASB-37, Balance Sheet Classification of Deferred Income Taxes).

Full disclosure must be made in the financial statements or footnotes thereto if a significant variation in the customary relationship between income tax expense and pretax accounting income occurs as a result of compliance with FASB-31.

GLOSSARY

Deferred taxes   Tax effects to be charged to expense in subsequent periods

Income tax expense   That amount of income tax chargeable to the current period, whether or not currently payable (or refundable)

Income tax liability   The amount of income tax due as calculated under the provision of the U.S. Internal Revenue Code

Income taxes   Taxes based on income as determined by the provisions of the U.S. Internal Revenue Code, as well as other foreign, franchising, state, and local taxes based on income

Indefinite reversal criteria   Sufficient evidence that a subsidiary has invested or will invest its undistributed earnings indefinitely, or such earnings will be remitted in a tax-free liquidation (In this event, income taxes need not be accrued on the undistributed earnings.)

Interperiod tax allocation   The process of using tax deferrals and accruals to balance the tax liability and expense among periods

Intraperiod tax allocation   The process of apportioning the tax expense within a period to the proper accounts, namely, income before extraordinary items, extraordinary items, prior-period adjustments, and direct entries to equity accounts

"Net-of-tax presentation"   Tax effects recognized under interperiod tax allocation which are considered to be adjustments of the valuation of the related asset or liability

Permanent differences   Differences between the taxable income and the pretax accounting income that are caused by different rules of recognition of items affecting net income (Permanent differences do not reverse themselves in subsequent periods.)

Pretax accounting income   Profit or loss for a period, exclusive of income tax expense, as determined under the guidelines of GAAP

Tax carrybacks or carryforwards   Losses in years other than the current year that can be applied to prior years (carrybacks) or future years (carryforwards) to reduce net taxable income

Tax effects   Differences between the tax liability and the tax expense that are caused by timing differences. Included in tax effects are tax carrybacks and carryforwards and taxable adjustments to equity accounts

Taxable income   Net excess (or deficiency) of revenues over deductions (not including tax carrybacks or carryforwards) as specified in the Code

Timing differences   Differences between the taxable income and the pretax accounting income that are caused by different periods of recognition of items affecting net income. Timing differences reverse themselves in subsequent periods, so the net long-term timing difference is zero.

INCOME TAXES
IMPORTANT NOTICE

In December 1987, FASB-96 (Accounting for Income Taxes) was issued to supersede APB-11 (Accounting for Income Taxes). FASB-96 was scheduled to become effective for fiscal years beginning after December 15, 1988, and earlier adoption was encouraged.

As a result of numerous complaints from major industrial enterprises regarding the complexity and cost of implementing the provisions of FASB-96, the Financial Accounting Standards Board (FASB) issued FASB-100, deferring the effective date of FASB-96 by one year to December 15, 1989. FASB-103 granted a further deferral of two years to December 15, 1991, with earlier application encouraged.

Two Exposure Drafts (ED) are outstanding as of the date of this publication. One of the outstanding EDs would defer the effective date of FASB-96 for one more year, until fiscal years beginning after December 15, 1992, with earlier application permitted. The other outstanding ED would supersede FASB-96 and would be effective for fiscal years beginning after December 15, 1992. If the FASB meets its own schedule for issuing final Statements based on these two outstanding EDs, FASB-96 will be superseded without ever having gone into effect, although some enterprises have elected its early application.

Until the FASB issues a new Statement superseding FASB-96, an enterprise may account for income taxes by (i) continuing to apply the provisions of APB-11 or (ii) electing early adoption of FASB-96.

This edition of the *GAAP Guide* contains coverage of both APB-11 and FASB-96. The provisions of APB-11 appear in chapter 19.01a and the provisions of FASB-96 appear in chapter 19.01b.

Highlights of the outstanding Exposure Draft are summarized at the end of chapter 19.01b and are noted in the Disclosure Index.

Because of the status of APB-11 and FASB-96, it was also necessary to include two chapters entitled "Investment Tax

Credit" in this issue of the *GAAP Guide*. Chapter 25.01a contains coverage of the accounting standards relating to investment tax credits as they existed prior to the amendments by FASB-96. Chapter 25.01a should be used by those enterprises that are continuing to apply the provisions of APB-11 to account for income taxes. Chapter 25.01b contains coverage of the accounting standards relating to investment tax credits as they existed after the amendments by FASB-96. Chapter 25.01b should be used by those enterprises that are electing early adoption of the provisions of FASB-96.

INCOME TAXES

Overview

FASB-96 supersedes APB-11 (Accounting for Income Taxes) and establishes new accounting and reporting standards for federal, state, local, and foreign income taxes. The provisions of FASB-96 are extended to (a) activities of not-for-profit organizations that are subject to income taxes and (b) regulated enterprises that meet the criteria for application of FASB-71 (Accounting for the Effects of Certain Types of Regulation). All domestic and foreign operations of an enterprise that are consolidated, combined, or accounted for by the equity method (APB-18) are covered by FASB-96. Other promulgated GAAP related to accounting for income taxes and covered in this chapter are:

APB-10 (paragraph 6), Tax Allocation Accounts—Discounts

APB-10 (paragraph 7), Offsetting of Securities Against Taxes Payable

APB-23, Accounting for Income Taxes—Special Areas

FASB Interpretation-18, Accounting for Income Taxes in Interim Periods

APB-10 was issued in December 1966, and paragraph 6 of that pronouncement addresses the problem of whether long-term tax allocation accounts should or should not be determined on a discounted basis (present value) as recommended by Accounting Research Study No. 9. APB-10 concludes that, pending further consideration of the broader aspects of discounting, deferred taxes should not be accounted for on a discounted basis.

Paragraph 7 of APB-10 addresses the problem of whether the offsetting of assets and liabilities in the balance sheet is or is not permissible. APB-10 concludes that unless a legal right of offset exists, offsetting of assets and liabilities in the balance sheet is not permitted by GAAP. However, when securities that are specifically acceptable as payment for taxes are purchased, a right of offset exists, and such securities may be deducted from the related taxes payable on the balance sheet.

APB-23 addresses the recognition of deferred taxes on the (a) undistributed earnings of a subsidiary, (b) investment in corporate joint ventures, (c) bad debt reserves of savings and loan associations, and (d) policyholders' surplus of stock life insurance companies. On including the undistributed earnings of a subsidiary in the pretax financial accounting income of a parent company, either through consolidation or accounting for the investment by the equity methods, APB-23 concludes that the results will produce, depending on the intent and actions of the parent company, either (i) a temporary difference, (ii) a difference that does not reverse until indefinite future periods, or (iii) a combination of both types of differences. APB-23 is discussed in further detail later in this chapter.

FASB Interpretation-18 provides guidance in accounting for income taxes in interim periods in accordance with the provisions of APB-28 (Interim Financial Reporting). APB-28 generally provides that an estimated annual effective tax rate be used by an enterprise to determine interim period income tax provisions. Income taxes for interim periods is discussed in more detail later in this chapter.

The following items are specifically *excluded* from the requirements of FASB-96:

a. *Accounting for the investment tax credit (ITC)*—APB-2 and APB-4 remain the current GAAP addressing the ITC. Under APB-2 and APB-4, the deferral method and flow-through method are both considered acceptable in accounting for the ITC. The deferral method requires that the ITC be amortized to income over the productive life of the acquired property. The flow-through method requires that the ITC be accounted for as a reduction of taxes for the period in which the credit arises.

b. *Discounting in income taxes*—Under APB-10, the present GAAP on discounting tax allocation accounts, deferred taxes should not be accounted for on a discounted basis.

c. *Allocation of income taxes*—FASB-96 does not address the allocation of income taxes among components of a business enterprise, other than the specific disclosures required by FASB-96.

d. *Accounting for income taxes in interim periods*—Except for the effects of enacted changes in tax laws or rates, FASB-96 does not affect APB-28, the present GAAP on interim period income tax accounting.

FASB-96 does not amend the requirements for the recognition of deferred taxes specified by APB-23 (Accounting for Income Taxes—Special Areas), which addresses (a) the undistributed earnings of a subsidiary, (b) investments in corporate joint ventures, (c) the bad debt reserves of savings and loan associations, and (d) the policy-holders' surplus of stock life insurance companies. In addition, FASB-96 (a) does not address recognition of deferred taxes for deposits in statutory reserve funds by U.S. steamship companies, (b) does not amend accounting for leverage leases as required by FASB-13 (Accounting for Leases) and FASB Interpretation-21 (Accounting for Leases in a Business Combination), and (c) prohibits recognition of a deferred tax liability or asset related to goodwill.

> **OBSERVATION:** *The FASB acknowledged that accounting for income taxes related to leveraged leases under the provisions of FASB-13 (Accounting for Leases) and FASB Interpretation-21 (Accounting for Leases in a Business Combination) is not consistent with the requirements of FASB-96. The FASB decided not to separately address accounting for income taxes pertaining to leveraged leases without complete reconsideration of the entire subject of leveraged leases.*

Background

The major criticism of the old rules on accounting for income taxes was the difficulty in applying the provisions of APB-11. FASB-96 (Accounting for Income Taxes) contains the new rules that are intended to increase the comparability of financial statements and reduce the complexity of accounting for income taxes. Although comparability of financial statements has been substantially achieved by FASB-96, the complexity of applying the rules still remains. Most enterprises will be required to keep more detailed records to support their deferred tax calculations than they are presently maintaining. Some enterprises may have to allocate much more time and effort to their tax planning strategies in order to maximize net deferred tax assets. However, as a practical matter, many of the complex calculations may become unnecessary based on the concept of materiality, but the prospects of having to make those calculations for all material income taxes imposed by all taxing jurisdictions could unnerve the most competent accounting professional.

FASB-96 states that the objective of accounting for income taxes on an accrual basis is to recognize the amount of current and deferred taxes payable or refundable at the date of the financial statements (a) as a result of all events that have been recognized in the financial statements and (b) as measured by the provisions of enacted tax laws. The old rules did not contain an objective of accounting for income taxes. Instead, APB-11 addressed the "principal problem" in accounting for income taxes. This was simply the fact that some transactions affected the determination of net income for financial accounting purposes in one reporting period and the computation of taxable income and income taxes payable in a different reporting period. APB-11 concluded that the amount of income taxes payable for a period does not necessarily represent the appropriate income tax expense for financial accounting purposes in that same period. Even if the new rules do not specifically say so, this conclusion still applies.

FASB-96 requires a *liability approach* to accounting for income taxes while prior GAAP (APB-11) required a *deferred approach*. The liability approach places emphasis on the accuracy of the balance sheet while the deferred approach emphasizes the correctness of the income statement. Under the liability approach, deferred taxes are computed based on the tax rates in effect for the periods in which *temporary differences* (*timing differences* under the old rules) are expected to reverse. An annual adjustment of the deferred tax liability or asset is made through the income statement for any subsequent changes in enacted tax rates.

Although the new rules are effective for fiscal years beginning on or after December 16, 1989, enterprises may elect an earlier adoption date. As a result of the lower tax rates enacted by the 1986 Tax Reform Act, most enterprises applying FASB-96 will have a substantial decrease in their deferred tax liability with a corresponding increase in income. If earlier adoption is elected, the increase in income could be included in 1987 as the cumulative effect of a change in an accounting principle.

It is important that an enterprise determine whether or not the data necessary for the complex deferred tax calculations required by FASB-96 can be easily obtained from its present record-keeping systems. Also, an enterprise must decide whether it is advantageous or not to make an early adoption of FASB-96, and whether it should restate its financial statements or report the adoption of FASB-96 by the *cumulative effect* method in accordance with APB-20 (Accounting Changes).

Differences in Pretax Financial Income and Taxable Income

One of the basic principles in accounting is that business entities are presumed to continue in existence unless liquidation is imminent (going-concern principle). Thus, a business currently subject to income taxes is expected to pay such taxes in the future. Income tax expense is an important determinant of net income and must be identified and measured with the appropriate accounting periods.

Because of the differences that arise between accounting standards (GAAP) and prevailing tax laws, the amount of an enterprise's taxable income and pretax financial accounting income for the same period is different. As a result, the amount of income tax liability (or refund) based on prevailing tax laws will be different from the amount of income tax liability (or refund) based on pretax financial accounting income. A difference between the amount of taxable income and the amount of pretax financial accounting income for the year may result from any of the following types of transactions:

- Income is included in taxable income after it has already been included in financial accounting income.

  Example: Installment sales may be reported for tax purposes as they are collected, but for financial accounting income purposes, the total income from the installment sale is recognized in the period the sale is made. Thus, collections on the installment sale are included in taxable income, after the entire sale has been recognized in financial accounting income in the year in which the sale was made.

- Income is included in taxable income before it is included in financial accounting income.

  Example: Under prevailing tax law, rents collected in advance must be included in taxable income, but such rents are recognized and included in financial accounting income only in the periods in which they are earned in accordance with GAAP.

- Expenses are deducted in computing taxable income after they have already been deducted in computing financial accounting income.

  Example: Under prevailing tax law, a provision for estimated product warranty is not deductible in computing taxable income, but such a provision is deductible in computing financial accounting income of the year in which the related sale is made.

- Expenses are deducted in computing taxable income before they are deducted in computing financial accounting income.

Example: Under prevailing tax law, an accelerated depreciation method may be used in computing taxable income, but in computing financial accounting income, the straight-line method may be used to more properly match revenue with expired costs.

Differences between accounting standards and prevailing tax laws may also create a difference between the tax base of an asset or liability and the reported amount of the same asset or liability in the financial statements. Sometimes this type of difference accumulates over more than one year. Each of the following results in a difference between the tax basis of an asset or liability and the reported amount of the same asset or liability in the financial statements:

- The tax basis of a depreciable asset is reduced by a tax credit.

  Example: Under prevailing tax law, a taxpayer may elect to take either (i) the full amount of its ACRS deduction (depreciation) and a reduced investment tax credit, or (b) the full investment tax credit and a reduced amount of ACRS deduction. In either circumstance, for financial reporting purposes, the amount recovered in the future for the asset will exceed the asset's remaining tax basis and the excess amount is taxable at the time the asset is recovered.

- Investment tax credit is accounted for by the deferral method in accordance with APB-2.

  Example: Under the deferral method allowed by APB-2, the cost of an asset is reduced by the amount of its related investment tax credit (ITC), and for financial reporting purposes, the amount of the ITC may be reported as deferred income. In this circumstance, for financial reporting purposes, the amount recovered in the future for the reduced asset will be less than the asset's remaining tax basis and the difference is tax deductible at the time the asset is recovered.

- The reporting currency and functional currency are the same in a foreign operation.

  Example: Under FASB-52 (Foreign Currency Translation), when the reporting currency and the functional currency are the same, historical exchange rates are used to remeasure certain assets and liabilities from the foreign currency into U.S. dollars. When a change occurs in exchange rates, a difference will arise between the foreign tax basis of those assets and liabilities and the foreign currency equivalent of their U.S. dollar historical cost. That difference, for foreign tax purposes, will become either taxable or deductible at the time of recovery and settlement of the reported amounts of those assets and liabilities.

- An inflation adjustment (indexing) that is required by a specific tax jurisdiction increases the tax basis of an asset.

  Example: An inflation adjustment of a depreciable or other asset may be required by a particular tax jurisdiction. When this occurs, future depreciation deductions for tax purposes and gain or loss on sale of the asset are based on the asset's inflation-adjusted tax basis. For financial reporting purposes, the amount recovered in the future for the asset will be less than the asset's remaining tax basis and the difference is tax deductible at the time the asset is recovered.

- Differences arise between values assigned and tax bases in purchase business combinations.

  Example: Under APB-16 (Business Combinations), differences usually arise between the tax bases of the assets and liabilities acquired in a business combination accounted for by the purchase method and the fair values assigned to those same assets and liabilities. Those differences, for financial reporting purposes, will become either taxable or deductible at the time of recovery and settlement of the reported amounts of the assets and liabilities.

Temporary Differences

Under FASB-96, differences that arise between the amount of taxable income and the amount of pretax financial accounting income for a period and/or differences between the tax basis of an asset or liability and the reported amount of that same asset or liability in the financial statements are collectively referred to as *temporary differences*. Under the provisions of FASB-96, temporary differences include what were previously referred to as *timing differences* under prior GAAP (APB-11), and also include other differences that arise between recorded amounts of assets and liabilities and their tax bases.

Appendix E of FASB-96 defines a temporary differences as, "A difference between the tax basis of an asset or liability and its reported amount in the financial statements that will result in taxable or deductible amounts in future years when the reported amount of the asset or liability is recovered or settled, respectively."

> **OBSERVATION**: *It is logical to assume that a temporary difference must be related to, and/or identified with, an asset or liability since the definition of a temporary difference in Appendix E of FASB-96 specifically states that "a temporary difference is a difference between the tax basis of an asset or liability and its reported amount. . ." Apparently, the definition is contradictory, because it goes on to say: "Some temporary differences cannot be identified with a particular asset or liability for financial reporting, but those temporary differences (a) result from events that have been recognized in the financial statements and (b) will result in taxable or deductible amounts in future years based on provisions in the tax law."*

A temporary difference is related to, or identified with, an asset or liability if reduction of that asset or liability would cause an increase or decrease in the amount of the temporary difference. In other words, the amount of the temporary difference would automatically increase or decrease as a result of the reduction in the related asset or liability. A reduction of the related asset can arise as a result of amortization, sale, or other realization of the asset. A reduction of the related liability can arise as a result of the amortization or other satisfaction of the liability. The following examples demonstrate how a temporary difference can be related to, or identified with, an asset or liability:

Example 1—For tax purposes, a company uses an accelerated method of depreciation for a fixed asset; but for financial statement purposes, the straight-line method is used.

Discussion—The sale of the fixed asset will cause a reduction in the fixed asset which will automatically decrease the underlying timing difference. In other words, the related temporary difference will reverse and become a taxable amount as a result of the reduction in the fixed asset. Thus, the temporary difference that resulted from the use of the two depreciation methods is related to a fixed asset.

Example 2—For tax purposes a company uses the installment sales method, but for financial statement purposes, sales are reported when the goods are delivered.

Discussion—The amount of the installment receivable (an asset) is reduced by the amount of the collections that results in a decrease in the amount of the related temporary difference. Thus, the temporary difference that resulted from the use of the installment sales method for tax purposes is related to an asset.

Example 3—For tax purposes, a company uses the completed contract method for reporting profits on construction contracts, but for financial statement purposes the percentage-of-completion method is used.

Discussion—The temporary difference (income on the contracts) that arises between the two methods of reporting profits will only become taxable (reverse) when the contracts are completed. Interim billing, collection, or retention of funds related to the contracts do not affect the temporary differences. Thus, the temporary difference between the two methods of reporting long-term construction contracts is not related to any asset or liability.

Permanent differences   Some differences between pretax financial accounting income and taxable income do not reverse themselves in subsequent periods. They arise from special tax laws regarding exempt income, dividend received exclusions, and certain other special deductions. Permanent differences are either (a) nontaxable, (b) nondeductible, or (c) special tax allowances. These differences are not considered temporary differences because they do not result in tax consequences and do not affect subsequent periods.

> **OBSERVATION:** *Income tax expense per books and income tax liability per tax return are both calculated on taxable items only. Thus, permanent differences are simply ignored in computing both income tax expense per books and income tax liability per the tax return.*

Bad debt allowances of savings and loan associations, and policyholders' surplus of stock life insurance companies that create a difference between taxable income and pretax financial accounting income, are usually considered permanent differences because the company controls the events that create the tax consequence. However, if circumstances dictate that income taxes will be paid because of a reduction in the bad debt allowance or in policyholders' surplus, a tax expense should be accrued on such reductions in the period they occur. In effect, these reductions do create a temporary difference when they occur and should not be accounted for as an extraordinary item.

Disclosure of bad debt allowances and policyholders' surplus should be made in the financial statements or in footnotes thereto, as follows:

Bad Debt Allowance (reserves)

1. The purpose of the allowance account and the rules and regulations pertaining thereto
2. The fact that income taxes may become payable if the allowance account is used for other purposes
3. The total amount of the allowance account for which income taxes have not been paid

Policyholders' Surplus

1. Treatment of the policyholders' surplus under the provisions of the IRC
2. The fact that income taxes may become payable if the company takes specific action, which should be appropriately described
3. The total amount of policyholders' surplus for which income taxes have not been paid

These disclosure requirements also apply to the parent company of the savings and loan association or the stock life insurance company.

Indefinite Reversal Criteria

Under GAAP, there is a presumption that all undistributed earnings of a subsidiary (domestic and foreign) will eventually be transferred to the parent. Unless this presumption is overcome, the undistributed earnings included in a parent's consolidated income will result in a temporary difference which should be recognized in the accounts. On the other hand, the presumption may be overcome by sufficient evidence that the subsidiary has or will invest its earnings indefinitely, or that the earnings will be remitted to its parent in a tax-free liquidation. To substantiate the *indefinite reversal criteria,* a parent company must have evidence of specific plans for the reinvestment of the undistributed earnings of its subsidiary that demonstrate remittance of the earnings will be postponed indefinitely. Under these circumstances, the parent company is not required to accrue deferred income taxes on the undistributed earnings of the subsidiary. If the plans of the parent company change and earnings will be remitted in the forseeable future, the parent company must accrue as an expense of the current period the appropriate income tax expense. If the reverse occurs, where income taxes had been accrued and the undistributed earnings will not be distributed in the forseeable future, the parent company should adjust income tax expense of the current period. In either case, the adjustment of income tax expense should not be accounted for as an extraordinary item.

The indefinite reversal criteria also applies to the tax effects of temporary differences resulting from differences between taxable income and pretax financial accounting income of corporate joint ventures that are essentially permanent in duration and that are accounted for by the equity method.

In a parent-subsidiary relationship, the parent has numeric control of the voting common stock of the subsidiary (50% or more), and thus, can decide whether the indefinite reversal criteria applies to its subsidiary. However, only the controlling interest (50% or more) of a corporate joint venture accounted for by the equity method can determine that undistributed earnings will be reinvested for an indefinite period. The fact that the equity method presumes that an investor has the ability to exercise significant influence over the investee if the investor owns 20% or more control is irrelevant in considering whether the indefinite reversal criteria applies to a particular investment.

Changes in investment   An investment of more than 50% in a subsidiary may change to the extent that a subsidiary relationship no longer exists, and the equity method (20% to 50% or less control) or the cost method (less than 20% control) must be applied. If an investment in a subsidiary changes to the extent that it must be accounted for by the equity method, the investor should recognize income taxes on its share of the current earnings of the investee in accordance with the equity method. If, prior to the change from a subsidiary to an investment accounted for by the equity or cost method, the parent had not accrued income taxes because of the indefinite reversal criteria, it should then accrue income taxes on the undistributed earnings in the period that it becomes apparent that part or all of the undistributed earnings will be remitted. This accrual should not be accounted for as an extraordinary item.

Deferred income taxes resulting from undistributed earnings of a subsidiary, corporate joint venture, and an investment in common stock accounted for by the equity method should be considered in accounting for a sale or other disposition of the underlying investment.

Railroad gradings and tunnel bores   Income tax benefits resulting from the amortization of railroad gradings and tunnel bores are temporary differences for which tax allocation must be made (FASB Interpretation-18).

U.S. steamship companies   Present promulgated GAAP do not cover deposits in capital construction funds or statutory reserves of U.S. steamship companies complying with the Merchant Marine Act of 1970.

Accounting for Temporary Differences

A temporary difference that arises during a period between pretax financial accounting income and taxable income will reverse itself in one or more future periods. A temporary difference that arises between the tax basis of an asset or liability and the reported amount of that same asset or liability in the financial statements will reverse itself at the time the asset is sold or disposed of otherwise, or the liability is settled. A temporary difference results in either taxable income or a tax deduction in the year in which it reverses. A temporary difference with a credit balance results in taxable income in the year in which it reverses, while a temporary difference with a debit balance results in a tax deduction in the year in which it reverses.

FASB-96 requires that an enterprise recognize a deferred tax liability (asset) for the tax effects of all temporary differences that arise during a period. A deferred tax liability is recognized for the tax effects of temporary differences that are expected to result in net taxable income in one or more future years, while a deferred tax asset is recognized for the tax effects of temporary differences that are expected to result in net tax deductions in one or more future years.

Under FASB-96, the *liability method* must be used to determine the amount of deferred taxes as of the date of an enterprise's financial statements. The liability approach assumes that the only items of future taxable income or tax deductions are the reversals of temporary differences. Under the liability method, deferred taxes are computed in accordance with the tax law and tax rates that are expected to be in effect for the period in which a temporary difference reverses. To determine the deferred tax liability (asset) for a particular future period, the tax rate that is expected to be in effect for that particular future year is applied to the net amount of temporary differences for that particular year. An enterprise shall base its tax computation on the tax elections it expects to make and the tax rates applicable to the type of net taxable amounts that are expected for each future year, such as ordinary income, capital gains or losses, dividend income, and so forth.

If the tax law requires that more than one method or system be used to determine the amount of tax due, an enterprise shall compute its deferred tax liability or asset by all the methods required by law. For example, if the tax law requires the computation of a tax liability by a regular method and by an alternative minimum tax method, the deferred tax liability shall be calculated by both methods.

> **OBSERVATION:** *The liability approach under FASB-96 assumes that the only items of future taxable income or tax deductions are the reversals of temporary differences. Any other assumption as to income or losses is prohibited by FASB-96. The deferred tax expense or credit that is shown in the income statement for the year is equal to the difference between the deferred tax liability (asset) at the beginning of the year and the end of the year.*
>
> *Under FASB-96, an enterprise must estimate the amount and timing of all future taxable income and tax deductions resulting from the reversal of temporary differences. The tax rates enacted for each future year are applied to each future year's net taxable income or net tax deductions to calculate the deferred tax liability or asset. If an enterprise is subject to the alternative minimum tax (AMT) in any of the future years in which temporary differences reverse, two computations of scheduled reversals of temporary difference may be necessary—one computation based on the regular tax method and the other based on the AMT, with the higher amount used to calculate the deferred tax liability at the end of the current year.*

Deferred tax asset   Under FASB-96, a net deferred tax asset may be recognized only to the extent that it can be realized, based on the loss carryback provisions of the tax law, by refund of taxes paid in the current year or a prior year. A claim of refund resulting from an operating loss carryback or unused tax credit of the current year is reported in the financial statements as an asset. Any additional net deductible amounts of temporary differences in future years are, in substance, treated the same as operating loss carryforwards.

> **OBSERVATION:** *Under FASB-96, fewer "naked" tax assets (net deferred tax assets) will be recorded because they are recognized only if an enterprise can obtain a refund of taxes previously paid. This mechanical method of recognizing net deferred tax assets is quite different from the **judgmental approach** permitted by APB-11. As a result of this mechanical approach, an enterprise will be able to verify the amount of its deferred tax liability or asset.*

Effects of changes in tax laws or rates   A deferred tax liability (asset) shall be adjusted for the effects of any changes in the tax laws or rates during a period. The amount of the adjustment shall be included in income from continuing operations for the period that includes the date of the enactment of the change.

> **OBSERVATION:** *Any change in enacted future tax rates or laws will be reflected in the income statement as part of income tax expense in the year in which the change is enacted. As a result, minor fluctuations in earnings from year to year may be somewhat magnified.*

Temporary differences for foreign assets and liabilities   A change in exchange rates will result in a temporary difference between the foreign currency carrying amount and the foreign currency tax basis of an enterprise's foreign assets and liabilities. Another type of temporary difference that arises as a result of a change in exchange rates is when the reporting currency (not the foreign currency) is the functional currency and certain assets and liabilities are remeasured from the foreign currency into the reporting currency using historical exchange rates. After a change in exchange rates, there will be a temporary difference between (i) the current foreign currency equivalent of the historical cost as measured in the reporting currency and (ii) the foreign currency tax basis of those assets and liabilities. Regardless of their source, temporary differences result in taxable or deductible amounts on an enterprise's foreign tax return in one or more future years. Temporary differences that result from a change in exchange rates must be accounted for in accordance with the provisions of FASB-96.

When the reporting currency (not the foreign currency) is the functional currency, remeasurement of an enterprise's deferred foreign tax liability or asset after a change in the exchange rate will result in a transaction gain or loss that is recognized currently in determining net income. When the foreign currency is the functional currency, translation of an enterprise's foreign assets and liabilities will result in a translation adjustment that is not included currently in determining net income. Although FASB-52 (Foreign Currency Translation) requires disclosure of the aggregate transaction gain or loss included in determining net income, it does not specify how to display that transaction gain or loss (or its components) for financial reporting. Accordingly, a transaction gain or loss that results from remeasuring a deferred foreign tax liability or asset may be included in the reported amount of deferred tax benefit or expense if the presentation is considered to be more useful. If reported in that manner, that transaction gain or loss is still included in the aggregate transaction gain or loss for the period which is required to be disclosed by FASB-52.

Operating Losses

Under present tax regulations an operating loss of a period may be carried back or carried forward and applied as a reduction of income in those periods permitted by the tax laws. The taxable income and the financial accounting income will change for those periods to which the loss is carried back or forward. Under FASB-96, an operating loss or tax credit carryforward that is allowable for tax purposes is recognized as a reduction of any net taxable income that is expected to arise *from the reversal of net temporary differences* in those future years that fall within the loss carryforward period allowed by the tax law.

Carryforwards of operating losses or tax credits may not be recognized as assets if they cannot be applied, because of limitations in the tax law, as reductions of net taxable income that arise from the reversal of temporary differences of any year. This is true regardless of the amount of estimated taxable financial income that an enterprise expects to generate in future years.

> **OBSERVATION:** *An enterprise may record a net deferred tax asset only when future net tax deductions can be carried back to reduce taxes paid for the current year or a prior year based on the*

> *provisions of the tax law. Thus, recoverability of future net tax deductions under FASB-96 is based on a mechanical computation, unlike the old rules under which judgment was required to estimate the availability of future earnings. Under the old rules (APB-11), a net tax deduction that could not be carried back for a refund could be used to offset future earnings if future earnings were expected to be available.*

For tax purposes, an operating loss carryforward is equal to the amount of tax deductions that exceed taxable gross income during a taxable year that may, under tax law, be carried forward to future years to reduce taxable income. *For financial reporting purposes,* an operating loss carryforward is the same amount as that for tax purposes reduced by any net taxable income arising from the reversal of temporary differences during the allowable carryforward period and increased by any net tax deductions arising from the reversal of temporary differences that have not been recognized in the financial statements. Where none exists for tax purposes, an operating loss carryforward for financial reporting purposes is equal to the net tax deductions arising from the reversal of temporary differences that have not been recognized in the financial statements.

Reporting tax benefits of operating losses   Except in a business combination or a quasi reorganization, the tax benefit of a particular carryforward operating loss shall be classified, reported, and included in the same type of income or loss of the current year that absorbs that particular carryforward operating loss. The original source of income or loss that established the carryforward operating loss does not affect the category of income or loss that the carryforward operating loss is reported as in the current year. For example, if income from continuing operations of the current year absorbs a carryforward loss of a prior year, the tax benefit of that carryforward loss is classified, reported, and included as income or loss from continuing operations. On the other hand, if extraordinary income of the current year absorbs a carryforward loss of a prior year, the tax benefit of that carryforward loss is classified, reported, and included as extraordinary income or loss.

> *OBSERVATION: Under FASB-96, earnings per share from continuing operations may be significantly affected by a carryforward operating loss that is absorbed in income from continuing operations of the current year. This provision of FASB-96 could affect how financial analysts will view the quality of an enterprise's earnings. Under the old rules (APB-11), the tax benefit*

of a carryforward operating loss that was recognized in a subsequent period did not affect an enterprise's earnings per share from continuing operations because it was always reported as an extraordinary item.

Operating losses in business combinations The tax benefits of acquired carryforward operating losses or tax credits may be recognized as of the date of a business combination or afterwards. In a purchase business combination, an operating loss or tax credit carryforward of one combining enterprise at the date of acquisition may be recognized as a reduction of any deferred tax liability of the other combining enterprise. This results in either (i) a reduction in goodwill or noncurrent assets of the acquired enterprise (except long-term investments in marketable securities) or (ii) an increase in negative goodwill.

If recognized subsequent to the date of acquisition, tax benefits of carryforward operating losses or tax credits shall be used to reduce to zero any goodwill and other noncurrent intangible assets that were acquired in the business combination. Any excess shall be recognized as a reduction of current income tax expense.

> **OBSERVATION:** *The tax benefits of realized unrecorded preacquisition loss carryforwards of purchased subsidiaries and other realized carryforwards must be applied first to reduce to zero any goodwill and other noncurrent intangible assets related to the acquisition and any balance must be applied as a reduction of income tax expense. Under prior GAAP (APB-11), realized unrecorded preacquisition loss carryforwards of purchased subsidiaries and other realized carryforwards were recognized as retroactive reductions of goodwill and other noncurrent assets.*

Operating losses in quasi reorganizations For financial reporting purposes, the tax benefit of an operating loss or tax credit carryforward that existed as of the date of a quasi reorganization and that was used in years subsequent to that date, is reported as a direct contribution to capital as of the date of the quasi reorganization. In the event that a quasi reorganization consists only of the elimination of a deficit in retained earnings and a corresponding reduction in contributed capital, the tax benefit of an operating loss or tax credit carryforward is included in the current year's income or loss and subsequently transferred from retained earnings to contributed capital.

In those circumstances where losses were previously charged directly to contributed capital, any tax benefit relating to a prior operating loss or tax credit carryforward shall be subsequently recognized, for financial reporting purposes, as a direct addition to contributed capital.

Computation of Deferred Tax Liability or Asset

For the purposes of FASB-96, a deferred tax liability is computed on the assumption that the only net taxable amounts subject to tax in each future year are from the reversal of temporary differences. However, the tax rate that an enterprise uses to compute its deferred tax liability for each future year is the same tax rate that the enterprise expects its other taxable income to be subject to in the same year. For example, if an enterprise expects to be subject to the highest tax rate in a particular future year, that highest tax rate must be used to compute any deferred tax liability for that particular year.

> **OBSERVATION**: *The tax law determines whether temporary differences that will result in taxable and deductible amounts in future years may be offset against each other. For example, if the tax law provides that capital losses are deductible only to the extent of capital gains, temporary differences that will result in future deductions in the form of capital losses cannot be offset against temporary differences that will result in future ordinary income for purposes of determining net taxable amounts in future years.*

Enterprises whose taxable income is seldom or never subject to the maximum tax rate may make aggregate calculations using an estimated average tax rate at which the aggregate net taxable amount would be subject to taxation in various future years. However, an enterprise may be required to prepare detailed schedules identifying unusual situations, such as a large amount of taxable income in a single future year.

The following procedure may be used to compute the amount of a deferred tax liability or deferred tax asset as of the date of the financial statements:

Step 1. *Schedule all temporary differences*—The following information should appear on the schedule: (a) original amount of each temporary difference; (b) the origination date of each temporary difference; (c) the future year(s) in which each temporary difference is expected to reverse (become taxable income or a tax deduction) and (d) the amount of the temporary difference that is expected to reverse.

Step 2. *Determine net taxable/deductible amounts*—Determine the estimated amount of net taxable income or net tax deduction for each future year that is expected to result from the reversal of all temporary differences by combining those temporary differences resulting in taxable income with those temporary differences resulting in tax deductions, into one net amount for each future year. (Provisions in the tax law may permit or require that a net deduction in a particular year offset net taxable amounts in certain earlier or later years.)

Step 3. *Deduct allowable operating loss carryforwards*—Operating loss carryforwards that are allowable for tax purposes are deducted from any future year within the allowable loss carryforward period in which there is net taxable income resulting from the reversal of temporary differences.

Step 4. *Carryback and carryforward*—Carryback (as permitted by tax law) an estimated net tax deduction resulting from the reversal of temporary differences in one future year to offset the estimated net taxable income resulting from the reversal of temporary differences of an earlier year. Carryforward (as permitted by tax law) an estimated net tax deduction resulting from the reversal of temporary differences in an earlier year to offset the estimated net taxable income resulting from the reversal of temporary differences in a subsequent year.

Step 5. *Recompute net taxable/deductible amounts*—After applying carrybacks and carryforwards, as permitted or required by tax law (Step 4), recompute the estimated amount of net taxable income or net tax deduction for each future year.

Step 6. *Compute deferred tax assets*—Compute and recognize a deferred tax asset for those future years, if any, that reflect an estimated net tax deduction but only if the tax benefit of the net tax deduction can be realized based on the loss carryback provisions of the tax law (i) to reduce a current deferred tax liability and (ii) to reduce taxes paid in the current or a prior year. (No asset is recognized for any other estimated net tax deduction of any future year.)

Step 7. *Compute deferred tax liabilities*—Compute and recognize a deferred tax liability for any future year that reflects estimated net taxable income. Compute the amount of any allowable tax credit carryforward for each future year that is included in the carryforward period. Subtract the allowable tax credit carryforward for each future year from the deferred tax liability for each future year. The difference is the amount of net deferred tax liability for each future year. (**Note**: The enacted tax rates and laws applicable to each future year are used to determine the amount of tax liability on the estimated net taxable income of each future year.)

Step 8. *Total deferred tax liability*—The total deferred tax liability of an enterprise is simply the total of all future years computed in Step 7 that reflect a deferred tax liability.

The following illustration demonstrates how the offsetting procedures of FASB-96 should be applied.

AAA Corporation had taxable income of $1,400 for the current year. Future recovery of taxable amounts of installment receivables (Taxable amount—A) is expected to be $400 per year from year 2 through year 6. In addition, the reversal of other temporary differences resulting in $200 per year taxable income from year 2 through year 6 is also expected (Taxable amount—B). A liability for warranty expense that has previously been recognized in the financial statements is expected to be paid in years 4 and 5 in the amount of $3,000 and $1,000 respectively. Enacted tax rates are listed below.

Year	Current	2	3	4	5	6
Taxable income	$1,400	$ –	$ –	$ –	$ –	$ –
Taxable amount—A		400	400	400	400	400
Taxable amount—B		200	200	200	200	200
Deductible amount—A				(3,000)		
Deductible amount—B					(1,000)	
	$1,400	$600	$600	($2,400)	($ 400)	$600
Carryback year 4 loss	(1,400)	(600)	(400)	2,400		
Net taxable/(deductible)	–	–	$200	–	($ 400)	$600
Carryback year 5 loss			(200)		200	
Net taxable/(deductible)					($ 200)	$600
Carryforward year 5 loss					200	(200)
Net taxable/(deductible)						$400
Enacted tax rates	50%	40%	30%	30%	30%	30%

- The $3,000 deductible amount—A in year 4 offsets the $600 taxable income of year 4 and the remaining $2,400 is carried back $1,400 to the current year; $600 to year 2; and the balance of $400 to year 3.

- The $1,000 deductible amount—B in year 5 offsets the $600 taxable income of year 5 and, of the remaining $400, $200 is carried back to year 3 and $200 is carried forward to year 6.

At the end of the current year, AAA Corporation should recognize:

- Income tax expense for the current year of $700 based on $1,400 taxable income (50% of $1,400).
- A deferred income tax benefit of $580. The $580 includes a $700 net deferred tax asset resulting from the net tax deductions of year 4 that offset (by loss carryback procedures) the taxable income of $1,400 for the current year, and the recognition of a net deferred tax liability of $120 for year 6 based on $400 net taxable amount and a 30% tax rate.

Total Income Tax Expense (Benefit)

In each year, an enterprise shall recognize a deferred tax expense or benefit in the amount of the net change in its deferred tax liability or deferred tax asset. The deferred tax expense or benefit recognized together with the amount of income taxes currently payable or refundable is the total amount of income tax expense or benefit for the year. The total amount of income tax expense or benefit for the year shall be allocated among (a) continuing operations, (b) discontinued operations, (c) extraordinary items, (d) the cumulative effect of accounting changes, (e) prior-period adjustments, (f) gains and losses included in comprehensive income but excluded from net income, and (g) capital transactions.

> *OBSERVATION: Under present accounting practice, the category of gains and losses that are included in comprehensive income but excluded from net income includes (1) certain changes in market values of investments in marketable equity securities classified as noncurrent assets, (2) certain changes in market values of investments in industries having specialized accounting practices for marketable securities, (3) adjustments from recognizing certain additional pension liabilities, and (4) foreign currency translation adjustments.*

Tax-Planning Strategies

An enterprise can use tax-planning strategies to minimize deferred tax liabilities by changing the nature and timing of future net taxable income or net tax deductions resulting from the reversal of temporary differences. For example, an enterprise can accelerate future taxable income by selling installment receivables in order to use a net operating loss carryforward before it expires.

The use of tax-planning strategies may allow an enterprise to change the years in which an amount becomes taxable or deductible. Changing the year in which an amount becomes deductible may provide an enterprise with a tax benefit by offsetting taxable amounts of the same year. In addition, a deductible amount may be converted to a tax benefit as a loss carryback. Changing the year in which an amount becomes taxable may provide an enterprise with a tax benefit by utilizing a loss or tax credit prior to its expiration.

A tax-planning strategy may be used by an enterprise for the purpose of estimating the years in which temporary differences will result in taxable or deductible amounts, provided that such a strategy meets both of the following conditions:

- The tax-planning strategy must make business sense and require prudent and feasible actions that management can control.
- The cost of the tax-planning strategy should be minor and incidental. The amount of the tax benefit cannot qualify as a reduction of the cost of the tax-planning strategy.

Changes in an Enterprise's Tax Status

The taxable/nontaxable status of an enterprise may change during the year, such as changing from a partnership to a corporation. In the event of a change in the tax status of an enterprise, temporary differences may be created or eliminated at the date of change. At the date a nontaxable enterprise becomes a taxable enterprise, a deferred tax liability shall be recognized in accordance with the provisions of FASB-96 for any temporary differences resulting from the change. On the other hand, when a taxable enterprise becomes a nontaxable enterprise, any existing deferred tax liability or deferred tax asset must be eliminated. The recognition or elimination of a deferred tax liability or asset as a result of a change in tax status is included in income from continuing operations of the period in which the change occurs.

Regulated Enterprises

Regulated enterprises (as defined by FASB-71 (Accounting for the Effects of Certain Types of Regulation)) must comply with FASB-96, including the following specific provisions:

a. The use of the net-of-tax accounting and reporting method is strictly prohibited.

> **OBSERVATION:** *Tax allocation under the net-of-tax method is a procedure whereby the tax effects (determined by either the deferred or liability methods) of temporary differences are recognized in the valuation of assets or liabilities and the related revenues and expenses. The tax effects are applied to reduce specific assets or liabilities on the basis that tax deductibility or taxability are factors in their valuation.*

b. A deferred tax liability is required to be recognized for the (i) tax benefits of originating temporary differences that are passed on to customers and (ii) equity component of the allowance for funds used during construction.
c. A deferred tax liability or asset must be adjusted for any enacted change in the tax laws or rates.

An asset shall be recognized by a regulated enterprise in the amount of the probable future revenue that will be received from customers if it is probable that the regulator will allow a future increase in rates for items (b) and (c) above. On the other hand, if it is probable that a future decrease in taxes payable for items (b) and (c) above will be returned to customers through a future decrease in rates, a regulated enterprise shall recognize a liability in the amount of the probable reduction in future revenue in accordance with FASB-71. In this event, the asset or liability recognized by the regulated enterprise also is a temporary difference, and a deferred tax liability or asset shall be recognized for the deferred tax effects of that temporary difference.

Business Combinations

Under FASB-96, the net-of-tax method of valuing assets and liabilities in a purchase business combination has been eliminated. Differences between assigned fair values and tax bases of acquired assets and liabilities in a purchase business combination shall be set up as a separate deferred tax liability or asset and shall not be accounted for as an adjustment of the related balance sheet account. Under FASB-96, deferred taxes are not recognized for temporary differences relating to goodwill, unallocated negative goodwill, or leveraged leases.

The Ace Company is acquired by the Spade Company for $40,000 in a business combination accounted for as a purchase. The fair value assigned to the assets acquired is $44,000 and the fair value of liabilities assumed was $20,000. The tax base of the assets acquired was $30,000 and there was no difference between the tax base and fair value of the assumed liabilities. The tax rate enacted for all future years is 40%. The allocation of the purchase price and computation of the deferred tax liability is as follows:

Fair value of assets acquired	$44,000
Value of liabilities assumed	(20,000)
Deferred tax liability [($44,000 – $30,000) x 40%]	(5,600)
Goodwill	21,600
Purchase price	$40,000

The journal entry to record the acquisition is:

Assets acquired	$44,000	
Goodwill acquired	21,600	
Cash		$40,000
Liabilities assumed		20,000
Deferred tax liability		5,600

Accounting for Income Taxes—Interim Periods

The promulgated GAAP for Interim Financial Reporting (APB-28) require that taxes for interim periods be determined in accordance with the existing promulgated GAAP for accounting for income taxes (FASB-96). At the end of each interim period, APB-28 requires an enterprise to make its best estimate of its annual effective tax rate that is expected to be applicable for the full fiscal year. The estimated annual effective tax rate should reflect all anticipated investment tax credits, foreign tax rates, percentage depletion, capital gain rates, and other available tax planning alternatives. At the end of each interim period during the year, this estimated annual effective tax rate is revised, if necessary, to the best current estimates of the annual effective tax rate.

At the end of each year, an enterprise shall recognize a deferred tax expense (benefit), if any, in the amount of the net change in its deferred tax liability (asset) from the beginning of the period to the end of the period. The deferred tax expense or benefit recognized in this manner together with the amount of income taxes currently payable or refundable is the total amount of income tax expense (benefit) for the year. Under FASB-96, the total amount of income tax expense (benefit) for the year shall be allocated among (a) continuing operations, (b) discontinued operations, (c) extraordinary items, (d) the cumulative effect of accounting changes, (e) prior-period adjustments, (f) gains and losses included in comprehensive income but excluded from net income, and (g) capital transactions.

> **OBSERVATION:** *Under present accounting practice, gains and losses that are included in comprehensive income but excluded from net income include (1) certain changes in market values of investments in marketable securities classified as noncurrent assets, (2) certain changes in market values of investments in industries having specialized accounting practices for marketable securities, (3) adjustments from recognizing certain additional pension liabilities, and (4) foreign currency translation adjustments.*

The interim-period tax is determined by applying the established estimated annual effective tax rate to the year-to-date ordinary income or loss, and subtracting the previous interim year-to-date tax on the ordinary income or loss. Ordinary income or loss is defined as income or loss from continuing operations before a provision for income taxes, excluding significant unusual or nonrecurring items. This excludes extraordinary items, discontinued operations, and cumulative effects of changes in an accounting principle. Income tax is defined to include both current and deferred taxes.

The tax effects of losses that arise in the early portion of a fiscal year (in the event carryback of such losses is not possible) should be recognized only if realization in subsequent interim periods of that year is assured beyond any reasonable doubt. The estimated annual effective tax rate shall include only the tax benefit of a loss that has already been realized, or future realization within the same fiscal period is assured beyond any reasonable doubt.

Under FASB-96, a net deferred tax asset may be recognized only to the extent that it can be realized, based on the loss carryback provisions of the tax law, by refund of taxes paid in the current year or a prior year. Therefore, an asset may not be recognized for a loss carryforward at the end of a fiscal year regardless of the probability that the enterprise will generate profits in future years. This limitation shall be applied in determining (i) the estimated tax benefit of an *ordinary* loss for the fiscal year, (ii) the estimated annual effective tax rate, and (iii) the year-to-date benefit of a loss.

APB-28 has been amended by paragraph 205(g) of FASB-96 to clarify the meaning of the term *future realization assured beyond any reasonable doubt*. FASB-96 states that this term shall have the same meaning as it had in the prior GAAP on accounting for income taxes (APB-11). Paragraphs 45 and 47 of ABP-11 concluded that the following conditions had to be met to substantiate that the future realization of a loss was assured beyond any reasonable doubt:

- The enterprise has been reasonably profitable over a long period or has experienced occasional losses that were subsequently offset by taxable income.
- The loss carryforward is the result of an isolated, nonrecurring, and identifiable source.
- Realization of future taxable income is large enough to offset the loss carryforward and will occur with the period allowed under tax law.

The following illustration reflects the computation of the estimated annual effective tax rate and its application.

A business estimates $1,000,000 of ordinary income for the year and anticipated realizable tax credits of $100,000. The income tax rate is 50%. Seasonable patterns in the fourth quarter assure the realization of the tax benefits beyond any reasonable doubt.

Tax on ordinary income (50%)	$500,000
Less: Anticipated credits	100,000
Net tax to be provided	$400,000
Estimated annual effective tax rate ($400,000 required tax divided by $1,000,000 income)	40%

Based on the estimated annual effective tax rate, the quarterly computations of taxes might appear as:

	Estimated Results		Estimated	Provision for Taxes	
Period	Quarter	Cumulative	Tax Rate	Quarter	Cumulative
1	($ 200,000)	($ 200,000)	40%	($ 80,000)	($ 80,000)
2	100,000	(100,000)	40%	40,000	(40,000)
3	150,000	50,000	40%	60,000	20,000
4	950,000	1,000,000	40%	380,000	400,000
	$1,000,000			$400,000	

If a reliable estimate cannot be made for the annual effective tax rate, the actual year-to-date annual effective tax rate should be used. If a reliable estimate of part of the ordinary income or loss, or of the related tax (or benefit) cannot be made, it should be reported in the interim period in which it actually occurs.

Significant, unusual, or extraordinary items that are reported separately net of their related tax effects are recognized in the interim period in which they occur. The related tax on these items is the difference between the tax on year-to-date ordinary income including the item, and the tax on year-to-date ordinary income excluding the item.

Assume the same facts as those in the preceding illustration; assume also that the business incurs a tax-deductible significant unusual extraordinary loss in the third quarter of $200,000 the benefit (50%) for which is assured beyond any reasonable doubt, because the loss can be carried back.

Since the estimated annual effective tax rate is unaffected under these circumstances, the tax on ordinary income or loss is the same, and the computation of the estimated annual effective tax rate is not reproduced.

	Income		Provision for Taxes	
Period	Ordinary	Extraordinary	Ordinary	Extraordinary
1	($ 200,000)		($ 80,000)	
2	100,000		40,000	
3	150,000	($200,000)	60,000	($100,000)
4	950,000		380,000	
	$1,000,000	($200,000)	$400,000	($100,000)

If the $200,000 tax-deductible unusual extraordinary loss in the third quarter was not realizable beyond any reasonable doubt, it would appear only in the third and succeeding periods to the extent that it could offset ordinary income for the year to date.

The tax benefit of a loss that results from a significant, unusual, and extraordinary item or a discontinued operation shall not be recognized until it is realized or realization is assured beyond a reasonable doubt. Realization is assured beyond a reasonable doubt by:

1. Offsetting year-to-date ordinary income
2. Offsetting taxable income from unusual, extraordinary, discontinued operations, or items credited directly to stockholders' equity accounts
3. Carrying back the loss to prior years
4. Future taxable income that is almost certain to occur shortly, especially from seasonable patterns of revenue

The provision for taxes on income or loss from the operation of a discontinued segment prior to measurement date, and the gain or loss on the disposal of the discontinued operation, is determined (as stated earlier) by computing the difference between the tax on year-to-date ordinary income or loss including the discontinued segment and the tax on year-to-date ordinary income or loss excluding the discontinued segment. Thereafter, the provision for taxes shall not be recomputed, but should be divided into two components: (i) for the remaining ordinary income or loss and (ii) for the income or loss from operations of the discontinued segment. A revised estimated annual effective tax rate and resulting tax benefits are then recomputed for the remaining ordinary income or loss.

The following illustration depicts how a discontinued segment is accounted for:

A business estimates ordinary income of $1,000,000 for the year and tax credits of $100,000 that are realizable beyond any reasonable doubt. Income tax rates are 50%. The estimated annual effective tax rate is as follows:

Tax on pretax ordinary income (50%)	$500,000
Less: Anticipated credits	(100,000)
Net tax to be provided	$400,000
Estimated annual effective tax rate ($400,000 ÷ $1,000,000)	40%

The first two quarters appear as:

	Estimated Results			Provision for Taxes	
Period	Quarter	Cumulative	Rate	Quarter	Cumulative
1	$200,000	$200,000	40%	$ 80,000	$ 80,000
2	250,000	450,000	40%	100,000	180,000

During the third quarter the decision to discontinue a division of the company was made. The results of operations for the continuing divisions of the company and for the discontinued division are as follows:

	Revised	Discontinued Division	
Quarter	Ordinary Income	Operations	Loss on Disposal
1	$ 250,000	($ 50,000)	
2	350,000	(100,000)	
3	500,000	(100,000)	($550,000)
4 (Estimated)	500,000		
Total for Year	$1,600,000	($250,000)	($550,000)

The only assumptions that have changed for the estimated annual effective tax rate is that $20,000 of the $100,000 in tax credits was related to the discontinued operations. The recomputation of the estimated annual effective tax rate is:

Tax on ordinary income (50% of $1,600,000)	$800,000
Less: Anticipated tax credits	80,000
Net tax to be provided	$720,000
Estimated annual effective tax rate ($720,000 ÷ $1,600,000)	45%

The quarterly amounts, based on the revised ordinary income and estimated annual effective tax rate, are:

	Estimated Results			Provision for Taxes	
Period	*Quarter*	*Cumulative*	*Rate*	*Quarter*	*Cumulative*
1	$ 250,000	$ 250,000	45%	$112,500	$112,500
2	350,000	600,000	45%	157,500	270,000
3	500,000	1,100,000	45%	225,000	495,000
4	500,000	1,600,000	45%	225,000	720,000
	$1,600,000			$720,000	

The computation of the tax benefit attributable to the discontinued division for the first two quarters is the difference between the tax on year-to-date ordinary income or loss including the discontinued division, and the tax on the year-to-date ordinary income or loss, excluding the discontinued division, as follows:

	Tax on Ordinary Income		
Quarter	*Previously Computed*	*Recomputed*	*Tax Benefit, Discontinued Div.*
1	$ 80,000	$112,500	($32,500)
2	100,000	157,500	(57,500)
Totals	$180,000	$270,000	($90,000)

The third-quarter tax benefits for (1) the loss from operations and (2) the provision for the disposal of the discontinued division are computed on the revised estimated annual income with and without the effects of the discontinued division, as follows:

	Discontinued Division	
	Loss on Operations	*Loss on Disposal*
Estimated revised ordinary income	$1,600,000	$1,600,000
Discontinued division loss on operations	250,000	
Discontinued division loss on disposal		550,000
Total	$1,350,000	$1,050,000

Tax at regular tax rate (50%)	$ 675,000	$ 525,000
Anticipated credits—continuing operations	(80,000)	(80,000)
Taxes—after effect of discontinued division	$ 595,000	$ 445,000
Previously computed taxes for year	720,000	720,000
Tax benefit—discontinued division	($ 125,000)	($ 275,000)
Less: Tax benefits recognized in first two quarters	(90,000)	—
Tax benefit for third quarter	($ 35,000)	($ 275,000)

The $20,000 in tax credits related to the discontinued division have not been recognized on the assumption that they will not be realized.

Except in a business combination or a quasi reorganization, FASB-96 requires that the tax benefit of a particular carryforward loss that is recognized in a subsequent year be included in, and reported as, the same category of income or loss of the current year that absorbs that particular carryforward loss. Thus, if the income or loss that absorbs the particular carryforward loss is income or loss from continuing operations, the tax benefit of the carryforward loss shall also be included in income or loss from continuing operations. That requirement shall also be observed in reporting the tax benefit of an operating loss carryforward in interim periods.

The tax benefit of an operating loss carryforward from prior years shall be included in the estimated annual effective tax rate computation if realization of the tax benefit as a result of *ordinary* income in the current year is assured beyond any reasonable doubt. Otherwise, the tax benefit shall be recognized in each interim period to the extent that income in the period and for the year to date is available to offset the operating loss carryforward.

The cumulative effect of a change in an accounting principle on the beginning-of-the-year retained earnings is reported in the first interim period of the fiscal year (FASB-3). The related income tax effects are computed as though the new accounting principle had been applied retroactively to all affected prior periods (APB-20). When the change is made in other than the first interim period, the prechange interim periods are restated, by applying the newly adopted accounting principle to those prechange interim periods. The tax or tax benefits for the prechange interim periods is then re-computed on the year-to-date and annual estimated amounts, modified only for the effect of the change in accounting principle. (See chapter entitled "Accounting Changes" for more detail.)

Businesses subject to tax in more than one taxing jurisdiction shall compute one overall estimated annual effective tax rate, except:

1. Ordinary income (loss) and related tax (benefit) shall be excluded in computing the estimated annual effective tax rate and interim-period tax (benefit) in any jurisdiction in which an ordinary loss is anticipated for the year, or in which there is an ordinary loss for the year-to-date, for which a tax benefit cannot be recognized.

2. Ordinary income (loss) and related tax (benefit) shall be excluded in computing the estimated annual effective tax rate and interim-period tax (benefit) in any foreign jurisdiction for which reliable estimates cannot be made. In this event, the tax (benefit) on ordinary income (loss) shall be recognized in the interim period in which it is reported.

Changes resulting from new tax laws should be reflected in a revised estimated annual effective tax rate for the first interim period affected.

Full disclosure should be made of any significant difference in the usual relationship between income tax expense and pretax accounting income, arising from the application of the promulgated GAAP for accounting for income taxes in interim periods.

> **OBSERVATION:** *FASB Technical Bulletin 79-9 reaffirms the fact that the effect of a change in tax rates during an interim period should be reflected in a revised estimated annual effective tax rate. The revised annual effective tax rate is applied to pretax income for the year-to-date at the end of the interim period in which the change in tax rate took effect.*

Financial Statement Presentation and Disclosure

In a classified statement of financial position, a deferred tax liability or asset shall be classified either as current or noncurrent depending on whether the temporary difference is related to an identifiable asset or liability. If the temporary difference is not related to an identifiable asset or liability, it is classified as current (i) if, upon reversal, it will result in net taxable income or a net tax deduction within the next year or (ii) if the operating cycle of an enterprise is longer than one year, the operating cycle is used to determine the current/noncurrent classification. Temporary differences that are related to an asset or liability are classified as current/noncurrent based on the classification of their related asset or liability.

Offsetting of deferred tax liabilities and assets that are attributable to different tax jurisdictions is not permitted by FASB-96. An enterprise is required to disclose the types of temporary differences that represent significant portions of a deferred tax liability or asset. The owners of S Corporations, partnerships, and similar entities are liable for the payment of any income taxes due on the income earned by these entities. *Public enterprises* of this type are required by FASB-96 to disclose that (i) they are not subject to income taxes and (ii) their owners are liable for payment of any income taxes due on income earned by the public enterprise. In addition, the enterprise must disclose the difference, if any, between the reported amounts of its assets and liabilities and their related tax bases.

APB-23 (Accounting for Income Taxes—Special Areas), addresses the accrual of deferred tax in regard to (a) the undistributed earnings of a subsidiary, (b) investments in corporate joint ventures, (c) the bad debt reserves of savings and loan associations, and (d) the policyholders' surplus of stock life insurance companies. Under APB-23, there is a presumption that all undistributed earnings of a subsidiary (domestic and foreign) will eventually be transferred to the parent company. Unless the presumption is overcome, the undistributed earnings included in a parent's consolidated income will result in a temporary difference, which should be recognized in the accounts. In addition, corporate joint ventures and investments in common stocks accounted for by the equity method present the same problem as a subsidiary in regard to temporary differences and should be accounted for in the same manner.

Under FASB-96, when a deferred tax liability is *not* recognized for any of the areas addressed by APB-23 or for deposits in statutory reserve funds by U.S. steamship enterprises, the following information shall be disclosed in the financial statements or notes thereto:

a. A description of the types of unrecognized temporary differences, the types of events that would trigger their taxability, and the cumulative amount of each type (Unrecognized temporary differences are those for which no deferred tax liability has been recognized.)

b. If practicable, the amount of any deferred tax liability that has not been recognized for unremitted earnings of the enterprise; if not practicable, a statement of that fact, and the amount of withholding tax due upon distribution of those earnings

c. Other than unremitted earnings [see (b)], the amount of deferred tax liability that has not been recognized for any other temporary differences, such as the (i) bad debt reserve of a stock/mutual savings and loan association or a mutual savings bank, (ii) policyholders' surplus of a life insurance enterprise, and (iii) statutory reserve funds of a U.S. steamship enterprise

The amount of income tax expense or benefit allocated to the following financial statement captions shall be disclosed for each year for which those items are presented: (a) continuing operations, (b) discontinued operations, (c) extraordinary items, (d) the cumulative effect of accounting changes, (e) prior-period adjustments, (f) gains and losses included in comprehensive income but excluded from net income, and (g) capital transactions.

An enterprise is required to disclose, for each year presented, the components of income tax expense relating to continuing operations. The components of income tax expense include: (a) current income tax expense or credit, (b) deferred income tax expense or credit, (c) investment tax credits, (d) government grants, (e) tax benefits of carryforward operating losses and (f) adjustments of a deferred tax liability or asset relating to a change in (i) the enacted tax laws or rates or (ii) an enterprise's tax status.

An enterprise shall disclose in its financial statements a reconciliation between income tax expense from continuing operations that is reported on the income statement with income tax expense from continuing operations based on statutory regular income tax rates. In the event there are alternative tax systems, the regular tax rates shall be presumed to be the *statutory rates*. An enterprise shall disclose the estimated amount and the nature of each reconciling item that is material, and the reconciliation shall be expressed in percentages or dollar amounts. A nonpublic enterprise may submit the reconciliation of income tax expense in narrative form but the disclosure of the nature of all significant reconciling items is still required.

> **OBSERVATION:** *The reconciliation of income tax expense on the income statement, with the income tax expense based on statutory rates which is required by the provisions of FASB-96, is similar to the reconciliation presently required by SEC rules.*

An enterprise shall disclose the amounts and expiration dates of operating loss and tax credit carryforwards for both financial reporting purposes and for tax purposes. The amounts disclosed for financial reporting purposes shall be those that have not yet been recognized as reductions of a deferred tax liability, and the amounts disclosed for tax purposes shall be those that are available to reduce taxes payable on tax returns in future years. An enterprise may disclose a reasonable aggregation of expiration dates in lieu of exact expiration dates. An enterprise must separately disclose any significant amounts of carryforward net operating losses or tax credits that are likely to be used as a reduction of acquired goodwill and other acquired noncurrent intangible assets.

Separately issued financial statements of enterprises that are members of a consolidated group filing a consolidated tax return shall disclose:

a. Current income tax expense and its deferred tax expense for each year presented and, as of the date of each statement of financial position presented, the amount of any tax-related balances between members of the same consolidated group

b. The method of allocating the consolidated income tax expense (current and deferred) to individual members of the group and the nature and effect of any changes in that method of allocation [Note: This disclosure must be made for the same years in which the disclosures for (a) above are made.]

Effective Date and Transition

FASB-96 is effective for fiscal years beginning on or after December 16, 1989. The initial application of FASB-96 shall be made as of the beginning of an enterprise's fiscal year.

Earlier application of the provisions of FASB-96 is encouraged and restatement of financial statements for fiscal years prior to the effective date, to conform with the provisions of FASB-96, is permitted, but not required. FASB-96 shall be applied to the amount of deferred charges or credits at the beginning of the fiscal year of adoption or at the beginning of the earliest year in which an enterprise elects to restate its financial statements, whichever is applicable. The effects of applying FASB-96 on the amount of deferred tax charges or credits shall be reported as the cumulative effect of a change in accounting principle, in accordance with paragraph 20 of APB-20 (Accounting Changes), except for the type of effects that are required by FASB-96 to be excluded from net income, such as the tax effect of an operating loss or tax credit carryforward for financial reporting purposes as of the date of a quasi-reorganization. Those latter effects shall be recognized in a manner consistent with the reporting requirements of FASB-96.

> **OBSERVATION:** *The transition rules for the application of FASB-96 are very flexible. Since the effective date of FASB-96 is for fiscal years beginning on or after December 16, 1989, an enterprise may wait for the mandatory date which would likely fall in 1990 to adopt FASB-96, or it may elect earlier adoption either 1987 or 1988, or 1989. Furthermore, upon adoption of FASB-96, an enterprise may elect to retroactively restate some or all of its financial statements or recognize the change in accounting principle (adoption of FASB-96) in accordance with APB-20. In this circumstance, the total effect of the adoption of FASB-96 is recognized in the income statement of the latest year presented.*

If the presentation of the financial statements does not contain the earliest year restated, the beginning balance of retained earnings for the earliest year that is presented, and any other components of stockholders' equity, shall be adjusted for the effect of the restatement as of that date. Pro forma effects of retroactive application in accordance with APB-20 are not required if statements of earnings that are presented for prior years are not restated.

The initial presentation of the financial statement for the year in which FASB-96 is first adopted shall disclose:

a. The effect of adopting FASB-96 on income from continuing operations, income before extraordinary items, and on net income (and on related per share amounts) for the year of adoption if restated financial statements for the prior year are not presented

b. The effect of any restatement on income from continuing operations, income before extraordinary items, and on net income (and on related per share amounts) for each year presented

If an enterprise elects to restate its financial statements for prior years, consummated purchase business combinations of those prior years must be remeasured in accordance with paragraph 23 of FASB-96. However, no remeasurement shall be made for purchase business combinations consummated prior to the beginning of the earliest year restated or, if no restatement is made, prior to the first year that FASB-96 is applied. In this event, remaining balances of assets and/or liabilities that were originally assigned values on a net-of-tax basis pursuant to paragraph 89 of APB-16 (Business Combinations) shall not be adjusted. The difference between those remaining balances and their tax bases (except leveraged leases), as of the beginning of the first year that FASB-96 is applied, are temporary differences for which a deferred tax liability or asset must be recognized. That adjustment and other effects of applying FASB-96 on the amount of deferred tax charges or credits at the beginning of the fiscal year shall be reported, as discussed above, as the cumulative effect of a change in accounting principle, in accordance with paragraph 20 of APB-20 (Accounting Changes).

> **OBSERVATION:** *The transition rules relating to prior business combinations accounted for by the purchase method are much more complicated. If the purchase business combination took place in a year in which financial statements are restated or in the year that FASB-96 is first applied, the acquired assets and liabilities are remeasured at pre-tax amounts and a separate deferred tax account must be set up. On the other hand, if the purchase business combination occurred in a year in which financial statements were not restated for the purposes of FASB-96, deferred taxes are recognized on the difference between the remaining book value and tax bases of those assets and liabilities.*

Construction in progress has been accounted for on a net-of-tax basis (or after-tax basis) by some entities that qualify as regulated enterprises under FASB-71 (Accounting for the Effects of Certain Types of Regulation). Enterprises that have followed this method of accounting shall, upon the initial application of FASB-96, adjust their construction in progress accounts to reflect the amounts that would have resulted if the provisions of FASB-96 had been applied to all prior years. No adjustment shall be made to the reported amount of plant in service at the beginning of the earliest year restated or at the beginning of the year in which FASB-96 is first applied, whichever is applicable. The difference, if any, between the reported amount of plant in service and the tax basis of that same plant in service is a temporary difference for which a deferred tax liability must be recognized. If it is probable that amounts required for settlement of that deferred tax liability will be recovered from customers through future rates, an asset and the related deferred tax liability for that additional temporary difference shall be recognized for that probable future revenue. The net effect of applying the provisions of this paragraph shall be reported (as discussed above), as the cumulative effect of a change in accounting principle, in accordance with paragraph 20 of APB-20 (Accounting Changes).

EXPOSURE DRAFT

The following material is based on two Exposure Drafts (ED), one entitled *Accounting for Income Taxes — Deferral of the Effective Date of FASB Statement No. 96: An Amendment of FASB Statement No. 96* and the other entitled *Accounting for Income Taxes*. These EDs are outstanding as of the date of this publication. There may be significant differences between the EDs discussed below and the official FASB Statements when they are promulgated. Thus, the reader is cautioned to compare carefully the material in these EDs with the official pronouncements when they become available.

Accounting for Income Taxes—Deferral of the Effective Date of FASB Statement No. 96: An Amendment of FASB Statement No. 96

This ED would defer the effective date of FASB-96 to fiscal years beginning after December 15, 1992. Earlier application would be permitted.

Although FASB-96 was originally scheduled to be effective for fiscal years beginning after December 15, 1988, it has not yet gone into effect. FASB-100 deferred the effective date of FASB-96 to fiscal years beginning after December 15, 1989, and FASB-103 provided a further deferral to fiscal years beginning after December 15, 1991.

Concurrently the FASB has issued another Exposure Draft, this one entitled *Accounting for Income Taxes,* which is discussed below. The ED on *Accounting for Income Taxes* would supersede FASB-96, and would be effective for fiscal years beginning after December 15, 1992. If the FASB meets its own schedule for issuing the new Statement on *Accounting for Income Taxes,* FASB-96 will be superseded without ever having gone into effect, although some enterprises have elected its early application.

Accounting for Income Taxes

The Exposure Draft entitled *Accounting for Income Taxes* would supersede FASB-96, which has the same title.

The FASB has received numerous requests to amend FASB-96. According to the ED, the requests emphasized two objectives: (1) to ease the restrictions on recognizing deferred tax assets arising from tax loss carryforwards, and (2) to simplify various calculations.

The ED, like FASB-96, would take the asset and liability approach to accounting for income taxes, but would depart from FASB-96 on a number of issues. The most significant changes are summarized below.

Tax Loss Carryforwards

The ED would allow recognition of a tax asset, based on the anticipated future tax savings from a loss carryforward. A valuation allowance would be used in order to reduce the carrying amount to the amount that would "more likely than not" be realized.

This would contrast sharply with FASB-96, which does not allow recognition of loss carryforwards. On this issue the ED also differs from APB-11, which allows recognition of loss carryforwards only if realization is assured beyond any reasonable doubt.

In support of this change, the FASB offers a new interpretation of FASB Concepts Statement No. 6 (FASB:CS-6) (Elements of Financial Statements). One of the characteristics of an asset, according to FASB:CS-6, is that a "transaction or other event giving rise to the entity's right to or control of the benefit has already occurred." In applying this concept to accounting for income taxes, it is necessary to identify the critical event which allows a potential tax benefit from a loss carryforward to qualify as an asset.

According to FASB-96, the critical event is the earning of income in a subsequent year, to which the loss carryforward can be applied. Consequently, FASB-96 does not allow a loss carryforward to qualify as an asset until the enterprise earns taxable income in a subsequent year.

Reflecting the FASB's reconsideration, the ED concludes that the critical event is the reporting of the loss which becomes available for carryforward. Thus the potential tax savings from a loss carryforward can qualify as a tax asset immediately upon the reporting of the tax loss. However, the tax asset should be recognized at the time of reporting the tax loss only if the enterprise is "more likely than not" to report future taxable income against which the loss carryforward can be applied.

In making this "more likely than not" decision, and in determining the amount of a valuation allowance if one is needed, the enterprise should consider all available evidence, both positive and negative. Among other factors, the enterprise should consider the potential effects of tax planning strategies, net of any related expenses or losses.

Tax Rate

To simplify calculations, the ED would adopt a convention to replace the more precise computations called for by FASB-96. The convention in the ED would use the marginal enacted tax rate that applies to the last dollars of taxable income in the periods in which the deferred tax asset or liability is expected to be settled or realized.

Classification

The ED would classify deferred tax assets and liabilities as current or noncurrent, based on the assets and liabilities to which they relate. If amounts are not related to a specific asset or liability, the ED would classify deferred tax assets and liabilities on the basis of the expected reversal date of the specific temporary difference.

The ED differs from FASB-96, which defines the current portion of a tax asset or liability as the portion relating to temporary differences that will result in deductible or taxable amounts during the following year (with special provisions if the operating cycle is longer than one year).

The approach to classification proposed by the ED is similar to the pre-FASB-96 treatment of the issue in FASB-37 (Balance Sheet Classification of Deferred Income Taxes).

Exemptions from Deferred Tax Accounting

The ED would reduce the list of special exemptions from the requirements of deferred tax accounting. According to the ED, the only fully-exempt areas would be the undistributed earnings of foreign subsidiaries or foreign joint ventures, if those earnings are or will be invested indefinitely. The other areas that are currently exempt would come within the coverage of the ED, but the new accounting standard would be modified with regard to these areas.

The areas that are currently exempt and would come within the coverage of the ED are, in summary:

1. Undistributed earnings of domestic subsidiaries or domestic joint ventures
2. Bad debt reserves of savings and loan associations
3. Policyholders' surplus of stock life insurance companies
4. U.S. steamship enterprises' deposits in statutory reserve funds

In these previously-exempt areas, the new accounting standard would apply with two modifications. First, coverage of these areas would not include temporary differences between tax and financial accounting which arose before the beginning of the year for which application of the new accounting standard is required. Second, recognition of deferred tax assets in these areas would be governed by special limitations.

Direct Addition to Contributed Capital

The ED would require an entity to report, as a direct addition to contributed capital, any tax benefits attributable to (a) carryforwards that existed and were not recognized at the date of a quasi-reorganization of any type, including one that involves no more than an elimination of a deficit in retained earnings, and (b) tax deductible dividends paid on unallocated shares of an ESOP.

FASB-96 deals differently with a quasi-reorganization which consists only of an elimination of a deficit in retained earnings. In this situation, FASB-96 requires the tax benefit of an operating loss or tax credit carryforward to be included in the current year's income or loss and subsequently transferred from retained earnings to contributed capital.

FASB-96 does not expressly deal with tax deductible dividends paid on unallocated shares of an ESOP.

Disclosure

In addition to the disclosures required by FASB-96, the ED would require disclosure of:

1. The total of all deferred tax liabilities
2. The total of all deferred tax assets
3. The total valuation allowance for deferred tax assets
4. Any net change in the valuation allowance
5. The nature and effect of significant matters affecting comparability of information for all periods presented (for example, the effect of a change in judgment regarding future realization of a deferred tax asset)

Transition

The ED includes an innovative provision on transition, regarding purchase business combinations which were consummated before the beginning of the year when the accounting standard is first applied, but this provision would not apply to leveraged leases or when the adjustment would be impracticable.

Goodwill would not be adjusted, but the remaining balances as of the date of initial application would be adjusted from net-of-tax amounts to pretax amounts. Any differences between those adjusted remaining balances and their tax bases would be temporary differences, to be recognized as deferred tax liabilities or assets as of the beginning of the year of first application. The net effect would be reported as the effect of a change in accounting principle.

FASB-96 does not allow this type of adjustment.

INSTALLMENT METHOD
OF ACCOUNTING

Overview

APB-10, paragraph 12, and ARB-43, Chapter 1A, paragraph 1, constitute the promulgated GAAP for the installment method of accounting and unrealized profit.

Background

Promulgated GAAP prohibit accounting for sales by any form of installment accounting except under exceptional circumstances where collectibility cannot be reasonably estimated or assured. The doubtfulness of collectibility can be caused by the length of an extended collection period or because no basis of estimation can be established. In such cases, a company can use either the cost recovery method or the installment sales method of accounting (APB-10).

Cost Recovery Method

The cost recovery method, also known as the sunk-cost theory, is used in situations where recovery of cost is undeterminable or extremely questionable. The procedure is simply that all cost is recovered before any gain is recognized. Once all cost has been recovered, any other collections are recognized as revenue. The only expenses remaining to be charged against such revenue are those relating to the collection process.

   For example, if a company sells for $100 an item that cost $40 and receives no down payment, the first $20 collected, regardless of the year collected, would be considered recovery of one-half the cost. The next $20 collected would be recovery of the balance of the cost, regardless of the year collected. The remaining $60 (all gross profit) would be recognized as income when received. The only additional expenses that could be charged against the remaining $60 would be those directly related to the collection process.

Recording Installment Sales

Under the installment sales method of accounting, each payment collected consists of part recovery of cost and part recovery of gross profit, in the same ratio that these two elements existed in the original sale. For example, assume that a furniture dealer sells for $100 a chair that cost him $70. The gross profit percentage for this sale is 30%. The dealer would recognize 70% of any payment as a recovery of cost and 30% as realized gross profit.

The entries to record the initial sale, assuming the use of a periodic inventory system and no down payment, are:

Accounts receivable—installment sales	$100	
Installment sales		$100
Cost of installment sales	$ 70	
Inventory		$ 70

At the end of the period, the company closes out the installment sales account and the cost of installment sales to unrealized gross profit on installment sales account, which in this example is $30. The entry is:

Installment sales	$100	
Cost of installment sales		$ 70
Unrealized gross profit on installment sales		30

In the period that the company collects $40, the entries are:

Cash	$ 40	
Accounts receivable—installment sales		$ 40
Unrealized gross profit on installment sales	$ 12	
Realized gross profit on installment sales		$ 12

The $40 collected includes $28 recovery of cost and $12 of realized gross profit on installment sales (70%/30% relationship).

Since gross profit ratios are different for most products and departments and fluctuate between years, it is necessary to keep a separate record of sales by year, product lines, and department. Separate accounts and records must be kept for receivables, realized gross profit, unrealized gross profit, and repossessions for each category of product. Under the installment sales method, selling and administrative costs are charged to expense in the period incurred.

Generally, the seller will protect its interest in an installment sale by retaining title to the goods through a conditional sales contract, lease, mortgage, or trustee. In the event of a default on an installment sales contract, the related account receivable and unrealized gross profit are written off. In many cases of default, the goods are repossessed by the seller. The loss (or gain) on a default of an installment sales contract is determined as follows:

$$
\begin{array}{c} \text{Loss} \\ \text{(or Gain)} = \end{array}
\begin{bmatrix} \text{balance of} \\ \text{account} \\ \text{receivable} \end{bmatrix}
\text{ less }
\begin{bmatrix} \text{unrealized} \\ \text{gross} \\ \text{profit} \end{bmatrix}
\text{ less }
\begin{bmatrix} \text{inventory value of} \\ \text{repossessed} \\ \text{merchandise} \\ \text{(if any)} \end{bmatrix}
$$

For example, continuing the preceding illustration, if the first payment of $40 was the only payment the company received and the goods were not repossessed, the journal entry to record the default and loss would be:

Unrealized gross profit	$18	
Loss on installment sales	42	
Accounts receivable—installment sales		$60

If the goods were repossessed and had an inventory value of $25, the journal entry would be:

Unrealized gross profit	$18	
Loss on installment sales	17	
Inventory	25	
Accounts receivable—installment sales		$60

When goods are repossessed, one of the major problems is determining the value of these inventory goods. Some of the methods of determining the value include:

1. Fair market value
2. Unrecovered cost (results in no gain or no loss)
3. Resale value less reconditioning costs plus a normal profit (net realizable value)
4. No value—a good method when no other method is appropriate, particularly when the actual value is minor

Deferred Income Taxes

The installment sales method is acceptable for tax purposes, because the government attempts to collect taxes when the taxpayer has the cash on hand rather than basing collection on a theoretical analysis of accounting principles. The use of installment accounting for tax purposes and normal accrual accounting for financial reporting purposes results in a timing difference and creates a deferred tax liability.

Disclosure

Accounts receivable on installment sales are shown separately in the balance sheet. They are classified as current assets in accordance with the normal operating cycle of the entity, which frequently extends for more than one year. Resources that are reasonably expected to be realized in cash, sold, or consumed (prepaid items) during the normal operating cycle of a business are classified as current assets. The amounts maturing each period for each class of installment receivable should also be disclosed.

Unrealized gross profit is presented in the balance sheet as a separate caption, immediately above stockholders' equity or as a contra account to the related installment receivable.

Since realized gross profit is recognized as a portion of each cash collection, a percentage relationship will always exist between the installment accounts receivable balance for a particular sales category and the related unrealized gross profit for that category. The percentage relationship will be the same as the gross profit ratio on the initial sale.

INTANGIBLE ASSETS

Overview

APB-17 establishes the promulgated GAAP for accounting for intangible assets. Accounting for intangible assets of motor carriers is covered by FASB-44. A good source of nonpromulgated GAAP is Accounting Research Study No. 10 (Accounting for Goodwill (AICPA)).

The promulgated GAAP (APB-17) cover both internally developed intangibles and those acquired in a business combination. However, the promulgated GAAP (APB-17) do not cover research and development costs included in FASB-2.

> **OBSERVATION**: *APB-17 is effective for intangible assets acquired after October 31, 1970, and provides that intangible assets acquired prior to November 1, 1970, could continue to be accounted for in accordance with the preceding GAAP (ARB-43, Chapter 5). Under Chapter 5 of ARB-43, an intangible asset with an indeterminate life (type b) could be capitalized and subsequent amortization was not required, unless it became reasonably evident that the life of the intangible asset had become limited. Thus, under Chapter 5 of ARB-43, it was possible to **permanently capitalize** a type b intangible asset. To this day, the balance sheet of some enterprises reflects the cost of type b intangible assets which have never been amortized.*
>
> *APB-17, the present promulgated GAAP, requires that all intangible assets be amortized over their estimated useful lives, which cannot exceed forty years.*

FASB-72 (Accounting for Certain Acquisitions of Banking or Thrift Institutions) is applicable to that portion of goodwill that arises from the excess of the fair value of assumed liabilities over the fair value of acquired identifiable assets that may result from the acquisition of a troubled banking or thrift institution. FASB-72 provides for a different method of amortization over a shorter period than that required by APB-17 (Intangible Assets). In addition, FASB Interpretation-9 provides guidance for recording the acquisition of a banking or thrift institution by the use of the net-spread method and the separate-valuation method. For a complete discussion of FASB-72 and FASB Interpretation-9, refer to Chapter 45.01, "Banking and Thrift Institutions," in the specialized industry accounting principles section of this guide.

Background

The term *intangible asset* refers to certain long-lived legal rights and competitive advantages developed or acquired by a business enterprise.

Intangible assets differ considerably in their characteristics, useful lives, and relationship to operations of an enterprise and may be classified as follows.

Identifiability Patents, copyrights, franchises, trademarks, and other similar intangible assets that can be specifically identified with reasonably descriptive names. Other types of intangible assets lack specific identification, the most common being goodwill.

Manner of Acquisition Intangible assets may be purchased or developed internally and may be acquired singly, in groups, or in business combinations.

Determinate or Indeterminate Life Patents are issued to inventors for a period of 17 years. Copyrights and most franchises also expire within a definite period. Other intangible assets such as organizational costs, secret processes, and goodwill have no determinable term of existence, or the expected period of benefit cannot be ascertained at the time of acquisition.

Transferability The rights to a patent, copyright, or franchise can be separately identified and bought or sold. Organizational costs are an inseparable part of a business, and it is unlikely that a purchaser would purchase the organizational costs without the business. Similarly, goodwill is inseparable from a business and is transferable only as an inseparable intangible asset of an enterprise.

Cost of Intangibles

A company should record as assets the cost of intangible assets acquired from other enterprises or individuals. Costs of developing, maintaining, or restoring intangible assets that are not specifically identifiable, have indeterminate lives, or are inherent in a continuing business and related to an enterprise as a whole, such as goodwill, should be deducted from income when incurred.

> **OBSERVATION:** *For a discussion of the net-spread method and the separate-valuation method used to record the acquisition of a banking or thrift institution, refer to Chapter 45.01, "Banking and Thrift Institutions."*

Cost of an intangible asset is measured by (1) the amount of cash disbursed or the fair value of other assets distributed, (2) the present value of amounts to be paid for liabilities incurred, and (3) the fair value of consideration received for stock issued (cost may be determined either by the fair value of the consideration given or by the fair value of the property acquired, whichever is more clearly evident).

The cost of unidentifiable intangible assets is measured by the difference between the cost of the group of assets or of the enterprise acquired and the sum of the assigned costs to identifiable assets acquired, less liabilities assumed. Cost of identifiable assets should not include goodwill.

The cost of an intangible asset, including goodwill acquired in a business combination, may *not* be written off as a lump sum to capital surplus or to retained earnings, or be reduced to a nominal amount at or immediately after acquisition.

Amortization

The cost of each type of intangible asset should be amortized by systematic charges to income over the period estimated to be benefited, but not to exceed 40 years.

Usually, all methods of amortizing goodwill are criticized as arbitrary, because the life of goodwill is indefinite and an estimated period of existence is not measurable.

Amortizing the cost of intangible assets, on arbitrary bases, in the absence of evidence of limited lives or decreased values may recognize expenses and decreases of assets prematurely. However, delaying amortization of the cost until a loss is evident may recognize the decreases after the fact.

Even if the estimated useful life of an intangible asset is more than 40 years, it must be amortized over 40 years or less.

A business enterprise should evaluate the periods of amortization continually to determine if later circumstances warrant revision of estimated useful lives. If estimates are changed, the unamortized cost should be allocated to the number of years in the revised useful life, but not to exceed 40 years after date of acquisition.

> **OBSERVATION:** *FASB-72 concludes that goodwill arising in the acquisition of a troubled banking or thrift institution should be amortized over a relatively short period because of the uncertainty about the nature and extent of the estimated future benefits related to the goodwill (see Chapter 45.01).*

Method The straight-line method of amortization should be applied unless a company demonstrates that another systematic method is more appropriate. The method and estimated useful lives of intangible assets should be adequately disclosed in the financial statements.

Income tax effect Amortization of acquired intangible assets not deductible in computing income taxes payable does not create a timing (temporary) difference, and allocation of income taxes is inappropriate. Only goodwill acquired after November 1, 1970, should be amortized, and retroactive amortization of previously unamortized goodwill acquired prior to November 1, 1970, is prohibited (APB-17).

Negative Goodwill

The measurement or valuation of cost in financial accounting usually means the historical or acquisition cost. The sum of the market or appraised values of identifiable assets less liabilities assumed may sometimes exceed the cost of the assets or business enterprise being acquired. Under these circumstances, the values assigned to the noncurrent assets being acquired should be reduced proportionately (except long-term investments in marketable securities) to absorb the excess value. A deferred credit for an excess of assigned values of identifiable assets over cost (*negative goodwill*) should not be recorded unless the noncurrent assets have been reduced to zero. If, after reducing the noncurrent assets (except long-term investments in marketable securities) to zero, a deferred credit still remains, it should be classified as a deferred credit—excess of acquired net assets over cost, and amortized systematically to income over the period expected to benefit, but not in excess of 40 years. The method and period of amortization should be adequately disclosed in the financial statements. No part of the excess of acquired net assets over cost (negative goodwill) should be credited directly to stockholders' equity at the date of acquisition.

Disposal of Goodwill

Goodwill is unidentifiable apart from a business and cannot be disposed of separately from the enterprise as a whole. However, a large segment or a separable group of assets of an acquired company may be sold or otherwise liquidated, and all or a portion of the unamortized cost of goodwill recognized in the acquisition should be included in the cost of the assets sold.

Step-by-Step Acquisitions

If an enterprise purchases, on a step-by-step basis, a subsidiary that is consolidated or an investment that is accounted for under the equity method, the fair value of the underlying assets acquired and the goodwill for each step purchased must be separately identified.

Assume that Company P acquired an interest in Company S in two steps: (1) It acquired 20% of the outstanding common stock for $200,000. (2) The following year it acquired an additional 60% for $500,000. At the dates of acquisition, the equity book values for Company S were $900,000 and $1,100,000 respectively.

Computation of Excess of Cost over Book Value

First Acquisition

Cost of 20% acquired	$200,000
20% of equity book value of $900,000	180,000
Excess of cost over book value (goodwill)	$ 20,000

Second Acquisition

Cost of 60% acquired	$500,000
60% of equity book value of $1,100,000	660,000
Excess of book value over cost (negative goodwill)	($160,000)

Actually, as of the date of the second acquisition, Company P had an investment of $700,000 for 80% of Company S. Company S at the second acquisition date had an equity book value of $1,100,000, and

Company P's 80% is $880,000, for which it paid $700,000. Had Company P been recording its first acquisition of 20% on the equity method, it would have recorded its 20% of the $200,000 increase in Company S's book value (assuming that no dividends or other distributions were made to Company P by Company S). Thus, the adjusted equity in Company S on the books of Company P would include the original $200,000 purchase price plus 20% of the $200,000 increase in book value (from $900,000 to $1,100,000), or a total of $220,000 ($180,000 + $40,000). The cost of the second acquisition of 60% for $500,000 and the adjusted basis for the 20% at $220,000 equals $720,000, which represents 80% of $1,100,000, or $880,000. The difference of $160,000 is the excess of book value over cost (negative goodwill), indicated by the computation for the second acquisition of 60%.

Disclosure

A description of intangible assets, method of amortization, and estimated useful lives should be appropriately disclosed in the financial statements or in footnotes.

In the event that a large part or all of the unamortized cost of an intangible asset is included as an extraordinary charge in the determination of net income, the reasons for the extraordinary deduction should be fully disclosed.

Intangible Assets of Motor Carriers

The cost of intangible assets of motor carriers may include (1) expected benefits from established routes, (2) marketing or operating efficiencies, (3) knowledge of business, (4) customer lists, (5) favorable leases, (6) operating rights, and (7) goodwill. Operating rights are franchises or permits issued by the ICC or a state agency that permit a motor carrier to transport specified commodities over a specified route. Operating rights usually result in limiting competition over a particular route. When issued by a federal agency, they are referred to as *interstate operating rights*, and when issued by a state agency, they are referred to as *intrastate operating rights*. FASB-44 covers only interstate operating rights and those intrastate operating rights in states which have enacted legislation similar to the Motor Carrier Act of 1980.

> **OBSERVATION**: *As a result of the Motor Carrier Act of 1980, the FASB has found that the value of an interstate operating right of a motor carrier has become permanently and substantially impaired, as evidenced by a significant decline in the value of these rights for sale or for use as collateral. The FASB has concluded that the unamortized cost of impaired operating rights should be completely written off by a charge to income in the year in which their value was impaired. FASB-44 applies to intrastate operating rights in those states that enact legislation similar to the Motor Carrier Act.*

The cost of previously acquired intangible assets of motor carriers must be separately identified and classified as (1) impaired operating rights, (2) other identifiable intangible assets, including unimpaired operating rights, and (3) goodwill. Cost is defined as the net carrying amount of the intangible asset on the date FASB-44 is first applied. However, net carrying amount shall include only the original or unamortized original cost of the intangible asset.

Costs of developing, maintaining, or restoring intangible assets after they were acquired must not be included in the cost of the intangible assets. In addition, those costs that are identified and assigned to previously acquired intangible assets shall not be merged with, or replaced by, any amounts relating to other identifiable intangibles or goodwill.

GAAP that existed on the date that the intangible assets were previously acquired should be used as the basis for identifying and assigning costs to (1) impaired operating rights, (2) other identifiable intangible assets, including unimpaired operating rights, and (3) goodwill.

If, for any reason, a motor carrier cannot separately identify and assign costs to its previously acquired intangible assets in accordance with FASB-44, it shall be presumed that all such costs relate to impaired operating rights.

Previously acquired intangible assets which are classified as impaired operating rights in accordance with FASB-44 shall be charged to income in the period in which FASB-44 is first applied, and if material, such amounts shall be reported as an extraordinary item in accordance with existing GAAP (APB-30).

After FASB-44 is first applied, any intangible assets that must subsequently be charged to income in accordance with the provisions of FASB-44 shall not be reported as an extraordinary item, even if such amounts are material.

Tax effects that arise from the application of FASB-44 should be accounted for in accordance with existing GAAP (FASB-96).

Motor carriers shall account for operating rights which do not have to be charged to income in accordance with FASB-44, and other identifiable intangible assets, including goodwill, in accordance with APB-17 (Intangible Assets) or ARB-43, Chapter 5 (Intangible Assets). In other words, after charging all impaired operating rights to income in accordance with FASB-44, the remaining unimpaired operating rights and other identifiable assets, including goodwill, shall be reported in accordance with the GAAP that existed at the time the asset was acquired. If the intangible asset was acquired at the time ARB-43 (Chapter 5) was in effect, the intangible asset should be reported on the balance sheet at its original unamortized cost. If the intangible asset was acquired after APB-17 went into effect (November 1, 1970), it should be reported on the balance sheet at its original cost, less amortization over a period of 40 years or less.

FASB-44 is effective for financial statements covering fiscal periods that end after December 15, 1980. Earlier application of FASB-44 is encouraged for fiscal periods prior to its effective date, providing that the financial statements had not been issued before December 19, 1980.

FASB-44 should not be applied retroactively to previously issued financial statements.

Comprehensive Illustrations

The following examples depict the computation of goodwill using different facts.

---

1. Company P acquires an 80% interest in the outstanding common stock of Company S for $725,000. At the date of acquisition, Company S has capital stock of $600,000 and retained earnings of $150,000.

As at the Date of Acquisition

Cost of investment in Company S		$725,000
Company S stockholders' equity:		
Capital stock	$600,000	
Retained earnings	150,000	
Total	$750,000	
Acquired by Company P	80%	
Equity acquired by Company P		600,000
Excess of cost over book value (goodwill)		$125,000

2. Company P acquires cash all the assets and liabilities of Company S for $500,000. An appraisal at the date of acquisition reflects the following values.

Accounts receivable (net)	$ 75,000
Inventories	125,000
Fixed assets	400,000
Long-term marketable securities	100,000
Total	$700,000
Liabilities assumed (present values)	250,000
Value of underlying assets	$450,000
Cost of assets acquired	500,000
Excess of cost over assets acquired (goodwill)	$ 50,000

In example 2 above, if the cost of the assets acquired was $400,000, creating negative goodwill of $50,000, only noncurrent assets, *except long-term marketable securities,* should be adjusted downward, but not below zero. The result in this case is that fixed assets are reduced to $350,000, and *no negative goodwill is recorded.* However, negative goodwill would have been recorded on the books if all the noncurrent assets (except long-term marketable securities) had been reduced to zero and a balance of the excess of book value over cost still remained.

3. When preferred stock is involved in an acquisition of a subsidiary, caution must be taken when (a) dividends are in arrears or (b) there is any preference in liquidation.

Company P acquires 75,000 shares of Company S common stock for $900,000. At the date of acquisition, Company S has 100,000 shares of common stock outstanding with a stated value of $1,000,000, and 5,000 shares of 5% preferred stock $100 par outstanding with dividends in arrears of $50,000; the preferred stock is entitled to $105 per share in the event of liquidation.

Computation of Excess of Cost over Book Value

	Preferred	Common
5,000 shares of preferred stock par $100	$500,000	
Stated value of common stock		$1,000,000
Dividends in arrears	50,000	(50,000)
Liquidation preference on preferred stock	25,000	(25,000)
Retained earnings		225,000
Paid-in capital		100,000
Totals	$575,000	$1,250,000
75% of common equity acquired by P		$ 937,500
Cost of 75%		900,000
Excess of book value over cost (negative goodwill)		$ 37,500

INTEREST ON RECEIVABLES AND PAYABLES

Overview

APB-21 is the main source of GAAP on imputing, if necessary, interest on receivables and payables. However, APB-21 excludes the following types of receivables and payables:

1. Arising in the ordinary course of business, which are due in approximately one year or less
2. Whose terms of payments are in property or services and not in cash
3. Representing security or retainage deposits
4. Arising in the ordinary course of business of a lending institution
5. Arising from transactions between a parent and its subsidiaries, or between subsidiaries of a common parent
6. Whose interest rate is determined by a governmental agency

The present value techniques used in APB-21 should not be applied to estimates of a contractual property or other obligations that are assumed in connection with a sale of property, goods, or services such as an estimated warranty for product performance.

> **OBSERVATION**: *Interest that is imputed on certain receivables and payables in accordance with APB-21 is eligible for capitalization under the provisions of FASB-34 (See chapter entitled "Interest Costs Capitalized").*

Background

Those receivables and payables that are not specifically excluded from the provisions of APB-21 and that are contractual rights to receive or pay money at a fixed or determinable date must be recorded at their present value if (1) the interest rate is not stated or (2) the stated interest rate is unreasonable. This is an application of the basic principle of substance over form.

A note issued or received solely for cash equal to its face amount is presumed to earn the interest stated. However, if rights or privileges are attached to the note, they must be evaluated separately. For example, a beer distributor lends $5,000 for two years at no interest to a customer who wishes to purchase bar equipment. There is, of course, a tacit agreement that the customer will buy the distributor's products. In this event, a present value must be established for the note receivable, and the difference between the face of the note ($5,000) and its present value must be considered an additional cost of doing business for the beer distributor.

There is a general presumption that the interest stated on a note, resulting from a business transaction entered into at arm's length, is fair and adequate. However, if no interest is stated or the interest stated appears unreasonable, the substance of the transaction must be recorded.

A note issued or received in a noncash transaction contains two elements to be valued: (1) the principal amount for the property, goods, or services exchanged and (2) an interest factor for the use of funds over the time period of the note. These types of notes must be recorded at their present value. Any difference between the face amount of the note and its present value is a discount or premium that must be amortized over the life of the note.

Determining Present Value

There is no predetermined formula for computing an appropriate interest rate. *However, the objective is to approximate what the rate would have been, using the same terms and conditions, if it had been negotiated by an independent lender.* The following guidelines are recommended:

1. Credit rating of the borrower
2. Restrictive covenants or collateral involved
3. Prevailing market rates
4. Rate at which the debtor could borrow funds

The appropriate interest rate will frequently depend upon a combination of the above factors.

Amortization of Discount or Premium

The difference between the present value and the face amount of the receivable or the payable represents the amount of premium or discount. A discount exists if the present value of the total eventual proceeds of the note (face amount plus stated interest), using the appropriate rate of interest, is *less* than the face amount of the note. A premium exists if the present value of the total eventual proceeds of the note (face amount plus stated interest), using the appropriate rate of interest, is *more* than the face amount of the note.

The premium or discount should be amortized over the life of the note, using a constant rate on any outstanding balance. This method is called the *interest method* and is reviewed in the comprehensive illustration at the end of this chapter.

Statement Presentation of Discount or Premium

The premium or discount that arises from the use of present values on cash and noncash transactions is inseparable from the related asset or liability. Therefore, such premiums or discounts are deducted from their related asset or liability on the balance sheet. Discounts or premiums resulting from imputing interest must not be classified as deferred charges or credits.

Disclosure

A full description of the receivable or payable, the effective interest rate, and the face amount of the note should be disclosed in the financial statements or footnotes thereto.

Issue costs should be reported separately in the balance sheet as deferred charges.

Comprehensive Illustrations

The following example indicates how interest is imputed on a non-interest-bearing note.

A manufacturer sells a machine for $10,000 and accepts a $10,000 note receivable bearing no interest for five years; 10% is an appropriate interest rate. The initial journal entry would be:

Note receivable	$10,000.00	
Sales (present value at 10%)		$6,209.00
Unamortized discount on note		3,791.00

End of 1st year:
    Unamortized discount on note $ 620.90
        Interest income $ 620.90
        (10% of $6,209)

End of 2nd year:
    Unamortized discount on note $ 682.99
        Interest income $ 682.99
        (10% of $6,829.90)

End of 3rd year:
    Unamortized discount on note $ 751.29
        Interest income $ 751.29
        (10% of $7,512.89)

End of 4th year:
    Unamortized discount on note $ 826.42
        Interest income $ 826.42
        (10% of $8,264.18)

End of 5th year:
    Unamortized discount on note $ 909.06
        Interest income $ 909.06
        (10% of $9,090.60)

In the example above, the manufacturer records the note at its face amount but records the sale at the present value of the note because that is all the note is worth today. The difference between the face amount of the note and its present value is recorded as *unamortized discount on note.*

The *interest method* is used to produce a constant rate which is applied to any outstanding balance. In the above example, the present value of $6,209 was recorded for the $10,000 sale using the appropriate interest rate of 10% for the five-year term of the note. The difference between the $10,000 sale and its present value of $6,209 is $2,791, which was recorded as unamortized discount on note. Since the present value was determined by using the 10% rate for five years, it stands to reason that the same 10% rate, when applied to each annual outstanding balance for the same five years, will result in full amortization of the discount on the note, as follows:

		Amortization of Discount on the Note
Original balance	$6,209.00	$3,791.00
Year 1, 10%	620.90	620.90
Remaining balance	$6,829.90	$3,170.10
Year 2, 10%	682.99	682.99
Remaining balance	$7,512.89	$2,487.11
Year 3, 10%	751.29	751.29
Remaining balance	$8,264.18	$1,735.82
Year 4, 10%	826.42	826.42
Remaining balance	$9,090.60	$ 909.40
Year 5, 10%	909.05	909.05
*Remaining balance	$9,999.65	$ 0.35

*Difference of $0.35 due to rounding.

The next example illustrates how a note with an unreasonable rate of interest should be recorded.

A company purchases a $10,000 machine and issues for payment a $10,000 four-year note bearing 2% compound interest per year; 10% is considered an appropriate rate of interest. The initial journal entry is:

Machine (present value of $10,824 @ 10%)	$7,393	
Unamortized discount on note	3,431	
Note payable		$10,000
Deferred interest payable		824

1st year:

Interest expense	$ 739	
Unamortized discount on note		$ 739

2nd year:

Interest expense	$ 813	
Unamortized discount on note		$ 813

3rd year:

Interest expense	$ 895	
Unamortized discount on note		$ 895

4th year:

Interest expense	$ 984	
Unamortized discount on note		$ 984

In the fourth year, when the note and the 2% interest are paid, the following journal entry is made:

Note payable	$10,000	
Deferred interest payable	824	
Cash		$10,824

In the above example, the company records a note payable ($10,000) and the deferred interest ($824) at their face amount. The total due in four years is $10,824, and the machine is valued at the present value of this amount ($7,393). This is because today the $10,824 is worth only $7,393, which is the amount at which the sale should be recorded. The difference between the total amount due in four years ($10,824) and its present value ($7,393) must be considered deferred interest ($3,431) for the use of the seller's funds.

INTEREST COSTS CAPITALIZED

Overview

FASB-34 (Capitalization of Interest Cost) covers the promulgated GAAP on the capitalization of interest costs on certain qualifying assets that are undergoing activities to get them ready for their intended use. FASB-42 (Determining Materiality for Capitalization of Interest Cost) is an amendment to FASB-34, which requires that the same materiality tests applied to regular GAAP be applied to the materiality of capitalizing interest cost.

FASB-58 (Capitalization of Interest Cost in Financial Statements that Include Investments Accounted For by the Equity Method) amends FASB-34 to provide for capitalization of interest cost on equity funds, loans, and advances made by investors to certain investees that are accounted for by the equity method (APB-18).

FASB-62 (Capitalization of Interest Cost in Situations Involving Certain Tax-Exempt Borrowings and Certain Gifts and Grants) amends FASB-34 to provide special treatment in capitalizing interest costs on qualifying assets that are acquired with (a) the proceeds of tax-exempt borrowings and (b) a gift or grant that is restricted for the sole purpose of acquiring a specific asset. In addition, FASB-62 supersedes FASB Technical Bulletin 81-5 (Offsetting Interest Cost to Be Capitalized with Interest Income).

FASB-34 (Capitalization of Interest Cost) supersedes the provisions for capitalizing interest costs that appear in the AICPA Industry Accounting Guide entitled "Retail Land Sales." Thus, enterprises involved in retail land sales must apply the provisions of FASB-34 to determine the amount of interest cost that must be capitalized.

FASB-34 includes the capitalization of interest imputed on receivables and payables in accordance with APB-21 (Interest on Receivables and Payables). In other words, interest costs that are imputed in accordance with existing GAAP may qualify for capitalization in accordance with FASB-34. In addition, FASB-34 permits the capitalization of interest costs that are related to a lease that is capitalized in accordance with FASB-13 (Accounting for Leases). Thus, interest costs that would otherwise ultimately be expensed under APB-21 and FASB-13 are eligible for capitalization in accordance with FASB-34.

Background

The basis of accounting for depreciable fixed assets is cost, and all normal expenditures of readying an asset for use should be capitalized. However, unnecessary expenditures that do not add to the utility of the asset should be charged to expense. An expenditure for repairing a piece of equipment that was damaged during shipment should be charged to expense.

Razing and removal costs (less salvage value) of structures located on land purchased as a building site are added to the cost of the land. Land itself is never depreciated.

> **OBSERVATION:** *Promulgated GAAP (ARB-43) require that assets be recorded at cost, except in the case of quasi-reorganizations (corporate readjustments) in which it is permissible to write up or write down assets to market values (APB-6).*

Expenditures that increase the capacity or operating efficiency of an asset, if they are substantial, should be capitalized. Minor expenditures are usually treated as period costs even though they may have the characteristics of capital expenditures. When the cost of improvements is substantial or when there is a change in the estimated useful life of an asset, depreciation charges for future periods should be revised on the basis of the new book value and the new estimated remaining useful life.

The revision of the estimated useful life of an asset is measured prospectively and accounted for in the current and future periods. No adjustment is made to prior depreciation.

Capitalization of Interest—General

The FASB has concluded that, under certain conditions, interest costs should be capitalized as part of the total acquisition cost of an asset. The interest costs are incurred only during the period of time that is required to complete and get the asset ready for its intended use. Intended use means *sale* or *use within the business*. Thus, there is usually a relationship between the length of the period necessary to acquire the asset and the amount of interest that will be capitalized.

The FASB has also concluded that a better measure of acquisition cost is achieved when certain interest costs are capitalized. This apparently results in a better matching of revenue and costs in future periods.

> **OBSERVATION:** *The basis of capitalizing certain interest costs is that the cost of an asset should include all costs necessary to bring the asset to the condition and location for its intended use. However, FASB-34 fails to mention that GAAP also provide that unnecessary expenditures that do not add to the utility of an asset should not be capitalized. Companies that are required to borrow funds to acquire an asset are placed on an equal basis as far as interest expense is concerned, as that of companies that do not have to borrow. The only difference is that the total cost of the asset to the company that borrows is increased by the amount of capitalized interest. For example, Company A and Company B both acquire an identical asset for $10 million that requires three years to complete for its intended use. Company A pays cash, and at the end of three years, the total cost of the asset is $10 million. In addition, assume that Company A also had net income of $2 million a year for each of the three years and had no interest expense at all. Assume also that Company B had $1.5 million net income for each of the three years after deducting $500,000 of interest expense per year. Assuming that Company B qualifies for capitalized interest costs under FASB-34, it would reflect $2 million per year net income and not show any interest expense. However, on the balance sheet of Company B at the end of three years, the same identical asset would appear at a cost of $11.5 million. Thus, Company A has a cost of $10 million for the asset, while Company B will reflect a total cost of $11.5 million for the identical asset. Although the interest cost may be necessary to Company B, it obviously does not add to the utility of the asset.*

Qualifying Assets—Acquisition Period

Interest cost must be capitalized for all assets that require an *acquisition period* to get them ready for their intended use. *Acquisition period* is defined as the period commencing with the first expenditure for a qualifying asset and ending when the asset is substantially complete and ready for its intended use. Thus, before interest costs can be capitalized, expenditures must have been made for the qualifying asset, and activities that are required to get the asset ready for its intended use must actually be in progress.

FASB-42 (Determining Materiality for Capitalization of Interest Cost) was issued to reaffirm that the usual rules of materiality embodied in GAAP must be followed in determining the materiality for the capitalization of interest costs. One of the purposes of FASB-42 was to eliminate language in FASB-34 which implies capitalization of interest costs could be avoided in certain circumstances. Thus, in applying the provisions of FASB-34, all the usual materiality tests used in applying other promulgated GAAP should also be used in determining the materiality for capitalization of interest costs.

Qualifying Assets—Intended Use

Certain interest costs, if material, must be capitalized and added to the acquisition cost of assets that require a period of time (acquisition period) to get them ready for their intended use. The cost of assets to which capitalized interest must be allocated include the cost of both (1) assets acquired for a company's own use and (2) assets acquired for sale in the ordinary course of business. Thus, inventory items that require a long time to produce, such as a real estate development, qualify for capitalization of interest costs. However, interest costs should not be capitalized for inventories that require a period of time to get them ready for their intended use if such inventories are routinely produced in large quantities on a repetitive basis.

> **OBSERVATION:** *The FASB concluded that the benefit of capitalizing interest costs on inventories that are routinely produced in large quantities does not justify the cost. Thus, interest costs should not be capitalized for inventories that are routinely produced in large quantities.*

FASB-34 does not allow the capitalization of interest cost (1) for assets that are ready for their intended use or that are actually being issued in the earning activities of a business and (2) for assets that are not being used in the earning activities of a business that are not undergoing the activities required to get them ready for use. In other words, interest costs cannot be capitalized (1) for completed assets and (2) for incompleted assets that are not undergoing activities to be completed. Also, FASB-34 specifically prohibits imputing interest costs on any equity funds.

Amount of Interest Cost to Be Capitalized

The maximum amount of interest cost that may be capitalized for any accounting period may not exceed the actual interest cost (from any source) that is incurred by an enterprise during that same accounting period. In other words, capitalizing interest cost may not create a credit balance in the interest expense account. In consolidated financial statements, this limitation on the maximum amount of interest cost that may be capitalized in a period should be applied on a consolidated basis.

> **OBSERVATION:** *Footnote 4 to paragraph 16 of FASB-87 states that, "The interest cost component of net periodic pension cost shall not be considered to be interest for purposes of applying FASB Statement No. 34, Capitalization of Interest Cost."*
>
> *Similarly, footnote 8 to paragraph 22 of FASB-106 states that: "The interest cost component of postretirement benefit cost shall not be considered interest for purposes of applying FASB Statement No. 34, Capitalization of Interest Cost."*

In order to compute the amount of interest cost to be capitalized for a particular accounting period, the average accumulated expenditures for the qualifying asset during the particular accounting period must be determined. To determine the average accumulated expenditures, each expenditure must be *weighted* for the time it was outstanding during the particular accounting period.

In the acquisition of a qualifying asset, a calendar year company expends $225,000 on January 1, 19X1; $360,000 on March 1, 19X1; and $180,000 on November 1, 19X1. The average accumulated expenditures for 19X1 are computed as follows:

Amount of Expenditure	Period from Expenditure to End of Year	Average Expenditure
$225,000	12 months	$225,000
360,000	10 months	300,000
180,000	2 months	30,000
$765,000		$555,000

If no specific borrowing is made to acquire the qualifying asset, the weighted-average interest rate incurred on other borrowings outstanding during the period shall be used to determine the amount of interest cost to be capitalized. Thus, the weighted-average interest rate is applied to the average accumulated expenditures for the period to calculate the amount of capitalized interest cost on the qualifying asset.

If a specific new borrowing is made to acquire the qualifying asset, the interest rate incurred on the new borrowing shall be used to determine the amount of interest costs to be capitalized. Thus, the interest rate on the specific new borrowing is applied to the average accumulated expenditures for the period to calculate the amount of capitalized interest cost on the qualifying asset. However, capitalized interest cost on average accumulated expenditures in excess of the amount of the specific new borrowing shall be calculated by the use of the weighted-average interest rate incurred on other borrowings outstanding during the period. In other words, the interest rate incurred on the specific new borrowing is used only on the average accumulated expenditures that are equal to, or less than, the amount of the new specific borrowing. The weighted-average interest rate is used on the average expenditures that exceed the amount of the new specific borrowing.

Progress payments received from the buyer of a qualifying asset must be deducted in the computation of the average amount of accumulated expenditures during a period. Nonetheless, the determination of the average amount of accumulated expenditures for a period may be reasonably estimated.

Judgment will be required to identify and select the appropriate specific borrowings that should be used in determining the weighted-average interest rate. The objective should be to obtain a reasonable cost of financing for the qualifying asset that could have been avoided if the asset was not acquired.

Capitalization Period

The interest capitalization period commences with the first expenditure for the asset and continues through the acquisition period. Interest is not capitalized during delays or interruptions, except for brief interruptions, which occur during the acquisition or development stage of the qualifying asset. When the qualifying asset is substantially complete and ready for its intended use, the capitalization of interest ceases. The qualifying asset may be completed in independent parts or in dependent parts. Interest capitalization ceases for an independent part when it is substantially complete and ready for its intended use. However, for dependent parts of a qualifying asset, interest capitalization does not stop until all dependent parts are substantially complete and ready for their intended use.

Before interest costs can be capitalized, expenditures must have been made for the qualifying asset and activities that are required to get the asset ready for its intended use must actually be in progress.

Investor's Qualifying Assets

Under the provisions of FASB-58, which amends FASB-34, an investor's qualifying assets, for the purposes of capitalizing interest costs under FASB-34, shall include equity funds, loans, and advances made to investees accounted for by the equity method, provided that the investee (a) is undergoing activities necessary to start its planned principal operations and (b) the activities include the use of funds to acquire qualifying assets for its operations. Thus, from the date of inception to the date that planned principal operations begin, an investor must capitalize interest costs on equity funds, loans, and advances made to an investee accounted for by the equity method if, during that period, the investee is undergoing activities necessary to start its planned principal operations and such activities include the use of funds to acquire qualifying assets for its operations. The investor cannot capitalize any interest costs on or after the date that the investee actually begins its planned principal operations. The term *planned principal operations*, under FASB-58, has the same meaning as used in FASB-7 (Accounting and Reporting for Development Stage Enterprises). Under the provisions of FASB-7, a development stage company is one which is devoting substantially all of its efforts to establishing a new business and (a) planned principal operations have not commenced or (b) planned principal operations have commenced, but there has been no significant revenue therefrom.

For the purposes of FASB-58, the term *investor* means both the parent company and all consolidated subsidiaries. Thus, all qualifying assets of a parent company and its consolidated subsidiaries which appear in the consolidated balance sheet are subject to the interest capitalization provisions of FASB-34 (as amended).

FASB-58 expressly states that it does not affect the accounting or reporting of capitalized interest cost in an investee's separate financial statements.

Capitalized interest costs on an investment accounted for by the equity method are included in the carrying amount of the investment. Up to the date on which the planned principal operations of the investee commence, the investor's carrying amount of the investment, which includes capitalized interest costs (if any), may exceed the underlying equity in the investment. If the investor cannot relate the excess carrying amount of the investment to specific identifiable assets of the investee, the difference is considered goodwill [paragraph 19(n) of APB-18]. Goodwill must be amortized to income over its estimated useful life, which may not exceed forty years (APB-17, Intangible Assets). The straight-line method of amortization must be used for goodwill unless another systematic and rational method can be justified.

Any interest cost capitalized under the provisions of FASB-58 shall not be changed in restating financial statements of prior periods. Thus, if an unconsolidated investee is subsequently consolidated in the investor's financial statements, as a result of increased ownership or a voluntary change by the reporting entity, interest costs capitalized in accordance with FASB-58 shall not be changed if restatement of financial statements is necessary.

FASB-58 is effective for investments (equity funds, loans, or advances) made by an investor to an investee accounted for by the equity method on or after July 1, 1982. Earlier application of the provisions of FASB-58 are encouraged, but are not required.

Contractual obligations existing on July 1, 1982, for investments not made may be accounted for in the same manner as they were prior to July 1, 1982, or the provisions of FASB-58 may be applied.

FASB-58 may be applied to unissued annual financial statements, but shall not be retroactively applied to previously issued financial statements.

Tax-Exempt Borrowings and Gifts and Grants

Under the provisions of FASB-34, capitalized interest cost for a qualifying asset is determined by applying either a specific interest rate or a weighted-average interest rate to the average accumulated expenditures during a particular period for the qualifying asset. The actual interest cost incurred on the qualifying asset is not used under the provisions of FASB-34, and it is not necessary to identify a specific borrowing or loan to a specific qualifying asset in order to capitalize interest costs. Thus, an underlying premise in FASB-34 is that borrowings usually cannot be identified with specific qualifying assets. The financing policies of most enterprises are planned to meet general funding objectives, and the identification of specific borrowings with specific assets is considered highly subjective.

FASB-62 concludes that different circumstances are involved in the acquisition of a qualifying asset with tax-exempt borrowings, such as industrial revenue bonds and pollution control bonds. The tax-exempt borrowings, temporary interest income on unused funds, and construction expenditures for the qualifying asset are so integrated that they must be accounted for as a single transaction. Thus, FASB-62 amends FASB-34 to provide for the capitalization of interest cost for any portion of a qualifying asset that is acquired with tax-exempt borrowings, as follows:

Capitalization Period

Interest cost shall be capitalized from the date of the tax-exempt borrowings to the date that the qualifying asset is ready for its intended use.

Amount of Capitalized Interest Cost

The amount of capitalized interest cost allowable under FASB-62 is equal to the total actual interest cost on the tax-exempt borrowing, less any interest income earned on temporary investments of the tax-exempt funds. In other words, the actual net cost of interest on the tax-exempt borrowing is capitalized and added to the acquisition cost of the related qualifying asset.

External Restriction Requirement

FASB-62 applies only where the qualifying asset is financed by tax-exempt borrowing, in which the use of the borrowed funds is restricted to acquiring the assets or servicing the related debt. The restriction must be *external*, that is, imposed by law, contract, or other authority outside the enterprise that borrows the funds.

After the qualifying asset is ready for its intended use and interest capitalization ceases, interest cost incurred on the related tax-exempt borrowing is eligible for capitalization on other qualifying assets of the enterprise.

As mentioned previously, FASB-62 supersedes FASB Technical Bulletin 81-5 (Offsetting Interest Cost to Be Capitalized with Interest Income). However, FASB-62 reaffirms that interest income earned on temporary funds that are earmarked for the construction of a qualifying asset cannot be used to offset the amount of interest cost that must be capitalized. As discussed above, the only exception to this rule is for qualifying assets that are acquired with tax-exempt borrowings.

Restricted gifts and grants   FASB-62 does not permit the capitalization of interest cost on any portion of a qualifying asset which is acquired with a gift or grant that is restricted to the acquisition of the specified qualifying asset. Restricted interest income on temporary investment of funds is considered an addition to the restricted gift or grant.

> *OBSERVATION: FASB-62 concludes that no interest cost should be capitalized on qualifying assets acquired by restricted gifts or grants, because there is no economic cost of financing involved in acquiring an asset with a gift or grant. In addition, any interest earned on temporary investment of funds from a gift or grant is, in substance, part of the gift or grant.*

FASB-62 is effective for tax-exempt borrowing transactions entered into on or after September 1, 1982, and for gifts and grants that are received on or after September 1, 1982. Earlier application of the provisions of FASB-62 is permitted in financial statements that have not been previously issued. FASB-62 expressly permits the retroactive application of its provisions to previously issued financial statements for fiscal years beginning on or after December 6, 1979. Any restated financial statements must include, in the year when FASB-62 is first applied, disclosure of the nature of the effects of the restatement on income before extraordinary items, net income, and related per share amounts for each restated year.

Disposition of Capitalized Interest

If capitalized interest costs are added to the overall cost of an asset, the total cost of the asset, including capitalized interest, may exceed the net realizable or other lower value of the asset that is required by GAAP. In this event, FASB-34 requires that the provision to reduce the asset cost to the lower value required by GAAP be increased. Thus, the total asset cost, including capitalized interest, less the provision, should equal the lower value for the asset that is required by GAAP.

> *OBSERVATION: Paragraph 19 of FASB-34 is apparently directed to those situations in which GAAP provide for a contra or provision account that, in effect, reduces an asset to a lower value. However, in the event an asset is permanently impaired, GAAP require that the carrying amount of the asset be reduced to its net realizable value. In this case, no contra or provision account is generally utilized. Evidently, paragraph 19 of FASB-34 does not contemplate these situations.*
>
> *Capitalized interest costs will increase the total cost of an asset acquired for a company's own use. As a result of the capitalized interest, the net carrying amount of the asset in a subsequent year may exceed its net realizable value. If the decline in value of the asset is other than temporary, the net carrying amount of the asset*

> *has become impaired. Under existing promulgated GAAP, the*
> *impaired amount must be removed from the net carrying amount,*
> *by a charge to net income in the period in which the impairment*
> *occurs. Thus, it is likely that excessive amounts of capitalized*
> *interest may be a direct cause of an impairment of the carrying*
> *amount of an asset in years subsequent to interest capitalization.*

Capitalized interest costs become an integral part of the acquisition costs of an asset and should be accounted for as such in the event of disposal of the asset.

Full Cost Method in Extractive Industries

FASB Interpretation-33 covers the application of FASB-34 (Capitalization of Interest Costs) to oil and gas producing activities that are being accounted for by the full cost method.

Unproved properties and major developments that represent unusually significant investments are assets which qualify for capitalization of interest costs, if the following conditions are met:

a. Exploration or development activities are in progress.
b. The assets are not currently being depreciated, depleted, or amortized.

Other assets that qualify for capitalization of interest costs, in accordance with FASB-34, are significant properties or projects within a nonproducing cost center on which exploration or development activities are in progress.

All assets that are currently being depreciated, depleted, or amortized are considered in use in the earning activities of the business and, in accordance with FASB-34, do not qualify for capitalization of interest costs.

FASB Interpretation-33 is effective for fiscal years beginning after December 15, 1979. Current and prior interim financial statements that are presented after the effective date must be restated to reflect the provisions of FASB Interpretation-33. In addition, the following disclosures shall be made in current and prior financial statements that are presented after the effective date:

a. The nature of the change in method of applying FASB-34
b. The effect of the change on income from continuing operations, net income, and related per share amounts for each current and prior period presented after the effective date

Disclosure, Effective Date, and Transition

The total amount of interest costs incurred and charged to expense during the period and the amount of interest costs, if any, which have been capitalized during the period, should be disclosed in the financial statements or footnotes thereto.

FASB-34 is effective for fiscal years beginning on and after December 15, 1979, although earlier application is permitted, but not required, for prior financial statements that have not been previously issued. Interest capitalization shall begin on December 15, 1979, for qualifying assets in existence at that time for which interest costs have not been previously capitalized. No adjustment need be made to qualifying assets for which interest costs have been capitalized prior to December 14, 1979. However, additional capitalized interest costs must be determined in accordance with FASB-34.

The provisions of FASB-34 shall not be applied retroactively for previously issued annual financial statements.

Comprehensive Illustration

The following is a comprehensive illustration of the application of FASB-34 (Capitalization of Interest Cost).

On January 1, Year One, Poll Powerhouse borrowed $300,000 from its bank at an annual rate of 18%. The principal amount plus interest is due on January 1, Year Three. The funds from this loan are specifically earmarked for the construction of a new plant facility. On February 1, Year One, Poll paid $15,000 for architects' fees and for fees for filing a project application with the state government.

On March 1, Year One, Poll received approval for the project from the state and construction of the plant was started. The following summarizes the costs incurred on this project.

Year One

February 1 (architects' and filing fees)	$ 15,000
April 1	150,000
September 1	60,000

Year Two

January 1	1,000
March 1	360,000
November 1	180,000
Total Project Cost	$766,000

The $1,000 is a miscellaneous cost and was expensed in Year Two, since it was determined by Poll to be immaterial.

The following schedule summarizes the borrowings of Poll as of December 31, Year Two.

Borrowing Date	Amount	Maturity Date	Annual Interest Rate
March 1, Year One	$1,000,000	Feb. 28, Year Three	17%
October 1, Year Two	500,000	Sept. 30, Year Four	14%

From February 1, Year Two, to March 31, Year Two, a major strike of construction workers was in effect. Therefore, all construction activity was halted during this period.

In August, Year Two, construction was voluntarily halted for the entire month by Poll. The chief executive officer did not want construction to continue without his supervision. Therefore, during his scheduled vacation construction was completely halted.

Solution to Problem

Poll's new plant facility is a qualifying asset under the provisions of FASB-34 and is subject to interest capitalization. The interest capitalization period begins on the first date that an expenditure is made by Poll, which was for architects' fees, February 1, Year One.

In order to compute the interest capitalization for Year One, the average accumulated expenditures for Year One must be calculated as follows:

Amount	Period from Expenditure to End of Year	Average Expenditure
$ 15,000	11 months	$ 13,750
150,000	9 months	112,500
60,000	4 months	20,000
$225,000		$146,250

The expenditures must be weighted by the period of time from the date they were made to the end of the year in order to determine the average expenditures for the entire year.

Next, the average expenditures must be multiplied by the interest rate on the borrowing (18%). This rate is used because Poll has specifically associated the borrowing with the construction of the new plant facility, and the average accumulated expenditures ($146,250) do not exceed the amount of the borrowing ($300,000). Therefore, the interest capitalized for Year One is computed as follows:

Average accumulated expenditures	$146,250
Interest rate	18%
Capitalizable interest cost—Year One	$ 26,325

The final step is to determine that Poll actually incurred at least $26,325 of interest costs in Year One. Since in Year One Poll incurred $195,667 of interest costs ($300,000 x 18% + $1,000,000 x 17% x 10/12), the full $26,325 must be capitalized.

The next step is to compute the average accumulated expenditures for Year Two, which are calculated as follows:

Amount	Period from Expenditure to End of Year	Average Expenditure
$225,000	12 months	$225,000
360,000	10 months	300,000
180,000	2 months	30,000
$765,000		$555,000

The $1,000 miscellaneous cost is not included, since Poll decided that this amount was immaterial and expensed it.

It is important to note that the expenditures for Year One are included as part of the base to compute Year Two capitalizable interest cost. FASB-34 requires that the average accumulated expenditures be calculated, and this would include those of prior accounting periods. Thus, the expenditures of $225,000 made by Poll in Year One are properly included in calculating the average accumulated expenditures for Year Two.

There is one further adjustment necessary to the above calculation of the average accumulated expenditures for Year Two. The plant facility was completed on December 31, Year Two, but there were two interruptions in construction in Year Two. Interest is not capitalized during delays or interruptions which are caused internally by an enterprise, unless they are brief. However, interest is capitalized during brief delays or interruptions which are externally imposed, or delays inherent in acquiring the qualifying asset. Thus, in this problem, the strike was an externally imposed interruption and interest capitalization continues during this period. However, the voluntary interruption in construction due to the supervisor's vacation is a period in which interest capitalization ceases. Therefore, interest is not capitalized during August, Year Two.

In order to give effect to the cessation of interest capitalization for the month of August, Year Two, it is necessary to adjust the calculation of the average accumulated expenditures for Year Two as follows:

Amount	Period from Expenditure to End of Year, Less One Month of Interruption	Average Expenditure
$225,000	11 months	$206,250
360,000	9 months	270,000
180,000	2 months	30,000
$765,000		$506,250

Note: The $180,000 was expended on November 1, Year Two, after the interruption, so no adjustment need be made to the average expenditure of $30,000.

If the average accumulated expenditures for the qualifying asset exceed the amount of the specific borrowing made to construct the asset, the capitalization rate applicable to the excess is the weighted average interest rate incurred on other borrowings. In this problem, the computation of the excess expenditures over the original loan amount is as follows:

Average expenditures through December 31, Year Two	$506,250
Less: Amount of original loan	300,000
Excess expenditures	$206,250

Thus, in Year Two, $206,250 of the $506,250 average expenditures must be capitalized using the weighted-average borrowing rate, and the balance of $300,000 is capitalized using the interest rate on the original loan made to specifically acquire the qualifying asset. The weighted-average rate on the other borrowings is computed as follows:

Amount	Weighted Amount	Rate	Annual Interest
$1,000,000	$1,000,000	17%	$170,000
500,000	125,000	14% (3 mos.)	$ 17,500
$1,500,000	$1,125,000		$187,500

$187,500
$1,125,000 = 16.67% weighted-average interest rate

The interest cost to be capitalized for Year Two can now be computed as follows:

$300,000	x	18.00%	=	$54,000
206,250	x	16.67%	=	34,382
				$88,382

The final step is to determine whether Poll incurred at least $88,382 of interest expense in Year Two. Since in Year Two Poll incurred $241,500 ($300,000 X 18% + $1,000,000 X 17% + $500,000 X 14% X 3/12) of interest, the full $88,382 is capitalizable as part of the acquisition cost of the asset in Year Two.

The total amount of interest which Poll must capitalize on the new plant facility is $114,707 ($26,325 for Year One and $88,382 for Year Two).

INTERIM FINANCIAL REPORTING

Overview

APB-28 covers the general promulgated GAAP for accounting and reporting on interim periods. This opinion provides the accounting and disclosure requirements necessary for interim reporting and establishes the minimum disclosures for interim reports of publicly traded companies.

Income taxes for interim reporting are discussed in the chapter entitled "Income Taxes;" accounting changes for interim reporting are discussed in the chapter entitled "Accounting Changes." Financial reporting for segments of a business enterprise is not required in interim financial statements (FASB-18).

Background

Interim financial reports may be issued quarterly, monthly, or at other intervals, and may include complete financial statements or summarized data. In addition, they usually include the current interim period and a cumulative year-to-date period with comparative reports on the corresponding periods of the immediately preceding fiscal year.

The procedures and disclosures expressed in the promulgated GAAP (APB-28) are applicable whenever an entity issues interim financial reports.

Accounting and Reporting

Each interim period must be viewed as an integral part of the annual period, and accounting principles and reporting practices should be based on those of the latest annual reports of the entity, unless there has been a change in an accounting principle. A change in an accounting principle during an interim period is discussed in the chapter entitled "Accounting Changes."

The accounting and reporting on the results of operation for interim financial statements is discussed in the following paragraphs.

Revenues are recognized as earned on the same basis as that for fiscal periods.

As closely as possible, product costs are determined as those for the fiscal period with some exceptions for inventory valuation, as follows:

1. Companies using the gross profit method to determine interim inventory costs, or other methods different from those used for annual inventory valuation, should disclose the method used at the interim date and any material difference from the reconciliation with the annual physical inventory.

2. A liquidation of a base-period LIFO inventory at an interim date that apparently will be corrected by the end of the annual period should be valued at the expected cost of replacement. Cost of sales for the interim period should include the expected cost of replacement and not the cost of the base-period LIFO inventory.

3. Inventory losses from market declines should be included in the interim period in which they occur, and gains in subsequent interim periods should be recognized in such interim period but should not exceed the losses included in prior interim periods.

   Temporary market declines that are expected to be made up by the end of the annual period need not be recognized in interim periods.

4. Inventory and product costs computed by the use of a standard cost accounting system should be determined by the same procedures used at the end of a fiscal year. Variances from standard costs that are expected to be made up by the end of the fiscal year need not be included in interim-period statements.

Other costs and expenses should be charged or allocated to produce a fair presentation of the results of operation, changes in financial position, and financial position for all interim periods. The following should apply in accounting for other costs and expenses:

1. The general rule in preparing interim-period financial statements is that costs and expenses that clearly benefit more than one period should be properly allocated to the periods affected. This procedure should be consistently applied.

2. Companies that have material seasonal revenue variations must avoid the possibility that interim-period financial statements become misleading. Disclosure of material seasonal revenue variations should be made in the interim-period fi-

nancial statements. In addition, it is desirable to disclose results for a full year, ending at the interim date.

3. Unusual and infrequent transactions that are material and not
   designated as extraordinary items, such as the effects of a
   disposal of a segment of business, should be reported separately in the interim periods in which they occur.

4. All other pertinent information, such as accounting changes,
   contingencies, seasonal results, and purchase or pooling transactions, should be disclosed to provide the necessary information for the proper understanding of the interim financial
   statements.

Interim reports should not contain arbitrary amounts of costs or
expenses. Estimates should be reasonable and should be based on all
available information applied consistently from period to period. An
effective tax rate is used for income tax provision in interim periods.
Income taxes for interim-period reports are discussed in the chapter
entitled "Income Taxes."

Material contingencies and other uncertainties that exist at an
interim date must be disclosed in interim reports in the same manner
as that required for annual reports. However, these contingencies
and uncertainties, at an interim date, should be evaluated in relation
to the annual report. The disclosure for such items must be repeated
in every interim and annual report until the contingency is resolved
or becomes immaterial.

Summarized Interim Financial Statements

Publicly traded companies reporting summarized financial information at interim dates should include the following minimum
information:

1. Gross revenues, provision for income taxes, extraordinary
   items, effects of accounting changes (principles or practice),
   and net income

2. Primary and fully diluted earnings-per-share data

3. Material seasonal variations of revenues, costs, or expenses

4. Contingent items and effects of the disposal of a segment of
   business

5. Material changes in financial position

Summarized interim financial statements based on these minimum disclosures *do not* constitute a fair presentation of financial

position and results of operations in conformity with GAAP.

In the event that fourth-quarter results are not issued separately, the annual report should include disclosures for the fourth quarter on the aggregate effect of material year-end adjustments and infrequently occurring items, extraordinary items, and disposal of business segments that occurred in the fourth quarter.

When summarized interim financial data are not presented, significant changes in liquid assets, working capital, long-term liabilities, and stockholders' equity should be disclosed and disseminated to the public.

INVENTORY PRICING AND METHODS

Overview

The main source of promulgated GAAP for inventories is ARB-43, Chapter 4 (as amended). Other promulgated GAAP relating to the subject of inventory are FASB Interpretation-1 (Accounting Changes Related to the Cost of Inventory) and FASB Interpretation-17 (Applying the Lower of Cost or Market Rule in Translated Financial Statements).

In addition to the above and other areas of promulgated GAAP, this chapter includes most of the nonpromulgated GAAP on inventories.

Background

Inventories of goods must be periodically compiled, measured, and recorded in the books of accounts of a business. Inventory includes the total amount of tangible personal property and is usually classified as (1) finished goods, (2) work in process, and (3) raw materials.

Inventories exclude long-term assets that are subject to depreciation or assets that will be classified as such.

Inventories are classified as current assets, except when there are excessive quantities which may not reasonably be expected to be used or sold within the normal operating cycle of a business. In this event, the excess inventory is classified as noncurrent.

The periodic preparation of financial statements requires that revenues and costs be matched (one of the basic [pervasive] principles of GAAP), and the valuation of inventories is a major objective in that matching principle.

Inventory Systems

Periodic system   The inventory is determined by a physical count as of a specific date. As long as the count is made frequently enough for reporting purposes, it is not necessary to maintain extensive inventory records. The inventory shown on the balance sheet is determined by the physical count and is priced in accordance with the inventory method used. The net change between the beginning and ending inventories enters into the computation of the cost of goods sold.

Perpetual system   With this system, inventory records are maintained and updated regularly. The system has the advantage of providing inventory information on a timely basis but requires the maintenance of a full set of inventory records. Theoretically, physical counts are not necessary, but they are normally taken to verify the inventory records. GAAP require that a physical check of perpetual inventory records be made periodically. The maintenance of the inventory information consists of posting each individual transaction.

Title to Goods

Legal title to merchandise usually determines whether or not it is included in the inventory of an enterprise. According to the Uniform Commercial Code, title to goods passes from the seller to the buyer in any manner and on any conditions explicitly agreed on by the parties. If no conditions are explicitly agreed on, title to goods passes from the seller to the buyer at the time and place at which the seller completes its performance with reference to the physical delivery of the goods. Title passes to the buyer at the time and place of shipment if the seller is required only to send the goods. However, if the contract requires delivery at destination, title passes when the goods are tendered at the destination. The following is the most commonly used terminology in passing title from the seller to the buyer:

> F.O.B.—means *free on board* and requires the seller, at its expense, to deliver the goods to the destination indicated as F.O.B.
>
> F.A.S.—means *free alongside* and is usually used in conjunction with a dock or a seaport. The seller must at its expense deliver the goods to the vessel indicated on the F.A.S.
>
> C.I.F.—means that the price of the goods includes the cost of the goods and the insurance and freight to the named destination.
>
> C & F—means that the price of the goods includes the cost of the goods and the freight to the named destination.
>
> C.O.D.—means *collect on delivery* and requires the buyer to pay for the goods at the time and place of delivery.

Costs

The basis of accounting for inventories is cost (basic principle), which has been defined as the price paid or consideration given to acquire an asset. In inventory accounting, cost is the sum of the expenditures and charges, direct and indirect, in bringing goods to their existing condition or location.

The principles of measuring inventory costs can be easily stated. However, the application of the principles, particularly to items in work in process and finished goods, is difficult because of the problem involved in allocating the various costs and charges. For example, idle factory expense, excessive spoilage, double freight, and rehandling costs can be so abnormal that they may have to be charged to the current period, rather than as a portion of the inventory costs. Selling expenses should not be considered as any part of inventory costs. *The exclusion of all overhead from inventory costs is an unacceptable accounting procedure* (direct or variable costing).

Departure from the Cost Basis

When the utility of the goods in the ordinary course of business is no longer as great as their cost, a departure from the cost basis principle of measuring the inventory is required. Whether the cause be from obsolescence, physical deterioration, changes in price levels, or any other, the difference should be recognized as a loss for the current period. This is usually accomplished by stating such goods at a lower level designated as market (lower of cost or market principle).

Lower of Cost or Market

In the phrase *lower of cost or market,* the term *market* means current replacement cost, whether by purchase or by reproduction, *but is limited to the following maximum and minimum amounts:*

1. *Maximum:* cannot exceed the estimated selling price less any costs of completion and disposal. The maximum cost is also the net realizable value.
2. *Minimum:* the maximum less an allowance for normal profit.

		Replacement	(1) Selling	(2) Cost of	(1 – 2)	(3) Normal	[(1 – 2) – 3]
Item	*Cost*	*Cost*	*Price*	*Completion*	*Maximum**	*Profit*	*Minimum*
1	$20.50	$ 19.00	$ 25.00	$ 1.00	$ 24.00	$ 6.00	$ 18.00
2	26.00	20.00	30.00	2.00	28.00	7.00	21.00
3	10.00	12.00	15.00	1.00	14.00	3.00	11.00
4	40.00	55.00	60.00	6.00	54.00	4.00	50.00
	$96.50	$106.00	$130.00	$10.00	$120.00	$20.00	$100.00

*The maximum is equal to the net realizable value.

The lower of cost or market for the above four items is:

Item 1	$19.00	Item 3	$10.00
Item 2	$21.00	Item 4	$40.00

If the lower of cost or market is applied to each individual item in the above illustration, items 1 and 2 must be written down by $1.50 and $5.00, respectively, or a total of $6.50. However, if the lower of cost or market is applied to the entire inventory, there is no write-down, because total cost of $96.50 is lower than market of $106.00.

The correct procedure in applying the lower-of-cost-or-market principle is first to determine what market is and then to compare it to cost. Market can be either replacement cost or the maximum or minimum restriction on replacement cost.

When market is lower than cost, the purposes of the maximum and minimum limitation are:

1. The maximum prevents a loss in future periods by at least valuing the inventory at its estimated selling price less costs of completion and disposal.
2. The minimum prevents any future periods from realizing any more than a normal profit.

The write-down of inventory to market is usually reflected in cost of goods sold, unless the amount is unusually material, in which case the loss should be identified separately in the income statement.

The journal entry to record the write-down to a separate account is:

Inventory loss due to decline in market $XXX
    Inventory $XXX

The lower-of-cost-or-market principle may be applied to a single item, a category, or the total inventory, provided that the method most clearly reflects periodic income.

The purpose of reducing inventory to the lower of cost or market is to reflect fairly the income of the period (matching-of-revenue-and-cost principle).

The basic principle of consistency must be applied in the valuation of inventory, and the method should be disclosed in the financial statements.

In the event that a significant change occurs in the measurement of inventory, adequate disclosure of the nature of the change and, if material (materiality principle), the effect on income should be disclosed in the financial statements.

Exceptions   Exceptional cases, such as precious metals having a fixed determinable monetary value with no substantial cost of marketing, may be stated at such monetary value. When inventory is stated at a value in excess of cost, this fact should be fully disclosed in the financial statements.

The prerequisites of this exception are (1) immediate marketability at quoted prices and (2) cost difficult to obtain.

Cost Methods

For inventory purposes, cost may be determined by specific identification or by the association of the flow of cost factors—first-in, first-out (FIFO), last-in, first-out (LIFO), and average.

In selecting an inventory cost method, the primary objective is the selection of the method that under the circumstances most clearly reflects periodic income. When similar goods are purchased at different times, it may not be possible to identify and match the specific costs of the item sold. Frequently, the identity of goods and their specific related costs are lost between the time of acquisition and the time of sale. This has resulted in the development and general acceptance of several assumptions with respect to the flow of cost factors (FIFO, LIFO, and average cost) to provide practical bases for the measurement of periodic income.

Inventory identification   In some lines of business, specific items or lots of inventory are clearly identifiable from the time of purchase through the time of sale and are costed on this basis. Usually, the identity of goods is lost between the time of acquisition and the time of sale, and inventories are identified on the flow-of-cost factors.

When a flow-of-cost method is used, the actual physical movement of the inventory is irrelevant.

Standard Costs

The use of standard costs is a management tool that identifies favorable or unfavorable variances from predetermined estimates established by past performance or time and motion studies. Inventory valuation by the use of standard costs is acceptable, if adjusted at reasonable intervals to reflect the approximate costs computed under one of the recognized methods, and adequate disclosure is made in the financial statements.

At the end of the reporting period the physical inventory is costed at LIFO, FIFO, or some other generally accepted method. Any variation between this result and the carrying value of the inventory at standard cost must be closed out to cost of goods sold and ending inventory such that the reported figure represents that which the generally accepted method would yield.

First-in, First-out Method (FIFO)

The *FIFO method* of identifying inventory is based on the assumption that costs should be charged against revenue in the order in which they occurred. The inventory remaining on hand is presumed to consist of the most recent costs. In other words, the first goods acquired are the first goods out, and the last goods acquired are in the ending inventory (assuming that there is an ending inventory).

Theoretically, FIFO approximates the results that would be obtained by the specific identification method.

Last-in, First-out Method (LIFO)

The last-in, first-out method of determining inventory (LIFO) requires that records be maintained as to the base year layer and additional layers that may be created or used up. An additional LIFO layer is created in any year in which the ending inventory is more than the beginning inventory. An additional LIFO layer is priced at the earliest or average costs of the year in which it was created, because the LIFO method matches the last costs incurred with current revenue, leaving the first cost incurred to be included in any inventory increase.

After an original LIFO layer is created (base year), it may decrease or additional layers may be created each year according to the quantity of ending inventory.

When the ending inventory is less than the beginning inventory, one or more LIFO layers may be used up. It is important to remember that once a LIFO layer is used up, any future new LIFO layer is priced at the cost of the year in which it is created, and not by reference to a prior LIFO layer cost.

In addition to the disclosure of significant accounting policies (APB-22) and of composition of inventories (ARB-43, Chapter 4), a business using the LIFO method of reporting inventory must disclose the following data, if it reports to the SEC:

1. Current replacement value of the LIFO inventories at each balance sheet date presented
2. The effect on the results of operations for any reduction of a LIFO layer

Dollar-Value LIFO

A variation of the conventional LIFO method is the dollar-value LIFO method. Under the regular LIFO method, units of inventory are priced at unit prices. Under the dollar-value LIFO method, the base-year inventory is priced in dollars; for inventories of all subsequent years, price indices are used, with the base year as 100.

Year	Inventory at Base-Year Prices	Price Index	$ LIFO Inventory Amount
1	$100,000	100	$100,000
2	20,000	105	21,000
3	10,000	110	11,000
4	20,000	120	24,000
5	20,000	125	25,000
Totals	$170,000		$181,000

Weighted-Average Method

The weighted-average method of inventory valuation assumes that costs are charged against revenue on the basis of an average of the number of units acquired at each price level. The resulting average price is applied to the ending inventory to find the total ending inventory value. The weighted average is determined by dividing the total costs of the inventory available, including any beginning inventory, by the total number of units, as follows:

	Units	Cost per Unit	Total Cost
Beginning inventory	10,000	$4.00	$ 40,000
Purchase, July 25	8,000	4.20	33,600
Purchase, August 15	5,000	4.13	20,650
Purchase, September 5	7,000	4.30	30,100
Purchase, September 25	12,000	4.25	51,000
Totals	42,000		$175,350

Total cost $175,350 ÷ total units 42,000 = $4.175 weighted-average cost per unit.

Assume that the ending inventory consisted of 14,000 units. Value of ending inventory = 14,000 units x $4.175 per unit, or $58,450.

Moving-Average Method

The moving-average method can be used only with a perpetual inventory. The cost per unit is recomputed after every addition to the inventory.

	Total Units	Total Cost	Unit Cost
Beginning inventory	1,000	$ 5,000	$5.00
Sale of 200 units	800	4,000	5.00
Purchase of 1,200 @ $6	2,000	11,200	5.60
Sales of 1,000 units	1,000	5,600	5.60
Purchase of 1,000 @ $5	2,000	10,600	5.30

Note: Only purchases change the unit price as sales are taken out at the prior moving-average unit cost.

Under the moving-average method, the ending inventory is costed at the last moving-average unit cost for the period.

Retail Inventory Method

Because of the great variety and quantity of inventory in some types of businesses, the reversed markup procedure of inventory pricing, such as the retail inventory method, may be both practical and appropriate.

It is necessary to maintain records of purchases at both cost and selling price and of sales at selling price in order to use the retail inventory method. With the information available, a ratio of cost to retail can be calculated and applied to the ending inventory at retail to compute the approximate cost.

	Cost	*Retail*
Inventory, at beginning of period	$ 100,000	$ 150,000
Purchases during the period	1,100,000	1,850,000
Totals	$1,200,000	$2,000,000
Sales during the period		1,800,000
Estimated ending inventory at retail		$ 200,000
Estimated ending inventory at cost (60% of retail)		$ 120,000

Computation of Ratio of Cost to Retail

$$\frac{\$1,200,000}{\$2,000,000} \; = \; 60\% \text{ of } \$200,000 \; = \; \$120,000$$

Physical inventories measured by the retail method should be taken periodically as a check on the accuracy of the estimated inventories.

The above illustration ignores the problem of changes made in selling prices after the original pricing of goods.

Original selling prices are revised or modified, thus necessitating an understanding of the following terminology:

Original retail: The first selling price at which goods are offered for sale

Markup: The selling price raised above the original selling price

Markdown: The selling price lowered below the original selling price

Markup cancellation: Markup selling price decreased, but not below the original selling price

Markdown cancellation: Markdown selling price increased, but not above the original selling price

Net markup: Markup minus markup cancellation

Net markdown: Markdown minus markdown cancellation

Markon: Difference between the cost and the original selling price, plus any net markups

Original cost	$100
Original selling price ($50 markon)	$150
Markup	50
Original selling price plus markup	$200
Markup cancellation	25
Original selling price plus net markup	$175
Markdown (consists of $25 markup cancellation and a $25 markdown)	50
Original selling price minus markdown	$125
Markdown	25
Original selling price minus markdown	$100
Markdown cancellation	25
Original selling price minus net markdown	$125
Markup (consists of a $25 markdown cancellation and a $25 markup)	50
Original selling price plus net markup	$175

Theoretically speaking, the last selling price consisted of:

$50	markup
25	markup cancellation
25	markup cancellation
25	markdown
25	markdown
25	markdown cancellation
25	markdown cancellation
25	markup
$25	net plus change

Now the goods are priced at the original selling price plus a net markup of $25, or a total of $175.

The purpose of the conventional retail inventory method is to produce an inventory valuation (measurement) closely approximating what would be obtained by taking a physical inventory and pricing the goods at the lower of cost or market.

In order to approximate the lower of cost or market in the computations, *markdowns and markdown cancellations are excluded in calculating the ratio of cost to retail and are added to the retail inventory after the ratio is determined.*

In calculating the cost-to-retail ratio, any adjustment to the retail value will necessarily affect the ratio and hence the resultant cost figure. Adjustments that decrease the denominator of the ratio increase the ratio and the value for ending inventory at cost, thus increasing gross profit. In the interests of conservatism, as well as for other reasons, adjustments that decrease the retail figure should be avoided. Markups, which increase the denominator, however, are included *net* of cancellations.

Net markdowns (markdowns less markdown cancellations) are an example of adjustments that decrease the denominator. Including them in the retail figure violates the lower-of-cost-or-market rule. As shown below, net markdowns are not included in the calculation of the ratio but *are* included in the determination of ending inventory after computing the ratio. The rationale for this is that the cost-to-retail ratio is presumed to be based on normal conditions, and markdown is not a normal condition. When *applying* the ratio, however, to conform to the lower-of-cost-or-market rule, the retail value must be reduced by the amount of the markdowns.

Employee discounts obviously apply only to goods sold, not those remaining on hand. A sale at less than normal retail price to an employee does not represent a valid reduction to lower of cost or market, nor does it represent a valid adjustment of the cost-to-retail ratio or the value of the ending inventory. Hence, employee discounts should not enter into any of the calculations, but are deducted from retail in the same way as markdowns after the computation of the cost-to-retail ratio.

Inventory spoilage and shrinkage affect the ending inventory figure but should not enter into the cost-to-retail ratio calculation. It is an obvious distortion to make cost a higher percentage of retail merely because some items are missing from the retail inventory. When arriving at the final figure for inventory at cost, the amount of shrinkage is deducted either at cost or at retail depending upon whether shrinkage is stated at cost or at retail.

Assume the following information:

	Cost	Retail
Inventory, beginning of the period	$200,000	$ 300,000
Purchases	550,000	800,000
Transportation-in	50,000	
Markups		100,000
Markup cancellations		20,000
Markdowns		70,000
Markdown cancellations		10,000

The calculations would be as follows:

	Cost	Retail
Inventory, at beginning of period	$200,000	$ 300,000
Purchases	550,000	800,000
Transportation-in	50,000	
Markups		100,000
Markup cancellations		(20,000)
Totals (ratio of cost to retail 67.8%)	$800,000	$1,180,000
Markdowns		(70,000)
Markdown cancellations		10,000
Total goods at retail		$1,120,000
Less: Sales during the period		860,000
Inventory, ending (at retail)		$ 260,000
Inventory, ending (67.8% of $260,000)*		$ 176,280

*At estimated lower of cost or market

LIFO application   The LIFO method of evaluating inventory can be applied to the retail inventory method by using procedures somewhat different from the conventional retail method. Basically two differences have to be taken into consideration:

1. Since the LIFO method produces a valuation approximating cost, and the conventional retail method produces a valuation approximating the lower of cost or market, to apply the LIFO concept to the conventional retail method, it is necessary to include all markdowns as well as markups in determining the ratio of cost to retail.

2. With the LIFO method, the quantity of inventory on hand is from the earliest purchases during the year or from prior years' LIFO layers. The cost-to-retail ratio considers the current relationship between cost and selling price. Therefore, the beginning inventory is omitted from the cost-to-retail ratio, because it may cause a distortion. In short, to apply the LIFO concept to the retail inventory method:

   a. All markdowns as well as markups are included in the cost-to-retail ratio.

   b. The beginning inventory data are not used to compute the cost-to-retail ratio.

	Cost	Retail
Inventory, beginning of period	omitted	omitted
Purchases	$550,000	$ 800,000
Transportation-in	50,000	
Markups		100,000
Markup cancellations		(20,000)
Markdowns		(70,000)
Markdown cancellations		10,000
Totals (ratio of cost to retail 73.2%)	$600,000	$ 820,000
Add: Inventory, beginning of period		300,000
Total goods at retail		$1,120,000
Less: Sales during period		860,000
Inventory, ending of period (at retail)		$ 260,000

Since the $260,000 ending LIFO inventory (at retail) is less than the $300,000 beginning LIFO inventory (at retail), it is obvious that a prior LIFO layer was partially depleted:

	Retail
Beginning inventory	$300,000
Ending inventory	260,000
LIFO layer depleted	$ 40,000

The $40,000 difference is multiplied by the beginning inventory cost-to-retail ratio (66.67%) and then subtracted from the beginning inventory at cost, as follows:

	Cost
Beginning inventory	$200,000
$40,000 x 66.67%	(26,668)
Ending inventory (at cost)	$173,332

If the ending LIFO inventory (at retail) had been greater than the beginning LIFO inventory (at retail), a new LIFO layer would have been created which would have been costed at the new cost-to-retail ratio (73.2%).

The basic assumption of the retail inventory method is that there exists an equal distribution of goods (high-cost ratio and low-cost ratio) between sales, beginning inventory, and ending inventory. In instances where this basic premise does not prevail, cost ratios should be determined by departments or small units. This requires keeping (by departments) separate sales, purchases, markups, markdowns, and beginning and ending inventories.

Base Stock Method

The base stock method is similar to the LIFO method. It assumes a continuous permanent stock of inventory that is, in effect, a fixed asset. Excesses over this base stock are considered temporary inventory and are priced at *current replacement cost*. Amounts below the base stock are similarly considered temporary and are charged against revenue at replacement cost. The essential difference between the base stock method and LIFO is that the former uses replacement cost whereas LIFO relies on actual costs exclusively. Since the base stock method is not allowed for tax purposes, it is seldom encountered in practice.

Relative Sales Value Costing

This method is used when costs cannot be determined individually. Joint products, lump-sum purchase of assets (basket purchase), and large assets that are subdivided (real estate tracts) are examples of items that would be costed by their relative sales value.

ABC Company purchases four large pieces of machinery for $100,000. At the time of purchase an appraisal discloses the following fair values:

Machine #1	$ 12,000
Machine #2	28,000
Machine #3	40,000
Machine #4	30,000
Total	$110,000

The machines are priced at their relative fair values, as follows:

Machine #1	12/110 x $100,000	=	$ 10,909
Machine #2	28/110 x $100,000	=	25,455
Machine #3	40/110 x $100,000	=	36,364
Machine #4	30/110 x $100,000	=	27,272
Total cost allocated			$100,000

Firm Purchase Commitments

Losses on firm purchase commitments for inventory goods should be measured in the same manner as inventory losses and, if material, should be recognized in the accounts and disclosed separately in the income statement.

The recognition of losses, which are expected to arise from firm, noncancelable commitments and which arise from the decline in the utility of a cost expenditure, should be disclosed in the current period income statement.

In addition, all significant firm purchase commitments must be disclosed in the financial statements or in footnotes, whether or not any losses are recognized.

Disclosure

The general disclosure requirements for inventories are:

1. A description of accounting principles used and the methods of applying those principles (APB-22)
2. Any accounting principles or methods that are peculiar to a particular industry (APB-22)
3. Classification of inventories (ARB-43)
4. Basis of pricing inventories (ARB-43)
5. Method of determining inventories (LIFO, FIFO, average, etc.) (ARB-43)

All the above disclosures must be consistent from year to year, and if a significant change occurs, the following additional disclosures are necessary:

1. The nature of the change
2. If the change is significant, the effect on net income

Businesses dependent upon a limited number of sources for raw material or inventory or upon precarious sources (labor problems, foreign governments, etc.) should disclose the pertinent facts in their financial statements or footnotes thereto.

Inventory of Discontinued Segments

Inventories used in discontinued segments of a business should be written down to their net realizable value and the amount of write-down included as part of the gain or loss recognized on the disposal of the discontinued segment. However, such a write-down should not be attributable to any inventory adjustment that should have been recognized prior to the measurement date of the loss on disposal. In this event, the loss on the write-down should be included in the operating results of the discontinued segment (APB-30).

Inventory for Interim Financial Reporting

Generally, the same principles and methods are used to value inventories for interim financial statements as are used for annual reports. However, for practical purposes or otherwise there are some exceptions.

An estimated gross profit is frequently utilized to determine the cost of goods sold during an interim period. This procedure is acceptable for GAAP, as long as periodic physical inventories are taken to adjust the gross profit percentage used. Companies using the gross profit method for interim financial statements should disclose that fact and any significant adjustments that may occur in amounts determined by a physical count (APB-28).

When the LIFO method is used for interim financial statements and a LIFO layer is depleted, in part or in whole, that is expected to be replaced before the end of the fiscal period, it is acceptable to use the expected cost of replacement for the depleted LIFO inventory in determining cost of goods sold for the interim period (APB-28).

Inventory losses from market declines, other than those which are expected to be recouped before the end of the fiscal year, should be included in the results of operations of the interim period in which the loss occurs. Subsequent gains from market price recovery in later interim periods should be included in the results of operation in which the gain occurs, but only to the extent of the previously recognized losses (APB-28).

Standard costs are acceptable in determining inventory valuations for interim financial reporting. Unplanned or unanticipated purchase price, volume, or capacity variances should be included in the results of operations of the interim period in which they occur. Anticipated and planned purchase price, volume, or capacity variances that are expected to be recouped by the end of the fiscal year should be deferred at interim dates. In general, the same procedures for standard costs used at the end of the fiscal year should be used for interim financial reporting (APB-28).

Inventories in Business Combinations

Inventory acquired in a business combination accounted for by the purchase method is valued as follows:

Raw materials—Current replacement cost
Finished goods—Net realizable value less a reasonable profit
Work in process—Net realizable value less a reasonable profit

Inventories acquired in a business combination accounted for as a pooling of interests are valued at the same cost as that to the acquired entity.

Inventory for Terminated Contracts

When inventory is acquired for a specific customer contract that is subsequently terminated for any purpose, the carrying value of such inventory should be adjusted to reflect any loss in value.

Inventories—Research and Development

Inventories of supplies used in research and development activities should be charged to expense unless they clearly have an alternative use or can be used in future research and development projects.

When research and development activities consume goods, supplies, or materials from other sources within an organization, the carrying value of such inventory should be charged to research and development expense. Goods produced by research and development activities that may be used in the regular inventory of the organization may be transferred physically to regular inventory, at which time a credit in the amount of the costs assigned to the goods should be made to the research and development department (FASB-2).

Inventories—General Price-Level Changes

When preparing general price-level financial statements, the inventory method (FIFO, LIFO, average, etc.) will dictate the price index that must be used to restate inventory amounts. (See the chapter entitled "General Price-Level Changes.")

Inventories—Intercompany Profits

Regardless of any minority interest, all (100%) of any intercompany profits in inventory must be eliminated for consolidated financial statements and investments in common stocks accounted for by the equity method. (See the chapter entitled "Consolidated Financial Statements.")

Inventories—Long-term Construction-Type Contracts

The construction in progress account used in both the completed-contract and percentage-of-completion methods of accounting for long-term construction-type contracts is in fact an inventory account.

Inventories—Tax Allocation

Inventories accounted differently for financial accounting and tax purposes may create temporary (timing) differences for which interperiod tax allocation may be necessary (FASB-96).

Inventories—Accounting Change

An accounting change involving inventories in interim or annual reports necessitates accounting for the cumulative effect of the change and/or restatement of prior-period reports, including certain required *pro forma* information (APB-20).

Inventories—Nonmonetary Exchanges

A nonmonetary exchange of inventory held for sale in the ordinary course of business for similar property to be held for the same purpose does not complete the earning process and no gain or loss is recognized. The inventory received in the nonmonetary exchange should be recorded at the book value of the inventory surrendered, unless cash is also involved in the transaction (APB-29).

Inventory Profits

Profits from the sale of inventory, whose cost and selling price have increased significantly since acquisition, will probably include *ghost profits* or *inventory profits*. These profits are considered fictitious, because the cost to replace the inventory has increased significantly and the normal gross profit on the inventory is considerably less than the gross profit containing the ghost or inventory profits.

During periods of rapid inflation, a significant portion of reported net income of a business may actually be ghost or inventory profits. The use of the LIFO method for pricing inventories may offset part or all of any ghost or inventory profits, because current purchases or production costs are matched against current revenue, leaving the earliest inventory on hand.

Certain publicly held companies are required by the SEC to disclose in a supplemental statement the current replacement cost for cost of goods sold, inventories, and resulting ghost or inventory profits.

Conclusion

Inventory is tangible personal property held for sale in the ordinary course of business. Inventory may be raw materials, in various stages of being produced (work in process), or finished goods.

Matching of revenue and costs is an important objective in accounting for inventory to ensure the proper determination of income in accordance with GAAP.

Accounting for inventories is cost (basic principle), which has been defined as the price paid or consideration given to acquire an asset. In inventory accounting, cost is the sum of the expenditures and charges, directly or indirectly, in bringing goods to their existing condition or location. For inventory purposes, cost may be determined by specific identification or by the association of the flow of cost factors such as LIFO, FIFO, or average. In selecting an inventory cost method, the primary objective is the selection of the method that under the circumstances most clearly reflects periodic income.

When the utility of the inventory, in the ordinary course of business, is no longer as great as its cost, a departure from the cost basis is required. This is accomplished by pricing the inventory at the lower of cost or market on an item-by-item basis or on the entire inventory.

Market is defined as current replacement cost, either by purchase or reproduction, except that a maximum and minimum limitation is imposed. The valuation of inventories at the lower of cost or market results in recording losses but not profits prior to the sale of the inventory. The reason that beginning and ending inventories are included in the computation of net income is to arrive at the cost of goods sold during the period of time covered by the statement.

FIFO and LIFO are inventory costing methods employed to measure the *flow of costs*. FIFO matches the first cost incurred with the first revenue produced, whereas LIFO matches the last cost incurred with the first revenue produced. In periods of changing prices, different costs are matched with revenue for the same quantity sold, depending on whether LIFO or FIFO is used.

The LIFO method matches current costs and current revenue. When prices are rising, higher costs are matched to current revenue; when prices are falling, lower costs are matched to current revenue. This minimizes recognition of inventory profits or losses that arise from fluctuations in the value of the inventory.

If the base of a LIFO inventory is substantially depleted after a long period of price increases, the cumulative effect of the old costs being matched against current revenue may distort net income for the period.

Comprehensive Illustration

To illustrate the application of FIFO, LIFO, and the weighted-average methods of inventory valuation, assume the following facts:

Units Purchased During the Year

Date	Units	Cost per Unit	Total Cost
January 15	10,000	$5.10	$ 51,000
March 20	20,000	5.20	104,000
May 10	50,000	5.00	250,000
June 8	30,000	5.40	162,000
October 12	5,000	5.30	26,500
December 21	5,000	5.50	27,500
Totals	120,000		$621,000

Beginning inventory consisted of 10,000 units at $5.
Ending inventory consisted of 14,000 units.

Under *FIFO*, the first units in stock are the first units out, which means that the ending inventory is of the units purchased last. Since the ending inventory is 14,000 units and the December purchases were only 5,000 units, we must go back to October's purchases for another 5,000 units; and in order to make up the 14,000 units in the ending inventory, we need to take 4,000 units from the June purchases, as follows:

December purchases	5,000 units	@	$5.50	=	$27,500
October purchases	5,000 units	@	5.30	=	26,500
June purchases	4,000 units	@	5.40	=	21,600
Ending inventory using FIFO	14,000 units				$75,600

Under *LIFO*, the last units in stock are the first units out, which means that the ending inventory is composed of the units purchased first. Using LIFO, we must go back to the earliest inventory to start our calculations. The earliest inventory available is the *beginning inventory* of 10,000 units at $5, but the ending inventory is 14,000 units. Thus, we must go to the next earliest purchase, which is January, and use 4,000 units at the January price to complete the ending inventory valuation, as follows:

Beginning inventory	10,000 units	@	$5.00	=	$50,000
From January's purchase	4,000 units	@	5.10	=	20,400
Ending inventory using LIFO	14,000 units				$70,400

Under the *weighted-average* method we must find out what the weighted-average cost per unit is and then multiply it by the 14,000 units in the ending inventory, thus:

	Units	Cost per Unit	Total Cost
Beginning inventory	10,000	$5.00	$ 50,000
Purchases:			
January 15	10,000	5.10	51,000
March 20	20,000	5.20	104,000
May 10	50,000	5.00	250,000
June 8	30,000	5.40	162,000
October 12	5,000	5.30	26,500
December 21	5,000	5.50	27,500
Totals	130,000		$671,000

Weighted average = Total costs divided by total units

= $671,000 divided by 130,000

= $5.1615 per unit

Ending inventory = 14,000 x $5.1615 per unit = $72,261

Comparison of Three Methods

Ending inventory, FIFO	$75,600
Ending inventory, LIFO	70,400
Ending inventory, weighted average	72,261

In periods of inflation, the FIFO method will always produce the highest ending inventory, resulting in the lowest cost of goods sold and the most gross profit. LIFO will produce the lowest ending inventory, resulting in the highest cost of goods sold and the least gross profit. The weighted-average method will yield results that will fall between those of LIFO and FIFO.

INVESTMENT TAX CREDIT
IMPORTANT NOTICE

In December 1987, FASB-96 (Accounting for Income Taxes) was issued to supersede APB-11 (Accounting for Income Taxes). FASB-96 was scheduled to become effective for fiscal years beginning after December 15, 1988, and earlier adoption was encouraged.

As a result of numerous complaints from major industrial enterprises regarding the complexity and cost of implementing the provisions of FASB-96, the Financial Accounting Standards Board (FASB) issued FASB-100, deferring the effective date of FASB-96 by one year to December 15, 1989. FASB-103 granted a further deferral of two years to December 15, 1991, with earlier application encouraged.

Two Exposure Drafts (ED) are outstanding as of the date of this publication. One of the outstanding EDs would defer the effective date of FASB-96 for one more year, until fiscal years beginning after December 15, 1992, with earlier application permitted. The other outstanding ED would supersede FASB-96 and would be effective for fiscal years beginning after December 15, 1992. If the FASB meets its own schedule for issuing final Statements based on these two outstanding EDs, FASB-96 will be superseded without ever having gone into effect, although some enterprises have elected its early application.

Until the FASB issues a new Statement superseding FASB-96, an enterprise may account for income taxes by (i) continuing to apply the provisions of APB-11 or (ii) electing early adoption of FASB-96.

This edition of the *GAAP Guide* contains coverage of both APB-11 and FASB-96. The provisions of APB-11 appear in chapter 19.01a and the provisions of FASB-96 appear in chapter 19.01b.

Highlights of the outstanding Exposure Draft are summarized at the end of chapter 19.01b and are noted in the Disclosure Index.

Because of the status of APB-11 and FASB-96, it was also necessary to include two chapters entitled "Investment Tax

Credit" in this issue of the *GAAP Guide*. Chapter 25.01a contains coverage of the accounting standards relating to investment tax credits as they existed prior to the amendments by FASB-96. Chapter 25.01a should be used by those enterprises that are continuing to apply the provisions of APB-11 to account for income taxes. Chapter 25.01b contains coverage of the accounting standards relating to investment tax credits as they existed after the amendments by FASB-96. Chapter 25.01b should be used by those enterprises that are electing early adoption of the provisions of FASB-96.

INVESTMENT TAX CREDIT

Overview

The present promulgated GAAP on accounting for the investment credit is APB-2, which has been amended by APB-4 and FASB Interpretation-25, Accounting for an Unused Investment Tax Credit. FASB Interpretation-32 (Application of Percentage Limitations in Recognizing Investment Tax Credit) represents an interpretation of APB-2, APB-4, and FASB Interpretation-25.

> **OBSERVATION:** *The regular 10% investment tax credit (ITC) has been generally repealed for property placed in service after December 31, 1985. The ITC carryover rules continue to apply for property placed in service prior to 1986.*
>
> *FASB Technical Bulletin 86-1 (FASB:TB 86-1), issued on October 27, 1986, provides guidance on recognizing and reporting the effects of the Tax Reform Act of 1986. FASB:TB 86-1 specifies that an enterprise should not adjust the amount of net deferred tax credits that were previously offset by investment tax credits, even though the Tax Reform Act of 1986 specifies a reduction in the amount of the allowable carryforward for investment tax credits. For further discussion of FASB:TB 86-1, see the chapter entitled "Income Taxes."*

Background

The investment credit may be a significant factor in influencing the determination of net income. The problem remains as to *when* the investment credit should be reflected in an operating statement.

The three suggested methods are (1) a direct contribution to capital, (2) a deduction of taxes for the period in which the credit arises, and (3) amortization over the life of the property.

The preferred method is to amortize the investment credit to net income over the productive life of the acquired property (deferral method).

An alternative method, but probably not as acceptable, is to treat the credit as a reduction of taxes of the year in which the credit arises (flow-through method). In practice today, the flow-through method is used by most companies.

The argument to amortize the investment credit to net income (deferral method) is based on the basic principle of matching costs with revenue. The theoretical support for deducting the investment credit from the tax liability in the year the credit arises is based on the literal translation of the IRC in that the investment credit is a credit against taxes due.

Using an investment credit as a direct contribution to capital is irrational and unacceptable, because it bypasses the income statement entirely.

The SEC has issued a statement (ASR 96) to the effect that the only two acceptable methods are (1) amortization of the credit over the life of the acquired property and (2) a direct reduction of taxes in the year in which the credit arose.

Accounting for Investment Tax Credits

The total amount of tax benefits which become available in a current period must be included in computing income tax expense (books) for that current period (FASB Interpretation-25). The deferral method of tax allocation must be used. Investment tax credits are recognized for financial accounting purposes even though the same investment tax credits have not yet been realized for tax purposes. The theory that apparently justifies this treatment is that investment tax credits recognized in this manner will subsequently be realized as a reduction of an income tax liability of a future period.

> **OBSERVATION**: *This promulgated GAAP (FASB Interpretation-25) requires that an investment tax credit be realized for financial accounting purposes before the same investment tax credit is realized for tax purposes. This is a violation of another existing promulgated GAAP (APB-2) which specifically prohibits the recognition of an investment tax credit before it is actually used as an offset against income tax liability.*
>
> *This conflict in GAAP can be apparently traced to the use of the "with and without" method used to compute deferred taxes. Under the "with and without" method, investment tax credits are recognized in computing deferred taxes. Thus, investment tax credits are recognized on timing differences for financial accounting purposes.*

FASB Interpretation-25 further requires that any excess available investment tax credits not used in determining income tax expense for the current period must be used to reduce any existing net deferred tax credits which will reverse during the allowable carryforward periods of the related investment tax credits. Those investment tax credits which are used to offset existing net deferred tax credits will eventually be realized, as a reduction of income taxes payable, during the allowable carryforward period(s). When this occurs, a corresponding amount of net deferred tax credits must be reinstated and amortized over the period of its related timing difference.

FASB Interpretation-25 requires that all available investment tax credits be first applied to the current year using the statutory percentage limitation in effect for the current year. However, if excess investment tax credits still remain, they should be used to offset any existing net deferred tax credits which will reverse during the allowable carryforward periods. The statutory percentage limitations that must be used under these circumstances are the limitations applicable to the years in which previously recorded deferred tax credits are expected to reverse (FASB Interpretation-32). In other words, the reversal of the deferred tax credits must be scheduled by years to determine the total amount that is expected to reverse in each year. The statutory percentage limitation for each year is then multiplied by the amount that is expected to reverse in each year.

As mentioned previously, unused investment tax credits can be carried back three years and carried forward fifteen years on a first-in, first-out basis. When investment tax credits are carried forward they are included in computing income tax expense (books) for the current period (FASB Interpretation-25). Any excess investment tax credits not used in computing income tax expense for the current period are used to offset existing net deferred tax credits (FASB Interpretation-25).

Any investment tax credits not used in computing income tax expense for the current period, or used to offset existing net deferred tax credits, should be disclosed, if material, in the financial statements by footnote (APB-4).

When investment tax credits are carried back to prior years, income tax expense (per books) is reduced in the current period by the amount of refund of federal income taxes previously paid. In addition, the amount of investment tax credits which is carried back must be added to the total amount of investment tax credits recognized (per books) for the current period. The two preferable methods of accounting for the investment tax credit in the income statement when a carryback is involved are (APB-4):

1. The tax credit attributable to the carryback or carryforward is included in the total tax expense and is disclosed parenthetically or in a footnote.

2. The tax credit attributable to the carryback or carryforward is deducted as a separate item from the total tax expense.

Companies that defer and amortize investment tax credits over the productive life of the related asset (deferral method) should only include as a tax benefit for a current period the amount of amortization for the current year.

The following example will illustrate the major requirements of FASB Interpretation-25.

Assume the following facts for XYZ Corporation for its calendar year ended December 31, 1981.

- $900,000 of available unused investment tax credits for the current period.
- $1,000,000 of pretax financial accounting income (per books).
- $200,000 of net timing differences which reduce taxable income.
- $800,000 of taxable income.
- 40% tax rate for current period.
- $900,000 of existing net deferred tax credits of which $600,000 will reverse (amortize) in the carryforward period of the unused investment tax credits.

  The $600,000 will reverse as follows: $200,000 in 1982, $200,000 in 1983, and $200,000 in 1984.

- For the purposes of this illustration, assume that the investment tax credit for 1981 is limited to the first $25,000 of tax liability, plus 80% of any tax liability in excess of $25,000. Also assume that the investment tax credit for tax years ending in 1982 and thereafter is limited to the first $25,000 of tax liability, plus 90% of any tax liability in excess of $25,000.

Discussion

Income tax expense is computed on all taxable items included in pretax financial accounting income. In this example, all items included in financial accounting income are eventually taxable.

There are no permanent differences in this example. However, in any event, permanent differences do not affect subsequent periods (they do not reverse) and no interperiod tax allocation (deferred taxes) need be made to account for them. Therefore, if a permanent difference is taxable it is included in computing income tax expense (books) for the period. If a permanent difference is nontaxable it is excluded in computing income tax expense for financial accounting purposes.

The first computation in solving this example is to determine income tax expense on pretax financial accounting income (per books) and the current income tax liability on taxable income (tax return), as follows:

Income Tax Expense on Pretax Financial Accounting Income:

Pretax financial accounting income	$1,000,000
Rate of tax	40%
Income tax expense before allowable investment tax credit	$ 400,000
Allowable investment tax credit [$25,000 plus 80% of ($400,000 – $25,000)]	325,000
Income tax expense (per books)	$ 75,000

Current Income Tax Liability on Taxable Income:

Pretax financial accounting income	$1,000,000
Less: Timing difference	200,000
Taxable income	$ 800,000
Rate of tax	40%
Income tax liability before allowable investment tax credit	$ 320,000
Allowable investment tax credit [$25,000 plus 80% of ($320,000 – $25,000)]	261,000
Current income tax liability	$ 59,000

The $16,000 difference between income tax expense of $75,000 (books) and the current income tax liability of $59,000 (tax return) is the deferred tax expense on the net timing differences of $200,000, computed as follows:

Net timing differences	$200,000
Rate of tax	40%
Income tax expense before allowable investment tax credit	$ 80,000
Allowable investment tax credit (80% of $80,000)	64,000
Deferred tax expense on timing difference	$ 16,000

The allowable investment tax credit for financial accounting income purposes is $325,000. The promulgated GAAP (FASB Interpretation-25) require that any excess available investment tax credits not used in the current period in determining income tax expense (books) must be used to reduce any net deferred tax credits which will reverse within the carryforward period of the available investment tax credit. From the information given, there are $900,000 of existing net deferred tax credits of which $600,000 will reverse (amortize) within the carryforward period. For financial accounting purposes, the maximum amount of existing net deferred tax credits which can be used to offset the excess available investment tax credit not used in the current period is $540,000. The $540,000 is arrived at by applying the statutory percentage limitation which is in effect in the year of reversal, to the net deferred tax credits that reverse (FASB Interpretation-32). Thus, the $200,000 that reverses in 1982 is multiplied by the statutory percentage limitation in effect for 1982 ($200,000 x 90% = $180,000). The $200,000 that reverses in 1983 is multiplied by the statutory percentage limitation in effect for 1983 ($200,000 x 90% = $180,000). And the $200,000 that reverses in 1984 is multiplied by the statutory percentage limitation in effect for 1984 ($200,000 x 90% = $180,000). The total of the three computations is $540,000 ($180,000 + $180,000 + $180,000). Therefore, the maximum investment tax credit which can be recognized in this current period for financial accounting purposes in accordance with FASB Interpretation-25 and FASB Interpretation-32 is as follows:

Allowable investment tax credit on pretaxed financial accounting income (see first computation)	$325,000
Allowable investment tax credit on existing net deferred tax which will reverse within the carryforward period (1982 = $180,000, 1983 = $180,000 and 1984 = $180,000)	540,000
Maximum investment tax credit which can be recognized for financial accounting purposes	$865,000
Available investment tax credits	$900,000

The journal entry to record the current income tax expense, deferred taxes for the current period and the offset of the excess available investment tax credits against the maximum amount of deferred tax credits is:

Income tax expense—deferred	$ 16,000	
Income tax expense—current	59,000	
Deferred tax credits	540,000	
Current tax liability		$ 59,000
Provision for deferred taxes		540,000
Deferred taxes		16,000

The credit to deferred taxes of $16,000 represents the deferred tax on the net timing difference which arose in the current period. The credit to the provision for deferred taxes is an income statement account and appears in the total provision for income taxes for the current period, as follows:

Provision for income taxes:	
Current	$ 59,000
Deferred	16,000
Provision for deferred taxes	(540,000)
Total provision for income taxes	$(465,000)

The balance in the net deferred tax credit account which will appear on the balance sheet is computed as follows:

Balance, beginning of period	$900,000
Add: Deferred tax on net timing difference for current period	16,000
Less: Net deferred tax credit offset against excess available investment tax credit	(540,000)
Balance, end of period	$376,000

The computation of the ending balance and changes in investment tax credits for financial accounting and tax purposes is as follows:

	Financial	*Tax*
Beginning balance	$ 900,000	$ 900,000
Used in determining current income taxes	(325,000)	(261,000)
Used to offset existing net deferred tax credits	(540,000)	
Ending balance	$ 35,000	$ 639,000

In accordance with FASB Interpretation-25, the $35,000 of unused investment tax credits for financial accounting purposes may not be recorded on the books as an asset. However, if unused investment tax credits are material they should be disclosed by footnote in the financial statements (APB-4).

FASB Interpretation-25 also requires that deferred tax credits, which have been offset by investment tax credits, be reinstated in the subsequent period in which the investment tax credits are realized. In continuing the example of XYZ Corporation for its next succeeding calendar year, we will assume the following additional data to demonstrate the reinstatement of deferred taxes previously offset by investment tax credits:

- $35,000 of available unused investment tax credits for financial accounting purposes (balance from previous year)
- $639,000 of available unused investment tax credits for tax purposes (balance from previous year)
- $100,000 of available unused investment tax credits arising in current year
- $376,000 of existing net deferred tax credits (balance from previous year)
- $1,000,000 pretax financial accounting income
- $200,000 of net timing differences which reduce taxable income
- $800,000 of taxable income
- 40% tax rate
- For the purposes of this illustration, assume that the investment tax credit for 1982 is limited to the first $25,000 of tax liability, plus 90% of any tax liability in excess of $25,000.

Income Tax Expense on Pretax Financial Accounting Income:

Pretax financial accounting income	$1,000,000
Rate of tax	40%
Income tax expense before allowable investment tax credit	$ 400,000
Allowable investment tax credit [$25,000 plus 90% of ($400,000 − $25,000) = $362,500. However, for book purposes there is only $135,000 available ($35,000 + $100,000)].	135,000
Income tax expense (per books)	$ 265,000

Current Income Tax Liability on Taxable Income:

Pretax financial accounting income	$1,000,000
Less: Timing difference	200,000
Taxable income	$ 800,000
Rate of tax	40%
Income tax liability before allowable investment tax credit	$ 320,000
Allowable investment tax credit [$25,000 plus 90% of ($320,000 – $25,000)]	290,500
Current income tax liability	$ 29,500

The $235,500 difference between income tax expense of $265,000 (books) and the current income tax liability of $29,500 (tax return) consists of $8,000 deferred tax expense on the current year's net timing difference of $200,000, and the balance of $227,500 represents net deferred tax credits that must be reinstated. The journal entry to record the current income tax expense, deferred taxes for the current period and to reinstate the deferred tax credits, is as follows:

Income tax expense—current	$ 29,500	
Provision for deferred taxes	227,500	
Income tax expense—deferred	8,000	
Current tax liability		$ 29,500
Deferred tax credits		235,500

The credit to deferred tax credits consists of $8,000 arising in the current period and $227,500 of deferred tax credits being reinstated. The debit to the provision for deferred taxes is an income statement account and appears in the total provision for income taxes, as follows:

Provision for income taxes:	
Current	$ 29,500
Deferred	8,000
Provision for deferred taxes	227,500
Total provision for income taxes	$265,000

The balance in the net deferred tax credit account which will appear on the balance sheet is computed as follows:

Balance, beginning of period	$376,000
Add: Deferred tax on net timing difference for current period	8,000
Deferred taxes reinstated for investment tax credits realized	227,500
Balance, end of period	$611,500

The computation of the ending balance and changes in investment tax credits for financial accounting and tax purposes is as follows:

	Financial	Tax
Beginning balance	$ 35,000	$639,000
New investment tax credits for current year	100,000	100,000
Used for determining current income taxes	(135,000)	(290,500)
Ending balance	$ NONE	$448,500

The tax benefit of a net operating loss carryforward may be recognized when future realization is assured beyond any reasonable doubt (APB-11). This same treatment is not allowed for an investment tax credit carryforward which may not be recognized even though future realization is assured beyond any reasonable doubt (FASB Interpretation-25).

Business combinations   When an unused investment tax credit is acquired in a business combination accounted for as a purchase transaction, no value is assigned to it (FASB Interpretation-25). This is because existing promulgated GAAP (APB-2) prohibits the recording of an unused investment tax credit as an asset under any circumstances. The treatment of unused investment tax credits acquired in a purchase transaction as promulgated by FASB Interpretation-25 is as follows:

1. At the date of the purchase transaction no value is assigned to any unused investment tax credits acquired in the transaction.
2. At the date that a tax benefit is realized from the acquired unused investment tax credit, any unamortized goodwill (positive or negative) which arose from the same purchase

transaction is reduced or increased by the amount of the tax benefit realized. The adjustment to goodwill is not made retro-actively but is made prospectively. That is, there is no restate-ment of previously issued financial statements. The adjust-ment to goodwill is made in the period in which the tax benefit is realized and future periods. This means that the remaining amount of unamortized goodwill at the beginning of the pe-riod in which the tax benefit is realized is adjusted and the new balance is amortized over the current and remaining periods of amortization.

3. In the event that there is no unamortized goodwill at the beginning of the period in which the tax benefit is realized, then the noncurrent assets, if any, acquired in the same pur-chase transaction are reduced proportionately by the amount of the realized tax benefit. The adjustment is made prospectively in the same manner as goodwill (see 2 above).

4. If there is no unamortized goodwill or balances of noncurrent assets acquired in the same purchase transaction as the un-used investment tax credit, or if the noncurrent assets are reduced to zero and realized tax benefits still exist, then any remaining realized tax benefits should be recorded as deferred credits and amortized to income over a period not to exceed forty years.

Other Considerations

Once a method of reporting the investment tax credit is selected, it should not be changed. A change may result in a consistency excep-tion in the auditor's report (APB-4).

Only one method should be established for consolidated state-ments even though the members of the consolidating group may employ several different methods (APB-4).

In accounting for leverage leases the lessor must use the deferral method of accounting for the investment credit, or else the lease must be accounted for as a direct financing lease (FASB-13).

Disclosure

The two most acceptable forms of balance sheet presentation for the investment tax credit are (1) as a deduction from the corresponding asset and (2) as a deferred credit.

In the first case, the income statement will show a lower deprecia-tion expense for the year, because the depreciable base of the asset has been reduced by the credit and so the credit will not appear on the income statement. If, however, this year's amount of the credit is shown directly on the income statement, then the depreciation expense for the year should be higher by the same amount.

Whatever method is used to account for the investment tax credit, full disclosure of the method and amounts involved should be made, as should material amounts of unused investment credits.

Conflict in GAAP

APB-2 and APB-4 require that investment tax credits be disclosed parenthetically or by footnote unless they can actually be used as an offset against the current income tax liability, or carried back to prior years for a claim of refund. In other words, investment tax credits are not to be recorded on the books of an enterprise, or be used as an offset against the income tax liability unless they can be actually realized for tax purposes and represent an available tax benefit. The justification for this treatment is apparently based on the limited life of the investment tax credit as provided by federal tax regulations. Under current tax regulations, an investment tax credit can be carried back three years and carried forward fifteen years, which are the same periods allowed for net operating losses.

The deferred tax method of interperiod tax allocation is required by APB-11 (Accounting for Income Taxes). APB-11 states that, "The tax effect of a timing difference should be measured by the differential between taxes computed with and without inclusion of the transaction creating the difference between taxable income and pretax accounting income." Thus, the "with and without" method of computing deferred taxes was established and investment tax credits are included in determining income tax expense (books) before the same investment tax credits are actually realized for tax purposes.

FASB Interpretation-25 condones the practice of recognizing investment tax credits for financial accounting purposes prior to their realization for tax purposes.

APB-11 permits the recognition, for financial accounting purposes, of a tax benefit resulting from an operating loss carryforward, providing that the realization of the tax benefit is assured beyond any reasonable doubt. Thus, income tax expense (books) can be reduced by the recognition of such an operating loss carryforward before the tax benefit is actually realized for tax purposes. However, FASB Interpretation-25 prohibits the recognition of a tax benefit resulting from an investment tax credit, even if the realization of the tax benefit is assured beyond any reasonable doubt. Thus, the tax benefit of an operating loss carryforward can be recognized for financial accounting purposes before the same loss is realized for tax purposes, but the tax benefit of an investment tax credit cannot be recognized under any circumstances prior to its realization for tax purposes.

To add further confusion, FASB Interpretation-25 requires that any excess available investment tax credits, not used to determine the current income tax expense (books), must be used to reduce any existing net deferred tax credits which will reverse in the available carryforward period. The journal entry to record the use of the excess available investment tax credits to reduce existing net deferred tax credits is as follows:

Deferred tax credits	$XX,XXX	
Provision for deferred taxes		$XX,XXX

The *provision for deferred taxes* appears in the income statement as part of the total current provision for income taxes. Thus, once again, current income tax expense is reduced by the tax benefits of investment tax credits which have not yet been realized for tax purposes.

INVESTMENT TAX CREDIT
IMPORTANT NOTICE

In December 1987, FASB-96 (Accounting for Income Taxes) was issued to supersede APB-11 (Accounting for Income Taxes). FASB-96 was scheduled to become effective for fiscal years beginning after December 15, 1988, and earlier adoption was encouraged.

As a result of numerous complaints from major industrial enterprises regarding the complexity and cost of implementing the provisions of FASB-96, the Financial Accounting Standards Board (FASB) issued FASB-100, deferring the effective date of FASB-96 by one year to December 15, 1989. FASB-103 granted a further deferral of two years to December 15, 1991, with earlier application encouraged.

Two Exposure Drafts (ED) are outstanding as of the date of this publication. One of the outstanding EDs would defer the effective date of FASB-96 for one more year, until fiscal years beginning after December 15, 1992, with earlier application permitted. The other outstanding ED would supersede FASB-96 and would be effective for fiscal years beginning after December 15, 1992. If the FASB meets its own schedule for issuing final Statements based on these two outstanding EDs, FASB-96 will be superseded without ever having gone into effect, although some enterprises have elected its early application.

Until the FASB issues a new Statement superseding FASB-96, an enterprise may account for income taxes by (i) continuing to apply the provisions of APB-11 or (ii) electing early adoption of FASB-96.

This edition of the *GAAP Guide* contains coverage of both APB-11 and FASB-96. The provisions of APB-11 appear in chapter 19.01a and the provisions of FASB-96 appear in chapter 19.01b.

Highlights of the outstanding Exposure Draft are summarized at the end of chapter 19.01b and are noted in the Disclosure Index.

Because of the status of APB-11 and FASB-96, it was also necessary to include two chapters entitled "Investment Tax

Credit" in this issue of the *GAAP Guide*. Chapter 25.01a contains coverage of the accounting standards relating to investment tax credits as they existed prior to the amendments by FASB-96. Chapter 25.01a should be used by those enterprises that are continuing to apply the provisions of APB-11 to account for income taxes. Chapter 25.01b contains coverage of the accounting standards relating to investment tax credits as they existed after the amendments by FASB-96. Chapter 25.01b should be used by those enterprises that are electing early adoption of the provisions of FASB-96.

INVESTMENT TAX CREDIT

Overview

The present promulgated GAAP on accounting for the investment credit is APB-2, which has been amended by APB-4.

Background

The investment credit may be a significant factor in influencing the determination of net income. The problem remains as to *when* the investment credit should be reflected in the income statement.

The three suggested methods are (1) a direct contribution to capital, (2) a deduction of taxes for the period in which the credit arises, and (3) amortization over the life of the property.

The preferred method is to amortize the investment credit to net income over the productive life of the acquired property (deferral method).

A less acceptable alternative method is to treat the credit as a reduction of taxes of the year in which the credit arises (flow-through method). In practice today, the flow-through method is used by most companies.

The argument to amortize the investment credit to net income (deferral method) is based on the basic principle of matching costs with revenue. The theoretical support for deducting the investment credit from the tax liability in the year the credit arises is based on the literal translation of the Internal Revenue Code (IRC) in that the investment credit is a credit against taxes due.

Using an investment credit as a direct contribution to capital is irrational and unacceptable, because it bypasses the income statement entirely.

The SEC has issued a statement (ASR 96) to the effect that the only two acceptable methods are (1) amortization of the credit over the life of the acquired property and (2) a direct reduction of taxes in the year in which the credit arose.

Accounting for Investment Tax Credits

Accounting for income taxes is addressed by FASB-96, which requires that the liability method be used to determine a deferred tax liability (asset). The liability approach assumes that the only items of future taxable income or tax deductions are the reversals of temporary differences. Any other assumption regarding income or losses is prohibited by FASB-96. The deferred tax expense or credit that is shown in the income statement for the year is equal to the difference between the deferred tax liability (asset) at the beginning of the year and the end of the year.

Under FASB-96, an enterprise must estimate the amount and timing of all future taxable income and tax deductions resulting from the reversal of temporary differences. The tax rates enacted for each future year are applied to each future year's net taxable income or net tax deductions to calculate the deferred tax liability or asset. Investment tax credits are recognized for financial accounting purposes in the year in which they are deductible for income tax purposes.

When investment tax credits are carried back to prior years, income tax expense (per books) is reduced in the current period by the amount of refund of federal income taxes previously paid. In addition, the amount of investment tax credits which is carried back must be added to the total amount of investment tax credits recognized (per books) for the current period. The two preferable methods of accounting for the investment tax credit in the income statement when a carryback is involved are:

1. The tax credit attributable to the carryback or carryforward is included in the total tax expense and is disclosed parenthetically or in a footnote.
2. The tax credit attributable to the carryback or carryforward is deducted as a separate item from the total tax expense.

Companies that defer and amortize investment tax credits over the productive life of the related asset (deferral method) should include as a tax benefit for a current period only the amount of amortization for the current year. This is because existing GAAP (APB-2) prohibits the recording of an unused investment tax credit as an asset under any circumstances.

Other Considerations

Once a method of reporting the investment tax credit is selected it should not be changed. A change may result in a consistency exception in the auditor's report (APB-4). Only one method should be established for consolidated statements even though the members of the consolidating group may employ several different methods (APB-4).

In accounting for leveraged leases, the lessor must use the deferral method of accounting for the investment credit, or else the lease must be accounted for as a direct financing lease (FASB-13).

> **OBSERVATION:** *The FASB acknowledged that accounting for income taxes related to leveraged leases under the provisions of FASB-13 (Accounting for Leases) and FASB Interpretation-21 (Accounting for Leases in a Business Combination) is not consistent with the requirements of FASB-96 (Accounting for Income Taxes). The FASB decided not to separately address accounting for income taxes pertaining to leveraged leases without complete reconsideration of the entire subject of leveraged leases.*

Disclosure

The two most acceptable forms of balance sheet presentation for the investment tax credit are to show it (1) as a deduction from the corresponding asset and (2) as a deferred credit.

In the first case, the income statement will show a lower depreciation expense for the year, because the depreciable base of the asset has been reduced by the credit and therefore the credit will not appear on the income statement. In the second case, the amount of the credit will be shown directly on the income statement and the depreciation expense should be higher by the same amount.

Whatever method is used to account for the investment tax credit, full disclosure of the method and amounts involved should be made, as should material amounts of unused investment credits.

APB-2 and APB-4 require that investment tax credits be disclosed parenthetically or by footnote unless they can actually be used as an offset against the current income tax liability, or carried back to prior years for a claim of refund. In other words, investment tax credits are not to be recorded on the books of an enterprise, or be used as an offset against the income tax liability, unless they can be realized for tax purposes and represent an available tax benefit. The justification for this treatment is apparently based on the limited life of the investment tax credit as provided by federal tax regulations. Under current tax regulations, an investment tax credit can be carried back three years and carried forward fifteen years, which are the same periods allowed for net operating losses.

LEASES

Overview

The main source of promulgated GAAP on accounting for leases is FASB-13 (Accounting for Leases), which has subsequently been amended or interpreted by the following:

FASB-22, Changes in the Provisions of Lease Agreements Resulting from Refunding of Tax-Exempt Debt

FASB-23, Inception of the Lease

FASB-27, Classification of Renewals or Extensions of Existing Sales-Type or Direct Financing Leases

FASB-28, Accounting for Sales with Leasebacks

FASB-29, Determining Contingent Rentals

FASB-91, Accounting for Nonrefundable Fees and Costs Associated with Originating or Acquiring Loans and Initial Direct Costs of Leases

FASB-98, Accounting for Leases:
- Sale-Leaseback Transactions Involving Real Estate
- Sales-Type Leases of Real Estate
- Definition of Lease Term
- Initial Direct Costs of Direct Financing Leases

FASB Interpretation-19, Lessee Guarantee of the Residual Value of Leased Property

FASB Interpretation-23, Leases of Certain Property Owned by a Governmental Unit or Authority

FASB Interpretation-24, Leases Involving Only a Part of a Building

FASB Interpretation-26, Accounting for Purchase of a Leased Asset by the Lessee during the Term of the Lease

FASB Interpretation-27, Accounting for a Loss on a Sublease

In addition, the staff of the Financial Accounting Standards Board has issued the following Technical Bulletins concerning leases:

79-10 Fiscal Funding Clauses in Lease Agreements

79-12 Interest Rate Used in Calculating the Present Value of Minimum Lease Payments

79-14 Upward Adjustment of Guaranteed Residual Values
79-15 Accounting for Loss on a Sublease Not Involving the Disposal of a Segment

79-16 Effect of a Change in Income Tax Rate on the Accounting for Leveraged Leases

79-17 Reporting Cumulative Effect Adjustment from Retroactive Application of FASB Statement 13

79-18 Transition Requirement of Certain FASB Amendments and Interpretations of FASB Statement 13

85-3 Accounting for Operating Leases with Scheduled Rent Increases

86-2 Accounting for an Interest in the Residual Value of a Leased Asset

88-1 Issues Relating to Leases:
- Time Pattern of the Physical Use of the Property in an Operating Lease
- Lease Incentives in an Operating Lease
- Applicability of Leveraged Lease Accounting to Existing Assets of the Lessor
- Money-Over-Money Lease Transactions
- Wrap Lease Transactions

FASB-13 defines a lease as an agreement that conveys the right to use assets (tangible or intangible) for a stated period. This broad definition includes certain transactions not generally considered leases and excludes leases of natural resources (oil, minerals, and timber) and licensing agreements for manuscripts, patents, motion pictures, and copyrights.

FASB-22 addresses an inconsistency between FASB-13 (Accounting for Leases) and APB-26 (Extinguishment of Debt) arising from refundings of tax-exempt debt, including advance refundings that are accounted for as early extinguishments of debt. FASB-22 is covered in more detail later in this chapter.

FASB-23 amends FASB-13 to specify that, if the leased property is yet to be constructed or acquired by the lessor at the inception of the lease, the lessor's criterion pertaining to "no important uncertainties of unreimbursable costs yet to be incurred by the lessor" shall not be applied at the inception of the lease but shall be applied at the date that construction of the property is completed or the property is acquired. FASB-23 amends FASB-13 to specify that any increases in the minimum lease payments that have occurred during the preacquisition or preconstruction period as a result of an escalation clause are to be considered in determining the fair value of the leased property at the inception of the lease. FASB-23 also amends FASB-13 to limit the amount that can be recorded by the lessor for the residual value of leased property to an amount not greater than the estimate as of the inception of the lease. FASB-23 is discussed more fully throughout this chapter.

FASB-27 modifies FASB-13 to require a lessor to classify a renewal or an extension of a sales-type or direct financing lease as a sales-type lease if the lease would otherwise qualify as a sales-type lease and the renewal or extension occurs at or near the end of the lease term. Otherwise, FASB-13 prohibits the classification of a renewal or extension of a sales-type or direct financing lease as a sales-type lease at any other time during the lease term.

FASB-28 amends FASB-13 to specify the appropriate accounting for sale-leaseback transactions depending on the percentage amount of the property that the seller-lessee leases back (substantially all of the property, a minor portion of the property, or more than a minor portion of the property but less than substantially all) and whether the lease is classified as a capital lease or an operating lease.

FASB-29 amends FASB-13 to provide a new definition for contingent rentals as those that cannot be determined at the inception of the lease because they depend on future factors or events. Rental payments based on future sales volume, future machine hours, future interest rates, and future price indexes are examples of contingent rentals. Contingent rentals can either increase or decrease lease payments (FASB-29).

FASB-91 establishes accounting and reporting standards for nonrefundable fees and costs associated with lending, committing to lend, or purchasing a loan or group of loans. Under FASB-91, direct loan origination fees and costs, including initial direct costs incurred by a lessor in negotiating and consummating a lease are offset against each other and the net amount is deferred and recognized over the life of the loan as an adjustment to the yield on the loan. The provisions of FASB-91 apply to all types of loans, including debt securities, and to all types of lenders, including banks, thrift institutions, insurance companies, mortgage bankers, and other financial and nonfinancial institutions. However, FASB-91 does not apply to nonrefundable fees and costs that are associated with originating or acquiring loans that are carried at market value.

FASB-98 amends FASB-13 to establish a new definition of *penalty* and *lease term* for all leasing transactions. FASB-98 specifies the appropriate accounting for a seller-lessee in a sale-leaseback transaction involving real estate, including real estate with equipment, such as manufacturing facilities, power plants, furnished office buildings, etc. FASB-98 establishes the appropriate accounting for a sale-leaseback transaction in which property improvements or integral equipment is sold to a purchaser-lessor and leased back by the seller-lessee who retains the ownership of the underlying land. FASB-98 also provides the appropriate accounting for sale-leaseback transactions involving real estate with equipment that include separate sale and leaseback agreements for the real estate and the equipment (a) with the same entity or related parties and (b) that are consummated at or near the same time, suggesting that they were negotiated as a package.

Substance over Form

Some lease agreements are such that an asset and a related liability should be reported on the balance sheet of an enterprise. The distinction is one of *substance over form* (basic principle) when then transaction actually *transfers substantially all the benefits and risks inherent in the ownership of the property.*

Established in GAAP are criteria to determine whether a lease transaction is in substance a transfer of the incidents of ownership. If, at its inception, a lease meets one or more of the following four criteria, the lease should be classified as a transfer of ownership:

1. By the end of the lease term, ownership of the leased property is transferred to the lessee.
2. The lease contains a bargain purchase option.
3. The lease term is substantially (75% or more) equal to the estimated useful life of the leased property.
4. At the inception of the lease, the present value of the minimum lease payments, with certain adjustments, is 90% or more of the fair value of the leased property.

The above four criteria are examined in more detail later in this chapter.

A lease that transfers substantially all the benefits and risks inherent in the ownership of property is called a *capital lease*. Such a lease should be accounted for by the lessee as the acquisition of an asset and the incurrence of a liability. The lessor should account for such a lease as a sale or financing. These leases are referred to as *sales-type* or *direct financing leases*. All other leases are referred to as *operating leases*.

Terminology

It is essential that the various terms used in accounting for leases be thoroughly understood.

Capital lease   A capital lease transfers substantially all the benefits and risks inherent in the ownership of the property to the lessee, who accounts for the lease as an acquisition of an asset and the incurrence of a liability.

Sales-type lease   A sales-type lease usually results in a manufacturer's or dealer's profit or loss to the lessor and transfers substantially all the benefits and risks inherent in the ownership of the leased property to the lessee; in addition, (1) the minimum lease payments are reasonably predictable of collection and (2) no important uncertainties exist regarding costs to be incurred by the lessor under the terms of the lease.
A lease involving *real estate* shall not be classified as a sales-type lease unless the title to the leased property is transferred to the lessee at or shortly after the end of the lease term (FASB-98, Sale-Leasebacks Involving Real Estate).

Direct financing lease   A direct financing lease does not result in a manufacturer's or dealer's profit or loss to the lessor, but does transfer substantially all the benefits and risks inherent in the ownership of the leased property to the lessee; in addition, (1) the minimum lease payments are reasonably predictable of collection and (2) no important uncertainties exist regarding costs to be incurred by the lessor under the terms of the lease.

Comparison of Sales-Type and Direct Financing Leases

Both sales-type and direct financing leases transfer substantially all the benefits and risks inherent in the ownership of the leased property to the lessee, who records the transaction as a *capital lease*.

A sales-type lease usually gives rise to a manufacturer's or dealer's profit or loss, whereas a direct financing lease does not give rise to a manufacturer's or dealer's profit or loss.

In a sales-type lease, the *fair value* of the leased property at the inception of the lease differs from the cost or carrying amount; in a direct financing lease, the fair value of the leased property at the inception of the lease is the same as the cost or carrying amount. This is because a manufacturer's or dealer's profit or loss usually exists in a sales-type lease and fair value is usually the *normal selling price* of the property. In a direct financing lease, fair value is usually cost.

It must be remembered that a lessor need not be a dealer or manufacturer to realize a profit or loss, if, at the inception of the lease, the fair value differs from the cost or carrying amount.

Fair value Fair value is the price the leased property could be sold for between unrelated parties in an arm's length transaction.

For the manufacturer or dealer, the fair value is usually the normal selling price less trade or volume discounts. However, fair value may be less than the normal selling price, and sometimes less than the cost of the property.

For others, the fair value is usually cost less trade or volume discounts. However, fair value may be less than cost, especially in circumstances where a long period elapses between the acquisition of the property by the lessor and the inception of a lease.

Fair rental Fair rental is the rental rate for similar property under similar lease terms and conditions.

Related parties Related parties are one or more entities subject to the significant influence over the operating and financial policies of another entity.

Executory costs Examples of executory costs include insurance, maintenance, and taxes paid in connection with the leased property.

Bargain purchase option A bargain purchase option is a lessee's option to purchase the leased property at a bargain price that makes the exercise of the option almost certain.

Bargain renewal option A bargain renewal option is a lessee's option to renew the lease at a bargain rental price that makes the exercise of the option almost certain.

Estimated economic life   Estimated economic life is the estimated remaining useful life of the property for the purpose for which it was intended, regardless of the term of the lease.

Estimated residual value   Estimated residual value is the estimated fair value of the leased property at the end of the lease term. The estimated residual value shall not exceed the amount estimated at the inception of the lease except for the effect of any increases that result during the construction or preacquisition period due to escalation provisions in the lease.

Unguaranteed residual value   Unguaranteed residual value is the estimated fair value of the leased property at the end of the lease term that is not guaranteed by either the lessee or a third party unrelated to the lessor. A guarantee by a third party related to the lessee shall be considered a lessee guarantee.

Lessee's incremental borrowing rate   The lessee's incremental borrowing rate is the rate of interest that the lessee would have had to pay at the inception of the lease to borrow the funds, on similar terms, to purchase the leased property.

> **OBSERVATION:** *FASB Technical Bulletin 79-12 precludes the use of the lessee's secured borrowing rate as a substitute for its incremental borrowing rate, as long as the incremental borrowing rate is determinable, reasonable, and consistent with the alternative financing the lessee could obtain.*

Inception of lease   The inception of the lease is the date of the lease agreement *or* the date of a written commitment signed by the parties involved that sets forth the principal provisions of the lease transaction. A written commitment which does not contain all of the principal provisions of the lease transaction does not qualify under the promulgated GAAP (FASB-23).

Interest rate implicit in the lease   The interest rate implicit in the lease is the discount rate that, when applied to certain items (enumerated below), results in an aggregate present value equal to the fair value of the leased property at the beginning of the lease term, less any investment credit expected to be realized and retained by the lessor. The items that the discount rate is applied to are (1) the minimum lease payments, excluding executory costs such as insurance, maintenance, and taxes (including any profit thereon) that are paid by the lessor and (2) the estimated fair value of the property at the end of the lease term, exclusive of any portion guaranteed by either the lessee or a third party unrelated to the lessor (unguaranteed residual value).

Initial direct costs (FASB-91)   The definition of initial direct costs in paragraph 5(m) of FASB-13, as amended by paragraph 24 of FASB-91, is as follows:

> *Initial direct costs.** Only those costs incurred by the lessor that are (a) costs to originate a lease incurred in transactions with independent third parties that (i) result directly from and are essential to acquire that lease and (ii) would not have been incurred had that leasing transaction not occurred and (b) certain costs directly related to specified activities performed by the lessor for that lease. Those activities are evaluating the prospective lessee's financial condition; evaluating and recording guarantees, collateral, and other security arrangements; negotiating lease terms; preparing and processing lease documents; and closing the transaction. The costs directly related to those activities shall include only that portion of the employees' total compensation and payroll-related fringe benefits directly related to time spent performing those activities for that lease and other costs related to those activities that would not have been incurred but for that lease. Initial direct costs shall not include costs related to activities performed by the lessor for advertising, soliciting potential lessees, servicing existing leases, and other ancillary activities related to establishing and monitoring credit policies, supervision, and administration. Initial direct costs shall not include administrative costs, rent, depreciation, any other occupancy and equipment costs, and employees' compensation and fringe benefits related to activities described in the previous sentence, unsuccessful origination efforts, and idle time.

> ———————

> *Initial direct cost shall be offset by nonrefundable fees that are yield adjustments as prescribed in FASB Statement No. 91, *Accounting for Nonrefundable Fees and Costs Associated with Originating or Acquiring Loans and Initial Direct Costs of Leases.*

In determining the net amount of initial direct costs in a leasing transaction under FASB-13, a lessor shall apply the provisions of paragraphs 5 through 9 of FASB-91 relating to loan origination fees, commitment fees, and direct loan origination costs of completed loans. Initial direct costs shall be accounted for by lessors as part of the investment in a direct financing lease.

OBSERVATION: *The recognition of a portion of the unearned income at the inception of a lease transaction to offset initial direct costs is not permitted (paragraph 23 of FASB-91).*

Contingent rentals   Contingent rentals are those which cannot be determined at the inception of the lease because they depend on future factors or events. Rental payments based on future sales volume, future machine hours, future interest rates and future price indexes are examples of contingent rentals. Contingent rentals can either increase or decrease lease payments (FASB-29).

Increases in minimum lease payments that occur during the preacquisition or construction period as a result of an escalation clause in the lease are not considered contingent rentals.

Lease Term

The lease term shall include all of the following time periods:

1. Any fixed noncancelable term
2. Any period(s) covered by a bargain renewal option
3. Any period(s) in which penalties are imposed in an amount that at the inception of the lease reasonably assures the renewal of the lease by the lessee
4. Any period(s) covered by ordinary renewal options during which a guarantee by the lessee of the lessor's debt that is directly or indirectly related to the leased property is expected to be in effect or a loan from the lessee to the lessor that is directly or indirectly related to the leased property is expected to be outstanding

    Note: The phrase *indirectly related to the leased property* is used to cover situations that in substance are guarantees of the lessor's debt or loans to the lessor by the lessee that are related to the leased property, but are structured in such a manner that they do not represent a direct guarantee or loan.

5. Any period(s) covered by ordinary renewal options preceding the date on which a bargain purchase option is exercisable
6. Any period(s) representing renewals or extensions of the lease at the lessor's option

Under no circumstances shall a lease term extend beyond the date a bargain purchase option becomes exercisable.

Noncancelable lease term A noncancelable lease term is a provision in a lease agreement that specifies that the lease may be canceled only (i) on some remote contingency, (ii) with permission of the lessor, or (iii) if the lessee enters into a new lease with the same lessor.

FASB Technical Bulletin 79-10 provides guidance concerning fiscal funding clauses that are frequently found in leases of governmental units. The fiscal funding clause permits cancellation of a lease by a governmental unit if the necessary governmental appropriations are not made to pay for the lease. FASB Technical Bulletin 79-10 reaffirms the definition in FASB-13 of a noncancelable lease term. Thus, if there is a remote possibility that a fiscal funding clause will be exercised by a governmental unit, the lease should be classified as noncancelable. On the other hand, if the possibility is more than remote, the lease should be classified as cancelable in accordance with the provisions of FASB-13.

Penalty The term *penalty* refers to any outside factor or provision of the lease agreement that does or can impose on the lessee the requirement to disburse cash, incur or assume a liability, perform services, surrender or transfer an asset or rights to an asset or otherwise forego an economic benefit or suffer an economic detriment.

Lessee's Minimum Lease Payments

Normal minimum lease payments include:

1. The minimum rent called for during the lease term
2. Any payment(s) or guarantee(s) that the lessee must make or is required to make concerning the leased property at the end of the lease term (residual value), including:
   a. Any amount stated to purchase the leased property
   b. Any amount stated to make up any deficiency from a specified minimum
   c. Any amount payable for failure to renew or extend the lease at the expiration of the lease term

When a lease contains a *bargain purchase option*, the minimum lease payments include only (1) the *minimum rental payments over the lease term* and (2) *the payment required to exercise the bargain purchase option*.

Under all circumstances, the following should be excluded in determining minimum lease payments:

1. A guarantee by the lessee to pay the lessor's debt on the leased property
2. The lessee's obligation (separate from the rental payments) to pay executory costs (insurance, taxes, etc.) in connection with the leased property
3. Contingent rentals

> **OBSERVATION:** *FASB Interpretation-19 clarifies certain guarantees of the residual value of leased property made by a lessee, as follows:*
>
> 1. *A guarantee by a lessee to make up a residual value deficiency caused by damage, extraordinary wear and tear, or excessive usage is similar to a contingent rental, since the amount is not determinable at the inception of the lease. Therefore, this type of lessee guarantee does not constitute a lessee guarantee of residual value for purposes of computing the lessee's minimum lease payments.*
>
> 2. *A lessee's guarantee to make up a residual value deficiency at the end of a lease term is limited to the specified maximum deficiency called for by the lease.*
>
> 3. *Unless the lessor explicitly releases the lessee, a guarantee of residual value by an unrelated third party for the benefit of the lessor does not release the obligation of the lessee. Therefore, such a guarantee by an unrelated third party shall not be used to reduce the lessee's minimum lease payments. Costs incurred in connection with a guarantee by an unrelated third party are considered executory costs and are not included in computing the lessee's minimum lease payments.*

Lessor's Minimum Lease Payments

The minimum lease payments to a lessor are the sum of:

1. The minimum lease payments under the lease terms
2. Any guarantee by a third party, unrelated to the lessee and lessor, of the residual value or rental payments beyond the lease term, providing such guarantor is financially capable of discharging the potential obligation

Classification of Leases by Lessees

If one or more of the following four criteria are present at the inception of a lease, it should be classified as a capital lease by the lessee.

I.   Ownership of the property is transferred to the lessee by the end of the lease term.

II. The lease contains a bargain purchase option.

III. The lease term, at inception, is substantially (75% or more) equal to the estimated economic life of the leased property, including earlier years of use. (Exception: This particular criterion cannot be used for a lease that begins within the last 25% of the original estimated economic life of the leased property. For example: A jet aircraft that has an estimated economic life of 25 years is leased for five successive five-year leases. If the first four five-year leases were classified as operating leases, the last five-year lease could not be classified as a capital lease because the lease would commence within the last 25% of the estimated economic life of the property and would fall under this exception.)

IV. The present value of the minimum lease payments at the beginning of the lease term, excluding executory costs and profits thereon to be paid by the lessor, is 90% or more of the fair value of the property at the inception of the lease, less any investment tax credit retained and expected to be realized by the lessor. (Exception: This particular criterion cannot be used for a lease that begins within the last 25% of the original estimated economic life of the leased property.)

Lessee's discount rate   A lessee's incremental borrowing rate should be used to determine the present value of the minimum lease payments, except that the lessor's implicit rate of interest should be used if it is known and it is lower.

Lessor's discount rate   A lessor shall compute the present value of the minimum lease payments, using the interest rate *implicit in the lease.*

Classification of Leases by Lessors

If, at inception, a lease meets any one of the four criteria indicating that substantially all the benefits and risks of ownership have been transferred to the lessee, and *meets both the following conditions,* the lease shall be classified by the lessor as a sales-type or direct financing lease, whichever is appropriate:

1. *Collection of the minimum lease payments is reasonably predictable.* A receivable resulting from a lease subject to an estimate of uncollectibility based on experience shall not be precluded from being classified as either a sales-type or a direct financing lease.

2. *No important uncertainties exist for unreimbursable costs yet to be incurred by the lessor under the lease.* Important uncertainties include extensive warranties and material commitments beyond normal practice. The necessity of estimating *executory costs*, such as insurance, maintenance and taxes, shall not be considered important uncertainties.

    Note: In the event the leased property is not acquired or constructed before the inception of the lease, this condition is not applied until such time as the leased property is acquired or constructed by the lessor (FASB-23).

A lease involving real estate shall not be classified by the lessor as a sales-type lease unless the title to the leased property is transferred to the lessee at or shortly after the end of the lease term (FASB-98).

Changing a Provision of a Lease

If a change in a provision of a lease results in a different lease classification at the inception of the lease because it meets different criteria, a new lease agreement is created that must be reclassified according to its different criteria. Renewal, extension, or a new lease under which the lessee continues to use the same property is not considered a change in a lease provision.

Any action that extends the lease term, except to void a residual guarantee, or a penalty for failure to renew the lease at the end of the lease term, shall be considered a new lease agreement that must be classified according to the different criteria.

Mere changes in estimates or circumstances do not cause a reclassification.

Refunding of tax-exempt debt   If a change in a lease occurs as a result of a refunding by the lessor of tax-exempt debt and (1) the lessee receives the economic advantages of the refunding, and (2) the revised lease qualifies and is classified either as a capital lease by the lessee or as a direct financing lease by the lessor, the change in the lease shall be accounted for on the basis of whether or not an extinguishment of debt has occurred (FASB-22), as follows:

1. Accounted for as an extinguishment of debt

    a. The lessee adjusts the lease obligation to the present value of the future minimum lease payments under the revised agreement, using the effective interest rate of the new lease agreement. Any gain or loss shall be treated as a gain or loss on an early extinguishment of debt.

    b. The lessor adjusts the balance of the minimum lease payments receivable and the gross investment in the lease (if affected) for the difference between the present values of the old and new or revised agreement. Any gain or loss shall be recognized in the current period.

2. Not accounted for as an extinguishment of debt

    a. The lessee accrues any costs connected with the refunding that are obligated to be reimbursed to the lessor. The interest method is used to amortize the costs over the period from the date of the refunding to the call date of the debt to be refunded.

    b. The lessor recognizes as revenue any reimbursements to be received from the lessee for costs paid related to the debt to be refunded over the period from the date of the refunding to the call date of the debt to be refunded.

Accounting and Reporting by Lessees

Initial recording   The lessee records a capital lease as an asset along with a corresponding liability. The initial recording value of a lease is the *lesser* of the fair value of the leased property or the present value of the minimum lease payments, excluding any portion representing executory costs and profit thereon to be paid by the lessor. Fair value is determined as of the inception of the lease, and the present value of the minimum lease payments is computed at the beginning of the lease term. The inception of the lease and the beginning of the lease term are not necessarily the same dates.

Since the definition of lessee's minimum lease payments *excludes* a lessee's obligation to pay executory costs (apart from the rental payments), any executory costs included in the minimum lease payments must be part of the rental payments, identified separately or not. Thus, there may be no executory costs at all to exclude from the minimum lease payments; or if such costs are included in the rental payments and are not separately identified (which is probably the most likely case), an estimate of the amount will be necessary.

A lessee's incremental borrowing rate should be used to determine the present value of the minimum lease payments unless the lessor's implicit rate of interest is known and is lower. A *lessor* shall compute the present value of the minimum lease payments using the interest rate implicit in the lease that results in a present value equal to the fair value.

Leases with escalation clauses In lease agreements or written commitments in which the leased property is to be acquired or constructed by the lessor, there may be a provision for the escalation of the minimum lease payments during the construction or preacquisition period. Usually, the escalation is based on increased costs of acquisition or construction of the leased property. A provision to escalate the minimum lease payments during the construction or preacquisition period can also be based on other measures of cost or value, including general price-level changes or changes in the consumer price index.

The relationship between the total amount of minimum lease payments and the fair value of a lease is such that when one increases so does the other. For example, assume that the total minimum lease payments of a particular lease are $100,000 payable in five equal annual installments, and the fair value of the same lease is $350,000. If the minimum lease payments are increased 20% to $120,000, it is quite likely that the fair value of the lease will increase correspondingly because the lease is then worth more money to an investor.

FASB-23 requires that increases in the minimum lease payments that occur during the preacquisition or construction period as a result of an escalation clause are to be considered in determining the fair value of the leased property at the inception of the lease for the purposes of the initial recording of the lease transaction by the lessee, or where fair value is used as a basis of allocation.

The initial recording value of a lease transaction by the lessee, which is required by FASB-13, is the lesser of the fair value of the leased property or the present value of the minimum lease payments. FASB-23 changes the lessee's determination of fair value for leases which contain escalation clauses from the fair value on the inception date to a fair value amount that includes the effect of any increases which have occurred as a result of the escalation clause. The changes embodied in FASB-23 are intended to create lease classifications that more closely reflect the substance of a lease transaction.

OBSERVATION: *The question arises as to when leases of this type should be recorded on the books of the lessee. FASB-23 appears to indicate that the initial recording should be made only after the effects of the escalation clause on the fair value of the leased property are determined. Otherwise, FASB-23 is silent in all respects as to when the lease transaction should be recorded. In the case of significant amounts of leases, it appears to be illogical to wait several years to record the transaction. However, if this is the only viable alternative, full disclosure of all pertinent facts pertaining to the lease agreement or commitment should be made in a prominent footnote.*

The other alternative is to record these types of lease transactions immediately at the inception of the lease, utilizing whatever information is available and subsequently adjusting the recorded amounts when the effects of the escalation clauses are known. This alternative does not appear to be viable because of the difficulties mentioned in the following paragraphs.

The last-enumerated criterion in FASB-13 for capitalizing a lease is when the present value of the minimum lease payments is 90% or more of the fair value of the leased property at the inception of the lease. When this criterion is considered for capitalizing a lease in conjunction with the alternative of recording lease transactions covered by FASB-23 at the inception of the lease and then subsequently adjusting the recorded amounts when the effects of the escalation clauses become known, the following problems arise, which are not addressed by either FASB-13 or FASB-23.

1. *If we assume that FASB-23 requires that the fair value of leases with escalation clauses be determined at a future date, what fair value should be used to determine whether the lease is or is not a capital lease in accordance with the criterion of whether the present value of the minimum lease payments is 90% or more of the fair value of the leased property at the inception of the lease?*

2. *What if a lease of this type is capitalized in accordance with the criterion that the present value of the minimum lease payments is 90% or more of the fair value at inception of the lease, and subsequently, as a result of the escalation clause, the present value becomes less than 90% of the fair value, so that the lease should not have been capitalized?*

3. *Suppose a lease with an escalation clause is properly classified as an operating lease at inception of the lease and subsequently, as a result of the escalation clause, the lease qualifies as a capital lease?*

The above are just a few of the complications that could arise in applying the provisions of FASB-23 to lease transactions. Some clarification must be forthcoming before this promulgated GAAP can be pragmatically applied.

FASB-23 also permits increases in the estimated residual value (see definition) that occur as a result of escalation provisions in leases in which the leased property is to be acquired or constructed by the lessor. For example, if the estimated residual value is 10% of the fair value at the inception of a lease and during the construction or preacquisition period of the leased property the effects of the escalation clause increase the fair value, then the estimated residual value is also allowed to increase above the amount which was estimated at the date of the inception of the lease.

Amortization   The asset(s) recorded under a capital lease shall be amortized in a manner consistent with the lessee's normal depreciation policy for other owned assets. The period for amortization is either (1) the estimated economic life or (2) the lease term, depending on which criterion was used to classify the lease. If the criterion used to classify the lease as a capital lease was either I (ownership of the property is transferred to the lessee by the end of the lease term) or II (lease contains a bargain purchase option), the asset is amortized over its estimated economic life. In all other cases, the asset is amortized over the lease term. Any *estimated residual value* is deducted from the asset to determine the amortizable base.

Interest expense: interest method   The interest method is used to produce a constant rate of interest on the remaining lease liability. A portion of each minimum lease payment is allocated to interest expense and/or amortization, and the balance is applied to reduce the lease liability. Any *residual guarantee(s)* by the lessee or penalty payments are automatically taken into consideration by using the interest method and will result in a balance at the end of the lease term equal to the amount of the guarantee or penalty payments at that date.

Jones Company leases a tractor-trailer for $8,000 per year on a noncancelable five-year lease. Jones guarantees to the lessor that the tractor-trailer will have a residual value of at least $5,000 at the end of the lease term.

Assume that all other assumptions have been eliminated and that a 12% interest rate is used.

Present value of $8,000 payments x 5 years   12%   = $28,838
Present value of $5,000 one payment   12%   =   2,837
    Total asset and lease obligation $31,675

> **Note:** The present value of the $8,000 series of annual rental payments is found in the present value of annuity tables, and the present value of the $5,000 residual guarantee (one payment) is found in the present value tables.

A schedule of interest expense, amortization, and reduction of the lease obligation of $31,675 to the $5,000 residual guarantee using the interest method, follows:

Book Value Lease Obligation Beginning of Year	Rental Payments	12% Interest on Beginning Book Value	Amortization	Book Value Lease Obligations End of Year
$31,675	$ 8,000	$ 3,801	$ 4,199	$27,476
27,476	8,000	3,297	4,703	22,773
22,773	8,000	2,733	5,267	17,506
17,506	8,000	2,101	5,899	11,607
11,607	8,000	1,393	6,607	5,000
	$40,000	$13,325	$26,675	

Accounting for Lease Changes—Lessee

If a guarantee or penalty is rendered inoperative because of a renewal or other extension of the *lease term*, or if a new lease is consummated in which the lessee continues to lease the same property, an adjustment must be made to the asset and lease obligation for the difference between the present values of the old and the revised agreements. In these cases, the present value of the future minimum lease payments under the new or revised agreement should be computed using the original rate of interest on the initial lease.

Other lease changes should be accounted for as follows:

1. If a lease change results in revised minimum lease payments, but is also classified as a capital lease, an adjustment is made to the asset and lease obligation for the difference between the present values of the old and the new or revised agree-

ment. The present value of the future minimum lease payments under the new or revised agreement should be computed using the original rate of interest used on the initial lease.

2. If a new or revised agreement results from a lease change and is classified as an operating lease, gain or loss is recognized and the asset and lease obligation is eliminated from the books of account.

3. A renewal, extension, or new lease under which the lessee continues to use the same property, except when a guarantee or penalty is rendered inoperative (see above), is accounted for as follows:

    a. *Renewal or extension classified as a capital lease:* an adjustment is made for the difference between the original and revised present values, using the original discount rate.

    b. *Renewal or extension classified as an operating lease:* the existing lease continues to be accounted for as a capital lease to the end of its lease term, and the renewal or extension is accounted for as an operating lease.

When leased property under a capital lease is purchased by the lessee, it is accounted for as a renewal or extension of a capital lease (FASB Interpretation-26). Thus, any difference between the carrying amount and the purchase price on the date of purchase is treated as an adjustment of the carrying amount of the property.

Termination of a Capital Lease—Lessee

Gain or loss, if any, is recognized on the termination of a capital lease, and the asset and lease liability must be removed from the books of account.

Lessee's Operating Leases

Leases that do not qualify as capital leases in accordance with the provisions of FASB-13 are classified as operating leases. The cost of property covering an operating lease is included in the lessor's balance sheet as property, plant, and equipment. FASB-13 and FASB

Technical Bulletin 85-3 require that rental income and expense relating to an operating lease must be amortized over the time periods in which the lessee derives benefit from the physical usage of the leased property. Thus, rental expense must be amortized over the lease term on a straight-line basis, unless some other systematic and rational basis is more representative of the time pattern in which the benefits of the leased property are derived by the lessee.

> **OBSERVATION:** *Care must be exercised when accounting for sales-type leases involving real estate. FASB-98 (Accounting for Leases) amended FASB-13 to require that a lease involving real estate shall not be classified by the lessor as a sales-type lease unless title to the leased property is transferred to the lessee at or shortly after the end of the lease term. As a result, a lessor may be required to classify a lease involving real estate as an operating lease, instead of a sales-type lease, because the lease agreement does not provide for the transfer of the leased property to the lessee by the end of the lease term. In this event, the lessor must recognize a loss at the inception of an operating lease involving real estate if the fair value of the leased property is less than its cost or carrying amount, whichever is applicable. The amount of loss is equal to the difference between the fair value of the leased property and its cost or carrying amount at the inception of the lease.*

Contingent rental expense   Some operating lease agreements provide for rental increases or decreases based on one or more future conditions, such as future sales volume, future machine hours, future interest rates, or future price indexes. Under FASB-13, these types of rental increases or decreases are classified as *contingent rentals*. Contingent rentals are defined as those which cannot be determined at the inception of the lease because they depend on future conditions or events. A lessee's contingent rental payments are deducted as an expense in the period in which they arise.

Scheduled rent increases or decreases   To accommodate the lessee, a lessor may structure an operating lease agreement to provide for smaller rental payments in the early years of the lease and higher rental payments toward the end of the lease. For example, a six-year operating lease agreement may provide for rental payments of $1,000 per month for the first two years; $1,500 per month for the next two years; and $2,000 per month for the last two years; for a total rental payment of $108,000 for the six years. Under this circumstance, FASB-13 requires that the $108,000 total rental payments be amortized over the six-year lease term on a straight-line basis. The monthly amortization for the first two years of the lease term is $1,500, even though only $1,000 per month is paid by the lessee under the terms of the lease.

It can be argued that in the early years of the above type of lease agreement, the lessee receives not only the use of the leased property, but also the temporary use of cash, equal to the excess of the fair rental value of the leased property over the actual rental payments. To recognize the economic substance of this lease transaction, both the lessee and the lessor should record imputed interest on the difference between the actual amount of rental payments and the computed amount of level rental payments. However, FASB Technical Bulletin 85-3 reconfirms that under the provisions of FASB-13 it is unacceptable to use the time value of money as a factor in recognizing rentals under operating leases.

Right to control physical use of leased property   In accounting for leases, there is a significant distinction between lease agreements that grant the lessee the right to control the use of the leased property at the beginning of the lease term and those lease agreements that do not. A lease agreement may contain a rent escalation clause that is based on the lessee's utilization of the leased property. For example, a lease agreement covering a 10,000 square foot warehouse provides for a rent increase at the time the lessee utilizes more than 5,000 square feet of the warehouse. In this example, the lessee has control of the entire leased property at the beginning of the lease term. On the other hand, a lease agreement may contain a rent escalation clause for property that was originally leased, which becomes effective at the time the lessee leases additional property from the lessor. For example, a master lease provides for an increase in rent on property that was originally leased, at the time the lessee leases additional property from the lessor. In this example, the lessee does not have control of the additional leased property at the beginning of the lease term.

FASB Technical Bulletin 88-1 concludes that the right to control the use of leased property is considered to be the equivalent of the physical use of the property. In a lease agreement that gives the lessee control of the use of the leased property from the beginning of the lease term, FASB Technical Bulletin 88-1 requires that the lessee and the lessor recognize as part of the minimum lease payments, rental expense and rental revenue, including escalated amounts, on a straight-line basis over the lease term. On the other hand, when the lease agreement provides for the lessee to gain control over additional property, FASB Technical Bulletin 88-1 provides that the escalated rent related to the original leased property should be accounted for by the lessee as rental expense on the original leased property and recognized in proportion to the additional leased property in the years that the lessee has control over the use of the additional leased property. The lessor shall recognize the escalated rents on the original leased property as additional rental revenue. The amount of rental expense or rental revenue recognized on the additional leased property should be proportionate to the relative fair value of the additional property, as determined at the inception of the lease, during those periods in which the lessee controls the use of the additional property.

FASB Technical Bulletin 88-1 is effective for transactions *entered into* on or after January 1, 1989. Earlier application of FASB:TB 88-1 is encouraged for unissued annual financial statements. (**Note**: In FASB:TB 88-1, the term *entered into* means the date of the lease agreement or commitment, if earlier. A commitment must contain the principal provisions of the transaction and be signed by the parties to the transaction. A commitment that does not contain the principal provisions of the lease agreement does not qualify.)

Lease incentives in operating leases   To induce a prospective tenant to lease property, a lessor may offer (a) to make cash payments directly to the prospective tenant, (b) to reimburse the prospective tenant's moving expenses, or (c) to assume the obligation of the prospective tenant to a third party under a preexisting lease. Under FASB Technical Bulletin 88-1, these inducements are accounted for as either (i) an incentive for the lessee and an incentive for the lessor or (ii) a reduction of rental expense by the lessee and a reduction of rental revenue by the lessor. Incentives or concessions that are paid to or incurred by the lessor on behalf of the lessee are accounted for as reductions of rental expense and/or rental revenue and recognized over the term of the new lease on a straight-line basis.

FASB Technical Bulletin 88-1 does not change current accounting policy relating to the lessee's immediate recognition of expenses or losses, such as moving expenses, losses on subleases, or the write-off of abandoned leasehold improvements. Under FASB Technical Bulletin 88-1, any loss incurred by the lessor as a result of entering into a lease is an incentive for the lessee to sign the new lease and should be accounted for as part of the new lease transaction.

On the other hand, losses incurred by the lessor as a result of assuming the lessee's obligation to a third party under a preexisting lease shall be accounted for as an incentive by both the lessor and lessee. In this circumstance, the lessee and the lessor shall independently estimate the amount of loss related to the assumption of the preexisting lease with a third party. The lessee may estimate the amount of loss related to the incentive by comparing the new lease to the prevailing market rate for similar leased property or by comparing the prevailing market rate for similar property reduced by the value of the lease obligation assumed by the new lessor. The lessor may estimate the amount of loss related to the incentive by subtracting from the total assumed obligation the expected benefits, if any, that the new lessor may derive from the use of the assumed leased property, including income from a sublease.

FASB Technical Bulletin 88-1 is effective for transactions *entered into* on or after January 1, 1989. Earlier application of FASB:TB 88-1 is encouraged for unissued annual financial statements. (**Note**: In FASB:TB 88-1, the term *entered into* means the date of the lease agreement or commitment, if earlier. A commitment must contain the principal provisions of the transaction and be signed by the parties to the transaction. A commitment that does not contain the principal provisions of the lease agreement does not qualify.)

As an incentive to execute a new operating lease for eight years, a lessor assumes the obligation on the lessee's preexisting lease which has four years remaining. The new lease payments are $8,000 per year and the lease payments on the lessee's preexisting lease are $6,000 per year. The estimated loss on the assumption of the lessee's preexisting lease is $2,400 based on the fact that the lessor can sublease the property for $450 per month for the remaining four years left on the lease. Based on a comparison with current market rates for similar leased property, the lessee calculates its amount of estimated loss as $1,600 for the remaining four years left on the lease.

The following are the lessor's and lessee's journal entries relating to this lease transaction:

Lessor Accounting

Incentive to lessee	$2,400	
Liability on sublease assumed		$2,400

To record deferred cost and liability
at the inception of the lease, related
to the loss on assumption of remaining
lease.

Liability on sublease assumed ($2,400/4 years)	600	
Sublease expense ($450 x 12 months)	5,400	
Cash		6,000

To record cash payment on sublease assumed and amortization of the liability on the sublease assumed.

[**Note:** The above journal entry is a recurring annual entry in years 1 through 4.]

Cash	5,400	
Sublease revenue ($450 x 12 months)		5,400

To record cash received from sublease of property.

[**Note:** The above journal entry is a recurring annual entry in years 1 through 4.]

Cash	8,000	
Rental revenue		7,700
Incentive to lessee ($2,400/8 years)		300

[**Note:** The above journal entry is a recurring annual entry in years 1 through 8.]

Lessee Accounting

Loss on sublease assumed by lessor	1,600	
Incentive from lessor		1,600

To record loss on sublease assumed by lessor in conjunction with new lease.

Lease expense	7,800	
Incentive from lessor ($1,600/8 years)	200	
Cash		8,000

To record cash payment on new lease and amortization of incentive over the new lease.

[**Note:** The above journal entry is a recurring annual entry in years 1 through 8.]

Lessee's Financial Statement Disclosure

Assets, accumulated amortization, and liabilities from capital leases should be reported separately in the balance sheet and classified as current or noncurrent in the same manner as other assets and liabilities.

Current amortization charges to income must be clearly disclosed, along with the additional information:

1. *Gross assets:* as of each balance sheet date presented, in aggregate and by major property categories (this information may be combined with comparable owned assets)
2. *Minimum future lease payments:* in total and for each of the next five years, showing deductions for executory costs, including any profit thereon, and the amount of imputed interest to reduce the net minimum lease payments to present values
3. *Minimum sublease income:* due in future periods under noncancelable subleases

Operating leases   The following financial statement disclosure is required for all operating leases of lessees having noncancelable lease terms in excess of one year:

1. *Minimum future rental payments:* in total and for each of the next five years
2. *Minimum sublease income:* due in future periods under noncancelable subleases
3. *Schedule of total rental expense:* showing the composition by minimum rentals, contingent rentals, and sublease income (excluding leases with terms of a month or less that were not renewed)

General disclosure   A general description of the lessee's leasing arrangements, including (1) basis of contingent rental payments, (2) terms of renewals, purchase options, and escalation clauses, and (3) restrictions imposed by lease agreements, such as additional debt, dividends, and leasing limitations. Following is an illustration of a lessee's financial statement disclosure.

Lessee's Financial Statement Disclosure

Lessee's Balance Sheet

	December 31	
Assets	*19X8*	*19X7*
Leased property:		
Capital leases, less accumulated amortization (Note——)	$XXX,XXX	$XXX,XXX
Liabilities		
Current:		
Obligations under capital leases (Note——)	$XXX,XXX	$XXX,XXX
Noncurrent:		
Obligations under capital leases (Note——)	$ XX,XXX	$ XX,XXX

Capital Leases
Gross Assets and Accumulated Amortization

	December 31	
Type of Property	*19X8*	*19X7*
Manufacturing plants	$ XX,XXX	$XX,XXX
Retail stores	X,XXX	X,XXX
Other	XXX	XXX
Total	$XXX,XXX	$XX,XXX
Less: Accumulated amortization	XX,XXX	X, XXX
Capital leases, net	$XXX,XXX	$XX,XXX

Capital Leases
Minimum Future Lease Payments and
Present Values of the Net Minimum Lease Payments

Year Ended
December 31

19X9	$ XX,XXX
19X0	X,XXX
19X1	X,XXX
19X2	X,XXX
19X3	X,XXX
After 19X3	XXX
Total minimum lease payments	$XXX,XXX
Less: Executory costs (estimated)	X,XXX
Net minimum lease payments	$XXX,XXX
Less: Imputed interest	XX,XXX
Present value of net minimum lease payments	$ XX,XXX

In addition to the foregoing statements and schedules, footnotes describing minimum sublease income and contingent rentals should be included, if required.

Operating Leases
Schedule of Minimum Future Rental Payments

Year Ended
December 31

19X9	$ XX,XXX
19X0	XXX,XXX
19X1	XX,XXX
19X2	XX,XXX
19X3	XX,XXX
After 19X3	XXX,XXX
Total minimum future rental payments	$XXX,XXX

In addition to the above information on operating leases, a footnote should be included describing minimum sublease income due in the future under noncancelable subleases.

Operating Leases
Composition of Total Rental Expense

	December 31	
	19X8	*19X7*
Minimum rentals	$XXX,XXX	$XXX,XXX
Contingent rentals	XX,XXX	XX,XXX
Less: Sublease rental income	(X,XXX)	(X,XXX)
Total rental expense, net	$XXX,XXX	$XXX,XXX

Note: The above schedule of total rental expense excludes leases with terms of one month or less that were not renewed.

In addition to the foregoing information on capital and operating leases, a footnote describing the general disclosure policy for the lessee's leases should be included, containing (1) general leasing arrangements, (2) basis of contingent rental payments, (3) terms of renewals, purchase options, and escalation clauses, and (4) restrictions imposed by lease agreements, such as additional debt, dividends, and leasing limitations.

Accounting and Reporting by Lessors

Leases are classified for the lessor as either (1) sales-type, (2) direct financing, or (3) operating.

Sales-type leases are usually used by sellers of property to increase the marketability of expensive assets. The occurrence of a manufacturer's or dealer's profit or loss is generally present in a sales-type lease.

Direct financing leases do not give rise to a manufacturer's or dealer's profit or loss, and the fair value is usually the cost or the carrying amount of the property.

Recording sales-type leases The lessor's *gross investment* in the lease is computed, which is equal to the (i) sum of the lessor's minimum lease payments less any executory costs and profit thereon to be paid by the lessor and (ii) any unguaranteed residual value accruing to the benefit of the lessor (this is the estimated fair value of the leased property at the end of the lease term, which is not guaranteed). (**Note**: If the residual value is guaranteed, it would be included in the minimum lease payments.)

The estimated residual value used to compute the unguaranteed residual value accruing to the benefit of the lessor shall not exceed the amount estimated at the inception of the lease.

Using the interest rate implicit in the lease, the lessor's gross investment in the lease is discounted to its present value. The present value of the lessor's gross investment in the lease represents the sales price of the property that is included in income for the period. (**Note**: When using the interest rate implicit in the lease, the present value will always be equal to the fair value.)

The cost or carrying amount of the property sold plus any initial direct costs (costs incurred by the lessor to negotiate and consummate the lease, such as legal fees and commissions) less the present value of the unguaranteed residual value (if any) accruing to the benefit of the lessor is charged against income in the period in which the corresponding sale is recorded.

The difference between the lessor's gross investment in the lease and the sales price of the property is recorded as unearned income, which is amortized to income over the lease term by the interest method. The unearned income is included in the balance sheet as a deduction from the related gross investment, which results in the net investment in the lease.

A lease involving real estate shall not be classified by the lessor as a sales-type lease unless the title to the leased property is transferred to the lessee at or shortly after the end of the lease term.

Recording direct financing leases The lessor's *gross investment* in the lease is computed, which is equal to the sum of (i) the lessor's minimum lease payments less any executory costs and profit thereon to be paid by the lessor and (ii) any unguaranteed residual value accruing to the benefit of the lessor (this is the estimated fair value of the lease property at the end of the lease term, which is not guaranteed). (**Note**: If the residual value is guaranteed, it would be included in the minimum lease payments.)

Under FASB-91, loan origination fees and direct loan origination costs, including initial direct costs incurred by the lessor in negotiating and consummating the lease, are offset against each other and the resulting net amount is deferred and recognized over the life of the loan as an adjustment to the yield on the loan.

The difference between the lessor's gross investment in the lease and the cost or carrying amount of the leased property, if different, is recorded as unearned income, which is amortized to income over the lease term by the interest method. The unearned income is included in the balance sheet as a deduction from the related gross investment, which results in the net investment in the lease.

> **OBSERVATION:** *The practice of recognizing a portion of the unearned income at the inception of the lease to offset initial direct costs is no longer acceptable (paragraph 5 of FASB-91).*

Other methods   Other methods of recognizing income may be used for both sales-type and direct financing leases, provided the results are not materially different from those produced by the method prescribed.

Balance Sheet Classification—Lessor

The resulting net investment in both sales-type and direct financing leases is subject to the same treatment as other assets in classifying as current or noncurrent.

Annual Review of Residual Values—Lessor

The unguaranteed residual values of both sales-type and direct financing leases should be reviewed at least annually to determine whether a decline, other than temporary, has occurred in their estimated values. If a decline is not temporary, the accounting for the transaction should be revised using the new estimate, and the resulting loss should be recognized in the period that the change is made. *Upward adjustments are not allowed.*

FASB Technical Bulletin 79-14 states that the prohibition of upward adjustments in residual values also applies to guaranteed residual values, even if the guaranteed residual value results from renegotiation of the value between the lessee and the lessor.

Accounting for Lease Changes—Lessor

The definition of lease term includes any periods in which penalties are imposed in an amount that reasonably assures the renewal of the lease by the lessee. The definition of minimum lease payments includes any payments or guarantees that the lessee is required to make concerning the leased property including any amount (1) to purchase the leased property, (2) to make up any deficiency from a specified minimum, and (3) for failure to renew or extend the lease at the expiration of the lease term. Guarantees and penalties such as these are usually canceled and become inoperative in the event the lease is renewed, is extended, or a new lease for the same property is consummated.

If a sales-type or direct financing lease contains a residual guarantee or a penalty for failure to renew and is rendered inoperative as a result of a lease renewal or other extension of the lease term, or if a new lease is consummated where the lessee continues to lease the same property, an adjustment must be made to the unearned income account for the difference between the present values of the old and the revised agreements. The present value of the future minimum lease payments under the new agreement should be computed by using the original rate of interest used for the initial lease. (**Note**: Care must be exercised in these circumstances to avoid an upward adjustment of any previously recorded residual values.)

In sales-type and direct financing leases which do not contain residual guarantees or penalties for failure to renew, an adjustment must be made to account for lease changes, renewals, or other extensions, including a new lease in which the lessee continues to lease the same property. If the classification of the lease remains unchanged or is classified as a direct financing lease and the amount of the remaining minimum lease payments is changed, an adjustment must be made to unearned income to account for the difference between the present values of the old and the new agreements. If a new classification results in a sales-type lease, it shall be classified and treated as a direct financing lease unless the transaction occurs within the last few months of the original lease, in which case it shall be classified as a sales-type lease (FASB-27).

If the classification of a lease is changed to an operating lease, the accounting treatment depends upon whether the operating lease starts immediately or at the end of the existing lease, as follows:

Starts immediately   The remaining net investment is eliminated from the accounts and the leased property is recorded as an asset using the lower of (1) original cost, (2) present fair value, or (3) present carrying amount. The difference between the remaining net investment and the new recorded value of the asset is charged to income in the period of change.

Starts subsequently   The existing lease continues to be accounted for as a sales-type or direct financing lease until the new operating lease commences, at which time the accounting treatment is the same as if the operating lease started immediately. Renewals and extensions usually commence at the end of the original sales-type or direct financing lease. Under these circumstances there should not be any remaining investment to eliminate from the books and the leased property is not recorded as an asset.

Termination of a Lease—Lessor

A termination of a lease is recognized in the income of the period in which the termination occurs by the following journal entries:

1. The remaining net investment is eliminated from the accounts.
2. The leased property is recorded as an asset using the lower of the (a) original cost, (b) present fair value, or (c) present carrying amount.

Lessor's Operating Leases

Leases that do not qualify as capital leases in accordance with the provisions of FASB-13 are classified as operating leases. The cost of the property leased to the lessee is included in the lessor's balance sheet as property, plant, and equipment. The lessor's income statement will normally include the expenses of the leased property (unless it is a net lease), such as depreciation, maintenance, taxes, insurance, and other related items. However, if material, initial direct costs (those directly related to the negotiation and consummation of the lease) should be deferred and allocated to income over the lease term.

FASB-13 requires that rental income from an operating lease be amortized over the time periods in which the lessor's benefits in the leased property are depleted. Thus, rental income must be amortized over the lease term on a straight-line basis, unless some other systematic and rational basis is more representative of the time pattern in which the benefits of the leased property are depleted.

FASB-98 amended FASB-13 to require that a lease involving real estate shall not be classified by the lessor as a sales-type lease unless title to the leased property is transferred to the lessee at or shortly after the end of the lease term. As a result, an enterprise may be required to classify a lease involving real estate as an operating lease, instead of a sales-type lease, because the lease agreement does not provide for the transfer of the leased property to the lessee by the end of the lease term. In this event, the lessor must recognize a loss at the inception of an operating lease involving real estate if the fair value of the leased property is less than its cost or carrying amount, whichever is applicable. The amount of loss is equal to the difference between the fair value of the leased property and its cost or carrying amount at the inception of the lease.

Contingent rental income   Some operating lease agreements provide for rental increases or decreases based on one or more future
conditions, such as future sales volume, future machine hours, future interest rates, or future price indexes. Under FASB-13, these
types of rental increases or decreases are classified as *contingent
rentals*. Contingent rentals are defined as those which cannot be
determined at the inception of the lease because they depend on
future conditions or events. A lessor's contingent rental income is
accrued in the period in which it arises.

Scheduled rent increases or decreases   To accommodate the lessee,
a lessor may structure an operating lease agreement to provide for
smaller rental payments in the early years of the lease and higher
rental payments toward the end of the lease. For example, a six-year
operating lease agreement may provide for rental payments of $1,000
per month for the first two years; $1,500 per month for the next two
years; and $2,000 per month for the last two years; for a total rental
payment of $108,000 for the six years. In this event, FASB-13 requires
that the $108,000 total rental income be amortized by the lessor over
the six-year lease term on a straight-line basis. The monthly amortization for the first two years of the lease term is $1,500, even though
only $1,000 per month is received by the lessor under the terms of the
lease.

It can be argued that in the early years of the above type of lease
agreement, the lessee receives not only the use of the leased property, but also the temporary use of cash, equal to the excess of the fair
rental value of the leased property over the actual rental payments.
To recognize the economic substance of this lease transaction, it
would appear that both the lessee and the lessor should record
imputed interest on the difference between the actual amount of
rental payments and the computed amount of rental payments
(straight-line or other systematic basis). However, under the provisions of FASB-13 it is unacceptable to use the time value of money as
a factor in recognizing rentals under operating leases (FASB Technical Bulletin 85-3).

Right to control physical use of leased property   FASB Technical
Bulletin 88-1 concludes that the right to control the use of leased
property is considered to be the equivalent of the physical use of the
property. In a lease agreement that gives the lessee control of the use
of the leased property from the beginning of the lease term, FASB
Technical Bulletin 88-1 requires that the lessee and the lessor recognize as part of the minimum lease payments rental expense and
rental revenue, including escalated amounts, on a straight-line basis

over the lease term. On the other hand, when the lease agreement provides for the lessee to gain control over additional property, FASB Technical Bulletin 88-1 provides that the escalated rent related to the original leased property should be accounted for by the lessee as rental expense on the original leased property and recognized in proportion to the additional leased property in the years that the lessee has control over the use of the additional leased property. The lessor shall recognize the escalated rents on the original leased property as additional rental revenue. The amount of rental expense or rental revenue recognized on the additional leased property should be proportionate to the relative fair value of the additional property, as determined at the inception of the lease, during those periods in which the lessee controls the use of the additional property.

FASB Technical Bulletin 88-1 is effective for transactions *entered into* on or after January 1, 1989. Earlier application of FASB:TB 88-1 is encouraged for unissued annual financial statements. (**Note**: In FASB:TB 88-1, the term *entered into* means the date of the lease agreement or commitment, if earlier. A commitment must contain the principal provisions of the transaction and be signed by the parties to the transaction. A commitment that does not contain the principal provisions of the lease agreement does not qualify.)

Money-over-money operating lease transactions   A money-over-money lease transaction is one in which an enterprise manufactures or purchases an asset, leases the asset to a lessee, and obtains nonrecourse financing in excess of the asset's cost using the leased asset and the future lease rentals as collateral. A money-over-money lease transaction may result either in (a) an operating lease, (b) a direct financing lease, or (c) a sales-type lease.

An enterprise shall account for a money-over-money lease transaction as (a) the purchase or manufacture of an asset, (b) the leasing of that asset under an operating lease, direct financing lease, or sales-type lease in accordance with the provisions of FASB-13, and (c) the borrowing of funds.

If a money-over-money transaction results in an operating lease, the lessor should record an asset and liability on its statement of financial position. If the transaction results in a direct financing lease or a sales-type lease, the lessor should record a lease receivable and a liability on its statement of financial position. Offsetting assets and liabilities in a statement of financial position is prohibited by GAAP, unless a legal right of setoff exists (paragraph 7 of APB-10).

In a money-over-money lease transaction, FASB Technical Bulletin 88-1 concludes that (a) an enterprise may recognize a manufacturer's or dealer's profit on a sales-type lease but any proceeds from the related borrowing may not be recognized as income at the inception of the lease and (b) an enterprise may not offset the resulting asset and liability in its statement of financial position, unless a legal right of setoff exists.

FASB Technical Bulletin 88-1 is effective for transactions *entered into* on or after January 1, 1989. Earlier application of FASB:TB 88-1 is encouraged for unissued annual financial statements. (**Note**: In FASB:TB 88-1, the term *entered into* means the date of the lease agreement or commitment, if earlier. A commitment must contain the principal provisions of the transaction and be signed by the parties to the transaction. A commitment that does not contain the principal provisions of the lease agreement does not qualify.)

Lease incentives in operating leases   To induce a prospective tenant to lease property, a lessor may offer (a) to make cash payments directly to the prospective tenant, (b) to reimburse the prospective tenant's moving expenses, or (c) to assume the obligation of the prospective tenant to a third party under a preexisting lease. Under FASB Technical Bulletin 88-1, these inducements are accounted for as either (i) an incentive for the lessee and an incentive for the lessor or (ii) a reduction of rental expense by the lessee and a reduction of rental revenue by the lessor. Incentives or concessions that are paid to or incurred by the lessor on behalf of the lessee are accounted for as reductions of rental expense and/or rental revenue and recognized over the term of the new lease on a straight-line basis.

FASB Technical Bulletin 88-1 does not change current accounting policy relating to the lessee's immediate recognition of expenses or losses, such as moving expenses, losses on subleases, or the write-off of abandoned leasehold improvements. Under FASB Technical Bulletin 88-1, any loss incurred by the lessor as a result of entering into a lease is an incentive for the lessee to sign the new lease and should be accounted for as part of the new lease transaction.

On the other hand, losses incurred by the lessor as a result of assuming the lessee's obligation to a third party under a preexisting lease shall be accounted for as an incentive by both the lessor and lessee. In this circumstance, the lessee and the lessor shall independently estimate the amount of loss related to the assumption of the preexisting lease with a third party. The lessee may estimate the amount of loss related to the incentive by comparing the new lease to the prevailing market rate for similar leased property or by comparing the prevailing market rate for similar property reduced by the value of the lease obligation assumed by the new lessor. The lessor may estimate the amount of loss related to the incentive by subtracting from the total assumed obligation the expected benefits, if any, that the new lessor may derive from the use of the assumed leased property, including income from a sublease.

FASB Technical Bulletin 88-1 is effective for transactions *entered into* on or after January 1, 1989. Earlier application of FASB:TB 88-1 is encouraged for unissued annual financial statements. (**Note**: In FASB:TB 88-1, the term *entered into* means the date of the lease agreement or commitment, if earlier. A commitment must contain the principal provisions of the transaction and be signed by the parties to the transaction. A commitment that does not contain the principal provisions of the lease agreement does not qualify.)

As an incentive to execute a new operating lease for eight years, a lessor assumes the obligation on the lessee's preexisting lease, which has four years remaining. The new lease payments are $8,000 per year and the lease payments on the lessee's preexisting lease are $6,000 per year. The estimated loss on the assumption of the lessee's preexisting lease is $2,400 based on the fact that the lessor can sublease the property for $450 per month for the remaining four years left on the lease. Based on a comparison with current market rates for similar leased property, the lessee calculates its amount of estimated loss as $1,600 for the remaining four years left on the lease.

The following are the lessor's and lessee's journal entries relating to this lease transaction:

Lessor Accounting

Incentive to lessee	$2,400	
Liability on sublease assumed		$2,400

To record deferred cost and liability at the inception of the lease, related to the loss on assumption of remaining lease.

Liability on sublease assumed		
($2,400/4 years)	600	
Sublease expense ($450 x 12 months)	5,400	
Cash		6,000

To record cash payment on sublease assumedand amortization of the liability on the sublease assumed.

[**Note**: The above journal entry is a re- curring annual entry in years 1 through 4.]

Cash	5,400	
Sublease revenue ($450 x 12 months)		5,400
To record cash received from sublease of property.		

[**Note**: The above journal entry is a recurring annual entry in years 1 through 4.]

Cash	8,000	
Rental revenue		7,700
Incentive to lessee ($2,400/8 years)		300

[**Note**: The above journal entry is a recurring annual entry in years 1 through 8.]

Lessee Accounting

Loss on sublease assumed by lessor	1,600	
Incentive from lessor		1,600
To record loss on sublease assumed by lessor in conjunction with new lease.		

Lease expense	7,800	
Incentive from lessor ($1,600/8 years)	200	
Cash		8,000
To record cash payment on new lease and amortization of incentive over the new lease.		

[**Note**: The above journal entry is a recurring annual entry in years 1 through 8.]

Residual Value of a Leased Asset

Lease brokers or other enterprises may acquire an interest in the residual value of a leased asset by the payment of cash, the assumption of liabilities, and/or the payment of other consideration, including services rendered by the lease broker.

FASB Technical Bulletin 86-2 (FASB:TB 86-2) provides guidance on accounting for an interest in the residual value of a leased asset that is either (i) acquired by a third party or (ii) retained by a lessor that sells the related minimum rental payments.

An interest in the residual value of a leased asset may be acquired by an enterprise in the form of an unconditional interest in the leased asset or the right to receive all, or a portion, of the proceeds from the sale of the leased asset at the end of the lease term without acquiring the related lease. For example, a lease broker may receive an interest in the residual value of a leased asset as a fee for services rendered. An interest in the residual value of a leased asset can also be acquired directly from a lessor. For example, a lessor may sell substantially all of the minimum rental payments associated with a sales-type, direct financing, or leveraged lease and retain an interest in the residual value of the leased asset.

The acquisition of an interest in the residual value of a leased asset generally includes the right to receive all or part of the future benefit that may be derived from the residual value of the leased asset. For example, an enterprise may acquire from a lessor the unconditional right to own and possess, at the end of the lease term, an asset subject to a lease; or an enterprise may acquire the right to receive all, or a portion, of the proceeds from the sale of a leased asset at the end of the lease term. Both of these transactions should be recorded as the acquisition of an asset, since both transactions involve the acquisition of an interest in the residual value of a leased asset.

Under FASB:TB 86-2, the cost of an interest in the residual value of a leased asset should be measured by (a) the amount of cash disbursed, (b) the fair value of other consideration given, and (c) the present value of liabilities assumed at the date the right is acquired. However, if more clearly evident, the fair value of the interest in the residual value of the leased asset at the date of the agreement should be used instead of the fair value of the assets surrendered, services rendered, or liabilities assumed.

An enterprise should account for the acquisition of an interest in the residual value of a leased asset at no more than the acquisition cost of the asset. Furthermore, an enterprise shall not recognize any increases in the residual value of the leased asset over the remaining term of the related lease, regardless of the lessor's classification and accounting for the leased asset.

If in subsequent periods there is a decline, other than temporary, in the fair value of the interest in the residual value of a leased asset, the carrying amount of the asset shall be reduced to the new fair value and the amount of write-down recognized as a current loss. In this event, the new fair value becomes the new carrying amount for the asset, and the new carrying amount shall not be increased in any subsequent period prior to the sale or other disposition of the interest in the residual value of the leased asset.

After the sale of substantially all of the minimum rental payments of a sales-type, direct financing, or leveraged lease, a lessor should report any remaining interest in the residual value of the lease at its carrying amount at the date of the sale of the lease payments. In addition, the lessor shall not recognize any increases in the residual value of the leased asset over the remaining term of the related lease.

If in subsequent periods there is a decline, other than temporary, in the fair value of the interest in the residual value of a leased asset, the carrying amount of the asset shall be reduced to the new fair value and the amount of write-down recognized as a current loss. In this event, the new fair value becomes the new carrying amount for the asset, and the new carrying amount shall not be increased in any subsequent period prior to the sale or other disposition of the interest in the residual value of the leased asset.

A guarantee of the residual value of a leased asset does not change the nature of an interest in the residual value of a leased asset or its historical acquisition cost.

FASB:TB 86-2 is effective December 17, 1986, for transactions entered into on or after June 18, 1986. Earlier application to transactions occurring in periods for which financial statements have not been issued is encouraged.

Financial information for transactions entered into on or after June 18, 1986, that was reported differently than specified by FASB:TB 86-2 should be restated to conform to the provisions of FASB:TB 86-2 when the interim or annual financial statements containing that information are subsequently presented.

Lease Sale or Assignment to Third Parties

Sale or assignment of a sales-type or a direct financing lease does not negate the original accounting treatment. Profit or loss is recognized at the time of sale or assignment, unless the seller assumes *substantial risks.*

Frequently, a sale of property *subject to an operating lease* is complicated by some type of indemnification agreement by the seller. The seller may guarantee that the property will remain leased or may agree to reacquire the property if the tenant does not pay the specified rent. These types of transactions cannot be accounted for as a sale because of the substantial risk assumed by the seller. The principle of *substance over form* must be applied to such situations and treated accordingly. Examples of *substantial risk* on the part of the seller are:

1. Agreements to reacquire the property or lease
2. Agreements to substitute another existing lease
3. Agreements to use "best efforts" to secure a replacement buyer or lessee

Examples of *nonsubstantial risk* situations on the part of the seller are:

1. Execution of a remarketing agreement that includes a fee for the seller
2. When the seller does not give priority to the releasing or other disposition of the property owned by a third party

If a sale to a third party purchaser is not recorded as a sale because of the substantial risk factor assumed by the seller, it should be accounted for as a *borrowing*. The proceeds from the "sale" are recorded as an obligation on the books of the seller. Rental payments made by the lessee under the operating lease are recorded as revenue to the seller, even if the rentals are paid to the third party. Each rental payment shall consist of imputed interest, and the balance of the payment shall be applied as a reduction of the obligation. Any sale or assignment of lease payments under an operating lease shall be accounted for as borrowings.

Lessor's Financial Statement Disclosure

The following financial statement disclosure is required by lessors whose *significant business activity is leasing* (not including *leveraged leasing*):

For sales-type and direct financing leases:

1. A schedule of the components of the *net investment* in leases, as of each balance sheet date, which shall include:

   a. Future minimum lease payments
   b. Executory costs
   c. Allowance for uncollectibles

    d. Unguaranteed residual values accruing to the benefit
       of the lessor
    e. Unearned income
    f. Contingent rentals

2. A schedule of the minimum lease payments, in total and for
   the next five years

For operating leases:

1. A schedule of the investment in property on operating leases,
   and property held for lease, by major categories, less accumulated depreciation, as of each balance sheet presented
2. A schedule of future minimum rentals on noncancelable operating leases, in total for the next five years
3. The amount of contingent rentals included in each income
   statement presented

General disclosure for leases of lessors: a general description of the
lessor's leasing arrangements.

Lessor's Financial Statement Disclosure

Lessor's Balance Sheet

	December 31	
Assets	*19X8*	*19X7*
Current assets:		
Net investment in sales-type and direct financing leases (Note___)	$ XXX,XXX	$ XXX,XXX
Noncurrent assets:		
Net investment in sales-type and direct financing leases (Note___)	$ XX,XXX	$ XX,XXX
Property on operating leases and property held for leases (net of accumulated depreciation of $X,XXX and $XX,XXX for 19X8 and 19X7, respectively) (Note___)	$ XX,XXX	$ XX,XXX

Schedule of Components—Net Investment in Leases
Sales-Type and Direct Financing Leases

	19X8	19X7
Total minimum lease payments receivable	$X,XXX,XXX	$X,XXX,XXX
Less: Estimated executory costs, including profit thereon	XX,XXX	XX,XXX
Minimum lease payments	$X,XXX,XXX	$X,XXX,XXX
Less: Allowance for uncollectibles	XXX,XXX	XXX,XXX
Net minimum lease payments receivable	$X,XXX,XXX	$X,XXX,XXX
Add: Estimated unguaranteed residual values of leased properties	XXX,XXX	XXX,XXX
	$X,XXX,XXX	$X,XXX,XXX
Less: Unearned income	XXX,XXX	XXX,XXX
Net investment in sales-type and direct financing leases	$X,XXX,XXX	$X,XXX,XXX

A footnote should be included for contingent rentals.

Lessor's Schedule of Minimum Lease Payments

Year Ended December 31	
19X9	$ XXX,XXX
19X0	XXX,XXX
19X1	XXX,XXX
19X2	X,XXX,XXX
19X3	XXX,XXX
After 19X3	X,XXX,XXX
Total minimum lease payments receivable	$X,XXX,XXX

*Lessor's Schedule of Investment in Property
on Operating Leases and Property Held
for Lease (by Major Class Categories)*

Data-processing equipment	$X,XXX,XXX
Transportation equipment	XXX,XXX
Construction equipment	XXX,XXX
Other	XX,XXX
Total	$X,XXX,XXX
Less: Accumulated depreciation	XXX,XXX
Net investment	$X,XXX,XXX

*Lessor's Schedule of Future Minimum Rentals
on Noncancelable Operating Leases*

*Year Ended
December 31*

19X9	$ XXX,XXX
19X0	XXX,XXX
19X1	XXX,XXX
19X2	XXX,XXX
19X3	XX,XXX
After 19X3	XXX,XXX
Total future minimum rentals	$X,XXX,XXX

A footnote should be included for contingent rentals.

Leases Involving Real Estate

Leases involving real estate are divided into the following lease categories:

1. Land only
2. Land and building(s)
3. Land, building(s), and equipment
4. Only part of a building(s)

Review of classification of leases by lessees A review of the classifications of leases by lessees is necessary because accounting for leases involving real estate depends primarily on the criteria for classifying leases.

If one or more of the following four criteria are present at the inception of a lease, it should be classified as a capital lease by the lessee:

I. Ownership of the property is transferred to the lessee by the end of the lease term.

II. The lease contains a bargain purchase option.

III. The lease term, at inception, is substantially (75% or more) equal to the estimated economic life of the leased property, including earlier years of use. [*Exception:* This particular criterion cannot be used for a lease that begins within the last 25% of the original estimated economic life of the leased property.]

IV. The present value of the minimum lease payments at the beginning of the lease term, excluding executory costs and profits thereon to be paid by the lessor, is 90% or more of the fair value of the property at the inception of the lease, less any investment tax credit retained by the lessor and expected to be realized by him. [*Exception*: This particular criterion cannot be used for a lease that begins within the last 25% of the original estimated economic life of the leased property.]

Leases involving land only A *lessee* shall account for a lease involving land only as a capital lease if either criterion I or criterion II are met. All other leases involving land only shall be classified as operating leases by the lessee.

A *lessor* shall classify a lease involving land only as a sales-type lease and account for the transaction as a sale under the provisions of FASB-66, if the lease gives rise to a manufacturer's or dealer's profit (or loss) and criterion I is met. A lessor shall classify a lease involving land only as a direct financing lease or a leveraged lease, whichever is applicable, if the lease does not give rise to a manufacturer's or dealer's profit (or loss), criterion I is met, and (a) the collection of the minimum lease payments is reasonably predictable and (b) no important uncertainties exist regarding costs yet to be incurred by the lessor under the lease. A lessor shall classify a lease involving land only as a direct financing lease, a leveraged lease, or an operating lease, whichever is applicable, if criterion II is met, and (a) the collection of the minimum lease payments is reasonably predictable and (b) no important uncertainties exist regarding costs yet to be incurred by the lessor under the lease. All other leases involving land only shall be classified as operating leases by the lessor.

Leases involving land and building(s)   Leases involving land and building(s) may be broken down into three categories, as follows:

1. Leases that meet criterion I or II
2. Leases in which the fair value of the land is less than 25% of the total fair value of the leased property at the inception of the lease
3. Leases in which the fair value of the land is 25% or more of the total fair value of the leased property at the inception of the lease

1. Leases that meet criterion I or II   Leases that meet either criterion I or criterion II are accounted for as follows:

Lessee   The present value of the minimum lease payments, less executory costs and profits thereon (to be paid by the lessor), is allocated between the land and building(s) in proportion to their fair value at the inception of the lease. The present value assigned to the building(s) is amortized in accordance with the lessee's normal depreciation policy.

Lessor   If a lease gives rise to a manufacturer's or dealer's profit (or loss) and criterion I is met, a lessor shall classify a lease involving land and building(s) as a sales-type lease and account for the transaction as a sale under the provisions of FASB-66. If a lease does not give rise to a manufacturer's or dealer's profit (or loss) and criterion I is met, a lessor shall classify a lease involving land and building(s) as a direct financing lease or a leveraged lease, whichever is applicable, providing that (a) collection of the minimum lease payments are reasonably predictable and (b) no important uncertainties exist regarding costs yet to be incurred by the lessor under the lease.
If a lease gives rise to a manufacturer's or dealer's profit (or loss) and criterion II is met, a lessor shall classify a lease involving land and building(s) as an operating lease. If the lease does not give rise to a manufacturer's or dealer's profit (or loss) and criterion II is met, a lessor shall classify a lease involving land

and building(s) as a direct financing lease or a leveraged lease, whichever is applicable, providing that (a) collection of the minimum lease payments is reasonably predictable and (b) no important uncertainties exist regarding costs yet to be incurred by the lessor under the lease.

All other leases involving land and building(s) shall be classified as operating leases by the lessor.

2. <u>Fair value of the land is less than 25% of the total fair value of the leased property at the inception of the lease</u> (When applying criterion III and criterion IV, both the lessee and lessor shall consider the land and building(s) as a *single unit*, and the estimated economic life of the building(s) shall be the estimated economic life of the single unit.) This type of lease is accounted for as follows:

Lessee   The land and building(s) are accounted for as a single capitalized asset and amortized in accordance with the lessee's normal depreciation policy over the lease term if either criterion III or criterion IV are met.

Lessor   If a lease gives rise to a manufacturer's or dealer's profit (or loss) and criterion III or criterion IV is met, a lessor shall classify a lease involving land and building(s), in which the fair value of the land is less than 25% of the total fair value of the leased property at the inception of the lease as an operating lease. If the lease does not give rise to a manufacturer's or dealer's profit (or loss) and criterion III or criterion IV is met, a lessor shall classify a lease involving land and building(s) in which the fair value of the land is less than 25% of the total fair value of the leased property at the inception of the lease as a direct financing lease or a leveraged lease, whichever is applicable, providing that (a) collection of the minimum lease payments is reasonably predictable and (b) no important uncertainties exist regarding costs yet to be incurred by the lessor under the lease. All other leases involving land and building(s) shall be classified as operating leases by the lessor.

3. <u>Fair value of the land is more than 25% of the total fair value of the leased property at the inception of the lease</u> [When applying criterion III and criterion IV, both the lessee and the lessor shall consider the land and building(s) *separately*. To determine the separate values of the land and building(s), the lessee's incremental borrowing rate is applied to the fair value of

the land to determine the annual minimum lease payments applicable to the land. The balance of the minimum lease payments remaining shall be attributed to the building(s).] This type of lease is accounted for as follows:

Lessee The building(s) portion is accounted for as a capital lease and amortized in accordance with the lessee's normal depreciation policy over the lease term if the building(s) portion meets either criterion III or criterion IV. The land portion shall be accounted for separately as an operating lease.

Lessor If a lease gives rise to a manufacturer's or dealer's profit (or loss) and criterion III or criterion IV are met, a lessor shall classify a lease involving land and building(s) in which the fair value of the land is 25% or more of the total fair value of the leased property at the inception of the lease as an operating lease. If the lease does not give rise to a manufacturer's or dealer's profit (or loss) and criterion III or criterion IV is met, a lessor shall classify the building(s) portion of a lease in which the fair value of the land is 25% or more of the total fair value of the leased property at the inception of the lease as a direct financing lease or a leveraged lease, whichever is applicable, providing that (a) collection of the minimum lease payments is reasonably predictable and (b) no important uncertainties exist regarding costs yet to be incurred by the lessor under the lease. The land portion shall be accounted for separately as an operating lease.

All other leases involving land and building(s) shall be classified as operating leases by the lessor.

Leases involving land, building(s), and equipment Equipment values, if material, should not be commingled with real estate values in leases. The minimum lease payments attributed to the equipment shall, if necessary, be appropriately estimated and separately stated. The criteria for the classification of leases should be separately applied to the equipment to determine proper accountability.

Leases involving only part of a building(s) If the cost and fair value of a lease involving only part of a building(s) can be objectively determined, the lease classification and accountability shall be the same for any other land and building(s) lease. An independent appraisal of the leased property or replacement cost can be made as a basis for the objective determination of fair value (FASB Interpretation-24). In the event that cost and fair value cannot be objectively determined, leases involving only part of a building(s) should be classified and accounted for as follows:

Lessee   The lessee shall classify the lease only in accordance with criterion III as follows: The lease term, at inception, is substantially (75% or more) equal to the estimated economic life of the leased property, including earlier years of use. [*Exception*: This particular criterion cannot be used for a lease that begins within the last 25% of the original estimated economic life of the leased property.]

In applying the above criterion, the estimated economic life of the building(s) in which the leased premises are located shall be used.

In the event the above criterion is met, the leased property is capitalized as a single unit and amortized in accordance with the lessee's normal depreciation policy over the lease term. In all other cases, the lease shall be classified as an operating lease.

Lessor   In all cases where the cost and fair value are indeterminable, the lessor shall account for the lease as an operating lease.

Sale-Leasebacks Involving Real Estate

Under the provisions of FASB-98, the definition of *sale-leaseback accounting* is analogous to the definition of the full accrual method of accounting. Under sale-leaseback accounting, the sale portion of a sale-leaseback transaction is recorded as a sale by the seller-lessee, the property sold and all of its related liabilities are eliminated from the seller-lessee's balance sheet, gain or loss on the sale portion of the sale-leaseback transaction is recognized by the seller-lessee in accordance with the provisions of FASB-13 (as amended by FASB-28, FASB-66, and FASB-98), and the lease portion of the sale-leaseback transaction is accounted for in accordance with the provisions of FASB-13 (as amended by FASB-28).

Under FASB-98, a seller-lessee shall apply sale-leaseback accounting only to those sale-leaseback transactions that include payment terms and provisions that provide for (i) a normal leaseback (as defined by FASB-98), (ii) an adequate initial and continuing investment by the purchaser-lessor (as defined by FASB-66), (iii) the transfer of all of the other risks and rewards of ownership to the purchaser-lessor, and (iv) no other continued involvement by the seller-lessee, other than the continued involvement represented by the lease portion of the sale-leaseback transaction.

Normal leaseback   A normal leaseback, under FASB-98, is one in which the seller-lessee actively uses substantially all of the leased property in its trade or business during the lease term. The seller-lessee may sublease a minor portion of the leased property, equal to 10% or less of the reasonable rental value for the entire leased property, and the lease will still qualify as a normal leaseback. Thus, to qualify as a normal leaseback under FASB-98, the seller-lessee must actively use substantially all of the leased property in its trade or business in consideration for rent payments, which may include contingent rentals that are based on the seller-lessee's future operations.

If occupancy by the seller-lessee's customers is transient or short-term, the seller-lessee may provide ancillary services, such as housekeeping, inventory control, entertainment, bookkeeping, and food service. Thus, active use by a seller-lessee in its trade or business includes the use of the leased property as a hotel, bonded warehouse, parking lot, or some other similar business.

Adequate initial and continuing investment by the purchaser-lessor   To qualify for sale-leaseback accounting under FASB-98, the purchaser-lessor's initial and continuing investment in the property must be adequate as prescribed by FASB-66. Under FASB-66, the purchaser's minimum initial investment must be made at or before the time of sale in cash or cash equivalents. A purchaser's note does not qualify for the minimum initial investment unless payment of the note is unconditionally guaranteed by an irrevocable letter of credit from an established unrelated lending institution. A permanent loan commitment by an independent third party to replace a loan made by the seller shall not be included in the purchaser's initial investment. Any funds that have been loaned or will be loaned, directly or indirectly, to the purchaser by the seller must be deducted from the purchaser's initial investment to determine whether the required minimum has been met. For the purposes of this provision, the seller must be exposed to a potential loss as a result of the funds loaned to the purchaser. For example, if a purchaser made an initial cash investment of $200,000 in a real estate transaction, $25,000 of which was a loan from the seller, the purchaser's minimum initial investment would be $175,000. However, if an unrelated reputable banking institution unconditionally guaranteed the timely repayment of the $25,000 to the seller, the entire $200,000 would be eligible as the purchaser's initial investment.

In determining whether the purchaser's minimum initial investment is adequate under the provisions of FASB-66, the *sales value* of the property is used and not the stated sales price that appears in the sales contract. The sales value is defined as the stated sales price of the property, increased or decreased for other considerations included in the sale that clearly represent additional or reduced proceeds to the seller on the sale (FASB-66).

There is a direct relationship between the amount of the purchaser's initial investment and the probability that the seller will eventually collect the balance due. The larger the down payment, the more likely the purchaser will pay the balance due. A reasonable basis for establishing the amount of a purchaser's initial investment is the prevailing practices of independent lending institutions. Thus, the difference between the amount of a primary mortgage that an independent lending institution would lend on a particular parcel of real estate and the *sales value* of the property is a realistic guide in determining the amount of the purchaser's initial investment.

In order to apply the full accrual method of accounting to a real estate transaction (other than a retail land sale), FASB-66 provides that the minimum initial investment (down payment) of the purchaser should be the greater of 1 or 2 below:

1. The percentage of the *sales value* of the property as indicated on the following table:

	Minimum Down Payment (% of Sales Value)
Land:	
Held for commercial, industrial, or residential development to commence within two years after sale	20%
Held for commercial, industrial, or residential development after two years	25%
Commercial and Industrial Property:	
Office and industrial buildings, shopping centers, etc.:	
Properties subject to lease on a long-term lease basis to parties having satisfactory credit rating; cash flow currently sufficient to service all indebtedness	10%
Single tenancy properties sold to a user having a satisfactory credit rating	15%
All other	20%

Other Income-Producing Properties (hotels, motels, marinas,
mobile home parks, etc.):

Cash flow currently sufficient to service all indebtedness	15%
Start-up situations or current deficiencies in cash flow	25%

Multi-Family Residential Property

Primary residence:

Cash flow currently sufficient to service all indebtedness	10%
Start-up situations or current deficiencies in cash flow	15%

Secondary or recreational residence:

Cash flow currently sufficient to service all indebtedness	15%
Start-up situations or current deficiencies in cash flow	25%

Single Family Residential Property (including condominium
or cooperative housing):

Primary residence of the buyer	5%*
Secondary or recreational residence	10%*

*If collectibility of the remaining portion of the sales price cannot be supported by reliable evidence of collection experience, a higher down payment is indicated and should not be less than 60% of the difference between the sales value and the financing available from loans guaranteed by regulatory bodies, such as FHA or VA, or from independent financial institutions. This 60% test applies when independent first mortgage financing is not utilized and the seller takes a receivable from the buyer for the difference between the sales value and the initial investment. When independent first mortgage financing is utilized, the adequacy of the initial investment on sales of single family residential property should be determined in accordance with FASB-66.

2. The lesser of the following:

   a. The difference between the *sales value* of the property and 115% of the maximum permanent mortgage loan or commitment on the property recently obtained from a primary independent lending institution,

   OR

   b. Twenty-five percent (25%) of the *sales value* of the property.

Even if the required minimum initial investment is made by the purchaser, a separate assessment must be made to determine the collectibility of the purchaser's receivable. In other words, there must be reasonable assurance that the receivable will be collected after the minimum initial investment is received by the seller, and if not, the sale should not be recorded by the full accrual method. The minimum initial investment must be made by the purchaser, and the seller must be reasonably assured that the balance of the sales price will be collected before the real estate sale is recorded and any profits are recognized. The assessment of the receivable by the seller should include credit reports on the purchaser and an evaluation of the adequacy of the cash flow from the property.

In addition to an adequate initial investment, FASB-66 also requires that the purchaser maintain a continuing investment in the property by increasing the investment each year. The purchaser's total indebtedness for the purchase price of the property must be reduced each year in equal amounts which will extinguish the entire indebtedness (interest and principal) over a specified maximum period. The specified maximum period for land transactions is twenty (20) years. The specified maximum period for all other real estate transactions is no more than that offered at the time of sale for first mortgages by independent financial institutions. The purchaser's commitment to pay the full amount of the indebtedness to the seller becomes doubtful if the total indebtedness is not to be paid within the specified maximum period.

Transfer of all other risks and rewards of ownership   In order to qualify for sale-leaseback accounting under FASB-98, the seller-lessee must transfer all of the other risks and rewards of ownership in the property to the purchaser-lessor.

No other continuing involvement   FASB-98 considers the lease-back portion of a sale-leaseback transaction to be a form of continued involvement with the leased property by the seller-lessee (paragraph 48 of FASB-98). Other than the continued involvement represented by the leaseback portion of the sale-leaseback transaction, a normal leaseback excludes any *other* continuing involvement in the leased property by the seller-lessee. Thus, sale-leaseback accounting cannot be used to account for a sale-leaseback transaction in which the seller-lessee has any other continuing involvement in the property other than that represented by the leaseback portion of the transaction.

An exchange of some stated or unstated rights or privileges is indicated in a sale-leaseback transaction if the terms of the transaction are substantially different from terms that an independent third-party lessor would accept. In this event, the stated or unstated rights or privileges shall be considered in evaluating the continued involvement of the seller-lessee. Terms or conditions that indicate that stated or unstated rights or privileges exist may involve the sales price, the interest rate, and terms of any loan from the seller-lessee to the purchaser-lessor.

Accounting for sale-leasebacks involving real estate   Once a sale-leaseback transaction qualifies for sale-leaseback accounting in accordance with the provisions of FASB-98, the following steps should be applied to determine the amount of gain (loss) and the time of recognition of the gain (loss):

Step 1.   Compute the *amount* of gain (loss) on the sale portion of the sale-leaseback transaction in accordance with the provisions of FASB-66. (Disregard the fact that the sale is part of a sale-leaseback transaction.)

> **Note**: A loss must be immediately recognized on the sale portion of a sale-leaseback transaction if the undepreciated cost of the property sold is more than its fair value. The maximum amount of loss that shall be recognized immediately cannot exceed the difference between the fair value of the property and its undepreciated cost. If the indicated loss exceeds the difference between the fair value of the property sold and its undepreciated cost, the loss is possibly, in substance, a prepayment of rent. Under this circumstance, it is appropriate to defer the indicated loss and amortize it as prepaid rent (paragraph 33c of FASB-13 as amended by paragraph 3 of FASB-28).

> *OBSERVATION: Paragraph 33c of FASB-13, as amended by paragraph 3 of FASB-28, states that the maximum indicated loss may not be more than the difference between the undepreciated cost of the property sold and its fair value. On the other hand, paragraph 18 of FASB-28 states that the maximum indicated loss may not be more than the difference between the carrying amount of the property sold and its fair value. Thus, it is not clear whether the undepreciated cost or the carrying amount of the property should be used in calculating the maximum loss that is recognized immediately.*

Step 2.   Classify the lease portion of the sale-leaseback transaction in accordance with the provisions of FASB-13, as amended by FASB-28. (Depending on the percentage amount of the property that the seller-lessee leases back, a lease may be classified under FASB-28 as a lease involving either (a) substantially all of the property, (b) a minor portion of the property, or (c) more than a minor portion of the property but less than substantially all.)

Note: Under the terms of the sale-leaseback, a seller-lessee may lease back a minor portion of the property sold to the purchaser-lessor, substantially all of the property, or a portion that is more than minor and less than substantially all. A minor portion of the property has been leased back if the present value of the total rents to be paid by the seller-lessee under the terms of the lease agreement is reasonable and equal to 10% or less of the fair value of the property at the inception of the lease. Substantially all of the property has been leased back if the present value of the total rents to be paid by the seller-lessee, under the terms of the lease agreement is reasonable and equal to 90% or more of the fair value of the property at the inception of the lease.

Step 3. Determine whether the lease portion of the sale-leaseback transaction qualifies as a capital lease or operating lease under the provisions of FASB-13.

Note: Under FASB-13, a lease is classified as a capital lease if it meets one or more of the following criteria:

a. Ownership of the property is transferred to the lessee by the end of the lease term.
b. The lease contains a bargain purchase option.
c. The lease term, at inception, is substantially (75% or more) equal to the estimated economic life of the leased property, including earlier years of use. [Exception: This particular criterion cannot be used for a lease that begins within the last 25% of the original estimated economic life of the leased property.]
d. The present value of the minimum lease payments at the beginning of the lease term, excluding executory costs and profits thereon to be paid by the lessor, is 90% or more of the fair value of the property at the inception of the lease, less any investment tax credits retained, and expected to be realized, by the lessor. [Exception: This particular criterion can-

not be used for a lease that begins within the last 25% of the original estimated economic life of the leased property.]

Step 4. Recognize the amount of gain (loss) computed in Step 1, based on the percentage amount of the property that the seller-lessee leases back in Step 2 (substantially all of the property, a minor portion of the property, or more than a minor portion of the property but less than substantially all) AND whether in Step 3, the lease is classified as a capital lease or an operating lease.

If, under Step 2, the lease portion of the sale-leaseback transaction is classified as *substantially all*:

Any gain (loss) on the sale must be deferred and amortized by the seller-lessee, according to whether the lease is classified, under Step 3, as a capital lease or as an operating lease, as follows:

Capital lease—If the lease is classified as a capital lease, the gain (loss) on the sale is amortized in proportion to the amortization of the leased property.

Operating lease—If the lease is classified as an operating lease, the gain (loss) on the sale is amortized in proportion to the gross rental charged to expense over the lease term.

If, under Step 2, the lease portion of the sale-leaseback transaction is classified as *minor*:

The sale and leaseback are accounted for as two independent transactions based on their separate terms. However, the lease must provide for a reasonable amount of rent, considering prevailing market conditions at the inception of the lease. The seller-lessee must increase or decrease the gain (loss) on the sale of the property by an amount which brings the total rental for the leased property to a reasonable amount. Any amount resulting from a rental adjustment shall be amortized as follows:

Capital lease—The deferred or accrued amount of rental adjustment is amortized in proportion to the amortization of the leased property.

Operating lease—The deferred or accrued amount of rental adjustment is amortized in proportion to the gross rental charged to expense over the lease term.

If, under Step 2, the lease portion of the sale-leaseback transaction is classified as *more than minor but less than substantially all*:

The seller-lessee shall recognize any excess gain determined at the date of the sale, according to whether the lease is classified under Step 3 as a capital lease or an operating lease, as follows:

Capital lease—The excess gain (if any) is equal to the amount of gain that exceeds the seller-lessee's recorded amount of the property as determined under the provisions of FASB-13 (the lesser of the fair value of the leased property or the present value of the minimum lease payments). For example, if the seller-lessee's recorded amount of the sale-leaseback property is $100,000 as determined under the provisions of FASB-13, and the amount of gain on the sale portion of the sale-leaseback transaction is $120,000, the excess gain that is recognized by the seller-lessee is $20,000. The balance of the gain ($100,000) is deferred and amortized in proportion to the amortization of the leased property.

Operating lease—The excess gain (if any) on a sale-leaseback transaction is equal to the amount of gain that exceeds the present value of the minimum lease payments over the term of the lease. The amount of gain on the sale portion of the sale-leaseback transaction that is not recognized at the date of the sale is deferred and amortized over the lease term in proportion to the gross rentals charged to expense.

Profit recognition other than full accrual method   The two most important factors in evaluating the economic substance of a real estate sale are (1) the transfer of the usual risks and rewards of ownership in the property and (2) the full performance by the seller of all acts required by the contract to earn the revenue. Generally, both of these factors must be accomplished before full profit may be recognized on a sale of real estate.

A sale-leaseback transaction must qualify under the provisions of FASB-98 and most of the provisions of FASB-66 before the full amount of the profit on the sale portion of the transaction can be recognized by the seller-lessee in accordance with the sale-leaseback accounting method (full accrual method).

When one or more of the criteria required by FASB-66 is not met for the sale portion of a sale-leaseback transaction, an alternative method of recognizing revenue from the sale must be used. The alternative method selected may be required by FASB-66 or may be a matter of professional judgment. The four alternative accounting methods recommended by FASB-66 for recognizing a sale of real estate that does not qualify for the full accrual method of accounting are (a) the deposit method, (b) the cost recovery method, (c) the installment sales method, and (d) the reduced profit method (FASB-66).

After an alternative method is adopted for the sale portion of a sale-leaseback transaction involving real estate, periodic evaluation should be made of the collectibility of the receivable. When it becomes apparent that the seller-lessee's receivable is reasonably assured of being collected, a change to the full accrual accounting method is appropriate. The change is not a change in an accounting principle (Statement of Position 78-4). When the change to the full accrual accounting method is made, any remaining deferred gross profit is recognized in full in the period in which the change is made. If the change creates a material effect on the seller's financial statements, full disclosure of the effects and the reason for the change should be appropriately made in the financial statements or footnotes thereto (Statement of Position 78-4). (For a complete discussion of profit recognition on real estate transactions, see FASB-66.)

Regulated enterprises sale-leaseback involving real estate   FASB-98 applies to regulated enterprises that are subject to FASB-71 (Accounting for the Effects of Certain Types of Regulation). The application of FASB-98 for financial accounting purposes (GAAP) may result in the recognition of income and expense in a different accounting period than that in which the same income and expense is recognized for regulatory purposes (rate-making). Under income tax accounting (FASB-96), this results in a temporary difference (timing difference under APB-11). If a temporary difference represents part or all of a phase-in plan, as defined by FASB-92, a specific method of accounting is prescribed by FASB-98. For all other types of temporary differences, a different method of accounting is specified.

If a temporary difference represents part or all of a phase-in plan, as defined by FASB-92, it shall be accounted for in accordance with the provisions of FASB-92. In all other circumstances, a temporary difference shall be modified to conform with FASB-71. For example, the sale portion of a sale-leaseback transaction may be recognized for regulatory purposes and not recognized for financial accounting purposes because the transaction is accounted for by the deposit method. In this event, amortization of the asset should be modified to equal the total amount of the rental expense and gain or loss that are allowable for regulatory purposes. Also, the sale portion of a sale-leaseback transaction may be recognized for regulatory purposes and not recognized for financial accounting purposes because the transaction is accounted for as a financing. In this event, amortization of the asset and the total amount of interest imputed under the interest method for the financing should be modified to equal the total rental expense and gain or loss that are allowable for regulatory purposes.

If it is not part of a phase-in plan, as defined by FASB-92, and its meets the criteria of FASB-71, a temporary difference between the amount of income or expense that is allowable for regulatory purposes, and the amount of income or expense that is recognized by the deposit method or as a financing shall be capitalized or accrued as a separate regulatory asset or liability.

Disclosure of sale-leasebacks involving real estate   The financial statements of the seller-lessee shall include a description of the terms of the sale-leaseback transaction, including future commitments, obligations, or other provisions that require or result in the seller-lessee's continuing involvement.

A seller-lessee who has accounted for a sale-leaseback by the deposit method or as a financing shall disclose in the aggregate and for each of the five succeeding fiscal years:

- The obligation for future minimum lease payments as of the date of the latest balance sheet presented
- The total of minimum sublease rentals, if any, to be received in the future under noncancelable subleases.

Effective date and transition   FASB-98 is effective for sale-leaseback transactions involving real estate *entered into* on or after July 1, 1988. Earlier application of the provisions of FASB-98 is encouraged for those transactions that occurred in periods for which annual financial statements have not been issued.

For the purpose of FASB-98, the term *entered into* means the date of the lease agreement or the date of a written commitment signed by the parties involved that sets forth the principal provisions of the lease transaction.

Sale-Leaseback Transactions (Non-Real Estate)

Sale-leaseback transactions involving real estate are addressed in FASB-98. All other sale-leaseback transactions are covered by FASB-28, which is discussed below.

Sale-leaseback   A sale-leaseback is a transaction in which an owner sells property and then leases back part or all of the same property. Such an owner is referred to as the seller-lessee.

Purchaser-lessor   The purchasor-lessor is the party who purchases the property and leases back the same property to the seller-lessee.

Profit or loss on the sale   Profit or loss on the sale is the amount which would have been recognized on the sale by the seller-lessee, assuming there was no leaseback.

Substantially all* or *minor   Under the terms of the lease, the seller-lessee may have a *minor* portion or *substantially all* of the rights to the remaining use of the property. This is determined by the present value of a total *reasonable rental* for the rights to the remaining use of the property retained by the seller-lessee. The seller-lessee has transferred *substantially all* of the rights to the remaining use of the property to the purchaser-lessor if the present value of the total *reasonable rental* under the terms of the lease is 10% or less than the fair value of the property sold at the inception of the lease. The seller-lessee has transferred a *minor* portion of the remaining rights to the purchaser-lessor if the terms of the leaseback include the entire property sold and qualify as a capital lease under FASB-13.

> *OBSERVATION: FASB-28 does not define **reasonable rental** or **fair value**. However, FASB-13 defines **fair value** as the price the leased property could be sold for between unrelated parties in an arm's length transaction. FASB-13 defines **fair rental** as the rental rate for similar property under similar lease terms and conditions.*

Accounting for Sale-Leasebacks

When an owner sells property and then leases the same property back again, the transaction is called a sale-leaseback. If the lease meets the criteria for capitalization, the purchaser-lessor records the acquisition of the property as a purchase and the lease as a direct financing lease. If the lease does not meet the criteria for capitalization, the acquisition of the property is recorded as a purchase and the lease as an operating lease.

Accounting for the sale-leaseback by the seller-lessee is determined by the degree of rights in the remaining use of the property the seller-lessee retains, as follows:

a.   Substantially all
b.   Minor
c.   More than minor but less than substantially all

Substantially all   If the entire property sold is leased back and the seller-lessee retains the rights to *substantially all* of the remaining use in the property, the seller-lessee records the lease as a capital lease, provided it meets the criteria for capitalization under FASB-13. If the lease does not meet the criteria for capitalization, the seller-lessee records it as an operating lease. Whether the lease is recorded as a capital lease or an operating lease, any profit or loss (see definition) on the sale by the seller-lessee must be deferred and amortized as follows:

Capital lease   For a capital lease, the deferred profit or loss on the sale is amortized in proportion to the amortization of the leased property.

Operating lease   For an operating lease, the deferred profit or loss on the sale is amortized in proportion to the gross rental charged to expense over the lease term.

Whether a capital lease or an operating lease, if the leased asset is land only, the amortization of the deferred profit or loss on the sale must be on a straight-line basis over the lease term.

Minor   If the seller-lessee retains the rights to a *minor* portion of the remaining use in the property, the seller-lessee shall account for the sale and leaseback as two independent transactions based on their separate terms. However, the lease must provide for a reasonable amount of rent, considering prevailing market conditions at the inception of the lease. The seller-lessee must increase or decrease the profit or loss on the sale by an amount, if any, which brings the total rental for the leased property to a reasonable amount. Any amount created by this adjustment shall be amortized, as follows:

Capital lease   For a capital lease, the deferred or accrued amount is amortized in proportion to the amortization of the leased property.

Operating lease   For an operating lease, the deferred or accrued amount is amortized in proportion to the gross rental charged to expense over the lease term.

Whether a capital lease or an operating lease, if the leased asset is land only, the amortization of the deferred or accrued amount must be on a straight-line basis over the lease term.

> *OBSERVATION: If the total rental on the lease is less than a reasonable amount compared to prevailing market conditions at the inception of the lease, a profit on the sale would have to be increased and a loss on the sale would have to be decreased.*
>
> *In the case of an operating lease, the journal entry would be a debit to prepaid rent and a credit to profit or loss. The prepaid rent is amortized in an amount which increases the periodic rental expense over the lease term to a reasonable amount. Conversely, if the total rental on the lease is more than a reasonable amount compared to prevailing market conditions at the inception of the lease, a profit on the sale would have to be decreased and a loss on the sale would have to be increased. The journal entry would be a debit to profit or loss and a credit to deferred rent. The deferred rent is amortized in an amount which decreases the periodic rental expense over the lease term to a reasonable amount.*
>
> *In the case of a capital lease, the debit to prepaid rent or the credit to deferred rent is not made. Instead, the debit or credit increases or decreases the amount which is recorded for the leased property. The leased property is then amortized in the usual manner.*

More than minor but less than substantially all   If the seller-lessee retains the rights to more than a minor but less than substantially all of the remaining use in the property, the seller-lessee shall recognize any excess profit (not losses) determined at the date of sale as follows:

Capital lease   The excess profit (if any) on a sale-leaseback transaction is equal to the amount of profit that exceeds the seller-lessee's recorded amount of the property as determined under the provisions of FASB-13 (the lesser of the fair value of the leased property or the present value of the minimum lease payments). For example, if the seller-lessee's recorded amount of the sale-leaseback property is $100,000 as determined under the provisions of FASB-13, and the amount of profit on the sale-leaseback transaction is $120,000, the excess profit that is recognized by the seller-lessee is $20,000. The balance of the profit ($100,000) is deferred and amortized in proportion to the amortization of the leased property.

Operating lease   The excess profit (if any) on a sale-leaseback transaction is equal to the amount of profit that exceeds the present value of the minimum lease payments over the term of the lease. The amount of profit on the sale-leaseback transaction that is not recognized at the date of the sale is deferred and amortized over the lease term in proportion to the gross rentals charged to expense.

Whether a capital lease or an operating lease, if the leased property is land only, the amortization of the deferred profit (if any) must be on a straight-line basis over the lease term.

Wrap Lease Transactions

FASB Technical Bulletin 88-1 provides guidance on accounting and reporting on wrap lease transactions. In a wrap lease transaction, a lessor leases equipment to a lessee and obtains nonrecourse financing from a financial institution using the lease receivable and the asset as collateral. The lessor sells the asset subject to the lease and the nonrecourse financing to a third-party investor and then leases the asset back. Thus, the original lessor remains the principal lessor who continues to service the lease. The transaction with the third-party investor may or may not occur at the same time as the original lease is executed with the original equipment user. As a matter of fact, it is not unusual, in a wrap lease transaction, for the subsequent nonrecourse financing or sale to a third-party to occur up to six months after the original lease agreement is executed.

In exchange for the sale of the asset to a third-party investor, the lessor may receive a combination of cash, a note, an interest in the residual value of the leased asset, and certain other rights or contingent rights, such as the right to remarket the asset at the end of the lease term. Depending on the terms of the specific transaction, (i) the lessor may or may not be liable for the leaseback payments if the primary lessee defaults, (ii) the lessor may or may not receive a fee for servicing the lease, (iii) payments under the leaseback may or may not approximate collections under the note and (iv) the terms of the leaseback may or may not correspond with the terms of the original equipment lease.

A wrap lease transaction consists primarily of a sale-leaseback of property and should be accounted for as such under FASB-13 (Accounting for Leases) or FASB-98 (Accounting for Leases), whichever is applicable. If the property involved in a wrap lease transaction is other than real estate, the provisions of FASB-13, as amended by FASB-28 (Accounting for Sales with Leasebacks) must be followed. On the other hand, if the property involved is real estate, the provisions of FASB-98 must be observed in accounting for the sale-leaseback transaction.

Under sale-leaseback accounting, the sale portion of a sale-leaseback transaction is recorded as a sale by the seller-lessee, the property sold and all of its related liabilities are eliminated from the seller-lessee's balance sheet, gain or loss on the sale portion of the sale-leaseback transaction is recognized by the seller-lessee in accordance with paragraph 33 of FASB-13, as amended by FASB-28, the lease portion of the sale-leaseback transaction should be classified as a capital lease or an operating lease in accordance with paragraph 6 of FASB-13 and accounted for by the seller-lessee in accordance with paragraph 33 of FASB-13.

The purchaser-lessor shall record a sale-leaseback transaction as a purchase and a direct financing lease, if the lease portion of the sale-leaseback meets the criteria of a capital lease under paragraph 7 of FASB-13. Otherwise, the purchaser-lessor shall record the transaction as a purchase and an operating lease (paragraph 34 of FASB-13).

The main difference in accounting for a sale-leaseback under FASB-13 and FASB-98 is that under the provisions of FASB-98, the sale portion of the sale-leaseback must meet all of the criteria for sales recognition under the provisions of FASB-66 (Accounting for Sales of Real Estate). FASB-98 prohibits a lease involving real estate from being classified as a sales-type lease unless the lease agreement provides for the title of the leased property to be transferred to the lessee at or shortly after the end of the lease term.

In reporting a wrap lease transaction, FASB Technical Bulletin 88-1 requires that an enterprise's statement of financial position reflect (a) the amount of the retained residual interest in the leased property, (b) the amount of the gross sublease receivable, (c) the amount of the nonrecourse third-party debt, (d) the amount of the leaseback obligation, and (e) amount of the note receivable from the investor. Offsetting the subleased asset and its related nonrecourse debt in the statement of financial position is prohibited by GAAP (APB-10), unless a legal right of setoff exists.

To illustrate the economics of wrap lease transactions, assume that a lessor leases an asset with an undepreciated cost of $1,000 to a lessee for five years at $19.12 a month. The residual value of the leased asset at the end of the lease term is estimated to be $164.53 and the interest rate implicit in the lease is 10%. The lessor would classify the lease as a direct financing lease under the provisions of FASB-13 (Accounting for Leases) and record the following journal entry:

Lease receivable	$1,147.20	
Residual value of leased asset	164.53	
Asset		$1,000.00
Unearned income—lease receivable		247.20
Unearned income—residual		64.53

> **Note:** For financial reporting purposes, FASB-13 requires that the lease receivable and residual value of the leased asset be combined and reported as the gross investment in the lease. In addition, the unearned income amounts must also be combined.

Using the lease receivable and the asset as collateral, the lessor enters into a nonrecourse financing arrangement with a financial institution for $900.00 (the present value of the $19.12 monthly lease payment for 60 months discounted at 10%) at a rate of 10%. The lessor would record the following journal entry to reflect the liability for the nonrecourse debt:

Cash	$900.00	
Nonrecourse debt		$900.00

The lessor then sells the asset subject to the lease and the nonrecourse debt to a group of equity partners and leases the asset back for five years at $19.12 a month (for simplicity, assume that the lease, the nonrecourse financing, and the sale to the equity partners occur at the same time). The lessor is now the lessee-sublessor and remains the obligor with the financial institution that financed the nonrecourse debt. In return for the asset, the lessor receives the following:

1. Cash of $50, representing the sale of 50% of the residual value of the leased asset.
2. An additional $103.66 in cash, representing the transfer of tax benefits. (For purposes of this illustration, the $103.66 represents the discounted tax benefits associated with the transaction using 1985 tax laws, and includes the investment tax credit (ITC).)

3. A note receivable for $900.00 bearing interest at 10% with 60 monthly payments of $19.12 (60 payments at $19.12 represent a gross note of $1,147.20 and unearned income of $247.20).
4. The right to receive a fee of $82.27 for remarketing the asset at the end of the initial lease term (the present value of an $82.27 payment 60 months in the future discounted at 10% equals $50.00).
5. In addition, the lessor retains a 50% interest in the proceeds of the residual value of the leased asset at the end of the lease term.

Accounting for Certain Losses on Sale-Leasebacks

Under any circumstances, if the fair value of the property at the time of the sale-leaseback is less than its undepreciated cost, the seller-lessee shall recognize immediately a loss in an amount not to exceed the difference between the fair value and the undepreciated cost of the property sold.

> **OBSERVATION**: *Paragraph 33c of FASB-13, as amended by paragraph 3 of FASB-28, states that the maximum indicated loss may not be more than the difference between the undepreciated cost of the property sold and its fair value. On the other hand, paragraph 18 of FASB-28 states that the maximum indicated loss may not be more than the difference between the carrying amount of the property sold and its fair value. Thus, it is not clear whether the undepreciated cost or the carrying amount of the property should be used in calculating the maximum loss that is recognized immediately.*

Subleases and Similar Transactions

Unless the original lease agreement is replaced by a new agreement, the original lessor shall continue to account for the lease as before.

A termination of a lease is recognized by a lessor in the income of the period in which termination occurs, by the following entries:

1. The remaining net investment is eliminated from the accounts.
2. The leased property is recorded as an asset using the lower of the (a) original cost, (b) present value at termination, or (c) present carrying amount at termination.

If an original lessee is relieved of the primary obligation under an original lease, the transaction should be accounted for by the lessee as follows:

Capital leases   Termination of the lease occurs and gain or loss is recognized in income of the period. A loss contingency should also be provided for if the original lessee remains secondarily liable on the lease.

Operating leases   A loss contingency should be provided for if the original lessee remains secondarily liable on the lease.

When a lessee subleases leased property, the original lease continues and a simultaneous new lease is created in which the lessee becomes a sublessor. The results are that the original lessee is both a lessee in the original lease and, at the same time, a sublessor in the new lease. In situations like this, the original lease continues to be accounted for as if nothing happened, but the new lease must be classified and accounted for separately.

If an original lessee is not relieved of the primary obligation under an original lease, the transaction should be accounted for by the original lessee-sublessor as follows:

1. If the criterion for the original lease was I (ownership of the property is transferred before the end of the lease term) or II (lease contains a bargain purchase option), the new lease shall be classified based on its own new criteria. If the new lease qualifies for capitalization, it shall be accounted for as a sales-type or a direct financing lease, whichever is appropriate, and the unamortized balance of the asset under the original lease shall be treated as the cost of the leased property to the sublessor (original lessee).

    In the event that the new lease does not qualify for capitalization, it shall be treated as an operating lease. [**Note:** As stated earlier, the original lease continues to be accounted for in the usual manner.]

2. If the criterion for the original lease was III (lease term is substantially—75% or more—equal to the estimated economic life of the leased property at the inception of the lease) or IV (present value of the minimum lease payments—excluding executory costs—is 90% or more of the fair value at inception), the new lease shall be capitalized only if it meets criterion III and (a) the collection of the minimum lease payments is reasonably predictable and (b) no important uncertainties

exist regarding costs yet to be incurred by the lessor under the lease. If the new lease meets the criteria above, it is accounted for as a direct financing lease, with the amortized balance of the asset under the original lease as the cost of the leased property.

If the new lease does not meet the specific conditions above, it is accounted for as an operating lease. [**Note:** As stated earlier, the original lease continues to be accounted for in the usual manner.]

In any event, if the original lease is an operating lease, the sublease is accounted for as an operating lease also.

Even though the sublessor (original lessee) remains primarily obligated under an original lease, a loss may be recognized on a sublease (FASB Interpretation-27). The loss is measured as the difference between the unamortized cost of the leased property (net carrying amount) and the present value of the minimum lease payments which will be received under the terms of the sublease.

> **OBSERVATION:** *FASB Interpretation-27 is silent as to recognition of any gain on subleases in which the sublessor (original lessee) remains primarily obligated under the original lease. However, FASB-13, paragraph 39, implies that both gain or loss may be recognized on sales-type and direct financing leases.*

FASB Interpretation-27 also reaffirms that estimated costs and expenses directly associated with a decision to dispose of a business segment should include future rental payments on long-term leases less any future rentals to be received from subleases of the same properties (APB-30). The gain or loss is measured as the difference between the unamortized cost of the leased property (net carrying amount) and the present value of the minimum lease payments which will be received under the terms of the sublease. The gain or loss is included in the overall gain or loss on the disposal of the business segment.

> **OBSERVATION:** *FASB Interpretation-27 is not clear on its coverage of subleases which are classified as operating leases. There is a strong argument that gain or loss on an operating sublease be included as part of the overall gain or loss on disposal of a business segment. APB-30 specifically states that all costs and expenses which are directly associated with the decision to dispose of a*

> business segment be included in the overall gain or loss on the disposal. If a business segment has a long-term operating lease which is subleased and classified as an operating lease as part of the overall disposal of the segment, then any gain or loss would obviously be directly associated with management's decision to dispose of the segment. The gain or loss would be measured as the difference between the present value of the future rental payments which must be paid on the original lease and the present value of the future rental receipts which will be collected on the operating sublease. The journal entry to record a loss would be a debit to the gain or loss account for disposal of the business segment and a credit to a deferred account. The deferred credit account would be amortized each year in an amount which would make up the difference between the payment made on the original lease and the rental collected on the operating sublease.

FASB Technical Bulletin 79-15 reaffirms that a loss on a sublease not connected with the disposal of a business segment should be accounted for as any other loss on a sublease in accordance with FASB-13.

Leases Involving Governmental Units

Leases with governmental units usually lack fair values, have indeterminable economic lives, and cannot provide for transfer of ownership. These special provisions usually prevent their classification as any other than operating leases.

However, leases involving governmental units are subject to the same criteria as any other lease unless all of the following conditions exist; and in that event, these leases are classified as operating leases:

1. A governmental unit or authority owns the leased property.
2. The leased property is operated by or on behalf of a governmental unit or authority and is part of a larger facility, such as an airport.
3. The leased property cannot be moved to another location because it is a permanent structure or part of a permanent structure.
4. Any governmental unit or authority can terminate the lease agreement at any time under the terms of the lease agreement, existing statutes, or regulations.

5. Ownership is transferred to the lessee and the lessee cannot purchase the leased property.
6. Equivalent property in the same area as the leased property cannot be purchased or leased from anyone else.

Related Party Leases

Except in cases where the substance of a lease transaction clearly indicates that the terms and conditions have been significantly influenced by the related parties, these types of leases are classified and accounted for as if the parties were unrelated.

It is important to note that generally a subsidiary whose principal business activity is leasing property to its parent must be consolidated with the parent's financial statements.

> **OBSERVATION:** *Specific financial statement disclosures pertaining to related parties are required by FASB-57 (Related Party Disclosures).*

Accounting and Reporting for Leveraged Leases

A lessee shall classify and account for *leveraged* leases in the same manner as *nonleveraged* leases. *Only a lessor* must classify and account for leveraged leases in the specific manner prescribed herein.

FASB-13 defines a *leveraged lease* as a lease having all the following characteristics:

1. A leveraged lease meets the definition of a direct financing lease as follows:

   A direct financing lease is a lease that does not result in a manufacturer's or dealer's profit or loss because the fair value of the leased property at the inception of the lease is the same as the cost or carrying amount. In a direct financing lease, substantially all the benefits and risks inherent in the ownership of the lease property are transferred to the lessee. In addition, the following requirements must be met:

   a. The minimum lease payments are reasonably predictable of collection.
   b. No important uncertainties exist regarding costs to be incurred by the lessor under the terms of the lease.

2. It involves at least three parties: (a) a lessee, (b) a lessor, and (c) a long-term creditor. (**Note:** The lessor is sometimes referred to as the *equity participant*.)
3. The financing is sufficient to provide the lessor with substantial leverage in the transaction and is nonrecourse as to the general credit of the lessor.
4. Once the lessor's net investment is completed, it declines in the early years and rises in later years before being liquidated. These fluctuations in the lessor's net investment can occur more than once in the lease term.

If the investment tax credit is accounted for as provided herein and a lease meets the preceding definition, it shall be classified and accounted for as a leveraged lease.

The initial and continuing investment of the lessor in a leveraged lease shall be recorded *net* of the nonrecourse debt, as follows:

1. Rentals receivable, net of that portion applicable to principal and interest on the nonrecourse debt
2. A receivable for the amount of the investment tax credit to be realized on the transaction
3. The estimated residual value of the leased property
4. Unearned and deferred income consisting of (a) the estimated pretax lease income or loss, after deducting initial direct costs of negotiating and consummating the lease transaction, that remains to be allocated to income over the lease term and (b) the investment tax credit that remains to be allocated to income over the lease term

FASB Technical Bulletin 79-16 requires that the effect of an income tax rate change be recognized in net income of the period in which the rate change occurs. If the effect of the income tax rate change creates a significant variation between the usual relationship of taxable income and pretax accounting income, disclosure should be made in accordance with FASB-96 (Accounting for Income Taxes).

The investment in a leveraged lease, less applicable deferred taxes, shall represent the lessor's net investment for purposes of computing periodic net income from the leveraged lease. The following method is used to compute periodic net income:

1. A projected cash flow analysis is prepared for the lease term.
2. The rate of return on net investment in the years it is positive is computed (usually by trial and error).

3. Every year the net investment is increased or decreased by the difference between the net cash flow and the amount of income recognized, if any.

The amount of net income that is recognized each year consists of:

1. Pretax lease income or loss (allocated from the unearned income portion of the net investment)
2. Investment tax credit (allocated from the deferred income portion of the net investment)
3. The tax effect of the pretax lease income or loss recognized (which is reflected in tax expense for the year)

Any tax effect on the difference between pretax accounting income or loss and taxable income or loss is charged or credited to deferred taxes.

All the important assumptions affecting the estimated net income from the leveraged lease, including any estimated residual values, should be reviewed at least annually.

If at the inception or at any time during the lease, the projected net cash receipts over the initial or remaining lease term are less than the lessor's initial or current investment, the resulting loss shall be immediately recognized.

Upward adjustments of the estimated residual value are not permitted.

The lessor's financial statement disclosure for leveraged leases shall include the amount of deferred taxes separately stated.

When leveraged leasing is a significant part of the lessor's business activity, a schedule of the components of the net investment in leveraged leases shall be fully disclosed in the footnotes to the financial statements.

Lessor's existing asset in a leveraged lease   Only a direct financing lease may qualify as a leveraged lease under the provisions of FASB-13 (paragraph 42a). One of the requirements of a direct financing lease is that it may not result in a manufacturer's or dealer's profit or loss. In other words, the cost or carrying amount, if different, must be the same as the fair value of the leased property at the inception of the lease. FASB Technical Bulletin 88-1 reaffirms the fact that this requirement is intended to be applied literally. Thus, it is difficult for an existing asset of a lessor to qualify for leveraged lease accounting because the carrying amount (cost less accumulated depreciation) of an asset previously placed in service is not likely to be the same as its fair value. However, an existing asset of the lessor may qualify for leveraged lease accounting, if its carrying amount is equal to its fair value, without any write-down or other adjustment to its fair value.

FASB Technical Bulletin 88-1 is effective for transactions *entered into* on or after January 1, 1989. Earlier application of FASB:TB 88-1 is encouraged for unissued annual financial statements. (**Note:** In FASB:TB 88-1, the term *entered into* means the date of the lease agreement or commitment, if earlier. A commitment must contain the principal provisions of the transaction and be signed by the parties to the transaction. A commitment that does not contain the principal provisions of the lease agreement does not qualify.)

Business Combinations

A business combination, in itself, does not affect the classification of a lease. However, if as a result of a business combination, a lease is revised or modified to the extent that under the promulgated GAAP (FASB-13) it is considered a new agreement, it should be reclassified on the basis of its revision or modification.

Ordinarily, under the purchase method or pooling-of-interests method of effecting a business combination, a lease retains its previous classification under FASB-13 and is accounted for in the same manner as it was prior to the combination.

The acquiring company in a business combination accounted for by the purchase method shall account for a leveraged lease by assigning a fair value (present value, net of tax) to the net investment in a leveraged lease based on the remaining future cash flows with appropriate recognition for any future estimated tax effects. After the fair value (present value, net of tax) of the net investment is determined, it should be allocated to net rentals receivable, estimated residual value, and unearned income. Thereafter, a company should account for the leveraged lease by allocating the periodic cash flow between the net investment and the lease income.

In a business combination where an acquired lease has not been conformed to FASB-13, the acquiring company should classify such a lease to conform retroactively to FASB-13.

Effective Date and Transition

FASB-13 is effective for leasing transactions entered into on or after January 1, 1977, and earlier application is encouraged. Leasing transactions entered into prior to January 1, 1977, and concluded after that date are excluded from FASB-13 if they are supported by a written commitment signed by the parties.

Financial statements presented for fiscal years beginning after December 31, 1980, shall be retroactively restated to the provisions of FASB-13.

> **OBSERVATION**: *The preceding discussion of the transitional procedures of FASB-13 is brief and incomplete. The reader is advised to refer to the actual transitional procedures enumerated in FASB-13. In addition, FASB Technical Bulletins 79-17 and 79-18 contain information relating to the transitional period in FASB-13.*

Comprehensive Illustration—Capital Lease

Paine Corporation leases a computer under a noncancelable five-year lease for annual rental payments of $10,000. The fair value of the computer at the inception of the lease is $36,048, and the incremental borrowing rate of Paine is 10%. There are no executory costs and no investment tax credit available. The annual rent of $10,000 is considered a fair rental as opposed to a bargain rental. The estimated economic life of the computer is ten years.

Classification of Lease by Paine as Lessee

A review is made of the criteria involved in the provisions of the lease to determine its classification.

1. Criterion I is not met, because there is no transfer of the ownership of the leased property before the end of the lease term.
2. Criterion II is not met, because the lease does not contain a bargain purchase option.
3. Criterion III is not met, because the lease term (five years) is not equal to 75% or more of the estimated economic life (ten years) of the leased property. [**Note**: There are not other provisions affecting the lease term other than the five-year noncancelable term.]

4. Criterion IV is met, because the present value ($37,980) of the minimum lease payments, excluding executory costs and profits thereon paid by the lessor, is 90% or more of the fair value ($36,048) of the leased property. [**Note:** The present value computations are given below.]

Paine Corporation should record the transaction as a capital lease.

Accounting for the Lease by Paine

The initial recording value of the leased property, at the inception of the lease, is the lesser of the fair value of the leased property or the present value of the minimum lease payments, excluding any portion that represents executory costs and profit thereon to be paid by the lessor.

The discount rate used by the lessee to find the present value of the minimum lease payments is its incremental borrowing rate of 10%, unless the lessee has knowledge of the lessor's implicit interest rate in the lease, and that rate is lower.

The lessor's interest rate implicit in the lease in this example is 12%. As a rule, the interest rate implicit in the lease is equal to the discount rate that, when applied to the minimum lease payments of $10,000 per year for five years and, if any, the unguaranteed residual value of the leased property, results in a present value equal to the fair value of the leased property at the inception of the lease. (For simplicity, this definition excludes any unusual factors that a lessor might recognize in determining its rate of return.)

This means that Paine must use its incremental borrowing rate of 10% to discount the minimum lease payments to their present value, which is $37,980.

The initial recording value of the leased property is the lesser of the fair value of the leased property at inception or the present value of the minimum lease payments using the lower interest rate. Therefore, the $36,048 fair value is less than the minimum lease payments of $37,980 (computed by using the lower incremental borrowing rate) and is used to initially record the lease, as follows:

Lease property, capital leases	$36,048	
Obligations, capital leases		$36,048

Amortization by Lessee

The asset(s) recorded under a capital lease shall be amortized in a manner consistent with lessee's normal depreciation policy for other owned assets. The period for amortization is either (1) the estimated economic life or (2) the lease term, depending on which criterion was used to classify the lease. If the criterion used to classify the lease as a capital lease was either criterion I (ownership of the property is transferred to the lessee by the end of the lease term) or criterion II (lease contains a bargain purchase option), the asset is amortized over its economic life. In all other cases, the asset is amortized over the lease term. Any residual value is deducted from the asset to determine the amortizable base.

Since the Paine Corporation's lease qualified under criterion IV (present value of the minimum lease payments, excluding executory costs and profit thereon paid by the lessor, is 90% or more of the fair value of the leased property), the amortization period must be over the lease term.

A schedule of amortization, interest expense, and lease obligation payments for Paine Corporation's computer lease, using the interest method, follows:

Book Value Lease Obligations Beginning of Year	Rental Payments	12% Interest on Beginning Book Value	Amortization	Book Value Lease Obligations End of Year
$36,048	$ 10,000	$ 4,326	$ 5,674	$30,374
30,374	10,000	3,645	6,355	24,019
24,019	10,000	2,882	7,118	16,901
16,901	10,000	2,028	7,972	8,929
8,929	10,000	1,071	8,929	—
	$50,000	$13,952	$36,048	

Note: The interest rate used is 12%, which is the interest rate implicit in the lease.

LONG-TERM CONSTRUCTION CONTRACTS

Overview

ARB-45 is the main source of promulgated GAAP on long-term construction-type contracts. Governmental contracts are specifically excluded from the promulgated GAAP and are discussed elsewhere in the chapter on government contracts.

> *OBSERVATION: The specialized accounting and auditing practices for construction contractors appear in the AICPA Industry Audit and Accounting Guide entitled "Construction Contractors." Specialized accounting practices also appear in the AICPA Statement of Position 81-1 (Accounting for Performance of Construction-Type and Certain Production-Type Contracts).*
>
> *The Construction Contractors Guide and SOP 81-1 were issued concurrently in 1981 and supersede the previous audit guide (Audits of Construction Contractors) issued in 1965. The Construction Contractors Guide primarily focuses on the construction industry, whereas SOP 81-1 makes recommendations on accounting issues that apply to a broad range of contracting activities.*
>
> *In the case of construction-type contracts, revenue may be recognized either by the completed-contract method or by the percentage-of-completion method. The percentage-of-completion method is preferable when the estimated cost to complete the contract and the extent of progress made on the contract are reasonably determinable. When estimates are unreliable, the completed-contract method should be used.*

Background

Because of the length of time involved in long-term construction contracts, the problem exists as to when income should be recognized. Two methods are generally followed to account for these long-term contracts: the completed-contract method and the percentage-of-completion method.

Completed-Contract Method

The completed-contract method recognizes income only on completion or substantial completion of the contract.

A contract is regarded as substantially complete if the remaining costs are insignificant.

Excess of accumulated costs over related billings should be reflected in the balance sheet as a current asset, and excess of accumulated billings over related costs should usually be reflected as a current liability. In the case of more than one contract, the accumulated costs or liabilities should be separately stated on the balance sheet. The preferred terminology for the balance sheet presentation should be *(Costs) (Billings) of uncompleted contracts in excess of related (billings) (costs)*.

In some cases, it is preferable to allocate general and administrative expenses to contract costs as opposed to period income. In years when no contracts are completed, a better matching of costs and revenues is achieved by carrying general expense as a charge to the contract. If a contractor has many jobs, however, it is more appropriate to charge these expenses to current periods.

In all cases, although income is not recognized until completion of the contract, a provision for an expected loss should be recognized when it becomes evident that a loss on the contract is apparent.

The primary advantage of the completed-contract method is that it is based on final results rather than on estimates. The primary disadvantage of the completed-contract method is that it does not reflect current performances when the period of the contract extends over more than one accounting period.

Accounting for the Completed-Contract Method

The following are important points to remember in accounting for contracts under the completed-contract method:

1. Charge applicable overhead and direct costs to a construction-in-progress account (an asset).
2. Credit billing and/or cash received to advances on construction-in-progress account (a liability).
3. At completion of the contract, gross profit or loss is recognized as follows:

   Contract price − total costs = gross profit or loss

4. At interim balance sheet dates, the excess of either the con-struction-in-progress account or the advances account over the other is classified as a current asset or a current liability. It is a *current* asset or a *current* liability because of the *normal operating cycle concept.*

5. An expected loss on the total contract is discovered by:

   a. Adding estimated costs to complete to the recorded costs to date to arrive at total contract costs

   b. Adding to advances any additional revenue expected to arrive at total contract revenue

   c. Subtracting b from a to arrive at total estimated loss on contract

Losses should be recognized in full in the year they are discovered.

Percentage-of-Completion Method

Revenues are generally recognized when (1) the earning process is complete or virtually complete and (2) an exchange has taken place.

Accounting for long-term construction contracts on the percent-age-of-completion method is an exception to the basic realization principle. This exception is based on the evidence that the ultimate proceeds are available and the consensus that a better measure of periodic income results (matching-of-revenue-and-cost principle).

The principal advantages of the percentage-of-completion method are the reflection of the status of the uncompleted contracts and the periodic recognition of the income currently rather than irregularly as contracts are completed.

The principal disadvantage of the percentage-of-completion method is the necessity of relying on estimates of the ultimate costs.

The percentage-of-completion method recognizes income as work progresses on the contract.

The recommended method for recognizing income is to deter-mine the percentage of estimated total income either (1) that incurred costs to date bear to total estimated costs based on the most recent costs information or (2) that may be indicated by such other measure or progress toward completion appropriate to the work performed.

During the early stages of a contract, all or a portion of items such as material and subcontract costs may be excluded if it appears that the results would produce a more meaningful allocation of periodic income.

When current estimates of the total contract costs indicate a loss, a provision for the loss on the entire contract should be made. However, when a loss is indicated on a total contract that is part of a related group of contracts, the group may be treated as a unit in determining the necessity of providing for losses.

Income to be recognized under the percentage-of-completion method at various stages should not ordinarily be measured by interim billings.

Accounting for the Percentage-of-Completion Method

The following are important points to remember in accounting for contracts under the percentage-of-completion method:

1. Journal entries and interim balance sheet treatment are the same as the completed-contract method *except* that the amount of estimated gross profit earned in each period is recorded by charging the construction in progress account and crediting realized gross profit.
2. Gross profit or loss is recognized in each period by the following formula:

$$\frac{\text{Total cost to date}}{\text{estimated total cost}} \times \frac{\text{total estimated}}{\text{gross profit or loss}} - \frac{\text{gross profit}}{\text{recognized to date}} = \frac{\text{realized gross profit}}{}$$

3. An estimated loss on the total contract is recognized immediately in the year it is discovered. However, any previous gross profit or loss reported in prior years must be deducted from the total estimated loss.

Choice of Method

The percentage-of-completion method is preferred when the estimated cost to complete and the extent of construction progress are reasonably determinable. When estimates are unreliable, the completed-contract method should be used.

Disclosure

Generally, long-term construction-type contracts require no special disclosure, since they are, in fact, the nature of the contractor's business. However, unusual extraordinary commitments should be fully disclosed in the financial statements or footnotes thereto.

Comprehensive Illustration

The following example demonstrates the accounting involved in both the completed-contract and percentage-of-completion methods:

The following data pertain to a $2,000,000 long-term construction contract:

	19X5	19X6	19X7
Costs incurred during the year	$ 500,000	$700,000	$ 300,000
Year-end estimated costs to complete	$1,000,000	$300,000	—
Billing during the year	$ 400,000	$700,000	$ 900,000
Collections during the year	$ 200,000	$500,000	$1,200,000

The journal entries for both the completed-contract method and the percentage-of-completion method for the three years are as follows:

19X5	Completed Contract		% of Completion	
Construction in progress	$ 500,000		$ 500,000	
Cash or liability		$ 500,000		$ 500,000
Accounts receivable	$ 400,000		$ 400,000	
Advance billings		$ 400,000		$ 400,000
Cash	$ 200,000		$ 200,000	
Accounts receivable		$ 200,000		$ 200,000
Construction in progress	no entry		$ 166,667	
Realized gross profit (P&L)				$ 166,667
19X6				
Construction in progress	$ 700,000		$ 700,000	
Cash or liability		$ 700,000		$ 700,000
Accounts receivable	$ 700,000		$ 700,000	
Advance billings		$ 700,000		$ 700,000
Cash	$ 500,000		$ 500,000	
Accounts receivable		$ 500,000		$ 500,000
Construction in progress	no entry		$ 233,333	
Realized gross profit (P&L)				$ 233,333
19X7				
Construction in progress	$ 300,000		$ 300,000	
Cash or liability		$ 300,000		$ 300,000
Accounts receivable	$ 900,000		$ 900,000	
Advance billings		$ 900,000		$ 900,000
Cash	$1,200,000		$1,200,000	
Accounts receivable		$1,200,000		$1,200,000
Construction in progress	no entry		$ 100,000	
Realized gross profit (P&L)				$ 100,000
Advance billings	$2,000,000		$2,000,000	
Construction in progress		$1,500,000		$2,000,000
Realized gross profit (P&L)		500,000		—

Computation of Realized Gross Profit
19X5

$$\frac{\$\ 500,000}{\$1,500,000} \quad \times \quad \$500,000 \quad - \quad 0 \quad = \quad \$166,667$$

19X6

$$\frac{\$1,200,000}{\$1,500,000} \quad \times \quad \$500,000 \quad - \quad \$166,667 \quad = \quad \$233,333$$

19X7

$$\frac{\$1,500,000}{\$1,500,000} \quad \times \quad \$500,000 \quad - \quad \$400,000 \quad = \quad \underline{\$100,000}$$

Total gross profit $\qquad\qquad\qquad$ $\underline{\underline{\$500,000}}$

LONG-TERM OBLIGATIONS

Overview

FASB-47 contains disclosure requirements for certain unconditional purchase obligations associated with financing arrangements that have not been recorded on the books, and separate disclosure requirements for (1) unconditional purchase obligations that have been recorded on the books, (2) maturities and sinking funds for long-term borrowing, and (3) redemptions of capital stock. The disclosure requirements in FASB-47 pertain to long-term obligations that have a remaining term in excess of one year. An unconditional purchase obligation is considered unconditional even if the agreement provides for cancellation in the event of some remote occurrence. FASB-47 encourages, but does not require, the disclosure of certain unconditional purchase obligations at their present values.

Background

Under existing accounting principles, exchanges between enterprises or individuals are usually recorded when the actual transfer of resources, services, and/or obligations occurs (APB Statement-4). However, unfulfilled purchase commitments for the future exchange of resources, services, and/or obligations are not recorded until the commitment is at least partially fulfilled by one of the contracting parties (APB Statement-4). Exceptions to the general rule for unfulfilled purchase commitments are certain leases and losses on firm noncancelable purchase commitments which are recorded under existing accounting principles. Commitments for leases that qualify for capitalization in accordance with FASB-13 are recorded for financial accounting purposes. In addition, losses on firm noncancelable purchase commitments are recognized in the accounts and, if material, disclosed separately in the income statement.

Enterprises and/or individuals frequently acquire assets or liabilities by written contract. A contract may contain unconditional rights and obligations or conditional rights and obligations. A right or obligation is unconditional when nothing but the passage of time is necessary for the right or obligation to mature. On the other hand, a conditional right or obligation is one that matures only on the occurrence of one or more events that are specified in the contract.

If a significant period elapses between the execution and subsequent performance of a contract, a problem may arise as to when, if at all, the asset and/or liabilities created by the contract should be recognized by the contracting parties. Under existing accounting practices, assets and/or liabilities that are created by a contract may not be recognized at all, or may be either recognized in the accounts or disclosed by footnote.

> **OBSERVATION:** *An FASB Research Report entitled "Recognition of Contractual Rights and Obligations," by Yuji Ijiri (December 1980), contains an excellent discussion on this topic.*

The disclosure of certain contractual rights or obligations is sometimes confused with the disclosure of a contingency. However, the disclosure of a contingency is necessary only when there is a contingent *gain* or *loss* in accordance with the provisions of FASB-5. If there is no contingent *gain* or *loss*, disclosure is not required. On the other hand, the disclosure of information on certain contractual rights or obligations may be required by GAAP to avoid misleading financial statements.

A situation may arise in which the disclosure of a contractual obligation is required by GAAP and, at the same time, a *loss contingency* may exist involving the same contractual obligation. In this event, the disclosure of the information concerning the contractual obligation would have to be presented in accordance with GAAP, and the disclosure of the loss contingency would also have to be made in accordance with GAAP.

Unconditional Purchase Obligations

For the purposes of FASB-47, an unconditional purchase obligation is one in which one party is required to transfer funds to another party in return for future delivery of specified quantities of goods or services at specified prices.

> **OBSERVATION:** *The definition of an unconditional purchase obligation, for the purposes of FASB-47, is one in which one party is required to make a transfer of funds to another party in return for specified quantities of goods or services at specified prices. Thus, an unconditional purchase obligation to transfer assets, other than funds, to another party in return for specified quantities of goods or*

services at specified prices, is not considered an unconditional obligation and, apparently, would not be covered by FASB-47.

Under FASB-47, the unconditional purchase obligation must be associated with the financing arrangements (a) for the facilities that will provide the contracted goods or services or (b) relating to the costs of the contracted goods or services (such as carrying costs, etc.). Unconditional purchase obligations that have a remaining term of one year or less are excluded from the provisions of FASB-47. In addition, an unconditional purchase obligation qualifies for FASB-47, even though it is cancelable, because of:

1. A remote contingency
2. Permission of the other party
3. A replacement agreement between the same parties
4. A provision for a penalty payment in an amount which reasonably assures the continuation of the agreement

The provisions in FASB-47 concerning unconditional purchase obligations cover the purchaser's disclosure requirements and are primarily directed to take-or-pay contracts and throughput contracts.

> **OBSERVATION:** *In a take-or-pay contract a buyer agrees to pay certain periodic amounts for certain products or services. The buyer must make the specified periodic payments, even though it does not take delivery of the products or services.*
>
> *In a throughput contract, one party agrees to pay certain periodic amounts to another party for the transportation or processing of a product. The periodic payments must be made, even though the minimum quantities specified in the agreement in each period have not been sent to the other party for transporting or processing.*
>
> *In a take-or-pay contract and a throughput contract, the periodic payments are unconditional and are not dependent on the occurrence of a specified event or the fulfillment of a condition.*

Minimum lease payments that are required to be disclosed in accordance with FASB-13 need not be disclosed in accordance with FASB-47. However, minimum lease payments that are not required to be disclosed in accordance with FASB-13 must be disclosed in accordance with FASB-47 if they meet the requirements for disclosure outlined in FASB-47.

> **OBSERVATION**: *Apparently, FASB-47 requires the disclosure of certain leases that were specifically excluded from FASB-13, if such leases are (1) substantially noncancelable, (2) part of the financing arrangements for the facilities that will provide specified goods or services, or related to the costs for the specified goods or services, and (3) for a remaining term in excess of one year. The following types of leases and similar agreements were expressly excluded from FASB-13 and may require disclosure under the provisions of FASB-47:*

> 1. *Natural resource leases, including oil, gas, minerals, and timber*
> 2. *Leases involving services only*
> 3. *Licensing agreements, including motion picture films, plays, manuscripts, patents, and copyrights*

> *Furthermore, despite the similarity to take-or-pay contracts, "nuclear fuel heat supply contracts" are specifically included in FASB-13 as leases and therefore are not covered by FASB-47.*

Disclosure of Unrecorded Unconditional Purchase Obligations

Unrecorded unconditional purchase obligations that are (1) substantially noncancelable, (2) associated with the financing arrangements (a) for the facilities that will provide the contracted goods or services or (b) relating to the costs of the contracted goods or services (such as carrying costs, etc.), and (3) for a remaining term in excess of one year must be disclosed by footnote in the purchaser's financial statements. The disclosures must include:

1. A description of the nature and term of the obligation
2. The total determinable amount of unrecorded unconditional purchase obligations as of the latest balance sheet date, and the total determinable amount of unrecorded unconditional purchase obligations for each of the five years after the latest balance sheet date
3. A description of the nature of any variable component of the unrecorded unconditional purchase obligations
4. For each income statement presented, the amounts actually purchased under the unconditional purchase obligations

> **OBSERVATION**: *An unconditional obligation may consist of a determinable portion and a variable portion. The determinable portion is quantified and disclosed in accordance with item 2 above. The variable portion need not be quantified, but the nature of such amounts must be disclosed in accordance with item 3 above.*

Similar or related obligations may be combined and disclosures are not required if the aggregate commitment of all unrecorded unconditional purchase obligations is immaterial.

FASB-47 does not require, but does encourage, the disclosure of the present value of the total determinable amounts of unrecorded unconditional purchase obligations for each of the five years after the latest balance sheet date (item 2 above). In computing the present value of an obligation, the discount rate is usually evident. In most cases, the discount rate is the effective interest rate at the inception of the borrowings that (1) financed the project or (2) are associated with the unrecorded unconditional purchase obligations. If it is not practical to determine the discount rate, or if there are no borrowings associated with the obligations, the discount rate that should be used is the purchaser's incremental borrowing rate. The purchaser's incremental borrowing rate is the rate the purchaser would have incurred at the inception of the obligation to borrow funds, on similar terms, to discharge the unconditional purchase obligation.

The disclosure of the present value of the total determinable amount of unconditional purchase obligations, and the disclosure of the nature of any variable component of the unconditional purchase obligations should be presented as follows:

Year	Total Required Payments
19X1	$ 100,000
19X2	100,000
19X3	200,000
19X4	200,000
19X5	200,000
Subsequent years	700,000
Total	1,500,000
Less: Imputed interest	350,000
Present value of required payments	$1,150,000

In addition to the determinable required payments presented above, the company is required to periodically pay 12% of the variable operating expenses of the plant of the X Corporation. (**Note:** For each income statement presented, the amounts actually purchased under the unconditional purchase obligations would also have to be disclosed.)

Disclosure of Other Unconditional Obligations

FASB-47 does not change prior GAAP related to recording as liabilities certain unconditional purchase obligations, or the accounting treatment of future obligations that are substantially the same as certain obligations that are recorded as liabilities. In addition, FASB-47 reaffirms that the economic substance of a transaction should be recorded, rather than the legal form of the transaction.

The following specific disclosures must be made as of the date of the latest balance sheet presented:

1. For each of the five years immediately following the latest balance sheet date, the amount of payments for recorded unconditional purchase obligations that meet the disclosure provisions of FASB-47. In addition, all amounts due after the fifth year shall be disclosed in a caption labeled "subsequent years" (see illustration #1 below). The disclosure provisions of FASB-47 require that an unconditional purchase obligation (a) be substantially noncancelable, (b) have a remaining term in excess of one year, and (c) be associated with the financing arrangements for facilities that will provide the contracted goods or services or relating to the costs of the contracted goods or services (such as carrying costs, etc.).

> **OBSERVATION:** *The above disclosure requirements cover unconditional purchase obligations that meet the criteria of paragraph 6 of FASB-47 and which have been recorded on the purchaser's balance sheet. Thus, the asset and corresponding liability is recorded on the books and in addition, the above disclosure requirements of FASB-47 must also be made.*

2. For each of the five years immediately following the latest balance sheet date, the combined total of maturities and sink-

ing fund requirements for all long-term borrowings (see illustration #2 below).

3. For each of the five years immediately following the latest balance sheet date, the total of required redemptions (separately or combined) for all classes of capital stock that are redeemable at determinable prices on determinable dates (see illustration #3 below).

Illustration #1—Take-or-Pay, Throughput, and Similar Contracts

X Company has entered into a long-term contract to purchase all of the widgets produced by a supplier. The contract expires in 1995, and X Company must make minimum annual payments to the supplier, whether or not it is able to take delivery of the widgets. The minimum total payments for each of the five years and later years succeeding December 31, 19X1, are as follows:

Year	Total Payments (in thousands)
19X2	$ 4,000
19X3	12,000
19X4	14,000
19X5	10,000
19X6	12,000
Subsequent years	28,000
Total	80,000
Less: Imputed interest	30,000
Present value of payments	$ 50,000

(**Note:** FASB-47 requires the disclosure of the above information for periods subsequent to the fifth year, as reflected in the above illustration.)

Illustration #2—Maturities and Sinking Fund Requirements

Maturities of long-term debt and sinking fund requirements on long-term debt for each of the five years succeeding December 31, 19X1, are as follows:

Year	Long-Term Debt and Sinking Fund Requirements
19X2	$ 50,000
19X3	50,000
19X4	100,000
19X5	100,000
19X6	50,000

(**Note:** FASB-47 does not require the disclosure of the above information for periods subsequent to the fifth year.)

Illustration #3—Redemption of Capital Stock

Mandatory redemption requirements for all classes of capital stock for each of the five years succeeding December 31, 19X1, are as follows:

Year	4% Preferred	7% Preferred
19X2	$ 200,000	$ 400,000
19X3	200,000	400,000
19X4	200,000	400,000
19X5	none	400,000
19X6	none	400,000

(**Note:** FASB-47 does not require the disclosure of the above information for periods subsequent to the fifth year.)

> **OBSERVATION:** *If an unconditional obligation is not recorded on the books of an enterprise, the disclosures required by FASB-47 may be misleading to readers of financial statements because the benefits, if any, that are associated with the disclosed obligations are not required to be disclosed. When a lease is capitalized in accordance with FASB-13, both the asset (benefit) and a liability (obligation) are recognized on the books. However, if the unconditional obligation is not recorded, an enterprise may be unconditionally obligated to pay millions of dollars over a specified period, under a take-or-pay contract, for a continuous supply of natural gas. Under FASB-47, the unconditional obligation would have to be disclosed. However, the associated benefits, such as an assured supply of natural gas at a fixed price, are not required to be disclosed.*

> *Paragraph 7(a) of FASB-47, which requires a statement about the nature and term of the obligation, may be the place for an enterprise to appropriately describe the associated benefits, if any. The last sentence of paragraph 19, Appendix A, of FASB-47 states that "The lack of explicit requirements to disclose associated benefits does not preclude an enterprise from describing those benefits."*

Effective Date

FASB-47 is effective for fiscal years ending on or after June 16, 1981, and earlier application is encouraged. However, the amounts actually purchased under unconditional purchase obligations for each income statement presented do not have to be disclosed for comparative purposes for periods that began prior to the effective date of FASB-47.

Product Financing Arrangements

FASB-47 contains specific disclosure requirements for recorded and unrecorded take-or-pay and throughput contracts. Both of these types of contracts are considered unconditional obligations under the provisions of FASB-47. However, a take-or-pay or throughput contract may, in substance, be a product financing arrangement. A product financing arrangement may also require unconditional periodic payments that are not dependent on the occurrence of a specified event or the fulfillment of a specified condition. The problem is that product financing arrangements that are unconditional obligations are accounted for much differently from take-or-pay and throughput contracts. Product financing arrangements are covered elsewhere in this publication in the chapter entitled "Product Financing Arrangements."

MARKETABLE SECURITIES

Overview

Accounting for certain marketable securities is covered by FASB-12 and four subsequent FASB Interpretations, as follows:

- 11—Changes in Market Value After the Balance Sheet Date
- 12—Accounting for Previously Established Allowance Accounts
- 13—Consolidation of a Parent and Its Subsidiaries Having Different Balance Sheet Dates
- 16—Clarification of Definitions and Accounting for Marketable Equity Securities that Become Nonmarketable

FASB-80 (Accounting for Futures Contracts) is discussed at the end of this section, after the discussion on marketable securities. FASB Technical Bulletin 85-2 (Accounting for Collateralized Mortgage Obligations [CMOs] is discussed at the end of the chapter entitled "Mortgage Banking Industry."

FASB Technical Bulletin 79-19 was issued to provide guidance to an investor in accounting for its proportionate share of an investee's valuation allowance account for noncurrent marketable securities.

The procedures enumerated herein apply to all companies, including mutual savings banks, that do not have specialized accounting practices in accounting for marketable securities. In addition, some of the promulgated GAAP apply to those companies in industries that do have specialized accounting practices in accounting for marketable securities.

Nonprofit organizations, mutual life insurance companies, and employee benefit plans are specifically excluded from complying with the promulgated GAAP. Nonmarketable securities are not covered and are completely excluded.

Investments accounted for by the equity method are generally not covered by FASB-12.

Background

The promulgated GAAP (FASB-12) differentiate between those industries having specialized accounting practices with respect to marketable equity securities and those that have no specialized practices.

An equity security is defined as any instrument that represents an ownership share or the right to acquire or sell an ownership share at a determinable price. This includes stock options, warrants, rights, puts, calls, and common, preferred, and other forms of capital stock. Preferred stock that is redeemable at the option of the owner or must be redeemed by the issuer is specifically excluded from the definition of an equity security for purposes of the promulgated GAAP, as are treasury stock and convertible bonds.

> *Realized gain or loss* is the difference between the net proceeds from the sale of a marketable security and its cost.
>
> *Unrealized gain or loss* is the difference between the market value and the cost of a marketable security.

Marketability

In order for a security to be classified as a marketable security, it must be marketable. Marketability is evidenced by whether a security can be readily bought or sold. A current *bid* and *ask* price is evidence of marketability for both over-the-counter stocks and stocks traded on a national exchange, except that over-the-counter quotations issued by the National Quotations Bureau, Inc., may not be used unless three quotations are available.

The determination of marketability is made as of the balance sheet date.

Marketability of equity securities traded on foreign markets is determined in the same way, provided the foreign market's trading volume and scope of activities are comparable to a U.S. counterpart.

Restricted or legend stock is not considered marketable unless it can qualify for sale within one year and is marketable as defined herein. Market prices for unrestricted shares of the same class of stock that is restricted can be used in determining marketability.

A temporary lack of market (no trades or quotations) at the balance sheet date does not render an equity security nonmarketable if a market closely precedes the balance sheet date. Moreover, if the balance sheet date falls on a day when markets are closed, the first trading day afterward should be used. Where the lack of quotations by NASDAQ or the lack of three quotations from the National Quotations Bureau, Inc., for the over-the-counter securities is temporary, a market price may be determined by the following:

1. The first quotation by NASDAQ preceding the balance sheet date

2. One quotation from the National Quotations Bureau, Inc., on the balance sheet date or on the first day preceding the balance sheet date that quotations are available

Industries Not Having Specialized Practices

Any company that does not account for marketable securities by a specialized industry practice should follow these procedures for accounting for them:

1. Marketable securities should be classified into two groups: (i) a current group and (ii) a noncurrent group. *In the case of unclassified balance sheets, all marketable securities are to be classified as noncurrent.*
2. The total cost and the total market for each group should be determined.
3. The carrying amount of each group is the lower of cost or market for each group.
4. Unrealized losses on the group classified as current are deducted on the income statement in determining net income for the period. The credit side of the entry is to a valuation account as follows:

Loss on marketable securities	$X,XXX	
Allowances for losses, marketable securities		$X,XXX

5. Unrealized losses on the group classified as noncurrent are reported separately as a reduction of stockholders' equity. The credit side of the entry is to a valuation account, as follows:

Stockholders' equity	$X,XXX	
Allowances for losses, noncurrent marketable securities		$X,XXX

6. Subsequent unrealized gains or losses are reported in the same manner (the current group through the income statement and the noncurrent group through the equity section of the balance sheet). *However, under no circumstances can either the current group or the noncurrent group be valued in excess of the original cost of the group.*

Unrealized losses on the noncurrent group of marketable securities are reported as a reduction of stockholders' equity, whereas unrealized losses on the current group are reported as a reduction of net income.

Allowance for losses accounts for both groups are *contra accounts* and are deducted from the related groups for balance sheet purposes.

Reclassification   Any change of a particular security from one group (current or noncurrent) to the other group (current or noncurrent) must be made at the lower of cost or market on the date of transfer. The lower of cost or market on the date of transfer becomes the new cost basis, and any gain (to the extent of prior realized or unrealized losses) or loss is accounted for as if realized and is included in the determination of net income for the period.

Subsequent unrealized gains or losses   Subsequent unrealized gains or losses are recorded by adjusting the allowance for losses account, except that under no circumstances can either group be valued in excess of its original cost.

Sale of a security   A sale of a security from either the current or the noncurrent group results in a realized gain or loss and is reported in the income statement for the period. The cost of the security sold will usually be its original cost unless it was transferred from one group to another or a security in the noncurrent group was written down as a result of a decline in market value that was not temporary.

> **OBSERVATION**: *Since unrealized losses in both the current and noncurrent portfolios are based on the aggregate cost or market of the entire portfolio, the original cost of each security in each portfolio is not changed. Therefore, when a security is sold, its original cost is deducted from the portfolio and the aggregate cost, market, and related valuation account are recomputed. The only time an original cost of a security is changed is when it is transferred from one group to another or if a security in the noncurrent group is written down as a result of a decline in its market price that is other than temporary.*

An entity that is consolidated with a parent shall first determine its total cost and market for its current group and its noncurrent group before combining those aggregate totals with the parent's aggregate totals.

In the consolidation of a parent's statements with a subsidiary's statements of a different balance sheet date, the following applies (FASB Interpretation-13):

1. The parent and each subsidiary comply with the promulgated GAAP as at the date of their own balance sheet, and then the aggregate totals are combined for consolidation purposes.

2. Intervening events occurring between the balance sheet date of the subsidiary and that of the parent which materially affect the financial position or the results of operations should be adequately recognized or disclosed in the consolidated financial statements (ARB-51).

The marketable securities of an investment accounted for by the equity method shall not be combined with those of the investor. Obviously, such an entity could, itself, be subject to the provisions of the promulgated GAAP (FASB-12).

> **OBSERVATION:** *Changes in the stockholders' equity of an investment accounted for by the equity method (APB-18), which is the result of a decline in the market value of noncurrent marketable securities, are not covered by FASB-12. APB-18 requires that an investor record its proportionate share of the capital transactions of an investment accounted for by the equity method. FASB Technical Bulletin 79-19 requires that an investor reduce its investment accounted for by the equity method, by its proportionate share of the investee's valuation allowance account for noncurrent marketable securities. In addition, the investor should include in its stockholders' equity its proportionate share of the investee's valuation allowance account.*

Disclosure The following disclosures for marketable securities shall be made in the financial statements or footnotes thereto by a company which does not follow specialized industry accounting practices for marketable equity securities.

1. As at the date of each balance sheet presented, the total cost and market value of marketable equity securities indicating which is the carrying value for:

    a. Total marketable securities

    b. Total current marketable securities

    c. Total noncurrent marketable securities

2. As at the date of the most recent balance sheet presented, the total gross unrealized gains and the total gross unrealized losses for:

    a. Total marketable securities

    b. Total current marketable securities

    c. Total noncurrent marketable securities

3. For each income statement presented:

    a. The net realized gain or loss included in net income

    b. The cost basis that was used in computing realized gain or loss

    c. The change in any valuation account that has been included in the equity section of the balance sheet, and the amount of any change that was included in the determination of net income

In unclassified balance sheets, the above disclosures for the current portfolio are omitted.

4. In consolidated balance sheets that contain both specialized and nonspecialized practices for accounting for marketable securities, the disclosure requirements for both should be made.

5. Significant net realized and net unrealized gains and losses on marketable securities arising after the date of the balance sheet and prior to their issuance should be disclosed.

Financial statements should not be adjusted for realized gains and losses or for changes in market values of marketable securities that occur subsequent to the balance sheet date. A special procedure is discussed later for permanent declines in the noncurrent portfolio of marketable securities.

Industries Having Specialized Practices

Investment companies, brokers, and dealers in securities, stock life and casualty insurance companies, and other industries that follow specialized practices in accounting for marketable securities must comply with the promulgated GAAP (FASB-12) to a limited extent, as follows:

1. Marketable equity securities must be carried at the lower of cost or market, except market has a broader definition in those industries which do have specialized practices for marketable securities.
2. Market value may be whatever is permitted in a specific specialized industry, such as appraised value or fair value.

> **OBSERVATION:** *In industries in which either the cost basis or the market basis is accepted practice, an election to use the market basis does not require justification as an accounting change APB-20) or compliance with the related disclosure requirements (FASB-12).*

3. Marketable securities should be classified into a current group and a noncurrent group. In unclassified balance sheets, all marketable securities are to be classified as noncurrent. This provision is exactly the same as that for industries which do not have specialized practices.
4. The aggregate carrying amount of a portfolio of marketable securities is the lower of cost or market (as defined herein) at the balance sheet date. A valuation account shall be used to record any excess of aggregate cost of a portfolio over aggregate market value. This provision is exactly the same as for industries which do not have specialized practices in accounting for marketable securities, except for the broader definition of market value.
5. Marketable securities portfolios of investments accounted for by the equity method should not be combined with portfolios of the investors.
6. Portfolios of entities that use the same specialized industry accounting practices for marketable securities should be combined into a single portfolio to determine the aggregate lower of cost or market value.
7. Specialized industry practices for reporting realized or unrealized gains or losses on marketable securities are not changed by the promulgated GAAP.
8. If a parent company recognizes realized gains or losses on marketable securities in determining net income, all subsidiar-

ies and investments accounted for by the equity method must conform to this practice for the purposes of consolidation. Otherwise, accepted accounting practices for marketable securities followed by a subsidiary or an investment accounted for by the equity method shall be retained in consolidating, even if such practices differ from those of the parent.

> **OBSERVATION**: *Since realized gains and losses are almost always recognized (GAAP), the only subsidiary or investment accounted for by the equity method that could logically be subject to conforming is one which follows a specialized industry practice that does not recognize realized gains or losses.*

9. When two or more subsidiaries do not follow specialized industry practices and are consolidated with a parent which does follow specialized industry practices, the current and noncurrent portfolios of such subsidiaries are kept separate from those of the parent in consolidating, for the purpose of determining carrying amounts.

Disclosures   The following disclosures for marketable securities shall be made in the financial statements or footnotes thereto by a company which follows specialized industry accounting practices for marketable equity securities.

1. For companies that include unrealized gains and losses on marketable securities in the equity section of the balance sheet and not in the determination of net income:

    a. As at the most recent balance sheet the gross unrealized gains and the gross unrealized losses
    b. For each income statement presented, the changes in net unrealized gains or losses

2. In consolidated balance sheets that contain both specialized and nonspecialized practices for accounting for marketable securities, the disclosure requirements for both should be made.

3. Significant net realized and net unrealized gains and losses on marketable securities arising after the balance sheet date and prior to their issuance should be disclosed.

Financial statements should not be adjusted for realized gains and losses or changes in market values of marketable securities that occur subsequent to the balance sheet date. A special procedure is discussed later for permanent declines in the noncurrent portfolio of marketable securities.

For the purpose of companies that follow specialized accounting practices, unrealized gains and losses are those which constitute the present accepted practice in a particular industry (FASB-12).

Other Than Temporary Declines—Noncurrent Group

The provisions in this section apply to all companies, whether or not they follow specialized industry practices in accounting for marketable equity securities.

As mentioned previously, a decline in one or more securities of the noncurrent group is handled as a reduction of the equity section of the balance sheet and does not enter into the determination of net income for the period. Under these circumstances, a permanent decline in a security of the noncurrent group would never be recognized in net income. However, FASB-12 provides an exception for declines in securities of the noncurrent group that are *other than temporary*. Under FASB-12, an other than temporary decline in a marketable security that exists on the balance sheet date must be recognized in the net income of the period in which the decline is discovered. The decline is usually equal to the difference between the recorded cost of the security and its current market price, or net realizable value, at the balance sheet date. *Thus, if a decline in one or more securities of the noncurrent group is other than temporary, the loss is recognized in the income statement for that period and not as a reduction of the equity section of the balance sheet.* The journal entry is:

Realized loss on marketable securities $XX,XXX

    Investment in marketable securities $XX,XXX

If a noncurrent marketable security is written down because of a loss that is other than temporary, and the security remains a part of the noncurrent group, any subsequent increase in value is not recognized in the income statement, but is used in the computation of the total unrealized gain or loss on the noncurrent group and is applied as a reduction or increase of the equity section of the balance sheet.

To determine whether a decline at the balance sheet date is permanent or temporary, reference to changes in market price or a realized gain or loss that occurs subsequent to the balance sheet date but prior to the issuance of the financial statements should be taken into consideration. However, the amount of permanent decline for an individual marketable security cannot exceed the amount that existed at the date of the balance sheet. Recoveries of a permanent decline in a marketable security after the balance sheet date and prior to the issuance of the financial statements should be taken into consideration, because such a recovery tends to indicate that all or part of the decline was, in fact, not permanent (FASB Interpretation-11).

FASB-12 does not discuss the difference between a decline in a current or noncurrent marketable security that is (a) permanent, (b) other than temporary, or (c) temporary. An Auditing Interpretation issued in January 1975 by the AICPA states that declines in marketable securities that reflect general market conditions may or may not be indicative of the ability of an enterprise to ultimately recover the carrying amount of an investment. However, the continued existence of a decline in a particular marketable security is indicative of an uncertainty, which may necessitate financial statement disclosure or a qualification of the auditor's opinion. If specific adverse conditions exist for a particular marketable security, a write-down in the carrying amount is necessary, unless persuasive evidence exists to the contrary.

The staff of the SEC takes the position that the phrase *other than temporary* in FASB-12 is not intended to mean *permanent impairment*, as that term is used elsewhere in professional accounting literature (SEC Staff Bulletin No. 59). The SEC staff believes that the following factors, individually or in combination, indicate that a decline is other than temporary and that a write-down of the carrying value of the noncurrent marketable security is required:

- The length of time and the extent to which the market value of the security has been less than its cost

- The financial condition and near-term prospects of the issuer, including any specific events which may influence the operations of the issuer, such as changes in technology that may impair the earnings potential of the investment or the discontinuance of a segment of the business that may affect the future earnings potential

- The intent and ability of the holder to retain its investment in the issuer for a period of time sufficient to allow for any anticipated recovery in the market value of the security

The SEC staff concludes that unless evidence exists to support a realizable value equal to or greater than the carrying value of the noncurrent marketable security, a write-down accounted for as a realized loss should be recorded.

Income Tax Effects

Tax effects of unrealized gains or losses entering into the determination of net income must be reflected in the computation of deferred income taxes. *However, the tax effects of unrealized capital losses should be recognized only when it is absolutely certain that the benefit will be realized by the offset of the capital losses against capital gains.*

Comprehensive Illustration

The following schedule of marketable securities was prepared for the LKM Corporation:

Schedule 1
MARKETABLE SECURITIES PORTFOLIO

		First Year			Second Year	
	Cost	Market	Unrealized Gain (Loss)	Cost	Market	Unrealized Gain (Loss)
Current Group:						
Security A	$1,000	$1,500	$ 500	$1,000	$1,500	$ 50
Security B	4,000	3,500	(500)	4,000	4,500	500
Security C	3,000	2,000	(1,000)	3,000	3,500	500
Totals	$8,000	$7,000	$(1,000)	$8,000	$9,500	$1,500
Noncurrent Group:						
Security X	$2,000	$2,500	$ 500	$2,000	$2,000	
Security Y	1,500	1,000	(500)	1,500	2,000	$ 500
Security Z	6,000	5,500	(500)	6,000	5,200	(800)
Totals	$9,500	$9,000	$ (500)	$9,500	$9,200	$(300)

At the end of the first year, the carrying amount of the current group is the total market value of $7,000. Since the original cost was $8,000, the $1,000 unrealized loss must be recorded, as follows:

Loss on marketable securities	$1,000	
Allowance for losses, current marketable securities		$1,000

The carrying value of the noncurrent group at the end of the first year is the market value of $9,000. Since the original cost was $9,500, the unrealized loss of $500 must be recorded, as follows:

Stockholders' equity	$ 500	
Allowance for losses, noncurrent marketable securities		$ 500

The unrealized loss of $500 on the noncurrent marketable securities is deducted from the equity section of the balance sheet and does not enter into the determination of net income for the period.

At the end of the second year, the carrying value of the current group is $8,000 (the original cost), even though the market value is $9,500, because *the valuation may never exceed the original cost*. The journal entry to adjust the valuation account is:

Allowance for losses, current marketable securities	$1,000	
Gain on marketable securities		$1,000

The gain on marketable securities appears in the income statement for the period.

The carrying value of the noncurrent group at the end of the second year is the market value of $9,200, which is $300 less than the original cost of $9,500. However, the net book value is $9,000 ($9,500 original cost, less allowance for losses account of $500), so the allowance for losses account must be reduced from $500 to $300, as follows:

Allowance for losses, noncurrent marketable securities	$ 200	
Stockholders' equity		$ 200

The unrealized gain of $200 on the noncurrent group is not reported in the income statement, but it reduces the allowance for losses account set up the previous year.

Reversals of previous year's writedowns are not considered as unrealized gains, but as a change in an accounting estimate of a prior realized loss. Actually, the original writedown represented a reduction in the net realizable value of the marketable securities, and any subsequent recovery reduces or eliminates the need for an allowance for losses account.

ACCOUNTING FOR FUTURES CONTRACTS

Overview

FASB-80 establishes the promulgated GAAP for reporting futures contracts that are traded on commodities and other exchanges. Neither foreign currency futures contracts nor forward placement or delayed delivery contracts are covered by FASB-80. Foreign currency futures contracts should be accounted for in accordance with FASB-52 (Foreign Currency Translation). Forward placement or delayed delivery contracts should be accounted for in accordance with prevailing accepted accounting principles and practices. FASB-80 applies to general purpose financial statements of all enterprises.

FASB-80 rescinds FASB Technical Bulletin 81-1 (Disclosure of Interest Rate Futures Contracts and Forward and Standby Contracts).

The thrust of FASB-80 is that changes in the market value of a futures contract must be recognized in the period of change, unless the futures contract qualifies as a hedge.

Background

Many types of commodities are traded on various commodity exchanges. Examples of some of the many types of commodities traded include grains such as wheat, barley, corn, oats, etc.; metals such as gold, silver, platinum, copper, lead, zinc, etc.; meats such as cattle, pork bellies, turkeys, etc.; financial instruments such as commercial paper, Treasury bills, bonds and notes, GNMA mortgages, etc.; and miscellaneous items such as cotton, plywood, eggs, soybeans, etc.

Commodities, like securities, may be purchased long or sold short. Each commodity contract involves a specified quantity of the commodity.

A commodity may be traded in the form of a spot contract or a futures contract. A spot contract is for the current month and usually involves paying cash and taking physical delivery of the commodity. However, the great majority of commodity transactions involve futures contracts. This is because most investors do not want actual delivery of the commodity and therefore *cover* their positions before the spot month (the month in which the commodity contract expires). Some commodity contracts, such as stock index futures and Eurodollar time deposit futures, do not involve the delivery of a commodity; and all outstanding contracts are settled for cash on their last day of trading. For every *buy* or *long* futures contract there must be a corresponding *sell* or *short* futures contract.

Futures contracts are traded on the basis that an investor agrees to buy or sell a certain quantity of a specific commodity in a specific future month and at a specific price. Thus, in June 19X1 an investor can agree to buy 100 ounces of gold in June 19X2 at a price that is agreed upon at the inception of the contract (June 19X1). If the price of gold rises six months later, the value of the June 19X2 gold futures contract will increase proportionately. In this event, the investor can make a profit by disposing of his *long* position. On the other hand, if the investor thought that the price of gold was going to decrease over the next year, a contract for 100 ounces of June 19X2 gold should be sold short. In this event, if the price of gold does decline, the investor can make a profit by disposing of his *short* position. The difference between the purchase price and selling price of a contract, less brokerage commission, is the investor's profit. If commodities are purchased or sold on margin, an investor's profit is decreased by the amount of interest paid on the margin account.

The commodity markets play an important role in the economy of the United States. The process of hedging is an integral part of many businesses and would not be possible without the existing commodity futures markets. Over the past few years, there has been a significant increase in the volume of futures transactions involving prime financial paper and future interest rates. Most of the increase in activity can be associated with hedging transactions. For example, savings and loan associations frequently hedge their actual position in GNMA mortgages by buying or selling futures contracts of GNMA mortgages which trade on the Chicago Board of Trade. Farmers, food processors, metal manufacturers, millers, and others who must store large quantities of commodities as inventory can minimize their exposure to price fluctuation by hedging their positions. For example, if a farmer believes that the price of his crop of corn is going to be substantially less at his expected harvest time, he can sell corn futures today and make actual delivery of the corn when his crop is ready for harvest. Alternatively, the farmer can close out his short position by purchasing spot contracts of corn in the month he is ready to sell his crop. The profit made on the commodity contracts will offset the decline in the market value of the farmer's corn.

Some commodities are regulated by the Commodities Exchange Act, and some commodities are not regulated. Most regulated commodities are in the agricultural industries, such as grains, eggs, potatoes, cotton, and soybeans. The most important federal regulations (a) require that commodity exchange members submit daily reports of their commodity trading activity and (b) limit the number of futures contracts in any one commodity that any one person or enterprise can acquire for speculation purposes.

Transactions on commodity exchanges are cleared and settled by a clearing association appointed by the exchange. Thus, all buy and sell transactions in futures commodity contracts are handled by a clearing association. A settlement price for all open commodity contracts is established at the close of business each day by all commodity exchanges. This process is referred to as *marking-to-market*. Each broker must settle his net difference on all open contracts in cash each day with the clearing association. On the broker's books the daily settlement is posted to a contract difference account, which is subsequently posted to each customer's account to reflect any gain or loss.

Accounting for Speculative Futures Contracts

The minimum contract deposit that is paid to a commodity broker for the purchase of a futures contract is usually recorded by an enterprise as an asset (due from commodity broker). The recorded asset is then increased or decreased during the period the futures contract is outstanding to take into account the changes in the market value of the futures contract. The changes in the market value of a futures contract that does not meet the hedge criteria established by FASB-80 (see below) must be reported by an enterprise as a gain or loss in the period in which the change occurs. A change in the market value of a futures contract is calculated by multiplying the size of the contract by the change in the contract's quoted market price.

> **OBSERVATION:** *Broker's commissions and related costs should be capitalized as part of the cost of acquiring the asset.*

Hedge Criteria Established by FASB-80

Under FASB-80, a futures contract that hedges an existing or anticipated exposure to price or interest rate changes shall qualify as a hedge if all of the following conditions are met:

Must be designated as a hedge   A futures contract must be designated by an enterprise as a hedge of identifiable assets, liabilities, firm commitments, or anticipated transactions. A futures contract cannot be accounted for as a hedge until the date it is designated as a hedge by the enterprise. In order to be designated as a hedge, a futures contract must effectively reduce the enterprise's exposure to the risk of changes in price or interest rates.

> *OBSERVATION: FASB-80 gives management the opportunity to choose how to report changes in the market value of futures contracts that relate to hedge situations. If management designates the contract as a hedge (and all the other criteria are satisfied), a change in the market value of the contract is not reflected in income until the related transaction is completed. On the other hand, if management does not designate the contract as a hedge, a change in the market value of the contract is recognized as gain or loss when it appears.*

Exposure to the risk of changes in price or interest rates   The hedged item must be exposed to the risk of changes in market prices or interest rates. Thus, in order for the transaction to qualify as an economic hedge, the hedged item must contribute to the enterprise's risk associated with changes in prices or interest rates. The existence of risk associated with changes in prices or interest rates and whether a futures contract reduces that risk may be apparent or may require extensive analysis and judgment. However, FASB-80 does not permit a futures contract to be accounted for as a hedge of any item that is already effectively hedged by other assets, liabilities, commitments, or other transactions of an enterprise.

The assessment of price risk may be done on a decentralized basis if an enterprise cannot otherwise assess such risk on the basis of the enterprise as a whole and the risk management activities can be assessed on a decentralized basis.

Must reduce exposure to the risk of changes in price or interest rates   The changes in the market value of a futures contract must be highly correlated, at the inception of the contract and throughout the hedge period, to the changes in the fair value of the hedged item(s). It must also be *probable* (likely) that changes in the market value of the futures contract will substantially offset the price changes or interest rate changes associated with the hedged item. Thus, the underlying commodity or financial instrument of a futures contract should be identical to the commodity or financial instrument which is hedged. However, the underlying commodity or financial instrument of a futures contract may differ from the underlying item being hedged, if (a) there is a clear economic relationship between the prices of the two commodities or financial instruments and (b) a high degree of price correlation is probable (likely).

Hedged items reported at fair value   For an item to qualify as an economic hedge under FASB-80, it must generally be accounted for at historical cost or the lower of cost or market, such as investments carried at cost, liabilities carried at historical proceeds, and inventories carried at the lower of cost or market. Thus, enterprises that hedge assets reported at fair value, in accordance with generally accepted accounting principles or specialized industry practices, are required to include the changes in value of both the hedged assets and the related futures contracts in income of the same accounting period.

Accounting for Hedges

Changes in the market value of a futures contract associated with a hedged item must not be recognized in income until the related change in the fair value of the hedged item is also recognized in income. To recognize a change in the market value of a futures contract in a different period from the related change in the fair value of the hedged item would negate the underlying economic effect of the hedging transaction. FASB-80 recognizes the underlying economic effect of a hedging transaction by providing for delayed income recognition of the changes in the market value of futures contracts that meet the hedge criteria. However, FASB-80 does not change current accounting principles or practices for assets, liabilities, or commitments.

Accounting for hedges of existing items   In order to qualify as a hedge, a futures contract must meet the hedge criteria established by FASB-80 (see above). If a futures contract qualifies under FASB-80 as a hedge of an existing asset, liability, or firm commitment, changes in the market value of the futures contract are recognized in income at the same time as the effects of the price or interest rate changes of the hedged item. Adjustments of the carrying amount of a hedged item must be accounted for in the same manner as the carrying amount of the item, except for hedged interest-bearing financial instruments that are otherwise reported at amortized cost. Adjustments of the carrying amount of hedged interest-bearing financial instruments that are otherwise reported at amortized cost must begin on the date the hedge is closed out and must be amortized as either interest income or interest expense over the expected remaining life of the instrument. If a futures contract qualifies under FASB-80 as a hedge of a firm commitment to purchase or sell a commodity or financial instrument at a fixed price, changes in the market value must be included in the ultimate gain or loss on the transaction.

If it is *probable* that both the hedged item and the futures contract will be retained to the delivery date specified in the futures contract, an enterprise may recognize the premium or discount on a hedge contract in income over the life of the contract. The premium or discount is computed at the inception of the hedge by reference to the contracted futures price and the fair value of the hedged item.

> **OBSERVATION:** *A futures contract may qualify as a hedge of a fixed-rate financial instrument which an enterprise intends to hold to maturity, if the funding for the enterprise's assets has been made with instruments having earlier maturities or repricing dates.*

Commodity dealers and others who use futures contracts to hedge a net exposure consisting of inventory held for sale and firm commitments to purchase and sell similar assets may find it impractical to associate specific futures contracts with related hedges, because of the volume and frequency of transactions. In this event, it is permissible to make reasonable allocations of the results of futures contracts between the assets on hand or specific commitments on hand at the end of a reporting period and the assets sold during the period.

Assessment of correlation   FASB-80 requires that an ongoing assessment be made of the correlation between the changes in the market value of a futures contract and the changes in the fair value of the related hedged item to determine the effectiveness of the hedged transaction. If a high correlation has not been achieved, the enterprise must cease to account for the futures contract as a hedge and must recognize, as a gain or loss in current income, the amount of change in the market value of the futures contract since inception that has not been offset by the change in the fair value of the hedged item.

Accounting for certain anticipated transactions   A futures contract may be used to hedge a purchase or sale transaction that an enterprise expects, but is not legally required, to enter into. This type of futures contract is referred to as an *anticipatory hedge*. In an anticipatory hedge, the futures contract does not relate to an enterprise's existing assets, liabilities, or firm commitments.

In order to qualify as an anticipatory hedge, a futures contract must meet the hedge criteria established by FASB-80 (see above). If a futures contract qualifies under FASB-80 as an anticipatory hedge, changes in the market value of the futures contract shall be included in the ultimate gain or loss on the hedged transaction. If gain or loss in the fair value of an asset or liability will be recognized in income subsequent to its acquisition or issuance, gain or loss on the related futures contract must be recognized at the same time. However, if the futures contract is closed out before the date of the anticipated transaction, the accumulated change in the market value of the contract must be carried forward and included in the ultimate gain or loss on the transaction. When it becomes *probable* that the quantity of the anticipated transaction will be less than originally identified, a pro rata portion of the changes in the market value of the futures contract must be recognized as a gain or loss and a pro rata portion must be included in the ultimate gain or loss on the transaction.

Subject to the limitations described above, changes in the market value of a futures contract which hedges an anticipated transaction that an enterprise expects to occur must be included in the ultimate gain or loss on the anticipated transaction if both of the following conditions are met:

Significant Terms are Identified   An enterprise must identify the significant terms of the anticipated transaction, including (a) the commodity or type of financial instrument involved, (b) the quantity to be purchased or sold, and (c) the expected date of the transaction. As long as all other conditions are met for each possible transaction, an enterprise may identify more than one similar transaction if identification of a single transaction is not possible.

Probable that the Anticipated Transaction Will Occur   It must be *probable* (likely) that the anticipated transaction will occur during the normal course of an enterprise's business. In other words, there must be a high level of assurance that the anticipated transaction will occur. The probability that the anticipated transaction will occur must be supported by observable facts and should not be based on management's intent (paragraph 56 of FASB-80). Under FASB-80, the likelihood that the anticipated transaction will occur is not sufficiently probable if the anticipated transaction can be abandoned by the enterprise with little cost or disruption of operations.

Disclosure and Effective Date

Enterprises that apply the accounting required by FASB-80 for hedges and anticipated transactions must disclose the following information in their financial statements:

- The nature of the items that are hedged or related to futures contracts
- The accounting method(s) used for the futures contracts
- A description of the events or transactions that will result in recognition in income of the changes in value of the futures contracts

Rescission of FASB Technical Bulletin 81-1   Upon the issuance of FASB-80, FASB Technical Bulletin 81-1 (Disclosure of Interest Rate Futures Contracts and Forward and Standby Contracts) was rescinded.

Effective date   The provisions of FASB-80 shall be applied to futures contracts entered into on or after January 1, 1985, and earlier application of FASB-80 is encouraged in annual financial statements that have not been previously issued. The disclosure requirements of FASB-80 must be complied with in financial statements for periods ending on or after December 16, 1984, for all open futures contracts that have been designated as hedges, whether or not other provisions of FASB-80 have been applied. Prospective application of the provisions of FASB-80 is permitted to all futures contracts owned by an enterprise on the date FASB-80 is first applied.

NONMONETARY TRANSACTIONS

Overview

The promulgated GAAP on nonmonetary transactions are APB-29 and FASB Interpretation-30 (Accounting for Involuntary Conversions of Nonmonetary Assets). The following types of transactions are specifically excluded from the promulgated GAAP:

1. Accounting for business combinations (purchase and pooling-of-interests methods)
2. A nonmonetary transfer of assets between companies or persons under common ownership control
3. Issuance of capital stock for the acquisition of nonmonetary assets or services
4. Stock dividends and stock splits, issued or received

FASB Technical Bulletin 85-1 (FASB:TB 85-1), issued on March 18, 1985, provides guidance to members of the Federal Home Loan Banking System (primarily savings and loan institutions) on accounting for the receipt of the new Federal Home Loan Mortgage Corporation (FHLMC) participating preferred stock.

Monetary Assets or Liabilities

Business transactions usually involve cash or monetary assets or liabilities that are exchanged for goods or services.

Monetary assets or liabilities are fixed in terms of currency and are usually contractual claims to fixed amounts of money. Examples of monetary assets and liabilities are cash, accounts and notes receivable, and accounts and notes payable.

Nonmonetary Assets or Liabilities

Some business transactions involve the exchange or transfer of nonmonetary assets or liabilities which are not fixed in terms of currency.

Nonmonetary assets or liabilities are those other than monetary assets or liabilities. Examples of nonmonetary assets and liabilities are inventory, investments in common stock, property, plant, and equipment, liability for advance rent collected, and common stock.

Under certain circumstances, a monetary asset or liability may become nonmonetary. For example, a marketable bond being held to maturity would qualify as a monetary asset because its face amount is fixed in terms of currency. However, if the same bond was being held for speculation, it would properly be classified as a nonmonetary asset because the amount that will be received when it is sold is not determinable and therefore not fixed in terms of currency.

Exchange (Reciprocal Transfer)

An exchange is a reciprocal transfer in which each party to the transaction receives and/or gives up assets, liabilities, or services. Exchanges can be either monetary or nonmonetary, or a combination of both. Nonmonetary exchanges are usually for the mutual convenience of two businesses. Examples include an exchange of inventory for trucking services or a trade of a starting quarterback for three linemen and a future draft choice.

Nonreciprocal Transfer

A nonreciprocal transfer is a transaction in one direction, in which one party to the transaction usually acquires either an intangible asset or nothing. Examples of nonreciprocal transfers are:

1. Declaration and distribution of a dividend
2. Acquisition of treasury stock
3. Sale of capital stock
4. Conversion of convertible debt
5. Charitable contributions

Fair Value

Accounting for the transfer or distribution of a nonmonetary asset or liability should be based on the fair value of the asset or liability that is received or surrendered, whichever is more clearly evident (APB-29). The only exceptions to this rule are (a) when fair value is not determinable, (b) certain nonreciprocal transfers to owners, and (c) when the earning process is not completed (APB-29). Fair value of the assets in a nonmonetary transfer should be determined by reference to the estimated realizable value of similar assets that are sold for cash, quoted market prices, independent appraisals, and other available evidence. If cash could have been received in lieu of the nonmonetary asset, then the amount of cash may be the basis for the valuation of the nonmonetary asset.

Fair Value not Determinable

Because of uncertainties, there may be situations where the fair value of the nonmonetary assets received and surrendered cannot be determined with reasonable accuracy. In these situations, the only valuation available may be the recorded book values of the nonmonetary assets (APB-29). Thus APB-29 suggests, but does not require, that the recorded amount of a nonmonetary asset be used in those situations in which fair value cannot be reasonably determined.

Nonreciprocal Transfers to Owners

If the fair value of the nonmonetary assets in a nonreciprocal transfer to owners can be objectively determined and realized in an outright sale at or near the date of transfer, the transfer shall be accounted for at fair value (APB-29). However, in a reorganization or liquidation (including spin-offs), or in a rescission of a business combination, the nonreciprocal transfer of nonmonetary assets shall be accounted for at their recorded amount, less any necessary reduction for impairment in values (APB-29). In other words, these types of nonmonetary transfers to owners must be accounted for either at the assets' recorded amount or at the assets' net realizable value, as follows:

1. If the recorded amount of the nonmonetary assets is less than fair value, the transfer is accounted for at the recorded amount because there is no reduction necessary for impairment.
2. If the recorded amount of the nonmonetary assets is more than fair value, the transfer is accounted for at net realizable value, which is equal to the recorded amount less a reduction for impairment.

A *pro rata* distribution to owners of the shares of a subsidiary or investee that is or will be consolidated or accounted for by the equity method is considered a spin-off for the purposes of APB-29.

FHLMC Participating Preferred Stock   On December 6, 1984, the Federal Home Loan Mortgage Corporation declared a distribution consisting of a new class of participating preferred stock, payable to the 12 district FHL banks in proportion to their respective holdings of FHLMC's nonvoting common stock. Between December 8, 1984, and December 14, 1984, each FHL bank declared a dividend of the new class of participating preferred stock to its stockholders of record (the *members*) as of the close of business on December 3, 1984. Shares of the new class of participating preferred stock were allocated to members in the same manner and on the same basis as cash dividends would be allocated to members as of such record date pursuant to 12 C.F.R. Sec. 522.6.

With certain exceptions, shares of the new class of participating preferred stock may be sold, transferred, pledged or otherwise disposed of *only* to and among members and the FHLMC.

Each member was treated as receiving a distribution in an amount equal to the fair market value of the shares of the new class of participating preferred stock received. The distribution was treated as a dividend to the extent of the earnings and profits of the FHL bank from which the distribution was received. No amount treated as a dividend was eligible for the dividends received deduction. Any remainder of the distribution was treated as an adjustment of the member's basis in its FHL bank stock to the extent of such basis, with any excess treated as a gain from the sale or exchange of FHL bank stock.

Under APB-29 (Nonmonetary Transactions), the distribution of the Federal Home Loan Mortgage Corporation's participating preferred stock to the savings and loan associations who are members of the Federal Home Loan Banking System represents a nonreciprocal transfer of a nonmonetary asset to owners. If the fair value of a nonmonetary asset in a nonreciprocal transfer to owners can be objectively determined and realized in an outright sale at or near the date of transfer, the transfer shall be accounted for at fair value (APB-29).

An independent appraisal of the price range at which the preferred stock was expected to trade on the New York Stock Exchange was obtained by the FHLMC before the stock began trading on January 23, 1985. Under FASB:TB 85-1, the preferred stock should be recognized by member institutions at its fair value on December 31, 1984, in accordance with APB-29.

Under FASB:TB 85-1, accounting for the preferred stock at fair value will result in income to a member institution, which should be reported as an extraordinary item (APB-30), because of the infrequency of occurrence, and unusual nature, of the distribution. The amount recorded by a member institution as fair value as at December 31, 1984, becomes the cost of the preferred stock. Under FASB:TB 85-1, the preferred stock should be reported in the financial statements of a member institution in accordance with FASB-12 (Marketable Securities).

> **OBSERVATION**: *Paragraph 3 of FASB:TB 85-1 states that the FHLMC preferred stock is a marketable equity security and should be reported in accordance with FASB-12. However, under FASB-12, restricted or legend stock is not considered a marketable security. The Distribution Circular, dated December 21, 1984, for the FHLMC preferred stock states that the preferred stock may be sold, transferred, pledged, or otherwise disposed of only to and among Freddie Mac and its member institutions and that each stock certificate will bear a conspicuous legend as to this restriction on transfer. Thus, reporting the FHLMC preferred stock as a marketable security under the provisions of FASB-12 may not be appropriate.*

FASB:TB 85-1 is effective for fiscal years and interim period financial statements ending after December 1, 1984, that are issued on or after April 1, 1985. If financial statements have been issued that did not report the distribution of the FHLMC preferred stock as required by FASB:TB 85-1, such financial statements should be retroactively restated when reissued. Earlier application of the provisions of FASB:TB 85-1 is encouraged, but not required.

Earning Process not Complete

A basic principle states that "When the earning process is complete and an exchange has taken place, only then is the realization of revenue recognized." There are two types of nonmonetary exchanges that do not result in completion of the earning process:

1. An exchange of property held for sale in the ordinary course of business for similar property to be held for the same purpose
2. An exchange of productive assets used in business but not held for sale for similar property to be held for the same purpose

In these two cases, the nonmonetary exchange should be based on the recorded amount (book value) of the nonmonetary asset surrendered, unless the exchange includes an amount of monetary consideration. The amount of the monetary consideration included in the nonmonetary exchange should be accounted for as follows:

Recipient of the monetary consideration The recipient of the monetary consideration should recognize realized gain on the exchange to the extent that the monetary amount exceeds a proportionate share of the recorded amount of the asset relinquished.

If the transaction results in a loss, the entire loss on the exchange should be recognized.

Payor of the monetary consideration The payor of the monetary consideration should not recognize any gain on the exchange and should record the cost of the nonmonetary asset received at the amount of the nonmonetary asset surrendered, plus the amount of the monetary consideration paid.

If the transaction results in a loss, the entire loss on the exchange should be recognized.

EITF consensus on nonmonetary transactions In Issue Number 86-29, the FASB Emerging Issues Task Force reached a consensus concerning an exchange of nonmonetary assets in which monetary consideration (boot) is involved. The consensus concluded that an exchange of nonmonetary assets in which a significant amount of monetary consideration is also involved should be accounted for as a monetary transaction instead of a nonmonetary transaction. The Task Force agreed that a significant amount of monetary consideration should be defined as at least 25% or more of the fair value of the exchange. As a monetary transaction, both parties would record the exchange at fair value. The Task Force consensus also stated that if the monetary consideration is less than 25%, the pro rata gain recognition guidance in paragraph 22 of APB-29 should be applied by the recipient of the boot and the payor of the boot would not recognize any gain.

> OBSERVATION: *This portion of the Task Force consensus view on Issue Number 86-29 requires that all of the gain on a nonmonetary transaction be recognized if amount of boot involved in the transaction exceeds 25% or more of the fair value of the exchange. Paragraph 22 of APB-29 requires that the recipient of the boot recognize gain on the exchange, but only to the extent that the amount of boot exceeds the proportionate share of the recorded amount of the asset exchanged. Thus, a conflict exists between the Task Force consensus view on Issue Number 86-29 and the provisions of paragraph 22 of APB-29.*

Formula for recognition of gains or losses The following formula may be used in determining the recognition of nonmonetary gains or losses.

1. The gain or loss on the transaction is the difference between the fair market value and the net book value of the asset surrendered.
2. Losses on any nonmonetary assets are always recognized in full.
3. Gains are recognized in full if the earning process has been completed.
4. If the earning process has not been completed, gains are recognized as follows:

    a. no boot involved = no gain recognized

    b. boot is given = no gain recognized

    c. boot is received = a portion of the gain is recognized as follows:

$$\frac{\text{Cash received}}{\text{cash received} + \text{fair market value of asset received}} \quad \times \quad \text{gain} = \begin{array}{c}\text{recognized amount}\\ \text{of gain}\end{array}$$

An asset with a $6,000 cost is exchanged for $4,000 in cash and an asset with a fair value of $8,000. Both assets were held for sale in the ordinary course of business, and except for the cash the earning process would not have been completed and no gain would be recognized. Using the formula for recognition of gain, the computation is as follows:

$$\frac{\$4,000}{\$4,000 + \$8,000} \quad \times \quad \$6,000 \;=\; \$2,000$$

Basis of acquired asset:

Original cost	$6,000
Less: Cash received	4,000
	2,000
Add: Recognized gain	2,000
Basis of acquired asset	$4,000

Losses are recognized in full (conservatism).

Gain or Loss

Gain or loss, when applicable, should be recognized in nonmonetary transactions. A difference in the gain or loss for tax purposes and that recognized for accounting purposes may constitute a timing difference in income tax provision.

Involuntary Conversion of Nonmonetary Assets to Monetary Assets

When a nonmonetary asset is involuntarily converted to a monetary asset, a monetary transaction results, and gain or loss must be recognized in the period of conversion (FASB Interpretation-30). The gain or loss is the difference between the carrying amount of the nonmonetary asset and the proceeds from the conversion.

Gain or loss from an involuntary conversion of a nonmonetary asset to a monetary asset should be classified as from continuing operations, extraordinary items, disposal of a segment, etc., according to the particular circumstances (APB-30). In addition, a gain or loss recognized for tax purposes in a period different from that for financial accounting purposes (books) creates a timing (temporary) difference, for which interperiod tax allocation may be necessary (FASB-96).

If the amount of proceeds that will be received from the involuntary conversion of the nonmonetary asset cannot be determined, the gain or loss shall be recognized and classified as a contingency (see chapter entitled "Contingencies").

The involuntary conversion of a LIFO inventory layer at an interim reporting date does not have to be recognized if the proceeds are reinvested in replacement inventory by the end of the fiscal year (FASB Interpretation-30).

> **OBSERVATION:** *This is the same treatment afforded a temporary liquidation of a LIFO inventory layer at interim dates which is expected to be corrected by the end of the annual period (see chapter entitled "Interim Financial Reporting").*

In the event the proceeds from an involuntary conversion of a LIFO inventory layer are not reinvested in replacement inventory by the end of the fiscal year, gain for financial accounting purposes need not be recognized, providing the taxpayer does not recognize such gains for income tax reporting purposes (FASB Interpretation-30).

Examples of involuntary conversion are the total or partial destruction of property through fire or other catastrophe, theft of property, or condemnation of property by a governmental authority (eminent domain proceedings).

Disclosure

Adequate disclosure of the nature of the nonmonetary transaction, the basis of accounting for assets transferred, and gains or losses recognized should be disclosed in the financial statements for the period.

Conclusion

All nonmonetary transactions except those for which fair value is undeterminable or for which the earning process is not complete are based on the fair value of the asset surrendered or received, whichever is more clearly evident. Gain or loss is recognized on nonmonetary transactions. In the event that fair value cannot be reasonably determined, the recorded book value may be used. In exchanges where the earning process is not complete, gain is recognized to the extent *boot* is received, and losses are recognized in full.

A gain or a loss recognized for tax purposes in a period different from that for financial accounting purposes creates a timing (temporary) difference, for which interperiod income tax allocation may apply (FASB-96).

EXPOSURE DRAFT

Accounting for Contributions Received and Contributions Made and Capitalization of Works of Art, Historical Treasures, and Similar Assets

An Exposure Draft (ED) entitled *Accounting for Contributions Received and Contributions Made and Capitalization of Works of Art, Historical Treasures, and Similar Assets* is outstanding as of the date of this publication. The ED is summarized in the chapter entitled "Revenue Recognition."

PENSION PLANS - EMPLOYERS

Overview

Financial accounting and reporting standards for employer's pension plans are established by FASB-87 (Employers' Accounting for Pensions). FASB-87 supersedes APB-8, as amended (Accounting for Costs of a Pension Plan); FASB-36 (Disclosure of Pension Information); and FASB Interpretation-3 (Accounting for the Cost of Pension Plans Subject to the Employee Retirement Income Security Act of 1974). In addition, FASB-87 amends APB-16 to provide that the purchase of the assets and liabilities of a pension plan shall no longer be accounted for in accordance with paragraph 88h of APB-16 (Business Combinations), but shall be accounted for in accordance with paragraph 74 of FASB-87, entitled "Business Combinations." FASB-87 also amends FASB-5 (Contingencies) to delete references to APB-8, and to provide for the recognition of a loss contingency when an employer withdraws as a member of a multiemployer pension plan, and it is *probable* or *reasonably possible* that, as a result of the withdrawal, the employer has incurred a liability for a portion of the plan's unfunded benefit obligation.

FASB-87 does not change or supersede any of the provisions of FASB-35 (Accounting and Reporting by Defined Benefit Plans).

> ***OBSERVATION***: *FASB Technical Bulletin 81-3 (FASB:TB 81-3) provides guidance on the accounting implications of the Multiemployer Pension Plan Amendments Act of 1980 (MPPAA). FASB:TB 81-3 makes reference to APB-8, FASB-36, and FASB Interpretation-3, all of which have been superseded by FASB-87. Furthermore, FASB:TB 81-3 suggests that employers participating in multiemployer plans that are deemed to be defined benefit plans subject to the MPPAA should look to FASB Interpretation-3 for guidance.*
>
> *It appears that FASB:TB 81-3 should have also been superseded by FASB-87, but was not. Although FASB:TB 81-3 remains technically effective, it obviously should not be relied upon.*

Deferred compensation plan A deferred compensation plan is a contractual agreement that specifies that a portion of the employee's compensation will be set aside and paid in future periods as retirement benefits. Only those deferred compensation plans that in substance are pension plans are covered by FASB-87.

Postemployment and postretirement benefits are generally considered a form of deferred compensation to an employee because these types of benefits are provided by an employer in exchange for an employee's services. Thus, these benefits must be properly measured and recognized in the financial statements and, if the amount is material, financial statement disclosure may be required.

> **OBSERVATION:** *For a detailed discussion of postemployment and postretirement benefits and their disclosure requirements, see chapters entitled "Deferred Compensation Contracts and Postretirement Benefits Other Than Pensions."*

Background

Employment between an employee and an employer is usually based on an exchange agreement. The employee agrees to provide services for the employer in exchange for a current wage, a pension benefit, and frequently other benefits such as death, dental, disability, etc. Although pension benefits and some other benefits are not paid currently, they represent deferred compensation that must be accounted for as part of the employee's total compensation package.

Pension benefits are usually paid on a periodic basis to retired employees or their survivors, but may be paid in a single lump sum. Other benefits, such as death, dental, disability, etc., may also be provided through a pension plan.

A pension plan may be contributory or noncontributory; that is, the employees may be required to contribute to the plan, or the entire cost of the plan may be borne by the employer. A pension plan may be funded or unfunded; that is, the employees and/or the employer may make cash contributions to a pension plan trustee, or the employer may make only credit entries on its books reflecting the pension liability under the plan. Pension plans are accounted for on the accrual basis, and any difference between net periodic pension cost charged against income and the amount actually funded is recorded as an accrued or prepaid pension cost.

Although interest cost on the pension liability and the return (or loss) on a pension plan's assets will increase or decrease net periodic pension cost, they are considered financial costs rather than employee compensation costs. Financial costs can be controlled by the manner in which the employer provides financing for the pension plan. An employer can eliminate interest cost by completely funding the plan or by purchasing annuity contracts to settle all pension obligations. The return on plan assets can be increased by the contribution of more assets to the pension fund.

Pension plan accounting   The assets of a pension plan are usually kept in a trust account, completely segregated from the assets of the employer. Contributions to the pension trust account are periodically made by the employer and, if the plan is contributory, by the employees. The plan assets are invested in stocks, bonds, real estate, and other types of investments. Plan assets are increased by earnings and gains on investments and are decreased by losses on investments and the payment of pension benefits. Plan assets placed in a trust account cannot usually be withdrawn by the employer. However, an exception arises when the plan assets exceed the pension obligation. In this event, most pension plan agreements permit the employer to withdraw the excess amount of plan assets, providing that all other existing pension plan obligations have been satisfied by the employer. Under GAAP, pension plan assets that are not effectively restricted for the payment of pension benefits or segregated in a trust are not considered pension plan assets.

Accounting and reporting for a pension plan (defined benefit plan) is covered by FASB-35.

Scope and Applicability of FASB-87

Most of the provisions of FASB-87 address *defined benefit pension plans* of single employers. A defined benefit pension plan is one that contains a "pension benefit formula," which generally describes the amount of pension benefit that each employee will receive for services performed during a specified period of employment. The amount of the employer's periodic contribution to a defined benefit pension plan is based on the total pension benefits earned by all eligible employees during a specified period of employment.

A *defined contribution pension plan* does not contain a pension benefit formula, but generally specifies the periodic amount that the employer shall contribute to the pension plan and how that amount shall be allocated to the eligible employees who perform services during that same period. Each periodic employer contribution is allocated among separate accounts maintained for each employee, and pension benefits are based solely on the amount available in each employee's account at the time of his or her retirement.

FASB-87 does not apply to a plan that provides only life and/or health insurance benefits to retirees. GAAP for such plans are established by FASB-106, discussed in the chapter entitled "Postretirement Benefits Other Than Pensions." Until an enterprise applies FASB-106, the enterprise should comply with the disclosure requirements of FASB-81, and may voluntarily use accrual accounting for postretirement benefit plans, similar to the accounting that is required for pension plans by FASB-87 and FASB-88.

Frequently, defined contribution pension plans provide for some method of determining defined benefits for employees, as may be the case with many "target benefit" plans. If, in substance, a plan does provide defined benefits for employees, it shall be accounted for as a defined benefit pension plan.

For the purposes of FASB-87, any plan that is not a defined contribution pension plan is considered a defined benefit pension plan (see definition of a defined benefit pension plan in Appendix D of FASB-87). FASB-87 does not supersede or change any of the requirements of FASB-35 (Accounting and Reporting by Defined Benefit Plans).

FASB-87 requires that its provisions be applied to any arrangement, express or implied, that is similar in substance to a pension plan, regardless of its form or method of financing. Thus, a pension plan arrangement does not have to be in writing if the existence of a pension plan is implied by company policy.

An employer's settlement of a defined benefit pension obligation, curtailment of a defined benefit pension plan, and/or the termination of pension benefits are covered by FASB-88 (Employers' Accounting for Settlements and Curtailments of Defined Benefit Pension Plans and for Termination Benefits).

The use of estimates, averages, and/or computational shortcuts is permitted by FASB-87 to reduce the cost of compliance, providing that the results are not significantly different from those that would be obtained by detailed application.

Actuarial Assumptions

Actuarial assumptions are factors that are used to calculate the estimated cost of pension plan benefits. Employee mortality, employee turnover, retirement age, administrative expenses of the pension plan, interest earned on plan assets, and the date on which a benefit becomes fully vested are some of the more important actuarial assumptions.

Under FASB-87, each significant actuarial assumption must reflect the best estimate for that particular assumption. In the absence of evidence to the contrary, all actuarial assumptions shall be made on the basis that the pension plan will continue in existence (going-concern concept).

Discount rates that are used in actuarial valuations shall reflect the rates at which the pension benefits could be effectively settled. In selecting appropriate interest rates, employers should refer to current information on rates used in annuity contracts that could be purchased to settle pension obligations, including annuity rates published by the Pension Benefit Guaranty Corporation, or the rates of return on high-quality fixed-income investments that are expected to be available through the maturity dates of the pension benefits.

An actuarial gain or loss is the difference between an actuarial assumption and actual experience. Under FASB-87, actuarial gains and losses are not included in net periodic pension cost in the year in which they arise, but may be subject to amortization in subsequent periods if certain criteria are met.

Pension Plan Assets

The resources of a pension plan may be converted into (a) plan assets that are invested to provide pension benefits for the participants of the plan, such as stocks, bonds, and other investments (paragraph 19 of FASB-87) or (b) plan assets that are used in the operation of the plan, such as real estate, furniture, fixtures, etc. (paragraph 51 of FASB-87). Plan assets must be segregated in a trust or otherwise effectively restricted so that they cannot be used by the employer for other purposes. Under FASB-87, plan assets do not include amounts accrued by an employer as net periodic pension cost, but not yet paid to the pension plan. Plan assets may include securities of the employer if they are freely transferable.

Pension plan assets that are held as investments to provide pension benefits shall be measured at fair value. Pension plan assets that are used in the operation of the plan shall be measured, for all purposes, at cost less accumulated depreciation or amortization (paragraph 51 of FASB-87). All plan assets shall be measured as of the date of the financial statements or, if used consistently from year to year, as of a date not more than three months prior to that date (paragraph 52 of FASB-87).

For the purposes of FASB-87, plan liabilities that are incurred, other than for pension benefits, may be considered reductions of plan assets (Appendix D of FASB-87, under definition of "Plan Assets").

Capsule Analysis of FASB-87

This capsule analysis offers an overall perspective of some of the major provisions of FASB-87. It is intended to simplify the material covered and to expedite the reader's understanding of FASB-87.

Under FASB-87, an enterprise must make at least two types of journal entries to record its pension cost, as follows:

(a) Net periodic pension cost $XXX
        Accrued pension cost payable $XXX
      To accrue pension cost for a specific period.

(b) Accrued pension cost payable $XXX
        Cash $XXX
      To record cash contribution to pension plan trustee.

Most of the provisions of FASB-87 pertain to the computation of the amount to be recorded in entry type (a) as net periodic pension cost. This computation requires numerous worksheet calculations which are illustrated throughout FASB-87.

In some but not all situations, an enterprise may also be required to make a third type of entry, as follows:

(c) Intangible asset $XXX
     Excess of additional pension liability over
         unrecognized prior service cost (an
           offset to net worth)   XXX
       Accrued pension cost payable $XXX

As is discussed later in this chapter, this third type of entry is generally required if the employer's pension liability exceeds the fair value of the pension plan assets.

FASB-87 also requires a schedule reconciling the funded status of an employer's pension plan with certain amounts reported in the employer's statement of financial position. The reconciliation schedule must be as of the date of the financial statements or, if used consistently from year to year, as of a date not more than three months prior to the date of the financial statements. The following illustrates such a reconciliation as of the date of initial adoption of FASB-87.

Reconciliation of Pension Plan Funded Status
with Amounts Reported on Statement of Financial Position
(as of the date of initial application of FASB-87)

(a)	Projected benefit obligation	$(100,000)
(b)	Fair value of plan assets	65,000
(c)	Funded status of plan	(35,000)
(d)	Unrecognized prior service cost	0
(e)	Unrecognized net (gain) or loss	0
(f)	Unrecognized net obligation or (net asset) at date of initial application of FASB-87	35,000
(g)	(Accrued) or prepaid pension cost	$ 0

Only item (g) is actually recorded on the books of the employer. The other items are usually recorded by the employer on worksheets.

Each item appearing in the above reconciliation schedule is discussed briefly below. Further details are provided in subsequent text and illustrations.

(a) *Projected benefit obligation*   is the actuarial present value, as of a specified date, of the total cost of all employees' vested and nonvested pension benefits that have been attributed by the pension benefit formula to services performed by employees to that date.

The projected benefit obligation includes the actuarial present value of all pension benefits (vested and nonvested) attributed by the pension benefit formula, whether the benefits are based on future employee compensation levels or not. Vested benefits are pension benefits that an employee has an irrevocable right to receive at a date specified in the pension agreement, even if the employee does not continue to work for the employer. In the event a pension plan is discontinued, a vested benefit obligation remains a liability of the employer.

Payments of pension benefits decrease both the projected benefit obligation and the fair value of plan assets, while contributions to a plan decrease accrued pension cost (or increase the prepaid pension cost), and increase the fair value of plan assets.

The projected benefit obligation appears on the books of the pension plan but not on the books of the employer. However, the employer should maintain a record of the projected benefit obligation on a worksheet.

The *accumulated benefit obligation* is calculated in the same way as the projected benefit obligation, except that current or past compensation levels are used to determine pension benefits instead of future compensation levels, even if the pension benefit formula requires the use of future compensation levels to determine pension benefits. Under FASB-87, an employer must recognize an additional minimum liability in its statement of financial position, if its accumulated benefit obligation exceeds the fair value of pension plan assets as of a specified date. The amount of the additional minimum liability must at least equal the employer's *unfunded accumulated benefit obligation*, which is the amount by which the accumulated benefit obligation exceeds the fair value of plan assets. In the event a pension plan is discontinued, the balance of any unfunded accumulated benefit obligation remains a liability of the employer.

(b) *Fair value of plan assets* is the amount that a pension plan could reasonably expect to receive from a current sale of plan assets, that are held to provide pension benefits, between a willing buyer under no compulsion to buy and a willing seller under no compulsion to sell. Plan assets that are used in the operation of the pension plan (building, equipment, furniture, fixtures, etc.) are valued at cost less accumulated depreciation or amortization.

Pension plan assets are recorded on the books of the pension plan. However, an employer should maintain worksheet records of the cost and fair value of all pension plan assets.

(c) *Funded status of plan* is the difference between the projected benefit obligation and the fair value of plan assets as of a given date. If the projected benefit obligation exceeds the fair value of the plan assets, a pension plan liability exists. If the fair value of plan assets exceeds the projected benefit obligation, a pension plan asset exists.

(d) *Unrecognized prior service cost* is the portion of prior service cost that has not been recognized by the employer in net periodic pension cost of any period. The amount of unrecognized prior service cost as of the date of initial application of FASB-87 is zero by definition.

Upon the initial adoption of a pension plan or through a plan amendment, certain employees may be granted pension benefits for services performed in prior periods. These retroactive pension benefits are referred to as "prior service costs," and are usually granted by the employer with the expectation that they will produce future economic benefits, such as reducing employee turnover, improving employee productivity, and minimizing the need to increase employee compensation. Under FASB-87, an employer is required to amortize any prior service cost in equal amounts over the future periods of each active employee who is expected to receive the benefits.

An employer does not record unrecognized prior service cost on its books but should maintain worksheet records of such amounts. The total amount of any prior service cost is recorded on the books of the pension plan, as an increase in the projected benefit obligation, in the period in which the retroactive benefits become effective.

(e) *Unrecognized net gain or loss* is the amount of actuarial gain or loss for a period that has not been recognized by the employer in net periodic pension cost of any period. The amount of unrecognized net gain or loss as of the date of initial application of FASB-87 is zero by definition.

Actuarial gains or losses arise from the difference between (a) the actual and expected amount of projected benefit obligation at the end of a period and/or (b) the actual and expected amount of the fair value of pension plan assets at the end of the period. Under FASB-87, actuarial gains or losses are not recognized by the employer in the period in which they arise, but may become subject to amortization in subsequent periods if certain criteria are met.

An unrecognized net gain or loss that, as of the beginning of the year, exceeds 10% of (a) the projected benefit obligation or (b) the market-related value of plan assets, whichever is greater, is subject to amortization. Amortization for the year is equal to the amount of unrecognized net gain or loss in excess of 10% divided by the average remaining service period of active employees expected to receive benefits under the plan.

Actuarial gains and losses are recognized on the books of a pension plan as they occur. However, an employer does not record actuarial gains or losses on its books but should maintain worksheet records of such amounts.

(f) *Unrecognized net obligation or net asset at date of initial application of FASB-87* is the difference between the projected benefit obligation and the fair value of plan assets plus previously recognized unfunded accrued pension cost or less previously recognized prepaid pension cost. In other words, the unrecognized net obligation or net asset is the difference between the funded status of a plan (projected benefit obligation less the fair value of plan assets), and the total amount of accrued or prepaid pension cost existing on the books of the employer as of the date of the initial application of FASB-87. Thus, if all contributions of prior periods were equal to all of the net pension cost of prior periods, there should be no accrued or prepaid pension cost on the books of the employer at the date of the initial application of FASB-87. In this event, the unrecognized net obligation or net asset is exactly equal to the funded status of the plan as of the date of the initial application of FASB-87.

The unrecognized net obligation or net asset as of the date of initial application of FASB-87 shall be amortized on a straight-line basis over the average remaining service period of employees expected to receive benefits under the plan, except (a) if the amortization period is less than 15 years, the employer may elect to use 15 years, and (b) if the plan is composed of all or substantially all inactive participants, the employer shall use those participants' average remaining life expectancy as the amortization period.

The amount of the employer's unrecognized obligation or net asset is included in the projected benefit obligation which is recorded on the books of the pension plan, as of the date of the employer's initial application of FASB-87. However, an employer does not record its unrecognized net obligation or net asset on its books as of the date of the initial application of FASB-87 but should maintain a worksheet record of such amount.

(g) *Accrued or prepaid pension cost*   Accrued pension cost is the total amount of net periodic pension cost that has been recognized but not funded. Prepaid pension cost is the total amount that has been funded in excess of the total amount of the net periodic pension cost that has been recognized.

Accrued or prepaid pension cost is recorded on the books of the employer.

Net Periodic Pension Cost

The employer's *net periodic pension cost* represents the net amount of pension cost for a specified period that is charged against income. Under FASB-87, the components of net periodic pension cost are (a) service cost, (b) interest cost on the projected benefit obligation, (c) actual return on plan assets, (d) amortization of unrecognized prior service cost (if any), (e) amortization of unrecognized net gain or loss (if required by FASB-87), and (f) amortization of the unrecognized net obligation or net asset existing at the date of initial application of FASB-87.

It is important to note that all of the components of net periodic pension cost are recognized on the books of the pension plan trustee in the period in which they arise, but the same components are not necessarily recognized on the books of the employer at the same time. For example, the total prior service cost that results from a plan amendment is recognized in full on the books of the pension plan in the period in which it arises as an increase in the projected benefit obligation. However, under the provisions of FASB-87, the employer recognizes the total prior service cost in equal amounts over the future service periods of each active employee who is expected to receive the benefits. The employer does not record any unrecognized prior service cost on its books but should maintain a worksheet record of such amounts.

The components of net periodic pension cost that are either partially recognized or not recognized at all on the employer's books in the period in which they arise are (a) unrecognized prior service cost, (b) unrecognized net asset gain or loss, and (c) unrecognized net obligation or net asset existing at the date of the initial application of FASB-87.

Net periodic pension cost is estimated in advance at the beginning of a period based on actuarial assumptions relating to (a) the discount rate on the projected benefit obligation, (b) the expected long-term rate of return on pension plan assets, and (c) the average remaining service periods of active employees covered by the pension plan. At the end of the period, adjustments are made to account for the differences (actuarial gains or losses), if any, between the estimated and actual amounts.

The same actuarial assumptions used to calculate the previous year's net periodic pension cost shall be used to calculate the net periodic pension cost in subsequent interim and annual financial statements, unless more current valuations of plan assets and obligations are available or a significant event has occurred, such as a plan amendment, which would usually require new valuations.

The following illustration shows how the different components of net periodic pension cost are estimated.

Computation of Net Periodic Pension Cost Accrual

Service cost component	$2,000
Interest cost component	3,000
Estimated return on plan assets	(2,500)
Amortization of unrecognized prior service cost	1,000
Amortization of unrecognized net (gain) or loss	1,000
Amortization of initial unrecognized net obligation (asset)	1,500
Total net periodic pension cost accrual	$6,000

For simplicity, it is assumed that there are no differences (actuarial gains or losses) between the estimated and actual amounts at the end of the period, and that the employer made no contributions to the pension fund during the period.

	Beginning of period	End of period
(a) Projected benefit obligation	$(115,000)	$(120,000)
(b) Fair value of plan assets	65,000	67,500
(c) Funded status of plan	$ (50,000)	$ (52,500)
(d) Unrecognized prior service cost	10,000	9,000
(e) Unrecognized net (gain) or loss	5,000	4,000
(f) Unrecognized net obligation or (net asset) at date of initial application of FASB-87	35,000	33,500
(g) (Accrued) or prepaid pension cost	$ 0	$ (6,000)

The following journal entry was made by the employer to record the net periodic pension cost accrual:

| Net periodic pension cost | $6,000 | |
| Accrued pension cost | | $6,000 |

The following is an explanation of the changes in the accounts that were affected by the net periodic pension cost accrual.

(a) *Projected benefit obligation*   The $5,000 increase in the projected benefit obligation, between the beginning and end of the period, consists of the service cost component ($2,000) and interest cost component ($3,000) of the net periodic pension cost accrual.

An increase in the projected benefit obligation of $5,000 will be recorded on the books of the pension plan, representing the service cost component of $2,000 and interest cost component of $3,000 for the period.

(b) *Fair value of plan assets*   The $2,500 increase in the fair value of plan assets, between the beginning and end of the period, represents the increase in the fair value of plan assets for the period.

An increase in the fair value of plan assets of $2,500 will be recorded on the books of the pension plan.

(c) *Funded status of plan*   The $2,500 increase in the funded status of the plan, between the beginning and end of the period, is the difference between the $5,000 increase in the projected benefit obligation for the period and the $2,500 increase in the fair value of plan assets for the period.

(d) *Unrecognized prior service cost*   The $1,000 decrease in the unrecognized prior service cost, between the beginning and end of the period, is the amount of amortization of prior service cost that has been recognized by the employer as a component of net periodic pension cost ($6,000).

As mentioned previously, unrecognized prior service cost is not recorded on the books of the employer, but worksheet records should be maintained for such amounts. Thus, the employer should reduce the worksheet balance of the unrecognized prior service cost by $1,000.

The $1,000 decrease in the unrecognized prior service cost is not recorded on the books of the pension plan because the total effects of the plan amendment were included, in full, in the projected benefit obligation in the year in which the plan amendment became effective.

(e) *Unrecognized net gain or loss*   The $1,000 decrease in the unrecognized net gain or loss (actuarial gain or loss), between the beginning and end of the period, is the amount of amortization that has been recognized by the employer as a component of net periodic pension cost ($6,000).

As mentioned previously, unrecognized net gain or loss (actuarial gain or loss) is not recorded on the books of the employer, but worksheet records should be maintained for such amounts. Thus, the employer should reduce the worksheet balance of the unrecognized net gain or loss by $1,000.

The $1,000 decrease in the unrecognized net gain or loss is recorded on the books of the pension plan because the total net gain or loss was included in the pension plan's records in the year in which the actuarial gain or loss occurred.

(f) *Unrecognized net obligation or net asset at date of initial application of FASB-87*   The $1,500 decrease in the unrecognized net obligation, between the beginning and the end of the period, is the amount of amortization which has been recognized by the employer as a component of net periodic pension cost ($6,000) for the period.

As mentioned previously, unrecognized net obligation or net asset is not recorded on the books of the employer, but worksheet records should be maintained for such amounts. Thus, the employer should reduce the worksheet balance of the unrecognized net obligation or net asset by $1,500.

The $1,500 decrease in the unrecognized net obligation or net asset is not recorded on the books of the pension plan because the total amount of the unrecognized net obligation or net asset was included in the funded status of the plan, as of the date of the initial application of FASB-87.

(g) *Accrued or prepaid pension cost*   The $6,000 increase in the accrued or prepaid pension cost, between the beginning and the end of the period, is the amount of the net periodic pension cost for the period which has not been funded by employer contributions.

Accrued pension cost is the total amount of net periodic pension cost that has been recognized to date but not funded by contributions to the pension plan. Prepaid pension cost is the total amount that has been funded by contributions to date, in excess of the total amount of net periodic pension cost that has been recognized.

Service Cost Component

A defined benefit pension plan contains a pension benefit formula that defines the pension benefit that an employee will receive for services performed during a specified period. FASB-87 requires that the terms in the pension benefit formula be used to determine the amount of pension benefit earned by each employee for services performed during a specified period. Under FASB-87, attribution is the process of assigning pension benefits or cost to periods of employee service, in accordance with the pension benefit formula.

The service cost component of net periodic pension cost is defined by FASB-87 as the actuarial present value of pension benefits attributed by the pension benefit formula to employee service during a specified period. For example, a pension benefit formula may state that an employee shall receive, at the retirement age stated in the plan, a pension benefit of $20 per month for life, for each year of service. To compute the total future value of the pension benefit for the year, the monthly benefit is multiplied by the number of months in the employee's life expectancy at retirement age. The number of months in the employee's life expectancy at retirement age is determined by reference to mortality tables. The actuarial present value of all employees' future pension benefits that are earned during a period is computed and included as the service cost component of the net periodic pension cost for the same period.

If the terms of the pension benefit formula provide for benefits based on estimated future compensation levels of employees, those estimated future compensation levels shall be used to determine the service cost component of net periodic pension cost. For example, if the pension benefit formula states that an employee's benefit for a period is equal to 1% of his or her final pay, an estimate of the employee's final pay shall be used to calculate the benefit for the period. Assumed compensation levels should reflect the best estimate of the future compensation levels of the employee involved and be consistent with assumed discount rates to the extent that they both incorporate expectation of the same future economic conditions (paragraph 202 of FASB-87). Thus, future compensation levels in final-pay plans or career-average-pay plans are reflected in the service cost component of net periodic pension cost. Assumed compensation levels shall also reflect changes due to general price levels, productivity, seniority, promotion, and other factors.

Changes resulting from a plan amendment that has become effective and automatic benefit changes specified by the terms of the pension plan, such as cost-of-living increases, shall be included in the determination of service cost for a period.

An employer's substantive commitment to make future plan amendments in recognition of employees' prior services may indicate pension benefits far in excess of those reflected in the existing pension benefit formula. Such a commitment may be evidenced by a history of regular increases in non-pay-related benefits, benefits under a career-average-pay plan, or other evidence. In this event, FASB-87 requires that the pension plan be accounted for on the basis of the employer's substantive commitment, and that appropriate disclosure be made in the employer's financial statements.

A plan's pension benefit formula may provide a nonvested benefit of $10 per month for life in the first 19 years of an employee's service and a vested benefit of $1,000 per month for life in the 20th year of an employee's service. If a pension plan benefit formula attributes all or a disproportionate portion of total pension benefits to later years, the employee's *total projected benefit* shall be calculated and used as the basis of assigning the total pension benefits under the plan. In this event, the employee's total projected benefit shall be assumed to accumulate in proportion to the ratio of the total completed years of service to date to the total completed years of service as of the date the benefit becomes fully vested. An employee's total projected benefit from a pension plan is the actuarial present value of the total cost of pension benefits that the employee is likely to receive under the plan. If the pension benefit formula is based on future compensation, the future compensation shall be used in calculating the employee's total projected benefit.

In the event a pension benefit formula does not indicate the manner in which a specific benefit relates to specific services performed by an employee, the benefit shall be assumed to be accumulated as follows:

If the Benefit Is Includable in Vested Benefits

The benefit shall be accumulated in proportion to the ratio of total completed years of service to date, to the total completed years of service as of the date the benefit becomes fully vested.

A vested benefit is a benefit that an employee has an irrevocable right to receive. For example, an employee is entitled to receive a vested benefit whether or not he or she continues to work for the employer.

If the Benefit Is Not Includable in Vested Benefits

The benefit shall be accumulated in proportion to the ratio of completed years of service to date to the total projected years of service. (An example of a benefit that is not includable in vested benefits is a death or disability benefit that is payable only if death or disability occurs during the employee's active service.)

Interest Cost Component

The two factors used to determine the actuarial present value of a future pension benefit are (a) the probability that the benefit will be paid to the employee (through the use of actuarial assumptions), and (b) the time value of money (through the use of discounts for interest cost). The probability that a pension benefit will be paid is based on actuarial assumptions such as employee mortality, employee turnover, and the date the benefits become vested. An employer's liability for a retirement fund of $56,520 that is due in ten years is not equal to a present liability of $56,620. At an 8% discount rate the $56,520 has a present value today of only $26,169. The $26,169 increases each year by the amount the employer's interest cost of 8%, and in ten years grows to $56,620 if the 8% interest rate does not change.

FASB-87 requires an employer to recognize, as a component of net periodic pension cost, the interest cost on the projected benefit obligation. The interest cost is equal to the increase in the amount of the projected benefit obligation due to the passage of time.

> **OBSERVATION**: *FASB-87 specifies that the interest cost component of net periodic pension cost shall not be considered to be interest for the purposes of applying the provisions of FASB-34 (Capitalization of Interest Cost).*

Actual Return on Plan Assets Component

The actual return on plan assets is equal to the difference between the fair value of plan assets at the beginning and end of a period, adjusted for employer and employee contributions (if a contributory plan) and pension benefit payments made during the period. Fair value is the amount that a pension plan could reasonably expect to receive from a current sale of an investment between a willing buyer under no compulsion to buy and a willing seller under no compulsion to sell. Plan assets that are used in the operation of the pension plan (building, equipment, furniture, fixtures, etc.) are valued at cost less accumulated depreciation or amortization.

A return on plan assets decreases the employer's cost of providing pension benefits to its employees, while a loss increases pension cost. Net periodic pension income can result from a significantly high return on pension plan assets during a period.

FASB-87 requires an employer to recognize, as a component of net periodic pension cost, the actual return (or loss) on pension plan assets.

> **OBSERVATION**: *FASB-87 requires the employer to recognize the actual return on plan assets, which may include both realized and unrealized gains and losses. One of the paradoxes of GAAP is that FASB-87 requires an employer to recognize the unrealized gains and losses on the assets of the pension plan trustee (an entity separate from the employer), but traditional GAAP prohibits the employer from recognizing any unrealized gains and losses on the employer's own investments.*

Amortization of Unrecognized Prior Service Cost Component

Upon the initial adoption of a pension plan or through a plan amendment, employees are granted pension benefits for services performed in prior periods. These retroactive pension benefits are usually granted by the employer in the expectation that they will produce future economic benefits, such as reducing employee turnover, improving employee productivity, and minimizing the need for increasing employee compensation. The cost of pension benefits that are retroactively granted to employees for services performed in prior periods is referred to as *prior service cost*.

Under FASB-87, only a portion of the total amount of prior service cost arising in a period, including retroactive benefits that are granted to retirees, is included in net periodic pension cost. FASB-87 requires that the total prior service cost arising in a period from an adoption or amendment of a plan be amortized in equal amounts over the future service periods of each *active* employee who is expected to receive the retroactive benefits.

> **OBSERVATION:** *Since retirees are not expected to render future services, the cost of their retroactive benefits cannot be recognized over their remaining service periods (paragraph 170 of FASB-87). Although not clear, FASB-87 appears to require that the total prior service cost arising from a plan adoption or amendment, including the cost attributed to the benefits of retirees, shall be amortized in equal amounts over the future service periods of only the active employees who are expected to receive benefits. (See below for exceptions.)*

If substantially all of the participants of a pension plan are inactive, the prior service cost attributed to the benefits of the inactive participants shall be amortized over the remaining life expectancy of those participants.

> **OBSERVATION:** *The last sentence of paragraph 25 of FASB-87 addresses the method of amortizing that portion of the cost of retroactive plan amendments that affect benefits of inactive participants of a plan composed of substantially all inactive participants, but does not address the method of amortizing the portion of the cost of the same retroactive plan amendments that affect benefits of the active participants of the same plan. Two assumptions can be made. The first is that the cost of the active participants' benefits is not amortized at all, and thus is charged to net income of the period. The second assumption is that the cost of the **active** participants' benefits is amortized in the same manner as if the plan were not composed of substantially all inactive participants. In this event,*

> *the cost attributed to the retroactive benefits of the **active** partici-*
> *pants of a plan composed of substantially all **inactive** participants*
> *is amortized in equal amounts over the future service periods of*
> *each active employee who is expected to receive the retroactive*
> *benefits.*

FASB-87 permits the consistent use of an alternative amortization approach which more rapidly reduces the amount of unrecognized prior service cost. For example, straight-line amortization of unrecognized prior service cost over the average future service period of active employees who are expected to receive benefits under the plan is acceptable. If an alternative method is used to amortize unrecognized prior service cost, it must be disclosed in the financial statements.

The period in which an employer expects to realize the economic benefits from retroactive pension benefits that were previously granted may be shorter than the entire remaining future service period of all active employees. Under this circumstance, FASB-87 requires that a more rapid rate of amortization be applied to the remaining balance of the unrecognized prior service cost, to reflect the earlier realization of the employer's economic benefits and to properly allocate the cost to the periods benefited.

An amendment to a pension plan usually increases the cost of employees' pension benefits and increases the amount of the projected benefit obligation. However, a pension plan amendment may decrease the cost of employees' pension benefits, which results in a decrease in the amount of the projected benefit obligation. Any decrease resulting from a pension plan amendment shall be applied to reduce the balance of any existing unrecognized prior service cost and any excess shall be amortized on the same basis as increases in unrecognized prior service cost.

Gains and Losses Component

Gains and losses are changes in the amount of either the projected benefit obligation or pension plan assets, resulting from the differences between estimates or assumptions used and actual experience. Thus, a gain or loss can result from the difference between (a) the expected amount and actual amount of the projected benefit obligation at the end of a period, and/or (b) the expected amount and actual amount of the fair value of pension plan assets at the end of a period. Technically, both of these types of gains and losses are considered *actuarial gains and losses.* However, under FASB-87, a gain or loss resulting from a change in the projected benefit obligation is referred to as an "actuarial gain or loss," while a gain or loss resulting from a change in the fair value of pension plan assets is referred to as a "net asset gain or loss." For the purposes of FASB-87, the sources of these gains and losses are not separately distinguished, and they include amounts that have been realized as well as amounts that are unrealized.

Under FASB-87, the gains and losses component of net periodic pension cost consists of (a) the difference between the actual return on pension plan assets and the expected return on pension plan assets ("net asset gain or loss"), and (b) if required, amortization of any unrecognized gain or loss from previous periods.

> **OBSERVATION:** *The difference between the actual return on pension plan assets and the expected return on pension plan assets ("net asset gain or loss") is not recognized in the period in which it arises, but is included in the gains and losses component of net periodic pension cost only as an offset or supplement to the actual return on pension plan assets which is also a separate component of net periodic pension cost (paragraph 54, footnote 13, of FASB-87).*

As discussed in a previous section, the actual return on pension plan assets is equal to the difference between the fair value of pension plan assets at the beginning and end of a period, adjusted for any contributions and pension benefit payments made during that period. Fair value is the amount that a pension plan could reasonably expect to receive from a current sale of an investment between a willing buyer under no compulsion to buy and a willing seller under no compulsion to sell.

The expected return on pension plan assets during the period is computed by multiplying the *market-related value* of plan assets by the *expected long-term rate of return.* The expected long-term rate of return is an actuarial assumption of the expected long-term interest rate that will be earned on plan assets during the period. Under FASB-87, the current rate of return earned on plan assets and the rates of return expected to be available for plan investments should be considered in estimating the long-term rate of return on plan assets. The expected long-term rate of return on plan assets should reflect the average rate of earnings expected on plan investments.

To reduce the volatility of changes in the fair value of pension plan assets and the resulting effect on net periodic pension cost,

FASB-87 requires the use of a market-related value for plan assets to compute the expected return on such assets during a period. Market-related value is used only to compute the expected return on pension plan assets for the period (expected return = market-related value multiplied by the expected long-term rate of return).

Under FASB-87, the market-related value of a plan asset can be either (a) the actual fair value of the pension plan asset or (b) a calculated value that recognizes, in a systematic and rational manner, the changes in the actual fair value of the pension plan asset over a period of not more than five years. Thus, in computing the market-related value of a pension plan asset, an enterprise may use actual fair value or a calculated value based on a five-year moving average of the changes in the actual fair value of the pension plan asset. In this event, the calculated market-related value would include only 20% of the total changes in the actual fair value of the pension plan asset that have occurred during the past five years. For example if the actual fair value of a plan asset at the end of each of the last six years was $8,000, $10,000, $12,000, $14,000, $16,000, and $13,000, the net gain for the five years is $5,000 ($2,000 + $2,000 + $2,000 + $2,000 less $3,000 = $5,000). In this event, only 20% of the $5,000 gain ($1,000) is included in computing the calculated market-related value of the pension plan asset for the current year.

The only difference between the actual fair value of a pension plan asset and its calculated market-related value is the amount of net gain or loss from previous years that has not yet been recognized in the calculated market-related value.

Market-related value may be computed differently for each class of plan assets, but the method of computing market-related value must be consistently applied from year to year for each class of plan assets. For example, fair value may be used for bonds and other fixed income investments, and a calculated market-related value for stocks and other equities.

The following illustrates one method of computing market-related value.

For computing the market-related value of a particular class of plan assets as of the end of each period, an employer uses a calculated value that includes 20% of the gains and losses on the plan assets that have occurred over the last five years. The total market-related value of this particular class of plan assets at the beginning of calendar year 19X6 was $100,000. The total fair value of the plan assets was $120,000 at the beginning of 19X6 and $130,000 at the end of 19X6. Actual gains and losses for the past five years as of the beginning of 19X6 were: 19X1 $10,000; 19X2 $(8,000); 19X3 $12,000; 19X4 $10,000; 19X5 $(4,000); which resulted in a net gain of $20,000 for the five years. Employer's contributions to the plan for 19X6 are estimated at $2,000 and benefit payments expected to be paid from the plan in 19X6 are also $2,000. The expected long-term rate of return on plan assets for 19X6 is 10%. The computation of the estimated market-related value as of December 31, 19X6, for this particular class of plans is determined as follows:

Market-related value at the beginning of period	$100,000
Add:	
Expected return on assets for 19X6 (market-related value, multiplied by expected long-term rate of return ($100,000 x 10%)	10,000
20% of the net gain or loss for the last 5 years (20% x $20,000)	4,000
Employer's contribution	2,000
Benefit payments made from plan	(2,000)
Estimated market-related value, Dec. 31, 19X6 (Note)	$114,000

Note: The difference between the fair value ($130,000) and market-related value ($114,000) of plan assets at the end of 19X6 is $16,000. This difference represents the amount of net gain from previous years that has not yet been recognized in the market-related value of plan assets.

The expected return on plan assets is based on market-related values, which do not include all of the net asset gains and losses from previous years (unless market-related values are equal to fair values). Thus, net asset gains and losses may include both (a) gains and losses of previous years that have been included in market-related value and (b) gains and losses of previous years that have not yet been included in market-related value.

As mentioned above, FASB-87 does not require the recognition of any gains and losses as components of net periodic pension cost of the period in which they arise, except to the extent that the net asset gain or loss for the period offsets or supplements the actual return of pension plan assets for the period. However, in subsequent years, all gains and losses, except those which have not yet been recognized in the market-related values of pension plan assets are subject to certain minimum amortization provisions of FASB-87.

FASB-87 requires amortization of unrecognized net gains or losses based on beginning-of-the-year balances. An unrecognized net gain or loss which, as of the beginning of the year, exceeds 10% of (a) the projected benefit obligation or (b) the market-related value of plan assets, whichever is greater, is subject to amortization. The minimum amortization for the year is calculated by dividing the average remaining service period of active employees, who are expected to receive benefits under the plan, into the amount of unrecognized net gain or loss which, as of the beginning of the year, exceeds 10 % of (a) the projected benefit obligation or (b) the market-related value of plan assets, whichever is greater. However, if substantially all of a plan's participants are inactive, the average remaining life expectancy of the inactive participants is divided into the excess unrecognized net gain or loss subject to amortization. The computation of the minimum amortization required by FASB-87 is made each year based on beginning-of-the-year balances of unrecognized net gains or losses.

In lieu of the minimum amortization of unrecognized gains and losses specified by FASB-87, an employer may use an alternative amortization method provided that the method (a) is systematic and applied consistently, (b) is applied to both gains and losses similarly, (c) reduces the unamortized balance by an amount greater than the amount that would result from the minimum amortization method provided by FASB-87, and (d) is disclosed in the financial statements.

The following is a comprehensive illustration of the gains and losses component of net periodic pension cost.

ABC Corporation elected to apply the provision of FASB-87 as of January 1, 19X7, and also elected to compute all pension-related amounts as of the end of the period. The unrecognized net obligation existing at the date of the initial application of FASB-87 was $400, of which $40 was amortized in 19X7. The net asset (gain) or loss for 19X7, resulting from changes in actuarial assumptions, was a loss of $400, which was deferred as an unrecognized net loss for the year. The market-related value of pension plan assets at 1/1/X8 is $1,600 and the average remaining service life of active employees is 10 years.

The expected net periodic pension cost for 19X8 is $340, broken down as follows: service cost $200; interest cost $240 (10%); amortization of unrecognized net asset loss $20; amortization of unrecognized net obligation $40; less a 10% expected return on plan assets of $160 (expected return = market-related value of plan assets of $1,600 multiplied by the expected long-term rate of return of 10%). No contributions were made to the pension plan in 19X8.

		Actual 12/31/X7	Expected 12/31/X8	Actual 12/31/X8
(A)	Projected benefit obligation	$(2,400)	$(2,840)	$(2,900)
(B)	Fair value of plan assets	1,640	1,800	1,750
	Funded status of plan	$ (760)	$(1,040)	$(1,150)
	Unrecognized prior service cost	0	0	0
	Unrecognized net (gain) or loss	400	380	490
	Unrecognized net obligation existing at 1/1/X7	360	320	320
	(Accrued)/prepaid pension cost	$ 0	$ 340	$ 340

(A) The difference between the actual projected benefit obligation for 19X7 and the expected projected benefit obligation for 19X8 is $440, which consists of the expected service cost of $200, and the expected interest cost of $240. However, the actual projected benefit for 19X8 increased $500 over the actual projected benefit for 19X7. The difference between the expected increase in the projected benefit obligation of $440 and the actual increase of $500 represents a $60 actuarial loss. The $60 loss occurred because the actuarial assumptions used were different from actual experience.

The $40 amortization of the unrecognized net obligation does not affect the projected benefit obligation because the full amount of the net obligation was recognized in the projected benefit obligation as of the date of the initial application of FASB-87.

(B) The difference between the actual fair value of plan assets for 19X7 and the expected fair value of plan assets for 19X8 is $160, which represents the 10% expected return on plan assets (market-related value of plan assets of $1,600 x 10%). However, the actual fair value of plan assets for 19X8 of $1,750 increased only $110 over the actual fair value of plan assets of $1,640 for 19X7. The difference between the expected increase in the fair value of plan assets of $160 and the actual increase of $110 represents a $50 net asset loss for the period. The loss occurred because the actual rate of return on pension plan assets was less than the expected rate of return.

Cost Components of Net Periodic Pension Cost for 19X8

FASB-87 requires the financial statement disclosure of the amount of net periodic pension cost for the period. The disclosure shall separately indicate the service cost component, the interest cost component, the actual return on plan assets for the period, and the net total of other components. The following illustrates this disclosure:

Service cost	$200
Interest cost	240
Actual return on plan assets	(110)
Net amortization and deferral (see below)	10
Net periodic pension cost for 19X8	$340
Net amortization and deferral computation:	
Amortization of unrecognized net obligation	$ 40
Amortization of unrecognized prior service cost	0
Amortization of unrecognized net (gain) or loss	20
Net asset gain or (loss) for 19X8 – deferred (Note 1)	(50)
Net amortization and deferral	$ 10

Note 1: A net asset gain or loss is not recognized in the period in which it arises (paragraph 29 of FASB-87), but is included in the gains and losses component of net periodic pension cost (paragraph 34 of FASB-87), but only as an offset or supplement to the actual return on pension plan assets, which is a separate component of net periodic pension cost (paragraph 54, footnote 13, of FASB-87).

Computation of the Amortization of the
Unrecognized Gain or Loss for 19X8

Unrecognized net (gain) or loss 1/1	$400
Add asset gain or subtract asset loss not yet recognized in market-related values at 1/1 (difference between fair value of plan assets ($1,640) and market-related value ($,1600))	40
Unrecognized net (gain) or loss subject to the minimum amortization provisions of FASB-87	440
10% of the greater of the projected benefit obligation or market-related value at 1/1	240
Unrecognized net (gain) or loss subject to amortization	200
Amortization for 19X8 (over the 10-year average remaining service life of active employees)	$ 20

Note: The unrecognized net (gain) or loss at 1/1 must be adjusted to exclude asset gains and losses not yet reflected in market-related values, because gains and losses are not required to be amortized (paragraph 31 of FASB-87).

Note: The $60 loss that occurred in 19X8 as a result of the difference between the expected and actual projected benefit obligation for 19X8, and the $50 loss that occurred in 19X8 as a result of the difference between the expected and actual fair value of plan assets for 19X8, will become subject to the minimum amortization provisions of FASB-87 as of 1/1/X9. The computation of the amount of unrecognized net (gain) or loss as of January 1, 19X9, is as follows:

Unrecognized net asset (gain) or loss 1/1/X8		$400
Less: Amortization for 19X8		20
Unrecognized net asset (gain) or loss 12/31/X8		380
Add: Actuarial net (gain) or loss for 19X8	$60	
Net asset (gain) or loss for 19X8	50	110
Unrecognized net (gain) or loss as of January 1, 19X9		$490

Amortization of the Unrecognized Net Obligation or Net Asset (as of the date of initial application of FASB-87)

The *funded status* of a pension plan is equal to the difference between the projected benefit obligation and the fair value of pension plan assets. The funded status indicates whether the employer has underfunded or overfunded the pension plan.

The unrecognized net obligation or net asset of a pension plan shall be determined by the employer as of the date of its financial statements of the beginning of the year in which FASB-87 is first applied, or, if used consistently from year to year, as of a date not more than three months prior to that date (see also section entitled "Transition and Effective Date"). The unrecognized net obligation or net asset is equal to the difference between the projected benefit obligation and fair value of pension plan assets, plus previously recognized unfunded accrued pension cost or less previously recognized prepaid pension cost. In the event there is no accrued or prepaid pension cost on the employer's statement of financial position as of the date of transition to FASB-87, the funded status of the pension plan and the unrecognized net obligation or net asset are exactly equal.

An unrecognized net obligation or net asset shall be amortized by the employer on a straight-line basis over the average remaining service period of employees expected to receive benefits under the plan, as of the date of initial application of FASB-87, except under the following circumstances:

a. If the amortization period is less than 15 years, an employer may elect to use 15 years, or

b. If the plan is composed of all or substantially all inactive participants, the employer shall use those participants' average remaining life expectancy as the amortization period

The above amortization method shall also be used to recognize, as of the date of the initial application of FASB-87, any unrecognized net obligation or (net asset) of a defined contribution pension plan.

Recognition of Liabilities and Assets

If an employer's total contribution to its pension plan for the period is not equal to the amount of net periodic pension cost required to be recognized under the provisions of FASB-87, the difference shall be recognized by the employer either as a liability or as an asset. A liability (unfunded accrued pension cost) shall be recognized if the amount of contribution is less than the amount of net periodic pension cost. If the amount of contribution is more than the amount of net periodic pension cost, an asset (prepaid pension cost) shall be recognized.

The *projected benefit obligation* is the actuarial present value of all employee benefits that are attributed by the pension benefit formula to employees' services performed prior to a specific date. The projected benefit obligation includes all pension benefits attributed by the pension benefit formula, whether the benefits are based on future employee compensation levels or not. The *accumulated benefit obligation* is the amount of the projected benefit obligation as of a specific date, reduced by the actuarial present value of any pension benefits attributed by the pension benefit formula that are based on future employee compensation levels, including the indirect effects of changes in future compensation levels, such as increases in the social security wage base. In lieu of estimates of future compensation levels, current and/or past compensation levels of employees should be used to calculate the accumulated benefit obligation.

An employer's *unfunded accumulated benefit obligation* is the amount of the accumulated benefit obligation that exceeds the amount of the fair value of plan assets as of a specific date. Under FASB-87, an additional minimum liability must be recognized in the employer's statement of financial position if an unfunded accumulated benefit obligation exists and (a) an asset has been recognized as prepaid pension cost, (b) a liability has been recognized as unfunded accrued pension cost in an amount that is less than the amount of the existing unfunded accumulated benefit obligation, or (c) no accrued or prepaid pension cost has been recognized. If an asset has been recognized as prepaid pension cost, the additional minimum liability is the amount of the existing unfunded accumulated benefit obligation plus the amount of the prepaid pension cost. If a liability has been recognized as unfunded accrued pension cost in an amount that is less than the amount of the existing unfunded accumulated benefit obligation, the additional minimum liability is the amount of the existing unfunded accumulated benefit obligation reduced by the amount of the unfunded accrued pension cost. If no accrued or prepaid pension cost has been recognized, the additional minimum liability is the amount of the existing unfunded accumulated benefit obligation.

If an additional minimum liability is required to be recognized, an intangible asset in the same amount as the additional minimum liability shall also be recognized, but the amount of the intangible asset shall not exceed the total amount of any existing unrecognized prior service cost and any unrecognized net obligation. In the event that the intangible asset exceeds the total existing unrecognized prior service cost and unrecognized net obligation, the excess shall be reported as a separate component of stockholders' equity (a reduction of equity), net of related tax benefits.

Unless more current amounts are available, the amount of additional minimum liability reported in interim financial statements shall be the same amount as reported by the employer in its previous year-end statement of financial position, adjusted for subsequent accruals and contributions.

The calculation of the additional minimum liability is reflected in the following illustration.

Calculation of the Additional Minimum Liability

	As of End of Period		
	Year 1	*Year 2*	*Year 3*
Accumulated benefit obligation	$(3,762)	$(4,884)	$(4,848)
Fair value of plan assets	3,495	4,515	4,866
(Unfunded) or over-funded accumulated benefit obligation	$ (267)	$ (369)	$ 18
Projected benefit obligation	$(5,637)	$(7,326)	$(7,272)
Fair value of plan assets	3,495	4,515	4,866
Funded status of plan	(2,142)	(2,811)	(2,406)
Unrecognized prior service cost	2,145	3,942	3,516
Unrecognized net (gain) or loss	(753)	(1,671)	(1,380)
Unrecognized net obligation at date of initial application of FASB-87	840	780	720
(Accrued) or prepaid pension cost	$ 90	$ 240	$ 450

(Accrued) or prepaid pension cost at beginning of period	$ 0	$ 90	$ 240
Less: Net periodic pension cost	912	1,005	1,191
Add: Contributions paid	1,002	1,155	1,401
(Accrued) or prepaid pension cost at end of period	$ 90	$ 240	$ 450
(Unfunded) or overfunded accumulated benefit obligation (computed above)	$ (267)	$ (369)	$ 18
Required adjustment for additional minimum liability	(357)	(252)	609
Intangible asset	357	252	(609)
Cumulative balance of the additional minimum liability	(357)	(609)	0

Note: The adjustment necessary to record the additional minimum liability is equal to the unfunded accumulated benefit obligation, plus the amount of any prepaid pension cost or minus the amount of any accrued pension cost (at the end of the period), less the previous balance of the additional minimum liability from the preceding year. Thus the adjustment in year 1 is $357, which is equal to the unfunded accumulated benefit obligation of $267, plus the prepaid pension cost of $90 at the end of the period (there was no previous balance of the additional minimum liability from the preceding year). The adjustment for year 2 if $252, which is equal to the unfunded accumulated benefit obligation of $369, plus the amount of prepaid pension cost of $240 at the end of the period, less the preceding year's balance of the additional minimum liability of $357.

In the third year, the balance of the unfunded accumulated benefit obligation was an $18 debit, which results in no unfunded accumulated benefit obligation. Thus, the adjustment consisted of simply eliminating the preceding year's balance of $609.

Note: The additional minimum liability that was required in all three years did not exceed the unrecognized prior service cost plus the unrecognized net obligation. Thus, no portion of the required additional minimum liability had to be reported as a separate component of stockholders' equity.

Measurement of Plan Assets

All pension plan assets that are held as investments to provide pension benefits shall be measured at their fair values as of the date of the financial statements or, if used consistently from year to year, as of a date not more than three months prior to that date (paragraph 49 of FASB-87). Fair value is the amount that a pension plan could reasonably expect to receive for a current sale of an investment between a willing buyer under no compulsion to buy and a willing seller under no compulsion to sell. If an active market exists for a plan investment, fair value shall be determined by the market price. If an active market does not exist for a particular plan investment, selling prices for similar investments, if available, should be appropriately considered. If no active market exists, an estimate of the fair value of the plan investment may be based on its projected cash flow, provided that appropriate consideration is given to current discount rates and the investment risk involved.

Pension plan assets that are used in the actual operation of a plan should be valued at amortized cost (paragraph 51 of FASB-87). Thus, buildings, leasehold improvements, furniture, equipment and fixtures that are used in the everyday operation of a pension plan should be valued at historical cost less accumulated depreciation or amortization.

Measurement Dates

For the purposes of FASB-87, plan assets and obligations shall be determined either (a) as of the date of the financial statements or (b) if used consistently from year to year, as of a date not more than three months prior to the date of the financial statements.

Unless more current amounts are available, the amount of additional minimum liability reported in interim financial statements shall be the same amount as reported by the employer in its previous year-end statement of financial position, adjusted for subsequent accruals and contributions.

The same assumptions used to calculate the previous year-end net periodic pension cost shall be used to calculate the net periodic pension cost in subsequent interim and annual financial statements, unless more current valuations of plan assets and obligations are available or a significant event has occurred, such as a plan amendment which would usually require new valuations.

Financial Statement Disclosure

The following financial statement disclosures shall be made by an employer who sponsors a defined benefit pension plan:

- A full description of the pension plan, including the employee groups covered, type of benefit formula, funding policy, types of assets held and significant nonbenefit liabilities (if any), and the nature and effect of significant matters affecting comparability of information for all periods presented.
- The amount of net periodic pension cost for the period detailing the separate amounts for the (a) service cost component, (b) interest cost component, (c) actual return on plan assets for the period, and (d) net total of other components.
- A schedule reconciling the funded status of the plan with amounts reported in the employer's statement of financial position, showing separately:

  (a) The fair value of plan assets.
  (b) The projected benefit obligation, separately identifying the accumulated benefit obligation and vested benefit obligation.
  (c) The amount of unrecognized prior service cost.
  (d) The amount of unrecognized net gain or loss, including asset gains and losses not yet reflected in market-related values.
  (e) The amount of any remaining unrecognized net obligation or net asset existing at the date of the initial application of FASB-87.
  (f) The amount of unconditional liability equal to either (i) the unfunded accumulated benefit obligation plus any prepaid pension cost, (ii) the unfunded accumulated

benefit obligation reduced by any unfunded accrued pension cost, or (iii) the amount of the unfunded accumulated benefit obligation

(g) The amount of the net pension asset or liability that has been recognized in the employer's statement of financial position. This amount must be equal to the total of items (a) through (f). For an illustration of a reconciliation schedule, see the Capsule Analysis of FASB-87, above.

- The weighted-average assumed discount rate and, if applicable, the rate of compensation increase used in determining the projected benefit obligation, and the weighted-average expected long-term rate of return on pension plan assets.

- If applicable, the amounts and types of securities of the employer and/or related parties that are included in plan assets, and the approximate amount of annual benefits of employees and retirees covered by annuity contracts issued by the employer and related parties. Also, if applicable, the alternative amortization method used for unrecognized prior service cost and the alternative amortization method used to reflect the substantive commitment of an employer to pay more employee benefits than its existing pension benefit formula indicates.

Employers with Two or More Pension Plans

If an employer sponsors more than one defined benefit pension plan, the provisions of FASB-87 shall be applied separately to each plan. An employer shall not apply the assets of one plan to reduce or eliminate the unfunded accrued pension cost and/or minimum additional liability of another plan, unless the employer clearly has the right to do so. An excess of plan assets over the accumulated benefit obligation or prepaid pension cost of one plan cannot be applied to reduce or eliminate a liability of another plan which is required to be recognized by FASB-87.

All of the disclosures required by FASB-87 for defined benefit pension plans of a single employer may be combined, or combined in particular groups to provide the most useful information, except for plans with assets that have a net pension plan liability or a net pension plan asset, which must be separately disclosed. Unless plans are based on similar economic assumptions, the required disclosures for plans outside the U.S. shall not be combined with U.S. plans.

Annuity Contracts

All or part of an employer's obligation to provide pension plan benefits to individuals may be effectively transferred to an insurance company by the purchase of annuity contracts. An annuity contract is an irrevocable agreement in which an insurance company unconditionally agrees to provide specific periodic payments, or a lump-sum payment to another party, in return for a specified premium. Thus, by use of an annuity contract, an employer can effectively transfer to an insurance company its legal obligation to provide specific employee pension plan benefits. For the purposes of FASB-87, an annuity contract is not considered an annuity contract if the insurance company is a captive insurer or there is reasonable doubt that the insurance company will meet its obligation. A captive insurer is one that does business primarily with the employer and its related parties.

An annuity contract may be participating or nonparticipating. In a participating annuity contract, the insurance company's investing activities with the funds received for the annuity contract are generally shared, in the form of dividends, with the purchaser (the employer or the pension fund). An annuity contract is not considered an annuity contract, for the purposes of FASB-87, unless all the risks and rewards associated with the assets and obligations assumed by the insurance company are actually transferred to the insurance company by the employer.

The cost incurred for currently earned benefits under an annuity contract shall be the cost of those benefits, except for the cost of participating rights of participating annuity contracts, which must be accounted for separately (see below). Thus, the service cost component of net periodic pension cost for the current period is the cost incurred for nonparticipating annuity contracts that cover all currently earned benefits. Pension benefits not covered by annuity contracts shall be accounted for in accordance with the provisions of FASB-87 that address accounting for the cost of pension benefits not covered by annuity contracts.

The projected benefit obligation and the accumulated benefit obligation shall not include the cost of benefits covered by annuity contracts. Except for the cost of participation rights (see below), pension plan assets shall not include the cost of any annuity contracts.

The difference in cost between a nonparticipating annuity contract and a participating annuity contract is usually attributable to the cost of the participation right. The cost of a participation right, at the date of its purchase, is recognized as a pension plan asset. In subsequent periods, a participation right is included in plan assets at its fair value, if fair value is reasonably determinable. If fair value is not reasonably determinable, a participation right is included in plan assets at its amortized cost and systematically amortized over the expected dividend period stated in the contract. In this event, amortized cost may not exceed the net realizable value of the participation right.

Other contracts with insurance companies   The purchase of insurance contracts that are, in substance, annuity contracts shall be accounted for in accordance with the provisions of FASB-87 (see previous section). The purchase of other types of insurance contracts shall be accounted for as pension plan assets and reported at fair value. The best evidence of fair value for some insurance contracts may be their contract values. Under FASB-87, the cash surrender value or conversion value of an insurance contract is presumed to be its fair value.

Defined Contribution Pension Plans

A defined contribution pension plan provides for employer contributions that are defined in the plan, but does not contain any provision for defined pension benefits for employees. Thus, a defined contribution pension plan does not contain a "defined benefit pension formula." However, based on the amount of the employer's defined contributions, pension benefits are provided in return for services performed by employees.

Under FASB-87, a defined contribution pension plan provides for individual accounts for each plan participant and contains the terms that specify how contributions are determined for each participant's individual account. Each periodic employer contribution is allocated to each participant's individual account in accordance with the terms of the plan, and pension benefits are based solely on the amount available in each participant's account at the time of his or her retirement. The amount available in each participant's account at the time of his or her retirement is the total of the amounts contributed by the employer, plus the returns earned on investments of those contributions, and forfeitures of other participants' benefits that have been allocated to the participant's account.

Under FASB-87, the net periodic pension cost of a defined contribution pension plan is the amount of contributions in a period which are made to the individual accounts of participants who performed services during that same period. Contributions for periods after an individual retires or terminates shall be estimated and accrued during periods in which the individual performs services.

The amount of the unrecognized net obligation or net asset of a defined contribution pension plan, at the date of initial application of FASB-87, shall be amortized on a straight-line basis over the average remaining service period of employees expected to receive benefits under the plan, except (a) if the amortization period is less than 15 years, the employer may elect to use 15 years, and (b) if the plan is composed of all or substantially all inactive participants, the employer shall use those participants' average remaining life expectancy as the amortization period.

> **OBSERVATION:** *The above amortization method is the same as that used to amortize the unrecognized net obligation or net asset of a defined benefit pension plan at the date of the initial application of FASB-87. Although not specified by FASB-87, this seems to imply that an employer who sponsors a defined contribution pension plan is also required to record an unrecognized net obligation or net asset at the date of the initial application of FASB-87.*

An employer who sponsors one or more defined contribution pension plans shall disclose the following information separately from its defined benefit pension plan disclosures:

- A description of the plan(s) including employee groups covered, the basis for determining contributions, and the nature and effect of significant matters affecting comparability of information for all periods presented
- The amount of pension cost recognized during the period

Frequently, defined contribution pension plans provide for some method of determining benefits for employees, as may be the case with many "target benefit" plans. If, in substance, a plan does provide defined benefits for employees, it shall be accounted for as a defined benefit pension plan in accordance with the appropriate provisions of FASB-87.

For the purposes of FASB-87, any plan that is not a defined contribution pension plan is considered a defined benefit pension plan (see definition of a defined benefit pension plan in the Glossary of Appendix D of FASB-87).

Multiemployer Plans

A multiemployer plan is a pension plan to which two or more unrelated employers make contributions, usually pursuant to one or more collective-bargaining agreements. In a multiemployer pension plan, assets contributed by one employer are not segregated in separate accounts or restricted to provide benefits only to employees of that employer. Thus, assets contributed by one employer in a multiemployer plan may be used to provide benefits to employees of other participating employers.

The net periodic pension cost of an employer participating in a multiemployer plan is the amount of the required contribution for the period. An employer participating in a multiemployer plan shall also recognize as a liability any of its contributions that are due and unpaid.

> **OBSERVATION:** *A withdrawal from a multiemployer pension plan may result in a loss contingency if the withdrawing employer has a potential liability to the plan for a portion of its unfunded benefit obligation. Under FASB-87, if it is **probable** or **reasonably possible** that the loss contingency will develop into an actual loss, the withdrawing employer shall account for the loss contingency in accordance with the provisions of FASB-5 (Contingencies).*

An employer participating in a multiemployer plan shall disclose the following information separately from disclosures for a single-employer plan:

- A description of the multiemployer plan(s) including employee groups covered, the types of benefits provided (defined benefit or defined contribution), and the nature and effect of significant matters affecting comparability of information for all periods presented.
- The amount of pension cost recognized during the period

> **OBSERVATION:** *FASB Technical Bulletin 81-3 (FASB:TB 81-3) provides guidance on the accounting implications of the Multiemployer Pension Plan Amendments Act of 1980 (MPPAA). FASB:TB 81-3 makes reference to APB-8, FASB-36, and FASB Interpretation-3, all of which have been superseded by FASB-87. Furthermore, FASB:TB 81-3 suggests that employers participating in multiemployer plans that are deemed to be defined benefit*

> *plans subject to the MPPAA should look to FASB Interpretation-3 for guidance.*
>
> *It appears that FASB:TB 81-3 should have also been superseded by FASB-87, but was not. Although FASB:TB 81-3 remains technically effective, it obviously should not be relied upon.*

Multiple-employer plans Some pension plans to which two or more unrelated employers contribute are not multiemployer plans, but are groups of single-employer plans combined to allow participating employers to pool assets for investment purposes and to reduce the cost of plan administration. Under FASB-87, multiple-employer plans are considered single-employer plans and each employer's accounting shall be based on its respective interest in the plan.

Non-U.S. Pension Plans

FASB-87 does not make any special provision for non-U.S. pension plans, except for a different effective date. FASB-87 is effective for employers who have non-U.S. pension plans for fiscal years beginning on or after December 16, 1988.

In some foreign countries it is customary or required for an employer to provide benefits for employees in the event of a voluntary or involuntary severance of employment. In this event, if the substance of the arrangement is a pension plan, it is subject to the provisions of FASB-87 (for example, benefits are paid for substantially all terminations).

Business Combinations

The total cost of a business combination accounted for by the purchase method must be allocated to the individual assets acquired and liabilities assumed (APB-16). Each identifiable asset is assigned a cost equal to its fair value. Liabilities are accounted for at the present value of the amount that will eventually be paid and, if certain criteria are met, appropriate consideration should be given to contingent assets and liabilities (FASB-38).

When a single-employer defined benefit pension plan is acquired as part of a business combination accounted for by the purchase method, an excess of the projected benefit obligation over the plan assets shall be recognized as a liability and an excess of plan assets over the projected benefit obligation shall be recognized as an asset.

The recognition of a new liability or new asset by the purchaser, at the date of a business combination accounted for by the purchase method, results in the elimination of any (a) previously existing unrecognized net gain or loss, (b) unrecognized prior service cost, and (c) unrecognized net obligation or net asset that existed at the date of initial application of FASB-87.

In subsequent periods, the differences between the purchaser's net pension cost and contributions will reduce the new liability or new asset recognized at the date of combination to the extent that the previously unrecognized net gain or loss, unrecognized prior service cost, or unrecognized net obligation are considered in determining the amounts of contributions to the plan. In addition, the effects of an expected plan termination or curtailment shall be considered by the purchaser in calculating the amount of the projected benefit obligation at the date of a business combination accounted for by the purchase method.

> **OBSERVATION**: *FASB-87 amends APB-16, to provide that the assets and liabilities of a pension plan acquired by the purchase method of accounting shall no longer be accounted for in accordance with paragraph 88h of APB-16 (Business Combinations), but shall be accounted for in accordance with paragraph 74 of FASB-87, which is discussed above.*

Transition and Effective Date

For defined benefit pension plans consisting of 100 or fewer participants that are sponsored by employers that are *nonpublic enterprises* (see definition below), and for pension plans located outside the United States, FASB-87 is effective for fiscal years beginning on or after December 16, 1988. For all other pension plans, FASB-87 is effective for fiscal years beginning on or after December 16, 1986, except for paragraphs 36, 37, and 38, which are effective for fiscal years beginning on or after December 16, 1988. Paragraphs 36, 37, and 38 require the recognition of an additional minimum liability in the employer's statement of financial position, if the unfunded accumulated benefit obligation exceeds the fair value of plan assets.

Retroactive application of the provisions of FASB-87 to previously issued annual financial statements is not permitted. However, if FASB-87 is initially applied in other than the first interim period of a fiscal year, previously issued interim financial statements of the same fiscal year shall be restated.

Definition of nonpublic enterprise   FASB-87 defines a nonpublic enterprise as "An enterprise other than one (a) whose debt or equity securities are traded in a public market, either on a stock exchange or in the over-the-counter market (including securities quoted only locally or regionally), or (b) whose financial statements are filed with a regulatory agency in preparation for the sale of any class of securities."

Recognition of unrecognized net obligation or net asset   The unrecognized net obligation or net asset of a pension plan shall be determined by the employer as of the date of its financial statements of the beginning of the year in which FASB-87 is first applied, or, if used consistently from year to year, as of a date not more than three months prior to that date. The unrecognized net obligation or net asset is equal to the difference between the projected benefit obligation and fair value of pension plan assets, plus previously recognized unfunded accrued pension cost or less previously recognized prepaid pension cost.

An unrecognized net obligation or net asset shall be amortized by the employer on a straight-line basis over the average remaining service period of employees expected to receive benefits under the plan, as of the date of initial application of FASB-87, except under the following circumstances:

a.   if the amortization period is less than 15 years, an employer may elect to use 15 years, or

b.   if the plan is composed of all or substantially all inactive participants, the employer shall use those participants' average remaining life expectancy as the amortization period

> **OBSERVATION:** *Recognition and amortization of the unrecognized net obligation or net asset is also discussed in the section entitled "Amortization of Unrecognized Net Obligation or Net Asset (as of the date of the initial application of FASB-87)."*

Change in Accounting Principle

After FASB-87 (Employers' Accounting for Pensions) was issued, the following article appears in *The CPA Letter*, which is published by the AICPA:

Many companies will have a change in accounting principle as a result of implementing FASB Statement no. 87, *Employers' Accounting for Pensions*. SAS no. 1, *Consistency of Application of Generally Accepted Accounting Principles*, section 420, requires the auditor's opinion to be modified for consistency when there is a change in accounting principle having a material effect on the financial statements.

According to the AICPA's auditing standards division, if the change is made on a piecemeal basis as permitted by FASB Statement no. 87 and each change is material, the auditor should modify his report as to consistency for each change. If the change does not have a material effect in the year it is made but may be expected to have such an effect in the future, no consistency modification is required in the auditor's report, but disclosure of the change, nevertheless should be made in the notes to the financial statements.

The above information should be verified before an enterprise reports a material change in accounting principle as a result of implementing FASB-87 on a piecemeal basis.

Change in method of accounting for certain postretirement benefits   FASB Technical Bulletin 87-1 (FASB:TB 87-1), issued April 9, 1987, provides guidance on accounting for the effects of a change in the method of accounting for (i) *postretirement life insurance benefits* that *are not* provided through an employer's pension plan or (ii) *postretirement health care benefits* that *are or are not* provided through an employer's pension plan (paragraph 13 of FASB:TB 87-1).

> **OBSERVATION:** *Postretirement is a narrower term than postemployment (footnote 1, FASB-81). Postretirement benefits are provided for an employee only after he or she has reached retirement age in accordance with the terms of a specific pension plan. Postemployment benefits are provided for any period after employment has been terminated, including the period from the date of termination to the date of retirement as well as any period after retirement.*

FASB-87 (Employers' Accounting for Pensions) established *mandatory* methods of accounting for certain types of pension benefits, and allowed enterprises to adopt similar accounting methods *voluntarily* for certain other types of benefits. The mandatory provisions of FASB-87 require that a change in accounting method be accounted for prospectively by including the amount of the effect of the change in the unrecognized net obligation or unrecognized net asset that is computed as of the date that FASB-87 is adopted by an enterprise. The unrecognized net obligation or unrecognized net asset is then amortized to income in subsequent periods.

The mandatory provisions of FASB-87 requiring that a change in accounting method be accounted for prospectively do *not* apply to (a) postretirement life insurance benefits not provided through a pension plan or (b) postretirement health care benefits, whether provided through a pension plan or a separate plan. These two types of postretirement benefits are, however, covered by the mandatory disclosure provisions of FASB-81 (Disclosure of Post-retirement Health Care and Life Insurance Benefits). Under FASB-87 and FASB-81 read together, therefore, enterprises have discretion as to how they account for these types of postretirement benefits, provided the financial statements include the disclosure required by FASB-81. Enterprises also have discretion to change their methods of accounting for these types of postretirement benefits, provided the new method is preferable to the one previously used (paragraph 16 of APB-20).

Under the provisions of FASB:TB 87-1, if an employer changes its method of accounting for postretirement life insurance benefits that are not provided through the employer's pension plan, or postretirement health care benefits whether provided through the employer's pension plan or a separate plan, the effects of such a change may be recognized either (i) prospectively, or (ii) by the cumulative effect method. In other words, FASB:TB 87-1 permits these types of changes to be recognized in the same manner as either a change in accounting estimate (prospectively), or a change in accounting principle (by the cumulative effect method).

> **OBSERVATION:** *FASB:TB 87-1 gives absolutely no guidance as to the circumstances in which the prospective method is preferable to the cumulative effect method, or vice versa. Thus, even if an enterprise can easily make the computations required for the cumulative effect method, the enterprise has complete discretion under FASB:TB 87-1 to use either the prospective method or the cumulative effect method.*

If the effect of a change in accounting principle or method is accounted for prospectively, the amount of the effect is recognized in the period of change and/or future periods (paragraph 3 of FASB:TB 87-1). Under FASB-87, the effect of a change in accounting principle or method is included in the amount of the unrecognized net obligation/asset that is recorded as of the date of the adoption of FASB-87. Prospective accounting is achieved through the amortization of the unrecognized net obligation/asset in the period of change and/or future periods.

If the effect of the change is accounted for by the cumulative effect method, the total effect of the accounting change on all prior years is shown in the income statement of the year of change as a separate item immediately above net income, and the newly adopted accounting principle is used in determining net income of the current period (paragraph 3 of FASB:TB 87-1).

If the accrual method adopted by an employer immediately recognizes any obligation at the date of plan adoption, the cost of plan amendments, and gains and losses, the cumulative effect of the accounting change will be the same amount as the unrecognized benefit obligation attributed to employee service to date (paragraph 17 of FASB:TB 87-1). In this event, the effect of the accounting change may be recognized, either in the current year as a cumulative adjustment, or accounted for prospectively in the current year and future periods through the periodic amortization of the unrecognized net obligation/asset.

Certain financial statement disclosure is required by FASB:TB 87-1, regardless of the method used to account for the effects of the change in accounting principle. Financial statement disclosure of the nature of, and justification for, an accounting change should be made in the period in which the change is adopted by an enterprise. The disclosure of the justification for the change in accounting principle should contain a clear explanation of why the newly adopted accounting method is preferable. The effect of adopting the new accounting method on income before extraordinary items, net income, and the related per share amounts of the period of the change should also be disclosed. These financial statement disclosures are similar to the disclosures required by APB-20 (Accounting Changes).

FASB:TB 87-1 also requires financial statement disclosures of a description of the new method of accounting that is being used by the employer to account for the effects of the change in accounting principle. The following information should also be disclosed:

If the Change Is Accounted for Prospectively—The effects of the change method of accounting for prospective recognition should be disclosed.

If the Change Is Accounted for by Cumulative Effect Method—The pro forma effects of retroactive application on income before extraordinary items and net income, including per share amounts, should be disclosed as required by paragraph 21 of APB-20.

FASB:TB 87-1 states that the disclosures required by FASB-81 (Disclosure of Postretirement Health Care and Life Insurance Benefits) should also be disclosed in the financial statements.

FASB Technical Bulletin 87-1 is effective for fiscal years beginning after December 15, 1986, and earlier application is permitted. Restatement of financial statements that have previously been issued is not permitted.

PENSION PLANS - SETTLEMENTS AND CURTAILMENTS

Overview

FASB-88 establishes accounting and reporting standards for settlements and curtailments of defined benefit pension plans and for termination benefits that are offered to employees. FASB-88 supersedes FASB-74 (Accounting for Special Termination Benefits Paid to Employees).

> **OBSERVATION:** *FASB-88 is effective for events occurring during and after the fiscal year in which FASB-87 (Employers' Accounting for Pensions) is first applied. FASB-87 is generally effective for fiscal years beginning on or after December 16, 1986, except for pension plans of nonpublic enterprises consisting of 100 or fewer participants and plans located outside of the United States.*
>
> *For discussion of settlements and curtailments of postretirement plans other than pensions, see the chapter entitled "Postretirement Benefits Other Than Pensions."*

Background

In connection with the operation of a defined benefit pension plan, FASB-87 (Employers' Accounting for Pensions) provides for the delayed recognition of actuarial gains and losses, prior service costs, and the net obligation or asset that arises at the date of the initial application of FASB-87. As a result, at any given date, an employer's pension plan records may reflect a balance of an (a) unrecognized net gain or loss, (b) unrecognized prior service cost, and/or (c) unrecognized net obligation or net asset. Part or all of these unrecognized balances may be recognized in a settlement or curtailment of a pension plan.

In a settlement of a defined benefit pension plan, the employer or the pension plan is irrevocably released from its primary responsibility for all or part of its pension plan obligation and all significant risks relating to the settlement are eliminated. For example, through the purchase of nonparticipating annuity contracts or cash payments to some or all of the plan participants in exchange for their pension benefits, an employer may be irrevocably released from the pension plan obligation related to the pension benefits involved in the exchange. After the settlement of a pension plan, an employer may continue to provide pension benefits in the same pension plan or a new plan.

The maximum gain or loss recognized at the date of a plan settlement is the total of the unamortized balance of any (a) unrecognized net gain or loss arising after the date of the initial application of FASB-87 and/or (b) unrecognized *net asset* that arose at the date of the initial application of FASB-87. The amount of gain or loss recognized depends on the percentage decrease or increase in the projected benefit obligation resulting from the plan settlement. If the projected benefit obligation is reduced by 40%, only 40% of the gain or loss is recognized. On the other hand, if the projected benefit obligation is completely discharged, 100% of the gain or loss on the plan settlement is recognized.

In a curtailment of a defined benefit pension plan some of the future pension benefits for present employees are significantly reduced, generally resulting in a net decrease (gain) or increase (loss) in the projected benefit obligation. For example, if employees are terminated as a result of a plan curtailment, some or all of their pension benefits based on future compensation levels may cease to be an obligation of the employer or pension plan. In this event, the projected benefit obligation is decreased (a gain) by the amount of the pension benefits that are no longer an obligation of the plan. On the other hand, if terminated employees who are eligible for subsidized early retirement benefits accept the benefits at a date earlier than expected, there is an increase (loss) in the projected benefit obligation. Gain or loss on a plan curtailment is based on the net decrease (gain) or increase (loss) in the projected benefit obligation.

An employer may have to recognize an additional loss that is not included in the gain or loss on a plan curtailment, but is recognized as part of the total effects of a plan curtailment. This loss is equal to the amount of decrease in the unrecognized prior service cost of the pension benefits that are reduced by the plan curtailment. A separate loss computation is necessary for the unrecognized prior service cost of each plan amendment.

The pension benefits that are reduced or eliminated in a plan curtailment may have been granted to some or all of the employees who were working for the employer as of the date of the initial application of FASB-87. For this reason, any unrecognized *net obligation* that arose at the date of the initial application of FASB-87 and that remains unamortized at the date of the plan curtailment is also treated as a separate unrecognized prior service cost.

A pension plan settlement and a pension plan curtailment may occur simultaneously or separately. If the expected years of future service for some employees are reduced but the pension plan continues in existence, a curtailment has occurred but not a settlement. If an employer settles all or a portion of its pension obligation and continues to provide defined benefits to employees for future services, either in the same plan or in a successor plan, a settlement has occurred, but not a curtailment. If an employer terminates its defined benefit pension plan without replacing it with another defined benefit pension plan, and settles its present pension plan obligation in full, a curtailment and settlement has occurred. Under these circumstances, it makes no difference whether or not some or all of the employees continue to work for the employer.

Termination benefits are frequently offered by employers as part of an overall plan to reduce employment levels, to increase productivity, or generally to decrease payroll costs. To induce certain groups of employees to terminate employment, many employers offer attractive termination benefits. This is particularly true for those employees who are close to, or have reached, the early retirement age specified in the employer's existing pension plan. Termination benefits may consist of periodic future payments, lump-sum payments, or a combination of both. The payment of termination benefits may be made from a new or existing employee benefit plan, from the employer's existing assets, or from a combination of these sources.

Under FASB-88, termination benefits are classified either as *special* or *contractual*. Special termination benefits are those that are offered to employees for a short period of time in connection with their termination of employment. Contractual termination benefits are those that are required by the terms of an existing plan or agreement and are provided only on the occurrence of a specified event, such as early retirement or the closing of a facility.

FASB-88 requires that the cost of termination benefits be recognized by an employer as a loss and a corresponding liability. The recognition date depends on whether the benefits are special or contractual.

Updating Pension Plan Records

Before applying the provisions of FASB-88, an employer should bring its defined benefit pension plan records up to date, preferably as of the day before the curtailment and/or settlement of the plan. The effects of the pending curtailment and/or settlement must be ignored in the updating process and all computations including the net periodic pension cost accrual must be consistent with prior periods. The updating process includes the measurement of the fair value of pension plan assets and the computation of the net periodic pension cost accrual.

> **OBSERVATION:** *Neither FASB-87 nor FASB-88 provides any guidance on the appropriate valuation of assets employed in the operation of a pension plan in the event such assets are disposed of as part of a curtailment and/or settlement of a plan. Under this circumstance, it appears appropriate to measure these assets at their fair value in spite of the fact that paragraph 51 of FASB-87 requires that such assets be measured, for all purposes, at their cost less accumulated depreciation or amortization.*

Settlements of Defined Benefit Pension Plans

Under FASB-88, a settlement of a defined benefit pension plan is an irrevocable transaction that (a) releases the employer or the pension plan from its primary responsibility for the payment of all or a portion of the pension plan obligation and (b) eliminates all of the significant risks associated with the assets and obligations used to effectuate the settlement. A settlement of a defined benefit pension plan does not require that the plan be completely terminated (paragraph 26 of FASB-88).

All or a part of an employer's obligation to provide pension plan benefits to individuals may be effectively transferred to an insurance company by the purchase of annuity contracts. An annuity contract is an irrevocable agreement in which an insurance company unconditionally agrees to provide specific periodic payments or a lump-sum payment to another party in return for a specified premium. For the purposes of FASB-87 and FASB-88, an annuity contract is not considered an annuity contract if the insurance company is a *captive insurer* or there is reasonable doubt that the insurance company will meet its obligation. A captive insurer is one that does business primarily with the employer and its related parties.

An annuity contract may be participating or nonparticipating. In a participating annuity contract the insurance company's investing activities with the funds received for the premium of the annuity contract are generally shared, in the form of dividends, with the purchaser of the contract (the employer or the pension fund). An annuity contract is not considered an annuity contract unless all the risks and rewards associated with the assets and obligations assumed by the insurance company are actually transferred to the insurance company by the employer.

Gain or loss on a plan settlement should be based on pension plan records that have been updated as of the day before the settlement (see above section entitled Updating Pension Plan Records). Under FASB-88, the maximum gain or loss on a settlement of a defined benefit pension plan is equal to the total balance of any (a) unrecognized net gain or loss arising after the date of the initial application of FASB-87 that remains unamortized at the date of the plan settlement, and (b) unrecognized *net asset* that arose at the date of the initial application of FASB-87 that remains unamortized at the date of the plan settlement.

If the total pension plan obligation is settled by the employer, the maximum gain or loss is recognized. If part of the pension benefit obligation is settled, the employer must recognize a pro rata portion of the maximum gain or loss, equal to the percentage reduction in the projected benefit obligation, unless the transaction qualifies as a "small settlement" (discussed below). Thus, if 40% of the pension plan obligation is settled, 40% of the maximum gain or loss on the settlement is recognized, and if 100% of the pension benefit obligation is settled, 100% of the maximum gain or loss is recognized.

If the employer purchases a participating annuity contract to settle a pension obligation, the cost of the contract must be allocated between the cost of the pure annuity feature and the cost of the participation right. The amount of cost allocated to the participation rights reduces gain (but not loss) that would otherwise be recognized on a plan settlement. However, the participation rights do not affect the determination of the amount of loss that is recognized on a plan settlement.

Reporting gain or loss on a plan settlement   Gain or loss on a plan settlement is reported as an ordinary gain or loss, unless it meets the criteria of an extraordinary item as specified in APB-30 (paragraph 48 of FASB-88).

Small settlements for the year   Part or all of a pension plan's obligation to an employee may be settled by the payment of cash or the purchase of an annuity contract which may be either participating or nonparticipating. An annuity contract is an irrevocable contract in which an insurance company unconditionally assumes a legal obligation to pay specific benefits to specific individuals in return for a premium.

The cost of a cash settlement of a pension plan obligation is the amount of cash paid to the employee. The cost of a settlement of a pension plan obligation involving a nonparticipating annuity contract is the cost of the contract. The cost of a settlement involving a participating annuity contract is the cost of the contract less the amount attributed to the participation rights.

If the total cost of all plan settlements for the year is small or insignificant, gain or loss recognition may not be required. Paragraph

11 of FASB-88 provides that an employer is not required, but is permitted, to recognize the gain or loss on all plan settlements for the year if the cost of all such settlements does not exceed the sum of the service cost and interest cost components of the net periodic pension cost for the current year. Once an accounting policy is adopted for small or insignificant settlements it must be consistently applied from year to year. Thus, an employer that initially elects nonrecognition of gain or loss on all small settlements during a year must continue that same accounting policy from year to year.

> **OBSERVATION:** *If the total cost of all plan settlements for the year is small or insignificant, the employer has absolute discretion to decide whether or not to recognize gain or loss, provided only that the accounting policy is followed consistently from year to year.*

Curtailment of Defined Benefit Pension Plans

Under FASB-88, a curtailment of a defined benefit pension plan results from an event in which (a) the expected years of future service arising from a prior plan amendment are *significantly* reduced for present employees who are entitled to receive pension benefits from that prior plan amendment or (b) the accrual of defined pension benefits is eliminated for some or all of the future services of a *significant* number of employees.

The total effects of a plan curtailment consist of (1) the decrease (loss) in the unamortized balance of unrecognized prior service cost (or unrecognized *net obligation*) that results from the significant reduction of the expected years of future service for present employees [see (a) above] and (2) the net decrease (gain) or increase (loss) in the projected benefit obligation that results from the elimination of the accrual of defined pension benefits for some or all of the future services of a significant number of employees [see (b) above]. Each of these two components that comprise the total effects of a plan curtailment are discussed separately below.

Decrease (loss) in unrecognized prior service cost   Retroactive pension benefits are sometimes granted by an employer, upon adoption of a plan or through a plan amendment, based on employees' services in prior periods. The costs of these retroactive pension benefits are referred to as prior service costs. Retroactive pension benefits are granted by an employer in expectation of future economic benefits, such as reduced employee turnover and higher productivity. FASB-87 requires that the prior service cost relating to a specific plan amendment be amortized in equal amounts over the expected years of future service of each active employee who is expected to receive benefits from the plan amendment. Periodic amortization for each expected year of future service is calculated by dividing the total expected years of future service into the total amount of unrecognized prior service cost. The total amount of unrecognized prior service cost represents the total cost of pension benefits that have been granted under the provisions of the plan amendment. If the expected years of future service are reduced as a result of a plan curtailment, the related unrecognized prior service cost must also be reduced and recognized as a loss by the employer.

The expected years of future service for present employees may be significantly reduced by the termination or suspension of pension benefits for future services so that employees are no longer allowed to earn additional benefits. In addition, the termination of some of the present employees earlier than expected may also result in a significant reduction in their total expected years of future service. As a result of the significant reduction in the expected years of future service, a loss is incurred by the employer, in the amount of the decrease in the balance of the related unamortized unrecognized prior service cost at the date of the plan curtailment. To compute the loss, the percentage reduction in the total remaining expected years of future service at the date of the plan curtailment must first be calculated (number of expected years of future service that are reduced, divided by, the total number of remaining expected years of future service before reduction). To determine the amount of the loss, the balance of the related unamortized unrecognized prior service cost at the date of the plan curtailment is multiplied by the percentage reduction in the total number of expected years of future service. For example, if the total remaining expected years of future service at the date of the plan curtailment is 1,000, and the number of years of future service that is reduced is 400, the percentage reduction is 40%. The balance of the related unamortized unrecognized prior service cost at the date of the plan curtailment is reduced by 40%, which represents the loss that the employer must recognize as part of the total effects of the plan curtailment.

For the purposes of FASB-88, the balance of any unrecognized *net obligation* that arose at the date of the initial application of FASB-87, which remains unamortized at the date of a subsequent plan curtailment, is also treated as a separate unrecognized prior service cost. Thus, if the expected years of future service are significantly reduced for those employees employed at the date of the initial application of FASB-87, a separate loss must be calculated and recognized by the employer. In this event, the loss is equal to the amount by which the unamortized unrecognized *net obligation* is reduced when multiplied by the percentage reduction resulting from the expected years of future service that are significantly reduced for those employees who were employed at the date of the initial application of FASB-87.

The total of all decreases (losses) in unamortized balances of unrecognized prior service costs and/or unrecognized *net obligation* is included in the total effects of a plan curtailment (illustration 3A of Appendix B of FASB-88, but is not included in the gain or loss on the plan curtailment (paragraph 40 of FASB-88).

The following are the steps necessary to compute each decrease (loss) in the balance of the unamortized unrecognized prior service cost at the date of a plan curtailment arising from a significant reduction in the expected years of employees' future service:

Step 1. Compute the percentage reduction in the total remaining expected years of future service, at the date of the plan curtailment, resulting from the expected years of future service that are significantly reduced. For example, if the expected years of future service that are reduced are 600 and the total remaining expected years of future service at the date of the plan curtailment is 1,000, the percentage reduction is 60%.

Step 2. Multiply the balance of the unamortized unrecognized prior service cost (or unamortized unrecognized *net obligation*) of each plan amendment affected by the plan curtailment by the percentage calculated in Step 1. The result is the amount of loss that must be recognized by the employer as part of the total effects of the plan curtailment. The balance of the unamortized unrecognized prior service cost (or unamortized unrecognized *net obligation*) is also reduced by the same amount.

(From a practical standpoint, the dollar amount of amortization for each expected year of future service can be multiplied by the total number of expected years of future service that is reduced.)

Step 3. The amount of loss recognized on the decrease in the balance of the unamortized unrecognized prior service cost (or unamortized unrecognized *net obligation*) is not part of the gain or loss on the plan curtailment (paragraph 40 of FASB-88), but is included in the total effects of the plan curtailment (illustration 3A of Appendix B of FASB-88).

Decrease (gain) or increase (loss) in the projected benefit obligation A plan curtailment may result in a net decrease (gain) or net increase (loss) in the projected benefit obligation. For example, if employees are terminated as a result of a plan curtailment, some or all of their pension benefits based on future compensation levels may cease to be an obligation of the employer or pension plan. In this event, the projected benefit obligation is decreased (a gain) by the amount of the benefits that are no longer an obligation of the plan. On the other hand, if terminated employees who are eligible for subsidized early retirement benefits accept those benefits at an earlier date than expected, there is usually an increase (loss) in the projected benefit obligation. Gain or loss on a plan curtailment is based on the net decrease (gain) or increase (loss) in the projected benefit obligation.

A plan curtailment may result from the closing of a facility or the disposal of a discontinued business segment. If the event that results in the plan curtailment is related to the disposal of a discontinued business segment, gain or loss on the plan curtailment must be included in the total gain or loss on the disposal of the discontinued business segment (APB-30).

The following steps are necessary to compute the gain or loss on a plan curtailment:

Step 1.   Determine the total net gain (decrease) or net loss (increase) in the projected benefit obligation resulting from the plan curtailment. Do not include any increase (loss) in the projected benefit obligation that arises in connection with termination benefits (paragraph 13 of FASB-88, footnote 4).

Step 2.   Combine the remaining balance of any unrecognized *net obligation* that arose at the date of the initial application of FASB-87, and that remains unamortized at the date of the plan curtailment, with the balance of any unrecognized net gain or loss that arose after the initial application of FASB-87, and that also remains unamortized at the date of the plan curtailment. (**Note**: The remaining balance of any unrecognized *net obligation* that arose at the date of the initial application of FASB-87, and that remains unamortized at the date of the plan curtailment is treated as an unrecognized prior service cost.)

The amount of gain or loss on the plan curtailment is determined as follows:

If the change in the projected benefit obligation is a net gain (Step 1) and there is an unrecognized net gain (Step 2)   Curtailment gain is recognized in the amount of the net gain in the projected benefit obligation. (The unrecognized net gain computed in Step 2 is not used.)

If the change in the projected benefit obligation is a net gain (Step 1) and there is an unrecognized net loss (Step 2)   If the net gain in the projected benefit obligation does not exceed the unrecognized net loss, no curtailment gain or loss is recognized. If the net gain in the projected benefit obligation exceeds the unrecognized net loss, curtailment gain is recognized in the amount of the excess of the net gain in the projected benefit obligation over the unrecognized net loss.

If the change in the projected benefit obligation is a net loss (Step 1) and there is an unrecognized net gain (Step 2)   If the net loss in the projected benefit obligation does not exceed the unrecognized net gain, no curtailment gain or loss is recognized. If the net loss in the projected benefit obligation exceeds the unrecognized net gain, curtailment loss is recognized in the amount of the excess of the net loss in the projected benefit obligation over the unrecognized net gain.

If the change in the projected benefit obligation is a net loss (Step 1) and there is an unrecognized net loss (Step 2)   Curtailment loss is recognized in the amount of the net loss in the projected benefit obligation. (The unrecognized net loss computed in Step 2 is not used.)

Recognition of the total effects of a plan curtailment   As mentioned previously, the total effects of a plan curtailment consist of (a) the decrease (loss) in the unamortized balance of unrecognized prior service cost and/or unrecognized net obligation that arose at the date of initial application of FASB-87, resulting from the significant reduction of the expected years of future service for present employees and (b) the net decrease (gain) or increase (loss) in the projected benefit obligation that results from the elimination of the accrual of defined pension benefits for some or all of the future services of a significant number of employees.

If the total effects of a plan curtailment result in a loss, the loss is recognized when it is *probable* that the curtailment will occur and the effects of the curtailment can be *reasonably estimated*. If the total effects of a plan curtailment result in a gain, the gain is recognized only when the related employees terminate or the plan suspension or amendment is adopted.

Reporting total effects of a plan curtailment   Gain or loss on the total effects of a pension plan curtailment is reported as an ordinary gain or loss, unless it meets the criteria of an extraordinary item as specified by APB-30 (paragraph 48 of FASB-88).

Comprehensive illustration   The following is a comprehensive illustration of the (a) computation of employees' expected years of future service under a new plan amendment and (b) computation of the loss from the decrease in the balance of the unamortized unrecognized prior service cost related to the expected years of future service that are significantly reduced by the plan curtailment.

Company X had 50 employees who were expected to receive pension benefits under a new pension plan amendment which became effective January 1, 19X1. In the computation of the expected years of future service for each employee who was entitled to receive benefits under the new plan amendment, the company assumed that 10% of the employees would either quit or retire during the next 10 years. The total amount of unrecognized prior service cost arising from the new pension plan amendment was $27,500.

Computation of Expected Years of Future Service and Loss from the Decrease in Unrecognized Prior Service Cost Resulting from the Expected Years of Future Service That Are Significantly Reduced by a Plan Curtailment

Employee Number	Expected Years of Future Service	Year									
		X1	X2	X3	X4	X5	X6	X7	X8	X9	X10
1-5	5	5									
6-10	10	5	5								
11-15	15	5	5	5							
16-20	20	5	5	5	5						
21-25	25	5	5	5	5	5					
26-30	30	5	5	5	5	5	5				
31-35	35	5	5	5	5	5	5	5			
36-40	40	5	5	5	5	5	5	5	5		
41-45	45	5	5	5	5	5	5	5	5	5	
46-50	50	5	5	5	5	5	5	5	5	5	5
	275										
Service years rendered		50	45	40	35	30	25	20	15	10	5
Amortization fraction		$\frac{50}{275}$	$\frac{45}{275}$	$\frac{40}{275}$	$\frac{35}{275}$	$\frac{30}{275}$	$\frac{25}{275}$	$\frac{20}{275}$	$\frac{15}{275}$	$\frac{10}{275}$	$\frac{5}{275}$

Amortization for each expected year of future service = $100 ($27,500 unrecognized prior service cost divided by 275 years of expected future service).

If, at the beginning of year 3, fifteen (15) employees are terminated which results in a reduction of 90 years of expected future service, the percentage reduction is 50% (remaining expected years of future service at the beginning of year 3 is 180 (275 less 50 for year 1 and 45 for year 2 = 180) and the reduction of 90 is equal to 50%). The remaining balance of unrecognized prior service cost relating to the new plan amendment at the beginning of year 3 was $18,000 (180 remaining years of expected future service multiplied by the $100 amortization rate per year). Thus, the pension plan curtailment, relating to the expected years of future service that were significantly reduced by the termination of fifteen (15) employees, results in a loss of $9,000 (50% of $18,000).

Termination Benefits

Under FASB-88, termination benefits are classified as either *special* or *contractual*. Special termination benefits are those that are offered to employees for a short period of time in connection with the termination of their employment. Contractual termination benefits are those that are required by the terms of an existing plan or agreement and that are provided only on the occurrence of a specified event, such as early retirement or the closing of a facility.

FASB-88 requires the recognition of the cost of termination benefits as a loss and corresponding liability. The recognition date depends on whether the benefits are special or contractual.

Special termination benefits   The recognition date on which the employer records the loss and corresponding liability for special termination benefits occurs when (a) the employees accept the offer of the special termination benefits and (b) the amount of the cost of the benefits can be reasonably estimated. (**Note:** This represents no change from the accounting specified by FASB-74, which has been superseded by FASB-88.)

Contractual termination benefits   The recognition date on which the employer records the loss and corresponding liability for contractual termination benefits occurs when (a) it is probable that employees will be entitled to the benefits and (b) the amount of the cost of the benefits can be reasonably estimated.

Reporting a loss on termination benefits   A loss on termination benefits is reported as an ordinary loss, unless it meets the criteria of an extraordinary item as specified in APB-30 (paragraph 48 of FASB-88).

Disposal of an Identifiable Business Segment

Under APB-30, severance pay, additional pension costs, and employee relocation expenses are all costs directly associated with the decision to dispose of an identifiable business segment and are properly includable in the total gain or loss on disposal. Gains and losses resulting from the application of FASB-88 that are directly related to the disposal of an identifiable business segment must be accounted for in accordance with APB-30.

The measurement date for determining a gain or loss on the disposal of an identifiable business segment is the date that management commits itself to a formal plan of action to sell or otherwise dispose of the segment. The disposal date is the date of closing in the case of a sale, or the date operations cease in the case of an abandonment.

Determination of gain or loss on disposal of a segment of business should be made as of the measurement date, based on estimates of net realizable values. The estimated loss on the disposal of a segment of business is recognized as of the measurement date. A gain on the disposal of a business segment should not be recognized until it is realized, which is usually the disposal date.

Although a gain or loss on the disposal of an identifiable business segment is not an extraordinary item, it is treated in a similar manner on the income statement.

Financial Statement Disclosure

An employer must disclose in its financial statements a description of the nature of the events and the amount of gain or loss resulting from the application of the provisions of FASB-88, regardless of whether the gain or loss is directly related to the disposal of a business segment.

Effective Date and Transition

FASB-88 is effective for events that occur in and after the fiscal year in which FASB-87 is first applied. FASB-87 is generally effective for fiscal years beginning on or after December 16, 1986, except for pension plans of nonpublic enterprises consisting of 100 or fewer participants, and plans located outside of the United States.

Retroactive application of the provisions of FASB-88 to previously issued annual financial statements is not permitted. However, if FASB-88 is initially applied in other than the first interim period of a fiscal year, previously issued interim financial statements of the same fiscal year shall be restated.

Asset reversion transactions Some employers are reporting deferred credits on their statements of financial position, resulting from asset reversion transactions in which they received plan assets in excess of plan obligations. Under prior practice, these credit balances have been systematically amortized by entries which reduce the net periodic pension cost of subsequent periods.

Under FASB-88, the entire balance remaining in the deferred credit account at the time of initial application of FASB-87 must be recognized as a gain by the employer, except that the recognized gain may not exceed the balance of any unamortized unrecognized net asset that arose at the date of the initial application of FASB-87. The recognized gain shall be reported in the income statement as a cumulative effect of a change in accounting principle, in accordance with the provisions of APB-20 (Accounting Changes).

Comprehensive Illustration

The following is a comprehensive illustration of a curtailment and settlement of a pension plan.

Complete Termination of a Defined Benefit Pension Plan and the Computation of the Gain or Loss on the Curtailment and Settlement

The updated records of a defined benefit pension plan reflect the following:

Vested benefits	$ (30,000)
Nonvested benefits	(50,000)
Accumulated benefit obligation	$ (80,000)
Effects of benefits based on future compensation levels	(20,000)
Projected benefit obligation	$(100,000)
Fair value of plan assets	95,000
Funded status of plan	$ (5,000)

Unrecognized prior service cost	1,000
Unrecognized net (gain) or loss	(1,000)
Unrecognized net obligation or (net asset) at date of initial application of FASB-87	2,000
Accrued pension cost	$ 3,000

Assume that the above plan is completely terminated without a successor plan. Under this circumstance, the effects of the pension benefits that are based on future compensation levels are no longer an obligation of the employer or the plan since all of the plan participants have been terminated. Assume also that the total projected benefit obligation was settled by the purchase of nonparticipating annuity contracts for $80,000, and the excess plan assets in the amount of $15,000 were withdrawn by the employer. The computation of the gain or loss resulting from the curtailment and settlement is as follows:

Computation of the total effects of a plan curtailment The total effects of a plan curtailment consist of (a) the total loss resulting from the decreases in the balances of any unamortized unrecognized prior service costs and/or the unamortized unrecognized *net obligation* that arose at the date of the initial application of FASB-87, relating to the expected years of future service that were significantly reduced for present employees and (b) the net decrease (gain) or increase (loss) in the projected benefit obligation resulting from the elimination of the accrual of defined pension benefits for some or all of the future services of a significant number of employees.

The loss resulting from the decrease in the balance of any unamortized unrecognized prior service costs (or unamortized unrecognized *net obligation*) is computed as follows:

Step 1. The percentage reduction, if any, in the balances of any unamortized unrecognized prior service cost and/or the unamortized unrecognized *net obligation* must be calculated (each loss must be computed separately, unless the pension plan is completely terminated). In the above illustration, the percentage reduction resulting from the significant reduction in the expected years of future service is 100%, because the plan is completely terminated. As a result, no separate computation is necessary.

Step 2. Multiply the unamortized balance of each unrecognized prior service cost and unrecognized *net obligation* by its percentage reduction, if any. In the above illustration, the unamortized balance of the unrecognized prior service cost of $1,000 is multiplied by 100%, and the unamortized balance of the unrecognized net obligation of $2,000 is multiplied by 100%, which results in a total loss of $3,000.

Step 3. The $3,000 computed in Step 2 is treated as an effect of the plan curtailment, not as part of the gain or loss on the plan curtailment.

The net decrease (gain) or increase (loss) in the projected benefit obligation is computed as follows:

Step 4. Calculate the net decrease (gain) or net increase (loss) in the projected benefit obligation resulting from the plan curtailment. Do not include any increase (loss) in the projected benefit obligation that arose in connection with termination benefits (paragraph 13 of FASB-88, footnote 4). In the above illustration, the effects of the pension benefits based on future compensation levels of $20,000 are no longer an obligation of the employer or the plan. This results in a $20,000 net decrease (gain) in the projected benefit obligation, because there are no other decreases or increases.

Step 5. Compute the total of (a) the balance of any unrecognized net gain or loss arising after the initial application of FASB-87 that remains unamortized at the date of the plan curtailment, and (b) the balance of any unrecognized *net asset* that arose at the date of the initial application of FASB-87 that remains unamortized at the date of the plan curtailment. In the above illustration the total is a gain of $1,000 (unrecognized net gain of $1,000 and no unrecognized *net asset*).

Step 6. Compute the gain or loss on the plan curtailment, as follows:

If Step 4 (projected benefit obligation) is a gain and Step 5 is also a gain, curtailment gain is recognized in the amount of Step 4 (the amount of gain in Step 5 is ignored).

If Step 4 (projected benefit obligation) is a loss and Step 5 is also a loss, curtailment loss is recognized in the amount of Step 4 (the amount of loss in Step 5 is ignored).

If Step 4 (projected benefit obligation) is a gain and Step 5 is a loss, curtailment gain is recognized in the amount by which the gain in Step 4 exceeds the loss in Step 5. If Step 5 exceeds Step 4, no gain or loss is recognized.

If Step 4 (projected benefit obligation) is a loss and Step 5 is a gain, curtailment loss is recognized in the amount by which the loss in Step 4 exceeds the gain in Step 5. If Step 5 exceeds Step 4, no gain or loss is recognized.

In the above illustration, the net decrease (gain) in the projected benefit obligation was $20,000 (Step 4) and the total unrecognized net gain or loss is a gain of $1,000 (Step 5). Since Step 4 and Step 5 both result in a gain, a gain on the plan curtailment in the amount of Step 4 is recognized, which is $20,000.

Settlement gain or loss   As in Step 5 above, compute the total of (a) the balance of any unrecognized net gain or loss arising after the initial application of FASB-87 that remains unamortized at the date of the plan settlement, and (b) the balance of any unrecognized *net asset* that arose at the date of the initial application of FASB-87 that remains unamortized at the date of the plan settlement.

If part of the pension obligation is settled, the employer must recognize a pro rata portion of the maximum gain or loss, equal to the total of the unrecognized net gain or loss and/or the unrecognized *net asset* multiplied by the percentage reduction in the projected benefit obligation. In the above illustration, there was an unamortized balance of an unrecognized net gain of $1,000 and no unamortized balance of any unrecognized *net asset*. Since the pension plan was terminated, the pension obligation completely settled, and the decrease in the projected benefit obligation was 100%, the pro rata portion that must be recognized is 100%, or $1,000. Thus, the gain on the settlement of the pension plan is $1,000.

Summary   The loss on the decrease in the unamortized balance of unrecognized prior service cost and unrecognized *net obligation* is $3,000, which was computed in Step 3. This loss is reported as a "Loss on Effects of Curtailment of Pension Plan." The net gain on the decrease in the projected benefit obligation is $20,000, which was computed in Step 6. This gain is reported as a "Gain on the Curtailment of Pension Plan." The "Gain on the Settlement of Pension Plan" is $1,000, which was computed separately above. Thus, the net gain on the pension plan curtailment and settlement was $18,000 ($3,000 loss, $20,000 gain, and $1,000 gain).

Journal entry   The journal entry and suggested financial statement presentation of the net gain on pension plan curtailment and settlement of $18,000 is as follows:

Cash (excess plan assets)	$15,000	
Accrued pension cost	3,000	
Gain from termination of pension plan		$18,000

Suggested financial statement presentation:

Gain on curtailment of pension plan	$20,000
Loss on effects of curtailment of pension plan	3,000
Total effects of plan curtailment	$17,000
Gain on settlement of pension plan	1,000
Net gain on pension plan curtailment and settlement	$18,000

PENSION PLAN FINANCIAL STATEMENTS

Overview

Financial reporting for defined benefit plans is covered in FASB Statement-35 (Accounting and Reporting for Defined Benefit Plans). FASB-35 does not require that financial statements be prepared and distributed for defined benefit plans. However, when financial statements of defined benefit plans are prepared and presented, they must comply with the provisions of FASB-35 in order to be in conformity with GAAP.

FASB-75 (Deferral of the Effective Date of Certain Accounting Requirements for Pension Plans of State and Local Governmental Units) supersedes FASB-59 and defers indefinitely the effective date of FASB-35, as it pertains to state and local governmental units.

A defined benefit plan is one that defines the method of determining employee benefits that are expected to be paid on retirement. Based on the benefits that are expected to be paid, the employer's contributions can be actuarially computed. A plan that specifies a fixed rate of employer contributions is considered to be a defined benefit pension plan for the purposes of FASB-35, if the employer's contributions are periodically adjusted to allow for payment of defined benefits which are described in the plan.

FASB-35 apparently covers all defined benefit pension plans including those of state and local governments and those subject to the provisions of the Employee Retirement Income Security Act of 1974 (ERISA). Government sponsored social security plans, temporary plans, and plans that are expected to be terminated are not covered by FASB-35.

Background

The main objective of financial statements of defined benefit pension plans is to provide financial information that may be utilized to assess the present and future ability of the pension plan to pay benefits as they become due. The financial statements should contain information about (1) the resources of the pension plan, (2) the accumulated plan benefits of participants, (3) the transactions affecting the plan's resources and benefits, and (4) other additional information, as necessary to provide clarity to the financial statement presentation.

FASB-35 requires that the annual financial statements of defined benefit pension plans include:

1. A statement of net assets available for benefits
2. A statement of changes in net assets available for benefits
3. Information on the actuarial present value of accumulated plan benefits
4. Information on the year-to-year changes in the actuarial present value of accumulated plan benefits (if significant)

All financial statements and information should be prepared and presented for the same fiscal or calendar period. Thus, net assets available for benefits and the actuarial present value of accumulated plan benefits must be presented as of the same date and the changes in both should be presented for the same period. Financial statements for the most recent year-end period are preferred by FASB-35. However, if the information on the actuarial present value of accumulated plan benefits is not available or cannot be reasonably determined for the most recent year-end period, then such information shall be presented as of the beginning of the year. In this event, all other financial statements and changes in financial statements must be presented for the same period.

The information concerning the actuarial present value of accumulated plan benefits and its year-to-year changes may be presented on the face of the financial statements, in a footnote thereto, or as a separate statement. However, each category of information must be presented in its entirety in the same location on the financial statements regardless of the format in which it is presented.

> **OBSERVATION:** *FASB-35 was adopted by a four-to-three vote of the Financial Accounting Standards Board. The basic area of disagreement that led to the three dissenting voters was the perceived accomplishment of including actuarial information in financial statements of pension plans. The affirmative voters believed that better comparability could be achieved among various pension plan financial statements. The dissenting group believed that the CPA's association with actuarial information may lead to an aura of unjustified reliability for financial statement users.*

Reasonable Approximation and Averages

Benefit information may become available during a fiscal year and not at the beginning or end of the year. In this event, FASB-35 allows the use of averages or approximations in determining benefit information at the beginning or end of the fiscal year. However, the method used to estimate benefit information must produce results similar to those required by FASB-35.

Net Assets Available for Benefits

The pension plan's resources should be identified in reasonable detail and presented on the accrual basis of accounting. The following illustrates the type of presentation suggested by FASB-35:

Statement of Net Assets Available for Benefits

December 31

Assets	1981	1980	Increase (Decrease)
Investments at quoted market values (NOTE):			
Federal and state securities	$ 000,000	$0,000,000	$ 00,000
Corporate debt securities	0,000,000	0,000,000	000,000
Preferred stock	000,000	000,000	(0,000)
Common stock	0,000,000	0,000,000	000,000
	$0,000,000	$0,000,000	$ 000,000
Investments at estimated fair value (NOTE):			
Corporate debt securities	$ 000,000	$ 000,000	$ (00,000)
Preferred stock	000,000	000,000	00,000
Mortgages	0,000,000	0,000,000	(000,000)
Real estate	000,000	000,000	0,000
	$0,000,000	$0,000,000	$ 000,000
Deposit administrative contract at contract value (NOTE):	0,000,000	0,000,000	000,000
Total investments	$0,000,000	$0,000,000	$ 000,000
Cash	000,000	000,000	(00,000)
Contributions receivable— employers	000,000	000,000	(00,000)
Accrued interest and dividends	00,000	00,000	00,000
Total assets	$0,000,000	$0,000,000	$ 000,000
Liabilities			
Accounts payable and accrued items	000,000	000,000	(00,000)
Net assets available for benefits	$0,000,000	$0,000,000	$ 000,000

> **OBSERVATION:** *The above illustrated statement and other illustrated statements to follow differ from the illustrations which appear in FASB-35 (Appendix), in the following respects:*
>
> 1. *There is no increase (decrease) column in any of the illustrations in FASB-35.*
>
> 2. *Comparison of the current year and immediate prior year is used in FASB-35 only when the benefit information date is at the beginning of the current year. Thus, only the current year is shown in the illustration provided in FASB-35 if the benefit information date is at the end of the current year. However, in footnote 1 of FASB-35, it is suggested that comparative financial statements for several plan years are more useful in assessing a plan's ability to provide future benefits.*

Assets that are used in the actual operation of a pension plan should be reported at amortized cost on the financial statements. Thus, buildings, leasehold improvements, furniture, equipment and fixtures which are used in the everyday operation of a pension plan should be presented at historical cost less accumulated depreciation or amortization.

All pension plan investments that are held to provide benefits for the plan's participants, excluding contracts with insurance companies, must be identified in reasonable detail and presented at fair value in the financial statements. Quoted market values, in an active market, should be used as fair value when available. If fair value is determined by some other method, the method should be adequately disclosed in the financial statements or footnotes thereto. FASB-35 defines fair value as the amount that could reasonably be expected to be received in a current sale between a willing buyer and willing seller, neither under compulsion to buy or sell. Plan investments include debt or equity securities, real estate, and other types of investments held to provide benefits for the plan's participants.

Contributions receivable from employees, employers, state or federal grants, and other sources should be separately identified in the financial statements. Contributions receivable should be reported on the accrual basis pursuant to actual legal or contractual obligations or formal commitments. The fact that an employer accrues a liability to a pension plan does not, by itself, provide a basis for a pension plan to record a corresponding receivable.

In order for a pension plan to record an employer contribution receivable, the receivable must be supported by a formal commitment or an actual legal or contractual obligation. However, FASB-35 states that evidence of a formal commitment may include (1) the formal approval of a specified contribution, (2) a consistent pattern of payments made after the pension plan's year-end pursuant to an established funding policy that attributes the payments to the preceding plan year, and (3) a federal tax deduction taken for the contribution by the employer for periods ending on or before the reporting date for the pension plan.

> **OBSERVATION:** *Many pension plans provide that a company may, at its discretion, discontinue contributions and/or the plan itself. The resulting legal position is that the company has no legal liability for future pension fund contributions, and employees have no rights to any benefits beyond those already provided for in the pension fund. However, the position of promulgated GAAP is one of substance over form and that a business is viewed as an entity which will continue to exist (going-concern concept). Therefore, GAAP require that the "no future legal liability clauses" of a pension plan be ignored for the purposes of determining the annual pension costs of employers.*

For the purposes of presenting contracts with insurance companies in the statement of net assets available for benefits, FASB-35 requires that all pension plans, including those not subject to ERISA, shall value such contracts in the same manner as that required by item 13 of the Federal Government's Form 5500 or 5500C (Annual Return/Report of Employee Benefit Plan). Form 5500 is for employee benefit plans with 100 or more participants, and Form 5500C is for employee benefit plans with fewer than 100 participants. Thus, the reader must refer to Form 5500 or 5500C to determine which insurance contracts are included in the presentation required by FASB-35, and which valuation method should be used. The instructions for item 13 of Forms 5500 and 5500C are identical and appear as follows:

---

13. Plan assets and liabilities at the beginning and the end of the plan year (list all assets and liabilities at current value). A fully insured welfare plan or a pension plan with no trust and which is funded entirely by allocated insurance contracts which fully guarantee the amount of benefit payments should check box and complete this item.. ☐

Note: *Include all plan assets and liabilities of a trust or separately maintained fund. (If more than one trust/fund, report on a combined basis.) Include all insurance values except for the value of that*

> *portion of an allocated insurance contract which fully guarantees the amount of benefit payments. Round off amounts to nearest dollar. Trusts with no assets at the beginning and the end of the plan year enter zero on line 13(h).*

An *allocated* insurance contract is one that has been purchased to provide an immediate or deferred annuity for a plan participant. In other words, an insurance company is paid a premium to assume certain specified benefits that must be paid to specified plan participants. An *unallocated* insurance contract is one that has not been used to purchase specific benefits for specific plan participants. The insurance company accumulates the unallocated funds in the unallocated insurance contract until it is instructed to pay specific benefits from the unallocated funds, or instructed to purchase an annuity to provide specified benefits. Unallocated funds of an unallocated insurance contract may usually be withdrawn and used for other purposes.

The instructions for item 13 of Form 5500 and 5500C affect FASB-35 in two main aspects. The first aspect is that allocated insurance contracts are not included in the financial statements that are required by FASB-35, except for some footnote disclosures. The second aspect is that unallocated insurance contracts (other than pooled separate accounts) must be broken down into (1) unallocated separate accounts, and (2) unallocated other accounts. These accounts should be valued at current value. Forms 5500 and 5500C define current value as the fair market value where available and otherwise as the fair value determined in good faith by a trustee or a named fiduciary pursuant to the terms of the plan, assuming an orderly liquidation at the time of such determination.

> **OBSERVATION:** *The financial information required by Forms 5500 and 5500C must be submitted at current values which is basically what is required by FASB-35. In addition, many of the financial disclosures required by FASB-35 also appear on Forms 5500 and 5500C. Thus, it may be advisable to prepare the Government forms before the financial statements required by FASB-35.*

Changes in Net Assets Available for Benefits

Significant changes in net assets available for benefits should be identified in reasonable detail in the Statement of Changes in Net Assets Available for Benefits. The following illustrates the type of presentation suggested by FASB-35.

Statement of Changes in Net Assets Available for Benefits
Year Ended December 31

	1981	1980	Increase (Decrease)
Investment Income:			
Interest	$ 00,000	$ 00,000	$ 0,000
Dividend	00,000	00,000	000
Rental	00,000	00,000	(000)
Increase (decrease) in investments at quoted market values (NOTE)	000,000	(00,000)	00,000
Increase (decrease) in investments at estimated fair values (NOTE)	00,000	000,000	$ 0,000
	$ 000,000	$ 000,000	$ 00,000
Less: Investment expenses	00,000	00,000	00,000
	$ 000,000	$ 000,000	$ 000,000
Contributions from employers (NOTE)	000,000	000,000	00,000
Contributions from federal agency	00,000	00,000	(00,000)
Total	$0,000,000	$0,000,000	$ 000,000
Less: direct benefit payments to participants	$ 000,000	$ 000,000	$ 00,000
Less: annuity contracts purchased (NOTE)	000,000	000,000	00,000
Less: expenses of administration	00,000	00,000	0,000
Total	000,000	000,000	00,000
Net increase in net assets	$ 000,000	$ 000,000	$ 00,000
Net assets available for benefits:			
Beginning of year	0,000,000	0,000,000	
End of year	$0,000,000	$0,000,000	

The minimum disclosures required by FASB-35, which should appear in the Statement of Changes in Net Assets Available for Benefits or its related footnotes, are as follows:

1. Investment income other than from realized or unrealized gains or losses on investments, should be separately disclosed in reasonable detail.

2. Realized and unrealized gains or losses on investments presented at quoted market values should be reported separately from those of investments presented at estimated fair value.

3. Contributions from employers, participants, and others, should be reported separately. Cash and noncash contributions from employers should be disclosed. Noncash contributions should be recorded at their fair value on the date of receipt and, if significant, they should be fully described in the financial statements or footnotes thereto.

4. Direct benefit payments to participants should be reported separately.

5. Purchases of insurance contracts that are excluded from the plan's assets should be separately reported. Dividend income on insurance contracts that are excluded from the plan's assets may be netted against the purchase of such contracts. The dividend income policy on insurance contracts should be disclosed in a footnote to the financial statements.

6. Expenses of administrating the plan should be separately reported.

Accumulated Plan Benefits of Participants

FASB-35 requires that certain specified information regarding the actuarial present value of accumulated plan benefits of participants must be disclosed as part and within the financial statements. The present value of the accumulated plan benefits must be determined as at the plan benefit information date. Thus, if the plan benefit information date is the beginning of the year, the present value of the accumulated plan benefits must be determined as at the beginning of the year.

In addition, financial statements as at the beginning of the year must also be included in the presentation. On the other hand, if the plan benefit information is dated as at the end of the year, the present value of the accumulated plan benefits must be determined as at the same date and financial statements as at the end of the year must also be included in the presentation. FASB-35 states a preference for the use of end-of-year benefit information.

FASB-35 allows considerable flexibility in presenting the actuarial present value of accumulated plan benefits and the changes therein from year to year. The following illustrates one type of presentation.

Statement of Accumulated Plan Benefits
December 31,

	1981	1980	Increase (Decrease)
Actuarial present value of accumulated plan benefits (Note):			
Vested benefits			
Participants currently receiving payments	$ 0,000,000	$ 0,000,000	$ 000,000
Other participants	0,000,000	0,000,000	000,000
	$00,000,000	$00,000,000	$0,000,000
Nonvested benefits	0,000,000	0,000,000	000,000
Total actuarial present value of accumulated plan benefits	$00,000,000	$00,000,000	$0,000,000
Net assets available for benefits	$ 0,000,000	$ 0,000,000	

FASB-35 requires that the total actuarial present value of accumulated plan benefits be broken down and presented in at least three categories: (1) vested benefits of participants currently receiving payments, (2) vested benefits of other participants, and (3) nonvested benefits. Vested benefits of participants currently receiving payments should include benefits due and payable as of the benefit information date. Disclosure of the accumulated contributions of present employees, including interest, if any, as of the benefit information date should be made in a footnote to the financial statements. In addition, the rate of interest, if any, should also be disclosed.

For the purposes of FASB-35 it is presumed that a pension plan will continue to exist (going-concern concept). The best estimates should be used in each actuarial assumption in order to reflect the pension plan's most likely expectations. The following specific assumptions, which must be applied, appear in FASB-35:

1. Assumed rates of return shall reflect the expected rates of return during the periods for which payment of benefits is deferred and shall be consistent with returns realistically achievable on the types of assets held by the plan and the plan's investment policy. To the extent that assumed rates of return are based on values of existing plan assets, the values used in determining assumed rates of return shall be the values presented in the plan's financial statements pursuant to the requirements of this Statement.

2. Expected rates of inflation assumed in estimating automatic cost-of-living adjustments shall be consistent with the assumed rates of return.

3. Administrative expenses expected to be paid by the plan (not those paid by the sponsor) that are associated with providing accumulated plan benefits shall be reflected either by appropriately adjusting the assumed rates of return or by assigning those expenses to future periods and discounting them to the benefit information date. If the former method is used, the adjustment of the assumed rates of return shall be separately disclosed.

An acceptable alternative in determining the actuarial present value of accumulated plan benefits as of the benefit information date, is to use the same assumptions as an insurance company would use if it were to issue an insurance contract to provide the same accumulated plan benefits to the same participants.

Accumulated plan benefits should be determined at the benefit information date in accordance with the provisions of the pension plan. Accumulated plan benefits should include those expected to be paid to (1) retired or terminated employees or their beneficiaries, (2) beneficiaries of deceased employees, and (3) present employees or their beneficiaries.

Pension plan benefits can usually be determined by reference to the provisions in the plan. In most pension plans, benefits are usually based on each year of service (employment) rendered by the employee. If the benefits are not clearly determinable from the provisions of the plan, FASB-35 requires the following computation to determine the accumulated benefits:

Benefits Includable in Vested Benefits

$$\frac{\text{number of years service completed}}{\substack{\text{number of years service that will} \\ \text{have been completed when the benefits} \\ \text{will first be fully vested}}} \quad \textbf{EQUALS} \quad \substack{\text{Percent} \\ \text{of plan benefits} \\ \text{accumulated}}$$

(The above computation is used to determine the amount of plan benefits that have been accumulated to the benefit information date. This computation is used for plan benefits that are classified as vested benefits.)

Benefits Not Includable in Vested Benefits

$$\frac{\text{number of years service completed to the benefit information date}}{\substack{\text{estimated number of years service} \\ \text{upon anticipated separation from covered} \\ \text{employment}}} \quad \textbf{EQUALS} \quad \substack{\text{Percent} \\ \text{of plan benefits} \\ \text{accumulated}}$$

(The above computation is used to determine the amount of plan benefits that are not includable in vested benefits which have been accumulated to the benefit information date. This type of plan benefit includes death or disability benefits that are payable only if death or disability occurs during active service.)

FASB-35 requires that the following procedures be applied in determining accumulated plan benefits:

1. Accumulated plan benefits shall be determined as at the benefit information date based on employees' history of earnings and service, and other appropriate factors.
2. In the case of periodic benefit increases, death benefits, early retirement benefits, and disability benefits, accumulated plan benefits should be based on the employees' projected years of service.
3. All automatic benefit increases that are specified in the plan, such as a cost-of-living increase, which are expected to occur subsequent to the benefit information date, shall be recognized in determining accumulated plan benefits.
4. Benefits that are covered by allocated insurance contracts which are not included as plan assets (in accordance with FASB-35) are not included in determining accumulated plan

benefits, provided that payment for the allocated insurance contract has been made to the insurance company.

5. Benefits arising from plan amendments adopted subsequent to the benefit information date shall not be included in determining accumulated plan benefits.

6. In computing Social Security benefits, employees' earnings as at the benefit information date shall be used to determine future compensation. Increases in Social Security benefits, or compensation base arising from present or future Social Security laws shall be excluded in determining future compensation.

Changes in Accumulated Plan Benefits

Certain factors that cause changes in the actuarial present value of accumulated plan benefits between the current and prior benefit information dates, if significant either individually or in the aggregation, shall be identified in the financial statements or the footnotes thereto. Significant changes that are caused by individual factors shall be separately identified. The minimum disclosure required by FASB-35 includes the effects of the following factors, if significant:

1. Plan amendments
2. Changes in the nature of the plan, such as a merger with another plan, or a spinoff of a plan
3. Changes in actuarial assumptions

> **OBSERVATION:** *As mentioned previously, an acceptable alternative permitted by FASB-35 to determine the actuarial present value of accumulated plan benefits as of the benefit information date, is to use the same assumptions as an insurance company would use if it were to issue an insurance contract to provide the same accumulated plan benefits to the same participants. If a pension plan uses this method, it should disclose, if practical, the effects of changes in the actuarial present value of accumulated plan benefits which are caused by changes in actuarial assumptions. If the effects cannot be separately disclosed, they should be included in determining accumulated benefits.*

Other factors that result in changes in the actuarial present value of accumulated plan benefits, if significant, may also be identified in the financial statements. Other factors that may cause significant changes in the actuarial present value of accumulated plan benefits are factors that affect (1) the amount of accumulated benefits, (2) the discount period, and (3) the amount of benefits paid. Actuarial gains and losses may be separately disclosed, or included with the effect of additional accumulated benefits.

Amounts paid to an insurance company for the purchase of insurance contracts are included in determining the amount of benefits paid. However, amounts paid by an insurance company for benefits, in accordance with an insurance contract which has been excluded from the plan's assets (in accordance with FASB-35), are not included in determining the amount of benefits paid.

Changes in actuarial assumptions that result from changes in a plan's expected experience, are treated as changes in accounting estimates. Accounting estimates are accounted for in the year of change and, if necessary, future years. Prior years' financial statements are not restated in accounting for a change in an accounting estimate (APB-20).

Changes in the actuarial present value of accumulated plan benefits may be presented in the form of a separate reconciliation statement, or elsewhere in the financial statements. If the reconciliation statement is used, it should reflect the actuarial present value of accumulated plan benefits at both the beginning and the end of the year. The amount of detail between the beginning and end of year depends on whether a full presentation is made, or only the required minimum disclosures. If a full presentation is made, then all changes are identified and disclosed. However, if only the required minimum disclosures are made, it will be necessary to include all other changes on one line to reconcile the beginning and ending balances.

Statement of Changes in Accumulated Plan Benefits

	Year ended December 31, 1980 Increase (Decrease)
Actuarial present value of accumulated plan benefits, at beginning of year	$ 000,000
Plan amendment	00,000
Changes in actuarial assumptions	00,000
Other factors	(0,000)
Actuarial present value of accumulated plan benefits, at end of the year	$ 000,000

As mentioned previously, the minimum disclosures of changes in the actuarial present value of accumulated plan benefits required by FASB-35 are (1) plan amendments, (2) changes in the nature of the plan, and (3) changes in actuarial assumptions. Thus, when the minimum disclosures are presented in a reconciliation statement, a separate line must be used for all "other" changes in order to balance the statement. When a full presentation is made in a reconciliation statement, all changes are identified and disclosed separately.

If the minimum required disclosures pertaining to the changes in the actuarial present value of accumulated plan benefits are made elsewhere in the financial statements and not in a reconciliation statement format, FASB-35 requires that the actuarial present value of accumulated plan benefits, as of the preceding benefit information date, also be disclosed.

Other Financial Statement Disclosures

In addition to the financial statement and footnote disclosures mentioned previously, FASB-35 requires two specific additional footnote disclosures and several other disclosures if they are applicable. The two required footnote disclosures must appear in the footnote disclosures of the pension plan's "significant accounting policies," which is usually the first footnote disclosure (APB-22). They are as follows:

1. The significant assumptions and method used to determine fair value of investments and the value of reported insurance contracts, must be adequately described.

2. The significant assumptions and method used to determine the actuarial present value of accumulated plan benefits must be adequately described. In addition, any significant changes in assumptions or methods that occur during the reporting period, must also be described.

Other financial statement disclosures that must be made, if applicable are as follows:

1. A brief description of the important provisions of the pension plan agreement. However, if this information is made generally available from sources other than the financial statements, reference to such sources may be made in the financial statements, instead of providing the brief description.

2. Significant amendments to the pension plan that are adopted on or before the latest benefit information date should be described. In the event that significant plan amendments are

adopted between the latest benefit information date and the end of the plan's year, disclosure should be made to the effect that the present value of accumulated plan benefits do not include the effects of those amendments.

3. A general description of the order of priority for plan partici-pants' claims to the assets of the plan upon termination of the plan. In addition, a description of any benefits guaranteed by the Pension Benefit Guaranty Corporation (PBGC). Also, a description of the applicability of any PBGC guaranty to any recent plan amendment.

    If the information required in the above paragraph is made generally available from sources other than the financial statements, reference to such sources may be made in the financial statements, providing that the following (or similar) disclosure is made in the financial statements.

    "Should the pension plan terminate at some future time, its net assets generally will not be available on a pro rata basis to provide participants' benefits. Whether a particular par-ticipant's accumulated plan benefits will be paid depends on both the priority of those benefits and the level of benefits guaranteed by the Pension Benefit Guaranty Corporation (a Federal Agency) at that time. Some benefits may be fully or partially provided for by the then existing assets and the Pension Benefit Guaranty Corporation, while other benefits may not be provided for at all."

4. Significant plan administration costs that are being absorbed by the employer should be disclosed, if any.

5. The policy for funding the pension plan and any changes in policy during the plan year should be described. The method for determining participants' contributions, if any, should be described and plans subject to ERISA must disclose whether ERISA minimum funding requirements have been met. The status of minimum funding waivers should be disclosed, if applicable.

6. The pension plan's policy concerning purchased insurance contracts that are excluded from the pension plan's assets should be disclosed.

7. Disclosure of whether or not a favorable "determination let-ter" has been obtained for federal income tax purposes should be made.

8. Disclosure of any plan investments that represent 5% or more of the net assets available for benefits, should be made.

9. Disclosure of any party-in-interest transactions between the plan and (1) the employer, (2) the sponsor, or (3) the employee organization.

10. The disclosure of unusual or infrequent events and the effects of such events, that occur subsequent to the latest benefit information date, but prior to the issuance of the financial statements, which may significantly affect the plan's present and future ability to pay benefits. In the event that the effects of such events are not reasonably determinable, all substantive reasons should be disclosed.

The following is a comprehensive illustration of many of the footnotes to the financial statements that are required or applicable under the provisions of FASB-35.

FINANCIAL STATEMENT NOTES

Summary of Significant Accounting Policies

Description of Pension Plan This pension plan is called the ABC Company Defined Benefit Pension Plan and covers substantially all of the employees of the ABC Company. The Plan is subject to the provisions of the Employee Retirement Income Security Act of 1974 (ERISA).

Annual pension benefits begin at the normal retirement age (65) for employees with 10 or more years of service to the company. The amount received at age 65 is equal to 1 1/2% of the final five-year average annual compensation for each year of service. Employees may elect to retire early from ages 55 to 64. The portion of the accumulated plan benefits attributable to the Company's contributions to an employee is forfeited if an employee discontinues employment before rendering 10 years of service. Several elections are available to employees for the distribution of pension benefits. Employees may elect to receive their pension benefits in the form of a joint and survivor annuity, single life annuity, or as a lump sum distribution upon termination or retirement. The minimum amount that an employee may receive upon electing a life annuity is the greater of the annuity for five years or the employee's accumulated contributions to the plan, plus interest.

Death benefits are paid to the beneficiary equal to the value of the employee's accumulated pension benefits if the active employee was 55 years or older. Annual disability benefits are paid to an active employee who has become disabled, equal to the normal retirement benefits that have been accumulated at the time of disability. At normal retirement age, the disabled employee would begin receiving normal retirement benefits computed as if he had retired at the date of disability.

Investment Valuation   Investments are valued at quoted market prices when available. Securities for which no quoted market price is available are valued at a fair value. Fair value is based upon a combination of different factors. In most cases, corporate bonds are valued through comparison of similar securities' yields. Restricted common stock, is usually valued at the quoted price of the issuers unrestricted stock, reduced by a discount to reflect the restriction. If neither a quoted market price is available nor an unrestricted stock of the issuer exists, then a value is determined on a multiple of current earnings reduced by comparison of similar companies' earnings with a quoted price.

Mortgages are valued at their present values based on prevailing interest rates applied to the future principal and interest payments. Real estate leased to third parties is valued at the present value of all future rental receipts and estimated residual values. The interest rate used to discount future values varies with the risks inherent in each real estate investment.

The value of the Plan's deposit administration contract with American Insurance Company is contract value. Contract value is determined by the contributions made plus interest at the rate specified in the contract less funds used to purchase annuities and pay expenses. The Plan's assets do not include those funds used to purchase annuities. When an annuity is purchased, American Insurance Company is required to pay all related pension benefits to a particular employee.

Actuarial Present Value of Accumulated Plan Benefits   All future periodic benefit payments, including any lump sum distributions provided for under the provisions of the Plan are included in Accumulated Plan Benefits. Accumulated plan benefits include all benefits which may be paid to present employees or beneficiaries, retired or terminated employees or beneficiaries, and beneficiaries of employees who have died. The plan provides for benefits which are based on the employees compensation during the last five years of eligible service. The basis of the accumulated plan benefits for active employees is the average compensation during the last five years of service. All benefits are included, up to the valuation date, providing that they are related to services rendered by the employee. Any benefits that are provided from assets that are excluded from the Plan's assets, are excluded from accumulated plan benefits.

The actuarial present value for the accumulated plan benefits is computed by American Appraisal Inc. Certain assumptions are utilized to adjust the accumulated plan benefits to reflect the present value of money and the probability of payment. Significant actuarial assumptions utilized in the valuations presented as of December 31, 1980 and December, 1979 are as follows: Participants' life expectancy based on mortality tables (_____), average retirement age of 62.

Termination of the Plan   In the event of termination, the net assets of the plan will be allocated, in accordance with ERISA and its related regulations. The order of priority is as follows:

1. Any benefits related to the contributions of the employees.
2. Any annuity benefits that have been received for at least the past three years to former employees or their beneficiaries or that employees eligible to retire for that three year period would have received if they would have retired with benefits under the Plan. The priority amount is the lowest benefit payable or paid during the five year period before termination of the Plan.
3. Insured vested benefits by the Pension Benefit Guaranty Corporation (PBGC) up to certain limitations.
4. All uninsured vested benefits.
5. All nonvested benefits.

Note: Annuity contracts for which the American Insurance Company is obligated to pay benefits, are not included in the above priority schedule.

PBGC insurance benefits include most vested normal age retirement benefits, early retirement benefits, and certain disability and survivor's pensions. However, all benefits under the Plan are not guaranteed by PBGC and certain limitations are placed on some of the benefits guaranteed. Vested benefits are guaranteed at the level in effect at the Plan termination date, but are subject to a statutory ceiling which limits individual monthly benefits. The ceiling in 1980 and 1979 was 000,000 and 000,000 respectively for employees who are 65 years old and elect a single life annuity. All other annuitants are subject to a downward adjustment. Benefit improvements as a result of a Plan amendment are not automatically fully guaranteed by PBGC. PBGC guarantees the greater of 20% or $20 for each year following the effective date of an amendment. Thus, the full increase in benefits would be completely guaranteed, within 5 years after an amendment assuming primary ceilings are in effect.

Investments Other Than Insurance Company Contract   All of the Plan's investments are held by a bank-administered trust fund, except for the deposit administration contract. The fair values of those investments for 1980 and 1979 were 000,000 and 000,000 respectively.

Insurance Company Contract   The company entered into a deposit administration contract with the American Insurance Company in 1977. The Plan deposits a minimum of $100,000 annually which is placed in an unallocated fund. American adds interest to the fund at a stated rate of 7%. The interest rate can be changed after 1985, but the different rate only affects deposits made after the date of change. Withdrawals are made from the fund under the direction of the Plan's administration in order to purchase an annuity. American Insurance Company premiums on purchased annuities is fixed for the term of the contract. Periodic dividends, if any, increase the unallocated fund. Dividends received in 1980 and 1979 were 000 and 000 respectively. These dividends are deducted from the purchased annuity contract payments on the Statement of Changes in Net Assets.

Plan Amendment   There is an amendment to the plan expected in 1983 which will increase the annual pension benefits for each year of service.

Changes in Accounting Methods   In 1980, FASB-35 was issued by the Financial Accounting Standards Board. The financial statements of ABC Defined Benefit Pension Plan comply with this pronouncement. Thus previously reported information pertaining to the years presented has been restated to allow comparability.

POSTRETIREMENT BENEFITS OTHER THAN PENSIONS

Overview

FASB-106, issued in December 1990, establishes employers' accounting and disclosure requirements for postretirement benefits other than pensions.

In general, FASB-106 is effective for fiscal years beginning on or after December 16, 1992. However, the effective date is extended for an additional two years, to fiscal years beginning on or after December 16, 1994, for (1) plans outside the United States and (2) defined benefit plans of nonpublic enterprises with no more than 500 participants in all of their plans in the aggregate. Earlier application is encouraged. Until an enterprise applies FASB-106, prior GAAP remain in effect.

The first part of this chapter covers the GAAP that remain in effect until an enterprise applies FASB-106. The second part of the chapter covers the GAAP according to FASB-106.

For convenient discussion, this chapter uses the term "postretirement benefits" to mean postretirement benefits other than pensions. The accounting literature sometimes uses the abbreviation "OPEB" (other postretirement employee benefits) with the same meaning. Pension plans are covered in other chapters of the *GAAP Guide.*

FASB-106 and the prior GAAP discussed in this chapter apply only to benefits payable after retirement. They do *not* apply to temporary benefits after a layoff, or to benefits offered after employment but not pursuant to retirement.

GAAP BEFORE APPLICATION OF FASB-106

Required Disclosure

FASB-81 (Disclosure of Postretirement Health Care and Life Insurance Benefits) remains in effect until an enterprise applies FASB-106. FASB-81 establishes standards of *disclosure*, but does not establish any standards of *accounting* for postretirement plans.

Voluntary Use of Accrual Accounting

FASB-87 (Employers' Accounting for Pensions) notes that employers may voluntarily use accrual accounting for postretirement benefit plans, similar to the accounting that is required for pension plans by FASB-87 and FASB-88 (Employers' Accounting for Settlements and Curtailments of Defined Benefit Pension Plans and for Termination Benefits).

Only a small number of employers have voluntarily adopted the accrual accounting standards of FASB-87 and FASB-88 as the standards of accounting for postretirement benefit plans. Most employers account for postretirement benefits on a cash basis (sometimes referred to as the "pay-as-you-go" method), and they make the financial statement disclosure required by FASB-81.

> **OBSERVATION:** *FASB Technical Bulletin 87-1 (FASB:TB 87-1) provided guidance on accounting for the effects of a change in accounting method, for an enterprise which voluntarily adopted the accrual accounting standards of FASB-87 and FASB-88 as its standards of accounting for postretirement benefits. FASB:TB 87-1 was rescinded upon the issuance of FASB-106. Any change in the method of accounting for postretirement benefit plans is governed by FASB-106.*

Disclosure According to FASB-81

FASB-81 provides for financial statement disclosure of plans which provide health care and life insurance benefits to employees after retirement. FASB-81 specifies the minimum disclosure requirements and encourages additional types of disclosures, as follows.

Minimum disclosures required   FASB-81 requires the following minimum financial statement disclosures:

1.   *Description of employee groups covered and benefits provided*   An employer must disclose the types of postretirement health care and life insurance benefits it provides for its employees and disclose the groups of employees covered by these benefits. The financial statement disclosures required by FASB-81 may be presented for the total of all postretirement health care and life insurance benefits provided by the employer, or for each type of benefit separately.

Under FASB-81, health care benefits include dental, hearing, vision, and all other health-related benefits.

2. *Description of the accounting and funding policies used for the benefits*   An employer must disclose the accounting and funding policies used to account for and fund its postretirement health care and life insurance benefits. The cost of postretirement health care and life insurance benefits that is included in net income of the period under disclosure requirement No. 3 below shall be based on these same accounting and funding policies.

3. *Cost of the benefits included in net income for the period*   An employer must disclose the cost of the postretirement health care and life insurance benefits that is included in its net income for the period. If the cost cannot be exactly determined, an employer is encouraged to use reasonable methods to approximate the amount. If the amount cannot be reasonably approximated or separated from the cost of providing benefits to active employees, the employer shall disclose (a) the total cost of providing health care and life insurance benefits to active and retired employees, and (b) the number of active and retired employees. For purposes of this disclosure requirement, an employee and members of his or her family are counted as one employee.

   The cost of postretirement health care and life insurance benefits that is included in net income of the period shall be based on the same accounting and funding policies that are described for these benefits (see disclosure requirement No. 2, above).

4. *Effect of significant items that affect comparability of benefit costs for all periods presented*   The cost of postretirement health care and life insurance benefits must be comparable for all periods presented. If an item affects the comparability of postretirement health care and life insurance benefit costs in any of the periods presented, the effect of that item must be disclosed, if significant.

Additional disclosures encouraged   FASB-81 encourages, but does not require, disclosure of other information such as the present value of estimated future health care and life insurance benefits for retirees, the amount of contributions to trusts established to pay retiree health care benefits, and the fair value of assets in trusts established to pay retiree health care benefits. In addition, paragraph 28 of FASB-81 suggests the following supplemental disclosures:

a. The average age and number of active employees potentially eligible for postretirement health care and life insurance benefits

b. The number of retirees covered by the employer's plan

c. Information concerning the significance of the potential future postretirement health care and life insurance benefits for both active and retired employees

d. The average benefits per retiree for the most recent year for which the information is available. According to FASB-81, the average benefits per retiree might be determined by dividing the total benefit payments for the year by the number of covered retirees.

> **OBSERVATION:** *Even before an enterprise applies FASB-106, financial statements filed with the Securities and Exchange Commission should disclose the impact FASB-106 is expected to have on the financial statements when the employer first applies it. This is the position of the SEC staff, based on SEC Staff Accounting Bulletin No. 74, issued in December 1987 (Disclosure of the Impact that Recently Issued Accounting Standards Will Have on the Financial Statements of the Registrant When Adopted in a Future Period).*

FASB-106 Supersedes FASB-81

As noted above, FASB-106 supersedes FASB-81. The remainder of this chapter discusses GAAP according to FASB-106.

GAAP ACCORDING TO FASB-106

FASB-106 (Employers' Accounting for Postretirement Benefits Other Than Pensions) brings about a drastic change by establishing *accounting* as well as *disclosure* standards for postretirement benefit plans.

FASB-106 supersedes FASB-81 (Disclosure of Postretirement Health Care and Life Insurance Benefits) and rescinds FASB Technical Bulletin No. 87-1 (Accounting for a Change in Method of Accounting for Certain Postretirement Benefits).

In addition, FASB-106 amends APB-12 (Omnibus Opinion — 1967), FASB-87 (Employers' Accounting for Pensions), and APB-16 (Business Combinations). These amendments are noted in the chapters entitled "Deferred Compensation," "Pensions," and "Business Combinations."

Postretirement benefits consist of all forms of benefits other than retirement income provided by an employer to retired workers, their beneficiaries, and dependents. The term does not include benefits paid after employment but before retirement, such as layoff benefits.

> **OBSERVATION**: *A separate FASB project will deal with benefits paid before retirement. Meanwhile, FASB-106 does not discourage the use of accrual accounting for those benefits (paragraph 1, footnote 2).*

Postretirement benefits may begin immediately on employees' termination of service or may be deferred until retired employees reach a specified age. Benefits such as health care, tuition assistance, or legal services are provided to retirees as the need arises. Other benefits, such as life insurance, are provided on the occurrence of specified events.

A postretirement benefit plan is one in which an employer agrees to provide certain postretirement benefits to current and former employees after they retire. A postretirement benefit plan may be *contributory*—that is, the employees may be required to contribute to the plan—or the entire cost of the plan may be borne by the employer.

A postretirement benefit plan may be *funded* or *unfunded*—that is, the employees and/or the employer may make cash contributions to a postretirement benefit plan trustee, or the employer may make only credit entries on its books reflecting the postretirement benefit liability under the plan. According to FASB-106, postretirement benefit plans should be accounted for on the accrual basis, and any difference between net periodic postretirement benefit cost charged against income and the amount actually funded is recorded as an accrued or prepaid cost.

General Approach of FASB-106 — Deferred Compensation

According to FASB-106, postretirement benefits are a type of *deferred compensation* that should be accounted for as part of an employee's total compensation package. A *deferred compensation plan* is an agreement specifying that a portion of an employee's compensation will be set aside and paid in future periods.

Accrual Accounting

FASB-106 requires employers to account for postretirement benefit plans on the accrual basis. Any difference between net periodic postretirement benefit cost charged against income and the amount actually funded is recorded as an accrued or prepaid cost.

Comparison of FASB-106 to FASB-87 and FASB-88

Although there are some important differences, many provisions of FASB-106 are similar to the accounting and reporting requirements for pension accounting established by FASB-87 and FASB-88.

In accounting for postretirement benefits under FASB-106, an employer makes at least two types of journal entries to record its cost of these benefits, as follows:

(a) Net periodic postretirement
        benefit cost $ XXX
      Accrued postretirement benefit
        cost payable $ XXX
     To accrue postretirement benefit
     cost for a specific period.

(b) Accrued postretirement benefit
        cost payable $ XXX
      Cash $ XXX
     To record cash contribution to
     postretirement plan trustee or to
     pay benefits.

These entries are similar to those required for pension accounting under FASB-87, except for obvious differences in the titles of the general ledger accounts.

Most of the provisions of FASB-87 and FASB-106 pertain to the computation of the amount to be recorded in journal entry type (a) above. This computation requires numerous worksheet calculations which are illustrated throughout FASB-87 and FASB-106.

OBSERVATION: A major difference between FASB-87 and FASB-106 is that under certain circumstances, FASB-87 requires the recognition of a minimum pension plan liability while FASB-106 does not require the recognition of a minimum liability for a postretirement benefit plan.

Financial statement disclosure under FASB-106 requires a reconciliation of the funded status of the postretirement benefit plan with certain amounts reported in the employer's statement of financial position. This reconciliation is similar to that required by FASB-87 for disclosure of pension plans.

SCOPE AND APPLICABILITY OF FASB-106

FASB-106 applies to any plan that satisfies five tests, relating to:

- Type of benefits
- Types of beneficiaries
- General rather than selective coverage of employees
- Source and form of payment
- Nature of the employer's undertaking

Type of Benefits FASB-106 applies to an employer's undertaking to provide various types of benefits to employees after they retire. The benefits may commence immediately on termination of the employee's active service, or may be deferred until the retired employee reaches a specified age.

The benefits include health care, life insurance outside of a pension plan, tuition assistance, day care, legal services, housing subsidies, and other types of postretirement benefits. However, FASB-106 does not apply to pension or life insurance benefits provided in a pension plan. The GAAP for pensions and life insurance benefits provided by pension plans are established by FASB-87 and FASB-88.

OBSERVATION: FASB-106 covers a broader range of benefits than FASB-81. Both FASB-106 and FASB-81 cover health care and life insurance benefits, but FASB-106 covers additional types of benefits, such as tuition, day care, legal services, and housing subsidies.

If an employer has established a plan to provide benefits to active employees as well as to retired employees, FASB-106 requires the employer to divide the plan into two parts for accounting purposes; one part covering benefits to active employees and the other part covering benefits to retired employees. The employer should use the accounting standards of FASB-106 only for the part covering benefits to retired employees.

Types of Beneficiaries The beneficiaries may be retired employees, disabled employees, any other former employees who are expected to receive benefits, or retirees' beneficiaries and covered dependents, pursuant to the terms of an employer's undertaking to provide such benefits. The beneficiaries may also be individuals who (1) have ceased permanent active employment because of disability, (2) have not yet completed formal procedures for retirement, and (3) are carried on nonretired status under the disability provisions of the plan so that they can continue accumulating credit for pensions or other postretirement benefits.

General Rather than Selective Coverage of Employees The plan should cover employees in general rather than individual employees. An employer's practice of providing postretirement benefits to selected employees under individual contracts with specific terms determined on an individual basis does not constitute a postretirement plan under FASB-106.

> **OBSERVATION**: *An employer's commitment to selected individual employees should be accrued in accordance with the terms of the individual contracts (see the chapter entitled "Deferred Compensation").*

FASB-106 does apply to contracts with individual employees if these contracts, taken together, are equivalent to a plan covering employees in general.

> **OBSERVATION**: *Professional judgment is required in any situation where contracts with individual employees may be equivalent to a general plan. FASB-106 provides no guidance on how to make the determination.*

Source and Form of Payment   A plan is covered by FASB-106 if it provides reimbursement or direct payment to providers for the cost of specified services as the need for those services arises, or if it provides lump sum benefits, such as death benefits. The plan may be either funded or unfunded.

> *OBSERVATION: The assets of a postretirement benefit plan are usually kept in a trust account, completely segregated from the assets of the employer. Contributions to the postretirement benefit plan trust account are made periodically by the employer and, if the plan is contributory, by the employees. The plan assets are invested in stocks, bonds, real estate, and other types of investments. Plan assets are increased by earnings, gains on investments and contributions by the employer (and employees if the plan is contributory), and are decreased by losses on investments and the payment of benefits.*

Nature of the Employer's Undertaking   FASB-106 applies to any arrangement that is in substance a plan for providing postretirement benefits, regardless of its form.

> *OBSERVATION: In a situation where the existence of a plan is not clear, professional judgment is required in determining whether a plan exists "in substance." FASB-106 provides only a limited amount of guidance on this issue.*

FASB-106 applies not only to written plans, but also to unwritten plans if the existence of these plans can be perceived on the basis of (1) the employer's practice of paying benefits, or (2) the employer's oral representations to current or former employees. Once an employer pays benefits or promises to pay benefits, FASB-106 presumes that the employer has undertaken to provide future benefits as indicated by the past payments or promises, unless there is evidence to the contrary.

> *OBSERVATION: In order to indicate the existence of a plan, it appears that the employer's oral representations (1) should refer to a plan that is general in its scope and (2) should be communicated to current or former employees in general, or to individual employees as representatives of the employees in general.*

One of the most important and controversial issues is whether FASB-106 applies only to legally enforceable obligations, or to a broader range of commitments including those that cannot be legally enforced.

> **OBSERVATION:** *This issue is highly significant. The ERISA law gives substantial legal protection to the expectations of employees under pension plans, but does not give the same level of protection to employee expectations of nonpension benefits. Courts have upheld the right of employers to terminate or curtail benefits under nonpension plans, unless the employers have entered into legally binding commitments to maintain benefits, such as collective bargaining agreements.*

FASB-106 "Basis for Conclusions" explains in more detail the type of employer's obligation that is covered by FASB-106. Although the "Basis for Conclusions" is not part of the formal pronouncement, it provides significant guidance. According to the "Basis for Conclusions," an employer's undertaking comes within the scope of FASB-106 if the undertaking is a "liability" under FASB Concepts Statement No. 6 (Elements of Financial Statements).

The "Basis for Conclusions" in FASB-106 relies on FASB:CS-6 for the proposition that an obligation can qualify as a liability whether or not the obligation is legally enforceable. The test is whether the obligation "is effectively binding on the employer because of past practices, social or moral sanctions, or customs." FASB-106 concludes that an employer, by paying benefits or promising to do so, incurs a liability as the term is explained in FASB:CS-6, and therefore incurs a liability to be accounted for under FASB-106, in the absence of evidence to the contrary.

> **OBSERVATION:**
>
> 1. *Employers will require expert legal advice to determine what is meant by "evidence to the contrary."*
>
> 2. *Accountants should obtain expert legal advice before (a) advising employers on the applicability of FASB-106 to existing plans, (b) advising employers on the structuring of new plans or the restructuring of existing plans if the structure of the plan may determine whether the plan is within the scope of FASB-106, or (c) auditing the financial statements of an employer if there is a serious question as to whether the employer's plan is within the scope of FASB-106.*

3. *Some employers may benefit by bringing their plans within the coverage of FASB-106. For example, the accrual requirements of FASB-106 may increase the employer's cost of goods sold or cost of operations, leading to a possible increase in (a) the sales price that the employer can charge for its products or services under cost-plus contracts or (b) the rate that regulatory agencies will allow the employer to charge for its services. The accrual requirements may also reduce the net income of an employer, benefitting an employer that is obligated to make payments computed on the basis of net income.*

4. *Other employers may prefer to place their plans beyond the scope of FASB-106. For example, an employer may be concerned that the presence of an accrued liability on its financial statements may create confusion about the nature of the employer's obligation to make future payments. This accrued liability may even be used as evidence against the employer if it modifies or terminates its plan. As another example, many employers want their financial statements to show the strongest possible financial condition, and may prefer to avoid reporting the expenses and liabilities required by FASB-106. Finally, an employer whose plan is beyond the scope of FASB-106 will avoid the burdensome accounting procedures that would be required under FASB-106.*

5. *If a plan is covered by FASB-106, the next question is whether the plan is a defined benefit plan or a defined contribution plan. FASB-106 prescribes significantly different accounting and reporting requirements for these two categories. FASB-106 deals primarily with defined benefit plans. For the distinctive accounting and reporting requirements applicable to defined contribution plans, see the section entitled "Defined Contribution Plans." When considering the structuring or restructuring of a plan, the employer and its advisors should therefore consider (a) whether the plan is covered by FASB-106 and, if so, (b) whether the plan is governed by the accounting and reporting requirements for defined benefit plans or for defined contribution plans.*

USE OF REASONABLE APPROXIMATIONS

FASB-106 allows an employer to use estimates, averages, or computational shortcuts, provided that the employer reasonably expects that the results will not be materially different from those which would have been reached by a fully detailed application of the provisions of FASB-106.

SINGLE-EMPLOYER DEFINED BENEFIT POSTRETIREMENT PLANS

FASB-106 deals primarily with an employer's accounting for a single-employer plan that provides defined benefits.

OBSERVATION:

1. *FASB-106 also briefly covers multiemployer plans, multiple-employer plans, and defined contribution plans. Each is discussed later in this chapter.*

2. *The accounting and reporting requirements for defined contribution plans differ significantly from those for defined benefit plans. If a plan has some characteristics of each type, FASB-106 calls for careful analysis of the substance of the plan. The difference in the accounting and reporting requirements, depending on whether the plan is a defined benefit plan or a defined contribution plan, may be a significant factor to be considered by employers attempting to structure or restructure their plans before the effective date of FASB-106.*

In a defined benefit plan, the benefit may be defined in terms of a specified monetary amount (such as a life insurance benefit), or a specified type of benefit (such as all or a percentage of the cost of specified surgical procedures). The benefits may be subject to a maximum (or "cap"), either per individual employee or for the plan as a whole, or the employer may agree to pay the full amount of benefits without regard to any maximum amount.

The employee's entitlement to benefits is expressed in the benefit formula, which specifies the years of service to be rendered, age to be attained while in service, or a combination of both, which must be met for an employee to be eligible to receive benefits under the plan. The benefit formula may also define the beginning of the period of service during which the employee earns credit toward eligibility, as well as the levels of benefits earned for specific periods of service.

The total amount of benefits depends not only on the benefit formula but also on actuarial factors, such as the longevity of the retired employee (and the longevity of the retiree's beneficiaries and covered dependents), and the occurrence of specific events entitling the individuals to benefits (such as illnesses).

Because of these factors, the employer cannot precisely calculate the amount of benefits to be paid in the future to any retired employee (or to the retiree's beneficiaries and covered dependents). The FASB is satisfied, however, that employers can make reasonable estimates useful for accounting purposes.

Accumulated Postretirement Benefit Obligation

FASB-106 requires the employer to accrue the accumulated postretirement benefit obligation. Once an employee has attained full eligibility, the amount of this obligation is the same as the employee's *expected* postretirement benefit obligation. Until then, the *accumulated* amount is the portion of the expected amount attributed to employee service rendered to a particular date.

The accumulated and the expected amounts represent the actuarial present value of the anticipated benefits. Measurement of these amounts is based on assumptions regarding such items as the expected cost of providing future benefits and any cost-sharing provisions under which the employee, the government, or others will absorb part of these costs. If the benefits or cost-sharing provisions are related to the employee's salary progression, the calculation of benefits and cost-sharing reflects the anticipated impact of this progression.

> **OBSERVATION:** *FASB-106 differs from the accounting for pensions in FASB-87 in this respect, because FASB-87 does not anticipate salary progression.*

The following example illustrates the relationship between estimated and accumulated postretirement benefit obligations.

A plan provides postretirement health care benefits to all employees who render at least 10 years of service and attain age 65 while in service. A 60-year-old employee, hired at age 45, is expected to terminate employment at age 67 and is expected to live to age 77. A discount rate of 8% is assumed.

At December 31, 19X2, the employer estimates the expected amount and timing of benefit payments for that employee as follows:

Age	Expected Future Claims	Present Value at Age	
		60	65
68	$ 2,322	$ 1,255	$ 1,843
69	2,564	1,283	1,885
70	2,850	1,320	1,940
71	3,154	1,353	1,988
72	3,488	1,385	2,035
73	3,868	1,422	2,090
74	4,274	1,455	2,138
75	4,734	1,492	2,193
76	5,240	1,530	2,247
77	7,798	2,108	3,097
	$40,292	$14,603	$21,456

At December 31, 19X2, when the employee's age is 60, the *expected* postretirement benefit obligation is $14,603, and the *accumulated* postretirement benefit obligation is $10,952 (15/20 of $14,603 because the employee has worked 15 of the 20 years needed for eligibility).

Assuming no changes in health care costs or other circumstances, the obligations at later dates are as follows:

- December 31, 19X7 (age 65), the expected and the accumulated postretirement benefit obligations are both $21,456. These amounts are the same, because the employee is fully eligible.

- December 31, 19X8 (age 66), the expected and the accumulated postretirement benefit obligations are both $23,172 ($21,456 the previous year, plus interest @ 8% for 1 year).

Measurement of Cost and Obligations

In discussing the measurement of cost and obligations of single-employer defined benefit plans, FASB-106 addresses the following issues:

- Accounting for the substantive plan
- Assumptions

Accounting for the Substantive Plan

According to FASB-106, the accounting and reporting should reflect the substantive plan; that is, the plan as understood by the employer and the employees. Generally, the substantive plan is accurately reflected in writing. However, the employer's past practice or communications of intended future changes may indicate that the substantive plan differs from the written plan.

> **OBSERVATION:** *If an independent auditor is faced with a situation where the substantive plan appears to be different from the written plan, the auditor should (1) seek expert legal advice, (2) consult with the highest levels of the employer's management, and (3) fully document the matter in the audit files.*

FASB-106 discusses some areas in which the substantive plan may differ from the written plan, as follows:

- Cost sharing
- Benefit changes
- Plan amendments

Cost Sharing In general, the employer's cost-sharing policy should be regarded as part of the substantive plan if (1) the employer has maintained a consistent level of cost-sharing with retirees, (2) the employer has consistently increased or decreased the share of the cost contributed by employees or retirees, or (3) the employer has the ability to change the cost-sharing provisions at a specified time or when certain conditions exist, and has communicated to plan participants its intent to make such changes.

However, an employer's past practice regarding cost sharing should not be regarded as the substantive plan if:

- The cost sharing was accompanied by offsetting changes in other benefits or compensation.
- The employer was subjected to significant costs, such as work stoppages, in order to carry out that policy.

Along similar lines, an employer's communication of its intent to change the cost-sharing provisions should not be regarded as the substantive plan if:

- The plan participants would be unwilling to accept the change without adverse results to the employer's operations.
- The plan participants would insist on other modifications of the plan, that would offset the change in cost sharing, in order to accept the proposed change.

In estimating the amount of contributions to be received by the plan from active or retired employees, the employer should consider any relevant substantive plan provisions, such as the employer's past practice of consistently changing the contribution rates. If the employer is obliged to return contributions to employees who do not become eligible for benefits (together with interest, if applicable), the estimated amount of this obligation should be (1) included in the employer's total benefit obligation and (2) factored into calculations of the contributions needed by the plan.

Benefit Changes The measurement of the obligation under the plan should include automatic benefit changes specified by the plan. An example is a plan that promises to pay a benefit in kind, such as health care benefits, instead of a defined dollar amount. The obligation to pay the benefit automatically changes in amount when the cost of the benefit changes.

Plan Amendments Measurement should also include plan amendments as soon as they have been contractually agreed on, even if some or all of the provisions become effective in later periods.

> **OBSERVATION:** *Even if a plan amendment has not been contractually agreed on, it appears that an employer should reflect the amendment if it can be regarded as a change in the substantive plan. In general, a substantive plan may differ from the written plan in either of two cases: (a) when the employer has communicated its intention to adopt the amendment or (b) when the employer has engaged in consistent past practice.*

Assumptions

An employer has to make numerous assumptions in order to apply FASB-106. Each assumption should reflect the best estimate of the future event to which it relates, without regard to the estimates involved in making other assumptions. FASB-106 describes this approach as the use of explicit assumptions.

> **OBSERVATION:** *The FASB finds the use of explicit assumptions preferable to an* **implicit** *approach to assumptions, under which the reliability of assumptions would be judged in the aggregate, not individually. "Basis for Conclusions," paragraph 181.*

All assumptions should be based on the expectation that the plan will continue in the absence of evidence that it will not continue. Some of the assumptions discussed in FASB-106 apply generally to all types of benefits, while other assumptions are unique to health care benefits.

General Assumptions

FASB-106 discusses the following general assumptions:

- Time value of money (discount rates)
- Expected long-term rate of return on plan assets
- Future compensation levels
- Other general assumptions

Time Value of Money (Discount Rates)   One of the essential assumptions relates to discount rates. Assumed discount rates are used in measuring the expected and accumulated postretirement benefit obligations and the service cost and interest cost components of net periodic postretirement benefit cost. Assumed discount rates should reflect the time value of money at the measurement date, as indicated by rates of return on high-quality fixed-income investments currently available with cash flows corresponding to the anticipated needs of the plan. If the employer could possibly settle its obligation under the plan by purchasing insurance (for example, nonparticipating life insurance contracts to provide death benefits), the interest rates inherent in the potential settlement amount are relevant to the employer's determination of assumed discount rates.

Expected Long-Term Rate of Return on Plan Assets Assumptions are also required in determining the expected long-term rate of return on plan assets. In general, plan assets should be investments that have been segregated and restricted, usually in trust, for the exclusive purpose of paying postretirement benefits.

The expected long-term rate of return on plan assets should reflect the anticipated average rate of earnings on existing plan assets and those expected to be contributed during the period.

> **OBSERVATION:** *This factor is used, together with the **market-related value** of plan assets, in computing the **expected return** on plan assets. The difference between the actual return and the expected return on plan assets is defined in FASB-106 as "plan asset gain or loss," discussed later.*

When estimating the rate of return on plan assets, the employer should consider the rate of return on (1) assets currently invested and (2) assets that will be reinvested. If the income from plan assets is taxable, the anticipated amount of taxes should be deducted to produce a net-of-tax rate of return. If a plan is unfunded or has no assets that qualify as plan assets under FASB-106, the employer has no basis on which to calculate an expected long-term rate of return on plan assets.

Future Compensation Levels If the benefit formula provides for varying amounts of postretirement benefits based on the compensation levels of employees, the employer has to make further assumptions about the impact of anticipated future compensation levels on the cost of benefits and the obligation to pay them.

Estimates of future compensation should be based on anticipated compensation of individual employees, including future changes arising from general price levels, productivity, seniority, promotion, and other factors. All assumptions should be consistent with regard to general factors such as future rates of inflation. The assumptions should also include any indirect effects related to salary progression, such as the impact of inflation-based adjustments to the maximum benefit provided under the plan.

Other General Assumptions Other general assumptions involved in applying FASB-106 include the following: participation rates for contributory plans; retirement age; factors affecting the amount and timing of future benefits (such as per capita claims cost by age, health care cost trend rates, and Medicare reimbursement rates); and the probability of payment (such as turnover of employees, dependency status, and mortality).

Assumptions Unique to Postretirement Health Care Benefits

Most postretirement benefit plans include health care benefits. These plans require some special types of assumptions in determining per capita claims cost, in addition to the general assumptions required by all postretirement benefit plans.

FASB-106 discusses the following assumptions unique to postretirement health care benefits:

- Per capita claims cost
- Assumptions about trends in health care costs
- Attribution

Per Capita Claims Cost   An employer should estimate the net incurred claims cost at each age at which a participant is expected to receive benefits. In order to estimate this net cost, the employer should first estimate the assumed per capita claims cost at each age, and then subtract the effects of (a) Medicare and other reimbursements from third parties, and (b) cost-sharing provisions which cause the participant to collect less than 100% of the claim. If plan participants are required to make contributions to the plan during their active service, the actuarial present value of the participants' future contributions should be subtracted from the actuarial present value of the assumed net incurred claims costs.

The *assumed per capita claims cost* is the annual cost of benefits from the time when an individual's coverage begins for the remainder of that person's life (or until coverage ends, when sooner). The annual benefit cost should be based on the best possible estimate of life expectancy that reflects age and other appropriate factors such as gender and geographical location. If the employer incurs significant costs in administering the plan, these costs should also be considered part of the assumed per capita claims cost.

If an employer does not have a reliable basis for estimating the assumed per capital claims cost by age, the employer may base its estimate on other reliable factors. For example, the estimate may be based on the claims costs that have actually been incurred for employees of all ages, adjusted by factors to reflect health care cost trends and cost sharing.

A number of assumptions are based on the estimated effects of inflation. The employer should use consistent methods of estimating inflation, whether the assumption relates to discount rates, compensation levels, or health care cost trend rates.

If the history of the plan is reliable enough to provide a basis for future estimates, the past and present claims data of the plan should be considered in calculating the assumed per capita claims cost. If the plan does not provide any reliable data, the employer may base its estimates on other employers' claims information, as assembled by insurance companies, actuarial firms, or employee benefits consulting firms.

> **OBSERVATION:** *The independent auditor should verify that any outside information comes from reliable and independent sources, and that the audit files fully identify these sources.*

The estimates derived from the experience of other employers should, however, be adjusted to reflect the demographics of the specific employer and the benefits available under its plan, to the extent they differ from those of the other employers. Relevant factors include, for example, health care utilization patterns, expected geographical locations of retirees and their dependents, and significant differences among the nature and types of benefits covered.

Assumptions about Trends in Health Care Cost Rates   Assumptions about the trend in health care cost rates represent the expected annual rate of change in the cost of health care benefits currently provided under the plan (due to factors other than changes in the demographics of participants) for each year from the measurement date until the payment of benefits. The trend rates should be based on past and current cost trends, reflecting such factors as health care cost inflation, changes in utilization or delivery patterns, technological advances, and changes in the health status of plan participants. Examples include the possible future need for technology that is now being developed, or the reduction of the need for benefits resulting from participation in wellness programs.

Different cost trend rates may be required for different types of services. For example, the cost trend rate for hospital care may differ from that for dental care. Further, the cost trend rates may fluctuate at different rates during different projected periods in the future. For example, there may be a rapid short-term increase, with a subsequent leveling off in the longer term.

The employer should assume that governmental benefits will continue as provided by existing law, and that benefits from other providers will continue in accordance with their existing plans. Future changes in the law should not be anticipated.

Attribution   Once the expected postretirement benefit obligation for an employee has been determined, an equal amount of that obligation should be attributed to each year of service in the attribution period, unless the benefit formula of the plan necessitates attribution on some other basis.

The attribution period starts when the employee begins earning credit towards postretirement benefits. This generally occurs on the date of hire, but may be at a later date if the benefit formula requires a significant waiting period before the employee can earn credit. In any event, the attribution period ends when the employee reaches full eligibility for benefits. Thus the cost of providing the benefits is attributed to the period during which the employee builds up full eligibility. The employer does not attribute any of the cost to any period after the employee has achieved full eligibility.

Under the postretirement benefit plan of Company Q, employees qualify by rendering at least 5 years of service and reaching age 65 while in service. The company hires an employee at age 61. Assume the expected postretirement benefit obligation regarding this employee is $10,000.

The employee's attribution period is 5 years. (Note that the employee will not become eligible at age 65, because the employee will not yet have completed 5 years of service.) For each of the first 5 years of service, the annual service cost will be $2,000 (1/5 of $10,000). No service cost will be attributed after the first 5 years, even if the employee remains in service.

The next example illustrates attribution under a "frontloaded" plan, in which a disproportionate share of the benefit obligation is attributed to the early years of an employee's service.

A life insurance plan provides postretirement death benefits of $200,000 for 10 years of service after age 45 and additional death benefits of $10,000 for each year of service thereafter until age 65. (The maximum benefit is therefore $300,000, consisting of the basic $200,000 plus 10 additional years @ $10,000.)

In this situation, the benefit obligation should be attributed to periods corresponding to the benefit formula, as follows:

- The actuarial present value of a death benefit of $20,000 (1/10 of $200,000) is attributed to each of the first 10 years of service after age 45.
- The actuarial present value of an additional $10,000 death benefit is attributed to each year of service thereafter until age 65.

Recognition of Net Periodic Postretirement Benefit Cost

The amount of net periodic postretirement benefit cost is derived from the net change in the amount of the accumulated postretirement benefit obligation, after ignoring those components of the net change that do not pertain to the cost of benefits.

The net periodic postretirement benefit cost recognized for a period consists of the following components:

- Service cost
- Interest cost
- Actual return on plan assets, if any
- Amortization of unrecognized prior service cost
- Gain or loss (to the extent recognized)
- Amortization of the unrecognized obligation or asset at the date of initial application of FASB-106.

> **OBSERVATION:** *The employer makes one entry to accrue the net periodic postretirement benefit cost, the amount of which is the total of the components listed above, determined by worksheet calculations.*

Basic Transactions and Adjustments

Company A's date of transition to the accounting requirements of FASB-106 was the beginning of Year 1. At that time, the accumulated postretirement benefit obligation was $300,000. The plan was unfunded.

At the end of Year 1, Company A paid $65,000 of postretirement benefits. Service cost attributed to Year 1 was $60,000. The assumed discount rate was 10%.

Worksheets as of the end of Year 1 are as follows:

	Accrued Postretirement Benefit Cost	Accumulated Postretirement Benefit Obligation	Unrecognized Transition Obligation
Beginning of year	$ -0-	$(300,000)	$ 300,000
Recognition of components of net periodic postretirement benefit cost:			
Service cost	(60,000)	(60,000)	
Interest cost (a)	(30,000)	(30,000)	
Amortization of transition obligation (b)	(15,000)		(15,000)
	(105,000)	(90,000)	(15,000)
Benefit payments	65,000	65,000	
Net change	(40,000)	(25,000)	(15,000)
End of year	$ (40,000)	$(325,000)	$ 285,000

(a) 10% (assumed discount rate) of $300,000 (accumulated postretirement obligation at beginning of year).

(b) 20-year straight-line amortization of transition obligation (discussed later in this chapter).

The amounts on this worksheet will be reflected in the reconciliation of the funded status of the plan with the amounts shown on the statement of financial position, as follows:

	Beginning of Year 1	Net Change	End of Year 1
Accumulated postretirement benefit obligation	$(300,000)	$(25,000)	$(325,000)
Plan assets at fair value	-0-		-0-
Funded status	(300,000)	(25,000)	(325,000)
Unrecognized transition obligation	300,000	(15,000)	285,000
Accrued postretirement benefit cost	$ -0-	$(40,000)	$ (40,000)

Service Cost Component

The *service cost component* of net periodic postretirement benefit plan cost is defined by FASB-106 as the portion of the expected postretirement benefit obligation attributed to employee service during a specified period, based on the actuarial present value of the expected obligation.

A defined benefit postretirement benefit plan contains a benefit formula that defines the benefit an employee will receive for services performed during a specified period (service cost). FASB-106 requires that the terms of the benefit formula be used to determine the amount of postretirement benefit earned by each employee for services performed during a specified period. Under FASB-106, attribution is the process of assigning postretirement benefits or cost to periods of employee service, in accordance with the postretirement benefit formula.

Interest Cost Component

FASB-106 requires an employer to recognize as a component of net periodic postretirement benefit cost the interest cost on the accumulated postretirement benefit obligation. The interest cost is equal to the increase in the amount of the obligation due to the passage of time, measured at a rate equal to the assumed discount rate. FASB-106 specifies that the interest cost component of net postretirement benefit cost should not be considered interest expense for purposes of applying FASB-34 (Capitalization of Interest Cost).

Actual Return on Plan Assets Component

If a plan is funded, one component of periodic postretirement benefit cost is the actual return on plan assets. The amount of the actual return on plan assets is equal to the difference between the fair value of plan assets at the beginning and end of a period, adjusted for employer contributions, employee contributions (if the plan is contributory) and postretirement benefits paid during the period.

> **OBSERVATION:** *In brief, plan assets are investments that have been segregated and restricted, usually in a trust, for the sole purpose of paying postretirement benefits.*

Fair value is the amount that could reasonably be expected to result from a current sale of an investment between a willing buyer and a willing seller, that is, a sale other than a forced liquidation. Plan assets that are used in the operation of the postretirement benefit plan (building, equipment, furniture, fixtures, etc.) are valued at cost less accumulated depreciation or amortization.

The actual return on plan assets should be shown net of tax expense if the fund holding the plan assets is a taxable entity.

A return on plan assets decreases the employer's cost of providing postretirement benefits to its employees, while a loss on plan assets increases postretirement benefit cost. Net periodic postretirement benefit income can result from a significantly high return on plan assets during a period.

An employer may determine its actual gain or loss on plan assets as follows:

Plan assets, beginning of year, at fair value	$ 200,000
Add: Assets contributed to plan	750,000
Less: Benefit payments from plan	(650,000)
	300,000
Less: Plan assets, end of year, at fair value	340,000
Actual (return) loss on plan assets	$ (40,000)

> **OBSERVATION:** *Actual return on plan assets is one of the components of net periodic postretirement benefit cost. As discussed later in this chapter, FASB-106 requires this component to be disclosed on the financial statements. Another component of net postretirement benefit cost is gains and losses (discussed later in this chapter). The "gains and losses" component includes, among other items, "plan asset gains and losses," defined as the difference between the actual return and the expected return on plan assets.*
>
> *The following example illustrates the combined effect on net periodic postretirement benefit cost of (1) actual return on plan assets and (2) plan asset gains and losses: If the actual return on plan assets is $1,000,000 and the expected return is $700,000, the plan asset gain is the $300,000 difference between the actual return and the expected return. This $300,000 plan asset gain is part of the "gains and losses" component of net periodic postretirement benefit cost, while the $1,000,000 actual return on plan assets is another component. The combined effect is a net decrease of $700,000 in net periodic postretirement benefit cost, the result of offsetting the $300,000 plan asset gain against the $1,000,000 actual return. This $700,000 is equal to the expected return on plan assets. The total amount of net postretirement benefit cost will include the $700,000 as well as other components, including service cost, interest cost, etc. The $300,000 plan asset gain will be taken into account in computing (1) the expected return on plan assets in the future and (2) amortization of deferred gains and losses. See discussion and illustration later in this chapter.*

Amortization of Unrecognized Prior Service Cost Component

When a postretirement benefit plan is initially adopted or amended, employees may be granted benefits for services performed in prior periods. The cost of postretirement benefits that are retroactively granted to employees is referred to as *prior service cost.*

Under FASB-106, only a portion of the total amount of prior service cost arising in a period is included in net periodic postretirement benefit cost. FASB-106 requires that the total prior service cost arising in a period from the adoption or amendment of a plan be amortized in a systematic manner. *Amortization* of prior service cost is a component of net periodic postretirement benefit cost.

Initiation of a Plan, or Amendment that Improves Benefits in an Existing Plan When an employer initiates a plan or adopts an amendment that improves the benefits in an existing plan, the amount of prior service cost is the amount of increase in the accumulated postretirement benefit obligation that can be attributed to service of employees in prior periods.

Plan Amendment Increasing Benefits

At the beginning of Year 2, Company A amended its plan, causing the accumulated postretirement benefit obligation to increase by $84,000. Active plan participants had an average of 12 remaining years of service before reaching full eligibility for benefits.

At the end of Year 2, the employer paid $60,000 in benefits. Service cost was $50,000.

The worksheets as of the end of Year 2 are as follows:

	Accrued Postretirement Benefit Cost	Accumulated Postretirement Benefit Obligation	Unrecognized Transition Obligation	Unrecognized Prior Service Cost
Beginning of year	$ (40,000)	$(325,000)	$285,000	$ -0-
Plan amendment		(84,000)		84,000
Recognition of components of net periodic postretirement benefit cost:				
Service cost	(50,000)	(50,000)		
Interest cost (a)	(40,900)	(40,900)		
Amortization of transition obligation (b)	(15,000)		(15,000)	
Amortization of prior service cost (c)	(7,000)			(7,000)
	(112,900)	(174,900)	(15,000)	77,000
Benefit payments	60,000	60,000		
Net change	(52,900)	(114,900)	(15,000)	77,000
End of year	$ (92,900)	$(439,900)	$270,000	$77,000

(a) 10% (assumed discount rate) of $325,000 (accumulated postretirement benefit obligation at beginning of year), plus 10% of $84,000 (increase in obligation by plan amendment).

(b) 20-year amortization of original $300,000 transition obligation.

(c) Straight-line amortization of prior service cost, based on average remaining years of service (12 years) of active plan participants before reaching full eligibility.

Reconciliation of funded status:

	End of Year 1	Net Change	End of Year 2
Accumulated postretirement benefit obligation	$ (325,000)	$(114,900)	$ (439,900)
Plan assets at fair value	-0-		-0-
Funded status	(325,000)	(114,900)	(439,900)
Unrecognized prior service cost	-0-	77,000	77,000
Unrecognized transition obligation	285,000	(15,000)	270,000
Accrued postretirement benefit cost	$ (40,000)	$ (52,900)	$ (92,900)

Methods of Amortizing Prior Service Cost   FASB-106 provides a number of rules regarding the amortization of prior service cost, as follows:

- General rule
- Special rule if all or most employees are fully eligible
- Simplified computation
- Accelerated amortization

General rule   The general rule requires amortization of prior service cost in equal installments during each employee's remaining years of service until that employee reaches full eligibility under the new or amended plan.

Special rule if all or most employees are fully eligible   If all or almost all employees are already fully eligible for benefits when the plan is initiated or amended, the employer should amortize prior service cost over the remaining life expectancy of these employees.

Simplified computation   FASB-106 allows a simplified form of computation, provided it amortizes prior service cost more quickly than the methods described above. For example, instead of basing its amortization on the period during which each individual employee reaches full eligibility, an employer may amortize prior service cost over the *average* remaining years of service of all active plan participants until they reach full eligibility.

Accelerated amortization   An enterprise should use an accelerated method of amortization if a history of plan amendments and other evidence indicates that the employer's economic benefits from the initiation or amendment of the plan will be exhausted before the employees reach full eligibility for postretirement benefits. In this situation, amortization should reflect the period during which the employer expects to receive economic benefits from the existence of the plan.

Plan Amendments that Reduce Obligation   If a plan amendment reduces the accumulated postretirement obligation, the reduction should be amortized in accordance with the above rules and should be applied (a) to reduce any existing unrecognized prior service cost and (b) to reduce any unrecognized transition obligation.

Gain or Loss Component

The approach to gains and losses in FASB-106 is similar to that in FASB-87 (Employers' Accounting for Pensions). Gains or losses consist of certain types of changes in (1) the accumulated postretirement benefit obligation and (2) the plan assets. The changes may result from either (a) experience different from that assumed or (b) changes in assumptions.

Gains and losses include amounts that have been realized (for example, the sale of a security) and amounts that have not been realized (for example, changes in the market value of plan assets).

Elements of the Gain or Loss Component

The gain or loss component of net postretirement benefit cost is the combination of three elements:

- Plan asset gains and losses
- Other gains and losses recognized immediately
- Amortization of deferred gains and losses

> **OBSERVATION:** *The gain or loss component of net postretirement benefit cost does not include the actual return on plan assets, which is another component of net periodic postretirement benefit cost, discussed earlier in this chapter.*

The gain or loss component does include, among other items, the difference between the actual return and the expected return on plan assets ("Plan Asset Gains and Losses," discussed under the next heading), since this difference falls within the general concept of gains and losses according to FASB-106—changes resulting from experience different from that assumed or from changes in assumptions.

Plan Asset Gains and Losses   Plan asset gains and losses are the difference between the actual return (including earnings and holding gains/losses) and the expected return (including earnings and holding gains/losses) for the same period.

The computation of plan asset gains and losses starts with determining the expected return on plan assets, which consists of two components: (1) earnings (the expected long-term rate of return on plan assets) and (2) holding gains or losses (changes in the market-related value of plan assets).

The market-related value may be either fair market value or a calculation that recognizes changes in fair market value systematically over a period of five years or less. The employer may use different methods of calculating market-related value for different categories of assets, but each category must be treated consistently during successive periods.

FASB-106 requires plan asset gains and losses to be included in net periodic postretirement benefit cost. For purposes of financial statement disclosure, plan asset gains and losses should be included in the "net total of other components" of net periodic postretirement benefit cost.

> **OBSERVATION:** *As noted earlier in this chapter, net periodic postretirement benefit cost includes (among other items): (1) plan asset gains and losses and (2) actual return on plan assets. The combined effect of these two items is equal to the expected return on plan assets.*
>
> *Plan asset gains and losses are taken into account in computing the expected return on plan assets in the future. This year's plan asset gains and losses will therefore be reflected, in the computation of the expected return on plan assets, in future years' net periodic postretirement benefit cost. Plan asset gains and losses are also taken into account in computing amortization of deferred gains and losses.*

Other Gains and Losses Recognized Immediately   Immediate recognition of other types of gains and losses is required in some situations and permitted in others.

Immediate recognition required   An employer should recognize an immediate gain or loss if it decides to deviate temporarily from its substantive plan, either by (1) forgiving a retrospective adjustment of the current or prior years' cost-sharing provisions as they relate to benefit costs already incurred by retirees or (2) otherwise changing the employer's share of benefit costs incurred in the current or prior periods.

Immediate recognition permitted   If immediate recognition of gains and losses is not required, an employer may elect to use a method that consistently recognizes gains and losses immediately, provided: (1) any gain that does not offset a loss previously recognized in income must first offset any unrecognized transition obligation, and (2) any loss that does not offset a gain previously recognized in income must first offset any unrecognized transition asset.

Amortization of Deferred Gains and Losses   Any gains and losses not recognized immediately are deferred gains and losses. FASB-106 establishes a special formula to determine (1) whether or not an employer is required to amortize deferred gains and losses, and (2) if amortization is required, the minimum amount of periodic amortization. FASB-106 allows other methods instead of those provided by the formula, if certain qualifications are met.

Determining whether amortization of deferred gains and losses is required   FASB-106 requires the employer to amortize unrecognized gains and losses if:

1.   The beginning-of-year balance of net unrecognized gain or loss (with a modification noted below) is more than

2.   A base figure used for comparison purposes.

The base figure is 10% of the greater of:

   a.   the accumulated postretirement benefit obligation, or

   b.   the market-related value of plan assets.

For purposes of this comparison, the unrecognized gain or loss is modified, so as to exclude any plan asset gains or losses that have not yet been reflected in market-related value.

> **OBSERVATION:** *If unrecognized gains or losses are not greater than the base figure, they come within the 10% "corridor" and the employer need not amortize them.*

Amount to be amortized   If amortization is required under the formula, the amount to be amortized is the difference between the beginning of year balance of net unrecognized gain or loss and the base figure.

Methods of amortizing deferred gains and losses   The minimum amortization is the amount to be amortized, determined as above, divided by the average remaining service period of active plan participants. If all or almost all of the plan's participants are inactive, divide instead by the average remaining life expectancy of the inactive participants.

Instead of using the minimum amortization method, an employer may use any other systematic method of amortization, provided that (a) the amortization for each period is at least as much as the amount determined by the minimum amortization method, (b) the method is used consistently, (c) the method applies consistently to gains and losses, and (d) the method is disclosed.

Gains and Losses

At the beginning of 19X5, Company L prepared the following projection of changes during that year:

	Prepaid Postretirement Benefit Cost	Accumulated Postretirement Benefit Obligation	Unrecognized Transition Obligation	Unrecognized Net Loss	Plan Assets
Beginning of year	$ 406,000	$(3,625,000)	$2,700,000	$ 302,500	$1,028,500
Recognition of compo-nents of net periodic post-retire-ment benefit cost:					
Service cost	(180,000)	(180,000)			
Interest cost	(326,250)	(326,250)			
Amortization of transi-tion obli-gation	(150,000)		(150,000)		
Amortization of unrecog-nized net loss					
Expected return on plan assets (a)	96,850				96,850
	(559,400)	(506,250)	(150,000)		96,850
Assets contri-buted to plan	956,250				956,250
Benefit pay-ments from plan		450,000			(450,000)
Net change	396,850	(56,250)	(150,000)		603,100
End of year—projected	$ 802,850	$(3,681,250)	$2,550,000	$ 302,500	$1,631,600

(a)   See Schedule 1.

As of the end of 19X5, Company L prepared the following worksheet and supporting schedules to reflect actual changes dur-ing the year:

	Projected 12/31/X5	Net Gain (Loss)	Actual 12/31/X5
Accumulated postretirement benefit obligation	$(3,681,250)	$118,630 (b)	$(3,562,620)
Plan assets at fair value	1,631,600	(110,180) (c)	1,521,420
Funded status	(2,049,650)	8,450	(2,041,200)
Unrecognized net (gain) loss	302,500	(8,450)	294,050
Unrecognized transition obligation	2,550,000	—	2,550,000
Prepaid postretirement benefit cost	$ 802,850	$ -0-	$ 802,850

(b) Liability at year-end was $118,630 less than projected, due to changes in assumptions not detailed here.

(c) See Schedule 1.

Net Periodic Postretirement Benefit Cost

Service cost	$180,000
Interest cost	326,250
Actual loss on plan assets (d)	13,330
Amortization of transition obligation	150,000
Net amortization and deferral (e)	(110,180)
Net periodic postretirement benefit cost	$559,400

(d) See Schedule 3.
(e) See Schedule 4.

Schedule 1 — Plan Assets

Expected long-term rate of return on plan assets	10%
Beginning balance, market-related value (f)	$ 968,500
Contributions to plan (end of year)	956,250
Benefits paid by plan	(450,000)
Expected return on plan assets	96,850
	1,571,600
20% of each of last 5 years' asset gains (losses)	(7,036)
Ending balance, market-related value	$ 1,564,564
Beginning balance, fair value of plan assets	$ 1,028,500
Contributions to plan	956,250
Benefits paid	(450,000)
Actual return (loss) on plan assets (g)	(13,330)
Ending balance, fair value of plan assets	$ 1,521,420
Deferred asset gain (loss) for year (h)	$ (110,180)
Gain (loss) not included in ending balance market-related value (i)	$ (43,144)

(f)   This example adds 20% of each of the last 5 years' gains or losses.

(g)   See Schedule 3.

(h)   (Actual return on plan assets) — (expected return on plan assets). *Note*: The term "deferred asset gain (loss) for year" follows the terminology in the illustrations attached to FASB-106, although the text of FASB-106 refers to the same item as "plan asset gains and losses."

(i)   (Ending balance, fair value of plan assets) — (ending balance, market-related value of plan assets).

Schedule 2 — Amortization of Unrecognized Net Gain or Loss

10% of beginning balance of accumulated postretirement benefit obligation	$362,500
10% of beginning balance of market-related value of plan assets (j)	96,850
Greater of the above	$362,500
Unrecognized net (gain) loss at beginning of year	$302,500
Asset gain (loss) not included in beginning balance of market-related value (k)	60,000
Amount subject to amortization	$362,500
Amount in excess of the corridor subject to amortization	None
Required amortization	None

(j) See Schedule 1.
(k) See Schedule 1.

Schedule 3 — Actual Return or Loss on Plan Assets

Plan assets at fair value, beginning of year	$ 1,028,500
Plus: Assets contributed to plan	956,250
Less: Benefit payments from plan	(450,000)
	1,534,750
Less: Plan assets at fair value, end of year	(1,521,420)
Actual (return) loss on plan assets	$ 13,330

Schedule 4 — Net Amortization and Deferral

Amortization of unrecognized net (gain) or loss (l)	$ -0-
Deferred asset gain (loss) for year (m)	(110,180)
Net amortization and deferral	$(110,180)

(l) See Schedule 2.
(m) See Schedule 1.

Amortization of Transition Obligation/Asset Component

The final component of net periodic postretirement benefit cost is amortization of the unrecognized obligation or asset at the date of initial application of FASB-106. This component is discussed later in this chapter, under the heading "Transition."

Measurement of Plan Assets

Plan assets are generally stocks, bonds, and other investments. Such assets may include the participation rights in participating insurance contracts, but not other rights in insurance contracts. The employer's own securities may be included as plan assets, but only if they are transferable.

Plan assets are increased by various means, including the employer's contributions, employees' contributions if the plan is contributory, and earnings from investing the contributed amounts. Plan assets are decreased by benefit payments, income taxes, and other expenses. The amount of plan assets at any time represents the balance remaining after subtracting the cumulative amount of decreases from the cumulative amount of increases.

All plan assets should be segregated and restricted for paying postretirement benefits. Usually, the assets are in a trust. Plan assets may be withdrawn only for the stated purposes of the plan. In limited circumstances, the plan may permit withdrawal when the plan's assets exceed its obligations and the employer has taken appropriate steps to satisfy existing obligations.

If assets are not segregated or effectively restricted in some other way, they are not plan assets even though the employer intends to use them for paying postretirement benefits. Assets that are accrued but not yet paid into the plan should not be regarded as plan assets.

For purposes of disclosure, FASB-106 requires the employer to use fair value as the measurement for all plan investments, including equity or debt securities, real estate, and other items. Fair value is the amount that could reasonably be expected to result from a current sale between a willing buyer and a willing seller. Value should not be based on the estimated proceeds of a forced or liquidation sale.

If an active market exists for the investment, fair value should be measured by the market value. If no active market exists for the specific investment, but an active market exists for similar investments, the market value of those similar investments may provide helpful guidance on the market value of the plan's investment. If no active market exists for the investment or a similar one, the employer should consider basing fair value on a forecast of expected cash flows, discounted at a current rate commensurate with the risk involved.

Plan assets used in plan operations, such as buildings, equipment, furniture and fixtures, and leasehold improvements, should be measured at cost less accumulated depreciation or amortization.

> **OBSERVATION:** *FASB-106 does not discuss the possible use of plan assets in the operations of the employer's business.*

Insurance Contracts

Benefits covered by insurance contracts (defined below) should be excluded from the accumulated postretirement benefit obligation. Insurance contracts should also be excluded from plan assets, except for the cost of participation rights in participating insurance contracts.

Definition of Insurance Contracts   FASB-106 defines an *insurance contract* as a contract in which the insurance company unconditionally undertakes a legal obligation to provide specified benefits to specific individuals in return for a fixed premium. The contract must be irrevocable, and must involve the transfer of significant risk from the employer (or the plan) to the insurance company. A contract does not qualify as an insurance contract under FASB-106 if (1) the insurance company is a *captive insurer* doing business primarily with the employer and related parties or (2) there is any reasonable doubt that the insurance company will meet its obligations under the contract.

Participating Insurance Contracts   Some contracts are *participating insurance contracts,* in which the purchaser (either the plan or the employer) participates in the experience of the insurance company. The purchaser's participation generally takes the form of a dividend that effectively reduces the cost of the plan. If, however, the employer's participation is so great that the employer retains all or most of the risks and rewards of the plan, the contract is not regarded as an insurance contract for purposes of FASB-106.

The purchase price of a participating contract is ordinarily higher than the price of a similar contract without the participation right. The difference between the price with and without the participation right is considered to be the cost of the participation right. The employer should regard this cost as an asset when purchased. At subsequent dates, the employer should measure the participation right at its fair value if fair value can reasonably be estimated. Otherwise, the participation right should be measured at its amortized cost, but this amount should not exceed the participation right's net realizable value. The cost should be amortized systematically over the expected dividend period.

Cost of Insurance   Insurance contracts, such as life insurance contracts, may be purchased during a period to cover postretirement benefits attributed to service by employees in the same period. In this situation, the cost of the benefits equals the cost of purchasing the insurance (after adjusting for the cost of any participation rights included in the contract).

Accordingly, if all postretirement benefits attributed to service by employees in the current period are covered by nonparticipating insurance contracts purchased during the same period, the cost of the benefits equals the cost of purchasing the insurance. If the benefits are only partially covered by nonparticipating insurance contracts, the uninsured portion of the benefits is accounted for in the same way as benefits under uninsured plans.

Insurance Company Not Fully Bound   If the insurance company does not unconditionally undertake a legal obligation to pay specified benefits to specific individuals, the arrangement does not qualify as an insurance contract for purposes of FASB-106. The arrangement should be accounted for as an investment at fair value.

Fair value is presumed to equal the cash surrender value or conversion value, if any. In some cases, the best estimate of fair value is the contract value.

Measurement Date

The measurement date for plan assets and obligations should be the financial statement date or an earlier date within three months, if such a date is used consistently from year to year. Information can be prepared ahead of the measurement date and projected forward to that date to adjust for events occurring between the preparation of the information and the measurement date.

Net periodic postretirement benefit cost, as shown on interim and annual financial statements, generally should be measured on the basis of the assumptions carried over to the beginning of the current year from the previous year-end measurements. If, however, more recent measurements of plan assets and obligations are available, the employer should use them. Recent measurements may become available, for example, when a significant event occurs that requires a remeasurement, such as a plan amendment, settlement, or curtailment. Once a remeasurement has been made, the assumptions underlying that remeasurement should be used to remeasure net postretirement benefit cost from the date of the significant event to the year-end measurement date.

Disclosures

In addition to the accrual accounting discussed above, FASB-106 requires elaborate disclosure of an employer's obligation to provide postretirement benefits and the costs of these benefits.

FASB-106 requires the employer to disclose the following information about a defined benefit postretirement plan:

Substantive Plan

A description of the substantive plan, including:

- The nature of the plan
- Any modifications of the existing cost-sharing provisions that are reflected in the substantive plan
- The nature of any commitment to increase monetary benefits provided by the plan
- Employee groups covered
- Types of benefits provided
- Funding policy
- Types of assets held and significant liabilities (other than liabilities to pay benefits)
- The nature and effect of significant matters affecting the comparability of information for all periods presented; for example, the effect of a business combination or divestiture

Net Postretirement Benefit Cost

The employer should disclose the amount of the net postretirement benefit cost, showing each of the following components separately:

- Service cost
- Interest cost
- Actual return on plan assets
- Amortization of unrecognized transition obligation/asset
- Net total of other components, generally consisting of:
    1. Net asset gain or loss arising during the period but deferred for later recognition;

    > **OBSERVATION:** *FASB-106, footnote 23 to par. 74, notes that this category is, "in effect, an offset or a supplement to the actual return on plan assets." The illustrations accompanying FASB-106 indicate that this category includes plan asset gains and losses.*

    2. Amortization of unrecognized prior service cost;
    3. Amortization of net gain or loss from prior periods; and
    4. Gain or loss recognized due to temporary deviation from substantive plan.

Reconciliation of Funded Status

The employer's disclosure should include a reconciliation of the funded status of the plan with amounts shown in the statement of financial position, showing each of the following items separately:

- Fair value of plan assets
- Accumulated postretirement benefit obligation, with separate identification of the portions of the obligation resulting from (1) retirees, (2) other fully eligible plan participants, and (3) other active plan participants
- Unrecognized prior service cost
- Unrecognized net gain or loss, including plan asset gains and losses not yet reflected in market-related value
- Unrecognized transition obligation/asset
- Net postretirement benefit asset or liability as shown in the statement of financial position (this amount should equal the net result of combining the five items listed above)

Assumed Cost Trend Rate

The employer should disclose the assumed health care cost trend rate (or rates) used to measure the expected gross eligible charges (that is, for benefits covered by the plan) for the next year, together with (1) a general description of the direction and pattern of change in subsequent years and (2) the ultimate assumed trend rate and the year when it is expected to be reached.

Other Assumptions

FASB-106 requires that the employer disclose the following assumptions:

- The weighted average of the assumed discount rates and the assumed rates of compensation increase (for pay-related plans) used to measure the accumulated postretirement benefit obligation
- The weighted average of the expected long-term rates of return on plan assets
- The estimated income tax rates included in the long-term rate of return on plan assets, if the income of the plan is segregated from the employer's investment income for tax purposes.

Effect of 1% Increase in Cost Trend Rate

The employer should disclose the effect of a 1% increase in the assumed health care cost trend rate for each future year, on each of the following (if all other assumptions remain constant, and the substantive plan remains unchanged):

- The combined total of the service cost component and the interest cost component of net periodic postretirement health care benefit cost
- The accumulated postretirement benefit obligation for health care benefits

Employer's Own Securities and Insurance

The employer should disclose the amount and types of securities of the employer and related parties included in plan assets, and the approximate amount of future annual benefits covered by insurance contracts issued by the employer and related parties.

Alternative Amortization

FASB-106 requires the employer to disclose any alternative amortization method used pursuant to par. 53 of FASB-106 (amortization of prior service cost more rapidly than general requirement) or par. 60 (amortization of unrecognized net gain or loss more rapidly than general requirement).

Gain or Loss from Settlement or Curtailment

The employer should disclose the amount of gain or loss recognized from a settlement or a curtailment during the period, together with a description of the nature of these events.

Termination Benefits

The employer should disclose the cost of providing special or contractual termination benefits recognized during the period, together with a description of these events.

Employers with Two or More Plans

FASB-106 deals with the questions of measurement and disclosure separately for an employer with two or more plans and for employers with one plan.

Aggregate Measurement FASB-106 generally requires an employer with two or more plans to measure each plan separately. However, an employer may measure its plans as an aggregate rather than as separate plans, if the plans meet the following criteria:

1. The plans provide postretirement health care benefits
2. The plans provide either of the following:
   a. Different benefits to the same group of employees
   b. The same benefits to different groups of employees
3. The plans are unfunded (without any plan assets)
4. The employer aggregates all of its plans that meet the preceding three tests.

An employer may make a separate aggregation of plans providing welfare benefits (that is, postretirement benefits other than health care), if requirements (2) through (4) above are met. However, a plan that has plan assets should not be aggregated with other plans, but should be measured separately.

Aggregate Disclosure Generally, an employer may make aggregate disclosure of all defined benefit plans, or may make disclosure of groups of aggregated plans, subject to the following standards:

- Disclosures for plans with plan assets that exceed the accumulated postretirement benefit obligation may generally be aggregated with disclosures for plans in which the obligations exceed the assets. However, the reconciliation of the funded status of the plans should separately show the aggregate plan assets and the aggregate obligations of any plans that are not fully funded.
- Plans that provide health care benefits should not be aggregated with plans that provide welfare benefits, if the accumulated postretirement benefit obligation of the welfare plans is significant in relation to the total.
- Plans inside the U.S. should not be aggregated with plans outside the U.S., if the accumulated postretirement benefit obligation of the plans outside the U.S. is significant in relation to the total.

MULTIEMPLOYER PLANS

Definition and Characteristics A *multiemployer plan* is one to which two or more unrelated employers contribute. Multiemployer plans generally result from *collective bargaining agreements*, and are administered by a board of trustees representing management and labor of all contributing employers. Sometimes these plans are called "joint trusts" or "union plans." An employer may participate in a number of plans; for example, the employees may belong to a number of unions. Numerous employers may participate in a multiemployer plan. Often the employers are in the same industry, but sometimes the employers are in different industries, and the only common element among the employers is that their employees belong to the same labor union.

The assets contributed by one employer may be used to provide benefits to employees of other employers, since the assets contributed by one employer are not segregated from those contributed by other employers. Even though the plan provides defined benefits to employees of all the employers, the plan typically requires a defined contribution from each participating employer, but the amount of an employer's obligation may be changed by events affecting other participating employers and their employees (Basis for Conclusions, par. 375).

A multiemployer plan can exist even without the involvement of a labor union. For example, a national non-profit organization may organize a multiemployer plan for itself and its local chapters.

Accounting for Multiemployer Plans Distinctive accounting requirements apply to an employer that participates in a multiemployer plan. The employer recognizes as net postretirement benefit cost the contribution required for the period, including cash and the fair value of noncash contributions. The employer recognizes as a liability any unpaid contributions required for the period.

> ### OBSERVATION:
> 1. *This accounting resembles that required for the single employer that has a **defined contribution plan** (see section entitled "Defined Contribution Plans").*
> 2. *By participating in a multiemployer plan, an employer that has a **defined benefit plan** accounts for it essentially as if it were a **defined contribution plan**. The financing of the plan is, in effect, off-balance-sheet.*

The employer should make the following disclosures about multiemployer plans, separate from disclosures for any single-employer plan:

- Description of each multiemployer plan, including categories of employees covered, type of benefits provided (for example, whether the plan is a defined benefit or defined contribution plan), and the nature and effect of significant matters affecting comparability of the information for all periods shown on the financial statements.

- Amount of postretirement cost recognized during the period, if this information is available.

> **OBSERVATION:** *The information may be unavailable if, for example, (1) a multiemployer plan provides health and welfare benefits to active employees as well as to retirees and (2) the employer is unable to determine how much of its contributions to the plan are attributable to postretirement benefits.*

If information about the amount of postretirement cost recognized during the period is not available, the employer should disclose the total required contribution for the period to the plan for general health and welfare benefits for active employees as well as retired employees.

Withdrawal from Multiemployer Plan   When an employer withdraws from a multiemployer plan, the employer may be contractually liable to pay into the plan a portion of its unfunded accumulated postretirement benefit obligation.

> **OBSERVATION:** *Contractual obligations are the only ones facing the employer that withdraws from a multiemployer **postretirement** benefit plan. In contrast, an employer that withdraws from a multiemployer **pension** plan is subject not only to contractual obligations, but also to statutory obligations under the Multiemployer Pension Plan Amendments Act of 1980.*

An employer should apply FASB-5 (Accounting for Contingencies) if withdrawal from the plan is probable or reasonably possible, and the employer will incur an obligation as a result.

Obligation under "Maintenance of Benefits" Clause   An employer should also apply FASB-5 (Accounting for Contingencies) if it is probable or reasonably likely that the employer's contribution to the multiemployer plan will increase during the remainder of the contract period under a "maintenance of benefits" clause, to make up for a shortfall in the funding of the plan in order to assure the full level of benefits described in the plan.

MULTIPLE-EMPLOYER PLANS

A multiple-employer plan is quite distinct from a multiemployer plan. In a *multiple-employer* plan, individual employers combine their single-employer plans for pooling assets for investment purposes, or for reducing the costs of administration. The participating employers may have different benefit formulas; each employer's contributions to the plan are based on that employer's benefit formula. These plans are generally not the result of collective bargaining agreements.

Each employer should account for its interest in a multiple-employer plan as if that interest were a single-employer plan.

> **OBSERVATION:** *If an employer is a participant in a multiple-employer plan, the employer should consider disclosing this fact, as well as the other information included in the required disclosures about single-employer plans.*

PLANS OUTSIDE THE UNITED STATES

FASB-106 applies to plans outside as well as inside the U.S., with only one exception: the effective date is extended to December 15, 1994, for plans outside the U.S. If the accumulated postretirement obligation of the plans outside the U.S. is significant in proportion to the total of all the employer's postretirement benefit plans, the employer should make separate disclosure of the plans outside the U.S. Otherwise, the employer may make combined disclosure of plans outside and inside the U.S.

> **OBSERVATION:**
> 1. *FASB-106 does not define "outside the U.S." The following factors, among others, may be relevant: (1) where all or most of the employees and beneficiaries are located, (2) where all or most of the plan assets are invested, (3) where all or most of the activity in administering the plan takes place, and (4) which country's law governs the relationships among employees, beneficiaries, and the employer.*
> 2. *If a plan is governed by the law of a foreign country that confers vested rights on employees, the employer may have to include this information in the description of the substantive plan, included in the disclosures required by FASB-106.*

BUSINESS COMBINATIONS

If an employer sponsors a single-employer defined benefit postretirement plan, and the employer is acquired in a business combination treated as a purchase, the allocation of the purchase price must reflect the existence of the plan, once FASB-106 is adopted. In order to do this, the allocation should reflect either (1) a liability (for the excess of the accumulated postretirement benefit obligation over the plan assets) or (2) an asset (for the excess of the plan assets over the accumulated postretirement benefit obligation).

For purposes of this allocation, plan assets are measured at fair value. The accumulated postretirement benefit obligation is measured on the basis of the benefits attributable to employee service rendered to the acquired employer before consummation of the business combination. This amount should be adjusted to reflect (1) any changes in assumptions based on the purchaser's assessment of future events and (2) any changes the purchaser makes in the substantive plan.

Benefit Improvements Attributed to Prior Service   If benefits of an existing plan are improved in connection with a business combination treated as a purchase, and all or part of the improvement is attributable to employee service prior to the consummation date of the purchase, the accounting depends on whether or not the improvement was a condition of the purchase agreement.

If the improvement was a condition of the agreement, the improvement should be accounted for as part of the purchase agreement, and not as prior service cost, even though all or part of the improvement is attributable to prior service. On the other hand, if the improvement was not a condition of the agreement, the improvement should be accounted for as prior service cost to the extent the improvement is attributable to prior service.

Termination or Curtailment   If a postretirement benefit plan is likely to be terminated or curtailed when an employer is acquired in a business combination accounted for as a purchase, the effect of the anticipated termination or curtailment should be taken into account in measuring the accumulated postretirement benefit obligation at the time of acquisition.

Anticipate Additional Liabilities Only if Certain or Probable   In connection with a purchase-type acquisition, the purchaser should anticipate additional liabilities only if their occurrence is either (1) certain (for example, when the additional liability is a condition of the acquisition agreement) or (2) probable (as indicated by the circumstances).

> **OBSERVATION:** *The "Basis for Conclusions" indicates that, in the context of purchase-type acquisitions, an enterprise participating in a **multiemployer** plan should not recognize additional liabilities to the plan, unless specific conditions exist that make additional liabilities probable. The FASB was not convinced that an obligation for future contributions to a multiemployer plan ordinarily exists, or that an employer should recognize any contractual withdrawal liability unless withdrawal is probable.*

Elimination of Unrecognized Items When an employer applies the preceding provisions for business combinations, the result will be the elimination of the following pre-existing items of the acquired employer:

- Unrecognized net gain or loss
- Unrecognized prior service cost
- Unrecognized transition obligation or transition asset

After the acquisition, the difference between the amount contributed and the net periodic postretirement benefit cost will reduce the liability or asset recognized at the time of the acquisition, to the extent the net obligation assumed or the net asset acquired is taken into account in determining the amount of contributions to the plan.

ACCOUNTING FOR SETTLEMENT OF A POSTRETIREMENT BENEFIT OBLIGATION

According to FASB-106, a *settlement* is a transaction that has the following characteristics:

- It is irrevocable.
- It relieves the employer (or the plan) of primary responsibility for the postretirement benefit obligation.
- It eliminates significant risks related to the obligation and the assets used to put the settlement into effect.

Settlements take place, for example, in the following situations:

- The employer makes lump-sum cash payments to plan participants, buying their rights to receive specified postretirement benefits.

- The employer purchases long-term nonparticipating insurance contracts to cover the accumulated postretirement benefit obligation for some or all of the participants in the plan (but the insurance company cannot be under the employer's control).

Settlements do *not* take place, however, in the following situations:

- The employer purchases an insurance contract from an insurance company controlled by the employer. This does not qualify as a settlement because the employer is still exposed to risk through its relationship with the insurance company.

- The employer invests in high-quality fixed-income securities with principal and income payment dates similar to the estimated due dates of benefits. This does not qualify as a settlement because (1) the investment decision can be revoked, (2) the purchase of the securities does not relieve the employer or the plan of primary responsibility for the postretirement benefit obligation, and (3) the purchase of the securities does not eliminate significant risks related to the postretirement benefit obligation.

Maximum Gain or Loss When a postretirement benefit obligation is settled, the maximum gain or loss to be recognized in income is the unrecognized gain or loss plus any unrecognized transition asset. This maximum gain or loss includes any gain or loss resulting from the remeasurement of plan assets and of the accumulated postretirement benefit obligation at the time of settlement.

Settlement Gain or Loss When Entire Obligation Is Settled If an employer settles the entire accumulated postretirement benefit obligation, a further distinction is made depending on whether the maximum amount subject to recognition is a gain or a loss.

If the maximum amount is a gain, the amount of this gain should first reduce any unrecognized transition obligation, then any excess gain should be recognized in income. If the maximum amount is a loss, the full amount of this loss should be recognized in income.

Settlement Gain or Loss when Only Part of Obligation Is Settled If an employer settles only part of the accumulated postretirement benefit obligation, the employer should recognize in income a pro rata portion of the amount of gain or loss that would have been recognized if the entire obligation had been settled. The pro rata portion equals the percentage by which the partial settlement reduces the accumulated postretirement benefit obligation.

Participating Insurance If an employer settles the obligation by purchasing a participating insurance contract, the cost of the participation right should be deducted from the maximum gain but not from the maximum loss, before the employer determines the amount to be recognized in income.

Settlements at Lower Cost than Current Cost of Service and Interest FASB-106 defines the *cost of a settlement* as follows:

- If the settlement is for cash, its cost is the amount of cash paid to plan participants.
- If the settlement uses nonparticipating insurance contracts, its cost is the cost of the contracts.
- If the settlement uses participating insurance contracts, its cost is the cost of the contracts minus the amount attributed to participation rights.

If the cost of all settlements during a year is no more than the combined amount of service cost and interest cost components of net postretirement benefit cost for the same year, FASB-106 permits but does not require the employer to recognize gain or loss for those settlements. The employer should apply a consistent policy each year.

ACCOUNTING FOR A PLAN CURTAILMENT

A *curtailment* is an event that either (1) significantly reduces the expected years of future service of active plan participants or (2) eliminates the accrual of defined benefits for some or all of the future services of a significant number of active plan participants.

The following events are examples of curtailments:

- Termination of employees' services earlier than anticipated. (This may or may not relate to the closing of a facility or the discontinuation of a segment of the employer's business.)

- Termination or suspension of a plan, so that employees no longer earn additional benefits for future service. (If the plan is suspended, future service may be counted toward eligibility for benefits accumulated on the basis of past service.)

Gain and Loss Recognition   Under the general provisions of FASB-106 for plans that continue without curtailment, the employer should recognize prior service cost on an amortized basis, on the theory that the employer receives economic benefits from the future services of employees covered by the plan.

When a plan is curtailed, the employer's expectation of receiving benefits from future services of its employees is reduced. Accordingly, curtailment requires the employer to recognize as a loss all or part of the remaining balance of unrecognized prior service cost. In this context, unrecognized prior service cost includes the cost of plan amendments and any unrecognized transition obligation.

Curtailment Resulting from Termination of Employees   If a curtailment occurs as the result of the termination of a significant number of employees who were plan participants, the curtailment loss consists of the following components:

1. The portion of the remaining unrecognized prior service cost (relating to this and any prior plan amendment) attributable to the previously estimated number of remaining future years of service of all terminated employees, **plus**

2. The portion of the remaining unrecognized transition obligation attributable to the previously estimated number of remaining future years of service, but only of the terminated employees who were participants in the plan at the date of transition to FASB-106.

Curtailment Resulting from Terminating Accrual of Additional Benefits for Future Services   If a curtailment results from terminating the accrual of additional benefits for the future services of a significant number of employees, the curtailment loss consists of the following components:

1. The pro rata amount of the remaining unrecognized prior service cost

> *This amount is based on the portion of the remaining expected years of service in the amortization period that originally was attributable to the employees (a) who were plan participants at the date of the plan amendment and (b) whose future accrual of benefits has been terminated, **plus***

2. The pro rata amount of the remaining unrecognized transition obligation

> *This amount is based on the portion of the remaining years of service of all participants who were active at the date of transition to FASB-106, that originally was attributable to the remaining expected future years of service of the employees whose future accrual of benefits has been terminated.*

Changes in Accumulated Postretirement Benefit Obligation A curtailment may cause a gain by decreasing the accumulated postretirement benefit obligation, or a loss by increasing that obligation.

If a curtailment decreases the accumulated obligation, the gain from this decrease should first be used to offset any unrecognized net loss, and the excess is a curtailment gain. If a curtailment increases the accumulated obligation, the loss from this increase should first be used to offset any unrecognized net gain, and the excess is a curtailment loss. In this context, any remaining unrecognized transition asset should be regarded as an unrecognized net gain, and should be combined with the unrecognized net gain or loss arising after transition to FASB-106.

When Curtailment Gains and Losses Should Be Recognized

Net loss If a curtailment produces a net loss as the combined effect of the above calculations regarding unrecognized prior service cost and the accumulated postretirement benefit obligation, this combined net loss should be recognized in income when it is *probable* that a curtailment will occur and the net effect of the curtailment is reasonably estimable.

Net gain If the curtailment produces a net gain as the combined result of the above calculations regarding unrecognized prior service cost and the accumulated postretirement benefit obligation, the net gain should be recognized in income when the affected employees terminate, or the plan suspension or amendment is adopted.

Curtailment

Company B reduced its workforce, including a significant number of employees who had been accumulating benefits under the postretirement benefit plan. An analysis of the terminated employees revealed:

a. At the time of curtailment, the terminated employees represented 22% of the *remaining years of expected service* of all employees who had been plan participants at the employer's date of transition.
b. At the time of curtailment, the terminated employees represented 18% of the *remaining years of service prior to full eligibility* of all employees who had been plan participants at the date of a prior plan amendment.

Company B's worksheet computation of the curtailment gain or loss is as follows:

	Before Curtailment	Curtailment	After Curtailment
Accumulated postretirement benefit obligation	$(514,000)	$108,000	$(406,000)
Plan assets at fair value	146,000		146,000
Funded status	(368,000)	108,000	(260,000)
Unrecognized net gain	(89,150)		(89,150)
Unrecognized prior service cost (a)	66,000	(11,880)	54,120
Unrecognized transition obligation (b)	390,000	(85,800)	304,200
(Accrued)/prepaid postretirement benefit cost	$ (1,150)	$ 10,320	$ 9,170

(a) Effect of curtailment is 18% of $66,000 (unrecognized prior service cost).
(b) Effect of curtailment is 22% of $390,000 (unrecognized transition obligation).

RELATIONSHIP OF SETTLEMENTS AND CURTAILMENTS TO OTHER EVENTS

An event may be either a settlement, or a curtailment, or both at the same time.

Curtailment, but not Settlement   A curtailment occurs, but not a settlement, if the expected future benefits are eliminated for some plan participants (for example, because their employment is terminated), but the plan continues to exist, to pay benefits, to invest assets, and to receive contributions.

Settlement, but not Curtailment   In contrast, a settlement occurs, but not a curtailment, if an employer purchases nonparticipating insurance contracts to cover the accumulated postretirement benefit obligation, while continuing to provide defined benefits for future service (either in the same plan or in a successor plan).

Settlement and Curtailment   Finally, if an employer settles its obligation and terminates the existence of the plan without establishing a successor defined benefit plan to take its place, the event is both a settlement and a curtailment. This occurs whether or not the employees continue to work for the employer.

Partial Settlement and Full Curtailment Resulting from Sale of Line of Business

Company C sold a line of business to Company D. In connection with the sale:

a. Company C terminated all employees of the sold division (a full curtailment).

b. Company D hired most of the employees.

c. Company D assumed an accumulated postretirement benefit obligation of $160,000 for postretirement benefits related to the former employees of Company C hired by Company D (a partial settlement).

d. The plan trustee transferred $200,000 of plan assets to Company D, consisting of $160,000 for the settlement of the accumulated postretirement benefit obligation and $40,000 as an excess contribution.

e. Company C determined that its gain on the sale of the division was $600,000, before considering any of the effects of the sale on the postretirement benefit plan.

Company C's accounting policy is to determine the effects of a curtailment before determining the effects of a settlement when both events occur simultaneously.

For Company C, the net loss from the curtailment is $456,000, which is recognized with the $600,000 gain resulting from the disposal of the division. The effect of the curtailment is determined as follows:

	Before Curtailment	Curtailment-Related Effects Resulting from Sale	After Curtailment
Accumulated postretirement benefit obligation	$(514,000)	$ (20,000) (a)	$(534,000)
Plan assets at fair value	220,000		220,000
Funded status	(294,000)	(20,000)	(314,000)
Unrecognized net gain	(99,150)	20,000 (a)	(79,150)
Unrecognized prior service cost	66,000	(66,000) (b)	—
Unrecognized transition obligation	390,000	(390,000) (c)	—
(Accrued)/prepaid postretirement benefit cost	$ 62,850	$(456,000)	$(393,150)

(a) Loss from earlier-than-expected retirement of fully eligible employees (not detailed here).

(b) Loss from unrecognized prior service cost attributable to terminated employees.

(c) Loss from unrecognized transition obligation attributable to terminated employees.

The $16,255 loss related to the settlement and transfer of plan assets that is recognized with the gain from the sale is determined as follows:

	After Curtailment	Settlement and Transfer of Plan Assets	After Settlement
Accumulated postretirement benefit obligation	$(534,000)	$160,000	$(374,000)
Plan assets at fair value	220,000	(200,000)	20,000
Funded status	(314,000)	(40,000)	(354,000)
Unrecognized net gain	(79,150)	23,745 (d)	(55,405)
Unrecognized prior service cost	—	—	—
Unrecognized transition obligation	—	—	—
Accrued postretirement benefit cost	$(393,150)	$ (16,255)	$(409,405)

(d) The unrecognized net gain is computed as follows:

Step 1. Compute the percentage of the accumulated postretirement benefit obligation settled to the total accumulated postretirement benefit obligation ($160,000/$534,000 = 30%).

Step 2. Maximum gain is measured as the unrecognized net gain subsequent to transition plus any unrecognized transition asset ($79,150 + $Ø = $79,150).

Step 3. The settlement gain is 30% of $79,150 = $23,745.

MEASUREMENT OF THE EFFECTS OF TERMINATION BENEFITS

If an employer offers postretirement benefits as special termination benefits that are not required by any pre-existing contract, the employer should recognize a liability and a loss when the employees accept the offer and the amount is reasonably estimable.

If the employer is contractually obliged to provide postretirement benefits as termination benefits, the employer should recognize a liability and a loss when it is probable that employees will be eligible and the amount is reasonably estimable.

If an employer offers special or contractual termination benefits and curtails the postretirement benefit plan at the same time, FASB-106 requires the employer to account separately for the termination benefits and the curtailment.

The amount of the liability and loss to be recognized when employees accept an offer of termination benefits in the form of postretirement benefits is determined as follows:

Step 1. Determine the accumulated postretirement benefit obligation for those employees (without including any special termination benefits), on the assumption that (a) any of those employees who are not yet fully eligible for benefits will terminate as soon as they become fully eligible, and (b) any of those employees who are fully eligible will retire immediately.

Step 2. Adjust the accumulated postretirement benefit obligation as computed in Step 1 to reflect the special termination benefits.

Step 3. Subtract the amount in Step 2 from the amount in Step 1.

DISPOSAL OF A SEGMENT

If an employer recognizes a gain or loss from settlement or curtailment of a postretirement benefit plan, or from offering postretirement benefits as special termination benefits, and the gain or loss is directly related to the disposal of a segment of a business or a portion of a line of business, the gain or loss should be included in determining the gain or loss from the disposal. The net gain or loss attributable to the disposal should be recognized in accordance with APB-30 (Reporting the Results of Operations).

DEFINED CONTRIBUTION PLANS

A *defined contribution plan* provides an individual account for each participant, and specifies how to determine the amount to be contributed to each individual's account. The plan does not specify the amount of postretirement benefits to be received by any individual. This amount is determined by the amount of contributions, the return on the investment of the amount contributed, and any forfeitures of the benefits of other plan participants that are allocated to the individual's account.

Accounting for Contributions   A defined contribution plan may require the employer to contribute to the plan only for periods in which an employee renders services, or the employer may be required to continue making payments for periods after the employee retires or terminates employment. To the extent an employer's contribution is made in the same period as the employee renders services, the employer's net postretirement benefit cost equals the amount of contributions required for that period. If the plan requires the employer to continue contributions after the employee retires or terminates, the employer should make accruals during the employee's service period of the estimated amount of contributions to be made after the employee's retirement or termination.

Disclosure   An employer should make the following disclosure of its defined contribution plans, separately from its disclosure of defined benefit plans:

- A description of each plan, including employee groups covered, the basis for determining contributions, and the nature and effect of significant matters affecting comparability of information for all periods presented
- The net postretirement benefit cost recognized during the period

If an employer has a postretirement plan that is a hybrid between a defined benefit plan and a defined contribution plan, the employer should carefully analyze the situation in order to determine which way to account for the plan. The plan should be treated as a defined benefit plan if its substance is to provide a defined benefit. This is the case, for example, with some "target benefit" plans.

> **OBSERVATION:** *The accounting and disclosure requirements for defined contribution plans are radically different from those for defined benefit plans. Some employers are likely to experiment with various types of hybrids, in order to achieve some of the economic characteristics of one type, while qualifying for the accounting and disclosure treatment of the other type.*

EFFECTIVE DATE

In general, FASB-106 is effective for fiscal years beginning on or after December 16, 1992. However, the effective date is extended for two additional years, to fiscal years beginning on or after December 16, 1994, in either of the following two situations:

- The plan is outside the U.S.
- The plan is a defined benefit plan of an employer that is a nonpublic employer with less than 500 participants in all of its plans in the aggregate

Earlier application of FASB-106 is encouraged. An employer may not restate *annual* financial statements that were issued before initial application of FASB-106, but an enterprise should restate any *interim* financial statements that were issued during the same fiscal year in which FASB-106 was first applied.

TRANSITION

FASB-106 includes intricate provisions on transition to FASB-106, and gives employers the choice between two very different methods of recognizing the net transition obligation or asset.

Transition—Postretirement Benefit Fund   On the date of transition to FASB-106, an employer may own assets in a postretirement benefit fund for the sole purpose of paying postretirement benefits. If any of these assets (1) have been excluded from the employer's statement of financial position and (2) do not qualify as plan assets under FASB-106, the employer should recognize these assets as the first step in making the transition adjustments.

At the date of transition, these assets are recognized at fair value as assets of the employer (but not as prepaid postretirement benefit cost), with an equal amount recognized as accrued postretirement benefit obligation. At later dates, the employer accounts for these assets as required by GAAP pertaining to whatever type of assets they happen to be. The fair value of these assets at the date of transition is used as their cost. The financial statements should show any restrictions on the use of these assets.

Net Transition Obligation or Asset   For a defined benefit plan, the employer should determine the net transition obligation or asset as of the *beginning* of the fiscal year in which FASB-106 is first applied. For this purpose, the employer may use either the first day of the fiscal year, or an alternative measurement within three months *before* the first day of the fiscal year, but the employer should use the same date consistently from year to year.

The net transition obligation or asset is determined as follows (in worksheet form):

Net Transition Obligation or Asset

1. Start with the accumulated postretirement benefit obligation.
2. Enter any accrued postretirement benefit cost that has previously been recognized.
3. Subtract (2) from (1).
4. Enter the fair value of plan assets
5. Enter any prepaid postretirement benefit cost that has previously been recognized.
6. Subtract (5) from (4).
7. Finally, subtract (6) from (3). This amount is the net transition obligation or asset.

For a defined contribution plan, the employer should recognize the transition obligation in the same manner.

Immediate or Delayed Recognition   Having determined the amount of the net transition obligation or asset, the employer may elect either immediate recognition or delayed recognition. If an employer maintains more than one postretirement benefit plan, the employer should elect a single method of transition for all defined benefit and defined contribution plans.

Immediate Recognition — Adjust for Events Occurring On or After December 22, 1990   If the employer elects immediate recognition, the amount to be recognized in income consists of the net transition obligation or asset subject to the following adjustments for events occurring on or after December 22, 1990, but before the transition date:

- Exclude the amount attributable to the effects of initiating a plan or improving the benefits on or after December 22, 1990 (but before the transition date), and treat this amount as unrecognized prior service cost.

- Adjust the accounting for any business combinations con-summated on or after December 22, 1990 (but before the transition date) that were treated as purchases, to reflect the accumulated postretirement benefit obligation incurred and the fair value of plan assets acquired. If reliable information for this purpose is not available as of the date the business combination was consummated, the purchaser should deter-mine the amount of the net obligation or asset as of the date of transition to FASB-106, and should use that information as the basis for retroactively adjusting the purchase price as of the date of consummation.

If the adjustments described above relate to fiscal years before the year of transition to FASB-106, they will affect prior years' income. For example, the first adjustment, which pertains to unrecognized prior service cost, requires the amortization of this prior service cost from the date of plan initiation or benefit improvement until the beginning of the transition year. The second adjustment, which per-tains to business combinations, requires the adjustment of the amount allocated to goodwill at the time of the business combination and, as a result, the adjustment of the amount amortized as goodwill from the date of the consummation until the beginning of the transition year. The cumulative effect on prior years' income of these adjust-ments should be recognized as part of the accounting change result-ing from transition to FASB-106.

Immediate Recognition — Effect of Change in Accounting Prin-ciple If an employer elects immediate recognition, the amount immediately recognized consists of the net transition obligation or asset adjusted for events occurring on or after December 22, 1990, combined with the cumulative effect of those adjustments. The amount immediately recognized should be treated as the effect of an accounting change. This amount should be presented, net of any related income tax effect, between "extraordinary items" and "net income" in the statement of income. The effect of this accounting change should be presented as part of the per share information in the statement of income.

> **OBSERVATION:** *In connection with the immediate recognition of the transition obligation or asset, FASB-106 does not mention the possibility of capitalizing part of the transition amount, to the extent it may be attributable to the cost of inventory or other assets. The lack of guidance on this point implies that capitalization is not*

permitted if an employer elects immediate recognition of the transition obligation or asset.

In contrast, if an employer elects delayed recognition of the transition obligation or asset, this delayed recognition is recorded as a component of net periodic postretirement benefit cost. Capitalization of this cost is appropriate, to the extent it pertains to inventory or other assets (FASB-106, par. 5, note 3).

Delayed Recognition — Amortization of Net Transition Obligation or Asset   If an employer elects delayed recognition, the employer should amortize the net transition obligation or asset as follows:

Generally, amortization should be straight-line, during the average remaining service period of active participants in the plan. This rule is subject to three exceptions.

- *Less than 20 years' average remaining service*   If the average remaining service period is less than 20 years, the employer may elect to amortize over a 20-year period.

- *All or almost all participants inactive*   If all or almost all plan participants are inactive, the employer should amortize over the average remaining life expectancy of those participants.

- *Cumulative payments after transition exceed cumulative accruals*   If the adjusted cumulative payments to plan participants after the transition date are greater than the amount accrued as cumulative postretirement benefit cost after that date, the employer should recognize an additional amount of the unrecognized transition obligation equal to the excess cumulative benefit payments over accrued cumulative benefit cost. For purposes of this provision: (a) cumulative payments to plan participants after the transition date are reduced by any plan assets or any recognized accrued postretirement benefit obligation at the transition date and (b) payments made pursuant to a settlement are included in the amount of cumulative benefit payments after the transition date.

Interim Financial Statements   An employer may have to determine how to amortize its unrecognized transition obligation in interim financial statements if the employer anticipates recognition of an additional amount of this transition obligation later in the year because cumulative payments are likely to exceed cumulative accruals after the transition date. The interim statements should be based on the estimated amount to be amortized during the year, including any additional amounts the employer expects to recognize during the year because of cumulative payments exceeding cumulative accruals after the transition, with the following exception: the effects of a settlement should be recognized when the settlement itself is recognized, and should not be anticipated in interim statements.

If the estimates reflected in an interim statement are revised by the time the next interim statement is prepared, the effects of the revision are recognized during the remainder of the fiscal year. The annual statement should reflect the employer's final determination of the amount of the unrecognized transition obligation to be amortized. Any difference between the year-end amount and the amounts shown in interim statements is recognized immediately.

PRODUCT FINANCING ARRANGEMENTS

Overview

FASB-49 contains the specialized accounting and reporting principles and practices that were originally published in the AICPA Statement of Position 78-8 (SOP 78-8) entitled "Accounting for Product Financing Arrangements."

FASB-49 indicates that the specialized accounting and reporting principles and practices were extracted from SOP 78-8 without significant change and that the Financial Accounting Standards Board did not contemplate a comprehensive reconsideration of the accounting issues in SOP 78-8.

Background

Product financing arrangements usually provide for one entity to obtain inventory or product for another entity (the sponsor), which agrees to purchase the inventory or product at specific prices over a specific period. The agreed-upon prices to be paid for the inventory or product, by the sponsor, usually include financing and holding costs. The following are a few of the more common types of product financing arrangements:

1. A sponsor sells inventory or product to another entity and in a related arrangement agrees to buy the inventory or product back.
2. Another entity agrees to purchase a product or inventory for a sponsor, who in a related arrangement agrees to buy the product or inventory from the other entity.
3. A sponsor by arrangement controls the product or inventory purchased or held by another entity.

In all of the above arrangements, the sponsor agrees to purchase, over a specified period, the product or inventory from the other entity at prearranged prices. The substance of a product financing arrangement, regardless of its legal form, reflects a financing arrangement and not a sale or purchase by the sponsor.

Other factors that frequently, but not always, exist in a product financing arrangement are as follows:

1. The entity that provides the financing arrangement to the sponsor is an existing trust, nonbusiness entity, credit grantor, or was formed for the sole purpose of providing the financing arrangement to the sponsor.
2. Small quantities of the product involved in the financing arrangement may be sold by the financing entity, but most of the product is ultimately used or sold by the sponsor.
3. The product is stored on the sponsor's premises.
4. The sponsor guarantees the debt of the other entity.

For the purposes of FASB-49, unmined or unharvested natural resources and financial instruments are not considered products. Thus, apparently, they are not covered by the provisions of FASB-49.

> **OBSERVATION**: *No mention is made in FASB-49 as to how a product financing arrangement involving unmined or unharvested natural resources should be accounted for. For example, X Company enters into a financing arrangement with Y Company wherein Y Company acquires 10,000 acres of unharvested timberlands for the sole benefit of X Company. X Company guarantees the bank loan that was necessary to acquire the timberlands and agrees to purchase the processed timber from Y Company at specified prices over a specified period. The specified prices include (1) the cost of the timber, (2) processing costs, (3) interest costs on the bank loan, and (4) a small handling fee. Only the standing timber was purchased and not the land.*
>
> *It appears that the provisions of FASB-49 should apply to the above transaction, but FASB-49 expressly does not cover it.*

In a product financing arrangement, the specified prices that the sponsor must pay cannot be subject to change except for fluctuations due to finance and holding costs. The specified prices may be stated or determinable by reference to the substance of the arrangement, such as (1) resale price guarantees or (2) options which, in substance, compel or require the sponsor to purchase the product. In addition, the cost of the product and related costs to the other entity must be substantially covered by the specified prices that the seller must pay for the product. Related costs include interest, holding costs, and other fees charged by the other entity.

Accounting for Product Financing Arrangements

An arrangement that, in substance, contains the characteristics of a product financing arrangement shall be accounted for by the sponsor of such an arrangement, as follows:

1. If another entity buys a product from a sponsor and in a related arrangement agrees to sell the product, or a processed product containing the original product, back to the sponsor, no sale should be recorded and the product should remain as an asset on the sponsor's books. Also, the sponsor should record a liability in the amount of the proceeds received from the other entity under the provisions of the product financing arrangement.

    Product financing arrangements are in substance a method of financing a product and should not be recorded as a sale and repurchase by the sponsor.

2. If another entity buys a product for a sponsor's benefit and the sponsor agrees, in a related arrangement, to buy the product, or a processed product containing the original product, back from the other entity, an asset and the related liability should be recorded by the sponsor at the time the other entity acquires the product.

Excluding processing costs, the difference between the regular product cost which the sponsor would have paid if there was no product financing arrangement, and the cost that the sponsor actually pays under the terms of the product financing arrangement, should be accounted for by the sponsor as financing and holding costs. These financing and holding costs should be recorded on the books of the sponsor in accordance with its regular accounting policies for such costs, even though the costs are incurred and paid directly by the other entity.

Separately identified interest costs which the sponsor pays as part of the specified prices may qualify for interest capitalization under FASB-34 (Capitalization of Interest Costs). If not, the separately identified interest costs actually paid by the sponsor would count toward the total interest costs incurred during the period, for the purposes of FASB-34. Under FASB-34, total capitalized interest costs for any particular period may not exceed the total interest costs actually incurred by an enterprise during that particular period.

Effective Date

FASB-49 is effective for product financing arrangements entered into on after June 16, 1981, and shall be applied to current and/or future periods (prospectively).

QUASI-REORGANIZATIONS

Overview

Current promulgated GAAP on quasi-reorganizations appear in ARB-43, Chapter 7A.

A quasi-reorganization is frequently referred to as a corporate readjustment.

Background

When a business reaches a turnaround point and profitable operations seem likely, a quasi-reorganization may be appropriate to eliminate the accumulated deficit from past unprofitable operations. The resulting financial statements will have more credibility, making it easier for the company to borrow money for its profitable operations. In addition, by eliminating the deficit in retained earnings, the possibility of paying dividends in the future becomes more likely.

Although the corporate entity remains unchanged in a quasi-reorganization, a new basis of accountability is established. Assets are usually restated downward to their fair values, and stockholders' equity is adjusted so that retained earnings has a zero balance. Retained earnings is adjusted to a zero balance by charging the deficit either (1) to capital contributed in excess of par or (2) to capital contributed other than for capital stock (usually donated capital). Obviously, this means that capital accounts (other than for capital stock) must be available to absorb the deficit in retained earnings (after all quasi-reorganization adjustments are made).

Although the capital stock account may not be used to absorb a deficit in retained earnings, it is permissible for a corporation to reduce the par value of its existing capital stock and to transfer the resulting excess to a capital contributed in excess of par account (paid-in capital). This procedure is frequently used in a quasi-reorganization.

The following types of situations justify a quasi-reorganization, provided that capital accounts (other than for capital stock) are available to absorb the resulting retained earnings deficit after all adjustments:

1. Historical cost of assets clearly requires adjustment so that realistic financial reporting is possible.
2. A quasi-reorganization is an acceptable alternative to legal proceedings resulting in a reorganization.
3. A large deficit from past operations exists.

In financial accounting, stockholders' equity is usually made up of the following:

1. Capital contributed for stock, to the extent of the par or stated value of each class of stock presently outstanding
2. a. Capital contributed in excess of par or stated value of each class of stock, whether as a result of original issues, any subsequent reductions of par or stated value, or transactions by the corporation in its own shares
   b. Capital received other than for stock, whether from shareholders or others (such as donated capital)
3. Retained earnings (or deficit), which represents the accumulated income or loss of the corporation.

Generally, items properly chargeable to current or future years' income accounts may not be charged to capital accounts. An exception to this rule occurs in accounting for quasi-reorganizations.

Accounting and Reporting

If a corporation elects to restate its assets and stockholders' equity through a quasi-reorganization, it must make a clear report of the proposed restatements to its shareholders and obtain their formal consent.

Assets should be written down to their fair values; and if fair values are not readily determinable, conservative estimates may be used. Estimates may also be used to provide for known possible losses prior to the date of the quasi-reorganization, when amounts are indeterminable.

If estimates are used and the amounts are subsequently found to be excessive or insufficient, the difference should be charged or credited to the capital account previously charged or credited and not to retained earnings.

The steps in the accounting procedure are as follows:

1. All amounts to be written off should be charged to retained earnings, irrespective of whether retained earnings has or will have a deficit.

2. After all amounts to be written off are recognized and charged to retained earnings, any debit balance in retained earnings may be transferred by journal entry to either (a) capital contributed in excess of par or (b) capital contributed other than for capital stock.

    It makes no difference whether the two capital accounts above were previously existing or were created as a result of the quasi-reorganization.

    It is important to remember that it is improper to increase a credit balance in retained earnings by an accounting or quasi-reorganization, but it is acceptable to eliminate a deficit.

3. If a deficit in retained earnings is transferred to an allowable capital account, any subsequent balance sheet must disclose, by dating the retained earnings, that the balance in the retained earnings account has increased since the date of reorganization. For example:

    Retained earnings, since July 1, 19XX $1,234,567

    The dating of retained earnings following a quasi-reorganization would rarely, if ever, be of significance after a period of ten years. There may be exceptional circumstances that could justify a period of less than ten years (ARB-46).

4. New or additional shares of stock may be issued or exchanged for other shares or existing indebtedness. For example, stockholders may agree to subscribe to additional shares, or bondholders may agree to accept capital stock in lieu of interest in arrears, in order to provide new cash for future operations. Accounting entries for these types of transactions are handled in accordance with GAAP.

5. Corporations with subsidiaries should follow the same procedures so that no credit balance remains in consolidated retained earnings after a quasi-reorganization where losses have been charged to allowable capital accounts.

    In those cases, where losses have been charged to the allowable capital accounts, instead of a credit balance in consolidated retained earnings, the parent company's interest in such retained earnings should be regarded as capitalized by the quasi-reorganization in the same way retained earnings of a subsidiary are capitalized on the date of its acquisition.

6. The effective date of the quasi-reorganization from which income of the corporation is thereafter determined should be as close as possible to the date of formal stockholders' consent and preferably at the start of a new fiscal year.

Under no circumstances should adjustments made pursuant to a quasi-reorganization be included in the determination of net income for any period.

If not previously recognized, a tax benefit arising prior to a quasi-reorganization, which is realizable beyond a reasonable doubt, should be recorded as an asset at the date of the reorganization. Such tax benefits may result from the amount of deficit in retained earnings that was applied to paid-in capital as a result of a quasi-reorganization, or from loss carryforwards that arose prior to the quasi-reorganization (FASB-96). However, the tax benefit of an unused investment tax credit may never be recorded as an asset (APB-2 and APB-4).

Disclosure

Adequate disclosure of all pertinent information should be made in the financial statements. A new retained earnings account dated as of the date of the quasi-reorganization should be established and reflected in subsequent financial statements. Usually, the dating of the new retained earnings account can be eliminated after ten years and in unusual circumstances earlier than ten years (ARB-46).

Comprehensive Illustration

The following example demonstrates the procedures which must be used in accounting for a quasi-reorganization.

The Centrex Company, founded in 1970, has experienced losses in each of its first six years of operation. In May 1976, however, the company acquired two patents on an advanced solar-heating unit, which in several months has become the standard for the industry. The quarter ended September 30, 1976, was extremely profitable, and the patent and accompanying licensing agreements indicate that continuing profitability is quite likely.

The company is closely held, and the stockholders have agreed in principle to a quasi-reorganization. Negotiations have been held with various creditors regarding capitalizing debts.

The balance sheet of the company at December 31, 1976, appeared as follows:

Assets	
Cash	$ 25,000
Accounts receivable (net)	410,000
Plant and equipment (net)	1,670,000
Other assets	80,000
Total assets	$2,185,000

Liabilities and Equity	
Accounts payable	$ 840,000
Notes payable—other	300,000
Equipment notes payable	240,000
Common stock	500,000
Paid-in capital—common stock	1,017,000
Retained earnings	(712,000)
Total liabilities and equity	$2,185,000

The stockholders and creditors have approved the following plan of informal reorganization effective January 1, 1977:

1. The current shareholders will exchange their 100,000 shares of $5 par stock for 100,000 shares of $1 par stock.
2. The creditors have agreed to accept $300,000 in a 5% preferred stock for $300,000 of accounts payable.
3. The plant and equipment will be written down to its fair value of $1,100,000.
4. Accounts receivable of $70,000 will be written off as uncollectible.
5. Other assets will be written down to their fair value of $50,000.

The first step in a quasi-reorganization is to write down all assets to their fair values. In the example, the journal entry would be:

Retained earnings	$ 670,000	
Plant and equipment		$570,000
Accounts receivable		70,000
Other assets		30,000

Next, the change in the par value of the common stock is recorded:

Common stock	$ 400,000	
Paid-in capital—common stock		$ 400,000

The following journal entry records the new preferred stock issued for $300,000 of accounts payable:

Accounts payable	$ 300,000	
5% preferred stock		$ 300,000

After all the quasi-reorganization adjustments are made, the deficit in retained earnings ($1,382,000) is eliminated against the paid-in capital—common stock, leaving a zero balance in retained earnings:

Paid-in capital—common stock	$1,382,000	
Retained earnings		$1,382,000

The Centrex Company balance sheet after giving effect to the reorganization appears as:

Centrex Company

Assets

Cash	$ 25,000
Accounts receivable (net)	340,000
Plant and equipment (net)	1,100,000
Other assets	50,000
Total assets	$1,515,000

Liabilities and Equity

Accounts payable	$ 540,000
Notes payable—other	300,000
Equipment notes payable	240,000
Common stock ($1 par)	100,000
5% Preferred stock	300,000
Paid-in capital—common stock	35,000
Retained earnings since January 1, 1977	-0-
Total liabilities and equity	$1,515,000

Retained earnings must be dated on the balance sheet after a reorganization.

REAL AND PERSONAL PROPERTY TAXES

Overview

ARB-43, Chapter 10A (as amended), provides the existing promulgated GAAP for accounting for real and personal property taxes.

Accounting and Reporting

Although many states have different laws or precedents as to when the legal liability accrues for real and personal property taxes, the general rule is that it accrues on the date the taxes are assessed. However, the exact amount of tax may not be known on the assessment date, and a reasonable estimate must be made. The inability to determine the exact amount of real and personal property taxes is not an acceptable excuse for failure to recognize the existing tax liability. In those cases where the accrued amount is subject to a great deal of uncertainty, the liability should be appropriately described as estimated.

Whether the amount of the accrued tax liability for real and personal property taxes is known or estimated, it should be reported as a current liability in the balance sheet.

A monthly accrual over the fiscal period of the taxing authority is considered the most acceptable basis for recording real and personal property taxes. This results in the appropriate accrual or prepayment at any closing date.

An adjustment to the estimated tax liability of a prior year must be made when the exact amount is determined. This adjustment is made in the income statement of the period in which the exact amount is determined, either as an adjustment to the current year's provision or as a separate item on the income statement.

It is sometimes proper to capitalize real estate taxes on property being developed for internal use or for sale to customers. However, in most circumstances, real and personal property taxes are considered an expense of doing business and are reported in the appropriate income statement (1) as an operating expense, (2) as a deduction from income, or (3) allocated to several expense accounts, such as manufacturing overhead and general and administrative expenses. As a general rule, real and personal property taxes should not be combined with income taxes.

OBSERVATION: *The promulgated GAAP do not describe the criteria for capitalizing or not capitalizing real estate taxes.*

The most important consideration for real and personal property taxes is consistency. The accounting treatment and reporting must be consistently applied from year to year.

RELATED PARTY DISCLOSURES

Overview

FASB-57 establishes the promulgated GAAP for the disclosure of material related party transactions. In general, a related party is one which can exercise control or significant influence over the management or operating policies of another party, to the extent that one of the parties is or may be prevented from fully pursuing its own separate interests.

Background

When performing an examination of financial statements, the auditor is responsible for identifying any related party transactions encountered during the course of the audit. Related parties include the reporting entity, its affiliates, principal owners, management, and members of their immediate families. Related parties may exist when one entity has the ability to *significantly influence* another entity, through management or otherwise.

Regulation S-X (SEC) requires a prescribed accounting treatment for related parties. However, most transactions between related parties should be accounted for on the same basis as if the parties were not related, unless the *substance* of the transaction is not arm's length. Substance over form is an important consideration when accounting for transactions involving related parties.

Under existing generally accepted auditing standards, the independent auditor exercises professional judgment in determining that related party transactions are adequately disclosed in the financial statements. Generally accepted auditing standards (SAS-45) require that significant related party transactions, individually or in the aggregate, be disclosed in the financial statements of the reporting entity in accordance with FASB-57.

Material Related Party Transaction Disclosures

Related parties consist of all affiliates of an enterprise, including (a) its management and their immediate families, (b) its principal owners and their immediate families, (c) its investments accounted for by the equity method, (d) beneficial employee trusts that are managed by the management of the enterprise, and (e) any party that may, or does, deal with the enterprise and has ownership of, control over, or can significantly influence the management or operating policies of another party to the extent that an arm's-length transaction may not be achieved.

FASB-57 requires that material related party transactions which are not eliminated in consolidated or combined financial statements must be disclosed in the financial statements of the reporting entity. However, related party transactions involving compensation arrangements, expense allowances, and similar items incurred in the ordinary course of business do not have to be disclosed.

If separate financial statements of an entity that has been consolidated are presented in a financial report which includes the consolidated financial statements, duplicate disclosure of the related party transactions is not necessary. Thus, disclosure of the material related party transactions in the consolidated statements is all that is required. However, disclosure of related party transactions is required in separate financial statements of (a) a parent company, (b) a subsidiary, (c) a corporate joint venture, or (d) an investee which is 50% or less owned.

The minimum financial statement disclosures required by FASB-57 for material related party transactions that (a) are not eliminated in consolidated or combined financial statements and (b) are not compensation arrangements, expense allowances, or similar items incurred in the ordinary course of business are as follows:

1. The nature of the material related party relationship. In addition, the name of the related party should be disclosed, if it is essential to the understanding of the relationship.

2. A description of the material related party transactions, including amounts and other pertinent information for each period in which an income statement is presented.

   Related party transactions of no or nominal amounts must also be disclosed. In other words, all information that is necessary to an understanding of the effects of the material related party transactions on the financial statements must be disclosed.

3. The effects of any change in terms between the related parties from terms used in prior periods. In addition, the dollar amount of transactions for each period in which an income statement is presented must be disclosed.

4. If not apparent in the financial statements, (a) the terms of related party transactions, (b) the manner of settlement of related party transactions, and (c) the amount due to or from related parties must all be disclosed.

5. If the operating results or financial position of a reporting entity can be altered significantly by the effects of common ownership or management control of the reporting entity and one or more other entities, even if there are no transactions between any of the entities, the nature of the ownership or management control must be disclosed in the financial statements. In other words, if the existence of the control relationship has the potential of producing operating results or financial positions that differ from those that would exist if there were no control relationship, disclosure must be made of the nature of such ownership or management control.

The amount of detail disclosed for related party transactions must be sufficient for the user of the financial statements to be able to understand the related party transaction. Thus, this disclosure of the total amount of a specific type of material related party transaction or of the effects of the relationship between the related parties may be all that is necessary.

One cannot assume that a related party transaction is consummated in the same manner as an arm's-length transaction, since free market competition is not the basis of related party transactions. Disclosures or other representations of a material related party transaction in financial statements should not imply that the transaction was made on the same basis as an arm's-length transaction, unless the disclosures or representations can be substantiated.

FASB-57 is effective for fiscal years ending on or after June 16, 1982.

RESEARCH AND DEVELOPMENT COSTS

Overview

The following pronouncements establish the promulgated GAAP for research and development costs:

FASB-2, Accounting for Research and Development Costs

FASB-68, Research and Development Arrangements

FASB-86, Accounting for the Costs of Computer Software to Be Sold, Leased, or Otherwise Marketed

FASB Interpretation-4, Applicability of FASB Statement No. 2 to Business Combinations Accounted for by the Purchase Method

FASB Interpretation-6, Applicability of FASB Statement No. 2 to Computer Software

FASB Technical Bulletin 84-1, Accounting for Stock Issued to Acquire the Results of a Research and Development Arrangement

FASB-2 is the primary GAAP that addresses the accounting for research and development costs. The following specific activities are not covered by the provisions of FASB-2:

- Activities that are unique to the extractive industries, such as prospecting, exploration, drilling, mining, and similar functions. However, research and development activities that are comparable in nature to other companies not in the extractive industry, such as the development or improvement of techniques and processes, are covered.
- Research and development performed under contract for others, including indirect costs which are specifically reimbursable under a contract.

FASB Interpretation-4 provides guidance in applying the provisions of FASB-2 to research and development costs acquired in a business combination accounted for by the purchase method. FASB Interpretation-6 provides some guidance in applying the provisions of FASB-2 to computer software, but very little text remains in this pronouncement since its amendment by FASB-86.

FASB-68 deals with research and development arrangements which are partially or completely funded by other parties. FASB-68 applies to the party who performs the research and development activities, whether that party is the enterprise, the funding party, or a third party. FASB-68 does not cover government-sponsored research and development projects.

> **OBSERVATION:** *FASB Technical Bulletin 84-1 concludes that the acquisition of the results of a research and development arrangement through the issuance of capital stock should be accounted for at the fair value of the stock issued, or at the fair value of the consideration received, whichever is more clearly evident.*

FASB-86 establishes accounting and reporting standards for costs incurred for computer software products that are sold, leased, or otherwise marketed by an enterprise. FASB-86 covers the costs incurred for separate computer software products and the costs incurred for integral parts of computer software products or processes, which are either purchased or internally developed and produced by an enterprise. FASB-86 does not cover the costs incurred for computer software that is (a) produced for others by an enterprise under a contractual arrangement or (b) created for the internal use of an enterprise.

Background

Research is the planned efforts of a company to discover new information that will help create a new product, service, process, or technique or vastly improve one in current use. Development takes the findings generated by research and formulates a plan to create the desired item or to improve the existing one. Development in the context of this area of GAAP does not include normal improvements in existing operations. The promulgated GAAP do not include market research and testing, because these items specifically relate to the selling and marketing operations of a company. In addition, general and administrative expenses not *directly* related to the R&D activities are also not included in the promulgated GAAP.

The underlying basic principle in accounting for R&D is conservatism, because of the high degree of uncertainty of any resulting future benefit. Since at the time of performing the R&D there is no possible method of determining any future success, the most conservative approach is to expense the item in the period incurred.

Accounting and Reporting R&D

All R&D costs covered by the promulgated GAAP are expensed when incurred except R&D machinery, equipment, and facilities which have alternative future uses either in R&D activities or otherwise. Machinery, equipment, and facilities, which have alternative future uses should be capitalized. However, depreciation or amortization on such capitalized R&D machinery, equipment, and facilities is charged to expense. All expenditures in conjunction with an R&D project, including personnel costs, materials, equipment, facilities, and intangibles, for which the company has no alternative future use beyond the specific project for which the items were purchased, are expensed. Indirect costs, including general and administrative expenses, which are *directly* related to the R&D are also expensed when incurred.

As mentioned previously, it is important to remember that R&D costs related to market research or testing, and general and administrative expenses that are not directly related to R&D activity, are costs not covered by the promulgated GAAP.

Research and development costs acquired by the purchase method in a business combination shall be assigned their fair values, if any, in accordance with existing promulgated GAAP (APB-16). The subsequent accounting by the acquirer of these R&D costs shall be made in compliance with the promulgated GAAP enumerated herein. Those R&D costs with future alternative use shall be capitalized and all others expensed (FASB Interpretation-4).

Disclosure

The amount of R&D charged to expense for the period must be disclosed in the financial statements for each period presented.

COMPUTER SOFTWARE TO BE SOLD, LEASED, OR OTHERWISE MARKETED

FASB-86 applies only to those costs incurred in purchasing or internally developing and producing computer software products that are sold, leased, or otherwise marketed by an enterprise. The costs covered by FASB-86 may be incurred (a) for separate computer software products or (b) for integral parts of computer software products or processes. FASB-86 does not cover those costs incurred for computer software that is (a) produced by an enterprise for others under a contractual arrangement or (b) created for the internal use of an enterprise.

Under FASB-86, the terms *computer software product, software product,* and *product* are used interchangeably to mean either (a) a computer software program, (b) a group of programs, or (c) a product enhancement. A product enhancement represents improvement to an existing product that significantly improves the marketability or extends the estimated useful life of the original product. A product enhancement almost always involves a new design or redesign of the original computer software product.

The primary activities that are involved in the creation of a computer software product are the (a) planning function, (b) design function, and (c) production function. The planning function of a computer software product generally includes preliminary product specifications and design and the development of a production and a financial plan for the product. In addition, the planning function should also include a marketing analysis and a marketing plan for the product. The planning function should generate sufficient documentation and detailed information for an enterprise to make a determination of the overall feasibility of the proposed computer software product.

The design function of a computer software product includes the product design and the detail program design. The production of a product master generally involves coding, testing, and the development of training materials. Coding is the process in which the requirements of the detailed program design are converted into a computer language. Testing includes the steps necessary to determine whether the computer software product works in accordance with its design specifications and documentation.

Computer software costs that must be expensed   FASB-86 specifies that all costs incurred in establishing the technological feasibility of a computer software product that is sold, leased, or otherwise marketed by an enterprise are research and development costs, which must be accounted for as required by FASB-2 (Accounting for Research and Development Costs). Thus, until technological feasibility is established in accordance with FASB-86 (see below), all costs incurred through the purchase or internal development and production of a computer software product that is sold, leased, or otherwise marketed must be accounted for as research and development costs in accordance with the provisions of FASB-2.

Under the provisions of FASB-2, all research and development costs must be expensed when incurred, except machinery, equipment and facilities, which have alternative future use in either the research and development activities of an enterprise or otherwise. Market research and testing are not considered research and development activities under the provisions of FASB-2, because these functions specifically relate to the selling and marketing operations of an enterprise. In addition, general and administrative expenses are not considered research and development costs, unless they are *directly* related to the research and development activities of an enterprise. Thus, the development costs of a computer system that improves an enterprise's administrative or selling procedures would not be considered research and development costs. However, all costs incurred for internally developed computer software products used in an enterprise's own research and development activities should be charged to expense when incurred, because the future alternative use test does not apply to such costs (FASB Interpretation-6, Footnote 2).

Under FASB-86, production costs incurred for integral parts of a computer software product or process must be expensed, unless (a) technological feasibility has been established for the computer software product or process and (b) all research and development activities have been completed for the other components of the computer software product or process.

Computer software costs that must be capitalized   After technological feasibility has been established, FASB-86 specifies that all costs incurred for a computer software product that is sold, leased, or otherwise marketed by an enterprise shall be capitalized. Thus, the costs of producing product masters for a computer software product, including costs for coding and testing, shall be capitalized, but only after technological feasibility has been established in accordance with FASB-86 (see below).

Production costs for computer software that is to be used as an integral part of a product or process shall be capitalized, but only after (a) technological feasibility has been established for the software and (b) all research and development activities for the other components of the product or process have been completed.

Capitalization of computer software costs shall be discontinued when the computer software product is available to be sold, leased, or otherwise marketed. Costs for maintenance and customer support shall be charged to expense when incurred or when the related revenue is recognized, whichever occurs first.

> **OBSERVATION:** *Under FASB-86, the amount of costs that an enterprise is required to capitalize depends primarily on its choice of production methods. Thus, an enterprise may control the amount of computer software costs that it capitalizes by establishing technological feasibility at a designated time during the production process.*

Establishing technological feasibility Technological feasibility is established when all of the activities that are necessary to substantiate that the computer software product can be produced in accordance with its design specifications have been completed, including functions, features, and technical performance requirements. Thus, all planning, designing, coding, and testing activities that are required to substantiate that the computer software product can be produced to meet its design specifications must be completed before technological feasibility can be established.

Under FASB-86, the method of establishing the technological feasibility of a computer software product depends on whether the process of creating the computer software product includes a detail program design or not. The following are the minimum requirements for establishing the technological feasibility of a computer software product:

Includes Detail Program Design

If the process of creating the computer software product includes a detail program design, an enterprise must comply with the following criteria to establish the technological feasibility of a computer software product:

1. An enterprise must complete the product design and detail program design for the computer software product and establish that it has available the necessary skills, hardware, and software technology to produce the product.
2. An enterprise must substantiate the completeness of the program design and its consistency with the product design by documenting and tracing the detail program design to the product specifications.
3. An enterprise must identify the high-risk development issues in the computer software product through review of the detail program design; and if any uncertainties relating to the

high-risk development issues are discovered, they must be resolved through coding and testing. High-risk development issues that may be encountered in the production of a computer software product may include novel, unique, or unproven functions and features, and/or technological innovations.

Does Not Include Detail Program Design

If the process of creating the computer software product *does not* include a detail program design, an enterprise must comply with the following criteria to establish the technological feasibility of a computer software product:

1. An enterprise must complete a product design and a working model of the computer software product.
2. An enterprise must substantiate the completeness of the working model and its consistency with the product design by testing the model.

Amortization of capitalized computer software costs   Amortization of capitalized computer software costs, on a product-by-product basis, shall begin when the product is available to be sold, leased, or otherwise marketed. Periodic amortization, on a product-by-product basis, shall be equal to the greater of (a) the amount computed by the straight-line method over the estimated useful life of the product or (b) the amount computed by using the ratio that current gross revenues bear to total estimated gross revenues (including current gross revenues).

Inventory costs   Inventory costs shall be capitalized on a unit-specific basis and charged to cost of sales when the related revenue from the sale of those units is recognized. Inventory costs include duplicate copies of the computer software product made from the product master, documentation, training materials, and the costs incurred for packaging the product for distribution.

Periodic evaluation of capitalized computer software costs   Unamortized computer software costs that have been previously capitalized in accordance with FASB-86 are reported at net realizable value on an enterprise's balance sheet. Net realizable value is determined on a product-by-product basis and is equal to the estimated future gross revenues of a specific product, less estimated future costs of completing and disposing of that specific product, including the costs of performing maintenance and customer support on a product-by-product basis as required by the terms of the sale.

The excess of any unamortized computer software costs over its related net realizable value at a balance sheet date shall be written down. The amount of write-down shall be charged to periodic income. Capitalized costs that have been written down as a charge to income shall not be capitalized again or restored in any future period.

Financial statement disclosures   The total amount of unamortized computer software costs that is included in each balance sheet presented shall be disclosed in the financial statements. The total amount of computer software costs charged to expense shall be disclosed for each income statement presented. The total amount of computer software costs charged to expense shall include amortization expense and amounts written down to net realizable value.

All computer software costs that are classified as research and development costs shall be disclosed as such in accordance with FASB-2 (Accounting for Research and Development Costs). These costs may include the costs of planning, product design, detail program design, and the costs incurred in establishing technological feasibility of a computer software product.

Effective date and transition   FASB-86 is effective for financial statements for fiscal years beginning on or after December 16, 1985, and shall also be applied to all computer software projects in progress at the time of the initial application of FASB-86. Earlier application of the provisions of FASB-86 is permitted in previously unissued annual financial statements.

The amount of capitalized and noncapitalized computer software costs that was incurred prior to the first application of FASB-86 shall not be changed. However, the amortization provisions of FASB-86 shall be applied to any unamortized balance of computer software costs that was capitalized prior to December 16, 1985 (the effective date of FASB-86).

> **OBSERVATION:** *In the period in which FASB-86 is first applied, an enterprise should disclose in its financial statements the effects of the change in accounting principle on income before extraordinary items, net income, and related per share amounts, in accordance with APB-20 (Accounting Changes).*

Research and Development Arrangements

FASB-68 covers research and development arrangements of an enterprise which are partially or completely funded by other parties. In this respect, the typical arrangement is for the parties to set up a limited partnership through which the R&D activities related to a specific project are funded. Although the limited partnership arrangement is used in FASB-68 for illustrative purposes, the legal structure of an R&D arrangement may take a variety of forms and is sometimes influenced by income tax implications and securities regulations.

In a typical R&D arrangement, an enterprise which has the basic technology for a particular project is the general partner and manages the R&D activities. The limited partners, who may or may not be related parties, provide all or part of the funds to complete the project. If the funds are not sufficient, the arrangement may allow or require the general partner to either (a) sell additional limited partnership interest or (b) use its own funds to complete the project. In addition, some funds may be provided in the form of loans or advances to the limited partnership. The repayment of the loans or advances may be guaranteed by the partnership.

The actual R&D activities are usually performed by the enterprise or a related party, under a contract with the limited partnership. The contract price is either fixed or cost plus a fixed or percentage fee and is performed on a *best efforts* basis, with no guarantee of ultimate success. The legal ownership of the results of the project vests with partnership. Frequently, the enterprise has an option to acquire the partnership's interest in the project or to obtain exclusive use of the results of the project. If the project is a success, the enterprise will no doubt exercise its option to acquire the project. However, under some circumstances, even if the project is unsuccessful, the enterprise may still have reason to acquire the project, in spite of the fact that it is not legally required to do so. For example, the enterprise may want to prevent the final results of the project from falling into the hands of a competitor.

Many of the liabilities and obligations which an enterprise undertakes in an R&D project which is funded by others are specified in the agreements. However, some liabilities and obligations may exist in substance but may not be reduced to writing. For example, future payments by the enterprise to other parties for royalties or the acquisition of the partnership's interest in the project may, in substance, represent (a) the repayment of a loan or (b) the purchase price of a specific asset.

Nature of R&D arrangement   In R&D arrangements that are partially or completely funded by other parties, accounting and reporting for R&D costs depend upon the nature of the obligation that an enterprise incurs in the arrangement. The nature of the obligation in such R&D arrangements can fall into one of the following categories:

1. The obligation is solely to perform contractual services.
2. The obligation represents a liability to repay all of the funds provided by the other parties.
3. The obligation is partly to perform contractual services and partly a liability to repay some, but not all, of the funds provided by the other parties.

No problem arises if the nature of the obligation incurred by an enterprise is solely to perform contractual services. In this event, all R&D costs are charged to *cost of sales*. Also, no problem arises if the nature of the obligation represents a liability to repay all of the funds provided by the other parties. In this event, all R&D costs are charged to *expense* when incurred.

If the nature of the obligation incurred by an enterprise is partly a liability and partly the performance of contractual services, R&D costs are charged partly to expense and partly to cost of sales. The portion charged to cost of sales is related to the funds provided by the other parties which do not have to be repaid by the enterprise. The portion charged to expense is related to the funds provided by the other parties which are likely to be repaid by the enterprise. Under FASB-68, the portion charged to expense is referred to as the enterprise's portion of the R&D costs. Under the provisions of FASB-68, an enterprise shall charge its portion of the R&D costs to expense in the same manner as the liability is incurred. Thus, if the liability arises on a pro rata basis, the enterprise's portion of the R&D costs shall be charged to expense in the same manner. If the liability arises as the initial funds are expended, the enterprise's portion of the R&D costs shall be charged to expense in the same manner.

FASB-68 provides guidance in determining the nature of the obligation that an enterprise incurs in R&D arrangements which are partially or completely funded by other parties. FASB-68 requires that an enterprise report in its financial statements the estimated liability, if any, incurred in an R&D arrangement which is partially or completely funded by other parties. The estimated liability shall include any contractually defined obligations and any obligations not contractually defined but otherwise reasonably evident. A critical factor in determining an enterprise's obligation is whether the financial risks involved in the R&D arrangement have been substantively and genuinely transferred to the other parties. To the extent that an enterprise retains any financial risk, the R&D costs are considered costs incurred by the enterprise on its own behalf and must, therefore, be expensed as incurred. Thus, if an enterprise contractually or otherwise obligates itself to repay any of the funds provided by others, regardless of the outcome of the R&D project, the financial risks have not been transferred and the enterprise's commitment to repay is evident. On the other hand, an enterprise does not undertake any financial risk when it obligates itself to repay the other parties, providing that the R&D project results in future economic benefit to the enterprise.

Under the provisions of FASB-68, if significant indications exist that the enterprise is *likely* to repay any funds, it is presumed that a liability has been incurred. This presumption can be overcome only by substantial evidence to the contrary. Circumstances in which significant indications exist that the enterprise is likely to repay funds and a liability is presumed are as follows:

1. Regardless of the success of the R&D project, the enterprise has indicated the intent to repay all or part of the funds provided by other parties.

2. If it failed to repay any of the funds, the enterprise would suffer a *severe economic penalty.* Under FASB-68, an economic penalty is *severe* if an enterprise would probably elect, under normal business circumstances, to repay the funds rather than to incur the penalty.

3. At the inception of the R&D arrangement, a material related party relationship (FASB-57) exists between the enterprise and any of the parties funding the R&D project.

4. At the inception of the R&D arrangement, the project is substantially complete. Under this circumstance, the financial risks involved in the R&D project are already known to all parties.

Under the provisions of FASB-68, an obligation may represent a liability whether it is payable in cash, securities, or by some other means.

Obligation for contractual services   If substantially all of the financial risks of the R&D project are transferred to the other parties and the enterprise is not committed to repay any of the funds provided by the other parties, the enterprise shall account for its obligation as contractual R&D services. If repayment by the enterprise of any of the funds provided by the other parties depends on the availability of a future economic benefit to the enterprise, the enterprise shall also account for its obligation as contractual R&D services. In these circumstances, the financial risks of the R&D arrangement have clearly been transferred to others and the enterprise is only obligated to perform contractual R&D services.

Frequently, an enterprise makes a loan or advance to the other parties, which is designated to be repaid as a reduction of the purchase price for the results of the project, or as a reduction of future royalty payments from the enterprise. In this event, the portion of the loan or advance which is designated to be repaid as a reduction of the purchase price for the results of the project, or as a reduction of future royalties, shall be accounted for by the enterprise as R&D expense, unless it can be attributed to activities other than R&D, such as marketing or advertising.

At or before the completion of the R&D project, the enterprise may elect to exercise its option to purchase the partnership's interest, or to obtain exclusive rights to the results of the project. The enterprise shall account for the purchase of the partnership's interest, or the exclusive rights, in accordance with existing GAAP. Thus, any asset that results from the R&D project shall be assigned its fair value (APB-16), and intangible assets shall be accounted for in accordance with APB-17 (Intangible Assets).

If an enterprise is required to issue warrants or similar instruments in connection with the R&D arrangements, a portion of the funds provided by the other parties shall be recorded as paid-in capital. The amount capitalized as paid-in capital shall be equal to the fair market value of the warrants or other instruments at the date the R&D arrangement is consummated.

Financial statement disclosure   Notes to the financial statements shall include the following disclosures for R&D arrangements which are accounted for as contracts to perform R&D services for others in accordance with FASB-68:

As of the Date of Each Balance Sheet Presented

- The terms of the significant agreements relating to the R&D arrangement, including (a) purchase provisions, (b) license agreements, (c) royalty arrangements, and (d) commitments to provide additional funds

For Each Income Statement Presented

- The amount of R&D costs incurred and compensation earned during the period for such R&D arrangements

Effective date   FASB-68 is effective for R&D arrangements covered by its provisions that are entered into on or after January 1, 1983. Earlier application of the provisions of FASB-68 is encouraged in previously unissued financial statements.

Retroactive application of the provisions of FASB-68 to previously issued financial statements is permitted, but not required. If retroactive application is elected, the financial statements of the year of change shall disclose the nature of any restatement and its effects on income before extraordinary items, net income, and related per share amounts, for each year presented.

RESULTS OF OPERATIONS

Overview

There are several separate promulgated GAAP in the area of reporting the results of operations, as follows:

APB-9 (as amended), Reporting the Results of Operations

APB-30 (as amended), Reporting the Results of Operations—Reporting the Effects of Disposal of a Segment of a Business, and Extraordinary, Unusual, and Infrequently Occurring Events and Transactions

FASB-16, Prior Period Adjustments

FASB Interpretation-27, Accounting for a Loss On a Sublease

APB-9 clearly indicates that it applies to general-purpose statements prepared in conformity with GAAP that present the results of operations. Investment companies, insurance companies, and certain nonprofit organizations which have developed special formats for income statements that differ from the typical commercial formats need not comply with the provision of APB-9, which requires that net income be presented as one amount. Otherwise, these entities are covered by APB-9. Both APB-30 and FASB-16 are silent in respect to these particular companies, so it is assumed that they must fully comply with these promulgated GAAP.

Background

Prior to the issuance of APB-9 there were differences in the accounting profession as to what should or should not be included in net income. Proponents of the *all-inclusive concept* believe that all items affecting net increases in owners' equity, except dividends and capital transactions, should be included in computing net income. These proponents support their position with the following reasons:

1. Extraordinary items are part of income, and annual income statements over the life of an entity when added together should represent total net income as reported.
2. Omission of extraordinary items will distort the total financial position of an enterprise.

3. Extraordinary items may be manipulated, or possibly over-looked, if they are not included on a regular basis.
4. An income statement that includes all charges or credits arising during the year is simple to prepare, easy to understand, and not subject to variations based on judgment.

Proponents of the *current operating performance concept,* who advocate excluding extraordinary items from net income, maintain the following position:

1. Net income should place emphasis on the normal operations of an enterprise and exclude nonrecurring extraordinary items.
2. The annual income statement's primary purpose is to inform interested parties as to what an entity was able to earn under the current year's operating conditions.
3. Net income for the year should reflect as clearly as possible what happened under that year's conditions, in order that comparability may be achieved with prior years and with the performance of other enterprises in the same industry.
4. Readers of financial statements are frequently unable to determine net income from normal operations when extraordinary items are included in the computation of net income.
5. A material extraordinary item included in net income may be so distorting in its effect as to lead to unsound judgment about the current operating performance of the company.

Although the two schools of thought still exist, present-day GAAP support the all-inclusive concept. Net income should include all items of income and loss during a reporting period, except prior-period adjustments, dividends, and capital transactions. All extraordinary items should be segregated and shown separately in the income statement.

APB-9 further describes capital transactions as follows:

1. Charges or credits arising from transactions in a company's own capital stock
2. Transfers to and from appropriated retained earnings
3. Adjustments made pursuant to a quasi-reorganization

Extraordinary Items

Extraordinary items are transactions and other events that are (1) material in nature, (2) of a character significantly different from the typical or customary business activities, (3) not expected to recur frequently, and (4) not normally considered in evaluating the ordinary operating results of an enterprise. Extraordinary items must be separately disclosed in the income statement, net of any related income tax effect.

Extraordinary items are usually determined by informed professional judgment, taking into consideration all the facts involved in a particular situation. However, some areas of promulgated GAAP require that an item be treated as extraordinary. The following are the more common items that, if material, should be reported as extraordinary items:

1. The profit or loss on disposal of a significant part of the assets, or a separate segment, of the previously separate companies of a business combination, when disposed of within two years after the date of the combination (APB-16)
2. Gains on restructuring payables (FASB-15)
3. Most gains or losses on the extinguishment of debt (FASB-4)
4. Most expropriations of property (APB-30)

The cumulative effect of an accounting change is reflected in the income statement, net of related tax effects, between extraordinary items and net income. On the other hand, a gain or loss on discontinued operations is reflected in the income statement, net of related income tax effects, between income from continuing operations and extraordinary items.

For reporting purposes, extraordinary items arising as part of the net income from an investment accounted for by the equity method are combined with extraordinary items of the investor.

If professional judgment dictates individual treatment of a material event or transaction that does not qualify as an extraordinary item, it may be separately reported as a component of income from continuing operations with appropriate footnote disclosure. However, in this event, the separately identified item should not be reported net of its related tax effects.

Prior-Period Adjustments

An SEC interpretation of GAAP questioned the use of prior-period adjustments to account for certain negotiated settlements of litigation. One criterion for a prior-period adjustment had been that the event which caused the adjustment depended primarily on the determination of persons other than management.

The two most common types of prior-period adjustments had been settlements of litigation and settlements of income taxes. The SEC concluded that management plays a significant role in any negotiated settlement and that these settlements do not meet the criteria for a prior-period adjustment.

Consequently the definition of a prior-period adjustment has been narrowly redefined by FASB-16 as either:

1. A correction of an error in a prior-period statement
2. An adjustment for the realization of the tax benefits of the preacquisition operating-loss carryforwards of purchased subsidiaries

All other items of profit and loss (including accruals for loss contingencies) shall be included in the determination of net income for the period. Items which previously had qualified for treatment as prior-period adjustments will now be included in net income and will require disclosure as necessary for conformity with other requirements of GAAP.

Interim-period adjustments   An adjustment of prior interim periods of a current fiscal year can include any of the following settlements:

1. Litigation or similar claims
2. Income taxes
3. Renegotiation
4. Utility revenues governed by rate-making processes

In adjusting interim periods of the current year, any adjustment of prior periods is made to the first interim period of the current year. Adjustments to the other interim periods of the current year are related to the interim period affected.

The effects (1) on income from continuous operations, (2) on net income, and (3) on earnings per share of an adjustment to a current interim period must be fully disclosed.

Accounting changes   Present promulgated GAAP are unaffected by the new narrow definition of prior-period adjustments.

The following accounting changes necessitate adjustments of prior periods for reporting purposes:

1. Reporting a change in an entity
2. An accounting change from the LIFO method to any other method
3. An accounting change in reporting long-term construction contracts
4. A change to or from the full-cost method used in the extractive industries
5. One-time change for closely held corporations in connection with a public offering of its equity securities, or when such a company first issues financial statements for obtaining additional equity capital from outside investors (see APB-20)
6. Change from the retirement-replacement-betterment method of accounting for railroad track structures to the depreciation method of accounting (FASB-73)

In addition, a change in accounting methods of constituents of a pooling-of-interest to conform with the parent company is still applied retroactively, and financial statements presented for prior periods should be restated.

In those rare material cases when prior-period adjustments are recorded, the resulting effects should be disclosed in the period in which the adjustments are made by *restating the balance of retained earnings at the beginning of such period.*

Both the gross and net effect (of related income taxes) of prior-period adjustments on net income should be disclosed in the year of adjustment and all years presented.

Discontinued Operations

Discontinued operations are identifiable segments of a business that have been or will be disposed of.

Identifiable entity   Segments of a business are components that represent a major class of a firm's business, usually taking the form of a subsidiary, division, department, or other identifiable entity.

Segments of a business have separate assets and results of operations and activities that can be clearly distinguished for financial reporting purposes.

Facts that indicate there is no separate identity suggest that the form of business should not be classified as a segment of a business.

Measurement date   The measurement date of the disposal of a segment of a business is the date management commits to a formal plan for action to sell or otherwise dispose of the segment.

> **OBSERVATION:**   *The plan of disposal should be carried out within one year from the measurement date. If a plan of disposal is estimated to be completed within one year and subsequently is not, any revision of the net realizable value of the segment should be treated as a change in an accounting estimate and should therefore be made prospectively.*

Disposal date   The disposal date is the date of closing, in the case of a sale, or the date operations cease, in the case of abandonment.

Determination of gain or loss   The estimated loss on disposal of a segment of business should be provided for as of the *measurement date.*

   In the case of a gain, it should not be recognized until it is realized (realization principle), which is usually the *disposal date.*

   Determination of gain or loss on disposal of a segment of a business should be made as of the measurement date, based on estimates of the net realizable value.

   Net losses from operations between the measurement date and the expected disposal date should be provided for in the determination of gain or loss.

   Estimates should be based on the amounts that can be projected with reasonable accuracy.

> **OBSERVATION:**   *Cost, expenses, and other adjustments associated with normal business activities which should have been recognized prior to the measurement date should not be included in the gain or loss on disposal of a segment but should be included in income (loss) from discontinued operations. Severance pay, additional pension costs, and employee relocation expenses are costs directly associated with the decision to dispose of the segment and are properly includable in the gain or loss on disposal.*

Long-term leases   FASB Interpretation-27 reaffirms that estimated costs and expenses directly associated with a decision to dispose of a business segment should include future rental payments on long-term leases less any future rentals to be received from subleases of the same properties (APB-30). The gain or loss is measured as the difference between the unamortized cost of the leased property (net carrying amount) and the present value of the minimum lease payments which will be received under the terms of the sublease. The gain or loss is included in the overall gain or loss on the disposal of the business segment.

> ***OBSERVATION:*** *FASB Interpretation-27 is not clear on its coverage of subleases which are classified as operating leases. There is a strong argument that gain or loss on an operating sublease be included as part of the overall gain or loss on disposal of a business segment. APB-30 specifically states that all costs and expenses which are directly associated to the decision to dispose of a business segment be included in the overall gain or loss on the disposal. If a business segment has a long-term operating lease which is subleased and classified as an operating lease as part of the overall disposal of the segment, then any gain or loss would obviously be directly associated with management's decision to dispose of the segment. The gain or loss would be measured as the difference between the present value of the future rental payments which must be paid on the original lease and the present value of the future rental receipts which will be collected on the operating sublease. The journal entry to record a loss would be a debit to the gain or loss account for disposal of the business segment and a credit to a deferred account. The deferred credit account should be amortized each year in an amount which would make up the difference between the payment made on the original lease and the rental collected on the operating sublease.*

Disclosure Notes to the financial statements for the period encompassing the measurement date should include:

1. Identity of the segment of business
2. Expected date of disposal
3. Manner of disposal
4. Description of the remaining assets and liabilities of the segment of business
5. Income and loss from operations and other proceeds from disposal of the segment of business, from the measurement date to the date of the balance sheet

Presentation of Net Income

The following is the preferred method of financial statement presentation of net income:

Income (loss) from continuing operations before provision for income taxes	$XXXXX	
Provision for income taxes	XXX	
Income (loss) from continuing operations		$XXXXX
Discontinued operations (note____)		
Income (loss) from operations of discontinued division A (less applicable income taxes $XX)	$ XXXX	
Loss (gain) on disposal of division A, including provision of $XX for operating losses during phase-out period (less applicable income taxes of $XX)	XXX	
Net income (loss) from discontinued operations		XXXX
Net income (loss) before extraordinary items		$XXXXX
Extraordinary items (note ____) (less applicable income taxes of $XX)		XX
Cumulative effect on prior years (to December 31, 19XX) of a change in an accounting principle (less applicable income taxes of $XX)		XXX
Net income		$XXXXX

Earnings per share (EPS) for extraordinary items is not required but is strongly recommended by APB-15 and APB-30. EPS for discontinued operations and the resulting gain or loss on the disposal of the segment may or may not be presented (APB-30).

When common stock equivalents or other dilutive securities cause a dilution in one of the EPS data presented on the face of the income statement, and at the same time cause an antidilution in another EPS data presented on the same income statement, all the EPS data presented should be computed using the common stock equivalents or other dilutive securities (APB-30).

Whenever prior-period adjustments have been recorded during any period included in a five- or ten-year historical financial summary, the reported amounts of net income and components thereof should be appropriately restated.

REVENUE RECOGNITION

Overview

FASB-48 contains the specialized accounting and reporting principles and practices that were originally published in the AICPA Statement of Position 75-1, entitled "Revenue Recognition When Right of Return Exists."

FASB-48 indicates that the specialized accounting and reporting principles and practices were extracted from SOP 75-1, without significant change, and that the Financial Accounting Standards Board did not contemplate a comprehensive reconsideration of the accounting issues covered in SOP 75-1.

FASB-48 does not cover real estate or lease transactions and does not apply to accounting for revenue of service industries.

> **OBSERVATION:** *FASB-48 covers only sales for which a "right of return exists." Thus, in a sale of $100,000 worth of merchandise, of which 30% can be returned, only $30,000 of the sale is subject to FASB-48. Since the balance of the sale ($70,000) is not subject to a right of return, it is not covered by FASB-48.*

FASB Technical Bulletin 90-1 specifies the appropriate method of recognizing revenue and related costs from separately priced extended warranty and product maintenance contracts.

Background

The realization principle requires that revenue be earned before it is recognized. Revenue is usually recognized when the earning process is complete and an exchange has taken place (APB Statement-4). The earning process is not complete until collection of the sales price is reasonably assured (APB-10).

It is common practice in some industries for dealers and distributors of personal property to have the right to return unsold merchandise. The right to return merchandise is usually an industry practice but also occurs as a result of a contractual agreement. The return period can last for a few days, as in the perishable food industry, or it can last for several years, which is not infrequent for some types of publishers. The rate of return of some publishers may be as high as

60%, while in other industries, such as perishable foods, the rate of return may be insignificant.

As long as a right of return exists and the returns could be significant, the seller is exposed to reacquiring the ownership of the property. In other words, the risks and rewards of ownership are not, in substance, passed on to the buyer.

Since the earning process is not complete until collection of the sales price is reasonably assured, certain accounting problems arise in recognizing revenue when the right to return exists.

Revenue Recognition for Returnable Merchandise

When a buyer has the right to return merchandise purchased, the seller may not recognize income from the sale, unless all of the following conditions are met:

1. The price between the seller and the buyer is substantially fixed, or determinable.
2. The seller has received full payment, or the buyer is indebted to the seller and the indebtedness is not contingent on the resale of the merchandise.
3. Physical destruction, damage, or theft of the merchandise would not change the buyer's obligation to the seller.
4. The buyer has economic substance and is not a front, straw party, or conduit, existing for the benefit of the seller.
5. No significant obligations exist for the seller to help the buyer resell the merchandise.
6. A reasonable estimate can be made of the amount of future returns.

If all of the above conditions are met, revenue shall be recognized on sales for which a right of return exists, provided that an appropriate provision is made for costs or losses which may occur in connection with the return of merchandise from the buyer. However, if one or more of the conditions prescribed by FASB-48 are not met, revenue cannot be recognized until the right of return privilege has substantially expired, or the provisions of FASB-48 are subsequently met.

> **OBSERVATION:** *An exchange of one item for a similar item of the same quality and value, regardless of size or color, is not considered a return for the purposes of FASB-48.*

If all of the conditions of FASB-48 are met, an appropriate provision for costs or losses which may occur in connection with the return of merchandise from the buyer must be made by the seller. The provision for costs or losses must be in accordance with the provisions of FASB-5 (Accounting for Contingencies). Under FASB-5, a determination must be made as to whether the costs or losses are (1) probable, (2) reasonably possible, or (3) remote. Under FASB-5, a provision for a loss contingency should be accrued, by a charge to income, providing that both of the following conditions exist:

1. It is *probable* that at the date of the financial statements an asset has been impaired or a liability incurred, based on subsequent available information prior to the issuance of the financial statements.
2. The amount of loss can be reasonably estimated.

The second requirement (above) for the accrual of a loss contingency under FASB-5 will always exist when all of the conditions of FASB-48 are met. This is because condition 6 of FASB-48 requires that a reasonable estimate can be made of the amount of future returns, which also means that the amount of loss on the returns, if any, should be reasonably estimable. Thus, if returns are *probable* and all of the conditions of FASB-48 are met, an accrual is required by FASB-5. This accrual will result in a reduction of sales revenue and related cost of sales in the income statement, which is exactly what FASB-48 requires. However, if returns are *reasonably possible* or *remote* and all of the conditions of FASB-48 are met, an accrual is not required by FASB-5. In this event, FASB-5 requires footnote disclosure only, and not an accrual. If there is no accrual, sales revenue and related cost of sales in the income statement will not be reduced to reflect estimated returns that are reasonably possible or remote. It is highly unlikely that these results were intended by FASB-48.

> **OBSERVATION:** *It certainly seems logical that an accrual be made for returns which meet all of the conditions of FASB-48, and all of the conditions of FASB-5 for the accrual of a loss contingency, except that they are classified as reasonably possible, instead of probable.*

When returns are probable and all of the conditions of FASB-48 are met, sales revenue and related cost of sales of expected returns, along with any estimated losses on reacquiring the returns, are, in substance, deferred. During this period of deferral the customer's receivable is overstated because it is unlikely that the customer will pay for merchandise that will probably be returned. Financial statements of the seller during the period of deferral will reflect (1) an overstatement of the customer's receivable, (2) an overstatement of deferred liability account (provision for expected returns), and (3) an understatement of inventory.

If all of the conditions of FASB-48 are not met, the seller cannot recognize the sales revenue until the right of return privilege has substantially expired or the provisions of FASB-48 are subsequently met. However, FASB-48 is not clear on how the seller should keep track of these types of transactions until they can be recognized. The seller has at least three different alternatives. First, the transaction may not be recorded at all on the books of the seller. Perhaps the seller could maintain a *memorandum account* for these types of transactions. Second, the transaction could be recorded as a debit to a deferred receivable account and a credit to a deferred sales account. Lastly, the seller could handle the transaction as a consignment. In any event, it appears logical that some sort of control be maintained for these types of transactions.

Reasonable Estimates of Returns

Reasonable estimates of returns depend on individual circumstances. An enterprise must take into consideration its individual customers and the types of merchandise involved in determining the estimated amount of returns that may occur. FASB-48 cites the following factors which tend to decrease the possibility of making a reasonable estimate of returns:

1. Possible technological obsolescence or changes in demand for the merchandise
2. The length of the period that the customer has to exercise the right of return
3. Little or no past experience in determining returns for specific types of merchandise
4. Little or no past experience in determining returns for similar types of merchandise
5. A good chance that future marketing policies of the seller and/or the relationship with its customers will change

The above factors should be considered in conjunction with the past experience with a specific customer and the individual product involved in the sale. One or more of these factors may or may not impair the ability of an enterprise to make a reasonable estimate of the amount of future returns.

Disclosure and Effective Date

FASB-48 is effective for fiscal years beginning on or after June 16, 1981. As with most promulgated GAAP, earlier application of FASB-48 is encouraged.

> **OBSERVATION:** *The Exposure Draft for FASB-48 required that gross sales and related accounting policies be disclosed by an enterprise, if product returns are a significant part of its operation. In spite of the fact that the final draft of FASB-48 makes no mention of this disclosure, it is probably still required by APB-22 (See the chapter entitled "Accounting Policies").*

An accounting change which results from the initial application of FASB-48 shall be made, if practical, by retroactive restatement of all comparative financial statements presented. In addition, the financial statements of the year of change shall disclose the nature of any restatement and its effect on sales, income before extraordinary items, net income, and related per share amounts, for each year presented.

If it is impractical to retroactively restate all of the individual financial statements for the comparative years presented, the following procedure must be used:

1. The new accounting principle (FASB-48) is used in determining net income of the year of change (current period).
2. As many consecutive prior years' financial statements as practical (which are presented for comparative purposes) are then retroactively restated.
3. The cumulative effect of the change to FASB-48 is then computed for any remaining prior years.
4. The cumulative effect is then included in determining net income for the earliest year restated.
5. Financial statements presented for years prior to the earliest year restated (which includes the cumulative effect) shall be presented for comparative purposes as they were originally reported.

In the event that it is impractical to retroactively restate any prior year, FASB-48 requires that the cumulative effect of the change in accounting principle be included in the net income of the year of change in accordance with APB-20. In any year in which the cumulative effect is used, the effect of the change to FASB-48 on sales, income before extraordinary items, net income, and related per share amounts shall be disclosed.

In applying the provisions of FASB-48 retroactively, reasonable estimates and approximations may be necessary. Available information on the amount of returns for prior years that have already occurred may be used as a basis for estimates and approximations.

Comprehensive Illustration

The right to return merchandise to a seller may only apply to a portion of a total sale. For example, X Company sells 100,000 widgets to Y Company on January 1 for $1 per widget (cost $0.65). In the sales agreement, X Company grants to Y Company the right to return up to a maximum of 30% of the widgets within six months from the date of sale. Under these circumstances, FASB-48 would only apply to the 30% of the widgets that can be returned by Y Company within six months. Assuming that all of the conditions imposed by FASB-48 are met and it is *probable* that one-half (50%) of the widgets subject to return will actually be returned and the estimated cost that X Company expects to incur in connection with the returns is $1,000, the computations would be as follows:

Total sale	$100,000
Less: Portion of the sale not subject to FASB-48	70,000
Balance of the sale subject to FASB-48	$ 30,000
Less: Provision for estimated returns (50% of $30,000), plus estimated cost to be incurred on reacquiring the returns ($1,000)	16,000
Balance of sale which is recognized	$ 14,000
Balance of sale not subject to FASB-48	70,000
Total revenue recognized at date of sale	$ 84,000
Provision for returnable merchandise	$ 15,000
Provision for related estimated costs	1,000
Total provision for expected merchandise returns and related costs	$ 16,000

Under FASB-48, X Company should report $84,000 of revenue on the date the title to the widgets passes to Y Company. X Company should also set up a provision for returnable merchandise and related costs of $16,000. Sales and related cost of sales should be reported at their gross amounts in the income statement and the sales and related cost of sales for the *probable* returns should be deducted from the gross amounts. After the return period (six months) has substantially expired for Y Company, X Company may recognize as revenue any remaining balance in the provision account. The journal entries to record the transactions on the books of X Company are as follows:

Accounts receivable	$100,000	
Sales		$100,000
To record the gross sales to Y Company		
Cost of sales	$ 65,000	
Inventory		$ 65,000
To record cost of sales for Y Company order		
Sales	$ 15,000	
Deferred cost of sales (65¢ per widget)	9,750	
Deferred cost of reacquiring returns	1,000	
Provision for estimated returns		$ 15,000
Cost of sales		9,750
Provision for cost of reacquiring returns		1,000
To defer sales of $15,000, related cost of sales of $9,750, and estimated cost of $1,000 to reacquire estimated returns (freight $600, handling $300, and insurance $100)		

Warranty and Maintenance Contracts

Many retailers offer extended warranty and product maintenance or service contracts as separately priced items along with the products they sell. These types of contracts provide the customer with certain services, replacement parts, or warranty coverage which is not provided by the manufacturer of the product that the retailers sell.

FASB Technical Bulletin 90-1 (FASB:TB 90-1) specifies the appropriate method of recognizing revenue and related costs from separately priced extended warranty and product maintenance contracts. For the GAAP on warranty and maintenance contracts that are *not* separately priced, see the chapter entitled "Contingencies."

Scope of FASB:TB 90-1

FASB:TB 90-1 applies only to contracts that are *separately priced*. This condition is met if the price of the contract is stated separately from the price of the product, and the customer can choose whether or not to purchase the contract.

As defined in FASB:TB 90-1, *an extended warranty contract* is an agreement to provide warranty protection in addition to the scope of the manufacturer's original warranty, if any, or beyond the duration of the manufacturer's original warranty.

A *product maintenance contract* is an agreement to perform certain services to maintain a product for a specified period of time. An enterprise may agree to perform maintenance services a certain number of times, or as needed during the term of the contract.

Recognition of Revenue   FASB:TB 90-1 requires that revenue from separately priced extended warranty and product maintenance contracts be deferred and recognized on a straight-line basis over the contract period. An exception applies if sufficient historical evidence indicates that the costs of performing services are incurred on a basis other than straight-line. In this case, revenue should be recognized over the contract period in proportion to the anticipated costs.

Recognition of Costs   FASB:TB 90-1 requires that incremental direct costs of separately priced extended warranty and product maintenance contracts be deferred and charged to expense in proportion to the revenue recognized. Incremental direct costs are those directly related to the acquisition of a contract, which would not have been incurred but for the acquisition of the contract.

All other costs related to separately priced extended warranty and product maintenance contracts should be charged to expense when incurred. Such costs include costs of services performed under the contract, general and administrative expenses, advertising expenses, and costs associated with the negotiation of a contract that is not consummated.

Losses   FASB:TB 90-1 requires that losses on separately priced extended warranty and product maintenance contracts be recognized if the anticipated costs of providing services under the contracts, plus the unamortized portion of acquisition costs, exceed the related unearned revenue. In making this determination, an enterprise should account for its contracts by grouping them in a consistent manner.

> **OBSERVATION**: *The Appendix to FASB:TB 90-1 states that its provisions on loss recognition include the pool of risk concept from FASB-60. Apparently this refers to the provision in FASB-60 which requires insurance contracts to be "grouped consistent with the enterprise's manner of acquiring, servicing and measuring the profitability" of contracts. FASB:TB 90-1 seems to advise enterprises to group the contracts in a pool of risk along the lines indicated by FASB-60 for loss recognition purposes, and not to recognize losses on the basis of individual contracts.*

Once the amount of a loss has been determined as indicated above, the enterprise should first recognize the loss by writing off any unamortized acquisition costs. If this write-off does not account for the entire amount of the loss, the enterprise should recognize a liability for the excess.

Effective date and transition   FASB:TB 90-1 is effective for contracts sold in fiscal years beginning on or after December 16, 1990. Earlier application is permitted.

The enterprise may also apply FASB:TB 90-1 to existing contracts, that is, contracts that were in existence on either (1) the first day of a fiscal year which began on or after December 16, 1990, or (2) an earlier date adopted by the enterprise for application of FASB:TB 90-1. If an enterprise applies FASB:TB 90-1 to existing contracts, it must disclose the cumulative effect of the change in accounting principle in accordance with paragraphs 19, 20, and 21 of APB-20 (Accounting Changes).

EXPOSURE DRAFT

Accounting for Contributions Received and Contributions Made and Capitalization of Works of Art, Historical Treasures, and Similar Assets

The following material is based on an Exposure Draft (ED) entitled *Accounting for Contributions Received and Contributions Made and Capitalization of Works of Art, Historical Treasures, and Similar Assets.* This ED is outstanding as of the date of this publication. There may be significant differences between the ED discussed below and the official FASB Statement when it is promulgated. Thus, the reader is cautioned to compare carefully the material in this ED with the official pronouncement when it becomes available.

This ED would establish accounting standards for contributions and would apply generally to all entities, whether for profit or not. With some exceptions, the ED would require that contributions received, whether in the form of cash, pledges, services, works of art, or other assets, be recognized as revenues. There would be a corresponding recognition of assets, expenses, or decreases of liabilities, depending on the form of the benefit received. Measurement would be at fair value. Works of art and other assets acquired in prior periods would be capitalized. Contributions made would be recognized as expenses in the period made, at fair value.

Pledges A pledge would be recognized, provided it was unconditional. If conditions were attached to a pledge, revenue would be recognized when the conditions were substantially satisfied.

Services Contributions of services would be recognized if they satisfied any one of the following tests:

1. The services create or enhance other assets.
2. The services are provided by entities which normally provide similar services for compensation.
3. The services are substantially the same as those normally purchased by the recipient.

An entity receiving contributed services would have to make the following disclosures:

1. The nature and amount of contributed services received and recognized as revenue.
2. The nature and amount of contributed services received but not recognized as revenue, with an explanation of the reasons why they were not recognized.
3. A general description of the programs or activities for which services were contributed.

Works of Art, Historical Treasures, and Similar Assets Contributions of works of art, historical treasures, and similar assets would be recognized as revenues unless (a) the entity had no intent to sell them and (b) there was no market in which they could be sold or exchanged. At the time of recognition, these assets would be capitalized. Similar assets acquired by purchase would also be capitalized.

Some Provisions Applicable Only to Not-for-Profit Entities The ED applies generally to all entities, whether for profit or not, but certain provisions apply only to not-for-profit entities. The financial statements of not-for-profit entities would have to distinguish among contributions which increase (a) permanently restricted net assets, (b) temporarily restricted net assets, and (c) unrestricted net assets. Not-for-profit entities would also have to recognize the expiration of donor-imposed restrictions in the appropriate period, which could be the period in which (i) the purpose of the restriction has been fulfilled, (ii) the stipulated time has elapsed, or (iii) another stipulated event has occurred.

Effective Date The ED would generally be effective for fiscal years beginning on or after May 16, 1992. Entities would have an additional three years to capitalize works of art, historical treasures, and similar assets acquired in prior periods. Capitalization would be at the cost or fair value of the assets at the acquisition date, or at current cost or current market value, whichever was the most practical.

SEGMENTAL REPORTING

Overview

The promulgated GAAP on segmental reporting are:

FASB-14, Financial Reporting for Segments of a Business Enterprise

FASB-18, Financial Reporting for Segments of a Business Enterprise—Interim Financial Statements

FASB-24, Reporting Segment Information in Financial Statements That Are Presented in Another Enterprise's Financial Report

In addition, FASB Technical Bulletins 79-4 and 79-5 have been issued to provide guidance in defining U.S. Territories and the term *customer* for the purposes of FASB-14.

Segmental information for each fiscal year presented is required of all enterprises that issue a complete set of financial statements in conformity with GAAP. However, segmental information is not required (FASB-24) in the following circumstances:

1. If a complete set of financial statements is consolidated or combined in the financial report of another enterprise, then the segmental information does not have to be disclosed in the accompanying separate complete set of financial statements when presented in the same financial report containing the consolidated or combined statements. However, segmental information would have to be disclosed for the consolidated or combined statements.

2. A complete set of financial statements for a foreign investee that is not a subsidiary need not disclose segmental information when presented in the same financial report of a primary reporting enterprise, unless the foreign investee's separately issued financial statements already disclose the required segmental data. In other words, if the non-subsidiary foreign investee's financial statements already contain the required segmental information, then it must be disclosed when such financial statements are presented in the same financial report of a primary reporting entity.

3. A complete set of financial statements of any enterprise which is presented in the financial report of a nonpublic enterprise need not disclose segmental information. A non-public enterprise is not required to disclose segmental information (FASB-21—see below).

> **OBSERVATION:** *FASB-24 differentiates between a complete set of financial statements being "presented" and a set which is "consolidated" or "combined." Although the distinction is not clear, it is assumed that being "presented" means that the complete set of financial statements is included in the financial report but is not "consolidated" or "combined."*

Disclosure of segmental information is required in a complete set of financial statements of an investment accounted for by the cost or equity method when such statements are presented in the financial report of another enterprise. However, all of the percentage tests required by FASB-14 are computed by excluding the amounts attributable to the investment accounted for by the cost or equity method. For example, the 10% revenue test to determine a reportable segment under FASB-14 must be computed on the total of all the enterprise's industry segments. When determining the same test for an investment accounted for by the cost or equity method, all revenue from such an investment is excluded and the 10% is computed only on the other industry segments of the primary reporting entity. All other percentage tests required by FASB-14 are determined in the same manner (that is, by excluding the amounts attributable to the investment accounted for by the cost or equity method).

The following definitions are used in segmental reporting (FASB-24):

Segmental information   Segmental information is required to be disclosed by FASB-14, namely, an enterprise's (1) operations in different industries, (2) foreign operations and export sales, and (3) major customers.

Complete set of financial statements   A complete set of financial statements includes financial position, cash flows, results of operations, all necessary footnotes and prepared in conformity with GAAP.

Financial report   A financial report includes one or more complete sets of financial statements and other information (annual reports, SEC filings, etc.).

Foreign investee not a subsidiary of the primary reporting enterprise An entity organized and domiciled in a foreign country of which fifty percent (50%) or more of its voting stock is owned by foreign residents is considered to be a foreign investee not a subsidiary of the primary reporting enterprise.

Nonpublic Enterprise (FASB-21)

A nonpublic enterprise is an enterprise other than one

1. Whose debt or equity securities are traded in a public market
2. That is required to file financial statements with the SEC

An enterprise loses its status as nonpublic when it issues financial statements in preparation for the sale of any class of securities in a public market.

A public market is a foreign or domestic stock exchange or an over-the-counter market.

A nonpublic enterprise is not required to disclose earnings per share (APB-15) or segment information (FASB-14) in a complete set of separately issued financial statements. The nonpublic enterprise may be a subsidiary, joint venture, or any other investee.

If the nonpublic enterprise elects to disclose earnings per share or segment information, it must comply with the disclosure requirements of GAAP. It may not disclose this information on an arbitrary basis.

Background

Promulgated GAAP (FASB-14) require that annual financial statements contain segmental information about a company's operations in (1) different industries, (2) foreign operations and export sales, and (3) major customers.

Financial reporting of segmental information of a business is not required in interim financial statements (FASB-18).

The required financial statement information is basically a disaggregation of the entity's regular financial statements. The accounting principles used in preparing the financial statements should be used for the segment information, *except* that many intercompany transactions that are eliminated in consolidation are included in segmental reporting.

It is not necessary to present segment data regarding unconsolidated subsidiaries or investees. However, identification must be made about the specific industry and geographic area in which these companies operate.

It is important to remember that transactions between the segments of an enterprise are not eliminated, as in consolidation; rather they are reported on a gross basis.

Terminology

The following terminology is used in segmental reporting:

Industry segment   A part of a company that sells primarily to outsiders for a profit is an industry segment. Vertically integrated operations of a company are not considered to be industry segments.

Reportable segment   A reportable segment is any part of a company for which segment reporting is required by the criteria explained herein.

Revenue   Revenue includes sales either to outsiders or to other segments of the company. Intersegmental sales should be based on sales or transfer prices used by the company. However, intersegmental sales should not include the cost of shared facilities or other joint costs.
Interest earned on intersegmental trade receivables is included in intersegmental sales, if the receivable or other asset is included in the industry segment's identifiable assets (see below). However, interest on advances or loans between industry segments is not included in intersegmental revenues.
Operating income or loss of an industry segment should include interest on loans or advances between industry segments, if the industry segment's principal operations are financial (banking, insurance, leasing, etc.).

Industry segment's operating profit or loss   An industry segment's operating profit or loss is revenue less operating expenses, as defined herein. Operating expenses include those related to intersegmental sales as well as those to unaffiliated customers. Operating expenses incurred by an enterprise that are not directly traceable to a specific industry segment shall be allocated on a reasonable basis to those industry segments for whose benefit the expenses were incurred. Intersegmental purchases are accounted for on the basis of transfer and sales prices used by the company. The operating profit or loss of an industry segment shall not include the following:

1. Revenue not derived from the operation of any industry segment
2. Revenue earned at the corporate level

3. General corporate expenses
4. Interest expense, except for an industry segment whose principal operation is financial
5. Foreign or domestic income taxes
6. Equity in the income or loss from an unconsolidated subsidiary or investee
7. Gain or loss on discontinued operations
8. Extraordinary items
9. Minority interests
10. Cumulative effect of a change in an accounting principle

Operating expenses of industry segments should be determined by their nature and not by the fact that they are recorded as general corporate expenses. If an expense would ordinarily be deducted in computing the operating profit or loss of an industry segment, then it should be so included, regardless of how it was entered on the records. In other words, the nature of the expense should determine its deductibility as an operating expense of an industry segment.

Identifiable assets   Identifiable assets are either the tangible and intangible assets used exclusively by a segment, or the allocated portion of assets used jointly by more than one segment. General corporate assets are not allocated to segments, and loan and investment accounts are not considered assets unless income from these accounts is included in segment profit or loss.

Goodwill, less any amortization, is included in an industry segment's identifiable assets. An industry segment's identifiable assets should be net of any valuation accounts, such as allowance for doubtful accounts, accumulated depreciation, etc.

Loans and advances between industry segments whose principal operations are financial (banking, leasing, insurance, etc.) and whose income is derived from such loans and advances should be included as an identifiable industry segment asset.

Determining Reportable Segments

There are three steps in determining the reportable segments of an enterprise:

1. Identifying the enterprise's products and services
2. Grouping the products and services into industry segments
3. Selecting the significant industry segments

Grouping Products and Services

Although several systems exist for classifying business activities, the determination of industry segments depends primarily on the judgment of management. Existing profit centers are useful in collecting segment data, unless they cross industry lines.

Industry segmentation of foreign operations should also be performed. However, those foreign operations for which segmentation is impractical should be reported as a single segment, and appropriately disclosed.

Selecting Reportable Segments

10% tests   A test is made each fiscal year to determine an enterprise's reportable segments. A reportable segment must satisfy one or more of the following tests:

1.   Its revenue (as defined herein to mean revenue both from intercompany and from outsiders) is at least 10% of all the enterprise's industry segments.
2.   Its operating profit or loss is 10% or more of the greater of *a* or *b* below.
     a.   The total of all the enterprise's industry segments that had operating profits
     b.   The total of all the enterprise's industry segments that had operating losses
3.   Its identifiable assets (as defined herein) are 10% or more of the enterprise's combined industry segments' identifiable assets.

> **OBSERVATION:** *To determine criterion 2 above, all losses of industry segments which had operating losses are totaled, and all profits of industry segments which had operating profits are totaled. The greater of the two totals (losses or profits) is then used to apply the 10% test, as follows:*

Segment	Losses	Profits
A	$ 1,000	
B		$2,000
C		1,000
D	3,000	
E	7,000	
Totals	$11,000	$3,000

Under the 10% rule, the $11,000 is used and the reportable segments are those which have losses or profits in excess of $1,100 (10% of $11,000). Therefore, industry segments B, D, and E qualify as reportable segments for this particular criterion.

In the event that it is impractical to disaggregate part or all of a foreign operation, it should be treated as a single industry segment and should be included in the combined revenue, combined operating profit or loss, and combined identifiable assets of the company's industry segments.

Comparability test   Since the determination of a reportable segment is made each fiscal year, a reportable segment of the immediate prior years may fail to meet the 10% test in the current year. However, if the reportable segment that fails to meet the current year's test is expected to satisfy the 10% test in future years, in order to satisfy the criterion of comparability it would have to be included in the current year, even though it failed to meet the test. On the other hand, if an industry segment that usually fails to qualify as a reportable segment happens to qualify because of an unusual event, it may be necessary to exclude the segment on the basis of distorting comparability.

75% test   Combined revenue from sales to outsiders, by all reportable segments, must be at least 75% of the total revenue of all the industry segments of an enterprise. If the 75% test is not met by the reportable segments which passed the 10% and comparability tests, additional industry segments must be added to meet the 75% test. These additional industry segments do not have to pass the 10% or comparability test. Within the framework described above, it is desirable to combine segments as necessary to keep the total number of segments at ten or less.

Dominant Segments

If the revenue, operating profit or loss, and identifiable assets of a segment all exceed 90% of the respective totals for the enterprise, and no other segment meets any 10% test, that segment is considered *dominant*. A dominant segment must be identified, but none of the detailed disclosures applying to multisegment enterprises need be reported.

Information to be Reported

The enterprise must report revenue, profitability, and identifiable assets for each business segment, total unsegmented foreign operations, and the aggregate of other business which is not by itself significant.

As for revenue, the enterprise should separately report sales to outsiders and intercompany transfers. Transfers should be costed at the rate used by the company for operating purposes, and that basis should be disclosed.

Operating profit or loss of each reportable segment and the amount of expenses allocated to that segment should be disclosed. The methods used to allocate expenses should be consistently applied. In addition to operating profit or loss, the company is free to present some other measure of profitability as long as the methods used in determining the amounts are disclosed.

The aggregate amount of identifiable assets must be disclosed for each segment and in total.

The company must also disclose the types of products and any significant segmental accounting policies not already disclosed in the regular financial statements.

Other disclosures required for each reportable segment include:

1. Depreciation, depletion, and amortization
2. Capital expenditures
3. Equity in unconsolidated but vertically integrated subsidiaries, and the geographic area in which they operate
4. The effect on operating profit of segments due to a change in accounting principle

> **OBSERVATION:** *The* pro forma *effects of the retroactive application of a change in an accounting principle, and the* pro forma *supplemental information relating to a business combination accounted for by the purchase method (APB-16), need not be presented for individual reportable segments.*

Reportable segment information may be presented in footnotes to the statements or in separate schedules.

The information presented for revenue, operating profit or loss, and identifiable assets must be reconciled to the related financial statements' amounts for revenue, pretax income, and total assets.

Foreign Operations and Export Sales

Information regarding operations outside the enterprise's home country or which generate revenue from sales or transfers between geographic areas should be included in the financial statements.

> **OBSERVATION:** *For purposes of FASB-14, Puerto Rico and other U.S. Territories are part of the United States and are not considered foreign countries (FASB Technical Bulletin 79-4).*

An enterprise should report segment information for each significant geographic area. A geographic area is a country or a group of countries that is treated as a homogeneous unit for segmental reporting purposes. A geographic area is significant if it meets either of the following tests:

1. Revenue from unaffiliated customers is 10% or more of consolidated revenue.
2. Identifiable assets are 10% or more of consolidated total assets.

The enterprise should disclose revenue, operating profit or loss (or net income, or some other measure of profitability), and identifiable assets.

When an enterprise has export sales to outsiders which are 10% or more of total sales to outsiders, these amounts should be disclosed.

The enterprise should identify the geographic areas for which it is presenting segment information, and may disclose the information in the statements, footnotes, or a separate schedule.

The amounts shown as revenue, operating profit or loss (or other measure of profitability), and identifiable assets must be reconciled to the related amounts shown in the financial statements for revenue, pretax income, and total assets.

Information about Major Customers

An enterprise that makes 10% or more of its revenue from sales to a single customer or government must disclose such facts. The required disclosures include the identity of the segment and the amount of revenue involved.

> **OBSERVATION:** *An insurer who makes payments for patients to a health care facility is not a "customer" for the purposes of FASB-14. The patient is the "customer" because he makes the decision as to the doctor, time, place, and type of service to be received (FASB Technical Bulletin 79-5). However, if the decision as to the doctor, time, place, and type of service is made by the insurer, then the insurer would be considered the "customer" for the purpose of*

FASB-14. In this respect, some Health Maintenance Organizations (HMOs) deny their beneficiaries the choice of doctor (provider) and/ or health care facility. Thus, an HMO can be an insurer, and may also be a "major customer" for the purposes of FASB-14 (Technical Bulletin 79-5).

Restatement of Previously Reported Segment Information

Since the reporting of segment information is required on a comparative basis, previously reported information must be restated when:

1. The statements of the company have been restated for a change in accounting principle or entity.
2. The company has changed the segment or geographic grouping of its operation, which results in changes in the information presented.

Comprehensive Illustration

The following segmental disclosure appeared in the annual report of Harcourt Brace Jovanovich, Inc.

The principal sources of the company's business are the following:

Segment	*Principal Activities*
School instructional materials	Publishing textbooks and related learning materials, and distributing supplies to elementary and secondary schools.
University and professional publishing and instruction	Publishing scientific and medical books and journals, college textbooks, reprint editions of scholarly works, books and other materials for use in conducting bar review courses and CPA accreditation courses; distributing professional books; publishing books and journals and conducting seminars for lawyers and other practitioners, including continuing education.

Segment	*Principal Activities*
Popular enterprises	Providing instructional entertainment at three marine parks, operating several restaurants and a number of fast-food outlets.
Periodical subscriptions and advertising	Publishing business and professional periodicals and directories, farm magazines and rural-county directories, a magazine for elementary schoolteachers, and magazines that have paid mail subscription or newsstand sales or both.
General books	Publishing books of general interest (including children's books) in hardcover, in trade paperback editions, and in mass-market paperback editions; operating book clubs; operating a general bookstore; publishing high-priced illustated books sold mainly by mail.
Tests and testing services	Publishing tests, and providing scoring services, to assess learning aptitudes and acheivements of students and others, and to furnish assessment skills to an executive management service.
Insurance	Selling accident and health and life insurance to individuals, primarily through a farm-magazine subscription sales force, and underwriting and servicing life insurace also generated thereby; acting as general insurance brokers and agents in New York City and its suburbs.

Sales and revenues and income from operations for each of these segments are shown on pages XX and XX. Segment sales and services provided to unaffiliated customers; intersegment sales are not material. Segment income from operations includes segment sales and other publishing income, less operating expenses directly traceable to the segment. General corporate expenses benefiting more than one segment, which include compensation of general corporate officers, certain occupancy costs, stockholder reporting expenses, general insurance, and legal and other corporate consulting fees and expenses, are not allocated to segments.

Consolidated Sales and Revenues By Sources, 19X1–19X5

	19X5		19X4		19X3		19X2		19X1	
	Amount	*%*	*Amount*	*%*	*Amount*	*%*	*Amount*	*%*	*Amount*	*%*
School instructional materials	$109,344,034	29.5	$ 96,746,532	35.8	$ 90,097,760	37.3	$ 77,325,681	37.8	$ 68,831,039	38.9
University and professional publishing and instruction	83,376,749	22.5	73,237,322	27.1	69,630,791	28.9	59,191,248	28.9	48,443,365	27.4
Popular enterprises	60,015,015	16.2	—	—	—	—	—	—	—	—
Periodical subscriptions and advertising	52,137,971	14.0	36,201,794	13.3	30,382,168	12.6	26,702,713	13.1	24,607,403	13.9
General books	31,015,468	8.3	31,584,892	11.7	21,832,971	9.0	13,528,937	6.6	11,571,782	6.5
Tests and testing services	24,925,939	6.7	23,746,824	8.8	21,303,087	8.8	20,814,978	10.2	17,321,338	9.8
Insurance	10,273,504	2.8	8,858,476	3.3	8,099,969	3.4	7,006,332	3.4	6,111,257	3.5
	$371,088,680	100.0%	$270,375,840	100.0%	$241,346,746	100.0%	$204,569,889	100.0%	$176,886,184	100.0%

Consolidated Income from Operations By Sources, 19X1–19X5

	19X5		19X4		19X3		19X2		19X1	
	Amount	*%*	*Amount*	*%*	*Amount*	*%*	*Amount*	*%*	*Amount*	*%*
School instructional materials	$ 16,202,661	38.6	$ 15,891,954	47.0	$ 16,916,880	54.7	$ 11,998,025	47.2	$ 10,601,534	47.9
University and professional publishing and instruction	11,161,632	26.6	10,355,444	30.6	11,105,255	35.9	8,374,741	33.0	5,282,409	23.9
Popular enterprises	10,409,911	24.8	—	—	—	—	—	—	—	—
Periodical subscriptions and advertising	4,593,876	10.9	3,679,302	10.9	2,731,988	8.8	2,576,287	10.1	2,800,010	12.7
General books	(603,577)	(1.4)	2,199,783	6.5	(1,575,778)	(5.1)	(419,354)	(1.6)	812,751	3.7
Tests and testing services	3,207,615	7.6	4,194,694	12.4	3,673,852	11.9	3,985,873	15.7	3,623,025	16.4
Insurance	2,899,595	6.9	2,626,616	7.8	2,474,197	8.0	2,645,864	10.4	2,413,033	10.9
Unallocated corporate overhead	(5,869,976)	(14.0)	(5,141,580)	(15.2)	(4,415,607)	(14.2)	(3,757,620)	(14.8)	(3,417,347)	(15.5)
	$ 42,001,737	100.0%	$ 33,806,213	100.0%	$ 30,910,787	100.0%	$ 25,403,816	100.0%	$ 22,115,415	100.0%

Note: Income from operation for 19X1 - 19X4 has been restated to exclude net interest expense.

Identifiable assets, capital expenditures, and depreciation and amortization by segment for the year ended December 31, 19X5,were as follows:

	Assets	Capital Expenditures	Depreciation and Amortization
School instructional materials	$ 74,809,678	$ 4,333,265	$ 2,153,768
University and professional publishing and instruction	59,664,933	7,159,186	3,757,840
Popular enterprises	73,921,849	10,425,400	3,836,850
Periodical subscriptions and advertising	25,361,552	1,282,076	528,510
General books	22,473,489	669,298	578,438
Tests and testing services	8,820,970	457,633	405,675
Insurance	8,923,162	70,740	33,346
General corporate	24,765,184	4,515,250	95,793
Total	$298,740,817	$28,912,848	$11,390,220

The company's export and foreign subsidiary sales are less than 10% of total revenues, and no single customer, including governmental agencies, accounts for 10% or more of total revenues.

STOCKHOLDERS' EQUITY

Overview

This chapter contains promulgated and nonpromulgated GAAP pertaining to items properly included or related to stockholders' equity. The specific promulgated GAAP included herein are:

ARB-43, Chapter 1A, Capital Surplus
ARB-43, Chapter 1A, Donated Stock
ARB-43, Chapter 1A, Treasury Stock
ARB-43, Chapter 1B, Profits or Losses on Treasury Stock
ARB-43, Chapter 7B, Stock Dividends and Splits
APB-6, Paragraph 12, Treasury Stock
APB-10, Paragraphs 10 and 11, Liquidation Preference of Preferred Stock
APB-12, Paragraphs 9 and 10, Capital Changes

FASB Technical Bulletin 85-6 provides guidance on (a) accounting for treasury shares that are acquired at a price significantly higher than their market price and (b) the income statement classification of costs incurred in consummating a *standstill* agreement and/or in defending against a takeover attempt.

Background

The various elements constituting stockholders' equity must be clearly classified according to source. Stockholders' equity may be broadly classified into (1) legal capital, (2) paid-in capital, (3) minority interests, and (4) retained earnings.

Legal Capital

Legal (or stated) capital is usually defined by state law. It refers to the amount of capital that must be retained by a corporation for the protection of its creditors. Legal capital may consist of common or preferred shares. Preferred shares may be participating or nonparticipating as to the earnings of the corporation, may be cumulative or noncumulative as to the payment of dividends, may have a claim as to assets on liquidation of the business, and may be callable for redemption at a specified price. Usually, preferred stock does not have voting rights.

Common stock usually has the right to vote, the right to share in earnings, a preemptive right to a proportionate share of any additional common stock issued, and the right to share in assets on liquidation.

Generally, preferred stock is issued at par value, but common stock may have a par or a no-par value. When no-par common stock is recorded at a particular amount, it is called the *stated value.*

Any difference between the par value or stated value of stock and the actual price paid is either a discount, if issued for less, or a premium, if issued for more, than par or stated value.

A corporation's charter contains the types and amounts of stock that it can legally issue, which is called the *authorized capital stock.* When part or all of the authorized capital stock is issued, it is called *issued capital stock.* Since a corporation may own issued capital stock in the form of treasury stock, the amount of issued capital stock in the hands of stockholders is called *outstanding capital stock.* In summary, capital stock may be (1) authorized, (2) authorized and issued, and (3) authorized, issued, and outstanding.

Frequently, a corporation sells its capital stock by subscriptions. An individual subscriber becomes a stockholder on subscribing to the capital stock; and upon full payment of the subscription, a stock certificate evidencing ownership in the corporation is issued. When the subscription method is used to sell capital stock, a subscription receivable account is debited and a capital stock subscribed account is credited. On payment of the subscription, the subscription receivable account is credited and cash or other assets are debited. On the actual issuance of the stock certificates, the capital stock subscribed account is debited and the regular capital stock account is credited. Obviously, if any discount or premium is involved (the difference between the par or stated value and the price received), a separate account must be set up that is usually designated as *premium (discount) on common (preferred) stock.* A premium is classified as paid-in capital, and a discount is deducted from the capital stock.

Legal Capital—Disclosures

When financial statements are prepared in conformity with GAAP, capital changes must be disclosed in a separate statement(s), or footnote(s) to the financial statement. This requirement is in addition to disclosure of the changes in retained earnings, although all capital changes may be included in one statement. Capital accounts that may have to be disclosed because of changes during the year are capital stock, paid-in capital, retained earnings, treasury stock, and other capital accounts in the particular circumstances (APB-12, paragraphs 9 and 10).

Numerous different types of disclosures pertaining to the components of stockholders' equity are required by GAAP. The usual disclosures are:

Capital stock   By each different class, the total number of shares authorized, issued, and outstanding; also, the number of shares reserved for stock options outstanding for future grants and the changes during the year. Any unusual voting rights should also be disclosed.

Paid-in capital   The total amount of paid-in capital (capital in excess of par) for each class of security.

Retained earnings   The total appropriated and unappropriated retained earnings.

Restrictions on dividends, participation rights, and liquidation preferences should be fully disclosed, as should the pertinent rights and privileges of the various classes of stockholders.

In the case of options, warrants, and convertible securities, the conversion rates and exercise prices must be disclosed.

Preferred or other senior securities that have preference in involuntary liquidation in excess of their par or stated value must be disclosed as follows (APB-10):

a.   Call price per share or in the aggregate at which the security may be called or redeemed through a sinking fund

b.   The amount per share and total of all cumulative preferred dividends in arrears

Paid-In Capital

All stockholders' equity that is not classified as legal capital, minority interests, or retained earnings is usually designated as paid-in capital. The common sources of paid-in capital result from:

1.   Excess of par or stated value paid for capital stock
2.   Sale of treasury stock
3.   The issuance of detachable stock purchase warrants (APB-14)
4.   Donated assets
5.   Capital created by a corporate readjustment or quasi-reorganization

ARB-43, Chapter 1A, paragraph 6 states the following in reference to donated stock:

> If capital stock is issued nominally for the acquisition of property and it appears that at about the same time, and pursuant to a previous agreement or understanding, some portion of the stock so issued is donated to the corporation, it is not permissible to treat the par value of the stock nominally issued for the property as the cost of that property. If stock so donated is subsequently sold, it is not permissible to treat the proceeds as a credit to surplus of the corporation.

Charges should not be made to paid-in capital, however created, that are properly chargeable to income accounts of the current or future years (ARB-43, Chapter 1A, paragraph 2).

Minority Interests

The *parent company theory* is used in practice almost exclusively for disclosing minority interests in a consolidated balance sheet. Under the parent company theory, minority interests are *not* considered part of stockholders' equity and are disclosed in the consolidated balance sheet between the liability section and the stockholders' equity section. Where minority interests are insignificant and do not warrant a separate classification in the consolidated balance sheet, some enterprises have disclosed minority interests among other liabilities. Minority interests in consolidated net income are shown as a deduction of consolidated net income.

Under the *entity theory*, minority interests are disclosed within and as part of the consolidated stockholders' equity section of the consolidated balance sheet. Although the entity theory has much theoretical support, it is seldom used in practice, because under GAAP, consolidated financial statements represent the results of operations, cash flows, and financial position of a single entity (ARB-51).

Retained Earnings

Appropriated retained earnings should be clearly distinguished from unappropriated retained earnings.

Treasury Stock

Treasury stock is not generally considered an asset, because it is widely held that a corporation cannot own part of itself. When reacquired by a corporation, the status of treasury stock is similar to that of authorized but unissued capital stock. Under no circumstances should a corporation include as income any dividend on its own treasury shares (Chapter 1A of ARB-43). However, paragraph 4 of Chapter 1A of ARB-43 and paragraph 12b of APB-6 provide that treasury stock may be reported as an asset under certain circumstances (not described), if adequately disclosed. Accordingly, some corporations in recent years have reported treasury stock as an asset if the treasury stock was held to liquidate a specific liability which appeared on the balance sheet.

> **OBSERVATION**: *Treasury stock should not be classified as an asset under any circumstances. The exception provided by paragraph 4 of Chapter 1A of ARB-43 and paragraph 12b of APB-6 has no foundation, because the definition of a liability under existing GAAP is any obligation whose liquidation is reasonably expected to require the use of assets or the creation of other liabilities. Therefore, any obligation that will be liquidated by the use of treasury stock cannot meet the definition of a liability, because of the fact that treasury stock is not an asset.*

Reacquisition of treasury stock   If treasury shares are reacquired for a purchase price significantly in excess of their current market price, it is *presumed* that the total purchase price includes amounts for stated or unstated rights or privileges (FASB Technical Bulletin 85-6). Under this circumstance, the total purchase price must be allocated between the cost of the treasury shares and the cost of the rights or privileges that are identified with the purchase of the treasury shares. The allocation of the total purchase price shall be based on the fair value of the rights or privileges, or the fair value of the treasury shares, whichever is more clearly evident. Fair value shall be determined as of the date on which the major terms of the purchase agreement were reached. If no rights or privileges can be identified, the entire purchase price shall be allocated to the cost of the treasury shares.

FASB Technical Bulletin 85-6 requires financial statement disclosure of the allocation and accounting treatment of amounts paid in connection with an enterprise's purchase of treasury shares for a price significantly in excess of the current market price.

Greenmail and standstill agreements   Payments to a shareholder or former shareholder for any agreement in which the shareholder or former shareholder agrees not to purchase additional shares of an enterprise's capital stock should be expensed as incurred, because such payments do not provide any future economic benefits (FASB Technical Bulletin 85-6).

Cost incurred by an enterprise to defend itself against a takeover attempt and costs relating to a standstill agreement do not meet the criteria of extraordinary items (FASB Technical Bulletin 85-6). However, if professional judgment dictates individual treatment of a material transaction that does not qualify as an extraordinary item, it may be separately reported as a component of income from continuing operations with appropriate footnote disclosure.

Accounting and reporting   Under GAAP, both the cost method and par value method of accounting for treasury stock are acceptable. Under the cost method, each acquisition of treasury stock is accounted for at cost. In addition, separate records are maintained to reflect the date of purchase of the treasury stock, the number of shares acquired, and the reacquisition cost per share. The inventory of treasury stock may be kept on the basis of any acceptable inventory method, such as specific identification, LIFO, FIFO, or average cost basis. Upon the sale or other disposition, the treasury stock account is credited for an amount equal to the number of shares sold, multiplied by the reacquisition cost per share. In other words, under the cost method, the amount credited to the treasury stock account upon sale or other disposition is exactly the same as the amount which was debited to the account when the treasury stock was acquired. The cost method of accounting for treasury stock is more commonly used in practice than the par value method.

Under the par value method of accounting for treasury stock, the treasury stock account is debited only for the par or stated value of each share reacquired. Any excess paid per share, over the par or stated value, is debited to additional paid-in capital, but only for the amount per share that was originally credited when the stock was issued. Any excess cost per share remaining over the par or stated value per share and the amount per share originally credited to additional paid-in capital is debited to retained earnings. If the cost per share of treasury stock is less than the par or stated value per share and the amount per share originally credited to additional paid-in capital, the difference is credited to paid-in capital from treasury stock. Under the par value method of accounting for treasury stock, all of the original capital balances related to the shares reacquired are removed from the books.

When treasury stock is acquired with the intent of retiring the stock (whether or not retirement is actually accomplished), the excess of the price paid for the treasury stock over its par or stated value may be allocated between (a) paid-in capital arising from the same class of stock and (b) retained earnings. However, the amount of excess that can be allocated to paid-in capital arising from the same class of stock shall be limited to the sum of (a) any paid-in capital arising from previous retirements and net gains on sales of the same class of treasury stock and (b) the pro rata portion of paid-in capital, voluntary transfers of retained earnings, capitalization of stock dividends, etc. on the same class of stock. For this purpose, any paid-in capital arising from issues of capital stock that are fully retired (formal or constructive) is deemed to be applicable on a pro rata basis to all shares of common stock. As an alternative, the excess of the price paid for the treasury stock over its par or stated value may be charged entirely to retained earnings, based on the fact that a corporation can always capitalize or allocate retained earnings for such a purpose (paragraph 12a(i) of APB-6).

When the price paid for the acquired treasury stock is less than its par or stated value, the difference shall be credited to paid-in capital.

When treasury stock is acquired for purposes other than retirement, it shall be separately disclosed in the balance sheet as a deduction from stockholders' equity; or, as mentioned previously, under certain circumstances the treasury stock may be shown as an asset, provided that it is adequately disclosed.

A gain on the sale of treasury stock acquired for purposes other than retirement shall be credited to paid-in capital from the sale of treasury stock. Losses may be charged to paid-in capital, but only to the extent of available net gains from previous sales or retirements of the same class of stock; otherwise, losses shall be charged to retained earnings.

If a state law prescribes the manner in which a corporation shall account for the acquisition of treasury stock, the state law shall be followed, even if the state law is in variance with existing GAAP (APB-6). Restrictions on the availability of retained earnings for the payment of dividends or any other restrictions required by state law shall be disclosed in the financial statements (APB-6).

If treasury stock is donated to a corporation and then subsequently sold, the entire proceeds shall be credited to paid-in capital from the sale of donated treasury stock.

Dividends

A dividend is a pro rata distribution by a corporation, based on shares of a particular class and usually represents a distribution of earnings.

Cash dividends Cash dividends are the most common type of dividend distribution. Preferred stock usually pays a fixed dividend, expressed in dollars or a percentage.

Three dates are usually involved in a dividend distribution:

1. *Date of declaration*: The date the board of directors formally declares the dividend to the stockholders
2. *Date of record*: The date the board of directors specifies that stockholders of record on a certain date are entitled to the dividend payment
3. *Date of payment*: The date the dividend is actually disbursed by the corporation or its paying agent

Dividends are recorded on the books of the corporation as a liability (dividends payable) on the date of declaration. Dividends are paid only on authorized, issued, and outstanding shares, thereby eliminating any dividend payment on treasury stock.

Stock dividends   A stock dividend is accounted for the same way as a cash dividend, except that since there is no tangible distribution, an amount equal to the fair market value of the stock dividend is transferred from retained earnings to capital stock and, if appropriate, to paid-in capital.

LPS Corporation declares a 5% stock dividend on its 1,000,000 shares of outstanding $10 par common stock (5,000,000 authorized). On the date of declaration, LPS stock is selling for $20 per share.

Total stock dividend (5% of $1,000,000)	50,000 shares	
Value of 50,000 shares @ $20 per share (market)	$1,000,000	

Journal entry:

Retained earnings	$1,000,000	
Capital stock, $10 par common		$500,000
Paid-in capital, $10 par common		500,000
To record declaration by the board of directors of a 5% stock dividend on the $10 par common capital stock.		

Stock split   It is important to differentiate between a stock dividend and a stock split, because the accounting treatment is radically different.

When a stock distribution is more than 20% to 25% of the outstanding shares immediately before the distribution, it is classified as a stock split (ARB-43, Chapter 7B). A straight stock split increases the number of shares of capital stock outstanding, and a reverse stock split decreases the number of shares of capital stock outstanding.

In either a straight stock split or reverse stock split, the total dollar amount of stockholders' equity does not change. However, the par or stated value per share of capital stock decreases or increases in proportion with the increase or decrease in the number of shares outstanding. For example, in a straight stock split of 4 for 1 of $40 par value capital stock, the new stock has a par value of $10 and the number of shares outstanding increases to 4 shares for each share of stock previously outstanding. In other words 1 share of old capital stock is equal to 4 shares of the new capital stock. In a reverse stock split of 1 for 4 of $40 par value capital stock, the new stock has a par value of $160 per share and the number of shares outstanding decreases to 1 share for each 4 shares of stock previously outstanding . In other words, 4 shares of old capital stock are equal to 1 share of the new capital stock.

A straight stock split is used by a corporation to reduce the market price of its capital stock in order to make the market price of the stock more attractive to buyers. Thus, in a 4 for 1 straight stock split, the new shares would probably sell for about one-fourth of the previous market price of the old shares prior to the split. Reverse stock splits are unusual and are used to increase the market price of a corporation's stock. For example, a reverse stock split of 1 for 4 of stock selling for $3 would probably increase the market price of the new shares to about $12 per share.

No journal entry is required to record a stock split except a memorandum entry in the capital stock account to indicate the new par or stated value of the stock and the number of new shares outstanding after the split.

Stock splits should not be referred to as dividends. Related corporate resolutions, notices, and announcements should use the term *split effected in the form of a dividend* or avoid the use of the word dividend at all.

Stock Rights

A shareholder's interest in a corporation does not change on account of a stock dividend or a stock split except as to the total number of shares representing his stock interest. The cost of a stockholder's original shares should be reallocated among the new number of shares after a stock dividend or split. Gain or loss is then recognized on the basis of the adjusted cost per share (ARB-43, Chapter 7B). Stock rights should be recorded by the recipient by allocating the original cost of the stock between the stock and the stock right, using the following formula:

$$\frac{\text{Market value of stock right}}{\text{market value} + \text{market value}} \quad \text{x} \quad \frac{\text{cost of}}{\text{stock}} \quad = \quad \frac{\text{value of}}{\text{right}}$$
$$\text{of stock right} \qquad \text{of stock}$$

Original cost of stock is $100. Market value of stock is $90, and the market value of the stock right is $6. At what price should the stock right be recorded?

$$\frac{\$6}{\$6 \ + \ \$90} \quad \text{x} \quad \$100 \quad = \quad \$6.25$$

Journal entry to record stock right:

Investment in stock right	$6.25	
Investment in stock		$6.25

No accounting entry is necessary for the entity issuing the stock right or warrant, except for detachable stock purchase warrants or similar rights which are accounted for separately and assigned a value (see the chapter entitled "Convertible Debt").

When a stock right or warrant is used to purchase the specified security, the cost of the right or warrant is treated as part of the investment in the new security.

STOCK ISSUED TO EMPLOYEES

Overview

APB-25 (generally applicable to most stock option plans initiated after December 31, 1972) and ARB-43, Chapter 13B (issued June 1953) establish the current promulgated GAAP for accounting for stock issued to employees. FASB Interpretation-28 (Accounting for Stock Appreciation Rights and Other Variable Stock Option or Award Plans) is an interpretation of APB-15 (Earnings per Share) and APB-25 (Stock Issued to Employees). FASB Interpretation-31 (Treatment of Stock Compensation Plans in EPS Computations) is also an interpretation of APB-15 and, in addition, modifies FASB Interpretation-28. FASB Interpretation-38 clarifies APB-25 regarding the measurement date for determining compensation cost for stock option, purchase, and award plans involving junior stock. ARB-43 originally established principles and procedures for accounting for *traditional* stock options. APB-25 applies these principles to the various types of stock options and plans that have been developed since the issuance of ARB-43. For instance, it specifies accounting principles for stock options and plans where future events determine the number of shares to be granted the employee and/or the exercise price. APB-25 specifically supersedes ARB-43 in establishing new criteria for measuring a company's compensation cost. APB-25 delineates the income tax treatment originating from any options, purchases, or award plans.

FASB Technical Bulletin 82-2 deals with the accounting implications involved in converting previously issued stock options into the new incentive stock options allowed under the provisions of the Economic Recovery Tax Act of 1981.

Similar to many other areas of accounting, GAAP apply to the substance of an option plan rather than its form. In accounting for an option plan, a company must comply with the GAAP applicable to the option's underlying substance.

A description of the more common types of plans follows:

Typical fixed plan   Terms are fixed at the date of grant to determine the number of shares of stock involved and the option price to the employee. Transferability of the stock acquired by the employee is usually restricted, and the plan generally provides that the employee must perform current and/or future services.

Stock option and purchase plan   An employee is granted the right to purchase a fixed number of shares at a certain price during a specified period.

Stock bonus and award plan   An employee is granted a bonus or award of a fixed number of shares or a specified dollar amount which is payable in shares. The employee usually makes no payment to receive the bonus or award of stock.

Shadow or phantom stock plan   The employee receives cash, stock, or a combination of both, in an amount equal to a specified increase in the market price of the employer corporation's stock or an amount equal to a specified increase in the dividend distributions of the employer corporation.

Combination and elective plan   The employee is granted rights to more than one plan, or the right to select alternatives under one plan. The separate rights may be granted at different intervals or simultaneously and may run concurrently or for different periods. These plans are sometimes referred to as tandem or alternate stock plans.

Background

A stock option can be compensatory or noncompensatory. A compensatory stock option involves services rendered to the employer corporation, and a noncompensatory stock option does not. Accounting for noncompensatory stock options presents few problems. However, when a stock option is compensatory, the compensation costs must be measured, which may involve some problems.

Noncompensatory Plans

Certain stock options and stock purchase plans are not intended to compensate employees. For example, a corporation's intent may be to raise additional capital or to diversify its ownership to include employees and officers. Usually, the terms of the option will clearly indicate the nature and purpose of the plan.

A plan is noncompensatory if the cash received per share is very close to the amount of cash that would be received if the same deal was offered to all shareholders. In these types of transactions, a company does not generally recognize any compensation costs.

The essential characteristics of noncompensatory stock options or stock purchase plans are:

1. Substantially all full-time employees meeting limited employment qualifications may participate. Excluded are officers and employees who own more than a specific amount of the outstanding stock in the corporation.
2. Stock is offered equally to eligible employees, but the plan may limit the total amount of shares that can be purchased.
3. The time permitted to exercise the rights is limited to a reasonable period.
4. Any discount from the market price is no greater than would be a reasonable offer of stock to shareholders or others.

Plans that do not contain these characteristics are usually classified compensatory plans. In a compensatory plan, the company receives cash or another asset in addition to an employee's services for the stock it issues.

Compensatory Plans

Stock options may give rise to compensation, usually out of an offer or agreement by a corporation to issue shares to one or more officers or employees (grantees) at a stated price less than the prevailing market. In some instances the grantees' options are exercisable under certain conditions, such as the length of employment of an employee. In other cases, the grantees may agree to take the shares only for investment purposes and not for resale.

Under traditional stock option and stock purchase plans, an employer corporation grants options to purchase shares of its stock, often at a price lower than the prevailing market, making it possible for the individual exercising the option to have at least a potential profit at the moment of acquisition. Most option agreements provide that the purchaser must retain the stock for a minimum period, thus eliminating the possibility of speculation.

Options that give rise to compensation result in compensation expense on the books of the corporation and in compensation income to the recipient. The cost of compensation is measured by the excess of the quoted market price of the stock over the option price on the measurement date.

> **OBSERVATION:** *Under the provisions of the Economic Recovery Tax Act of 1981, a corporation can modify existing stock options to conform with the conditions for new incentive stock options. In meeting the pricing requirements of the new incentive stock option*

plan, an enterprise must increase the exercise price (option price) at the date of the grant or last amendment of the exercise price to an amount equal to or in excess of the fair-market value of the underlying stock. This in effect converts the stock option from compensatory to noncompensatory. Thus, any compensation expense and related deferred taxes that an enterprise had previously recorded in connection with the stock option must be adjusted in the period in which the option plan is modified. FASB Technical Bulletin 82-2 provides that this adjustment is accounted for as a change in an accounting estimate, and any compensation expense and related deferred taxes are decreased in the period of change by the amount previously recorded.

Measurement Date

The quoted market price of the shares granted under an option may vary considerably over the period of the option. This creates a problem in determining a date that may be used to measure the cost of compensation if the shares are offered at less than market. At least six dates can be considered:

1. Date of adoption of the option plan
2. Date on which the option is granted to an employee
3. Date on which the grantee has performed any conditions precedent to the exercise of the option
4. Date on which the grantee may first exercise the option
5. Date on which the option is exercised by the grantee
6. Date on which the grantee disposes of the stock acquired

The measurement date for determining compensation costs in stock options is the first date on which the following is known, which is usually the date the option is granted:

1. *Number of shares an employee is entitled to receive*
2. *Option or purchase price*

Plans that have variable terms which are dependent on events that will occur after the grant date will have a measurement date different from the grant date.

In a stock option for current services the measurement date may be the end of the fiscal period if the following conditions are met:

1. An established formal plan provides the terms of the award.
2. The plan details how to determine the total dollar amount due to an employee. It is possible that the *actual* amount will be indeterminable at the end of the period because it is dependent on an item, such as net income, which will not be known at that time.
3. The employee is being compensated for services rendered in the current period.

If a company transfers stock to a trustee, agent, or other third party, the measurement date becomes the date of transfer to the trustee if the following items are irrevocable:

1. Transfer of the stock to the trust
2. Terms of the trust agreement
3. Specified employee(s) who will receive the stock

In essence, if all three of the above are met, the company has given up any alternative use of the shares except for the ones specifically stipulated in the stock option agreement.

If treasury stock is distributed in a stock option plan, it is unacceptable to measure compensation costs by the amount paid to reacquire such treasury stock. The only exception to this rule is when a company meets all the conditions in a stock option for current services (above). In this event, the company may elect to measure its compensation costs by the amount paid to reacquire treasury stock, provided the treasury stock is reacquired during the current period in which the award is made and distribution to the employee occurs shortly after the close of the period.

The measurement date for stock options consisting of convertible securities can be determined only after the conversion ratio is known. Compensation is measured on the measurement date by the market price of the convertible security or the security into which it is convertible, *whichever is higher*.

If a company renews a stock option or extends the period during which the recipient can exercise the option, then a new measurement date is established as if a new option had just been granted.

The measurement date does not change merely because the agreement stipulates that termination of employment alters the number of shares an employee will receive.

Variable awards   Under *variable plan awards* the number of shares of stock which an employee can acquire or the exercise price, or both are not determinable until after the date of grant (FASB Interpretation-28). *Variable plan awards* include stock appreciation rights and other variable plans in which the number of shares, exercise price, or both are contingent on a future event.

The vesting period in variable plan awards usually runs from the date of grant to the exercise date. For the purposes of GAAP, the variable plan awards become vested on the date that the employee's right to receive the benefits under the plan are not contingent on any additional services to be performed by the employee (FASB Interpretation-28).

Compensation expense is charged to the *service period* which is the period(s) in which the related services are performed by the employee (FASB Interpretation-28). If the service period cannot be determined by the terms of the plan or otherwise, then the service period is presumed to be the same as the vesting period (FASB Interpretation-28). If the variable plan award is for past services, compensation costs are charged as an expense of the period in which the plan was granted.

When the service period of a variable plan award covers more than one fiscal period, compensation costs between the date of grant and the measurement date must be estimated as follows:

1. In the year of grant or first fiscal period, compensation costs must be measured with whatever information is available. If the number of shares are known but not the exercise price, then an exercise price must be estimated. If the exercise price is known but not the number of shares, then the number of shares must be estimated. If both the number of shares and the exercise price are unknown, then reasonable estimates must be made based on all information available.

2. Compensation costs are initially measured as the difference between the quoted market price and the option price multiplied by the number of shares involved.

3. In subsequent periods, compensation costs are adjusted, but not below zero, for any increase or decrease in the quoted market price. The adjustment is made to compensation expense of the period in which the change in the quoted market price occurs.

4. The accrued compensation costs for a right which is cancelled or forfeited shall be adjusted by decreasing compensation expense in the period of cancellation or forfeiture. Such adjustments are considered as changes in accounting estimates and are made in the period of change and/or future periods.

5. Accrued compensation costs should be charged to expense over the periods (service period) in which the employee performs the related services.

Junior stock plans   Junior stock is a separate class of stock sold to employees for a fraction of the price of the company's regular common stock. The junior stock pays a lower dividend and has less voting rights than the company's common stock and is usually not transferable, except back to the issuing company. The junior stock is convertible into the company's regular common stock if certain performance goals, such as specified levels of sales or profits, are met.

FASB Interpretation-38 requires that all junior stock options be accounted for as variable stock options because at the date of grant of a junior stock option there is no way to determine the number of shares of regular common stock that will ultimately be issued on the date the junior shares are converted by an employee. Thus, under the rules for variable stock options, the date for measuring compensation cost for junior stock plans is the first date on which is known (a) how many shares of regular common stock an employee is entitled to receive in exchange for the junior stock and (b) the option or purchase price, if any, that the employee pays for the junior stock.

> **OBSERVATION:** *Restricted junior stock that is issued to employees and becomes unrestricted when certain performance goals are achieved is also subject to the provisions of FASB Interpretation-38.*

Compensation cost is calculated on the measurement date as the difference between (a) the quoted market value of the shares of regular common stock that an employee is entitled to receive upon conversion of the junior stock and (b) the amount paid or to be paid by the employee for the junior stock. Compensation cost must be charged to expense over the service period specified in the option agreement, which is the period(s) in which the related services are performed by the employee (FASB Interpretation-28). However, in junior stock options, accrual of compensation cost cannot begin until the date it becomes *probable* that the employee will qualify for conversion of the junior stock to regular common stock, through the achievement of performance goals or the occurrence of transactions specified in the plan (FASB Interpretation-38). Once it has become *probable* that an employee will qualify for conversion of junior shares to regular common shares, compensation cost must be accrued. If the plan specifies a period during which performance must occur, the accrual of compensation cost must be allocated to that same period.

If no period is specified in the plan, compensation cost should be accrued over the period that starts on the date that performance becomes *probable* and ends on the date that performance is *most likely* or when a required service period ends.

> **OBSERVATION:** *As used in FASB Interpretation-38 "probable" has the same meaning as it has in FASB-5 (see the chapter entitled "Contingencies"), namely, that it is "likely" that the events will take place. However, the meaning of "most likely" is not clear. Evidently "most likely" is a higher degree of probability, although not explained in either FASB Interpretation-38 or FASB-5.*

If, as a result of vesting provisions, junior stock becomes convertible to regular common stock after the measurement date, compensation cost shall be recognized during the period from (a) the first date that performance becomes *probable* or the date that performance occurs to (b) the date that the junior stock becomes convertible or the end of the service period, whichever occurs first. If cash is paid to the employee to reacquire previously issued junior stock, compensation cost is equal to the excess of the amount of cash paid to the employee, over the amount of cash or other assets received from the employee for the junior stock.

For the purpose of determining earnings per share (APB-15), junior stock options are considered common stock equivalents, to the extent they are convertible into the employer's regular common stock.

FASB Interpretation-38 is effective for grants made to employees on or after March 14, 1984, under stock option, purchase, and award plans involving junior stock. Earlier application in previously unissued financial statements is encouraged, but not required.

Measuring Compensation Costs

The amount of compensation, or the value of the stock option, is the excess of the unadjusted quoted market price of the stock at the measurement date over the amount the employee must pay in cash or other assets. Often, the market quotations for a closely held or nonpublic corporation are not available, and other methods of valuation must be used. No compensation would be recorded if the employee purchases the stock for an amount equal to or greater than the market price.

> **OBSERVATION:** *The value of a stock option may be affected by many factors, such as transferability, and other restrictions. In spite of the recognition of these factors, the promulgated GAAP*

require (as a practical solution) the use of a quoted market price to measure compensation costs relating to both restricted or unrestricted stock. Only if a quoted market price is not available can an estimate be used.

Compensation costs related to options for convertible stock are based on the higher market price of either the convertible stock awarded or the underlying security for which the convertible stock can be exchanged.

Cash paid to settle an earlier option right with an employee is the measure of compensation, and the earlier measure of compensation (date the option was granted) should be adjusted.

If a company uses cash to reacquire stock shortly after the stock was issued to an employee through a stock option plan, then the cash paid is used to measure the compensation cost.

If a principal stockholder (one with an interest greater than 10%) establishes a stock option for an employee, the company should recognize compensation costs in accordance with the plan, as long as it derives benefits from the transaction. Stated differently, if the principal stockholder's actions benefit the company by keeping a valuable employee or attempting to improve employee service to the firm, then compensation costs should be recognized in accordance with GAAP. However, if the plan is granted because of a special relationship between an employee and the principal, a prior obligation unrelated to the company, or the company obviously does not benefit, then no compensation costs should be recognized. Obviously, the donated compensation costs by the principal stockholder should be credited to a capital account.

If compensation costs are to be measured at a date in the future, a company must make a reasonable estimate of what the compensation costs will be. Since the measurement date is unknown, the price of the stock at the end of each period should be used. If the number of shares is also unknown, a reasonable estimate, given the known facts, must be made.

> **OBSERVATION:** *Adjustments to estimates in future periods should be made as a change in an accounting estimate. A change in an accounting estimate is made in the period of change and/or in future periods. No restatement of prior financial statements is made.*

When a stock option plan combines two or more plans, compensation cost for each subplan may be measured separately. If the plan gives the employee a choice as to which section of the plan is to be exercised, the measurement at the end of each period should be based on an estimate of which part of the plan the employee is most likely to elect at that point in time.

Related Tax Effects

A company usually realizes a tax deduction for any amount the employee declares as ordinary income. The tax deduction is taken in the year in which the employee includes the benefits from the stock option in gross income. This corporate tax reduction results in a temporary (timing) difference, because on the company's books the compensation cost is reflected as an expense during the period of related employee service, but is recognized on the tax return in the year the employee includes the benefit in gross income. In such cases deferred taxes should be recorded.

If a tax reduction exists above and beyond that which is recognized as a deferred tax, it should be added to paid-in capital in excess of par in the period of the tax deduction.

It is also possible that recorded compensation cost will be greater than the allowable tax reduction. In such cases a company may deduct the difference from paid-in capital in the period of the tax reduction. This reduction is limited to the amount that the tax reduction for the same plan previously increased paid-in capital.

A company can incur additional compensation costs by reimbursing an employee for the tax benefit derived from the stock option plan. This reimbursement should be recognized as an additional expense against income.

Recognition of Compensation Costs

Compensation costs should be recognized as an expense over the period of employment attributable to the option. If this period is not stated, a reasonable estimate must be made, taking into account the circumstances implied by the terms of the agreement.

Stock issued in accordance with a plan for past and future services of an employee must be allocated between expired costs and future costs. Future costs should be charged to the periods in which the employee performs services. In the event stock options are exercised before the related compensation costs are actually incurred, a deferred or prepaid compensation account is set up. Unearned compensation costs should be written off to the period(s) in which they were actually earned, and any balances at a reporting date should be deducted from stockholders' equity.

Recognition of a stock option is made in accordance with the substance of the transaction. Therefore, if an employee gives an employer a nonrecourse note as consideration for stock issued with the stock as collateral, the transaction may be in substance the grant of a stock option. In this event, compensation costs should be measured and the nonrecourse note should be reported as a reduction of stockholders' equity and not as an asset.

Common Stock Equivalents

To the extent that they are payable in common stock, stock options, rights, and other award plans are common stock equivalents for the purposes of determining earnings per share (APB-15). Stock options, rights, and other awards which are payable solely in cash are not common stock equivalents.

In applying the treasury stock method to determine the dilutive effect of stock options, rights, and other award plans, the exercise proceeds consist of (1) the exercise price, if any, that the employee must pay, (2) the amount of compensation, if any, to be charged to future periods, and (3) an adjustment, if any, for related tax effects. Under no circumstances should the exercise proceeds include any compensation for past services of an employee (FASB Interpretation-31).

The exercise price that the employee must pay is usually stipulated in the option agreement. Generally, the exercise price must be paid when the employee exercises the options. The amount of compensation to be charged to future periods must be measurable and must not have been previously expensed. Measurable compensation to future periods is the difference between the aggregate compensation and the amount of compensation that has been accrued to date. The aggregate compensation is equal to the difference between the market price at the end of the year and the market price at the beginning of the year, multiplied by the number of shares that the employee would be entitled to at the end of the vesting period. The vesting period in variable plan awards, as mentioned previously, usually runs from the date of grant to the exercise date. For the purposes of GAAP, variable plan awards become vested on the date that the employee's right to receive the benefits under the plan are not contingent on any additional services to be performed by the employee (FASB Interpretation-28).

The adjustment, if any, for related tax effects may arise because the tax deduction for compensation expense may be more or less than the compensation expense recognized for financial accounting purposes. If the market price of the stock under option increases from the measurement date to the date on which the tax deduction for compensation expense is determined, a tax benefit will result. The reason why a tax benefit results is that the deduction for compensation expense on the tax return is larger than the deduction for compensation expense that was used for financial accounting purposes. Thus, this tax benefit is included as part of the exercise proceeds (FASB Interpretation-31). When the compensation expense for tax purposes is less than that for financial accounting purposes, the opposite will occur—the exercise proceeds are reduced by the additional tax liability. The tax effects are determined by the *with-and-without* method that is also used to compute deferred income taxes (see chapter entitled "Income Taxes").

For stock appreciation rights and other variable plan awards, the average aggregate compensation and average market price are used to determine the dilutive effect on primary EPS. The dilutive effect on fully diluted EPS is determined in the same manner as for primary EPS except when the ending market price is higher. In this event, the ending market price and the ending aggregate compensation are used (FASB Interpretation-31). Issuable shares must be weighted in the event that stock appreciation rights and other variable plan awards are granted during a current period.

A combination plan usually grants the employee the right to receive either stock or cash for stock appreciation. However, there is a presumption in GAAP that the plan will be paid in stock (FASB Interpretation-31). If past experience or company policy reasonably indicates that payment will be made in cash, the presumption may be overcome. Compensation expense and earnings per share data for a current period must be computed on the same basis. In other words, if it is assumed that an employee will receive stock in a combination plan, then EPS data must be computed on the same basis.

On January 1, 1980, the General Potato Company granted stock appreciation rights to certain employees in tandem with stock options. The rights entitled the employees to the appreciation in the market price of the stock over the market price at the date of grant which was the same as the exercise price ($10.00). The appreciation in market price is payable in stock, cash, or a combination of both, at the election of the employees. Exercise of the stock options automatically cancels the equivalent number of rights, and exercise of the rights cancels the options for an equivalent number of shares of stock. There were 10,000 shares of stock under option which will become fully vested in four years (December 31, 1983). The rights and options expire on December 31, 1989, and no related tax effects are expected to arise. The following is a summary of the pertinent data:

Date of grant	January 1, 1980
Vesting period	100% in 1983
Expiration date	December 31, 1989
Number of shares	10,000
Exercise price	$10.00
Quoted market price—grant date	10.00
Market price—December 31, 1980	14.00
Market price—December 31, 1981	16.00
Market price—December 31, 1982	18.00
Market price—December 31, 1983	20.00
Market price—December 31, 1984	22.00

Discussion

At the end of the first year (December 31, 1980) the market price of the stock is $14.00 per share, and the market price at the beginning of the year was $10.00 per share. Thus, there has been a $4.00 per share market appreciation, which equals $40,000 for the 10,000 shares under option. The $40,000 would all be compensation expense for 1980, for accounting purposes, if the vesting period was only one year. However, the vesting period is four years and only one-fourth (25%) of the $40,000 should be accrued, for accounting purposes, as compensation expense for the year 1980. The balance of $30,000 is compensation to be charged to future periods. The legal agreement would dictate when the employees could actually exercise the rights or options. However, for accounting purposes, compensation expense is charged to the *service period*, which is the period in which the related services are performed by the employee. If the service period cannot be determined by the terms of the plan, the service period is presumed to be the same as the vesting period (FASB Interpretation-28).

If the vesting period was 25% each year for four years, instead of 100% in four years, the calculations would differ significantly. Instead of accruing 25% of the stock appreciation ($40,000) in the first year as compensation expense, it would be necessary to accrue 52.08%. The 52.08% in the first year consists of 25% vested in one year; 1/2 of the 25% (12.5%) vested in year two; 1/3 of the 25% (8.33%) vested in year three; and 1/4 of the 25% (6.25%) vested in year four (25 + 12.5 + 8.33 + 6.25 = 52.08). In other words, compensation expense in year one consists of all the 25% vested in year one;

1/2 of the 25% vested in year two because it is earned over years one and two; 1/3 of the 25% vested in year three because it is earned over three years; and 1/4 of the 25% vested in year four because it is earned over all four years. The following chart illustrates the percentages that should be used when the vesting period is 25% each year for four years, instead of 100% in four years:

	Service Period			
Vesting Period	*Year One*	*Year Two*	*Year Three*	*Year Four*
1	25.00%	25.00%	25.00%	25.00%
2	12.50	25.00	25.00	25.00
3	8.33	16.67	25.00	25.00
4	6.25	12.50	18.75	25.00
Total	52.08%	79.17%	93.75%	100.00%

For earnings per share (EPS) calculation, exercise proceeds are the total of (1) the exercise price, if any, that the employee must pay, (2) the amount of compensation, if any, to be charged to future periods, and (3) an adjustment, if any, for related tax effects. Since the employees are not exercising any rights or options in the first year, there are no exercise proceeds for employees. The problem states that there are no related tax effects, so there are no exercise proceeds from related tax effects. The only exercise proceeds are $30,000 of compensation that will be charged to future periods. Thus, for both primary and fully diluted EPS, the exercise proceeds are $30,000.

For stock appreciation rights and other variable plan awards, the average aggregate compensation and average market price are used to determine the dilutive effect on primary EPS. The dilutive effect on fully diluted EPS is determined in the same manner as for primary EPS except when the ending market price is higher. In this event, the ending market price and the ending aggregate compensation are used (FASB Interpretation-31). The total aggregate compensation is $40,000, and the average aggregate compensation is $20,000 because this is the first year and the beginning balance of aggregate compensation is zero ($40,000 + zero, divided by 2 = average for year). The average market price of the stock is $12.00, because at the beginning of the year it was $10.00 per share and at the end of the year it was $14.00 per share ($10.00 + $14.00 = $24.00, divided by 2 = $12.00). The average market price of $12.00 per share is divided into the average aggregate compensation of $20,000 to determine the amount of issuable shares (1,667) for primary EPS.

Under the treasury stock method, the next step is to determine the number of shares that can be reacquired with the exercise proceeds. This is accomplished by dividing the average market price ($12.00) into the average exercise proceeds which is $15,000. (Beginning exercise proceeds are zero and ending exercise proceeds are $30,000.) Thus, the number of shares that can be reacquired for primary EPS with the exercise proceeds is 1,250 ($15,000 divided by $12.00). If we subtract the 1,250 shares that can be reacquired with the exercise proceeds from the 1,667 issuable shares, the balance of 417 shares must be added to the outstanding shares for primary EPS computations. These shares are called incremental shares.

The dilutive effect on fully diluted EPS is determined in the same manner as for primary EPS except when the ending market price is higher than the average market price for the year, in which case, the ending market price and the ending aggregate compensation are used. The market price is higher ($14.00) at the end of the year than the average market price ($12.00). Thus, the ending market price of $14.00 is divided into the ending aggregate compensation of $40,000 to yield issuable shares of 2,857 for fully diluted EPS. The next step is to determine the number of shares that can be reacquired with the exercise proceeds. This is accomplished by dividing the market price at the end of the year ($14.00) into the end of the year exercise proceeds ($30,000) which results in 2,143 shares. The 2,143 shares that can be reacquired with the exercise proceeds are subtracted from the 2,857 issuable shares, which leaves 714 incremental shares that must be added to outstanding shares for computing fully diluted EPS.

All of the above information, along with the remaining years, is summarized in the following illustration:

Computation of Accrued Compensation

| | | | | | Compensation | |
| | Market | Aggregate | % | Accrued To | To Be Charged To | Exercise |
Date	Price	Compensation	Accrued	Date	Future Periods	Proceeds
1980	$14.00	$40,000	25%	$10,000	$30,000	$30,000
1981	16.00	60,000	50%	30,000	30,000	30,000
1982	18.00	80,000	75%	60,000	20,000	20,000
1983	20.00	100,000	100%	100,000	None	None
1984	22.00	120,000	100%	120,000	None	None

Computation of EPS Data

	Primary EPS			Fully Diluted EPS		
Exercise Proceeds	*Issuable Shares*	*Assumed Repurchased*	*Incremental Shares*	*Issuable Shares*	*Assumed Repurchased*	*Incremental Shares*
$30,000	1,667	1,250	417	2,857	2,143	714
30,000	3,333	2,000	1,333	3,750	1,875	1,875
20,000	4,117	1,470	2,647	4,444	1,111	3,333
None	4,737	526	4,211	5,000	None	5,000
None	5,238	None	5,238	5,454	None	5,454

Explanation of Terminology Used

Aggregate Compensation	= The difference between the market price at the beginning of the year and the market price at the end of the year multiplied by the number of shares that the employee would be entitled to at the end of the vesting period
% Accrued	= The percentage amount of the aggregate compensation which is vested for the current period
Compensation Accrued to Date	= The dollar amount of the aggregate compensation which is vested for the current period
Compensation to Be Charged to Future Periods	= The difference between the aggregate compensation for the period and the amount of aggregate compensation accrued to date
Exercise Proceeds	= (1) The exercise price, if any, that the employee must pay, (2) the amount of compensation, if any, to be charged to future periods, and (3) an adjustment, if any, for related tax effects

PRIMARY EPS

Issuable Shares = Average aggregate compensation divided by the average market price

Assumed Repurchased = Average exercise proceeds divided by the average market price

Incremental Shares = The difference between the issuable shares and the assumed repurchased shares

FULLY DILUTED EPS

Issuable Shares = Average aggregate compensation divided by the average market price, UNLESS THE ENDING MARKET PRICE IS HIGHER, in which case, the end of the year aggregate compensation is divided by the end of the year market price

Assumed Repurchased = Average exercise proceeds divided by the average market price, UNLESS THE ENDING MARKET PRICE IS HIGHER, in which case, the end of the year exercise proceeds are divided by the end of the year market price

Incremental Shares = The difference between the issuable shares and the assumed repurchased shares

Note: The above computations are usually done on a more frequent interval than annually (monthly, quarterly, etc.).

Disclosure

When a company issues financial statements, it must adequately disclose the status of all option plans at the end of the period being reported. This disclosure should include:

1. Number of shares covered by each option
2. Exercise price
3. Number of shares that could be exercised
4. Number of shares exercised
5. Option price of exercised shares

Companies filing with the SEC must meet additional disclosure requirements (Regulation SX).

Comprehensive Illustrations

The following examples demonstrate the accounting treatment for stock options.

An officer of a corporation is granted an option to purchase 100 shares of $20 par value stock for $30 when the market price is $40.

Compensation—officers	$1,000	
Outstanding stock options		$1,000

Subsequently, when the stock option is exercised, the journal entry is:

Cash	$3,000	
Outstanding stock options	1,000	
Common stock		$2,000
Paid-in capital		2,000

Outstanding stock options are part of the stockholders' equity and are usually classified as paid-in capital until they are exercised.

In more complex situations (such as those where stock options are granted on the basis of performance over a number of years) it becomes necessary to estimate compensation costs for reporting purposes between the date of grant and the measurement date.

Moreover, deferred taxes must be recognized when the corporation expenses the compensation costs for reporting purposes but not for tax purposes. This is because the compensation costs based on a stock option are not usually deductible until the employee exercises the option.

An example of a more complex situation follows:

An officer of a corporation is granted an option to purchase up to 1,000 shares of stock ($50 par value) at the end of two years at 80% of the then market price. The amount of the option will be determined by the total net income of the corporation for the two years in accordance with the following schedule:

Number of Shares	*Net Income*
200	0 to $500,000
500	$500,001 to $1,000,000
700	$1,000,001 to $1,500,000
1,000	above $1,500,000

At the end of the first year, assume the following facts:

Market price of stock	$ 100
Corporate net income	$700,000
Corporate tax rate	50%

What is the accrual for the compensation costs at the end of the first year?

Compensation costs at the end of the first year:

$$500 \text{ shares } \times 20\% \times \text{market price} = \$10,000$$
or
$$500 \times \$20 = \$10,000$$

The journal entry at the end of the first year is:

Deferred taxes	$ 5,000	
Compensation costs	10,000	
Outstanding stock options		$10,000
Income tax expense		5,000

At the end of the second year, corporate net income is $400,000 and the market price of the stock is $110.

The journal entry at the end of the second year to record the stock option is:

Deferred taxes	$2,700	
Compensation costs	5,400	
Outstanding stock options		$5,400
Income tax expense		2,700

The compensation costs and deferred taxes were found by valuing the entire option at the end of two years and subtracting the previous year's compensation costs and related deferred taxes.

The journal entry when the officer exercises the stock option is:

Cash ($110 x 0.80 x 700 shares)	$61,600	
Outstanding stock options	15,400	
Common stock ($50 par x 700 shares)		$35,000
Paid-in capital		42,000

TRANSFER OF RECEIVABLES WITH RECOURSE

Overview

FASB-77 establishes the promulgated GAAP for transfers of receivables that are subject to recourse provisions. Transfers of receivables that are subject to recourse must be reported as sales if specified conditions in FASB-77 are met. Otherwise, the proceeds received from a transfer of receivables subject to recourse must be reported by the transferor as a liability. The provisions of FASB-77 cover only the seller's (transferor's) accounting and reporting practices and not the buyer's (transferee's) accounting and reporting practices.

FASB-77 covers the transfer of receivables that are subject to recourse and other comparable transfers of receivables with recourse, including the following:

- Participation agreements in a particular receivable or pool of receivables which provide for recourse
- Factoring agreements with recourse
- Sales or assignments of sales-type and direct financing leases that provide for recourse
- Sales or assignments of property subject to sales-type or direct financing leases that provide for recourse

FASB-77 amends paragraph 20 of FASB-13 (Accounting for Leases), which deals with a lessor's sale or assignment of a lease, or property subject to a lease, that was accounted for as a sales-type or direct financing lease. The thrust of this amendment is that if the sale or assignment is with recourse, it shall be accounted for by the lessor in accordance with the provisions of FASB-77.

FASB-77 is effective for all transfers of receivables subject to recourse, which occur on or after January 1, 1984. Thus, transactions entered into prior to January 1, 1984, that are consummated on or after January 1, 1984, are covered by FASB-77. Earlier application of the provisions of FASB-77 are encouraged in annual or interim financial statements that have not been previously issued.

Background

Businesses frequently sell receivables to financial institutions and others to raise cash. When receivables are sold on a recourse basis, the purchaser has a contractual right to demand payment from the seller, in the event of a default by a debtor. Upon receipt of payment for the defaulted receivable, the purchaser returns the defaulted receivable to the seller.

Many different types of arrangements are employed in the sale of receivables. Factoring is a process by which a company can convert its receivables into cash by assigning them to a factor either with or without recourse. *With recourse* means that the assignee (buyer) can return the receivable to the assignor (seller) and get back the amount paid if the receivable turns out to be uncollectible. *Without recourse* means that the assignee assumes the risk of any losses incurred on the collection of the receivables. Under factoring arrangements, the customer (debtor) may or may not be notified of the assignment of receivables.

One type of recourse arrangement for the sale of receivables provides for the purchaser to retain a percentage of the total amount paid for the receivables. This safety cushion retained by the purchaser until the receivables are collected is called a *hold back* or *dealer's reserve*. The agreement for the sale of receivables may contain a provision for the purchaser to automatically charge defaulted receivables to the reserve account. Any amount remaining in the reserve account after all, or a specified percentage, of the receivables have been collected is then remitted to the seller.

Pledging is the process whereby the company uses existing accounts receivable as collateral for a loan. The company retains title to the receivables but pledges that it will use the proceeds from the receivables to repay the loan.

> **OBSERVATION:** *A sale of receivables subject to recourse is negotiated between the buyer and seller on the basis of (a) the volume of receivables involved, (b) the stated interest rates, service charges, or finance charges on the receivables, (c) the prevailing interest rates at the date of the transaction, (d) the credit rating of the seller, and (e) other similar financial and economic factors.*

The actual process used to dun customers and collect the outstanding receivables is called *servicing*. The sales agreement for the receivables should specify whether the seller will continue servicing the receivables or whether the purchaser will assume the servicing function. A *servicing fee* for either the seller or purchaser may be stipulated in the sales agreement. If a servicing fee is not included in the sales agreement, the ultimate price paid for the receivables will, no doubt, include an amount for the additional costs involved in servicing the receivables.

The face amount of a receivable may include amounts for unperformed portions of executory contracts, such as a contract to repair and maintain the property purchased. For example, a $600 receivable for a washing and drying machine may include a $100 contract to provide maintenance of the appliance for a specified period. Unused portions of executory contracts are frequently refundable to the buyer in the event of cancellation or default. Thus, the purchaser of receivables will take executory contracts into consideration when determining the amount that is paid for the related receivables.

Sale or Liability

A transfer of receivables that is subject to recourse must be reported as either a sale or a liability, according to (a) each party's rights and obligations arising from the transfer and (b) which party controls the future economic benefits of the receivables. The future economic benefits of receivables consist of the rights to exchange or sell the receivables, use the receivables to produce goods or services, or use the receivables to settle liabilities. Legal title or ownership of the receivables does not always include control of the future economic benefits of the receivables. This is especially true where a seller (transferor) of receivables retains the right to repurchase the receivables. Under these circumstances, the seller controls the future economic benefits as a direct result of being able to repurchase the receivables.

FASB-77 requires that a transfer of receivables that are subject to recourse be reported as a sale, if all of the following conditions are met:

1.   The seller unequivocally surrenders to the buyer the control of the future economic benefits of the receivables. If the seller has an option to repurchase the receivables from the buyer, control of the future economic benefits of the receivables has not been unequivocally surrendered. However, a right of first refusal, granted to the seller, to reacquire the receivables based on a bona fide offer by an unrelated third party is not considered an option to repurchase.

2. The seller's remaining obligations to the buyer under the recourse provisions of the transfer agreement must be subject to reasonable estimation on the date of the sale of the receivables. In order to determine the remaining obligations under the recourse provisions of a transfer agreement, the seller will be required to make a reasonable estimate of (a) the amount of bad debts and related costs of collection and repossession, (b) the amount of prepayments, and (c) the validity of the transferred receivables. If the seller cannot make a reasonable estimate of the collectibility of the transferred receivables and the related costs of collection and repossession, a transfer of receivables shall not be reported as a sale.

3. The seller cannot be required to repurchase the receivables from the buyer except in accordance with the recourse provisions of the transfer agreement. Insignificant repurchases of receivables by the seller in accordance with the recourse provisions of the transfer agreement do not preclude the recognition of a transfer of receivables from being a sale. However, the amount of receivables repurchased by the seller must be minimal.

If all of the above conditions are met, the seller must report the transfer of receivables as a sale. If all of the above conditions for a sale of receivables subject to recourse are not met, the seller shall report the proceeds received from the buyer of the receivables as a liability.

Gain or loss on transfer   Gain or loss on the sale of receivables subject to recourse is equal to the difference between the sales price of the receivables (less *probable adjustments*) and the *net receivables*.

Net receivables, for the purposes of FASB-77, does not have the same meaning as is commonly used in accounting literature, which is gross receivables less a provision for doubtful accounts. For the purposes of FASB-77, *net receivables* are equal to gross receivables, including recorded finance and service charges and other fees, less the related amount of unearned finance and service charges and other fees.

Probable adjustments are those which result from (a) the failure of the debtor to make timely payments, such as estimated bad debt losses and related costs of collection and repossessions, (b) the estimated effects of prepayments by debtors, and (c) the defects in the validity of the transferred receivables, such as a defect in the title or ownership of a receivable. For the purposes of FASB-77, all *probable adjustments* incurred in connection with a transfer of receivables that qualifies as a sale shall be accrued in accordance with FASB-5. Under FASB-5, a contingency exists, if at the date of its financial statements, an enterprise does not expect to collect the full amount of its accounts receivables. Under this circumstance, an accrual for a loss contingency must be charged to income, if *both* of the following conditions are met:

- It is *probable* that as of the date of the financial statements an asset has been impaired or a liability incurred, based on subsequent available information prior to the issuance of the financial statements, and
- The amount of the loss can be *reasonably estimated*.

If both of the above conditions are met, an accrual for the estimated amount of uncollectible receivables must be charged to income, even if the uncollectible receivables cannot be specifically identified. An enterprise may base its estimate of uncollectible receivables on its prior experience, the experience of other enterprises in the same industry, the debtor's ability to pay, and an appraisal of current economic conditions. If an enterprise is unable to reasonably estimate the amount of its uncollectible accounts, there may be significant uncertainty as to the ultimate collection of the receivables. If a significant uncertainty exists in the collection of accounts receivable, the installment sales method, cost recovery method, or some other method of revenue recognition should be used (paragraph 12 of APB-10).

> **OBSERVATION:** *FASB-5 requires certain financial statement disclosures for a loss contingency that is reasonably possible but does not meet both conditions for accrual. However, FASB-77 does not contain any similar disclosure requirement for a probable adjustment that is **reasonably possible** but does not meet both conditions for accrual.*

If the transfer agreement provides for the buyer to service the receivables, no adjustment is necessary. Also, if the transfer agreement requires the seller to service the receivables and provides for a reasonable (normal) servicing fee, no adjustment is necessary. However, if the transfer agreement requires the seller to service the receivables and does *not* provide for a reasonable (normal) servicing fee, the sales price of the transfer of receivables must be adjusted. The amount of adjustment to the sales price is the amount that is required to provide a reasonable (normal) servicing fee. In other words, the amount provided in the transfer agreement for servicing income to the seller, plus the amount of the adjustment shall equal a reasonable servicing fee which shall be amortized over the term of the related receivables. In this event, the seller shall record the total amount provided for a reasonable servicing fee as deferred servicing income, which shall be amortized to income over the servicing period.

Change in interest rates   The sales price of a qualified transfer of receivables subject to recourse may be based on a floating interest rate. In this event, the interest rate used to calculate the sales price at the date of transfer shall be determined in accordance with APB-21 (Interest on Receivables and Payables).

> **OBSERVATION:** *APB-21 states that there is no predetermined formula for computing an appropriate interest rate for any transaction. However, the objective is to approximate the interest rate that would be negotiated, under the same terms and conditions, by an independent lender. In evaluating the appropriate interest rate to be used, the following guidelines are recommended by APB-21:*
>
> a. *The credit rating of the borrower*
> b. *The restrictive covenants or collateral involved*
> c. *The prevailing interest rates at the date of the transaction*
> d. *The interest rate at which the debtor could borrow funds*
>
> **Note:** *The appropriate interest rate will frequently depend upon a combination of one or more of the above factors.*

After the date of transfer of the receivables subject to recourse, a change in interest rates shall be accounted for as a change in accounting estimate (APB-20, see the chapter entitled "Accounting Changes"). APB-20 requires that a change in accounting estimate be accounted for prospectively (a) in the period of change, if the change affects only that period or (b) in the period of change and future periods, if the change affects both periods. Thus, after the date of transfer of the receivables, a change in interest rates is reported in income of the period of change as an increase or decrease in the original sales price of the receivables.

Financial Statement Disclosures

FASB-77 requires the following disclosures concerning the transfer of receivables subject to recourse which are reported as sales in the transferor's financial statements:

- The amount of proceeds received from the transfer of receivables during each period for which an income statement is presented
- If the information is available, the amount of receivables that remain uncollected at the date of each balance sheet presented

Note: The disclosures of similar transfers may be aggregated where appropriate.

There may be other disclosures relating to the transfer of receivables subject to recourse that are required by existing GAAP. Some of the more important disclosures required by existing GAAP are discussed below.

FASB-5 (Contingencies)   Even if they have a remote chance of materializing, FASB-5 requires the disclosure of (a) guarantees to repurchase receivables under recourse provisions, (b) guarantees to repurchase the repossessed property underlying the receivables subject to recourse, (c) guarantees of specific yields on the transferred receivables, including *floating interest rate provisions*, and (d) assets pledged as security for a loan. Thus, if a transaction involving any transfer of receivables subject to recourse contains any of the aforementioned contingencies, even if they are remote, the following disclosures must be made in the transferor's financial statements or footnotes thereto:

- The specific nature of the contingency
- The amount of the contingency

APB-30 (Reporting Results of Operations)   The nature and financial effects of a material gain or loss on the sale of receivables subject to recourse that occurs infrequently may have to be disclosed as a separate component of income from continuing operations. The disclosure must appear on the face of the income statement, or in a footnote thereto, in accordance with APB-30.

APB-20 (Accounting Changes)   The effects of a change in accounting estimate that covers several future accounting periods, such as a change in interest rates relating to a floating interest rate provision, must be disclosed. In this event, the effect of the change in accounting estimate on income before extraordinary items, net income, and related per share amounts of the current period must be disclosed in the financial statements in accordance with paragraph 33 of APB-20.

FASB-57 (Related Party Disclosures)   A sale of receivables subject to recourse which occurs between related parties must be disclosed in accordance with the provisions of FASB-57. Thus, a transaction between a parent company or an affiliate and an unconsolidated finance subsidiary would have to be disclosed.

TROUBLED DEBT RESTRUCTURING

Overview

FASB-15 (Accounting by Debtors and Creditors for Troubled Debt Restructuring) contains the promulgated GAAP on this subject and supersedes FASB Interpretation-2 (Imputing Interest on Debt Arrangements Made Under the Federal Bankruptcy Act). FASB Technical Bulletin 81-6 reaffirms that FASB-15 applies to debtors in bankruptcy, as long as most of the debts of the debtor are not *generally restated*.

> **OBSERVATION:** *Three FASB Technical Bulletins (79-6, 79-7, and 80-2) have been issued to provide guidance in applying FASB-15. Each Technical Bulletin is covered in its appropriate place in this chapter.*

Early extinguishment of debt (APB-26) arising from a troubled debt restructuring is now covered by FASB-15 and excluded from APB-26.

For the purposes of the promulgated GAAP (FASB-15), troubled debt restructuring does not include the following:

1. Changes in lease agreements (FASB-13)
2. Employment-related agreements, such as deferred compensation contracts or pension plans
3. A debtor's failure to pay trade accounts that do not involve a restructure agreement
4. A creditor's legal action to collect accounts that do not involve a restructure agreement

Troubled debt restructuring arranged under any provision of the Federal Bankruptcy Act is covered by the promulgated GAAP unless the debtor generally restates its liabilities, as in the case of a corporate readjustment or quasi-reorganization.

The promulgated GAAP generally establishes standards for accounting and reporting, by both the debtor and creditor, for a troubled debt restructuring.

Background

A troubled debt restructuring is one in which the creditor allows the debtor certain concessions that he would not normally consider. The concessions *must be* made in light of the debtor's financial difficulty, and the objective of the creditor *must be* to maximize recovery of his investment. Troubled debt restructurings are often the result of legal proceedings or of negotiation between the parties.

FASB Technical Bulletin 81-6 reaffirms that the provisions of FASB-15 are applicable to troubled debt restructurings arranged under any provision of the Federal Bankruptcy Act, except those provisions in which the debtor generally restates most of its liabilities. In other words, if most of a debtor's liabilities are being restated, FASB-15 does not apply. A debtor is usually permitted to restate most of its liabilities with the approval of the court and most of its creditors in a quasi-reorganization, corporate readjustment, and similar situations.

A troubled debt restructuring by a debtor in bankruptcy proceedings would be permitted under FASB-15 provided that the restructuring did *not* constitute a *general restatement* of the debtor's liabilities.

Troubled debt restructures include situations in which:

1. The creditor accepts a third-party receivable or other asset(s) of the debtor, in lieu of his receivable from the debtor.
2. The creditor accepts an equity interest in the debtor in lieu of his receivable. (This is not to be confused with convertible securities, which are *not* troubled debt restructurings.)
3. The creditor accepts modification of the terms of the debt including but not limited to:
    a. Reduction in stated interest rate
    b. Extension of maturity at a favorable interest rate
    c. Reduction in face amount of the debt
    d. Reduction in accrued   interest

The reductions mentioned in a, c, and d can be either absolute or contingent.

> **OBSERVATION:** *FASB Technical Bulletin 80-2 reaffirms that a debtor and the related creditor in a troubled debt restructuring must independently account for the debt restructure. Thus, a debtor may account for the debt restructure as* **troubled,** *whereas the related creditor may not necessarily account for the debt restructure as* **troubled.**

Definition of Terms

A *receivable* (or *payable*) is defined as a contractual right to receive or pay money that is already recorded on the debtor's or creditor's balance sheet and includes accrued interest, premiums, discounts, issue costs, and any related valuation allowances. Although transactions affecting these accounts take on a variety of forms, it is the *substance*, not the form, that should govern the accounting treatment.

The *time of restructuring* is defined as the date an agreement to restructure is consummated.

Not all debt restructuring can be considered troubled, even though the debtor is in financial difficulty. Circumstances in which the restructuring is not troubled include:

1. The debtor satisfies the debt by giving fair value of assets or equity that at least equals either:
   a. The creditor's recorded receivable, or
   b. The debtor's carrying amount of the payable
2. The creditor reduces the interest rate primarily in response to changes in market rates.
3. The debtor issues at or near the current market new marketable securities in exchange for the old securities. (The fact that the debtor can obtain at similar rates and conditions funds from other sources is evidence that the restructuring is not troubled.)

Accounting and Reporting by Debtors

A debtor accounts for a troubled debt restructuring by the type of restructuring. Types of restructuring include:

1. Transfer of assets(s) in full settlement
2. Granting an equity interest in full settlement
3. Modification of terms of the debt
4. Combinations of the above three types

Transfer of asset(s)   The debtor will recognize a gain in the amount of the excess of the carrying amount of the payable (and accrued interest, premiums, etc.) over the fair value of the asset(s) given up. Fair value is, of course, an arm's-length purchase or sale price. The gain, or loss, is reported in net income of the period.

> **OBSERVATION:** *Fair value may be determined either by the assets given up or the amount of payable, whichever is more clearly evident. However, in the case of a partial settlement, the value of the asset(s) given up must be used. This eliminates the need to allocate the fair value of the payable between the settled portion and the remaining outstanding balance.*

The excess of the carrying amount of the debt over the fair value of the asset(s) given up is the gain on debt restructuring. However, the difference between the fair value and the carrying amount of the asset(s) given up is the gain or loss on the transfer of asset(s), which is included in net income in the period the transfer occurs.

Transfer of equity interest The difference between the fair value of the equity interest and the carrying amount of the payable is recognized as gain or loss. As a practical matter, the difference will always be a gain since it is unlikely the debtor would exchange fair value in *excess* of his obligation to satisfy his creditors.

The difference between the fair value and the carrying amount of the equity interest given up is the gain or loss on the transfer asset(s), which is included in net income in the period the transfer occurs.

Modification of terms A restructuring that does not involve the transfer of assets or equity will often involve the modification of the terms of the debt. In a modification, the debtor accounts for the effects of the restructuring prospectively and does not change the carrying amount unless the carrying amount exceeds the total future cash payments specified by the new terms. The *total future cash payments* are the principal and any accrued interest at the time of the restructuring which continues to be payable by the new terms. *Interest expense* is computed by a method which causes a constant effective rate (such as the interest method). The new effective rate of interest is the discount rate at which the carrying amount of the debt is equal to the present value of the future cash payments.

When the total future cash payments are less than the carrying amount, the debtor should reduce the carrying amount accordingly and recognize the difference as a gain. When there are several related accounts (discount, premium, etc.), the reduction may need to be allocated among them. All cash payments after the restructuring go toward reducing the carrying amount, and *no* interest expense is recognized after the date of restructure.

When there are indeterminate future payments, or anytime the future payments might exceed the carrying amount, the debtor recognizes no gain. The debtor should assume that the future contingent payments will have to be made at least to the extent necessary to obviate any gain.

In estimating future cash payments for any purpose *in this area*, it is assumed that the maximum amount of periods (and interest) is going to occur.

Combination of types   When a restructuring involves combinations of asset or equity transfers and modification of terms, the fair value of any asset or equity is used first to reduce the carrying amount of the payable. The difference between the fair value and the carrying amount of any asset(s) transferred is recognized as gain or loss. No gain on restructuring can be recognized unless the carrying amount exceeds the total future cash payments.

Repossessions and foreclosures shall be accounted for in the same manner as satisfaction by surrender of assets.

All gains on debt restructure are aggregated and included in net income for the period. If substantial, the gains are reported as an extraordinary item (net of tax effects).

Contingently payable accounts   Amounts contingently payable in future periods are recognized as payable and as interest expense in accordance with the treatment of other contingencies. The criteria for contingencies are:

1.   It is probable that the liability has been incurred.
2.   The amount must be reasonably estimable.

If any contingently payable amounts were included in the total future cash payments, they must now be deducted from the carrying amount of the restructured payable to the extent they originally prevented recognition of a gain at the time of the restructuring.

In estimating future payments subject to fluctuation, estimates should be based on the interest rate in effect at the time of restructure. A change in future rates is treated as a change in an estimate. The accounting for these fluctuations cannot result in an immediate gain. Rather, the future payments will reduce the carrying amount, and any residual value shall be considered gain.

Incidental cost of restructure   In an issuance of equity the incidental costs are charged against the equity issued. All other direct costs are either deducted from recognized gains, or, if no gain exists, they are expensed in the period.

Disclosure by debtors   The debtor must disclose the following regarding any debt restructuring during a period:

1.   Description of the terms of each restructuring
2.   Aggregate gain on restructure and related tax effect
3.   Aggregate net gain or loss on asset transfer
4.   Per share amount of aggregate gain on the restructuring and the related tax effect

The debtor should also disclose contingently payable amounts included in the carrying amount of restructured payables, and the total of contingently payable amounts and the conditions under which the amounts become payable or are forgiven.

Accounting by Creditors

The creditor accounts for restructure by the same categories as the debtor. The treatment of each type of restructure is explained below.

Receipt of assets or equity   When the creditor receives either assets or equity as full settlement of a receivable, he should account for these at their fair value at the time of the restructuring. The fair value of the receivable satisfied can be used if it is more clearly determinable than the fair value of the asset or equity acquired. In partial payments the creditor *must* use the fair value of the asset or equity received.

The excess of the recorded receivable over the fair value of the assets received is recognized as a loss. The creditor accounts for these assets as if they were acquired for cash.

Modification of terms   When the creditor accepts a modification of terms, he accounts for the restructuring prospectively and does not change the recorded investment *unless* it exceeds the total future cash payments (as defined in the terms of the new agreement).

The creditor recognizes interest income at a constant rate of effective interest. For the effective rate, the creditor uses the discount rate at which the present value of the future cash receipts is equal to the recorded investment.

If the total future cash receipts are less than the recorded investment, the investment should be reduced and a loss recognized. All subsequent cash received is applied to reduce the balance of the recorded investment, and none is considered interest.

When the restructured receivable involves indeterminate future cash receipts, the creditor recognizes a loss to the extent that the minimum future cash receipts are less than the recorded investment. As for contingently receivable amounts, the creditor excludes them from the total future cash receipts unless they are *probable* and can be *reasonably estimated*. If exclusion results in a deficiency, it is recognized as a loss. Flexible payments should be estimated on the basis of the minimum allowable length of time.

The provisions of FASB-15 do not affect the requirements of FASB-5 (see the chapter entitled "Contingencies") to provide for probable losses on modified debt restructuring that can be reasonably estimated (FASB Technical Bulletin 79-6).

Naturally, contingently receivable interest should not be recognized until it is earned *and* the contingency has been resolved. However, before these amounts can be recognized as income, they must first be used to reduce the recorded investment *to the extent* that contingent receipts (which were considered receivable) avoided recognition of a loss on restructuring.

> **OBSERVATION:** *When future cash receipts exceed the recorded investment in a receivable whose terms have been modified, the excess should be accounted for as interest income. If recognition of excess receipts results in a higher than normal return on investment, the nature of the excess receipts should be disclosed (FASB Technical Bulletin 79-7).*

Combination of types   The creditor shall reduce his recorded investment by the fair value of assets received. Any loss recognized is limited to the excess of the remaining recorded investment over the total future cash receipts. Any future interest income is recognized at a constant effective rate of interest (interest method) or other accepted specialized industry practice that is used for receivables.

Related matters   Foreclosures are accounted for in the same manner as the receipt of assets or equity. Losses, to the extent that they were not previously recognized by valuation allowances, enter into net income for the period.

If a loss from a troubled debt restructuring has been previously provided in a valuation allowance account, such a loss shall be deducted from its related valuation allowance and not charged directly to net income.

Fluctuation in interest rates after a restructuring are accounted for as changes in an accounting estimate in the period they occur. A creditor shall recognize a loss and reduce its restructured receivable when fluctuations in interest rates cause the minimum future cash receipts to fall below the recorded investment in the restructured receivable.

Legal fees and other direct costs resulting from a troubled debt restructuring shall be expensed by the creditor when incurred.

Creditor disclosure   The creditor shall disclose the following regarding troubled debt restructurings:

1. Restructured receivables, by major category:
    a.   Aggregate recorded investment
    b.   Gross interest income that would have been earned if there had been no restructuring
    c.   Gross interest income on restructured receivables that is included in net income for the period (Modified receivables with a rate of interest greater than or equal to the rate the creditor would require for similar risk receivables need not be included in the disclosures above.)
2. Amount(s) of any commitment(s) to lend additional funds to any debtor who is a party to a restructuring

These disclosures may be made in aggregate by major category.

Substitution of debtors   When a restructuring involves the addition of or substitution of a new debtor for the old debtor, the substance of the transaction determines the correct treatment.

Banking and Thrift Institutions

BANKING AND THRIFT INSTITUTIONS

Overview

The specialized industry GAAP for banking and thrift institutions are as follows:

FASB Interpretation-9, Applying APB Opinion Nos. 16 and 17 When A Savings and Loan Association or a Similar Institution is Acquired in a Business Combination Accounted for by the Purchase Method

FASB-72, Accounting for Certain Acquisitions of Banking or Thrift Institutions

Nonrefundable fees and costs associated with originating or acquiring loans are addressed by FASB-91 (Accounting for Nonrefundable Fees and Costs Associated with Originating or Acquiring Loans and Initial Direct Costs of Leases).

> **OBSERVATION:** *In a special supplement to* The CPA Letter, *dated February 10, 1986, the AICPA Accounting Standards Executive Committee (AcSEC) issued a four-page notice that provides guidance in determining the proper accounting that should be applied to real estate acquisition, development, or construction (ADC) arrangements of financial institutions. This notice applies only to those ADC arrangements in which the lender participates in expected residual profit, which is defined as the amount of profit, whether called interest or another name such as equity kicker, above a reasonable amount of interest and fees expected to be earned by the lender.*
>
> *A copy of the above AcSEC notice should be obtained by those financial institutions that enter into ADC arrangements.*

FASB Interpretation-9 concludes that the net-spread method should not be used in determining the amount of goodwill or other intangible assets that are acquired in a business combination accounted for by the purchase method. FASB Interpretation-9 also discusses the circumstances in which goodwill recorded in an acquisition of a banking or thrift institution can be amortized by accelerated methods.

FASB-72 is applicable to the acquisition of a troubled banking or thrift institution, and specifically to that portion of goodwill that arises from the excess of the fair value of assumed liabilities over the fair value of acquired identifiable assets. In respect to this portion of goodwill, FASB-72 provides for a different method of amortization from that required by APB-17 (Intangible Assets). Although a shorter period of amortization is generally provided for the portion of goodwill covered by FASB-72, the amortization period can still be as much as 40 years. Any other goodwill that arises in the acquisition of a troubled banking or thrift institution is accounted for in accordance with existing GAAP.

FASB-72 also covers accounting and reporting for financial assistance that may be granted by a regulatory authority in connection with an enterprise's acquisition of a troubled banking or thrift institution.

FASB-72 is applicable to acquisitions of commercial banks, savings and loan associations, mutual savings banks, credit unions, and other similar depository institutions.

FASB-72 is an amendment and interpretation of APB-17 (Intangible Assets), an interpretation of APB-16 (Business Combinations), and an amendment of FASB Interpretation-9 (Applying APB Opinion Nos. 16 and 17 When a Savings and Loan Association or a Similar Institution Is Acquired in a Business Combination Accounted for by the Purchase Method).

> **OBSERVATION:** *A provision in a final rule regarding Delegated Merger Approvals, issued in 1985 by the Federal Home Loan Bank Board, states, "Where goodwill has been included in the resulting association's assets (as a consequence of a merger), the applicant must submit an opinion of a certified public accountant . . ." Apparently, an opinion must be submitted, satisfactory to the principal supervisory agent, that the goodwill's use and value are accounted for in accordance with generally accepted accounting principles. The effective date of the rule is December 23, 1985.*

Background

Certain economic and competitive conditions may adversely affect the financial position of savings and loan associations and mutual savings banks. High interest rates may erode profit margins, and as a result many financial institutions could report losses.

The long-term interest-bearing assets of banking and thrift institutions may produce significantly lower interest yields than that which can be earned under current market conditions. High cost of funds to a financial institution may exceed lower interest yields on long-term interest-bearing assets, which frequently produces operating losses.

When a troubled banking or thrift institution is acquired and accounted for by the purchase method, the excess of the fair value of the liabilities assumed over the fair value of the individual identifiable assets acquired is accounted for as goodwill (FASB-72). The amount of goodwill recorded by the purchaser is very likely to approximate the discount on the acquired long-term interest-bearing assets.

Under existing GAAP (APB-17, Intangible Assets), goodwill must be amortized over its estimated life, which may not exceed 40 years. In addition, APB-17 requires that the straight-line method be used for amortizing goodwill, unless another systematic and rational method can be justified.

The FASB concluded that goodwill arising in the acquisition of a troubled banking institution should be amortized over a relatively short period because of the uncertainty about the nature and extent of the estimated future benefits related to the goodwill (paragraph 32 of FASB-72). Some of the factors that support this conclusion are:

1. Goodwill has always been related to the excess future profits a business is likely to earn. It is extremely difficult to justify goodwill in the acquisition of a troubled banking institution which has been incurring large losses.

2. FASB Statement of Financial Concepts No. 3 defines an asset as a probable future economic benefit obtained or controlled by an entity as a result of a past transaction or event. It is extremely doubtful whether goodwill resulting from the acquisition of a troubled banking institution can be properly classified as a *probable future economic benefit.*

OBSERVATION: *The above factors could lead to the conclusion that any goodwill arising in the acquisition of a troubled banking institution should be written off to expense at the time of acquisition. The FASB prefers a special amortization period and method as a middle ground between the two extremes of (a) complete write-off immediately upon acquisition and (b) 40-year amortization as provided by APB-17.*

> *The solution adopted in FASB-72 is characterized by the Board as "a rapid and pragmatic resolution of the problem" (paragraph 31).*

Since goodwill is usually related to future excess profits and profitable operations, a more palatable method of accounting for the goodwill which arises in the acquisition of a troubled banking or thrift institution may be to treat it as a *preacquisition contingency* (FASB-38).

FASB-38 requires that a portion of the total acquisition cost under the purchase method be allocated to contingent assets, liabilities, and impairments. If it is *probable* that the contingent item existed at the consummation date of the combination and the amount of the contingent item can be *reasonably estimated*, FASB-38 requires that it be recognized.

Paragraphs 5 and 6 of FASB-72 are applicable only to acquisitions of banking and thrift institutions in which the fair value of the liabilities assumed exceeds the fair value of all identifiable assets acquired. Paragraphs 5 and 6 provide for a different amortization method for goodwill from the method that is permitted under APB-17. The provisions of paragraphs 4, 7, and 8 through 11 apply to all acquisitions of banking or thrift institutions. Although FASB-72 does not specify, apparently paragraphs 12, 13, 14, and 15 of FASB-72 also apply to all acquisitions of banking and thrift institutions.

Net-Spread Method and Separate-Valuation Method

The two methods available to record the acquisition of a savings and loan association are the net-spread method and the separate-valuation method. Under the net-spread method, the spread between interest paid on deposits and interest received on mortgages is used to evaluate whether the difference is normal, subnormal, or above normal for a particular market area. If the spread is normal, the principal assets and liabilities that are being acquired are recorded at the carrying amounts shown on the financial statements of the association being acquired. If the spread is subnormal or above normal, an adjustment is made to compensate for the difference. In other words, the acquisition is viewed as the purchase of an entire business and not of separate individual assets. The net-spread method is not acceptable for the purposes of GAAP.

The separate-valuation method is based on recording the acquired identifiable assets at fair value at the date of purchase (APB-16), which is the usual method called for by GAAP. Any difference between the fair value of assets acquired less liabilities assumed is recorded as purchased goodwill.

Fair value of assets is influenced by the ability of the assets to generate future income and/or new business within the territory served. Therefore, if the amount paid for the assets to generate future income or new business can be reliably determined, it shall not be recorded as goodwill, but recorded as a separate identifiable intangible asset and amortized over its estimated life. Any portion of the purchase price that cannot be specifically allocated to identifiable tangible or intangible assets shall be recorded as goodwill (FASB Interpretation-9).

Goodwill recorded in an acquisition of a savings and loan association may be amortized by accelerated methods (contrary to the general rule) if both of the following circumstances exist:

1. Included in goodwill is an indeterminable amount for the acquired assets to generate future income or new business, but these factors cannot be separately valued.
2. The expected benefits from such factors are expected to decline over their useful lives.

Acquisitions of Troubled Banking Institutions

At the date of acquisition of a banking or thrift institution, the excess of the fair value of liabilities assumed over the fair value of the acquired identifiable assets should be classified as goodwill (FASB-72).

> **OBSERVATION:** *Under the purchase method of accounting for a business combination, goodwill is the difference between the cost of the acquisition and the fair value of the net assets acquired. However, FASB-72 does not necessarily apply to the amount of goodwill computed in this manner. FASB-72 applies only to the excess of the fair value of the liabilities assumed over the fair value of the identifiable tangible and intangible asset acquired.*

Allocating the cost of an acquisition Independent appraisals and/or subsequent sales of acquired assets may provide evidence of fair value (APB-16). Each identifiable tangible and intangible asset acquired is assigned a portion of the acquisition cost, equal to its fair value at the date of acquisition (APB-16). The fair value of a long-term interest-bearing asset is the present value of the amount that will be received, less an allowance for uncollectible accounts (APB-16). The fair value of an assumed liability is its present value at the prevailing interest rates at the date of acquisition (APB-16). A portion of the total acquisition cost must be allocated to contingent assets, contingent liabilities, and contingent impairments of assets, if any, provided that the following conditions are met:

1. It is probable that the contingent item existed at the consummation date of the business combination accounted for by the purchase method.
2. After the consummation date, but prior to the end of the *allocation period*, the facts in item 1 above are confirmed.
3. The amount of the asset, liability, or impairment can be reasonably estimated.

If the above conditions are met, the purchase method requires that a portion of the total cost of acquiring a banking institution must be allocated to any contingent items (FASB-38). The allocation period is the period that is required by the purchaser to identify and quantify the acquired assets and assumed liabilities for the purposes of allocating the total cost of the acquisition in accordance with APB-16. The allocation period usually will not exceed one year from the closing date of the purchase transaction (FASB-38).

Identifiable intangible assets   Identifiable assets include intangible assets which can be identified and named, including contracts, patents, franchises, customer and supplier lists, and favorable leases, at appraised values (APB-16). Identifiable intangible assets of a banking or thrift institution may include existing depositor or borrower relationships, such as the capacity of existing savings and loan accounts to generate future income and/or additional business or new business (FASB Interpretation-9). The fair value of these types of identifiable intangible assets must be reliably determined on the basis of existing facts at the date of acquisition without regard to future events (FASB-72). If an acquisition of a banking or thrift institution includes any of these types of identifiable intangible assets which can be reliably determined, a portion of the cost of the acquisition should be assigned to such assets and amortized over their estimated useful lives, in accordance with APB-17.

Maximum amortization period   The amount of goodwill and the related periodic amortization, computed in accordance with FASB-72, should be calculated at the date of acquisition. The periodic amortization expense should not be adjusted in subsequent periods, except as provided by FASB-72 (see below). The maximum period of amortization should not exceed the lesser of 40 years or the estimated remaining life of the long-term interest-bearing assets with maturities in excess of one year, if any, which were acquired in the transaction. If a significant amount of long-term interest-bearing assets with maturities of over one year is not acquired as part of the acquisition, goodwill should be amortized over the estimated average remaining life of the acquired existing customer deposit base.

Method of amortization   Amortization must be calculated by the use of a constant percentage rate applied to the carrying amount of the long-term interest-bearing assets, which is expected to be outstanding at the beginning of each period. The carrying amount that is expected to be outstanding at the beginning of each period should be determined by reference to the terms of the long-term interest-bearing assets. If any prepayment assumptions are used to calculate the fair value of the acquired long-term interest-bearing assets at the date of acquisition, the same prepayment assumptions must be used to determine the expected carrying amount of long-term interest-bearing assets that will be outstanding in each subsequent period.

> **OBSERVATION:** *The carrying amount of long-term interest-bearing assets is equal to their face amount, increased or decreased by any related unamortized premium or discount (FASB-72).*

Subsequent revision of amortization   In periods subsequent to the date of acquisition, an enterprise must continually evaluate the remaining periods of amortization of its unamortized intangible assets to determine whether revision of such amortization periods is necessary (APB-17, paragraph 31). If the remaining amortization period is revised, the unamortized cost of the intangible asset must be allocated to the revised period. However, the total amortization period for an intangible asset can never exceed 40 years from the date of its acquisition. New estimates of value and future benefits may indicate the necessity of reducing significantly the carrying amount of an unamortized intangible asset (APB-17, paragraph 31). Under these circumstances, a charge to net income is made in the year in which the reduction is indicated by the new estimates.

If a significant portion of a segment or separable group of the operating assets of an acquired banking or thrift institution is subsequently sold or otherwise disposed of, a proportionate amount of the unamortized goodwill must be allocated and charged to the cost of the sale (FASB-72). The loss of a significant and valuable customer base of an acquired banking or thrift institution may result from the sale or liquidation of a major portion of the acquired long-term interest-bearing assets, if such assets are not replaced with similar assets. If the estimated value or benefits of the related unamortized goodwill are significantly reduced as a result of such a sale or liquidation, the reduction must be recognized as a charge to income in the year of sale or liquidation.

The amount of goodwill which results from the application of FASB-72 may not be revised upward under any circumstances (FASB-72).

> **OBSERVATION:** *If there is a permanent impairment in the value of an unamortized intangible asset, its carrying amount should be reduced to net realizable value by a charge to income in the year in which the impairment is discovered.*

Additional goodwill   In the acquisition of a banking or thrift institution, the amount of goodwill may exceed the difference between the fair value of the liabilities assumed and the fair value of the assets acquired. In this event, additional goodwill is recognized and accounted for in accordance with the provisions of APB-17.

Accounting for Regulatory Assistance

In connection with the acquisition of a banking or thrift institution, an enterprise may receive financial assistance from a regulatory agency such as the Federal Deposit Insurance Corporation (FDIC) or the Federal Savings and Loan Insurance Corporation (FSLIC). The financial assistance may be immediate, or may be granted in periods subsequent to the date of acquisition of the banking or thrift institution. In addition, as part of the financial assistance, assets and/or liabilities may be transferred to the regulatory agency.

Additional interest   A regulatory agency often provides periodic financial assistance which is approximately equal to the difference between the average yield on the long-term interest-bearing assets acquired in the acquisition and the current interest cost of carrying such assets. Under FASB-72, the computation of this type of financial assistance is made at the date of acquisition and is based on the difference between the average yield on the long-term interest-bearing assets and the current interest cost of carrying such assets. The amount thus computed is treated as additional interest on the long-term interest-bearing assets. The additional interest is included in determining the present value (fair value) of the long-term interest-bearing assets at the date of acquisition. The additional interest is reported in income of the period in which it is accrued. No other adjustment shall be made in the carrying amount of the long-term interest-bearing assets for subsequent changes in the estimated amount of financial assistance.

Long-term interest-bearing assets that the acquiring enterprise intends to sell must be reported at an amount which does not exceed the current market value of such assets.

Other types of financial assistance   Under FASB-72, other types of financial assistance granted by a regulatory agency must be accounted for as part of the combination if (a) the assistance is probable and (b) the amount of assistance can be reasonably estimated. Thus, under the purchase method, assets that are, or will be, received as a result of regulatory financial assistance must be assigned a portion of the total acquisition cost of the banking or thrift institution.

> **OBSERVATION:** *FASB-72 does not cover a situation in which the amount of financial assistance by a regulatory agency exceeds the amount of goodwill that would otherwise be recorded in the transaction. In this event, the fair value of the assets acquired will exceed the fair value of the liabilities assumed. Under the purchase method, the excess of acquired assets over assumed liabilities shall be accounted for as* **negative goodwill.** *Under APB-16 (Business Combinations), negative goodwill is not recorded unless the fair values of the noncurrent assets acquired, if any, except long-term investments in marketable securities, are proportionately reduced to zero. If a credit still remains after the noncurrent assets have been reduced to zero, the credit should be classified as a deferred credit and amortized to income over the period that is expected to benefit, but not to exceed 40 years (APB-17).*

Transfer of assets or liabilities   Assets and/or liabilities may be transferred to a regulatory agency as part of the plan of financial assistance. In this event, the fair value of the assets and/or liabilities that are transferred to the regulatory agency shall be excluded from the fair market value of the assets and liabilities acquired in the transaction.

Financial assistance after date of acquisition   Financial assistance may not be recognized at any time, unless (a) it is probable and (b) the amount of assistance can be reasonably estimated. Financial assistance may become probable and the amount reasonably estimable after the date of acquisition of the banking or thrift institution. In this event, the financial assistance must be recognized in the financial statements of the period(s) in which it becomes probable and the amount reasonably estimable. When this occurs, the financial assistance must be reported as a reduction of the balance of the unamortized goodwill; and amortization for subsequent periods must be adjusted proportionately.

> **OBSERVATION:** *All types of regulatory financial assistance, except assistance in the form of additional interest, must be **probable** and the amount **reasonably estimable** before such assistance is recognized and reported in the financial statements of an enterprise (FASB-72). This leads to the conclusion that financial assistance in the form of additional interest is recognized in accordance with existing GAAP and that all other types of financial assistance are recognized only if they are probable and the amounts are reasonably estimable.*
>
> *Under existing GAAP, the accounting recognition of financial assistance depends on the substance of the transaction or the contractual agreement between the parties. Thus, financial assistance may represent (a) a bona fide receivable, (b) a gain contingency, or (c) a contingent asset. A bona fide receivable is recognized when an exchange takes place, collection of the amount is reasonably assured, and the earning process is complete (APB Statement-4). A gain contingency should not be recognized prior to its realization, and financial disclosure is necessary (FASB-5). Under the purchase method of accounting, a contingent asset is allocated a portion of the total acquisition cost if certain conditions are met (FASB-38).*
>
> *Most technicians will likely agree that the concepts of **probable** and **reasonably estimable** are already embodied in the recognition principles of existing GAAP.*

Repayment of financial assistance   An enterprise may agree to repay, based on the attainment of future profitability levels, all or part of the financial assistance granted by a regulatory agency. Repayment of financial assistance must be recognized as a liability and a charge to income of the period in which the repayment is probable and the amounts can be reasonably estimated, in accordance with FASB-5 (Accounting for Contingencies).

Disclosure of financial assistance The nature and amount of financial assistance received by an enterprise from a regulatory agency in connection with the acquisition of a banking or thrift institution must be disclosed in the financial statements.

Effective Date

FASB-72 is effective for business combinations initiated on or after October 1, 1982, and earlier application is encouraged. Retroactive application of the provisions of FASB-72 to business combinations initiated prior to October 1, 1982, is permitted but not required.

If financial statements issued prior to March 1, 1983, omit the application of FASB-72 to business combinations initiated and consummated after September 30, 1982, and prior to March 1, 1983, the financial statements in subsequent periods must be restated; or, if not restated, the retained earnings for the subsequent period must be appropriately adjusted.

> **OBSERVATION:** *The initiation date of a business combination involving a **mutual** banking or thrift institution is the date on which notification is given to the board of directors or to the owners. The initiation date of a business combination involving other types of entities is the earlier of:*
>
> a. *The date of public announcement, or notification to the shareholders of any one of the combining companies, of the major terms of the plan, including the ratio of exchange or a formula which provides for the ratio of exchange, or*
>
> b. *The data on which shareholders of the company being acquired are notified directly or by newspaper advertisement of the exchange offer (APB Interpretation of APB-16).*

Loan and commitment fees Loan origination and commitment fees and direct loan origination costs shall be accounted for as prescribed in FASB-91 (Accounting for Nonrefundable Fees and Costs Associated with Originating or Acquiring Loans and Initial Direct Costs of Leases). (**Note:** A full discussion of FASB-91 can be found in the chapter entitled "Mortgage Banking Industry.")

Entertainment Industry

BROADCASTERS

Overview

FASB-63 (Financial Reporting by Broadcasters) contains the specialized accounting and reporting principles and practices that were originally published in the AICPA Statement of Position 75-5 (Accounting Practices in the Broadcasting Industry).

FASB-63 defines a *broadcaster* as an entity that transmits radio or television program material. Program material acquired by a license agreement should be accounted for as a *purchase of rights* by a broadcaster (licensee), provided that certain conditions are met.

A significant change from the specialized accounting principles in SOP 75-5 has been made in FASB-63 concerning the application of APB-21 (Interest on Receivables and Payables) to license agreements for program material rights of broadcasters. Under SOP 75-5, the licensor and licensee were required to apply the provisions of APB-21 to license agreements for program material rights. Under FASB-63, the application of APB-21 is optional.

Background

A broadcasting station may be completely independent or may be affiliated with a network. Independent broadcasters must purchase or otherwise provide for all of their programming, while a network affiliated broadcaster obtains much of its programming from its affiliated network.

Revenues of broadcasters arise from the sale of advertising time. Independent broadcasters must sell all of their advertising time, whereas much of an affiliated broadcaster's advertising time is sold by the network. When the broadcaster airs the sponsor's advertising, revenue is recognized. Network affiliated broadcasters receive revenue from their affiliated networks on a monthly basis. The revenue is based on a formula, and the networks submit weekly reports of revenue to their affiliates.

Advertising rates are usually based on the size of the estimated audience reached by the broadcaster and the quality of the station's programming. Rates vary significantly from market to market. Local and regional rates are generally less than national advertising rates. Rate cards that contain the advertising rates of a broadcaster are determined during rating periods in which the size and demographics of the broadcaster's audience are measured along with the quality of the broadcaster's programming. Rate cards are usually broken down into broadcasting time periods and are revised on a regular basis.

A broadcaster may exchange advertising time for services or products. Such barter transactions should not conflict with a broadcaster's regular advertising business.

Programming costs are usually the largest expense of television broadcasters. Independent broadcasters must obtain all of their programming, while network affiliated broadcasters obtain much of their programming from their affiliated networks. Programming costs are generally higher for independent broadcasters than they are for network affiliated broadcasters. Program material for television broadcasters is purchased under television licenses from producers and distributors. These producers and distributors generally package several films and license the broadcaster for one or more exhibitions or for a specified period, at which time the license expires. The license agreement usually provides for installment payments over a period which is almost always less than the license period. Thus, the producer or distributor receives all of its money for the license prior to the expiration of the license.

Many television broadcasters produce some of their programming material either live or on videotape. Local news broadcasts and local interview shows are popular programs produced by television broadcasters.

Television and radio broadcasters are regulated by the Federal Communications Commission (FCC). Broadcasters are licensed periodically to use frequencies in a specific area which are assigned by the FCC. In licensing a broadcaster, the FCC may consider the (1) financial position of the broadcaster, (2) advertising policies, (3) quality of the programming, and (4) contribution made to the community in which the broadcaster operates. Advertising rates are not regulated by the FCC, but guidelines have been established for advertising rates by the National Association of Broadcasters.

The major assets of a broadcaster are its FCC license and its network affiliation. Thus, network affiliated broadcasters are usually more valuable than independent broadcasters.

FASB-63 covers three specific aspects of the broadcasting industry: (a) program material license agreements, (b) barter transactions, and (c) intangible assets.

Program Material License Agreements

FASB-63 requires that broadcasters record the assets and liabilities that are involved in a program material license agreement as a purchase of a right or group of rights. The license agreement shall be reported in the financial statements of the licensee when the license period begins and all of the following conditions are met:

1. The cost of each license fee for each program is known or is reasonably determinable.
2. The broadcaster has accepted the program material in accordance with the terms of the license agreement.
3. The licensor can deliver the program material rights, and the broadcaster can exercise the rights. Availability of the program material rights exists when they can be shown or telecast by the licensee for the first time under a licensing agreement, regardless of restrictions on the timing of subsequent showings or telecasts.

FASB-63 requires that the balance sheet of broadcasters be classified. Thus, assets and liabilities shall be classified as current or noncurrent based on the normal operating cycle of the enterprise.

> **OBSERVATION:** *SOP 75-5 (Accounting Practices in the Broadcasting Industry) specifies that one year should be used as the normal operating cycle in the broadcasting industry. Thus, program material rights should be classified as current if they are expected to be used within one year. Liabilities should be classified as current if they are expected to be paid within one year.*

The asset and liability that arise from the purchase of program material rights shall be reported by the licensee or licensor at either (a) the gross amount of the liability or (b) the present value of the liability computed in accordance with APB-21 (Interest on Receivables and Payables). Under the provisions of APB-21, the present value of the liability (over one year) is reported as an asset, and the difference between the present value and the face amount of the liability is reported as deferred interest expense. The deferred interest expense is amortized to income in proportion to the payments made on the liability.

> **OBSERVATION:** *The thrust of APB-21 is to require the imputation of interest on liabilities (over one year) that bear an unreasonable rate of interest or no interest at all. Thus, if a reasonable rate of interest is charged on a liability, the provisions of APB-21 would not apply and the liability would be recorded at its gross amount. In addition, APB-21 does not apply to receivables or payables with terms of less than one year.*
>
> *APB-21 was based on the pervasive principle of **substance over form**. Allowing the licensee or licensor to report the liability or receivable either **gross** or at **present value** is equivalent to permitting the licensee or licensor to report either the **substance** or the **form** of the transaction.*
>
> *In addition, FASB-63 represents an amendment of APB-21, in that it provides an exemption from compliance with APB-21 for receivables and payables arising from licensing agreements involving program material rights.*

Amortization of program material rights shall be computed on the estimated number of times that the program will be aired by the broadcaster. An accelerated method of amortization must be used when the first broadcast of a program is more valuable than its reruns, which is usually the case. Thus, the straight-line method of amortization shall be used only when each broadcast is expected to produce approximately the same amount of revenue.

Feature programs shall be amortized on an individual basis. However, series programs shall be amortized on a series basis. Program rights purchased for unlimited broadcasts shall be amortized over the term of the license agreement. The cost of rights to a package of programs shall be allocated to each program right in the package, based on the relative value of each program right to the broadcaster.

Unamortized program rights shall not exceed their net realizable value. In the event that program rights do exceed their net realizable value, they shall be written down to net realizable value by a charge to current income. Program rights shall be reported in the balance sheet at the lower of their unamortized cost or their estimated net realizable value.

Barter Transactions

FASB-63 requires that all barter transactions be recorded in accordance with existing GAAP (APB-29, Accounting for Nonmonetary Transactions). The transaction shall be reported at the time the broadcaster airs the commercial. If the services or products have not been received at the date the commercial is aired, a receivable shall be reported. On the other hand, if services or products are received before the date the commercial is aired, a liability shall be reported.

APB-29 requires that nonmonetary exchanges be accounted for at the fair value of the assets or services received or surrendered, whichever is more clearly evident. If fair value is indeterminable, the only valuation available may be the recorded book value of the nonmonetary assets exchanged. When barter revenue is significant, SOP 75-5 suggests that it be disclosed in the financial statements or footnotes thereto.

A broadcaster that is affiliated with a network does not usually record barter transactions consummated by the affiliated network. Compensation to the broadcaster, if any, on these types of barter transactions is usually included in the periodic report from the affiliated network.

Intangible Assets

FASB-63 requires that intangible assets in the broadcasting industry shall be accounted for in accordance with existing GAAP (APB-17, Intangible Assets). Thus, intangible assets in the broadcasting industry must be amortized by the straight-line method over a period not to exceed 40 years.

If a network affiliation is terminated, any unamortized network affiliation costs shall be charged to expense unless a replacement agreement exists. In this event, if the fair value of the replacement agreement exceeds the unamortized network affiliation cost of the terminated agreement, no gain is recognized. However, if the fair value of the replacement agreement is less than the unamortized network affiliation cost of the terminated agreement, a loss is recognized to the extent of the difference.

Under the provisions of APB-17, a company shall record as assets the cost of intangible assets acquired from other enterprises or individuals. Costs of developing, maintaining, or restoring intangible assets that are not specifically identifiable, have indeterminate lives, or are inherent in a continuing business and related to an enterprise as a whole, such as goodwill, shall be deducted from income when incurred.

> **OBSERVATION:** *SOP 75-5 states that a change in network affiliation is not, by itself, justification to support a change in the amortization method used by a broadcaster. FASB-63 is silent on this point.*

Disclosure and Effective Date

Unrecorded program material license agreements that have been executed and do not meet the criteria of FASB-63 must be disclosed in the notes to the financial statements.

> **OBSERVATION:** *FASB-63 is silent on the extent of footnote disclosure that is necessary for unrecorded license agreements that have been executed but do not meet the criteria of FASB-63. However, it appears that the provisions of FASB-47 (Disclosure of Long-Term Obligations) may apply to some unrecorded license agreements that have been executed. FASB-47 requires that unrecorded unconditional purchase obligations that (a) are substantially noncancellable, (b) are related to the costs of the specific goods or services in the contract, or are part of the financing arrangement for the facilities that will provide the specified goods or services in the contract, and (c) are for a remaining term in excess of one year must be disclosed by footnote in the purchaser's financial statements. The disclosures include:*
>
> 1. *A description of the nature and term of the obligation*
> 2. *The total determinable amount of unrecorded unconditional purchase obligations as of the latest balance sheet date, and the total determinable amount of unrecorded unconditional purchase obligations for each of the five years after the latest balance sheet date*
> 3. *A description of the nature of any variable component of the unrecorded unconditional purchase obligations*
> 4. *For each income statement presented, the amounts actually purchased under the unconditional purchase obligations*

FASB-63 is effective for fiscal years beginning on or after December 16, 1982, and earlier application is encouraged. Retroactive restatement of previously issued annual financial statements is permitted but not required. If retroactive restatement of previously issued annual financial statements presented for comparative purposes is not elected by an entity, the cumulative effect of the change to FASB-63 shall be included in net income of the year of change in accordance with the provisions of APB-20 (Accounting Changes). In this event, the effect of the change to FASB-63 on income before extraordinary items, net income, and related per share amounts shall be disclosed in the financial statements of the period in which the change occurs.

If retroactive restatement of all comparative financial statements presented is elected by an entity, the financial statements of the year of change shall disclose the nature of any restatement and its effects on income before extraordinary items, net income, and related per share amounts, for each year presented.

If it is impractical to retroactively restate all of the individual financial statements for the comparative years presented, the following procedure must be used:

1. The new accounting principle (FASB-63) is used in determining net income of the year of change (current period).

2. As many consecutive prior years' financial statements as practical (which are presented for comparative purposes) are then retroactively restated.

3. The cumulative effect of the change to FASB-63 is then computed for any remaining prior years.

4. The cumulative effect is then included in determining net income for the earliest year restated.

5. Financial statements present for years prior to the earliest year restated (which includes the cumulative effect) shall be presented for comparative purposes as they were originally reported.

OBSERVATION: *Simply put, an enterprise has a choice in reporting the effects of the accounting change arising from FASB-63. An enterprise may report the effects of the change by the* **cumulative effect method** *or by the* **retroactive restatement method.**

CABLE TELEVISION COMPANIES

Overview

FASB-51 (Financial Reporting by Cable Television Companies) contains the specialized accounting and reporting principles and practices that were originally published in the AICPA Statement of Position 79-2 (Accounting by Cable Television Companies).

Background

Cable television (CATV) systems are organized and built to provide uninterrupted program entertainment, usually not available on regular commercial television. The distribution of the television programs by a CATV system is usually made over coaxial cables or satellites to a defined area. A CATV system network may cover a small community or a major metropolitan area.

Ordinarily, a cable TV company obtains a franchise from a local governmental authority which permits the distribution of CATV programs in a specified area. The franchise agreement usually provides for payment of fees to the granting authority and contains, among other provisions, the maximum fees that the company can charge a subscriber. In addition, franchise agreements may include many provisions pertaining to the type and quality of service that must be provided, number of TV channels, type of construction, and duration of the franchise. If all of the terms of the franchise agreement are not met, the governmental authority may retain the right to terminate the contract with the cable TV company.

The operation of a CATV system begins with the purchase of program entertainment from a cable service company or a production company. Program entertainment is usually acquired on a long-term contract with one or more cable service companies. The transmission signals of the cable service company are picked up by the CATV system by microwave relay, antennas, or satellite, then amplified and distributed to subscribers via coaxial cables. The subscriber usually pays an initial hookup charge and thereafter, a monthly subscription fee.

The size of the franchise area and the density of the population will usually determine the construction period required to install a CATV system. However, the type of system being built may also affect the period of construction. For example, if the coaxial cables must be installed underground rather than on utility poles, the period of construction will likely take longer. The construction period is completed when all of the equipment used to receive transmissions (head-end equipment) is installed, all main (head-end) and distribution cables are in place, and most subscriber drops (installation hardware) are installed. The CATV system is *energized* when the first transmission is made to subscribers. It is not unusual to energize part of a CATV system before the entire system is built because large CATV systems are generally built in sections over several years. When this occurs, a *prematurity period* is established. A prematurity period begins when the first subscriber's revenue is earned and ends when construction of the system is completed or when the first major stage of construction is completed. The prematurity period will vary in direct relation to the size of the franchise and the density of the population.

The capital investment that is necessary, even for a small CATV system, is quite substantial. The acquisition of a franchise and the cost of the physical facilities are expensive, and the operating overhead during the construction period requires a great deal of working capital. Space on utility poles or underground ducts is usually leased from utility companies.

Generally accepted accounting principles which have been promulgated for commercial companies are also used in reporting on cable television companies. However, FASB-51 contains the specialized methods of applying existing GAAP to cable TV companies.

Initial Recording of Assets

In the construction of a cable TV company the *prematurity period* begins on the date that subscribers' revenue is earned and ends on the date that the construction of the CATV system is completed or when the first major stage of construction is completed. However, some cable TV companies have determined that the prematurity period begins on the date that subscribers' revenue is earned and ends on the date that a predetermined number of subscribers is reached.

The prematurity period must be determined by management prior to the recognition of any earned revenue from the first subscriber. Generally, the prematurity period will rarely exceed two years, except in large major market areas. FASB-51 contains a presumption that the prematurity period usually should not exceed two years. Unless very unusual circumstances arise, a prematurity period shall not be changed after it is established by management.

A clearly identifiable portion of a cable TV system which is in a prematurity period should be accounted for separately from the rest of the system. A clearly identifiable portion of a system is distinct from the rest of the system in that it meets most of the following conditions:

1. It is a separate franchise area or different geographic area.
2. It has separate equipment or facilities.
3. It has a separate construction period, break-even point, and/or separate accountability.
4. It has a separate budget and/or separate accountability.

FASB-51 distinguishes between capitalized costs attributable to the main cable television plant and other related capitalized costs of a fully operational system, such as the cost of leases on utility poles or underground ducts, leases on satellite or microwave installations, property taxes, and capitalized interest costs. FASB-51 requires that these other related capitalized costs of a fully operational system be amortized over the same period used to depreciate the main cable television plant.

All costs of constructing the physical facilities of a CATV system should be capitalized. However, during the prematurity period some subscribers are receiving service while construction continues on the system. Thus, during the prematurity period a distinction must be made between costs related to (1) the current period, (2) future periods, and (3) both current and future periods.

Costs related to current period   Selling, marketing, administrative expenses, and all costs related to current subscribers should be accounted for as period costs.

Costs related to future periods   During the prematurity period, all costs of constructing the physical facilities of the CATV system should continue to be capitalized.

Costs related to both current and future periods   Tangible and intangible costs which are incurred and capitalized or deferred during the prematurity period are related to both current and future periods. Capitalized costs of the main cable television plant and other related capitalized costs of a fully operational system (such as the cost of leases on utility poles or underground ducts, leases on satellite or microwave installations, property taxes, and capitalized interest costs) must be amortized or depreciated over their estimated useful lives or the life of the franchise, whichever is less. Thus, during the prematurity period a portion of these costs must be *matched* with current revenue from subscribers.

FASB-51 requires that during the prematurity period charges for capitalized costs, other than those of the main cable television plant, should be allocated to both current and future periods based on a fraction. The denominator of the fraction is the total expected subscribers at the end of the prematurity period; the numerator of the fraction is the estimated number of subscribers at the end of each month of the prematurity period. The fraction results in the amount of amortization which is charged to expense in the current period.

During the prematurity period, depreciation of the cost of the main cable television plant of the CATV system should also be allocated by the same fraction. However, instead of computing depreciation on the costs incurred to date, the total depreciable base of the main cable television plant is estimated, and the total amount of depreciation is determined by applying the depreciation method normally used by the company. After the total amount of depreciation is computed, the fraction described in the previous paragraph is applied to arrive at the amount of depreciation expense that should be charged to the current period.

Under the provisions of FASB-34 (Capitalization of Interest Cost) certain interest costs, if material, must be capitalized and added to the acquisition cost of assets that require a period of time to get ready for their intended use. The cost of assets to which capitalized interest should be allocated includes the cost of both those assets acquired for a company's own use and those acquired for sale in the ordinary course of business.

FASB-34 does not allow the capitalization of interest for (1) assets that are ready for their intended use or are actually being used in the earning activities of a business and (2) assets that are not being used in the earning activities of a business and that are not undergoing the activities required to get them ready for use.

The interest capitalization period commences with the first expenditure for the asset and continues through the acquisition period. Interest is not capitalized during delays or interruptions, other than brief, which occur during the acquisition or development stage of the qualifying asset. When the qualifying asset is substantially complete and ready for its intended use, the capitalization of interest ceases.

Total capitalized interest costs for any particular period may not exceed the total interest costs actually incurred by an enterprise during that particular period. In consolidated financial statements, this limitation on the total amount of interest costs which may be capitalized in a period should be applied on a consolidated basis.

Capitalized interest costs for a particular period are determined by applying an interest rate to the average amount of accumulated expenditures during the period for the qualifying asset. The interest rate paid on borrowings during a particular period should be used to determine the amount of interest costs which should be capitalized for the period. Where a qualifying asset is related to a specific new borrowing, the allocated interest cost is equal to the amount of interest incurred on the new borrowing. However, if the average accumulated expenditures outstanding for the period exceed the amount of the related specific new borrowing, interest cost should be computed on the excess. The interest rate that should be used on the excess is the weighted average interest rate for other borrowings of the company.

Thus, interest cost must be capitalized during the prematurity period on that portion of the CATV system which is undergoing activities to get it ready for its intended use and is not being used in the earning activities of the system.

Hookup Revenue and Franchise Costs

Hookup revenue should be included in current revenue, but only to the extent of direct selling costs. Direct selling costs include those costs which are incurred in obtaining and processing new subscribers. Hookup revenue in excess of direct selling costs should be deferred and amortized to revenue over the estimated average subscription period.

Initial hookup costs for subscribers should be capitalized, and subsequent disconnects and connects shall be charged to expense as incurred. The depreciation period for initial hookup costs for subscribers should not exceed the depreciation period of the main cable television plant.

Usually, a CATV company makes a formal franchise application to a local governmental unit to provide cable television service in its geographical area. The costs associated with any successful application may be significant and are accounted for in accordance with APB-17 (Intangible Assets). These successful franchise costs are capitalized and amortized to income over the lesser of their estimated useful life or the life of the franchise, but in no event longer than 40 years (APB-17). The straight-line method is used for amortization purposes unless a different method can be justified.

The costs associated with unsuccessful franchise applications and abandoned franchises are charged to expense in the period in which it is determined that they cannot benefit any future period.

Periodic Review of Recoverability

Capitalized assets not only benefit a future period, but their costs should be recoverable from expected future revenue. Thus, a periodic review of the capitalized costs of a cable TV company must be made to determine whether the costs are recoverable through future successful operations or future sale of the assets. Capitalized costs shall be written down to recoverable values by the use of a contra account. Thus, the asset account should be debited with all additions; and the contra account, when deducted from the asset account, will equal the recoverable value of the asset.

Effective Date

FASB-51 is effective for fiscal years beginning on or after December 16, 1981, and earlier application is allowed, but not required. In addition, FASB-51 states that its provisions may be, but are not required to be, applied retroactively. Thus, comparative financial statements presented for prior years may be, but are not required to be, restated. Actual historical subscriber data may be used for restatement purposes if estimates of subscribers are not available.

MOTION PICTURE FILMS

Overview

FASB-53 contains the specialized accounting and reporting principles and practices that were originally published in the AICPA industry accounting guide entitled "Accounting for Motion Picture Films" and the AICPA Statement of Position 79-4 (Accounting for Motion Picture Films). The specialized accounting and reporting principles and practices are directed primarily to licensors of motion picture films. In addition, a licensor should account for a license agreement as a sale of a right or a group of rights.

FASB-53 indicates that the specialized accounting and reporting principles and practices were extracted from the AICPA publications without significant change.

Background

The exhibition rights to a film are usually licensed by the licensor who may be the original producer of the film or a distributor of the film. The rights licensed may be for one showing of the film or for multiple showings of the film over a specified period. Generally, only one first-run telecast of a film is licensed in a given market at a given time.

A film starts with the acquisition of a story property (book, stage play, original screenplay, etc.), goes through the various stages of film production, and is then distributed for exhibition. The production-to-distribution cycle can be as short as a few months and sometimes exceeds three years, depending on the nature and length of the film. Films can be produced for television or theaters, or eventually they can be exhibited in both media.

Revenue Recognition

Revenue for motion picture film rights is recognized in accordance with the basic realization principle embodied in GAAP. However, FASB-53 requires that certain events occur before revenue may be recognized. Revenue recognition from theatrical exhibitions is discussed separately from television exhibitions.

Theatrical exhibitions In larger markets, exhibition rights are sold on a percentage of box office receipts, sometimes with a nonrefundable guarantee. In smaller markets, the film rights are usually sold on a flat-fee basis. In foreign markets, nonrefundable guarantees are generally considered outright sales because additional revenues based on percentage of box office receipts are seldom, if ever, remitted to the licensor. This is particularly true in foreign markets where the licensor has no control over distribution. Thus, nonrefundable guarantees, which are essentially outright sales, should be recognized as revenue on the execution of a noncancellable agreement.

Under normal conditions, revenue should be recognized for percentage and flat-fee contracts on the date the film is exhibited by the licensee. Normal nonrefundable guarantees against a percentage of box office receipts should be deferred and recognized as revenue on the date of the exhibition of the film.

Television exhibitions Exhibition contracts of film rights for television usually provide for more than one exhibition over a specific period. In addition, most television contracts include a package of several films. These types of contracts expire on the date of the last authorized telecast, or on a specific date, if it occurs sooner. Payment for the contract is usually made in installments over a period which is shorter than that of the licensing agreement. Under FASB-53, revenue can be recognized on a television exhibition contract, when the license period begins and all of the following conditions are met:

1. The license fee for each film is known.
2. The cost of each film can be reasonably determined.
3. Collection of the full contract is reasonably assured.
4. The licensee has accepted the film in accordance with the conditions of the license agreement.
5. Availability of the film exists. The licensor can deliver the right and the licensee can exercise the right. Availability of the film exists when a film may be shown for the first time under a licensing agreement.

Revenue recognition should be postponed if an option or any other condition creates a doubt as to the ability or obligation of both parties to perform.

If a receivable from the sale of film rights extends over a long period and is either noninterest bearing or has an unreasonable rate of interest, the provisions of APB-21 (Interest on Receivables and Payables) should be applied. Thus, the present value of the long-term receivable will be recorded as a sale, and the difference between the present value and face amount of the receivable will be recorded as deferred interest income.

Costs and Expenses

The production costs of motion picture films usually consist of (1) costs for acquisition of story rights, (2) pre-production costs, (3) principal photography costs, and (4) post-production costs. Production costs are generally accounted for on a film-by-film basis. Production costs include all items that are required and necessary to complete a film. Production overhead is part of completing a film and should be allocated on a systematic and rational basis in accordance with GAAP.

Motion picture film talent is sometimes compensated, in part or all, by participation in the revenues produced by the film. A percentage amount from all or from specific revenues or profits is the usual arrangement. The total participation is estimated and then amortized in the same manner as the amortization of production costs (see below).

A film may have a primary and secondary market. The first market in which the film is exhibited is the primary market and is probably the market for which the film was produced.

Amortization of production costs and other amortizable amounts should commence with the release of the film for exhibition purposes. FASB-53 recommends the *Individual Film Forecast Computation Method* for amortizing film production costs. This method amortizes the costs in the same ratio that current revenues bear to total estimated gross revenues. The computation is similar to the percentage-of-completion method used in long-term construction-type contracts. The following formula does not appear in FASB-53 but may be used:

$$\frac{\text{Total Revenue to Date}}{\text{Total Estimated Gross Revenues}} \times \frac{\text{Total}}{\text{Amortizable}} - \frac{\text{Prior Period}}{\text{Amortization}} = \frac{\text{Current}}{\text{Amortization}}$$

Care must be exercised in determining the *total estimated gross revenues* because long-term non-interest bearing revenues can be included only to the extent of their present values (APB-21). Thus, the difference between the present value of the estimated long-term gross revenue and its face amount is recorded as deferred interest income at the inception of the contract. The *total revenues to date* in the fraction (numerator) must also exclude any interest income collected to date. In other words, both the numerator and denominator of the fraction do not include any imputed interest.

Periodic reviews should be made of the total estimated gross revenue, and appropriate revisions made when current information dictates. Revisions should be made prospectively as a change in accounting estimate (APB-20).

FASB-53 states that periodic table computations may be used to determine amortization providing that the results approximate those computed under the Individual Film Forecast Computation Method.

Inventory Adjustments

The inventory of motion picture films consists of the unamortized production and other properly capitalized costs. A periodic review must be made of each individual film to determine whether the total estimated gross revenues for the film are enough to recover the unamortized costs, talent participation percentages, and all direct distribution expenses. When total estimated gross revenues are insufficient, an inventory write-down to net realizable value is necessary.

If the estimate of future gross revenues for a particular film is subsequently increased during the same fiscal period in which the film was written down to net realizable value, the film may be written back up in an amount that does not exceed the current year write-down. Any film costs that have been reduced to net realizable value at the end of a fiscal period may not be written back up in subsequent fiscal periods.

It may become necessary to reduce unfinished and/or unreleased films to their net realizable value. This can occur in situations where the film costs have significantly exceeded budgeted costs, or where major downward revisions of estimated gross revenue are required because of existing circumstances.

The inventory of story costs (rights to books, stage plays, etc.) must be reviewed periodically to determine whether they will be used in the production of a motion picture film. Industry practices dictate that story costs held for more than three years, which have not been set for production of a film, should be charged off to current production overhead. After being charged off, story costs should not be reinstated even if they are set for production.

Loans and Interest Costs

Loans, guarantees, and advances by motion picture companies to independent producers should be recorded to reflect the substance of the transaction. Loans and/or advances to independent producers for the production of motion picture films should be recorded as film cost inventory by the motion picture film company. All other items of revenue and expense should be accounted for in accordance with the provisions of FASB-53.

> **OBSERVATION:** *Although the original AICPA industry accounting guide specifically covered the interest costs incurred in the production of a motion picture film, FASB-53 does not. However, FASB-34 (Capitalization of Interest Cost) does allow the capitalization of interest costs for qualifying assets which require a period of time to be completed for their intended use. The cost of assets to which capitalized interest may be allocated includes the cost of both those assets acquired for a company's own use and those acquired for sale in the ordinary course of business. Thus, interest costs may be capitalized in the production of motion picture films that qualify under the provision of FASB-34.*

Financial Statements

FASB-53 allows a motion picture company to use a classified or unclassified balance sheet for reporting purposes. Motion picture companies that segregate assets and liabilities between current and noncurrent classifications (classified balance sheet) should use the following guidelines:

1. Unamortized film inventory in release to a primary market; completed films not released, reduced by secondary market allocations, if any; and television films in production that are under contract for sale should all be classified as current assets.
2. Secondary market allocations of films which will not be realized within 12 months and all related film production costs should be classified as noncurrent.
3. Production costs that are allocated to secondary television markets should be classified as noncurrent. These costs should be amortized as revenues are recorded from secondary television markets. (**Note**: This treatment of production costs allocated to secondary television markets is expected to avoid

reclassification of items, back and forth, between current and noncurrent classifications.)
4. Liabilities should be recorded in accordance with existing GAAP. Thus, current liabilities are obligations whose liquidation is reasonably expected to require the use of current assets or the creation of other current liabilities (ARB-43).
5. From the time of execution to the time of revenue recognition, license agreements for the sale of television film rights are to be considered as executory and should not be reported on the balance sheet until revenues are recognized. Amounts received on such agreements should be reported as advance payments and be classified as current or noncurrent according to the circumstances.

Home Market

Motion picture films licensed for use at home on video cassettes, video disks, or through cable television should be accounted for in accordance with the provisions of FASB-53.

Disclosure and Effective Date

FASB-53 requires disclosure of film inventories, including films (1) released, (2) completed but not released, and (3) in process. In addition, the amount of story rights should also be disclosed.

> **OBSERVATION:** *The industry accounting guide entitled "Accounting for Motion Picture Films" required that accounting policies peculiar to the industry be disclosed in accordance with APB-22 (see the chapter entitled "Accounting Policies"); it also required that a description of the amortization methods of film costs used by a company be disclosed in accordance with APB-17 (Intangible Assets). Although FASB-53 does not mention these disclosures, it is apparent that they are still required by existing GAAP.*

FASB-53 is effective for fiscal years beginning after December 15, 1981, and earlier application is encouraged. In addition, FASB-53 encourages entities to apply its provisions retroactively. Thus, comparative financial statements presented for prior years may be restated.

RECORD AND MUSIC

Overview

FASB-50 (Financial Reporting in the Record and Music Industry) contains the specialized accounting and reporting principles and practices that were originally published in the AICPA Statement of Position 76-1 (Accounting Practices in the Record and Music Industry).

Background

Music publishers usually control the copyright on their music and most music publishers are frequently owned by an artist-composer. On the other hand, record companies must usually depend on an artist who is employed under a personal service contract to produce the record master that is used in manufacturing the ultimate product. As a general rule, the caliber and reputation of the recording artist has a direct effect on the success of any album or individual record.

The more successful recording artists are paid a nonrefundable advance against future royalties. Lesser known recording artists are not paid any advance and frequently must bear some of the cost of producing the record master.

A record master is produced by an expert sound engineer. Each instrument and voice is first recorded separately on magnetic tape. The sound engineer then combines each instrument and voice, emphasizing and deemphasizing as he deems appropriate. This process is called mixing and is probably the most important phase of manufacturing a record. The mixing process produces a record master, which is used to make acetate discs that are coated with metal. The metal coated disc is used to produce the mold that is eventually used to make the final product. Record masters are also utilized to produce tapes for the manufacturer of tape cartridges and cassettes. The following costs are usually incurred in the production of a record master:

a. Costs for the recording studio
b. Costs for engineers, mixing experts, directors, and other technical talent

   c. Costs for musicians, arrangers, vocal background, and other similar talent

   d. Costs for producing the record master itself

Music publishers usually license others, on a royalty basis, to use their music. Additional sources of income for music publishers include royalties from public performances, revenue from the music used in motion picture films, and revenue from the sale of sheet music.

Music publishers are usually members of ASCAP (American Society of Composers, Authors, and Publishers) or some other society or association. These organizations act as collection agencies for music publishers and composers by monitoring radio and TV stations and live performances. Copyright laws provide that each time that music is played publicly, the publisher and/or composer are entitled to a minimum royalty. By monitoring radio and TV stations and live performances, ASCAP collects the royalties due to various publishers and/or composers. After collecting the royalties, ASCAP makes periodic remittances to the publisher and/or composer.

One of the major accounting problems in the record and music industry is the timing of the recognition of a sale. This is because of the return privileges that manufacturers and distributors must make to their customers. In addition, some manufacturers create discounts by including a certain number of free records in proportion to the size of the order.

> **OBSERVATION:** *Accounting and reporting for revenue when a right of return exists is covered by FASB-48.*

Licensor Accounting

Owners of music copyrights or record masters usually enter into license agreements based on a minimum guarantee, which is generally paid in advance by the licensee. The licensor should record the receipt of a minimum license guarantee as deferred income (liability), which should be recognized as it is earned in accordance with the license agreement. If the license agreement is unclear as to when the guarantee is earned, the only alternative may be to recognize the guarantee over the term of the license agreement.

Fees that are not fixed in amount by the terms of the license agreement cannot be recognized as revenue by the licensor until a reasonable estimate can be made of such fees or the license agreement expires.

A license agreement must be examined carefully to determine whether an outright sale was consummated or a license was granted. An outright sale of specific rights must be distinguished from a minimum license agreement. When a licensee receives from the licensor a noncancelable contract for a specified fee granting specific rights to the licensee, who may use these rights at any time without restriction, an outright sale has been consummated. In this event, the earning process is complete and revenue should be recognized if collectibility of the balance of the fee, if any, is reasonably assured.

> **OBSERVATION:** *Promulgated GAAP prohibit accounting for revenue by any form of installment accounting except under exceptional circumstances where collectibility cannot be reasonably assured. In such cases, a company can use either the cost recovery method or the installment sales method of accounting (APB-10).*

Royalties paid to artists should be accounted for on the accrual basis of accounting. Thus, royalty advances should be recorded as prepaid royalties when evidence is available that such advances will be recouped from future earned royalties.

Future royalty guarantees and commitments, if material, should be disclosed in the financial statements.

The cost of a record master should be recorded as an asset if it is reasonably assured that such cost will be recovered from expected future revenue. The cost of a record master should be amortized to income in proportion to the net revenue that is expected to be realized.

Any portion of the cost of a record master which is recoverable from the artist should be accounted for appropriately. Any portion of the cost of a record master that is recorded as an asset shall be disclosed separately in the financial statements.

Licensee Accounting

As mentioned previously, license agreements are usually based on a minimum guarantee that is generally paid in advance to the licensor by the licensee. The licensee should record this minimum payment as a deferred charge. The deferred charge should be amortized to income over the periods that are benefited, which is usually the term of the license agreement.

The last sentence of paragraph 15 of FASB-50 requires that fees not fixed in amount by the terms of the license agreement before the agreement expires "shall be estimated and accrued on a license-by-license basis by the licensee."

Effective Date

FASB-50 is effective for fiscal years beginning on or after December 16, 1981, and earlier application is encouraged. The provisions of FASB-50 are to be applied retroactively. Thus, financial statements presented for prior periods shall be restated to reflect the provisions of FASB-50.

Franchise Fee Revenue

FRANCHISE FEE REVENUE

Overview

FASB-45 (Accounting for Franchise Fee Revenue) contains the specialized accounting and reporting principles and practices that were originally published in an AICPA industry accounting guide entitled "Accounting for Franchise Fee Revenue." This industry accounting guide was published in 1973 and is devoted solely to the accounting problems of the party granting the franchise (franchisor).

FASB-45 indicates that the specialized accounting and reporting principles and practices were extracted from the franchise fee revenue guide and that the FASB did not contemplate a comprehensive reconsideration of the accounting issues covered in the guide.

Background

In brief, a franchise agreement usually transfers certain rights (the franchise), which are owned by the franchisor, to a franchisee. The rights transferred for a specified period may include the use of patents, secret processes, trademarks, and trade names. Payment for the franchise rights may include an initial franchise fee and/or continuing fees or royalties. The agreement should also provide for any continuing services which are to be rendered by the franchisor, and any inventory or purchases which may be required of the franchisee. In addition, the franchise agreement should clearly set forth the procedure for cancellation, resale, or reacquisition of the franchise by the franchisor.

Conventional accounting practices and methods, including existing promulgated GAAP, should be used in accounting for franchise revenue. However, the timing and classification of franchise revenues and the association of franchise costs to related franchise revenues may create unique accounting problems.

Revenue Recognition—Individual Franchise Fees

The two major accounting problems in revenue recognition of initial franchise fees are (1) the time the fee is properly regarded as earned and (2) the assurance of collectibility of any receivable resulting from unpaid portions of the initial fee.

> **OBSERVATION**: *These accounting problems are not unique to franchise accounting and merely represent a rehash of the basic realization of revenue principle. The realization principle requires that revenue be earned before it is recorded. GAAP require that the realization of revenue be recognized in the accounting period in which the earning process is substantially completed and an exchange has taken place (APB Statement 4). In addition, revenue is usually recognized at the amount established by the parties to the exchange except for transactions in which collection of the receivable is not reasonably assured (APB Statement 4). In the event that collection of the receivable is not reasonably assured, the installment method or cost recovery method may be used (APB-10).*

FASB-45 requires that revenue on individual franchise fees be recognized on the consummation of the transaction, which occurs when all material conditions of the sale have been substantially performed. Substantial performance by the franchisor occurs when the following conditions are met:

1. The franchisor is not obligated in any way (trade practice, law, intent, or agreement) to excuse payment of any unpaid notes or to refund any cash already received.
2. The initial services required of the franchisor by contract or otherwise have been substantially performed.
3. All other conditions have been met which affect the consummation of the sale.

It is presumed that substantial performance does not usually occur prior to the commencement of operations by the franchisee. In other words, the earliest that substantial performance is presumed to occur under FASB-45 is when the franchisee actually commences operations of the franchise. However, this presumption may be overcome if the franchisor can demonstrate that substantial performance occurs at an earlier date.

Another accounting problem involved in the recognition of individual franchise fees is the collectibility of any receivable resulting from unpaid portions of the initial franchise fee. An adequate provision for estimated uncollectible amounts from individual franchise fees must be established, if necessary. If the collection of long-term receivables from individual franchise fees is not reasonably assured, the cost recovery or installment sale accounting methods should be used to recognize revenue.

Cost recovery method   The cost recovery method, also known as the sunk-cost theory, is used in situations where recovery of cost is undeterminable or extremely questionable. The procedure is simply that all cost is recovered before any gain is recognized. Once all cost has been recovered, any other collections are recognized as revenue. The only expenses remaining to be charged against such revenue are those relating to the collection process. For example, if a company sells for $100 an item that cost $40, and receives no down payment, the first $20 collected, regardless of the year collected, would be considered recovery of one-half the cost. The next $20 collected would be recovery of the balance of the cost, regardless of the year collected. The remaining $60 (all gross profit) would be recognized as income when received. The only additional expenses that could be charged against the remaining $60 would be those directly related to the collection process.

Installment sales method   Under the installment sales method of accounting, each payment collected consists of part recovery of cost and part recovery of gross profit, in the same ratio that these two elements existed in the original sale. For example, assume that a furniture dealer sells for $100 a chair that cost him $70. The gross profit percentage for this sale is 30%. The dealer would recognize 70% of any payment as a recovery of cost and 30% as realized gross profit.

Continuing franchise fees   In the event that the continuing franchise fees appear to be insufficient to cover the costs and reasonable profit of the franchisor for the continuing services required by the franchise agreement, a portion of the initial franchise fee, if any, should be deferred as appropriate and amortized over the term of the franchise. The amount deferred should be sufficient to cover all the costs of the continuing services plus a reasonable profit.

> **OBSERVATION:** *Apparently, FASB-45 assumes that continuing services required by the franchisor always coincide with the term of the franchise and amortization should be based on the term of the franchise. A more realistic approach would be to relate the amortization period to the period in which the continuing services will be provided by the franchisor, which may not necessarily be the entire term of the franchise.*
>
> *Also, it may be desirable to replace "reasonable profit" with "normal profit." Normal profit for a product, service, or industry, is more precise and determinable than a reasonable profit.*

Revenue Recognition—Area Franchise Fees

Revenue recognition from an area franchise is accounted for exactly the same as that for individual franchise fees. The only difference is that substantial performance of the franchisor may be more difficult to determine. The terms of the franchise agreement must be used to determine when substantial performance has occurred. In addition, it may be necessary to use the percentage-of-completion method of recognizing revenue in some franchise agreements. For example, an area franchise agreement may require the franchisor to provide specific initial services to any franchise opened in the area. In this event, the franchisor should reasonably estimate the number of franchises that are expected to be opened in the area and should recognize a portion of the total area franchise fee as a substantial performance occurs for each franchise in the area. Thus, it is necessary to determine the cost of servicing each individual franchise within the area and the total cost of all individual franchises that are expected to be opened in the area. The next step is to determine the percent of costs that have been substantially performed to the total costs of all individual franchises that are expected to be opened in the area. The resulting percent is applied to the total initial area franchise revenue to determine the amount of area franchise revenue that can be recognized.

> **OBSERVATION:** *The percentage-of-completion method of recognizing revenue should be used only in those situations in which costs can be reasonably estimated with some degree of reliability.*

Estimates of the number of franchises that are expected to be opened in an area franchise should be determined by reference to the significant terms and conditions of the franchise agreement.

If the franchisor's substantial performance under the terms of the franchise agreement is related to the area franchise, and not to the individual franchises within the area, revenue recognition occurs when all material services and conditions relating to the area franchise have been substantially performed. Thus, this type of area franchise is treated similarly to an individual franchise.

Any portion of the franchise revenue that is related to unperformed future services which may have to be refunded shall not be recognized by the franchisor until the right to refund has expired.

Franchisee and Franchisor—Unusual Relationships

Unusual relationships may exist between the franchisee and the franchisor, besides those created by the franchise agreement. The franchisor may guarantee debt of the franchisee, or contractually control the franchisee's operations to the extent that an affiliation exists. In all these circumstances, FASB-45 requires that all material services and conditions relating to the franchise be substantially performed by the franchisor before revenue is recognized.

> **OBSERVATION:** *The above requirements for unusual relationships between the franchisee and franchisor are no different than those for an individual or area franchise. That is, substantial performance must occur before the franchisor may recognize any revenue.*

> **OBSERVATION:** *The conclusions reached by FASB-45 relating to unusual relationships between the franchisee and franchisor are not in complete agreement with the conclusions reached in the industry accounting guide entitled "Accounting for Franchise Fee Revenue." The guide's conclusions are that "Revenue should not be recognized if these relationships overcome the concepts of revenue recognition referred to above." In other words, the guide's position is that if the unusual relationships overcome the concepts of recognizing revenue when substantial performance occurs, revenue should not be recognized. Thus, the substance of the franchise transaction must be viewed in the context of the unusual relationships between the franchisee and the franchisor before revenue can be recognized.*

According to FASB-45, the initial franchise fee shall be deferred if it is probable that the franchisor will acquire the franchise back from the franchisee because of an option, or other understanding. In this event, the deferred amount is accounted for as a reduction of the cost of reacquiring the franchise when the option or understanding is exercised.

Tangible Assets Included in the Franchise Fee

Besides the initial services of the franchisor, the initial franchise fee may include the sale of specific tangible property, such as inventory, signs, equipment, or real property. Thus, a portion of the initial franchise fee must be allocated to such tangible property. FASB-45 requires that the amount allocated shall be the fair value of the property. The fair value of the tangible property shall be recognized as revenue when title to such property passes to the franchisee, even though substantial performance has not occurred for other services included in the franchise agreement.

> **OBSERVATION:** *FASB-45 does not mention the date on which fair value of the tangible property must be determined. It is assumed that the fair value should be determined at the date of the franchise agreement, which ordinarily establishes the date of the sale.*

The franchise agreement may also allocate a portion of the initial franchise fee to specific services that the franchisor will provide. If the various services that the franchisor will provide are interrelated to the extent that objective segregation is impossible, FASB-45 prohibits the recognition or revenue for any specific service until all the services required under the franchise agreement have been substantially performed. However, if actual prices are available for a specific service, through recent sales of the specific service, FASB-45 does permit recognition of revenue based on substantial performance of the specific service. In other words, if the franchisor has established objective prices for specific service, a portion of the total franchise fee may be recognized on completion of substantial performance of the specific services.

Continuing Franchise Fees

Continuing franchise fees are consideration for the continuing rights granted by the franchise agreement and for general and specific services during the life of the franchise agreement. Continuing franchise fees are recognized as revenue when actually earned and receivable from the franchisee. This is true, even if the continuing franchise fee is designated for a specific purpose. However, if an agency relationship is established by the franchise agreement and a designated portion of the continuing franchise fee is required to be segregated for a specific purpose, the designated amounts shall be recorded as a liability. Any costs incurred for the specific purpose would be charged against the liability. All other costs relating to continuing franchise fees are expensed as incurred.

> **OBSERVATION:** *There is apparently a conflict between paragraphs 14 and 17 of FASB-45. Paragraph 14 (second sentence) indicates that all direct and indirect costs relating to continuing franchise fees be expensed as incurred. Paragraph 17 (first sentence) indicates that direct costs related to all franchise sales be deferred and recognized at the time that the related revenue is recognized.*
>
> *The industry accounting guide entitled "Accounting for Franchise Fee Revenue" (page 15) clearly indicates, in the first para-*

graph under Continuing Franchise Fees, that expenses related to such fees be recorded on the accrual basis. However, the third paragraph indicates that costs which are related to a portion of a continuing franchise fee that has been designated for a particular purpose should be expensed as they are incurred.

Continuing Product Sales

If the terms of the franchise agreement allow the franchisee to obtain equipment and supplies from the franchisor at bargain purchase prices, a portion of the initial franchise fee must be deferred. The portion of the initial franchise fee that must be deferred is either (1) the difference between the normal selling price of the equipment and supplies and the bargain purchase price or (2) an amount which will enable the franchisor to recover all costs and provide a normal profit. The deferred amount is accounted for as an adjustment of the initial franchise fee and an adjustment of the selling price of the bargain purchase items.

> **OBSERVATION:** *The sale of equipment and supplies by the franchisor at normal selling prices, which should include a reasonable profit for the franchisor, is accounted for at the time that the sale is complete. The amount of sale is found by reference to the franchise agreement, and the cost of the sale is the cost of the equipment or supplies to the franchisor. If it is apparent that the franchisor is not making a reasonable profit on the equipment or supplies, then the rules for "bargain purchases" must be followed.*

Agency Sales

Some franchise arrangements in substance establish an agency relationship between the franchisor and the franchisee. The franchisor acts as agent for the franchisee by reselling inventory, equipment, and supplies at no profit. In other words, the franchisor orders items for the franchisee and then resells the same items to the franchisee at no profit. FASB-45 requires that these transactions be accounted for on the franchisor's books as receivables and payables, and not as profit or loss items.

Matching of Revenue and Costs

Direct franchising costs should be matched to their related franchise revenue in accordance with the accrual basis of accounting. This may necessitate the deferral of direct costs incurred prior to revenue recognition and the accrual of direct costs, if any, not yet incurred through the date on which revenue is recognized.

Total direct costs that are deferred or accrued must not exceed their estimated related revenue.

Selling, general, administrative, and other indirect costs that occur on a regular basis regardless of the sales volume are required by FASB-45 to be expensed when incurred.

Repossessed Franchises

In repossessing a franchise, the franchisor may, or may not, refund the consideration previously paid by the franchisee. If a refund is paid by the franchisor, the accounting treatment is equivalent to a cancellation of the original sale. Any revenue previously recognized is treated as a reduction of the revenue of the current period in which the franchise is reacquired.

> **OBSERVATION:** *Since substantial performance is required before any revenue may be recognized, it is unlikely that a franchisor would grant a refund in the event that the revenue had already been recognized. Instead, it is more likely that the franchisor would enforce collection of any balance due rather than cancel the sale.*

If a refund is not paid by the franchisor, the transaction is not considered a cancellation of the sale and no adjustment is made to the previously recorded revenue. However, if a balance is still owed by the franchisee, it may be necessary to review the allowance for uncollectible amounts for the transaction. Also, any deferred revenue on the original sale should now be recognized in full.

Business Combinations

When a franchisor acquires the operations of one of its own franchises in an arm's length transaction, FASB-45 requires that the acquisition be accounted for in accordance with APB-16 (see the chapter entitled "Business Combinations").

Pooling-of-interests method   If the acquisition of one of its own franchises is accounted for as a pooling-of-interests, the financial statements of the two entities are combined as of the beginning of the year and all intercompany transactions are eliminated in the combined financial statements. Thus, the original sale of the franchise and any other sales of products or services do not appear on the combined financial statements. In addition, any prior years' financial statements which are presented would have to be retroactively restated to reflect the business combination.

Purchase method   If the acquisition of one of its own franchisees is accounted for as a purchase, the financial statements of the two entities are combined as of the date of the acquisition and no prior intercompany accounts are eliminated in the combined financial statements. In addition, details of the results of operations for each separate company prior to the date of combination that are included in the current combined net income, must be disclosed by footnote.

Disclosures

FASB-45 requires that the following disclosures be made in the financial statements or footnotes thereto:

1. The nature of all significant commitments and obligations of the franchisor, including a description of the services that have not been substantially performed
2. If the installment or cost recovery method is being used to account for franchise fee revenue, the following must be disclosed:
    a. The sales price of franchises being reported on the installment or cost recovery method
    b. The revenue and related deferred costs (currently and cumulative)
    c. The periods in which the franchise fees become payable
    d. The total revenue that was originally deferred because of uncertainties and then subsequently collected because the uncertainties were resolved
3. If significant, separate disclosure for (a) initial franchise fees and (b) other franchise fee revenue
4. Revenue and costs related to non-owned franchises, as opposed to franchises owned and operated by the franchisor.
5. If significant changes in the ownership of franchises occurs during the period, the following shall be disclosed:

a. The number of franchises sold during the period
b. The number of franchises purchased during the period
c. The number of franchised outlets in operation during the period
d. The number of franchisor-owned outlets in operation during the period

The following disclosures, while not required, are considered desirable:

1. A statement of whether initial franchise fee revenue will probably decline in the future because sales will reach a saturation point
2. If not apparent in the financial statements, the relative contribution to net income of initial franchise fee revenue

Effective Date

FASB-45 is effective for fiscal years beginning on or after June 16, 1981, and earlier application is encouraged. Financial statements presented for prior periods shall be restated to reflect the provisions of FASB-45.

Insurance Industry

INSURANCE ENTERPRISES

Overview

The following promulgated GAAP contain the current accounting and reporting standards for insurance enterprises:

- FASB-60, Accounting and Reporting by Insurance Enterprises
- FASB-61, Accounting for Title Plant
- FASB-91, Accounting for Nonrefundable Fees and Costs As sociated with Originating or Acquiring Loans and Initial Direct Costs of Leases
- FASB-97, Accounting and Reporting by Insurance Enterprises for Certain Long-Duration Contracts and for Realized Gains and Losses from the Sale of Investments
- FASB Technical Bulletin 84-3, Accounting for the Effects of the Tax Reform Act of 1984 on Deferred Income Taxes of Stock Life Insurance Enterprises

FASB-60 contains the specialized accounting and reporting principles and practices that were originally published in the following AICPA publications:

- Audits of Stock Life Insurance Companies
- Audits of Fire and Casualty Insurance Companies
- Statement of Position 79-3, Accounting for Investments of Stock Life Insurance Companies
- Statement of Position 80-1, Accounting for Title Insurance Companies

The provisions of FASB-60 cover general purpose financial statements for stock life insurance companies and property and liability insurance companies (stock and mutual), including reciprocal or interinsurance exchanges. Title insurance companies are also covered by FASB-60, with the exception of accounting for a *title plant*, which is covered by FASB-61. In addition, mortgage guaranty insurance companies are covered by FASB-60, except for premium revenue recognition, claim costs, and acquisition costs. Mutual life insurance companies, assessment enterprises, and fraternal benefit societies are expressly excluded from the provisions of FASB-60.

FASB-91 amended FASB-60 to establish accounting and reporting standards for nonrefundable fees and costs associated with lending, committing to lend, or purchasing a loan or group of loans. FASB-91 also specifies the appropriate accounting for fees and initial direct costs associated with leasing transactions.

The provisions of FASB-91 apply to all types of loans, including debt securities, and to all types of lenders, including banks, thrift institutions, insurance companies, mortgage bankers, and other financial and nonfinancial institutions. FASB-91 is discussed in detail in the chapter entitled "Mortgage Banking Industry."

FASB-97 amends FASB-60 to establish accounting and reporting standards for interest-sensitive and flexible premium long-duration insurance contracts, which include the popular type of insurance referred to as universal life and certain single premium annuity insurance contracts. Since these types of long-duration insurance contracts were developed in recent years, they were not addressed by the original GAAP for insurance enterprises.

FASB-97 also amends FASB-60 to specify that realized gains and losses of insurance enterprises be included as a component of *other income* on a pretax basis. Under FASB-97, realized gains and losses may not be deferred to future periods. Under FASB-60, realized gains and losses were reported net of taxes in a separate income statement caption after operating income.

FASB-97 does not establish accounting and reporting standards for limited-payment and universal life-type contracts that address (a) loss recognition (premium deficiency), (b) accounting for reinsurance, and (c) financial statement disclosure. The provisions of FASB-60 that apply to these specific items also apply to limited-payment and universal life-type contracts.

FASB Technical Bulletin 84-3 was issued to establish the appropriate accounting for the effects of the Tax Reform Act of 1984 on deferred income taxes of stock life insurance enterprises.

BACKGROUND

Property and Liability Insurance Companies

Property and liability companies are very similar to life insurance companies. The main difference is that property and liability insurance companies cover risks incurred on property or liability and life insurance companies cover risks involving the death or disability of the insured. Both types of insurance companies collect premiums and usually pay commissions to agents or sales personnel. In addition, both types of insurance companies have underwriting departments and use other insurance companies to spread excess or specialized risks (reinsurance).

A property and liability insurance company may be organized as (1) a stock company, (2) a mutual company, or (3) a reciprocal or interinsurance exchange.

Stock Company—A stock property and liability insurance company is owned by its stockholders and is organized as a corporation. Because of the corporate form, stockholders' liability is usually limited to the amount of their investment in capital stock.

Mutual Company—In a mutual property and liability insurance company the current policyholders are the owners at any given time and they share in the earnings and have the right to vote for the members of the board of directors. Upon liquidation of a mutual company, the current policyholders receive any remaining assets after payment of all liabilities. Most mutual companies issue nonassessable insurance policies that limit the liability of the policyholders in the event of bankruptcy or lack of capital.

Reciprocal or Interinsurance Exchange—A reciprocal insurance exchange is comprised of subscribers who sign subscribers' agreements. The subscribers' agreements provide, among other things, for an attorney-in-fact who has the power to underwrite insurance for the subscribers. However, each subscribers' liability is several and not joint. Thus, the liability of each subscriber is limited by the amount stated in the subscriber's agreement. Subscribers may be individuals, corporations, trusts, or partnerships. Compensation is paid to the attorney-in-fact based on either a percentage of premium income or some other appropriate method.

A property and liability insurance company may underwrite one line of insurance business, or it may be licensed to sell multiple lines of insurance. The lines of property and liability insurance are usually grouped as (1) fire and similar perils, (2) general liability, (3) marine perils, (4) automobile liability and property damage, (5) homeowners' insurance, (6) accident and health, (7) workmen's compensation, (8) fidelity, (9) theft, (10) glass, (11) surety, (12) boiler and equipment, and other miscellaneous commercial insurance.

From an economic standpoint, insurance is a method used to spread a specific risk among policyholders. The insurance company assumes the specific risk and charges a premium based on past loss experiences for the specific risk. The premiums collected by the insurance company are used to pay current losses and operational costs, and the balance is invested. Thus, the two main sources of income for a property and liability insurance company are (1) premiums and (2) investment income.

Insurable interest   An owner of an insurance contract must have an insurable interest in the subject matter of the policy in order for the contract to be valid. An insurable interest in life insurance need only exist at the time the policy is issued, while an insurable interest in property insurance must exist at the time of the loss.

An insurable interest is a test of financial relationship. A wife may insure the life of her husband, an employer the life of an employee, a creditor the life of his debtor, and a partner the life of his copartners. In life insurance the insurable interest must exist only at the time the policy is issued and if subsequently the relationship is broken (divorce of a marriage, dissolution of a partnership) the owner may still collect the benefits of the insurance contract.

A landlord may insure his property and a homeowner his home. However, in property insurance the insurable interest must exist at the time a loss is incurred. If a landlord sells his property, he has no further insurable interest and is not entitled to collect for any losses on the property sold.

Departmental functions   The departmental functions of a typical property and liability insurance company would usually consist of (1) an agency department, (2) an underwriting department, (3) a policy service department, and (4) an investment department.

The agency department is responsible for the marketing functions of the insurance company. Supervision and training of sales personnel, sales promotion, and other selling activities are handled by the agency department.

The underwriting department is responsible for evaluating the risks which are undertaken by the insurance company, and also controls the issuance of all policies. Premium rates are determined by past loss experiences for specific types of risks. In addition, the underwriting department determines all reinsurance arrangements.

The policy service department is responsible for bookkeeping activities, such as premium notices and collection, changes in address, beneficiary and similar changes, and the payment of loss claims.

The insurance company's investments are managed by the investment department.

Cash basis   Usually, insurance companies keep their general ledgers on a cash basis, because this is exactly how they do business. Another reason why the cash basis is used is that some reports required by regulatory agencies must be prepared on a cash basis, particularly details of income and expense. Assets that have been recorded on the books of an insurance company are called *ledger assets*. Assets that are not recorded on the books are called *nonledger assets*. Nonledger assets arise from the adjusting journal entries which are necessary to convert the cash basis trial balance to the accrual basis. Liabilities are referred to in the same manner, so those that are recorded on the books are called *ledger liabilities*, and those not recorded on the books are called *nonledger liabilities*.

Because insurance companies use the cash basis, very few liabilities are recorded, and consequently most liabilities are nonledger. An insurance company will have few nonledger assets because most of its assets arise from cash transactions.

When adjusting journal entries are made for workpapers to convert the cash basis trial balance to the accrual basis, they are not posted to the books. Therefore, the books of insurance companies are always on the cash basis. This procedure makes it necessary for the insurance company to keep certain other records, such as a *claims register*, so that information is available to adjust easily to the accrual basis. The claims register keeps track of claims pending, paid, negotiated, and rejected, while the cash basis trial balance reflects only the claims actually paid. The claims register is used to prepare some of the necessary adjusting journal entries for conversion to the accrual basis.

Reinsurance   All insurance companies theoretically have a maximum financial capacity or limit as to the amount of insurance they should underwrite. In addition, many insurance companies set their own limit on the amount of risk they are willing to undertake and, thus, the amount of insurance they will underwrite. However, even if an insurance company has reached its theoretical financial capacity or self-imposed limit, the company can still write additional business and utilize reinsurance to keep within its established limits. Reinsurance is the transfer of one or more policies from one insurance company (the ceding company) to another (the reinsurer). The reinsurer charges the ceding company a premium for the amount of risk it has assumed and agrees to pay its share of any losses. In practice, some insurance companies have entered into agreements with other insurance companies for automatic reinsurance. Automatic reinsurance means that a specific portion or percentage of the total business written by the ceding company is automatically reinsured by one or more insurance companies. On the other hand, *facultative reinsurance* means that the ceding company submits each individual risk or portion of risk to the reinsurer, who then has the choice of accepting or rejecting each individual risk.

Another form of reinsurance occurs when one insurance company sells all or part of its insurance in force to another insurance company. However, this form of reinsurance almost always includes the transfer of policy service responsibilities to the assuming company. Thus, the assuming company takes over the actual bookkeeping responsibilities, such as premium notices and collections. Frequently, a sale of insurance policies in force will require the approval of local regulatory agencies.

Regulation of the industry   Every state has statutory laws governing the insurance industry. The insurance department of each state is charged with the responsibility of making sure that insurance companies remain solvent and deal fairly with policyholders. In addition, most states require some sort of periodic uniform financial report from insurance companies. Insurance companies are also restricted as to the types of investments that they can make.

The National Association of Insurance Commissioners (NAIC) is an organization composed of the insurance commissioners from each state. The NAIC meets semi-annually and makes recommendations for new rules and procedures which are almost always adopted by all of the states. The NAIC is very concerned with financial reporting and auditing of insurance companies. The results have been the establishment of uniform annual reports and the development of an examiner's manual which is written in the form of an audit program for insurance companies.

Sales and personnel   Property and liability insurance companies obtain their business through (1) direct writing, (2) brokers, (3) local and regional agents, and (4) general agents. In obtaining its business through direct writing, an insurance company usually has salaried or commission sales personnel who do not have the power to bind the company on any insurance risks. The sales personnel who work directly for the company must submit all policies sold to a branch or home office for approval. Insurance brokers are usually independent agents who represent many insurance companies. Brokers can submit policies which they have sold to any insurance company they wish and the insurance company may accept or reject the broker's business as they see fit. Local and regional agents usually report to a branch or home office and are appointed on a nonexclusive territory basis. They are generally paid a commission based on a percentage of the premiums that they produce. General agents are also compensated on a percentage of the premiums that they produce. However, the percentage is almost always higher for a general agent than for any other type of insurance solicitor. General agents usually sign contracts with the insurance company and agree to maintain a sales force and promote the insurance company's business. In addition, a general agent agrees to pay its own expenses and often agrees to obtain subagents. In exchange, the insurance company usually grants an exclusive territory to the general agent.

Many property and liability insurance companies handle their own policy claims through salaried employees. These employees often investigate a claim and propose a settlement with the claimant. However, in most cases, settlements must be approved by the home office.

Another method used by insurance companies to investigate, adjust, and settle policy claims is through an adjustment bureau. Adjustment bureaus consist of several insurance companies which are all members of the adjustment bureau. The expenses of a bureau are paid by the members, usually based on the number of claims handled or the dollar value of the claims. The right of final approval of all settlements made by an adjustment bureau is usually exercised by the insurance company. Members are not obligated to use the bureau.

Independent insurance adjustors, who work on a fee basis, are another alternative an insurance company may use to investigate, adjust, and settle policy claims.

Most of the accounting and statistical data used by a property and liability insurance company appears in the *daily reports*. A daily report is a copy of a section of the insurance policy that was sold, and it contains practically all of the accounting and statistical data necessary to record the transaction. Copies of the daily reports are distributed to several departments at the home office of the insurance company. The underwriting department receives a copy of the daily report from which the correct premium for the policy is computed.

Stock Life Insurance Companies

The proceeds of a life insurance policy usually provide some degree of financial security to one or more beneficiaries named in the policy. Upon death of the insured, the insurance company pays the face amount of the policy, less any outstanding indebtedness, to the beneficiary. However, the proceeds of the insurance policy are not always paid in a lump sum at the time of death of the insured. Many different choices are available as to how the proceeds will be paid. For example, an election can be made by a policyholder to have the insurance company pay certain periodic amounts to the beneficiary, or to pay the proceeds when the beneficiary reaches a specified age. In this event, the proceeds are held by the insurance company and usually will earn interest. Almost any type of arrangement can be made with a life insurance company for the payment of a policy's proceeds.

An owner of an insurance contract must have an insurable interest in the subject matter of the policy in order for the contract to be valid. An insurable interest in life insurance need only exist at the time the policy is issued, while an insurable interest in casualty insurance must exist at the time of the loss.

From an economic standpoint, insurance is a method which is used to spread a specific risk among many individuals. The insurance company assumes the specific risk, such as death, and charges a premium based on actuarial calculations. In the case of death, mortality tables have been established which take into consideration the frequency of deaths among individuals in various age groups. The premiums collected by the insurance company are used to pay current benefits and costs, and the balance is invested to yield investment income. Theoretically, if an individual dies in the year that the mortality tables predict, the accumulated net premiums collected by the insurance company, plus the investment earned on the accumulated premiums, should be sufficient to pay the face amount of the policy and still leave a profit. These accumulated premiums and investment income are reflected on the balance sheet of an insurance company as *policy reserves*.

An annuity insurance policy is one that the insured does not have to die to collect. It is more like a fixed compulsory saving plan. The insured pays premiums for a stated period, after which the insurance company makes fixed payments to the insured either for a specified time or for the balance of the insured's life.

Accident and health insurance policies are issued on an individual or group basis. In these types of policies the insurance company pays for hospital and medical care, and sometimes for the loss of income during periods that the insured is incapacitated.

The important thing to remember is that revenues of an insurance company are usually derived from premiums and investment income.

The two most common types of insurance companies are (1) stock companies and (2) mutual companies. Stock companies are formed to earn profit for their shareholders. A stock life insurance company may issue participating and nonparticipating insurance policies.

Participating policyholders share in the earnings created by their policies. These earnings, if any, are returned to the participating policyholders in the form of dividends. Nonparticipating policyholders do not share in any earnings of the company.

As a general rule, mutual insurance companies issue only participating policies. Thus, all of the policyholders share in the earnings and all have the right to vote for the members of the board of directors.

The departments of a typical life insurance company would include (1) an agency department, (2) an underwriting department, (3) a policy service department, (4) an actuarial department, and (5) an investment department.

The agency department is responsible for the marketing functions of the insurance company. Supervision and training of sales personnel, sales promotion, and other selling activities are handled by the agency department.

The underwriting department is responsible for evaluating the risks which are undertaken by the insurance company and also controls the issuance of all policies.

Determining premium rates and calculating the dividends on participating policies are functions of the actuarial department. Long range planning and the calculation of the adequacy of policy reserves are also the responsibility of the actuarial department.

The policy service department is responsible for bookkeeping activities, such as premium notices and collection; changes in address, beneficiary and similar changes; and the payment of claims or benefits.

The insurance company's investments are managed by the investment department.

Generally, life insurance companies are exempt from registration under the Securities Exchange Act of 1934. However, many insurance companies have established holding companies, which are not considered life insurance companies and, thus, must be registered under the 1934 Act. In addition, some insurance companies have registered their shares under the 1934 Act so that the shares can be listed and traded on a national stock exchange. Public offerings of life insurance companies' stock must be registered under the Securities Act of 1933.

If an insurance company has registered under either of the securities acts, it must comply with annual and periodic reporting requirements and proxy solicitation rules.

An insurance company receives its revenues from premiums and investment income. Premium income may be derived directly from the owner of the policy or from reinsurance agreements with other insurance companies. Investment income is regulated by insurance statutes which set forth the types of investments that may be made.

Life insurance companies generally sell (1) life insurance, (2) annuity contracts, and (3) accident and health contracts. There are many different types of life insurance coverage. The more common are discussed below.

Whole-life policies   Benefits are paid upon death of the insured. Benefits are usually equal to the face amount of the policy, less loans or indebtedness owed to the insurance company. Whole-life policies usually accumulate a cash surrender value which increases as each year passes. The owner of the policy can usually borrow from the insurance company or a bank using the cash surrender value as collateral.

Premiums for whole-life insurance are generally level, that is, they are the same amount each year. They are payable annually, but more frequent payments can be made by payment of a small service fee. A whole-life policy can be paid in one lump-sum payment at the beginning of the policy term, but this is an exception, as most policies are paid either quarterly, semi-annually, or annually. A *straight-life* policy (also called *ordinary life*) requires that premiums be paid during the entire life of the insured. A limited-payment policy requires that premiums be paid over a specified period, which is usually ten, twenty, or thirty years. As a result, the premiums on a limited-payment policy are always higher than those of a straight-life policy, but the total cost of the policy is usually less.

Term insurance policies   Term insurance policies are issued for a specific period, and death benefits are paid only if the insured dies during the specified period. Benefits are usually equal to the face amount of the policy. Term insurance policies generally do not accumulate any cash surrender value, and thus, no loans can be made against them.

Term insurance policies are written for short periods, usually one to five years. However, in most cases the policyholder is granted the right to renew a term insurance policy up to a maximum age (60 or 65) without having to submit additional evidence of insurability. The term policy may also grant the right to the policyholder to convert the term insurance to whole-life or some other type of coverage.

Premiums for term insurance policies usually increase with the age of the insured. Payments must be made annually, but they may be made at interim periods during the year for an additional service charge.

Since term insurance does not usually accumulate any cash value, the premiums constitute payment for insurance protection only. Thus, most people feel that term insurance is best in those cases where protection is sought.

Besides individual term policies, an insurance company may issue group term life insurance policies. A group term policy insures a specific group of individuals under a single master contract, usually for one year. Premiums are calculated on the basis of the ages of the individuals in the group.

Endowment insurance policies   Endowment policies are issued for a specific time, called the *endowment period*, and have a maturity date on which the insured receives the face amount of the policy, less any indebtedness owed to the insurance company. However, if the insured dies during the endowment period, the insurance company pays the face amount, less any indebtedness, to the beneficiary of the policy. Thus, the insured has insurance protection during the endowment period and, if living at the maturity date, receives the face amount of the policy, less any indebtedness due to the insurance company. Endowment policies accumulate a cash value which increases with time. The cash value may be used as collateral for a loan.

Premiums for endowment policies can be on a single lump-sum payment or on a limited-payment basis, but are generally payable over the endowment period specified in the policy.

Basic insurance policies can be expanded by the use of riders which are attached to, and made part of, the insurance contract. A nonforfeiture rider can be attached to a policy which provides that in the event the policyholder fails to make a premium payment, the insurance company may use the cash value of the policy to make the premium payment. Another type of nonforfeiture rider provides for the entire policy to be converted to a term insurance policy in the event that a premium payment is not made on time. Thus, the policyholder is given extended protection instead of having the insurance protection lapse.

Still another type of common rider provides for the waiver of all premiums during periods of disability that the insured might experience. An accidental death benefit rider (double indemnity) provides that the insurance company will pay twice the face amount of the policy, if the insured dies by accidental means.

Obviously, each rider has its price, which increases the overall premium on the insurance policy.

In an annuity contract, the insurance company guarantees to pay a periodic sum of money to one or more annuitants over a specified period. The annuity can begin immediately or at some specified future date. Annuity contracts can be issued on an individual or group basis, and group annuities are often utilized to fulfill a company's pension plan obligations. Premiums for annuities are based on the amount of the periodic payment, the date the payments begin, and the age of the annuitant.

Straight-life annuity   Under a straight-life contract, the annuitant receives guaranteed periodic payments as long as he or she lives. No further payments are made by the insurance company after the date of death of the annuitant.

Life annuity—period certain   Life annuity—period certain is exactly the same as a straight-life annuity except that the insurance company agrees to make the guaranteed payments for a specified time. Thus, if the annuitant dies before the end of the specified time, the annuitant's beneficiary continues to receive the guaranteed payments until the specified time comes to an end.

Joint and survivorship annuity   A joint and survivorship contract involves two or more annuitants and provides for guaranteed periodic payments to any surviving annuitant.

Variable annuity   The periodic annuity payment from a variable annuity varies in accordance with investment experience. Investments for variable annuities are kept in a separate fund, and the amount of the periodic annuity is based on the performance of the investments. Variable annuities may or may not include a minimum death benefit during the accumulation period.

There are many types of accident and health insurance policies available today. However, most of the coverage is provided by group contracts. The more common types provide for reimbursement of medical expenses and for loss of income during periods of partial or total disability. Medical coverage is frequently broken down into hospital expenses and reimbursement for doctor bills. Health insurance policies almost always contain a *deductible clause,* which requires that the insured pay a stipulated amount of losses before coverage is effective.

Title Insurance Companies

The main business activity of a title insurance company is to issue title insurance policies. Title insurance provides protection against loss or damage that results from liens or defects in the ownership document to a parcel of real estate. Thus, if a buyer obtains title insurance on real estate that is being purchased and subsequently a loss is incurred because of a lien or defect in the title to the property, the title insurance company will pay any loss or damage. Generally, every mortgage lender will require a title insurance policy on the property being purchased before they will lend any funds as a mortgage.

A title insurance policy is very unique because the premiums are usually not refundable and the term of the policy is indefinite. However, the amount of title insurance and the date of title search are stated in the policy. Thus, any loss in excess of the amount of title insurance and any loss which occurs because of a lien or defect that did not exist up to the date of the title search will not be covered by the policy.

When an application for title insurance is received by the insurance company, a title search is made. A title search consists of reviewing and scrutinizing the chain of ownership of the property being insured up to the date of the title search. Some title searches may go back several hundred years. Each change of ownership is examined to make sure it was properly made and that no unpaid liens or defects exist against the title to the property. If a lien or defect is discovered, the title insurance policy is still usually issued but the discovered lien or defect is cited in the policy and not covered. In this event, the buyer may be able to cancel the purchase of the property or compel the seller to take care of the existing lien or defect. Most contracts for the sale of real property contain a provision to the effect that the property is being sold free of any liens and/or defects and that the buyer has a specified period to determine whether any liens or defects do exist against the property being purchased.

The records that a title insurance company uses to search the chain of ownership of a parcel of real estate is called the *title plant.* The title plant consists of the public records of a specific geographic area (town, city, county, etc.) that have been appropriately indexed and integrated so that an individual parcel of real property may be easily located. From the title plant, the insurance company can prepare an abstract on any piece of real estate in the particular geographic area. An abstract is a short summary of the ownership history of a specified parcel of real property.

A title plant is usually kept up-to-date on a daily basis. A well-maintained title plant usually increases in value over time and seldom, if ever, decreases in value. In addition, the estimated useful life of a title plant is generally indefinite. These unusual characteristics make a title plant quite unique.

CLASSIFICATION OF INSURANCE CONTRACTS

FASB-60 requires that insurance policies be classified as either short-duration contracts or long-duration contracts. A short-duration contract is not expected to cover an extended period, and a long-duration contract is expected to cover an extended period. In a short-duration contract, the insurance carrier primarily provides insurance protection, while in a long-duration contract the insurance company provides other services and functions in addition to insurance protection. Other services and functions that an insurance company may provide to a policyholder include loans secured by the insurance policy and various options for the payment of policy benefits.

In determining whether an insurance contract is of short duration or long duration, FASB-60 requires that the following factors be considered.

Short-duration contract The amount of premiums charged, the amount of coverage provided, or other provisions of the contract can be adjusted or canceled by the insurance company at the end of any contract period. A short-duration insurance contract provides insurance protection and is issued for a short, fixed period.

Long-duration contract The contract is usually noncancelable, guaranteed renewable, or otherwise not subject to unilateral changes in its provisions. A long-duration insurance contract provides insurance protection for an extended period and includes other services and functions which must be performed.

Most property and liability insurance contracts and some specialized short-term life insurance contracts are classified as short-duration contracts. Most life insurance contracts and title insurance contracts are classified as long-duration contracts. Accident and health insurance contracts may be of short duration or long duration, according to their expected term of coverage.

PREMIUM REVENUE RECOGNITION

As mentioned previously, FASB-60 requires that insurance policies be classified as either short-duration contracts or long-duration contracts according to whether or not the coverage is for an extended period. Premium revenue recognition is based on whether the insurance policy is classified as a short-duration contract or a long-duration contract, as follows:

Short-duration contracts   FASB-60 requires that premium revenue from short-duration contracts be periodically recognized in proportion to the insurance company's performance under the contract. The insurance company's performance under the contract is the coverage of the risks that are insured. Thus, in those insurance policies in which coverage is provided evenly over the term of the insurance, the premiums should be recognized evenly over the term of the insurance. However, if the period of coverage (risk) is different from the term of the insurance contract, then the premium should be recognized over the period of coverage. In other words, the premium income must be *matched* to the period of risk (coverage) during which the insurance company is exposed to potential loss. In the event the amount of insurance declines over the term of the insurance, the premium should be recognized in proportion to the amount of insurance over the term of the insurance.

In some types of insurance, such as workmen's compensation, the final premium is not determined until after the term of the insurance contract because the premium is based on the total amount of compensation paid to employees. The insurance company receives a premium deposit at the inception of the policy, and a premium adjustment is made after the term of the insurance. In this event, an estimate of the final premium adjustment is necessary in order to recognize the total premium revenue over the term of insurance coverage. If the final total premium cannot be reasonably estimated, the cost recovery method or the deposit method of accounting may be used until the final total premium is known.

Over the term of an insurance policy, the premiums are expected to pay for losses, if any, and operational expenses and still provide the insurance company with a profit. The amount of losses that a single insurance policy may incur is based on the law of averages. In other words, the possible loss that a single policy may incur is based on the loss experience of many policies. As long as an insurance policy is outstanding, there may be a claim for a loss. Thus, the unearned portion of a premium, at any time, should be sufficient to pay losses, operational expenses, and a margin for profit. Statutory laws, in most states, provide that insurance companies must maintain reserves for possible losses equal to the unearned premiums of all insurance policies outstanding. The most common method used to determine unearned premiums is the *monthly pro rata fractional basis*. This method assumes that the same dollar amount of insurance business is written each day of every month. Thus, the mean of all insurance business written in any month is the middle of the month. One year is divided into 24 periods, and a fraction is assigned to each month as follows: January 1/24, February 3/24, March 5/24, April

7/24, May 9/24, June 11/24, and so forth. The appropriate fraction is then applied to the total original premium to determine the amount of earned and unearned premium.

Most state statutes require that insurance companies maintain their records in a manner in which a determination can be made annually on December 31 of the (1) premiums in force on direct insurance business and any reinsurance business and (2) premiums in force on insurance business that has been ceded on a reinsurance basis to other insurance companies.

Long-duration contracts   FASB-60 requires that premium revenue from long-duration contracts be recognized when due from the policyholder. Thus, premiums for whole-life, endowment, renewable term, and other long-duration contracts are recognized as revenue when the premiums are due from the policyholders.

Title insurance premiums are considered due from policyholders and recognized as revenue when the title insurance company is legally or contractually entitled to the premium. Either the effective date of the title insurance policy or the date of the binder is the likely date on which the title insurance company is legally or contractually entitled to collect the premium.

> **OBSERVATION:** *The reasoning behind recognizing the entire title insurance premium on the effective date of the policy is because the insurance company has performed all of the acts necessary to earn the revenue. If a subsequent loss occurs, it will be because the insurance company did not uncover the cause of the loss at the time of the title search.*

INVESTMENT, LIMITED-PAYMENT, AND UNIVERSAL LIFE-TYPE CONTRACTS

The accounting specified by FASB-60 is designed for long-duration insurance contracts that generally provide for (a) insurance protection, (b) level premium payments, and (c) contract terms that are fixed and guaranteed. The long-duration insurance contracts addressed by FASB-97 are referred to as (a) investment contracts, (b) limited-payment contracts, and (c) universal life-type contracts.

Interest-sensitive and flexible-premium long-duration insurance contracts do not have fixed and guaranteed terms that are typical of most traditional insurance contracts. Instead, the terms of this type of contract usually allow the insurer to vary the amount of charges and credits made to the policyholder's account, and more often than not, the terms allow the policyholder to vary the amount of premium paid. FASB-97 concludes that the accounting methods established by FASB-60 for the recognition of revenue, based on a percentage of premiums, are not appropriate for insurance contracts in which the insurer has the discretion of varying amounts charged or credited to the policyholder's account or the policyholder has the discretion of varying the amount of premium paid.

An *investment contract* is one that does not subject the insurer to any significant risk of death or disability. Under FASB-97, investment contracts are accounted for in the same manner as other interest-bearing contracts. Payments received by the insurer are not reported as revenue.

A *limited-payment contract* is one that subjects the insurer to risk over a period longer than the premium payment period. Under FASB-97, income from limited-payment insurance contracts is recognized over the period covered by the contract rather than the period that payments are received.

A *universal life-type contract* is one that contains terms that give the policyholder significant discretion over the amount and timing of premium payments and allows the insurer to vary the amounts charged or credited to the policyholder's account. FASB-97 requires the use of the retrospective deposit method of accounting for universal life-type contracts. Under this method, an insurer is required to record a liability for policyholder benefits equal to the amount of the policyholder's account balance. Premiums are not accounted for as revenue under this method.

FASB-97 specifies that when a traditional insurance policy is surrendered and replaced by an interest-sensitive or flexible-premium insurance contract, the balance of any unamortized deferred policy acquisition costs related to the surrendered policy and any difference between the liability for policyholder benefits and the cash surrender value should be charged to operations.

FASB-97 does not establish accounting and reporting standards for limited-payment and universal life-type contracts that address loss recognition (premium deficiency), accounting for reinsurance, and financial statement disclosure. The provisions of FASB-60 that apply to these items shall also apply to limited-payment and universal life-type contracts.

Accounting for Investment Contracts

FASB-97 defines an investment contract as one that does not expose the insurance enterprise to significant risks arising from policyholder mortality or morbidity. Since the risk of loss from death or disability is almost nonexistent, an investment contract is viewed more as an investment instrument than as an insurance contract. Under FASB-97, an insurance enterprise shall account for an investment contract in the same way as other financial institutions account for most other types of interest-bearing financial instruments. Amounts received by an insurance enterprise as payments for investment contracts shall be reported as liabilities and not reported as revenue.

Some long-duration insurance contracts contain terms that permit the policyholder to purchase an annuity at a guaranteed price on settlement of the contract. Under FASB-97, there is no mortality risk involved in this type of contract until the right to purchase the annuity contract has been executed.

An insurance enterprise may be required to make annuity payments regardless of whether the beneficiary lives or dies, and additional payments beginning on a specified date if the beneficiary is alive on that date. These types of policies are accounted for as insurance contracts, under both FASB-60 and FASB-97, unless (a) there is a remote chance that the beneficiary will be alive on the date that the additional payments begin or (b) the present value of the estimated additional payments is immaterial when compared with the present value of all payments that are estimated to be made under the contract.

Accounting for Limited-Payment Contracts

FASB-97 defines a limited-payment insurance contract as one in which the terms are fixed and guaranteed, and for which premiums are paid over a period shorter than the period over which benefits are provided. Under FASB-97, the benefit period includes the period during which (a) the insurance enterprise is subject to risk from policyholder mortality and morbidity and (b) the insurance enterprise is responsible for administration of the contract. The period in which the policyholder or beneficiary elects to have settlement proceeds disbursed is *not* included in the benefit period.

The period in which an insurance enterprise is exposed to mortality and morbidity risks in connection with a limited-payment contract extends beyond the period in which premiums are collected. This occurs because premiums are paid over a period shorter than the period over which benefits are provided by the insurance enterprise. The liability for policyholder benefits for this type of limited-payment insurance contract shall be set up and accounted for in accordance with FASB-60. Under this circumstance, the earnings process is not completed by the mere collection of premiums. The excess of gross over net premiums received must be deferred and amortized by a constant method over the period that the insurance enterprise provides services. Thus, for life insurance contracts, the deferred premiums are amortized in relationship to the amount of insurance in force, and for annuity contracts, the deferred premiums are amortized in relationship to the estimated amount of benefits that are expected to be paid.

FASB-97 does not establish accounting and reporting standards for limited-payment insurance contracts that address (a) loss recognition (premium deficiency), (b) accounting for reinsurance, and (c) financial statement disclosure. The provisions of FASB-60 that apply to these specific items shall also apply to limited-payment insurance contracts.

Accounting for Universal Life-Type Contracts

Universal life insurance contracts do not have fixed and guaranteed terms that are typical of the types of insurance contracts for which the accounting specified in FASB-60 was designed. However, as discussed below, certain types of conventional forms of participating and nonguaranteed-premium contracts may be, in substance, universal life-type contracts. Policyholders of universal life-type insurance contracts are frequently granted significant discretion over the amount and timing of premium payments. In addition, insurers are frequently granted significant discretion over amounts that accrue to and that are assessed against policyholders. Insurance contracts that provide death or annuity benefits and have one or more of the following features are referred to by FASB-97 as universal life-type insurance contracts:

- The terms of the contract do not fix and guarantee the amounts assessed by the insurer against the policyholder for mortality coverage, contract administration, initiation, or surrender.
- Interest and other amounts that accrue to the benefit of the policyholder are not fixed and guaranteed by the terms of the contract.
- Without consent of the insurer, the policyholder may change the amount of premium within certain limits set forth in the contract.

FASB-60 prescribed the appropriate accounting for conventional forms of participating and nonguaranteed-premium contracts.

However, as mentioned above, some conventional forms of participating and nonguaranteed-premium contracts may be, in substance, universal life-type contracts, which are accounted for in accordance with the provisions of FASB-97. For the purposes of FASB-97, a *participating contract* is considered a universal life-type contract if, without the consent of the insurer, the policyholder can change the amount of the premium, within limits set forth in the contract. In addition, both *participating* or *nonguaranteed-premium* insurance contracts are considered universal life-type contracts if they contain any of the following features:

- Under the terms of the contract, the insurer maintains a stated account balance for the policyholder which is credited with premiums and interest and assessed for contract administration, mortality coverage, and initiation or surrender fees. The amounts credited to, or assessed against the policyholder's account balance are not fixed and guaranteed.

- Changes in interest rates or other market conditions are expected to be the primary cause of changes in any contract element. It is not expected that the primary cause of changes in any contract element will be related to the experience of a group of similar contracts or the enterprise as a whole.

Under FASB-60, a liability for future policy benefits relating to long-duration contracts, except title insurance contracts, is accrued when premium revenue is recognized by the insurance enterprise. The liability is based on actuarial assumptions at the time the insurance contracts are consummated and is presented in the balance sheet at present value. In subsequent periods, changes in the original actuarial assumptions which result in changes in future policy benefits or related costs and expenses are recognized in net income of the period of change.

The liability for future policy benefits consists of the present value of future policy benefits and related expenses, less the present value of related future net premiums. Net premium is that portion of the gross premium which is necessary to cover future payments of all policy benefits and related costs and expenses. Gross premium is the amount the policyholder pays and is equal to the net premium plus the profit made by the insurance enterprise.

Under FASB-97, an insurance enterprise shall compute its liability for policy benefits for universal life-type contracts as the sum of the following:

1. Any amounts that have been accrued to the benefit of policyholders at the date of the financial statements
2. Any amounts assessed against policyholders to compensate the insurance enterprise for services to be performed over future periods
3. Any amounts previously assessed against policyholders that the insurance enterprise must refund if the contract is terminated
4. Any loss that will probably (likely) occur as a result of premium deficiency (computed in accordance with FASB-60)

In determining its liability for policy benefits, an insurance enterprise shall not anticipate amounts that may be assessed against policyholders in future periods. In the event that no other amount can be established, the policyholder's cash surrender value in the insurance contract, at the date of the financial statements, shall represent the insurance enterprise's liability for policy benefits. The liability for policy benefits shall not include a provision for the risk of adverse deviation.

An insurance enterprise shall not report premiums collected on universal life-type contracts as revenue in its statement of earnings. Revenue on universal life-type contracts is assessed against policyholders and reported in the period of assessment, unless it is evident that the assessed amount represents compensation to the insurance enterprise for future services to be provided over more than one period.

Amounts assessed against policyholders' balances for future services to be provided by the insurance enterprise over more than one period are reported as unearned income in the period in which they are assessed. In addition, amounts assessed against policyholders' balances as initiation or front-end fees are also unearned revenue. Unearned revenue shall be amortized to income over the periods benefited based on the same assumptions and factors that are used to amortize capitalized acquisition costs.

An insurance enterprise shall not report as an expense in its statement of earnings any payments to policyholders that represent a return of policyholder balances. The cost of contract administration, amortization of capitalized acquisition costs, and benefit claims that exceed related policyholder balances shall be reported as expenses.

Under FASB-97, the amortization of capitalized policy acquisition costs is recognized at a constant rate based on the present value of the gross profit that is expected to be generated by a book (group) of universal life-type insurance contracts. The same interest rate used to accrue interest on a policyholder's account shall be used to compute the present value of the gross profit that is expected to be realized on a book of universal life-type contracts. In those periods in which material amounts of negative gross profits arise, the present value of estimated gross profits, gross costs, or the balance of insurance in force shall be used as a substitute allocation base for calculating amortization.

Estimated gross profit shall include the best estimate of each of the following individual items, over the life of the book of universal life-type contracts, without provision for adverse deviation:

- Assessments for mortality, minus benefit claims in excess of related policyholder balances
- Assessments for contract administration, minus costs incurred
- Investment income from, minus interest credited to, policyholder balances
- Assessments against policyholder accounts upon termination
- All other assessed amounts and credits

Under FASB-97, amortization of capitalized acquisition costs is based on the present value of estimated gross profits, while under FASB-60, amortization of capitalized acquisition costs is based on expected premium revenues. Under FASB-60, acquisition costs that are directly related to the production of insurance business include all direct costs and indirect costs, such as underwriting and policy issuance expenses. Collection expenses, professional fees, depreciation, and general and administrative expenses are not directly related to, nor do they vary directly with, the production of new or renewal insurance business, and should be expensed as incurred. Under FASB-97, acquisition costs that vary in a constant relationship to *premiums or insurance in force*, are recurring in nature, or tend to be incurred in a level amount from period to period shall be charged to expense in the period incurred.

The computation of amortization under FASB-97 includes the accrual of interest on the unamortized balance of capitalized acquisition costs and the balance of any unearned income, at the same interest rate used to discount expected gross profits. Under FASB-97, estimates of expected gross profit must be periodically evaluated and if earlier estimates indicate that revision is necessary, total amortization to date shall be adjusted by a charge or credit to the statement of earnings. To compute the present value of revised estimates of expected gross profits, an insurance enterprise shall use either (a) the rate in effect at the inception of the book of universal life-type contracts or (b) the latest revised interest rate applied to the remaining benefit period. The method used to determine the present value of revised estimates of expected gross profit shall be consistently applied in subsequent revisions.

FASB-97 does not establish accounting and reporting standards for universal life-type insurance contracts that address (a) loss recognition (premium deficiency), (b) accounting for reinsurance, and (c) financial statement disclosure. The provisions of FASB-60 that apply to these specific items shall also apply to universal life-type insurance contracts.

Internal replacement transactions A policyholder may use the cash surrender value of an old insurance contract to pay the initial lump-sum premium for a new universal life-type contract. This is sometimes referred to as an internal replacement transaction. FASB-97 specifies that when a traditional insurance policy is surrendered and replaced by an interest-sensitive or flexible-premium insurance contract, the balance of any unamortized deferred policy acquisition costs related to the surrendered policy and any difference between the liability for policyholder benefits and the cash surrender value should be charged to operations.

Effective Date and Transition of FASB-97

FASB-97 is effective for fiscal years beginning on or after December 16, 1988, with earlier application encouraged. Unless restatement of all years is not practical, accounting changes resulting from the adoption of FASB-97 shall be accounted for by the retroactive restatement of all previously issued financial statements that are presented for comparison purposes. In the year that FASB-97 is first applied, the financial statements shall disclose the nature of the restatement and its effect on income before extraordinary items, net income, and related per share amounts for each year presented.

If retroactive restatement of all previously issued financial statements is not practicable, the cumulative effect of applying FASB-97 in accordance with APB-20 (Accounting Changes) shall be computed and included in the net income of the year of adoption. In the year of adoption, the financial statements shall disclose the nature of the cumulative adjustment and the effect of applying FASB-97 on income before extraordinary items, net income, and related per share amounts.

CLAIM COSTS AND FUTURE POLICY BENEFITS

Property and liability insurance companies must pay claims to policyholders who incur losses which have been insured. At any given time, claims may (1) be reported to the insurance company and be in the process of settlement or (2) be incurred but not reported to the insurance company.

As mentioned previously, a title insurance company insures ownership to real property. The title company scrutinizes the chain of title to uncover any defects. Presumably, if a title company does its job properly, there should be no claims for losses. In practice, however, claims do occur and the title company does incur losses.

Life insurance companies also incur costs in the form of policy benefits that are paid to the beneficiary in accordance with the terms of the insurance policy.

FASB-60 contains specific promulgated GAAP for claim costs and future policy benefits, as follows:

Claim Costs

Title insurance companies should accrue estimated claim costs at the time the related insurance premiums are recognized as revenue. Claim costs for other types of insurance contracts shall be accrued as they occur. Thus, a provision for claim costs (liability) should include (1) reported losses in the process of settlement and (2) estimated losses incurred but not reported. The provision for reported claims in the process of settlement may be made by estimating each reported claim on an individual basis. However, because of their large number, smaller reported claims may be estimated by an average dollar loss per claim. Thus, the provision for smaller claims is frequently made by multiplying the number of smaller claims by the estimated average loss per claim.

Claims incurred but not reported are more difficult to determine and are usually estimated on a formula basis. Formulas are usually determined on the basis of statistics on actual claim experience for prior years, which is then adjusted for current trends and other factors. This is usually accomplished by examining specific types of insurance policies for a selected period and then relating the loss experience to the premiums in force for the specific type of insurance policies. Formulas are only used for normal losses which are expected to recur. Large losses resulting from catastrophes are not included in the statistics used in determining formulas but are estimated separately, usually on the basis of judgment. Thus, a formula will usually consist of the loss experience determined for a prior period, adjusted for current trends, and a factor for large catastrophic losses.

Statutory Formula Reserves are required by most states for bodily injury, liability, and workmen's compensation insurance. In addition, several states require minimum reserves for unreported losses incurred on surety and fidelity insurance policies.

FASB-60 requires that a liability be accrued in the financial statements for reported losses in the process of settlement and unreported losses incurred but not reported. The liability for unpaid losses should not include the effects of inflation and other economic factors, and should be based on the best estimate of the cost of settlement, arrived at by using past loss experience adjusted for current trends. The cost of settlement may be reduced by an estimated salvage and/or subrogation expected to be recovered from the claim. Amounts of salvage and subrogation should be deducted from the liability for unpaid losses in the balance sheet, and the amount deducted should be disclosed in a footnote to the financial statements.

Differences in and adjustments to estimates and actual claim payments, which result from periodic reviews, shall be recognized in net income of the period in which the differences or adjustments occur.

> **OBSERVATION:** *An insurance company may elect to report its liability for unpaid claims and the related claim adjustment expense for short-duration contracts at their present value. In this event, the amount of the effects of such a presentation must be disclosed in the financial statements.*

Title insurance companies and mortgage guaranty companies sometimes acquire real property as a result of settling a claim. Real property acquired in settlement of a claim should be reported at estimated fair value. Subsequent adjustments to the reported fair value and realized gain or loss on the final disposition of the real property shall be reported in the financial statements as an increase or decrease of claim costs. Real property acquired in settling a claim should not be classified as an investment but should be reported separately in the balance sheet.

Claim adjustment expense   Figuring the liability for reported claims in the process of settlement and for claims incurred but not reported involves the calculation of the amount of claim that will be paid to the policyholder. The claims adjustment expense represents the estimated expenses that are related to, and will be incurred in, settling the claims of policyholders. Claims adjustment expense may be classified as allocated or unallocated. *Allocated claims adjustment expenses* are those that can be directly associated with a specific claim. *Unallocated claims adjustment expenses* are those that cannot be associated with a specific claim and include indirect salaries, stationery, postage, rent, travel, and other similar expenses of the claims department.

The liability for the claims adjustment expense is generally determined by a formula based on expenses incurred in the settlement of claims in prior periods. In other words, the formula is based on past experience which may be adjusted for current trends.

FASB-60 requires that a liability for claims adjustment expense for short-duration contracts be accrued for all reported claims in the process of settlement and all claims incurred but not reported.

Future Policy Benefits

An insurance company pools the risks of many individuals and businesses. Thus, the undertaking of risks is the primary business of an insurance company. However, the real risk that an insurance company takes is that actual experience will be worse than the actuarial assumptions used in calculating the premium. When this occurs, the insurance company loses money. Thus, it is important that insurance companies be reasonably conservative in their basic assumptions, which should include a provision for the *risk of adverse deviation*.

The normal costs of an insurance company include the payment of policy benefits and the expenses of doing business. These costs must be matched to their related premium revenue.

FASB-60 requires that a liability for future policy benefits on long-duration insurance contracts be accrued at the time that premium revenue is recognized. The liability includes the present value of future policy benefits and related expenses, less the present value of related future net premiums. Stated another way, the liability for future policy benefits for a particular group of insurance contracts is the excess of the total amount of net premiums collected over the total amount of related policy benefits paid to date. *Gross premium* is the total cost of the insurance contract to the policyholder. When accumulated with investment income, the gross premium is supposed to create a fund which will be sufficient to pay all policy benefits and related costs and expenses and provide a profit for the insurance company. *Net premium* is that portion of the gross premium which is necessary to cover all policy benefits and related costs and expenses. In other words, net premium is supposed to represent the gross premium, less a profit for the insurance company.

Future policy benefits and related expenses are calculated by the use of actuarial assumptions, such as investment yields, mortality and morbidity rates, and estimated terminations or withdrawals. The liability for future policy benefits and related expenses is based on actuarial assumptions existing at the time the insurance contract is consummated, and is presented in the balance sheet at its present value. The liability for future policy benefits should include a provision for unfavorable deviations from the original actuarial assumptions. This provision is referred to as the *risk of adverse deviation*. Changes in the original actuarial assumptions in subsequent periods are recognized in net income of the period of change.

OTHER COSTS

Since the matching concept is applied to the recognition of premium revenue, it is only logical that the same principal be used in accounting for the costs incurred in obtaining the premium revenue. Thus, variable acquisition costs that are directly or indirectly related to the production of new or renewal premium revenue should be deferred and amortized as a charge against income as the related premium revenue is earned. Acquisition costs that are directly related to the production of insurance business include all direct costs and indirect costs, such as underwriting and policy issuance expenses. Collection expenses, professional fees, depreciation, and general and administrative expenses are not directly related to, nor do they vary directly with, the production of new or renewal insurance business, and should be expensed as incurred.

Deferred acquisition costs should be amortized as a charge to income in the same manner as the related premium revenue is earned. The method of amortization should be consistently applied from year to year. Unamortized acquisition costs are classified in the balance sheet as assets.

Actual acquisition expenses for long-duration contracts should be compared to those used in the actuarial assumptions and, when possible, the actual acquisition expenses should be used in the actuarial assumptions instead of estimates. When estimates are used to determine the acquisition expenses which should be deferred, it is necessary to adjust such estimates to actual amounts if the differences are significant.

> **OBSERVATION:** *Under regulatory accounting practices, all acquisition expenses are charged against income in the period incurred. Thus, a significant difference between regulatory accounting practices and GAAP is the deferral and amortization of acquisition expenses. This difference is reflected in stockholders' equity and net income determined under regulatory accounting practices, and stockholders' equity and net income determined under GAAP.*

Other expenses of insurance companies are treated in accordance with existing GAAP. Thus, if an expenditure benefits future periods, it may be deferred and charged to the periods benefited. However, all other expenses, such as policy maintenance, investment expenses, and general overhead, which are not directly related to the production of new or renewal insurance business should be charged to operations in the period incurred.

DEFICIENCY IN PREMIUMS OR LIABILITY FOR FUTURE POLICY BENEFITS

Insurance companies may incur losses on short-duration and long-duration contracts. For the purposes of FASB-60, premium deficiencies shall be determined by reasonable grouping of similar insurance policies which is consistent with a company's usual system of acquiring, servicing, and measuring profitability for its insurance business. Each of these types of deficiencies is discussed separately below.

Short-Duration Contracts

Premium revenue is supposed to be sufficient to cover expected claim costs, claim adjustment expenses, acquisition costs, policy maintenance costs, and estimated dividends to policyholders and provide a margin of profit for the insurance company. Whenever unearned premiums are less than (1) the related liability for unpaid claim costs and claim adjustment expenses, (2) related unamortized acquisition costs, (3) related estimated policy maintenance costs, and (4) related dividends to policyholders, a premium deficiency exists.

Premium deficiencies should be recognized in the financial statements. Recognition should be made by reducing unamortized deferred acquisition costs by a charge to income in the amount of the deficiency. If the unamortized deferred acquisition costs are smaller than the amount of premium deficiency, all of the unamortized deferred acquisition costs should be charged to income, and an additional separate liability for the balance of the premium deficiency should be recorded by a charge to income.

> **OBSERVATION**: *A provision for anticipated premium deficiencies should be provided when unearned premiums are insufficient to cover all related costs and expenses. Related costs and expenses should include expected claims and claims adjustment expenses, expected policyholder dividends, unamortized deferred acquisition costs, and any anticipated expenses that are expected to be incurred subsequent to the inception date of the policy. If a cost, subsequent to the inception date of the policy, is direct or can be attributed to maintaining the policy in force, it should be included in the determination of the premium deficiency.*

If an insurance company includes anticipated investment income in the determination of a premium deficiency, FASB-60 requires that the effects, and the amount of the effects on the financial statements, be disclosed.

Long-Duration Contracts

As mentioned previously, FASB-60 requires that the liability for future policy benefits for long-duration contracts be accrued at the time that the premium revenue is recognized. The liability is based on actuarial assumptions at the time the insurance contracts are consummated, and is presented in the balance sheet at present value. In subsequent periods, changes in the original actuarial assumptions which result in changes in future policy benefits or related costs and expenses are recognized in net income of the period of change.

The liability for future policy benefits consists of the present value of future policy benefits and related expenses, less the present value of related future net premiums. Net premium is that portion of the gross premium which is necessary to cover future payment of all policy benefits and related costs and expenses. Gross premium is the amount the policyholder pays and is equal to the net premium plus the profit made by the insurance company.

At any given time, the present value of future gross premiums for a particular group of insurance contracts may be insufficient to cover (1) the present value of future policy benefits and related expenses and (2) the remaining unamortized acquisition costs. In this event, a gross premium deficiency occurs. The gross premium deficiency is usually the result of significant changes in the original actuarial assumptions. The procedures to determine a gross premium deficiency are as follows:

1. Compute the present value of future policy benefits and related settlement and maintenance expenses using revised assumptions and updated experience.
2. Compute the present value of future gross premiums using revised assumptions and updated experience.
3. Subtract 1 from 2 to arrive at the new liability for future policy benefits based on revised assumptions and updated experience.
4. Compare the new liability for future policy benefits determined in 3 with the actual recorded liability for future policy benefits, reduced by the actual remaining unamortized acquisition costs. A deficiency exists if the newly computed liability exceeds the actual liability, reduced by the actual remaining unamortized acquisition costs.

A deficiency in the liability for future policy benefits must be recognized in net income by either increasing the liability for future policy benefits, or by decreasing unamortized acquisition costs. The revised assumptions and updated experience shall be used subsequently to determine changes in the liability for future policy benefits. Under no circumstances should a deficiency be reported if its effect is to create income in future periods.

A deficiency in the liability for future policy benefits is usually determined by groups or blocks of similar insurance policies. However, if a group or block of insurance contracts does not indicate a deficiency, but the aggregate liability for an entire line of insurance business does indicate a deficiency, the deficiency should be recognized.

REINSURANCE

When one insurance company reinsures part or all of an outstanding policy with one or more other insurance companies, it is called *reinsurance*. If a loss is incurred on a policy that has been reinsured, the reinsurers will have to pay their proportionate share of the settlement. Thus, amounts recoverable from reinsurers should be included in the determination of (1) the liability for unpaid claims in the process of settlement, (2) the liability for unpaid claims incurred but not reported, and (3) the liability for claim adjustment expenses.

FASB-60 requires that amounts recoverable from reinsurers be reported as follows:

1. Amounts recoverable for claims and claim adjustment expenses that have already been paid should be accounted for as a receivable (asset) from the reinsurers.
2. Amounts recoverable for claims and claim adjustment expenses that have not been paid should be deducted from the liability for unpaid claims and claim adjustment expenses.
3. Collectible premiums that have been ceded to a reinsurer are not considered receivables, and they should be netted against their related unearned premiums.
4. Receivables and payables to the same reinsurer should be offset against each other.
5. Premiums ceded to a reinsurer should be deducted from the related earned premiums in the income statement.
6. Recovery of claims from reinsurers should be deducted from the related incurred claims in the income statement.

A liability for estimated future servicing costs shall be accrued if a ceding insurance company agrees to service, without reasonable compensation, insurance contracts that have been ceded to a reinsurer. If a reinsurance contract does not shift the risk of loss to the reinsurer, the ceding insurance company shall account for the premiums paid by the insured, less the premium paid to the reinsurer, as a deposit.

POLICYHOLDER DIVIDENDS

Policyholder dividends must be accrued and reported in the financial statements. If the amount is not known, the use of reasonable estimates is required by FASB-60.

The amount of current income allocated to participating insurance contracts must be excluded from stockholders' equity by a charge to current operations and a credit to a liability account. The liability account is reduced when dividends are subsequently declared or paid. Dividends declared or paid to participating insurance contracts in excess of the liability should also be charged to current operations.

Life insurance companies do not usually pay or declare dividends on participating insurance policies during the first two years, because of the high initial policy acquisition costs. In determining the amount of dividends on participating insurance policies, consideration must be given to any restrictions on such amounts which may be imposed by the terms of the insurance contract, governing law, or company policy. Where participating policy dividends are specified in the policy or projected at the time the policy is issued, they should be accrued ratably over the periods in which premiums are collected.

CONTINGENT COMMISSIONS

Insurance companies usually agree to pay additional commissions to their brokers and agents if the business they generate results in a favorable loss experience. Therefore, these additional commissions are contingent on whether or not a favorable loss experience occurs.

FASB-60 requires that contingent commissions (receivable or payable) be appropriately accrued and appear in the income statement of the periods in which the related profits are recognized.

INVESTMENTS

FASB-60 contains specific guidance in the valuation of investments of insurance companies.

Bonds If the insurance company has the ability and intent to keep bonds to maturity, the bonds should be carried at amortized cost, providing that there has been no permanent decline in the market value of the bonds below amortized cost. Bonds held for speculation should be carried at market value, and unrealized gains or losses should be periodically recognized.

Common and nonredeemable preferred stock Common and nonredeemable preferred stock should be carried at market value. If the insurance company has the ability and intent to keep redeemable preferred stock until redemption, the preferred stock should be carried at amortized cost, providing that there has been no permanent decline in the market value of the preferred stock below amortized cost.

Mortgages   Mortgages should be carried at the balance of the unpaid principal. Mortgages purchased at a discount or premium should be carried at amortized cost. An allowance for estimated uncollectible mortgage loans should be used, if necessary, and changes in the allowance account should be included in realized gains and losses.

Real estate investments   Real estate investments should be carried at depreciated cost. Amortization, depreciation, and other related costs or credits should be included in the determination of investment income.

Loan and commitment fees   Loan origination and commitment fees and direct loan origination costs shall be accounted for as prescribed in FASB-91 (Accounting for Nonrefundable Fees and Costs Associated with Originating or Acquiring Loans and Initial Direct Costs of Leases).

Reporting Realized Gains and Losses   FASB-97 amends FASB-60 to eliminate the practice of reporting realized investment gains and losses in the statement of earnings, below operating earnings. An insurance enterprise is required by FASB-97 to report realized gains and losses as a component of other income, on a pretax basis, above earnings from operations in the statement of earnings. In addition, FASB-97 does not permit the direct or indirect deferment of realized investment gains and losses.

Unrealized investment gains and losses should not be included in the determination of net income, but are recognized, net of related taxes, as an addition to, or reduction of, stockholders' equity.

Permanent declines in security investments, below cost or amortized cost, should be recognized as realized losses. These security investments should be written down to their net realizable values, which subsequently become their new cost basis. Recovery in market value above the new cost basis shall not be recognized until sale, maturity, or other disposition of the security.

REAL ESTATE USED IN BUSINESS AND SEPARATE ACCOUNTS

Real estate should be classified in accordance with its predominant use as either property used in business or as an investment. Real estate operating expenses, including depreciation, should be classified in a manner consistent with the related asset, as either investment expenses or operating expenses. Real estate that is used in business by the insurance company should not be accounted for as investment income with a corresponding charge to operations for rental expense. In other words, an insurance company cannot include rental income in its financial statements for property it uses in the regular course of business.

> **OBSERVATION:** *Real estate is always classified as an investment for regulatory accounting purposes, regardless of its use. Rental expense is charged to operations, and rental income is included in investment income for real estate used by the insurance company in its own business.*

As a fiduciary, an insurance company may maintain assets and liabilities in separate accounts for the purposes of funding fixed-benefit plans. In this capacity, the insurance company usually receives a fee and does not assume any investment risk. Except for long-term separate accounts in which the insurance company has guaranteed a specific investment return, investments in separate accounts shall be valued at market. Long-term separate accounts with guaranteed returns shall be valued in the same manner as any other investment of the insurance company. Assets and liabilities of separate accounts shall be reported in the financial statements in summary totals.

DEFERRED INCOME TAXES

The Life Insurance Company Act of 1959 covers the taxation of life insurance companies for federal tax purposes. For the purposes of GAAP, life insurance companies must comply with existing promulgated pronouncements, and thus must determine deferred income taxes when appropriate.

If circumstances indicate that the current tax effects of a temporary (timing) difference will not reverse in subsequent periods, an insurance company does not have to accrue deferred income taxes. However, deferred taxes shall be accrued if the reversal of the temporary difference cannot be reasonably determined. Deferred income taxes shall be accrued in accordance with existing GAAP.

Once a determination is made as to whether deferred income taxes should or should not be provided on the tax effects of temporary differences, circumstances may change. In this event, if deferred taxes have not previously been provided, they should be accrued and reported as an income tax expense in the period of correction. Deferred taxes accrued under these circumstances should not be reported as an extraordinary item. Regardless of whether the gross change or net change method is used, previously accrued deferred income taxes should be included in income as the related temporary differences reverse, if the previously determined tax effects are expected to be different from those originally anticipated.

Policyholders' surplus of stock life insurance companies that create a difference between taxable income and pretax financial accounting income are usually considered permanent differences, because the company controls the events that create the tax consequence. However, if circumstances dictate that income taxes will be paid because of a reduction in policyholders' surplus, an income tax expense should be accrued on such reductions in the period in which they occur. In effect, these reductions do create a temporary difference when they occur, and they should not be accounted for as an extraordinary item.

> **OBSERVATION:** *The Tax Reform Act of 1984 requires life insurance enterprises with assets of $100 million or more to recompute their policy reserves as of the beginning of the first taxable year beginning after December 31, 1983. Insurance companies with assets of less than $100 million may make a special election not to have their reserves recomputed. The computation of the new policy reserves, as of the beginning of the first taxable year beginning after December 31, 1983, shall be based on the recomputation of each existing insurance contract, as if the provisions of the Act had applied to the contract when it was issued.*
>
> *If an insurance enterprise changes its method of accounting solely for the purpose of complying with the Act, the change will not be treated as a change in the method of accounting under the provisions of the Internal Revenue Code. Furthermore, any change in the method of accounting for policy reserves will not be treated as such, if the change is made solely to comply with the provisions of the Act. A change in the method of accounting and/or a change in the method of computing policy reserves between an insurance company's first taxable year beginning after December 31, 1983, and the preceding year, shall not give rise to any taxable income or loss, if the change is made solely to comply with the provisions of the Act. This provision of the Act is referred to as the "fresh start adjustment," because it is likely that most insurance companies will permanently escape taxation on the decrease in the amount of their policy reserves.*

If the recomputation required by the Act results in a decrease in the amount of policy reserves, deferred income taxes that have been recorded on the books by an insurance enterprise will have to be adjusted. FASB Technical Bulletin 84-3 provides that the adjustment to deferred taxes should be recognized as a reduction of income tax expense in one interim period of the current year. The effect of the adjustment on income tax expense should be disclosed and may be shown as a separate component of income tax expense.

FASB Technical Bulletin 84-3 is effective for financial statements and interim financial information issued after September 30, 1984, for fiscal years ending after July 18, 1984 (the enactment date of the Tax Reform Act of 1984). Earlier application is permitted, but not required. Interim financial information issued after September 30, 1984, for fiscal years ending after July 18, 1984, should be retroactively restated, if necessary.

DISCLOSURE

FASB-60 requires specific disclosures in the financial statements of insurance companies. These disclosures are listed below.

1. The basis for estimating
   a. The liability for unpaid claims
   b. The liability for claim adjustment expenses
2. The methods and assumptions used in calculating the liability for future policy benefits (In addition, FASB-60 encourages, but does not require, the disclosure of the average rate of assumed investment yields that are in effect for the current period.)
3. Capitalized acquisition costs
   a. The nature of such costs
   b. The method of amortizing such costs
   c. The amount of amortization of such costs for the current period
4. If the liabilities for unpaid claims and claim adjustment expenses for short-duration contracts are reported at their present values in the financial statements
   a. The carrying amount of those liabilities
   b. The range of interest rates used to discount those liabilities

5. If estimated investment income is used in calculating a premium deficiency for short-duration contracts
   a. If yes, a statement disclosing that fact
   b. If no, no disclosure necessary
6. Reinsurance transactions of an insurance company
   a. The nature and significance of such transactions
   b. Estimated amounts recoverable from reinsurers that are related to unpaid claims and claim adjustment expenses
7. Participating insurance of an insurance company
   a. The relative percentage of participating insurance
   b. The method of accounting for participating insurance policyholder dividends
   c. The amount of such dividends
   d. The amount of any additional income allocated to participating insurance policyholders
8. Stockholders' equity, statutory capital, and surplus
   a. The amount of statutory capital and surplus
   b. The amount of statutory capital and surplus required for regulatory purposes, if significant to the enterprise's total statutory capital and surplus
   c. The nature of statutory restrictions on dividends and the amount of retained earnings not available for dividends to stockholders
9. Policyholders' surplus of life insurance companies (When an insurance company is consolidated or accounted for by the equity method, these disclosures also apply to the parent company.)
   a. The treatment of the policyholders' surplus under the provisions of the Internal Revenue Code
   b. The fact that income taxes may become payable if the company takes specific action, which should be appropriately disclosed
   c. The total amount of policyholders' surplus for which income taxes have not been provided
10. If no current or deferred federal income taxes have been provided by a life insurance company for any retained earnings in excess of policyholders' surplus
    a. The amount of such retained earnings
    b. The reasons for not accruing deferred federal income taxes

> **OBSERVATION:** *SEC-reporting companies should refer to Accounting Series Release 301 (October 21, 1981) for a complete list of disclosures required by the SEC for insurance companies.*

EFFECTIVE DATE AND TRANSITION

FASB-60 is effective for fiscal years beginning on or after December 16, 1982. As with most promulgated GAAP, earlier application of FASB-60 is encouraged.

An accounting change which results from the initial application of FASB-60 shall be made, if practical, by retroactive restatement of all comparative financial statements presented. In addition, the financial statements of the year of change shall disclose the nature of any restatement and its effect on income before extraordinary items, net income, and related per share amounts, for each year restated. The individual effects of changing to conform with FASB-60 must also be disclosed.

If it is impractical to retroactively restate all of the individual financial statements for the comparative years presented, the following procedure must be used:

1. The new accounting principles (FASB-60) are used in determining net income of the year of change (current period).
2. As many consecutive prior year's financial statements as practical (which are presented for comparative purposes) are then retroactively restated.
3. The cumulative effect of the change to FASB-60 is then computed for any remaining prior years.
4. The cumulative effect is then included in determining net income for the earliest year restated.
5. Financial statements presented for years prior to the earliest year restated (which includes the cumulative effect) shall be presented for comparative purposes as they were originally reported.

In the event that it is impractical to retroactively restate any prior year, FASB-60 requires that the cumulative effect of the change in accounting principle be included in the net income of the year of change, in accordance with APB-20 (Accounting Changes). In any year in which the cumulative effect is used, the effect of the change to FASB-60 on income before extraordinary items, net income, and related per share amounts shall be disclosed.

OBSERVATION: The specialized accounting principles and practices which have been extracted from various AICPA insurance publications and which are included in FASB-60 have been in effect for several years. As a result, it is highly unlikely that many insurance companies will be subject to the transition provisions of FASB-60 because they have probably been applying the specialized accounting principles and practices since they were promulgated by the AICPA.

In addition, the cumulative effect of a change in an accounting principle may be omitted under APB-20 if it is impossible to compute. In this event, the effects of the change, in the year of change, must be disclosed, along with an explanation as to why the cumulative effect was omitted.

OTHER SIGNIFICANT INFORMATION

There are significant differences in accounting principles and practices used in reporting to insurance regulatory agencies and generally accepted accounting principles. The following are some of the more important exceptions to GAAP which are used in regulatory accounting practices:

1. Increasing the *policy reserves* account by a direct debit to unassigned surplus (retained earnings) instead of a charge to income
2. Charging unassigned surplus with prior service costs of pension plans instead of a charge to income
3. Netting liabilities against related assets
4. Debiting unassigned surplus for only the par value of certain stock dividends

Mandatory securities valuation reserve   In most states, a Mandatory Securities Valuation Reserve (MSVR) must be established in accordance with a formula. Unassigned surplus is debited, and a reserve account is credited. This procedure is unacceptable under GAAP.

Under GAAP, the MSVR represents an appropriation of retained earnings (surplus) which should be included in the equity section of the balance sheet.

Nonadmitted assets   It is not permitted to show certain assets on the balance sheet of an insurance company under regulatory accounting practices. Nonadmitted assets are charged to surplus and thus eliminated from the regulatory balance sheet. The following is a list of the more common nonadmitted assets:

1. Furniture and equipment
2. Automobiles
3. Prepaid and deferred expenses
4. Goodwill and other intangible assets
5. Unauthorized investments
6. Investments in excess of authorized amounts
7. Receivables from agents (debit balances)
8. Receivables from employees and officers
9. Accrued income on investments in default
10. Receivables from unauthorized reinsurers

Nonadmitted assets must be restored in presenting financial statements in conformity with GAAP. This is accomplished by debiting the various assets and crediting retained earnings (surplus). However, care must be exercised in determining the collectibility of receivables which are restored.

Stockholder's equity   It may be necessary to reclassify an insurance company's equity account for the purposes of financial statements presented in conformity with GAAP. As mentioned previously, nonadmitted assets must be restored by a credit to retained earnings. If an insurance company has increased its policy reserves by a direct charge to surplus, the transaction will have to be redone to be in conformity with GAAP. Care must also be exercised in segregating appropriated surplus from unassigned surplus for financial statement purposes.

TITLE PLANT

Overview

FASB-61 contains the specialized accounting principles and practices for title plants that were originally published in the AICPA Statement of Position 80-1 (Accounting for Title Insurance Companies).

The provisions of FASB-61 are directed to companies that utilize title plants in their operations, such as title abstract companies, title agents, and title insurance companies.

Background

The main business activity of a title insurance company is to issue title insurance policies. Title insurance provides protection against loss or damage to a parcel of real estate that results from liens or defects in the ownership document. Thus, if a buyer obtains title insurance on real estate that is being purchased and subsequently a loss is incurred because of a lien or defect in the title to the property, the title insurance company will pay any loss or damage. Generally, every mortgage lender will require a title insurance policy on the property being purchased before they will lend any funds as a mortgage.

A title insurance policy is unique because the premiums are usually not refundable and the term of the policy is indefinite. However, the amount of title insurance and the date of title search are stated in the policy. Thus, any loss in excess of the amount of title insurance and any loss which occurs because of a lien or defect that did not exist up to the date of the title search will not be covered by the policy.

When an application for title insurance is received by the insurance company, a title search is made. A title search consists of reviewing and scrutinizing the chain of ownership of the property being insured up to the date of the title search. Some title searches may go back several hundred years. Each change of ownership is examined to make sure it was properly made and that no unpaid liens or defects exist against the title to the property. If a lien or defect is discovered, the title insurance policy is still usually issued but the discovered lien or defect is cited in the policy and not covered. In this event, the buyer may be able to cancel the purchase of the property or compel the seller to take care of the existing lien or defect. Most contracts for the sale of real property contain a provision to the effect that the property is being sold free of any liens and/or defects, and that the buyer has a specified period to determine whether any liens or defects do exist against the property being purchased.

The records that a title insurance company uses to search the chain of ownership of a parcel of real estate are called the *title plant*. The title plant consists of the public records of a specific geographic area (town, city, county, etc.) that have been appropriately indexed and integrated so that an individual parcel of real property may be easily located. From the title plant the insurance company can prepare an abstract on any piece of real estate in the particular geographic area. An abstract is a short summary of the ownership history of a specific parcel of real property.

A title plant is usually kept up-to-date on a daily basis. A well-maintained title plant will usually increase in value over time and seldom, if ever, decrease in value. In addition, the estimated useful life of a title plant is generally indefinite. These unusual characteristics make a title plant unique.

Capitalization of Title Plant

Up until the time that a title plant is ready for its intended use, all direct costs incurred to acquire, organize, or construct the title plant shall be capitalized.

> **OBSERVATION:** *A title plant may be constructed or purchased by an enterprise. In either case, costs directly identified with the title plant are capitalized. A purchase may consist of (a) a copy of the title plant, (b) an undivided interest in the title plant, or (c) the exclusive ownership (outright purchase) of the title plant. In any event, the costs directly related to the title plant are capitalized.*

A title plant that is constructed or otherwise acquired will cover a definite period of time. For example, an enterprise may purchase a title plant of a particular geographic area, which covers the period January 1, 1940 through December 31, 1981. Subsequently, the enterprise may construct or otherwise acquire a title plant for the same geographic area which covers the period from January 1, 1900 through December 31, 1939. This type of title plant is sometimes referred to as an *antecedent title plant* or *backplant*. The same rules for capitalization of direct costs apply to this type of title plant. Thus, costs incurred to construct or otherwise acquire a backplant are capitalized if they can be directly identified to the acquisition of the backplant.

FASB-61 expressly states that capitalized costs of a title plant should not ordinarily be depreciated or otherwise charged to income. Thus, unless there is an impairment in the carrying amount of the title plant, the undepreciated capitalized costs are reported as an asset indefinitely on the balance sheet. The impairment of a title plant below its carrying amount is recognized in the income of the period in which the impairment is discovered.

The carrying amount of a title plant may become impaired if any of the following conditions exist:

1. The title plant is not properly maintained on a current basis.
2. The title plant may become partially or completely obsolete.
3. The title plant may be abandoned or severely neglected.
4. Economics, competition, or legal factors may result in a decline in the value of the title plant.

Maintenance and Operating Expenses

Costs incurred to modernize or modify a title plant may be expensed or separately deferred, but may not be added to the carrying amount of the title plant. If such costs are separately deferred, they should be amortized over their estimated useful lives in a systematic manner.

FASB-61 requires that all title plant maintenance and operational costs be expensed in the period incurred. Thus, the cost to update or maintain the title plant on a current basis and the cost of performing title searches to issue title policies are expensed as they are incurred.

Sale of Title Plant

A sale of a title plant may consist of (a) an outright sale, (b) a sale of an undivided interest, or (c) a sale of a copy, or the right to use, the title plant. FASB-61 requires that gain or loss on any sale of a title plant be reported separately in the financial statements.

Gain or loss on the sale of a title plant depends on the type of sale consummated by the seller. In the event of an outright sale of the title plant, gain or loss is the difference between the selling price and the net carrying amount of the title plant on the date of sale. In the event of the sale of an undivided interest in a title plant, gain or loss is the difference between the selling price and the pro rata portion of the title plant which is attributable to the sale of the undivided interest.

However, in a sale of a copy, or the right to use the title plant, no cost is allocated to the sale unless the value of the title plant decreases as a result of the sale. Thus, in the sale of a copy or the right to use the title plant, the sales price usually represents the gain on the sale.

Effective Date

FASB-61 is effective for fiscal years beginning on or after December 16, 1982. As with most promulgated GAAP, earlier application of FASB-61 is encouraged.

An accounting change which results from the initial application of FASB-61 shall be made, if practical, by retroactive restatement of all comparative financial statements. In addition, the financial statements of the year of change shall disclose the nature of any restatement and its effect on income before extraordinary items, net income, and related per share amounts, for each year presented.

If it is impractical to retroactively restate all of the individual financial statements for the comparative years presented, the following procedure must be used:

1. The new accounting principle (FASB-61) is used in determining net income of the year of change (current period).
2. As many consecutive prior years' financial statements (which are presented for comparative purposes) are then retroactively restated.
3. The cumulative effect of the change to FASB-61 is then computed for any remaining years in accordance with APB-20 (Accounting Changes).
4. The cumulative effect is then included in determining net income for the earliest year restated.
5. Financial statements presented for years prior to the earliest year restated (which include the cumulative effect) shall be presented for comparative purposes as they were originally reported.

In the event that it is impractical to retroactively restate any prior year, FASB-61 requires that the cumulative effect of the change in accounting principle be included in the net income of the year of change, in accordance with APB-20. In any year in which the cumulative effect is used, the effect of the change to FASB-61 on income before extraordinary items, net income, and related per share amounts shall be disclosed.

OBSERVATION: *The cumulative effect of a change in an accounting principle may be omitted under APB-20 if it is impossible to compute. In this event, the effects of the change, in the years of change, must be disclosed, along with an explanation as to why the cumulative effect was omitted.*

Mortgage Banking Industry

MORTGAGE BANKING INDUSTRY

Overview

FASB-65 contains the specialized accounting and reporting principles and practices that were originally published in the AICPA Statement of Position 74-12 (Accounting Practices in the Mortgage Banking Industry) and Statement of Position 76-2 (Accounting for Origination Costs and Loan and Commitment Fees in the Mortgage Banking Industry). FASB Technical Bulletin 85-2 (Accounting for Collateralized Mortgage Obligations [CMOs]) is discussed at the end of this chapter.

FASB-65 has also been amended by FASB-91 (Accounting for Nonrefundable Fees and Costs Associated with Originating or Acquiring Loans and Initial Direct Costs of Leases).

FASB-65 establishes the promulgated GAAP for (a) an enterprise or (b) that portion of an enterprise's operations engaged primarily in originating, marketing, and servicing mortgage loans for other than its own account. Thus, a financial institution or other enterprise that has operations which consist of originating, marketing, and servicing mortgage loans for others must apply the provisions of FASB-65 to those operations.

FASB Technical Bulletin 87-3 (FASB:TB 87-3), issued December 31, 1987, provides guidance on accounting for mortgage servicing fees and rights. The primary issue in this Technical Bulletin is what constitutes a normal servicing fee rate when an enterprise sells loans with servicing retained. Normal servicing fee rates are discussed more fully later in this chapter.

Accounting for Mortgage Loans

One of the more difficult problems in accounting for mortgage loans receivable and mortgage-backed securities of an enterprise engaged in mortgage banking activity is their valuation for reporting purposes. The valuation of mortgage loans receivable and mortgage-backed securities depends upon whether they are held for sale or for long-term investment. However, it should be noted that most mortgage loans and mortgage-backed securities are usually held for sale in the ordinary course of the business of a mortgage banker. Valuation of mortgage loans receivable and mortgage-backed securities for reporting purposes shall be determined as of the balance sheet date.

Held for long-term investment   Before a mortgage loan or a mortgage-backed security can be classified as a long-term investment, the intent and ability of an enterprise to hold the loan to maturity or for an extended period must exist. When a mortgage loan receivable or security held for sale is reclassified as a long-term investment, the transfer must be made at the lower of cost or market on the date of transfer. In the event of a permanent impairment in the value of a mortgage loan or security classified as a long-term investment, its carrying value shall be further reduced to net realizable value. The amount of reduction shall be reported in net income of the period in which the impairment is discovered. In subsequent periods, any market recovery from the net realizable value shall be realized only at the time of sale, maturity, or other disposition of the mortgage loan or security.

Any difference between the carrying amount of the loan or security and its outstanding principal balance shall be recognized as an adjustment to yield and amortized to income by the interest method over the estimated life of the loan. The interest method shall be applied in accordance with paragraphs 18 and 19 of FASB-91 (Accounting for Nonrefundable Fees and Costs Associated with Originating or Acquiring Loans and Initial Direct Costs of Leases).

> **OBSERVATION**:   *SOP 74-12 (Accounting Practices in the Mortgage Banking Industry) requires that mortgage loans and mortgage-backed securities held for long-term investment be reported at cost for financial statement purposes. FASB-65 does not specify or indicate the basis of valuation which should be used to record mortgage loans or mortgage-backed securities that are held for long-term investment. There is no apparent explanation for this omission.*
>
> *In addition, SOP 74-12 requires a number of conditions to exist at the time a mortgage loan or mortgage-backed security is classified as a long-term investment, so as to substantiate the intent and ability of the enterprise. The conditions spelled out in SOP 74-12 are:*
>
> a.   *The accounting records and financial reports of the enterprise must reflect these mortgage loans and mortgage-backed securities separately as long-term investments.*

  b. *Documentary evidence should exist, such as a corporate resolu-tion, that these mortgage loans and mortgage-backed securities will be held for an extended period of time or to maturity.*

  c. *In classified balance sheets of the enterprise, if any, the mort-gage loans and mortgage-backed securities will be reflected as noncurrent assets.*

  d. *Evidence of financial strength of the enterprise should exist to substantiate that the mortgage loans and mortgage-backed se-curities can be held for an extended period or until maturity.*

Only the last of the above conditions is mentioned in FASB-65. There is no apparent explanation for the omission of the other three conditions. Since FASB-65 purports to extract the specialized ac-counting principles from SOP 74-12 without significant change, the unexplained omission of (a) a valuation basis for reporting long-term investments in mortgage loans and mortgage-backed securities and (b) the other three conditions which substantiate the intent and ability of the enterprise causes uncertainty as to whether these omitted provisions of SOP 74-12 are still applicable.

Held for sale   All mortgage loans receivable and mortgage-backed securities held for sale shall be valued at the lower of cost or market as defined by FASB-65, according to the type of mortgage loan or mortgage-backed security. Write-downs of a mortgage loan or mort-gage-backed security to the lower of cost or market shall be included in net income of the period in which the adjustment occurs. After write-down, write-ups to market values in subsequent periods shall be recorded, but total recorded market value may not exceed cost. The journal entry to record the recovery of market value is a debit to mortgage loans or mortgage-backed securities and a credit to an income account.

For the purposes of disclosure, mortgage loans and mortgage-backed securities shall be classified in at least the following two categories: (a) residential (one to four units) and (b) commercial. Lower of cost or market can be determined on the total of all mort-gage loans in a particular category or for each individual mortgage loan or mortgage-backed security.

Discounts resulting from the purchase of mortgage loans that are held for sale shall not be realized as income until the loans are actually sold.

Lower of cost or market shall be determined in accordance with the type of mortgage loan receivable or mortgage-based security, as follows:

Loans and Securities Covered by Commitments

Mortgage loans and mortgage-backed securities that are covered by commitments shall be valued as specified in the commitment, in other words, the actual prices specified in the commitments. The reason for this is that the mortgage banker is, at least, guaranteed those prices agreed upon in the commitment.

Mortgage loans and mortgage-backed securities that do not conform to the required specifications in the commitments must be classified as loans and securities *not* covered by commitments.

Loans Not Covered by Commitments

Market value for loans not covered by commitments is the market value of the loans as determined by reference to the normal market in which the mortgage banker operates.

Quotations supplied by GNMA or the FNMA Free Market System or other public markets should be used when appropriate. If no established market quotations are available, market prices should be determined by the enterprise's normal market outlets.

Mortgage-Backed Securities Not Covered by Commitments

GNMA Mortgage-Backed Securities may be held by a mortgage banker for the purpose of trading on the open market. The current market value of the underlying mortgage loans which are pledged by the mortgage banker as collateral for the GNMA securities is usually the same as the current market value of the securities themselves. In other words, the market value of the mortgage loans held in trust as collateral for the GNMA securities should certainly be approximately the same as the value at which the GNMA securities are being traded.

Market value for GNMA Mortgage-Backed Securities for the purposes of lower of cost or market depends upon whether the trust agreement which covers the mortgage banker's underlying mortgage loans can be terminated on short notice and the mortgage loans sold on the open market. In this event, market value for the GNMA securities is either the current market value of the GNMA securities or the current market value of the underlying mortgage loans. The choice of which current market to use should be based on whether or not the mortgage banker intends to terminate the trust. If the mortgage banker does not intend to terminate the trust, market value for the purposes of lower of cost or market should be the current market value of the GNMA securities. If the mortgage banker intends to terminate the trust, market value for the purposes of lower of cost or market should be the current market value of the underlying mortgage loans.

If the trust cannot be terminated on short notice by the mortgage banker, market value of the GNMA securities for the purposes of lower of cost or market should be based on the published GNMA securities yield.

Block purchases of mortgage loans   Block purchases of mortgage loans have been made by mortgage bankers from GNMA or other investors. Certain costs incurred in block purchases of mortgage loans which can be associated with future servicing income are capitalized and amortized over the estimated average term of the mortgage loans. When these costs are appropriately capitalized in accordance with FASB-65, they shall be added to the valuation of the loans, after cost or the lower of cost or market is determined. However, if the costs have been inappropriately capitalized, they must be included as part of cost, or the lower of cost or market, of the mortgage loans.

Repurchase agreements   Frequently, a mortgage banking enterprise will enter into formal or informal repurchase agreements (repos) with a lending institution. In a repurchase agreement, the mortgage banking enterprise will give the lending institution a block of mortgage loans and/or mortgage-backed securities as collateral for a loan. On the surface, the transaction may appear as a sale of the mortgage loans and/or mortgage-backed securities to the lending institution, with an agreement, formal or otherwise, that the mortgage banking enterprise will repurchase the loans and/or securities at an agreed-upon price, which usually is equal to the amount of the loan. If the mortgage banking enterprise fails to repurchase the mortgage loans and/or mortgage-backed securities in accordance with the agreement, the lending institution exercises ownership of the loans and/or securities. The mortgage banking enterprise pays an agreed-upon rate of interest for the use of the funds.

Formal and informal repurchase agreements shall be accounted for by the mortgage banking enterprise as a financing, and no sale shall be recorded.

Historically, short-term interest rates have always been less than long-term interest rates. Thus, when a mortgage banker paid interest on short-term warehouse loans, the interest received on the pledged mortgage loans always exceeded the amount paid to carry them on a short-term basis. The difference between the short-term and long-term interest rates creates a *positive spread* for the mortgage banker. However, sometimes interest rates reverse, and short-term rates exceed long-term rates. This results in a *negative spread* in interest rates for the mortgage banker. Since the cost of warehousing mortgage loans by a mortgage banker is primarily a financing activity, negative spreads in interest rates should be charged to current operations as they are incurred.

Mortgage servicing fees All types of mortgage loans must be serviced. The process of collecting, sending notices, maintaining mortgage records, and other related chores are referred to as *servicing*. The owner of a loan or portfolio of loans may perform the *servicing function*, or it may engage someone else to perform such services. An entity which performs the servicing for mortgage loans usually charges a fee based on a percentage of the unpaid principal balance of the loans. Servicing revenue can be quite substantial.

As a general rule, most mortgage bankers service their own outstanding loans, and they may also service a large number of mortgage loans for others.

A problem may arise when a mortgage banker sells a loan or a portfolio of loans and agrees to continue servicing the loans at a fee which is significantly different from prevailing servicing rates.

Ordinarily, when a loan or portfolio of loans is sold and the buyer assumes the servicing function, no problem arises. Gain or loss on the sale of loans is the difference between the sales price and the net carrying amount of the loans. However, when loans are sold and the seller continues the servicing function for the buyer, a problem arises if the servicing fee charged is significantly different from prevailing service rates and the result is expected to materially affect current or future operating results. In this event, gain or loss on the sale of the mortgage loans must be increased or decreased to provide a normal profit on future servicing income, based on estimated prevailing servicing fee rates. The amount of adjustment shall be calculated on the date of sale and is equal to the difference between total servicing fee income based on the current prevailing servicing fee rate and total servicing fee income based on the contractually agreed-upon servicing fee rate. In the event that the contractually agreed-upon servicing fee rate is significantly lower than the current prevailing rate, the journal entry to record the adjustment is a debit to the gain or loss on the sale of mortgage loans and a credit to deferred servicing fee revenue. The deferred servicing fee revenue is amortized to income over the life of the related loans, so that each future period will include servicing fee revenue equal to the prevailing servicing fee rate at the date of sale of the mortgage loans.

Occasionally, estimated servicing costs may be expected to exceed normal servicing income over the estimated life of the related mortgage loans. In this event, the resulting loss shall be accrued on the date of sale or the date on which the loss is discovered.

It is important to note that the adjustment of future servicing fees is only made when (a) the agreed-upon servicing fee rate at the date of sale is materially different than the current prevailing servicing fee rate and (b) the agreed-upon servicing fee rate is expected to significantly affect current or future operating results.

Normal servicing fees   FASB Technical Bulletin 87-3 (FASB: TB 87-3) was issued to provide guidance on what constitutes a normal servicing fee rate when an enterprise sells loans and retains the servicing function.

Under FASB-65, a current (normal) servicing fee rate is representative of servicing fee rates most commonly used in comparable servicing agreements covering similar types of mortgage loans. Federally sponsored secondary market makers for mortgage loans, such as Government National Mortgage Association (GNMA), Federal Home Loan Mortgage Corporation (FHLMC), and Federal National Mortgage Association (FNMA), set minimum servicing fee rates for transactions with them. For purposes of determining gain or loss on mortgage loans sold to those agencies with servicing retained, servicing fee rates that are specified in servicing agreements with GNMA, FHLMC, and FNMA are generally considered normal servicing fee rates, as that term is used in FASB-65.

> **OBSERVATION:**   *At the June 1986 meeting of the FASB Emerging Issues Task Force (EITF) a discussion was held concerning the interpretation of what constitutes a normal servicing fee as defined in paragraph 11 of FASB-65 (Accounting for Certain Mortgage Banking Activities). Although a consensus was not reached on the definition of a normal servicing fee, the Task Force did reach a consensus that the use of a normal service fee that is developed as a function of the servicer's cost of servicing is not appropriate.*

If a seller-servicer sells mortgage loans directly to private-sector investors and retains the servicing of those loans, the seller-servicer should charge the private-sector investors a current (normal) servicing fee rate as defined in FASB-65. In this event, the seller-servicer should consider the normal servicing fee rates currently being charged by federally sponsored secondary market makers in comparable servicing agreements for similar types of mortgage loans.

If the servicing fee rate charged by the seller-servicer is not a normal servicing fee rate, an adjustment must be made to the sales price of the mortgage loans to the private-sector investors. In this event, gain or loss on the sale of the mortgage loans is adjusted to provide a normal profit on future servicing income, based on estimated prevailing normal servicing fee rates. The amount of adjustment shall be calculated on the date of sale and is equal to the difference between total servicing fee income based on current prevailing normal servicing fee rates and total servicing fee income based on the contractually agreed-upon servicing fee rate.

Prepayments of mortgage loans are generally taken into consideration at the time servicing rights are recorded on the books of a servicer of mortgage loans. In other words, the servicer sets up an allowance for anticipated future prepayments that may occur from refinancings or other sources. In this event, when an anticipated prepayment materializes, no adjustment to the recorded amount of the servicing right is necessary. On the other hand, if the mortgage loan servicer did not set up an allowance for prepayments at the time the servicing right was originally recorded, an adjustment to the servicing right asset would be required when a prepayment is made.

FASB Technical Bulletin 87-3 is effective for transactions entered into on or after December 31, 1987. Earlier application of the provisions of FASB:TB 87-3 is encouraged for those transactions that occurred in periods for which financial statements have not been issued.

Transactions with affiliates   In separate financial statements of mortgage banking enterprises, special treatment is afforded sales of mortgage loans and/or mortgage-backed securities which are made to affiliated enterprises. The selling affiliate must first adjust the carrying amount of the mortgage loans and/or mortgage-backed securities to the lower of cost or market before computing gain or loss on the sale. Any adjustment is charged or credited to income by the selling affiliate. Thus, the gain or loss on the sale of mortgage loans and/or mortgage-backed securities to an affiliated enterprise is the difference between the sales price and the lower of cost or market of the loans and/or securities.

Gain or loss on the sale or mortgage loans and/or mortgage-backed securities is determined as of the measurement date. The measurement date is the first date that management decides that the sale shall take place. The measurement date must be supported by formal approval of the sale by the purchasing affiliate and the issuance of a binding commitment. The binding commitment must be approved and accepted by the selling mortgage banker.

A mortgage banker may act in the capacity of an agent, for an affiliated company. In the capacity of an agent the mortgage banker will originate certain specified types of loans for the affiliated company. Under these circumstances the mortgage banker may charge an origination fee for services rendered in acquiring the loans. However, all risks of ownership must be assumed by the affiliated company in order to constitute an agency relationship. The affiliated company should record the loans acquired at the mortgage banker's acquisition cost.

Agreements, or arrangements which do not bind the affiliated company to purchase the loans originated by the affiliated mortgage banker such as *right of first refusal* contracts, do not establish an agency relationship.

> **OBSERVATION:** *This section on transactions with affiliates is applicable only to the separate financial statements of mortgage banking enterprises. Also, in separate financial statements of mortgage banking enterprises, material transactions with affiliates are subject to the disclosure provisions of FASB-57 (Related Party Disclosures).*

> **OBSERVATION:** *SOP 74-12 states that in the sale of mortgages from an affiliated mortgage banker to another affiliated enterprise, there is a presumption that the purchasing affiliate is acquiring the mortgage loans for long-term investment purposes. Thus, if a repurchase or similar agreement exists between the affiliated mortgage banker and the affiliated purchaser, the presumption that the mortgage loans are being acquired for long-term investment purposes cannot be supported. In this event, the transaction between the two affiliates may have to be accounted for as an intercompany loan, collateralized by the mortgage loans. FASB-65 does not cover this point.*

Issuance costs for GNMA securities   A mortgage banking enterprise may use either the concurrent dates method (15 days) or the internal reserve method (45 days) to pay the holder(s) of GNMA Mortgage-Backed Securities. Under the internal reserve method the mortgage banking enterprise is required to deposit one month's interest on the mortgage loans with a trustee. There is no such requirement under the concurrent dates method.

Under the provisions of FASB-65, the one month's interest required by the internal reserve method shall be capitalized and amortized by a mortgage banking enterprise. Amortization of any amount deferred must be over the period of, and in proportion to, the estimated net servicing income expected to be earned from the related underlying mortgage loans.

The total amount deferred by a mortgage banking enterprise for issuance costs or under any other provision of FASB-65 may not exceed the present value of the future net servicing income. Future net servicing income is the difference between estimated future servicing revenue and the estimated future related servicing costs.

Accounting for Servicing Rights

Mortgage banking enterprises sometimes acquire blocks of mortgages in bulk purchases from GNMA, FNMA, and others. Part of the purchase price may be attributable to the right to receive future servicing income. In addition, in a business combination, part of the purchase price may be properly allocable to the right to receive future servicing income. In either event, the amount directly attributable to the right to receive future servicing income shall be deferred with certain limitations. The first limitation is that the amount deferred for the right to receive future servicing income shall not be more than the difference between the market value (excluding servicing rights) of the mortgage loans at the date of purchase and the total purchase price paid for the loans, plus transfer fees, if any. Market value of the mortgage loans at the date of purchase must be determined in accordance with the provisions of FASB-65 (lower of cost or market), which have been discussed earlier. In addition, the following conditions must be met:

1. Prior to the date of purchase, the mortgage banker must obtain commitments from investors to purchase the mortgage loans or related mortgage-backed securities, or obtain such commitments no later than 30 days after the date of the purchase. The commitments must provide for the mortgage banker to continue servicing the mortgage loans.

2. If the sales price to the permanent investors exceeds the market value of the mortgage loans at the date of purchase, the difference must be applied to reduce any amount deferred for the right to receive future servicing income.

3. Other than those costs identified above, no other costs relating to the purchase of mortgage loans can be deferred.

> **OBSERVATION:** *If the above conditions are not met, the cost of the right to receive future servicing income is usually included as part of the cost of the mortgage loans for the purposes of determining lower of cost or market.*

The second limitation is that under no circumstances shall the amount allocated to the right to receive future servicing income exceed the present value of the estimated future *net* servicing income. A long-term interest rate is considered appropriate in calculating the present value of the estimated future *net* servicing income. The future *net* servicing income is the difference between the estimated future servicing revenue and the estimated future servicing costs. Probable late charges and other ancillary revenue shall be included in the estimated future servicing revenue, and direct costs and appropriate allocations of other costs related to the servicing function shall be included in the estimated future servicing costs. Servicing costs may be determined on an incremental cost basis.

The amortization of the right to receive future servicing income shall be made over the period of, and in proportion to, the estimated future *net* servicing income.

Financial Statement Disclosure

Balance sheet presentations of mortgage banking enterprises for reporting purposes may be classified or unclassified. In other words, segregation between current and noncurrent items is optional. However, mortgage loans receivable and mortgage-backed securities must be separately disclosed as to (a) those held for sale and (b) those held for long-term investment. In addition, disclosure must be made of the method used to determine the lower of cost or market value of mortgage loans receivable and mortgage-backed securities.

In connection with the capitalization of any *servicing rights* acquired by purchase during the period, the following disclosures must be made:

1. The amount capitalized
2. The method of amortization used
3. The amount of amortization

> **OBSERVATION:** *Under FASB-65, the above disclosures pertain only to servicing rights acquired by bulk purchases made during the current period. Since servicing rights are intangible assets, they*

are subject to the provisions of APB-17 (Intangible Assets). Thus, servicing rights acquired during the current period in a business combination and all servicing rights acquired in prior periods must be disclosed, if material, in accordance with APB-17. APB-17 generally requires that a description of intangible assets, method of amortization, and estimated useful lives be appropriately disclosed in the financial statements or in footnotes. In the event that a large part or all of the amortized cost of an intangible asset is included as an extraordinary charge in the determination of current net income, APB-17 requires that the reasons for the extraordinary deduction be fully disclosed.

The provisions of FASB-65 relating to (a) lower of cost or market (paragraph 4) and (b) disclosures (paragraph 28, 29, and 30) are effective for fiscal years beginning on or after December 16, 1982, and earlier application is encouraged. All other provisions of FASB-65 shall be applied prospectively to transactions entered into on or after January 1, 1983, and earlier application is also encouraged.

ACCOUNTING FOR NONREFUNDABLE FEES AND COSTS ASSOCIATED WITH ORIGINATING OR ACQUIRING LOANS (FASB-91)

Background

Loan origination fees and commitment fees represent a primary source of revenue to a mortgage banking enterprise. In addition, a mortgage banker may pay a fee to a permanent investor for a commitment by a permanent investor to purchase certain specified mortgage loans from the mortgage banker during a specified term.

FASB-91 establishes accounting and reporting standards for nonrefundable fees and costs associated with lending, committing to lend, or purchasing a loan or group of loans. FASB-91 also specifies the appropriate accounting for fees and initial direct costs associated with leasing transactions.

The provisions of FASB-91 apply to all types of loans, including debt securities, and to all types of lenders, including banks, thrift institutions, insurance companies, mortgage bankers, and other financial and nonfinancial institutions. However, FASB-91 does not apply to nonrefundable fees and costs that are associated with originating or acquiring loans that are carried at market value.

Appendix C of FASB-91 contains the following definitions of terms used in FASB-91:

Commitment fees   Fees charged for entering into an agreement that obligates the enterprise to make or acquire a loan or to satisfy an obligation of the other party under a specified condition. For purposes of this Statement [FASB-91], the term *commitment fees* includes fees for letters of credit and obligations to purchase a loan or group of loans and pass-through certificates.

Credit card fees   The periodic uniform fees that entitle cardholders to use credit cards. The amount of such fees generally is not dependent upon the level of credit available or frequency of usage. Typically the use of credit cards facilitates the cardholder's payment for the purchase of goods and services on a periodic, as-billed basis (usually monthly), involves the extension of credit, and, if payment is not made when billed, involves imposition of interest or finance charges. For the purposes of this Statement [FASB-91], the term *credit card fees* includes fees received in similar arrangements, such as charge card and cash card fees.

Incremental direct costs   Costs to originate a loan that (a) result directly from and are essential to the lending transaction and (b) would not have been incurred by the lender had that lending transaction not occurred.

Origination fees   Fees charged to the borrower in connection with the process of originating, refinancing, or restructuring a loan. This term includes, but is not limited to, points, management, arrangement, placement, application, underwriting, and other fees pursuant to a lending or leasing transaction and also includes syndication and participation fees to the extent they are associated with the portion of the loan retained by the lender.

Accounting for Direct Loan Origination Costs

Under FASB-91, there are only two categories of direct loan origination costs on completed loans that may be offset against any related loan origination fees or any related commitment fees. The first category of direct loan origination costs of a completed loan include those incremental direct costs that are incurred in originating loan transactions with independent third parties. Incremental direct costs are costs that are incurred to originate loans that (a) result directly from and are essential to the lending transaction and (b) would not have been incurred by the lender had that lending transaction not occurred.

The second category of direct loan origination costs includes certain costs that are directly related to the following specified activities performed by the lender in connection with a loan or a loan commitment:

 a. Evaluating the prospective borrower's financial condition
 b. Evaluating and recording guarantees, collateral, and other security arrangements
 c. Negotiating the terms of the loan
 d. Preparing and processing loan documents
 e. Closing the transaction

Direct loan origination costs shall include only that portion of the lender's total employee compensation, including payroll-related fringe benefits, that is directly related to time spent performing the above activities for a specific loan and other costs related to those activities that would not have been incurred but for that specific loan. In other words, direct loan origination costs shall not include any portion of the lender's total employee compensation, including payroll-related fringe benefits, that is not directly related to time spent performing the above activities for a specific loan.

All other lending-related costs shall be expensed by the lender as incurred. Costs related to activities performed by the lender for advertising, soliciting potential borrowers, servicing existing loans, and other ancillary activities related to establishing and monitoring credit policies, supervision and administration shall be charged to expense as incurred. Employees' compensation and fringe benefits related to those activities, unsuccessful loan origination efforts, and idle time shall be charged to expense as incurred. Administrative costs, rent, depreciation, and all other occupancy and equipment costs are considered indirect costs and shall be charged to expense as incurred.

Accounting for Loan Origination Fees

An enterprise may acquire an individual loan contract by originating a loan directly with the borrower or by purchasing a loan from a party other than the borrower. Although the provisions of FASB-91 must generally be applied to each individual loan contract, similar individual loan contracts may be grouped together for the purpose of recognizing net fees or costs and purchase premiums or discounts provided that the amounts do not differ materially from the amounts that would have been recognized on an individual loan-by-loan basis.

> **OBSERVATION**: *Individual loan contracts that are grouped together must have sufficiently similar characteristics and have approximately the same level of net fees or costs to permit the recalculation of the carrying amount of individual loan contracts. Thus, if an individual loan contract in the group is sold, its carrying amount must be recalculable.*

Loan origination fees and direct loan origination costs that are incurred on a specific loan shall be offset against each other and accounted for as follows:

If Loan Is Held for Resale—The loan origination fee and the related direct loan origination costs shall be deferred and recognized at the time the loan is sold.

If Loan Is Held for Investment—The net difference between the loan origination fee and the related direct loan origination cost shall be deferred and recognized over the life of the loan as an adjustment of the yield on the loan. The interest method shall be used to amortize the net fee or cost over the life of the loan.

Accounting for Commitment Fees

A loan commitment is a written representation from a lender to a borrower to lend funds for a specific purpose and term. A commitment term may be as short as one week or possibly as long as one year or longer. A *floating rate commitment* is one in which the interest rate to be charged on the loan is determined by the prevailing rate of interest at the time the loan is drawn upon. A *fixed rate commitment* is one in which the interest rate is specified in the commitment.

The recognition of revenue from loan commitment fees varies with the type and substance of the commitment. Obviously, income is recognized on all commitments if the loan is not made and the term of the commitment expires. In this event, the lender has no further obligation to perform, and the loan commitment fee is earned.

If a loan commitment is exercised before the expiration of the commitment period, the related commitment fee and direct loan origination cost shall be deferred and recognized over the life of the loan as an adjustment of the yield on the loan. The interest method shall be used to amortize the net fee or cost over the life of the loan.

If only a remote (unlikely) possibility exists that a commitment will be exercised based on an enterprise's past experience with similar types of commitments, the commitment fee shall be recognized as service fee income on a straight-line basis over the commitment period. In the event that the commitment is exercised before the end of the commitment period, the balance of the remaining unamortized commitment fee on the date the commitment is exercised shall be recognized over the life of the loan as an adjustment of the yield on the loan.

The commitment fee shall be recognized as service fee income as of the determination date if (1) the amount of a commitment fee is determined retrospectively as a percentage of an available line of credit unused in a previous period, (2) the percentage is nominal in relation to the stated interest rate on any related borrowing, and (3) borrowing will bear a market interest rate at the date the loan is made.

Credit card fees   Credit card fees that are periodically charged to cardholders' accounts are considered loan commitments. Under FASB-91, credit card fees are deferred and recognized on a straight-line basis over the period in which the cardholder is entitled to use the card. Other similar card arrangements that involve the extension of credit by a card issuer shall be accounted for in the same manner.

Syndication Fees

Loan syndication fees shall be recognized upon completion of the syndication loan, unless a portion of the syndication loan is retained by the syndication manager. In this event, the yield on the portion of the syndication loan retained by the syndication manager shall not be less than the average yield of all syndication loans, including fees, that are held by the other syndication participants. If the yield on the portion of the loan retained by the syndication manager is less than the average yield to the other syndication participants, the syndication manager shall defer a portion of the syndication fee in an amount that will produce a yield on the portion of the loan retained that is not less than the average yield of the loans held by the other syndication participants.

Fees and Costs in Refinancings or Restructurings

A refinanced loan, other than a troubled debt restructuring (FASB-15), shall be accounted for as a new loan if its terms are at least as favorable to the lender as the terms for comparable loans to other customers with similar collection risks who are not refinancing or restructuring a loan with the lender. This means that the effective yield of the new loan should be at least equal to the effective yield of comparable loans of other customers with similar collection risks who are not refinancing.

> **OBSERVATION:** *The comparison of effective yields takes into consideration the level of nominal interest rate, commitment and origination fees, and direct loan origination costs. In addition, the comparison of other factors, such as compensating balance arrangements, should be considered where appropriate.*

Any unamortized net fees or costs and any prepayment penalties from the original loan shall be recognized in interest income when the new loan is granted.

If the terms of a refinancing or restructuring are not at least as favorable to the lender as the terms for comparable loans to other customers with similar collection risks who are not refinancing or restructuring loans with the lender, or if only minor modifications are made to the original loan contract, the unamortized net fees or costs from the original loan and any prepayment penalties shall be carried forward as a part of the net investment in the new loan. Thus, the investment in the new loan shall consist of (a) the remaining net investment in the original loan, (b) any additional amounts loaned, (c) any fees received, and (d) any direct loan origination costs that are associated with the refinancing or restructuring. The remaining net investment in the original loan consists of the unpaid loan principal, any remaining unamortized net fees or costs, any remaining unamortized purchase premium or discount, and any accrued interest receivable.

For the purposes of applying paragraph 30 of FASB-15 (Accounting by Debtors and Creditors for Troubled Debt Restructurings), fees received in connection with a modification of terms of a troubled debt restructuring shall be applied as a reduction of the recorded investment in the loan. All related costs, including direct loan origination costs, shall be charged to expense as incurred.

Purchase of a Loan or Group of Loans

The initial investment in a purchased loan or group of loans shall include the amount paid to the seller plus any fees paid or less any fees received. The difference between the initial investment in a purchased loan or group of loans and the principal amount at the date of purchase shall be recognized as an adjustment of the yield over the life of the loan or group of loans. All other costs incurred in connection with acquiring purchased loans or committing to purchase loans shall be charged to expense as incurred.

For the purposes of FASB-91, the initial investment made for loans purchased as a group may be accounted for in the aggregate or may be allocated to the individual loans in the group. The cash flows generated by the payment terms of the underlying loan contracts shall be used to calculate the constant effective yield necessary to apply the interest method. Prepayments of principal shall not be anticipated in calculating the constant effective yield, unless the conditions specified by FASB-91 are met. If prepayments of principal are not anticipated and prepayments occur or a portion of the pur-chased loans is sold, a proportionate amount of the related deferred fees and purchase premium or discount shall be recognized in in-come so that the effective interest rate on the remaining portion of loans continues unchanged.

Application of the Interest Method

Except for *demand loans* and *revolving lines of credit* (see following discussion), the interest method shall be used to amortize net fees or costs that are required under FASB-91 to be recognized as yield adjustments over the life of their related loans. The interest method produces a constant effective rate of interest income on the remain-ing net investment in the loan receivable. The net investment in the loan receivable consists of the principal amount of the loan receivable adjusted for any unamortized fees or costs and purchase premium or discount. The amount of periodic amortization is equal to the difference between the stated interest on the outstanding principal amount of the loan receivable and the amount of periodic interest income calculated by the interest method.

During those periods in which interest income on a loan is not being recognized because of concerns about realization of the loan principal or interest, deferred net fees or costs shall not be amortized (paragraph 17 of FASB-91).

Under FASB-91, when the stated interest rate is not constant throughout the term of a loan, the interest method shall be applied as follows:

Interest Rate Increases   If the stated interest rate increases during the term of the loan, the amount of interest accrued in the early periods under the interest method will exceed the stated amount of interest for the same periods. In this event, the net investment in the loan could increase to an amount greater than the amount at which the borrower could settle the obligation. Under FASB-91, no interest income shall be recognized during any period in which the borrower can settle the obligation for less than the amount of the net investment in the loan. In determining the amount at which the borrower can settle the obligation, prepayment penalties shall be considered only to the extent that such penalties are imposed throughout the loan term.

Interest Rate Decreases   If the stated interest rate decreases during the term of the loan, the amount of periodic interest accrued in the early periods under the interest method will be less than the stated amount of interest received for the same periods. In that circumstance, the excess stated interest received during the early periods of the loan shall be deferred and recognized in those future periods when the constant effective yield under the interest method exceeds the stated interest rate.

Interest Rate Varies   The stated interest rate on a loan may be based on the future changes that occur in an independent factor, such as the prime interest rate, the London Interbank Offered Rate (LIBOR), or the U.S. Treasury bill weekly average rate. In this event, the calculation of the constant effective yield necessary to recognize fees and costs shall be based either on the independent factor in effect at the inception of the loan or on the independent factor as it changes over the life of the loan.

Prepayments of principal anticipated The cash flows generated by the payment terms of the underlying loan contracts shall be used to calculate the constant effective yield necessary to apply the interest method, and prepayments of principal shall not be anticipated to shorten the loan term. However, if an enterprise holds a large number of similar loans for which prepayments are probable (likely) and the timing and amount of prepayments can be reasonably estimated, an enterprise may consider estimates of future principal prepayments in calculating the constant effective yield necessary to apply the interest method.

> **OBSERVATION:** *Individual loan contracts that are grouped together must have sufficiently similar characteristics and have approximately the same levels of net fees or costs to permit the recalculation of the carrying amount of individual loan contracts. Thus, if an individual loan contract in the group is sold, that loan's carrying amount must be recalculable.*

If the enterprise anticipates prepayments in applying the interest method and a difference arises between the prepayments anticipated and actual prepayments received, the enterprise shall recalculate the effective yield to reflect the actual payments received to date and the remaining anticipated future payments. In this event, the net investment in the loans shall be adjusted to the amount that would have existed had the new effective yield been applied since the acquisition of the loans. The investment in the loans shall be adjusted to the new balance with a corresponding charge or credit to interest income.

Enterprises that anticipate prepayments shall disclose that policy and the significant assumptions underlying the prepayment estimates. The practice of recognizing net fees over the estimated average life of a group of loans shall no longer be acceptable.

> **OBSERVATION:** *Most of the above information is included in paragraph 19 of FASB-91, which sets forth the conditions that must exist for an enterprise to anticipate prepayments of principal in calculating the constant effective yield necessary to apply the interest method. Absent a reasonably large number of loans with similar characteristics, the FASB believes the reliability of reasonably projecting cash flows is diminished to an unacceptable level (paragraph 58 of FASB-91). When the conditions of paragraph 19 are not met, the FASB concluded that anticipation of prepayments is not appropriate and that recognition of fees and costs and purchase premiums or discounts should be in accordance with the repayment terms provided in the loan contract, with any unamortized amount recognized in income if and when prepayment occurs. In this respect, the practice of recognizing net fees over the estimated average life of a group of loans shall no longer be acceptable (paragraph 19 of FASB-91).*

Demand loans and revolving lines of credit A demand loan does not have scheduled repayment terms because it is payable on demand. A revolving line of credit usually grants the borrower the option of making multiple borrowings up to a specified maximum to repay portions of previous borrowings, and then to reborrow more funds under the same contract. As mentioned above, net fees or costs that are incurred in connection with demand loans and revolving lines of credit are not recognized by the interest method (paragraph 18 of FASB-91) but are recognized as follows:

> *Demand Loans* Net fees or costs on demand loans may be recognized as an adjustment of yield on a straight-line basis over a period that is consistent with (a) the understanding between the borrower and lender and (b) if no understanding exists, the lender's estimate of the period in which the loan will remain outstanding. At the time the loan is paid in full, any unamortized balance of net fees or costs shall also be recognized in full.

> *Revolving Lines of Credit* Net fees or costs on revolving lines of credit or similar arrangements shall be recognized in income on a straight-line basis over the period in which the revolving line of credit is active, provided that borrowings are outstanding for the maximum term specified in the loan agreement.
>
> At the time all borrowings are repaid in full by the borrower, and no additional funds can be borrowed under the terms of the loan agreement, the balance of any unamortized net fees or costs shall be recognized in income.
>
> When the loan agreement specifies a repayment schedule for the funds borrowed and no additional funds can be borrowed under the terms of the loan agreement, the interest method shall be used to recognize any net unamortized fees or costs.

Balance Sheet and Income Statement Classifications

Under FASB-91, the unamortized balance of loan origination, commitment, and other fees and costs and purchase premiums and discounts that are being recognized as an adjustment of yield shall be reported on the balance sheet of an enterprise as part of the related loan receivable balance.

Amortization of loan origination, commitment, and other fees and costs recognized as an adjustment of yield shall be reported as part of interest income. Amortization of commitment fees and other fees that are being amortized on a straight-line basis over the commitment period or included in income when the commitment expires shall be reported in the income statement as service fee income.

Effective Date and Transition

FASB-91 shall be applied prospectively to commitments granted and lending and leasing transactions that are entered into in fiscal years beginning after December 15, 1987, and in the interim periods that are included in those fiscal years. Retroactive restatement of all prior-period financial statements that are presented for comparative purposes is encouraged but not required. Earlier application of the provisions of FASB-91 to financial statements of those fiscal years for which financial statements have not previously been issued is also encouraged but not required. In the year that FASB-91 is first applied, the financial statements shall disclose the nature of accounting changes that result from applying the provisions of FASB-91 and their effect on income before extraordinary items, net income, and related per share amounts for the current year and for each restated year presented. If adopted prospectively, disclosure of the accounting change and the prior accounting policies shall be continued in financial statements of subsequent years in which outstanding loans accounted for under the prior policy are material.

ACCOUNTING FOR COLLATERALIZED MORTGAGE OBLIGATIONS (CMOs)

Overview

FASB Technical Bulletin 85-2 (FASB:TB 85-2) provides guidance on the issuer's accounting for certain types of bonds that are collateralized by pools of real estate mortgages and are commonly referred to as collateralized mortgage obligations (CMOs).

Background

A security whose payment is guaranteed by a specific pool of real estate mortgages is referred to as a mortgage-backed security. Generally, a mortgage-backed security is issued either as a pass-through certificate or a fixed-rate bond, which is commonly referred to as a *collateralized mortgage obligation.*

In addition to its payment being guaranteed by a specific pool of mortgages, the payment of a mortgage-backed security may also be guaranteed by the Government National Mortgage Association (GNMA), an agency of the United States government. GNMA guarantees, with the full faith and credit of the United States government, the timely payment of principal and interest to the registered holders of the securities.

A mortgage lender must apply to GNMA for approval to become an issuer of GNMA mortgage-backed securities and for a commitment for GNMA to guarantee a particular mortgage-backed security. An approved GNMA mortgage lender originates or acquires government insured or guaranteed mortgages (VA and FHA) and assembles them into a specific pool or loan package of mortgages. The mortgages within a specific pool must be of the same type, have similar maturities, be less than 12 months old and, in the case of GNMA I pools, all have the same interest rate. Mortgages in GNMA II pool may have interest rates that vary within a one-percent range. The minimum pool size is typically one million dollars.

GNMA reviews the documents submitted by the issuer and authorizes its transfer agent to prepare and deliver securities to investors. The issuer is fully responsible for the marketing and administration of the securities. In the GNMA I program, the issuer makes the monthly payment of principal and interest directly to the investors. In the GNMA II program, the issuer remits the principal and interest payments to GNMA's central paying agent, which in turn pays the holders of the securities. The issuer in both programs carries out mortgage servicing and prepares periodic reports to GNMA.

GNMA securities are modified pass-through securities. This means that holders of the securities receive monthly pass-through payments of interest at the rate shown on the securities, plus principal as scheduled on the pooled mortgages, whether or not such payments are made by the mortgagors. Holders of securities also receive pass-throughs of any early (unscheduled) recoveries of principal and, ultimately, the full repayment, at par, of all principal outstanding on the securities. All of these payments are guaranteed to the issuer by GNMA.

The Federal National Mortgage Association (Fannie Mae) and the Federal Home Loan Mortgage Corporation (Freddie Mac) are quasi-government agencies which issue securities backed by conventional mortgages that are not government insured or guaranteed. Fannie Mae and Freddie Mac securities are not backed by the full faith and credit of the United States government, but usually carry an AAA bond rating.

The irregular flow of income from a pass-through certificate does not appeal to all investors. Some Wall Street brokerage firms have responded with the *collateralized mortgage obligation* (CMO), which provides a more predictable cash flow. A CMO consists of a series of bonds that mature in approximately five, ten, twenty, and thirty years and that are collateralized by a specific pool of real estate mortgages. Maturity dates are approximate because they depend on how promptly the mortgagors make their mortgage payments and the number of mortgages that are paid off before their maturity date. Each series of bonds is periodically paid a fixed rate of interest, usually every one, three, or six months. As they are collected, all principal payments received from the mortgagors are deposited in an escrow account. The funds in the escrow account are used to retire the principal amount of the bonds in the order of their maturity. Thus, the principal amounts of the five-year bonds are paid off first, then the ten-year bonds, and so forth.

As a conduit for marketing the CMOs, one or more sponsors form a special purpose corporation, which is usually minimally capitalized. The special purpose corporation originates or acquires the mortgages, which are then pledged to an independent trustee, under the terms of the bond indenture. The obligations of the special purpose corporation are enumerated in the bond indenture.

If an enterprise has issued mortgage-backed securities and the amount is material, disclosure of the amount, type, interest rate, and all other pertinent facts should be made in the financial statements or footnotes thereto (FASB-65).

Accounting for CMOs

Under FASB Technical Bulletin 85-2, collateralized mortgage obligations (CMOs) are presumed to be borrowing transactions and should be recorded as liabilities in the financial statements of the issuer. However, a CMO shall not be accounted for as a borrowing transaction if (a) all but a nominal portion of the future economic benefits inherent in the associated collateral have been irrevocably passed to the investor and (b) no affiliate of the issuer can be required to make any future payments with respect to the obligation.

If each of the following conditions exists at the issuance date of the CMOs, they would generally indicate that the borrowing presumption has been overcome, and the obligation and its related collateral should be eliminated from the financial statements of the issuer:

1. The future economic benefits in the collateral securing the obligation are irrevocably surrendered by the issuer and/or its affiliates.

    a. The right or obligation to substitute or reacquire the collateral is irrevocably surrendered by the issuer and/or its affiliates. (Under FASB:TB 85-2, the CMO may contain a *call* provision, provided that the amount of reacquired collateral is expected to be minor.)

    b. The expected residual interest, if any, in the collateral is nominal. This condition would not be met if an affiliate of the issuer retained a partial ownership interest in the CMO or its related collateral.

        The expected residual interest in the collateral is equal to the present value of all amounts expected to revert to the issuer or its affiliates, including reinvestment earnings and servicing fees in excess of normal servicing fees.

2. No affiliate of the issuer can be required to make any future payments with respect to the obligation. (Under FASB:TB 85-2, an affiliate of the issuer may retain the servicing rights to the pooled mortgages.)

    a. The investor agrees to look solely to the segregated assets of the issuer, insurers, guarantors, or other third parties for repayment of the obligation, and the issuer's sponsor or affiliates cannot be secondarily liable for the payment of the obligation.

    b. The issuer and its affiliates cannot be required to redeem the obligation prior to its maturity date.

If the above conditions are met, the borrowings for the CMOs and the related collateral should be eliminated from the issuer's financial statements, and all other costs associated with the offering transaction should be charged to expense. The expected residual interest in the collateral, if any, should not be recorded until it accrues to the benefit of the issuer or its affiliates.

Servicing rights   If the servicing rights are retained by an affiliate of the issuer, and the servicing fee rate is less than the prevailing market servicing fee rates, the proceeds from an offering of collateralized mortgage obligations must be adjusted to provide a normal profit on future servicing income. The amount of adjustment shall be calculated on the issuance date of the CMOs and is equal to the difference between the total servicing fee income based on the current prevailing service fee rate and the total servicing fee income based upon the contractually agreed-upon servicing fee rate. In the event that the contractually agreed-upon servicing fee rate is significantly lower than the current prevailing rate, the journal entry to record the adjustment is a debit to the gain or loss on the CMO offering and a credit to deferred servicing fee revenue. The deferred servicing fee revenue is amortized to income over the life of the related mortgages so that each future period will include servicing fee income equal to the prevailing market servicing fee rate on the issuance date of the CMOs.

Consolidated statements   Usually the issuer of the CMO is a minimally capitalized special-purpose corporation that has been established by one or more sponsors. FASB:TB 85-2 concludes that since the majority-owned special-purpose corporation simply acts as a conduit for the sponsor, the financial statements of the special-purpose corporation should be consolidated with those of the sponsor in order to present more meaningful information.

Offsetting   As a general rule, the offsetting of assets and liabilities in the balance sheet is unacceptable unless a right of offset exists.

Collateralized mortgage obligations that do not meet the conditions of FASB:TB 85-2 shall be recorded as liabilities in the financial statements of the issuer. In respect to those CMOs, the pledging of collateral against the related liability is not equivalent to prepayment as described in paragraph 7 of APB-10. Thus, CMOs do not qualify as an exception to APB-10, and offsetting the associated collateral against the liability in the issuer's financial statements is not appropriate.

Effective date and transition   The provisions of FASB:TB 85-2 are effective for collateralized mortgage obligations issued after March 31, 1985. Earlier application is encouraged, but not required, for interim or annual financial statements that have not been previously issued. The provisions of FASB:TB 85-2 may be retroactively applied to financial statements that have been previously issued.

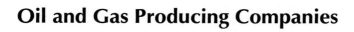
Oil and Gas Producing Companies

OIL AND GAS PRODUCING COMPANIES

Overview

The promulgated GAAP on accounting and reporting by oil and gas producing companies is FASB-19, which superseded FASB-9, and was to be effective for fiscal years beginning after December 15, 1978. Because the SEC rejected the successful efforts accounting method embodied in FASB-19 for a current-value method, FASB-19 was subsequently amended in February 1979 by FASB-25. Nonpromulgated GAAP, in the form of industry practices, exist for alternative methods (full-cost, current-value, and discovery-value accounting methods).

FASB-69 establishes comprehensive financial statement disclosures for oil and gas producing companies. Portions of the disclosure requirements in FASB-69 appeared in FASB-19 (Financial Accounting and Reporting by Oil and Gas Producing Companies), as amended by FASB-25 (Suspension of Certain Accounting Requirements for Oil and Gas Producing Companies). FASB-69 supersedes the disclosure requirements of both FASB-19 and FASB-25 and also incorporates some of the disclosure requirements for oil and gas producing activities which are required by the SEC.

FASB-89 (Financial Reporting and Changing Prices) amends paragraphs 35 through 38 of FASB-69, which had required the disclosure of supplementary current cost information by oil and gas producing companies. Thus, the disclosure of supplementary current cost information by oil and gas producing companies is no longer required.

The promulgated GAAP (FASB-19) covers only producing activities and specifically excludes the transporting, refining, and marketing of oil and/or gas. In addition, the promulgated GAAP does not cover the following:

1. Production of other wasting (nonregenerative) natural resources
2. Production of geothermal steam
3. Extraction of hydrocarbons as a by-product of the production of geothermal steam (Geothermal Steam Act of 1970)
4. Extraction of hydrocarbons from shale, tar sands, or coal
5. Accounting for interest on funds borrowed to finance oil and/ or gas producing activities.

Effects of FASB-25

The effective date of FASB-19 has been suspended indefinitely insofar as it requires the use of the successful efforts method of accounting (FASB-25). In other respects, the effective date of FASB-19 has been changed to fiscal years ending after December 25, 1979, although earlier application is encouraged.

The definitions of reserves used in FASB-19 were completely rescinded by FASB-25. The definitions that shall be used are those adopted by the SEC for its reporting purposes and which are in effect on the date reserve disclosures are made. Revision of previously reported reserves do not have to be made in the event the SEC changes its definitions of reserves.

Other disclosures required by FASB-25 have since been superseded by the comprehensive disclosure requirements of FASB-69.

Furthermore, FASB-25 specifically states that for the purposes of the promulgated GAAP on accounting changes (APB-20) the provisions of FASB-19 pertaining to the successful efforts method remain in effect. Since FASB-19 expresses a preference for the successful efforts method of accounting and rejects other methods, an enterprise that changes to any method other than the successful efforts will have the burden of justifying such change (APB-20).

The income tax allocation requirements of FASB-19 were not changed by FASB-25 and therefore remain in effect.

Background

FASB-19 supports and advocates the traditional historical cost accounting approach to accounting for oil and gas companies. The major problem is in understanding the activities and related terminology pertaining to the oil and gas producing industry.

Properties   Properties include any ownership in, or an interest representing the right to, or the participation in, the extraction of oil and/or gas. The term *properties* also includes a nonoperating interest, such as royalty interests, or production interests payable in oil and/or gas. Properties exclude contracts representing the right to purchase oil and/or gas (supply contracts).

Reservoir   Reservoir refers to a separate confined underground formation containing a natural accumulation of producible oil and/or gas.

Field   Field refers to one or more reservoirs related to the same individual geological structural feature and/or stratigraphic condition.

Proved area   A proved area is that part of the property in which proved reserves have been specifically attributed.

Proved reserves   The following definitions of proved reserves are those adopted by the SEC on December 19, 1978 (ASR-257), and were current at the date of publication. These definitions were developed by the Department of Energy for its financial reporting purposes.

Proved oil and gas reserves   Proved oil and gas reserves are the estimated quantities of crude oil, natural gas, and natural gas liquids which geological and engineering data demonstrate with reasonable certainty to be recoverable in future years from known reservoirs under existing economic and operating conditions; that is, prices and costs as of the date the estimate is made. Prices include consideration of changes in existing prices provided only by contractual arrangements, but not on escalations based upon future conditions.

1.   Reservoirs are considered proved if economic productibility is supported by either actual production or conclusive formation test. The area of a reservoir considered proved includes (a) that portion delineated by drilling and defined by gas–oil and/or oil–water contacts, if any, and (b) the immediately adjoining portions not yet drilled, but which can be reasonably judged as economically productive on the basis of available geological and engineering data. In the absence of information on fluid contacts, the lowest known structural occurrence of hydrocarbons controls the lower proved limit of the reservoir.

2.   Reserves which can be produced economically through application of improved recovery techniques (such as fluid injection) are included in the *proved* classification when successful testing by a pilot project, or the operation of an installed program in the reservoir, provides support for the engineering analysis on which the project or program is based.

3.   Estimates of proved reserves do not include the following: (a) oil that may become available from known reservoirs but is classified separately as *indicated additional reserve*; (b) crude oil, natural gas, and natural gas liquids, the recovery of which is

subject to reasonable doubt because of uncertainty as to geology, reservoir characteristics, or economic factors; (c) crude oil, natural gas, and natural gas liquids that may occur in undrilled prospects; and (d) crude oil, natural gas, and natural gas liquids that may be recovered from oil shales, coal, gilsonite and other such sources.

Proved developed oil and gas reserves   Proved developed oil and gas reserves are reserves that can be expected to be recovered through existing wells with existing equipment and operating methods. Additional oil and gas expected to be obtained through the application of fluid injection or other improved recovery techniques for supplementing the natural forces and mechanisms of primary recovery should be included as *proved developed reserves* only after testing by a pilot project or after the operation of an installed program has confirmed through production response that increased recovery will be achieved.

Proved undeveloped reserves   Proved undeveloped oil and gas reserves are reserves that are expected to be recovered from new wells on undrilled acreage, or from existing wells where a relatively major expenditure is required for recompletion. Reserves on undrilled acreage shall be limited to those drilling units offsetting productive units that are reasonably certain of production when drilled. Proved reserves for other undrilled units can be claimed only where it can be demonstrated with certainty that there is continuity of production from the existing productive formation. Under no circumstances should estimates for proved undeveloped reserves be attributable to any acreage for which an application of fluid injection or other improved recovery technique is contemplated, unless such techniques have been proved effective by actual tests in the area and in the same reservoir.

Wells, related equipment and facilities   include the cost of drilling and equipping *completed* wells, access to proved reserves, and facilities for extracting, treating, gathering, and storing the oil and/or gas.

Uncompleted wells, equipment and facilities   include the costs of all uncompleted wells, equipment, and facilities.

Support equipment and facilities   include the cost of support equipment and facilities used in producing oil and/or gas. Examples are construction and grading equipment, seismic equipment, vehicles, repair shops, warehouses, camps, and division, district, or field offices.

Stratigraphic test wells (expendable wells) are generally drilled without the intention of being completed for production, and are a geological drilling effort to gather information about specific geologic conditions. Core tests and other expendable holes are classified as stratigraphic test wells.

A stratigraphic test well drilled in a proved area is called a *development-type stratigraphic test well*. When drilled on an unproved area, these wells are called exploratory-type stratigraphic test wells.

Service wells are wells drilled to service or support production in an existing field. Examples are injection wells (gas, water, steam, air, etc.) and observation wells.

Development wells are wells drilled for producing oil and/or gas in a proved area known to be productive.

Exploratory wells are wells drilled for exploration or discovery, usually on unproved areas. If a well is classified as a development, service, or stratigraphic test well, it cannot be an exploratory well.

Supply agreements are long-term contracts or similar agreements that represent the right to purchase oil and/or gas, including those with foreign governments.

Discovery-value accounting refers to estimated methods used to determine the value of oil and/or gas reserves, either when discovered or at a later date when developed. The most common estimated valuation methods are:

1. *Current cost*—The amount of cash that currently would have to be paid to acquire the same asset. Similar to current reproduction cost or current replacement cost.

2. *Current exit value in orderly liquidation*—The net amount of cash that would be received in the current orderly liquidation of the asset.

3. *Expected exit value in due course of business*—The nondiscounted amount of cash the asset is expected to bring in the due course of business, less any direct costs incurred in its disposal (net

realizable value). Under this method, the oil and/or gas reserves would be valued at an amount equal to the estimated net cash flow from the reserves.

4. *Present value of expected cash flow*—The present value of the expected cash inflows from the reserves, less the present value of the expected related cash outflows to produce the cash inflows. Various different discount rates have been recommended, such as the prime rate, company's cost of capital, and the rate on long-term government bonds.

Under the discovery-value accounting method, property acquisition and other prediscovery expenditures would be deferred and written off when the areas to which the costs apply have been explored and the reserves, if any, determined and valued.

Under the promulgated GAAP (FASB-19), the discovery-value accounting method is unacceptable.

Current-value accounting   One of the four valuation methods mentioned above in discovery-value accounting is applied on a continuous basis, and oil and/or gas reserves are revalued at each financial statement date using the most current information available. Property acquisition and other prediscovery expenditures are deferred and written off when the areas to which the costs apply have been explored and the oil and/or gas reserves, if any, determined and valued.

The uncertainties and inherent unreliability in using estimates to value oil and/or gas reserves render the discovery-value and current-value methods as undesirable.

Under the promulgated GAAP (FASB-19) both the discovery-value and current-value methods are unacceptable.

Full-cost accounting   considers all costs of unsuccessful and successful property acquisition and exploration activities as a cost of discovering reserves. Thus, all costs are considered an integral part of the acquisition, discovery, and development of oil and/or gas reserves; and costs that cannot be directly related to the discovery of specific reserves are nonetheless capitalized.

In full costing, a country is usually selected as a cost center, and all costs incurred within the cost center are capitalized and subsequently amortized against the oil and/or gas reserves produced within the cost center. There is a limitation that capitalized costs of a cost center should not exceed the value of the oil and/or gas reserves of the same cost center.

Under the promulgated GAAP (FASB-19), the full-cost accounting method is unacceptable.

Successful-efforts costing   A cause-and-effect relationship between costs incurred and the discovery of specific reserves is required. The incurrence of a cost with no identifiable future benefit is usually expensed under the successful-efforts method.

The two major variations in the successful-efforts costing method are (1) the use of a small *area of interest* cost center and (2) the accounting treatment of an item is determined by its nature. When a small *area of interest* cost center, such as a field, lease, or reservoir, is used, costs relating to the cost center are capitalized and subsequently amortized against the oil and/or gas reserves discovered within the cost center. When the nature of the expenditure is used as the method for capitalizing or expensing an expenditure, the nature of the expenditure determines its treatment. As a result, geological and geophysical costs and unsuccessful exploratory wells (dry holes) are immediately charged to expense. In addition, some companies use a combination of both variations to determine whether an expenditure is capitalized or expensed.

Under successful-efforts costing, all property acquisition costs are capitalized when incurred, though different methods may subsequently be used to dispose of these costs.

Under present tax law, intangible drilling costs are generally deductible as an expense in the year incurred.

The promulgated GAAP (FASB-19) is generally based on the successful-efforts costing method.

Background Information

In 1975, the Energy Policy and Conservation Act, public law 94-163, was enacted by Congress. Title V, Section 503, of the act grants the following powers to the Securities and Exchange Commission:

> ...to prescribe rules applicable to persons engaged in the production of crude oil or natural gas, or make effective by recognition, or by other appropriate means indicating a determination to rely on, accounting practices developed by the Financial Accounting Standards Board, if the Securities and Exchange Commission is assured that such practice will be observed by persons engaged in the production of crude oil or natural gas to the same extent as would result if the Securities and Exchange Commission had prescribed such practices by rule.

In addition, the Energy Policy and Conservation Act of 1975 requires that certain information about national energy be compiled for both domestic and foreign operations, and consist of the following data:

1. The separate calculation of capital, revenue, and operating cost information pertaining to:

    a. Prospecting
    b. Acquisition
    c. Exploration
    d. Development
    e. Production

    The calculation of capital, revenue, and operating cost information includes geological and geophysical costs, carrying costs, unsuccessful exploratory drilling costs, intangible drilling and development costs on productive wells, the cost of unsuccessful development wells, and the cost of acquiring oil and gas reserves by means other than development. Any such calculation shall take into account disposition of capitalized costs, contractual arrangements involving special conveyance of rights and joint operations, differences between book and tax income, and prices used in the transfer of products or other assets from one person to any other person, including a person controlled by, controlling, or under common control with such person.

2. The full presentation of the financial information of persons engaged in the production of crude oil or natural gas, including:

    a. Disclosure of reserves and operating activities, both domestic and foreign, to facilitate evaluation of financial effort and result
    b. Classification of financial information by function to facilitate correlation with reserve and operating statistics, both domestic and foreign

3. Such other information, projections, and relationships of collected data as shall be necessary to facilitate the compilation of such data base

Securities Act Release No. 5706, issued on May 12, 1976, requires that certain information relating to oil and/or gas properties, reserves, and production be disclosed in registration statements, proxy statements, and reports filed with the Commission.

Securities Act Release No. 5801, issued on January 31, 1977, states that the Commission, consistent with its policy established in Accounting Series Release No. 150, will look to the FASB to provide leadership in setting forth accounting standards and principles for the producers of oil and/or gas.

Securities Act Release No. 5837, issued on June 30, 1977, solicits comments from interested parties with respect to the Commission's responsibility under the Energy Policy and Conservation Act of 1975. The release also states that the Commission will attempt to coordinate the reporting requirements promulgated by the FASB in its own disclosure and reporting requirements.

Securities Release No. 5861 and Securities Release No. 5877, issued on August 31, 1977, and October 26, 1977, respectively, generally adopt as a Commission regulation the accounting standards and disclosures that are contained in FASB-19. These releases apply to filings with the SEC and to reports filed with the Department of Energy.

Securities Release No. 5878, also issued on October 26, 1977, deals with replacement cost information (ASR 190) for certain registrants. In lieu of replacement cost information, the release requires the disclosure of the present value of future net revenues estimated to be received in the future from the production of proved oil and/or gas reserves. This release becomes effective for filings covering fiscal years ending after December 24, 1978.

On August 31, 1978, the SEC issued ASR-253 which included the following:

1. Adopted the successful efforts accounting method and disclosure requirements of FASB-19.

2. Indicated that a form of full-cost accounting for oil and gas producing companies will be developed by the SEC as an acceptable reportable alternative for the SEC.

3. Concluded that the full-cost and successful efforts methods based upon historical costs fails to provide sufficient information for gas and oil producing companies and that the SEC would take steps to develop an accounting method based on current valuation of proved oil and gas reserves.

4. Adopted disclosure rules for certain information regardless of the accounting method used.

5. Adopted the definition of proved reserves which differed from those prescribed by FASB-19.

On December 19, 1978, the SEC issued ASR-257 and ASR-258 which included the following:

1. Reaffirmed the conclusions the SEC prescribed in ASR-253 (enumerated above).
2. Adopted definitions of proved reserves developed by the Department of Energy for its reporting purposes.
3. Described the form of full-cost accounting for gas and oil producing companies that would be acceptable as an alternative to the successful efforts method for reporting to the SEC.

In 1982, the SEC issued ASR-300, adopting the disclosure requirements of FASB-69, discussed later in this chapter. The SEC issued Financial Reporting Release (FRR)-14 in 1983 and FRR-17 in 1984, clarifying the full-cost method of accounting.

Accounting Principles—Basic Concepts

The promulgated GAAP (FASB-19) does not address the transporting, refining, and marketing aspects of oil and/or gas production. The functions covered by the promulgated GAAP are (1) acquisition of properties, (2) exploration, (3) development, and (4) production.

Generally, the incurrence of a cost that results in the acquisition of an asset is capitalized and subsequently amortized, unless the asset becomes impaired or worthless, in which case it is reduced in value or written off. Costs that do not result in the acquisition of an asset, such as carrying costs of undeveloped properties, geological and geophysical (G&G) costs, and the costs of drilling exploratory wells that do not find proved reserves, are charged to expense when incurred.

Costs incurred to operate and maintain producing wells, related equipment, and facilities become part of the total production costs (also known as lifting costs). The other part of production costs comprise depreciation, depletion, and amortization of the costs capitalized as property acquisition, exploration, and development costs.

Before the accounting treatment of a cost can be determined, it must be first classified as a cost of acquiring properties, exploring, developing, or producing. For example, support equipment and labor can be classified as any of the functional activities in the oil and gas industry. Labor used in developing a producing well is capitalized and subsequently amortized, whereas labor costs incurred in operating producing wells become part of production costs.

The following is a brief discussion of the accounting principles and basic concepts involved in each function of the oil and gas industry:

Acquisition of properties   includes all costs to purchase, lease, or otherwise acquire a proved or unproved property, including brokers' fees, legal fees, and recording fees, and other costs incurred in acquiring properties. The acquisition of properties may include the transfer of all or part of the rights and responsibilities of operating the properties (operating interest) or none of the rights or responsibilities of operating (nonoperating interest).

If the interest in the property acquired is in substance a borrowing repayable in cash or its equivalent, it should be treated as a borrowing and not as the acquisition of an interest in the property.

If part or all of an interest in a property is sold and substantial uncertainty exists in the recovery of the applicable costs involved or if the seller has a substantial future performance obligation to drill a well or to operate the property without reimbursement, no gain should be recognized on these types of conveyances.

As in all nonmonetary exchanges of like property, gain or loss is recognized only to the extent of any "boot" received, as follows:

1. Exchange of assets used in oil and gas producing activities for other assets used in oil and gas producing activities

2. A joint pooling of assets to find, develop, or produce oil and/or gas from a particular property

Unproved properties should be reclassified to proved properties when proved reserves are attributed to the property. Periodic assessment of unproved properties should be made to determine whether they have been impaired. Impairment is likely if a dry hole has been drilled and there are no future plans to continue drilling, or if the end of a lease approaches and drilling has not commenced on the property. Losses for impairment of unproved properties are made by a charge to income and a credit to a valuation account in the year the impairment occurs.

If an unproved property is abandoned or becomes worthless, all related capitalized costs should be charged first against any related allowance for impairment account, and any excess charged to income of the period that the unproved property is abandoned or becomes worthless. If only a small portion of an amortization base is abandoned or becomes worthless, then that portion should be considered fully amortized and its cost charged to the accumulated depreciation, depletion, or amortization account, and no gain or loss is recognized.

The unit-of-production method is used to amortize (deplete) all capitalized property acquisition costs of proved properties. As stated previously, this amortization (depletion) becomes part of the production costs (lifting costs). Amortization rates should be reviewed at least annually and revisions should be accounted for prospectively as changes in accounting estimates (APB-20).

In proved properties that contain both oil and gas reserves, a common unit of measure based on the approximate relative energy content of the oil and gas should be used as the unit of production in the current period. Amortization is then based on the converted common unit of measure. In the event that either oil or gas dominates the content of both reserves and current production, unit-of-production amortization may be computed on the dominant mineral only.

Exploration includes all costs relating to the search for oil and/or gas reserves, including depreciation and applicable costs of support equipment and facilities, drilling exploratory wells, and exploratory-type stratigraphic test wells. Exploration costs may be incurred before the actual acquisition of the property, and in this sense they are sometimes referred to as prospecting costs.

Some exploration costs do not represent the acquisition of an identifiable asset, and are therefore charged directly to expense when incurred. The cost of carrying and maintaining undeveloped properties is an expense, because such costs do not increase the potential that the properties will contain proved reserves. Examples of these types of expenses are delay rentals, taxes on properties, legal costs, and loan maintenance.

Geological, topographical, and geophysical studies (G&G costs) and related salaries and other expenses are also expensed, because they do not represent the acquisition of an identifiable asset. The studies are frequently made before the acquisition of the property and represent research or information costs. More frequently than not, G&G costs are incurred and the properties are never acquired.

Pending the determination of whether a well has proved reserves, all costs of drilling exploratory wells are capitalized and are classified as uncompleted wells, equipment and facilities. The disposition of exploratory wells and their related costs is usually made shortly after completion, and if the well has proved reserves, the costs are capitalized and reclassified as wells, related equipment and facilities. However, if no proved reserves are found, the capitalized costs of drilling the well, less any salvage value, is charged to expense.

Sometimes an exploratory well cannot be classified as having found proved reserves on completion of drilling, because justification for major capital expenditures, such as a trunk pipeline, must be made, which may depend on the success of additional exploratory wells in the same area. In this event, the exploratory well and its related costs may be carried on the books as an asset for a period not exceeding one year, providing both of the following conditions are met:

1. A sufficient quantity of reserves was found to justify the completion as a producing well if the required capital expenditures are made.
2. Drilling of other exploratory wells has commenced or is firmly planned for the near future.

If the above conditions are not met, the exploratory well and all its related costs are charged to expense.

Costs incurred for an exploratory well or stratigraphic test well, net of salvage value, shall be charged to expense for the period, if the following conditions exist:

1. The well is in progress (uncompleted) at the end of the period.
2. A determination has been made prior to the issuance of the financial statements that the well has not located any proved reserves. In other words, the well has proved to be dry.

FASB Interpretation-36 requires that only the costs incurred through the end of the reporting period, net of any salvage value, need be charged to expense. The amount charged to expense should include costs incurred during the current period, as well as costs that were incurred and capitalized in prior periods. Thus, estimated costs to complete the uncompleted "dry well," if necessary, should not be accrued, since they will be charged to expense when incurred in subsequent periods.

The unit-of-production method is used to amortize all capitalized exploration costs, including support equipment and facilities. As stated previously, this amortization becomes part of the cost of production (lifting costs).

Development includes all costs incurred in creating a production system of wells, related equipment and facilities, on proved reserves so that the oil and/or gas can be lifted (produced). Development costs are associated with specific proved reserves; exploration costs are associated with unproved reserves. The cost of building a road to gain access to proved reserves is a development cost, as is the cost of providing facilities for extracting, treating, gathering, and storing the oil and/or gas. Development costs also include depreciation and operating costs of support equipment and facilities used in development activities.

Development costs are associated with previously discovered proved reserves with known future benefits. Therefore, under the promulgated GAAP, unsuccessful development wells (dry holes) are capitalized as a cost of creating the overall production system for proved reserves.

The unit-of-production method is used to amortize (deplete) all capitalized development costs. As stated previously, this amortization (depletion) becomes part of the production costs (lifting costs). Amortization rates should be reviewed at least annually, and revisions should be accounted for prospectively as changes in accounting estimates (APB-20).

In proved properties that contain both oil and gas, a common unit of measure based on the approximate relative energy content of the oil and gas should be used as the unit of production for the purpose of determining the number of units produced in the current period. Amortization is then based on the converted common unit of measure. In the event that either oil or gas dominates the content of both reserves and current production, unit-of-production amortization may be computed on the dominant mineral only.

Production   includes all costs incurred in lifting the oil and/or gas to the surface, and gathering, treating, field processing, and field storage. FASB-19 provides that the production function terminates at the outlet valve on the leased property or the field production storage tank, or under unusual circumstances, at the first point at which the oil and/or gas is delivered to a main pipeline, refinery, marine terminal, or a common carrier.

Production costs include labor, fuel, and supplies needed to operate the developed wells and related equipment, repairs, property taxes, and insurance on proved properties, and wells, related equipment and facilities.

Costs incurred to operate and maintain the production system become part of the total production costs (lifting costs). The other part of the production costs consists of the depreciation, depletion, and amortization of the costs capitalized as acquisition of properties, exploration, and development costs.

Support Equipment and Facilities

Costs for support equipment and facilities may be incurred for exploration, development, or production activities. Generally, these costs are capitalized and depreciated over their estimated useful lives or the life of the lease, whichever is appropriate. The depreciation expense and related costs of operating the support equipment and facilities is charged to the related activity (exploration, development, or production). When support equipment and facilities are utilized for more than one activity, the depreciation expense and operating costs should be allocated between the activities on a reasonable basis.

Residual salvage values and estimated costs of dismantlement, restoration, and abandonment should be considered in determining depreciation and amortization rates.

Balance Sheet—Subsequent Information

The promulgated GAAP require that information that becomes available subsequent to the balance sheet date and prior to the issuance of the financial statements should be taken into consideration in determining conditions that existed at the balance sheet date. The determination at the balance sheet date of whether an exploratory well has found proved reserves, the impairment of unproved properties, and similar conditions may be based on information that becomes available subsequent to the balance sheet date and prior to the issuance of the financial statements.

Income Tax Considerations

Comprehensive interperiod income tax allocation (FASB-96) should be applied for items that enter into the determination of pretax accounting income and taxable income in different periods (temporary differences). However, a future tax benefit arising from an excess of statutory depletion over cost depletion is not treated as a temporary difference but is accounted for as a permanent difference in the period in which it is allowed as a deduction for income tax purposes.

Segmental Reporting

Segmental reporting (FASB-14) is not necessary for oil and/or gas producing companies, because the functional activities of property acquisition, exploration, development, and production are not considered industry segments. However, promulgated GAAP does require some disclosure information based on geographic areas.

DISCLOSURES (FASB-69)

Most of the disclosure requirements of FASB-69 pertain to *publicly held enterprises,* as that term is defined in FASB-89 (Financial Reporting and Changing Prices). FASB-89 defines a public enterprise as "a business enterprise (a) whose debt or equity securities are traded in a public market on a domestic stock exchange or in a domestic over-the-counter market (including securities quoted only locally or regionally), or (b) that is required to file financial statements with the Securities and Exchange Commission. An enterprise is considered to be a public enterprise as soon as its financial statements are issued in preparation for the sale of any class of securities in a domestic market."

General Disclosures

Interim financial reports are not required to contain the disclosures mandated by FASB-69. However, interim financial reports are required to contain disclosure of favorable or adverse events concerning an enterprise's proved oil and gas reserves. A major oil or gas discovery is the type of favorable event that must be disclosed in interim financial reports. A major accident, such as a fire, that consumes significant quantities of proved oil and gas reserves is the type of adverse event that must be disclosed in interim financial reports.

> *OBSERVATION: APB-28 (Interim Financial Reporting) encourages the disclosure of significant events which affect the interim financial results.*

The method of accounting for costs incurred in oil and gas producing activities and the manner of disposing of capitalized costs must be fully disclosed by both public and nonpublic enterprises that are engaged in oil and gas producing activities.

> *OBSERVATION: Disclosure of accounting policies is required by APB-22 which states a preference for the presentation of disclosing accounting policies in the first footnote to the financial statements under the caption "Summary of Significant Accounting Policies."*
>
> *Under APB-22, both the accounting principle and the method of applying the principle should be disclosed, but accounting principles and their methods of application in the following areas are considered particularly important:*

a. A selection from existing acceptable alternatives
b. The areas that are peculiar to a specific industry in which the entity operates
c. Unusual and innovative applications of GAAP

When a complete set of annual financial statements is presented, publicly held enterprises that have significant oil and gas producing activities shall also disclose, as supplementary information to the financial statements the following information relating to gas and oil producing activities:

a.   Proved oil and gas reserve quantities
b.   Capitalized costs
c.   Costs incurred for property acquisition, exploration, and development activities
d.   Results of operations
e.   A standardized measure of discounted future net cash flows

The above supplementary information should be disclosed in complete sets of annual financial statements by publicly traded enterprises that have significant oil and gas producing activities. The test of whether an enterprise has significant oil and gas producing activities must be applied separately for each year that a complete set of annual financial statements is presented.

Generally, an enterprise has significant oil and gas producing activities if its oil and gas producing activities qualify as an industry segment under the provisions of FASB-14 (Segmental Reporting). Thus, if an enterprise satisfies one or more of the following tests, it is considered as having significant oil and gas producing activities:

1.   Its revenue from oil and gas producing activities (defined below) is at least 10% of the total revenue from all of the enterprise's industry segments (defined below).
2.   Its operating profit from oil and gas producing activities is at least 10% of the total operating profit of all of the enterprise's industry segments which reflect operating profits.
3.   Its operating loss from oil and gas producing activities is at least 10% of the total operating losses of all of the enterprise's industry segments which reflect operating losses.
4.   Its identifiable assets (defined below) relating to oil and gas producing activities are at least 10% of all of the identifiable assets of all of the enterprise's industry segments.

The following definitions are used in applying the above tests for significant oil and gas producing activities:

Revenues   shall include sales to unaffiliated organizations in connection with (a) net working interests, (b) royalty interests, (c) oil payment interests, and (d) net profit interests of the reporting enterprise. Intercompany sales or transfers shall also be included as revenue, based on appropriate market prices which are equivalent to an arm's length transaction at the point of delivery from the producing unit. Excluded from gross revenue are (a) royalty payments and (b) net profit disbursements. Production or severance taxes are included as part of production costs and shall not be deducted in determining gross revenue.

Industry segment   is a component of an enterprise that sells its products or services primarily to outsiders for a profit.

Identifiable assets   are tangible and intangible assets used exclusively by a segment of an enterprise, or the allocated portion of assets used jointly by more than one segment. General corporate assets are not allocated to segments and loan and investment accounts are not considered assets unless income from them is included in segment profit or loss.

Goodwill, less any amortization, is included in an industry segment's identifiable assets. An industry segment's identifiable assets are computed net of any valuation account, such as allowance for doubtful accounts, accumulated depreciation, etc.

Loans and advances between industry segments whose principal operations are financial (banking, leasing, insurance, etc.) and whose income is derived from such loans and advances, should be included as an identifiable industry segment asset.

Disclosures—Proved Oil and Gas Reserve Quantities

Publicly held enterprises shall disclose as supplementary information to each of their annual financial statements presented, the net quantities of proved reserves and proved developed reserves of crude oil and natural gas.

The net quantities of crude oil which includes condensate and natural gas liquids should be stated in barrels. The net quantities of natural gas should be stated in cubic feet. Net quantities of crude oil and gas, if significant, should be reported for the company's home country and each foreign geographic area (country or group of countries) in which significant reserves are located.

In determining net quantities the following rules shall apply:

1. Net quantities shall exclude oil and gas subject to purchase under long-term supply, purchase, or similar agreements including those with governments. However, if the company participates in the operation of the oil and/or gas producing properties or otherwise acts as a producer, this information is reported separately (see below).

2. Companies issuing consolidated financial statements shall include all the net quantities attributable to the parent company and all the net quantities attributable to the consolidated subsidiaries whether or not wholly owned.

   A significant portion of the net quantities at the end of the year may be attributable to a consolidated subsidiary that has a significant minority interest. In this event, disclosure of these facts and the approximate portion attributable to the consolidated subsidiary is required by FASB-69.

3. Net quantities of investments that are proportionately consolidated shall include the proportionate share of the investee's net quantities of oil and gas reserves.

4. Net quantities of investments that are accounted for by the equity method shall be excluded. (This information is separately reported; see below.)

5. Net quantities shall include any from royalty interest owned if the information is available. If the information is not available, a statement of that fact must be made and net quantities *produced* attributable to the royalty interest must be disclosed for each period presented.

6. Net quantities include operating and nonoperating interest in properties.

7. Net quantities shall not include interest of others in properties.

Beginning and ending net quantities in proved reserves and proved developed reserves of crude oil (including condensate and natural gas liquids) and natural gas and net changes during the year must be reported at the end of each year in which a complete set of financial statements is presented.

The following chart illustrates the method of disclosing net quantities recommended in the promulgated GAAP.

	Total Worldwide		United States		Other Foreign Geographic Area A		Foreign Geographic Area B		Foreign Geographic Areas	
	Oil	*Gas*	*Oil*	*Gas*	*Oil*	*Gas*	*Oil*	*Gas*	*Oil*	*Gas*
Proved developed and undeveloped reserve:										
1. Beginning of year	X	X	X	X	X	X	X	X	X	X
2. Revisions of previous estimates	X	X	X	X	X	X	X	X	X	X
3. Improved recovery	X	X	X	X	X	X	X	X	X	X
4. Purchases of minerals-in-place	X	X	X	X	X	X	X	X	X	X
5. Extensions, discoveries and other additions	X	X	X	X	X	X	X	X	X	X
6. Production	(X)	(X)	(X)	(X)	(X)	(X)	(X)	(X)	(X)	(X)
7. Sales of minerals-in-place	(X)	(X)	(X)	(X)	(X)	(X)	(X)	(X)	(X)	(X)
8. End of year	X	X	X	X	X	X	X	X	X	X
9. Proved developed reserves:										
Beginning of year	X	X	X	X	X	X	X	X	X	X
End of year	X	X	X	X	X	X	X	X	X	X

	Total Worldwide		United States		Foreign Geographic Area A		Foreign Geographic Area B		Foreign Geographic Areas	
	Oil	*Gas*	*Oil*	*Gas*	*Oil*	*Gas*	*Oil*	*Gas*	*Oil*	*Gas*
Oil and gas applicable to long-term supply agreements with foreign governments or authorities in which the company acts as producer:										
10. Proved reserves at end of year	X	X	X	X	X	X	X	X	X	X
11. Received during the year	X	X	X	X	X	X	X	X	X	X
12. Company's proportionate interest in reserves of investees accounted for by the equity method, end of year	X	X	X	X	X	X	X	X	X	X

An explanation of each item in the chart follows:

1. *Beginning of year*—The total net quantities at the beginning of the year

2. *Revisions of previous estimates*—Upward or downward revision of proved reserves resulting from new information or changes in economic factors

3. *Improved recovery*—Changes during the year resulting from new recovery techniques

4. *Purchases of minerals-in-place*—Purchases during the year of proved developed and undeveloped reserves

5. *Extensions, discoveries, and other additions*—Proved reserves resulting from the extension of previously discovered reservoirs, discovery of new fields or new reservoirs in old fields, and other additions

6. *Production*—The total amount of net quantities produced for the year

7. *Sales of minerals-in-place*—Sales during the year of proved developed and undeveloped reserves

8. *End of year*—The total net quantities at the end of the year (All items above this item should add up to this item.)

9. *Proved developed reserves*—Net quantities of proved developed reserves only for the beginning and ending of the year. Proved developed reserves include oil and/or gas expected to be recovered through existing wells using existing equipment and operation methods. Proved undeveloped reserves are those where oil and/or gas is expected to be recovered from new wells on undrilled acreage or from existing wells that require major expenditures for completion.

Net quantities subject to purchase under long-term supply agreements with governments or authorities and net quantities received during the year under such agreements must be separately disclosed as indicated in items 10 and 11.

An investor's share of net quantities of an investment accounted for by the equity method shall be separately disclosed at the end of the year (as indicated in item 12).

If important economic factors or significant uncertainties are involved in any of the net quantities reported by an enterprise, an explanatory note should accompany the supplementary oil and gas information. Important economic factors or significant uncertainties would include (a) exceptionally high future development or lifting expenditures and (b) contractual obligations requiring the enterprise to sell significant quantities of oil or gas at substantially lower prices than the expected market price at the time of production.

If a government restricts or prohibits the disclosure of any of the net quantities of oil and gas reserves required by FASB-69, or requires disclosure of a different nature than required by FASB-69, an enterprise must disclose the fact that (a) the net quantity reserves from that particular country are excluded from the supplementary information, or (b) the net quantity reserves from that particular country are not reported in accordance with the FASB-69.

Disclosures—Capitalized Costs

Publicly held enterprises shall disclose in each of their annual financial statements presented the total amount of capitalized costs and related accumulated depreciation (depletion) (amortization) and valuation allowances relating to oil and gas producing activities. Under FASB-19, capitalized costs are classified as follows:

1. Mineral interest in properties which must be classified as (a) proved properties or (b) unproved properties

2. Wells, related equipment and facilities

3. Support equipment and facilities used in oil and gas producing activities

4. Uncompleted wells, equipment and facilities

Existing GAAP (APB-12) require that the balances of major classes of depreciable assets, by nature or function, be disclosed in the financial statements of an enterprise. Thus, to comply with existing GAAP, it would appear appropriate to use the above classifications for capitalized costs relating to oil and gas producing activities. However, FASB-69 states that it often may be appropriate to combine one or more, or two or more, of the classifications of capitalized costs and offers the following illustration:

	Total
Unproved oil and gas properties	$XXX,XXX
Proved oil and gas properties	XXX,XXX
	$XXX,XXX
Less: Accumulated depreciation, depletion amortization, and valuation allowances	XX,XXX
Net capitalized costs	$XXX,XXX
Proportionate share of capitalized costs of investments accounted for by the equity method	$ XX,XXX

FASB-69 expressly requires that capitalized costs of unproved properties, if significant, be separately disclosed.

Under the provisions of FASB-69, capitalized costs of support equipment and facilities may be disclosed separately or included as appropriate with capitalized costs of proved and unproved properties.

An enterprise's proportionate share of the total capitalized costs relating to oil and gas producing activities of an investment accounted for by the equity method must be separately disclosed in each annual financial statement presented.

Disclosures—Incurred Functional Costs

Publicly held enterprises shall disclose in each of their annual financial statements presented the total capitalized or expensed costs for the following functional activities of oil and gas producing companies:

1. Property acquisition costs
2. Exploration costs
3. Development costs

Exploration and development costs shall include the depreciation expense of support equipment and facilities, but exclude the expenditures to acquire such equipment and facilities. Any of these functional costs which are incurred in a foreign country shall be separately disclosed by geographic areas in the same manner that net quantities of oil and gas are disclosed.

An enterprise's proportionate share of the total property acquisition, exploration, and development costs relating to oil and gas producing activities of an investment accounted for by the equity method must be separately disclosed, in total and by geographic area, in each annual financial statement presented.

The following illustrates the disclosure of the property acquisition, exploration, and development costs required by FASB-69:

	Total Worldwide		United States		Foreign Geographic Area A		Foreign Geographic Area B		Other Foreign Geographic Areas	
	Oil	*Gas*	*Oil*	*Gas*	*Oil*	*Gas*	*Oil*	*Gas*	*Oil*	*Gas*
Property acquisition costs	X	X	X	X	X	X	X	X	X	X
Exploration costs	X	X	X	X	X	X	X	X	X	X
Development costs	X	X	X	X	X	X	X	X	X	X
Proportionate share of the property, acquisition, exploration, and development costs from investments accounted for by the equity method	X	X	X	X	X	X	X	X	X	X

If costs to acquire mineral interest in proved reserves are significant, FASB-69 requires that they be disclosed separately from costs to acquire interests in unproved reserves.

Disclosures—Results of Operations

Publicly held enterprises shall disclose in each of their annual financial statements presented the results of operations (as defined below) for oil and gas producing activities. However, if the enterprise is subject to the segmentation provisions of FASB-14 (Segmental Reporting), the results of operations shall be included with the other segment information required by FASB-14.

Results of operations shall include an enterprise's interest in proved oil and gas reserves and oil and gas subject to purchase under long-term supply contracts and similar agreements.

Under FASB-69, results of operations for oil and gas producing activities shall be disclosed in total and for each geographic area for which related reserve quantities are disclosed.

The following information shall be disclosed for results of operations for oil and gas producing activities:

Revenues shall include sales to unaffiliated organizations in connection with (a) networking interests, (b) royalty interests, (c) oil payment interests, and (d) net profit interests of the reporting enterprise.

Intercompany sales or transfers shall also be included as revenue, based on appropriate market prices which are equivalent to arm's length transactions at the point of delivery from the producing unit.

Excluded from gross revenue are royalty payments and net profit disbursements. Production or severance taxes are included as part of production costs and shall not be deducted in determining gross revenue.

Production includes all costs incurred in lifting the oil and/or gas to the surface, and gathering, treating, field processing, and field storage. The production function terminates at the outlet valve on the leased property or the field production storage tank, or under unusual circumstances, at the first point at which the oil and/or gas is delivered to a main pipeline, refinery, marine terminal, or a common carrier.

Production costs include labor, fuel, and supplies needed to operate the developed wells and related equipment, repairs, property taxes, and insurance on proved properties, and wells, related equipment and facilities.

Costs incurred to operate and maintain the production system become part of the total production costs (lifting costs).

Depreciation, depletion, amortization, and valuation allowances related to capitalized costs are excluded from production costs and disclosed under a separate caption (see below).

Exploration includes all costs relating to the search for oil and/or gas reserves, including applicable costs of support equipment and facilities, drilling exploratory wells, and exploratory-type stratigraphic test wells. Exploration costs may be incurred before the actual acquisition of the property, and in this sense they are sometimes referred to as prospecting costs.

Some exploration costs do not represent the acquisition of an identifiable asset, and are therefore charged directly to expense when incurred. The cost of carrying and maintaining undeveloped properties is an expense, because such costs do not increase the potential that the properties will contain proved reserves. Examples of these types of expenses are delay rentals, taxes on properties, legal costs and land maintenance.

Geological, topographical, and geophysical studies (G&G costs) and related salary and other expenses are also expensed, because they do not represent the acquisition of an identifiable asset. The studies are frequently made before the acquisition of the property and represent research or information costs. More frequently than not, G&G costs are incurred and the properties are never acquired.

Depreciation, depletion, amortization, and valuation allowances related to capitalized costs are excluded from exploration expenses and disclosed under a separate caption (see below).

> **OBSERVATION:** *Enterprises using methods of accounting other than the successful efforts method will usually have no exploration costs to disclose. In this event, all exploration costs are usually capitalized and subsequently charged to net income as depreciation, depletion, amortization, and valuation allowances.*

Depreciation, depletion, amortization, and valuation allowances related to oil and gas producing activities, except that which is part of general overhead and financing costs, are disclosed separately under this caption.

> **OBSERVATION:** *Interest capitalized under the provisions of FASB-34, on qualifying assets used in oil and gas producing activities, will be charged to net income as depreciation, depletion, or amortization of the cost of the related asset.*

Income tax expense The statutory tax rate for the period shall be applied to the results of operations (as defined herein) to determine the income tax expense for the period. The determination of income tax expense shall reflect any permanent differences relating to oil and gas activities, provided that such permanent differences are appropriately reflected in the enterprise's consolidated income tax expense for the period.

Results of operations are equal to revenues, less (a) production costs, (b) exploration expenses, (c) depreciation, depletion, amortization, and valuation allowances, and (d) income tax expense. Results of operations for oil and gas producing activities shall not include general corporate overhead and financing costs. However, corporate overhead or expenses incurred at a central administrative office may include operating expenses of oil and gas producing activities and should be accounted for as such. In determining whether an expenditure is or is not an operating expense of oil and gas producing activities, the nature of the expense governs. The location in which the expense is recorded or paid is irrelevant.

Results of operations do not include an enterprise's proportionate share of the results of operations (as defined herein) of oil and gas producing activities from investments accounted for by the equity method. An enterprise's proportionate share of the results of operations (as defined herein) from an investment accounted for by the equity method must be separately disclosed, in total and by geographic area, in each annual financial statement presented.

The following illustrates the disclosure of results of operations (as defined herein):

	Total Worldwide	*United States*	*Foreign Geographic Area A*	*Foreign Geographic Area B*	*Other Foreign Geographic Areas*
Revenues	$ X	$ X	$ X	$ X	$ X
Production costs	(X)	(X)	(X)	(X)	(X)
Exploration expenses	(X)	(X)	(X)	(X)	(X)
Depreciation, depletion, and amortization, and valuation provisions	(X)	(X)	(X)	(X)	(X)
	X	X	X	X	X
Income tax expense	(X)	(X)	(X)	(X)	(X)
Results of operations for producing activities (excluding corporate overhead and financing costs)	$ X	$ X	$ X	$ X	$ X
Enterprise's share of equity method investees' results of operations for producing activities (excluding corporate overhead and financing costs)	$ X	$ X	$ X	$ X	$ X

Disclosures—Discounted Future Net Cash Flows

Publicly held enterprises shall disclose, in each of their annual financial statements presented, a statement of the present value of future net cash flows, in total and by geographic area, from (a) the net quantities of proved reserves and proved developed reserves of crude oil and natural gas, and (b) the net quantities of oil and gas subject to purchase under long-term supply contracts and similar agreements, and contracts in which the enterprise participates in the operation of the oil or gas producing properties or otherwise acts as a producer. Items (a) and (b) may be combined into one statement of the present value of future net cash flows.

Under the provisions of FASB-69, a standardized measure of discounted future net cash flows is achieved by utilizing a 10% discount rate. The statement of the present value of future net cash flows must include the following detail:

Future cash inflows are calculated by multiplying the current year-end net quantities of oil and gas reserves (items (a) and (b) above) by their respective current year-end prices. Future price changes shall be considered, but only to the extent of existing contractual agreements. In other words, prices that appear in existing agreements may be used, but only to the extent of the quantities involved in the agreement.

Future development and production costs are estimated expenditures which should be incurred in producing the future cash inflows. Future development and production costs shall be estimated based on current year-end costs and existing economic environment. If significant, future development costs shall be separately disclosed.

Future income tax expenses are calculated by applying the current year-end statutory income tax rates to the total pretax future cash flows from the net quantities of oil and gas reserves, less (a) the tax basis of the properties involved and (b) the tax effects of any permanent differences, such as investment tax credits and the excess of statutory depletion over the tax basis.

Future tax rates should be used if legislated before issuance of the financial statements.

Future net cash flows are calculated by deducting future development and production costs and future income tax expenses from the future cash inflows.

Discount is calculated by applying a standardized 10% rate per year, which shall reflect the timing of the receipts of the future net cash flows from the net quantities of oil and gas reserves.

Standardized measure of discounted future net cash flows is calculated by deducting the discount from the future net cash flows.

A significant portion of the consolidated standardized measure of discounted future net cash flows may be attributable to a consolidated subsidiary that has a significant minority interest. In this event, disclosure of these facts and the approximate portion attributed to the consolidated subsidiary is required by FASB-69.

The standardized measure of discounted future net cash flows does not include an enterprise's proportionate share of the standardized measure of discounted future net cash flows from investments accounted for by the equity method. An enterprise's proportionate share of the standardized measure of discounted future net cash flows from investments accounted for by the equity method must be separately disclosed, in total and by geographic area, in each annual financial statement presented.

An enterprise shall disclose in each of its annual financial statements presented a statement of the changes in the standardized measure of discounted future net cash flows, in total and by geographic area. The factors which cause the changes in the standardized measure of discounted future net cash flows shall be separately disclosed, if significant, under the following categories:

1. Sales and transfers of oil and gas produced during the period, net of production costs
2. Net changes in sales and transfer prices, and changes in future development and production (lifting) costs
3. Previously estimated future development costs incurred during the period
4. Net changes for extensions, discoveries, additions, and improved recovery, less related future development and production costs
5. Net changes for revisions in quantity estimates
6. Net changes due to purchases and sales of minerals in place
7. Accretion of discount
8. Net changes in income taxes
9. Other (including the effect of changes in estimated rates of production)

> **OBSERVATION:** *Accretion of discount (item 7 above) is a term used by the SEC, which refers to the annual amount of imputed interest that is calculated on the standardized measure of discounted future net cash flows (see illustration below).*

A newly formed oil company spends $200,000 to drill for oil and discovers a commercially exploitable well. At year-end it is estimated that this well will produce 10,000 barrels of oil for the next three years, or a total of 30,000 barrels. The year-end price of oil is $35 per barrel and future development and production costs and future income tax expenses are estimated at year-end prices to be $5 per barrel. The standardized measure of discounted future net cash flows (present value) at 10% is $30 ($35 - $5) x 10,000 = $300,000 x 2.48685 = $746,055. The amortization table for the three-year period is as follows:

Year	Present Value (A)	Interest (B)	Total	Net Cash Flow	Present Value Balance
1	$746,055	$74,606	$820,661	$300,000	$520,661
2	520,661	52,066	572,727	300,000	272,727
3	272,727	27,273	300,000	300,000	-0-

(A) = Standardized measure of discounted future net cash flows
(B) = Accretion of discount

In computing the changes in the standardized measure of discounted future net cash flows, the effects of price changes shall be calculated before the effects of quantity changes, so the latter will be priced at year-end prices. The effect of changes in income taxes shall include the effect of the income taxes incurred during the period and the effect of changes in future income tax expenses. All other changes except the accretion of discount and income taxes shall be reported pretax.

Footnotes shall be provided for any additional information which is necessary to prevent the disclosures from being misleading.

> **OBSERVATION:** *FASB-19 requires information that becomes available after the balance sheet date and before the issuance of the financial statements to be taken into consideration in determining conditions that existed at the balance sheet date. The determination at the balance sheet date of whether an exploratory well contains proved reserves, the impairment of unproved properties, and similar factors may be based on information that becomes available after the balance sheet date and before the issuance of the financial statements.*
>
> *A four-to-three vote of the FASB adopted paragraphs 30-34 of FASB-19 (Disclosure of a Standardized Measure of Discounted Future Net Cash Flows Relating to Proved Oil and Gas Reserves). The three dissenting Board members described this measurement as "completely lacking in reliability."*

The following is an illustration of the disclosure of the standardized measure of discounted future net cash flows and changes therein:

	Total	United States	Foreign Geographic Area A	Foreign Geographic Area B	Other Foreign Geographic Areas
Future cash inflows*	$ X	$ X	$ X	$ X	$ X
Future production and development costs*	(X)	(X)	(X)	(X)	(X)
Future income tax expenses*	(X)	(X)	(X)	(X)	(X)
Future net cash flows	X	X	X	X	X
10% annual discount for estimated timing of cash flows	(X)	(X)	(X)	(X)	(X)
Standardized measure of discounted future net cash flows relating to proved oil and gas reserves	$ X	$ X	$ X	$ X	$ X
Enterprise's share of equity method investees' standardized measure of discounted future net cash flows relating to proved oil and gas reserves	$ X	$ X	$ X	$ X	$ X
Beginning of year	$ X	$ X	$ X	$ X	$ X
Changes resulting from:					
Sales and transfers of oil and gas produced, net of production costs	(X)	(X)	(X)	(X)	(X)
Net changes in prices, and development and production costs	X	X	X	X	X
Extensions, discoveries additions, and improved recovery, less related costs	X	X	X	X	X
Development costs incurred during the period	X	X	X	X	X
Revisions of previous quantity estimates	X	X	X	X	X
Net change in purchases and sales of minerals in place	X	X	X	X	X
Accretion of discount	X	X	X	X	X
Net change in income taxes	X	X	X	X	X
Other	X	X	X	X	X
End of year	$ X	$ X	$ X	$ X	$ X

*Future net cash flows were computed using year-end prices and costs and year-end statutory tax rates (adjusted for permanent differences) that relate to existing proved oil and gas reserves in which the enterprise has mineral interests, or for which the enterprise has long-term supply, purchase, or similar agreements where the enterprise serves as the producer of the reserves.

Real Estate Transactions

REAL ESTATE COSTS
AND INITIAL RENTAL OPERATIONS

Overview

FASB-67 contains the specialized accounting and reporting principles and practices that were originally published in the following AICPA publications:

- Statement of Position 78-3, Accounting for Costs to Sell and Rent, and Initial Rental Operations of Real Estate Projects
- Statement of Position 80-3, Accounting for Real Estate Acquisition, Development, and Construction Costs

In addition, FASB-67 includes those portions of the industry accounting guide entitled "Accounting for Retail Land Sales," which cover costs of real estate projects.

FASB-67 establishes the promulgated GAAP for the acquisition, development, construction, and selling and rental costs which are related to real estate projects. In addition, FASB-67 covers (a) accounting for initial rental operations and (b) the rules for ascertaining when a real estate project is substantially completed and available for occupancy.

The following items are expressly excluded from the provisions of FASB-67:

1. Real estate projects that are not for sale or rent and are developed by an entity for its own use. This includes real estate reported in consolidated financial statements that was developed by one affiliated member of the group for use in the operations of another member of the group.
2. Initial direct costs of leases
3. Direct costs that are related to commercial activities such as manufacturing, merchandising, or service-oriented activities
4. Real estate rental periods of less than one month in duration

Background

Real estate acquisition costs may be broken down into (a) preacquisition costs and (b) postacquisition costs. Preacquisition costs are those which are incurred prior to the acquisition of the property, such as appraisals, surveys, legal fees, travel expenses, and costs to acquire options to purchase the property. Postacquisition costs are those which are incurred after the property has been acquired, such as development and construction costs. Postacquisition costs may be further broken down into (a) direct costs, (b) indirect costs, (c) costs of amenities, and (d) incidental operational costs.

Direct costs are those that can be directly identified with the real estate project. Indirect costs may or may not be related to a specific real estate project. Indirect costs of several real estate projects may be allocated to each project on a reasonable allocation basis.

Golf courses, swimming pools, tennis courts, clubhouses, and other amenities are frequently included in the overall plans of a real estate project. Ownership of these types of amenities may be retained by the real estate developer or may be included in the sale of individual units within the project. When the ownership of an amenity is included in the individual sales within a real estate project, the net cost of the amenity is considered a common cost of the project. Common costs of a real estate project are allocated on a reasonable basis to the individual components within the project. The net cost of an amenity is equal to the total cost of the amenity, less any anticipated proceeds. When a developer retains ownership of an amenity for resale or operations, the cost of the amenity is capitalized in an amount not to exceed its estimated fair value at the date of substantial completion of the amenity. Costs in excess of the estimated fair value of the amenity at the date of substantial completion are accounted for as common costs of the real estate project. After it is substantially completed and ready for its intended use, the cost of the amenity should not be revised.

Incidental operations of a real estate project occur during the development stage of the project and are intended to reduce the cost of the real estate project. Incidental operations do not include activities that result in a profit or return on the use of the real property. If the incremental revenues from incidental operations exceed the incremental costs, they are accounted for as a reduction of the capitalized costs of the project. However, if the incremental costs of incidental operations exceed the incremental revenue, they are charged to expense as incurred.

Capitalized costs of a real estate project must be allocated to the individual components within the project. The allocation is usually accomplished by the specific identification method, if the individual components within the project can be specifically identified. If specific identification is not possible, capitalized land cost and all other common costs, including common costs of amenities, shall be allocated on the basis of the relative fair value of each land parcel benefited prior to any construction. Capitalized construction costs are allocated on the basis of the relative sales value of each individual component within the real estate project. Individual components of a real estate project may consist of lots, acres, or some other identifiable unit.

Estimates are used extensively in the acquisition, development, and construction of a real estate project. As a result, revisions of estimated costs occur frequently and past, present, and future accounting periods may be affected by the revisions.

Revisions of estimates that occur in the acquisition, development, and construction stages of a real estate project are accounted for as changes in accounting estimates (APB-20). The effects of a change in accounting estimates should be accounted for (a) in the period of change, if the change affects only that period or (b) in the period of change and future periods, if the change affects both. A change in an accounting estimate caused in part or entirely by a change in accounting principle should be reported as a change in accounting estimate (APB-20). APB-20 (Accounting Changes) requires that disclosure be made in current-period financial statements of the effects of a change in an accounting estimate on (a) income before extraordinary items, (b) net income, and (c) related per share data.

Ordinary accounting estimates for uncollectible accounts or inventory adjustments, made each period, do not have to be disclosed, unless they are material.

Sometimes there is a significant change in the use of the property in a real estate project, or the project is completely abandoned. In the event that the project is abandoned, all capitalized costs of the project should be expensed immediately. Under no circumstances should capitalized costs of an abandoned real estate project be allocated to other real estate projects. In addition, if a portion of a real estate project is abandoned, the related capitalized costs should be expensed and not allocated to other portions of the same or other projects which are not abandoned.

The cost of land donated to governmental units should not be classified as abandoned if the donated land benefits part or all of the real estate project. Under these circumstances, the donated land shall be accounted for as a common cost of the real estate project.

Capitalized costs incurred prior to the change in use of all or part of the property in a real estate project are charged to expense, except in the following circumstances:

1. The change in use of all or part of the property in the real estate project is supported by a formal plan which indicates that a higher economic yield will result from the change in use. In this event, the capitalized costs incurred prior to the change and the estimated capitalized costs expected to be incurred to substantially complete the project are capitalized to the extent that the total capitalized costs do not exceed the estimated value of the completed revised project. Capitalized costs in excess of the estimated value of the completed revised project, if any, are charged to expense.

2. The change in use of all or part of the property in the real estate project is *not* supported by a formal plan, but the change in use is expected to produce a higher economic yield for the project. In this event, capitalized costs incurred prior to the change are capitalized to the extent that they do not exceed the net realizable value of the project based on the assumption that, on the date of the sale, the property will be sold *as is.*

Costs incurred to sell real estate projects may be accounted for as (a) project costs, (b) prepaid expenses, or (c) period costs, according to the accounting periods which are benefited.

Costs to rent real estate projects under operating leases are either chargeable to future periods or chargeable to the current period, according to whether their recovery is reasonably expected from future rental revenue.

Initial rental operations commence at the time a real estate project is substantially completed and available for occupancy. A real estate rental project is considered substantially completed and available for occupancy when tenant improvements have been completed by the developer, but in no event later than one year after major construction activity has been completed, excluding routine maintenance and clean-up.

Some portions of a real estate rental project may still require major construction for completion, and other portions of the same project may be substantially completed and available for occupancy. In this event, each portion should be accounted for as a separate project.

Suspension of major construction activity may occur because of a decline in rental demand. In this event, the carrying costs of the real estate project may be permanently impaired and a provision for losses may be required. Impairment of the carrying cost of a real estate project may occur from insufficient rental demand even if construction is not suspended.

Once a real estate rental project is substantially completed and available for occupancy, depreciation on the entire project should be appropriately recorded.

Preacquisition Costs of Real Property

Frequently, costs are incurred prior to the actual date on which a parcel of real property is acquired. These costs are referred to by FASB-67 as preacquisition costs. Practically any type of cost may be classified as a preacquisition cost if it is incurred prior to the date of acquisition of a parcel of real property. The cost of an option to purchase real property at a future date is a preacquisition cost and is usually capitalized. However, if the option is not exercised on or before its expiration date, the option becomes worthless and should be expensed.

All other types of preacquisition costs are expensed when incurred, unless they can be specifically identified to the real property being acquired and:

1. The preacquisition costs would be capitalized if the property were acquired.
2. The acquisition of the property is likely to occur.

> **OBSERVATION:** *Likely to occur implies that the property is available for sale, the purchaser is currently trying to acquire the property, and the necessary financing is apparently available.*

Thus, preacquisition costs of a real estate project consist of (a) unexpired options to purchase real property and (b) other costs which meet all of the above conditions. Preacquisition costs that do not qualify for capitalization should be expensed when incurred.

After a parcel of real property is acquired, preacquisition costs should be reclassified as project costs. In the event that the property is not acquired, capitalized preacquisition costs shall not exceed the amount recoverable, if any, from the sale of options, developmental plans, and other proceeds. Capitalized preacquisition costs in excess of recoverable amounts shall be charged to expense.

Taxes and Insurance on Real Property

FASB-67 requires that property taxes and insurance be capitalized as project costs only during periods in which activities necessary to get the property ready for its intended use are in progress.

> **OBSERVATION:** *Frequently, a land company will purchase a tract of land that will not be developed for several years. Apparently, under the provisions of FASB-67, real estate taxes, insurance, and interest related to the tract of land cannot be capitalized unless activities necessary to get the property ready for its intended use are in progress. However, this position apparently differs from the AICPA industry accounting guide entitled "Accounting for Retail Land Sales." Paragraph 51 of this guide states that "Costs directly related to inventories of unimproved land . . . are properly capitalizable until a salable condition is reached." Paragraph 51 further states that "Those costs would include interest, real estate taxes, and other direct costs incurred during the inventory and improvement periods."*

FASB-67 requires that property taxes and insurance costs be expensed as incurred, if the real property is not undergoing activities necessary to get it ready for its intended use.

> **OBSERVATION:** *Obviously, FASB-67 requires that the cost of a three-year insurance policy on a tract of land be expensed when incurred, if the land is not undergoing activities necessary to get it ready for its intended use. However, the accrual basis for accounting would require that the insurance policy be capitalized and amortized over the periods benefited.*

After real property is substantially completed and ready for its intended use, FASB-67 also requires that property taxes and insurance costs be expensed as incurred.

Project Costs of Real Property

Project costs of real estate projects may be direct or indirect. Direct costs that are related to the acquisition, development, and construction of a real estate project shall be capitalized as project costs.

Indirect costs of real estate projects that can be clearly identified to specific projects under development or construction shall be capitalized as project costs. Indirect costs that are accumulated in one account, but clearly relate to several real estate projects under development or construction, should be allocated on a reasonable basis to each of the projects.

Indirect costs on real estate projects not under development or construction must be expensed as incurred. In addition, indirect costs that cannot be clearly identified with specific projects such as general and administrative expenses should be charged to expense when incurred.

Amenity Costs of Real Property

Golf courses, swimming pools, tennis courts, clubhouses, and other types of amenities are frequently included in the overall plans of a real estate project. However, the ultimate disposition of an amenity may vary from one real estate project to another. Thus, accounting for the costs of amenities is based on the developer's (management) ultimate plans for the disposition of the amenity. In this respect, a developer may decide to retain ownership of the amenity and to either (a) operate the amenity or (b) eventually sell the amenity. On the other hand, the developer may be required under the terms of the individual sales agreements to sell or otherwise transfer ownership of the amenity to the purchasers of the individual components within the project. In this event, the purchasers of the individual components within the project usually form an *association* for the purposes of taking title to the amenity and operating the amenity for the common benefit of all owners of individual components within the project.

Accounting for the costs of amenities under the provisions of FASB-67 is as follows:

Ownership Not Retained by Developer

When the ownership of an amenity is to be transferred to the individual components within the real estate project, the net cost of the amenity is accounted for by the developer as a capitalized common cost of the project. The capitalized common cost of an amenity is allocated to the individual components within the project which are expected to benefit from the use of the amenity. Thus, the total cost of each individual component in the project which benefits from the amenity will include a proportionate share of the costs of the amenity.

The developer's net cost or gain that is accounted for as a common cost (reduction) of the real estate project may include the sales price, if any, and all other proceeds, if any, from the transfer of the amenity, less the following items:

1. Direct costs that are clearly identifiable to the amenity
2. Indirect costs that are clearly related to the amenity
3. The developer's cost of operating the amenity until the amenity is transferred to the individual components in the project in accordance with the sales contract or other contractual agreement
4. Common costs of the project that are appropriately allocated to the amenity

If an amenity clearly benefits specific individual components within a real estate project, the common cost (reduction) of the amenity should be allocated only to those specific individual components.

Ownership Retained by Developer

When a developer retains ownership of an amenity, the total cost of the amenity is capitalized as a separate asset. The total cost of an amenity includes direct costs, indirect costs, and the allocation of common costs, including operating results of the amenity prior to its date of substantial completion and availability for its intended use. However, under FASB-67 the amount capitalized cannot exceed the estimated fair value of the amenity at its expected date of substantial completion. Any costs in excess of the estimated fair value of the amenity at the expected date of its substantial completion are accounted for as common costs of the real estate project.

After it is substantially completed and ready for its intended use, further revision of the final capitalized cost of an amenity not in excess of its estimated fair value is not permitted. This cost becomes the basis of the amenity for any future sale. The subsequent basis for determining gain or loss on the sale of the amenity is the capitalized cost of the amenity not in excess of its estimated fair value at its date of substantial completion, less any allowable depreciation to the date of the sale.

After its date of substantial completion and availability for its intended use, the operational results of an amenity that is owned by the developer shall be included in the developer's current net income.

Incidental Operations of Real Property

Incidental operations of a real estate project usually occur during the holding or development stage of the project and are intended to reduce the cost of the project. Incidental operations do not include activities that result in a profit or return from the proposed development of the real property. For example, revenue received from billboard advertisements placed on the property or miscellaneous concession income would be classified as incidental operations.

If the incremental revenue received from incidental operations exceeds the related incremental costs, the difference is accounted for as a reduction of the capitalized costs of the real estate project. Thus, when incidental operations of a real estate project result in a profit, the capitalized costs of the project are reduced by the amount of profit. However, under FASB-67 the same does not hold true if the incidental operations result in a loss. Under FASB-67, if the incremental costs of incidental operations exceed the related incremental revenue, the difference is charged to expense when incurred.

Allocation of Capitalized Costs

All capitalized costs of a real estate project must be allocated to the individual components within the project. If practicable, FASB-67 requires that capitalized costs be allocated by the specific identification method. Under this method, capitalized costs are specifically identified with the individual components within the real estate project. However, if it is impractical to use the specific identification method to allocate capitalized costs, FASB-67 requires that allocation be made, as follows:

Land Costs

Only capitalized costs associated with the land prior to any construction are allocated as land costs. Land costs prior to any construction include capitalized land costs and other preconstruction common costs related to the land, including preconstruction common costs of amenities.

Total capitalized land costs are allocated on the basis of the relative fair value of each land parcel prior to any construction. A land parcel may be identified as a lot, an acre, acreage, a unit, or a tract.

Construction Costs

Capitalized construction costs are allocated on the basis of the relative sales value of each individual structure or unit located on a parcel of land. In the event capitalized costs of a real estate project cannot be allocated by the specific identification method or the relative sales value method, the capitalized cost shall be allocated on area methods or other methods appropriate under the circumstances.

Revisions of Estimates

Estimates are used extensively in the acquisition, development, and construction of a real estate project. As a result, revisions of estimated costs occur frequently and past, present, and future accounting periods may be affected by the revisions.

Revisions of estimates that occur in the acquisition, development, and construction stages of a real estate project are accounted for as changes in accounting estimates (APB-20). The effects of a change in accounting estimate should be accounted for (a) in the period of change, if the change affects only that period or (b) in the period of change and future periods, if the change affects both. A change in an accounting estimate caused in part or entirely by a change in accounting principle should be reported as a change in accounting estimate (APB-20). APB-20 (Accounting Changes) requires that disclosure be made in current period financial statements of the effects of a change in an accounting estimate on (a) income before extraordinary items, (b) net income, and (c) related per share data. However, ordinary accounting estimates for uncollectible accounts or inventory adjustments, made each period, do not have to be disclosed, unless they are material.

Abandonments and Changes in Use

Occasionally a real estate project is partially or completely abandoned, or there is a significant change in the use of the property in the project. Under the provisions of FASB-67, if part or all of a real estate project is abandoned, the related capitalized costs must be expensed immediately. Under no circumstances should the capitalized costs of an abandoned real estate project be allocated to other real estate projects.

The cost of land donated to a governmental authority should not be accounted for as abandoned. Under these circumstances, the cost of the donated land should be accounted for as common costs of acquiring the project. Thus, the cost of the donated land is allocated to the other land in the project, based on the relative fair value of each parcel of land prior to construction of any buildings or structures.

After significant development and construction costs have been capitalized in a real estate project, there may be a change in the use of part or all of the land within the project. Under the provisions of FASB-67, capitalized costs incurred prior to a change in use of all or part of the land within a real estate project are charged to expense, except in the following circumstances:

1. The enterprise has developed a formal plan which indicates that the change in use of the land will result in a higher economic yield than was originally anticipated. In this event, the maximum costs that can be capitalized must not exceed the estimated value of the revised project at the date of substantial completion and availability for its intended use. Capitalized costs in excess of the estimated value of the revised project when substantially completed, if any, are charged to expense.

2. The enterprise has not developed a formal plan, but the change in use of the land is expected to yield a higher economic return than was originally anticipated. In this event, the maximum cost that can be capitalized at the date of change in use cannot exceed the net realizable value of the project based on the assumption that, on the date of the sale, the property will be sold *as is*. Capitalized costs incurred prior to the change in use which exceed the net realizable value must be expensed.

Selling Costs of Real Estate Projects

Costs incurred to sell real estate projects should be accounted for as either (a) project costs, (b) prepaid expenses, or (c) period costs.

Project costs   Project costs are capitalized as part of the construction costs of the real estate project provided that both of the following conditions are met:

1. They are incurred for tangible assets which are used as marketing aids during the marketing period of the real estate project, or for services performed in obtaining regulatory approval for real estate sales in the project.
2. The costs incurred are reasonably expected to be recovered from sales.

Costs to sell real estate that qualify as project costs, less recoverable amounts from incidental operations or salvage value, include legal fees for prospectuses, sales offices, and model units, with or without furnishings.

Costs to sell real estate projects that qualify as project costs become part of the capitalized cost of the project and are allocated to the individual components of the project as common costs.

Prepaid expenses   Prepaid expenses, which are sometimes called *deferred charges,* are capitalized and amortized over the period that is expected to benefit from the expenditure. However, if the prepaid item can be identified with certain future revenue, it should be amortized to the periods in which the future revenue is earned. Costs incurred as prepaid expenses to sell real estate projects must meet the following conditions:

1. They do not qualify as project costs.
2. They are incurred for goods or services that will be used in future periods.

Advances on commissions, future advertising costs, and unused sales brochures are examples of costs to sell real estate projects which qualify as prepaid expenses.

Period costs   Period costs are charged to expense in the period incurred because they do not meet the criteria for project costs or prepaid expenses. Costs to sell real estate projects which do not benefit future periods should be expensed in the period incurred as period costs. Grand opening expenses, sales salaries, sales overhead, and used advertising costs are examples of period costs.

Rental Costs of Real Estate Projects

Costs incurred to rent real estate projects under operating leases are either chargeable to future periods or chargeable to the current period.

Chargeable to future periods   If the costs can be identified to, and reasonably expected to be recovered from, specific revenue, such costs should be capitalized and amortized to the periods in which the specific revenue is earned. If the costs are for goods not used or services not received, such costs should be charged to the future periods in which the goods are used or services are received.

If deferred rental costs can be associated with the revenue from a specific operating lease, such costs should be amortized over the lease term. The amortization period commences when the rental project is substantially completed and available for occupancy. On the other hand, if deferred rental costs cannot be identified with the revenue from a specific operating lease, such costs should be amortized over the periods benefited. The amortization period commences when the rental project is substantially completed and available for occupancy.

Unamortized rental costs that subsequently become unrecoverable from future operations should be expensed when they are determined to be unrecoverable. For example, unamortized rental costs related to specific leases which have been, or will be, terminated should be charged to expense.

Chargeable to the current period   If the costs to rent real estate projects under operating leases do not qualify as chargeable to future periods, they should be accounted for as period costs and expensed as incurred.

Initial Rental Operations

Initial rental operations commence at the time when a real estate project is substantially completed and available for occupancy. A real estate project is considered substantially completed and available for occupancy when tenant improvements have been completed by the developer, but in no event later than one year after major construction activity has been completed, excluding routine maintenance and clean-up.

The actual rental operation of a real estate project shall commence at the time the project is substantially completed and available for occupancy. At this time, rental revenues and related operating costs shall be recognized on an accrual basis. Operating costs shall include amortization of deferred rental costs, if any, and depreciation expense.

Some portions of a real estate rental project may still require major construction for completion, and other portions of the same project may be substantially completed and available for occupancy. In this event, each portion should be accounted for as a separate project.

Recoverability

Under the provisions of FASB-67, the net carrying amount of a real estate project under development or held for sale shall not exceed its estimated net realizable value. In the event that the net carrying amount of a real estate project exceeds its estimated net realizable value, a provision to reduce the net carrying amount of its estimated net realizable value shall be established in the books of account. The difference between the net carrying amount of the project and the provision, or allowance account, should equal the estimated net realizable value of the real estate project. Each individual project shall be separately analyzed to determine whether its net carrying amount exceeds its estimated net realizable value. An individual project is considered to consist of similar components within the real estate project, such as (a) individual residences, (b) individual apartments or condominiums, or (c) individual lots, acres, or tracts. Thus, a real estate project which includes 50 individual residences, 10 condominium buildings, 20 multifamily buildings, and 100 residential lots would be accounted for as four separate projects for the purposes of determining net realizable values. The net carrying amount of the 100 residential lots may exceed their net realizable value, while the individual net carrying values of the 50 individual residences, 10 condominium buildings, and 20 multifamily buildings may not exceed their individual estimated net realizable values.

Suspension of major construction activity may occur because of a decline in rental demand. In this event, the carrying costs of the real estate rental project may be permanently impaired and a provision for losses may be required. Impairment of the net carrying amount of a real estate project may occur from insufficient rental demand even if construction is not suspended.

Amendments and Effective Data

FASB-32 (Specialized Accounting and Reporting Principles and Practices in AICPA Statements of Position and Guides on Accounting and Auditing Matters) is amended by FASB-67, by deleting Statement of Position 78-3 from Appendix A, and deleting Statement of Position 80-3 from Appendix B.

FASB-67 is effective for costs of real estate projects incurred in fiscal years beginning on or after January 1, 1983. Earlier application of the provisions of FASB-67 is not required, but is encouraged.

REAL ESTATE—RECOGNITION OF SALES

Overview

FASB-66 and FASB-98 address the recognition of profit on real estate sales. FASB-98 specifically addresses sale-leaseback transactions involving real estate and FASB-66 contains the specialized accounting and reporting principles and practices that were originally published in the following AICPA publications:

- Industry Accounting Guide (Accounting for Profit Recognition on Sales of Real Estate)
- Industry Accounting Guide (Accounting for Retail Land Sales)
- SOP 75-6 (Questions Concerning Profit Recognition of Sales of Real Estate)
- SOP 78-4 (Application of the Deposit, Installment, and Cost Recovery Methods in Accounting for Sales of Real Estate)

FASB-66 does not include those portions of the industry accounting guide entitled "Accounting for Retail Land Sales," which cover costs of real estate projects. These costs of real estate projects are covered in FASB-67 (Accounting for Costs and Initial Rental Operations of Real Estate Projects).

FASB-66 establishes the promulgated GAAP for the recognition of profit on all real estate transactions for any type of accounting entity. In this respect, FASB-66 provides separate criteria for the recognition of profit on (a) all real estate transactions, except retail land sales, and (b) retail land sales. The following items are expressly excluded from the provisions of FASB-66:

1. Exchanges of real estate for other real estate
2. Sales and leasebacks

In extracting the specialized accounting principles and practices from the various AICPA publications, the FASB has made the following changes:

1. Sales of "Time-Sharing Interests in Real Estate" that represent fee simple ownership, or are sales-type leases under FASB-13, are accounted for as sales of real estate and are included in the provisions of FASB-66.

2. The discount rate which is applied to the total contract price of a retail land sale has been changed to a rate that produces an amount at which the receivable could be sold on a volume basis without recourse to the seller.

3. The disclosure requirements of the Retail Land Sales Guide have been condensed and certain disclosures omitted because of duplication with other existing GAAP.

FASB-98 contains financial accounting and reporting standards that establish:

- A new definition of *lease term* for all leasing transactions

- The appropriate accounting for a seller-lessee in a sale-leaseback transaction involving real estate, including real estate with equipment, such as manufacturing facilities, power plants, furnished office buildings, etc.

- The appropriate accounting for a sale-leaseback transaction in which property improvements or integral equipment is sold to a purchaser-lessor and leased back by the seller-lessee who retains the ownership of the underlying land

  Note: The term *property improvements or integral equipment* refers to any physical structure or equipment attached to the real estate, or other parts thereof, that cannot be removed and used separately without incurring significant cost.

- The appropriate accounting for sale-leaseback transactions involving real estate with equipment that include separate sale and leaseback agreements for the real estate and the equipment (a) with the same entity or related parties and (b) that are consummated at or near the same time, suggesting that they were negotiated as a package

Sale-leaseback transactions are addressed by FASB-28 and FASB-13, except for sale-leaseback transactions involving real estate, which are addressed by FASB-98. A *sale-leaseback* transaction is one in which an owner sells property and leases the same property back again from the purchaser. The parties to a sale-leaseback transaction are the *seller-lessee* and the *purchaser-lessor.*

If the lease portion of a sale-leaseback transaction meets the criteria for capitalization under FASB-13, the purchaser-lessor records the acquisition of the property as a purchase and the lease as a direct financing lease. If the lease portion of a sale-leaseback transaction does not meet the criteria for capitalization under FASB-13, the purchaser-lessor records the acquisition of the property as a purchase and the lease as an operating lease.

The seller-lessee accounts for the lease in a sale-leaseback transaction based on the portion of the property that is leased back. Under FASB-28, a seller-lessee can lease back (a) a minor portion of the property, (b) substantially all of the property, or (c) somewhere between more than a minor portion of the property and less than substantially all of the property.

Prior to the issuance of FASB-98, some enterprises recorded a sale of real estate in a sale-leaseback transaction ignoring the provisions of the sale-leaseback agreement, while other enterprises considered the provisions of the sale-leaseback agreement in evaluating whether the sale recognition criteria of FASB-66 were met. This difference in recording the sale portion of a sale-leaseback agreement resulted from different interpretations of paragraph 40 of FASB-66. Paragraph 40 of FASB-66 required that the *amount* of profit recognized on a sale-leaseback transaction was to be determined at the date of the sale in accordance with the provisions of FASB-66, but the amount of profit determined in this manner was to be accounted for in accordance with the provisions of FASB-13 and FASB-28. FASB-98 solves this problem by requiring that a sale-leaseback involving real estate, including real estate with equipment, be accounted for as a sale only if it qualifies as a sale under the provisions of FASB-66, and the seller makes active use of the leased property during the lease term.

Under FASB-66, a real estate sale must be consummated before it qualifies as a sale. Consummation of a real estate sale usually requires the seller to transfer title to the buyer. Prior to the issuance of FASB-98, FASB-13, as amended by FASB-26, provided that a sale of real estate could be recognized in a sales-type lease even if the title is never transferred. This resulted in a conflict between FASB-66 and FASB-13, which FASB-98 eliminates by prohibiting leases involving real estate to be classified as sales-type leases, under the provisions of FASB-13, unless the lease agreement provides for the title to the property to be transferred to the lessee at or shortly after the end of the lease term.

Under FASB-13, the lease term may be affected if the lessee provides financing to the lessor and the loan is interpreted as a *guarantee of the lessor's debt*. The lease term may also be affected by the interpretation of the term *economic penalty* which appears in FASB Technical Bulletin 79-11 (Effect of a Penalty on the Term of a Lease). To eliminate diversity in current accounting practice, FASB-98 contains a new definition of *lease term* that clarifies the meaning of a guarantee of the lessor's debt by the lessee and provides a clearer interpretation of the term *economic penalty.*

Background

The "matching" concept requires that revenue and related costs be "matched" in determining net income for a specific period. If revenue is deferred to a future period, the associated costs of that revenue must also be deferred. Frequently, it is necessary to estimate revenue and/or costs in order to achieve a proper "matching." The result of using the matching concept in determining income or loss is called the *earning process.* When the earning process is complete and an exchange has taken place, only then is the realization of revenue recognized. The realization principle requires that revenue be earned before it is recorded.

GAAP require that the realization of revenue be recognized in the accounting period in which the earning process is substantially completed and an exchange has taken place (APB Statement-4). In addition, revenue is usually recognized at the amount established by the parties to the exchange except for transactions in which collection of the receivable is not reasonably assured (APB Statement-4). In the event that collection of the receivable is not reasonably assured, the installment method or cost-recovery method may be used (APB-10). Alternatively, collections may be properly recorded as deposits in the event that considerable uncertainty exists as to their eventual collectibility.

Under the provisions of FASB-66, real estate transactions are broken down into (a) all real estate transactions, except retail land sales and (b) retail land sales.

All real estate transactions, except retail land sales   More often than not, in a real estate sale, a significant portion of the sales price is represented by a long-term receivable which is not backed by the full faith and credit of the buyer. Usually, the seller can only recover the property in the event of default by the buyer. Another unusual facet of real estate sales is the possible continuing involvement in the property by the seller. For instance, the seller may be legally bound to make certain improvements to the property or to adjacent property.

In order to assure the collection of the long-term receivable which is usually part of a real estate transaction, FASB-66 requires minimum down payments for all real estate sales before a seller may recognize a profit. FASB-66 emphasizes the timing of the recognition of profits but does not cover other aspects of real estate accounting.

Real estate transactions that are not considered "retail land sales" include the following:

1. Sales of homes, buildings, and parcels of land
2. Sales of lots to builders
3. Sales of corporate stock or a partnership interest where the economic substance of the transaction is actually a sale of real estate
4. Sales of options to acquire real estate
5. Sales of time-sharing interests in real estate

Retail land sales The development of a large tract of land usually over several years is typical of a company in the retail land sales industry. Master plans are drawn for the improvement of the property which may include amenities, and all necessary regulatory approvals are obtained. Large advertising campaigns are held at an early stage which frequently result in substantial sales prior to significant development of the property. In most retail land sales, a substantial portion of the sales price is financed by the seller in the form of a long-term receivable secured by the property. Interest and principal are paid by the buyer over an extended number of years. In the event of default, the buyer usually loses his entire equity and the property reverts back to the seller. Frequently, the retail land sales contract or existing state law provides for a period in which the purchaser may receive a refund of all or part of any payments made. In addition, the seller may be unable to obtain a deficiency judgment against the buyer because of operation of the law. Finally, many project-wide improvements and amenities are deferred until the later stages of development when the seller may be faced with financial difficulties.

Because of the small down payments, frequent cancellations and refunds, and the possibility that the retail land sales company may not be financially able to complete the project, certain specific conditions must be met before a sale can be recognized.

REAL ESTATE SALES, EXCEPT RETAIL LAND SALES

In order for a seller to report the total profit on a sale of real estate by the full accrual method, FASB-66 requires that the transaction meet specific criteria. The criteria are as follows:

1. A sale must be completed (consummated).
2. The initial and continuing payments (investment) made by the buyer must be adequate.
3. The seller's receivable shall not be subject to future subordination, except to (a) a primary lien on the property existing at the date of sale, or (b) a future loan, or existing permanent loan commitment of which the proceeds must first be applied to the payment of the seller's receivable.
4. All of the benefits and risks of ownership in the property must be substantially transferred to the buyer by the seller.
5. The seller must not have a substantial continued involvement with the property after the sale.

If a sale of real estate, other than a retail land sale, meets all of the above criteria, the seller must recognize the entire profit on the sale in accordance with the full accrual method of accounting. In the event a real estate sale fails to meet all of the above criteria, profit on the sale must be recognized by either (a) the deposit method, (b) the installment sales method, (c) the cost-recovery method, or (d) the reduced profit method. The method that must be used for profit recognition is determined by the specific circumstances of each real estate sale.

First, FASB-66 reviews in detail each of the specific criteria that must be present if the full accrual method is to be used.

When a Real Estate Sale Is Consummated

FASB-66 contains four criteria that must be met for a sale of real estate to be considered "consummated." The criteria are as follows:

1. The contracting parties are legally bound by the contract.
2. All consideration required by the terms of the contract has been paid.
3. If the seller is responsible by the terms of the contract to obtain permanent financing for the buyer, the seller must have arranged for such financing.
4. The seller has performed all of the acts required by the contract to earn the revenue.

Under FASB-66, all of the above criteria must be met before the sale of real estate is considered "consummated." As a general rule, the above criteria are met at the time of, or after, the closing of the real estate sale. These criteria are rarely met prior to closing or at the time a sales agreement is executed.

An exception to the "consummation rule" may occur if, after the date of sale, the seller has continued involvement with the property to construct office buildings, condominiums, shopping centers, or other similar improvements on the land which take a long time to complete. As will be discussed later, FASB-66 permits some profit recognition under certain circumstances even if the seller has this type of substantial continued involvement with the property.

Buyer's Initial and Continuing Investment

In determining whether the buyer's minimum initial investment (down payment) is adequate under the provisions of FASB-66, the *sales value* of the property is used and not the stated sales price in the contract. The *sales value* is defined as the stated sales price of the property, increased or decreased for other considerations included in the sale that clearly represent more or less proceeds to the seller on the sale. Thus, any payments made by the buyer that are not included in the stated sales price in the contract and which represent additional proceeds to the seller should be included as part of the buyer's minimum investment. These additional proceeds enter into the determination of both the buyer's minimum investment and the *sales value* of the property. Examples of additional proceeds to the seller are (a) the exercise price of a real estate option to purchase the property, (b) management fees, (c) points to obtain financing, (d) prepaid interest and principal payments, (e) payments by the buyer to third parties which reduce previously existing indebtedness on the property, and (f) any payments made by the buyer to the seller which will be applied at a future date against amounts due the seller. However, payments by the buyer to third parties for improvements to the property or payments which are not verifiable cannot be considered as additional proceeds to the seller.

Decreases in the stated sales price that are necessary to arrive at the *sales value* of the property may include, but are not limited to, the following:

1. The amount of discount, if any, necessary to reduce the buyer's receivable to its present value. Thus, if the buyer's receivable does not bear interest or the rate of interest is less than the prevailing rate, a discount would be required to reduce it to its present value (APB-21).

2. The present value of services that the seller agrees to perform without compensation or, if the seller agrees to perform

services at less than prevailing rates, the difference between (a) the present value of the services at prevailing rates and (b) the present value of the agreed upon compensation.

The effects of an underlying land lease must also be included in computing the *sales value* of the property. If a seller sells improvements to a buyer to be built on property subject to an underlying land lease, the present value of the lease payments must be included in the *sales value* of the property. The present value of the lease payments should be computed over the actual term of the primary indebtedness of the improvements, if any, or over the usual term of primary indebtedness for the type of improvements involved. The present value of the land lease payments is tantamount to additional indebtedness on the property. If the land lease is not subordinated, the discount rate to determine the present value of the land lease payments should be comparable to interest rates on primary debt of the same nature. However, if the land lease is subordinated, a higher discount rate comparable to secondary debt of the same nature, should be used.

XYZ, Inc. agrees to build improvements for ABC Company for a total price of $1,750,000. The improvements are to be built on land leased by ABC from a third party. The payments on the land lease are $18,000 per year, payable monthly in advance, and the lease term is for 45 years. ABC Company will pay for the improvements as follows:

Cash down payment	$ 250,000
10% unsecured note payable in five annual payments of $20,000 plus interest	100,000
Primary loan from insurance company secured by improvements to the property, payable in equal monthly payments over 28 years at 8 1/2% interest	1,400,000
Total Stated Sales Price of Improvements	$1,750,000

The computation of the *sales value*, as required by FASB-66, is as follows:

Present value of land lease payments for 28 years, payable $1,500 monthly, discounted at 8 1/2% interest	$ 193,361
Primary loan from insurance company	1,400,000
Total equivalent primary debt	$1,593,361
Unsecured note from buyer to seller	100,000
Cash down payment	250,000
Sales value*	$1,943,361

*The adequacy of the buyer's minimum initial investment in the property is based on the *sales value* of the property and not on the stated sales price.

If a land lease exists between the buyer and a third party, its effects on the sales value of the property are used only to determine the adequacy of the buyer's initial investment. However, when the seller of the improvements is also the lessor of the land lease, the computation of the profit on the sale of the improvements is also affected. Since it is impossible to separate the profits on the improvements from the profits on the underlying lease, FASB-66 requires a special computation limiting the amount of profit that can be recognized. The amount of profit which can be recognized on the improvements is equal to the *sales value* of the property less the cost of improvements and the cost of the land. However, the present value of the lease payments in the sales value may not exceed the actual cost of the land.

The result of the limitation on the amount of profit which can be recognized on the sale of improvements is to defer any residual profit on the land from being recognized until the land is sold or the future rental payments are actually received.

If a land lease between a buyer and a seller of improvements on the land is for a term of less than 20 years or does not substantially cover the economic life of the improvements being made to the property, the transaction should be accounted for as a single lease of land and improvements.

The buyer's minimum initial investment must be made at or before the time of sale in cash or cash equivalency. A buyer's note does not qualify for the minimum initial investment unless payment of the note is unconditionally guaranteed by an irrevocable letter of credit from an established unrelated lending institution. A permanent loan commitment by an independent third party to replace a loan made by the seller shall not be included in the buyer's initial investment. Any funds that have been loaned or will be loaned, directly or indirectly, to the buyer by the seller must be deducted from the buyer's initial investment (down payment) to determine whether the required minimum has been met. For the purposes of this provision, the seller must be exposed to a potential loss as a result of the funds loaned to the buyer. For example, if a buyer made an initial cash investment of $200,000 in a real estate transaction, $25,000 of which was a loan from the seller, the buyer's minimum initial investment under the provisions of FASB-66 would be $175,000. However, if an unrelated reputable banking institution unconditionally guaranteed the timely repayment of the $25,000 to the seller, the entire $200,000 would be eligible as the buyer's initial investment.

There is a direct relationship between the amount of the buyer's initial investment (down payment) and the probability that the seller will eventually collect the balance due. The larger the down payment, the more likely the buyer will pay the balance due. A reasonable basis for establishing the amount of a buyer's initial investment is the prevailing practices of independent lending institutions. Thus, the difference between the amount of primary mortgage an independent lending institution would lend on a particular parcel of real estate and the *sales value* of the property is a realistic guide as to the amount of the buyer's initial investment.

In order to apply the full accrual method of accounting to a real estate transaction (other than a retail land sale), FASB-66 provides that the minimum initial investment (down payment) of the buyer should be the greater of 1 or 2 below:

1. The percentage of the sales value of the property as indicated on the following table:

	Minimum Down Payment (% of Sales Value)
Land:	
Held for commercial, industrial, or residential development to commence within two years after sale	20%
Held for commercial, industrial, or residential development after two years	25%

Commercial and Industrial Property:

  Office and industrial buildings, shopping centers, etc.:

Properties subject to lease on a long-term lease basis to parties having satisfactory credit rating; cash flow currently sufficient to service all indebtedness	10%
Single tenancy properties sold to a user having a satisfactory credit rating	15%
All other	20%

Other Income-Producing Properties (hotels, motels, marinas, mobile home parks, etc.):

Cash flow currently sufficient to service all indebtedness	15%
Start-up situations or current deficiencies in cash flow	25%

Multi-Family Residential Property:

  Primary residence:

Cash flow currently sufficient to service all indebtedness	10%
Start-up situations or current deficiencies in cash flow	15%

  Secondary or Recreational Residence:

Cash flow currently sufficient to service all indebtedness	15%
Start-up situations or current deficiencies in cash flow	25%

Single Family Residential Property (including condominium or cooperative housing):

Primary residence of the buyer	5%*
Secondary or recreational residence	10%*

*If collectibility of the remaining portion of the sales price cannot be supported by reliable evidence of collection experience, a higher down payment is indicated and should not be less than 60% of the difference between the sales value and the financing available from loans guaranteed by regulatory bodies, such as FHA or VA, or from independent financial institutions. This 60% test applies when independent first mortgage financing is not utilized and the seller takes a receivable from the buyer for the difference between the sales value and the initial investment. When independent first mortgage financing is utilized, the adequacy of the initial investment on sales of single family residential property should be determined in accordance with FASB-66.

  2. The lesser of the following:

    a. The difference between the *sales value* of the property and 115% of the maximum permanent mortgage loan or commitment on the property recently obtained from a primary independent lending institution, OR

    b. Twenty-five percent (25%) of the *sales value* of the property

The following illustrates how the buyer's minimum initial investment (down payment) is determined in accordance with FASB-66.

The *sales value* of property being sold is $200,000, and the maximum permanent mortgage loan recently placed on the property from an independent lending institution is $150,000. The property being sold is commercial land, which will be developed by the buyer within two years after the date of sale. In order to apply the full accrual method of accounting to this real estate transaction, FASB-66 provides that the minimum initial investment (down payment) of the buyer should be the greater of 1 or 2 below:

1. The percentage of the *sales value* of the property as indicated on the table is $40,000 (20% of $200,000),

2. a. The difference between the *sales value* of the property and 115% of the recently placed permanent mortgage loan is $27,500 (115% of $150,000 = $172,500 and the difference between $200,000 [sales value] and $172,500 is $27,500).

   b. 25% of the sales value ($200,000) is $50,000.

   The lesser amount between 2a ($27,500) and 2b ($50,000) = $27,500
   The greater amount between 2a ($27,500) and 1 ($40,000) = $40,000

Thus, the minimum down payment of the buyer is $40,000.

OBSERVATION: *The above method of determining the buyer's initial minimum investment (down payment) is described differently in the AICPA industry accounting guide entitled "Accounting for Profit Recognition of Sales of Real Estate." The AICPA Guide permits the use of two independent methods to determine the minimum initial investment (down payment) of the buyer. The first and by far the simplest is that the minimum initial investment of the buyer be not less than 25% of the sales value of the property. The other method is that the minimum initial investment of the buyer be the greater of:*

1. *The difference between the* sales value *of the property and 115% of the primary permanent commitment or loan on the property, or*

2. *The percentage of the* sales value *of the property as indicated on the table*

> *Apparently, in extracting the specialized accounting principles from the AICPA Guide, the FASB concluded that the method promulgated in FASB-66 either (a) is a better method than that in the Guide or (b) produces the same results as the method described in the AICPA Guide.*

Even if the required minimum initial investment is made by the buyer, a separate assessment must be made to determine the collectibility of the receivable. In other words, there must be reasonable assurance that the receivable will be collected after the minimum initial investment is received by the seller, and if not, the sale should not be recorded by the full accrual method. The minimum initial investment must be made by the buyer, and the seller must be reasonably assured that the balance of the sales price will be collected before the real estate sale is recorded and any profits are recognized. The assessment of the receivable by the seller should include credit reports on the buyer and an evaluation of the adequacy of the cash flow from the property.

In addition to an adequate initial investment, FASB-66 also requires that the buyer maintain a continuing investment in the property by increasing his investment each year. The buyer's total indebtedness for the purchase price of the property must be reduced each year in equal amounts which will extinguish the entire indebtedness (interest and principal) over a specified maximum period. The specified maximum period for land transactions is twenty (20) years. The specified maximum period for all other real estate transactions is no more than that offered at the time of sale for first mortgages by independent financial institutions.

The buyer's commitment to pay the full amount of his indebtedness to the seller becomes doubtful if the total indebtedness is not to be paid within the specified maximum period.

A buyer's payments on his indebtedness must be in cash or cash equivalency. Funds provided directly or indirectly by the seller cannot be used in determining the buyer's continuing investment in the property.

Release Provisions

Real estate agreements involving land frequently provide for the periodic release of part of the land to the buyer. The buyer obtains the released land free of any liens. The conditions for the release usually require that sufficient funds have previously been paid by the buyer to cover the sales price of the released land and often an additional sum is required to effectuate the release. In these types of transactions involving released land, the requirements for a buyer's initial and continuing investment must be determined on the basis of the *sales value* of property not released or not subject to release. In other words, for a seller to recognize profit at the time of sale, a buyer's investment must be enough to pay any amounts for the release of land and still meet the specified initial and continued investment required by the provisions of FASB-66. If the buyer's initial and continuing investment is not sufficient, then each release of land should be treated as a separate sale and profit recognized at that time.

Future Subordination

If, at the time of sale, a seller's receivable is subject to future subordination, other than (a) to a primary lien on the property existing at the date of sale or (b) to a future loan, or existing permanent loan commitment, the proceeds of which must first be applied to the payment of the seller's receivable, no profit should be recognized because the effect of future subordination on the collectibility of a receivable cannot be reasonably evaluated. The cost-recovery method should be used to recognize profit at the time of sale if the seller's receivable is subject to future subordination, other than the two exceptions noted above.

Nontransfer of Ownership and Seller's Continued Involvement

Real estate transactions must be carefully analyzed to determine their economic substance. Frequently, the economic substance of a real estate sale is no more than a management fee arrangement or an indication that the risks and benefits of ownership have not really been transferred in the agreement. Therefore, accounting for a real estate transaction can become quite complicated because of the many types of continuing relations that can exist between a buyer and a seller. The substance of the real estate transaction should dictate the accounting method which should be used.

As a general rule, before a profit may be recognized, a sale must occur, collectibility of the receivable must be reasonably assured, and the seller must perform all of the acts required by the contract to earn the revenue. Profit may also be recognized, at the time of the sale, on contracts which provide for the continued involvement of the seller if the maximum potential loss of the seller is expressly limited and defined by the terms of the contract. In this event, the total profit on the sale, less the maximum potential loss which could occur because of the seller's involvement, is recognized at the time of the sale.

The two most important factors in evaluating the economic substance of a real estate sale are (1) the transfer of the usual risks and rewards of ownership in the property and (2) the full performance by the seller of all acts required by the contract to earn the revenue. Generally, both of these factors must be accomplished before full profit may be recognized on the sale of real estate. The more common types of real estate transactions and how they should be accounted for are discussed in the following paragraphs.

Profit Recognition Other Than Full Accrual Basis

As mentioned previously, in order for a seller to report the total profit on a sale of real estate by the full accrual method of accounting, FASB-66 requires that all of the following criteria be met:

1. A sale is consummated.
2. The initial and continuing payments (investment) made by the buyer must be adequate.
3. The seller's receivable shall not be subject to future subordination, except to (a) a primary lien on the property existing at the date of sale, or (b) a future loan, or existing permanent loan commitment of which the proceeds must first be applied to the payment of the seller's receivable.
4. All of the benefits and risks of ownership in the property must be substantially transferred to the buyer by the seller.
5. The seller must not have a substantial continued involvement with the property after the date of sale.

If a sale of real estate, other than a retail land sale, meets all of the above criteria, the seller must recognize the entire profit on the sale in accordance with the full accrual basis of accounting.

When one or more of the above criteria is not met in a real estate sale, an alternative method of recognizing revenue from the sale must be used. The alternative method selected may be required by FASB-66 or may be a matter of professional judgment. The four accounting methods recommended by FASB-66 are (a) the deposit method, (b) the cost-recovery method, (c) the installment sales method, and (d) the reduced profit method.

Deposit accounting   The uncertainty about the collectibility of the sales price in a real estate transaction may be so great that the effective date of the sale should be deferred and any cash received by the seller should be accounted for as a deposit. However, cash received that is designated by contract as nonrefundable interest may be applied as an offset to existing carrying charges on the property, such as property taxes and interest, instead of being accounted for as a deposit.

All cash received except that appropriately used as an offset to the carrying charges of the property must be reflected in the seller's balance sheet as a liability (deposit on a contract for the sale of real estate). No change is made in accounting for the property subject to the contract and its related mortgage debt, if any. However, the seller's financial statements should disclose that these items are subject to a sales contract. Depreciation expense should continue as a period cost, in spite of the fact that the property has been legally sold. Until the requirements of FASB-66 are met for profit recognition, the seller does not report a sale and continues to report all cash received either as a deposit or in the case of nonrefundable interest, as an offset to the carrying charges of the property involved. In the event that the buyer forfeits a nonrefundable deposit, or defaults on the contract, the seller should reduce the deposit account appropriately and include such amounts in income of the period.

Cost recovery method   If a seller's receivable is subject to subordination which cannot be reasonably evaluated, or uncertainty exists as to the recovery of the seller's cost on default by the buyer, the cost recovery method should be used. Even if cost has been recovered by the seller but additional collections are highly doubtful, the cost-recovery method would be appropriate. Frequently, the cost recovery method is initially used for transactions which would also qualify for the installment sales method.

> **OBSERVATION**: *The cost recovery and installment sales methods both defer the recognitions on the sale until collections are actually received.*

Under the cost recovery method, all collections are applied first to the recovery of the cost of the property, and only after full cost has been received is any profit recognized. The only expenses remaining to be charged against the profit are those relating to the collection process. When the cost recovery method is used, the total sales value is included in the income statement for the period in which the sale is made. From the total sales value in the income statement, the total cost of the sale and the deferred gross profit on the sale are deducted. On the balance sheet the deferred gross profit is reflected as a reduction of the related receivable. Until full cost is recovered, principal payments received are applied to reduce the related receivable and interest payments received are added to the deferred gross profit. At any given time, the related receivable less the deferred gross profit equals the remaining cost which must be recovered. After all cost is recovered, subsequent collections reduce the deferred gross profit and appear as a separate item of revenue on the income statement.

Installment sales method Promulgated GAAP prohibit accounting for sales by any form of installment accounting except under exceptional circumstances where collectibility cannot be reasonably estimated or assured. The doubtfulness of collectibility can be caused by the length of an extended collection period or because no basis of estimation can be established. In such cases a company can use either the cost-recovery method or the installment sales method of accounting (APB-10).

The installment sales method is frequently more appropriate for real estate transactions in which collectibility of the receivable from the buyer cannot be reasonably assured because defaults on loans secured by real estate usually result in the recovery of the property sold.

Under the installment sales method of accounting, each payment collected consists of part recovery of cost and part recovery of gross profit, in the same ratio that these two elements existed in the original sale. In a real estate transaction, the original sale is equal to the *sales value* of the property. Thus, under the installment sales method, profit is recognized on cash payments made by the buyer to the holder of the primary debt assumed, and cash payments to the seller. The profit recognized on the cash payments is based on the percentage of total profit to total *sales value*.

Jones Company sells real property to Smith for $2,000,000. Smith will assume an existing $1,200,000 first mortgage and pay $300,000 in cash as a down payment. The balance of $500,000 will be in the form of a 12% second mortgage to Jones Company payable in equal payments of principal and interest over a ten-year period. The cost of the property to Jones is $1,200,000.

Computation of Sales Value and Gross Profit

Cash	$ 300,000
Second mortgage	500,000
First mortgage	1,200,000
Total sales value (which happens to be the same as the stated sales price)	$ 2,000,000
Less: Cost of property sold	1,200,000
Total gross profit on sale	$ 800,000
Gross profit percentage	40.0%
Profit to be recognized on down payment (40% of $300,000)	$ 120,000

Assuming that the $300,000 down payment is insufficient to meet the requirements of full profit recognition on the sale (accrual basis of accounting), Jones would recognize $120,000 gross profit at the time of sale. Assume that several months later Smith makes a cash payment of $100,000 on the first mortgage and $50,000 on the second mortgage. The amount of gross profit which Jones would recognize on these payments would be as follows:

Payment of first mortgage	$100,000
Payment of second mortgage	50,000
Total cash payments	$150,000
Gross profit realized (40% of $150,000)	$ 60,000

The point is that even though Jones does not receive any cash on the payment of the first mortgage by Smith, gross profit is still realized because the gross profit percentage was based on the total *sales value* which included the first mortgage liability.

When the installment sales method is used, the total sales value is included in the income statement of the period in which the sale is made. From the total sales value in the income statement, the total cost of the sale and the deferred gross profit are deducted. On the balance sheet the deferred gross profit on the sale is deducted from the related receivable. As cash payments are received, the portion allocated to realized gross profit is presented as a separate item of revenue on the income statement and deferred gross profit is reduced by the same amount. At any given time, the related receivable less the deferred gross profit represents the remaining cost of the property sold. Since realized gross profit is recognized as a portion of each cash collection, a percentage relationship will always exist between the long-term receivable and its related deferred gross profit. This percentage relationship will be the same as the gross profit ratio on the initial sales value.

Reduced profit method   The buyer's receivable is discounted to the present value of the lowest level of annual payments required by the sales contract. The discount period is the maximum allowed under the provisions of FASB-66, and all lump-sum payments are excluded in the calculation. The discount rate cannot be less than that stated in the sales contract, if any, or the prevailing interest rate in accordance with existing GAAP (APB-21). The buyer's receivable discounted as described above is used in determining the profit on the sale of real estate and usually results in a "reduced profit" from that which would be obtained under normal accounting procedures. Lump-sum and other payments are recognized as profit when they are received by the seller.

Change to full accrual method   After the cost-recovery or installment sales method is adopted for a real estate transaction, a periodic evaluation should be made of the collectibility of the receivable. When it becomes apparent that the seller's receivable is reasonably assured of being collected, a change to the full accrual accounting method should be made by the seller. The change is not a change in an accounting principle (Statement of Position 78-4). When the change to the full accrual accounting method is made, any remaining deferred gross profit is recognized in full in the period in which the change is made. If the change creates a material effect on the seller's financial statements, full disclosure of the effects and the reason for the change should be appropriately made in the financial statements or footnotes thereto (Statement of Position 78-4).

Profit Recognition When Sale Is Not Consummated

If a real estate sale has not been consummated in accordance with the provisions of FASB-66, the deposit method of accounting shall be used until the sale is consummated.

As mentioned previously, an exception to the "consummation rule" occurs if the terms of the contract require the seller to sell a parcel of land and also construct on the same parcel a building which takes an extended period to complete. In other words, the seller is still involved with the property after the sale because he must construct the building. In most jurisdictions a "certificate of occupancy" must be obtained for a building or other structure. The certificate of occupancy indicates that the building has been constructed in accordance with the local building regulations and is ready for occupancy. Thus, a certificate of occupancy is usually necessary to consummate the real estate transaction. However, FASB-66 contains a special provision for profit recognition when a sale of real estate requires the seller to develop the property in the future. If the seller has contracted (a) for future development of the land, (b) to construct buildings, amenities, or other facilities on the land, or (c) to provide offsite improvements, partial recognition of profit may be recognized if future costs of development can be reasonably estimated at the time of sale. In this event, profit can be recognized for any work performed and finished by the seller when (a) the sale of the land is consummated and (b) the initial and continuing investments of the buyer are adequate. In other words, if the sale of the land meets the first two criteria for the use of the full accrual method of accounting, any profit allocable to (a) the work performed prior to the sale of the land and (b) the sale of the land can be recognized by the percentage-of-completion method. Thus, the total profit on the sale may be allocated to work performed prior to the sale of the land and to future construction and development work. The allocation of the total profit is based on the estimated costs for each activity using a uniform rate of gross profit for all activities. However, if significant uncertainties exist or costs and profits cannot be reasonably estimated, the completed contract method should be used.

If a buyer has the right to defer until completion payments due for developmental and construction work, or if the buyer is financially unable to pay these amounts as they come due, care should be exercised in recognizing any profits until completion or satisfactory payment.

The terms of a real estate transaction accounted for by the deposit method may indicate that the carrying amount of the property involved is more than the sales value in the contract and that a loss has been incurred. Since the seller is using the deposit method, no sale is recorded and thus no loss. However, the information indicates an impairment of an asset which should be appropriately recorded by the seller in the period of discovery by a charge to income and the creation of a valuation allowance account for the property involved.

Profit Recognition When Buyer's Investment Is Inadequate

If all of the criteria for the full accrual method of accounting are met except that the buyer's initial investment is inadequate, the seller shall account for the sale by the installment sales method, provided that the seller is reasonably assured of recovering the cost of the property if the buyer defaults. If the seller is not reasonably assured of recovering the cost of the property upon default by the buyer, or if cost recovery has been made but future collections are uncertain, the cost-recovery method or the deposit method shall be used by the seller to account for the sale.

If all of the criteria for the full accrual method of accounting are met, except that the buyer's continuing investment is inadequate, the seller shall account for the sale by the reduced profit method, provided that the buyer's periodic payments cover both of the following items:

1. Amortization of principal and interest based on the maximum primary mortgage that could be obtained on the property.

2. Interest, at an appropriate rate, on the excess amount, if any, of the total actual debt on the property over the maximum primary mortgage that could be obtained on the property.

If both of the above conditions are not met, the reduced profit method shall not be used by the seller. In this event, the seller should account for the sale either by the installment sales method or the cost-recovery method, whichever is more appropriate under the specific circumstances.

Profit Recognition—Subordinated Receivable

As mentioned previously, the cost-recovery method shall be used to recognize profit at the time of sale if the seller's receivable is subject to future subordination, except in the following situations:

1. Subordinated to a primary lien on the property existing at the date of sale.

2. Subordinated to a future loan, or existing permanent loan commitment, the proceeds of which must first be applied to the payment of the seller's receivable.

Profit Recognition—Seller's Continued Involvement

In some real estate transactions the seller does not transfer the benefits and risks of ownership to the buyer, or the seller maintains a substantial continued involvement with the property after the date of sale. These types of real estate transactions require careful examination to determine the appropriate method of accounting that should be applied.

In legal form a real estate transaction may be a sale, but in substance the contract may be a profit-sharing, financing, or leasing arrangement. If in substance the transaction is a profit-sharing, financing, or leasing arrangement, no sale or profit is recognized. If a real estate contract contains any of the following provisions, it should be accounted for as a profit-sharing, financing, or leasing arrangement:

1. The return of the buyer's investment in the property is guaranteed by the seller.
2. The buyer can compel the seller to repurchase the property.
3. An option or obligation exists for the seller to repurchase the property.
4. The seller is required to operate the property at its own risk for an extended period.
5. The seller, as general partner, holds a receivable from the limited partnership as a result of a real estate sale. The collection of the receivable depends on the successful operation of the limited partnership by the general partner who is also the seller and holder of the receivable.
6. A specific return on the buyer's investment is guaranteed by the seller for an extended period of time.

In real estate transactions in which the seller guarantees for a limited period (a) to return the buyer's investment or (b) a specific rate of return to the buyer, the seller shall account for the sale by the deposit method of accounting. After the operations of the property become profitable, the seller may recognize profit on the basis of performance. After the limited period has expired and all of the criteria for the full accrual method of accounting are met in accordance with FASB-66, the seller may recognize in full any remaining profit on the sale of real estate.

Initiating and supporting operations As part of a real estate transaction, the seller may be required to initiate or support the operations of the property for a stated period of time or until a certain level of operations has been achieved. In other words, the seller may agree to operate the property for a certain period or until a certain level of rental income has been reached.

Even if there is no agreement, there is a presumption that a seller has an obligation to initiate and support operations of the property he has sold in any of the following circumstances:

1. An interest in property is sold by the seller to a limited partnership in which he is a general partner.

2. An equity interest in the property sold is retained by the seller.

3. There is a management contract between the buyer and seller which provides for compensation that is significantly higher or lower than comparable prevailing rates and which cannot be terminated by either the buyer or the seller.

4. The collection of the receivable from the sale held by the seller is dependent on the operations of the property and represents a significant portion of the sales price. A significant receivable is defined as one in excess of 15% of the maximum primary financing that could have been obtained from an established lending institution.

If the seller has agreed to the initiating and supporting operations for a limited period, the seller may recognize profit on the sale on the basis of the performance of the required services. The measurement of performance shall be related to the cost incurred to date, and the total estimated costs to be incurred for the services. However, profit recognition may not start until there is reasonable assurance that estimated future rent receipts will cover (a) all operating costs, (b) debt service, and (c) any payments due the seller under the terms of the contract. For this purpose, the estimated future rent receipts shall not exceed the greater of (a) leases actually executed or (b) two thirds of the estimated future rent receipts. The difference between the estimated future rent receipts and the greater of (a) the signed leases or (b) two thirds of the estimated rent receipts shall be reserved as a safety factor.

In the event the sales contract does not specify the period for which the seller must initiate and support operations of the property, a two-year period shall be presumed. The two-year period shall commence at the time of initial rental, unless rent receipts cover all operating cost, debt service, and other commitments before the time of initial rental.

Services without compensation   As part of the contract for the sale of real estate, the seller may be required to perform services related to the property sold without compensation or at a reduced rate. In determining profit to be recognized at the time of sale, a value should be placed on such services at the prevailing rates and deducted from the sales price of the property sold. The value of the compensation should then be recognized over the period in which the services are to be performed by the seller.

Sale of real estate options   Proceeds from the sale of real estate options shall be accounted for by the deposit method. If the option is not exercised by its expiration date, the seller of the option shall recognize profit at that time. If an option is sold by the owner of the land and subsequently exercised, the proceeds from the sale of the option are included in determining the *sales value* of the property sold.

Sales of partial interests in property   A seller may continue to be involved in property sold by retaining an interest in the property and by giving the buyer preference as to profits, cash flow, return on investment, or some other similar arrangement. In this event, if the transaction is in substance a sale, the seller shall recognize profit to the extent that the sale proceeds, including receivables, exceed the seller's total cost in the property.

A seller may retain a partial interest in the property sold, such as an undivided interest or some other form of equity. If a seller sells a partial interest in real estate property and the sale meets all of the criteria for the full accrual method, except for the seller's continued involvement related to the partial interest in the property, the seller shall recognize the proportionate share of the profit that is attributable to the outside interests in the property. However, if the seller controls the buyer, profit on the sale shall not be recognized until realized from transactions with outside individuals, or through the sale of the property to outside parties.

A seller may sell single-family units or time-sharing interests in a condominium project. If the units or interests are sold individually, the seller shall recognize profit on the sales by the percentage-of-completion method, provided that all of the following conditions are met:

1. Construction has progressed beyond the preliminary stage, which means that the engineering and design work, execution of construction contracts, site clearance and preparation, and excavation or completion of the building foundation have all been completed.

2. The buyer cannot obtain a refund, except for nondelivery.
3. The property will not revert to rental property as evidenced by the number of units or interests that have been sold. In determining the sufficiency of the number of units or interests sold, reference shall be made to local and state laws, the provisions of the condominium or time-sharing contract, and the terms of the financing agreements.
4. Total sales and costs can be reasonably estimated in accordance with the percentage-of-completion method of accounting.

Until all of the above conditions are met, the seller shall account for the sales proceeds from the single-family units or time-sharing interests by the deposit method of accounting.

Disclosures FASB-66 does not contain any specific disclosure requirements for the sale of real estate, other than retail land sales. However, professional judgment may require that a significant sale of real estate be appropriately disclosed in the financial statements.

If interest is imputed on a receivable arising out of a real estate sale, certain disclosures are required by APB-21 (Interest on Receivables and Payables). In addition, if commitments or contingencies arise in a real estate sale, disclosure may be required by FASB-5 (Contingencies).

SALE-LEASEBACKS INVOLVING REAL ESTATE (FASB-98)

As mentioned earlier in this chapter, FASB-66 establishes standards of accounting and financial reporting for the recognition of profit or loss on *all* real estate transactions. Under FASB-66, the profit on a sale of real estate may be reported by the seller on the full accrual method only if the sale transaction meets all of the following criteria:

a. *The sale is consummated.*
b. *The buyer's initial and continuing investment is adequate.*
c. *The balance due the seller, if any, must not be subordinated, except to:*
   (i) *A primary lien on the property existing at the date of sale or*
   (ii) *A future loan, or existing permanent loan, the proceeds of which must be applied first to reduce any balance due to seller.*

d. *All of the benefits and risks of ownership in the property are transferred by the seller to the buyer.*

e. *The seller cannot have any substantial continued involvement with the property, after the sale is consummated.*

Under FASB-66, a sale of real estate is *consummated* at the time that (i) all the parties are bound by the terms of the contract, (ii) all consideration has been exchanged, (iii) any permanent financing for which the seller is responsible has been arranged, and (iv) all conditions precedent to closing have been performed.

If all of the above criteria have *not* been met, the seller is not permitted to recognize the profit on the sale of real estate by the full accrual method. Instead, the seller must recognize the profit on a sale of real estate either by (i) the deposit method, (ii) the installment method, (iii) the cost-recovery method, or (iv) the reduced profit method. Under all of these methods, the full amount of profit on a sale of real estate is deferred to a latter date. The specific circumstances of each sale of real estate dictate the method of accounting that must be used for profit recognition.

Sale-Leaseback Accounting

Under FASB-98, the sale portion of a sale-leaseback transaction involving real estate can be accounted for as a sale only if it qualifies as a sale under the provisions of FASB-66 (The provisions of FASB-66 pertaining to sales of real estate have ben discussed earlier in this chapter.) In addition, FASB-98 prohibits a lease involving real estate from being classified as a sales-type lease unless the lease agreement provides for the title of the leased property to be transferred to the lessee at or shortly after the end of the lease term.

Under *sale-leaseback accounting*, the sale portion of the sale-leaseback transaction is recorded as a sale by the seller-lessee, the property sold and all of its related liabilities are eliminated from the seller-lessee's balance sheet, gain or loss on the sale portion of the sale-leaseback transaction is recognized by the seller-lessee in accordance with the provisions of FASB-13 (as amended by FASB-28, FASB-66, and FASB-98), and the lease portion of the sale-leaseback transaction is accounted for in accordance with the provisions of FASB-13 (as amended by FASB-28). Sale-leaseback accounting under FASB-98 is analogous to the full accrual method under FASB-66.

Under FASB-98, a seller-lessee shall apply sale-leaseback accounting only to those sale-leaseback transactions that include payment terms and provisions that provide for (i) a normal leaseback (as defined by FASB-98), (ii) an adequate initial and continuing investment by the purchaser-lessor (as defined by FASB-66), (iii) the transfer of all of the other risks and rewards of ownership to the purchaser-lessor and (iv) no other continued involvement by the seller-lessee, other than the continued involvement represented by the lease portion of the sale-leaseback transaction.

Normal leaseback   A normal leaseback, under FASB-98, is one in which the seller-lessee actively uses substantially all of the leased property in its trade or business during the lease term. The seller-lessee may sublease a minor portion of the leased property, equal to 10% or less of the reasonable rental value for the entire leased property, and the lease will still qualify as a normal lease. Thus, to qualify as a normal leaseback under FASB-98, the seller-lessee must actively use substantially all of the leased property in its trade or business in consideration for rent payments, which may include contingent rentals that are based on the seller-lessee's future operations.

If occupancy by the seller-lessee's customers is transient or short-term, the seller-lessee may provide ancillary services, such as housekeeping, inventory control, entertainment, bookkeeping, and food service. Thus, active use by a seller-lessee in its trade or business includes the use of the leased property as a hotel, bonded warehouse, parking lots, or some other similar business.

Adequate initial and continuing investment by the purchaser-lessor   To qualify for sale-leaseback accounting under FASB-98, the purchaser-lessor's initial and continuing investment in the property must be adequate as prescribed by FASB-66. In determining whether the purchaser's minimum initial investment is adequate under the provisions of FASB-66, the *sales value* of the property is used and not the stated sales price that appears in the sales contract.

In addition to an adequate initial investment, FASB-66 also requires that the purchaser maintain a continuing investment in the property by increasing the investment each year. The purchaser's total indebtedness for the purchase price of the property must be reduced each year in equal amounts that will extinguish the entire indebtedness (interest and principal) over a specified maximum period. The specified maximum period for land transactions is twenty (20) years. The specified maximum period for all other real estate transactions is no more than that offered at the time of sale for first mortgages by independent financial institutions. (The purchaser's initial investment, continuing investment, and the stated sales price in the property have been fully discussed earlier in this chapter.)

Transfer of all other risks and rewards of ownership   In order to qualify for sale-leaseback accounting under FASB-98 the seller-lessee must transfer all of the risks and rewards of ownership in the property to the purchaser-lessor.

No other continuing involvement   FASB-98 considers the lease-back portion of a sale-leaseback transaction to be a form of continued involvement with the leased property by the seller-lessee (paragraph 48 of FASB-98). Other than the continued involvement represented by the leaseback portion of the sale-leaseback transaction, a normal leaseback excludes any *other* continuing involvement in the leased property by the seller-lessee. Thus, sale-leaseback accounting cannot be used to account for a sale-leaseback transaction in which the seller-lessee has any other continuing involvement in the property other than that represented by the leaseback portion of the transaction. (The continuing involvement of the seller in the property has been fully discussed earlier in this chapter.)

An exchange of some stated or unstated rights or privileges is indicated in a sale-leaseback transaction if the terms of the transaction are substantially different from terms that an independent third-party lessor would accept. In this event, the stated or unstated rights or privileges shall be considered in evaluating the continued involvement of the seller-lessee. Terms or conditions that indicate that stated or unstated rights or privileges exist may involve the sales price, the interest rate, and terms of any loan from the seller-lessee to the purchaser-lessor.

Recognition of Profit By Full Accrual Method

A sale-leaseback transaction must meet the criteria of FASB-98 before the seller-lessee can account for the transaction by the sale-leaseback accounting method (full accrual method). As mentioned above, under the sale-leaseback accounting method, the seller-lessee (a) records a sale, (b) removes the sold property and its related liabilities from the balance sheet, (c) recognizes gain or loss on the sale portion of the transaction in accordance with FASB-66, and (d) classifies the lease portion of the transaction either as a capitalized lease or an operating lease in accordance with the provisions of FASB-13, as amended by FASB-28.

Once a sale-leaseback transaction qualifies for sale-leaseback accounting in accordance with the provisions of FASB-98, the following steps should be followed to determine the amount of gain (loss) and the time of recognition of the gain (loss):

Step 1. Compute the *amount* of gain (loss) on the sale portion of the sale-leaseback transaction in accordance with the provisions of FASB-66. (Disregard the fact that the sale is part of a sale-leaseback transaction.)

Note: A loss must be immediately recognized on the sale portion of a sale-leaseback transaction if the undepreciated cost of the property sold is more than its fair value. The maximum amount of loss that shall be recognized immediately cannot exceed the difference between the fair value of the property and its undepreciated cost. If the indicated loss exceeds the difference between the fair value of the property sold and its undepreciated cost, the loss is possibly, in substance, a prepayment of rent. Under this circumstance, it is appropriate to defer the indicated loss and amortize it as prepaid rent (paragraph 33c of FASB-13 as amended by paragraph 3 of FASB-28).

OBSERVATION: Paragraph 33c of FASB-13, as amended by paragraph 3 of FASB-28, states that the maximum indicated loss may not be more than the difference between the undepreciated cost of the property sold and its fair value. On the other hand, paragraph 18 of FASB-28 states that the maximum indicated loss may not be more than the difference between the carrying amount of the property sold and its fair value. Thus, it is not clear whether the undepreciated cost or the carrying amount of the property should be used in calculating the maximum loss that is recognized immediately.

Step 2. Classify the lease portion of the sale-leaseback transaction in accordance with the provisions of FASB-13, as amended by FASB-28. (Depending on the percentage amount of the property that the seller-lessee leases back, a lease may be classified under FASB-28 as a lease involving either (a) substantially all of the property, (b) a minor portion of the property, or (c) more than a minor portion of the property but less than substantially all.)

Note: Under the terms of the sale-leaseback, a seller-lessee may lease back a minor portion of the property sold to the purchaser-lessor, substantially all of the property, or a portion that is more than minor and less than substantially all. A minor portion of the property has been leased back if the present value of the total rents to be paid by the seller-lessee under the terms of the lease agreement is reasonable, and equal to 10% or less of the fair value of the property at the inception of the lease. Substantially all of the property has been leased back if the present value of the total rents to be paid by the seller-lessee under the terms of the lease agreement, is reasonable, and equal to 90% or more of the fair value of the property at the inception of the lease.

Step 3. Determine whether the lease portion of the sale-leaseback transaction qualifies as a capital lease or operating lease under the provisions of FASB-13.

Note: Under FASB-13, a lease is classified as a capital lease if it meets one or more of the following criteria:

a. Ownership of the property is transferred to the lessee by the end of the lease term.

b. The lease contains a bargain purchase option.

c. The lease term, at inception, is substantially (75% or more) equal to the estimated economic life of the leased property, including earlier years of use. [Exception: This particular criterion cannot be used for a lease that begins within the last 25% of the original estimated economic life of the leased property.]

d. The present value of the minimum lease payments at the beginning of the lease term, excluding executory costs and profits thereon to be paid by the lessor, is 90% or more of the fair value of the property at the inception of the lease, less any investment tax credits retained, and expected to be realized, by the lessor. [Exception: This particular criterion cannot be used for a lease that begins within the last 25% of the original estimated economic life of the leased property.]

Step 4. Recognize the amount of gain (loss) computed in Step 1, based on the percentage amount of the property that the seller-lessee leases back, in Step 2 (substantially all of the property, a minor portion of the property, or more than a minor portion of the property but less than substantially all) AND whether in Step 3, the lease is classified as a capital lease or an operating lease.

If, under Step 2, the lease portion of the sale-leaseback transaction is classified as *substantially all*:

Any gain (loss) on the sale must be deferred and amortized by the seller-lessee, according to whether the lease is classi-fied, under Step 3, as a capital lease or as an operating lease, as follows:

Capital lease—If the lease is classified as a capital lease, the gain (loss) on the sale is amortized in proportion to the amortization of the leased property.

Operating lease—If the lease is classified as an operating lease, the gain (loss) on the sale is amortized in proportion to the gross rental charged to expense over the lease term.

If, under Step 2, the lease portion of the sale-leaseback transaction is classified as *minor*:

The sale and leaseback are accounted for as two indepen-dent transactions based on their separate terms. However, the lease must provide for a reasonable amount of rent, considering prevailing market conditions at the inception of the lease. The seller-lessee must increase or decrease the gain (loss) on the sale of the property by an amount which brings the total rental for the leased property to a reasonable amount. Any amount resulting from a rental adjustment shall be amortized as follows:

Capital lease—The deferred or accrued amount of rental ad-justment is amortized in proportion to the amortization of the leased property.

Operating lease—The deferred or accrued amount of rental adjustment is amortized in proportion to the gross rental charged to expense over the lease term.

If, under Step 2, the lease portion of the sale-leaseback transaction is classified as *more than minor but less than substantially all*:

The seller-lessee shall recognize any excess gain determined at the date of the sale, according to whether the lease is classified under Step 3 as a capital lease or an operating lease, as follows:

Capital lease—The excess gain (if any) is equal to the amount of gain that exceeds the seller-lessee's recorded amount of the property as determined under the provisions of FASB-13 (the lesser of the fair value of the leased property or the present value of the minimum lease payments). For example, if the seller-lessee's recorded amount of the sale-leaseback property is $100,000 as determined under the provisions of FASB-13, and the amount of gain on the sale portion of the sale-leaseback transaction is $120,000, the excess gain that is recognized by the seller-lessee is $20,000. The balance of the gain ($100,000) is deferred and amortized in proportion to the amortization of the leased property.

Operating lease—The excess gain (if any) on a sale-leaseback transaction is equal to the amount of gain that exceeds the present value of the minimum lease payments over the term of the lease. The amount of gain on the sale portion of the sale-leaseback transaction that is not recognized at the date of the sale is deferred and amortized over the lease term in proportion to the gross rentals charged to expense.

For a complete discussion of sale-leaseback transactions, see also "Accounting for Sale-Leasebacks" in the chapter entitled "Leases."

Profit Recognition Other than by the Full Accrual Method

A sale-leaseback transaction must qualify under the provisions of FASB-98 and most of the provisions of FASB-66 before the full amount of the profit on the sale portion of the transaction can be recognized by the sale-leaseback accounting method (full accrual method).

When one or more of the criteria for recognizing the full amount of profit on the sale portion of a sale-leaseback transaction is not met, an alternative method of recognizing revenue from the sale must be used. The alternative method selected may be required by FASB-66 or may be a matter of professional judgment. The four accounting methods recommended by FASB-66 are (a) the deposit method, (b) the cost-recovery method, (c) the installment sales method, and (d) the reduced profit method. (The four alternative methods have been fully discussed earlier in this chapter.)

A periodic evaluation of the collectibility of the receivable should be made and when it becomes apparent that the seller's receivable is reasonably assured of being collected, a change to the full accrual accounting method should be made by the seller. (Change to the full accrual method has been fully discussed earlier in this chapter.)

Regulated Enterprises—Sale-Leaseback Transactions

FASB-98 applies to regulated enterprises that are subject to FASB-71 (Accounting for the Effects of Certain Types of Regulation). The application of FASB-98 for financial accounting purposes (GAAP) may result in the recognition of income and expense in a different accounting period than that in which the same income and expense is recognized for regulatory purposes (rate-making). Under income tax accounting (FASB-96), this results in a temporary difference. If a temporary difference represents part or all of a phase-in plan as defined by FASB-92, a specific method of accounting is prescribed by FASB-98. For all other types of temporary differences a different method of accounting is specified.

If a temporary difference represents part or all of a phase-in plan, as defined by FASB-92, it shall be accounted for in accordance with the provisions of FASB-92. In all other circumstances, a temporary difference shall be modified to conform with FASB-71. For example, the sale portion of a sale-leaseback transaction may be recognized for regulatory purposes and not recognized for financial accounting purposes because the transaction is accounted for by the deposit method. In this event, amortization of the asset should be modified to equal the total amount of the rental expense and gain or loss that are allowable for regulatory purposes. Also, the sale portion of a sale-leaseback transaction may be recognized for regulatory pur-poses and not recognized for financial accounting purposes because the transaction is accounted for as a financing. In this event, amortization of the asset and the total amount of interest imputed under the interest method for the financing should be modified to equal the total rental expense and gain or loss that are allowable for regulatory purposes.

If it is not part of a phase-in plan as defined by FASB-92 and it meets the criteria of FASB-71, a temporary (timing) difference between the amount of income or expense that is allowable for regulatory purposes and the amount of income or expense that is recognized by the deposit method or as a financing shall be capitalized or accrued as a separate regulatory asset or liability.

Financial Statement Disclosure and Presentation

The financial statements of the seller-lessee shall include a description of the terms of the sale-leaseback transaction, including future commitments, obligations, or other provisions that require or result in the seller-lessee's continuing involvement.

A seller-lessee who has accounted for a sale-leaseback by the deposit method or as a financing shall disclose in the aggregate and for each of the five succeeding fiscal years:

- The obligation for future minimum lease payments as of the date of the latest balance sheet presented, and
- The total of minimum sublease rentals, if any, to be received in the future under noncancelable subleases.

Effective Date and Transition

FASB-98 is effective for transactions *entered into* on or after July 1, 1988. Earlier application of the provisions of FASB-98 is encouraged for those transactions that occurred in periods for which annual financial statements have not been issued. For the purposes of FASB-98, the term *entered into* means the date of the lease agreement or the date of a written commitment signed by the parties involved which sets forth the principal provisions of the lease transaction.

RETAIL LAND SALES

Profit Recognition

FASB-66 requires that profit on all retail land sales within a project shall be recognized by a single accounting method. As conditions change for the entire project, the method of profit recognition shall change in accordance with the provisions of FASB-66. The provisions of FASB-66 require that the profits on a retail land sales project be recognized either (a) by the full accrual method, (b) by the percentage-of-completion method, (c) by the installment sales method, or (d) by the deposit method. FASB-66 contains specific criteria which must be met before a particular profit recognition method can be used.

A retail land sales project is defined as a "homogeneous, reasonably contiguous area of land that may, for development or marketing, be subdivided in accordance with a master plan."

Profit Recognition—Full Accrual Method

All of the following conditions must be met for the entire retail land sales project before the full accrual method of accounting can be used for the recognition of profit on retail land sales:

1. The down payment and all subsequent payments have been made by the buyer, through and including any period of cancellation, and all periods for any refund have expired.
2. The buyer has paid a total of 10% or more in principal or interest of the total contract sales price.
3. The seller's collection experience for the project or prior projects indicates that 90% of the receivables in force for six months after the sale is recorded will be collected in full. A down payment of 20% or more is an acceptable substitute for this experience test.

   OBSERVATION: Profit may be recognized before the end of six months if collection experience is based on a prior project. The six-month period is an eligibility test for the full accrual method of accounting.

   The collection experience of a prior project may be used if (a) the prior project was similar in characteristics to the new project and (b) the collection period was long enough to determine collectibility of receivables to maturity dates.
4. The seller's receivable for the property sold is not subject to subordination of new loans. However, subordination is allowed for construction of a residence providing the project's collection experience for such subordinated receivables is approximately the same as that for those receivables which are not subordinated.
5. The seller is not obligated to construct amenities or other facilities, or complete any improvements for lots which have been sold.

If all of the above conditions are met for the entire retail land sales project, the seller shall recognize profits by the full accrual method of accounting.

The actual procedures that must be used to record retail land sales under the full accrual method of accounting are as follows:

1. The total contract price of the retail land sale, before any deductions, is recorded as a gross sale. The total contract price includes the total amount of principal and interest which is expected to be received from the sale.
2. The down payment on the sale is recorded. The difference between the total contract price of the retail land sale and the down payment is the gross receivable.
3. The gross receivable is discounted at the date of sale to yield an amount at which it could be sold on a volume basis without recourse to the seller. The discount on the gross receivable is referred to as a "valuation discount."
4. The valuation discount is amortized to income over the life of the retail land sales contract. The interest method should be used to produce a constant rate of amortization.
5. An allowance for contract cancellations is established based on estimates of contracts that are not expected to be collected in subsequent periods. Cancelled contracts are charged directly to the allowance account.

    For the purpose of determining the adequacy of the allowance for contract cancellations in subsequent periods, all receivables which do not conform to the criteria in the following table shall be considered uncollectible and the allowance account shall be appropriately adjusted:

Percent contract price paid	Delinquency period
Less than 25%	90 days
25% but less than 50%	120 days
50% and over	150 days

If a buyer is willing to assume personal liability for his debt and apparently has the means and ability to complete all payments, the delinquency periods in the above table may be extended.

6. The following items represent deductions from the gross sale to arrive at net sales for the period:

   a. Valuation discount

   b. Allowance for contract cancellations

   c. Deferred portion of gross sale (to be matched with future work or performance of the seller)

7. Cost of sales should be computed on net sales for the period.

8. A sale which is made and cancelled in the same reporting period should be included in and also deducted from gross sales or appropriately disclosed in some other manner.

9. The unamortized valuation discount (discount on receivables) and the allowance for contract cancellations are shown on the balance sheet as deductions from the related receivables.

10. Deferred revenue, less any related costs, is shown on the balance sheet as a liability. Deferred revenue should be recognized in future periods as the work is performed by the seller.

Profit Recognition—Percentage-of-Completion Method

If the first four criteria for applying the full accrual method of accounting are met for the entire retail land sales project and the fifth criterion is not met, the seller shall recognize profits by the percentage-of-completion method of accounting, provided that the following additional criteria are met for the entire project:

1. Progress on the entire project has passed the preliminary stages and tangible evidence exists to indicate that the project will be completed according to plans. Tangible evidence of such progress includes the following:

   a. Expenditure of funds has actually been made.

   b. Work on project improvements has been initiated.

   c. Engineering plans and construction commitments pertaining to lots that have been sold are in existence.

   d. There has been substantial completion of access roads and amenities.

   e. There is no evidence of any significant delay to the project and dependable estimates of costs to complete the project and extent of progress are reasonable.

2. At the end of the normal payment period it is reasonably expected that the property will clearly be useful for its intended purposes as represented by the seller at the time of sale.

If the above criteria are met for the entire project and the first four criteria for applying the full accrual method of accounting are met for the entire project, the seller shall recognize profits on retail land sales by the percentage-of-completion method.

Profit Recognition—Installment Sales Method

If the first two criteria for applying the full accrual method of accounting are met for the entire project and the other three criteria are not met, the seller shall recognize profits by the installment sales method, provided that the following additional criteria are met for the entire project:

1. The current and prospective financial capabilities of the retail land sales company (seller) must reflect with reasonable assurance that the company is capable of completing all of its obligations under the sales contract and master plan.

2. Indications of the seller's financial capabilities include (a) the sufficiency of equity capital, (b) borrowing capacity, and (c) positive cash flow from present operations.

If the above criteria are met for the entire project and the first two criteria for applying the full accrual method of accounting are met for the entire project, the seller shall recognize profits on retail land sales by the installment sales method.

Profit Recognition—Deposit Accounting Method

If the criteria for the full accrual method, percentage-of-completion method, or installment sale method are not met, the seller shall account for all proceeds from retail land sales by the deposit method of accounting. Under the deposit method of accounting, the effective date of the sale is deferred and all funds received, including principal and interest, are recorded as deposits on retail land sales.

Change in Accounting Method

If a retail land sales entity has been reporting sales for the entire project by the deposit method and subsequently the criteria for the installment sales method, percentage-of-completion method, or the full accrual method are met for the entire project, the change to the new method shall be accounted for as a change in accounting estimate. Thus, the effects of the change shall be accounted for prospectively in accordance with APB-20 (Accounting Changes). If the effects of the change in an accounting estimate are significant, disclosure of the effects on (a) income before extraordinary items, (b) net income, and (c) the related per share data should be made in the financial statements of the period of change.

Retail land sales may initially be accounted for by the installment sales method and subsequently the criteria for the percentage-of-completion method may be met for the entire project. In this event, the percentage-of-completion method may be adopted for the entire project. The effects of the change to the percentage-of-completion method are accounted for as a change in accounting estimate and, if material, disclosure of the effects on (a) income before extraordinary items, (b) net income, and (c) related per share data should be made in the financial statements of the period of change.

In reporting the change from the installment sales method to the percentage-of-completion method, the following procedures should be observed:

1. If required, the receivables should be discounted to their present values at the date of change in accordance with APB-21.
2. The liability for the remaining future performance of the seller should be discounted to its present value at the date of the change.
3. The amount of discount, if any, on the receivables and the amount of discount, if any, on the liability for remaining future performance by the seller are deducted from the unrealized gross profit on installment sales at the date of the change to arrive at the net credit to income resulting from the change.

Disclosure—Retail Land Sales

Retail land sales companies, diversified entities with significant retail land sales operations, and investors who derive a significant portion of their income from investments involved in retail land sales must comply with specific financial statement disclosures, as follows:

1. The maturities of the receivables from retail land sales for each of the five years following the date of the financial statements
2. The amount of delinquent receivables and the method used to determine delinquency
3. The weighted average and range of stated interest rates on receivables from retail land sales
4. Estimated total costs and anticipated expenditures to improve major areas of the project from which sales are being made, for each of the five years following the date of the financial statements
5. The amount of recorded obligations for improvements

Effective Date

FASB-66 is effective for all real estate transactions entered into and for all accounting changes that result from such transactions, on or after January 1, 1983. Financial statements for accounting periods ending on or after December 16, 1982, must contain the disclosures required by FASB-66 for retail land sales. Earlier application of the provisions of FASB-66 is not required but is encouraged.

Regulated Industries

REGULATED INDUSTRIES

Overview

FASB-71 (Accounting for the Effects of Certain Types of Regulation) establishes the promulgated GAAP for enterprises that are regulated by regulators who have the power to approve and/or regulate the rates that enterprises may charge customers for services or products. FASB-90 amends FASB-71 to specify the appropriate accounting for abandonments of plants and the disallowances of costs of recently completed plants. FASB-90 also amends FASB-71 to provide that an allowance for interest on funds used during the construction stage of an asset should be capitalized only if it is *probable* (likely) that such an allowance will be subsequently included by the governing regulatory authorities as an allowable cost of the constructed asset. In addition, footnote 6 to FASB-71 is superseded by the following:

> The term *probable* is used in this Statement consistent with its use in FASB Statement No. 5, *Accounting for Contingencies.* Statement 5 defines *probable* as an area within a range of the likelihood that a future event or events will occur. That range is from probable to remote, as follows:
>
> > *Probable*—The future event or events are likely to occur.
> >
> > *Reasonably possible*—The chance of the future event or events occurring is more than remote but less than likely.
> >
> > *Remote*—The chance of the future event or events occurring is slight.

The provisions of FASB-90 must be applied to all abandoned plants and disallowed plant costs, regardless of whether those events occurred before or will occur after the effective date of FASB-90 (paragraph 73 of FASB-90).

An enterprise may delay the application of FASB-90 until fiscal years beginning after December 15, 1988, and interim periods within those fiscal years if (a) application of FASB-90 would cause a violation or probable future violation of a restrictive clause in an existing loan indenture or other agreement and (b) the enterprise is actively seeking to obtain modification of that restrictive clause (paragraph 76 of FASB-90).

FASB Technical Bulletin 87-2 (FASB:TB 87-2), provides clarification on computing a loss on an abandonment in accordance with the provisions of FASB-90. As originally issued, FASB-90 contained an error in the method of amortization used in the example in paragraphs 16-25. FASB:TB 87-2 was issued to correct this error and to clarify the computation of deferred taxes and certain other matters. FASB:TB 87-2 is effective for fiscal years beginning on or after December 16, 1987, for all losses on abandonments recognized in accordance with FASB-90. Earlier application of the provisions of FASB:TB 87-2 is encouraged, but not required.

Enterprises that initially implemented the provisions of FASB-90 after October 31, 1987, and before the beginning of the enterprise's fiscal year beginning on or after December 16, 1987, shall adjust existing assets resulting from abandonments to comply with FASB:TB 87-2. Enterprises that initially implemented the provisions of FASB-90 before November 1, 1987, are not required to comply with the provisions of FASB:TB 87-2, but may do so if they wish. Existing assets that have already been recognized in accordance with FASB-90 may comply with FASB:TB 87-2 by retroactively restating the previously reported amounts or by an adjustment, in the year that FASB:TB 87-2 is first applied, for the cumulative effect of an accounting change along with appropriate disclosure.

> **OBSERVATION:** *The FASB agreed with some respondents who urged that they not be required to apply the provisions of FASB:TB 87-2 because they had already applied the provisions of FASB-90. Thus, the provisions of FASB:TB 87-2 need not be applied by enterprises that initially applied FASB-90 prior to November 1, 1987. November 1, 1987, is the date by which affected enterprises should have received a copy of the proposed Technical Bulletin.*

FASB-92 (Regulated Enterprises–Accounting for Phase-in Plans) amends FASB-71 to specify the accounting for phase-in plans. FASB-92 specifically addresses those phase-in plans ordered by a regulator in connection with a plant on which construction was started before January 1, 1988.

FASB-101 (Accounting for the Discontinuation of Application of FASB Statement No. 71) establishes the appropriate accounting that should be applied when an enterprise discontinues the application of the provisions of FASB-71.

For the purposes of FASB-71, a regulator may be an independent third party, or may be a governing board of the regulated enterprise that has been empowered by statute or contract. FASB-71 supersedes the Addendum to APB-2 (Accounting Principles for Regulated Industries). Paragraph 108 of FASB-71 amends APB-30 (Reporting the Results of Operations) to specify that utility refunds to customers be disclosed net of their tax effects, as a separate line item in the income statement. APB-30 generally prohibits net-of-tax disclosure of unusual or infrequently occurring items that do not qualify as extraordinary items.

FASB-71 does not change the fact that companies in regulated industries must comply with all existing and future authoritative accounting pronouncements. However, if a conflict arises between an authoritative accounting pronouncement and FASB-71, a regulated enterprise shall apply the provisions of FASB-71 instead of the conflicting pronouncement. The following conditions govern the application of FASB-71:

1. FASB-71 applies only to financial statements issued for external general purposes. Thus, FASB-71 does not apply to financial statements submitted to a regulatory agency.

    OBSERVATION: *FASB-71 is silent as to whether its provisions apply to financial statements for other than annual periods. Thus, it is unclear whether or not FASB-71 must be applied to interim financial statements.*

2. FASB-71 shall be applied only to regulated enterprises or those portions of the operations of a regulated enterprise which meet the specific criteria established by FASB-71.
3. FASB-71 does not apply to emergency governmental actions that are imposed under unusual circumstances, such as price controls during periods of high inflation.

Background

Over the years, regulatory agencies have been established by governmental authorities to regulate certain industries that provide essential services to the general public, such as public utilities, railroads, insurance companies, airlines, and so forth. One of the primary functions of most regulatory agencies is to establish the rates that the regulated enterprise can charge its customers for its services or products. In connection with their regulatory authority, most agencies prescribe the types of accounting records and reports that the regulated enterprise must maintain. Frequently, the accounting rules prescribed by these regulatory agencies conflict with GAAP.

The Addendum to APB-2 (Accounting Principles for Regulated Industries) required that financial statements of a regulated business intended for public use should be based on existing GAAP, with appropriate recognition given to the rate-making process established by the regulatory agency. Under GAAS, an independent auditor must comply with the first standard of reporting, which requires that financial statements be presented in accordance with GAAP.

Many different methods are used by regulatory agencies to set rates for regulated enterprises. However, the many different methods can be classified into (a) individual cost-of-service, (b) group rate-setting, and (c) a combination of both individual cost-of-service and group rate-setting.

Under the individual cost-of-service method of rate setting, the *allowable costs* that an enterprise is usually permitted to recover are all actual and/or estimated costs that are required to provide the service to the public, including a return on investment to compensate sources of long-term debt and equity capital. The rate or rates charged to different classes of customers are designed, but not guaranteed, to produce total revenue for the enterprise equal to the allowable costs. The individual cost-of-service method is usually used in setting rates for public utilities. An enterprise is more assured of cost recovery under the individual cost-of-service method than any other method.

Under the group rate-setting method, the allowable costs that an enterprise may recover are based on rates established on an industrywide, areawide, or some other aggregate basis. Group rate-setting is usually utilized in more competitive industries than those in which the individual cost-of-service method is used, such as airlines, motor carriers, railroads, insurance companies.

Under the combination of individual cost-of-service and group rate-setting methods, the allowable costs that an enterprise can recover are based on some combination of both methods. However, under the combination method, allowable costs do not usually include a provision for a return on investment, but may include an allowance for inflation or working capital.

Through the regulatory process, an enterprise is substantially assured of recovering its allowable costs by the collection of revenue from its customers. It is important to bear in mind that under some methods of rate-setting, allowable costs include a return on investment for the regulated enterprise. The economic effect of regulation is the substantiation that an asset exists or does not exist. Thus, as allowable costs are incurred by a regulated enterprise they should be capitalized as assets. On the other hand, costs that are not allowable under the regulatory process are not substantially assured of being recovered and should be expensed as incurred.

FASB-71 contains the criteria that an enterprise must meet to be classified as a *regulated enterprise* and also establishes the promulgated GAAP for the capitalization of allowable costs.

Criteria for Regulated Operations

FASB-71 applies to financial statements that are issued for general purposes by an enterprise which has regulated operations and meets all of the following criteria:

1. An independent third party regulator or a governing board of the regulated enterprise that has been empowered by statute or contract establishes or approves the rates the enterprise can charge its customers for its services or products.
2. The established or approved rates of the independent third party regulator or governing board of the regulated enterprise are intended to recover the specific costs of the regulated services or products.
3. The rates set by the independent third party regulator or governing board of the regulated enterprise to recover the costs of the regulated enterprise are reasonable and likely to be collected. In applying this criterion, consideration must be given to the demand for the services or products and the level of direct and indirect competition.

The thrust of FASB-71 is that the regulatory process can provide a basis for the regulated enterprise to recognize a specific asset. In this respect, FASB-71 requires that the following conditions be met for a regulated enterprise to recognize an incurred cost as a specific asset:

1. It must be clear that the regulator's intent is to provide recovery of a specific incurred cost.
2. On the basis of available evidence, it is expected that the regulated rates will produce revenue about equal to the specific incurred cost.

Thus, first an enterprise must qualify as a regulated enterprise by meeting the specified criteria of FASB-71, and then both of the above conditions must be met before an incurred cost can be capitalized as an asset.

FASB-71 does not identify any specific industry as *regulated*. Instead, the focus of FASB-71 is on the nature of regulation and its resulting financial effects on a specific enterprise. Thus, any enterprise in any industry which meets all of the criteria of FASB-71 must comply with its provisions.

The essence of the first criterion in FASB-71 is the existence of a regulator that can approve and/or regulate the rates that the enterprise can charge its customers for its services or products. The regulator may be an independent third party or a governing board of the enterprise empowered by statute or contract to approve and/or regulate the rates that the enterprise can charge its customers for its services or products. A contractual arrangement between an enterprise and its sole or principal customer may create the appearance of *regulation*. However, the sole or principal customer of the enterprise is also responsible for payment of the services or products and thus is not, in a strict sense, an independent third party regulator or governing board empowered by statute or contract. Therefore, Medicare, Medicaid, and similar contractual arrangements are excluded from the scope of FASB-71.

The principal economic effect of the regulatory process covered by FASB-71 is that it can provide substantiation that an asset does or does not exist at the time a regulated enterprise incurs costs to provide services or products.

> **OBSERVATION:** *FASB-71 reaches this conclusion by reasoning that the essence of an asset is its potential for future economic benefit. Some Financial Accounting Standards Board members disagree with the notion that regulatory action can create an asset.*

Under the provisions of FASB-71 the regulated rates must be designed to recover the specific costs of the regulated services or products. This is usually best accomplished by the individual cost-of-service method of rate-setting. Thus, the second criterion of FASB-71 requires that there be a cause-and-effect relationship between costs and revenues. A cause-and-effect relationship does not usually exist if regulated rates are based on industrywide costs. However, the cause-and-effect relationship is intended to be applied to the substance of the regulation and not the form of the regulation. Thus, if regulated rates are based on the costs of a particular group of companies and there is a dominant company within the group, the costs of the dominant company may represent the costs of the entire group. In this event, the second criterion of FASB-71 would be met.

The third criterion of FASB-71 requires that the regulated rates which are sufficient to recover incurred costs are reasonable to the ultimate consumer and likely to be collected.

If the regulatory process is based on the recovery of future costs and not on specific incurred costs, the provisions of FASB-71 are not met. If a *rate order* authorizing regulated rates for an enterprise does not clearly specify the recovery of specific incurred costs, the provisions of FASB-71 are not met. In other words, the rate order must clearly indicate the specific incurred costs that are designated for recovery. These specific incurred costs that are designated for recovery are referred to as allowable costs.

Sometimes the nature of an incurred cost, such as the abandonment of part or all of a particular facility, cannot be anticipated by the regulated enterprise or the regulator. Under these circumstances, the intent of the regulator may be inferred based on available evidence, and, as a result, it may be probable that the future rate increases will be provided by the regulator for the specific recovery of the unanticipated future cost.

On the other hand, the regulatory process may indicate the reduction or elimination of an existing asset or substantiate the existence of a new liability. If a cost or related asset is not classified as an allowable cost by the regulator, it will not produce future revenue through the regulatory process. In this event, the cost or related asset must be accounted for under existing GAAP which are applied to other enterprises in general.

> **OBSERVATION:** *If the regulatory process can create an asset, it appears that deregulation may result in the permanent impairment of an asset that owes its existence to regulation. This conclusion is consistent with FASB-44 (Accounting for Intangible Assets of Motor Carriers).*

A regulated enterprise may be required by the regulator to refund revenue that was collected in prior periods; or the regulator may include in its regulated rates amounts that are intended to recover specific costs that may be incurred in the future, with the understanding that if the costs are not incurred, an adjustment will be made to future regulated rates. In either instance, the regulator has substantiated the existence of a liability. In the event of customer refunds, FASB-71 requires that they be recorded as liabilities if they can be reasonably estimated and either (a) ordered by the regulator and are unpaid or (b) are likely to occur and are not yet recorded. In the event that the regulator includes in its regulated rates amounts that are intended to recover expected future costs which must be accounted for, a liability is created equal to the amount of revenue collected for the expected future costs.

The amount of revenue collected for the expected future costs is recorded as unearned revenue until the expected future costs are actually incurred or an adjustment is made by the regulator. For example, a regulator may include in its regulated rates an amount for expected future uninsured storm damages. In this respect, the regulator may require that any amounts not actually incurred in the future for storm damages must be refunded to customers in the form of a future adjustment in the regulated rates. As the revenue attributable to the future storm damage is collected, FASB-71 requires that it be recorded as a liability and included in income only when the actual storm damage costs are incurred.

A regulator can substantiate the existence of another type of liability by requiring the regulated enterprise to credit customers over a future period for gains or other reductions of net allowable costs. The gains or other reductions in net allowable costs would usually be amortized over the related future periods by a corresponding reduction in the approved regulated rates. In this event, FASB-71 requires that a liability be recorded in the amount of the future amortization.

If a liability is recorded because of the regulatory process, it can only be reduced or eliminated by the regulatory process. In other words, if a liability is created and recorded by the actions of the regulator, it can only be reduced or eliminated through the same process.

An enterprise subject to FASB-71 must comply with all of its provisions. If there is a conflict between FASB-71 and existing GAAP, the provisions of FASB-71 must be applied. However, in all other circumstances existing GAAP must be followed and applied by a regulated enterprise. Thus, if a regulated enterprise is required by court order to capitalize and amortize a particular cost and the cost does not qualify for capitalization under existing GAAP or FASB-71, the regulated enterprise cannot capitalize the cost in financial statements purported to be presented in accordance with GAAP. In other words, the capitalized cost would not be in conformity with GAAP.

ACCOUNTING FOR ABANDONMENTS (FASB-90)

Historically, utilities that have abandoned plants have usually done so in early stages of construction, rather than after incurring major construction costs. Prior to the issuance of FASB-71, most regulated enterprises accounted for the costs of abandoned plants on a cost-recovery basis; that is, no loss was recorded if revenues promised by a regulator were expected to recover the recorded costs.

The cost-recovery approach of accounting for abandonments is based on the view that the regulator is disallowing future earnings, rather than disallowing a portion of the cost of the abandoned plant. Thus, the effect of the cost-recovery approach is to delay the recognition of losses that are known to have been incurred.

Originally, FASB-71 required that an abandoned plant be reported at the lesser of its cost or the probable *gross revenue* expected to be allowed on the portion of the cost of the abandoned plant that the regulator included in allowable costs for rate-making purposes. Thus, FASB-71 did not change the practice of accounting for the cost of an abandoned plant on a cost-recovery basis.

FASB-90 amended FASB-71 to require that the future revenue that is expected to result from the regulator's inclusion of the cost of an abandoned plant in allowable costs for rate-making purposes be reported at its *present value* when the abandonment becomes *probable*. If the carrying amount of the abandoned plant exceeds that present value, a loss would be recognized.

Under FASB-90, the probability that an enterprise will abandon an asset may be classified as either (a) probable, (b) reasonably possible, or (c) remote. For purposes of FASB-90, probable means that the abandonment is *likely to occur,* remote means that the abandonment is *not likely to occur*, and reasonably possible means that the probability of the abandonment occurring is *somewhere between probable and remote*.

On the date it becomes probable (likely) that an enterprise will abandon an operating asset or an asset under construction, the total cost of that asset shall be removed from the books of account (plant-in-service or construction work-in-process) and reclassified as a new asset. The amount of cost assigned to the new asset will depend on the amount of the total cost of the abandoned plant that the enterprise estimates will be allowed by the governing regulatory authorities, and whether recovery of the allowed cost is likely to be provided with a full return on investment, a partial return on investment, or no return on investment during the period from the date the abandonment becomes probable through the date recovery is completed. Based on its estimate of allowed and disallowed costs and its expected return on investment, an enterprise should account for the total cost of the abandoned plant as follows.

If it is probable (likely) that all or part of the cost of the abandoned plant will be disallowed by the governing regulatory authorities and the amount of the disallowed cost can be reasonably estimated, the disallowed cost shall be recognized as a current loss and deducted from the total cost of the abandoned plant.

> **OBSERVATION:** *If only a range of the amount of the disallowed cost (similar to a minimum-maximum) can be established, then the minimum amount in the range should be used, unless some other amount within the range appears to be a better estimate (FASB Interpretation-14).*

If Full Return on Investment Is Expected   The total cost of the abandoned plant, less the amount of the probable disallowed cost that is recognized as a loss, shall be recorded and reported as a separate asset.

If Partial or No Return on Investment Is Expected   The present value of the expected future revenue to be generated from the allowable cost of the abandoned plant, plus any return on investment, shall be reported as a separate new asset. Any excess of the total cost of the abandoned plant reduced by the amount of disallowed cost reported as a loss, *over* the amount of the separate new asset, shall be reported as an additional loss.

An enterprise shall use its incremental borrowing rate to compute the present value of the expected future revenue to be generated from the allowable cost of the abandoned plant. An enterprise's incremental borrowing rate is the rate that an enterprise would have to pay to borrow an equivalent amount for a period equal to the expected recovery period.

To compute the present value of expected future revenue to be generated from the allowable cost of the abandoned plant, an enterprise may be required to estimate the probable time period before recovery is expected to begin and the probable time period before recovery is expected to be provided. If the estimate of either of these periods is a range (similar to a minimum-maximum), the present value shall be based on the minimum amount in the range, unless some other amount within the range appears to be a better estimate (FASB Interpretation-14).

Subsequent period adjustments to the separate new asset   In accounting for the abandonment of a plant, the following are some of the estimates that may be used by an enterprise to calculate and record the amount of the separate new asset:

a.   The amount of any probable disallowed cost of the abandoned plant that can be reasonably estimated

b.   Whether recovery of the allowed cost of the abandoned plant is likely to be provided with a full return on investment, a partial return on investment, or no return on investment

c.   The period from the date the abandonment becomes probable through the date recovery is completed

d.   The probable time period before recovery is expected to begin and the probable time period over which recovery is expected to be provided

If in subsequent periods, new information indicates that all or some of the estimates used by an enterprise to record the amount of the separate new asset have changed, FASB-90 requires that an adjustment be made to the recorded amount of the new asset. The amount of the adjustment shall be recognized as a gain or loss in the net income of the period in which the adjustment arises. However, no adjustment shall be made to the recorded amount of the separate new asset for changes in the enterprise's incremental borrowing rate.

Accrued carrying charges on the separate new asset   A carrying charge shall be accrued and added to the carrying amount of the recorded separate new asset during the period between the date on which the new asset is recognized by an enterprise and the date on which recovery begins. The rate of the carrying charge shall be based on whether a full return on investment is likely to be provided, or a partial or no return on investment is likely to be provided, as follows:

> *If Full Return on Investment Is Expected*   A rate equal to the allowed overall cost of capital in the jurisdiction in which recovery is expected to be provided shall be used to calculate the amount of the accrued carrying charge, during the period between the date on which the new asset is recognized and the date on which recovery begins.

If Partial or No Return on Investment Is Expected   The same rate that was used to compute the present value of the expected future revenue to be generated from the allowable cost of the abandoned plant shall be used to calculate the amount of the accrued carrying charge, during the period between the date on which the new asset is recognized and the date on which recovery begins.

Amortization of separate new asset during recovery period   The separate new asset shall be amortized during the recovery period, based on whether a full return on investment is likely to be provided, or a partial or no return on investment is likely to be provided, as follows:

If Full Return on Investment is Expected   The separate new asset shall be amortized during the recovery period in the same manner as that used for rate-making purposes.

If Partial or No Return on Investment Is Expected   The separate new asset shall be amortized during the recovery period at the same rate that was used to compute the present value of the expected future revenue to be generated from the allowable cost of the abandoned plant. (**Note**: This method of amortization will produce a constant return on the unamortized investment in the new asset equal to the rate at which the expected revenues were discounted.)

> *OBSERVATION:* *The example in paragraphs 16-25 of FASB-90 is not correct. The new asset in the example is not amortized in a manner that produces a constant return on the unamortized investment in the new asset equal to the rate at which net revenues were discounted, which is required by FASB-90. Thus, the example does not correctly reflect the intent of FASB-90.*

Adjustments to previously recorded assets   The provisions of FASB-90 must be applied to all abandoned plants, regardless of whether the abandonment occurred before or will occur after the effective date of FASB-90 (paragraph 73 of FASB-90). Thus, the initial application of FASB-90 will require certain adjustments to previously recorded assets with corresponding adjustments to reported net income of prior years or to the cumulative effect of an accounting change in the year of change (see "Effective date and transition").

Amounts that were recorded in prior years for recoverable costs of abandoned plants shall be adjusted in accordance with the provisions of FASB-90. If partial or no return on investment is likely to be provided, the discount rate used to compute the present value of the future revenues expected to be generated from the allowable cost of the abandoned plant shall be the regulated enterprise's incremental borrowing rate at the date on which the abandonment became probable.

Accounting for Disallowances of Plant Costs

Paragraph 10 of FASB-71 addresses the disallowance of costs by a regulator. That paragraph indicates that when a disallowance occurs, "...the carrying amount of any related asset shall be reduced to the extent that the asset has been impaired. Whether the asset [of a regulated enterprise] has been impaired shall be judged the same as for enterprises in general."

An enterprise's estimate of the cost of the abandoned plant that will be allowed should be based on the facts and circumstances related to the specific abandonment and should also consider the past practice and current policies of the governing regulatory authorities.

Under FASB-90, if it becomes probable (likely) that part of the cost of a recently completed plant will be disallowed by the governing regulatory authorities and the amount of the disallowed cost can be reasonably estimated, the disallowed cost shall be recognized as a current loss and deducted from the total cost of the recently completed plant.

> **OBSERVATION:** *If only a range of the amount of the disallowed cost (similar to a minimum-maximum) can be established, then the minimum amount in the range should be used, unless some other amount within the range appears to be a better estimate (FASB Interpretation-14).*

If part of the cost of the recently completed plant is explicitly, but indirectly, disallowed, such as an explicit disallowance of return on investment on a portion of the plant, an equivalent amount of cost shall be deducted from the reported cost of the recently completed plant and recognized as a loss.

Adjustments to previously recorded assets   The provisions of FASB-90 must be applied to all disallowed costs of recently completed plants, regardless of whether the disallowance of the costs occurred before or will occur after the effective date of FASB-90 (paragraph 73 of FASB-90). Thus, the initial application of FASB-90 will require certain adjustments to previously recorded assets with corresponding adjustments to reported net income of prior years or to the cumulative effect of an accounting change in the year of change (see "Effective date and transition").

Amounts that were recorded in prior years as disallowed costs of recently completed plants shall be adjusted in accordance with the provisions of FASB-90. Disallowed costs are deducted from the reported cost of the related plant.

Effective date and transition   Except as provided below, the provisions of FASB-90 shall be effective for fiscal years beginning after December 15, 1987, and for interim periods within those fiscal years, with earlier application encouraged.

Retroactive restatement of previously issued financial statements to include the provisions of FASB-90 is encouraged. In the year that FASB-90 is first applied, the financial statements shall disclose the nature of any restatement and its effect on (a) income before extraordinary items, net income, and related per share amounts for each period presented and (b) retained earnings at the beginning of the earliest period presented.

If an enterprise does not elect to retroactively restate previously issued financial statements to include the effects of the provisions of FASB-90, the provisions of APB-20 (Accounting Changes) shall be applied. In this event, the total effect of applying the provisions of FASB-90 to all prior periods is reflected as the "cumulative effect of a change in accounting principle" in the income statement of the year of change. In addition, the financial statements of the year of change shall also disclose the nature of the accounting change and the effect of adopting FASB-90 on income before extraordinary items, net income, and the related per share amounts.

Delaying the application of FASB-90   An enterprise may delay the application of FASB-90 until fiscal years beginning after December 15, 1988, and interim periods within those fiscal years if (a) application of FASB-90 would cause a violation or probable future violation of a restrictive clause in an existing loan indenture or other agreement and (b) the enterprise is actively seeking to obtain modification of that restrictive clause (paragraph 76 of FASB-90). If an enterprise delays the application of FASB-90, it shall disclose the following information in its financial statements for the first fiscal year beginning after December 15, 1987, and interim periods within that fiscal year:

a. The effects that the application of FASB-90 would have had on assets, retained earnings at the end of that fiscal year or interim period, income before extraordinary items, net income, and related per share amounts,

b. The nature of the violation or probable future violation that would result from the application of FASB-90, and

c. The steps that the enterprise is taking to eliminate the restrictions

Required adjustments for initial application of FASB-90   The provisions of FASB-90 must be applied to all abandoned plants and disallowed plant costs, regardless of whether those events occurred before or will occur after the effective date of FASB-90 (paragraph 73 of FASB-90). Thus, the initial application of FASB-90 will require certain adjustments to previously recorded assets with corresponding adjustments to reported net income of prior years or to the cumulative effect of an accounting change in the year of change.

Amounts that were recorded in prior years for recoverable costs of abandoned plants shall be adjusted in accordance with the provisions of FASB-90. If partial or no return on investment is likely to be provided, the discount rate used to compute the present value of the future revenues expected to be generated from the allowable cost of the abandoned plant shall be the regulated enterprise's incremental borrowing rate at the date on which the abandonment became probable.

Amounts that were recorded in prior years as disallowed costs of recently completed plants shall be adjusted in accordance with the provisions of FASB-90. Disallowed costs are deducted from the reported cost of the related plant.

ACCOUNTING FOR PHASE-IN PLANS (FASB-92)

Under traditional rate-making procedures, a utility is granted an increase in rates to provide for the recovery of the allowable costs of a newly completed utility plant that is placed in service. However, in recent years, the high cost of nuclear plants and the high cost of capital have resulted in *rate spikes*. A rate spike is an unusually high, one-time increase in the rates of a regulated enterprise. To solve the problem of rate spikes, regulatory authorities and utilities have developed phase-in plans.

Several different types of phase-in plans have been developed, all of which are designed to reduce the impact of rate spikes by (a) deferring a portion of the initial rate increase to future years and (b) providing the regulated enterprise with a return on the amounts deferred. Thus, instead of the traditional pattern of an increase in allowable costs followed by decreasing allowable costs for utility plants after the plants are placed in service, phase-in plans create a pattern of gradually increasing allowable costs for the initial years of the plant's service life.

Accounting for Phase-in Plans

The *allowable costs* that a regulatory authority usually permits a regulated enterprise to recover from the rates it charges to its customers include actual and/or estimated costs that are incurred to provide a product or service to the public, including a return on investment to compensate sources of long-term debt and equity capital. The rates that are approved by a regulatory authority are designed, but not guaranteed, to produce total revenue for a regulated enterprise that is approximately equal to its allowable costs.

Under the provisions of FASB-92, a phase-in plan is any method used to recognize allowable costs in the rates charged by a regulated enterprise to its customers that also meets all of the following criteria:

a. The phase-in plan was adopted by the regulator in connection with a major plant of the regulated enterprise, or of one of its suppliers, that is newly completed or scheduled for completion in the near future.

b. The method defers the rates approved to recover the allowable costs of the regulated enterprise beyond the period in which those allowable costs would have been charged to expense under GAAP applicable to enterprises in general.

c. The method defers the rates approved to recover the allowable costs of the regulated enterprise beyond the period in which those rates would have been ordered by the enterprise's regulator under the rate-making method routinely used prior to 1982 for similar allowable costs of the same regulated enterprise.

> **OBSERVATION:** *The definition of a phase-in plan under FASB-92 focuses on methods of rate making that defer recognition of allowable costs (a) that would not be deferred under GAAP applicable to enterprises in general and (b) that would not have been deferred in the past under the methods of rate-making used by a regulated enterprise's regulator (paragraph 47 of FASB-92).*

Under FASB-92, accounting for the deferment of the allowable costs of a plant in connection with a phase-in plan ordered by a regulator depends on whether or not the physical construction of the plant was substantially completed *before* January 1, 1988.

> **OBSERVATION:** *Paragraph 4 of FASB-92 addresses those phase-in plans ordered by a regulator in connection with a plant on which no substantial physical construction had been performed before January 1, 1988, while paragraph 5 of FASB-92 addresses those phase-in plans ordered by a regulator in connection with a plant on which substantial physical construction had been performed before January 1, 1988. Other than by implication, neither paragraph 4 nor 5 of FASB-92 appears to address phase-in plans ordered by a regulator in connection with a plant on which construction was started after January 1, 1988.*

Plant not substantially completed before January 1, 1988 If no substantial physical construction had been performed on a plant before January 1, 1988, *none* of the allowable costs that are deferred for future recovery under any phase-in plan ordered by a regulator may be capitalized for *financial reporting purposes*. (**Note**: In this context, allowable costs that are deferred for future recovery are those that are deferred beyond the period in which they would otherwise be charged to expense under GAAP applicable to enterprises in general.)

Plant completed or substantially completed before January 1, 1988 If a plant had been completed or substantially completed before January 1, 1988, all allowable costs that are deferred for future recovery under any phase-in plan ordered by a regulator, shall be capitalized as a separate asset (a deferred charge) for *financial reporting purposes*, providing that all of the following criteria are met (**Note**: Under FASB-92, these criteria are used to determine whether or not capitalization is appropriate.):

a. The regulator has agreed, in a formal plan, to the deferral of the allowable costs.

b. The timing of the recovery of all allowable costs that are deferred to future periods is specified in the formal plan agreed to by the regulator.

c. The recovery of all allowable costs deferred to future periods is scheduled to occur within ten years of the date on which the deferrals began.

d. The percentage increase in rates scheduled under the phase-in plan for each year cannot exceed the percentage increase of the immediately preceding year. Thus, the percentage increase in rates for year two of the phase-in plan cannot exceed the percentage increase in rates for year one of the phase-in plan, and the percentage increase in rates for year three cannot exceed the percentage increase for year two, and so forth.

If all of the above criteria are not met, none of the allowable costs that are deferred for future recovery under the regulator's formal plan shall be capitalized for *financial reporting purposes.* (**Note**: In this context, allowable costs that are deferred for future recovery are those that are deferred beyond the period in which they would otherwise be charged to expense under GAAP applicable to enterprises in general.)

Modification, replacement, or supplement of an existing phase-in plan When an existing phase-in plan is modified or a new plan is ordered to replace or supplement an existing plant, the specific criteria required by FASB-92 to determine whether capitalization of allowable costs is appropriate for *financial reporting purposes* (discussed above) shall be applied to the combination of both the original plan and the new plan. The date when deferrals begin, for the purpose of recovering all deferred allowable costs within ten years (criterion c above), is the date of the earliest deferral under either the new or the old plan, and the final recovery date is the date of the last recovery of all amounts deferred under the plan.

Capitalization of Earnings on Shareholders' Investment

Paragraph 17 of FASB-71 (Accounting for the Effects of Certain Types of Regulation) requires that an enterprise capitalize an allowance for the funds used during the construction stage of an asset in lieu of capitalizing interest in accordance with FASB-34 (Capitalization of Interest Cost). The capitalized interest usually includes interest costs on borrowing, or interest costs on a designated portion of equity funds, or on both. The cost of the constructed asset is increased by the amount of the capitalized interest.

FASB-90 (Regulated Enterprises—Accounting for Abandonments and Disallowances of Plant Costs) amends FASB-71 to specify that an allowance for funds used during the construction stage of an asset should be capitalized only if it is *probable* (likely) that the allowance for funds will be subsequently included by the governing regulatory authorities as an allowable cost of the constructed asset. If it is *not probable* (not likely) that the allowance for funds used during the construction stage of an asset will be included as an allowable cost for rate-making purposes, a regulated enterprise may not alternatively capitalize interest cost in accordance with FASB-34 (paragraph 66 of FASB-90).

A disallowance of a cost is the result of a rate-making action that prevents a regulated enterprise from recovering either some amount of its investment or some amount of return on its investment. Some existing phase-in plans have deferred allowable costs for recovery in future periods for rate-making purposes and have not provided a return on the investment on those deferred costs during the deferral period. This type of phase-in plan is in substance partially a deferral and partially a disallowance.

After the initial application of FASB-92, any allowance for earnings on shareholders' investment that is capitalized for rate-making purposes other than for an asset during its construction stage or as part of a phase-in plan may not be capitalized for *financial reporting purposes* (paragraph 9 of FASB-92).

Capitalized Amounts—Classification and Disclosure

Cumulative amounts that are capitalized under phase-in plans shall be reported as a separate asset in the balance sheet. The net amount that has been capitalized in each period or the net amount of previously capitalized allowable costs that are recovered during each period shall be reported as a separate item of other income or expense in the income statement. Allowable costs that have been capitalized shall not be reported as reductions of other expenses.

The terms of any phase-in plans in effect during the year or ordered for future years shall be disclosed in the financial statements. If allowable costs have been deferred for future recovery by a regulator for rate-making purposes, but not for *financial reporting purposes*, FASB-92 requires the financial statement disclosure of the net amount of such allowable costs that have been deferred for future recovery, and in addition, the disclosure of the net change in the related deferrals for those plans during the year. FASB-92 also requires the financial statement disclosure of the nature and amounts of any allowance for earnings on shareholders' investment that has been capitalized for rate-making purposes but not capitalized for *financial reporting purposes.*

Effective date and transition   FASB-92 is effective for fiscal years beginning on or after December 16, 1987, and for interim periods within those fiscal years, except that the application of FASB-92 to existing phase-in plans may be delayed provided that both of the following conditions are met:

- The enterprise has filed a rate application, or intends to do so as soon as practicable, to have its existing plan amended to meet the criteria of FASB-92.
- It is reasonably possible that the enterprise's regulator will change the terms of the phase-in plan so that it will meet the criteria of FASB-92.

If both of the above conditions are met, the provisions of FASB-92 shall not be applied to an existing phase-in plan until the earlier date on which either (a) one of the above conditions ceases to be met or (b) a final rate order is received, amending or refusing to amend the phase-in plan. Nonetheless, if an application for an amendment to a phase-in plan is delayed by the regulated enterprise or the application is not processed in the normal amount of time by the regulator, the application of FASB-92 shall not be delayed any further.

As mentioned previously, if a plant was completed or substantially completed before January 1, 1988, all allowable costs that are deferred for future recovery under any phase-in plan ordered by a regulator shall be capitalized as a separate asset (a deferred charge) for *financial reporting purposes*, providing that the following criteria are met:

a.   The regulator has agreed in a formal plan to the deferral of the allowable costs.
b.   The timing of the recovery of all allowable costs that are deferred to future periods is specified in the formal plan agreed to by the regulator.
c.   The recovery of all allowable costs deferred to future periods is scheduled to occur within ten years of the date on which the deferrals began.

d. The percentage increase in rates scheduled under the phase-in plan for each year cannot exceed the percentage increase of the immediate preceding year. Thus, the percentage increase in rates for year two of the phase-in plan cannot exceed the percentage increase in rates for year one of the phase-in plan, and the percentage increase in rates for year three cannot exceed the percentage increase for year two, and so forth.

In applying the above criteria to a plan that was in existence prior to the first fiscal year beginning on or after December 16, 1987, and which was revised to meet the criteria of FASB-92, the 10-year criterion (c above) and the requirement that the percentage increase in rates scheduled under the plan in each future year be no greater than the percentage increase scheduled under the plan for each immediately preceding year (d above) shall be measured from the date of the amendment of the plan rather than from the date of the first scheduled deferrals under the original plan.

Existing phase-in plans shall be evaluated to determine whether or not they meet the criteria of FASB-92 at the date of its initial application. As mentioned previously, if an existing phase-in plan does not meet the criteria of FASB-92, none of the allowable costs that are deferred for future recovery may be capitalized for *financial reporting purposes*. (**Note**: In this context, allowable costs that are deferred for future recovery are those that are deferred beyond the period in which they would otherwise be charged to expense under GAAP applicable to enterprises in general.)

Retroactive application of the provisions of FASB-92 that address accounting for phase-in plans is permitted in those fiscal years for which financial statements have previously been issued. In the event of retroactive application of the provisions of FASB-92, the financial statements of all prior periods presented for comparison purposes shall also be retroactively restated. In the year of the initial application of FASB-92, the restated financial statements shall disclose the nature of any restatement and its effect on income before extraordinary items, net income, and related per share amounts for each period presented and on retained earnings at the beginning of the earliest period presented.

If financial statements for prior fiscal years are not restated, the effects of applying FASB-92 to existing plans shall be reported as the cumulative effect of a change in accounting principle in accordance with APB-20 (Accounting Changes). In this event, the effect of adopting FASB-92 on income before extraordinary items, net income, and related per share amounts shall be disclosed in the financial statements. Earlier application of the provisions of FASB-92 is encouraged.

The provisions of FASB-92 that relate to the capitalization of an allowance for earnings on shareholders' investment, other than during construction or as part of a phase-in plan, do not apply to any amount capitalized in fiscal years prior to the initial application of FASB-92 (paragraph 14 of FASB-92).

SPECIFIC STANDARDS FOR REGULATED ENTERPRISES

Regulated enterprises subject to the provisions of FASB-71 must comply with the following specific standards.

Capitalization of interest   In the construction or acquisition of plant and equipment, a regulator may require a regulated enterprise to capitalize certain interest as part of the cost of the asset. The capitalized interest usually includes interest costs on borrowing, or interest costs on a designated portion of equity funds, or on both. The cost of the plant and equipment is increased by the amount of capitalized interest; and, for regulatory purposes, subsequent depreciation expense is based on the total cost of the asset. In other words, the depreciation is classified as an allowable cost. Under these circumstances, an allowance for interest on funds used during the construction stage of an asset should be capitalized only if it is *probable* (likely) that such an allowance will be subsequently included by the governing regulatory authorities as an allowable cost of the constructed asset (FASB-90). Thus, regardless of the amount of capitalized interest required by FASB-34 (Capitalization of Interest Cost), a regulated enterprise cannot capitalize interest on funds used during the construction stage of an asset that exceeds the amount that the governing regulatory authorities is likely to approve. If it is *not probable* (not likely) that an allowance for funds used during the construction stage of an asset will be included as an allowable cost for rate-making purposes (i.e., approved by the governing authorities), a regulated enterprise may not alternatively capitalize interest cost in accordance with FASB-34 (paragraph 66 of FASB-90).

The amount of interest that is required to be capitalized by the regulator shall be included in the income statement of the regulated enterprise as either (a) an item of other income, (b) a reduction of interest expense, or (c) as both an item of other income and a reduction of interest expense. In addition, the income statement shall indicate the basis for the amount of capitalized interest.

Intercompany profits   Under existing GAAP, 100% of any intercompany profits must be eliminated in consolidated financial statements (ARB-51) and investments accounted for by the equity method (APB-18). However, under the provisions of FASB-71, a regulated enterprise shall not eliminate intercompany profits on sales to regulated affiliates if the following conditions are met:

1. The sales price is reasonable, as evidenced by the acceptance of the sales price by the enterprise's regulator, or in light of the specific circumstance, and
2. It is expected, based on available evidence, that the approximate sales price which resulted in the intercompany profit will be recovered as an allowable cost.

If the above conditions are met, the realization of the intercompany profits are reasonably substantiated by the regulatory process. Thus, the intercompany profits shall not be eliminated because they are reasonably assured of being realized.

Deferred income taxes   Regulated enterprises (as defined by FASB-71) must comply with FASB-16 (Prior Period Adjustments), including the following specific provisions:

a. The use of the net-of-tax accounting and reporting method is strictly prohibited.

    OBSERVATION: *Tax allocation under the net-of-tax method is a procedure whereby the tax effects (determined by either the deferred or liability methods) of temporary differences are recognized in the valuation of assets or liabilities and the related revenues and expenses. The tax effects are applied to reduce specific assets or liabilities on the basis that tax deductibility or taxability are factors in their valuation.*

b. A deferred tax liability is required to be recognized for (i) the tax benefits of originating temporary differences that are passed on to customers and (ii) the equity component of the allowance for funds used during construction.
c. A deferred tax liability or asset must be adjusted for any enacted change in the tax laws or rates.

An asset shall be recognized by a regulated enterprise in the amount of the probable future revenue that will be received from customers if it is probable that the regulator will allow a future increase in rates for items (b) and (c) above. On the other hand, if it is probable that a future decrease in taxes payable for items (b) and (c) above will be returned to customers through a future decrease in rates, a regulated enterprise shall recognize a liability in the amount of the probable reduction in future revenue in accordance with FASB-71. In this event, the asset or liability recognized by the regulated enterprise is also a temporary difference, and a deferred tax liability or asset shall be recognized for the deferred tax effects of that temporary difference.

Disclosure of customer refunds   Disclosure shall be made of any refunds that have a material effect on net income and which are not recognized in the same period as the related revenue. Disclosure shall include the effect on net income and indicate the years that the related revenue was recognized. The material effect on net income, net of related income taxes, may be disclosed as a separate line item in the income statement, but may not be presented as an extraordinary item.

Disclosure of certain unamortized costs   Generally, a regulated enterprise recovers its allowable costs through a rate base established by a regulator. The rate base usually includes an amount for recovery of specific incurred costs plus a return based on the net equity of the regulated enterprise. Once the rate base is established, it is converted into specific prices that the regulated enterprise can charge for its services, such as X dollars per kilowatt hour.

A regulator may allow the recovery of a specific cost over the current and future periods, but not allow a return on equity for the same specific cost. In other words, a regulator may exclude a specific cost in calculating the return on equity for a regulated enterprise, but may allow recovery of the actual cost over the current and future periods. For example, severe storm damage may be incurred for which the regulator allows the recovery over the current and future periods. However, the storm damage is not allowed to be included in determining the rate of return on equity for the regulated enterprise. Thus, the regulator allows recovery of the actual cost, but no profit is made on the incurred storm damage cost. The following disclosures are required by FASB-71 for major costs that do not provide a return on investment and are required to be amortized over the current and future periods:

1. The unamortized amount of such costs
2. The remaining period of amortization

> **OBSERVATION:** *The thrust of the above disclosure re-*
> *quirements of FASB-71 is that if a cost is recoverable over an*
> *extended period and the regulator does not allow a return on*
> *investment (profit) for that specific cost, the unamortized balance*
> *of such costs must be disclosed along with the remaining amorti-*
> *zation period.*

Amendments to Existing GAAP

As mentioned previously, FASB-71 supersedes the Addendum to APB-2 (Accounting Principles for Regulated Industries). FASB-71 specifically amends all existing GAAP in which reference is made to the Addendum to APB-2. Thus, the reference to the Addendum to APB-2 in all existing GAAP is deleted by FASB-71.

Effective Date

FASB-71 is generally effective for fiscal years beginning on or after December 16, 1983, with earlier application encouraged. Except for refunds and leases, the provisions of FASB-71 shall be retroactively applied, if practicable.

Changes in accounting for refunds which result from the initial application of FASB-71 shall not be made by retroactive restatement of previously issued financial statements.

> **OBSERVATION:** *The two methods for recognizing a change in*
> *accounting principle are the (a) retroactive restatement method*
> *and (b) the cumulative effect method. Since FASB-71 prohibits the*
> *use of the retroactive restatement method for changes in accounting*
> *that result from the initial application of FASB-71, the cumulative*
> *effect method should be applied to account for the change.*

Commencing with the initial application of FASB-71, leases with inception dates subsequent of December 31, 1982, shall be classified in accordance with FASB-13. Leases with inception dates prior to January 1, 1983, can either be classified in accordance with FASB-13 or classified as they would have been prior to the issuance of FASB-71. However, FASB-71 requires that for fiscal years beginning on or after December 16, 1986, leases must be either:

1. Retroactively reclassified in the financial statements in accordance with FASB-13, or

2. Disclosure must be made in the financial statements of the amount of additional capitalized leased assets and lease obligations that would result from the retroactive reclassification made in accordance with FASB-13.

All other accounting changes which result from the initial application of FASB-71 shall be made, if practical, by retroactive restatement of all comparative financial statements presented. In addition, the financial statements of the year of change shall disclose the nature of any restatement and its effect on income before extraordinary items, net income, and related per share amounts for each year presented. However, related per share amounts need not be disclosed if an enterprise does not disclose earnings per share.

If it is impractical to retroactively restate all of the individual financial statements for the comparative years presented, the following procedure must be used:

1. The new accounting principle (FASB-71) is used in determining net income of the year of change (current period).

2. As many consecutive prior years' financial statements as practical (which are presented for comparative purposes) are then retroactively restated.

3. The cumulative effect of the change to FASB-71 is then computed for any remaining prior years.

4. The cumulative effect is then included in determining net income for the earliest year restated.

5. Financial statements presented for years prior to the earliest year restated (which includes the cumulative effect) shall be presented for comparative purposes as they were originally reported.

In the event that it is impractical to retroactively restate any prior year, FASB-71 requires that the cumulative effect of the change in accounting principle be included in the net income of the year of change in accordance with APB-20 (Accounting Changes). In any year in which the cumulative effect is used, the effect of the change to FASB-71 on income before extraordinary items, net income, and related per share amounts shall be disclosed. However, related per share amounts need not be disclosed if an enterprise does not disclose earnings per share.

OBSERVATION: The cumulative effect of a change in an accounting principle may be omitted under the provisions of APB-20 if it is impossible to compute. In this event, the effects of the change, in the year of change, must be disclosed, along with an explanation as to why the cumulative effect was omitted.

Discontinuing Application of FASB-71

FASB-101 (Accounting for the Discontinuation of Application of FASB Statement No. 71) establishes the appropriate accounting that should be applied when an enterprise discontinues the application of the provisions of FASB-71. Under FASB-101, an enterprise shall discontinue the application of the provisions of FASB-71 as of the date it determines that its "regulatory" operations in a particular regulatory jurisdiction cease to meet the criteria of FASB-71.

If the application of FASB-71 is discontinued for one separable portion of "regulatory" operations in a particular regulatory jurisdiction there is a presumption that the application of FASB-71 should be discontinued for all other "regulatory" operations within that same particular regulatory jurisdiction. However, an enterprise shall continue to apply the provisions of FASB-71 to any separable portion of "regulatory" operations that continues to meet the criteria of FASB-71, regardless of whether or not the other separable portions within the same particular regulatory jurisdiction meet the criteria of FASB-71.

Reporting the discontinuance of FASB-71　FASB-101 requires an enterprise to record the net effects of discontinuing the application of the provisions of FASB-71. At the time an enterprise ceases to meet the criteria for applying FASB-71, assets or liabilities that were recognized as a result of the actions of a regulator must be removed from the enterprise's statement of financial position. Carrying amounts of plant, equipment, and inventory as reported under the provisions of FASB-71, shall not be adjusted for (a) an allowance for funds used during construction of an asset, (b) intercompany profits on sales to regulated affiliates, and (c) disallowances of costs of recently completed plants. On the other hand, carrying amounts of plant, equipment, and inventory shall be adjusted for any other amounts that are excluded under GAAP for enterprises in general, such as impairment and postconstruction operating costs capitalized pursuant to paragraph 9 of FASB-71. Impairment of the carrying amounts of plant, equipment, and inventory shall be accounted for in the same manner as for enterprises in general.

After all adjustments required by FASB-101 are recorded, the net effect of these adjustments shall be included in the income of the period in which the application of FASB-71 is discontinued and the net amount shall be reported in the financial statements as an extraordinary item in accordance with APB-30 (Reporting the Results of Operations).

Disclosures and amendment to APB-30   The following financial statement disclosures shall be made in the period in which an enterprise discontinues the application of FASB-71 to all or any portion of its regulated operations:

1. The reason(s) for the discontinuation of applying FASB-71
2. The identification of the portion(s) of operations to which the application of FASB-71 is being discontinued
3. The net adjustment, less related taxes, resulting from the discontinuation of the application of FASB-71 shall be separately disclosed as an extraordinary item in the statement of operations

APB-30 contains the criteria for classifying an amount as an extraordinary item in the financial statements of an enterprise. FASB-101 amends APB-30 by requiring the net adjustment resulting from the discontinuation of FASB-71 to be classified as an extraordinary item regardless of the criteria in paragraph 20 of APB-30 for classifying an extraordinary item.

Effective date and transition   FASB-101 is effective for those enterprises that report the discontinuation of the application of FASB-71 in fiscal years ending on or after December 16, 1988. Enterprises that have reported the discontinuation of the application of FASB-71 in fiscal years ending prior to December 15, 1988, may retroactively restate their financial statements for the period that includes the date of discontinuation and periods subsequent to the date of discontinuation, but are not required to do so. Enterprises that have reported the discontinuation of the application of FASB-71 for the fiscal year that includes December 15, 1988, but have not applied the provisions of FASB-101 shall restate their financial statements for the interim period of the discontinuation and subsequent interim periods within that fiscal year.

Financial statements that are restated to reflect the application of FASB-101 shall disclose for each period restated, the nature of the restatement and its effect on (a) income before extraordinary items, (b) extraordinary items, (c) net income and (d) related per share amounts. FASB-101 does not permit the restatement of interim and annual financial statements for periods ending prior to the date on which an enterprise discontinues the application of FASB-71.

Enterprises may delay adopting the provisions of FASB-101 if they discontinue the application of FASB-71 in fiscal years that include December 15, 1988, or December 15, 1989. In this event, the discontinuation shall be reported in the annual financial statements for the fiscal year that includes December 15, 1989. Subsequently, when reporting the adoption of FASB-101, these enterprises shall restate interim and annual financial statements for the period including the date of the discontinuation and periods subsequent to that date. As mentioned previously, financial statements that are restated to reflect the application of FASB-101 shall disclose for each period restated the nature of the restatement and its effect on (a) income before extraordinary items, (b) extraordinary items, (c) net income and (d) related per share amounts.

Disclosure Index

DISCLOSURE INDEX

This Disclosure Index contains both required and recommended disclosures that are currently in use. Although the utmost care has been exercised in the preparation of this Index, it is not meant to be a substitute for professional judgment. There are circumstances in which disclosure is not required or recommended, but because of special factors, professional judgment may dictate that disclosure is necessary for a fair presentation.

This Disclosure Index has been designed to assist the preparer or reviewer of financial statements in determining whether necessary disclosures have been made. Its proper use can expedite the preparation or review of financial statements.

BALANCE SHEET

Cash

1. Withdrawal restrictions on funds
2. Segregation of funds to be used for specific purposes

Financial Instruments (FASB-105)

For each class (category) of financial instrument with off-balance-sheet risk of accounting loss subject to the provisions of FASB-105, the following financial statement disclosures should be made:

1. The face or contract amount (or the notional amount if there is no face or contract amount)
2. The nature and terms, including at a minimum, a discussion of credit and market risk, cash requirements of the instrument, and the related accounting policies
3. The maximum amount of accounting loss that would be incurred if any party failed completely to perform according to the terms of the financial instrument with off-balance-sheet risk, even if this is a remote possibility, and the collateral or other security for the amount due, if any, was absolutely worthless (in other words, a "worst case" scenario)

4. The entity's existing policy for determining the amount of collateral or other security required to support financial instruments subject to credit risk, information about the entity's access to that collateral or other security, and the nature and a brief description of the collateral or other security (in other words, an entity's policy for requiring security and a brief description of the security supporting financial instruments with off-balance-sheet risk of accounting loss)
5. FASB-105 encourages the disclosure of additional information about the extent of the collateral because it may provide a better indication of the extent of credit risk.

EXPOSURE DRAFT

Disclosures About Market Value of Financial Instruments

An Exposure Draft (ED) entitled *Disclosures About Market Value of Financial Instruments* is outstanding as of the date of this publication. There may be significant differences between the ED discussed below and the official FASB Statement when it is promulgated. Thus, the reader is cautioned to compare carefully the material in this ED with the official pronouncement when it becomes available.

The ED would require disclosure of the market value of all financial instruments for which it is practicable to estimate market value, whether or not the financial instruments are recognized in the statement of financial position.

The ED would exempt certain types of financial instruments from this disclosure requirement, including obligations under pension or other postretirement benefit plans, but would preserve pre-existing requirements for disclosure of the market value of these financial instruments.

If it is not practicable to estimate market value, the ED would require disclosure of the carrying amount, interest rate, maturity, and other characteristics of the financial instrument.

The ED is discussed further at the end of the chapter entitled "Financial Instruments."

Marketable Securities

1. Specialized industry practices
2. Method of valuation

3. Aggregate cost and market for current portfolio and noncurrent portfolio
4. Carrying value of each portfolio
5. Gross unrealized gains and losses for each portfolio
6. Net realized gain or loss included in determining net income of the period
7. Amount of change in valuation allowances
8. Significant net realized and unrealized gains and losses subsequent to the balance sheet date
9. Significant net realized and unrealized gains and losses occurring between a parent company and a subsidiary with different balance sheet dates
10. Investments accounted for by the equity method should not be combined with current or noncurrent portfolios of marketable securities
11. Financial statements that contain entities which have specialized industry practices and which do not have specialized industry practices must include the necessary disclosure of FASB-12 for both circumstances
12. Investments accounted for by the equity method may not be combined with current or noncurrent portfolios of marketable securities
13. Investments in affiliated companies should be separately identified
14. It may be desirable to identify government securities separately
15. Futures contracts:
    a. The nature of the items that are hedged or related to futures contracts
    b. The accounting method(s) used for futures contracts
    c. A description of the events or transactions that will result in recognition in income of changes in value of the futures contracts

Notes Receivable

1. Trade notes receivable
2. Nontrade segregated by type:
    a. From subsidiaries or affiliates
    b. From officers or employees

3. Installment notes receivable
4. Equity in accounts sold
5. Due from factors
6. Pledged as collateral
7. Face amount of notes
8. Effective interest rates
9. Notes discounted—contingent liability
10. Repayment terms and dates
11. Amounts of unearned income, discounts, premiums, finance charges, and interest deducted from related notes receivable
12. Allowance for possible losses
13. Noncurrent portions properly classified
14. Significant balances with one customer
15. Government contracts (CPFF) properly disclosed

Imputed Interest on Notes Receivable (Payable)

1. Description of note
2. Effective interest rate
3. Face amount of note
4. Value of any rights or privileges exchanged
5. Fair value of nonmonetary transaction except in those cases in which the earning process is not culminated
6. Unearned interest and finance charges deducted from related notes

Accounts Receivable

1. Trade accounts receivable
2. Nontrade segregated by type:
   a. From subsidiaries or affiliates
   b. From officers or employees
   c. Tax refunds
   d. Claims against government contracts (CPFF)
3. Allowance for uncollectible accounts
4. Accounts sold (contingent liability)
5. Equity retained in accounts sold
6. Accounts receivable—discounted

   7. Accounts receivable—pledged
   8. Accounts receivable—factored
   9. Significantly large balances
 10. Unbilled receivables shown separately from billed receivables
 11. Possible provision for sales returns, allowances, or discounts
 12. Amounts from affiliates or subsidiaries properly classified as current or noncurrent

Inventories

  1. Basis of valuation and method of costing
  2. Significant changes and effect on net income
  3. Amounts by major categories
  4. Amounts pledged as collateral
  5. Amounts valued in excess of cost, such as precious metals, minerals, etc.
  6. Substantial or unusual losses separately disclosed
  7. Losses on firm purchase commitments
  8. Principles particular to a given industry
  9. Replacement cost and effect on net income of depleted LIFO layer
 10. SEC filings—current replacement costs
 11. Oil and gas producing companies must comply with special disclosure requirements
 12. Consignments
 13. Product financing arrangements

Prepaid Items

  1. Segregated into types
  2. Properly classified as current or noncurrent

Depreciable Assets and Depreciation

  1. Basis for valuation
  2. Balances of major classes of depreciable assets by nature or function

   3. Accumulated depreciation, either by major classes or in total
   4. Description of depreciation methods used by major classes
   5. Depreciation expense for the period
   6. Significant commitments for depreciable assets
   7. Significant sale-and-leasebacks
   8. Segregation of depreciable assets not used in trade or business (idle facilities, investments, etc.)
   9. Pledged as collateral

Unconsolidated Investments

   1. Name of each investment
   2. Percentage of ownership
   3. Accounting policies with respect to each investment
   4. Differences between the carrying value and underlying equity in net assets and the treatment of such difference
   5. Quoted market value of each investment (not required for subsidiaries)
   6. Summary of assets, liabilities, and results of operation for each significant investment
   7. Effect on the investor of any outstanding conversions or dilutive securities of the investee
   8. If investment is 20% or more and the equity method is not used, the reason(s) must be disclosed
   9. If investment is less than 20% and the cost method is not used, the reason(s) must be disclosed
  10. Changes in the status of an investment
  11. Declaration of intent to reinvest the undistributed earnings of a subsidiary (nonaccrual of income taxes)
  12. Declaration of intent that undistributed earnings will be in the form of a tax-free liquidation (nonaccrual of income taxes)
  13. The cumulative amount of undistributed earnings on which a parent company or investor has not recognized income taxes
  14. Significant tax credits and deductions resulting from investments

Intangible Assets

   1. Method of amortization and estimated useful life

2. Carrying basis of intangibles
3. Explanation of the nonamortization of pre-11/1/70 intangibles
4. Intangible assets of motor carriers

Deferred Income Taxes

1. Segregated between net current amount and net noncurrent amount
2. Operating-loss carryforwards not used, including expiration dates
3. Significant other unused tax credits or deductions including expiration dates
4. Reason(s) for significant differences in the customary relationship between income tax expense and pretax accounting income
5. Nature of significant differences between pretax accounting income and taxable income
6. Components of income tax expense for the period (intraperiod tax allocation)
7. Tax effects of adjustments to prior periods
8. Amount of operating-loss carryback applied during the period

Leases—Lessee

1. Description of lessee's leasing arrangements:
   a. Basis of contingent payments
   b. Renewal or purchase options
   c. Escalation clauses
   d. Restrictions on dividends, further leasing, additional debt, etc.

2. Capital leases:
   a. Gross amount of assets by major classes under capital leases in accordance with their nature and/or function
   b. Aggregate future minimum lease payments for the period and for each of the five succeeding fiscal years, less executory costs (including profit thereon) included in the minimum lease payments

      c. Amount of imputed interest necessary to reduce the net minimum lease payments to its present value

      d. Total minimum sublease rentals to be received under noncancelable subleases

      e. Total amount of contingent rentals actually incurred during each period presented

3. Operating leases:

      a. Aggregate future minimum rental payments for the period and for the next succeeding five fiscal years

      b. Total minimum rentals to be received under noncancelable subleases

      c. Total rental expense for each period presented

Leases—Lessor

Where leasing, excluding leveraged leases, is a significant portion of a lessor's business in terms of net assets, revenue, or net income, the following is required for both sales-type and direct financing leases:

1. The components of the net investment in leases, including:

      a. Future minimum lease payments less executory costs (and profits thereon) included in the minimum lease payments

      b. Accumulated allowance for uncollectible minimum lease payments

      c. Unguaranteed residual values accruing to the lessor

      d. Unearned income

2. Future minimum lease payments to be received for each of the five succeeding fiscal years

3. Total contingent rentals included in income for each period presented

4. For direct-financing leases only: the amount of unearned income used to offset initial direct costs charged to income for each period presented

5. For operating leases:

      a. By major classes of property on lease or held for lease and according to nature or function; (1) cost, (2) carrying amount, and (3) accumulated depreciation in total

    b. Minimum future rentals on noncancelable leases in the aggregate and for each of the five succeeding fiscal years

    c. Total contingent rentals included in income for each period presented

6. General description of the lessor's usual leasing arrangements

Leveraged Leases

1. Deferred taxes related to leveraged leases should be separately disclosed

2. A separate presentation of pretax income from leveraged leases should be made in the income statement or footnote thereto to include (1) pretax income, (2) the tax effect on pretax income, and (3) the amount of investment tax credit recognized during the period

3. When leveraged leasing constitutes a significant portion of a lessor's business activity in terms of assets, revenue, or net income, the following components of the net investment balance in leveraged leases should be disclosed by footnote:

    a. Rentals receivable, net of rentals applicable to principal and interest on nonrecourse debt

    b. Estimated residual value of the leased property

    c. Unearned or deferred income, including (1) estimated pretax lease income less initial direct costs and (2) investment tax credit remaining to be allocated to income over the lease term

    d. The amount, if any, remaining to be collected for the investment tax credit realized on the transaction

Sale-Leaseback Transactions

Accounting for sale-leaseback transactions is addressed by FASB-13 and FASB-28. Accounting for all sale-leaseback transactions is determined by the degree of rights that the seller-lessee retains in the transaction, as follows:

    a. Substantially all

    b. Minor

    c. More than minor but less than substantially all

Financial statement disclosure for sale-leaseback transactions, other than real estate, shall include a full description of the terms of the sale-leaseback transaction.

Accounting for a sale-leaseback of real estate is addressed by FASB-98. Financial statement disclosures for sale-leaseback transactions involving real estate shall include a description of the terms of the sale-leaseback transaction, including future commitments, obligations, provisions, or circumstances that require or result in the seller-lessee's continuing involvement.

Unbilled Costs

1. Expenditures billable to customers
2. Unreimbursed costs and fees (CPFF contracts)
3. Costs and estimated earnings in excess of billings on uncompleted contracts

Notes Payable

1. Description of note
2. Amount of note
3. Effective interest rate
4. Segregation of type of notes:
    a. Trade
    b. Banks
    c. Items collateralized
    d. Related parties—stockholders, directors, officers, or employees
    e. Intercompany
5. Nonmonetary transaction:
    a. Imputed interest
    b. Premium or discount
    c. Face amount
    d. Effective interest rate
    e. Valuation of rights or privileges

Accounts Payable

1. Segregation by types:

      a. Trade
      b. Nontrade
      c. Related parties
      d. Intercompany
  2. Accounts collateralized

Income Taxes Payable (FASB-96)

In a classified statement of financial position, a deferred tax liability or asset shall be classified either as current or noncurrent. The current amount of a deferred tax liability or asset is equal to the net deferred tax effects of temporary differences:

  a. That will result in net taxable or deductible amounts during the next year
  b. Related to an asset or liability that is classified for financial reporting purposes as current because of an operating cycle that is longer than one year
  c. For which there is no related, identifiable asset or liability for financial reporting purposes whenever other related assets and liabilities are classified as current because of an operating cycle that is longer than one year

Under FASB-96, when a deferred tax liability is *not* recognized for any of the areas addressed by APB-23 or for deposits in statutory reserve funds by U.S. steamship enterprises, the following information shall be disclosed in the financial statements or notes thereto:

  a. A description of the types of temporary differences for which a deferred tax liability has not been recognized and the types of events that would cause those temporary differences to become taxable
  b. The cumulative amount of each type of temporary difference
  c. The amount of the unrecognized deferred tax liability for any unremitted earnings if determination is not practicable and the amount of withholding taxes that would be payable upon remittance of those earnings
  d. The amount of the unrecognized deferred tax liability for temporary differences other than unremitted earnings (that is, the bad debt) reserve of a stock or mutual savings and loan association or a mutual savings bank, the policyholders' sur-

plus of a life insurance enterprise, and the statutory reserve funds of a U.S. steamship enterprise

The amount of income tax expense or benefit allocated to the following financial statement captions shall be disclosed for each year for which those items are presented: (a) continuing operations, (b) discontinued operations, (c) extraordinary items, (d) the cumulative effect of accounting changes, (e) prior period adjustments, (f) gains and losses included in comprehensive income but excluded from net income, and (g) capital transactions.

For each year presented, an enterprise shall disclose in its financial statements or notes thereto, the significant components of income tax expense attributable to continuing operations. Those components would include, for example:

a. Current tax expense or benefit (Note: Interest penalties assessed on income tax deficiencies, such as underpayment or improper computation shall not be reported as income tax expense.)

b. Deferred tax expense or benefit, exclusive of adjustments of a deferred tax liability or asset for enacted changes in tax law or rates or a change in the tax status of an enterprise (see (f) below)

c. Investment tax credits

d. Government grants (to the extent recognized as a reduction of income tax expenses)

e. Benefits of operating loss carryforwards

f. Adjustments of a deferred tax liability or for enacted changes in tax laws or rates or a change in the tax status of an enterprise

An enterprise shall reconcile the amount of income tax expense it reports for the year from continuing operations, to the amount of income tax expense computed by applying the domestic federal statutory tax rates to pretax income from continuing operations. In the event there are alternative tax systems, the regular tax rates shall be used as the "statutory" tax rates. An enterprise shall disclose the estimated amount and the nature of each significant reconciling item, and the reconciliation shall be expressed in percentages or dollar amounts. A nonpublic enterprise may omit a numerical reconciliation, but must disclose the nature of all significant reconciling items.

FASB-103 defers the effective date of FASB-96 (Accounting for Income Taxes) for a period of two years, in addition to the one-year deferral announced in FASB-100 (Accounting for Income Taxes—Deferral of the Effective Date of FASB Statement No. 96). As a result, FASB-96 will be effective for fiscal years beginning on or after December 16, 1991.

An enterprise shall disclose the amounts and expiration dates of operating loss and tax credit carryforwards for both financial reporting purposes and for tax purposes.

An enterprise that is part of a group that files a consolidated tax return shall disclose in its separately issued financial statements:

a. The amount of current and deferred tax expense for each statement of earnings presented and the amount of any tax-related balances due to or from affiliates as of the date of each statement of financial position presented

b. The principal provisions of the method by which the consolidated amount of current and deferred tax expense is allocated to members of the group and the nature and effect of any changes in that method (and in determining related balances to or from affiliates) during the years for which the disclosures in (a) are presented

EXPOSURE DRAFT

Accounting for Income Taxes

An Exposure Draft (ED) entitled *Accounting for Income Taxes*, which would supersede FASB-96, is outstanding as of the date of this publication. There may be significant differences between the ED discussed below and the official FASB Statement when it is promulgated. Thus, the reader is cautioned to compare carefully the material in this ED with the official pronouncement when it becomes available.

The ED entitled *Accounting for Income Taxes* would require the following disclosures in addition to those required by FASB-96:

1. The total of all deferred tax liabilities.
2. The total of all deferred tax assets.
3. The total valuation allowance for deferred tax assets.
4. Any net change in the valuation allowance.
5. The nature and effect of significant matters affecting com parability of information for all periods presented.

> The ED is discussed further at the end of the chapter entitled "Income Taxes (FASB-96)."

Other Current Liabilities

1. Current accruals
2. Current portion of long-term obligations
3. Customers' advances or deposits
4. Guarantees, warranties, etc.
5. Billings in excess of costs and estimated earnings on uncompleted contracts
6. Compensated absences

Long-Term Obligations

1. Description of terms and interest rates
2. Assets pledged, restriction on dividends or retained earnings, sinking fund requirements, etc.
3. Current portions shown as current
4. Capitalized lease obligations
5. Convertibility
6. Nonmonetary transactions:
   a. Imputed interest
   b. Premium or discount
   c. Face amount
   d. Effective interest rates
   e. Valuation of rights and privileges
7. Unrecorded unconditional purchase obligations
8. Other unconditional obligations
9. Product financing arrangements
10. Pensions
11. Postretirement benefits other than pensions

Unrealized Gross Profits on Installment Sales

Stockholders' Equity

1. Common stock:
   a. Title of each class

b. Par or stated value

c. Number of shares authorized, issued, and outstanding

d. Reserved shares and purpose

2. Preferred stock:
    a. Title of each class
    b. Par or stated value
    c. Number of shares authorized, issued, and outstanding
    d. Reserved shares and purpose
    e. Convertibility
    f. Call price
    g. Cumulative or noncumulative
    h. Dividends in arrears
    i. Participating or nonparticipating
    j. Preference in liquidation

3. Stock subscriptions:
    a. Description
    b. Details of amounts

4. Additional capital:
    a. Segregated by source
    b. Restrictions

5. Retained earnings:
    a. Appropriated and unappropriated
    b. Dividend restrictions
    c. Stock dividends
    d. Treasury stock restrictions where required by charter or state law
    e. Dated, in case of quasi-reorganization

6. Treasury stock:
    a. Number of shares
    b. Basis of valuation
    c. Reserved shares and purpose

STATEMENT OF CAPITAL CHANGES

A statement of changes in the separate accounts of stockholders' equity, including retained earnings, is necessary when financial position, changes in financial position, and results of operations are presented in conformity with GAAP. This disclosure may be presented as a separate statement, as part of the basic financial statements, or in footnotes thereto.

STATEMENT OF CASH FLOWS

FASB-95 (Statement of Cash Flows) requires that a statement of cash flows be included as part of a full set of general purpose financial statements that are externally issued by any business enterprise.

Under the provisions of FASB-95, a statement of cash flows shall clearly specify the amount of net cash provided or used by an enterprise during a period from (a) operating activities, (b) investing activities, and (c) financing activities. The statement shall clearly indicate the net effect of those cash flows on the enterprise's cash and cash equivalents.

A reconciliation of beginning and ending cash and cash equivalents shall be included in the statement of cash flows. FASB-95 also requires that the statement of cash flows contain separate related disclosures about investing and financing activities of an enterprise that affect its financial position but do not directly affect its cash flows during the period.

FASB-104 makes two amendments to FASB-95 (Statement of Cash Flows). These amendments allow enterprises to make a choice in reporting certain cash flows and classifying cash flows from hedging transactions. Enterprises may continue to apply FASB-95, which itself provides some optional methods, or they may use one or both of the new optional methods provided in FASB-104.

Under the first of the new options allowed by FASB-104, the statement of cash flows of a bank, savings institution, or credit union may show net amounts of cash flows for (a) deposits with other financial institutions, (b) time deposits, and (c) loans to customers.

Under the second new option allowed by FASB-104, the statement of cash flows of any enterprise may classify cash flows from certain hedging transactions in the same category as the cash flows from the hedged item, provided this accounting policy is disclosed and the enterprise uses hedge accounting to account for the transaction.

INCOME STATEMENT

1. Substantial sales to one customer or a few customers
2. Method of recognizing long-term construction-type contracts

3. Method of reporting revenues for cost reimbursement contracts

4. Method of reporting income from leases

5. Proportionate share of income from investees

6. Depreciation expense separately shown

7. Significant interest income or expense

8. Amount of investment tax credit, accounting method, and carryovers

9. Method of foreign exchange conversion

10. Gain or loss on foreign exchange

11. Significant losses on firm purchase commitments

12. Unusual or infrequently occurring items other than extraordinary should be separately shown

13. Research and development costs

14. Bad debt reserves of savings and loan associations

15. Policyholders' surplus of stock life insurance companies

16. Pension plan expense

17. Postretirement benefits other than pensions

18. Discontinued operations

19. Gain or loss from extinguishment of debt

20. Cumulative effect of an accounting change

21. Extraordinary items

22. Intraperiod income tax allocation

23. Reasons for significant variations between income tax expense and pretax accounting income

24. Material differences between pretax accounting income and taxable income

25. Earnings per share (primary and fully diluted for complex capital structures)

EXPOSURE DRAFT

Accounting for Contributions Received and Contributions Made and Capitalization of Works of Art, Historical Treasures, and Similar Assets

An Exposure Draft (ED) entitled *Accounting for Contributions Received and Contributions Made and Capitalization of Works of*

Art, Historical Treasures, and Similar Assets is outstanding as of the date of this publication. There may be significant differences between the ED discussed below and the official FASB Statement when it is promulgated. Thus, the reader is cautioned to compare carefully the material in this ED with the official pronouncement when it becomes available.

The ED would require an enterprise to disclose:

1. The nature and amount of contributed services received and recognized as revenue for the period.
2. The nature and extent of contributed services received but not recognized as revenue and the reasons why they were not recognized.
3. A general description of the programs or activities for which services were contributed.

The ED is discussed further in the chapter entitled "Revenue Recognition."

GENERAL

Accounting Policies

1. Description of all significant accounting policies (Summary of Significant Accounting Policies)
2. Methods of applying accounting principles:
    a. Selection of acceptable alternatives
    b. Peculiar to a particular industry
    c. Unusual application of GAAP

Accounting Changes

1. Description of change
2. Nature and justification
3. Effect of change:
    a. Cumulative effect
    b. Restatement of financials
4. Reason for omitting cumulative effect and *pro forma* information
5. Change in method of amortizing new assets:

    a. Nature of change and method

    b. Effect on net income in period of change

    c. Related per share data

6. Change in reporting entity (restatement)

7. Correction of error in previous financial statements:

    a. Nature of error

    b. Effect on components of net income

    c. Related per share data

Business Combinations

1. Purchase method:

    a. Name, description, and total cost of acquisition

    b. Method of accounting (purchase)

    c. Period in which results of operations are included

    d. Amortization of goodwill

    e. Other pertinent information

    f. Contingent payments

    g. *Pro forma* results for current period as if acquisition had been combined from the beginning of fiscal year, and comparative year, if presented

    Disclosure g. above is not required for a nonpublic enterprise as described in FASB-79.

2. Pooling-of-interests:

    a. Name and brief description of companies combined

    b. Basis of presentation in current period and restatements of prior periods

    c. Method of accounting (pooling)

    d. Description and amount of shares issued

    e. Separate results of operation for each combining company

    f. Nature of adjustments to net assets of each combining company in order to adopt the same accounting policies

    g. Change in fiscal year

    h. Reconciliation of revenue and earnings previously reported by acquiring company with combined amounts presented in the financial statements

    i. *Pro forma* information of proposed pooling to stockholders

    j. Gain or loss on disposal of significant portions of the assets or segments of combining companies

    k. Pooling consummated after balance sheet date but before issuance of financial statements

    l. Earning of separate companies where new corporation is formed to effectuate combination

Commitments and Contingencies

1. Probable and reasonably possible losses where liability can be ascertained
2. Nature and range of loss
3. Remote losses on guarantees and similar items
4. Pending litigation
5. Guarantees of subsidiaries or affiliates
6. Tax contingencies
7. Accounts sold with recourse
8. Renegotiation of governmental contracts
9. Losses after balance sheet date but before issuance of financial statements
10. All material commitments
11. Gain contingencies that are not misleading as to likelihood of realization
12. Unused letters of credit
13. Information on noncancelable leases which are not capitalized
14. Indirect guarantees of indebtedness of others
15. Franchise commitments and obligations

Consolidated Financial Statements

ARB-51 requires that an enterprise's consolidation policy be fully disclosed in its financial statements or footnotes thereto.

Under the "parent company" theory, minority interests are not considered part of stockholders' equity and are disclosed in the consolidated balance sheet between the liability section and stockholders' equity section. Minority interests in consolidated net income are shown as a deduction of consolidated net income.

Under the "entity" theory, minority interests are disclosed within and as part of the consolidated stockholders' equity section of the consolidated balance sheet.

Development Stage Enterprises

1. Cumulative net losses
2. Cumulative income statement
3. Cumulative statement of changes in financial position
4. Date and number of shares of stock issued for cash or other consideration
5. Nature and valuation of noncash consideration received for stock issued
6. Description of development stage enterprises

Extraordinary Items

1. Nature and amount of each item with related tax effects
2. Unamortized cost of intangible assets included as extraordinary charge
3. Tax benefit of any operating-loss carryforward reported as an extraordinary item in the period realized
4. Investor's share of investee's extraordinary items
5. Extinguishment of debt

Extinguishment of Debt

1. Description of extinguishment
2. Gain or loss
3. Related tax effects
4. Assets placed in an irrevocable trust:
    a. A general description of the transaction
    b. The total amount of debt outstanding at the end of the period
    c. The total amount of debt that is considered extinguished at the end of the period

Foreign Currency Exchange

1. Aggregate transaction gain or loss
2. Analysis of changes in separate component of stockholders' equity which must include

    a. Beginning and ending cumulative balances
    b. Aggregate increase or decrease for the period from translation adjustments and gains and losses from (i) hedges of a net investment in a foreign entity and (ii) long-term intercompany transactions
    c. Amount of income taxes allocated to translation adjustments
    d. Amount of translation adjustment of a sale or substantial liquidation of a foreign investment
3. Exchange rate changes and effects on foreign currency transactions subsequent to balance sheet date, if material

Government Contracts

1. Advance payments as offsets
2. Inability to provide for renegotiation
3. Significant portion of a company's business
4. Basis of provisions for renegotiations
5. Reasonable estimate of termination not possible
6. Material termination claims
7. Controversial items
8. Claims against government segregated

Interest Costs Capitalized

1. The total amount of interest costs incurred and charged to expense during the period
2. The amount of interest costs that have been capitalized during the period

Interim Financial Reporting

1. Interim inventory cost method
2. Material contingencies

3. Significant seasonable variations in revenue
4. Disposal of a segment
5. Changes in accounting principle or estimate
6. Significant variations between income tax expense and pre-tax accounting income

Pension Plans—Employers

FASB-87 requires the disclosure of the following pension plan information:

1. A full description of the pension plan, including the employee groups covered, type of benefit formula, funding policy, types of assets held and significant nonbenefit liabilities (if any), and the nature and effect of significant matters affecting comparability of information for all periods presented

2. The amount of net periodic pension cost for the period detailing the separate amounts for the (a) service cost component, (b) interest cost component, (c) actual return on plan assets for the period, and (d) net total of other components

3. A schedule reconciling the funded status of the plan with amounts reported in the employer's statement of financial position, showing separately:

   a. Fair value of plan assets
   b. Projected benefit obligation, separately identifying the accumulated benefit obligation and vested benefit obligation
   c. Amount of unrecognized prior service cost
   d. Amount of unrecognized net gain or loss, including asset gains and losses not yet reflected in market-related values
   e. Amount of any remaining unrecognized net obligation or net asset existing at the date of the initial application of FASB-87
   f. Amount of additional minimum liability equal to either (i) the unfunded accumulated benefit obligation plus any prepaid pension cost, (ii) the unfunded accumulated benefit obligation reduced by any unfunded accrued pension cost, or (iii) the amount of the unfunded accumulated benefit obligation

    g. Amount of the net pension asset or liability that has been recognized in the employer's statement of financial position. This amount must be equal to the total of items a. through f.

4. The weighted-average assumed discount rate and, if applicable, the rate of compensation increase used in determining the projected benefit obligation, and the weighted-average expected long-term rate of return on pension plan assets.

5. If applicable, the amounts and types of securities of the employer and/or related parties that are included in plan assets and the approximate amount of annual benefits of employees and retirees covered by annuity contracts issued by the employer and related parties. Also, if applicable, the alternative amortization method used for unrecognized prior service cost and the alternative amortization method used to reflect the substantive commitment of an employer to pay more employees benefits than its existing pension benefit formula indicates.

6. Postretirement life insurance that is not provided through an employer's pension plan and all postretirement health care benefits, including:

    a. Nature and justification for any accounting change

    b. Why new method is preferable

    c. Effects on income before extraordinary items, net income, and per share amounts for the period

    d. Description of the new method

    e. Accounted for prospectively or by the cumulative effect method

        i. Prospectively—Effects of the change and method of accounting for prospective recognition

        ii. Cumulative Effect Method—Pro forma effects of the retroactive application on income before extraordinary items, net income, and per share amounts for the period

Pension Plans—Settlements and Curtailments

FASB-88 requires that a description of the nature of the events and the amount of gain or loss resulting from the settlement or curtailment of a pension plan be disclosed in the financial statements, regardless of whether the gain or loss is directly related to the disposal of a business segment.

Pension Plan—Financial Statements

1. Statement of net assets available for benefits
2. Statement of changes in net assets available for benefits
3. Actuarial present value of accumulated plan benefits
4. Year-to-year changes in the actuarial present value of accumulated plan benefits (if significant)

Postretirement Benefits Other Than Pensions

FASB-106 supersedes FASB-81 (see chapter entitled "Postretirement Benefits Other Than Pensions" for effective dates). Until an enterprise applies FASB-106, the following disclosures relating to postretirement benefits are required by FASB-81:

1. Description of employee groups covered and benefits provided
2. Description of the accounting and funding policies used for the benefits
3. Cost of the benefits included in net income for the period
4. Effect of significant items that affect comparability of benefit costs for all periods presented

FASB-81 encourages the disclosure of the following information:

1. Present value of future health care and life insurance benefits for retirees
2. Contribution to and fair market value of trusts to pay retiree health care benefits
3. The average age and number of active employees potentially eligible for postretirement health care and life insurance benefits
4. The number of retirees covered by the employer's plan
5. Information concerning the significance of the potential future postretirement health care and life insurance benefits for both active and retired employees
6. The average benefits per retiree for the most recent year for which that information is available

Once an enterprise applies FASB-106, the following disclosures are required:

1. Description of the substantive plan, including:

a. The nature of the plan

b. Any modifications of the existing cost sharing provisions that are reflected in the substantive plan

c. The nature of any commitment to increase monetary benefits provided by the plan

d. Employee groups covered

e. Types of benefits provided

f. Funding policy

g. Types of assets held and significant liabilities (other than liabilities to pay benefits)

h. The nature and effect of significant matters affecting the comparability of information for all periods presented, for example, the effect of a business combination or divestiture

2. The amount of net postretirement benefit cost, showing each of the following components separately:

   a. Service cost

   b. Interest cost

   c. Actual return on plan assets

   d. Amortization of unrecognized transition obligation/asset

   e. Net total of other components, generally consisting of (1) net asset gain or loss arising during the period but deferred for later recognition, (2) amortization of unrecognized prior service cost, (3) amortization of net gain or loss from prior periods, and (4) gain or loss recognized due to temporary deviation from substantive plan

3. Reconciliation of funded status with amounts shown in the statement of financial position, showing each of the following items separately:

   a. Fair value of plan assets

   b. Accumulated postretirement benefit obligation, with separate identification of the portions resulting from (1) retirees, (2) other fully eligible plan participants, and (3) other active plan participants

   c. Unrecognized prior service cost

   d. Unrecognized net gain or loss, including plan asset gains and losses not yet reflected in market-related value

    e. Unrecognized transition obligation/asset

    f. Net postretirement benefit asset or liability as shown in the statement of financial position (this amount should equal the net result of combining the five items listed above)

4. The assumed health care cost trend rate (or rates) used to measure the expected gross eligible charges for benefits covered under the plan for the next year, together with:

    a. A general description of the direction and pattern of change in subsequent years, and

    b. The ultimate assumed trend rate and the year when it is expected to be reached

5. The weighted average of the assumed discount rates and the assumed rates of compensation increase (for pay-related plans) used to measure the accumulated postretirement benefit obligation

6. The weighted average of the expected long-term rates of return on plan assets

7. The estimated income tax rates included in the long-term rate of return on plan assets, if the income of the plan is segregated from the employer's investment income for tax purposes

8. The effect of a 1% increase in the assumed health care cost trend for each future year, on each of the following (assuming no other changes):

    a. The combined total of the service cost component and the interest cost component of net periodic postretirement benefit cost

    b. The accumulated postretirement benefit obligation for health care benefits

9. The amount and types of securities of the employer and related parties included in plan assets, and the approximate amount of future annual benefits covered by insurance contracts issued by the employer and related parties

10. Any alternative amortization method used pursuant to par. 53 of FASB-106 (amortization of prior service cost more rapidly than general requirement) or par. 60 (amortization of unrecognized net gain or loss more rapidly than general requirement)

11. The amount of gain or loss recognized from a settlement or a curtailment during the period, together with a description of the nature of these events.

12. The cost of providing special or contractual termination benefits recognized during the period, together with a description of these events.

Quasi-Reorganizations

1. Disclose all pertinent information
2. Date retained earnings accounts

Research and Development

FASB-2 requires the financial statement disclosure of the amount of R&D charged to expense for each period presented.

FASB-86 requires that all computer software costs classified as R&D costs shall be disclosed as such in accordance with FASB-2. These costs may include the cost of planning, product design, detail program design, and the costs incurred in establishing technological feasibility of a computer software product.

The total amount of unamortized computer software costs that is included in each balance sheet presented shall be disclosed in the financial statements.

The total amount of computer software costs charged to expense shall be disclosed for each income statement presented. Computer software costs charged to expense shall include amortization expense and amounts written down to net realizable value.

Related Party Disclosures

1. The nature of the material related party relationship. In addition, the name of the related party should be disclosed, if it is essential to the understanding of the relationship.

2. A description of the material related party transactions, including amounts and other pertinent information for each period in which an income statement is presented.

   Related party transactions or no, or nominal, amounts must also be disclosed.

3. The effects of any change in terms between the related parties from terms used in prior periods. In addition, the dollar amount of transactions for each period in which an income statement is presented must be disclosed.

4. If not apparent in the financial statements, (a) the terms of

related party transactions, (b) the manner of settlement of related party transactions, and (c) the amount due to, or from, related parties, must all be disclosed.

5. If the operating results or financial positions of a reporting entity can be altered significantly by the effects of common ownership or management control of the reporting entity and one or more other entities, even if there are no transactions between any of the entities, the nature of the ownership or management control must be disclosed in the financial statements.

Segmental Reporting

1. Nonpublic companies are not required to disclose EPS data and segmental information
2. Industry segments and foreign operations
3. Sales and revenue:
    a. To unaffiliated customers
    b. To intercompany segments
    c. Types of products
    d. Revenue of each reportable segment
    e. Accounting policies
4. Operating profit or loss:
    a. Allocation of common operating costs and expenses
    b. Exclude revenue not derived from operations
    c. Exclude general corporate overhead, interest expense, income taxes, earnings from unconsolidated subsidiaries, discontinued operations, minority interests, extraordinary items, and cumulative effect of a change in an accounting principle
5. Other measures of profitability may be used
6. Tangible and intangible identifiable assets:
    a. By industry segments or foreign operations
    b. Exclude assets for general corporate use which are not used in any reportable segment
7. Other reportable segment information (by industry segments):
    a. Depreciation, depletion, or amortization
    b. Capital expenditures

     c. Net income from unconsolidated subsidiaries and investees whose operations are vertically integrated

     d. Nature and amount of unusual or infrequently occurring items included in the operating profit or loss of a reportable segment

     e. Effect on a reportable segment's operating profit or loss of a change in an accounting principle

     f. Method(s) used to allocate common costs between reportable segments

8. Export sales

9. Significant sales to one customer

10. Significant sales to governments if they exceed 10% of consolidated sales

11. All segmental information reconciled to financial statements

Stock Options

1. Status of all option plans:

     a. Number of shares covered by each option and date of grant

     b. Exercise price

     c. Number of shares that can be exercised

     d. Number of shares exercised

     e. Option price of exercised shares

     f. Expiration dates

2. All pertinent information about stock option plan, etc.

Short-Term Obligations Expected to Be Refinanced

1. General description of irrevocable financing agreement

2. Terms of new obligation or details of equity securities to be issued

3. Amount excluded from current liabilities as a result of refinancing

Supplementary Information on Changing Prices

FASB-89 encourages large enterprises to disclose certain minimum supplementary information for each of their five most recent years (Five-Year Summary of Selected Financial Data). In addition, if income from continuing operations as shown in the primary financial statements differs significantly from income from continuing operations determined on a current cost/constant purchasing power basis, certain additional disclosures relating to the components of income from continuing operations for the current year should also be disclosed.

The minimum supplementary information encouraged by FASB-89 should be disclosed in average-for-the-year units of constant purchasing power. The Consumer Price Index for All Urban Consumers (CPI-U) should be used to restate the current cost of an item in average-for-the-year units of constant purchasing power equal to that of dollars of the base period used in calculating the CPI-U (currently 1967). The level for the CPI-U used for each of the five most recent years should be disclosed.

An enterprise is encouraged to disclose the following minimum supplementary information for the five most recent years:

a. Net sales and other operating revenue

b. Income from continuing operations on a current cost basis

c. Purchasing power gain or loss on net monetary items

d. Increase or decrease in the current cost or lower recoverable amount of inventory and property, plant, and equipment, net of inflation

e. Aggregate foreign currency translation adjustment on a current cost basis, if applicable

f. Net assets at the end of the year on a current basis

g. Income per common share from continuing operations on a current cost basis

h. Cash dividends declared per common share

i. Market price per common share at year-end

j. Average level of the Consumer Price Index for All Urban Consumers

If income from continuing operations as shown in the primary financial statements differs significantly from income from continuing operations determined on a current cost/constant purchasing power basis, certain other disclosures for the current year are encouraged by FASB-89 in addition to the minimum supplementary information. The additional disclosures for the current year are as follows:

a. Income from continuing operations for the current year on a current cost basis
b. Separate amounts for the current cost or lower recoverable amount at the end of the current year of (a) inventory, and (b) property, plant, and equipment
c. Increase or decrease in current cost or lower recoverable amount before and after adjusting for the effects of inflation of (i) inventory, (ii) property, plant, and equipment
d. The principal types and sources of information used to calculate current costs for the current year
e. The differences, if any, in depreciation methods, useful lives, and salvage values used in the primary financial statements and the depreciation methods, useful lives, and salvage values used in the disclosure of current cost information for the current year

Tax Examinations

1. Examination or litigation in progress
2. All pertinent information
3. Settlement of examination or litigation

Transfers of Receivables With Recourse

1. The amount of proceeds received from the transfer
2. If the information is available, the amount of receivables that remain uncollected
3. Concentration of credit risk

Troubled Debt Restructuring

1. Debtor's troubled debt restructuring:
    a. Description of terms of restructuring
    b. Aggregate gain and related tax effect
    c. Aggregate gain or loss on transfer of assets
    d. Per share data on aggregate gain on restructure (net of related tax)

e. Contingent payable amounts with description of terms

2. Creditor's troubled debt restructuring:
    a. Restructured receivables by major categories
    b. Aggregate recorded investment
    c. Gross interest income not earned as a result of debt restructuring
    d. Gross interest income on restructured receivables included in current net income
    e. Commitments to lend additional funds to debtor

AUDITOR'S REPORT

Scope Limitation

1. Time constraints
2. Insufficient competent evidence:
    a. Inability to observe inventory
    b. Inability to confirm receivables
    c. Client restrictions
    d. Restrictions on the use of audit procedures
3. Inadequate records

Other Auditor's Report

1. Report being based in part on another auditor's report
2. Sharing of responsibility

Departure from GAAP

1. Lack of conformity to GAAP
2. Material departure
3. Inadequate disclosure

Consistency

1. Exception to change in accounting principle
2. Inconsistency in accounting principles

Uncertainties

1. Recurring losses (going concern principle)
2. Deficiency in working capital
3. Inability to obtain financing
4. Failure to comply with loan agreement

SPECIALIZED INDUSTRY DISCLOSURES

Banking or Thrift Acquisitions

FASB-72 requires that an enterprise disclose the nature and amount of financial assistance that it receives from a regulatory agency in connection with the acquisition of a banking or thrift institution.

Entertainment Industry

Broadcasters

1. Unrecorded program material license agreements that have been executed not meeting the criteria for recording in the financial statements

Motion Picture Films

1. Film inventories, including films released, completed and in process
2. Amount of story rights

Franchises

1. Nature of franchise agreement
2. Initial franchise fee
3. Other franchise fee revenue
4. Changes in owners of franchises

Insurance Industry

1. The basis for estimating:

a. The liability for unpaid claims

b. The liability for claim adjustment expenses

2. The methods and assumptions used in calculating the liability for future policy benefits. In addition, FASB-60 encourages, but does not require, the disclosure of the average rate of assumed investment yields that are in effect for the current period.

3. Capitalized acquisition costs:

   a. The nature of such costs

   b. The method of amortizing such costs

   c. The amount of amortization of such costs for the current period

4. If the liabilities for unpaid claims and claim adjustment expenses for short-duration contracts are reported at their present values in the financial statements:

   a. The carrying amount of those liabilities

   b. The range of interest rates used to discount those liabilities

5. If estimated investment income is used in calculating a premium deficiency for short-duration contracts:

   a. If yes, a statement disclosing that fact

   b. If no, no disclosure necessary

6. Reinsurance transaction of an insurance company:

   a. The nature and significance of such transactions

   b. Estimated amounts recoverable from reinsurers that are related to unpaid claims and claim adjustment expenses

7. Participating insurance of an insurance company:

   a. The relative percentage of participating insurance

   b. The method of accounting for participating insurance policyholder dividends

   c. The amount of such dividends

   d. The amount of any additional income allocated to participating insurance policyholders

8. Stockholder's equity, statutory capital, and surplus:

   a. The amount of statutory capital and surplus

   b. The amount of statutory capital and surplus required

for regulatory purposes, if significant to the enterprise's total statutory capital and surplus

c. The nature of statutory restrictions on dividends and the amount of retained earnings not available for dividends to stockholders

9. Policyholders' surplus of life insurance companies (when an insurance company is consolidated or accounted for by the equity method, these disclosures also apply to the parent company):

a. The treatment of the policyholders' surplus under the provisions of the Internal Revenue Code

b. The fact that income taxes may become payable if the company takes specific action, which should be appropriately disclosed

c. The total amount of policyholders' surplus for which income taxes have not been provided

10. If no current or deferred federal income taxes have been provided by a life insurance company for any retained earnings in excess of policyholders' surplus:

a. The amount of such retained earnings

b. The reasons for not accruing deferred federal income taxes

Mortgage Banking Industry

1. Mortgage loans receivable and mortgage backed securities must be separately disclosed as those held for sale and those held for investment

2. Method used to determine lower of cost or market value of mortgage loans receivable and mortgage backed securities

3. The amount of capitalized servicing rights including method and amount of amortization

Oil and Gas Producing Companies

1. Reserves and operating activities—domestic and foreign

2. Oil and gas properties, reserves, and production

3. Present value of future net revenues from production of proved oil and gas reserves

4. Quantities of crude oil and natural gas
5. Proportionate share of investee's quantities
6. Quantities from royalties
7. Long-term supply agreements with foreign governments
8. Capitalized costs, related depreciation, depletion, amortization, and valuation allowances:

   a. Mineral interests in property
   b. Wells, related equipment and facilities
   c. Support equipment and facilities
   d. Uncompleted wells, equipment and facilities

9. Functional costs:

   a. Property acquisitions
   b. Exploration
   c. Development
   d. Production

10. Economic factors and significant uncertainties for proved reserves

Regulated Industries

FASB-71 requires the financial statement disclosure of the following:

1. Any refunds that have a material effect on net income and which are not recognized in the same period as the related revenue. Disclosure shall include the effect on net income and indicate the years that the related revenue was recognized. The material effect on net income, net of related income taxes, may be disclosed as a separate line item in the income statement, but may not be presented as an extraordinary item.

2. Major allowable costs that do not provide for a return on investment and are required to be amortized over the current and future periods, including:

   a. The unamortized amount of such costs
   b. The remaining period of amortization

FASB-92 requires the disclosure of the following information relating to phase-in plans:

1. The terms of any phase-in plans in effect during the year or ordered for future years.

2. Net amount of any allowable costs relating to phase-in plans that have been deferred for future recovery by a regulator for rate-making purposes, but not for financial reporting purposes. In addition, the disclosure of the net change in the related deferrals for those plans during the year.

3. Nature and amounts of any allowance for earnings on shareholders' investment that has been capitalized for rate-making purposes but not capitalized for financial reporting purposes.

The following financial statement disclosure shall be made in the period in which an enterprise discontinues the application of FASB-71 to all or any portion of its regulated operations:

1. The reason(s) for the discontinuation of applying FASB-71

2. The identification of the portion(s) of operations to which the application of FASB-71 is being discontinued

3. The net adjustment, less related taxes, resulting from the discontinuation of the application of FASB-71 should be separately disclosed as an extraordinary item in the statement of operations

APB-30 contains the criteria that must be met for classifying an amount as an extraordinary item in the financial statements of an enterprise. FASB-101 amends APB-30 to permit the net adjustment resulting from the application of FASB-101 to be classified as an extraordinary item, regardless of the criteria in paragraph 20 of APB-30 that must be met for an amount to be classified as an extraordinary item.

Topical Index

TOPICAL INDEX

1992 HBJ Miller Compilation and Review Guide

The *HBJ Miller Compilation and Review Guide* identifies the four essential engagement stages — acceptance, planning, procedures, and report writing — giving you critical step-by-step guidance along the way. All standards that apply to these engagements are restated and thoroughly analyzed. Looseleaf binder format - $75.

1992 HBJ Miller GAAS Guide

The *HBJ Miller GAAS Guide* is the most accurate, authoritative source for answers on Generally Accepted Auditing Standards. This one handy volume reference contains all promulgated and many of the nonpromulgated standards, practices, and procedures that must be applied in the performance of an audit or other professional engagement. Paperback - $45. deluxe hardcover edition - $65.

1992 HBJ Miller Single Audit Guide

The *Single Audit Guide* thoroughly examines the Single Audit Act of 1984, the Act's effects on all promulgated standards, and the differences between single audits and other governmental audits. The *Guide* also provides step-by-step procedures that ensure your compliance with the single audit's unique sampling, testing and reporting reqirements. Looseleaf binder format - $75.

1992 HBJ Miller S Corporation Tax Guide

The *1992 S Corporation Tax Guide* clarifies the complex rules of S corporation taxation, with special attention to tax planning and tax saving strategies. Recent legislative changes are cited and interpreted to help you attain the best tax position. The *Guide* is topically organized and includes the Code, regulations, and key IRS and court rulings. Binder format - $75.

HBJ Miller European Accounting Guide

The *European Accounting Guide* provides crucial information about the accounting systems of 22 European countries. Expert evaluations are given on the legal and economic environments, and the statutory and self-regulatory agencies that govern each country's financial system are examined in great detail. Concrete examples will show you how to handle routine and unusual accounting situations in each country. Paperback - $65.

Accountants' Legal Liability Guide

Accountants' Legal Liability Guide explains in a clear and insightful manner how to mitigate exposure to legal liability. Written specifically for the professional accountant, this guide highlights high-risk engagements, and discusses sound practice management strategies and procedures that accounting firms should implement to avoid liability. Paperback - $40.

1992 HBJ Miller Update Services

When you subscribe to *HBJ Miller Update Services,* you will receive a complete restatement and analysis of official FASB or GASB pronouncements within weeks of their issuance. Subscriptions include a softcover copy of the *GAAP Guide* or the *Governmental GAAP Guide*, and a cloth-covered binder to store your updates. GAAP Guide Update Service - $150. Governmental GAAP Guide Update Service - $150.

(See next page for ordering information)